Contemporary
Literary Criticism

Guide to Gale Literary Criticism Series

For criticism on	Consult these Gale series
Authors now living or who died after December 31, 1959	*CONTEMPORARY LITERARY CRITICISM (CLC)*
Authors who died between 1900 and 1959	*TWENTIETH-CENTURY LITERARY CRITICISM (TCLC)*
Authors who died between 1800 and 1899	*NINETEENTH-CENTURY LITERATURE CRITICISM (NCLC)*
Authors who died between1400 and 1799	*LITERATURE CRITICISM FROM 1400 TO 1800 (LC)* *SHAKESPEAREAN CRITICISM (SC)*
Authors who died before 1400	*CLASSICAL AND MEDIEVAL LITERATURE CRITICISM (CMLC)*
Black writers of the past two hundred years	*BLACK LITERATURE CRITICISM (BLC) AND BLACK LITERATURE CRITICISM SUPPLEMENT (BLCS)*
Authors of books for children and young adults	*CHILDREN'S LITERATURE REVIEW (CLR)*
Dramatists	*DRAMA CRITICISM (DC)*
Hispanic writers of the late nineteenth and twentieth centuries	*HISPANIC LITERATURE CRITICISM (HLC)*
Native North American writers and orators of the eighteenth, nineteenth, and twentieth centuries	*NATIVE NORTH AMERICAN LITERATURE (NNAL)*
Poets	*POETRY CRITICISM (PC)*
Short story writers	*SHORT STORY CRITICISM (SSC)*
Major authors from the Renaissance to the present	*WORLD LITERATURE CRITICISM, 1500 TO THE PRESENT (WLC)*
Major authors and works from the Bible to the present	*WORLD LITERATURE CRITICISM SUPPLEMENT (WLCS)*

ISSN 0091-3421

Volume 120

Contemporary Literary Criticism

Criticism of the Works
of Today's Novelists, Poets, Playwrights,
Short Story Writers, Scriptwriters, and
Other Creative Writers

Jeffrey W. Hunter
Timothy J. White
EDITORS

Angela Y. Jones
Daniel Jones
Deborah A. Schmitt
Polly A. Vedder
Kathleen Wilson
ASSOCIATE EDITORS

GALE GROUP

Detroit
San Francisco
London
Boston
Woodbridge, CT

STAFF

Jeffrey W. Hunter, Timothy J. White, *Editors*

Angela Y. Jones, Daniel Jones, Deborah A. Schmitt,
Polly Vedder, and Kathleen Wilson, *Associate Editors*

Maria Franklin, *Permissions Manager*
Kimberly F. Smilay, *Permissions Specialist*
Kelly Quin, *Permissions Associate*
Erin Bealmear, and Sandy Gore, *Permissions Assistant*

Victoria B. Cariappa, *Research Manager*
Corrine Boland, Wendy Festerling, Tamara Nott, Tracie A. Richardson, *Research Associates*
Tim Lehnerer, Patricia Love, *Research Assistants*

Mary Beth Trimper, *Production Director*
Cindy Range, *Production Assistants*

Barbara J. Yarrow, *Graphic Services Manager*
Sherrell Hobbs, *Macintosh Artist*
Randy Bassett, *Image Database Supervisor*
Robert Duncan and Mikal Ansari, *Scanner Operators*
Pamela Reed, *Imaging Coordinator*

Library of Congress Catalog Card Number 76-46132
ISBN 0-7876-3195-7
ISSN 0091-3421

Printed in the United States of America
10 9 8 7 6 5 4 3 2 1

Contents

Preface vii

Acknowledgments xi

Preface

A Comprehensive Information Source
on Contemporary Literature

Named "one of the twenty-five most distinguished reference titles published during the past twenty-five years" by *Reference Quarterly,* the *Contemporary Literary Criticism (CLC)* series provides readers with critical commentary and general information on more than 2,000 authors now living or who died after December 31, 1959. Previous to the publication of the first volume of *CLC* in 1973, there was no ongoing digest monitoring scholarly and popular sources of critical opinion and explication of modern literature. *CLC,* therefore, has fulfilled an essential need, particularly since the complexity and variety of contemporary literature makes the function of criticism especially important to today's reader.

Scope of the Series

CLC presents significant passages from published criticism of works by creative writers. Since many of the authors covered by *CLC* inspire continual critical commentary, writers are often represented in more than one volume. There is, of course, no duplication of reprinted criticism.

Authors are selected for inclusion for a variety of reasons, among them the publication or dramatic production of a critically acclaimed new work, the reception of a major literary award, revival of interest in past writings, or the adaptation of a literary work to film or television.

Attention is also given to several other groups of writers—authors of considerable public interest—about whose work criticism is often difficult to locate. These include mystery and science fiction writers, literary and social critics, foreign writers, and authors who represent particular ethnic groups.

Format of the Book

Each *CLC* volume contains individual essays and reviews taken from hundreds of book review periodicals, general magazines, scholarly journals, monographs, and books. Entries include critical evaluations spanning from the beginning of an author's career to the most current commentary. Interviews, feature articles, and other published writings that offer insight into the author's works are also presented. Students, teachers, librarians, and researchers will find that the generous critical and biographical material in *CLC* provides them with vital information required to write a term paper, analyze a poem, or lead a book discussion group. In addition, complete bibliographical citations note the original source and all of the information necessary for a term paper footnote or bibliography.

Features

A *CLC* author entry consists of the following elements:

■   The **Author Heading** cites the author's name in the form under which the author has most commonly published, followed by birth date, and death date when applicable. Uncertainty as to a birth or death date is indicated by a question mark.

- A **Portrait** of the author is included when available.

- A brief **Biographical and Critical Introduction** to the author and his or her work precedes the criticism. The first line of the introduction provides the author's full name, pseudonyms (if applicable), nationality, and a listing of genres in which the author has written. To provide users with easier access to information, the biographical and critical essay included in each author entry is divided into four categories: "Introduction," "Biographical Information," "Major Works," and "Critical Reception." The introductions to single-work entries—entries that focus on well known and frequently studied books, short stories, and poems—are similarly organized to quickly provide readers with information on the plot and major characters of the work being discussed, its major themes, and its critical reception. Previous volumes of *CLC* in which the author has been featured are also listed in the introduction.

- A list of **Principal Works** notes the most important writings by the author. When foreign-language works have been translated into English, the English-language version of the title follows in brackets.

- The **Criticism** represents various kinds of critical writing, ranging in form from the brief review to the scholarly exegesis. Essays are selected by the editors to reflect the spectrum of opinion about a specific work or about an author's literary career in general. The critical and biographical materials are presented chronologically, adding a useful perspective to the entry. All titles by the author featured in the entry are printed in boldface type, which enables the reader to easily identify the works being discussed. Publication information (such as publisher names and book prices) and parenthetical numerical references (such as footnotes or page and line references to specific editions of a work) have been deleted at the editor's discretion to provide smoother reading of the text.

- Critical essays are prefaced by **Explanatory Notes** as an additional aid to readers. These notes may provide several types of valuable information, including: the reputation of the critic, the importance of the work of criticism, the commentator's approach to the author's work, the purpose of the criticism, and changes in critical trends regarding the author.

- A complete **Bibliographical Citation** designed to help the user find the original essay or book precedes each critical piece.

- Whenever possible, a recent **Author Interview** accompanies each entry.

- A concise **Further Reading** section appears at the end of entries on authors for whom a significant amount of criticism exists in addition to the pieces reprinted in *CLC*. Each citation in this section is accompanied by a descriptive annotation describing the content of that article. Materials included in this section are grouped under various headings (e.g., Biography, Bibliography, Criticism, and Interviews) to aid users in their search for additional information. Cross-references to other useful sources published by The Gale Group in which the author has appeared are also included: *Authors in the News, Black Writers, Children's Literature Review, Contemporary Authors, Dictionary of Literary Biography, DISCovering Authors, Drama Criticism, Hispanic Literature Criticism, Hispanic Writers, Native North American Literature, Poetry Criticism, Something about the Author, Short Story Criticism, Contemporary Authors Autobiography Series,* and *Something about the Author Autobiography Series.*

Other Features

CLC also includes the following features:

- An **Acknowledgments** section lists the copyright holders who have granted permission to reprint material in this volume of *CLC*. It does not, however, list every book or periodical reprinted or consulted during the preparation of the volume.

- Each new volume of *CLC* includes a **Cumulative Topic Index,** which lists all literary topics treated in *CLC, NCLC, TCLC,* and *LC 1400-1800.*

- A **Cumulative Author Index** lists all the authors who have appeared in the various literary criticism series published by The Gale Group, with cross-references to Gale's biographical and autobiographical series. A full listing of the series referenced there appears on the first page of the indexes of this volume. Readers will welcome this cumulated author index as a useful tool for locating an author within the various series. The index, which lists birth and death dates when available, will be particularly valuable for those authors who are identified with a certain period but whose death dates cause them to be placed in another, or for those authors whose careers span two periods. For example, Ernest Hemingway is found in *CLC,* yet F. Scott Fitzgerald, a writer often associated with him, is found in *Twentieth-Century Literary Criticism.*

- A **Cumulative Nationality Index** alphabetically lists all authors featured in *CLC* by nationality, followed by numbers corresponding to the volumes in which the authors appear.

- An alphabetical **Title Index** accompanies each volume of *CLC*. Listings are followed by the author's name and the corresponding page numbers where the titles are discussed. English translations of foreign titles and variations of titles are cross-referenced to the title under which a work was originally published. Titles of novels, novellas, dramas, films, record albums, and poetry, short story, and essay collections are printed in italics, while all individual poems, short stories, essays, and songs are printed in roman type within quotation marks; when published separately (e.g., T. S. Eliot's poem *The Waste Land),* the titles of long poems are printed in italics.

- In response to numerous suggestions from librarians, Gale has also produced a **Special Paperbound Edition** of the *CLC* title index. This annual cumulation, which alphabetically lists all titles reviewed in the series, is available to all customers. Additional copies of the index are available upon request. Librarians and patrons will welcome this separate index: it saves shelf space, is easy to use, and is recyclable upon receipt of the next edition.

Citing *Contemporary Literary Criticism*

When writing papers, students who quote directly from any volume in the Literary Criticism Series may use the following general forms to footnote reprinted criticism. The first example pertains to material drawn from periodicals, the second to material reprinted in books:

[1]Alfred Cismaru, "Making the Best of It," *The New Republic,* 207, No. 24, (December 7, 1992), 30, 32; excerpted and reprinted in *Contemporary Literary Criticism,* Vol. 85, ed. Christopher Giroux (Detroit: Gale, 1995), pp. 73-4.

[2]Yvor Winters, *The Post-Symbolist Methods* (Allen Swallow, 1967); excerpted and reprinted in *Contemporary Literary Criticism,* Vol. 85, ed. Christopher Giroux (Detroit: Gale, 1995), pp. 223-26.

Suggestions Are Welcome

The editors hope that readers will find *CLC* a useful reference tool and welcome comments about the work. Send comments and suggestions to: Editors, *Contemporary Literary Criticism,* The Gale Group, 27500 Drake Rd., Farmington Hills, MI 48333-3535.

Acknowledgments

The editors wish to thank the copyright holders of the excerpted criticism included in this volume and the permissions managers of many book and magazine publishing companies for assisting us in securing reproduction rights. We are also grateful to the staffs of the Detroit Public Library, the Library of Congress, the University of Detroit Mercy Library, Wayne State University Purdy/Kresge Library Complex, and the University of Michigan Libraries for making their resources available to us. Following is a list of the copyright holders who have granted us permission to reproduce material in this volume of *CLC*. Every effort has been made to trace copyright, but if omissions have been made, please let us know.

COPYRIGHTED MATERIALS IN *CLC*, VOLUME 120, WERE REPRODUCED FROM THE FOLLOWING PERIODICALS:

American Indian Culture and Research Journal, v. 17, 1993. Copyright © 1993 The Regents of the University of California. Reproduced by permission.—*The American Poetry Review*, v. 18, July-August, 1989 for "Pattern of Flux: The 'Torsion Form' in Gary Snyder's Poetry" by Tom Lavazzi. Copyright © 1989 by World Poetry, Inc. Reproduced by permission of the author.—*The Antioch Review*, v. 53, Fall, 1995. Copyright © 1995 by the Antioch Review Inc. Reproduced by permission of the Editors.—*Ariel: A Review of International English Literature*, v.. 24, January, 1993 for "Revolutionary Developments: Michelle Cliffs 'No Telephone to Heaven,' and Merle Collin's 'Angel,'" by Maria Helena Lima; v. 25, January, 1994 for "Race and Gender in Louise Erdrich's 'The Beet Queen,'" by Susan Meisenhelder. Copyright © 1993, 1994 The Board of Governors, The University of Calgary. Both reproduced by permission of the publisher and the respective authors.—*The Armchair Detective*, v. 22, Winter, 1989. Copyright © 1989 by *The Armchair Detective*. Reproduced by permission.—*Artforum*, v. XXIV, December, 1990 for "The Cave" by Michael Tarantino; v. XXXIV, May, 1996 for "Auteur Tricolore" by Georgia Brown. Both reproduced by permission of the publisher and the respective authors.—*Belles Lettres: A Review of Books by Women*, v. 4, Summer, 1989; v. 5, Summer, 1990; v. 7, Fall, 1991; v. 9, Spring, 1994. All reproduced by permission.—*Book World--Washington Post*, v. XVI, October, 1986 for "Neil Bissoondath: Tales of the New World" by Bob Shacochis; v. XIX, January, 1989 for "Going to Extremes and Other Tales of the New World" by Mervyn Morris; June, 1991 for "By the Rivers of Babylon" by Edward Hower. © 1986, 1989, 1991 Washington Post Book World Service/Washington Post Writers Group. All reproduced by permission of the respective authors.—*Books in Canada*, May, 1985, for "Continental Drifters" by Douglas Glover; v. XIX, October, 1990 for "A Safe Place" by Merna Summers; v. XXII, Fall, 1993, for "Urban Logos" by Carole Giangrande; v. XXIII, Fall, 1994, for "The Center: Can it Hold?" by Janice Kulyk Keefer. All reproduced by permission of the respective authors.—*Callaloo*, v. 16, Winter, 1993. Copyright © 1993 by Charles H. Rowell. Reproduced by permission of The Johns Hopkins University Press.—*Canadian Book Review Annual*, 1994. Reproduced by permission.—*The Canadian Forum*, February/March, 1989 for "Hopes or Illusions" by Marc Cote. Reproduced by permission of the author.—*Canadian Literature*, Spring, 1992, for "A review of the author's writing," by Frank Birbalsingh; Spring, 1993, for "Uncertainty" by Thomas Hastings; Winter, 1995, for "Building on Common Ground—An interview with Neil Bissoondath" by Penny Van Toorn; Winter, 1996, for "Shaping Ethnicity" by Marilyn Iwama. All reproduced by permission of the respective authors.—*CEA Critic*, v. 54, Fall, 1991. Copyright © 1991 by the College English Association, Inc. Reproduced by permission.—*Chicago Reader*, December, 1994. Reproduced by permission.—*Chicago Tribune -Books*, July, 1990 for "Hollywood's Left Twisting in the Plot" by Linda Stewart; November 14, 1993 for "Louise Erdrich Revisits the Complex World of the Chippewa" by Roberta Rubenstein; November, 1995, for "Sisterly Bonds," by Penelope Mesic. © copyrighted 1990, 1993, 1995 Chicago Tribune Company. All rights reserved. All reproduced by permission of the respective authors.—*The Christian Science Monitor*, January, 1987. © 1987 The Christian Science Publishing Society. All rights reserved. Reproduced by permission from *The Christian Science Monitor*./ v. 81, April, 1989 for "Chinese-American 'Bridge' Club" by Merle Rubin. © 1989 by Merle Rubin. All rights reserved. Reproduced by permission of the author./ March, 1994 for "Through the Lense of a Polish Filmmaker" by Marilynne S. Mason.(c) 1994 by Marilynne S. Mason. All rights reserved. Reproduced by permission of the author.—*Cinema Journal*, v. 34, Winter 1995. © 1995 by the University

1975; August, 1986; February, 1989; May, 1991; June, 1991; December, 1992; January 16, 1994; November, 1994; April 16, 1995; October, 1995. Copyright © 1975, 1986, 1989, 1991, 1992, 1994, 1995 by The New York Times Company. All reproduced by permission.—*The New Yorker*, Vol. LXXII, September 1996 for "Elmore's Legs" by Alec Wilkinson. © 1996 by Alec Wilkinson. All rights reserved. Reproduced by permission of the author.—*North Dakota Quarterly*, v. 55, Fall, 1987; v. 59, Fall, 1991; v. 61, Summer, 1993; v. 62, Fall 1994-95; v. 63, Fall, 1996. Copyright 1987, 1991, 1993, 1994-95, 1996 by The University of North Dakota. All reproduced by permission.—*The Observer*, April, 1997. © William Fiennes. Reproduced by permission of The Observer Limited, London.—*PMLA*, v. 109, October, 1994. Copyright © 1994 by the Modern Language Association of America. Reproduced by permission of the Modern Language Association of America.—*Poetry*, v. 164, June, 1997 for "Review of No Nature" by David Barber. © 1997 by the Modern Poetry Association. Reproduced by permission of the Editor of *Poetry* and the author.—*The Polish Review*, v. XL, 1995. Reproduced by permission.—*Quill & Quire*, v. 60, November, 1994, for "Debating the M-Word" by Sandra Martin. Reproduced by permission of the author.—*The Review of Contemporary Fiction*, v. 11, Spring, 1991. Copyright, 1991. Reproduced by permission.—*Sagetreib*, v. 2, Spring, 1993. Reproduced by permission.—*San Francisco Review of Books*, v. 16, Summer, 1991 for "Amy, Angst, and the Second Novel" by Elgy Gillespie. Reproduced by permission of the author.—*Sight and Sound*, v. 50, Spring 1981; v. 59, Summer 1990; v. 3, November 1993; v. 4, May 1994; v. 4, June 1994; v. 6, May, 1996; v. 6, August, 1996. Copyright © 1981, 1990, 1993, 1994, 1996 by The British Film Institute. All reproduced by permission.—*Studies in American Indian Literature*, v. 8, Fall, 1996 for "Blurs, Blends, Berdaches: Gender Mixing in the Novels of Louise Erdrich" by Julie Barak; v. 8, Winter, 1996 for "Women Aging into Power: Fictional Representations of Power and Authority in Louise Erdrich's Female Characters" by Susan Castillo. Both reproduced by permission of the respective authors.—*Substance*, v. X111, 1984. for "Translating Infante's Inferno" by Suzanne Jill Levine. © Suzanne Jill Levine. Reproduced by permission of the author. *The Times Literary Supplement*, January, 1989; March 6, 1992; October, 1993; December, 1994. © The Times Supplements Limited 1989, 1992, 1993, 1994. All reproduced from *The Times Literary Supplement* by permission.—*Western American Literature*, v. 18, Summer, 1983. Copyright, 1983, by the Western Literature Association. Reproduced by permission.—*Western Humanities Review*, v. XLI, Spring, 1997. Copyright, 1997, University of Utah. Reproduced by permission.—*Women's Review of Books*, v.5, November, 1987 for a review of "No Telephone to Heaven" by Erika Smilowitz; v. VIII, September, 1991 for "The Second Time Around" by Helen Yglesias; v. XI, July, 1994 for "Taking Liberties with History" by Deborah McDowell. Copyright © 1987, 1991, 1994. All rights reserved. All reproduced by permission of the respective authors.—*World Literature Today*, v. 61, Autumn, 1978; v. 61, Autumn 1987; v. 65, Spring, 1991; v. 67, Spring, 1993; v. 70, Autumn, 1996. Copyright © 1978, 1987, 1991, 1993, 1996 by the University of Oklahoma Press. All reproduced by permission.

COPYRIGHTED MATERIALs IN *CLC*, VOLUME 120, WERE REPRODUCED FROM THE FOLLOWING BOOKS:

Braendlin, Bonnie. From "Mother/Daughter Dialog(ic)s in, around, and about Amy Tan's The Joy Luck Club" in *Private Voices, Public Lives: Women Speak on the Literary Life*. Edited by Nancy Owen Nelson. University of North Texas Press, 1996. © 1996 by the University of North Texas Press. Reproduced by permission.—Coates, Paul. From "Exile and Identity: Kieslowski and His Contemporaries" in *Before the Wall Came Down: Soviet and East European Filmmakers Working in the West*. Edited by Graham Petrie and Ruth Dwyer. University Press of America, 1990. © 1990 by University Press of America. All rights reserved. Reproduced by permission.—Foster, M. Marie Booth. From "Voice, Mind, Self: Mother-Daughter Relationships in Amy Tan's The Joy Luck Club and The Kitchen God's Wife" in *Women of Color: Mother-Daughter Relationships in 20th-Century Literature*. Edited by Elizabeth Brown-Guillory. University of Texas Press, 1996. © 1996 by the University of Texas Press. All rights reserved. Reproduced by permission.—Shen, Gloria. From "Born of a Stranger: Mother-Daughter Relationships and Storytelling in Amy Tan's The Joy Luck Club" in *International Women's Writing: New Landscapes of Identity*. Edited by Anne E. Brown and Marjanne Gooze. Greenwood Press, 1995. © 1995 by Anne E. Brown and Marjanne E. Gooze. Reproduced by permission of Greenwood Publishing Group, Inc., Westport, CT.—Tharp, Julie. From "Women's Community and Survival in the Novels of Louise Erdrich" in *Communication and Women's Friendships: Parallels and Intersections in Literature and Life*. Edited by Janet Doubler Ward and Joanna Stephens Mink. Bowling Green State University Popular Press, 1993. Copyright © 1993 by Bowling Green State University Popular Press. Reproduced by permission.

PHOTOGRAPHS AND ILLUSTRATIONS APPEARING IN *CLC*, VOLUME 120, WERE RECEIVED FROM THE FOLLOWING SOURCES:

Neil Bissoondath
1955-

(Full name Neil Devindra Bissoondath) Trinidadian-born Canadian novelist, short story and nonfiction writer.

The following entry provides an overview of Bissoondath's career through 1996.

INTRODUCTION

Neil Bissoondath's writing typically focuses on the lives of characters displaced by political violence. In addition to immigrants and refugees, Bissoondath also explores the lives of those marginalized within their own societies, people alienated by their own culture. As Jim Shephard writes, "That spectrum of human response, from the selfless to the despairing, is what Neil Bissoondath writes about. In doing so, he speaks for the silenced voices that continue to fill the margins of our societies, the voices of those so overworked and under rewarded that the term 'disadvantaged' is inadequate to describe them."

Biographical Information

Born in 1955 in Arima, Trinidad, Bissoondath comes from a literary family: his uncles are V. S. Naipaul and the late Shiva Naipaul. His family lived in the town of Sangre Grande, where his father worked at the family store, until Bissoondath reached the age of fourteen. At that time his father built a house in Port of Spain, to be closer to the high school Bissoondath would attend, St. Mary's College. Although Bissoondath was from a Hindu tradition, he was able to adapt to a Catholic high school. Bissoondath describes himself as not very religious and distrustful of dogma. In the early Seventies, political upheaval and economic collapse had created a climate of chaos and violence in the island nation. In a situation similar to Germany in the Thirties, wherein Jews became a convenient scapegoat for the disintegrating economy, the East Indian merchant class became the target of persecution in Trinidad. In 1973, at the age of eighteen, Bissoondath left Trinidad. He settled in Canada, where he studied at York University, receiving a B. A. in French in 1977. Bissoondath taught English and French at the Inlingua School of Languages and the Toronto Language Workshop. He won the McClelland and Stewart award and the National Magazine award, both in 1986, for the short story "Dancing."

Major Works

Bissoondath's fist book was the short story collection, *Dig-

ging Up the Mountains* (1985). The title story is set on a Caribbean island which recently gained its independence and is in the throes of political and social upheaval. The story's protagonist, Harry Beharry, wants only to work in his garden and die in his own home. But the escalating violence forces him to flee. "Dancing," told in an autobiographical style, is the story of a Caribbean maid who voyages to Canada with the hopes of bettering herself. Through her a bewilderingly different world is revealed, with skyscrapers, automatic doors, and a coldness of climate and spirit. In "An Arrangement of Shadows," a white schoolteacher from England finds herself, after many years in the Caribbean, suddenly made an outcast by political changes. No longer comfortable but unable to leave, she finds herself stereotyped by others with many traits she despises. Bissoondath's first novel, *A Casual Brutality* (1988), is again set in a troubled Caribbean nation. Casaquemada, the island nation in the book, is a mixture of the politics and history of Guyana, Trinidad, Jamaica, and Grenada. Dr. Raj Ramsingh studied and married in Canada. But friends convince him that the intelligentsia owe something to their homeland, and although he knows the political situation is volatile, he returns to

Casaquemada. Growing violence claims the lives of his wife and son, and he returns to Canada. Bissoondath's next book is another collection of short stories, *On the Eve of Uncertain Tomorrows* (1990). In the title story, a group of refugees from various parts of the world wait together in a boarding house for decisions on their requests for political asylum in Canada. "Security" is a sequel to the story "Uncertainty" from Bissoondath's first collection. The principal character of both stories, Mr. Ramgoolam, has become alienated from his family. His wife now works outside the home, and his sons have become accustomed to the Canadian culture, even eating pork and beef. Seeking a sense of belonging, Mr. Ramgoolam retreats into his religion. But the more he immerses himself in his religious practices and listens to the Hindu radio programs (which he does not understand), the more alienated he becomes. In "Goodnight, Mr. Slade," the caretaker of an apartment building is being evicted and placed in a nursing home. The experience reminds him of his previous displacement, when he was sent to Nazi concentration camps. Instead of once again surrendering his life to the will of others, he commits suicide. The culture conflict of the immigrant is also the subject of Bissoondath's novel, *The Innocence of Age* (1994). The middle-aged Pasco, still grieving over the death of his wife, longs nostalgically for the past. But his son Danny rejects the past, seeing life only in terms of money and power. Danny works for a greedy slumlord whom Pasco despises. Their conflict is brought to a head when Danny begins to renovate Pasco's home, thinking more in terms of future profit than Pasco's comfort. In his nonfiction book, *Selling Illusions* (1994), Bissoondath argues that governmental promotion of a Multiculturalism policy actually harms those it hopes to protect. He suggests that government intervention focuses on superficial differences, at the expense of the more profound similarities people share. Bissoondath makes the case that cultural heritage is best protected by individual efforts.

Critical Reception

Early criticism of Bissoondath's work often compared his work to the writings of his uncles V. S. Naipaul and the late Shiva Naipaul. Most agreed that he shared their sense of linguistic style and attention to detail. Several critics felt Bissoondath's precise attention to surface details was subverted by an emotional detachment to his characters' inner lives. David Evans referred to this in his criticism of *A Casual Brutality,* saying that the narrative style is "replacing emotion with a near-photographic rendering of surface detail." Several critics laud Bissoondath's use of contrasting past and present to illuminate a character's inner conflict. As Merna Summers stated, "Present and past repeatedly illuminate each other in Bissoondath's stories, and the meaning often comes out of the tension between them." Although Bissoondath's stories often focus on the themes of the marginalized and dispossessed, he is frequently praised for

the broad range of protagonists. Not surprisingly, the controversial thesis of *Selling Illusions* generated criticism that examined the policy of Multiculturalism more than treating Bissoondath's ideas. However, many critics appreciated Bissoondath's courage for taking on a politically-charged, complex issue.

PRINCIPAL WORKS

Digging Up the Mountains (short stories) 1985
A Casual Brutality (novel) 1988
On the Eve of Uncertain Tomorrows (short stories) 1990
The Innocence of Age (novel) 1992
Selling Illusions: The Cult of Multiculturalism in Canada (nonfiction) 1994

CRITICISM

Douglas Glover (review date May 1985)

SOURCE: "Continental Drifters," in *Books in Canada,* Vol. 14, No. 4, May, 1985, p. 14.

[*In the review below, Glover praises* Digging Up the Mountains *and comments on several of the stories.*]

In his first story collection, **Digging Up the Mountains,** Neil Bissoondath reveals an impressive gift for writing prose that is precise and vivid, full of striking turns of phrase and exciting, many-fingered images.

Take, for example, the opening of his story **"An Arrangement Of Shadows":**

> The clock struck once and it was eight o'clock.
>
> Two pigeons, symmetrical slices of black on the blue sky, swooped and touched down abruptly on the red roof of the clock tower. The hands of the clock—broadswords of a brass long tarnished—were locked as always at four seventeen.

"All fine prose," in the words of F. Scott Fitzgerald, "is based on the verbs carrying the sentences." These lines of Bissoondath's are so alive that you race through them, scarcely noticing their technical virtuosity, yet they have colored the whole story—the striking, slicing, swooping, tarnishing, and locking is going on before your eyes.

Born in Trinidad in 1955, Bissoondath came to Canada 12 years ago as a university student. While his style bespeaks a sound British colonial school education, his stories reflect what one assumes is a personal sense of uprootedness and betrayal at the economic decline and social and ideological turmoil of post-independence Trinidad.

In **"There Are a Lot of Ways to Die"** Joseph Heaven, a successful immigrant with a rug installation business in Toronto, returns to Port of Spain expecting "a kind of fame, a continual welcome, the prodigal son having made good, having acquired skills, returning home to share the wealth." Instead, he finds that the shantytown workers don't want regular employment, that the new politics have endowed a class of insufferable nouveau bureaucrats, that old friends have died or lapsed into despair, that even the humid, rainy climate gives the lie to his memories of an idyllic island paradise.

"Might it not," thinks Joseph, referring to the story's central image, a dilapidated mansion symbolic of Trinidad itself, "have been always a big, open, empty house, with rooms destined to no purpose, with a façade that promised mystery but an interior that took away all hope." Finally, he decides to return to Canada, fearing that, in his absence, his memories of Toronto's civility may have turned into lies as well.

Joseph Heaven is the quintessential Bissoondath protagonist, with a foot in two continents, two worlds, each shifting subtly away from him as time passes, as memory becomes hallucination. In lesser souls, this alienation can cause bitterness, a theme that Bissoondath explores in several stories: **"The Revolutionary"** with its shambling, scarecrow ideologue; **"A Short Visit to a Failed Artist,"** a savage caricature of a woman-hating ("Women are shit") self-styled artist (who photocopies his face) living in a crowded, subsidized Toronto apartment; and **"Dancing,"** which ends in an explosion of anti-white, anti-Canadian racism.

Fearlessly, Bissoondath moves off his own turf, trying his themes on other nationalities—Japanese, Russian, Anglo-Canadian—but with less success than in his Trinidad stories. In **"Continental Drift"** a young Canadian hitch-hiking in Europe meets two Spanish migrant laborers in a hostel and feels "life suddenly electrified." Although the author's craftsmanship is evident, it seems wasted here on a trivial cliché about "real" experience and the noble working man. (This tepid effort is balanced by a couple of striking Central American atrocity stories **"In The Kingdom Of The Golden Dust"** and **"Counting The Wind"** which, though thematically unrelated, are among the best in the book.)

Sometimes, too, a certain stridency or one-sidedness invades Bissoondath's prevailing tone of bewildered fatalism. This is especially evident when he lapses into the old authorial lie of the uninvolved narrator. In **"Christmas Lunch"** the

"I" narrator watches an immigrant man basely torment an unwitting white woman from Newfoundland. The "I" doesn't protest, doesn't attempt to intervene; he flees as soon as politeness permits.

The strength of this fiction (and others like it) trades on the narrator's supposed detachment, his objectivity. Appalled by the cruelty, yet secure in his superior courtesy (smug, bourgeois) and narrative neutrality, he makes a subtly insidious pact with the reader that, yes, man, these are awful degenerate people, not like us. Yet this easy verdict betrays a moral ambiguity, a failure on the part of the "I" to engage his own demons. Silence is complicity.

These reservations aside, however, the publication of *Digging Up the Mountains* ushers in a ripe, new talent, a welcome addition to the CanLit émigré pantheon. Bissoondath combines deft prose, major themes, exotic peoples and locales to create a work of surpassing emotional impact.

John Sutherland (review date 19 June 1986)

SOURCE: "Fuentes the Memorious," in *London Review of Books*, Vol. 8, No. 11, June 19, 1986, pp. 19-20.

[*In the following excerpt, Sutherland lauds Bissoondath's writing but criticizes the "radical anger" that infuses several of his stories.*]

Neil Bissoondath's *Digging Up the Mountains* is a first book and a collection of short stories. The separate pieces are linked by an embittered sense of expatriation. Bissoondath himself was born in colonial Trinidad in 1955 and emigrated to Canada in 1973 after Independence. The title story records the government campaign against the Indian middle class which sanctioned murder, Bissoondath alleges, and eventually drove people like him into exile. The ruling West Indian blacks are generally portrayed by Bissoondath as arrogant and brutal. At home they are grossly incompetent and violent. Abroad they are vulgar and absurd. **"Dancing"** is the autobiographical account of a former fifty-dollar-a-month black maid, Sheila. She comes to Toronto, where she is picked up by a sponsoring relative who takes her to a blues party. A white neighbor complains at the din, and the West Indians insult and threaten him with the "Untarryo Human Right Commission." The "racialists," they explain, "owe us. And we going to collect." Another more spiteful story portrays a black "revolutionary" studying in Canada who cannot read the name "Lenin" or spell "proletariat." More effective is the gentler piece **"Insecurity,"** the comic portrait of an Indian merchant vacillating about whether to buy a house in distant Canada. When Bissoondath comes to terms with his racial anger he will be a writer worth watching.

Hanif Kureishi (review date 17 August 1986)

SOURCE: "Allistair Ramgoolam Does Well to be Uneasy," in *New York Times Book Review,* August 17, 1986, Sec. 7, p. 10.

[*Below, Kureishi favorably assesses the collection* Digging up the Mountain, *describing his favorite stories in the book.*]

The superb short stories in Neil Bissoondath's first collection are alive with movement and flight, leaving and returning, insecurity and impermanence. Peopled by exiles and immigrants, deracines and runaways—perhaps the true representatives of the mobile 20th century—these are tales of two worlds, usually the Caribbean and Canada—and of those who are stretched between the two.

Like his uncles, V. S. Naipaul and the late Shiva Naipaul, he has much to tell us about areas that have not been written about before. His stories recall theirs in subject matter, though he promises to have more range than V. S. Naipaul, and he can write plausible women characters.

The title story, **"Digging Up the Mountains,"** is set on a recently independent Caribbean island during a state of emergency. Hari Beharry is a successful businessman who wants nothing more than to tend his garden and die in his own house. But the island's former simplicity "had been replaced by the cynical politics of corruption that plagued all the urchin nations scrambling in the larger world." Friends are inexplicably taken away; others are shot; there are anonymous phone calls and letters. Finally there is more violence, followed by flight.

In another story, **"Insecurity,"** Alistair Ramgoolam, a similar self-made businessman, the sort who had attended the farewell ball for the last British Governor, is trying to escape by buying a house in Toronto through his son. On this island there are policemen with guns and "students parading Marx and Castro." The walls of his store have been daubed with slogans: "Socialism" and "Black Communism." "His life at the fringe of events, he felt, had given him a certain authority over and comprehension of the past. But the present, with its confusion and corruption, eluded him. The sense of drift nurtured unease." Here the pattern is like that of the title story: decent people who have worked hard are threatened by the smoldering volcano of colonial resentment and disorder. Once more the wrong people will be in charge: independence will have failed and one tyranny, usually the

British variety, will be replaced by the Caribbean kind of autocracy.

What is missing in both stories is also the same: an attempt to explain and understand the revolutionaries and what their grievances and politics are, and to say how their bitter resentments came to be forged.

The shorter piece called **"The Revolutionary"** does present us with Eugene Williamson, a militant student from Trinidad attending a university someplace else. Williamson has a baby son called Tarot, admires Che and Fidel and speaks of "the glorious, liberating path" of what he calls "socialist-proletarian" revolution. But Mr. Bissoondath's contempt for his character is too obvious and the caricature too grotesque for the story to succeed. This is partly because the shorter pieces in the book often drift; they are even more pointless than the lives of his characters. Mr. Bissoondath is a better writer when he is more expansive, when he can combine his marvelous gift for mood and detail with his ability to create character and drama.

These gifts coincide in the long story **"An Arrangement of Shadows."** Miss Victoria Jackson, a white teacher, leaves factory-gray England for the Caribbean only to find herself, years later, marooned on a stifling island where she cannot stay and which she cannot leave. Hemmed in by nationalist resentment, a rejected lover and provincial sexual hypocrisy, she suddenly finds herself an objective enemy of the island: an unwilling representative of everything she hates. She hears a dead colleague's voice say: "Our time is long gone. We are of a different age. We are not, none of us, wanted here. We are not required. We don't belong." Scrupulously selecting details of light, landscape and personality, Mr. Bissoondath builds his story relentlessly to a shattering climax.

In **"Dancing"** he once more tells us what it is like to be a harried stranger. An uneducated Caribbean woman, "just a ordinary fifty-dollar-a-month maid" in Trinidad, suffering from uppityness, joins her relatives in Canada. We get a terrifying, dizzy sense of what our own surroundings—automatic doors, high-rise apartment blocks, subways—are like to the uninitiated.

Mr. Bissoondath left Trinidad to study French at York University in Toronto and has taught both English and French. His scrupulousness and control mean much can be said quickly. Thus each of the longer stories seems full but not crowded, giving the sense of an embryo novel. And the novel will, I think, suit his talent.

In much recent North American writing the tone is insular, self-regarding, even self-obsessed. It is a relief then to run up against Neil Bissoondath's broad outlook and seriousness.

He has startling news from a changing world to tell us. At ease writing about France and Japan, as well as about the Caribbean and Canada, he has the fresh catholicity that is a welcome feature of third-world writing today.

It is also his ability to build the pressures of political context into the attempt of ordinary people to live reasonable lives that gives his work its power, its complexity and its contemporary relevance.

At the age of 10, Neil Bissoondath made a startling discovery—his uncle V. S. Naipaul was a writer. "I started reading when I was very young, but it hadn't occurred to me before then that all those people I enjoyed reading were professional writers," he said. "I saw V. S. as a kind of role model. I started writing stories and I realized that what I was doing could be a profession."

Those first stories, written as he grew up in Trinidad, were "usually pretty bad." But he didn't feel intimidated by being a member of a literary family that also included V. S. Naipaul's brother, Shiva, who died last year. "I don't carry the name Naipaul and that's a blessing," he said in a telephone interview from his home in Toronto. "And I don't view writing as a competition. Shiva's writing was very different from V. S.'s and mine is different from theirs." The short stories in *Digging Up the Mountains,* his first book, present a dark picture of life in the third world. Yet his own childhood in the West Indies was happy. "There wasn't a sense of threat," he said, "just a feeling that there was more to the world."

His tales also tell of demons, real or imagined, facing strangers in strange lands. But he adapted easily when he moved to Toronto 13 years ago at the age of 18 to attend York University. "As soon as I arrived I felt at home," he said, adding that V. S. Naipaul had warned him, "England was a place without a future" and the United States "was too big and would swallow me up."

He is working now on a novel. "It's nice to have so much space to explore. With a short story I'm always reining myself in."

Bob Shacochis (review date 19 October 1986)

SOURCE: "Neil Bissoondath: Tales of the New World," in *Washington Post Book World,* Vol. XVI, No. 16, October 19, 1986, p. 6.

[*Shacochis is an American writer and the 1985 winner of the American Book Award. Below, he examines the thematic relations of the stories in* Digging Up the Mountains.]

Bloodlines can function like a diplomatic passport for a writer making his or her debut, but they can just as easily be excess baggage, the constant unwanted weight of a destiny preordained for shortcomings. Neil Bissoondath, a Trinidad-born writer who emigrated to Toronto in 1973 at the age of 18, is the second-generation prince of an island-bred literary aristocracy, and thus is in the ostensible position of upholding a family's reputation. As nephew of V. S. Naipaul and the late Shiva Naipaul, Bissoondath is *de facto* an object of our curiosity. We want to know if he has inherited the gift, and the courage to develop it into a talent worthy of his genes. The answer is yes; Bissoondath is as deserving of praise as his uncles. He shares their fearless regard for complexity, and their inability to fool around. His psychological and historical insights are similarly dark, and as accurate as a laser scalpel.

So much for genetic luggage. Perhaps it is ultimately trivial, akin to eye color or shoe size. And yet I hesitate to say that because these stories have too much authority to be thought of as coincidental or derivative, and I realize that as I attempt to isolate the unique strength's of Bissoondath's work, I am identifying family trademarks as well.

The first recognizable trait to impress itself upon the reader is an extraordinary range of mobility. *Digging Up the Mountains,* Bissoondath's first publication, is a frustrating book to discuss in this respect. Its 14 stories seem to be the combined effort of a half-dozen authors, each writing from and about different parts of the planet. There are, of course, stories about life in contemporary Trinidad and the experiences of West Indian immigrants in Canada, powerfully compressed tales of distorted nationalism and cultural divorce. But Bissoondath assumes the freedom to kidnap any culture that intrigues him. Consequently, we have the first-person accounts of Mishi, a young Japanese woman suffocating in the thin male-dominated atmosphere of her ancestors, and Maria Luisa, a Central American teen-age girl about to be crowned Police Queen in the story **"In the Kingdom of Golden Dust."** In a tone of stunned passivity that may momentarily burst into hysteria, Maria Luisa daydreams of her dead boyfriends as their murderer emcees the bleak pageant, hallucinating their bloody resurrection. In **"An Arrangement of Shadows,"** Bissoondath dredges the enigmatic depths of the misguided and doomed Victoria Jackson, an expatriate schoolteacher from North America who sexually colonizes her black students. **"Continental Drift"** chronicles the sad fellowship of European migrant workers in France, and in **"Counting the Wind,"** the collection's end piece, a good-hearted graveyard keeper and his family become the unwilling hosts to daily executions during a conflict reminiscent of the Spanish Civil War.

Bissoondath sets loose enough diverse personalities and voices to turn any book into a self-contained Babylon, yet the collection is quietly unified by its underlying concerns. There is a clear sense of a central command post, an over-riding omniscience that continuously braids disparate realities into one hard, glistening cable of universal humanity. By not allowing his vision to anchor in one class, one race, one nation, or one ideology, Bissoondath has freed his imagination for the challenge of heterogeneity, the myths and frontiers of the *other*. It's not the only way, this global embrace of experience, for a writer to make big connections, but it is unquestionably the richest. The novelist Russell Banks has spoken of New World Writers, syncretic artists who feel entirely at ease borrowing from and transforming all the cultural traditions they can get their hands on—European, African, Latin, Caribbean, Indian, Asian, rural and urban, high and low. Bissoondath matches the description. Blending a variety of elements to construct an ecumenical and truly American literature, these are writers, in Banks' words, with "a powerful belief in fiction's essential role in the creation of a moral history of the hemisphere."

The profound thematic structuring of the stories in ***Digging Up the Mountains*** is an extension of this belief. The most poignant and disturbing pieces in the collection are the Trinidad/Canada set, which dramatize the bitter Third World landscape of post-colonial muddle. In the title story, Hari Beharry, son of an immigrant to the island and owner of a chain of profitable boutiques, has built himself a luxurious house. The house, and its view of the mountains, is Hari's tangible symbol of permanence: here he will entertain his grandchildren and their children, and from here, when the time comes, he will be buried.

"The island, however, was no longer that in which his father had lived. Its simplicity, its unsophistication, had vanished over the years and had been replaced by the cynical politics of corruption that plagued all the urchin nations scrambling in the larger world. Independence—written ever since with a capital I, small I being considered a spelling mistake at best, treason at worst—had promised the world. It had failed to deliver, and the island, in its isolation, blamed the world."

Hari, like the majority of Bissoondath's characters, is a member of a transitional generation, torn and without peace, unable to gather any meaningful sense of cultural identity out of "the black hole" of the island's history. They are nostalgic for an idealized past, victims of a volatile present, and outcasts, from a future that's already begun to shut them out from the tradition-laden lives of their parents and the new lives of their children. They represent a fall from consciousness that produces moral confusion and a society at the mercy of political opportunism. They become a parody of stability and status, not only people without virtue, but without an awareness of its existence in the world.

On Hari's island, suffering becomes a political craft. He gives up trying to determine which way the wind blows—it blows, like a hurricane, from contrary directions. The only recourse is to evacuate: "Flight had become necessary, and it would be penniless flight . . . he could leave with nothing. It was the price for years of opulent celebrity in a little place going wrong."

We can pity Hari, but that's about it. He is guilty of taking his success, and others' lack of it, for granted. He has, in his blindness, emulated the old colonial sins, a legacy adopted by the elite classes and cynically admired by too many of its victims who aspire to power.

Bissoondath is wise to make the causes and effects of dislocation his primary concern. We are largely a hemisphere of immigrants and refugees, the difference between the two categories sometimes less one of motivation than a degree of urgency. Something has happened, however, that's altered the dynamics of the flow. The cities of the Western world, destinations of hope, are gradually becoming Third World mini-states approaching critical mass. In **"Veins Visible,"** the most alarmingly prophetic story in the collection, Vern, a West Indian immigrant in Canada, has endured a winter witnessing the slow deaths of his friends from alienation and dissipation, lethally homesick for a place and a time that no longer exist. Vern concludes that "the whole world, everybody's a refugee, everybody's running from one thing or another."

This is revelation as over-simplification, but Bissoondath permits his character to make the more fundamental connection: "And then another thought chilled him: But it's happening here too. This country around him was beginning to crack. The angry words, the petty hatreds, the attitude not of living off the land but of raping it. He had seen it before, been through it before, and much more, more that was still to come, until a time when, even from here, the haven now, people would begin to flee. . . . He thought, Where to next, Refugee?"

There is, believe it or not, smart humor in some of these stories, but they are never merry journeys. I suppose Bissoondath will be criticized for his dark reports, and for his fascination with spiritual ugliness. More important, I think, is that he cannot be counted among those writers—and those readers—who have abandoned issues and values for posturing or moral fatigue. A Naipaul to his esthetic bones, he has engaged his art to the dangerous forces that sweep the world. If there are any more writers in the family I wish they'd hurry along.

Michael Gorra (review date Spring 1987)

SOURCE: A review of *Digging Up the Mountains*, in *The Hudson Review*, Vol. 40, Spring, 1987, pp. 139-40.

[*Below, Gorra feels some of Bissoondath's stories reach too far in an attempt to create personae different from himself, but lauds the writing and Bissoondath's potential.*]

Many of the stories in the Trinidadian writer Neil Bissoondath's first collection are also cast as dramatic monologues, often in the voices of those who are for one reason or another exiled from or disenfranchised by their homelands. But his attempts to speak in the voice of a peasant girl living under a Latin American dictatorship in **"In the Kingdom of the Golden Dust,"** or in that of a Japanese girl from a traditional family in **"The Cage,"** ring false to me: Here is the latter story's first paragraph:

> My father is an architect. Architects are good at designing things: stores, houses, apartments, prisons. For my mother, my father, not an unkind man, designed a house. For me, my father, not a kind man, designed a cage.

Too neat, too carefully calculated, this attempt to be Japanese; the writer is too conscious of trying this particular voice on to see how it feels. But sometimes one's new clothes don't fit, and I don't believe in this voice any more than I'd believe in Cary Grant in overalls.

But what an anxiety of influence Bissoondath must work under! He is the nephew of V. S. Naipaul, and so often in reading these stories, one is aware, too aware, of the uncle's work, whose prose Bissoondath's echoes:

> At first it had seemed like a joke: simple people—simplicity then viewed as a virtue, when they were truly simple, playing at the world until the wider corruption inexorably attracted them—eager to be duped by a greater sophistication. Yet Vernon had always felt that more than a simplicity had been involved, more than an island naivety.

This passage from **"Veins Visible"** feels like a footnote to the uncle's work, to *The Mimic Men* in particular, an exploration of territory he has already fully mapped, and which Bissoondath has not yet been able to make fully his own. Like most of the stories in the volume, it is neatly crafted, but I feel I've read it before, and not as I've read the latest *New Yorker* story before. For Bissoondath writes in that window of time in which such an attitude toward history and toward the psychic region of exile that history creates is still the property of an individual writer, and not of the house of fiction as a whole. And I suspect he's tried to compensate for that by attempting to extend that sense, in stories like **"The Cage,"** to situations that are quite different, perhaps too different, from his own.

Maybe this is unfair. Perhaps if the book came without a biographical note I wouldn't think these stories so derivative; perhaps, too, a summer-long saturation in Naipaul of my own has made me too conscious of any such echoes. Bissoondath works best in charting the lives of Trinidadians now living in Canada, as he does himself, writing about those who've traded the warmth of the islands, in every sense, for an economic opportunity whose cost in dislocation seems increasingly not worth paying; one such story, **"Dancing,"** told in the voice of a black Trinidadian housemaid newly come to Toronto, is far and away the most successful of the collection's dramatic monologues. And yet in one piece with the grandiose title **"Man as Plaything, Life as Mockery,"** Bissoondath does succeed not only in making his uncle's sense of placelessness his own, but in providing the sort of generalized statement about modern history that Naipaul only reached with *In a Free State*, after a decade and a half of work. In it a doctor of unspecified—one suspects East Asian—origin waits in a North American airport for the wife he left behind twenty years ago, and in remembering how he and his infant daughter had escaped the revolution that had caught his wife, comes to see his family in the terms the title suggests. The highest praise I know for this story is that it justifies that title, and makes one think that Bissoondath might, in the end, create a world of his own to write about.

Evelyn J. Hawthorne (review date Autumn 1987)

SOURCE: A review of *Digging Up the Mountains*, in *World Literature Today*, Vol. 61, No. 4, Autumn, 1987, pp. 673-4.

[*Below, Hawthorne lauds Bissoondath as a voice of marginalized peoples.*]

Digging Up the Mountains, a collection of fourteen short stories by the Trinidadian-born Canadian writer Neil Bissoondath, focuses with narrative urgency on themes of displacement, marginality, and political victimization. The protagonists of the stories are racially and ethnically diverse, such as the Japanese heroine of **"The Cage"** and the Latin Americans of **"In the Kingdom of the Golden Dust"** and **"Counting the Wind."** The majority of them however, are East Indian-Caribbeans who in many respects are the twentieth century's Wandering Jews. The stories about them put on view their status, actual and metaphorical, as exiles, especially their more recent evictions from (or pressured abandonment of) the Caribbean homeland. Bissoondath clearly blames politics and revolutionary ideas of the post-colonial, independent West Indies for the social disruptions.

In the stories **"Digging Up the Mountains," "Insecurity,"** and **"There Are a Lot of Ways to Die"** Bissoondath reveals the East Indian character under siege. His characters are dramatized as victims of ruthless and violent island politics which force them to flee the islands for their safety. One protagonist is bullied into a decision to leave Trinidad; he will thus forfeit rights to his considerable property. Another, gradually unhinged by political occurrences, marks time before he will need to leave the island but miserably hordes his money and unlawfully deposits it in a Canadian bank abroad. A third East Indian protagonist ill-advisedly returns to his island home; after becoming acutely aware of his isolation, however, and fearful about the future, he quickly decides to abandon the island for northern societies.

Migration does not provide the secure haven that East Indians and other racial groups hope for. Several stories reveal the disillusionment of these new immigrants. East Indians find that their feelings of insecurity and displacement have not abated and that, moreover, their spiritual disintegration has been hastened. Afro-Caribbeans are shown to react to their new situation with belligerence, though their stories seem less able to present their characters empathetically, their behavior made largely to seem headstrong and antisocial.

Exploring the condition of rootlessness and alienation felt by a new vintage of displaced persons, Bissoondath's stories are important to an understanding of these marginalized groups. Important too is their attempt to unmask the efficient cause of this problem—Third World political violence and turmoil, First World indifference—and thus to open a way to a dialogue. Though Bissoondath's judgments hamper narrative development and intrude upon his characterizations, his book is a thoughtful literary contribution.

Hanif Kureishi (review date 16 September 1988)

SOURCE: "Return to Casaquemada," in *New Statesman and Society,* September 16, 1988, p. 42.

[*In the following, Kureishi gives a mixed review of the novel.*]

I thought Neil Bissoondath's first collection of short stories, *Digging Up the Mountains,* was excellent. So it fascinated me to see whether this writer who had attained such cool ease over 200 meters could raise the stamina, distance and kicks of speed required for the 10,000 meters of his first novel. The answer is yes and no.

A Casual Brutality is the story, told in carefully assembled fragments, of Raj Ramsingh, a young and intelligent man of Indian extraction, growing up on the Caribbean island—"shaped like an inverted tear drop"—of Casaquemada. As a sort of wild suburb of the first world after years of colonial rule, Casaquemada is a place to leave, not a place to take over your grandfather's store. Raj, brought up by his grandparents (beautifully drawn by Bissoondath) decides to go west, to Canada, and learn to be a doctor.

It was to Toronto that Bissoondath himself went, on his uncle Vidia's advice; and it is with V. S. Naipaul's imprimatur that his nephew's book unsurprisingly comes. Apparently uncle Vidia warned young Neil against England as "a place without a future" and said "the United States is too big and will swallow you up."

In Canada Raj lives in the house of a French-Canadian woman neglected by her racist children. In this prosperous, democratic country, the old are criminally neglected. There is a powerful, moving scene in the Pleasure Dome, a glorified old people's home, where the old woman ends up, when Raj goes to visit her. He is jolted by how unfeeling the west is, by how merely functional people are.

Nearby, in a girlie bar, Raj meets his future wife Jan and she seduces him at a party. Raj himself seems to want nothing; things just happen to him. Consequently he never has much feeling for Jan and she has little for him; in fact Raj never has much feeling for anyone and is an irritatingly reserved person.

Raj fails, as well, to connect with Canada and, under the influence of a reformer who argues that the intelligent should return and do what they can for the nascent nation, the native returns to Casaquemada with wife and child. A once flourishing place, after a sugar and then an oil boom, the island is now firmly in the throes of a bad case of Naipaulitis: there is decay, corruption, sordor, filth and revolution everywhere.

Bissoondath brilliantly brings this alive through a range of characters: the old school friend now turned policeman and connoisseur of torture; Grappler, his much loved disillusioned uncle and member of the oddly absent government, once a man of independence who now says, "maybe independence for us just meant the right to loot ourselves"; and an assortment of no-good gun-toters, amateur astrologers and politicians fond of electric sex-dolls. The island, perhaps "a failed experiment in nationhood", is a sinister place, violent and out of control due to an army revolt. Things start to close in on Raj and his family. In this burning place where to have integrity is to be radically foolish, where honesty is impossible, not required, the book builds to a shattering climax.

Like Naipaul, Bissoondath is excellent at atmosphere, at place, at detail, but—again like Naipaul—he is not good at creating convincing women. This is unfortunate: a terrible marriage getting worse is bang at the center of this novel and Bissoondath just lacks, say, Updike's ability to give the tedious intricacies of love's failure some resonance and humor. (It's interesting that in an essay on Naipaul, Updike points out that "love affairs in Naipaul's fiction tend to culminate in some physical abuse of the woman", which is precisely what happens here too.)

The foreground of *A Casual Brutality* is curiously unpeopled and flat, the writing stern and overcontrolled, but the background teems with life. As a result, this novel, so full, so dramatic and necessary, seems too long and frequently unfocused.

John Lanchester (review date 5 January 1989)

SOURCE: "Foreigners," in *London Review of Books,* January 5, 1989, p. 22.

[*In the following excerpt, Lanchester feels the narrative style in* A Casual Brutality *occasionally rings false, but generally praises the novel.*]

Admirers of Neil Bissoondath's collection of stories, *Digging Up the Mountains,* who were eagerly scanning their newspapers for tidings of his first novel might be forgiven for not noticing that it had been published. But it has: and *A Casual Brutality* is a very impressive debut. Perhaps Bissoondath will have been warned not to expect too much attention by his uncle, V. S. Naipaul.

A Casual Brutality is narrated by Dr Raj Ramsingh, an Indian from the Caribbean island of Casaquemada, who has returned home after qualifying in Toronto. He brings with him his wife Jan—who rapidly starts to dislike the island and the extended-family life in which she is immersed—and his son. Dr Ramsingh's motives for returning to Casaquemada aren't entirely pure: the country is enjoying an oil boom, and some people are starting to make a lot of money. "Economics as buying spree," comments Ramsingh's uncle. "All the money did was sharpen our evils." The social structure of the island is fragile, and compromised by its history: the British who colonized Casaquemada "had other, more valuable lessons to teach, but they had paid only lip-service to their voiced ideals, had offered in the end but the evils of their actions, had propagated but the baser instincts, which took root and flourished so effortlessly in this world they called, with a kind of black humor, *new.*" The polity of Casaquemada begins to collapse and violence, both random and politically-motivated, becomes common.

Bissoondath's delightful talent for the evocation of charac-

ter and place carries the story along rapidly, and he displays an ability for elegant encapsulation—Ramsingh's shop-owning grandfather is, "in his taciturn way, a happy victim of the dictatorship of small business"—as well as for vivid *oratio recta.* (I liked the grandmother, forever boasting about her diabetes: "I sufferin from sugar.") He does, however, have another manner—a much less successful one—in which an impulse towards aphorism is given full reign. "There are times," runs the first line of the novel, "when the word *hope* is but a synonym for *illusion:* it is the most virile of perils." In the attempt to be lapidary that sentence has become tangled and fussy: nor does it help to establish an impression of Ramsingh's character. Compare the opening of a novel with which *A Casual Brutality*—deliberately?—has much in common, V. S. Naipaul's *A Bend in the River:* "The World is what it is; men who are nothing, who allow themselves to become nothing, have no place in it."

There the manner is a voice and the voice is a character. In *A Casual Brutality* I sometimes felt that the tragic events of the narrative, and the background chaos of Casaquemada, were being used as a way of setting up another excursion into world-weary sententiousness. "I have spent my life polishing shadows," the doctor says, after he has suffered the novel's central catastrophe. These unsuccessful episodes, however, are concentrated at the beginning and end of the book, when its view of life is at its bleakest and most explicit: for the most part Ramsingh-passive, weak, intelligent-is a memorable example of that tricky breed, the likeable unlikeable narrator. And anyone in this country who does read first novels will find, if they read this one, that its portrayal of a greedy, violent society, squandering once-and-for-all oil revenue, has a certain resonance.

Mervyn Morris (review date 22 January 1989)

SOURCE: "Going to Extremes and Other Tales of the New World," in *Washington Post Book World,* Vol. XIX, No. 5, January 22, 1989, p. 4.

[*In the following excerpt, Morris gives qualified praise for* A Casual Brutality.]

The narrator of *A Casual Brutality* is Raj Ramsingh, an "East Indian", born in Casaquemada (a fictional island not far from Trinidad). He has qualified as a doctor in Canada, and has married a white Canadian. Although he knows that the socio-political situation in Casaquemada (Spanish for burnt house) is unstable, Ramsingh persuades himself he must return. He goes back to the island, with his Canadian wife, Jan, and their infant son. Jan must adapt to an unfamiliar culture, which includes her husband's extended family; and Raj Ramsingh finds himself increasingly entangled in the racial and political complications of Casaquemada, a society on the edge of anarchy.

Neil Bissoondath was born in Trinidad in 1955 but left in 1973 and is now a Canadian citizen. His first book, **Digging Up the Mountains,** a collection of short stories, was published some three years ago, with a promotional quote from his uncle, V. S. Naipaul, who professed himself "staggered by the talent . . . already so developed."

A Casual Brutality, Bissoondath's first novel, captures and holds our interest through the carefully handled suspense of an eventful storyline, the emotional force of many episodes, and the sensitive presentation of several characters and various worlds.

Through the intricate structure of the work, Casaquemada gradually unfolds in historical depth and social detail. People on this island—mostly Indian or black—interact with varying degrees of tolerance, affection, hostility; and, as one character remarks, "sometimes you just can't tell who is your enemy and who is your friend." With the oil boom ended and the country in economic trouble, some who are well-off are resented by some who are not. Corruption spreads, internal authority disintegrates.

But this is not only a novel about political trouble in a third-world country. It is about the personal formation of Raj Ramsingh, about his family and other aspects of his Casaquemadan context and also about his Canadian experience. There is critical comment on Canada as well as on Casaquemada; and, like the island, Toronto is vividly presented: student lodgings, a girlie club, snow, an overnight dance party, the menace of racism, the desolation of an old people's home—all are made memorable.

Giving many instances, some of them in Canada, the novel implies that casual brutality is a regrettable constant in human experience and that self-deception will be punished. The narrative begins:

> There are times when the word *hope* is but a synonym for *illusion:* it is the most virile of perils. He who cannot discern the difference—he whose perception of reality has slipped from him, whose appreciation of honesty has withered from within—will face, at the end, a fine levied, with no appeal, with only regret coating the memory like ash.

But the novel is at its least convincing in passages such as this, when Ramsingh presents himself as having learned something generally meaningful about his profession or life, small countries or the world. Much to Bissoondath's disadvantage, they recall V. S. Naipaul narrators such as

Kripalsingh or Salim. For instance, Salim begins A *Bend in the River:* "The world is what it is; men who are nothing, who allow themselves to become nothing, have no place in it." Though the strategy is similar in the opening paragraph of *A Casual Brutality,* Ramsingh—unlike Salim—sounds mannered and self-important, and noticeably different from the Ramsingh we hear in most of the book.

Thomas Keneally (review date 26 February 1989)

SOURCE: "Home is Where the Death Squads Are," in *The New York Times Book Review,* February 26, 1989, Sec. 7, p. 14.

[*Keneally is the best-selling author of numerous books, including the widely acclaimed* Schindler's List. *Below, he finds* A Casual Brutality's *language sometimes strained and stilted, but feels Bissoondath is a writer of great potential.*]

Neil Bissoondath is a Canadian writer, born in Trinidad. He is also a nephew of the brothers V. S. and Shiva Naipaul, though he makes little of it. After all, this first novel shows he has his own fish to fry, even though they might derive from that same broad, blue, troubled sea, the Caribbean.

And like his uncles, Mr. Bissoondath writes well about the contingencies that brought Indians as indentured laborers to the West Indies, that saw the more enterprising of them become small businessmen living in awkward conjunction with former African slaves. "So there we were, African and Indian, a curious hybrid living in Spanish Casaquemada, using French poignards, dealing in offices with English clerks, driving along American highways." The children of successful Indians sent their children off to Britain, America, Canada for university education, but then the islands soured and the children became exiles abroad. It's an old story, but one that never ceases to tease the mind, especially the mind of a creative exile like Neil Bissoondath.

Casaquemada (in Spanish, burnt house) is the ominously named, fictional, exquisite island in which Dr. Raj Ramsingh, grandson of a self-improved Indian cane laborer, spends his childhood. He travels to Canada to study medicine, marries a Canadian under the pressure of having made her pregnant, has a son. "I am, by birth, Casaquemadan; by necessity disguised as choice, Canadian." His marriage is not as passionate as that of his aging Casaquemadan grandparents; it is in fact a model of what he sees as Canada's detachment and strange inverse probity: "Do not do unto others as you would not have them do unto you." Out of an amalgam of family loyalty, self-interest and the implorings of his friends, Raj returns to Casaquemada just when all its peculiarly Caribbean problems are coming to a head.

The British are long gone. "On the day that Marilyn Monroe died and Nelson Mandela was arrested, Casaquemada received its independence." The Casaquemadan prime minister is a shadowy old man who may not even be alive; the cabinet members are venal; death squads, their ranks including Raj Ramsingh's old schoolmate, summarily execute the restless. Sugar no longer commands a price, tourism has been undermined by civil unrest and the oil that gave all these grandchildren of African slaves and Indian laborers a brisk flush of affluence has also gone sour. Smoke rises from businesses torched by the mob. The air is alive with rumors that the British will send warships, the Americans the Marines, the Cubans paratroopers. Florida, so close, and Canada, so safe, seem to be the foreordained destinations on which every Casaquemadan with the price of a plane fare has his attention fixed. Yet in Toronto's steely seasons, even illegal immigrants grow wistful about the lost sweetness of Caribbean life.

In *A Casual Brutality* the equation seems to be: you can have safety, but the cost is Canadian chilliness and dispassion.

Again, Mr. Bissoondath has a wonderful sensibility for capturing the complexities and paradoxes of island life. Who could think that so many subtleties could be fitted within the boundaries of one small Caribbean island? Raj is educated by priests but performs Hindu prayers in his grandfather's garden. He is taught subtly by his grandparents, who have raised him since the death of his parents, to treasure his uncharacteristically lighter, "fair-fair" complexion and to despise those Indians who have not risen above the laborer status of their ancestors: the status, that is, of the black West Indians. He learns through the pores of his skin how to push black gardeners around. Yet he venerates the international champion West Indian cricket team, in which Indians are barely represented and in which all the cleverness is African.

Raj's complicated childhood is very appropriately brought into play as supporting evidence for the terrors of the present, as a foreshadowing of the contemporary crisis and tragedy of Casaquemada.

Yet, in the face of all the vigor and talent of this book, Mr. Bissoondath is a young writer and displays to wholehearted excess a lot of the problems of the young writer. It is specifically because this book will generate a lot of justifiable attention in the English-speaking world that these problems ought to be acknowledged.

When the narrator turns portentous, he's frightful. "The threshold between remembering and forgetting is but a membrane of transience. Yesterday was. Now is—but only for a second." Raj's admirable uncle, Grappler, an island bureau-crat, sometimes has the most awesomely wooden dialogue placed in his mouth. "Even with all the development expertise available here or abroad, we acted like a nouveau-riche nation. . . . We're a failed experiment in nationhood, Raj, one among many. We haven't matured, we still view criticism as attack." Raj's Canadian wife, Jan, is so consistently and wrongheadedly cold toward his Casaquemadan family that she becomes—to an extent far greater than the book's argument about island warmth and North American coldness demands—hateful. When the death squads come calling on her, however intellectually appalled we might be, we find it hard to weep for her.

Then there are the frankly irksome aspects of Mr. Bissoondath's energy. For example, we find occasional disorienting blasts of alliteration. "The pigeons strutted stiffly, collapsed in clucking confusion in their confining wire cages."

All these weaknesses are consistent throughout the book. They are—unhappily—as habitual as Mr. Bissoondath's powerful literary imagination. Yet, once more, when he writes of the genuinely complicated human phenomenon, he is as impeccable as any reader could desire. Raj's friend and relative Kayso, a crusading lawyer, is found dead, electrocuted in apparent commerce with a life-size sex doll. Even members of the family take the story as a viable version, one that exempts them from further action, one that settles the ghost. And as for the general population of Casaquemada, Raj reflects, "The man was dead, and the manner of his death had importance now only in its entertainment value."

The problem in this novel is that we know we have been in these tropics already, and in the hands of experts, including those of Neil Bissoondath's kinsmen and of Graham Greene. Through the egregious flaws of "A Casual Brutality," Mr. Bissoondath goes to undue trouble to remind us of that fact. But through his rough talent he fills us with hope for his future books.

Marc Côté (review date February/March 1989)

SOURCE: "Hopes or Illusions," in *The Canadian Forum*, February/March, 1989, pp. 31-2.

[*Below, Côté gives strong praise for the tone and content of* A Casual Brutality.]

In his first novel published three years after the remarkable collection of short stories *Digging Up the Mountains,* Neil Bissoondath has forged a powerful story of exploitation and violence set on a West Indian colonial island, recently proclaimed independent. First novels often show the greatest strengths and weaknesses of writers: often the style is uneven, the content overworked. *A Casual Brutality* carries none of these flaws; it is the work of a sure hand and disciplined mind.

A kind of double helix forms the structure of the novel beginning with the end of the novel in the departures room of the small Casaquemada airport. The first storyline is the present: a story without hope of the last days the narrative character, Raj Ramsingh, spends on Casaquemada. In counterpoint to this, the second storyline recounts the history of young Raj, growing up an orphan in the comfortable upperclass home of his grandparents and going to university in Toronto. Alternating between these two halves of the novel, Bissoondath compares the innocence of the boy with the alienation from self and the surrender to outside forces of the man.

Departure, alienation and surrender are not weak positions—as is cynicism which implies involvement in a conflict—these are the signifiers of defeat, of a loss of hope. From the first line of the novel, Bissoondath makes clear what hope means to his characters and story: "There are times when the word hope is but a synonym for *illusion*: it is the most virile of perils." Writing about people without hope, a story about "regret coating the memory like ash" is dangerous and difficult, even for the most experienced of writers. What saves *A Casual Brutality* from possible drone of boredom is the back and forth between past and present, the shifts in tone from innocence to experience.

Raj's story can be divided up into even thirds: life as a child in Casaquemada, pre- and medical school in Toronto, life as a husband and father back in the Caribbean.

In the Canadian section Bissoondath is extremely perceptive about our nation and its people. Raj boards with Mrs. Perroquet, widowed mother of two grown sons, in the first of several makeshift homes. The married son who lives in Guelph is good; the other is ne'er do well Andy who calls Raj a "nigger" and who forces Raj out of his mother's home when she has a stroke. Both sons, both good and bad, show little respect or concern for their mother, something Raj does not understand. While in medschool, Raj hangs out occasionally at a stripper bar and there he meets Jan, who after one night with Raj—against his will, in a way—gets pregnant and marries him. The child is miscarried, but the marriage continues of its own involuntary inertia. Through Jan, Raj is given insights into the people of his new home: "Hey, my folks are typical Canadians, man. You know, do not do unto others as you would not have them do unto you. My mum and I once went to get tickets to a show at the O'Keefe. Two windows were open. There was nobody at one, and a line of about thirty people at the other. Mum joined the line. I couldn't believe it, she joined the fucking line. I grabbed the money from her, went up to the other window. Had the tickets in a minute. You should've seen the dirty looks I got from the people in the line. And not one of them moved". In the same way, Raj and Jan remain married and Jan becomes pregnant again.

At the time of the second pregnancy the couple decide, without saying so that they are moving to Casaquemada. That nation, which received its independence "on the day that Marilyn Monroe died and Nelson Mandela was arrested", has for the years Raj has been living in Toronto experienced a false economic boom based entirely on foreign money invested in oil. Corruption isn't rampant, it's common and accepted. When one of Raj's friends—risen to the heights of fame as a civil rights lawyer—challenges a ministry of the government, he is murdered. The comment passed: the fellow was getting too big for his britches. Not sarcasm but common sense under the circumstances. All the more frightening because of the understatement.

Casaquemada's economic boom collapses just before Raj arrives with his family and the country begins its descent into the unrest of citizens suddenly expelled from paradise. Not a Caribbean problem: Algeria in October of 1988 had identical riots in the streets because its economy, based 97% on foreign investment in oil, has faltered. By a little extrapolation, the observation of what happens in fictitious Casaquemada and real Algeria can be extended to a possibility of the United States in a time when the American government has created an unreal boom based entirely on borrowed money.

Although it may seem that the politics of Casaquemada are at the core of this novel, the story never gives way to tract or heavy didactic passages. Nothing about *A Casual Brutality* is obvious or predictable: it is full of twists and turns. The characters are all likeable in indefinable ways. Raj is not a wimp, though he's powerless; Jan is not a conniving bitch, though she has manipulated Raj into marriage.

In the dedication to Anne Marcoux, Bissoondath thanks her for teaching him "among many other things/perspective"—and it is this that is Bissoondath's greatest talent.

Few successful authors are able to bring together politics, economics and creative talent to write fiction well worth reading. Neil Bissoondath is, however, a rare author who is able to write unforgettably well about a political situation without the sacrifice of his art to his beliefs. In the case of many political writers, Right and Wrong are writ large, loud and clear, beyond the reason of didactic purpose, characters and situations are made too simple; Bissoondath's story contains the complexities of good and evil as they exist everyday, mundane, soft and cloudy.

Merna Summers (review date October 1990)

SOURCE: "A Safe Place," in *Books in Canada*, Vol. XIX, No. 7, October 1990, p. 35.

[*Below, Summers reviews* On the Eve of Uncertain Tomorrows, *praising all but two of the stories.*]

A flock of pigeons flutters down toward the balcony of a Toronto apartment. An aging man, whose family duty it is to shoo them away, lets them settle, even though he knows they will foul the balcony.

> Mr. Ramgoolam figured that everybody—even birds—needed a safe place to land. Surely their wings would tire, he thought. Surely even pigeons, with their innate sense of direction, occasionally needed a point of reference from which they could reassure themselves of their place in the world.

This need for a place in the world, both physical and psychic, is a question that recurs in several of the 10 stories in Neil Bissoondath's new collection. It is seen in its most basic aspect in the title story, which concerns the world of the political refugee. A torture victim awaiting his Canadian immigration hearing, the main character visits a restaurant frequented by illegal immigrants. He thinks of the restaurant:

> It is like a closet for the soul, built for containing dusty memories of lives long past, for perpetuating the resentments of politics long past. Here, he thinks, there is no tomorrow; here, yesterday becomes forever.

The difficulty of creating a tomorrow also troubles Mr. Ramgoolam, the main character of **"Security."** Once a respected businessman in the Caribbean, he has come to Toronto to live with sons who have become "Canadian to the point of strangeness," and a wife who changes when she takes a job in an Indian restaurant, "stirring pots not her own." Mr. Ramgoolam has been unable to find work.

> Most frightening of all, though, was the realization that he too had grown away, not just from his sons, not just from his wife, but from himself. He no longer recognized himself, no longer knew who Alistair Ramgoolam was.

Mr. Ramgoolam's way of creating a space and an identity for himself is to become punctilious in the performance of Hindu religious rituals he has previously ignored, to listen to Hindi radio programs, "paying full attention to the programs, not understanding a word that was said or sung."

"Security" is a masterly story, one of the richest in the collection. Another fine story, **"Cracks and Keyholes,"** introduces the reader to an assortment of characters whose lives contain less happiness than humiliation. Again, the main character is a Caribbean immigrant, and the story, told in his voice, really sings. Lenny is a man who drifts from one minimum-wage job to another, and who at the moment is washing dishes in a strip joint on Yonge Street. The time is Christmas, and Lenny, looking at the tacky and worn street decorations, reflects that "it have few things more depressin' in this world than decorations that doesn't decorate."

> **This need for a place in the world, both physical and psychic, is a question that recurs in several of the 10 stories in Neil Bissoondath's new collection. It is seen in its most basic aspect in the title story, which concerns the world of the political refugee.**
> **—*Merna Summers***

This is a story about people trapped in their lives, about how some lives are very hard to get out of. Lenny thinks, "It ain't really a dog-eat-dog world, as my granma use to say. Is more a cat-eat-mouse world."

The title comes from a Caribbean Christmas story. In the tropics, where there are no chimneys, Santa is said to be able to get in and out by making himself very small, so that he can pass through the cracks and keyholes.

"The Arctic Landscape High Above the Equator" is set in an unnamed Latin American country, where American policy is concentrated on undermining stability. It is an attempt to investigate the conflict between the sacred impulses of the individual soul and the conditioned sense of duty. A diplomat, knowing that his lover's father is about to be assassinated, does not warn her because "he is too well trained for that."

Present and past repeatedly illuminate each other in Bissoondath's stories, and the meaning often comes out of the tension between them. In **"Goodnight, Mr. Slade,"** an old man, Mr. Goldman, is being evicted from the apartment building where he has been the caretaker, to be put into a nursing home. As the story moves along, we become aware that this is the second time that Mr. Goldman has been robbed of his world. A survivor of the Nazi death camps, he finally chooses suicide over entering the nursing home, refusing, as he sees it, "to allow my life to be turned once more into nonsense."

It is unfortunate that the two stories that seemed to me not to work very well—the ambitious **"Kira and Anya"** and the rather slight and inept **"Smoke"**—should have been placed immediately after the opening story. Putting them so near the beginning of the book may mislead readers into thinking that this is the best Bissoondath can do, and that would be a pity. Fine stories lie ahead. The best that Bissoondath can do is very good indeed.

Branko Gorjup (review date Spring 1991)

SOURCE: A review of *On the Eve of Uncertain Tomorrows,* in *World Literature Today,* Vol. 65, No. 2, Spring, 1991, pp. 353-54.

[*Below, Gorjup favorably assesses* On the Eve of Uncertain Tomorrows. *He notes that Bissoondath expands the concept of "immigrant" to include the "internal immigrant," defined as the individual isolated from a sense of belonging in his or her own land.*]

Immigrant writing has long been a staple of North American literature, enjoyed and studied for its wealth of powerful drama. Originating in the individual's conflict between a haunting memory of the past and an uncertain vision of the future, this drama has assumed different manifestations encompassing a wide range of issues, from escape and exile to a search for an alternative homeland. In addition, it has brought to our attention the complexity of the individual in a state of crisis, when such questions as survival, identity, loyalty, dignity, self-esteem, and self-affirmation begin to dominate an embattled psyche.

Neil Bissoondath's new collection of stories, *On the Eve of Uncertain Tomorrows,* deals with the precarious and fragile world of the immigrant, a world occupying the narrow and barren territory that extends somewhere between "departures" and "arrivals." However, in some of the selections Bissoondath stretches the meaning of the word *immigrant* beyond its sociological significance—usually denoting uprooted and displaced humans from other geocultural regions of the world—to symbolize a condition of not belonging to one's "own" country. Alicia in **"A Life of Goodbyes"** is such an "internal" immigrant. After twenty years of "itinerant life," she discovers with a sense of bitterness and resignation that she can no longer "reinsert" herself into a place which she had called her hometown. She also realizes that her "wanderings had come so easily largely because of that vague notion of a center, a place to go back to," but in her absence the center "grew fluid" and eventually "erased itself." With the illusion of the "center" thus shattered, what is left for Alicia is a life of circumference.

The majority of the stories, however, focus on "external"

immigrants, those individuals who had seen Canada as a possible destination where a life of normalcy, after a life of economic hardship and political degradation, could be reinstated. Such a life of normalcy, as Bissoondath's characters quickly find out, is not easily realized. Most of them fall victim to a crippling sense of despair and anxiety, as their identities disintegrate in the face of an incomprehensible present and an uncertain tomorrow. The chief reason for much of their spiritual turmoil, besides the host country's inhospitable and insensitive response, comes from their inability to break with the past. In **"Security,"** for example, Mr. Ramgoolam becomes more obsessed with his ancestral gods as the traditional role of the head of the family begins to slip away from him. The further he withdraws into his religion, though only into its ceremonial and histrionic dimension, the more intensely he experiences alienation from his wife and sons, whose determination to become integrated into the new society collides with his disjointed vision of a past that never was.

Hope may be illusory, but it is, as Bissoondath's characters experience it, a potent force, sometimes even miraculous, in helping us confront the unexpected.
—Branko Gorjup

An overwhelming sense of loneliness, futility, and resignation, depicted in a variety of images suggesting enclosure and entrapment, runs as a leitmotiv through the entire collection and is nowhere more disturbingly presented than in the title story. **"On the Eve of Uncertain Tomorrows"** recalls the atmosphere of Dante's limbo, of a world without meaningful coordinates in which individuals are destined to an undefinable and aimless life and whose only hope of escape is, if they are strong enough, into an uncertain tomorrow, if not—and unlike in Dante—into death. The central image of enclosure in the story is a cafe, appropriately called "La Barricada," in which a group of immigrants gather for the comfort of being together and to relive in silence their memories of torture. It is a place that, as Joaquin, the protagonist, describes, "emphasizes somehow its sense of spirit broken into timidity. It is like a closet for the soul, built for containing dusty memories of lives long lost." It is in this decrepit hollow that Joaquin, a victim of brutal torture, together with other compatriots from Latin America, awaits the day he will be "processed" by the immigration office, knowing that his only hope of remaining in Canada lies in his severely mutilated body. In spite of the fact that La Barricada is the only place in an uncomprehending and indifferent world where people like Joaquin can experience a sense of belonging, it is also a place where there is no tomorrow, where "yesterday becomes forever." Joaquin, like so many characters in other stories, becomes aware that the real prisons are in our heads and that consequently "we must learn how to make the keys for when our tomorrow comes."

Hope may be illusory, but it is, as Bissoondath's characters experience it, a potent force, sometimes even miraculous, in helping us confront the unexpected. In this sense the remarkable new collection by one of Canada's most respected young writers shows us how we can, even in moments of greatest uncertainty, learn the vital lesson of, ultimately, who we are.

Janice Vaudry (review date March 1991)

SOURCE: A review of *On the Eve of Uncertain Tomorrows,* in *A Reviewing Journal of Canadian Materials for Young People,* March, 1991, p. 114.

[*Below, Vaudry praises* On the Eve of Uncertain Tomorrows *as a compendium of the immigrant experience.*]

"It is the violence of beating wings that attracts Joaquin's attentions"; and so begins **On the Eve of Uncertain Tomorrows,** Neil Bissoondath's third fictional work. It is, however, the solid, consistent and moving writing that attracts *our* attention and holds it through this collection of short stories. The ten stories included cover a wide range geographically, emotionally and experientially. While one would expect V. S. Naipaul's nephew to write of the immigrant experience, concentrating on those from the Caribbean, he has gone beyond.

The first story, which bears the same title as the collection, reveals to us the extent of his intended scope as it treats of the emotional rollercoaster suffered by seven awaiting word on their refugee status in Canada. It drives home to us the absurdity of weighing up against each other the experiences of those who have escaped hardship, pain and suffering. Are we any less cruel by allowing them to stay in Canada until we decide that no, they have not suffered quite enough or that no, the danger in their homeland is not as imminent as believed? Bissoondath shows us that we all face uncertain tomorrows, some filled with physical dangers, others with emotional or social upheaval and change.

While we might expect Bissoondath's characters all to come from his Trinidadian/Canadian background they are drawn from a varied pool. He takes us from Montreal to Toronto and from Spain to South America to World War II Paris. In so doing he reveals to us the link of our experiences, that we all carry vestiges of our past and of our parents' pasts with us, and that change is a constancy. Whether it be Mr. Slade contemplating the move into a retirement home or Monica's realization that life in Toronto is unlike that on the

island, Bissoondath's characters all speak to us of their strength.

This is a highly recommended book for senior levels. It could be used on its own to generate discussion at several levels including the immigrant experience, the diversity of Canadian culture and of the changes and decisions that face each of us in our lifetime. It could also be contrasted with the experiences of immigrants in other countries, for example Samuel Selvon's *Lonely Londoners.*

"Here under this web of convention, [is] gold." The attraction of this work is immense, forcing us out of our shells of safety to confront all our uncertain tomorrows.

Jim Shephard (review date 26 May 1991)

SOURCE: "Keeping It Short: A Season of Stories; Trading One World for Another," in *New York Times Book Review,* May 26, 1991, p. 3.

[*Below, Shephard feels that Bissoondath's sensibilities intrude too much into the narrative of* On the Eve of Uncertain Tomorrows, *but the stories are important statements about the disenfranchised.*]

The Polish poet Adam Zagajewski, in his poem "Song of an Emigre," has his exiles begin their address to us in this way: "We come into being in alien cities. / We call them native but not for long. / We are allowed to admire their walls and spires. / From east to west we go, and in front of us / rolls the huge circle of a flaming / sun through which, nimbly, as in a circus, / a tamed lion jumps."

Neil Bissoondath's **On the Eve of Uncertain Tomorrows,** concerned as it is with that spiritual and material anguish of exiles, seems both an impressive collection of stories and a persuasive document of historical witness. Mr. Bissoondath, who was born in Trinidad in 1955 and emigrated to Canada in 1973, has written before on this subject, in a previous story collection, **Digging Up the Mountains,** and a novel, **A Casual Brutality,** but in this new book the focus on the plight of the exile seems more persistent. Much of this collection's power comes from the reader's sense that these fictions will not let go of their subject until we have acknowledged a whole people's pain. Even the stories' titles suggest the relentlessness with which these concerns are addressed: **"Security," "Cracks and Keyholes," "A Life of Goodbyes," "Things Best Forgotten"** and, of course, the title story.

Mr. Bissoondath's characters range from the dispossessed to those who have never possessed much in the first place, all living with the enervation and the resentment of having been forced by political or economic necessity to trade one world for another. Most of the stories locate characters cherishing a past warmth—emotional and meteorological—in a dismal, cold and low-rent Toronto, a world of "balconies cluttered with discards or strung with laundry lines," of "Yuffies and Vuffies, young urban failures and veteran urban failures."

For nearly all these characters, Canada and the West stand in for a dream denied, and for nearly all of them there is no going back. They find themselves working for people who "lived by only their own, deeply held priorities," people in whom "the spirit of slavery was not quite extinguished." They contrast a past life in which they demanded little, and usually got more than expected, with a present life that seems a barrage of promises, an ever-growing complex of dissatisfactions. They watch their families break apart into different and independent lives. They know they are not unusual.

They have what they recognize as "acute immigrant obsessions: success, provision, a gentle invisibility." They are dealing with the cruelties of context—living in situations that make them, they feel, everything they are. Most frightening of all is their realization that they have grown away not only from sons and daughters, wives and husbands, old homes and old ways, but also from themselves.

In the title story, a former electrician and union organizer named Joaquin, hands destroyed by torture, shares his holding pen of a rooming house with an Arab, a Vietnamese couple, a Haitian, a Sikh and a Sri Lankan while they all await word from their lawyer as to the fate of their requests for political asylum. In another story, **"Kira and Anya,"** two young women writing for magazines at opposite ends of the ideological spectrum together interview the man who wrecked their families, the old despot who caused their exile and, finally, his own. And in **"Things Best Forgotten,"** a father and son return to Spain to confront an old man who served on the firing squad that killed the son's grandfather.

The situation of Mr. Ramgoolam in **"Security"** is typical: "On the island, someone had always been there: his mother, his wife, a maid. But now—curious thought—his wife went out to work. His eldest son—after years of residence here, Canadian to the point of strangeness—was at his desk in a big, black office tower downtown, a telephone receiver plastered to one ear, a computer terminal sitting luminescent on his desk."

Typical also of this passage are some of the strengths and weaknesses of the stories as a whole: the honest directness of their exploration of the emotional situation, as well as the often unremarkable, workmanlike quality of the prose. One cheers the rich mix of sympathy and indictment embodied in that parenthetical "curious thought," even as one laments

the unsubtle familiarity of the thematic point of that telephone "plastered" to an ear, or that desk, that office and that computer terminal.

There is throughout the collection, despite its focus on the dispossessed, a heartening range of protagonists, of voices: a 65-year-old building superintendent, supplanted from Vienna to Paris to Toronto, comparing all three cities; a young schlemiel of a salesman with only enough self-awareness to manage a dim and distressed understanding of his life as a "map of conventionality"; a C.I.A. spook tracking within himself the signs of a conscience that seems to him ill directed, both bureaucratically threatening and ideologically treasonous; a half-black, half-Indian dishwasher in a strip joint, streetwise but still more idealistic than he realizes; a restive, middle-aged loner who at 37 abruptly effaced her old life (mother, husband) for a solitary life of travel; an utterly exhausted mother of five who worked as a nanny while having to neglect her own children, and who now works as a cleaning woman while having to neglect her own house.

But while the moral insight behind the stories seems admirable, the social urgency that propels them at times seems to hinder the esthetic shaping we expect. Thus a story like the title one seems determined to lay out for us the full spectrum of anxieties and hurdles that confront the illegal immigrant, whatever its effect on our sense of the form and persuasiveness of the central characters' experience.

And while there's a commendable straightforwardness in the stories' attempts to further explore and articulate the various characters' emotional complexities, that impulse occasionally slips into an intrusive kind of authorial prompting that calls to mind 19th-century novels in its desire to do the reader's interpretive work: "Did she dare? How could she tell him that part of her still loved him or, at least, still loved the man he had once been?" A character musing upon some pigeons "in fluttering desperation" against a wall of chicken wire, while he himself is trapped in a rooming house awaiting news of possible deportation, is, we're told, "the one confined, by the chicken wire and by so much more." This same character's apartment is like "a closet for the soul, built for containing dusty memories of lives long lost, for perpetuating the resentments of politics long past. Here, he thinks, there is no tomorrow; here, yesterday becomes forever."

That desire on the part of a governing intelligence to take over the stories, to insure proper interpretive response, at times makes the fiction seem more manifesto than felt experience. One can sense that guiding hand most often with the stories' attempts at closure, when the ironies underline rather than expand our sense of what we've been coming to learn, when those ironies are a bit too crashing: an old torturer who dreams of the kind of peace he finds in a painting of a Venetian canal is killed while standing before it; a mediocre young man's obsessive pursuit of a woman is transformed in a revelatory moment when he discovers that her overlooked friend will do just as well; an exile reduced to contemplating the wreck of his life while gazing upon the spectacle of "The Price Is Right" imagines himself exhorted to "come on down!" when he suffers a fatal heart attack; an old survivor of the Holocaust, faced with abandonment in a nursing home, chooses to do what the Nazis failed to.

But the best stories overcome such weaknesses and provide us with those moments—glimpses into the heartbreaking and resilient worlds of these exiles—that are generous enough, and tender enough, to form the heart of what we carry away from the collection, what we remember. The torture victim waiting to hear whether or not he will be sent back to his own country gazes again upon those pigeons and notes that their "lack of beauty denies them his sympathy." The wife of an old torturer appears in early photographs as a solemn bride, "as if already doubting her luck." That same torturer, after a flare-up, reassumes control "as if shrugging into a coat."

A man remembers his emigre father standing before the bathroom mirror, "quietly working on his pronunciation of *with*—'vis, vis, vit, vith, ou-iss, ou-ith.'" A cleaning woman recalls the humiliation of being instructed by her employer concerning the right way to shut the front door and decides, every lunchtime, to eat her meager meal from her employer's best crystal and silverware. A mother refuses to take pride "solely in what she has been able to provide for her children," since "as accomplishment it is too selfless; as autobiography, too despairing."

That spectrum of human response, from the selfless to the despairing, is what Neil Bissoondath writes about. In doing so, he speaks for the silenced voices that continue to fill the margins of our societies, the voices of those so overworked and underrewarded that the term "disadvantaged" is inadequate to describe them. At one point, one of the collection's characters, the victim of torture, recognizes that his destroyed hands are understood by his friends "as simply part of the universal damage." It is often Mr. Bissoondath's achievement that we are given a sense of the scope of that damage without losing sight of the individuals who are forced to endure it.

Edward Hower (review date 30 June 1991)

SOURCE: "By the Rivers of Babylon," in *Washington Post Book World,* June 30, 1991, p. 10.

[*Edward Hower is the author of three novels and of* The Pomegranate Princess, *a book of Indian folktales. Below, he favorably reviews* On the Eve of Uncertain Tomorrows.]

Displaced persons, the exiles among us, have always been popular figures in fiction. Looking through their eyes, we are given a vivid, unfamiliar perspective on our familiar world that forces us to evaluate our lives in ways we have never considered before.

Most of the characters in Neil Bissoondath's superb collection of 10 stories, **On the Eve of Uncertain Tomorrows,** are outsiders of one kind or another, and all have something important to tell us about ourselves and our assumptions. The author, a Trinidadian of East Indian ancestry who has lived in Canada since 1973, has a special feeling for people struggling to hang onto the traditions of their homelands while learning to survive in an alien urban environment.

Some of his characters manage to sustain themselves with small triumphs of humanity. In one story, the janitor of a strip-joint wins a dancer's friendship with his tales of a Caribbean Santa Claus slipping through cracks and keyholes of chimneyless tropical houses, though he can't find the magic to convince her to stop throwing away her life. A West Indian maid, working in the luxurious flat of a solitary young woman executive, finds the strength to assert herself within her own family.

Other outsiders don't fare so well. A once-prosperous East Indian merchant, trying to sell noisy vacuum cleaners in Canada, remembers how his house was cleaned on his native Caribbean island with a coconut-branch broom that "made a sweet, soft sound, a soothing swish that evoked in its trail the clucking of chickens and the distant bleat of a grazing goat." When he tries to light bowls of oil to observe a Hindu religious ceremony, the clouds of smoke bring the fire department crashing into his apartment. Finally, he is reduced to watching television game shows while his formerly submissive wife finds a new life as a restaurant cook. The author's sympathetic view of his character transcends the story's sadness, and the merchant's defeat becomes an eloquent tragedy.

Bissoondath's collection is full of variety—of characters, moods, styles, situations. All his stories show an awareness of Life's cruelty, but in some, humor is the best way to deal with it. A lonely Canadian salesman takes up smoking in order to have something in common with a beautiful woman in his French class; when she rebuffs him he has only his new addiction for consolation, until he takes a fresh look at his teacher.

In another story, a woman returns from her travels to her ex-husband's house, bringing along her current lover, a young South Sea islander. He is dismayed to learn that the tropical fish he once caught for export are being mistreated in pet shops. She has something to be dismayed about, too—she discovers, that she still loves her husband, though he has found happiness in a homosexual relationship. Somehow, the visit is concluded amicably, with the woman better understanding her compulsive search for new adventures.

When fiction leaves us less secure with what we think we know about the world, the effect can be painfully illuminating. In the powerful title story, two refugees await a court's decision about whether they are to be granted asylum or deported. Amin, an Arab, is determined to become "Amin Thompson, Canadian" in order to escape certain execution if he is sent home. His friend Joseph has been so brutally tortured in a Latin-American prison that he has become mute. When Amin's fate is decided, Joaquin briefly finds his voice again, but has nothing but rage to express with it. Life's only certainty, we discover, is that knowing where we belong and where we will live tomorrow can never be taken for granted.

The characters in *On the Eve of Uncertain Tomorrows,* the author's third book, are all memorable and beautifully drawn, even in the couple of stories whose plotting goes astray. Like Salman Rushdie, V. S. Naipaul, Bharati Mukherjee, Hanif Kureishi and other writers of what might be called the East Indian diaspora, Neil Bissoondath has learned to turn his exile to his advantage. This story collection is finally neither Canadian nor of the "Third World," but universal in its appeal and absolutely original. This is a work of compelling integrity and compassion.

Frank Birbalsingh (review date Spring 1992)

SOURCE: A review of the author's writing in *Canadian Literature,* No. 132, Spring, 1992, pp. 101-02.

[*In the following review, Birbalsingh gives a concise overview of Bissoondath's fiction.*]

One writer who should have no complaints about being neglected is Neil Bissoondath from Trinidad. From the appearance of his first book *Digging up the Mountains,* (1985) a collection of stories, Bissoondath has established himself as the most important South Asian writer of Indo-Caribbean origin, although he would reject such a label of himself, and claim that he is merely a Canadian writer. Since *Digging up the Mountains,* Bissoondath has written a novel *A Casual Brutality* (1988) and another collection of stories *On the Eve of Uncertain Tomorrows* (1990).

Bissoondath's writing stands out by its self-confidence and critical sharpness. The stories in his first volume, for instance, advance the view that after settling in the Caribbean

for one hundred and fifty years, Indians may be forced to emigrate, in which case the Caribbean would have to be regarded just as a stopover for them, on their journey from India to other destinations. Stories such as **"Insecurity"** and **"Digging up the Mountains"** illustrate a real threat to Indian security in the Caribbean, and this is no doubt one factor motivating Indians to emigrate from the region. Obviously, this is not a view that would endear Bissoondath to Caribbean governments, especially those in Guyana and Trinidad.

But all the stories in *Digging up the Mountains* are not as political as this. **"The Christmas Lunch"** for instance, is set in Canada, and exposes the suppressed frustration and puzzlement of Caribbean immigrants when first confronted with some Canadian habits and customs. The result is a feeling of not belonging—to Canada, the Caribbean, or anywhere. Bissoondath reveals a similar feeling in stories involving East European and Japanese characters, the implication being that insecurity leading to emigration and a sense of homelessness are phenomena of modern twentieth century life. This is what links his fiction to that of his uncle V. S. Naipaul, whose writing provides perhaps the most complete fictional study of exile and homelessness in the postcolonial era.

Bissoondath's novel centers on Raj Ramsingh an Indo-Caribbean doctor who moves between Canada and the Caribbean, surrounded by events of violence and terror, and images of chaos and collapse. In the end, after the death of his Canadian wife and their son, he flees from his home island, which, at that stage, is bracing itself for an apparent invasion by American forces similar to the American invasion of Grenada in 1984. *A Casual Brutality* has more overtly political implications than the author's short stories: its portrait of the Caribbean is one of decay and disintegration, and the recurrent images in the novel are those of brutality, insensitivity, forlornness and annihilation.

The stories in *On the Eve of Uncertain Tomorrows* offer further meditation on brutality and disorder leading to emigration and exile, except that the focus is on immigrants living in Canada. The immigrants come from equally inhospitable backgrounds, whether of Caribbean chaos and brutality, or Latin American political persecution. For example, the title story recounts the interaction of several refugees—a Haitian, Sikh, and Sri Lankan, as well as a Vietnamese couple—living together in one house in a Canadian city. They are all forced into homelessness by a shared background of starvation, civil war, forced conscription and economic, deprivation, and their common fate is summed up by the unnerving sense of loss, uncertainty and feeble vulnerability that consumes one protagonist, as he awaits deportation from Canada, and possible death in his homeland.

The story **"Security"** in Bissoondath's second collection is a sequel to **"Insecurity"** in his first. In the earlier story Ramgolam was living in fear of persecution and death in the Caribbean. In the later story he is an immigrant living with his wife and sons in Toronto. He is no longer in fear of his life, but he is bored at home, aimlessly watching television and burdened by thought about his sons being transformed by living in Canada into barbarians who eat beef and pork, despite being brought up as Hindus. The fact is that Ramgolam is just as insecure as he was in the Caribbean, only in a different way. His situation compares with that of V. S. Naipaul's hero Ralph Singh who, in *The Mimic Men* escapes from the disorder of his Caribbean island to London, the supposedly stable center of Empire, only to find "a greater disorder" there. Through characters like Ramgolam, Bissoondath illustrates the futility of immigration and the essential inadequacy of being human.

Among South Asian Canadian writers from the Caribbean, Bissoondath may be regarded as the most perceptive and skilled commentator on characteristic themes of disorder and persecution leading to flight or displacement, and ultimately to uncertainty or inner disorder. Bissoondath's success is due partly to an Atwoodian grasp of topical issues, an analytic intelligence reminiscent of V. S. Naipaul, and a technical fluency all his own. His stories are packed with authoritative detail presented with naturalness and conviction. At the same time, this very perfection of technique carries a touch of perfunctory professionalism. This is most true of some non-Caribbean stories, but it may also be seen in **"Power of Reason"** (in his second volume) in which we are given a wonderfully exact portrait of the West Indian protagonist Monica, including excellent descriptions of her jobs, personal relationships and domestic circumstances. Yet the power of the technique itself contributes to Monica's inability to cope, and her eventual victimization: it makes it less likely that she will triumph over her circumstances. By the same token, it is the studied technique that increases the impact of stories like **"Insecurity"** and **"Security."**

Thomas Hastings (review date Spring 1993)

SOURCE: "Uncertainty," in *Canadian Literature*, Spring 1993, pp. 146-7.

[In the following, Hastings reviews several stories from On the Eve of Uncertain Tomorrows.*]*

In **"Cracks and Keyholes,"** perhaps the best story in Neil Bissoondath's recent collection of short fiction, *On the Eve of Uncertain Tomorrows,* Lenny, a Caribbean immigrant who has lived in Canada for fifteen years and presently finds himself washing beer mugs at a run-down strip-joint in Toronto, proclaims, "I's livin' proof that not every immigrant is a multicultural success story." For Lenny, as for a number of characters in this uneven collection of ten stories, life doesn't always work out the way it is supposed to. Consequently, the individual effort to take control of the future by making sense of the present moment is an important theme in these stories. As the collection's title suggests, Bissoondath's characters stand precariously on the eve of a better tomorrow.

What that tomorrow will bring is, however, never clear. In the title story, for example, a political refugee waiting for landed immigrant status dreams at one moment about "fantasies of tomorrow" and then admits a short while later that "there is no tomorrow . . . yesterday is forever." For a number of characters the only future that awaits them is death, or what one character calls "glances of uncertainty."

Images of death and dying permeate the collection. Three of the stories conclude with the central character losing consciousness in the throes of death. **"The Arctic Landscape High above the Equator"** ends as the protagonist "feels himself beginning to shatter" and **"Security"** ends with the protagonist "blinded by the light." While offering a significant narrative challenge, such episodes also imbue Bisoondath's stories with a darker ethos than any of his earlier writing. The word "uncertainty," or variations of it, appears in almost every story.

While the injustice of everyday living, from the inevitability of death to the insidiousness of immigration lawyers and the disrespect of children for their parents, is a common concern in these stories, the effort of the human will to triumph over the tyranny of everyday living is equally important. In the excellent story **"The Power of Reason,"** Monica, a single mother with five children, overcomes the feeling of stagnation that has infected her life by correcting the sense of alienation that has developed between her and her three sons. Although she understands her sons when they are at home because they speak with an "island accent" that she is familiar with, she does not know who they are when she hears them on the street as "they speak in a dialect not of the island, not even of Canada, which would not have surprised her, but of black America." Eventually Monica kicks her sons out of her small apartment. In doing so she not only stops their freeloading but forces them to take responsibility for their own lives as their sisters have. In this small act of defiance Monica relearns the power both to reason and to love.

Although **"Smoke"** and **"Kira and Anya"** are uninspired, bordering on banality, and **"A Life of Goodbyes"** is inexcusable for its homophobic presentation of a gay male couple, the best stories in this collection, **"Crack and Keyholes," "The Power of Reason"** and **"On the Eve of Un-**

certain Tomorrows," are those which chronicle the inequities of a world irreparably fractured along numerous class, gender and racial lines and the efforts of individuals to mend those ruptures.

Carole Giangrande (review date Fall 1993)

SOURCE: "Urban Logos," in *Books in Canada,* Vol. XXII, No. 1, Fall, 1993, pp. 43-4.

[*In the following review, Giangrande describes* The Innocence of Age *as "a book with a strangely engrossing mix of banality and wisdom."*]

Faced with the distressing truths of racism, poverty, and crime, city dwellers find insight and wisdom in short supply these days. Neil Bissoondath's latest novel, *The Innocence of Age,* appears to offer some of both. It tells the story of a father-son conflict that embodies the clash of old, genteel Toronto and the new multicultural city of cold glitz and destitution.

It's a good, readable tale, and Bissoondath tells it with honesty and sensitivity. Yet it's only occasionally moving, and too often falls into trite and predictable ruts. It's possible that the author harbored some back-of-the-mind anxieties about whom he might offend—no small worry in a novel with a multiracial cast of characters, set in a city where touchiness rivals baseball as a pastime.

Some of the male characters are no more than rapacious stereotypes. And it seems churlish to complain about Lorraine, a good-as-gold '90s gal who handles hammers and popovers with equal dispatch. Nevertheless, readers of Bissoondath's previous work know he can create characters who are more vivid and less clichéd than these.

Pasco, the central character, is a long-time Toronto resident, the owner of a greasy spoon and five years a widower. His life consists of work, the friendship of cronies at a nearby pub, and the lonely sifting-through of memories and unfinished conversations with his late wife, Edna. Pasco's son Danny has no use for his dad's crowd, or for the city's unfortunates, people he derides as losers. He's a yuppie creep who prattles on about bucks and business to his staid old man. With true Toronto hubris, Danny decides to renovate Pasco's house for the eventual resale value and his dad offers scant resistance to a disruption he hates. It's hard to sympathize with Danny, and at this point in the story, it's equally hard to respect Pasco, who plays doormat to his son's Gucci shoes.

Gradually we learn that Pasco is driven by guilt to pander to a kid whose values he despises. It turns out he'd never

paid back the nest egg he'd borrowed from Edna to open his restaurant—money that should have gone toward his son's education. Never mind that; Danny's managed to get an education of another kind. He's a protégé of Mr. Simmons, a real-estate developer and archetypal Toronto villain, who pontificates on the value of "profit, profit and more profit" and the joys of rent-gouging. The man functions as a signpost directing the traffic of the plot around him; an urban logo of evil, but hardly a fleshed-out character.

Mr. Simmons has a seamy—yet quite predictable—hidden life. His maltreatment of Sita, a tenant who is an illegal immigrant, provides the novel with its most gripping and horrific scene. When Danny overhears them, it forces his mothballed conscience out of drydock and into troubled waters.

Meanwhile Pasco has gotten chummy with his widowed neighbor Lorraine, who's as good-hearted in her own way as Simmons is awful. As a friend of Pasco's late wife, she's an anchor to the past and to some of its less savory truths. All these she tells us as she cooks comfort food, dashes off to her job at the crisis center, and struggles to come to terms with her daughter's lesbian lifestyle. It seems the only thing she doesn't do is sleep.

Lorraine puts Pasco in a better frame of mind as he tries to be of help to one of his drinking buddies. Montgomery, an immigrant from Grenada, is (along with Sita) the most vital character in the novel. He's a minor character, but when he speaks, his words carry the weight of his soul. He is ultimately a tragic figure who seems capable of both love and foolishness. Likewise, Sita combines fear and terror with survivor's grit, and a glance or a word from her alludes to depth that's just below the surface.

More often than not, the book has too much awkward dialogue, too many wooden statements of opinion that keep us from feeling the heart at work. Yet Bissoondath effectively conveys a sense of Danny's emptiness as a component of his larger, soulless city. He has an exacting eye for the character and detail of Toronto and its street life. Best of all, he shows a subtle and genuine sense of the process of grieving, and of the long, meandering road it takes through one man's life. Pasco finally frees himself of grief through a symbolic act that joins his past to present suffering and hope. It's a satisfying ending for *The Innocence of Age,* a book with a strangely engrossing mix of banality and wisdom.

Sandra Martin (review date November 1994)

SOURCE: "Debating the M-Word," in *Quill & Quire,* Vol. 60, No. 11, November, 1994, p. 27.

[*In the following review, Martin praises Bissoondath for having the courage to speak against the politically correct dogma of multiculturalism in his book* Selling Illusions.]

Some people will say that Neil Bissoondath's *Selling Illusions: The Cult of Multiculturalism in Canada* is a brave book. Many will say that only somebody like Bissoondath—a writer of color—could get away with writing it. Both of those statements should be irrelevant to any discussion of the merits of Bissoondath's thesis and its articulation. The fact that they aren't is an indication of the fear that can stifle debate in this country. That fear makes us hesitate to express views that might be controversial, unpalatable, or distasteful because we are afraid that those who disagree, or who find our opinions offensive, will condemn not only our ideas, but us—for having the temerity to voice them.

Bissoondath acknowledges this problem in the first few pages of his polemic about the shortcomings of multiculturalism as a public policy. He claims that "the countering of criticism with accusation is a tactic not unfamiliar to me. My own attempts to contribute to public discourse have been met with nervous silence, a certain vilification and, finally, the explicit demand at one conference that I *Shut up!* since criticism of multicultural policy, I was told, served only 'to encourage racists like the Reform Party.'" He argues that a free and healthy society must be wary of all orthodoxies. In his view, orthodoxy is itself a form of tyranny, "with ideology—political, social, racial, financial—as its angry deity."

Bissoondath, the author of two books of short stories and two novels, *A Casual Brutality* and *The Innocence of Age,* is celebrated as a fiction writer. *Selling Illusions* is his first nonfiction book. On one level it is a diatribe against a public policy that he finds bankrupt, but on another, more personal, level it is the story of his own experience living under that policy. It is hard to separate the two, for naturally Bissoondath's experience has influenced his thinking about multiculturalism. Another person with a different background, set of talents, aspirations, connections, or luck, might well have a different reaction—or, indeed, no reaction at all.

Multiculturalism became official government policy in 1971 to "support and encourage the various cultures and ethnic groups that give structure and vitality to our society," as then-Prime Minister Pierre Trudeau said at the time. "They will be encouraged," Trudeau continued, "to share their cultural expression and values with other Canadians and so contribute to a richer life for us all."

Two years later, Bissoondath, aged 18, left his native Trinidad and arrived at York University in Toronto as an undergraduate. From the beginning he wanted to belong. For him, this country "offered hope" and was "a land worthy of commitment." What he found, though, was that he wasn't being asked to make any sacrifices, or to abandon old traditions to fit in with new ways. To his chagrin, "you did not have to adjust yourself to the society, the society was obligated to accommodate itself to you."

Bissoondath blames multiculturalism. He argues that Trudeau introduced multiculturalism not only as a sop to solicit immigrant votes, but as a means of putting Quebec in its place. He quotes *Le Devoir* publisher Lise Bissonette on why multiculturalism has never been as popular in Quebec as elsewhere in Canada. "Carried over into Quebec this multiculturalism would be suicidal, since it tends to make francophones a minority like the others."

And that, essentially, is Bissoondath's main complaint about multiculturalism. He believes that it highlights our superficial differences and undermines our essential sameness. By encouraging us to stress our cultural differences, Bissoondath argues, multiculturalism promotes divisiveness rather than solidarity.

Our sameness, he says, is that we all want to be Canadians, and that except for Native Peoples, we all came here—whether it was 200 years ago or last week—because we didn't want to be where we were anymore. We were looking for something better for ourselves and our children. He thinks multiculturalism is preventing us from realizing this dream and argues eloquently that we should remove personal culture and ethnicity from public policy. Heritage, he believes, belongs to the individual, and should be celebrated privately and unofficially.

What I like best about *Selling Illusions* is that it exists. I admire the cogent, forceful, and well-documented argument Bissoondath has engaged that multiculturalism leads to the simplification of culture, not its enhancement. His book has made me re-examine a policy that I had accepted as one of the benefits of being Canadian. He may be a little over-sensitive when he says that anybody critical of multicultural policy is immediately branded "racist," but I share his anxiety that he and not his arguments will be debated in the weeks following the book's publication.

I thought a lot about *Selling Illusions* when I went to the University of New Brunswick to a conference called "When Rights Collide," late in September. It was organized in the aftermath of the 1993 Matin Yaqzan debacle. He's the math professor who supplied an article to the student newspaper in which he argued that the date rape of a "promiscuous" girl was much less serious than the violation of a virgin. Yaqzan suggested that a sexually experienced young woman who was the victim of unwanted sexual intercourse should seek monetary redress for her "inconvenience" and "discomfort" and leave the moral outrage to others.

Yaqzan elicited so much moral outrage himself for his absurd views that he was suspended, barred from the UNB campus, and subjected to a performance review of his entire career, which spanned nearly 30 years. That decision by the university administration created its own furor on the editorial pages and talk shows of the nation, and Yaqzan was subsequently re-instated, and then offered an early retirement package that he seemed unable to refuse.

The Yaqzan incident—the appearance of his date rape article, his suspension, and re-instatement—all took place within 14 days. The speed with which it occurred astonished me. It sometimes takes longer to send a letter across the country. The university administration reacted so quickly that it didn't have time to isolate the issues, let alone think them through. As a result, the university damaged its own reputation—a reputation that it was still trying to cleanse almost a year later at a conference in which freedom of speech was pitted against the protective tenets entrenched in UNB's sexual harassment code.

It is indeed scary to live in a society in which one can be condemned for expressing thoughts and ideas that unwittingly give offense. There is little recourse today from the pernicious charge of being a racist or a sexual harasser. Those terms carry with them such a presumption of guilt that even if the accusation is eventually withdrawn, the damage has been done. Let's hope it doesn't happen to Neil Bissoondath.

As a postscript, let me add that while I was in Fredericton I read *The Coffin Tree* and *Irrawaddy Tango,* two novels by Wendy Law-Yone, the American writer who was to read in October at the International Festival of Authors in Toronto. Law-Yone was born in Burma (now Myanmar)—she relates the story of her escape from that tragic and terribly repressive country in the recently published *Without A Guide: Contemporary Women's Travel Adventures,* edited by Katherine Govier. Law-Yone's novels are psychological and political case sheets about torture and corruption. They are not in the least sentimental or self-pitying, but they are harrowing. If nothing else, they are a powerful reminder that in this country you can, if you have the courage, still say what you want. You may be criticized, you may be ostracized, but at least you won't be hauled off to the torture chamber.

Janice Kulyk Keefer (review date November 1994)

SOURCE: "The Center: Can it Hold?" in *Books in Canada,* Vol. XXIII, No. 8, November, 1994, pp. 32-3.

[*Below, Keefer argues against the premise of Bissoondath's* Selling Illusions.]

Neil Bissoondath has discovered the root of all evil in contemporary Canada: not economic collapse or the devastation of our environment, but multiculturalism. Bissoondath contends that multiculturalism has cost Canadians any fixed sense of who we collectively are by eradicating that center that we yearn to have "bind" us. Equating multiculturalism with apartheid, racialism, and ethnic ghettoization, he accuses it of destroying that unifying, Anglo-centric "old Canada" so many of us supposedly found so comforting. The only alternative to multiculturalism Bissoondath deigns to sketch out, however, is a vaguely envisioned Canada

> where inherent differences and inherent similarities meld easily and where no one is alienated with hyphenation. A nation of cultural hybrids, where every individual is unique, every individual distinct. And every individual is Canadian, undiluted and undivided.

The trouble with *Selling Illusions* is not only that Bissoondath, despite his claims to be free of ideology, is pushing a liberal and *laissez-faire* individualism that went out about the time of the Great Depression; he also never defines for us in any persuasive or significant manner just what it means to be pure "Canadian," other than to possess a colder climate and to be quieter and more peace-loving than Americans. His exemplary Canadian immigrant experience turns out to be that of the Ignatieff family, whom he turns into Slavic Horatio Algers. Yet it's his own attitudes toward both his country of birth and country of adoption that Bissoondath is really trying to sell, and this leads him into some slippery maneuvers. Thus he attacks other Canadian writers, notably activist members of the Black, Asian, and Native communities, for attempting to curtail or destroy freedom of expression and imagination, while he himself is unaccepting of writers whose imaginations are energized by a sense of double belonging to here and "there"—artists who may be third-generation Canadians, but for whom ethnicity has everything to do with an inexpungeable historical and cultural awareness of the countries their families chose to or were forced to abandon. One of the most puzzling aspects of *Selling Illusions* is, in fact, Bissoondath's blindness to the fact that Canada's embrace of multi- rather than bi-culturalism has greatly assisted the emergence and positive reception of writers such as Kogawa, Ondaatje, Mistry, and Ricci, who have explored cultural difference and the dynamic of ethnicity with all the power, sophistication, and vision that Bissoondath's caricature of multiculturalism, Toronto's "Caravan," lacks.

There is nothing particularly new or inspiring in this book, which is more a compendium of right-of-center truisms and the multicultural equivalent of suburban myths than a vigorous polemic. Parts of the book are difficult to digest, not because of the complexity of Bissoondath's ideas, but because of the infelicity of his prose. Mixed metaphors abound; his diction is sometimes faulty, as when he uses the term "corollary" where "opposite" would be the logical choice, or describes the fears of certain Canadians regarding non-European immigrants as "legitimate" when one would hope he means "strong" or "real." His vision of Canadian campuses being invaded by the equivalent of Nazi stormtroopers who shut down free discussion is bizarrely exaggerated, and his presentation of certain antimulticulturalists disingenuous: Doreen Kimura, for example, he introduces as the eminent neuropsychologist she is, but he neglects to inform us that as the president of the Society for Academic Freedom and Scholarship, a neo-conservative organization opposing the post-structuralist "paradigm shift" in the humanities, and linked to right-wing American organizations like the National Association of Scholars, she is of precisely that species of "ideologue" he otherwise excoriates.

While Bissoondath does acknowledge that the "old Canada" had its virulently racist moments, and while he occasionally makes valid points about the excesses of some present-day anti-racists, his presentation of multiculturalism is badly flawed by his inability to distinguish between what Linda Hutcheon has called the ideal and the ideology of multiculturalism. The ideal I would describe as a global phenomenon that, far from being Trudeau's brain child, is as much a part of the late-20th-century *Zeitgeist* as is postmodernism. It has been discussed as a positive and necessary development by thinkers of the caliber of Adam Michnik and Jürgen Habermas. The ideology as we know it in Canada can be linked to the state's attempts to control and trivialize the efforts of those formerly marginalized or silenced to empower themselves. Debunked the latter must certainly be—junked the former should not and cannot be. In trying to throw out the baby with the bathwater, Bissoondath himself ends up sailing down the drain, while the baby cries out, as lustily as ever, for some truly enlightened attention.

John Stanley (review date 1994)

SOURCE: A review of *Selling Illusions: The Cult of Multiculturalism in Canada,* in *Canadian Book Review Annual,* edited by Joyce M. Wilson, 1994, pp. 354-55.

[*In the following, Stanley negatively critiques the premise of* Selling Illusions.]

Multiculturalism has been an object of attack since its conception in 1967, in the report of the Royal Commission on Bilingualism and Biculturalism. As an important literary figure, and as one of the "ethnics" who presumably benefits

from multicultural policies and programs, Neil Bissoondath carries weight as a critic.

Unfortunately, his book is marred by minor slips (Elaine, not Diane, Ziemba is the Ontario Minister of Citizenship), sleights of hand, misleading juxtapositions, and simple ignorance. Bissoondath discusses Prime Minister Trudeau's introduction of a multiculturalism policy but immediately quotes from the Canadian Multiculturalism Act (1988), legislation from Mulroney, not the Trudeau government. Moreover, Bissoondath accepts without question the Quebec nationalist explanation for Trudeau's policy; he does not even mention the view that Trudeau introduced Multiculturalism in order to balance a bilingualism policy for Quebec with a multiculturalism policy for the West, a region with a very different history of settlement and almost no francophones.

Bissoondath also boldly states that Canada, a country without a state religion, is devoted to the separation of church and state. Any reader of the British North America Act (1867), or the Act incorporating Newfoundland into Confederation, would recognize that this American doctrine has almost no role in Canada. In discussing the famous 1993 advertisement for an Ontario government senior management position aimed exclusively at equity groups, the author confuses employment equity and anti-racism policies with multiculturalism, which was hardly favored by Ontario's NDP government. Somehow, even book-banning in Alberta school boards and the "culture of victimhood" get tied to multiculturalism!

Ultimately, critics of multiculturalism, whether from the right or from the left, are in the same camp, refusing to acknowledge the diversity inherent in Canadian cultures. Policies of multiculturalism, employment equity, and anti-racism are designed to ensure social justice and to promote the "peace, order, and good government" that are among the traditions all Canadians cherish. The importance of Bissoondath's book lies not in its inconsistent arguments but in its reflection of our difficult times.

Penny Van Toorn (interview date Winter 1995)

SOURCE: "Building on Common Ground: An interview with Neil Bissondath," in *Canadian Literature,* No. 147, Winter, 1995, pp. 127-35.

[*In the interview below, Bisoondath discusses his family history and other influences on his writing.*]

[*Van Toorn:*] *Tell me about your family history.*

[Bissoondath]: Both sides of the family left India to come to Trinidad as indentured laborers to work in the sugar cane plantations. It would have been my great grandparents, around the turn of the century. And they decided to stay. The Naipaul side were from the state of Madhya Pradesh. My uncle [V. S. Naipaul] has written about a sad trip he made to the village in *An Area of Darkness*.

And you've never attempted such a trip?

No, I have no particular attraction to India.

As the eldest child in a literary family, was there pressure on you to do something or be somebody?

When it comes to my immediate family, there was never any pressure in particular to do anything. There was simply the idea that you would leave Trinidad, you *would* move to another country to live, and there was a good chance you would not return. I left Trinidad willingly, happily, looking forward to a new kind of life. The idea of being a writer, which was one that came to me at a very early age—around nine or ten—was something that I could not do in Trinidad, and was something that I was looking forward to trying to do in this country. But there was never any pressure. There was a sort of passive support. It was simply a question of "You do what you have to do." They let me do it with their fingers crossed. Certainly with my mother there were fingers crossed. My mother died in 1983, in fact just a few months before my first book was published, which is something that I'll never quite get over, the fact that she never saw it. After my mother died, about a year or a year and a half later, my father remarried and they then moved to Toronto, but not long after arriving in Toronto my father discovered that he had cancer. So he returned to Trinidad and died there in 1990.

You've written a good deal about parents and children, and the tensions that exist beside strong bonds of gratitude and loyalty and love.

Leaving Trinidad at eighteen, I never really got to meet my parents as an adult. My mother died before any of that could be done. And so when my father moved to Toronto, I thought, this is my opportunity to try to get to know him directly, as one adult to another, and to talk about things openly and honestly and without rancor of any kind, and with love. But of course, we could not meet on that level. My father was not the kind of man who was capable of discussing things other than politics and sports. It simply wasn't possible to meet him on the emotional level that I wanted. He was shaped by his own life. It was not a society in which people talked to each other in the way I wanted to talk to my father. But at least I had the opportunity to try. I'm hoping that I won't fall into the same traps as my father, and

that I'll be able to have a different kind of relationship with my daughter.

Is Alistair Ramgoolam based on your father?

The Alistair Ramgoolam in **"Insecurity"** was not based directly on my father. He was based on a kind of businessman that I knew in Trinidad. Whereas the Alistair Ramgoolam in **"Security"** *was* informed more by my father, and the kind of life I saw him leading in Toronto. It was not a successful move to Toronto. He had come out of one kind of society and tried to insert himself into another, and I don't think he was happy in the end. He started to move towards a kind of Hinduism, a kind of ritual belief, or a belief in ritual.

Was that Hindu element present in your home when you were growing up in Trinidad?

No, it was not a religious household. My grandparents practiced Hinduism. My parents never did. I am very skeptical about religious belief and mysticism in general. It's not something that I understand. So many people just seem to depend on the ritual, in a hollow gesture that's unsupported by any kind of philosophy.

From your account of your father's inability to communicate certain ranges of feeling and experience, would it be valid to infer that Trinidadian society is very much a male-dominated society?

Yes, Trinidad is a very macho society. Canada was different. It was a kind of liberation. I grew up in Trinidad never really feeling quite at home there. I grew up in a family that read—which was my mother, and her sisters, the Naipaul family—but very few people in Trinidad enjoyed reading or the things that concerned me. So it was a society from which I felt fairly alienated. I was born in Arima, but I never actually lived there. My parents lived in a town called Sangre Grande, and that's where I grew up. My grandfather, like all his brothers, owned a store, so my father worked for him. The store was in Sangre Grande, and I went to Presbyterian primary school that had been started by Canadian missionaries. When I was about 13 or 14, my parents decided to build a house in Port of Spain, so that we would be closer to school. I went to Catholic high school, St. Mary's College. The school in **"An Arrangement of Shadows"** is based on St. Mary's.

I gather that your family were in relatively comfortable circumstances financially.

That's right. There are a substantial number of East Indians who have risen into the professions, so have become doctors and lawyers, and particularly businessmen. But I would think that the vast majority remain field workers. They cut the sugar cane.

Did you feel, as an East Indian, that you were part of a racial/political minority in Trinidad, despite your family's relatively privileged financial position?

There was the knowledge that politics would be divided along racial lines. But you also grow up with the attitude or belief that everybody's a thief. And it didn't matter really who formed the government or who formed the opposition. It just gave you greater opportunity to steal, and whoever was in power would steal. I suppose we were very cynical about politics. Everybody knows who is stealing politically, And then, in the class, in the circles in which we grew up, we were not really aware of the rural Indians. Although my grandparents started off life working in the rice paddies and the sugar cane fields, by the time my generation was growing up, we were traveling the world. We were thinking professionally, and that cut us off from the kind of life my grandparents had known, and that the majority of Indians still know in Trinidad.

A Casual Brutality *reads at times like autobiography.*

There's an autobiographical connection in almost everything that I've written, but it's autobiographical on different levels. It's not the story of my family, which remains to be written I think. But the people I've depicted are based on a variety of people that I knew when I was growing up in Trinidad. The grandmother, for example, is the archetypal Hindu Trinidadian grandmother. Everybody had one.

One of the things that novel seems to do is say farewell to Trinidad. Was there any sense in which you wrote **A Casual Brutality** *to explain to yourself, or to anybody else, why you left?*

That's a very interesting question. I've never thought of that. I felt when I'd finished that book that I had written it out. I was dealing there with things which had obsessed me for a long time throughout my growing up to the age of 18 in Trinidad. And then after that too, just hearing from family what was going on there. It's also things like the invasion, the takeover, on Grenada.

So you're running various places together.

Yes, Casaquemada is not simply Trinidad. It's mixture of Guyana, Trinidad, Jamaica, Grenada. What I've tried to do in creating Casaquemada is to create an island that will remind people of many places. The reason I didn't use a real island in the West Indies was to get away from any particular identification with one island and its particular problems, to try to internationalize it.

A Casual Brutality *has been criticized for precisely this lack of historical specificity.*

That would have come from someone who assumed that I had some kind of political agenda. I have no political agenda.

Has your experience of Trinidadian society and politics shaped your views on Canadian multiculturalism?

Absolutely. Absolutely. When you look at the kind of life that I had in Trinidad, the kind of upbringing, the attitudes that were offered of other races, the way various races viewed each other, I understand the kind of vision that creates apartheid, and I abhor it. I have seen people insist on dividing themselves for racial reasons, and religious reasons, and ethnic reasons, and I reject any idea of division. My reading of multiculturalism as practiced here in Canada is that it is a policy of division. It's a policy that falsifies the vision it pretends it wants to preserve. I find it simpleminded at best and I think it holds some dangers for us if we continue with it.

But surely the political implications of division depend on whether it is voluntary or imposed, and even then, the outcome can be ambivalent. Secession can be a way of avoiding being swallowed up by another society, but it can also trap people on a lower stratum of the vertical mosaic.

Yes, it's very complicated. I have to say that the criticisms that Bharati [Mukherjee] has leveled at Canadian multiculturalism I wholeheartedly agree with. I disagree, though, with her view of the United States and the melting pot. The American system likes to pretend that it is possible for individuals to shrug off their past, to pretend that it does not exist, and assume a new identity. Whereas the Canadian one says that it is possible to freeze the past, and maintain it as it used to exist, while the country one left, by the way, continues to evolve. The melting pot and the mosaic—they're equally false. There has to be a middle way. And the first part is to have governments and bureaucrats get out of it. I feel very strongly about that. And so my attitude, simply put, is leave it to the individual. Tradition is all very important, but it is up to the individuals and their families to preserve these things. When you start getting Government policy shaping this, we're entering some very dangerous waters.

You view Canadian society in a more positive light than, say, Himani Bannerji or Aruna Srivastava. Do you see the racism they speak of as being bound up with sexism?

That's very difficult for me to say. It may be. It's very difficult for me to talk about, because racism exists. I know it does. I keep thinking, my God, I grew up with more racism in Trinidad than you would find in this entire country. I have seen racism. I have lived with it. I grew up with racism. I know what racism is about. One of the areas in which I disagree with Bharati Mukherjee is where she talks about her preference for the United States because Canadian racism is always so polite—"You'd never know he's racist." Whereas the American racist is up front and direct. But my response to that is that I would rather have a racist who ignores me, or who says "Good morning" and then turns away, than one who puts a gun to my head and kills me.

You've seen that in Trinidad.

Exactly. I have seen the brutality, and I would rather live in a society where racism is unacceptable enough that even racists are not quite prepared to proclaim it openly. That isn't to deny that racism exists but that's how you deal with it.

Having grown up in a highly racist society, do you ever find yourself falling into racist patterns of thought?

Yeah, I do at times. We all catch ourselves at different moments. Sometimes I hear my father's voice in myself. I don't like it, but I know where it comes from. For example, when you hear reporting from the Middle East and I think, my god, those damned Arabs. And I think, No, wait a minute, think about this.

One critic has accused you of turning your back on your people.

Who are my people? I fear the automatic assumption of racial allegiance. My friends are of different colors, genders, sexual preferences, religions and so on.

As a writer, do you see yourself as part of any group of community, or as participating in any particular school or tradition?

I think I'm on my own path. When you get right down to it, when you're sitting in front of the typewriter or computer, you are working on your own path and no other path matters. Yet at the same time I've rather enjoyed belonging to one group I've been put into, and that is the group of writers who have emerged from the former British colonies. What is it—the empire strikes back? Although the only thing that unites us is the fact that we have a certain similarity of historical background. Apart from that, when I'm asked how I describe myself, I respond, "I am a Canadian writer," for the simple reason that that entails so much. It's a wonderful big box. You can put just about anything into that. Anything smaller would make me feel, I suppose, sort of enclosed.

You once mentioned that you dislike experimental writing.

I don't know why people would bother to not use periods or commas for example. I rather like paragraphs. I like a page that looks like a page. When people start using visual tricks on the page, I feel I'm being cheated, and I feel that this is somebody who has to stand on his head to transmit what he wants to say, and I don't think that's really necessary. I get irritated very easily by these kinds of things. And I cannot now read most of the Latin American writing. Mario Vargas Llosa is one exception. I love his work.

What are you trying to accomplish in your detailed descriptions of houses, streetscapes, and landscapes?

In the descriptive passages I'm trying to get as precise a feel for the place in which my character is as it's possible to get. What I'm interested in is individuals in a context, and the context is as important to me as the individual. The context informs the individual, and so the description is important to understanding the character, because what you're seeing is description not through Neil Bissoondath's eyes but through the character's eyes. How the character sees things tells you a lot about the character.

Do you see your descriptions functioning on symbolic or metaphorical levels as well?

No, I don't think on those levels at all. I'm not aware of them.

How do you think your work has changed or evolved since the stories of **Digging Up the Mountains?** *In* **The Innocence of Age,** *your immediate focus moves away from the Caribbean, yet some of your earlier themes and preoccupations—things apparently derived from your Trinidadian background—remain.*

Well yes, there are universal themes. The universality of human emotion in the end will inform all of my writing. The writer in Afghanistan whose son is killed by a Russian bullet, she feels the same pain as the mother in Latin America whose son is killed by an American bullet. That pain is the same. And where the damn bullet is made makes no difference. And this is the universality. When you strip away all the exoticism of different societies, you come down to the same basic naked emotions.

When so many people are striving to assert social difference, you're working in the other direction, looking for the common ground.

I think it's very easy to split people apart. I'd like to think I'm looking for the common ground. And I think that's more difficult. I get accused of all kinds of things. I've been called all kinds of nasty names. There's this controversy over appropriation of voice. What is amazing to me is that a lot the people who are saying that one does not have the right to appropriate another voice—to use their word—are also the people who march against apartheid. Those who would keep voices apart in literature are the ones who want to bring them together by getting rid of apartheid. There are basic contradictions in this stand. We spend our lives appropriating. And it's a basic human thing to do. It's one of the ways we learn from each other, and we learn to get along.

Some of your critics have taken issue with your portrayal of women. They say the women in your stories aren't real.

Well, I disagree with that. I like to think that my women are very real. A number of women—most of my readers seem to be women—have come up to me at readings and various functions, to talk to me about my women characters. A story like **"The Cage"** for example, about a Japanese woman, it's one that people still comment on continuously and positively. After reading that story, one woman from Malaysia told a friend of mine "I've never met him but it's as if he understood something of my own life." Now all I can do is go on that kind of reader reaction. I like women, and in fact I think that sometimes my female characters are more convincing than my males.

In **The Innocence of Age,** *the women were more real. I guess I found Jan in* **A Casual Brutality** *a little less . . .*

Yes. Jan has brought up a lot of adverse comment. One person said, "God, what would Canadian women think of the portrait of themselves through Jan in **A Casual Brutality?** But my point is I am not writing about Canadian capital-W Woman. I'm writing about one woman, and I insist on that always, that my characters are individuals unto themselves. They are not representative of any group, any race, any culture, any more than any of us is. I'm not a representative of my gender. I'm not a spokesman for my race, and my characters aren't either. Jan happens to be the kind of person she is. She may not be a very nice person, but, hey, I've met some people who aren't very nice, and some of them are Canadian women. Some of them are West Indian women, or West Indian men, or American. The problem is that this kind of criticism is almost a misunderstanding of what fiction, from a novelist's point of view, is all about. I'm writing about individuals.

Has having a daughter changed your perception of what it means to be a female in this world?

I don't think it's changed it. I think it's sharpened it. I don't think I ever had any illusion about what it means to be a female in this world. And I think every man continues to learn. You can't live in Montreal where the Polytechnic massacre took place without appreciating what it is like. You can't grow up in a family of women as I did—with many aunts and a working mother—and not realize what it's like in a society like Trinidad. When our daughter grows up I want her to learn karate, because I want her to be able to kick the balls out of any guy that tries to take advantage of her. I have lots of friends who are female and professional and you hear lots of stories of what goes on. It's unbelievable what goes on even among the most supposedly educated and liberal and open and professional people. I am determined that our daughter will do whatever she wants to do, will have none of these barriers put in her place, otherwise I'm going to have to kick a few balls myself.

Do you confer with anybody when you write?

I write completely alone. But the first person to read it once I've done it and am completely happy with it is Anne, my partner. And I listen to her very carefully. She's a very good reader. I trust her opinion. It's wonderful to have someone that you can actually trust. It's indispensable. I've made some significant changes on her advice.

Where do your ideas about writing and literary value come from?

I think they have just come up from my own reading and writing—being forced to think about it because people like you ask me questions. There's no formal thought behind it. It just evolved. I never studied English literature at university. In high school in Trinidad, the teaching of English literature was horrendous. There are writers I still cannot read. Like Henry James. The teachers at high school took these books, these things that I loved, and forced us to do autopsies on them, and of course you know what happens at the end of an autopsy. What are you left with? Certainly not anything that's living and breathing. And so when it came time to decide what to major in at university I decided to go for French for the simple reason that I liked the language. I'd studied it in high school, and I was determined never to take the chance again of having my love of English writing destroyed.

You studied Spanish at high school as well.

That's right.

And English was always your first language?

That's right.

Was Hindi ever spoken in your home?

Not a word. Never. The only people who spoke Hindi in Trinidad when I was growing up were my grandparents' generation.

When were you last in Trinidad?

In 1983 at my mother's funeral.

Ten years ago.

God yes, ten years. A long time ago now.

Marilyn Iwama (review date Winter 1996)

SOURCE: "Shaping Ethnicity," in *Canadian Literature,* No. 151, Winter 1996, pp. 171-72.

[*Below, Iwama criticizes the logic of* Selling Illusions.]

Neil Bissoondath describes *Selling Illusions* as his "personal attempt to grapple with" the policy of multiculturalism in Canada. The personal nature of this text is palpable. Complementing Bissoondath's views on multiculturalism are the story of his immigration to Canada from Trinidad, a chat about his family and friends, and a detailed rendering of the "creative process" of his writing. The reader learns Bissoondath's opinions on a constellation of topics surrounding politics and art, including his lengthy rebuttal of certain criticisms of his own art. For the reader concerned with the decontextualized interplay of writer, text, and critic, *Selling Illusions* is, then, a helpful volume.

But the policy of multiculturalism affects all Canadians, and by also promising "to look at where we are and how we got there," Bissoondath engages in a more public discourse, if not analysis, of Canadian political and social history as they relate to ethnicity. Regrettably, Bissoondath's discussion is constrained by a simplification of ethnicity heavily dependent on media sources and isolated quotations, sometimes uncited or selected from John Colombo's *Dictionary of Canadian Quotations* (1991). It is at this level that *Selling Illusions* flounders.

A strong component in critical discussions of ethnicity over the past two decades has been the substantial interdisciplinary effort invested in observing and articulating the process of racialization. Bissoondath acknowledges the entrance of the term "racialization" into the discourse on racism, claiming not to know the word, either, he says, through na-ivete, or his "distance from racial concepts and politics." Earlier in the text, he muses that racialization "seems to imply . . . to see life and all its ramifications through the color of one's own skin." Resting on his definition, Bissoondath's commentary skirts the complexities of racialization, and diminishes historical injustices it has caused. Simultaneously, his conviction that a racialized subjectivity is simply a matter of individual choice allows Bissoondath to subsume—as he does—individuals with a racialized sense of self under categories like the Nazi regime, and "the architects and defenders of apartheid."

Throughout *Selling Illusions,* Bissoondath links ethnicity with geography, the undeveloped imagination, the past, and an "ethnic" nationalism which entails patriotism, empire and exclusion. Bissoondath describes the dominant center of the "old Canada" as having been made "void" by the country's present "multicoloured" social reality. His desire is that Canadians fill this national void with a controlled "multiplicity of voices and visions," a center that would be, nonetheless, "distinct and firm and recognizably Canadian." This Canada would enjoy the inclusive "civit" nationalism that Bissoondath finds in Quebec.

The polemic of *Selling Illusions* rests on Bissoondath's equation of ethnicity with the subjection of mature selfhood to the "confines" of one's cultural past and skin color. Just as he asserts that the individual can choose to be racialized, Bissoondath stresses that each Canadian is free to choose between "continuing to be what one's parents have been" and the "psychological revolution" he has enjoyed, in coming to a lighter dependence on one's heritage "to guide or succor." Because Bissoondath constructs ethnicity and "race" as an individual matter of choice, multiculturalism as public policy is, *a priori,* flawed.

More ominous is Bissoondath's corollary that voices identifying systemic racism in Canada are "crying wolf," and that the most effective way to eliminate racism is for individuals to counter it with "an immediate challenge." Bissoondath decries the "culture of victimhood . . . the threads of which stitch themselves through the ideas of multiculturalism." Having constructed parameters of ethnicity that do not exceed individual responsibility Bissoondath must then denounce the social reality of victimization. Such a construction also facilitates his comparison of the call for "punitive" redress of past injustices with "arguing that the victims of torture must be allowed to torture their torturers."

Additional coverage of Bissoondath's life and work is contained in the following sources published by Gale: *Contemporary Authors,* **Vol. 136; and** *DISCovering Authors: Canadian.*

Guillermo Cabrera Infante

1929-

(Has also written under pseudonym of G. Cain) Cuban-born novelist, short story writer, essayist, critic, sketch writer, journalist, and translator.

The following entry presents an overview of Cabrera Infante's career through 1996. For further information on his life and works, see *CLC*, Volumes 5, 25, and 45.

INTRODUCTION

Cabrera Infante is a Cuban-born writer noted for his word-play, his use of humor and sexual imagery, and his opposition to the Communist regime that took power in Cuba in 1959. Initially a supporter of Fidel Castro's revolution and an official of the regime, Cabrera Infante left Cuba in 1965. Two years later he published *Tres tristes tigres* (1967; *Three Trapped Tigers*) his most critically acclaimed work. Like most of Cabrera Infante's fiction, the novel has a setting in pre-revolutionary Cuba, and makes extensive use of humorous and erotic wordplay. Cabrera Infante began his writing career as a film reviewer in the 1950s and continues to write essays, sketches, and nonfiction ranging from the whimsical to the somber.

Biographical Information

The son of a journalist, Cabrera Infante grew up in Cuba during the 1930s and 1940s. He attended the University of Havana, and graduated in 1956. By that time he had already begun to publish film reviews under the pseudonym G. Cain, a shortened version of his own name. An opponent of Cuba's dictator, Fulgencio Batista, Cabrera Infante spent a brief period in prison for using "English profanities" in a short story published in the literary journal *Bohemia*. He later supported the Castro revolution against Batista. After the new government took power in 1959, Cabrera Infante received a post on the Bureau of Cultural Affairs, and became director of the journal *Lunes de Revolución*. In 1961 Castro censored a film by Cabrera Infante's brother depicting Havana's night life during the Batista era and Cabrera Infante's revolutionary fervor cooled. He left Cuba for a diplomatic assignment in Belgium in 1965, and did not return. At about the same time, Cabrera Infante won Spain's Biblioteca Breva Prize for an unfinished novel that would be published, in greatly changed form, as *Three Trapped Tigers* in 1967. Cabrera Infante, who became a naturalized British citizen, participated in the translation of several of his works, and in 1986 published his first book written in English, *Holy Smoke*. Most of his work, however, has maintained its Cuban focus.

In 1993 he produced *Mea Cuba,* a collection of essays and other short fiction pieces on the subject of his homeland. In the same year he presented for the first time in English a collection of short stories called *Writes of Passage* that he had published in Havana three decades earlier.

Major Works

Cabrera Infante's most well-known work is the novel *Three Trapped Tigers,* which he described to Rita Guibert in 1973 as "a joke lasting about five hundred pages." Written in the Cuban Spanish vernacular as it is spoken on the streets of Havana, the book is a narrative of the city's night life in the pre-Castro era. It is a tale filled with puns, double entendre, and other forms of wordplay, often humorous and sexual in nature. Cabrera Infante's second novel, *La Habana para un infante difunto* (1979; *Infante's Inferno*) also employed linguistic acrobatics, erotic themes, and a semi-autobiographical tale of a youth's initiation into sexual mysteries. Cabrera Infante has published several short-story collections in Spanish and English, as well as a number of nonfiction works. Among the latter are *Un oficio del siglo XX* (1963; *A Twen-*

tieth-Century Job*), a book of film reviews; *Vista del amanecer en el trópico* (1974; *A View of Dawn in the Tropics*), a collection of sketches that chronicles the history of repression in Cuba; and *Holy Smoke* (1986), a lighthearted look at the history of the cigar. Among his most notable works in the 1990s was *Mea Cuba* (1993), a collection of essays, criticism, and letters.

Critical Reception

The rich linguistic material in *Three Trapped Tigers* made it a success with reviewers. Cabrera Infante's portrayal of a nighttime world in the novel earned comparisons to the "Nighttown" episode of James Joyce's *Ulysses,* and his whimsical use of language invited references not only to Joyce, but to Lewis Carroll. Cabrera Infante's continued reliance on intricate puns in his later work has subjected him to charges of literary indulgence. Alma Guillermoprieto, reviewing *Mea Cuba,* referred to the author as a "bombastic punster"; and Richard Eder, in a review of the same work, observed that Cabrera Infante's penchant for wordplay "energizes him, perhaps, but it depletes the reader." As one who has written in English and translated several of his works into that language, Cabrera Infante has been likened to Josef Conrad and Vladimir Nabokov, and has often been cited for his facility with a language not his own. His outspoken opposition to the Castro regime has invited equal helpings of praise and blame, and even those not overtly sympathetic to the regime have faulted Cabrera Infante for his tendency to use his writings as a platform for his political views.

PRINCIPAL WORKS

Así en la paz como en la guerra [*In Peace as in War*] (short stories) 1960
*Un oficio del siglo XX [*A Twentieth-Century Job*] (criticism) 1963
Tres tristes tigres [*Three Trapped Tigers*] (novel) 1967
Vista del amanecer en el trópico [*A View of Dawn in the Tropics*] (sketches) 1974
Exorcismos de esti(l)o [*Exorcizing a Sty(le)*] (prose) 1976
Arcadia todas las noches (criticism) 1978
La Habana para un infante difunto [*Infante's Inferno*] (novel) 1979
Holy Smoke: Anatomy of a Vice (nonfiction) 1986
Mea Cuba (essays, criticism, and letters) 1993
†Writes of Passage (short stories) 1993
Delito por bailar el chachachá (novellas) 1996

*Under pseudonym G. Cain. English edition published 1992.
†First published in Havana in 1960.

CRITICISM

Claudia Cairo Resnick (essay date Fall/Winter 1976)

SOURCE: "The Use of Jokes in Cabrera Infante's *Tres Tristes Tigres* [*Three Trapped Tigers*]," in *Latin American Literary Review,* Vol. V, No. 9, Fall/Winter, 1976, pp. 14-21.

[*In the following essay, Resnick explores themes of humor and sexuality in* Tres tristes tigres.]

Cabrera Infante's *Tres Tristes Tigres* [*Three Trapped Tigers*] continually underlines the interrelation of humor, language and sexuality. The humor in this novel is immediately evident to any reader, and has received some attention in several critical studies, most of which tend to emphasize its linguistic aspects. One article discusses the problems of translating not only the jokes, puns, and anagrams but the whole atmosphere of the novel. Another posits the text as a novel about language and literature in which verbal games serve to point out, among other things, an underlying sexual obsession in which masturbation is a recurrent theme. A third critic suggests the importance of masturbation in its relation to the verbal games in *Tres Tristes Tigres* but does not develop the idea further. To my knowledge, the only study to attempt an analysis of the humor in its relation to the subconscious or to sexual motifs is that of José Sánchez Boudy, but it is often inaccurate, myopic and unsatisfactory. A few examples will show why this is so.

In a section entitled "Meanings of importance for the understanding of *Tres Tristes Tigres*" Boudy interprets some of the text's best jokes, but his comments are often misleading. For the expression *forro romano* [Roman condom] he simply lists beside it *foro romano* [Roman forum]. This reveals nothing. He does not deal with the play on the two words, where *forro* [condom] is substituted for *foro* [forum], although the context shows that the Master of Ceremonies has intentionally used the term. As Siemens has indicated, the opening monologue in which this "joke" appears can be construed as a perverted genesis which from the outset is doomed; he cites the inherent contradiction of a name such as Minerva Eros (a minor character) as evidence. Perhaps this view of the Tropicana Club (where the action begins) as a giant Cuban condom is also a manifestation of the unrealized human potential and of the sterility in the lives of its actors/spectators/characters. The same joke serves to point out another of the great themes of the book, much discussed by the critics: that of *traduttori-traditori* [translator-betrayer]. The Master of Ceremonies does not translate his own joke although throughout his monologue he has been providing the English version for the benefit of his American audience. This suggests the constant betrayal which even an author is forced to perform to his own text. On a third level, the joke simply contains an obscene reference to the activities which the darkness of the nightclub facilitates.

Under the category of "Parodies," which he does not care to define, Sánchez Boudy states that La Estrellas's pathetic cry, *"Ay, negro, qué dolor, qué dolor"* ["Oh, Black man, such pain, such pain"] is a parody of a very popular Cuban children's song, which runs *"Mambrú se fue a la guerra, qué dolor, qué dolor, qué pena."* ["Mambrú went to war, such pain, such pain, such sorrow"]. That song is French in origin and is common throughout Latin America. But beyond that, what is the sense of making La Estrella's sorrow into a parody? She is physically obscene and emotionally pathetic; are we to believe that she is capable of self-parody? The clarification makes as much sense as stating that *"qué dolor"* is a free Spanish rendition of *Oy veh*!

In explaining another joke, Boudy interprets *"los melones pal mercado"* ["take the melons to market"] as a reference to the green uniforms worn by the Communist forces. Perhaps there is some expression in Cuba in which melons mean Commies, but such a reading is absolutely useless in this particular context. (*Tres Tristes Tigres*, p. 76) The phrase is shouted out to Codac as he speeds by a well-lit intersection; next to him is seated Manolito el Toro [Manolito the Bull] who has unbuttoned her shirt and is exposing her huge breasts. The 'melons' are a reference to the size of her breasts; any reader could grasp that without Boudy's help. For Boudy the unconscious is nothing more than a memory retrieval bank; he merely adopts a few Freudian terms, such as 'the subconscious' and cites Freud's work on jokes, but does not apply his theory.

What does Freud really say about jokes? He first enumerates various models on which innocent jokes are built, categorizing them according to their techniques. Thus he describes such techniques as word or thought condensation, allusion, representation through the opposite, play on words, puns, shift of emphasis, and nonsense. The section of *Tres Tristes Tigres* entitled "Bachata," and in particular Chapters XVI through XVIII, have an abundance of such innocent jokes. Here Arsen and Silvestre pick up Beba and Magalena and proceed to irritate them by using a language which is incomprehensible to the two women. Arsenio and Silvestre use puns, changes of emphasis, lots of nonsense, shifts into English and even word plays in English:

> Banks closed now. Only banks left are river banks, because park *bancos* are called benches in English. Hold-up impossible. (*Tres Tristes Tigres*, p. 373)

Before that they have tried to be polite and sweet:

—¿A dónde dirigimos esta carabela?

—O esta cara bella—dije yo aludiendo a Magalena (*Tres Tristes Tigres*, pp. 371-2)

["Where shall we direct this caravel?"

"Or this pretty face," I said, referring to Magalena.]

They soon change their approach, and they subject the two bewildered women to two contentless jokes: one is a story which never gets told because the narrators cannot decide who was present at the original event and other is a song which never gets sung although there is a long discussion about its title, name and lyrics. (*Tres Tristes Tigres*, pp. 387-90)

The most noticeable difference between the jokes presented by Freud and those of Cabrera Infante lies in their particular frame. Each joke cited by Freud depends on a story or brief plot in order to generate or justify the punch line. In the novel, however, we often come across accumulations of 'one-liners' that have a very weak thematic frame to hold them together. It is perhaps for this reason that the readers (as well as the two women who are listening to all this within the novel) often respond with uneasiness, and finally the effect of the humor is diminished and undermined. The joke, in a sense, is on Arsen and Silvestre, for their loquacity has impeded communication with Beba and Magalena: the two women are not seduced.

Other innocent jokes in the novel belong to the type described by Freud as "condensation accompanied by formation of a substitute, which is a composite word." Among these we find all of the created names: Ionescue, Beba Gardner, Ezra Pound-quake, Arsenius Cuetullus, Gary Cuéper and countless others. Arsen and Silvestre make extensive use of nonsense jokes, one of which is rather interesting. It is attributed to their friend Rine Leal as one more of the totally useless inventions with which he is credited: *"el cuchillo sin hoja que perdió el mango"* ["the bladeless knife, which lost its handle"]. (*Tres Tristes Tigres*, p. 383) In a footnote added to his work in 1912, Freud notes that

> a similar nonsensical technique appears if a joke seeks to maintain a connection which seems to be excluded by the special conditions implied in its content. Such, for instance, is Lichtenberg's knife without a blade which has no handle.

The function of this continuous use of language games by Arsen and Silvestre can be perceived more clearly if one examines another passage by Freud on nonsensical jokes. He states that such jokes are presenting something that is stupid and nonsensical, the sense of which lies in the revelation and demonstration of something else that is stupid and nonsensical.

It would now seem that the purpose of the verbal attack is to underline the stupidity of the two women, their lack of imagination, their unsophisticated literalness. Arsen and Silvestre establish their superiority over Beba and Magalena.

Innocent jokes are not the only kind to appear in this section of the novel: many jokes are tendentious; others are obscene. The scene where Arsen introduces the two women to Silvestre already contains sexual references:

> Encantado. Mucho gusssto. E un plasel. El busto es mío . . .

> [Delighted. I'm so pleazed to meat you. It's a pleazure. Noo,

> I'll meazure you now and pleazure you later]. (***Tres Tristes Tigres***, p. 397)

And in the poem recited by the ardent Arsen to Beba we find several obscenities, such as

> O si me hicieras un mudrá
> Con el dedo del medio erguido, parado,
> Y el anular y el otro, índice se llamará,
> Los dos, los cuatro, todos los demás,
> Acostados o postrados. (***Tres Tristes Tigres***, p. 398)

> [Or if you'd make a mudra for me
> with your middle finger upright,
> and your ring finger and the other, index it is called,
> the two, the four, all the rest on their sides, prostrated there]. (***Tres Tristes Tigres***, p. 410)

The function of this kind of joking obscenity is considered by Freud in his description of 'smut' (his translator's term). Freud states smut to be a form of verbal sexual aggression that is necessary sometimes in order to arouse a woman. When a third party is present at such an exchange, he effectively inhibits the woman and keeps her from acquiescing. At this point, the inactive third person (a male in Freud's model) becomes a listener, the recipient of the verbal assault, and "owing to this transformation it (the smutty comment) is already near to assuming the character of a joke." Freud later adds that such a joke will "evade restrictions and open sources of pleasure that have become inaccessible"; and also that the joke can be consummated only when the woman, who is the object of desire, leaves the room.

We now begin to comprehend the dynamics of the verbal assault on the two women in "Bachata." The hostility of Arsen and Silvestre is initially a form of sexual aggression aimed at arousal. However, Beba and Magalena each acts as a third party, hence neither will succumb to sexual demands in front of the other. Therefore, the two men, seeing that avenue of 'pleazure' shut off, turn to the lesser satisfaction offered by laughter with the added pleasure of showing off their own intellectual prowess. As such, the model is a reversal of the one proposed by Freud since it is women who act as deterrents. This variation may be accounted for by cultural differences, the distinction between Cuban night-people of the fifties and Viennese bourgeoisie at the turn of the century, and by the shift from psycho-analytic theory to literary text.

There is another woman at whom the verbal aggression is also directed: Laura Díaz, the one whom Arsenio had been in love with and whom Silvestre eventually marries. Her importance has been sufficiently studied. She is also the object of their desires, but since she is absent ('has left the room' in the Freudian model) the men indulge in obscene jokes, which would otherwise be directed at her in the form of smut. Laura is present in their minds and therefore in their discourse, although she is not in the car. Beba and Magalena are riding in the car with the two men, but they are absent in and to the discourse. In this situation it could also be argued that, true to the Freudian model, the two men are acting as third parties to each other in their attempts to seduce Beba and Magalena, thus explaining their lack of success.

In Mehlman's reading of Freud, the distinction between innocent and tendentious jokes disappears. He finds the "desire for masked repetition" present in any joking situation that attempts to recapture a feeling of pleasure from the telling itself, rather than from the content of the joke. Thus all the humor spent on the two women becomes perverse, an attempt to attain through other means some of the satisfaction that is unavailable, both because of the presence of the two dull women and because of the absence of the one woman who really matters to both Arsen and Silvestre.

Mehlman goes on to consider the auto-erotic qualities of fantasy and the triangular configuration of the 'sign system' which enables the joke to be actualized. He then points up an apparent contradiction in Freud's thinking. The joke is made by the joker in order to derive pleasure through channels which have not been restricted to him (by the presence of a third party). At the same time, the listener, who is inactive, is the one who laughs at the joke, thus presumably also deriving pleasure from it. The listener's pleasure is self-contained and auto-erotic. Thus the fulfillment of the pleasure of the joker takes place in the silent third party. In Cabrera Infante's text, Arsen and Silvestre are both engaged in giving and deriving pleasure from each other through their verbal calisthenics. This is indeed an act of mutual auto-eroticism, and is supported by the text's own references to verbal masturbation.

> Well, I'll talk to myself instead. To masturdebate. In the idiom of the mastur race. Thus masturspake Zarathustra. Make a solution of pollution. The solution of a sage is to pollute a page. Or a pageboy. Bring a boy to the boil. Bugger the little boys that come unto me. It is harder for a camel to enter a needle's eye than to have its prick up your neighbor's asseye. (*Tres Tristes Tigres*, p. 391)

What nobody seems to want to point out are the obvious homosexual implications of two willing male adults engaging in mutual intellectual and verbal masturbation.

This implication is natural if we examine some of the predominant types of relationships and characters throughout the novel. Magalena, who may well be mad, accuses Beba and her husband of abusing her sexually. (397-8) Earlier in the text, Codac (a photographer) runs into Magalena and sees her kissing Manolito el Toro, the buxom lesbian. Later on that same evening, Magalena and the woman of a Greek Jew (not identified by name) leave Codac in order to go to the bathroom. Codac has the sudden realization that this woman too is a lesbian; he tells himself that Cuba is the Isle of Lesbos. (pp. 128-9) At this point, Magalena's accusations of Beba and her husband begin to sound more plausible and her madness more understandable. In the third section of "Los Debutantes" ["The Debutantes"], a character named Magalena Crús (clearly the same Magalena) has a fight with another woman. Rodríguez Monegal incorrectly describes this episode as the monologue of a young woman who tells of her mother and her leaving home. In the course of that monologue Magalena denies the mother-daughter relationship:

> y por mi madre santa te lo juro que . . .
> [and I swear to you on my mother's grave . . .]
> (*Tres Tristes Tigres*, p. 34)

Then she relates that the other woman answered

> que yo no te voy paral ni ponel freno:
> por fines que yo no soy tu madre, me oíte.
> [That I won't stop you or rein you in;
> After all, I'm not your mother, you hear]. (*Tres Tristes Tigres*, p. 34)

The other woman could be Beba; her speech seems to as educated as that of the Beba we encounter later; however, one must keep in mind that this is Magalena's rendition of it, and it could be distorted in that 'translation.' Also, an unspecified period of time has elapsed between one scene and the other: Beba's speech could have evolved. To return to

the scene in "Bachata," we have the poem which Arsen creates for Beba, with its spoofs of Martí, Góngora, and Catullus, dedicated to *Lésbica Beba* (Lesbic Beba) and with references to lesbians and to the Isle of Lesbos.

Laura Díaz too had homosexual experiences as a little girl, according to the first section of "Los Debutantes." Rodríguez Monegal quotes a letter sent to him by Cabrera Infante, in which the author leaves no doubt as to the identity of the two little girls who "play together" under the truck. Thus all the female characters involved in "Bachata," be they present or absent, have had some link with homosexuality.

Laura Díaz' first husband was a homosexual, if we are to believe her ninth psychoanalytic hour and not her seventh. So are several other minor characters: Alex Bayer and his lover, the singer Cuba Venegas, and the unnamed girl with whom she visits Delia Doce. (*Tres Tristes Tigres*, P. 33) Arsenio and Silvestre indicate their fascination in homosexuals when they go to a gay nightclub to ogle the couples. (*Tres Tristes Tigres*, p. 110) Someone, perhaps Boustrophedon (another important character, although he never appears in direct dialogue or monologue) screams out at two passing women

> que sólo las lesbianas acaricien mi cara
> [let only lesbians caress my face] (*Tres Tristes Tigres*, p. 139)

The joking and vicarious thrills of oral-aural masturbation must come to an end as the two men consider their future: Silvestre's future marriage to Laura, their integration into straight society, and consequent betrayal of the carefree friendship between the two men. The joking ends when Laura, the woman who was absent from their discourse, is allowed symbolically to re-enter the room: once conversation centers on her, all joking ceases.

The complexity in the language of *Tres Tristes Tigres*, and the unorthodox time and plot structures demand what has been known since Cortázar's *Hopscotch* as a *lector cómplice* [an accomplice reader], an accomplice of the writer. Cortázar defined the *lector hembra* [female reader] as one who expects logically ordered progressions towards goals, idylls, marriages; this type of reader would be repulsed by a work such as *Hopscotch*, and perhaps Cortázar is repulsed by this sort of reader. Jokingly, the term *lector macho* [macho reader] has been used to refer to the accomplice reader, one who is active and willing to participate in the novel and collaborate with the writer in the final creation of a literary text. If we allow this equivocal use of the word *macho*, and we apply Freudian theory, we discover that the reader of *Tres Tristes Tigres* is left to participate explicitly in its ultimate joke. The naive female reader (or passive reader) leaves 'the room' created by the text, allowing Cabrera Infante and his *macho* readers to engage in mutual and auto-eroticism, a strange new form of vicarious masturbation through time and space.

Ardis L. Nelson (essay date Autumn 1978)

SOURCE: *"Holy Smoke: Anatomy of a Vice,"* in *World Literature Today,* Vol. 61, No. 4, Autumn, 1978, pp. 590-93.

[*In the following essay, Nelson explores Cabrera Infante's application of a "menippean" form of satire in* Holy Smoke.]

An ongoing controversy has been brewing regarding Guillermo Cabrera Infante's outrageously inventive and irreverent writing, from **Un oficio del siglo XX** (*A Twentieth-Century Job*; 1963) up to the present, as to whether a given work is an autobiography, a novel, a satire, a collection of fragments, or just a book. With the publication of **Holy Smoke,** a humorous narrative account of the history of tobacco and cigar-smoking and their presence in popular culture, Cabrera Infante guarantees himself a place in the Menippean mainstream along with such venerable offbeat authors as Petronius, Burton, Sterne, and Carroll. The menippea is impossible to define neatly or to categorize—in this respect it is like a cigar's *vitola*—but it has a decidedly unique and unmistakably oxymoronic and dialogic thrust. We can also say with certainty that the menippea or anatomy tends toward parody and burlesque in tone, a philosophical or intellectual posture in theme, and the encyclopedic accumulation of fact and erudition in form. Menippean satire is always innovative, but there are certain recurring patterns that reflect an attitude and approach to literature, and to the represented word in particular, that can be traced as far back as antiquity and the original generic features of the *spoudogeloios,* "serious-smiling." For Mikhail Bakhtin, the seriocomic genres, especially the Menippean satire and the Socratic dialogue, are dialogic, open and questing, in contrast with the serious genres—the epic, tragedy, history, and classical rhetoric—which are monologic and present a closed and stable world.

The serious forms comprehend man; the Menippean forms are based on man's ability to know and contain his fate. To any vision of a completed system of truth, the menippea suggests some element outside the system. Seriocomic forms present a challenge, open or covert, to literary and intellectual orthodoxy, a challenge that is reflected not only in their philosophic content but also in their structure and language.

It is interesting to note that these opposing literary categories are reflected in two major conflicting philosophical schools of thought: the epistemological and the hermeneutic. The epistemological, which corresponds to the monologic, asserts that there is one preferred view of reality (in recent Western history this view has been theological, succeeded by the scientific). The hermeneutic naturally corresponds to the dialogic and holds that there is no specific correct view, but rather that there is dialogue between any number of differing views.

> An ongoing controversy has been brewing regarding Guillermo Cabrera Infante's outrageously inventive and irreverent writing, from *Un oficio del siglo XX* up to the present, as to whether a given work is an autobiography, a novel, a satire, a collection of fragments, or just a book.
> —*Ardis L. Nelson*

According to Bakhtin, the essential characteristics of the seriocomic realm in literature include a new relationship to reality, which is centered on the living present and motivated by personal experience and creative invention rather than being based on myth and legend. Another essential characteristic is a "radically new relationship to the word as the material of literature" (MB, 108), which encompasses a broad spectrum of stylistic features, all of which reject the monologic nature of the traditional genres. These traits are the source for the Menippean satire and Socratic dialogue—products of the third and fourth century B.C. respectively—both of which have provided a reservoir of vitality for modern narrative. This essay will focus on elucidating these and other more specific Menippean features in **Holy Smoke.**

If we follow Bakhtin's line of thinking, the oxymoronic configuration lies at the heart of the menippea, with its roots in carnivalistic folklore. The very essence of the carnivalesque involves "the *joyful relativity* of all structure and order, of all authority and all (hierarchical) position, . . . the central carnivalistic act [being] the mock crowning and subsequent decrowning of the carnival king" (MB, 124). Beginning with its oxymoronic title, **Holy Smoke** is prolific in the apparently contradictory, in sharp contrasts and misalliances, both in the verbal pattern of the oxymoron and in incongruities on a number of planes. The noun *smoke* is entirely justifiable in the title of a book that has everything to do with smoking, but it demands further scrutiny in its titular role. On the one hand, *smoke* conjures up images of addiction, an unhealthy, profane activity that has upon occasion even been associated with the devil, at least for the Spanish Inquisition. Not surprisingly, Rodrigo de Xeres was thought to have been possessed by the devil when he demonstrated smoking in Seville (*HS,* 13), for if hell is fire and brimstone, smoke cannot be far away. Negative attitudes toward smoking through the ages represent a monologic viewpoint: the

Inquisition sponsored by the Catholic Church was later to be followed by the scientific inquisition of the modern-day Western world, which indicts smoking from a factual, absolutist point of view.

How, then, can smoke be "Holy"? Smoke may suggest the ecstasy of *religious* ritual, with which it was originally associated in the New World, where the shaman often inhaled smoke from a mind-altering weed. The implication is that smoking in and of itself is divine, and knowing the high value that Cabrera Infante has always placed on memory in his writings, we are inclined to believe that the close association attributed to memory and smoking lends a sacred quality to the latter as well: "What Wilde said of music is also true of smoking: it always makes you remember a time that never was. Though that past sometimes really existed. . . . [But] memory has no time" (*HS,* 28-29). Perhaps that is why he insists, "I believe with Casanova that most of the pleasure in smoking is, of course, in the smoke" (*HS,* 30). Another example of Menippean play is his presentation of the extremes to which people go to live out their favorite vices. The sale of pre-Castro Cuban cigars in New York City in 1983, for example, is described as a "religious experience" for some.

> Well put—and better sold. Soon all the cigars were gone (with the smoke?). 'Price estimates in the catalogue,' said the *New York Times,* 'showed that the auction house expected to get $2 to $12 for each cigar.' Wow! 'But Arlam Ettinger had a wide grin as a bidder who identified himself as Al Goldstein', a true gold nugget of a smoker, publisher of *Cigar* and, what else?, *Screw Magazine,* outbid a standing-room-only crowd of several hundred people for the first lot of 25 cigars. His bid was $2,100 or $84 a cigar. The rest was not silence but shaking of hands, rattling of money and rolling of eyes. (*HS,* 129)

The oxymoronic construct is a natural manifestation of a dialogic relationship. In *Holy Smoke* we have a world turned upside down, the inversion of hierarchies, a mixture of the high and the low, the serious and the comic. Although the cigar is *usually* spoken of in relatively glowing terms ("A cigarette is a dangling particule in your lips and the pipe is all clenched teeth and no fury. But a good cigar is like a passion. . . . A cigar is woman, to smoke divine!" *HS,* 30-31), it is also described in naturalistic or grotesque terms: "Between the mask or the naked face of the wrapper and the entrails of the filler, the binder is the leaf that keeps the bowels in check. The peritoneum as it were. This vegetal sac contains the guts" (*HS,* 35). Other manifestations of the oxymoronic pattern typical in the menippea, such as a mixture of genres, dialogic or multivoiced and multitoned narration, are readily identifiable in *Holy Smoke.*

Inserted genres, including poetry, quotes from historical and botanical texts, letters, films, interviews, newspapers, signs, billboards, books on tobacco etiquette, and literary selections, offer a compendium of information on smoking from every conceivable source. Similarly to Robert Burton in his *Anatomy of Melancholy,* Cabrera Infante here aspires to an encyclopedic approach, with a seemingly haphazard mixture of styles in which history, folklore, and scholarly research on tobacco and film blend with personal stories and commentary. Although the inserted materials are diverse in their original function, their inclusion in *Holy Smoke* becomes tantamount to homogeneity in that all are subjected to the "double-voiced" effect of irony and parody. These techniques are multivoiced because they introduce into the discourse "a semantic intention that is directly opposed to the original one. The second voice . . . clashes hostilely with its primordial host and forces him to serve directly opposing aims" (MB, 193). Ironic discourse involves the use of someone else's words to create a hostile effect.

The distancing and humor imparted by the narrator's commentaries on people, films, books, and events throughout *Holy Smoke* have the dialogic function of providing that irony and parody. Due in large part to the ridiculous and incongruous nature of much of the "impossible" dialogue, the solemn and "finalized quality" of man and his works is thrown into comic relief. Whereas in his earlier works Cabrera Infante's narrators made editorial comments on their *own* writing, the narrative voice in *Holy Smoke* comments on the works of *other* writers, "correcting" Defoe, for example—"Please, let's have an instant rewrite"—and remarking on the latter's discourse on tobacco in brackets: "But I tried several experiments with it, as if I was resolved it should hit one way or the other. [What you would call the hit-and-miss system or Crusoe subject to random.] I first took a piece of a leaf. . . . " (*HS,* 250).

One of the narrator's many roles in *Holy Smoke* is just this sort of dialogic relationship with the "external" materials assembled in the text. The first-person-singular narrator is also identified more closely with Cabrera Infante than ever before, as he recounts autobiographical information about himself and his family, including his personal reminiscences on cigar-smoking (*HS,* 24-31). The conversational tone of the narration gives the sensation of a dialogic relationship between narrator and reader as well, a relationship which is more or less familiar, depending on the context: "Groucho, *let me tell you,* was not talking of the quality of his cigar but. . . . " (*HS,* 61; emphasis mine). The setting which comes to mind most frequently is that of a stand-up comedian in a club, entertaining his audience.

Multilingualism offers another aspect of heterovoicing in *Holy Smoke,* Cabrera Infante's first book written in English rather than Spanish. In this way Cabrera Infante has adroitly converted a practical necessity—because *Holy Smoke* grew out of a suggested article for a U.S. magazine—into a Menippean vehicle, perfect for a writer who has been known as a master of the pun since his *Tres tristes tigres* (1964; Eng. *Three Trapped Tigers,* 1971) Cabrera Infante's capacity for paronomasia is no less brilliant in English than in Spanish, with lots of mixed metaphors, jumbled proverbs, and verbal ideas, techniques all that draw attention to the words being played upon, at the expense of any possibility for a logical sequence of thoughts. In *Holy Smoke* we learn that although cigarettes have been targeted for warnings by the surgeon general, cigars are not subject to this labeling: "In fact a corona has less to do with a coronary than a piece of buttered toast. . . . That's cigars and the heart. Now for the cigar and the arts" (*HS,* 200). *Holy Smoke*'s syntax carries over a distinctly Latinate quality from Spanish, and Cabrera Infante continues his practice of sprinkling untranslatable words and phrases in Spanish, French, Latin, and even Catalan throughout the text, along with offering numerous etymologies. Multilingualism is explicit proof that there is more than one view.

Another variant of "joyful relativity," anachronism—or the oxymoronic juxtaposition of past and present—is plentiful in *Holy Smoke.* In rejecting the monologic or absolute past of myth and legend, the Menippean subject is presented "in a zone of immediate and even crudely familiar contact with living contemporaries" (*MB,* 108). Cabrera Infante has always believed that our modern-day myths and heroes are made in Hollywood. In *Holy Smoke* movie stars are removed from their element and treated informally and out of context, as they are quoted and referenced solely in relation to their portrayal of smoking in the movies. One instance of playful anachronism is when the narrator claims that a movie, *Heaven Can Wait,* might help sell *Holy Smoke:* "Charles Coburn at his jolliest: every now and then he exclaims boisterously, 'Holy smoke!' and puffs at his perennial Partagas. The best plug ever for this book" (*HS,* 200). Although many an actor and actress from the old days is treated with awe in comparison with more recent stars, as heroes they are dethroned and placed in the service of an anatomy of an addiction. Joan Crawford, for example, is said to have had much more class in her handling of cigarettes than Geraldine Chaplin in a 1980 remake of a 1940 melodrama. No one and nothing is sacred. Historical facts and figures are contemporized via a jocular tone, a running punning commentary engaged in continually by the narrator. A quote from a historical source is followed by playful banter, as if it were a humorous reaction to the serious, monologic fact as recorded by history. The narrator's lines represent an imaginative "reader response" to the stilted historical version of a grand event, thus trivialized through layer upon layer of paronomasia, editorial quips in parentheses, inventions on the historical verging on disrespect—in short, total literary license. As a general rule, the first sentence or a paragraph will be a serious statement, followed with a quote, usually

referenced. The remainder of the paragraph is anyone's guess, but it is surely an exemplar of the unbridled freedom of invention and multiplicity of style indigenous to the Menippean satire.

The narrative composition of the first and largest section of *Holy Smoke* is framed by stories about Christopher Columbus, as discoverer of the New World and of tobacco. Columbus, characterized as the first European nonsmoker, is trivialized and contemporized through a tone of impudence and burlesque: "As to cigars Columbus must be praised or blamed for it too" (*HS,* 2). Treated with less than due respect—"This sailor who couldn't sail . . . came only for the money. Or rather for the gold"—Columbus is even discussed in terms of "crude slum naturalism": he is said to have reformed a streetwalker and to have been a hustler of sorts, who "ate, drank and pissed gold. (Freud would say later that he defecated it.)" (*HS,* 6).

The "dialogue of the dead," actually a formalization of the type of anachronism we are seeing in *Holy Smoke,* is a genre of Menippean origin that brings together people and ideas from different epochs to discuss important issues. Cabrera Infante's narrator conducts just this sort of parodic dialogue with Columbus and other historical figures. Columbus is presented as an ethnocentric and disdainful character in his dealings with the smoking Indians, with Cabrera Infante putting words in his mouth, as it were.

Columbus was instantly mistrustful of the strange artifact with which the witchdoctor made clouds over the meeting. Could he make rain too? It was all a futility rite. Besides, the contraption really looked like a musket! The Admirable Admiral took de Xeres aside to ask concerned: 'Are you sure this thing is safe?' Was he afraid of being blown sky high? De Xeres was about to explain about the safety valve in the *brujos*'s mouth but all he did was to answer his superior almost with disrespect: 'An *exploding* cigar? Ridiculous!' (*HS,* 6-7)

Here Cabrera Infante invents an "eccentric" dialogue between de Xeres and Columbus, the type which Bakhtin credits with disrupting the expected and acceptable in human behavior. The inappropriate verbal reaction to the shaman attributed to Columbus is made to appear all the more scandalous because of the following denigrating dialogic commentary of our modern-day narrator: "Columbus leapt like a lizard being smoked out . . . and gold sounded like God in his Italianate accent" (*HS,* 7).

As we can see, the oxymoronic bouncing back and forth of the menippea serves as a substitute for character development and plot development, with much more concern for topical or profoundly human issues than for history or legend. In Cabrera Infante's earlier works we have already evidenced a Menippean vision of the world in terms of an ulti-mate question or issue in life: in **Un oficio del siglo XX** a film critic examines his career and decides to leave it be-hind for a more creative endeavor, thus exorcising an aspect of his self-identity. In **Tres tristes tigres** the idea of betrayal in language, literature, and love is played out as an adven-ture on all levels of the text. In **La habana para un infante difunto** (1979; Eng. **Infante's Inferno,** 1984) the Don Juan figure and his sexual exploits are burlesqued. The narrator of **Holy Smoke** also fulfills the Menippean function of pro-voking and testing an idea or truth. Here all aspects of an addiction are discussed by a narrator who presents himself essentially as a seeker of knowledge. As researcher-narra-tor he may be seen as the wise man who gathers together all supporting evidence and demonstrates its applicability to his theme that smoking a cigar is a way to be *somebody* in this life. The epigraph that opens the book, taken from *Pete Kelly's Blues,* is: "Here, have a cigar. Light it up and be somebody!" Or his topic may be seen in Menippean terms as the adventure of an idea—or of an ultimate question in life: to smoke or not to smoke? If you answer affirmatively, he provides the living testimony of experts on how to choose a cigar, how to light it, how to smoke it and when, where and how long to smoke it. If you answer negatively, you will be taking a calculated risk in reading the book. As Enrique Fernandez suggests, "Is literature conducive to substance abuse? I'm here to tell you it is."

As an anatomy of a vice, **Holy Smoke** has something for ev-eryone. It presents the story of the rise of tobacco: its his-torical roots, its popularity, and the many forms of use and abuse it has taken; its demise in terms of health-related ef-fects; and its actual and symbolic presence in art forms, es-pecially in cinema and literature. **Holy Smoke** displays a wealth of dialogic Menippean qualities, thus reflecting the modern thrust toward the hermeneutic and away from the epistemological view and confirming Cabrera Infante's keen awareness of the prevailing spirit of the times.

William L. Siemens (essay date May-September 1979)

SOURCE: "Mirrors and Metamorphosis: Lewis Carroll's Presence in *Tres tristes tigres,*" in *Hispania,* Vol 62, No. 3, May-September, 1979, pp. 297-303.

[*In the following essay, Siemens discusses Cabrera Infante's use of literary devices in* Tres Tristes Tigres *that are simi-lar to those employed by Lewis Carroll in* Alice in Wonder-land.]

In an interview with Emir Rodriguez Monegal, Guillermo Cabrera Infante indicates the way in which he has incorpo-rated subtle allusions to the works of Lewis Carroll into *Tres tristes tigres:* "Hay un momento en *Tres tristes tigres,* en el final, en 'Bachata,' en que Cué y Silvestre contemplan una tempestad eléctrica tropical y Silvestre—que es el que se supone que sea mi *alter ego* en el libro—dice que parece un homenaje a un 4 de julio olvidado. . . . Por supuesto . . . que el 4 de julio de 1862 fue cuando Lewis Carroll, cuando el reverendo Dodgson . . . se fue de picnic con [Alicia] por el río Oxford." In recent Cuban prose fiction the name of the game is play itself, and when this comes to mean spe-cifically word play it is not surprising that the name of Lewis Carroll should crop up in some significant context. Cabrera Infante has stated, in fact, "Tengo una *enorme* admiración por Lewis Carroll. Tanto que creo que es el verdadero iniciador de la literatura moderna como la conocemos hoy dia."

The tone of his novel is set in an epigraph drawn from *Alice in Wonderland,* which reads, "Y trató de imaginar cómo se vería la luz de una vela cuando está apagada." For Alice in her context the question appears to be one of immortality, for it occurs to her when she is wondering what will become of her if she continues shrinking until she goes out altogether like a candle, but my impression is that Cabrera Infante has in mind a different primary frame of reference for the quo-tation. He has said on various occasions that he considers his novel to be fundamentally a collection of "voices": this is what gives it much of its peculiar character and has led to several errors in interpretation. In the "Advertencia" at the beginning of the book he remarks, "La escritura no es más que un intento de atrapar la voz humana al vuelo" (p. 9), and it would appear that, in asking the question concern-ing the nature of the flame after the candle is out, he is al-luding to an intention to examine the phenomenon of the spoken word after the sound of the voice is lost.

However, there is perhaps more similarity to Alice's thought than is immediately apparent because the spoken word may be Cabrera Infante's main point of reference in the search for immortality which becomes the major concern of at least three of the characters. Not only does Silvestre feel that Bustrófedon, the principal word-player of the novel, "ahora podia ser inmortal" (p. 318), but he himself accepts Arsenio Cué's characterization of him—Silvestre—as one who means to impose a sort of order on the mortal chaos through the word (p. 334). The whole point for this circle of friends is, as stated by Silvestre, "la sabiduría total, la felicidad, ser inmortales" (p. 318).

Bustrófedon, in point of fact, is nothing less than a logical extension of Carroll's tendency to play with words. Cabrera Infante's opinion concerning his unique style is that, as a stut-terer, Carroll "echaba al papel las palabras que le quedaban en la punta de la lengua, o quizá más atrás," and the Cuban has carried the obsession with metamorphic, kaleidoscopic language beyond what the earlier author ever dared. Bustrófedon (whose very name is that of a rhetorical device) "quiso ser el lenguaje" (p. 318), and we have every reason to believe that he achieved his aim, on the basis of his behavior in the section "Rompecabeza." There he takes on the proportions of an antichrist, in that he—in contrast to the "Word made flesh"—is the fleshly man who has become the word. The point is that what began with Carroll as an active obsession with language has culminated in Cabrera Infante with language incarnate.

It is especially in this "Rompecabeza" section that the reader encounters frequent references and allusions to Carroll and his works. When a restaurant proprietor is cowed by Bustrófedon's menacing him and thereby seemingly growing until he reaches the ceiling, the former begins to shrink and finally disappears into a hole which is an "o" or a zero, as the type itself grows smaller and the lines are shortened. Códac, who is the narrator at this point, remarks,

> Y me cordé [sic] de Alicia en el País de las Maravillas y se lo dije al Bustroformidable y él se puso a recrear, a regalar: Alicia en el mar de villas, Alicia en el país que más brilla, Alicia en el Cine Maravillas, Avaricia en el País de las Malavillas, Malavidas, Mavaricia, Marivia, Malicia, Milicia Milhizia Milhinda Milindia Milinda Malanda Malasia Malesia Maleza Maldicia Malisa Alisia Alivia Aluvia Alluvia Alevilla y marlisa y marbrilla y maldevilla . . . . (p. 209)

The form into which Códac puts the incident which leads to the outburst is what Martin Gardner calls "emblematic, or figured, verse: poems printed in such a way that they resemble something related to their subject matter" (*Alice,* p. 50). He has reference to Alice's imagination of the form of a mouse's "tale" as the shape of his tail, so that the speech is printed in that form.

Another example of figured verse in *Tres tristes tigres* appears in the "Casa de los espejos" section, as "una palabra que sube por ella misma así

> r
> r
> do
> a
> a
> a
> v
> v
> elee e (p. 143)

We are reminded of Thomas Pynchon's statement that

"words are only an eye-twitch away from the things they stand for," another major author's comment upon the growing autonomy of language.

Carroll's Humpty Dumpty anticipates Octavio Paz and Cabrera Infante in conceiving words as not only having substance and personality, but being rather cantankerous as well. Humpty Dumpty says, "They've a temper, some of them—particularly verbs: they're the proudest—adjectives you can do anything with, but not verbs—however, *I* can manage the whole lot of them!" (*Alice,* p. 269). Paz, for his part, is an admirer of the Marquis de Sade, as we see in the beginning of "Las palabras": "Dales la vuelta, / cógelas del rabo (chillen, putas), / azótalas." Nevertheless, Humpty Dumpty at least concedes that he pays his words extra when he forces them to work extra hard (*Alice,* p. 270). In the hands of Humpty Dumpty words tend to mean what their users want them to mean, but the next step is that of words acting on their own in the material sphere, and Bustrófedon is born.

The question of whether a word as it arrives within the hearer's perception necessarily has an "accepted" meaning, or whether it has only the meaning the speaker (or writer) chooses to give it, is a fundamental one for both of these writers. In 1852 Gustave Flaubert had already expressed his desire to write a book entirely free of subject matter, and of course our concern is closely related to that—the concept of meaning as dependent only upon the author's intention. "'When *I* use a word,' Humpty Dumpty said, in rather a scornful tone, 'it means just what I choose it to mean—neither more nor less'" (*Alice,* p. 269), and his creator reiterates, "I maintain that any writer of a book is fully authorized in attaching any meaning he likes to any word or phrase he intends to use" (*Alice,* p. 269). Similarly, Bustrófedon, the character who "empezó a cambiar el nombre de las cosas" (p. 220), had a growth on his spinal column, "y le hacía decir esas maravillas y jugar con las palabras y finalmente vivir nombrando todas las cosas por otro nombre como si estuviera, de veras, inventando un idioma nuevo" (p. 222). Later in *Tres tristes tigres,* it is mentioned that Bustrófedon may have managed to write a page of a book using only one word (perhaps attaching a different meaning to it each time he placed it on the page), and Cué mentions an antecedent or two. The next page confronts the reader with the lyrics of a *guaracha,* consisting only of the word "blen" (pp. 331-32).

The "Rompecabeza" section of *Tres tristes tigres* is largely dominated by Lewis Carroll. Not only does it contain the features previously mentioned but also such Carrollian favorites as *portmanteau* words, nonsense verse ("Váyala fiña de Viña/deifel Fader fidel fiasco/falla mimú psicocastro/alfú mar sefú más phinas," p. 210), metaphysical play with mathematical concepts (pp. 217-18), and twisted allusions to

Carroll's work, as in the case of the comic name "Ruth de Loukin-Glass" (p. 267).

Throughout the book there is a constant use of mirrors in all possible forms. An example is found on the page which Códac has had specially printed for Bustrófedon (who at this point in the narrative is dead and thus on the other side of the mirror): it is an exact mirror image of the preceding page (pp. 264-65). But perhaps the most sophisticated case of the Carrollian use of mirrors is found in the section appropriately entitled "Casa de los espejos." In it Arsenio Cué is invited to come up to the apartment of two girls named Laura and Livia, and he does so. He stresses his ascent up the "metaphysical stairs," as if he, like the author of the Apocalypse, had been chosen to receive a major revelation. And indeed, this is the case, for much of the book has to do with the unveiling of the artificial, and what he sees demonstrates to him just how deep is the beauty of his lady friends. While mouthing one of the novel's refrains about Cué—"No cambias"—Livia places on the bed a set of photographs of herself in the nude, which Cué takes as a disappointing case of substitution. Many of the interpersonal transactions in this passage take place through the mirror, and Cué watches as the two rather imperfect girls are "put together" by the use of more or less cheap cosmetics. When one of them is finished Cué remarks, "De verdad que está muy bien: es otra mujer," and at the conclusion of the chapter he has become a veritable magic mirror. When he is asked, "¿Verdad que estoy como nunca?" he replies, "Sí, ama, pero en Alturas del Bosque vive Blancanieves." To the repeated remark, "Tú siempre igual"—to which Cué assigns a different meaning than the speaker intended—he answers, "No, en serio estás bellísima. Están bellísimas" (pp. 145-56). The verb *ser* has been avoided throughout.

The mirror image of the story is related by Silvestre a few pages farther on, in the next section (pp. 165-68). He speaks of a date with another superficial beauty, one who has adopted a garbled version of the name of her favorite movie star and thus is known as Ingrid Bérgamo. The entire story is narrated in cinematic terms ("Veo en big close-up su mano," "a lo Cary Grant," "mi co-star," "la cámara ubicua"). Silvestre manages to spend the night in the same bed with Ingrid, but nothing more happens. In the morning he is startled by the sight of her wig, which he sees lying next to him, "como un abismo de falsedad": she is totally bald. He feigns sleep as she rushes to the bathroom to rearrange herself; Silvestre remarks, "Cuando sale es otra mujer" (pp.165-68), the last three words being identical to those uttered by Cué. Cué has watched how some Cuban beauties are put together, while Silvestre has seen how they can come apart.

An even more striking Carrollian use of mirror-image experiences is seen in an earlier "Ella cantaba boleros" segment (pp. 75-79). In it Códac speaks first of picking up—at

her request—an attractive girl wearing a man's shirt. She reveals that she calls herself Manolito el Toro, and leaves the automobile at a cabaret, where she meets and becomes intimate with a striking girl she refers to as Pepe. Finally convinced of this character's lesbianism, Códac moves on. The narration then proceeds to Códac's encounter with a character named Alex Bayer (also known as Alex Aspirina), a male homosexual who lives with a doctor. The significant point is in the transition between the two mirror-image encounters: Códac meets a black singer whom he knows, and comments, "Rolando se veía muy bein, muy cantante, muy cubano, muy muy habanero all con su traje de dril 100 blanco y su sombrero de paja, chiquito, puesto como solamente se lo saben poner los negros . . . " (p. 77). This is the transition through the mirror, by way of Códac's meeting with the opposite of what one would normally expect to see—a white man in a black suit.

It should be borne in mind as well that Códac (like Lewis Carroll) is a photographer and tends to view phenomena in terms of light and shadow, or positive and negative imagery. The latter point is evident in the description of his first view of La Estrella, who quickly becomes an obsession with him. It is plain to see here the concerns of Lewis Carroll the photographer, since Códac is very much in the photographer's role in this episode. Not only does he mention in passing his attempt to hide "las manchas amarillas del hipo" (from photo developer's acid), but he is introduced to a girl named Irenita by a dealer in pornographic pictures who apparently feels Códac can provide some free publicity. Códac says the pornographer "sacó a Irena por un brazo come si la pescara del mar de la oscuridad," and describes her as looking like a miniature Marilyn Monroe—that is, very small and blonde. The next portion of the description must be given in full so that the effect may be appreciated: "La rubita se rió con ganas levantando los labios y enseñando los dientes como si se levantara el vestido y enseñara los muslos y tenía los dientes más bonitos que yo he visto en la oscuridad: unos dientes parejos, bien formados, perfectos, sensuales como unos muslos, y nos pusimos a hablar y a cada rato ella enseñaba sus dientes sin ningún pudor y me gustaban tanto que por poco le pido que me dejara tocarle los dientes" (p. 62).

In her subsequent appearances Irenita never simply walks on the scene as would an ordinary person; she always seems to materialize suddenly out of the darkness. I think the allusion is clear: this is Cabrera Infante's tribute to Lewis Carroll's Cheshire Cat, which appears and disappears at will, at times leaving only its smile behind. Cué makes a palindrome of her name and underscores her in-and-out character when he introduces her to Silvestre as "Irenita Atineri" (p. 412).

Códac becomes involved in a love scene with her in the darkness of the night club. As they are leaving he notices something in the light of the stage that he has not seen before: "Era una mulata enorme, gorda gorda, de brazos como muslos y de muslos que parecían dos troncos sosteniendo el tanque de agua que era su cuerpo" (p. 63). In terms of light and shadow this too is a mirror experience: the small, light Irenita, met in the darkness, is about to be replaced by the huge, black Estrella, first seen in the light.

These two characters are opposites, but in the book there are also two sets of characters who seem to reflect Carroll's Tweedledum and Tweedledee. The first pair is formed by Cué's artificial beauties, who are inseparable. Cué remarks, "Livia y Laura eran más que compañeras de cuarto, amigas ahora y salían juntas a todas partes y trabajaban juntas . . . y acabaron por ser una pareja: Laura y Livia / Livia y Laura / Lauriliva: una sola cosa" (pp. 148-49).

The other pair to which I have reference comprises Silvestre and Cué, who, significantly, are the embodiments of two aspects of Carroll's personality, the mathematical and the verbal. Silvestre is described as a disciple of Bustrófedon and spends a great deal of time in word play as he narrates the "Bachata" section, which makes up the last third of the book. Cué, on the other hand, distrusts words (seemingly because they are so changeable) and puts his faith in numbers. He comments, "Hay quienes ven la vida lógica y ordenada, otros la sabemos absurda y confusa. El arte (como la religión o como la ciencia o como la filosofia) es otro intento de imponer la luz del orden a las tinieblas del caos. Feliz tú, Silvestre, que puedes o crees que puedes hacerlo por el verbo" (p. 334). Earlier Silvestre has asked him,"¿Tú crees verdaderamente en los números?" and received the reply, "Es casi en lo único que creo. Dos y dos serán siempre cuatro y el día que sean cinco es hora de echarse a correr" (p. 312). The irony of the situation is that on the next page he narrates a dream in which he runs, and he runs several more times before the end of the novel.

In the eleventh division of the "Bachata" section are found the "Confesiones de un comedor de gofio cubano" (*comer gofio* in Cuban jargon means to be a fool), which Silvestre says are Cué's complete works (pp. 321-22). There is a good deal of word play here, since even Cué is attracted to Bustrófedon in spite of himself, but where he shines is in his complex games with numbers, including a magic square with nine numerals which add up to fifteen in any direction (p. 329). His favorite number is three (a very important one for the book as a whole, from the title on), but he also makes the point that "9 sumado por si es 18 y multiplicado por si mismo es 81. Al revés y al derecho, el número en el espejo" (p. 328), which presumably would be doubly pleasing to Lewis Carroll. Silvestre, in contrast, likes the concept of *words* in the mirror, or palindromes, of which there are numerous examples in the text.

Another aspect of Lewis Carroll's character is revealed in an incident at the beach and also serves to unify Silvestre and Cué in this regard. Cué is speaking to a little girl named Angelita, and Silvestre remarks to his reader, "No me gustan los nifios, pero me encantan las nifias. Me habria gustado hablar con ella, sentir de cerca su gracia" (p. 353). Carroll's own famous comment on the subject is "I am fond of children (except boys)" (*Alice*, p. 11). The child has given Cué a white stone, and it is worth noting that Lewis Carroll marked with white stones many of his pleasant days spent with little girls.

Códac addresses his two friends as "Silvestre Ycúe" (p. 222), and it appears that they form a parallel with the feminine grouping of "Laurilivia." But it is curious to note that at the end of the novel both pairs are about to be broken up as a result of Silvestre's marriage to Laura (p. 434).

Cué himself, like Alice, has an experience in which he passes through the looking glass to become a different person. He narrates the first part of the experience near the beginning of the text and the conclusion near the end. He arrives at the home of a famous entrepreneur as a poor boy from the country, hoping to be discovered as a writer. As he enters the apartment he sees before him a shabby-looking person; he tells the reader, "Levanté la mano para dársela, al tiempoque inclinaba un poco la cabeza y él hizo lo mismo. Vi que sonreia un poco y sentí que yo también sonreía: los dos comprendimos al mismo tiempo: era un espejo" (p. 54). Evidently this is the meeting with the double which in some Romantic literature was a presage of one's death. Cué is apparently shot by the entrepreneur, thinks he is dead, and is "resurrected" by the man, though as an actor, not a writer. The latter part is told to Silvestre near the end of the book (pp. 423-24), and Silvestre later refers to the entire story as "su muerte y su nuevo nacimiento: su resurrección metafisica" (p. 431). Cué continually insists that he is no longer himself but his *Doppelgänger*, his mirror image: "Soy mi imagen de espejo. Eucoinesra. Arsenio Cué en el idioma del espejo" (p. 400).

One incident in the novel grows directly out of another in Lewis Carroll's life, and it is interesting to see how Cabrera Infante varies the details to fit it into his scheme. The model case is as follows, described by Martin Gardner: "On one occasion a pretty fifteen-year-old actress named Irene Barnes . . . spent a week with Charles Dodgson at a seaside resort . . . [She remarks,] 'His great delight was to teach me his Game of Logic [this was a method of solving syllogisms by placing black and red counters on a diagram of Carroll's own invention]. Dare I say this made the evening rather long, when the band was playing outside on the parade, and the moon shining on the sea?" (*Alice*, pp. 13-14).

Cabrera Infante is convinced that the man's behavior is rather abnormal. This belief is undoubtedly the basis for one portion of Silvestre's and Cué's evening together as described by the former in "Bachata." From the car they spy two available-looking girls, one of whom—like Irene Barnes—is very young. Silvestre remarks, when Cué stops and walks back to speak to them, "Lo vi alejarse por la acera izquierda, por donde ellas venian en la calle del espejo" (p. 365).

Once they are in the car, the two men make little attempt to seduce them in the normal manner. Rather, they regale them with a series of wild linguistic jokes, at times in multiple foreign languages. Silvestre wonders why, but says, "Ya no habia quien nos detuviera" (p. 384). Later he comments, "No tenian dientes para estas risas. Sin embargo, seguiamos haciéndoles cosquillas, ligando bromas de Falopio, hilarando un chiste-tras-otro. ¿Por qué? Quizá porque Arsenio y yo estábamos divertidos" (p. 386). After a few more pages he wonders again if it might not be easier simply to seduce them, and the four go out—significantly in the light of the Carroll story—into the moonlight, but still nothing happens (p. 391). It gives one the impression that the author is forcing his characters to play the role of Lewis Carroll almost against their will and without their understanding why they must do it.

Thus far we have considered individual cases of references, allusions or other reflections of the preoccupations of Lewis Carroll's work in that of Cabrera Infante. But on a much grander level it becomes evident that the entire novel may be conceived as a pair of roughly antithetical halves arranged each on its respective side of the "mirror" which is the center. In view of the fact that the work has been widely held to have no structure at all, however, it would be well to note a pertinent comment of the author. In introducing a chapter which failed to appear in *Tres tristes tigres* but was subsequently published in a journal known as *Alacrán Azul,* he mentions that his original intention had been to include it at the end, but that if he had done so it *would have disturbed the symmetry* of the novel. As pointed out by Emir Rodriguez Monegal, several stories have their beginnings in the first half and are concluded in the second. An example already dealt with above is that of Cué's "death" and his "resurrection," one of the opposites appearing in each half. Again in connection with his story, Beba Longoria, one of the girls he and Silvestre picked up, disappears from the narration at a point almost exactly the same number of pages from the end of the book as her first appearance to Cué is from the beginning.

Another example of some importance is the unit narrated by Silvestre between pages 36 and 42. Approximately fifteen pages from the end (pp. 436-37) he tells the reader fundamentally the same story but with some significant details not only altered but inverted. Then he comments, "Algún día escribiré este cuento." Obviously by the time of the publi-

cation of *Tres tristes tigres* he has done so, but presumably that comment to the reader was made previous to the writing.

In addition, in that same story, we find the young Silvestre—in an interesting twist on Don Quixote's sale of his land to buy books—selling the family library to be able to attend the cinema (pp. 36-42), while in the second half he is a writer. Furthermore, his opposite number, Arsenio Cué, begins his first-half story in the belief that he is a writer and ends it in the second as an actor.

It is clear that in the second half there are several reversals of situations introduced in the first, not the least of which is seen in the fact that the novel which begins with a great deal of noise issuing from the mouth of the emcee of the Tropicana night club ends with the manifold repetition of the phrase "en silencio" (p. 444).

Moreover, it would appear that the character I have described as the incarnation of Carrollian word play, Bustrófedon, serves as the mirror between the halves. The "Rompecabeza" section, which concentrates on his life and death, occupies the center of the text. Cabrera Infante refers to this character as "the two-way man," a sort of Janus-figure. His name, that of the device of alternating directions in writing, confirms this notion, and it is mentioned that he spends a good deal of time around O Street (p. 139). (While this represents the *letter* O in Havana's street nomenclature, Cabrera Infante apparently intends it to stand for the zero which divides thesis from antithesis.) Just as Jesus Christ divides history into B.C. and A.D., this "antichrist" divides the world of the novel into two halves which, to some extent at least, are mirror images of each other.

The imagery Cabrera Infante borrowed from Lewis Carroll is of the sort usually associated with modern apocalyptic literature. *Tres tristes tigres* is unquestionably an apocalyptic novel, reflecting as it does a world poised to receive its death-blow and experience rebirth under Fidel Castro.
—*William L. Siemens*

The imagery Cabrera Infante borrowed from Lewis Carroll is of the sort usually associated with modern apocalyptic literature. *Tres tristes tigres* is unquestionably an apocalyptic novel, reflecting as it does a world poised to receive its death-blow and experience rebirth under Fidel Castro. The term "apocalypse" means "unveiling," not only of some divine plan for the cosmos but also of the hidden sins of a generation. This, I believe, is why certain kinds of imagery are important both to Carroll, living in an age with much to hide prior to its jarring encounter with modern realities, and to Cabrera Infante, who lived in a country created largely for the tourist trade, an artificial paradise whose superficial glamor was about to be exposed. Thus we find the stress on mirrors, which create illusion and bring about a reversal of reality, and the emphasis on the breakdown and rebuilding of language and mathematics, which are fundamental to our understanding of reality. Viewed in this way, the high praise heaped upon the Victorian by the modern Cuban becomes more understandable: both writers were members and prophets of terminal generations.

Stephanie Merrim   (essay date Spring-Summer 1980)

SOURCE: "A Secret Idiom: The Grammar and Role of Language in *Tres tristes tigres*," in *Latin American Literary Review*, Vol. VIII, No. 16, Spring-Summer, 1980, pp. 96-117.

[*In the following essay, Merrim examines the rhetorical forms and figures of speech employed by Cabrera Infante in* Tres tristes tigres.]

> Tú, que me lees, ¿estás serguro de entender mi lenguaje?
>
> —Borges
> "La biblioteca de Babel"

Since even before entering the text proper, the reader of *Tres tristes tigres* [*Three Trapped Tigers*] is warned (in the "Advertencia") that the whole novel is written in an "idioma secreto," the nocturnal jargon of Havana, it comes as no surprise to find critics saying that "a new language is created in the space of the text itself." This kind of statement, however, tells us nothing in particular: all literary works create private languages; a text is as much a linguistic as a fictional universe. Instead, we should ask what is different and "secret" about the language of *Tres tristes tigres*? How does it surpass the mere recording of a dialect? What are its rules and grammar? These questions have been difficult to answer because *Tres tristes tigres* is so disjointed a text, a collage of so many styles and genres that there seems to be no binding force. I believe, however, that there can be found a consistency and development of style which would justify calling this odd pastiche of materials a cohesive language or, indeed, a metalanguage—a comment on the workings of language itself.

Bearing in mind this continuity, I should like to investigate the *role* of language in the text as a whole by examining the novel section by section in serial fashion, to show that since the theme of language so totally pervades the novel and ties in with diverse themes, each section either captures or further elucidates a different aspect of Cabrera's literary sign or his concept of language and thereby progressively builds—on the scale of the novel—a secret language.

Unlikely as it may seem, the loosely jointed features of *Tres tristes tigres* do respond to a generic impulse, that of the carnivalesque novel or menippean satire, for since the text's two most direct models, Petronius's *Satyricon* ("*Tres tristes tigres* es una traducción fallida del *Satiricon*") ["*Three Trapped Tigers* is an unsuccessful translation of the *Satyricon*"] and Lewis Carroll's *Alice* novels participate in this genre, one can expect to find carnivalesque traits in Cabrera's novel. It is well known that the structure of a carnivalesque work is characterized by an extraordinary freedom of composition which manifests itself in a multi-generic or collage texture, by the lack of a finalizing authorial presence which allows characters to evolve their own truth in a Socratic conversation of divergent voices, and by an apparent shattering of the customary novelesque logic of narrative, although "the appearance of carelessness that results reflects only the carelessness of the reader or his tendency to judge by a novel-centered concept of fiction." By debunking traditional narrative plot and character development and pushing them into the background, menippean satire permits intellectual freeplay—or in our case, intellectual wordplay—to come to the foreground. We shall explore these structural features in the course of this study; for now, I should like to focus on the characteristics of carnivalesque language.

M. Bakhtin, who first elaborated the concept of the carnivalesque as such, believes that the language of the carnival work—characterized by *skaz,* stylization and parody—falls outside the bounds of linguistics, being a metalinguistic phenomenon, double-edged or dialogical: "A single trait is common to all of these phenomena, despite their essential differences: in all of them the word has a double-directedness—it is directed both toward the object of speech, like an ordinary word, and toward *another* word, toward *another person's speech.*" In other words, the prime feature of the dialogical word is that it is *never equal to itself.* Each type of carnival discourse stands in a different relationship to the 'other' word hidden inside it. *Skaz,* from the Russian *skazal* (to say, to tell), indicates an orientation towards another person's spoken language: when the author reproduces someone else's speech, not his or her own, this is double-edged *skaz.* Stylization extends another person's style by means of exaggeration. Faithful to the tones and intentions of another author's style, stylization merely makes that style double-edged by inserting it into a foreign body of work. Parody, on the other hand, "introduces a semantic direction into that word which is diametrically opposed to its original direction." If in stylization the two voices merge, parody sets them against one another in hostile conflict. Considering the wide range of double-edged discourse, Bakhtin concludes that dialogical language lies at the foundation of prose, as versus poetic, language: "The possibility of employing within a single work words of various types in their extreme expressions without reducing them to a common denominator is one of the most essential characteristics of prose. Herein lies the most profound distinction between prose style and poetic style." In effect, Bakhtin is saying that prose language is essentially intertextual, bearing the traces of the other literary contexts through which it has passed.

Monological or single-voiced language is virtually absent from *Tres tristes tigres*. In order to convert spoken into literary language, Cabrera states, he transferred speech from the horizontal to the vertical plane, increasing the resonances of the word:

> uno de mis experimentos . . . era tratar de llevar este lenguaje básico, convertir este lenguaje oral en un lenguaje literario válido. Es decir, llevar este lenguaje si tú quieres horizontal, absolutamente hablado, a un plano vertical, a un plano artistico, a un plano literario.

> [one of my experiments . . . was to try to turn this basic language—to convert this oral language—into a valid literary language. In other words, to take this, if you will, horizontal, absolutely spoken, language, onto an artistic plane, a literary plane.]

The end product of the transfer was to replace monological language by dialogical *skaz,* intertextuality, parody, and a further double-edged form, translation, making Cabrera's language eminently self-conscious—literary—referring less to a real context than to an intertext.

It is no accident that while *Tres tristes tigres* starts off with a barrage of oratorical rhetoric in its prologue, Petronius' *Satyricon* commences with a fierce diatribe against exactly this same rhetoric. Thinking anachronistically, one might consider the opening chapter of the *Satyricon* as an implicit response to, and criticism of, the high-blown rhetoric of Cabrera's emcee, which grossly distorts the image of Cuba it sets forth. His is a rhetoric of the old Spanish school— sonorous, romantic, clichéd, with little meaningful connection to the underlying reality. However, when the lights fail to go on, the emcee forgets himself and says "coño": here, then, we encounter the first debunking of canonized culture, an attack on its language which illustrates *Tres tristes tigres's* anti-rhetorical stance.

There are various kinds of translation in the prologue, and all are betrayals. The greatest distortion takes place in the translation of Cuban reality into language, for the announcer filters Cuba not only through rhetoric but also through ste-

reotypes, the result being a version of Cuba whose only reality is found in the glossy blurbs of travel brochures. Brazil suffers the same misrepresentation, transformed into a Hollywood paradise, the "*Brazil* de Carmen Miranda y de Jose Carioca" (15). These are actually inter-cultural translations which shape foreign realities to accord with tourists' preconceptions, or rather, misconceptions. Whenever the narrator provides an instantaneous translation from English to Spanish, or vice-versa, he perpetuates the fraud. Passing from one class of false discourse to another, with each 'literary,' and thus non-literal, translation he adds new rhetorical flourishes. At the same time, he is guilty of serious translational boners, through mispronunciation ("Brazuil terra dye nostra felichidade" [15]), misrepresentation (William Campbell, we learn later, is not the heir to the soup fortune), and mistranslation ("Discriminatory public" [19]). Oral neologisms, reproducing the announcer's speech patterns, heighten the absurdity of his translations ("Amableypacientepublicocubanoes MisterCambellelfamosomillionarioherederodeunafortunadesopas" [17]). Yet auguring the change in language which follows the prologue, the narrator concludes by nullifying his own language: "Sin traduccion . . . *without translation* . . . sin palabras pero con música y sana alegria y esparcimiento. . . " (19).

The emcee has presented the reader with an entirely verbal reality, one which exists only in his words. Accordingly, if not conversely, what assumes great importance is the negative space, what is *not* said, but will be said later. For behind the eloquent rhetorical facade lies the true language of Cuba, the spontaneous oral speech which dominates the rest of the novel, beginning with "Los debutantes."

Because the narrations of "Los debutantes" appear to be straight monologues with no wordplays or literary allusions, and because, after all, much of "Los debutantes" represents the characters' first steps *towards* the nightworld, one might be tempted to equate these monologues (and here I am referring primarily to the women's voices, because the men's have more 'literary' features) with monological language. From the very first, however, the language of *Tres tristes tigres* is dialogical, characterized by polyphony and *skaz*.

In the carnivalesque novel, the author abdicates to the characters the right to a definitive word or style. Each character becomes a voice articulating one point of view, and in his words coexist two voices: the voice or *skaz* of the character, and the voice of the author which tries to reproduce the character's voice and which always stands at a certain remove—different with each character—from its object. Similarly, the wide range of verbal textures in *Tres tristes tigres,* more noticeable in "Los debutantes" than in any other section (since the male narrators of the remaining chapters tend to speak something of a common language), evinces the author's surrender of his voice to other voices as he attempts to faithfully record the oral *skaz* of each character. Far from monological then, each seeming monologue contains a hidden dialogue between the voice of the author and that of the speaker.

"Los debutantes" most explicitly contributes to the *idioma secreto* by capturing "los diferentes dialectos del espanol que se hablan en Cuba," ["the different dialects of Spanish spoken in Cuba"], the whole range of Cuban speech. One barometer of its striking assortment of voices is the presence of oral neologisms, created to simulate the characters' oral pronunciation or dialect. Already in the Prologue oral neologisms were employed to produce an ironic perspective on the announcer's rhetoric; here, appearing in greater abundance and variety, they serve to distinguish between the several, often unidentified voices. If, as has been said, *Tres tristes tigres* combines the detective story with semiology, then these special signs, the neologisms, provide an important clue to (or sign of) the speaker's identity.

For example, although Delia Doce's letter to her friend Estelvina (pp. 28-33) is written, its neologisms derive from oral pronunciation. Most of her neologisms are either simple spelling mistakes playing on the few nonsound/symbol correspondences of Spanish (i.e. interchanging v and b; s, c, and z; ll and y; omitting h's); misspellings based on pronunciation ("rialidá," "yegârá"); or the conjoinings of words according to pronunciation ("Mariasantisima"). In the narrative about Magalena Cruz (34-35) we find the highest incidence of neologisms. While the speech of its mysterious narrator (is it Beba Longorio, who later is seen in Magalena's company and has some peculiar hold over her?) may appear to be the most lower-class or unregenerated, it is nevertheless the most uniquely Cuban, displaying several traits characteristic of Cuban Spanish: exchange of the liquid consonants *r* and *l* ("hablal," "coldel"); apocope of the final syllable ("na ma" for "nada" más"); suppression or aspiration of S's ("asi mimo," "etás"); dropping of the intervocalic consonants ("vestia" for "vestida"), and so on. If indeed Beba Longorio is the narrator of this monologue, her next monologue (43-45) reveals a language in the process of transformation. Characterized by the same features of Cuban Spanish just mentioned, her speech has now gravitated towards a more sophisticated tone, acquiring the mannerisms of what she believes to be upper-class speech: a 'feminine' emphasis on words, indicated by italics ("Bueno, *menos* en eso, *Creo*"), or their elongation ("ma-ra-billo-sa"); creation of high-sounding neologisms ("la visconversa"); use of foreign words ("trusó," "*senkiu*"), and so on. Here, as earlier in the Prologue, the use of *skaz* borders on parody, with the author using the character's voice to hostile purposes.

Oral neologisms entail a making strange of language and as such signify the first step towards wordplay. Unfamiliar to the eye and mind, but not to the ear, the distortion of a word's orthographical representation constitutes, in essence, a separation of the signifier from the signified in order to accentuate the word's sound. Unlike the wordplays and allusions which begin to emerge in seminal form with the male narrators' monologues, oral neologisms are pure sound. Their signifiers neither hide nor create unsuspected signifieds; they are self-reflexive, referring back only to the oral dimensions of the word. Orality, therefore, is at the root of all of *Tres tristes tigres's* neologisms, but in wordplay the neologisms acquire a metaphorical depth, an intra-or intertextual dimension. In sum, this making strange of language indicates the path that the novel will take: by substituting the oral for the written and emphasizing sound over meaning, *Tres tristes tigres* defines itself as a large-scale tongue-twister.

> **Orality . . . is at the root of all of *Tres tristes tigres's* neologisms, but in wordplay the neologisms acquire a metaphorical depth, an intra-or intertextual dimension. In sum, this making strange of language indicates the path that the novel will take: by substituting the oral for the written and emphasizing sound over meaning, *Tres tristes tigres* defines itself as a large-scale tongue-twister.**
>
> **—Stephanie Merrim**

In many ways, Laura's story represents the "other" of *Tres tristes tigres,* both in terms of point of view—hers is another, outside perspective on the tigers' nightworld—and in terms of its implications for language. Thematically, Laura's story, told through her monologue in "Los debutantes" and through the eleven sessions with a psychiatrist interpolated throughout the novel, supplies both the woman's point of view on the male-dominated novel, and a different temporal perspective, for her first monologue takes place before she has entered the nightworld, and the sessions occur after she has married Silvestre, thereby bringing to a close both their participation in the nightworld. Consequently, her monologues are our only outside view of the nightworld and, importantly, its aftermath, and they form another novel in miniature, a whole other series within this polyphonic novel.

Significantly enough, the novel proper commences with Laura's statement; "Lo que no le dijimos *nunca* a nadie fue que nosotras también hacíamos cositas debajo del camión" [But what we *never* told anyone was that we too used to play with each other's things under the truck.] (23). What she never told, simply put, was the truth, because the truth was too shameful for Laura and her friend Aurelita to tell. Instead, they displace what was too shameful to tell, the homosexual nature of their activities, onto a more acceptable form, their story exposing the (heterosexual) activities of

Petra and her lover. And further, with each performance of their tale, the two children enlarge upon the details of the story, distorting even that truth. Their translation is thus a betrayal, both of the event and of themselves, and the avoidance of the truth engenders a series of periphrastic lies, lies which come to represent not only a false language, but repression itself. Normal discourse, the truth, is replaced by an "other" language, one with negative connotations.

When we next meet Laura in the first session, the game has become life and the need to tell all that she has repressed is overwhelming. Faced with a stifling lack of communication with her husband, Laura describes herself as "la esfinge ajita de secretos" ["the sphinx that had its bellyful of secrets"] (67) and turns to the psychiatrist in the attempt finally to unburden herself. Yet she has no words to impart her feelings: nothing that Laura says in the first session is her own; she speaks with her husband's words. The inability to speak the truth has installed itself as the center of Laura's life, making her an inveterate liar who translates her life into a series of falsehoods. Only by the seventh appointment does Laura endeavour to undo the lies she has told the psychiatrist ("El viernes le dije una mentira, doctor. Grandisima" ["I told you a lie on Friday, doctor. A really big lie."] (209) Peeling away the layers of falsehood, Laura grasps for a mode of genuine communication, but in the last, eleventh, session, she is on the verge of total breakdown.

"Seseribó" and "Casa de los espejos" further develop the counterpoint between men and women in *Tres tristes tigres.* While *Tres tristes tigres*'s male characters find an outlet for political and sexual frustration in verbal humor, its female characters are denied that outlet and thereby condemned to madness and artificiality, forced to play Ophelia to the men's Hamlets. Women are seen as dangerous and taboo ("Seseribó") and exposed as fakes of monstrous proportions when they pass through the "cámara del detector de mentiras" [lie detector] which strips them of their disguises ("casa de los espejos"). At the same time, in both chapters whenever women are present, we note a surge of wordplay or "masturhablarse" on the men's part, in defense against the women. This curious attraction and repulsion that the female characters exercise over the males can, on the one hand, be attributed to the fact that the female characters in *Tres tristes tigres* represent the baser plane of sensuality while the males strive for a higher, intellectual plane. In other words, whereas the closely knit circle of "tigers" postulate the nightworld, largely a mental construct, as a pure space removed from time, their women, who operate on a physical and sensual level, resort to grotesque extremes of make-up and disguises to ward off the ravages of time. Derided and scorned by the male characters (consider, in this regard, also the episode in "Bachata" with Beba and Magalena), the women—disallowed the gift of humor—serve as victims who must be sacrificed in order to preserve the intellectual purity of the

nightworld. On the other hand, but analogously, the true surrender of oneself to a woman (as in the case of Silvestre) would bring an end to the nightworld, hence the tigers' insistence on their masturbatory verbal continence which precludes the need for (the opposite) sex.

It is thought that macaronic or polyglot literature, with its monstrous verbal exuberance, may originally have been developed to celebrate the crowning of those real monsters, the carnival king and queen. Be that as it may, there is certainly a carnival impulse in the polyglot nature of *Tres tristes tigres,* which transforms the normally unilingual stylistic surface of a text into a polyphonic Babel of languages. This plurality of languages echoes the plurality of styles which make of *Tres tristes tigres* a collage of heterogeneous materials.

Not only different languages, but different kinds of languages—negative and positive—coincide in the novel. The polyglot conversation in English and French of the third section of "Seseribo" where Cué and his girlfriend show off their sophistication is ridiculed: "Ellos dos parecian muy preocupados en demostrar que podian hablar franglés y besarse al mismo tiempo" ["They were both deeply absorbed in showing they could speak French and kiss at the same time."] (94) Eribó complains that the two of them "quieren convertir al español en una lengua muerta" ["want to turn Spanish into a dead language."] (96): the use of foreign languages is one more negative product of Cuba's cultural "barroquismo" and hence receives a parodic treatment in *Tres tristes tigres.* At the same time, there figure in the text specialized languages or professional jargons, which fulfill a positive function as alternative languages. Already in *Un Officio del Siglo XX,* the *mundo al inverso* of movies is equated with its specialized languages, as in the section entitled "La lengua de Cain es el lenguaje del cine." ["Cain's language is the language of the movies."] Here, each tiger chooses a particular art upon which to base his private *mundo al inverso,* a gateway to the absolute, and each field has its own jargon. Eribó speaks the language of music (in "Seseribó"), Silvestre the language of the movies, Códac of photography and Cué, whose conversation is a weave of quotations, of the theatre. Beginning with "Seseribó," then, and extending throughout the text, we encounter a variety of alternative languages giving voice to the several underground worlds which converge in the nightworld.

To the eye, "Ella cantaba boleros" and the other narrative sections present a smooth narrative surface, unbroken by dialogue, short paragraphs or typographic play. But although the surface may look homogeneous, like all else in *Tres tristes tigres* it is woven of a heterogeneous body of stuff, encompassing many layers. Codac's narratives avail themselves of the technique, used by Beat Generation writers such as Jack Kerouac, of framing massively long sentences—often the length of a paragraph—into which are drawn many thoughts, sentences, points of view and voices, Dialogue enters only indirectly, without quotation marks, creating, almost imperceptibly, a tissue of alternating voices, such as the following:

> y al poco rato el griego que me dice ¿Por qué no saca a bailar a mi mujer? y yo le digo que no bailo y él me dice que cómo es posible que hay a un cubano que no baile y Magalena que le dice, No hay uno, hay dos, porque yo tampoco bailo . . . (129).

> [and soon the Greek is saying to me, Why don't you ask my wife for a dance? and I tell him I don't dance and he says, It's not possible, a Cuban who doesn't dance? and Magalena says, There's two of them because I can't dance either . . . (127)]

Ostensibly a monologue, in reality Códac's narratives are a melting pot of voices, a polyphonic dialogue. Cué's contribution to "casa de los espejos" also partakes of these twisting polyphonic sentences, supplementing the dialogical interplay of characters' voices with literary allusions or quotations. Once again, as with the *skaz* of "Los debutantes," but in a different way, the monologue proves to enclose a dialogue.

While in "Ella cantaba boleros" there is a little verbal distortion through wordplays, we do find innovative distortion in terms of the sentence. The polyphonic phrases of **Tres tristes tigres** represent an opening up of language, for certain techniques allow the sentences to continue almost indefinitely. Cabrera employs existing linguistic means such as parataxis, hypotaxis, semi-colons and colons to extend the sentence, while adding a technique of this own—slashes ("un si es no es falsa/trabajada/viril" [147]).

However, within this framework it is through a more far-reaching means of re-organization that the sentences succeed in perpetuating themselves at such great length. Metaphorical construction is the important and all-pervasive structuring technique of Cabrera's prose and usually takes the form of paradigmatic overlapping—repetition with change:

> Y alargaba una pierna sepia, tierra ahora, chocolate ahora, café ahora, tabaco ahora, azúcar, prieto ahora . . . (66).

> [and she stretched out a leg sepia one moment, then earth-brown, then chocolate, tobacco, sugar-colored, black . . .] (61)

> ella puso sus cinco chorizos sobre mi muslo, casi sus cinco salami que adornan un jamón sobre mi muslo, su mano sobre mi muslo . . . (70)

> [she put her 5 *chorizos,* five sausages, on my thigh, almost like five salamis garnishing a ham on my thigh, she put her hand on my thigh . . .] (65)

The omnipresent devices of repetition, slash constructions and anaphora also create metaphorical planes of equivalence:

> nunca la vi más hermosa que en aquella penumbra—excepto desnuda excepto desnuda excepto desnuda (150).

> [I have never seen her more beautiful than she was that evening—except naked except naked except naked.] (150)

> fabricó la gana/ el ansia/la necesidad de que la viera desnuda (150).

> [/Livia/ was manufacturing the desire, the anxiety, the necessity for me to see her naked . . .] (150)

> Es la salvaje belleza de la vida, sin que me oyera naturalmente, sin que me entendiera si me había oido, naturalmente . . . (64)

> [She's the savage beauty of life, without Irenita hearing me, naturally, not that she would have understood if she had heard me, naturally . . .] (my translation)

Most often, several of these metaphorical techniques will appear in conjunction, converting the sentence into a syntactically orchestrated instrumental solo which generates its own varying rhythm of repetitions.

Carrying our investigation beyond stylistic analysis to the narrative organization of the text as a whole, we can point out certain similarities between style and narrative structure which reveal **Tres tristes tigres** to be what might be called an "aphasic" text. All of its narrative structure obeys a non-traditional, non-linear logic and development. Each section is situated in a time/space different and discontinuous from the next: for example, on page 276, the reader is surprised to learn that Bustrófedon had already died by the time the opening scene of the novel takes place, a fact which implies that the majority of the text deals with the last sparks of the nightworld. Further, as stated earlier, **Tres tristes tigres** features a collage-like construction, binding together generically heterogeneous materials and obliterating the linear development of a plot. These multi-generic elements (such as "Los visitantes," "La muerte de Trotsky," etc.) are linked to the more narrative sections only through association, for they extend and often define the novel's major themes. In fact, the narrative sections themselves are organized associatively and not linearly, following cinematic techniques of flashback and montage. The end product is a non-linear text which works on a new associative logic, and whose structure reflects Bustrófedon's particular kind of aphasia: a contiguity disorder that impedes the metonymic organization of discourse.

The story on which "Los visitantes" is based is purposely banal and cliché-ridden. Therefore, with the subject matter so trivial, the reader's attention is automatically shifted to *how* the story is told or presented. And since the story is presented through a series of translations which become travesties of an (absent) original text, it is the process of translation that comes to the fore. Translation, as we shall see, gives rise to a new kind of double-edged word, one in which the translated word struggles to remain faithful to the original voice inside it, but often falls, inadvertently, into parody.

"Los visitantes" explicitly illustrates the problematics of translation with several cases in point in which, at every stage, the *traduttore* is a *tradittori* who betrays both reality and language. As in the "Prólogo," there are two kinds of translation to be found here—intercultural and intralingual; as the first is quite obvious, let us turn to the second.

Upon first reading, Silvestre's appears to be a "good" translation; it reads well, the Spanish is colloquial; in sum, the translation seems to stand up as well as an original might. But only when we read Rine's "Pésima" [awful] translation do we realize what has happened. This second translation, and, obviously, the original story, abounds with cultural references, wordplays, and foreign languages, many of which Rine finds untranslatable and resorts to footnotes to explain. (Perhaps this is a comment on the untranslateability of the text itself, which features the same traits.) Then, returning to Silvestre's version, we find that he has merely left out the untranslatable elements, flattening the polyphonic texture into a single dimension. Silvestre thereby sacrifices accuracy for style, achieving a "readable" text by betraying the original.

However, it is a toss-up which translation, Silvestre's or Rine's, is the greater betrayal, for they illustrate the two possible extremes of translation. While Silvestre's version undermines its double-edgedness, being good Spanish, by disregarding the original, Rine's is patently double-edged, a literal translation. In a literal translation the original language shines through, determining the lexicon and syntax of the new product; such translations in effect are little more than a linguistic pony to aid the reader whose knowledge of the foreign language is insufficient, but who nevertheless wishes to sample the original flavor. The paradox, then, is that a literal translation, while faithful to the original language, is a betrayal of the original text and its stylistic integrity. In other words, the most faithful double betrays its

own image, as Cué makes clear: "O estabas pensando en la traición o tradicióon o traducción de Rine, siempre leal, al pie de la letra as í?" (440) [Or were you thinking of the treason or tradition or translation of Rine Leal, always loyal, to the letter of the law?] (my translation)

Built into the story itself is another kind of translation, a critique taking the form of Mrs. Campbell's "Reparos" or "Correcciones." Mrs. Campbell criticizes both her husband's style and his portrayal of the events; demanding realism or journalistic accuracy, she unmasks the fictional character of her husband's narrative. However, at the same time as she adopts the stance of a literary critic finding fault with the inaccuracy of his style, she endows her own narrative with a recognizably "literary" style in phrases such as: "Navegamos por entre edificios de espejos, reverberos que comían los ojos . . . Un muelle se acercó lenta, inexorablemente" (181). [We sailed between buildings that were more mirrors than buildings, reflections that could swallow the eyes of those who gazed at them . . . Slowly, inevitably, a pier moved toward us.] (185-6) By positing this contradiction, Cabrera seems to suggest that any written form is a style—that there is no "zero" degree style—and that objectivity is simply an illusion. Yet the greatest illusion of all is Mrs. Campbell's mere existence. At the end of the novel we learn that there is no real Mrs. Campbell, that the paper tiger wife of "Los visitantes" is only a fictional projection of the author's personality onto a different persona, as are all characters. In this case, language gives rise to an illusion which betrays not only reality, but also the reader.

Although "Rompecabeza," with its subordination of the narrative to wordplay, seems to stand apart from the body of the novel, it actually comprises a key or *scholium* as vital to the text as "Bachata." When read word by word, to paraphrase Gertrude Stein, this writing that is anything becomes something—more specifically, wordplay reveals itself as the matrix for **Tres tristes tigres's** *idioma secreto*. We shall examine, as space permits, certain salient characteristics of wordplay.

Throughout this elegiac text, as we repeatedly see, much is made of the fact that all translation is a betrayal and that any language proves insufficient to carry out **Tres tristes tigres's** ecological task of recapturing the nightworld lost. Viewed in this light, wordplay appears as a substitute or *anti*-language evolved in the face of the betrayal of conventional language. As a result of the failure of language to successfully translate reality or a given message, wordplay de-emphasizes the signifier, centering its discourse on the actual physical properties of the sign—its plastic and musical dimensions—and not, as one critic aptly notes, on the conveying of a message:

La comunicación ha sido no sólo pospuesto sino

inexorablemente conmutada por una devaluación del carácter racional del lenguaje en una exaltación del la palabra como signos musicales o plásticos.

[Communication has not only been postponed, but inexorably switched, by means of a devaluation of the rational character of language, into a exaltation of words as musical or plastic signs.]

By taking recourse to the signifier and the phonically deter-mined associations of signifiers, this new oral idiom attains to what can be seen as an autonomous, non-referential lan-guage, giving (at least) the *illusion* of an absolute structure, independent of reality and complete in and of itself. Under these conditions, language can no longer be accused of be-traying reality or even meaning, since it is faithful only to its own origins—the linguistic code—and any 'meaning' it produces will be found in the relationship between signifiers.

Cabrera's special wordplays most often combine the char-acteristics of the anagram and pun, for a single sign (such as "Dádiva" [213]) proves anagramatically to harbour a se-ries of signifiers (Dádiva—ávida, vida, ida, David) related by sound and not by meaning. Carlos Fuentes has praised Cabrera for destroying "la fatal tradición de univocidad de nuestra prosa" ["the lethal tradition in our prose of univocality"] and for revealing the word as "un nudo de significados." ["a knot of meanings"] Such an opening up of language, in which one word engenders many, results in an excess of signifiers, an "intratextuality" of the word. And this intratextuality, in turn, reveals wordplay as an eminently *dialogical* form.

Now one of the most serious objections levied against the word-within-wordplay series is that they rupture the met-onymic story-telling flow of the narrative. However, a closer look at the relationship between signifiers reveals another structuring principle at work as binding as metonymy. As in the narrative sections, here we encounter the *metaphorical* technique of paradigmatic overlapping, repetition with change. A good illustration of this technique is the follow-ing wordplay progression where the paradigm (Bustro- or Bus-) is added to a (syntagmatic) series of qualifiers:

y nosotros en el más acá muertos de risa en la orilla del mantel, con este pregonero increíble, el heraldo, Bustrófeno, éste, gritando, BustrofenóNemo chico eres un Bustrófonbraun, gritando bustrórriba ma-rina, gritando, Bustifón, Bustrosimún, Busmonzón, gritando, Viento Bustrófenomenal, gritando a diestro y siniestro y ambidiestro (208).

[and we're still there in the hereafter drowning of laughter on the shores of the tablecloth . . . with this unbelievable public proclaimer BustrophenoNemo,

a Bustrofonbraum, crying out loud, Bustyphoon, Bustornado, Bustrombone, out-crying himself, Bustrombamarina, crying to left and right . . .] (214-15)

The concatenation of names is paratactic and metaphorical, relating disparate terms not through conjunctions but by the prefixation of Bus- or bustro-.

The various properties of wordplay suggested here, which make of it an anti-language, have been criticized as purpose-less and self-indulgent. Yet how can they be purposeless when Cabrera has stated that "the book's sense and sound is the book's language and the book's language is the book's meaning"? Given the unsuspected continuity between word-play and the *idioma secreto* of the text, might not these self-indulgences be said to comprise a pure core or model of the linguistic axis of the text? If *Tres tristes tigres's* protago-nists are indeed the nightworld and language, the correspon-dence is exact: world and language/anti-world and anti-language.

Whereas in "Los visitantes," the devaluation of the story's content brought matters of translation to the fore, the fact that "La muerte de Trotsky" repeats the same story in sev-eral versions allows questions of parody and style to surface. There are two possible ways of looking at "La muerte de Trotsky": we can consider each story separately as a parody of a particular author, or we can take all the stories globally as a fan of stylistic permutations or translations of a single ideal (and thus absent) story, as an excess of signifiers for one signified. From the first standpoint we shall see that parody functions as a translation of style, to which is added an explicit measure of irony (in translation proper, we re-peat, the ironic or parodic element is unintentional, though perhaps inevitable), irony which links up with iconoclasm. With regard to the second standpoint, I believe that Cabrera aspired to include the whole gamut of Cuban literary cul-ture, showing how Cuban writers might adapt themselves to the demands of socialist literature. The result is a series of diverse styles in which each literary language entails another modulation of Cuba's polyglot voice.

While it is truly remarkable that one country should have produced the many, disparate literary voices we find when we take each piece separately, one further tie besides Cuba unites them: representatives of sanctioned culture, they are all debunked by Cabrera's parodies. Parody joins with icono-clasm on more than one front to dethrone the powerful. The task of parody is ridicule and reform, an ironic literary criti-cism. By attaching this "song sung beside" to the works of all major Cuban writers, Cabrera aims a blow not only at the writers but at the Cuban establishment which sanctions them. Another important factor in "La muerte de Trotsky," this time a thematic one, is that of generational conflict, in which a second generation of revolutionaries kills off the first, symbolized by Trotsky himself. Much the same conflict comprises a defining characteristic of parody: one generation of writers figuratively kills off the previous generation or generations, their parodies furnishing an antithetical completion of the previous writers' works. Lastly, this parodying of a political action, Trotsky' murder, not only mocks but also neutralizes that action. Anything threatening that enters the nightworld must be de-activated, often through humor. Here political action, history, is first transformed into literature and then neutralized by parody: a monological form is rendered impotent by a dialogical form.

There is further irony in the fact that these examples of Socialist literature, a genre so committed to the transparent representation of reality, should here produce so great a variety of styles. That the infinite variety of style represents one of Cabrera's central concerns is reflected in *Exorcismos de esti (l) o*, "La muerte de Trotsky," and, indeed, in the collage-like structure of *Tres tristes tigres*. As the similarity in titles indicates, *Exorcismos* obviously takes its cue from Raymond Queneau's *tour de force, Exercises de Style,* a unique "essay" on style in which a single, unexceptional anecdote is told ninety-nine different ways. As in "La muerte de Trotsky," in Queneau's text the content of the story remains unchanged while the style permutes itself around a central axis, thereby giving rise, in both texts, to a large-scale configuration of paradigmatic overlapping.

However, there is a cardinal difference between Queneau's exercises and those of Cabrera: while Queneau's work is constructive, forming a unique dictionary of literary styles, Cabrera's is destructive, an exorcism of style. Both authors utilize a process of deconstruction (of discourse into its various components) and hyperbolic accumulation (of a single technique, or techniques in the case of Cabrera) to create a product which is recognizable as a style or *écriture*. But whereas Queneau's exercises tend more to stylization, i.e. simple exaggeration, Cabrera's fall squarely in the realm of parody. Through parody, like is turned on like as style destroys—or exorcises style. "La muerte de Trotsky" thus mirrors a prime intention of this whole text, which elevates oral language and parodically debunks literary style.

> —No puedes oir cómo el viejo Bach juega en la tonalidad en re, cómo construye sus imitaciones, cómo hace las variaciones imprevisiblemente pero donde el tema lo permite y lo sugiere y no antes, nunca después, y a pesar de ello logra sorprender? No te parece un esclavo con toda la libertad? (295)

> [—Can't you hear how old Bach plays on the tonality in D, how he builds up his imitations, how he makes his variations always unpredicatable but only when the theme allows and suggests it and

never before, never after, and how despite that he always manages to take you by surprise? Doesn't he seem like a slave with all the freedom in the world?] (320)

This remark, a key within a key, tells us certain crucial things about "Bachata," the self-styled scholia and longest section of *Tres tristes tigres*. Its first sentence refers to Bach's serial compositions, "The Art of the Fugue," along the lines of which "Bachata" is structured. Defining a fugue as,

> A polyphonic composition constructed on one or more short subjects, or themes, which are harmonized according to the laws of counter-point, and introduced from time to time with various contrapuntal devices,

we can see how polyphony informs the structure of "Bachata," with its discussions and variations of several philosophical themes. Indeed, polyphony stands out as the foremost characteristic of "Bachata," and especially of its language, for here is found the culmination of the dialogical word, in concentrations of wordplay (intratextual and intertextual) denser even than those of "Rompecabeza." The second sentence of the quote evokes the concept of game, in which the fixing of rules affords the player a special kind of freedom. A key to those special games, the text and the nightworld, "Bachata" clarifies their rules. But, as we shall see with particular respect to language, the principles of the game assert themselves only to fall apart as the nightworld dissolves, because "the center cannot hold."

In "Bachata," where the dialogical word reaches its peak, we encounter the whole range of oral and paragrammatic forms previously discussed. Silvestre, Bustro's most dedicated disciple, carries on his friends' wordplays in homage to him. And a rival "Rompecabeza," Cué's "Confesiones de un comedor de gofio cubano," features number puzzles, projects for aleatory literature and typographical games. Parody plays as important a role as before: Silvestre stylizes Borges' "Tema del traidor y del héroe," and Cué's poem, "Si te llamaras Babel y no Beba Martínez" parodies Neruda's "Bacarola." Cué's specialty as an actor, however, is to speak in quotations. All manner of quotations, be they direct ("Yo soy yo y mi circumstancia"—[335]; deformed (the vast majority, e.g. "El joder corrompe, el joder total corrompe totalmente" [326]); or disguised ("Pero no quiero conocerla, que no quiero verla" [325]), figure in his speech, endowing it with a paragrammatic, or plagiaristic texture. Since what Cué plagiarizes are cultural commonplaces, his paragrams acquire a parodic edge through two techniques. First, like puns, they are non-contextual: quoted out of context, the phrases form a kind of *bricolage*, bits and pieces gathered without regard to their specific function. Second, they are almost invariably distorted, turned into parodic doubles of themselves. If, as Lautréamont said, "Le plagiat est nécessaire," then Cué's speech represents that intertextual dialogue latent in every literary word.

A feast of dialogical language, "Bachata" celebrates the nightworld on all levels, affirming it one final time in the face of ever-encroaching reality. "Bachata," which along with the reference to Bach means "spree," is exactly that, an afternoon-through-morning of carousing, drinking, eating, driving, attempted womanizing and, most of all, conversation. Since in Bustro's "Geometrias del espíritu" a circle symbolizes perfect happiness, the concentric construction of "Bachata"—variations and returns to a theme all the while encircling the Malecón in the car—suggest the characters' desire to keep their happiness intact. But even in the neutralized space of the nightworld there enter threats, both negative and positive, to its existence. Fierce negative images, such as references to death, Silvestre's horror movie fantasies, nightmares of apocalyptic visions, and so on, abound in "Bachata." More and more the nightworld is invaded by a reality of dark, menacing aspect: Silverstre may be going blind, he is unable to write, Cué's artificial posturing alienates his friend, Magalena is either mad or being tortured by Beba, Bustro is dead. On the other hand, betrayal of the nightworld and of each other is imminent as Cué and Silvestre prepare to abandon their Hamlet-like passivity and take positive action, Silvestre by marrying Laura, and Cué by joining Fidel. Its existence rendered extremely precarious by these invasions on either side, the nightworld asserts itself one last time in full force, exposing its true nature as a defense against reality.

As the threat of reality causes the nightworld to affirm itself, so, on the level of language, do the presence of truth and danger give rise to wordplay as a defense. Like Laura, Silvestre is unable to tell the truth and avoids doing so with a series of periphrastic substitutions—not with lies, but with allusions and wordplay. Many of Silvestre's allusions (to Shakespeare, horror movies, literature) are ruled by Laura, with the hidden meaning implied but not stated. Yet allusions do not suffice, for Cué will avoid understanding Silvestre's confession at all costs; unable to convey his message obliquely, Silvestre breaks into compensatory wordplay:

> No entendió o no quiso entender. Al entendedor renuente no le bastan las palabras. Hay que hacerle cifras, mostrarle los numeritos. Lástima, podía haberle hablado ahora. Lo haré para mí. Masturhablarme. Solución que es polución. La solution d'un sage n'est que la polution d'un page . . . (362)

> [He didn't hear or he didn't want to hear. Words are not enough for the Pythagorean listener. It needs fig-

ures. I'd have to show him some prime numbers. A pity. I could have spoken to him just now. Well, I'll talk to myself instead. To masturdebate. . . . Make a solution of pollution. The solution of a sage is to pollute a page . . .] (391)

At other points in the text dense wordplay, either by one character or in a dialogue between characters, is set off by dangerous elements: Silvestre alternates between wordplay and narrative in his meditations on death (343-45); watching Cué look at himself in the mirror after his confession about going to the Sierra reminds Silvestre of the theme of the betrayal of doubles and incites wordplay (348-49); the presence of women, now particularly threatening because it recalls Laura, spurs a long exchange of wordplay between the men, to the exclusion of Beba and Magalena. Here, more than ever, we are given to understand wordplay as an alternate or compensatory language, explicitly called an "anti-lenguaje" [anti-language] (393) by Silvestre.

When, at these points, wordplay does take over, it comprises a fully self-sufficient language with its own structure and logic. In "Bachata" we can see the full-scale workings of *Tres tristes tigres's* dialogical language in dense pages of wordplay such as those of Silvestre (365-66), which are motivated by Beba and Magalena's entrance. Here any pretensions to a narrative, story-telling logic are abandoned as the discourse moves onto an associative plane ruled entirely by sound rather than meaning. The separation of the signified from the signifier, along with refuge in the signifier found in wordplay, once again manifests itself as the central organizing principle of *Tres tristes tigres's* language. Effacing, at once, the pole of the signified and the monological word, all the forms of dialogical language which have appeared separately until now, from the intratextual to the intertextual, converge and work together to the exclusion of non-carnivalesque elements. Related by sound, any one dialogical form can induce another or others, for they bounce off each other as well as combine to work together. Though apparently the most "self-indulgent," such pages as this nevertheless represent the culmination and conquest of the text's *idioma secreto,* its defeat of monological discourse.

Yet, ironically, this culmination of dialogical language at the same time bespeaks its downfall; deforming a quote from Yeats, Cué remarks, "The *Beast* lacks all convictions, while the words are full of passive insanity" (354). Cué's and Silvestre's words are indeed suffused with a "passive insanity" which derives from the desperate, ultimately futile, attempt to avoid truth and ward off threats to the nightworld. If before, as in "Rompecabeza," the nightworld and language held strong, here they are crumbling, with the infiltration of reality transforming wordplay into a pathetic avoidance of the truth. To ward off danger (in the form of the two women), Cué and Silvestre contrive to speak a language unknown to the women, thereby purposely alienating them; the men and the women are in effect speaking two different languages, and the Babelic breakdown of communication precludes any seduction of the women. Trapped between two conflicting impulses, of attraction and repulsion, Cué and Silvestre lose command of themselves, uncontrollably persisting in their solipsistic game:

> Creo que fue entonces cuando nos preguntamos, tácitamente . . . por qué hacerlas reír. ¿Qué éramos? ¿Clowns, el primero y el segundo, enterradores entre risas o seres humanos, personas corrientes y molidas, gente? ¿No era más fácil enamorarlas? (391).

> [I think it was at this point that we began wondering tacitly . . . whether it was worth making them laugh. What were we? Clowns, 1st and 2nd gravediggers when we weren't laughing or human beings, common and guarded persons, people? Wouldn't it be easier to make love to them?] (424)

Rather than succumbing to madness, Cué and Silvestre commence their re-entry of reality on positive, though divergent courses. Cué's theory of *contradictorios,* based on Ortega y Gasset's theory of tragedy, heralds their abandonment of the nightworld. In Cué's conception, *contradictorios,* who historically were warriors so brave that they were allowed to break all tribal rules in times of peace, are people with the courage to challenge society's norms, or, according to Ortega y Gasset, people who carry their ideal project into the world and defend that project. At first, after exhaustively listing figures whom they believe were *contradictorios,* Cué and Silvestre confess that they themselves are not. Later, however, Cué admits that Silvestre is indeed: "Un contradictorio. ¿Del cine, de la literatura o de la vida real? O hay que esperar todavía . . . el último capítulo? Titulado como, Desenmascarado o Evilly the Kid Strikes Back?" (429) [A contradictory. Of movies, literature or real life? Or do we have to wait for the final episode, like in those old Monogrammed serials? Unmasked or Evilly the Kid Strikes Back?] (464) An unmasking, a striking back which would allow Cué and Silvestre to become *contradictorios,* entails assuming a course of positive action which would carry the utopian core of the nightworld into the outside reality. And while the last chapter falls outside *Tres tristes tigres* (though perhaps in the realm of *Vista del Amanecer en el Trópico*), each character's choice represents one pole of a possible ideal project: Silvestre's, personal fulfillment, and Cué's, social fulfillment through political action.

The re-entry into reality also entails an annihilation of the secret language. When at last Silvestre discloses the truth about Laura, he is forced to cut his way through the ruins of the game language:

> Me quedé callado. Traté de encontrar algo más que refranes y frases hechas, una frase por hacer, palabras, alguna oración regada por aquí y por allá. No era ni pelota ni ajedrez, era armar un rompecabezas. (434)

> [I fell silent. I tried looking for something better than the usual pat sayings and catchphrases. A phrase to catch. Words and sentences scattered here and there. It wasn't either baseball or chess, it was a seesaw puzzle. Crisscrosswords.] (470)

Eschewing all double entendres, he finally states quite simply, *"Me voy a casar con ella"* (*434*) [*"I'm going to marry her"*] (*470*) thereby nullifying the periphrases and signalling his re-entry into monological discourse. And although Silvestre's crucial remark, "una frase por hacer," ["a phrase to catch"] symbolizes a search for the word to be carried over into the absent "último capítulo," ["last chapter"] perhaps language's double, silence, will replace the much-sought word: at the end of "Bachata" "en silencio" is obsessively interpolated between the pieces of Silvestre's discourse. Here, as throughout the novel, when language cedes to silence, talk cedes to action.

That madness which Silvestre and Cúe must needs avoid, but whose presence lurks in their words and in the nightworld, gains a voice in the Epilogue. Like Laura's psychoanalytic sessions, the Epilogue takes us, for one final moment, beyond the sphere of the text proper; both inside and outside the novel, it provides a picture of the madness and the language of madness which hover at the extremities of the nightworld. *La loca* sits in the park and talks to herself; running uncontrollably through the same monologue each time, endlessly, like a pianola score, she is unable to translate the world except into broken scatological images. Fragmented, oral, repetitive, metaphorically structured, ruled by a hermetic and unfathomable logic and thus robbed of its communicative function, her language resembles a crude distillation of wordplay carried to its ultimate extremes— the game become life. A Dorian Gray portrait of wordplay turned to ruin, the epilogue draws the fine line between anti-language and the language of madness.

With this cruel touch, the Epilogue adds one final dimension to *Tres tristes tigres*'s secret language. In the course of our discussion we have witnessed the development of a new language: its inception in the *skaz* of "Los debutantes," its infiltration of style and syntax, its assuming of various dialogical shapes (parody, translation and *bricolage*) and progressive acquisition of paragrammatic depth, its culmination and takeover of the verbal space in "Bachata," and finally, the secret idiom''s annihilation when threatened by its analogue, the language of madness. Polyphony, emphatic dialogism and metaphorical logic, among other techniques, bind this idiom to the text's grammar, making of the work a cohesive language and of *Tres tristes tigres* an orderly, if otherly, textual universe.

Suzanne Jill Levine (essay date 1984)

SOURCE: "Translating *Infante's Inferno*," in *Substance*, Vol. XIII, No. 1, 1984, pp. 85-94.

[*In the following essay, Levine describes the difficulties of translating Cabrera Infante's linguistically complex work from Spanish to English.*]

A romantic is usually afraid, isn't he, in case reality doesn't come up to expectations.

—Graham Greene, *Our Man in Havana*

I. Word Play

"Faithful poetic translation is an exercise of parallel reveries in two languages," it has been said. My collaboration with the Cuban (and now British) writer Guillermo Cabrera Infante as his faithfully unfaithful translator (how else can one translate traduttore traditore?) started out as an exercise of parallel *repartees,* reparteasing one another in English and Spanish, in a two-faced monologue of compulsive punsters. It all began in London where Cabrera Infante was in the throes of destroying *Tres tristes tigres* (1965) with his British collaborator in order to create a young Frankenstein, *Three Trapped Tigers* (1971), a version more than a translation or—as all translations are—another book. The English version of the Joyceful recreation of spoken Havanese had to be written, spoken rather, in American English, an idiom full of sounds more in tune with crude Cuban than bloody British, just as Havana was closer geographically, culturally, even racially to New York than to the island-city of Cabrera Infante's exile, exotic London.

As Aristotle in the *Poetics* dictates (in the words of his translator), "a good metaphor implies an intuitive perception of the similarity in dissimilars." If *Three Trapped Tigers* is a "good metaphor" of *Tres tristes tigres,* it is perhaps because verbal, stylistic affinities between author and collaborator transcended the inevitable language barrier. As Cabrera Infante once said, I brought to the translation of *Tres tristes tigres* "that sense of humor characteristic of New York Jews, which is based on play upon words and confronts reality with strict verbal logic." We had Marx in common, Julius of course: our shared language was the city-wise humor of the American movies, as well as Lewis Carroll's universe of nonsense: subversive wordplay was our common, if not sacred, ground. As Francis Steegmuller's Flaubert writes, "Don't we,

at bottom, feel just as Chinese as English or French? Aren't all our dreams of foreign places?" ("If you prick us, do we not bleed, etc.?") As translator (traduttora), I was the willing apprentice of Count Dracula Infante, ready to tread upon his dread Transylvania, to follow him unfaithfully (traditora) into that dimension of the Living Dead, the world of writing. To serf on the surface.

A correspondence, a resemblance despite difference, still holds true as we progress through a third translation (the second was *View of Dawn in the Tropics,* [1978]): *La habana para un infante difunto* (1979). Literally "Havana for a Dead Infant," it will become in English *Infante's Inferno,* an opportune title because of its parodical, allusive alliteration: this book is a Dantesque voyage into the Havana of Infante's youth, in search of not one but many Beatrices, in search of love, or rather sex: the dead *infante* remains caught in the circles of the hell and heaven of Havana, a memory, a book, an infinite Proustian discourse (which began perhaps in *Tres tristes tigres*) in which the discourse of the memory of Havana (and of the Infante that was) is all that remains. The unfaithful English title is faithful and fateful: Dante antè Infante. On the same note, the treasonous transformation of a female character named Dulce Espina (Sweet Thorn) into Honey Hawthorne alludes faithfully to her essential qualities—sweetness, thorniness, whore(Haw)ishness. "Hawthorne" also brings to bloom other buds: the book's rich allusions to the universe of literature. Cabrera Infante's *Inferno* can be seen as an ironic comment on the tradition of romance, within which Hawthorne's Puritan fable on the wages of love (or sex) is inscribed. There is Hawthorne, the absurd British agent in *Our Man in Havana* (the inversion of another absurdist, our Havanan in London perhaps?). And also the thorny motif of the "Hawthorne lane" in the English translation of *À la Recherche de Temps Perdu,* the *locus amenus* where Marcel first sees Gilberte, which then becomes a nostalgic refrain throughout the volumes: the whore thorns of love is certainly a motif Cabrera Infante shares with Proust.

The following excerpt from *Infante's Inferno* is another example (any essay on translation can become an infinite list of examples since theory must be subordinated to practice and since one metaphor inevitably leads to another!) of the seeking of the similar in the dissimilar, where wordplay is inscribed in the language of the translation and yet brings to life the language of the original.

Those were the days when Roberto, born Napoleon, Branly, who joined the group as a specialist in vitreous humor, was said to have a friend named Leo Tiparillo, and another called Chinchilla, and we couldn't tell the surnames from the nicknames, doubting that Chinchilla's hide was genuine and wondering how many matches it would take to light Tiparillo. I remember the day Branly became notably noticed by Olga

Andreu. He came to see her bowl of brand new goldfish, and asked with almost scientific curiosity: "Are they adults?" But Olga (christened Volgar by Branly) made Branly's game into a set from her settee, a repartee à la Satie:

"Adulterers"—said Olga. "They're fiendish fish."

"What are their names?"—asked double Branly "Daphne and Chloe?"

"No," said Olga, "Debussy and Ravel."

"Oh, I get it," said Branly, approaching the golden bowl but not bowled over. "Debussy must be the one with the flaxen scales."

"Algae."

"Olgae?"

"Vegetal filaments that float, vaguely."

"Are they from the impressionist school of fish?" asked Branly.

"Yes, Debussy even composed *La mer,* an impression."

"Quite impressive," Branly said. "Though I doubt he did it. Nobody at sea composes *La mer* and a goldfish wouldn't compose *The Fishbowl* either, I hasten to add."

Olga wanted to scare Branly:

"The other one, Ravel, a composer of waltzes and boleros, wrote the *Pavane for a Dead Punster.*"

Branly pretended not to feel the hook and had the last word-fish:

"I suppose that one afternoon Debussy will write *L'après-midi d'un poisson d'or.*"

Branly and Olga's *pasodoble* brings again to your ear's attention this book's alluring alliteration. If the pun was the "lowly form of wit" that permeated *Tres tristes tigres,* the main "game" here is alliteration (the translator's typewriter alliterates, driven by the text to write wet wag instead of wet rag, for instance!). An early structural principle in poetry, alliteration has mostly been employed as an emphatic or comic device, as in *Love's Labours Lost.* It is generally considered a lowly device in English poetry and proper prose even more so than in Spanish, a language whose musical exuberance encourages such license. In the baroque esthet-ics of writers like Lezama Lima, Severo Sarduy, and Cabrera Infante, alliteration and wordplay are part of a Dionysian destruction of language as transparent communicator: to al-literate is to mock conventions of propriety and to glorify words as mysterious objects: subverting the semantic, putting sound before sense, is a kind of liberation.

Alliteration expresses, frees the impulsive, rhythmic nature of language as music—which it is to the child and to the poet. In poetry, feeling is the meaning. In verbal humor, language's impulsive force is what dominates, moving the speaker to express what is repressed. Since *Infante's Inferno* is about memory, mostly erotic memories, alliteration—a common mnemonic device for fixing our memories, as in founding fathers and dancing daughters—harmonizes perfectly with its erotic content: alliterating words literally copulate with one another: the repetition of sounds produces a sensual effect, making the reader/translator conscious of an unconscious tendency to use language as music, as children or *infantes* do.

Music, "the universal language," is what poetic writing aims to be; as Cabrera Infante's narrator says à la Walter Pater at one point, "all writers aim to be musicians." Thus he mentions those "great great" impressionist composers Debussy and Ravel and the avant-garde Satie—Dada's *enfant terrible avant la lettre*—and thus he pays homage to Ravel's title *Pavane pour une infante défuncte.* Just as Cabrera Infante, a reveling Ravel of the unraveling word, seeks the music in words, the rumbling rumba rhythm of Havana in his books, so Ravel, a musician, reveals the music in the verbal reality of his title. It was not in homage to any dead Spanish *infanta,* but was chosen for its lilting alliteration, the sonorous beauty of the title reflecting the nostalgic beauty of the parodical pavana.

Maybe Cabrera Infante is a reincarnation of Ravel, Debussy, and Satie all rolled up in one, or perhaps he is their D'Artagnan: he makes fun of Ravel and Debussy in the corny semi-classical Cuban context, because, like Marx and Engels, they could be confused at times, their musical impressions sounding like one long wave—Debussy's Sea bubbling out of Ravel's fountain pen by mistake or Ravel's *Valse* being a more strident version of Debussy's *La plus que lente.* But precisely because their parodies or "translations" of popular forms are both carnivalesque and nostalgic is why they have so much in common with the Infante of this Inferno, who mocks the Latin male's Don Juan past and his Doñas, but is nostalgic for a lost paradise, which the past always is. As the impressionists created, paradoxically, a very artificial art in their imitations of nature and of popular art, so is this book about how real memories become self-conscious memoirs, more reminiscent of Casanova or *My Secret Life* than of life itself. The repartee à la Satie salutes the wit of Satie, the composer as prankster, the unique and eccentric inventor of strange titles, the musician as writer, or vice versa.

This little repartee, filled with those necessary substitutions of one joke for another, of one play of sounds for another, also sums up the continuous battle of words and wits and, metaphorically, of the sexes that is the process of collaboration which we began in *Tres tristes tigres.* It is no small coincidence that of all the women in *Infante's Inferno,* one might identify, as traduttora, with Olga Andreu, practically the only female in the book who gets to reveal a knack for verbal wit. Many of the other women are more than a match for the male hunter on the sexual battlefield, and at least one is infinitely more clever in the art of emotional manipulation, but Olga is the only, as they say, "wise guy." She is a distant dissonant and even dissident observer—and one of the few female characters who are not objects of the narrator's often obscure desire. Thus she is a kind of feminine counterpart of the first-person narrator who is more of a near-sighted voyeur than an active participant in his own history as a Cuban Casanova. But more later.

II. Marginality

> "New forms in art are created by the canonization of peripheral forms"
>
> —Viktor Shklovsky

Since it is at the level of language that the translator can be most creative, inventive, even subversive, I have preferred to translate writers like Cabrera Infante, Manuel Puig, and Severo Sarduy, who play with language, exposing its infidelity to itself, writers who create a new literature by parodying the old. Translation, another form of parody, is for a writer like Cabrera Infante "a more advanced stage" of the writing of the book, as Jorge Luis Borges once said. Thus, I have had the freedom to exaggerate the parodical elements (such as alliteration) when translating writers like Infante and Puig, particularly because they have been actively involved in the "subversion" of their originals. (Alliteration is also "contaminating" another book I am translating, Sarduy's neobaroque *Maitreya,* bubbling with courtly curtseys, mortified mourners, stark stages, and impeccable arecas.)

Though writers like Garcia Marquez and Vargas Llosa seem more obviously dissident because of their political postures, the more marginal writers, like Puig, Infante, Sarduy, and Reinaldo Arenas, are dissident in a more corrosive manner, digging into the root (route) of hypocrisy, into the very matter in which our consciousness is inscribed, that is, language. Like Lewis Carroll, father of the absurd, Infante, especially the Infante of *Tres tristes tigres,* twists words inside out, revealing their hollow center. Puig exposes our everyday languages, even the language we dream in, as suspect, as

concealing what it most intends to reveal. Sarduy renews the avant-garde tradition of poetic prose and obliges us to read a novel as if it were a poem, to surrender to the pleasure of suggestion instead of seeking sense, dancing as he does between the "earthy feast" of prose and the "lyrical voyage" of poetry.

Marginality and dissidence are also words that have been used to define the feminine place in history and culture. Julia Kristeva sees woman's inevitable marginality as an advantage; she aligns woman with the artist, particularly with avant-garde artists. Kristeva claims importance for woman's privileged contact with the mother's body, with the semiotic impulse preceding verbal development and therefore preceding the phase in which, as Lacanians have put it, the phallus becomes the transcendental signifier (in Hitchcockian terms, the Trans-Siberian Express). The term "mother-tongue" is a deceptive metaphor: mother may be the first to teach the infant speech, but she is only passing onto him or her the father-tongue. Once in the realm of verbal discourse, whether or not we are dissident (woman, artist, etc.), we all have to use the "matter and methods" of the so-called patriarchal code, even if our intention is to question, to parody, to destroy, and to make it over. But even though the dissident may contradict or compromise her/himself by using the very discourse of oppression, as Domna Stanton has written, the "feminist eye/I can find dissident strands, and combine them in a texture that exposes the phallic intentionality of . . . texts." To a certain extent, the same could be said for some dissident writing by men: Puig stands out as a writer who exposes the sexual politics implicit in the linguistic code that manipulates us. Kristeva seems to conclude that while some women writers like Hélène Cixous are trying "to shatter language, to find a specific discourse closer to the body and emotions," the existence of such a discourse is questionable. She finally opts for woman's dissidence, for feminine subversion as process of becoming, of deferring rather than differing: each individual woman must discover the multiplicity of her possible identifications.

Deferral, diffuseness, plurality, openness are some of the terms used to define uniquely feminine (subversive) writing, as in Gertrude Stein's radical re-inventions of literary language or in the Brazilian Clarice Lispector's novelistic portrayals of deferral, of an idealized feminine voice. However, these same terms could apply to the inventions of Laurence Sterne, Macedonio Fernández, Lezama Lima, Severo Sarduy, and Cabrera Infante. In this sense one could say that the translator of writers like these is producing pluralistic, open, diffuse texts much like the "woman text" of which Cixous has spoken. There is, of course, a difference: *Infante's Inferno,* for example, is a book in which man speaks while woman merely talks.

III. Men Speak, Women Talk, But Both Chat

In *Infante's Inferno,* woman is essentially an archetype: the mysterious other, a mirror in which Narcissus reflects himself or a screen upon which he projects himself. The final erotic encounter occurs in the Fausto movie theater, the place of screens, that is, of the silver screen and of "screen women," the phantom women in movie theaters whom throughout the book the narrator is trying to seduce or be seduced by. ("Screen woman" is an expression Shoshana Felman has used to characterize the female character in a Balzac story: the girl is a screen for the male protagonist's narcissistic, incestuous fantasies.) The screen-gazing *infante's* final encounter is with a woman who suddenly expands—like Alice when she eats the Wonderland biscuit—into a giant. This giant has been foreshadowed in an early chapter by a huge motherly woman whom the skinny adolescent tries to seduce, only to be interrupted by his brother who informs him that "this is where we came in," meaning they had already seen the whole movie. But in this last daydream, which becomes a nightmare, the rite of passage from adolescence to manhood is reversed: the narrator literally enters the vagina, descends into the speculum, crashes through the looking glass, and is swallowed up by this terrifying "sphinx without a sphincter" (to quote *Tres tristes tigres*). He becomes unborn, a dead infant, to finally be born again upon a "horizontal abyss," into the text, as a writer.

This infinite female is, of course, the mother, the gray eminence ruling over the *Inferno.* The mother (as Emir Rodriguez Monegal has suggested) is the one who, unlike the apparent austere father (the son finds out, when he's old enough to know better, that the father has a secret sex life), teaches the *infante* the pleasure of the text, that is, of reading, of movies, music, and conversation. What's more, she gives him his last name, Infante. Just like the mother in Puig's *Betrayed by Rita Hayworth* (also in contrast with an apparently austere father), she is both the source of his language and his introduction to pleasure. If (as Monegal notes) *Tres tristes tigres* is the adult vision/version of Cabrera Infante's Havana and *Inferno* is the adolescent vision, then it is also fitting that the silent or absent center of *Tres tristes tigres* be Laura Díaz, the girl both Arsenio Cue and Silvestre secretly loved, while in *Inferno,* despite all the visible and naked women, the mother, always in the background, is the unifying chord, the ultimate Beatrice. As irreverent as he may be with himself and the women he desires, he always reveres his mother, his ideal woman in every way (even physically). This adult versus adolescent comparison functions on the level of language as well: while *Tres tristes tigres* is curiously elliptical in dealing with the actual sex act, *Infante's Inferno* is unabashedly pornographic, like the language of the adolescent, eager to speak all, less afraid to describe than to experience sex. (One should add, of course, that *Tres tristes tigres*'s elliptical aspect was also the result of Spanish censorship at the time the book was published).

In *Infante's Inferno* the final manipulation of reality (and women) is through language. Like the mythic Narcissus who rejects Echo's caresses, this modern Narcissus only wishes to listen to his Echo. In this sense Cabrera Infante is explicitly exposing the sterility of the archetypal relationship between man and woman: the narrator is a supremely solitary figure, like the *pavo real,* the peacock from which the *pavane,* a courtly and often solo dance, originates. He is enclosed in his book, in his lonely hall of mirrors like King Christophe; the greatest moment of love, or, rather, orgasm, he experiences, as he says, is through masturbation.

Woman's absence, or silence, and man's speech, however, takes us back to the difference between speech and talk. The metaphoric mother-tongue, the language the mother teaches the infant, is actually a "screen" for the father-tongue (just as, on another plane, the father's austerity is a screen for his sexuality, the mother may just be all talk): certainly the Cuban *relajo* which threads through *Infante's Inferno* is a proto-male speech. As Hélène Cixous has suggested, man, out of a double fear of his mother, the fear of losing her and the fear of being castrated by her, has relegated woman to silence, metaphorically decapitating her. She has been consigned to being a mystery, a Sphinx; Cixous writes: "*Chienne chanteuse* ("Watchbitch") the Sphinx was called: she's an animal and she sings out. She sings out because women do . . . they do utter a little, but they don't speak. Always keep in mind the distinction between speaking and talking. It is said, in philosophical texts, that women's weapon is the word, because they talk endlessly, chatter, overflow with sound . . . : but they don't actually *speak,* they have nothing to say" (p. 49). Though the narrator in *Infante's Inferno* insists that he prefers the talk of women (beginning with his mother's sewing circle chatter), it is clear that it is women's talk and not speech he prefers. Indeed, those who do sometimes speak, like Olga, are too terrifying for words.

As to that other alternative, singing, it is interesting that the most significant female character in *Tres tristes tigres* is a singer, La Estrella, just as Sarduy's star transvestite is La Tremenda, an opera singer, a Cuban *chienne chanteuse.* *Maitreya* swings rhythmically between two poles: singing and "zingando" (fornication in Cuban slang). La Tremenda is either singing hysterically (or being hysterically silent—silence is the mark of hysteria, says Cixous—because her enemies have silenced her) or seeking the great transcendental signifier. Though for both Sarduy and Cabrera Infante the singer and singing are positive signs of the artist and of music as writing, they both satirize the feminine in the form of a singer. The Inferno's Infante mocks women and their words by satirizing, by reversing the archaic mother in the figure of the fatal Faustine who swallows up the *infante* in the Faust cinema, he perhaps triumphs over his fear of her: the rebirth of the *infante* as a writer is certainly a resolution of sorts.

The word is my *apparatus belly* (sic) is what the umbilical narrator might be finally saying.

Where does this leave a woman as translator of such a book? Is she not a double betrayer, to play Echo to this Narcissus, repeating the archetype once again? All who use the mother's father-tongue, who echo the ideas and discourse of great men are, in a sense, betrayers: this is the contradiction and compromise of dissidence. Just as Cabrera Infante must use the father-tongue to expose it, to parody it. And . . . just as he must learn speech to talk. Because more than anything, **Infante's Inferno** is a chatty, gossipy book. A bumbling Don Juan's jaded talk, the verbal fireworks of Cuban male *relajo* is silly chatter, defying the codes of formal speech. The narrator of this book—which is really a chain of anecdotes—reincarnates finally his mother, the story teller, the digresser, the pleasure seeker seeking pleasure only in the telling.

IV. Traduttora Traditora

If the metaphor "mother-tongue" is deceptive, so is the myth of the *Ursprach,* the original speech (explored by George Steiner in *After Babel*). And just as the existence of that original language is highly problematic, so is the concept of the original text. At least this is what Borges seems to be saying again and again in his fictions, particularly in "Pierre Menard, Author of the Quijote." Cabrera Infante confirms this in his **Tres tristes tigres:** there are no originals, only translations. Memory is a text translated into another text. If the sign of translation, of betrayal, ruled over **Tres tristes tigres,** the sign of passage, and therefore translation in a very concrete sense, marks his **Inferno.** Havana is the past, that is, "another country"; the infant is dead (or there never was one, as in Ravel's *Pavane*); what remains is the telling or the translating.

That **Infante's Inferno** is a version, a subversion, is already apparent in the title. What is alive in **La habana para un infante difunto** would become truly dead in the literal *Havana for a Dead Infant.* Because of what is lost and can be gained in crossing the language barrier, because of the inevitable rereading that occurs in transposing a text from one context to another, a translation must subvert the original. When the Havana narrator makes the jaded statement "no one man can rape a women," the infernal translator undermines this popular myth with the book's own corrosive mechanism of alliteration and writes: "no wee man can rape a woman." Since **La habana para un infante difunto** mocks popular sexual mythology, subverts traditional narrative, and sets verbal reality above all others, the more subversive **Infante's Inferno** is, the better. Verbal logic supplants fidelity when "fines de siglo" is translated not as "turn of the century" but as the "gay nineties," or when "Amor Propio" (the title initiating a chapter in praise of masturbation) is translated not as *amour-propre,* self-esteem or self-love, but as

"Love Thyself." (After all, the Bible is the book of books!) And the text continues to metamorphose blasphemously into another text when the following chapter (about the narrator's pursuit of women in movie theaters) is titled "Love Thy Neighbor" instead of false love, a literal translation of the Spanish saying "Amor trompero" (the original chapter title).

A final example of this crafty craft of transferring metaphors from the Cuban to American English is the translation of the chapter title "Mi último fracaso" ("My Last Failure") into "You Always Can Tell." This section deals with the common theme of an adolescent's sexual initiation, in this case the narrator's misadventures in strip-tease joints and brothels and his final quasi-successful intercourse with a streetwalker. As he takes leave of this girl, she is saying to him that she didn't think she'd have any customers that night, and he answers "you see?" so that she can complete the phrase with the line from a song (in Spanish): "You never know," and then he thinks an answer to her answer, but doesn't say it: it's another line from another *bolero:* "You will be my last failure." In the Spanish, "My Last Failure," corresponding to the popular theme of the chapter, is the perfect title. In English, however, "My Last Failure" does not have the same resonance, does not evoke a song or singer (in this case, Olga Guillot) that the Cuban reader would immediately recognize in the Spanish version. A literal translation would betray the intention of these words. "Better Late Than Never" was considered since it is a cliché, a popular saying which could epitomize the character's final participation in sexual intercourse after talking about it for 300 pages. "This Is Where I Came In" could also have been a double entendre with a single sense, but neither worked as a casual phrase at the end of the chapter, thus serving as a *leitmotive* that would give unity to the chapter. Then came the possibility of "You Never Can Tell," which works well as the phrase the girl utters at the end (changing "You never know" to "You never can tell"). But since the final phrase has to be the character's mental repartee, "you always can tell" works well as an ironic echo, the narrator being a constant Echo of his own narcissistic obsessions. Again, "You Always Can Tell" covers a multitude of sins: the character automatically approaches the streetwalker not knowing, but somehow instinctively knowing, that she is a streetwalker, thus, "you always can tell." Second, "Mi último fracaso" is an ironic title because his encounter with her is and is not a failure; like "Mi.último fracaso," "You Always Can Tell" is an affirmation which counterpoints the negative "You Never Can Tell" and the uncertainties of sexual initiation. Finally, "Mi último fracaso" recalls another text, a song, just as the title of *La habana* recalls the Ravel title, thus asserting the precedence of the verbal, of the literary, over a reality being described. You always can *tell,* a mis-quotation from the lexicon of clichés, very much emphasizes the *telling* of this story of sexual initiation in which the narrator tells all he can, and he can always *tell* (even when he cannot always *do*): the verbal precedes, substitutes, is the action.

Renato Poggioli expressed most aptly the reason for translating modern works when he remarked that "the modern translator, like the modern artist, strives after self-expression, although the self-expression may well be a not too literal expression of the self." *Infante's Inferno,* a book whose content is oppressively male, could never be a literal expression of this translator's self. However, translation—an activity caught between the scholarly and the creative, between the rational and the irrational—is a route, a voyage if you like, through which a writer/translator may seek to reconcile fragments: fragments of texts, of language, of oneself. More than a moment of interpretation, translation is an act of passage.

Lydia D. Hazera   (excerpt date July-December 1985)

SOURCE: "Strategies for Reader Participation in the Works of Cortázar, Cabrera Infante and Vargas Llosa," in *Latin American Literary Review,* Vol. XIII, No. 26, July-December, 1985, pp. 25-28.]

[*In the following excerpt, taken from an essay comparing Cabrera Infante's works with those of two other well-known Latin American authors, Hazera investigates Cabrera Infante's use of "fragmentary structures".*]

Like Cortázar, Cabrera Infante resorts to a fragmentary structure to provoke reader participation. While *Hopscotch* is a collage of written texts, *Three Trapped Tigers* is a collage of spoken texts. Unlike Cortázar, who orients the reader in the arrangement of the parts by providing a table of instructions, Cabrera Infante guides the reader by maintaining the same title, the same narrative point of view, and the same mode of speech in all sections of the novel dealing with a given subject. For instance, all sections entitled "I Heard Her Sing" deal with Códac's chronological narrative of Estrella Rodriguez, the nightclub singer. These sections can easily be extracted from the novel to form a short story. The psychiatric sessions are consecutively numbered and may also be put together to form a coherent narrative sequence. Though both "I Heard Her Sing" and the numbered psychiatric sessions are dispersed throughout the work, the point of view and mode of speech facilitate identification of the narrator. Other sections like "Mirrormaze" and "Bachata" consist of ongoing conversations between Silvestre and Cué and serve as a framework for narratives from other points of view. The reader soon becomes aware that there is no traditional plot, no individual psychology, only voices to render the nightclub reality of pre-Castro Havana.

Among the strategies considered previously, negation is one which an author may use to stimulate reader participation. Cabrera Infante uses negation to introduce his reader to his text. In his "Advertencia" he informs the reader that this book is written in Cuban, a Spanish dialect, that it is not a book to be read but one to be heard, thereby putting the reader on notice that his is an unliterary book, a book of the spoken language, instead of a literary one. The fact that he stresses that it is written in a dialect announces to the reader the author's antirhetorical stance. By denying literariness, Cabrera Infante predisposes the reader to counter the negation and substitute a positive view, to discover the potential of the spoken language as literature.

> **Like Cortázar, Cabrera Infante resorts to a fragmentary structure to provoke reader participation. While *Hopscotch* is a collage of written texts, *Three Trapped Tigers* is a collage of spoken texts. Unlike Cortázar, who orients the reader in the arrangement of the parts by providing a table of instructions, Cabrera Infante guides the reader by maintaining the same title, the same narrative point of view, and the same mode of speech in all sections of the novel dealing with a given subject.**
> **—Lydia D. Hazera**

In her perceptive article on *Three Trapped Tigers* Stephanie Merrim stresses the polyphonic qualities of the novel and points to features belonging to the carnivalesque novel:

It is well-known that the structure of a carnivalesque work is characterized by an extraordinary freedom of composition which manifests itself in a multi-generic or collage texture, by the lack of a finalizing authorial presence which allows characters to evolve their own truth in a Socratic conversation of divergent voices, and by an apparent shattering of the customary novelesque logic of narrative. . . .

Citing Mikhail Bakhtin, Merrim points to another feature of the carnivalesque novel, *skaz* (from the Russian *to show* or *to tell*). According to Bakhtin, *skaz* is "first of all the orientation toward the *speech of another person* . . . and as a consequence of that fact is also the orientation toward spoken language." Josefina Ludmer refers to the language used in some sections of *Three Trapped Tigers* as parodic *skaz*. Parodic *skaz* is an appropriate denomination, for often the author introduces into the speech of the character a semantic direction which is opposed to the original one.

There are different levels of parody in *Three Trapped Tigers:* a style of speech, a person's social and cultural manner of seeing, thinking, and speaking, and literary styles of well-known writers are parodied. Bakhtin observes that " . . . parody can be more, or less, deep: one can parody only superficial verbal forms, or one can parody the deepest principles of the other person's word. Furthermore, the parodistic word itself can be employed by the author in various ways: parody can be an end in itself (the literary parody as a genre, for example) . . . " In *Three Trapped Tigers* parody of different verbal forms and at varying levels may very well be the most salient tool for inciting reader participation. The work begins with a skillful parody of the Master of Ceremonies in the Tropicana Nightclub. Most readers are familiar with this stereotype. No doubt most have seen and heard him in the nightclubs of Vegas, Atlantic City, New York, London, Paris, or on a television special. Stylization will instantly provoke laughter in the reader. For instance, the exaggerated intrusions of English into the Spanish dialect will incite laughter and a questioning attitude. Exaggeration, an important aspect of stylization, essentially distorts reality, and distortion is the very essence of parody. This distortion conveys the author's critical view of the hybridization of the native tongue.

The language of Bustrófedon, the novel's absent character, incorporates several ingredients present in parody: humor, distortion, and satire. Though Bustrófedon is physically absent, his vocal presence permeates the novel in the form of tape recordings reproduced by Códac and the quotation of his ideas and opinions by Silvestre and Cué. His iconoclastic attitude toward language is expressed in endless verbal play and in parodies of the literary styles of consecrated Cuban writers. According to Merrim, wordplay centering on the physical properties of the sign de-emphasizes the signifier. By divesting the sign of semantic direction and converting it into a sonorous nonreferential sign the author creates a parody of language as a means of communication. This is confirmed in the parodies of the literary styles. In narrating one event, "The Death of Trotsky," in the literary styles of seven writers, Cabrera Infante not only parodies their styles but also communicates the ambiguity of language. The possibility that one event will provoke such different versions sustains his view that language is fraught with deception. This pervading view provokes in the reader a continuous questioning attitude toward language.

In literary parody the author reveals his role as reader and writer, for in parody he must read (decode) and write (encode). He is both critical and sympathetic toward his target. Because Cabrera Infante parodies style instead of meaning, his intention differs from that of the literary parodist whose intent is oriented toward distortion of meaning. Cabrera Infante's parodies underline the extent to which the style of these writers has become part of the oral tradition: for what he stylizes is rhythm, vocabulary, syntax. For instance, in "Los hachacitos de rosa," a parody of José Marti's style, he

distorts the title of a well-known children's poem, "Los zapaticos de rosa," published in *La edad de oro,* a magazine dedicated to the children of America. Instead of parodying the poem, he imitates Marti's modernist ornamental style. Trotsky's assassination, retold in this familiar style, provides, because of its political associations, an opening for other interpretations besides that of debunking literariness. Merrim posits a second possibility: that Cabrera Infante aspired to "include the whole gamut of Cuban literary culture, showing how Cuban writers might adapt themselves to the demand of socialist literature." This is quite probable, but within the tone and attitude that prevail throughout the book the parodies are essentially an attempt to demythify literature, divest it of exclusivity and integrate it into the linguistic system of Cuba. It is not surprising that Códac, commenting on Bustrófedon's taped parodies, says that he is now returning them to their rightful owner, folklore.

The incorporation of Bustrófedon's tapes into Códac's narrative and into Cué's and Silvestre's dialogues and the comments of all three protagonists about what Bustrófedon says, make them listeners and writers as well as protagonists. Códac, Cué and Silvestre, by mirroring Bustrófedon in their speech, also reflect and comment on his oral text, thereby inviting the reader to formulate his own views on the text. In so doing, the reader begins the creation of his own metafiction.

Bustrófedon is an appropriate mask for the author who, like him, negates written reality. Therefore, it follows that the section entitled "Some Revelations" consists of blank pages: for Bustrófedon, "alter ego of the author, never wrote a page: he only spoke them, in the same way that the novel attempts to speak . . . "

When Cabrera Infante uses the blank page to signify "revelation," he is using graphics to parody and attributing an aesthetic function to the page. The page and its graphic form an inseparable part of the overall design. Because of this view, Cabrera Infante incorporates graphic design into his novel to help the reader visualize form and meaning. In addition to visual images (graphic and verbal), he uses auditory images (verbal) to orient and stimulate reader participation. Indeed, the mode of speaking of each of the four protagonists (Eribó, Cué, Códac, and Silvestre) is characterized by a predominance of either visual or auditory images. Throughout his work, Cabrera Infante reveals a penchant for stimulating the reader through sense perceptions.

Mary E. Davis (essay date Autumn 1987)

SOURCE: "The Mind's Isle: An Introduction to Cabrera

Infante," in *World Literature Today,* Vol. 61, No. 4, Autumn, 1987, p. 512.]

[*In the following essay, Davis offers a short introduction to the study of Cabrera Infante's work with reference to several other writers, most notably James Joyce.*]

As the twentieth century draws to an uneasy close, we can begin to consider the novels, poems, movies, music, architecture, and celebrations that are its artifacts, and we are immediately struck by the persistence of memory (to steal a phrase from Dalí). As our understanding of history has become fainter, our dependence upon interior history, memory, has grown more obsessive. [Cabrera Infante] might be called the Bach of memory, and each of his texts adds variations to the central fugue. Borges, in a poem that re-creates the house of his childhood ("Androgué"), calls memory the fourth dimension, and it is into this realm that we travel with Cabrera Infante.

For those of us born into English, it is appropriate to consider Cabrera Infante in light of the prose of James Joyce. Indeed, there has been in this century a fascinating correspondence between the history, the exploration of language, and the sheer exuberance of imagination in Ireland and in Latin America. Cabrera Infante has reversed the order of Joyce's texts. He published his own *Finnegans Wake* in his first major novel, **Tres tristes tigres.** The importance of Joyce's stories in the collection *Dubliners* is assumed by **Vista del amanecer en el trópico.** Cabrera Infante's **Habana para un Infante difunto** presents the work that in Joyce's canon is paralleled by *Ulysses.* For Joyce, the only mode of entry into his world was through words, words that soared into epiphanies.

Joyce forced us to realize, for the first time in English, that prose has all the weapons in the arsenal of poetry, and he taught a whole generation of writers—Faulkner, Hemingway, Dos Passos, Fitzgerald—to use the entire arsenal. Nowadays, we who inhabit the realms memorialized by these poets of prose are more likely to see their inheritors' work at the movies than in other written texts.

In the cultural world that arises from Spanish, Cabrera Infante reminds us of the delightful conversations between dogs in Cervantes, of Sancho's island, of the words that become dragons and windmills. Quevedo's dust is as long-lasting as are the images from the movies. Cabrera Infante founds his poetry upon images no less gritty than Machado's interior country. Within Spanish America, Cabrera Infante must be considered as a member of the group of founders who insist that reality must endure a new foundation in the word itself. In Borges's Sur and in his infernal library, in García Márquez's Macondo, in Cortázar's Paris, in Fuentes's

Terra Nostra the world is begun again, and each new founding rests on a shimmering surface of words.

Another Irishman, Seamus Heaney, has written a fine essay on the sense of place (included in *Pre-occupations: Selected Prose,* 1968-1978), in which he explains:

Irrespective of our creed or politics, irrespective of what culture or subculture may have coloured our individual sensibilities, our imaginations assent to the stimulus of the names, our sense of the place is enhanced, our sense of ourselves as inhabitants not just of a geographical country but of a country of the mind is cemented. It is this feeling, assenting, equable marriage between the geographical country and the country of the mind, whether that country of the mind takes its tone unconsciously from a shared oral inherited culture, or from a consciously savoured literary culture, or from both, it is this marriage that constitutes the sense of place in its richest possible manifestation. (132)

Cabrera Infante places his Havana in the heart of the universe, in Conrad's heart of darkness, and through the hypnotic speech of his characters he dares us to enter his labyrinth. His inferno constantly reminds us of another *Commedia,* wherein Dante was recognized in Hell itself by the Florentine accent of his voice (Heaney, 137).

As Heaney maintains: "We are no longer innocent; we are no longer just parishioners of the local. We go to Paris at Easter instead of rolling eggs on the hill of the gable. . . . Yet those primary laws of our nature are still operative. We are dwellers, we are namers, we are lovers, we make homes and search for our history" (148-49).

In his memorial history Cabrera Infante gives us a priceless gift: his own island, his own Havana, his own epiphany. The joy of words exchanged among friends, sung in *boleros,* and transformed into images on the screen—this joy survives the tragedy of history, of change, of death itself.

José Miguel Oviedo (essay date Autumn 1987)

SOURCE: "Nabokov/Cabrera Infante: True Imaginary Lies," in *World Literature Today,* Vol. 61, No. 4, Autumn, 1987, pp. 559-67.

[*In the following essay, Oviedo explores "connections and convergences" between Cabrera Infante's work and that of Vladimir Nabokov.*]

Around 1970, in the prologue to his collection of essays *Extraterritorial,* George Steiner recognized that the language revolution that immediately preceded and followed World

War I—particularly in Central Europe—had produced among certain contemporary writers a phenomenon which he called *unhousedness,* a term we could paraphrase as "linguistic uprooting." Almost as if they had lost their sense of a center, these writers, to a greater or lesser degree, passed through various languages, making their relation to them a major theme of their works. Having fled the "maternal house" of their own language, they came to dwell precariously in an "international hotel" of languages containing many rooms, entrances, and exits. Steiner chose three authors—Nabokov, Borges, and Beckett—as models of this class of writer and pointed out that they were possibly "the three representative figures in the literature of exile—which is, perhaps, the main impulse of current literature." Moreover, he dedicated the first three essays of the volume to them, and the title of the collection was inspired by none other than Nabokov himself. Steiner concluded his titular essay with this paragraph:

> A great writer driven from language to language by social upheaval and war is an apt symbol for the age of the refugee. No exile is more radical, no feat of adaptation and new life more demanding. It seems proper that those who create art in a civilization of quasi-barbarism which has made so many homeless, which has torn up tongues and peoples by the root, should themselves be poets unhoused and wanderers across language. Eccentric, aloof, nostalgic, deliberately untimely as he aspires to be and so often is, Nabokov remains, by virtue of his extraterritoriality, profoundly of our time, and one of its spokesmen. (11)

Rereading these lines, it occurred to me that they applied not only to Nabokov but to Guillermo Cabrera Infante as well and that the relations and contacts between the two, which had always seemed evident to me, remained, to the best of my knowledge, generally unexplored. After examining the text for a while, I discovered that the connections and convergences between the Cuban and the Russian-American were so numerous and so complex that they deserved a study of greater depth than I was able to undertake at that time. The pages that follow should be considered as providing, at best, merely an approach to the theme, one that has vast implications and requires a rethinking of Hispanic American literature within the broader context of comparative literature and an understanding for what it truly is: namely, a literary language that has been fertilized by opening itself up to contact with other contemporary languages. In simultaneously overcoming the fate of the regional imperative and the fear of using the most radical forms of verbal invention—two superstitions that have long dominated a certain narrow "Hispanic" focus—this "extraterritorial" literature not only denies the inevitable character of the objective world but also questions internally the act of creation and even the creator himself. This supreme irony of imagination is based on our knowledge of language and on what we know of ourselves through language, a knowledge whose esthetic, moral, and ideological repercussions cannot be ignored if we are to understand literature as an activity that will continue to hold meaning for us at the end of the twentieth century.

I believe that a fundamental question which lies at the heart of all of Cabrera Infante's work is that of identity. I refer as much to authorial identity as to textual identity. This has as much to do with the relation he maintains with his books as with the relation his books maintain with us and with their own characters; these relations could not be more ambiguous and deceptive, because the *yo* or "I" of his stories, whoever it is, is always a precarious and suspicious identity that is reflected in others of equally questionable credibility.

—*José Miguel Oviedo*

I believe that a fundamental question which lies at the heart of all of Cabrera Infante's work is that of identity. I refer as much to authorial identity as to textual identity. This has as much to do with the relation he maintains with his books as with the relation his books maintain with us and with their own characters; these relations could not be more ambiguous and deceptive, because the *yo* or "I" of his stories, whoever it is, is always a precarious and suspicious identity that is reflected in others of equally questionable credibility. Cabrera Infante's texts always pose the same question—who really is this "I" who says "I"?—but never resolve it irrefutably, and what's more, from this reticence they create a game, an artifice, or a scheme whose validity lies in its uncertainty. There are many passages and texts in which Cabrera Infante has made clear the importance the matter has for him as a writer. There is one passage in *Exorcismos de esti(l)o,* however, which seems to me the most pertinent here; it is almost a poetic discourse on the literary persona and begins with a litany of questions.

> ¿Quién escribe? ¿Quién habla en un poema? ¿Quién narra en una novela? ¿Quién es el "yo" de las autobiografías? ¿Quién cuenta un cuento? ¿Quiénes conversan en esa imaginada pieza de sólo tres paredes? ¿Qué voz, activa o pasiva, habla, narra, cuenta, charla, instruye—se deja ver escrita? ¿Quién es ese ventrílocuo oculto que habla en este mismo momento por mi boca—o más bien por mis dedos?

(Who is writing? Who speaks in a poem? Who narrates in a novel? Who is the "I" in autobiographies? Who tells the story in a short story? Who converses in this imagined room with only three walls? What voice, active or passive, speaks, narrates, tells, discusses, instructs—allows itself to be seen in writing? Who is this hidden ventriloquist who is speaking at this very moment through my mouth or, better yet, through my fingers?)

The passage concludes with an affirmation corrected by a new query.

> Una segunda mirada sonora, escuchar otra vez ese silencio nos revelará—a mí en este instance; a ti lector, enseguida—que esa voz inaudita, ese escribano invisible es el lenguaje. Pero la última duda es también la primera—¿de qué voz original es el lenguaje el eco?

> (A closer, second look, listening again to this silence, will reveal to us—to me at this moment, to you, reader, momentarily—that this extraordinary voice, this invisible scribe, is language. The last doubt, however, is also the first: of what original voice is language the echo?)

This means, I suppose, that the author does not speak in the text, but rather that the text speaks through him or, better yet, that his words speak *through* him, that the author is a medium or instrument that operates with the forces of language, thereby creating a generative entity of meaning. The first invention of the author is the author himself, that word to which all other words of the text are attributed. He who writes is a phantasmagoric figure, a verbal echo of the person who emanates from his mouth (or better still, from his fingers or the typewriter, as he suggests) and says "I."

When this "I" operates within a text, it proceeds like omnivorous machinery which reactivates every memory, act, idea, or understanding that pertains to the real subject, converting it into imaginary reality and, more concretely, into words that capture lived experience and shape it into a story.

Cabrera Infante's stories are usually situated somewhere near the intersection of autobiography, memoir, and fiction, without corresponding exactly to any of these categories. To say that they are "autobiographical fictions" or "novelized autobiographies" does not help much, not only because these expressions present the problem of determining the proportion to which each element intervenes in the text, but also because these expressions seem to suggest a dependence between the story of a life and the real referent to which they allude, something quite beyond Cabrera Infante's intention; for him everything is a kind of word game. Perhaps it would

be more appropriate to invoke here a single literary genre, that of the "imaginary biography," with the added element that in his case the biography is, or appears to be, his own. Instead of narrating his life by trying to find the correspondence between the one who revives experience and the one who writes about it, Cabrera Infante frequently speaks of himself as if he were someone else and others him. He does not tell us his life story but instead draws from his life to invent yet another and writes about it—or, to be more precise, he writes about the life he lives while he is writing it. Certainly the antecedents of this genre are well known: Laurence Sterne, Marcel Schwob, Gertrude Stein, and of course Borges. I would like to add, with regard to Cabrera Infante, another illustrious name: that of Nabokov, whose work maintains in this respect interesting parallels with the Cuban's.

Nabokov must be one of the most ambiguous and astute (almost shrewd) writers of our century: his books always offer us some kind of trick, whose delicateness and artful skill can very well be likened to the net with which the lepidopterist catches a butterfly—a tenuous disguise that acts as a mortal prison, a mesh that allows us to see the beauty of the prey it destroys. Nabokov's novels usually betray their appearance, frequently their readers, and even their protagonists; one must expect from them the unexpected. The suspicious nature of their fictional world is underscored by the fact that many of them adopt a narrative mold which appears to coincide with the story of a life. We realize immediately that this life is completely imaginary (after all, these books are presented as novels); but sooner or later we discover that this life reflects the life of the narrator in a sort of somber parody and also like a lighted mirror before which he examines and recomposes passages of his own life. There is no autobiographical confession per se; what exists is a false biography composed as a pure esthetic object, whose secret function is that of recounting and giving meaning to certain moments already lived. It is the mediation of art that allows—or promises—the illumination of a truth that life has apparently left forgotten; outside of that, it is nothing. The memory of what was lost is one of the great obsessions of the imaginary world of Nabokov and serves as the principal reason for his predominant tone, which is both nostalgic and elegiac. This I shall try to illustrate by first using the novelistic model offered by *Pnin* (1957).

The book essentially narrates the North American academic life of Professor Timothy Pnin, a Russian exile whose physical appearance and domestic misadventures give him an air of resigned nobility not lacking in comicalness. The story is a fairly objective and detailed account related by a third-person narrator who remains anonymous almost to the end. The narrator not only knows Pnin's life in depth (in reality, what he is doing is telling us Pnin's life story or what appears to be such, anyway, with the detail of a professional biographer), but he also knows details about him not even Pnin knows or perhaps cares to remember. In a word, he is in absolute control of the other's existence. This is noticeable from the beginning: Pnin is seated in a train coach and is on his way to a lecture. In describing the situation, the narrator comments: "Thus he might have appeared to a fellow passenger; but except for a soldier asleep at one end and two women absorbed in a baby at the other, Pnin had the coach to himself."

This poses a dual question: if there is no other person in the coach, who and where is this narrator who is able to view the protagonist without being seen? The deceptive narrative perspective uses the approach of the detective novel: an anonymous figure knows all of Pnin's secrets and dispenses his information in a calculated manner. What immediately follows after the passage cited above reveals the first mystery: "Now a secret must be imparted. Professor Pnin was on the wrong train" (*P,* 8). Later we learn that the truth is even worse: Pnin has also placed in his pocket the wrong lecture and is headed straight for disaster. The only one who knows this is, again, the narrator. Progressively, several suggestions from the text bring to light that the narrator is a friend of Pnin, is probably Russian, most likely helped him emigrate to Europe, et cetera. The coincidences between the two lives and the objective distance the narrator tries to maintain have the paradoxical effect of making us feel—as Dabney Stuart says—that at work here is "a first-person point of view masquerading as the third."

Skillfully, the narrator finds a way to alternate the details concerning Pnin's present situation with frequent flashbacks to certain scenes of the Russian life of the protagonist. These scenes alter or parody facts and dates known perfectly well to be pertinent to the real life of Nabokov. For example, he informs us that Pnin's birthday was "on February 3, by the Julian calendar into which he had been born in St. Petersburg in 1898," which he no longer celebrated because, "after his departure from Russia, it sidled by in a Gregorian disguise (thirteen—no, twelve days late)" (*P,* 67). It is well known that Nabokov was born in that city on 22 April—or on the tenth or the twenty-third, depending on what calendar is used—in 1899, which would make him one year younger than Pnin. In the prologue to his autobiography *Speak, Memory* (1951) Nabokov refers to this circumstance in an ironic tone: "I find 'April 23' under 'birth date' in my most recent passport, which is also the birth date of Shakespeare, my nephew Vladimir Sikorski, Shirley Temple and Hazel Brown (who, moreover, shares my passport)."

Similarly, Pnin's memories, which are awakened by the physical contact with a book, by the sound of a word, or by a fragrance, appear constantly to allude to the personal recollections of Nabokov. The final chapter of the book, however, provides a great surprise to those who have been attentive to certain clues which the story has disseminated. Here we find out that the narrator has known Pnin from childhood, when the latter's father took care of him as a doctor in St. Petersburg. The narrator's recollections of this period are still accurate, *suspiciously* accurate, we could say, for Pnin himself, who has no memory of them, categorically denies them. Is the narrator inventing Pnin's life? Is he a reliable witness or at least disinterested? Whom should we believe? With a certain elegant cynicism, the narrator reveals to us that Liza had been his lover before becoming the wife of Pnin, whose conjugal misadventures have been one of the principal themes of the story; that Liza discussed with him Pnin's marriage proposal to her; and that he still keeps the love letter containing that proposal. Pnin, on the other hand, relates to another character his opinion concerning the narrator's credibility: "Now, don't believe a word he says, Georgiy Aramovich. He makes up everything. He once invented that we were schoolmates in Russia. . . . He is a dreadful inventor" (*P,* 185).

The final six pages of the novel imply an even greater change concerning the value of the information we had received in the preceding chapters: the narrator informs us that he is going to inherit the position at Waindell College they had just taken from poor Pnin, and we begin to understand that the image the narrator has projected of him is tied to so many complex interests and profound tensions that there is no way of believing in the portrait he has traced. Instead of reconstructing Pnin's life, he has invented one that is caricaturish and certainly vile. In the final scenes that caricature is multiplied: a colleague of Pnin, Professor Cockerell, takes advantage of a meeting with the narrator to perform cruel imitations of "Pnin teaching, Pnin eating, Pnin ogling a coed" (*P,* 187). This duplication or falsification, which seems so much like the narrator's own story, is reiterated by Pnin himself, who again pretends to be someone else when he answers the telephone just before leaving so as not to be humiliated by having to talk to the narrator. The last scene presents the narrator and Cockerell eating breakfast, with the latter telling the former something that causes the reader to recall the very beginning of the novel: "And now," he said, "I am going to tell you the story of Pnin rising to address the Cremona Women's Club and discovering he had brought the wrong lecture" (*P,* 191).

Cockerell's crude imitation, as well as the insidious image of Pnin composed by the narrator, is *not* Pnin. That Pnin's past is full of memories which belong to the real Nabokov makes things more ambiguous. What the book seems to be telling us is that there is nothing beyond the words that makes up for a life (real or imagined), that he who tells it substitutes its subject and imposes his prejudices and points of view, making it completely improbable, fictitious—an art object. Words always betray the facts, and there is no biography that could be innocent.

This narrative game which creates an ambiguous relation between the textual "I" and the presumed referential "I" is basically the same one we find in *La habana para un infante difunto.* Critics have argued at length the nature of the book: is it an autobiography that is not explicitly presented as such, or is it a novel that freely re-creates events from the personal life of the author? What exact purpose do memory and imagination serve in the book? How do the two interact in the text, and how does the reader perceive them? The argument, although interesting, is perhaps a bit academic, for it is precisely this ambiguity that appears to be an essential part of Cabrera Infante's literary intent, of which the very beginning of the story can provide a good example. *La Habana* opens with the following scene:

> Subí, subimos, la que era para mí entonces suntuosa escalera. Era la primera vez que subía una escalera: en el pueblo había muy pocas casas que tuvieran más de un piso y las que lo tenían eran inaccesibles. Este es mi recuerdo inaugural de La Habana, ir subiendo unas escaleras con escalones de mármol. . . . Están, además un jardín elaborado y una casa de rocalla, al pasar, que luego se revelarían como otra estación, la estación de policía, lugar de cuidado, por lo que tiendo a olvidarlo. Así mi verdadero primer recuerdo habanero es esta escalera lujosa que se hace oscura en el primer piso (tanto que no recuerdo el primer piso, sólo la escalera que tuerce una vez más después del descanso) para abrirse, luego de una voluta barroca, al segundo piso, a una luz differente, filtrada, casi malva, y a un espectáculo inusitado.

> ([I went up, we went up, what was for me at that time a sumptuous staircase.] It was the first time I climbed a staircase. Few houses in our town had more than one floor, and those that did were inaccessible. This is my inaugural memory of Havana: climbing marble steps. . . . Before the staircase there's the memory of the bus station and the Plaza del Vapor market across the street, both arcades, but there were colonnades in our town too. Thus, my first real memory of Havana is of this sumptuous staircase, which is dark until you reach the second floor (so that I don't recall the first floor, only the staircase winding once again after the landing), opening beyond a baroque whorl onto the third floor, into a different, filtered, almost mauve light, and an unexpected sight. [*II,* 1])

At the outset, the unprepared reader can take the phrase "Subí, subimos" (I went up, we went up) as a simple and natural reference to the fact that the narrator is not alone but is instead accompanied by his family, which is immediately clarified afterward. To be content with this interpretation of

"Subí, subimos," however, would be to ignore the subtle composition of the passage and the ambivalent narrative focus it introduces. In the first place, "Subí, subimos" proposes, already in the first line of the book, the duplicity of the voice that narrates: the *yo* of memory is not exactly the same *yo* who writes, in spite of the fact that the subject of those memories constitutes the life of the same person. The dual perspective of the one who recalls what he lived and the one who relives what he now recalls are implied by this plurality, which separates at the same time that it unites the respective subjects. The self-referential character of all autobiography is negated by the breach that is opened there: he who contemplates himself from the perspective of the present is not really referring to the person he *was,* but rather to the person who *exists right now* in the present of the narrator. The question of identity introduces here, as in the case of *Pnin,* the problem of time and memory: to write about oneself is to play constantly with those two elements and to rework them in accordance with esthetic standards that question one's own reality and accuracy.

The selection and reporting of memories therefore become crucial. The narrator not only manages both with a very clear intention but also transforms them into a subject that is discussed explicitly within the story. Shortly after having begun to tell his story in the manner we have seen, the narrator very clearly indicates what his book is *not* going to deal with and, by doing so, again evokes the initial scene.

> Pero no es de la vida negative que quiero escribir (aunque introducirá su metafísica en mi felicidad más de una vez) sino de la poca vida positiva que contuvieron esos a os de mi adolescencia, comenzada con el ascenso de una escalera de mármol impoluto, de arquitectura en voluta y baranda barroca. (*H,* 15)

> (But I don't want to write about the negative life [though its metaphysics will intrude upon my happiness more than once] but about the bit of positive life contained in those adolescent years, begun when ascending a solid marble staircase of convoluted design and baroque banisters. [*II,* 3])

Apart from the fact that it is precisely here in this passage in which appear for the first time the paronomastic segments that characterize Cabrera Infante's creation ("impoluto," "en voluta," "baranda barroca")—which underscores the ritual and literary nature of reconstructed memory—the quote allows us to know with precision that the subject of the book is only one of the many sides to the narrator, his "positive" side: that is, that which has to do with pleasure and eroticism. This other life does not coincide with chronology and has its own time frames, which the narrator also points out in great detail. The introduction of the erotic life is like a second birth of the evoked *yo,* a re-creation of itself in which its imagination intervenes, just as it intervened in the past in order to make the discovery of sex an adventure of fantasy and individual conscience, what the book directly associates with the discovery of a city by a provincial youth. What the long list of women obsessively maintained in the mind of Don Juan Habanero tells us is something nostalgic and mysterious: they help make him the adult he is now and who writes. In the first chapter, significantly titled "La casa de las transfiguraciones" (Eng. "The House of Changes"), the narrator notes:

> Muchas personas hablan de su adolescencia, sue an con ella, escriben sobre ella, pero pocos pueden se alar el día el que comenzó, la ni ez extendiéndose mientras la adolescencia se contrae—o al revés. Pero yo puedo decir con exactitud que el 25 de julio de 1941 comenzó mi adolescencia. (*H,* 12)

> (Many people talk, dream, or even write about their adolescence, but few can pinpoint the day it began, childhood expanding into a shrinking adolescence or vice versa. I can say precisely that on July 25th, 1941, my adolescence began. [*II,* 1])

The erotic life is presented as a life chosen as much on the level of "real" existence as on that of literary experience, a dual invention that the work continually reiterates, as when it declares: "That Sunday of expectations and revelations (it had to be Sunday, and if it wasn't, memory declares it a holiday)" (*II,* 11). The allusion to "revelations" is suggestive because it refers to another discovery of adulthood and fantasy: that of the cinema, a new invention that parodies literature with its fictitious images of reality. The cinema is the model—in the dual sense of stimulus and esthetic standard—that the narrator follows to revise his life and give it form; like a film director, the narrator creates a montage from the testimony of his own memory, which leaves a trace of its intervention through cuts, flashbacks, diversions, and self-criticism of the narrative flow. More than a writer who has already chosen a secure course, the narrator proceeds as a film editor or arranger of his erotic life; we experience, more than the product, the creative process. Moreover, this force is a constant desire to re-create memory freely without losing the thread that connects it to the past. In a passage from chapter 5 the presence of a certain Virginia is evoked, and, creating a similar effect to that of the zoom lens, the old memory is placed directly in the present, modified by the same act that revived it.

> Hoy se veía bella, con su melena corta, rubia y lacia (sí, ya sé: me contradigo: antes dije que tenía permanente, pero es con el pelo corto y lacio como yo la recuerdo esa segunda vez que la vi: tal vez nunca llevó permanente, tal vez nunca tuvo el pelo

lacio, pero tengo que ser fiel a mi memoria aunque ella me traicione.) (*H,* 278)

> (I saw Virginia again, of course. . . . She looked beautiful that day with her short, straight blond hair. [Yes, I know I'm contradicting myself: I said before that she had a permanent, but I remember her with short, straight hair the second time I saw her. Perhaps she never had a permanent or straight hair, but I have to be faithful to my memory even though it may betray me.] [*II,* 136])

The epilogue of the book, appropriately titled "Función continua," (Continuous Performance), offers an admirable example of how these different levels of autobiographical narration function. It is a passage that presents a revealing contrast with the previously mentioned scene at the beginning: here as before, the narrator attributes his second and true birth to his arrival in Havana to initiate there his sentimental education. In the epilogue we attend another kind of birth, one that is like a grotesque and parodic culmination of all erotic fantasies: in a movie house we again meet Margarita, possibly the woman with whom the narrator has come to establish the most intense personal relationship, and through a complicated and delirious erotic handling of matters he returns to the uterus; he returns to be born from the same body as that of the woman he loved.

The scene is certainly worthy of analysis. As it opens, the narrator mentions that he sees a girl buying a "ticket to paradise" ("to the gods" in the English edition, p. 392—*Tr.*), which certainly alludes to the movie but also, in a more disguised manner, to the access to her body that she will allow him to realize later. Further along, he parodies the insult that someone casts at her with the play on words, "Me voy a la miel—dando a entender que perseguía, que seguía aquella dulzura, bombón o caramelo que entró en ese recinto encantado que es un cine" (*H,* 690; "I was pursuing . . . Ambrosia Belle Candycunt—both entering now the charmed circle of the cinema" [*II,* 393-94]). The parallel nature of the actions—the present of entering the cinema and the future of entering the girl—is certainly ironized by the placard the narrator sees at the entrance to the theatre house: "INFANTES NO ADMITIDOS" (Infants not admitted). The narrator initiates his advance, descent, or entrance by painful force, by which he ultimately loses his wedding ring, watch, and cuff links. Guided by the light of a flashlight that the girl herself loans him and which serves as a rough imitation of a movie projector, he discovers that her entire body has become a kind of uterus, which he describes as a cave that is both welcoming and frightening at the same time and from which he knows he will be expelled: "Al recorrer el salón paso a paso y trazar su topografía supe que estaba en una pieza en forma de pera. Mi éxito será mi salida" (*H,* 704; "Upon carefully examining the area, bit by bit, and tracing its exact topography I knew I was inside a pear-shaped salon. . . . My success would be my exit" [*II*, 404]). Suddenly he discovers not the objects that he has lost but something inexplicable: a book that contains a travel log that is like an epic version of his own interuterine adventure. The logbook is signed only with the initials A.S., a mystery the narrator tries to unravel: "¿Esas iniciales no serían acaso . . . ? ¡Claro! ¡Eso era! ¡Ábrete Sésamo! La A y la S eran una indicación de Arriba la Salida" (706; "Weren't those the initials of— Of course! That was it! Why didn't I think of it before? Open Sesame! [In Spanish, naturally: *Abrete Sesamo*]" [*II*, 405]).

The book/birth connection should cause us to recall that the narrator associated one with the other at the beginning of his story: the objective of an autobiography is not to relate a life story but rather to create a book that can create its own protagonist. On the final page of the novel the narrator tells of (though it would be more appropriate to say that he dreams about) his own birth, the one event that is always denied to someone who writes his autobiography.

> Otro temblor todavía mayor me acostó sobre una alfombra acogedora. Luego hubo otro espasmo en la caverna y otro y otro más, cada vez más fuertes. ¡Era un cataclismo! Mi cuerpo (y yo con él) comenzó a moverse, a desplazarse sobre el suelo, primero a la derecha, luego a la izquierda, después volvimos a su centro para resbalar enseguida hacia adelante y finalmente salir despedidos con fuerza de despegue—¡hacia atrás! ¡Santos cielos!, ¿adónde iremos a parar? (*H*, 711)

> (But the tremor had now laid me out upon a cushioned carpet. Then there was another wave in the cavern and yet another, each time stronger. It was a cataclysm! How many richters had it reached? Now, believe you me, my body [and I with it] began to move along the floor! First to the right, then to the left, then we returned to the center—to immediately slip forward and finally fly out, as if we were, yes, airborne! I had always longed since childhood to fly on a carpet, but I was far from elated flying all by myself—backward. Good heavens! Where will we end up? [*II*, 409])

Observe that again the story uses the first-person plural (*volvimos, despedimos, iremos*) in order to accommodate the duplication of the narrative subject indicated by the phrase "Mi cuerpo (y yo con él)" (My body [and I with it]): he is simultaneously inside and outside the uterus, witnessing and describing his birth. The narrator tells us that at this precise moment he loses the travel log but not the flashlight and that he finally falls "libremente en un abismo horizontal" (*H*, 711; "freely into a horizontal abyss" [*II*, 410]). The last phrase of the novel is "Aquíllegamos" (*H*, 711; "Here's where I

came in" [*II*, 410]; lit. "Here's where *we* came in—*Tr.*). This is exactly the same phrase Eloy Santos, a character who introduces the narrator to the world of the cinema and to the mystery of the continuous performance, proclaimed "that Sunday of expectations and revelations," to which I referred earlier. "Aquíllegamos" signals the end of the movie and the beginning of its rerun, just as the epilogue concludes with the biological birth of the narrator and brings a final end to his fictitious interuterine adventure. One well understands then the ironic play on words in the title: *La Habana* is a *pavana* for an *infante difunto*, a new-born whose preadolescent life does not at all figure into this book.

This is not the only case in which Cabrera Infante buries one life while inventing another, as he proves in **Un oficio del siglo XX** (**A Twentieth-Century Job**), which collects the film criticism he wrote for *Carteles* and *Revolución* under the pseudonym G. Caín. The book is far more than a mere compilation of magazine articles, for the author uses the work as a vehicle to practice his habitual inventions of narrative voices and characters. In the first place, one must note that the book's cover declares that the work has two authors: Cabrera Infante and G. Caín. In addition, the latter appears in a larger typeface along with the dates 1954-1960 printed below; these dates refer to the period during which the notes appear, but they also seem to suggest the chronological limits of a fictitious life that partially coincides with the active life of the author. The chronicles of Caín are grouped into two large sections divided by three plates of color pages (blue, yellow, pink) in which the author speaks in order to establish his ambiguous relations with his alter ego, to relate to us passages from the life of one of the two or both, and to pass judgment on his critical work. Caín is not, then, a mere pseudonym; it is a *yo* that is complex and difficult, different and even the opposite of its creator—a living and autonomous being whom the other (Cabrera Infante) habitually mixes with his Habanero friends. In reality, it is Caín himself who demands, for the sake of his intellectual reputation, that the author write those texts that serve as prologue to and commentary for his chronicles. The resultant text is a transaction of the two wills.

> ¿Sería mucho decir, decir que este prólogo se debe no tanto a la insistencia de G. Caín en que lo escribiera como a mi resistencia a complacerlo? Hay un hecho cierto: toda relación es siempre un doble camino. Entre Caín y yo . . . siempre ha habido el mismo violento intercambio que entre el verdugo y su víctima, César y Cleopatra, el café y la leche, Roldán y Caturla. (13)

> (Would it be too much to say that this prologue owes less to the persistence with which G. Caín wrote it than to my resistance to accommodate him? One thing is certain: every story is a two-way street.

Between Caín and me . . . it has always been the same violent exchange as between the executioner and his victim, Caesar and Cleopatra, coffee and cream, Roldán and Caturla.)

These frankly hostile relations become more complicated because the alter ego never uses the first person in his chronicles, but rather the third person (14)—that is, he writes as if he were someone else, as if it were *the* other one. Caín is a literary thief, a usurper who does not respect the pact with his creator.

> Caín fue un maestro del enga o literario, un artífice de la mentira inocente, un aficionado a la bola fantástica, un fanático de la falsificación audaz y siempre imaginativa, y un pésimo artista del fraude, porque cultivé el *hoax* que regaba con su ingenio fecundo y abonaba con su brillantez verbal. (23)

> (Caín was a master of literary deception, a crafts-man of the white lie, an enthusiast of the fantastic rumor, a fanatic of bold and always imaginative forgery, and a very bad con artist because he culti-vated the hoax, which he sprinkled with his abun-dant inventiveness and fertilized with his verbal brilliance.)

As a critic of Caín, Cabrera Infante is equally severe; he con-fesses that "con el tiempo he llegado a detestar estas crónicas: tengo de ellas no una opinión justa, pero justiciera" (38; "With time I have come to detest these chronicles. I don't have a very just opinion of them, but rather one that is righteous"). As a person, Caín usually inspires disdain in Cabrera Infante: "Detestaba la suficiencia de Caín, su pedantería elefantina, su empe o en la mentira organizada, su juventud y su egolatría—su constante referirse a sí mismo en tercera persona no es más que un formidable disfraz de su egoísmo" (39; "I detested Caín's arrogance, his elephan-tine pedantry, his systematic lying, his youth and self-idola-try—his constant reference to himself in the third person is nothing more than a formidable disguising of his egoism").

These opinions are constantly present in the notes the au-thor places in his chronicles to clarify, point out discrepan-cies, or deny authority to Caín: "Las notas, pues, tendrían que revisar las crónicas—fue así como muchos textos pacientemente construidos se vinieron al suelo por una sola frase mía" (38; "Thus the notes would have to review the chronicles—this way many texts patiently constructed fell to the ground because of one single phrase of mine"). The notes question or oppose the chronicles in order to empha-size how different the writers are from each other and how their initial affinity—Cabrera Infante was once G. Caín, whose name is wrought from the former's—has been trans-

formed into an uncomfortable coexistence which seems closer to enmity and distrust: "Quizás yo sea un Caín para Caín. . . . No puedo sustraerme a la influencia de Caín, que cual sombra en pena puebla mis sue os y mis días. . . . Quizás este dilatado prólogo sea la muerte de Caín, pero ¿y si fuera a su vez mi propia muerte?" (46; "Perhaps I am Cain to Caín. . . . I cannot get away from Caín's influence, which in-habits my dreams and my days like a haunting shadow. . . . Perhaps this extensive prologue marks the death of Caín. What if it were, however, at the same time, my own death?")

The third section, signed by the author and titled "Requiem por un alter ego," is precisely that: the final farewell to a creature with whom its creator no longer wants to be asso-ciated. By parodying and inverting biblical history with cold irony, Cabrera Infante acknowledges the death of Caín.

> Creo que nadie mejor que yo para despedir a Caín: si le vi nacer, bien puedo verlo morir. . . . [Caín] ha decidido suicidarse en el silencio: Caín muere para que viva su alter ego, que tiene cosas más importantes que hacer. (468-69)

> (I believe that there is no one better than I to bid farewell to Caín. If I saw him being born, I can well see him die. . . . [Caín] has decided to kill himself in silence. Caín dies to ensure the survival of his alter ego, who has more important things to do.)

Later he adds a revealing detail: upon his death, someone comments, "Era un hombre extra o" (470; "He was a strange man"), and he reflects: "Entonces entendí *nombre por hombre*" (Then I understood *nombre* [name] for *hombre* [man]). That is, both levels (name and being) are inter-changeable in his intention, because Cabrera Infante does not want to publish a book of G. Caín's film criticism, but rather to fictionalize his alter ego as much as his chronicles; he treats them as *literature,* as a dialogue between different texts, voices, and authors without making a distinction be-tween those that are invented and those that are real, or those that are a mixture of the two. As the author explains: "It is not a novel because the main characters—there were sev-eral in the book, many more fictional characters by now, in-cluding myself, a false biographer—were real. At least the reader believed Caín to be a real critic. His criticism had been published without any fictional connections, and he had a name. To name something is to bring it into reality. As Adam shows us."

This close relationship between the real and fictional char-acters and the names that designate them, which allows for the textual games and allusions on the order of Caín/Cabrera Infante, is a major element in Nabokov's work. For Nabokov too, *nombres* are *hombres* and words shape destinies both on and off the page. In a passage from *Speak, Memory* he writes that he represents a fine case of "colored hearing," which is produced "by the very act of my orally forming a given letter while I imagine its outline" (34). Nabokov later explains the precise characteristics of the phenomenon.

> The long *a* of the English alphabet (and it is this alphabet I have in mind . . .) has for me the tint of weathered wood, but a French *a* evokes polished ebony. This black group also includes hard g (vulcanized rubber) and *r* (a sooty rag being ripped). Oatmeal *n*, noodle-limp *l*, and the ivorybacked mirror of *o* take care of the whites. (Ibid.)

This long lyrical passage demonstrates something more than the sensuality with which Nabokov perceives the sounds and physical suggestions of words: verbal reality is for him a form of magical perception, filled with nostalgia and memories, which he grants the same consistency as living beings and therefore the properties of the subjects of fiction. It should not seem surprising, then, that immediately afterward, the memoirist (Nabokov prefers to use the term *sunesthete*) evokes a scene from a time when he was seven years old: he was trying to build a tower with a set of alphabet blocks, only to discover that "their colors were all wrong" (*SM,* 35), for they made no sense with regard to the perceptions of form, sound, and chromatic values which he associated with letters. Words (their tonality and emotive aura) are what create memories and not the opposite. Therefore, in the first line of *Speak, Memory* the author declares, in a way very similar to Cabrera Infante, that the book is less the story of the facts of his life than its artistic composition—literally, an imagined autobiography: "The present work is a systematically correlated assemblage of personal recollections" (*SM,* 9). In the first chapter there is an episode which reveals that in a book of memoirs Nabokov also disposes his motifs much like a novelist or a musician. In this episode a character entertains a young boy with some matches; many years later, when the latter's father flees from Russia, a disguised man asks him for a match, and the stranger turns out to be the same man from happier times. Nabokov comments, "What pleases me is the evolution of the match theme. The following of such thematic designs through one's life should be, I think, the true purpose of autobiography" (*SM,* 27).

The way that language interacts with memory and identity, the curious portrayal of the characters through their names, can also be observed in other books by the two authors. Bustrófedon of *Tres tristes tigres* offers a good example. More than a character, Bustrófedon is the incarnation of the parodic and ludic powers of language; in a certain sense, he is language itself, a living verbal archive always in action, and therefore embodies the creative energy of the novel. Due to his constant linguistic games and his burlesque intention, he appears to be a new version of G. Caín, who was distinguished by the same traits. Since his nature is verbal, the se-

cret of his identity resides in his own name, which alludes to the reversibility of the written word, as if it were read in a mirror.

> ¿Quién era Bustrófedon? ¿Quién fue quién será quién es Bustrófedon? ¿B? Pensar en él es como pensar en la gallina de los huevos de oro, en una adivinanza sin respuesta, en la espiral. *Él era Bustrófedon para todos y toda era Bustrófedon para él* [énfasis del autor]. (207)

> (Who was Bustrófedon? Who was he, who will he be, who is Bustrófedon? B? To think of him is like thinking of the chicken that laid the golden eggs, a riddle without an answer, a spiral. *He was Bustrófedon to everyone and everything was Bustrófedon to him* [author's emphasis].)

The reader will immediately call to mind the tautological Humbert Humbert in *Lolita* (1955), a name whose comic duplication makes about as much sense to those who have read the novel and which Nabokov has described as "a hateful name for a hateful person." No less evocative is the name Lolita itself, which provokes the first outburst of sensuality in the novel, a waterfall of alliterations that reminds us at the same time of *Three Trapped Tigers:* "My sin, my soul. Lolee-ta: the tip of the tongue taking a trip of three steps down the palate to tap, at three, on the teeth. Lo. Lee. Ta" (*L,* 11). In *Pale Fire* (1962), perhaps his most elaborate and ambiguous novel, Nabokov plays this game on many levels. Once again we have the story of a life told by a man who knows it better than the one who lived it, but the difference is that he does so through an extensive commentary of a poem by the latter. The commentator and critic is named Charles Kinbote, and the name of the poet is John Shade. One must pay attention to these names because throughout the story we learn that the critic expects Shade's poem to reflect the passionate flight of Kinbote as a fantastic émigré from the fantastic kingdom of Zembla. Shade is, in effect, Kinbote's shadow, in the same way that the latter shares, to a certain degree, the real destiny of Nabokov. One again thinks of the pair Caín/Cabrera Infante, camouflaging the one in the other. In an unfinished draft of the poem, also titled "Pale Fire," there is a passage that reads: "I like my name: Shade, *Ombre,* almost 'man' / In Spanish" (*PF,* 174).

Shade is quite a ways from having satisfied the aspirations of Kinbote, who thinks that the poetic text without his scholarly annotations is not worth much: "Let me state that without my notes Shade's text simply has no human reality at all" (*PF,* 28). If Shade is merely a vaguely fixed projection in a somewhat confused text, the identity of Kinbote, who maintains with him a relation similar to that of the narrator and Pnin, is even more disquieting: in reality it hides another personality, that of Charles the Beloved, the last king of

Zembla. This adds an intriguing touch to the novel, which culminates with the assassination of Shade due to a confusion of identities: his assassin takes him for another person who physically resembles him (*PF,* 267). In the same conversation among professors in which this fact is mentioned, we find out the other secret the name Kinbote conceals.

> Professor Pardon now spoke to me: "I was under the impression that you were born in Russia, and that your name was a kind of anagram of Botkin or Botkine."
>
> Kinbote: "You are confusing me with some refugee from Nova Zembla"—sarcastically stressing "Nova"—.
>
> "Didn't you tell me, Charles, that *kinbote* means regicide in you language?" asked my dear Shade.
>
> "Yes, a king destroyer," I said (longing to explain that a king who sinks his identity in the mirror of exile is in a sense just that). (*PF,* 267)

Kinbote's name contains, then, multiple possibilities: it is a symbol of his exile, an obscure premonition of Shade's tragic ending, and alludes (in code) to his assassin. At the same time, the name of the latter, Gradus, gives rise, like Bustrófedon's, to a series of analogies and phonetic games that allude to his criminal activity: some of his aliases are "Jack Degree, De Grey, D'Argus, Vinogradus, Leningradus" (*PF,* 307). As is customary with Nabokov, references of this kind weave a system that extends from a particular book to other parts of his literary production. For example, the poet-commentator relation that is established between Shade and Kinbote is symmetrical to that established between Pushkin and Nabokov in the latter's famous annotated English translation of *Eugene Onegin,* published two years after *Pale Fire*; and if one reads an old poem by Nabokov, "An Evening of Russian Poetry," one will find verses that seem to project from that novel: "My back is Argus-eyed. I live in danger. False shadows turn to track me as I pass" (*Lolita,* 322).

Examining all this does not exhaust the theme of the similarities and connections between Nabokov and Cabrera Infante. Apart from the fact that GCI has acknowledged that the origin of **"To Kill a Foreign Name"** (published in this same issue of *WLT*) is a quote from Nabokov, "who is always right in terms of literature," there are other paths to explore, paths I can only point out here. Still to be studied is the influence of film, especially the so-called commercial cinema (Hitchcock above all), in their respective works and its connection with erotic sensibility: the importance that both concede to translation, pastiche, academic language, and the clichés of modern civilization as providers of images of almost constant irony; the invention of cities from

memory based on real cities—Havana of the fifties, St. Petersburg at the beginning of the century—in which they continue to live through imagination; polyglotism, which includes translation (and even retranslation) of each of the writers and the acquisition of new literary languages (proof of which for the Cuban came with the original publication in English of **Holy Smoke,** 1985); the interest in Cervantes which they share and which is reflected in the novelistic composition of *double fondo* (double frame), which characters who are readers of their own adventures, or books that imitate or contain books (like *The Real Life of Sebastian Knight,* 1941); the reiteration of certain geometric figures as symbols of the human adventure, especially the spiral, with its suggestion of reiteration and change; the pedantry common to many of their characters, filled with illustrious quotes, erudite ridicule, and bookish echoes; the ideological intransigence toward the revolutionary processes which, by denying them a country, altered forever their relations with their respective languages, cultures, et cetera.

Perhaps if at some time these common lines are traced and studied, one could prove not only that the literary works of Nabokov and Cabrera Infante have profound similarities, but *why* they do. We would understand, finally, that their works coincide because their literary lives are, at more than one point, parallel, in spite of the world of differences that exist between the tropical Havana of the one and the frozen St. Petersburg of the other. Imaginary lives, parallel lives, or perhaps, as Cabrera himself would say, "lives worth reading."

Nicholas Rankin (review date 20-26 January 1989)

SOURCE: A review of *View of Dawn in the Tropics* in *Times Literary Supplement,* No. 4477, January 20-26, 1989, p. 54.

[*In the following review, Rankin highlights the poignant qualities of the tales in* View of Dawn in the Tropics.]

View of Dawn in the Tropics is a brief and poignant history of Cuba, related in 117 sections. These vignettes, fables and snapshot descriptions vary in length from a paragraph to four pages, and their first lines are logged in the index as if they were prose poems. This post-modern technique of making a history from a mosaic of fragments has been employed by the Uruguayan Eduardo Galeano in his epic trilogy *Memory of Fire,* but in G. Cabrera Infante's hands the method is also reminiscent of the *Extraordinary Tales* collated by the Argentines, Borges and Bioy Casares. Here factual history is worn down into fictive myth; the clutter of names and dates and elaborate particularity have been polished away to leave emblematic figures such as "the black general", "the old soldier" and "the comandante", whose violent fates are laconically described.

Key to the book is the first word of the title. As one would expect from this pun-loving writer, "view" has several meanings. In the sense of "opinion", the exiled Cabrera Infante's view of his native land since Fidel Castro took power thirty years ago is clear: Cuba is a tyrannical dictatorship, a black joke far from any "dawn" of progressive enlightenment. Many of the vignettes are distanced by a cool style ("the senator was eating bread when they killed him, and his white linen suit was stained with blood and spilled coffee") which pretends to objectivity. Other sketches are already at one remove, being verbal descriptions of scenes depicted in other media: engravings, a map, photographs, a film. It is an exile's perspective, contemplating the leaves of a scrap-book of oppression and failed revolutions. And in the long view of Cuba's dire history—colonization by great powers, massacre of Indians, enslaving of blacks—the latest régime, with its persecution of dissidents and homosexuals, is regarded as quite consonant with what has gone on before.

The tone of the book does change, however, as chronology brings us up to date. The dead bodies and the gaol-bars become more bitterly personal than ironically picturesque. Three of the last nine vignettes have first-person narrators: a fugitive on a plank-and-tyre raft; a hungry convict in a labour camp; and a "disappeared" prisoner's mother raging with grief. The book is dedicated to one man who was shot by a firing squad and to another who shot himself.

Guillermo Cabrera Infante is perhaps the only naturalized British author who writes in Spanish. *Vista del amanecer en el tropico,* originally published in 1974, is here translated by Suzanne Jill Levine, but has been revised by the author. His hand is apparent in the English puns ("a joke is closer to a yoke than you think"), but they are fewer and less laboured than usual; appropriate to a book about a land which appears more sombre than sunny:

And it will always be there. As someone once said, that long, sad, unfortunate island will be there after the last Indian and after the last Spaniard and after the last African and after the last American and after the last Russian and after the last of the Cubans, surviving all disasters, eternally washed over by the Gulf Stream: beautiful and green, undying, eternal.

John King (review date 6 March 1992)

SOURCE: A review of *A Twentieth-Century Job,* in *Times Literary Supplement,* No. 4640, March 6, 1992, p. 17.

[*In the following review, King establishes the relevance of the film essays in* A Twentieth-Century Job.]

Readers acquainted with Guillermo Cabrera Infante's major works—*Three Trapped Tigers, Infante's Inferno, Holy Smoke*—will be aware of his pervading interest in film. As a young man, he had a regular movie column in Cuba, first in the journal *Carteles,* 1954-60, and later in the short-lived but extremely lively magazine of the Revolution, *Lunes de Revolución,* 1959-60. The bulk of *A Twentieth-Century Job* (which first appeared in Spanish in 1963) is made up of film criticism for those years, signed with the pseudonym G. Cain (G, CAbrera INfante). These pages are framed by the comments of another narrator who is, supposedly, the editor and annotator of the collected works and who criticizes and engages with his friend Cain. *Alter egos* or, as Cabrera Infante would have it, *alter egotists.*

The fictional frame allows Cabrera Infante the punster plenty of scope. Just the title of the book and the pseudonym of the author take us into a world teeming with allusions: Cain of biblical fame, *East of Eden, Citizen Kane,* sugar-cane (he's a Cuban after all, although he has lived in Britain for nearly thirty years). Film criticism is very much a twentieth-century job, but it requires the patience of Job to select the best of all those movies. There is a lot of fun, mixed with serious comment in these sections, which are written in Italics, and the device allows Cabrera Infante to get some critical distance from the enthusiastic film critic of the 1950s. The translation throughout is extremely good: Cabrera Infante himself, in collaboration with Kenneth Hall, makes the best of the association of ideas and the phonetic association that the English language can offer.

But it is the collection of film criticism, however ironically framed, that commands the reader's attention. How well does this stand the test of time; why translate this book after nearly thirty years? There are many levels of interest. Students of Latin American cultural history are given an engaging portrait of Cuban intellectual life in the 1950s. Cabrera Infante's colleague and fellow movie fanatic from the 1950s, Néstor Almendros (who is now perhaps the world's most inventive cinematographer), has described Cuba in that decade as a privileged place to see movies. "First, unlike the Spanish, the Cubans knew nothing about dubbing, so all the films were shown in their original versions with subtitles. Second, since this was a free market with almost no state controls, the distributors brought in many different kinds of films. I got to see all the American productions there, even the B movies. . . . I also saw Mexican, Spanish, Argentine, French and Italian films. . . . Havana was paradise for a film buff, but a paradise with no critical perspective." It was this critical perspective that Cabrera Infante, Almendros and other friends such as Germán Puig and Ricardo Vigón fostered by opening a film society and a Cinemathèque and by attempting to raise the status of film to an art form. Their mentors were, among others, André Bazin and the early *Cahiers du cinéma* critics such as Truffaut and Rivette, as Cabrera

Infante acknowledges: "We had talked a lot about Truffaut, about his reviews in *Cahiers.* . . . We, like him, believed that American movies, Hollywood and all those classics were the most important cinematography in the history of cinema, he and we fought for all the *films maudits,* for the forgotten directors, for the new directors with talent and against false reputations, the literary cinema and the lies of the technicians." Cain's film criticism, like *Cahiers'*, was conscious of raising the level of cinema in general, and North American cinema above all, by considering directors as artists, as *auteurs* rather than *metteurs en scène.*

There is also in this volume a great deal for the film buff to enjoy. Cabrera Infante, in short notes or in longer reviews, charts the development of movies in the 1950s and earlier. He deals with key directors: Welles, Huston, Hitchcock, Hawks, Minnelli and Wilder as well as the comic genius of Chaplin and Jacques Tati. A range of Hollywood genres from the musical to the Western are also considered. He shares in the excitement of the New Wave cinemas of the 1950s, the decline of neo-realism and the rise of European directors. Some reference is also made to Spanish and Latin American films, in particular the work of Buñuel. He retells and recreates the films through evocative descriptions and finely-drawn portraits. Here is *Rio Bravo:*

> the wait in jail and the growing tension; the rounds of the town, charged with humour and fear; the arrival of Lou Burdette, dashing on his white horse, the unpolluted villain; the song played by the mariachis, Spanish and terrific, that one of the characters explains is "El degüello", the tune that Santa Anna ordered played day and night before crushing the American resistance at the Alamo: its wailing sound in the night, its repeated macabre insolence; the fatal glass of beer in which the blood of the fugitive killer falls, when Dude is just about to let himself give in to the alcohol and the exacting death of the outlaw in the old style, updated here by that geometry of suspense that one thought Hitchcock had cornered for himself and that is now seen transplanted with easy success to the country of the six-shooter and the stagecoach.

Only on rare occasions do the observations seem threadbare, dated, or just wrong-headed, as when Cain steamily reviews Cacoyannis's *The Girl in Black:* "The widow is still young, and need and loneliness have made her clutch at sex with the desperation that reaches women when they are near to the death of sex that is the menopause."

David Elliott (review date 20 September 1992)

SOURCE: A review of *A Twentieth-Century Job,* in *Los Angeles Times Book Review,* September 20, 1992, p. 15.

[*In the following review, Elliott takes exception to aspects of* A Twentieth-Century Job, *but commends the book as a rare collection of reviews that one can read "in large gulps."*]

American film reviewing has widely become a fandango of fools, of wagging thumbs and swaggering blurbs. Guillermo Cabrera Infante's *A Twentieth-Century Job* arrives like a bottle tossed into the ocean of film 30 years ago, one with a message for anyone not taking their film pleasures seriously: Wake up, stupid.

This bracingly smart ensemble of reviews is from the Cuban novelist who since the 1960s has lived in London in voluntary exile from the land of The Beard. As a young intellectual, Infante, now 63, planted this garden of barbed flowers during the waning Batista era, and then briefly during the ruddy dawn of Castro. His hopes for a free cinema died quickly.

> **This bracingly smart ensemble of reviews [*A Twentieth Century Job*] is from the Cuban novelist who since the 1960s has lived in London in voluntary exile from the land of The Beard. As a young intellectual, Infante, now 63, planted this garden of barbed flowers during the waning Batista era, and then briefly during the ruddy dawn of Castro. His hopes for a free cinema died quickly.**
> **—David Elliot**

A Groucho Marxist, funny and impudent, Infante brought to these pieces the vervy bravura of an Otis Ferguson, François Truffaut, Dwight Macdonald or Pauline Kael. His reviews have a slash and scintillation that are grounded in thought. Though at moments preening or purple-prolix, Cabrera was a master of swift delight and demolition. Of the latter, savor his sinking of wooden, water-logged Howard Keel in "Floods of Fear": "Wouldn't it have been easier to provide Esther Williams with a moustache?"

Infante clearly had one eye on the Parisian pot of Cahiers du Cinéma during its '50s ferment. He shared many of its American enthusiasms (for Vincente Minnelli, Howard Hawks, Robert Aldrich) but seldom fell into auteurist fever at the drop of a name. This cinephile knew how to toss hot pepper into torpid eyes, but also had the maturity to campaign for worthy favorites and to revise judgment (downward with "The Red Shoes," movingly upward with "La

Grande Illusion"). As in Truffaut's collected reviews, here is a true critic, wings radiant, right out of the chrysalis.

Traveling to Mexico and New York, more often ducking into the cool dark of Havana cine-clubs and movie houses, Infante negated provincialism. Today, we can envy his calendar of films, the storm front of his enthusiasm. He swooped down hawkishly (Hawksishly in a rousing defense of "Rio Bravo"), seizing the French New Wave's treasure and that of the last classic Hollywood, that "immense factory of gilded pills," but also Mexican documentaries, Garbo revivals, the arrival in Cuba of Soviet films.

Infante, whose mind is a cyclotron of pun-and-stun wordplay, uses the framing device of a narrator. "Job" is the friend, editor and sparring alter-ego of "Cain" (Infante's old *nom de critique*, alluding to the Bible, to filmdom's most famous citizen, and to Cabrera Infante). Job cheers and jeers, sniping at young Cain's "execrable egotism," excoriating a "vile phrase," or commending a prophetic insight. His italicized intrusion, a postmodernist gig that often giggles up its sleeve, is lively but pretentious.

Why the revisionist stunt work? These reviews stand well alone and rarely seem old; some dated comments are part of the value. Job, a picador jabbing his torero, lays on many bad jokes (such as "robbing poor Borges blind") and becomes a pest. Young Cain devours light from the screens of Old Havana, while Job the jaded wise guy hangs out in the lobby, picking popcorn from his dentures.

No book of reviews can be read straight through, but Infante's can be consumed in large gulps. His calling Hitchcock's *Vertigo* the first romantic work of the century is a tab of excess worth paying to savor his vertiginous thrill with the film (which pulled him back on three more nights). Infante's demolition of *The Old Man and the Sea* is Carthaginian, and has there ever been a funnier rave than his squib on *The Court Jester*?

In one howler, Infante declares that in *Paths of Glory* director Stanley Kubrick "puts away his technical brilliance." Far from it! More easily forgiven is the four-page ramble around *Around the World in 80 Days,* which rather smartly restores to interest the dumb rush generated by Mike Todd's vast whimsy. And with the fabled work like *The Gold Rush* or an obscure one like *Wind Across the Everglades,* Cain achieved true poetry of praise.

There are some blind spots about actors. To write so well on *The Horse's Mouth* but ignore Alec Guinness is perverse (and why so little on James Dean in *East of Eden*?) Yet Infante also sagely noted that Guinness in *Father Brown* acted "with the scant sympathy Lutherans feel for Catholics" (never mind that Guinness later became Catholic), and

plumbed in Rock Hudson "the defect of saying his lines as if he were an actress and not an actor."

Ever the skeptic, Infante brought sympathy of rare grace to Bresson's *The Diary of a Country Priest.* Though Latin, he disliked bullfighting, until *Torero* stirred him with its bloody mystique. Not a sentimentalist, he yet wrote of *La Strada* with a tender gravity worthy of Fellini. As with the best critics, in the celluloid DNA of Infante's soul is a generosity born of hope and dreams, not the fuddy "correctness" of a culture commissar.

Despite some squirming from Job, this book is the open diary of a romance recollected in lust: Man pursues movies, man "gets" movies, man marries movies to smart criticism. Shortly before exile, Cain eagerly believed that Truffaut's *The 400 Blows* would spark a new era, would change the show for good and forever. He was largely wrong about that, but the zeal of his hope is cherishable.

Will H. Corral (review date Spring 1993)

SOURCE: A review of *Mea Cuba,* in *World Literature Today,* Vol. 67, No. 2, Spring, 1993, pp. 342-43.

[*In the following review, Corral criticizes Cabrera Infante's penchant for wordplay, as well as his attacks on Castro's system and other intellectuals.*]

Guillermo Cabrera Infante, ever the punster, has gathered here articles, essays, notes, speeches, and letters published in various international newspapers, magazines, and literary journals. They cover the period 1968-1992 yet do not include or represent all his cultural or political writings. Divided into three sections—"A propósito" (on his role in Cuban culture), "Vidas para leerlas" (purportedly biographies of Cuban authors), and "Vida única" (on Cuban and other topics)—the book is really a passionate, albeit flawed biographical assessment of Cuban cultural politics since the midsixties. Inimitable in style, obviously self-revealing, full of information, insight and gossip, hilariously combative, **Mea Cuba** may well become a definitive view of one side of the t(r)opic that Cuba has become.

When this book was published in mid-November 1992, Juan Goytisolo praised it in the Spanish press as an ironic homage to Fidel Castro, the "real" father of all Cubans, whether they be in Cuba, the cemetery, prison, or exile. This sort of obsession, akin to arguing that José Martí might be the only true Cuban-American, is the source of Cabrera Infante's greatest strength and weakness in the collection. From its allusive title (which can refer either to whatever faults the author represses or to a bodily function command that his homeland is carrying out without his ranting and raving) to the now tiresome infinite play on words, these texts cover a wide and pathetic state of intellectual affairs and persecutions.

Cabrera Infante's book includes divisive propaganda parading in the guise of concerned essayistic discourse. In this sense, it is no different from the concerned scholarship published in Cuba and in the United States. However, the difference is that Cabrera Infante would never entertain a dialogue. His texts are monologues, and frequently lengthy onanisms whose irreverence is also tiresome. Thus, in the second section of the book, his portraits of Lezama Lima, Virgilio Pi era, Lydia Cabrera, Labrador Ruiz, Carpentier, Almendros, Arenas, and others are vehemently negative. It is difficult for Cabrera Infante to see wholesomeness or goodness, even among those he considers friends. The piece on Calvert Casey, for example, is representative of the homophobia the author dare not speak. Nevertheless, the telling of these unparalleled lives is the best part of the book. In spite of the author's wishes, his texts read as the ideal format for what is bandied about the United States as cultural studies. Despite one's differences with his politics, Cabrera Infante's knowledge of Cuban literariness is the broadest, liveliest, and nastiest to date.

In this regard, if we limit ourselves to the many and still ongoing imbroglios about the infamous Padilla affair, Cabrera Infante's "Mordidas del caimán barbudo" (Bites from the Bearded Crocodile) is the fullest accounting of that fiasco. This essay, the longest in the first section (and the book), shows Cabrera Infante at his best, his cruelest, and his poorest—poorest in that his puns, which somehow work better in English, have now been retranslated. Thus, many of his Groucho Marx borrowings will be lost to the general Hispanic reading public that may buy *Mea Cuba* once the academics are done with it. Among the various immigrant groups in the U.S. the reaction could well be *dame un break, chico,* since of the many Latin phrases with which he sprinkles his text, *in situ* (as in his not being *in* Cuba for twenty-seven years) never appears. The first part of the book is as historically schizophrenic and myopic as Arenas's recent sexual autobiography *Antes que anochezca.* Cabrera Infante traces and reviews (at times supplying contemporary addenda to pieces published in previous decades) his problems with Castroite Cuba. Trying to decide between self-hagiography and diatribe, he opts for both, with frequent dashes of invective. There should be no doubt in anyone's mind that his mastery of the Spanish language is always present, but it could be put to better use. One can sympathize with his protestations, and academic Cuban exiles may be the first to rush to his defense; but he doth protest too much, in the worst way. Nevertheless, his own defense of Latin America's "Hispanicity" in the third section of the book is well wrought and incontestable, especially from one

of the only tried-and-true bilingual authors Spanish America has produced and read.

Mea Cuba is a Who's Who, What's What, Where's Where of contemporary Cuban letters. The author's eyewitness (and hearsay) account of what many of us are still fighting and writing about is difficult to circumvent or ignore.
—Will H. Corral

Mea Cuba is a Who's Who, What's What, Where's Where of contemporary Cuban letters. The author's eyewitness (and hearsay) account of what many of us are still fighting and writing about is difficult to circumvent or ignore. Cabrera Infante, star-struck, provides his readers with a cast of thousands; but some, like Carpentier, are struck by millions of his poisonous writerly shards, and the evidence could not be more damaging. Much like the main crystal in a kaleidoscope, Cabrera Infante manages to direct that cast of thousands for our and his enjoyment, and pain. From the very start, and throughout his book, the author states that these texts are political in nature. In this sense, paradoxically, I cannot think of a better overview of what Jorge Edwards has called "Cuban messes," but I also cannot think of a better or more personal collection of cheap shots on which to waste an extraordinary amount of talent and black humor. One will miss the exclusion of Cabrera Infante's morsels about Spanish American soap operas, popular music, or his troubles with Spanish censors (winked at here), but *Mea Cuba* should be read, if only to see how its protagonist became an inorganic intellectual, the author of really one well-known novel. This is so because, in naming or calling names, either feigning discretion or showing cowardice, he is seductively selective; and at times convincing.

Will Eaves (review date 22 October 1993)

SOURCE: A review of *Writes of Passage*, in *Times Literary Supplement,* No. 4725, October 22, 1993, p. 22.

[*In the following review, Eaves critiques* Writes of Passage, *a translation of a story collection first published in Cuba in 1960, as "repackaging."*]

"Language is my business", writes G. Cabrera Infante in an explanatory epilogue to this, his first book of short stories, published in Havana in 1960 but hitherto unavailable in Britain. The Chandleresque pose may be safely assumed to be ironic: language, as far as Batista's secret police were concerned in 1952, when the literary journal *Bohemia* carried a short story called "A Ballad of Bullets and Bull's Eyes", is also trouble; and the author's description of his detention inside El Principé Castle prison, for publishing a fiction peppered with "English profanities", is chilling. Banged up with a group of veteran rebel detainees, Infante finds his story—about a botched assassination attempt—has been taken literally by the convicts who upbraid him for its inaccuracies: "You don't know what you're talking about, man. That's not how you go about knocking off the opposition."

The "Ballad" itself seems almost unremarkable, as do many suppressed literary texts after the context of suppression has changed. A posse of political thugs sets up a routine murder which goes wrong when an innocent man is shot. Their only misgivings are over the amount of time wasted. In the build-up to the bathetic bullet, police officers and drifters track in and out of shot—Infante the screen dramatist is never far away—and a drunk, American tourist sings an obscene ditty before waddling away into the night. It is, Infante implies, pointless looking for any special degeneracy; the real offence, committed equally by convicts and the secret police, lies in denying a fiction its right to connote rather than denote. In this kind of closed mythology, everything must refer (and defer) to one thing: the state or the self. The problem is that Infante himself is implicated in this monomania, or "imprisoned by his own myth" as he might put it. The island of Cuba, that territorial expression of the ego from which there is no escape, brings him home every time on its "immovable raft".

The island is the anti-hero of the collection. A sense of the geographically implacable under-pins each story. In the first, **"Gobegger Foriu Tostay"**; a six-year-old girl prattles artlessly as her family faces eviction and her sister, Marieantonieta, resorts to prostitution to save the home. Terrible passions are caught up in the naming spree of infantile observation and Infante's camera weighs elation and dejection alike with the same photographic rigour.

Yet the family stays in place—an irony Infante makes sure we do not forget, and a frustrated pose which the best story, **"Josefina, Take Good Care of the Senores"**, turns into paralysis. Its narrator, a ghastly madame equal parts Grendel and Sweet Sue, gushes puns and malapropisms in praise of her prize whore, the permanently sedated amputee, Josefina. Popularity with a US senator guarantees Josefina's continued employment, but her choices are circumscribed by disaster. She cannot move from her bed and has gone mad after aborting a monstrous foetus. Even so, notes the madame, "she came to be called Josefina of her own violation".

Other stories seek to relieve the tension of island-bound immobility. A woman in desperate straits, hemmed in by her abusive brothers, wrecks her house chasing flies. Parched with thirst and anger, she is revived by a storm—relief rainfall; of course—and finds a fly dead in a glass of milk. In another narrative of interrupted cadences, an English teacher strips naked for her student before resuming instruction. There are also rites of passage dealing with familiar, comic themes of adolescence and infatuation, although these, too, are fretted with yearning: "All I wanted", murmurs a lovesick medical student, "was memory, the fragrance of memory."

One sympathizes. Like his miraculous narrative collage *View of Dawn in the Tropics,* Infante's *Writes of Passage* is essentially a photo-album of culture and memory stuck in the developing tray. There seems no way off the island of image reproduction; nothing really develops at all. And yet Infante exerts himself to break out of the photographic background with word-play that announces his continuing proficiency as a virile linguist. This would be fine if he did not also acknowledge the age of these stories in an introduction which snubs literature without pedigree: "I, who used to search and devour, read so very few modern novels. Otherwise I'd have to use a stomach pump." Language is Infante's business, no doubt of that. But is repackaging?

Richard Eder (review date 27 November 1994)

SOURCE: A review of *Mea Cuba*, in *Los Angeles Times Book Review,* November 27, 1994, p. 3.

[*In the following review, Eder cites weaknesses that blunt the impact of* Mea Cuba, *a book he calls "powerful at times."*]

For the first two years after Fidel Castro's triumphant entry into Havana, Cuba's artistic and literary life bubbled vigorously. It had not really been stagnant under Fulgencio Batista, who took no interest in what artists did unless they engaged in political resistance; nevertheless, the dictator's overthrow released an exuberant energy.

It was an energy of the left, of course, since that was where most writers, painters, musicians and filmmakers placed themselves anyway. It was also libertarian, ungovernable and unrestrained. Its voice was found most particularly in "Lunes de Revolucion," the weekly literary supplement of the newspaper Revolution, whose director, Carlos Franqui, embodied the violent idealism of the revolution's first years.

In its brief life, *Lunes* was a meteor, and by far the most vital literary publication in Latin America. Its editor, a young novelist, critic and hopeless Hollywood buff, thought of himself as an "anarcho-Surrealist." That amounts to cultural gourmandizing; the equivalent of sitting through a triple feature with chocolate peanuts as well as popcorn and butter.

It took less than two years for the chill of repression to be felt in other aspects of the Cuban revolution; for Castro's totalitarian elan to devour his revolutionary elan—allying itself at first with the Communists and then devouring many of them as well. Guillermo Cabrera Infante writes in **Mea Cuba** of the months in early 1961 when the freeze reached the artists and closed down his "Lunes."

His brother and a collaborator had made a short feature, "PM," that toured the smoky bars and dives of Havana in the best bittersweet film-noir manner. The authorities banned it as decadent. "Lunes," with the support of dozens of artists and writers, was about to publish an indignant protest when the government organized a three-day meeting to forestall it. President Osvaldo Dorticos urged the intellectuals to speak their minds without fear; Castro made a speech assuring them that "within the Revolution all things are possible."

Virgilio Piñero, a timid, shrunken, flamboyantly gay writer, made his way hesitantly to the microphone. "I only want to say that I'm very frightened. I don't know why I'm so frightened but that is all I have to say."

As it turned out, there was not much more to say. *Lunes* was shut down, ostensibly for a shortage of newsprint; Revolucion lasted only a little longer. Franqui went to live in Paris, Cabrera Infante was given a diplomatic job in Brussels, and a number of *Lunes* writers found brief employment in the government cultural agency.

It was gradual but relentless removal from the intellectual and artistic life of the country. Except for homosexuals—among whom were a number of the most talented Cuban artists—there were few harsh individual measures (the jailing of the poet Heberto Padilla was a notable exception). The punishment was exile or silence.

Mea Cuba gives the silence a clamorous voice: eloquent and powerful at times, and at others wordy, repetitive, strident and eventually hoarse. It is steadily obsessed with the wreckage of Cuba's material, moral and cultural values by one man's will to power; whose various manifestations the author refers to with such epithets as "Castro Convertible" and "Castroenterology."

Cabrera Infante, who has lived in London since breaking with Castro and publishing his satirical novel **Three Trapped Tigers** (a favorable review was one of the things that landed Padilla in jail), is addicted to puns and word games. It energizes him, perhaps, but it depletes the reader.

There are more serious weaknesses in **Mea Cuba.** It is a collection of about 60 articles written over a quarter-century and printed in a number of different periodicals. Many of them borrow or repeat from each other; no effort has been made to edit the repetitions out. Furthermore the translation, in which the author took a hand, is clumsy; at times ludicrously so.

It is a pity because it makes Cabrera Infante's strengths less accessible. Through the personal recollections, portraits, polemics and accounts of the recent and more remote past, he has put together something of a history of the Cuban imagination and character.

There is an exploration of Cuban suicide, for example. Castro's hopeless attack on the Moncada fortress early in his revolutionary career was virtually a kamikaze action. The author mentions the suicide of an opposition politician as climax to a radio speech (he didn't realize that the station had already switched to a commercial), and of a mayor unable to fulfill a campaign promise. He writes of the suicides of Haydee Santamaria, one of Castro's closest associates, and of Dorticos, whom Castro had deposed. Could 35 years of putting up with revolutionary decline amount to a national suicidal instinct? Far-fetched, perhaps, but suggestive.

His polemics range from petty—his anger at the pro-Castro Gabriel Garcia Marquez is such that he calls him an inferior writer—to splendid. Even better are some of his portraits.

He gives evocative accounts of Lezama Lima, the defiantly decadent writer whom the government all but starved, of Piñero and his timid valor, of Nicolas Guillen, proud of his official favor until one day Castro, perhaps in passing, called him lazy. "He's worse than Stalin," the shocked Guillen complained to the author, who was still in Cuba at the time.

The most memorable portrait is of Gustavo Arcos, the man who would not bend. He fought with Castro during the Moncada assault, joined him in Mexico to prepare the Sierra Maestra campaign; today, after many years in prison he is one of the country's much-persecuted civil rights leaders.

It is an extraordinary story of a man who lost favor with Castro because of his insistence on speaking his mind. Named ambassador to Belgium, to get him out of the country, he was being considered for the Rome embassy when he was arrested. Released, he tried to leave Cuba to see his desperately ill son in Miami. He was sentenced to 14 years more; at the same time, Castro brought his family back, lodged them in a luxury hotel and got the finest available medical care for the son. At one point he offered Arcos his freedom if he would promise not to try to leave. Arcos refused and served many years longer.

In exile, Cabrera Infante worked hard but in vain to enlist literary and intellectual figures in a fight for Arcos. The trouble was that he wasn't a writer, an artist or an intellectual. And Cabrera Infante concludes brilliantly with an account of refusing an invitation to a London human rights conference entitled, with would-be mordancy: "They Kill Writers, Don't They?"

"I told them that the title was not true. I told them that in totalitarian countries like Cuba, the last thing they kill is writers. They kill workers, peasants, leaders of the clandestine movement, Jehovah's Witnesses, whites and blacks. Everyone. But what they least kill is writers. Those shut up or get scared or their silence is bought with a house and a car and several trips to Europe. Or they leave the country as exiles. They don't kill writers. They kill, precisely, men without imagination like Gustavo Arcos. They kill their heroes."

Alma Guillermoprieto (review date 27 November 1994)

SOURCE: A review of *Mea Cuba,* in *New York Times Book Review,* Vol. CXLIV, No. 49,893, November 27, 1994, p. 9.

[*In the following review, Guillermoprieto commends Cabrera Infante's profiles of several gay Cuban poets who became victims of the Castro regime, but also notes his "endless petty settling of accounts."*]

Those who are familiar with the Cuban novelist and essayist Guillermo Cabrera Infante (his best-known work in this country is the novel *Three Trapped Tigers*) will be pleased to find him in full form in this collection of essays: irritable and irreverent, generous and catty, indignant and wistful and harsh, and of course—of curse! a desperate reader might wail—endlessly punning. The titles of the sections and essays are a fair representation of what our man from Havana is up to: **"Hey Cuba, Hecuba?"**; **"Have a Havana"**; **"Quiet Days in Cliché"**; **"Castroenteritis,"** and so forth.

The earliest essays gathered in *Mea Cuba* date from shortly after the author left his job as a cultural attaché in the Cuban Embassy in Brussels and, declaring himself an exile, settled in Europe in 1965. (He now lives in London.) The most recent essay is from 1992. The subjects of most of them, and certainly of the most interesting, are the lives, travails and various exquisite martyrdoms of Cuban intellectuals under the regime of Fidel Castro, as reflected on by the author for an eclectic assortment of publications, including Octavio Paz's magazine *Vuelta* and *The London Review of Books*.

Cuba, an island of lush growth and claustrophobic politics, could be expected to produce only the hothouse variety of intellectuals. With rare exceptions (or perhaps none, if one does not consider Nicolas Guillén a major poet or Virgilio Piñera a genius of the theater), the highest achievements of Cuban literature are baroque. From *Paradiso,* by José Lezama Lima, to *The Lost Steps,* by Alejo Carpentier, to *Three Trapped Tigers* itself (or even *El Monte,* the ground breaking study of the religion of Santeria by Lydia Cabrera, which Mr. Cabrera Infante terms "anthropoetry"), plots and sentences twist back upon themselves and spiral and branch out in an attempt to reproduce the intricate density of the world.

It is an intricate and a mannered life the intellectuals lead, too, and—at least in Mr. Cabrera Infante's telling of it—it is dominated by those he calls, in hothouse fashion, "pederasts." (Rarely the gentleman, the author is nevertheless discreet in his treatment of Lydia Cabrera, the anthropoet, referring to her female lover merely as a "constant companion.") The subject of homosexuality and its repression in revolutionary Cuba has recently surfaced in a number of ways (outstandingly, in the great Cuban director Tomas Gutierrez Alea's latest film, *Strawberry and Chocolate*).

There are reasons why the subject is compelling. Gay intellectual life in Cuba was once not a simple matter of attraction to the same sex, or of creating paintings, or of reading books and writing them, but an elaborate routine that encompassed orchestrated social encounters, devout attention to fashion or willful sartorial neglect, intricate, passionately literary conversations, defiant crossing of class boundaries, and extravagant, or extravagantly frustrated, sex. In 1959, gay intellectual Havana was perhaps one of the last great holdouts of the romantic vision. Then Fidel Castro came to power.

Early on, the revolution decided to round up homosexuals into camps. Although the camps were shortlived, the macho persecution of homosexuals endured. In what is perhaps the finest essay in this book, Mr. Cabrera Infante traces the fate of two homosexual writers under the revolutionary regime: the playwright Virgilio Piñera and the poet and novelist José Lezama Lima, the author of *Paradiso*. Piñera was skinny and fey, Lezama Lima ponderous and large. The playwright made it a point of pride to have no books in his almost barren beachside house; the poet's library was legendary. Piñera went for rough trade and Lezama Lima went after effete young men. Unlike a great many other writers, gay and straight, who wanted with equal desperation to be loyal to the revolution and to themselves, and who were caught like hares in the headlights of the regime's nighttime advance on their freedom, both Piñera and Lezama Lima were, essentially, apolitical. Both were suffocated by the revolution.

Piñera was arrested with a ludicrous display of force one day in 1964, and released thanks only to the intercession of his more respectable friends (Mr. Cabrera Infante included). Following this traumatic event he obtained permission to travel, but in Paris, Mr. Cabrera Infante writes, "he insisted that he wanted to go back to Cuba, that it didn't matter to him what could happen to him, that he could stand confinement, prison, the concentration camp—but not being far away from Havana. I understood his attachment to this city, that was once like a spell." Back in his beloved city, Piñera turned into a wraith, skinnier, less productive and more terrified each day, until death caught up with him in 1979.

Lezama Lima was never arrested; his reputation matched his enormous girth, and protected him. His artistic murder was more subtle: his masterpiece, *Paradiso,* has been out of print on the island since shortly after it was first published, in 1966. (According to legend, Government agents were deployed to Havana bookstores to buy up the first edition.) Mr. Cabrera Infante says that Lezama Lima was also systematically denied permission to travel abroad even as his health worsened. "His life became more difficult than it had ever been, and after writing steadily more pathetic letters in which he asked his sister for medicines and communication with the same rhythm, not hesychastic but indeed asthmatic, he died of a pulmonary edema in a nondescript hospital, in an anonymous room, without being recognized as the greatest poet Cuba has produced."

Mr. Cabrera Infante narrates these crushing events with a sober fury that serves him, and his subjects, well. Topics that wound him less deeply get the full fireworks of his brilliant carnivalesque style, and they are entertaining. Referring to the Colombian poet, Porfirio Barba Jacob, he writes: "The mention of a mariner, even a metaphorical one, leads us to the great amorous transport of Barba. It is said that the poet of Modernist decadence found his sinning sailor when he, literally, covered the waterfront. Littorally they found each other on the docks. The sailor became the lover of the pederast and pessimist rhymester . . . and, beneath it all, a poor poet. It was 1930 when the bard Barba was showing off his freshly caught mariner."

But despite the dazzling writing—in an occasionally lumbering, sometimes inspired translation by Kenneth Hall and the author—the style sometimes overwhelms the chronicle, and one finds oneself wishing for a respite from the shrill delivery and the endless petty settling of accounts. In a polemic against Argentine leftists, Mr. Cabrera Infante notes that the daughter of the leftist intellectual David Vinas was "disappeared" by the murderous right-wing dictatorship of the Argentine generals. He says, "Another patriot of those times who now are not the same was David Vinas, who did not dig his grave . . . but that of his daughter, to take refuge later—who would have thought!—in the capitalist paradise."

At his worst the bombastic punster's salvos are not meaningful but mean. At his best, he provides a moving chronicle of love and despair for the country he lost to Castro. "Mea Cuba," says Guillermo Cabrera Infante, whose words never have a single meaning, or even a single language. Where he has written "My Cuba" one must read, in Latin and Spanish, My Country, My Potion, My Measure, My Guilt and above all, vaster than all the puns in the title of this collections of essays written with the blood of exile, My Love, Cuba, My Love.

David Gallagher (review date 30 December 1994)

SOURCE: A review of *Mea Cuba* in *Times Literary Supplement,* No. 4787, December 30, 1994, p. 7.

[*In the following review, Gallagher cites examples of repression by the Castro regime in both* Mea Cuba *and Reinaldo Arenas's* Before Night Falls.]

How does Fidel Castro get away with it? He has presided for thirty-five years over one of the most oppressive regimes ever known, only a few miles off the coast of Florida. Until recently, he seemed to be surviving thanks only to subsidies from the Soviet Union, but there are no obvious signs of his imminent demise. This despite the fact that life in Cuba is so awful that about one-fifth of all Cubans have left the island, among them most of the country's intellectuals. Guillermo Cabrera Infante, Cuba's finest novelist, has lived in exile in London for nearly thirty years. Reinaldo Arenas, the best of the younger novelists who started writing under Castro, escaped to Florida among more than 100,000 boat people who fled from the Cuban port of Mariel in 1980. He subsequently committed suicide after ten years in exile. Through all this, Castro, whom Cabrera Infante has described as the only free man in Cuba, survives and thrives. In just these past few weeks, while the US administration was ordering the occupation of neighbouring Haiti allegedly to restore democracy, it was at the same time practically begging Castro not to allow any more Cubans to leave. Castro graciously agreed, after savouring the panic of US immigration officials.

Despite the spectacle—just before that agreement—of thousands of boat people trying to leave the island, no one seems to regard Castro as a monster. People may think of him as garrulous, a bit mad perhaps, but not really evil. He is apparently perceived as being so much larger than life that he is simply not to be judged by normal standards. People talk about "Castro's Cuba", as though it were quite natural for a man to own an island. Many Western intellectuals still idolize him, in exchange for the lavish hospitality he reserves for them. Gabriel García Márquez, for instance, remains rigidly loyal to his Cuban Caribbean holidays.

Recently, despite the US embargo, Cuba has become a destination for tourists and, more remarkably, for foreign investors, who talk and act as though Cuba had become fashionably post-Communist, like the Czech Republic. In the meantime, the millions of Cubans who are unable to leave have become so hungry that cats and dogs have almost disappeared from the island. So how does Castro deploy such a relatively benign image? Churchill and Nixon were hams, but "Churchill was a great ham and he knew it". De Gaulle was the finest French actor since Molière. And Castro? In Cabrera Infante's words, Castro is "perhaps the best television actor in the world", an important asset if you want to control your people. He is like a "Circe in uniform", whose most gullible victims are Western journalists, although there is recent evidence of even supposedly hardened Miami exiles being seduced during their exploratory visits to the island. Some of them have ended up investing in Cuba, doing "deals with Castro".

Though neither **Mea Cuba** nor Arenas's *Before Night Falls* are novels, they could only have been written by novelists. **Mea Cuba** is a selection of occasional pieces written over a period of nearly thirty years' exile. Although self-confessedly political, they are memorable for their intimate, nostalgic and often bravely comic anecdotes of the private life of Cubans under Castro. *Before Night Falls* is Arenas's posthumous autobiography: an account of his peasant childhood in rural Cuba, an early homosexual awakening, a brief, boyish flirtation with Castro's guerrillas, a period of Communist indoctrination, and finally his struggle to become a writer under a regime which despises literature and relentlessly persecutes homosexuals. Arenas incurred the regime's wrath by allowing friends to smuggle his manuscripts to France, as well as by his defiantly promiscuous homosexuality. He went into hiding, and although the whole Cuban police force seemed to be looking for him, Arenas managed to remain concealed for several months in the woods of Lenin Park. A few trusted friends took him food under cover of night. Following his inevitable capture, he was submitted to various stages of imprisonment over several years. He did a stint at the brutal Castillo del Morro, the colonial fortress by the sea that is one Havana's picture-postcard landmarks. He was then moved to Villa Marista, the secret police's torture centre, and later to an open prison. He was finally released in 1976, and took the boat from Mariel in 1980.

Many of the memorable anecdotes told by Cabrera Infante and Arenas are not necessarily political. In one splendid essay on the two homosexual writers José Lezama Lima and Virgilio Piñera, Cabrera Infante describes a chance meeting between them outside a plush male brothel, just opposite Havana's baroque cathedral. In another anecdote, the mulatto poet Nicolas Guillén has to put up with a mob shouting outside his house that he is lazy. The rent-a-mob assembles following a public complaint by Castro that Guillén's poetic output is too low (one poem per month) to justify his salary. Cabrera Infante also evokes some magnificent scenes from a four-month visit he made to Cuba in 1965, after spending three years away as cultural attaché in Brussels. He arrived just in time to attend his mother's funeral. In only six years of Communism, Havana has already suffered a mutation. The streets are dingy. There is nothing to buy. Roses have been torn out of elegant Vedado gardens and replaced with bananas. The language has changed. Public beaches are now called "Workers' leisure circles", buses are "rolling units".

One of the most moving stories Cabrera Infante tells is of Gustavo Arcos, a hero of Castro's revolution, who had participated in the assault on the Moncada barracks in 1952. Castro seems to have always held a personal grudge against him. Arcos was arrested in 1966 for no discernible reason and given the opportunity to confess, but he declined on the grounds that he couldn't confess to a crime he had not committed. Arcos spent twenty-two years in prison. Maybe he initially fell into disfavour because he did not stand the test of the so-called *parametraje*. According to Arenas, Cubans live in dread of being "parametered" or being told that they no longer "fulfill the necessary parameters" for the job they hold or the room they use or the freedom they have been enjoying.

Cabrera Infante and Arenas describe various stratagems to deal with Castro's tyranny. One of them is humour. Cabrera Infante has long been the wittiest writer in the Spanish-speaking world. Arenas writes a brutal, desperate prose which is not at all funny, but he too values humour and sees it as a last refuge against the revolution. He also understands that for the revolution, humour is a threat, as is anything spontaneous:

> One of the most nefarious characteristics of tyrannies is that they take everything too seriously and destroy all sense of humour. Historically, Cubans have found escape . . . through satire and mockery, but with the coming of Fidel Castro the sense of humour gradually disappeared until it became illegal. With it the Cuban people lost one of their few means of survival; by taking away their laughter, the Revolution took away their deepest sense of the nature of things. Yes, dictatorships are prudish, pompous, and utterly dreary.

Another stratagem to cope with dictatorship, certainly its prudishness and dreariness, is sex. In an essay called "Reinaldo Arenas, or Destruction by Sex", Cabrera Infante points out that for centuries, tyrannies have tried to curb Cubans' love of sex. A royal decree condemned their licentiousness as early as 1516, citing their excessive bathing as particularly dangerous. In *Infante's Inferno* (1979), Cabrera Infante's narrator has one blissful sexual adventure after another. No woman is able to resist him. *Before Night Falls* is Arenas's homosexual answer to *Infante's Inferno.* Arenas claims to have made love to "some five thousand men". Sometimes he has "ten, eleven or twelve" at a time. According to Arenas, homosexual activity proliferates in Cuba all the more for being banned by Castro (concentration camps were set up for homosexuals within a few years of Castro's takeover.)

Another stratagem favoured particularly by Cabrera Infante is the deployment of memory, to keep alive all that the dictatorship seeks to obliterate. In his novel *Three Trapped Tigers* (1967) he tried to bring to life a whole world that the puritan regime had suppressed: the life of pre-revolutionary Havana by night. Many of the writers and friends whom Cabrera Infante's memory rescued from oblivion chose the ultimate stratagem against the dictatorship: suicide (It would seem that suicide is many Cubans' last best hope.) Maybe in a collectivist society, it is the one free, individual act the régime cannot stop. There is a mind-boggling number of suicides in the two books. Arenas, who killed himself at the end of a long battle with AIDS, had already made several attempts to commit suicide when still in Cuba and healthy, and he describes each of them in *Before Night Falls.*

It remains for one to wonder what fate could be in store for Fidel Castro himself. How will the great actor go? In considering his options, Castro may occasionally think of his friend, the former Chilean president, Salvador Allende, who shot himself with a machine-gun that Castro had given him. Will Castro be able to beat that?

Alastair Reed (review date 2 February 1995)

SOURCE: A review of *Mea Cuba,* in *New York Review of Books,* Vol. XLII, No. 2, February 2, 1995, pp. 14-16.

[*In the following review, Reed chronicles Cabrera Infante's career, and praises him for "stand[ing] quite obstinately apart" from "the literature of frustration" employed by other Cuban exiles.*]

To be Cuban is to be born in Cuba. To be Cuban is to go with Cuba everywhere. To be Cuban is to carry Cuba like a persistent memory. We all carry Cuba within like an unheard music, like a rare vision that we know by heart. Cuba is a paradise from which we flee by trying to return.

In *Mea Cuba,* Guillermo Cabrera Infante gathers together all the separate writings on Cuba—articles, essays, memoirs, portraits, reflections, prepared talks—that he has produced since October 3, 1965, the day he left Cuba on a flight to Belgium (where he had been serving as cultural attaché) on the understanding of the authorities that he would not return for two years. His own understanding was different. As the plane passed the point of no return, he says,

> I knew then what would be my destiny: to travel without returning to Cuba, to care for my daughters and to occupy myself by/in literature. I don't know whether or not I pronounced the magic formula—"silence, exile, cunning"—but I can say that it is easier in this time to adopt the literary style than to copy the lifestyle of James Joyce.

Cabrera Infante's exile has lasted just short of thirty years by now, in the course of which he has become an enduringly original literary presence, unquestionably Cuba's most important living writer, and one who, more than the other Latin American writers of his generation, has intruded himself into the English language, writing occasionally in an English as startling and original as his Spanish, and masterminding the translations of his own work into English.

Inevitably, since *Mea Cuba* is as personal as its title suggests, its underlying theme, its underlying reality, is that of exile. When Cabrera Infante left Cuba, he first came to rest in Spain, but, denied permanent residence there, he moved to London, where he has lived steadily since 1966, in about as un-Cuban a setting as can be imagined. In an interview he gave a few years ago, he said: "I inhabit three islands: the British Isles, of which I am now a citizen; Cuba, which is always in my being and my memory; and the top of my desk, which is my active, everyday island." Most tellingly, however, exile for him meant exile from his language, not just Spanish, but Cuban Spanish, with its quickness of tongue, wryly admired in Spanish America. In the short memoir, **"Two Died Together,"** in *Mea Cuba,* Cabrera Infante writes of Cubans talking:

> A *tasca* in old Madrid on a November afternoon in 1976. Two middle-aged men are talking seated at a table. One of them is an imposing black who could easily play Othello, the other is white, short, with protruding eyes that seem to see everything. He could be played by Peter Lorre in *Casablanca.* Both are Cuban, both exiles and they have been talking louder than the Madrileños around them—and that's saying a lot. . . . They are, from right to left, Gastón Baquero and Enrique Labrador Ruiz. They are talking their way downhill. When there is a clearing in their conversation, one hears an unusual thunder: the whole *tasca* applauds. They are still applaud-

ing the two Cubans who talked. They heard them as one hears rain at first, then they listened attentively, then they applauded deafeningly. The Madrileños, who know about *tasca* talk, recognized the two foreigners for what they were: masters of conversation. . . . The two friends in the *tasca* were both exiles and the only thing left to them in life was their art. In which figured, prominently, conversation.

There are many parallels between his situation and that of Vladimir Nabokov—it was in his writing, too, that Cabrera Infante could recover and keep alive the country he had left, with no prospect of returning. Without choosing, he had become, to himself, an outpost of the Cuban language in London, something like a literary embassy, without portfolio. As a consequence, language became his reality. Language, insofar as he could keep it alive, was all he had of Cuba, all that he could take with him.

Born in 1929, three years younger than Fidel Castro, Cabrera Infante, whose parents were founding members of the Cuban Communist Party, came of age with the Revolution. In *Mea Cuba,* in the long essay **"Bites from the Bearded Crocodile,"** on the effect of the Revolution on Cuban writers, he recalls its first days:

> When Fidel Castro entered Havana in January 1959 like a larger Christ (as Severo Sarduy wrote from Paris with love), some of us saw him as some kind of younger, bearded version of Magwitch: a tall outlaw emerging from the fog of history to make political Pips of us all. However, the outlaw never became an in-law, only a law unto himself: the Redeemer was always wearing a gun on his hip.

Almost immediately Cabrera Infante was appointed editor of *Lunes de Revolución,* the literary supplement of the newspaper *Revolución* that served as the main voice of the new government. As editor, he gave the necessary support to his brother Saba to complete a short documentary film, *P.M.,* an excursion into the night life in the bars and clubs of Havana at the time. Submitted to the official censorship, the film was accused of being counter-revolutionary, and banned. Outraged, Cabrera Infante used *Lunes* to protest, and brought down on his head something of a show trial, at which Fidel Castro himself addressed the assembled intellectuals on their duties to the Revolution. Soon afterward, *Lunes* was closed down, and Cabrera Infante found himself in the kind of limbo many Cuban writers of his generation were to inhabit in succeeding years, forbidden to publish. "Within the Revolution, everything! Against the Revolution, nothing!" as Fidel "thundered like a thousand Zeuses." It was the fate that was to overtake the poet Heberto Padilla in 1971, when he was forced to make a ludicrous public confession of the anti-revolutionary bent of his writing. His case caused many writers throughout Latin America to break openly with the cause of Cuba.

Cabrera Infante was sent to Brussels as cultural attaché; but when he returned to Cuba in 1965 to attend his mother's funeral, he was made to realize the precariousness of any continuing Cuban existence under an imposed silence, and he accepted the inevitability of exile. The greatest deprivation of exile for Cabrera Infante turned out to be his isolation from the living, shifting language of everyday Havana; but that very circumstance did much to form his prose from that time on. The work-in-progress he carried with him when he left Cuba, the book later published as *Tres tristes tigres* in 1967, was written almost exclusively in a spoken language, spoken Cuban.

Cabrera Infante has resisted calling it a novel. It is a vast linguistic flight through the nightlife and night-happenings of a group of young Cubans, as meticulously set in a real Havana as was Joyce's *Ulysses* in Dublin, a spontaneous native Havana-by-night that would soon be forced underground. Its antecedents are the *Satyricon* of Petronius and the Nighttown chapter of *Ulysses*. The events, encounters, characters, conversations, arguments, and musings of five Cubans pass through all manner of linguistic modes, and the characters play throughout with many forms of public language—literature, advertising, popular song, local legend, propaganda, the movies, the comics. The spoken language, with its jokes, puns, antic quotations, and irreverent parody, is also playing with the dire realities behind it—the point is that in the spoken language alone the characters are alive and have their being. Living speech, free to run wild, is life-giving; the pathos lies in the inevitable return, at the night's end, to silence.

It had been Cabrera Infante's intention when he began the book to offset the passages of nighttime extravagance and excess with scenes from Cuba's new daytime reality, the revolutionary zeal that ran directly counter to the irreverences of the night: he would thus suggest the contradictions he lived through as a writer in Cuba. Once in exile, however, he saw that the life of his book lay in the spoken nighttime exuberances of his characters, although the Revolution is ever-present as backdrop and circumstance; and he finished the book accordingly. None of the very substantial novels that were being published in Latin America at the time came anything close to its originality and verbal agility; and few works in Spanish are as hilariously and irreverently funny. It is literature as performance—it can be read on different levels of attention, although language itself is its constant subject-matter. It is also a book to be heard as well as read.

Tres tristes tigres is Cabrera Infante's seminal work, and it greatly helped to set for Cabrera Infante the mode and manner of the writing that was to follow, as he faced the blank silence of exile. In many passages like this one from *Tres tristes tigres,* the Revolution intrudes into reverie:

> He made a muffled sound. What does a sound look like in its muffler? Idiocy of the folk. Muffled noises. Empty vessels make muffled sounds. Sounds to all deaf. Deaf words falling on silk purposes. Till deaf do us part. The early bird catches the first post. You can lead a horse to the water but you can't make him think. (Though you can make him sink.) Too many cocks spoil the brothel. We need a revolution among proverbs, for God's sake. Proverbs a la lanterne. Anyone who says a proverb should be shot. Ten sayings that shook the workers. Marx, Marx-Mao, Mao-Mao. It's a Mao's world. Soldiers, from the height of this sentence twenty centuries and Big Brother are watching you. Wiscondom of the folk. A phantom is hunting Europe, it is the phantom of Stalin. Crime, how many liberties have been taken in thy name. One must tend socialist man, as one would tend a tree. Ready. Aim. Timmmmmmbeeerrrrr! A call of duty is a beast forever. Isn't it true? Isn't it true? Isn't it? True.

The sheer fact that spoken language shifts constantly, makes sudden connections, plays with itself, asks and answers with a rapidity and an immediacy that a written language is at slow pains to match led Cabrera Infante to write from that point on deliberately in a spoken language, a language of sheer nerve, one that was free to play, to pun, to make spontaneous connections, to tease a subject, to go at times where language led, to perform a written language that at every point drew attention to itself as language, deceptive and unreliable as it might be clarifying. As a writer, he chose to become a speaking voice, varying between the reportorial and the wry, as here, in an essay called **"Actors and Sinners"**:

> Fidel Castro is perhaps the best television actor in the world, with a mastery of the medium and an absolute control not only of his voice and his gestures but of his temper. I remember having seen him one day in the waiting room of a television studio about to go on the air. Meanwhile, he killed time joking, strolling around calmly as he slowly smoked his habitual Havana, talking about cows and green pasturage and milk production, smiling satisfied: the agreeable agronomist. But no sooner had they introduced him to the well-lit studio and the camera had focused on him, than he came on the air transformed into a true Zeus thundering terrible traumas against an invisible opposition. He was not the elder Marx but the young Jupiter.

At the same time, however, Cabrera Infante was living in English, entering the language, writing (in English) the screenplay for the film *Vanishing Point,* and supervising the enormous task of turning the untranslatable flights of *Tres tristes tigres* into English, becoming in fact a bilingual being. As happened in Nabokov's case, exile had the effect of intensifying and heightening language for him, and the books he wrote from now on were all destined to have an English existence, masterminded by him. He wore both languages easily, and they cross-fertilized each other. In England especially, his command of the language has brought him both respect and attention.

Tres tristes tigres is Cabrera Infante's seminal work, and it greatly helped to set for Cabrera Infante the mode and manner of the writing that was to follow, as he faced the blank silence of exile.
—*Alastair Reed*

In 1981, he published in the *London Review of Books* his long essay on Cuban writers, **"Bites from the Bearded Crocodile,"** his first deliberate writing in English (he had later to translate it for the Spanish edition of *Mea Cuba,* as he did the hilarious memoir, *Holy Smoke,* which he wrote soon after in English). He did not, however, follow Conrad and Nabokov in becoming an English writer, although he was already wittily present as one. Cuba was still what he was composed of, and he determinedly remained a "writer of Cuban." All his work, consequently, skirts on autobiography, but while it feeds freely on past realities, it also sends them up, burlesquing them, peering at them from new and startling sides. In *Infante's Inferno,* the picaresque erotic memoir he wrote of his earlier years in Havana, puns abound, ever more energetically, each one a tugging reminder that we are at the mercy of language and the surprise turns it takes.

Mea Cuba gathers together pieces written irregularly over twenty-four years, close to seventy in all, some of them long, free-ranging essays, some of them short and pithy retorts to critics, some of them written addresses, some of them short reflections. The cast of characters is vast and recurring— friends and colleagues dead or exiled or silent, or caught up in the mechanism of the Revolution. Since Cabrera Infante was bent on preserving his Havana in writing, the detail is sharp, although the ironies are never far away, the tone increasingly sardonic as the book progresses. As opposed to its gleeful predecessors, *Mea Cuba* is in a sense a reluctant book, one that he would hardly have chosen to write had it not more or less accrued through time.

When he first settled in England, Cabrera Infante kept silent on matters Cuban for some time (silence, exile, cunning). In August of 1968 he was officially expelled from the Union of Writers and Artists of Cuba, as a traitor to the revolutionary cause, and he simultaneously broke his silence on Cuba, in articles and interviews in the press, in Spain and Latin America, and also in occasional lectures. He asks in his preface,

> What's a man like me doing in a book like this? Nobody considers me a political writer nor do I consider myself a politician. But it happens that there are occasions when politics is intensely transformed into an ethical activity.

The voice throughout these pieces is an essentially ethical one, withering and sardonic in its denouncing of human wrongs, bitter in its ironies, fierce in its dismissals. At the same time, however, he chronicles his time and situation in Cuba with enlivening recall, and peoples it with the lost friends and enemies who defined him then, particularly the writers who inevitably found themselves in the same stifling position that had forced him into exile, wondering whether anyone in Cuba would see their work. In an address he delivered in Madrid in 1990, reprinted in *Mea Cuba,* Cabrera Infante makes the observation:

> According to an English writer who visited Havana last year my books were the object of a strange cult among the ruins. Smuggled into the country, they were sold under the counter for the price of—ten tins of condensed milk! *La habana para un infante difunto* was then on the list of the best milked books. In the first slot, uncomfortably placed, was a book about perestroika (which in Havana is pronounced "*la espera estoica*"—the stoic wait), its author called, he is still called, Mikhail Gorbachev. It was the first time that in Communist Cuba a Soviet author collected his officially tax-exempt royalties not in pesos but in barter.

Asides on the ambiguous state of exile are threaded throughout the book.

> Cuba is the country that has produced the most exiles during more than a century and a half of American history . . . for us Cubans this is the century of exile. . . . A million and a half Cubans have already taken the landless road.

Such a diaspora has made inevitable an outpouring of writing on Cuba over the last thirty years, a whole literature of frustration. It seems to me that Cabrera Infante stands quite obstinately apart from that writing, in his stoical acceptance of "the violation of geography by history," and in his sardonic independence of mind and manner. It is the island of

his desk that is his true territory. His fierce exercise of his freedom to write more than compensates for the pain of exile, and the accompanying running guilt at being "here rather than there."

Most of the essays in *Mea Cuba* re-create the characters and lived circumstances during the years of descending limbo in Cuba, between 1959 and 1965, and the two people who figure most prominently in these chronicles are José Lezama Lima, the poet of Gongoresque density who was acknowledged as master of Cuban letters at the time of the Revolution, and Virgilio Piñera, the Cuban playwright, both of who served as mentors to Cabrera Infante. Both were homosexual; neither of them was at all adept at reading the changing political climate of the Revolution. They were doomed to be its victims, driven to a kind of internal emigration, to an enforced silence.

Cabrera Infante's re-creation of them, affectionate in detail and abundant in anecdote, dramatizes painfully and compassionately their inevitable suffocation. When the hearings against *Lunes* were being held, attended by Castro himself, Lezama Lima, who had himself been attacked in *Lunes,* nevertheless made a speech invoking the eternity of art and the permanence of culture. This was a characteristic imprudence, since Castro followed by denouncing all cultural divergence in the name of art (which applied even to long hair), by excoriating homosexuals in particular, and eventually persecuting them actively. Anything at all that smacked of the "degenerate" Cuba of Batista, any vestige of the nightworld Cuba Cabrera Infante was at such pains to document and preserve in *Tres tristes tigres,* had to be obliterated, cleansed, rehabilitated by the Revolution, and writers and artists, dangerously unreliable in such a light, had no choice but to surrender their lives, in one sense or the other.

Since this realization set clearly and implacably in Cabrera Infante's mind, his position on Cuba has never wavered. Cuba has been since the Sixties a tyranny, the Revolution long since perverted and betrayed. Illusions about the regime and justifications for it are to be revealed and exploded. He has also kept strenuously clear of the factionalism of Cuban exiles. His own stern and sardonic eye has been enough for him. Literature, the act of writing, has been for him life-giving, life-sustaining.

Cabrera Infante's writings stand out sharply from other writings on Cuba from the outside. They are fiercely personal and they have no particular case to make, no cause to argue. The numerous lives they summon up are anything but case studies—they are real people, rounded out and intricately remembered. Scorn there is in abundance, most of the rampant ridicule reserved for Fidel Castro, whom Cabrera Infante knew and observed in adolescence. In *Mea Cuba,* he is mostly referred to, for simplicity's sake, as The Tyrant.

He is variously to Cabrera Infante a figure become prehistoric by now, an actor who has totally consumed the stage, but who has survived in power only through creating a web of informers so vast as to sow distrust into the texture of everyday life in Cuba. In a long review-essay on Robert E. Quirk's biography of Fidel Castro, Cabrera Infante writes:

> Nevertheless Fidel Castro went on swamping the land with slogans concocted by this Maximum Publicist. See some samples: "Join the War Against All Weeds," "Land or Death!" To bigger billboards urging all Cubans to the joys of "Artificial Insemination—Not One Cow Left Barren!" It was a campaign that lasted two generations of Cubans. Not two years ago he exhorted all good men and true to do battle for the potato. "This is a battle we must win," he said on the May Day parade. "We will win the battle for the potato." It was more Groucho than Karl: "Potatoes of the country, unite! You have nothing to lose but your roots!" Potatory.

One of the studies in the book that show Cabrera Infante at his very best as a chronicler is his account of the life and times of Capablanca, the Cuban chess master, which begins with a three-year-old Cabrera Infante being taken by his mother to see the catafalque of the Great Cuban. The unwinding of Capablanca's character, career, and chess prowess through anecdote and aside, the range of reference and analogy Cabrera Infante sneaks into the text, the relish in the prose, give the whole essay the quality and completeness of a film.

> *Could Fischer have defeated Capablanca*? Fischer sought always to demolish his opponent, physically and mentally. The only way that Fischer would have been able to finish off Capablanca would have been to take advantage when Capa pressed the button of his timer to have, behind Fischer's back, a parade of chorus-girls, models and stripteasers to distract the naked eye of the Cuban.

There is a richly funny essay, **"Actors and Sinners,"** on politicians-as-actors-as politicians. There is also a moving essay of farewell to Néstor Almendros, the Spanish cinematographer who had become an "honorary Cuban" in Cabrera Infante's eyes, and who remained a constant friend in all Cabrera Infante's close ties with cinema. The pieces in *Mea Cuba* can so often shift in mood, go grave or antic by stages, turn a subject on its ear, reduce a gravity to absurdity, that the reader has to remain on his toes.

In bringing his work into English, Cabrera Infante has had the collaboration of a variety of translators, the most notable and durable of them being Suzanne Jill Levine, who trans-

lated *Three Trapped Tigers, View of Dawn in the Tropics,* and *Infante's Inferno.* She elaborates on the experience in her own book, *The Subversive Scribe,* a careful and exuberant account of the meticulous exchanges with the author in bringing certain complex passages, certain treacherous titles, into a satisfactory English equivalence. The translator of *Mea Cuba,* Kenneth Hall, has also performed valiantly. Comparing the English and Spanish versions, I find many small instances where a figure in the text, generally a pun, apparently untranslatable, has been neither lamely rendered nor dropped entirely, but has been recast so as to produce an almost equivalent effect in English. The ability to do so is the stamp of the master, and that stamp is everywhere recognizable in the pages of *Mea Cuba.*

Whatever the deprivations and invisibilities of exile, and quite apart from the remarkable literature he has produced, Cabrera Infante has by now earned for himself an unusual position, that of a small and ferociously independent outclave of Cuba, something of a conscience to Cubans, particularly those in exile. His view of Cuba is as clear as it is relentless, and he has Cuba at heart. His writings reveal that he is a Cuban to be trusted. It is not every Cuba-in-the-making these days that will be able to look a book like *Mea Cuba* in the eye.

"After scientific analysis only prophecy, it seems to me, is left," he writes in the essay **"And of My Cuba, What?"**

> When tyrannies succumb they leave behind the enormous weight of the past and no visible, foreseeable future—only the present can be creative. Thus one will have to extend the present of all Cubans to the immediate future, tomorrow, to wonder, and of my Cuba, what? To hear the echo that answers as if a sonorous mirror, *"What Cuba?"*

Adan Quan (review date Fall 1995)

SOURCE: A review of *Mea Cuba,* in *Antioch Review,* Vol. 53, No. 4, Fall, 1995, pp. 494-95.

[*In the following review, Quan faults Cabrera Infante for failing to note "the positive aspects of the Cuban revolution."*]

This wide-ranging collection of essays, articles, talks, and book reviews is by one of the foremost Cuban writers of this century. Written after his defection from Cuba in 1965, these pieces cover such topics as Lorca's sojourn in Cuba, a speculation on what the world would be like had there been no Columbus, and the acting careers of famous politicians. The principal topic, however, is the cultural politics of Cuba after the 1959 revolution. These political essays offer much fascinating detail about the lives of Cuban intellectuals. Many of the pieces will be of interest primarily to area scholars. Nevertheless, the book contains many gems of interest to the general reader, and the author's characteristic and always entertaining wordplay is faithfully translated.

From 1959-61, Infante served as editor-in-chief of the literary supplement of the Cuban government's official newspaper, *Revolución.* Differences with Castro led to his removal from this position, and eventually he was assigned as cultural attaché to the Cuban Embassy in Belgium. Returning to Cuba in 1965 for his mother's funeral, he found revolutionary Havana had become "like the wrong side of hell." He defected that year.

Not surprisingly, many of the essays criticize Castro's regime, and there are many poignant histories of exile, imprisonment, and suicide among Cuba's writers and artists. Infante never misses a chance to point out the social problems and hardships in post-revolutionary Cuba. Although his insights into these problems cannot be denied, he studiously ignores the positive aspects of the Cuban revolution (in health care and education, for example). Nevertheless, he convinces us that Castro is indeed a first-rate tyrant. A frequently recurring theme is the writer in exile; according to Infante, Cuba has produced more than its share of exiles in this century, and Cuban literature was born in exile. As with José Martí, exile has spurred Infante's productivity, leading to such novels as the masterful ***Three Trapped Tigers.*** At least, he can thank Castro for that.

Cesár Ferreira (review date Autumn 1996)

SOURCE: A review of *Delito por bailar el chachachá* in *World Literature Today,* Vol. 70, Autumn, 1996, pp. 921-22.

[*In the following review, Ferreira takes issue with Cabrera Infante for his numerous attacks on the Castro regime, which Ferreira says belong in a memoir rather than a collection of stories.*]

It is no secret to any reader of the works of Guillermo Cabrera Infante that, although he has lived in exile in London since the 1960s, the center of this Cuban writer's fictional universe has always been Havana. In fact, his masterpiece, *Tres tristes tigres* (1967), is a vast exploration of that city's once-upon-a-time intense bohemian nightlife. But whereas in *Tres tristes tigres* memory and nostalgia play a major role in the portrayal of Cuba's capital in the 1950s, a bittersweet tone permeates Cabrera Infante's latest sentimental journey to his homeland, ***Delito por bailar el chachachá.***

The book is a collection that includes a brief prologue and epilogue along with three short stories: **"En el gran ecbó,"** **"La mujer que se ahoga,"** and the title story, **"Delito por bailar el chachachá."** All three could be read as samples of the writer's unique uses of language: in the first two stories a brief, minimalist style reminiscent of Hemingway's best dialogue; in the third story an exuberant, transgressive prose.

In the prologue and epilogue Cabrera Infante points out that all three texts originate from the same scenario: a couple dining at a restaurant in Havana in the late 1950s, with music's playful digressive virtues serving as the hidden motif of all three pieces. For example, the intense emotions that Cuban bolero music evokes, such as passion, guilt, and betrayal, serve as the backdrop for the first two stories. These are brief pieces, in which amid the tightly crafted dialogue between the characters Cabrera Infante includes carefully described symbolic elements that define Cuban identity. However, more often than not, *santeria,* food, and tobacco overshadow the psychological tension between the couples who converse in the restaurant. The presence of music and other elements of everyday Cuban life is manifest, and even the witty use of language for which Cabrera Infante is well known partially comes alive. In the long run, however, in spite of the author's early attempt to justify his work, **"En el gran ecbó"** and **"La mujer que se ahoga"** are flat, trivial narratives that diminish the book's coherence.

One possible explanation for such a problem is Cabrera Infante's real intention behind the project: to expose the faults of Fidel Castro's regime, the focus of **"Delito por bailar el chachachá."** This is a lengthy piece, occupying over half of the volume, and, unlike the previous two, is narrated in the first person. Its anonymous protagonist (a Cuban intellectual) is arguably the author's alter ego. As he awaits the return of his lover at a restaurant, the narrator describes his surroundings inside and outside the restaurant. He soon reveals himself as an odd voyeur of the communist regime in the early days of Cuba's revolution. As he observes many women enter and leave the restaurant, commenting on their physical attributes, he also disinterestedly holds interviews with bureaucrats of the regime, individuals who prove to be nothing but caricatures.

The protagonist's obvious disenchantment with the political environment that surrounds him leads to candid reflections about Cuban society. Amid an imaginative and humorous prose, the reader is confronted with a variegated commentary on Cuban cultural identity, history, literature, film, music, and sex. At center stage are the author's recurring, sarcastic views on the limitations of Marxism, an ideology he sees as foreign to the problems of Cuba, one as simpleminded as the bureaucrats who try to implement it. Perhaps this is Cabrera Infante's personal *delito* here: trying to express his ideological differences with Castro's regime in a narrative that would have been better served in a memoir rather than in a collection of short stories.

Delito por bailar el chachachá is Cabrera Infante's attempt to bring together his many voices through the use of history, politics, and music. However, in all three stories his best prose flows in an uneven manner, leaving the reader with a disappointing glimpse of the Cuban author's true talent.

FURTHER READING

Bibliography

Feal, Rosemary Geisdorfer. "Works Cited." In her *Novel Lives: The Fictional Autobiographies of Guillermo Cabrera Infante and Mario Vargas Llosa,* pp. 170-75. No. 226, *North Carolina Studies in the Romance Languages and Literatures*. Chapel Hill: Department of Romance Languages, University of North Carolina, 1986.

> An extensive bibliography of works about Cabrera Infante and Mario Vargas Llosa.

Biography

Janes, Regina. "Ta(l)king Liberties: On Guillermo Cabrera Infante." *Salmagundi* 82-83 (Spring/Summer 1989): 222-37.

> Discusses Cabrera Infante's career, his opposition to Castro, two of his novels (*Three Trapped Tigers* and *Infante's Inferno*), and aspects of his personality.

Criticism

Alvarez-Borland, Isabel. "*La Habana para un Infante difunto:* Cabrera Infante's Self Conscious Narrative." *Hispania* 68, No. 1 (March 1985): 44-48.

> Provides a framework for understanding *La Habana para un Infante difunto* as a series of episodes that "oscillate . . . between [the narrator's] collective" and "individual" experiences.

Feal, Rosemary Geisdorfer. "The Duchamp Effect: G. Cabrera Infante and Readymade Art." *Criticism* XXXI, No. 4 (Fall 1989): 401-20.

> An examination of *Exorcismos de esti(l)o,* with an attempt to show similarities between Cabrera and the artist Marcel Duchamp with regard to their "attitude of indifference . . . toward 'high' art and literature. . . . "

Fox, Lorna Scott. "Castration." *London Review of Books* 16, No. 22 (24 November 1994): 22-23.

> A review of *Mea Cuba,* as well as *Before Night Falls*

by Reinaldo Arenas, which highlights ways that both writers dramatize tyranny under Castro.

Horne, Philip. "Wasps and All." *London Review of Books* 10, No. 22 (8 December 1988): 22.

> In a review of *View of Dawn in the Tropics* Horne commends Cabrera Infante for keeping "the pun count . . . pretty low" and "doing justice to each sufferer" he depicts.

Janes, Regina. "Speaking with Authority." *Salmagundi* 100 (Fall 1993): 86-96.

> Briefly discusses Cabrera Infante in a review of works by Edward Said, Conor Cruise O'Brien, and P. J. Marshall.

Kadir, Djelal. "Stalking the Oxen of the Sun and Felling the Sacred Cows: Joyce's *Ulysses* and Cabrera Infante's *Three Trapped Tigers*." *Latin American Literary Review* IV, No. 8 (Spring/Summer 1976): 15-22.

> Examines *Three Trapped Tigers,* James Joyce's *Ulysses,* and Homer's *Odyssey* as works that embody "the Spirit of Literature" and put their readers to "the task of decoding accumulated stores of eclectic materials which often extend much further than the authors might have been aware."

Malcuzynski, M.-Pierrette. "*Tres tristes tigres,* or the Treacherous Play on Carnival." *Ideologies & Literature* III, No. 15 (January-March 1981): 33-56.

> Applies theories of Mikhail Bakhtin on "carnivalization of literature" to a study of *Tres tristes tigres* in light of Cabrera Infante's anti-Communist political perspective.

Mitchell, Phyllis. "The Reel Against the Real: Cinema in the Novels of Guillermo Cabrera Infante and Manuel Puig." *Latin American Literary Review* VI, No. 11 (Fall/Winter 1977): 22-29.

> A discussion of Cabrera Infante and Puig as writers who, despite their differences in style, both owe a debt to the cinema for its influence on their work.

Perez, Gilberto. "It's a Wonderful Life." *The Nation* 256, No. 11 (4/11 January 1993): 24-28.

> Perez, who teaches film and grew up in Havana, reviews several film books, including *A Twentieth-Century Job.*

Prieto, René. "A Womb with a View: Sex and the Movies." *World Literature Today* 61, No. 4 (Autumn 1987): 584-89.

> An investigation of *La Habana para un Infante difunto* as a work which illustrates a particular relationship of literature, film, and the erotic as established by Roland Barthes and others.

Additional coverage of Cabrera Infante's life and career is contained in the following sources published by Gale: *Contemporary Authors,* Vols. 85-88; *Contemporary Authors New Revision Series,* Vol. 29; *Dictionary of Literary Biography,* Vol. 13; *DISCovering Authors Modules: Multicultural Authors; Hispanic Literature Criticism; Hispanic Writers;* and *Major Twentieth-Century Writers.*

Michelle Cliff
1946-

American poet, novelist, short story writer, and essayist.

The following entry provides an overview of Cliff's career through 1997.

INTRODUCTION

Cliff is a novelist, short story writer, and poet whose works illumine the plight of the culturally dispossessed and have been widely anthologized. Her writings chart the development of personal identity and reveal the various ways that familial relations, communal politics, societal norms, and economic conditions influence and determine an individual's sense of self. Cliff's quasi-autobiographical fiction centers on conflicts arising from issues related to race, gender, and class, reflecting an awareness of the consequences of intraracial prejudice that she experienced first-hand as a mixed-race, light-skinned, middle-class woman of Jamaican heritage. Although she considers herself a "political novelist" rather than a Caribbean writer, Cliff brings a multicultural perspective to her work, which addresses not only the oppression of women by patriarchal ideology but also the discrimination against (and even among) Third World peoples and societies due to the historical effects of European colonization. In addition, many of Cliff's writings include sexuality and homophobia as a subtext. Critics often have cited her dexterous blending of Creole *patois* and standard English as well as her disjointed narrative technique as stylistic hallmarks that exemplify postcolonial literature. Cliff explained that "part of my purpose as a writer of Afro-Caribbean—Indian, African, European—experience and heritage and Western experience and education has been to reject speechlessness, a process which has taken years, and to invent my own peculiar speech, with which to describe my own peculiar self, to draw together everything I am and have been."

Biographical Information

Born in Kingston, Jamaica, Cliff moved with her family to New York City in 1949 and attended public schools. In 1969 she graduated from Wagner College with a bachelor's degree in European history and accepted a position at the New York publisher W. W. Norton in 1970. The next year Cliff went to England and entered the Warburg Institute at the University of London, which granted her a master of philosophy degree with a specialization in languages and comparative historical studies of the Italian Renaissance. Returning to work at Norton in 1974, Cliff assumed the re-

sponsibilities of copy editor and eventually manuscript and production editor. She left the publishing firm in 1979 to concentrate on her first book, *Claiming an Identity They Taught Me to Despise* (1980). From 1981 to 1983 Cliff served as editor and co-publisher (with Adrienne Rich) of the feminist journal *Sinister Wisdom,* and from 1980 to 1989 she was a member of the editorial board of the journal *Signs.* During the 1980s, Cliff turned her attention to novel-writing and published *Abeng* (1984) and *No Telephone to Heaven* (1987). In addition to her work as a writer and editor, Cliff has taught at several American colleges and universities and has contributed regularly to various feminist and literary periodicals. She published *Bodies of Water,* her first collection of short stories, in 1990 and her third novel, *Free Enterprise,* in 1993. Since then, Cliff was named the Allan K. Smith Professor of English Language and Literature at Trinity College in Hartford, Connecticut, and has been a contributing editor to the journal *American Voice.*

Major Works

"In my writing I am concerned most of all with social issues and political realities and how they affect the lives of people," Cliff has remarked. Her works expose the intersections of various types of oppression stemming from differences based on race, gender, and class, illuminating the personal conflicts that inevitably ensue. The title prose poem of *Claiming an Identity They Taught Me to Despise,* for instance, explores the feelings of displacement and confusion of a Jamaican woman, who struggles with the consequences of being the lightest-skinned member of her family. Other poems in the volume scrutinize the impact of colonialism in Jamaica, particularly the special social privileges accorded light-skinned Creoles. Autobiographical on many levels, Cliff's writings feature female protagonists who, like the author herself, possess attributes that allow them to live simultaneously in two disparate cultures. *Abeng,* a female *bildungsroman,* centers on the trials and tribulations of the friendship between two girls, twelve-year-old Clare Savage and her playmate, Zoë. Through her bond with Zoë and a series of personal actions with painful consequences, Clara learns about the economic and racial barriers regulating the rural Jamaican community in which she lives with her grandmother. The poetry and prose comprising *The Land of Look Behind* (1985) address prejudice and colonialism, most notably in the section entitled "If I Could Write This in Fire, I Would Write This in Fire," which depicts the alienation imposed upon Jamaican mulattos. The novel *No Telephone to Heaven,* a sequel to *Abeng* set in Jamaica during the 1970s, traces the experiences of the adult Clare Savage as she attempts to find a connection with her Jamaican heritage after living abroad for many years. Finding her native island immersed in great political and social upheaval, Clare yearns for closure of her painful past and encounters others facing similar circumstances, including Harry/Harriet, a homosexual cross-dresser. He/she articulates the pain of ridicule and rejection through self-deprecatory jokes and frank assessments of the political, economic, and social strife affecting his/her life. Unified by intertextual references that resonate throughout the book, the stories in *Bodies of Water* are set in the United States and feature dispossessed children and psychologically shattered adults, who seek fulfillment and completion in an unintelligible world riddled by homophobia, racism, and sexism. *Free Enterprise* relates the story of Mary Ellen Pleasant, the largely forgotten woman entrepreneur who financed John Brown's doomed raid of Harper's Ferry just before the Civil War began. Through letters, poems, prose, and dialogues that shed light on other people involved with the raid, this novel narrates an account of the event that differs from the official record in various ways.

Critical Reception

Critics have praised Cliff for narrating multicultural stories that resonate with readers regardless of their cultural background, economic status, or gender, yet simultaneously offer incisive critiques on issues defined by and related to such categories. In addition, commentators have admired Cliff's technical skills in developing her characters, often citing the dialect-infused dialogues that range from standard English to Jamaican *patois* to Caribbean slang. Françoise Lionnet has observed that "this move from Standard English to Creole speech is meant to underscore class and race differences among protagonists, but it also makes manifest the double consciousness of the postcolonial, bilingual, and bicultural writer who lives and writes across the margins of different traditions and cultural universes." Many critics also have applauded the manner in which Cliff's family- and community-centered narratives transcend the boundaries of race, gender, and class by giving voice to individuals who often are silenced by "official" history. This feature has invited comparison of Cliff's writings to those of Toni Morrison. Cliff's "imaginative recovery of the past gives voice to the resistances that have been erased from history," Ann E. Green has remarked, adding that she "continues to write important stories, stories that reveal the multi-faceted nature of what any one culture may hold up as 'history.'"

PRINCIPAL WORKS

The Winner Names the Age: A Collection of Writing by Lillian Smith [editor] (prose) 1978
Claiming an Identity They Taught Me to Despise (prose poems) 1980
Abeng (novel) 1984
The Land of Look Behind: Prose and Poetry (poetry and prose) 1985
No Telephone to Heaven (novel) 1987
Bodies of Water (short stories) 1990
Free Enterprise (novel) 1993
The Store of a Million Items (short stories) 1998

CRITICISM

Frank Smilowitz (review date November 1987)

SOURCE: A review of *No Telephone to Heaven,* in *Women's Review of Books,* Vol. 5, No. 2, November, 1987, p. 13.

[*In the following excerpt, Smilowitz outlines Cliff's approach to the question of a Caribbean identity in* No Telephone to Heaven.]

Jamaican-born Michelle Cliff's latest novel, *No Telephone to Heaven,* touches on some of the themes of *Summer Lightning.* Cliff herself has lived outside of Jamaica for many years, and she writes knowingly about life in the "borrowed countries"—as she calls them—of American and England, about classism, and the clash of generations as it exists in Jamaica. This novel focuses, however, on what may be termed the pre-emptive concern of the entire region's literature: the question of a Caribbean identity.

The main character, Jamaican-born Clare Savage, is a divided person, as her name aptly signifies. ("Clare" or "clear" means light skin.) Her family has moved to Brooklyn, New York, where her father passes for white while her darker-skinned mother desperately grasps at tokens of the culture she has left behind. Eventually the mother returns home, taking one daughter with her and leaving Clare with her father. The duality is made overt: two sisters, the darker one in Jamaica and the lighter one in New York.

Clare is taken for white wherever she goes, but as a non-white Jamaican, proud of her homeland, her life becomes a tightrope, filled with perceived slights, self-imposed silences and an overriding sense of hypocrisy. As she travels in Europe and eventually enrolls at university in London, she is lonely and isolated: "I feel like a shadow . . . like a ghost . . . ," she admits, "like I could float through my days without ever touching . . . anyone . . . Locked off."

Her divided self is artfully paralleled in her Jamaican friend Harry/Harriet, a man/woman. He/she understands the problem: "Cyaan live split," he/she tells Clare, "Not in this world." Clare isn't even sure, for example, with which character to identify in *Jane Eyre.* "Was she not heroic Jane? Betrayed, left to wander. Solitary. Motherless . . . No, she told herself. No, she could not be Jane . . . No, my girl, try Bertha. Wild-maned Bertha . . . Captive. Ragout. Mixture. Confused. Jamaican." Eventually, like Harry/Harriet, who becomes Harriet, Clare makes her choice and returns home to Jamaica, literally reclaiming her roots in the form of her grandmother's abandoned property.

> **The abundant symbolism and obvious erudition—quotations from European and Caribbean sources open each chapter—are impressive, but the novel's general appeal may suffer as a result.**
> —*Frank Smilowitz*

The narrative passes back and forth in time as it details the experiences of two generations. The novel begins with a group of men and women, dressed in khaki, riding in a truck to an unknown destination, then moves to describe the violent machete murder of a wealthy Jamaican family by their yardboy. We learn of Clare's family, and the events that ultimately place Clare on that moving truck, and of the yardboy's poverty-stricken, inhuman existence. Finally the two narratives mesh into a unified whole. Even the narra-

tive structure works towards Cliff's intended point: the need for wholeness.

While this highly literary novel focuses on Clare Savage's personal dilemma, it also confronts the political future of Jamaica. Colonial exploitation is symbolized by the rape of Harry/Harriet by an English officer, which also parallels the rape of Harry/Harriet's black mother by his/her white father. At another point Clare thinks she may be pregnant by Bobby, an American Vietnam deserter who, significantly, has a sore that refuses to heal. She has a possible miscarriage and later finds an infection has made her sterile. Images of sterility, barrenness, impotence—the inability to create and sustain life—are all here and all speak for the political situation Cliff vividly and terrifyingly describes.

The abundant symbolism and obvious erudition—quotations from European and Caribbean sources open each chapter— are impressive, but the novel's general appeal may suffer as a result. While there are evocative sections filled with strong rhythmic language and passages of insightful description ("Like his labour, his connections to other people were casual," is the description of the yardboy), dialogue is at times stilted. It is hard to think of the characters as flesh and blood. But Cliff's use of Jamaican *patois* is perfect. She deftly uses it to reveal the deep understanding between Clare and Harry/ Harriet and moves in and out of the vernacular with unselfconscious ease. (She provides a glossary of Jamaican terms.)

As the title implies, ***No Telephone to Heaven*** provides no easy answers to the serious problems which confront Jamaica and its peoples, and other colonized peoples as well. What Cliff does offer is a provocative novel, rich in both story and substance.

Laura Frost (review date Spring 1991)

SOURCE: A review of *Bodies of Water,* in *The Review of Contemporary Fiction,* Vol. 11, No. 1, Spring, 1991, pp. 317-18.

[*In the following review, Frost applauds the characterization and style of* Bodies of Water.]

A nun avenges seventy-five years of abuse by torching her family's Winnebago; a black woman bleaches herself into a checkerboard sideshow freak; a Vietnam vet wearing a hat of yesterday's news wanders in a forest of shell-shocked men: such is Michelle Cliff's landscape of fragmented souls in her short story collection, ***Bodies of Water.***

Jamaican-born Cliff has shifted her focus from the West Indian setting of her outstanding novel *No Telephone to Heaven* (1980) to America. Just as Cliff herself has relocated to and "adopted" the U.S., her characters move as visitors in a strange land, not quite at ease with their surroundings or understanding their circumstances. The ten stories in *Bodies of Water* show remarkable range both in geography and tone, but they all share a common theme—the struggle to define the self in an essentially incomprehensible world.

Many of the stories feature abandoned children and disoriented adults, somehow set apart by a deeply wounding experience. Operating on a continually shifting foundation, where broken homes are more the rule than the exception, the characters often violate traditional social mores in their restless search for validation and wholeness. Rich intertextual references enliven the stories and illustrate how an individual's history can encompass many lives, as references from one "life" intrude into another. In **"A Woman Who Plays Trumpet Is Deported,"** set in the 1930s and '40s, an African-American female musician travels to Paris, where "They pay her to play. She stays in their hotel. Eats their food in a clean, well-lighted place. Pisses in their toilet. . . . No strange fruit hanging in the Tuileries."

The narrative voices in *Bodies of Water* are quietly scattered, carefully avoiding certain disclosures, and Cliff's writing not only accommodates but even simulates this quality. Her sentences are choppy prose-poems, alternatively flowing with the ease of free association and halting as pain becomes too sharp for conscious articulation: the effect is a sort of syntactical breakdown reflecting the internal state of her characters. If the reader is often puzzled and must struggle to piece together these narratives, it is a confirmation of Cliff's success at portraying characters who mystify even themselves.

The penultimate story, **"Bodies of Water,"** brings several of the characters from previous stories together in the form of an epistolary dialogue between a brother and sister. The recognition that there is some sort of connective tissue, however tenuous, among these lives, is a relief, and ultimately affirmative. Even if there are no triumphs, no dazzling epiphanies, even if these characters' lives only touch one another rather than interlock, it is somehow enough.

M. Stephanie Ricks (review date Winter 1991)

SOURCE: "Tales of the 'Other,'" in *Belle Lettres*, Vol. 6, No. 2, Winter, 1991, p. 15.

[*In the excerpt below, Ricks focuses on Cliff's representa-tion of isolation, alienation, and loss in several stories of Bodies of Water.*]

Michelle Cliff and Jamaica Kincaid, two writers from the Caribbean islands of Jamaica and Antigua, respectively, have crafted works that expertly and eloquently address themes of isolation, alienation, and loss. Kincaid's novel *Lucy* and Cliff's collection of short stories *Bodies of Water* adeptly introduce the life of the "other" navigating the customs, attitudes, and social contracts that define life in America. Included are the anonymous brown women seen on urban streets handling white children; the displaced Vietnam veterans, forced back into a society that no longer welcomes nor accommodates them; or a carnival's self-styled Hottentot Venus.

In *Bodies of Water,* Michelle Cliff draws from both historical and modern sources to zoom in on the individual as outsider in the United States. Her stories are spare, their rhythm staccato. The details sometimes overlap in stories and offer multilayered passages that are slowly peeled away as the narrative progresses.

In **"Columba,"** the only story to take place in the Caribbean, the story's unnamed narrator relates the tale of Columba, a fourteen-year-old sold by his mother as a house servant, to Charlotte, a middle-aged woman of means. Charlotte shares her home with her one-time lover Juan Antonio, a Cuban expatriate. Living frugally in dilapidated splendor, Charlotte spends most of her time in bed, in a room that reeks with the smell of urine, bay rum, and wet sugar from the tamarind balls she favors.

Although forbidden to talk to the servant, the narrator and Columba develop a friendship during Charlotte and Juan Antonio's absences. Columba is hungry for news from the States and asks and asks the narrator, a former New Jersey resident, pointed questions that show his infatuation with American pop culture. Questions like: "every detail about Duke Ellington, Marilyn Monroe, Stagger Lee, Jackie Wilson, Ava Gardner, Billy the Kid, Dinah Washington, Tony Curtis, Spartacus, John Wayne." And "What is life like for a Black man in America? An ordinary Black man, not a star?" The narrator, who has lived in a cloistered bourgeois community, does not know how to answer him.

Columba has found a 1930s Rover on Charlotte's property, located off in the fields, that is now populated with doves. It is there that he spends his free time, sitting amongst the birds. When Charlotte needs to repair her car, she remembers the abandoned Rover in the field and sends Juan Antonio for a replacement part. Juan Antonio chops his way through the overgrowth to Columba's sanctuary only to return with the tale of the doves. Charlotte, pleased with the news that once again her property has shown itself to be full of bounty, orders Columba to kill, pluck, dress, and freeze the doves. **"Columba"** ends with "'Sorry, man, you hear?' he said softly as he wrung the neck of the next one. He was weeping heavily. Heaving his shoulders with the effort of execution and grief. I sat beside him in silence, my arm around his waist. This was not done."

In **"A Hanged Man,"** Cliff uses two historical details to tell the story of a slave's flight to freedom. One is the story of a man who hung himself in a building used to punish slaves. These whipping houses, as they were called, were typically situated along the periphery of the plantation so that when northern Abolitionists came south to investigate reports of the owners' brutality to their slaves, they would not find the physical evidence. The second is the story of Peg-leg Joe, a conductor on the Underground Railroad, which is used to relate how a slave follows the tracks of a human foot and the circle of a peg to freedom. This unseen companion in front of her and the lifeless presence of the hung man behind propel her in her journey.

"A Woman Who Plays Trumpet Is Deported," is dedicated to Valaida Snow, a concentration-camp survivor who played the trumpet. It begins with abrupt, terse prose, its rhythm analogous to a solo trumpet riff. "A woman. A black woman. A black woman musician. A black woman musician who plays trumpet. A bitch who blows. A lady trumpet-player. A woman with chops."

In language that is piercing, clear, and fluid, the story follows the progress of this woman musician from America to Europe. Happy for the solitude and the opportunity to play, the woman is eventually picked up on a Copenhagen street in 1942 and lined up with other women and children with her trumpet clasped to her side.

The story of the book's title, **"Bodies of Water"** opens with Jess, an older woman fishing on a frozen lake. She is singing to attract the fish and to keep herself awake. Recently widowed by her lover and companion, Jess ultimately reflects on a childhood incident that continues to haunt her.

Michelle Cliff's writing whooshes like the breeze through autumn leaves, making the air crackle and the leaves quiver. Her stories are sometimes rich in details, other times painfully bare but always full of humanity, feeling, and truth. Cliff successfully weaves the divergent themes of oppression and empowerment, with all of the many shadings in between, into an enriching literary endeavor.

Michelle Cliff with Meryl F. Schwartz (interview date 2 April 1992)

SOURCE: An interview with Michelle Cliff, in *Contemporary Literature,* Vol. 34, No. 4, Winter, 1993, pp. 595-619.

[*In the following interview, originally conducted on April 2, 1992, Cliff discusses her multicultural self-identity, her political stance on gender, class, and race issues, the autobiographical origins of her writings, and the popularity of books by people of color.*]

Novelist, poet, and essayist, Michelle Cliff has spent the past decade and a half creating a body of resistance literature that describes and formally enacts the struggle for cultural decolonization. Originally from Jamaica, Cliff was educated in Jamaica, the United States, and England. She has written repeatedly of her struggle to claim her own voice, noting that "part of my purpose as a writer of Afro-Caribbean—Indian, African, European—experience and heritage and Western experience and education has been to reject speechlessness, a process which has taken years, and to invent my own peculiar speech, with which to describe my own peculiar self, to draw together everything I am and have been." As a light-skinned daughter of colonialism, Cliff was raised to reject her "colored" heritage, but after completing a dissertation on the Italian Renaissance at the University of London, she began a sustained examination of the Anglocentric education she had received. Partly as a result of her involvement in the women's movement, she had begun trying to use language to represent herself, and she discovered that in internalizing colonialist ideology, she had lost access to crucial parts of her identity. Thus her career as a writer began as a process of trying to reclaim the self through memory, dreams, and history. This project informs Cliff's first book, *Claiming an Identity They Taught Me to Despise* (1981), a characteristically fragmented and lyrical text that Cliff describes as "halfway between poetry and prose." Concerned that her use of language and imagery in this volume allowed the reader to "ignore what [she] was saying while admiring the way in which it was said," Cliff went on to develop a heteroglossic language and form that resist containment by apolitical reading strategies.

Cliff's first book was followed by *The Land of Look' Behind* (1985), a collection of poems and essays that includes selections from *Claiming an Identity They Taught Me to Despise,* and the novels *Abeng* (1984) and *No Telephone to Heaven* (1987). Together these novels chronicle a young woman's quest for the suppressed history of Jamaica and the process by which she comes to commit herself to anticolonialist politics. More recently, Cliff has published a collection of short fiction, *Bodies of Water* (1990), and a new novel, *Free Enterprise* (1993). Building on historical records of Mary Ellen Pleasant, who funded and helped plan the enterprise that came to be known as John Brown's raid on Harper's Ferry, *Free Enterprise* imaginatively recovers stories of the centuries-long resistance to the slave trade, centering on women who devoted their lives to "the cause." Cliff's essays, short stories, and poems have appeared in numerous periodicals and anthologies, including *Critical Fictions, Voice Literary Supplement, Ms., Caribbean Women Writers, New Worlds of Literature, American Voice, I-kon, Frontiers,* and *Heresies.* Set in the United States, the Caribbean, and England, Cliff's work reflects her own experience of diaspora while representing a wide range of imperialism's manifestations and effects. Her texts explore the ways in which colonialism's racist ideology intersects with a variety of oppressive ideological systems, including those based on class, gender, and sexual orientation. As one form of resistance to experiences of silencing as both colonial subject and woman, Cliff's fictions give imaginative life to the suppressed history of women's anticolonialist activism.

When we met on April 2, 1992, Cliff had just completed a poem about a newly emerged piece of her personal history. She was in good humor; laughter mixed easily with more contemplative moments as we spoke in her sunny office at Trinity College in Hartford, Connecticut, where she was the Allan K. Smith Visiting Writer, teaching fiction writing and a course on black women writers. Since 1990, Cliff has spent three spring semesters teaching writing and literature at Trinity, where she is presently Allan K. Smith Professor of English Language and Literature.

[Meryl F. Schwartz:] *At the moment I'm working on the development of a Caribbean studies program at the University of Hartford, and one of the first questions we've had to ask is "who is a Caribbean writer?" One of my colleagues insists that we cannot include writers who are not currently resident in the Caribbean.*

[Michelle Cliff:] How are you not going to count them? You diminish the literature enormously by eliminating those of us who are outside the borders. First of all, the Caribbean doesn't exist as an entity; it exists all over the world. It started in diaspora and it continues in diaspora.

Do you see yourself as participating in a community of Caribbean exile writers in particular, or does that category not mean anything to you in the context of a cultural diaspora?

Well, I'm in touch with some of us, but I don't think of myself as belonging to a community. I think it's just emerging now, especially with women. I grew up both here and in Jamaica, and it's as if I grew up in the nineteenth as well as the twentieth century, because the Jamaica of my childhood was very paternal, Victorian. I didn't know any women writers. The only woman Jamaican writer that I read was Sylvia Wynter, whom I've since met—she teaches at Stanford. There's been a burgeoning of Caribbean women writers as far as I'm concerned. Not that there weren't any—there were quite a few actually—but they weren't available to me. I

think Selwyn Cudjoe's conference at Wellesley in 1988 on Caribbean women writers was very helpful in getting us in touch with each other.

In 1990 I went to a conference called "Critical Fictions" at the Dia Center for the Arts in New York. The community there wasn't limited to Caribbean or African or Latin American or whatever; it was a community of political novelists. And I see myself much more in that category. We're writing out of different origins, perhaps, but we have a lot of the same interests. Angela Carter was there as a political novelist; I was there as a political novelist; Arturo Islas, a Chicano novelist who died of AIDS a year later; Luisa Valenzuela, Nawal El Saadawi from Egypt, Ama Ata Aidoo from Ghana; and they were much more my community, I felt. I grew up partly in the United States, I was educated in London, and I originated in Jamaica, so I can't limit myself to just one place.

That multicultural sense of identity seems to contradict some of the things you've written.

But I'm coming into myself as I write. The person I was while writing **Abeng** is not the person I am now. I reread **Abeng** the other day when I was home; I haven't read it in years. It's a good novel, but I've gone beyond that. When I started writing **Abeng** I was really trying to construct myself as a Jamaican. I was able then to claim the rest of the people that I happen to be as well, as I write.

One of the things that struck me when you gave the reading here at Trinity College was that the parts of **Free Enterprise** *that you read were set in the United States.*

It's also set in the Caribbean. The whole novel is about resistance. It has a Jew from Surinam, a woman who becomes a Maroon, and a freedom fighter, and it talks about the Inquisition and the Expulsion of the Jews in 1492. And then there's a Jamaican woman like myself—but it's not me—who joins forces with abolitionists in this country to fight slavery, leaving behind Jamaica because she thinks it's hopeless to struggle there, so she comes to the United States to become a freedom fighter and ends up in a leper colony in Louisiana. The leper colony is not really a leper colony; it's a colony of political activists who have been incarcerated. They spend their days telling each other their histories. One is a Hawaiian and one is from Tahiti. Then Rachel, the Jew, is there, and Annie who is from Jamaica, and they all sit around telling stories to keep history alive. It's much more diverse than my earlier work. It's a historical novel and it's set primarily in the past, but it's much more diverse than the other novels.

So you're moving toward a conception of affiliation based on political allegiance rather than origins?

Political enthusiasms.

The title of your recent essay, "Caliban's Daughter," suggested to me that you were still writing out of a sense of Jamaican identity.

I am, in a way. That's a very personal essay. I started it for the Caribbean Women Writers Conference, talking about myself, defining myself through the protagonist of *No Telephone to Heaven*, Clare Savage, by explaining why she is as she is. It's grown a bit more, but it is more of a Jamaican essay. And it's about England and Bertha Rochester and Jean Rhys and the usual suspects. Heathcliff . . .

I loved your suggestion in "Clare Savage as Crossroads Character" that somebody write Heathcliff a life.

I've done even more with that, because Angela Carter and I had this wonderful conversation at the Dia conference, and we both were convinced that Heathcliff was black, that he was meant to be black, and I went back and did some research. At the time in the novel when Earnshaw goes to Liverpool, Liverpool was the center of the slave trade and there were discarded slaves, so-called, all over the city. And Heathcliff is described as dark. Angela was working on a new edition of *Wuthering Heights,* and I don't know if she was able to finish it [before her death in 1992]. She was going to put that in there.

It's hard for me to imagine the Earnshaws integrating Heathcliff into the family to the extent that they did if he was African.

Because they're not told. He's a monster and what happens is he gets tamed, but not really, and I said to Angela or she said to me, I don't remember who came up with this first, that he disappears for three years from the narrative, just like Toni Morrison's character Sula disappears for ten years. You never know what's happened to him, but he comes back worse than ever but very, very rich. Angela said—this was her idea—there's only one place a man like Heathcliff could have made a fortune in those days so fast, and that was the slave trade. And she's absolutely right. And the Brontës knew all about that. So Heathcliff comes back completely damned because he's literally sold his own people, and it's probably his mother—my theory was that Earnshaw could have been his father and he had him by a slave woman. Something like that, and he goes to Liverpool, the mother's dead, and he brings the boy back. It really does fit.

Getting back to our discussion of your changing sense of identity, how would you respond at this point to these passages from **The Land of Look Behind***? The first is from "If I Could Write This in Fire, I Would Write This in Fire":*

I and Jamaica is who I am. No matter how far I travel—how deep the ambivalence I feel about ever returning.

The second passage is from "Love in the Third World." Addressing Jamaica, you say:

I wonder if I will ever return—I light a cigarette to trap the fear of what returning would mean. And this is something I will admit only to you. I am afraid my place is at your side. I am afraid my place is in the hills. This is a killing ambivalence. I bear in mind that you with all your cruelties are the source of me, and like even the most angry mother draw me back.

Is that a position you have moved on from? Is that ambivalence finished for you?

No, I don't think it will ever be finished.

I'm struck by your statement that you're afraid your place is in the hills, which is where your character Clare Savage ends up, as a member of a band of guerrilla fighters.

Well, that's what I meant by that. I meant that if I went back seriously, the only proper position for me to take would be as somebody who would be dedicated to extreme political change. And I don't see that degree of change as a possibility in Jamaica. I think things have gone beyond that. I could be wrong.

Due to the extent of neocolonialism?

Exactly. I don't see myself as a landowner in Jamaica—my family were and are landowners—I gave that up a very long time ago.

Did you feel that giving Clare the opportunity to go back made it easier for you to make the choice to remain here, to take on the role of intellectual activist as opposed to the armed resister?

That's probably true, but I see Clare's return as tragic. She's a fragmented character, and she doesn't get a chance to become whole at all. The most complete character in *No Telephone to Heaven* is Harry/Harriet. And I did that purposely because Jamaica is such a repellently homophobic society, so I wanted to have a gay hero/heroine.

Abeng *is full of suggestions that Clare is going to grow up to be a lesbian, and yet that theme seems to get dropped and displaced onto Harry/Harriet in* **No Telephone to Heaven.**

That's because Clare can't claim her sexuality. She's not in a place where she can. It's a very interesting thing, because the lesbian subtext in *Abeng* was unconscious, at least I think it was. The poet Dionne Brande raises the issue of the difference between being a lesbian in Europe and a lesbian in the Caribbean, and in the essay **"Caliban's Daughter"** I talk about this. Clare's access to lesbianism in Europe would be similar to the access Nadine Gordimer's character Rosa Burger has, and also the character Merle Kinbona in Paule Marshall's *The Chosen Place, the Timeless People*—where lesbianism is seen as a Eurocentric, eccentric, upper-class behavior, for the most part. Decadent and exploitative of Third World women. Whereas for Clare to claim her lesbianism in the Caribbean would be to become a complete woman. That's the way I read it. If Clare had had an affair in Britain with Liz, which is suggested very strongly in the novel, it wouldn't have led her back to herself. It would have made her more foreign to the place she came from. But her love for Harry/Harriet is a step towards herself. And if she wasn't killed she probably would have gone the whole way.

Harry/Harriet is the novel's lesbian in a sense; he's a man who wants to be a woman, and he loves women, which is complicated.

When you talk about the ending in "Clare Savage as Crossroads Character" you seem to feel positive about that ending as an achievement of wholeness because she's burned into the ground of her homeland.

Right, that's one way of becoming whole, but she's still dead.

So her death is not a moment of a consummate coming together; it is premature?

I think so, but you can go back and forth about that ending.

What I like to do with it is to argue that the ending leaves readers with a sense of incompletion that may motivate them to continue the struggle in which Clare was engaged.

That's good. Also, we don't know that Harry/Harriet dies, so there is always a possibility that he's going to go on. He's the real revolutionary in the book.

Related to that is the whole question of the way gender politics intersects with other issues in both **Abeng** *and* **No Telephone to Heaven**. *In* **Abeng** *Clare's political awakening is tied into her sexual awakening and her awareness of gender discrimination; she first menstruates at the same time she first acquires some knowledge of Jamaica's history—*

And realizes her love for Zoe.

There's clearly a moment of sexual awakening between the girls, and it's so fascinating that Clare's assertion of resistance to the sexual harassment of herself and Zoe is the very moment when she asserts her class and race privileges. And yet Clare's awareness of gender politics does not seem to be what propels her further into anticolonialist politics.

No, it doesn't.

What happens there?

I don't know. You know, so much of writing is unconscious. I wanted to make **No Telephone to Heaven** a book that stood by itself; I didn't want to necessarily write a sequel to **Abeng**. In the context of Jamaica, when Clare is thirteen years old, which is her age in **Abeng,** the only way she can deal with the racial oppression around her is by reading about the Holocaust. It's not until she moves to the United States that she begins to really deal with antiblack oppression. I think that's what happened to me. The Birmingham bombing, for example, was a huge event in my life. I was in high school in New York when it happened. Clare's reading the newspaper to her homeroom was what I did. The teacher asked me to read the *New York Times* every morning to the students, and I remember two things from those newspapers: one was the Birmingham bombing and the second was the death of Lorraine Hansberry. Both of those events really got to me. I didn't know then on how deep a level, but they obviously had an incredible effect, particularly the bombing. And I started to get more and more involved in racial politics here; it was the period of the civil rights movement. I was brought up to think that Jamaica was not a racist society, but America was. And England. And so my experience with the world at that time was much more through racial politics than gender politics.

So the change of emphasis in Clare's development from gender politics to racial politics is autobiographical.

Yes. But then it comes together later in my life. I'm writing about myself back then, and I think I've managed to put those things together. I hope to God I have. And now I find I'm writing more about being gay.

Where? In your fiction or in essays and poetry?

Well, I just finished a long poem. I had an interesting thing happen. I had a flashback about an incident that happened when I was twelve and still in Jamaica. It's a pretty awful story, actually. I was in a private girls' school, and my mother and father were living in Montego Bay, I was at school in Kingston, and there was this other house on the other side of the island where we used to go for weekends. And one weekend my parents came from Montego Bay to Kingston. It's a long schlep from Montego Bay to Kingston; it involves crossing the interior. My parents went into the house where

I was living while we were away at the country home with an aunt. They went through my bureau, found my diary, literally broke it open. They read it, then drove with it to the country house. They sat me on the verandah and read the diary out loud to me in front of my relatives and my sister. It was a silencing, what Tillie Olsen calls a silencing event. It silenced me for almost twenty years. I started to write when I was thirty-something.

The title story of **Bodies of Water** is about a boy who is gay, and he writes in his diary that he is gay. Now, when I wrote that story I did not connect it consciously to my own diary incident at all. But then when I went and looked back, I said, "Gee, this is interesting, because you're transferring yourself into a gay boy." Flashbacks are very strange events. I had remembered the incident of the reading of the diary. What had happened was I went back to school and I had a breakdown, and my parents had to take me out of school. And now, after having conversations with friends, I've remembered what was in the diary, which was that I was in love with another girl. She was taken out of school and sent to a boarding school, and we were never allowed to see each other again.

So the school or your family had been aware of the relationship.

I think both must have been. It's all very fragmented in my mind right now, but I'm remembering more and more. I can remember her name, I can remember what she looked like. Just like this relationship between two girls, the murder in **No Telephone to Heaven** actually happened to a family I knew, but I had forgotten it. I had blocked it out of my mind until I wrote the chapter, and then it all came back that this had actually happened. But now I've written about myself and this other girl—and about being girls in love on this island that was so wild but also so repressed, and just how destructive, how deadening that is. The effect it's had on me has been very good because I feel that much of the internalized homophobia that I have, that anybody gay has, is falling away, which is good. Up until now my sexuality hasn't been in my writing much, although it has been by implication.

And its absence from your writing has been very striking.

It *is* there, but as a subtext.

But it's not the focus.

I think part of it is self-censorship. I have to be honest. I think it is. And I think it's having grown up in a society that is enormously homophobic and the fact that my mother disowned me for being gay. At first when she did this, which is about ten years now, I thought I was the one to blame—

for years I felt I was the one to blame. So this was going on while I was writing **Abeng** and **No Telephone to Heaven.** But now that I've remembered, I'm feeling very angry and justified, and that's very good for me.

*I'd like to ask you about the incident with your cousin Henry in London. In **"If I Could Write This in Fire, I Would Write This in Fire,"** Henry visits you and joins with his friends in making homophobic remarks about a waiter shortly after being the victim of a racist snub in another establishment. You seem to be exploring the question of conflicting allegiances. Like Clare, you seem to be trying to decide where to align yourself. It seems that in your earlier work you felt that your fundamental allegiance was to anticolonialist politics.*

I think it is, but I think I can integrate it more now into my other concerns. I was thinking last night that this incident from my girlhood, even though I blocked it out, was something that worked to make me into someone who thinks in a revolutionary or political way—that that was my experience of oppression and silencing, which gave me the ability to realize other examples around me.

Internalized homophobia is a problem I have had. I have to be perfectly honest about that. It comes from where I came from. I didn't know a lesbian in my childhood, that I was aware of. The only gay person I knew was a gay man who worked for a relative as a butler/houseman who was very effeminate and who ended up going to London to become a dancer, which was really wonderful. And he was partly the basis for Harry/Harriet.

You've been living and working in a community of lesbian-feminist writers for years. Has that been nurturing in terms of your writing? Is that community partly what's allowing you to have these recollections now?

No, I don't think so. I have supportive friends; some are lesbian and some aren't. I guess they're all feminists, depending on how you define it. I think it's a very personal process. The support of women like that has been extremely helpful, but I can't do it until I'm ready to do it.

*I'd like to get back to Clare Savage and your relationship to her. In your 1982 article **"Object into Subject,"** you talk about the importance for characters of defining themselves through art. You talk about Alice Walker and about Toni Morrison's novel* Sula, *and yet you deny that particular power of self-definition to Clare. Would she have gone on to become an artist if she had lived?*

I don't know. She becomes an art historian; she's studying art history. She's an observer. The thing with Clare is that because she's disintegrated, she really goes through life as an observer. Now, the period that I was writing about in *No Telephone to Heaven* corresponds to the time in my life when I was studying the Italian Renaissance. So that's somewhat autobiographical . . . But the novel isn't completely autobiographical because I'm more of a survivor than she is. But I killed her off before I came out!

The connection between Clare's coming into herself and knowing her history permeates the novels. She can't come into herself until she knows her history, and clearly that dynamic has been part of your personal quest as well.

Well sure. Just remembering this incident is knowing part of my history, which is making me more complete. It's both personal and political history.

The connection between the two is one of the things I like about your work. One question that comes out of that is, to what extent do you see yourself as permanently marked by having received a colonialist education?

How can you not be marked? But you work with it. I was quite privileged in my education, in a sense, but I will always be marked by the fate of people like Zoe [a dark-skinned, economically disadvantaged character in *Abeng*], who were my friends and whom I loved and whom I saw damaged and deeply hurt. That's another kind of colonial education.

It's so interesting that in **No Telephone to Heaven,** *Clare will never come into contact with the itinerant laborer Christopher, whose story fragments the narrative of Clare's development.*

That's absolutely intentional. They have parallel lives, and they only meet in two incidents of violence—when he kills Paul and Paul's family and at the very end of the novel, where he's transformed into the movie monster.

This raises questions about what it means for relatively privileged readers and writers to make a political commitment to fight privilege. You talk, in **"If I Could Write This in Fire, I Would Write This in Fire,"** *about how for you it's not a question of relinquishing privilege. You say, "it's a question of grasping more of myself." I hear in that a response to people who are saying, "well, why are you giving up privilege?" You're saying that's not the issue for you, and yet there's always some kind of divide there, such as the distrust with which the other members of the resistance group initially meet Clare.*

Well, they would. How could they not?

Can you talk about how that relates to your personal experience?

It's tough. I was reading an anthology of West Indian women writers, a prose anthology called *Her True True Name*. There's a nasty swipe at me in the introduction. They say something to the effect that I am light enough that I might as well be white, which is not true. It's one thing to look x and to feel y, rather than to look x and feel x, and that's part of the difficulty being light-skinned: some people assume you have a white outlook just because you look white. You're met immediately on that level. But it varies a great deal. I felt I was included in that anthology because they couldn't exclude me, but to put me in they had to make a crack about me. The introduction ends with something like "not many of us are called Clare Savage," words to that effect. It was just plain bitchy, if you want my reading of that remark. And it goes back to very old and very painful stuff.

But it does vary from group to group. It's just something I live with. I was giving a reading on Monday of this week at Camden, New Jersey, at an inner-city community college. It was a wonderful experience. The audience was all people of color, though there were two apparently white people in the audience. I read from my new novel, and I talked about revolution and oppression. As soon as I started to speak, the audience, which could have been incredibly distrusting of me, wasn't. We really got down and talked about a lot of stuff. So it does vary. Most African-American people know somebody in their family who looks like me. There's a very wide spectrum of racial types. I think in Jamaica how one is perceived is not based just on skin color, but on property and privilege, and if some people see somebody like me, they assume that my alliance is with the colonizer. That is the usual assumption. So that they could make that kind of remark, even having read *No Telephone to Heaven.* They could still seem to assume that my alliance would be with the colonizer. It's something I'm addressing less and less, because, frankly, I'm too old to keep talking about that. I just have to accept that people are like that.

And in this country as well—

Oh, please, very much in this country. I know most of my students at Trinity don't believe I'm black—the white students. The black students don't seem to have a problem with who I say I am.

The whole question of political alliance is crucial in Clare's development. Your use of the image of the abeng *emphasizes the fact that Clare has the choice to become an instrument of oppressive or resistant forces.*

She can leave the island. Somebody like Zoe will never leave unless she goes to work as a domestic someplace, to live and die in somebody else's kitchen or nursery.

There's no getting away from that distinction between the

two girls, but it's Clare who has to come to recognize her relative privilege, where it is always obvious to Zoe. I really like the way you say that the choice of allegiance is Clare's to make, that political allegiance isn't necessarily based on how you look, and yet I think there is an awful lot of distrust of privileged people who align themselves with resistance movements. I felt that you were responding to that distrust in "If I Could Write This in Fire," that you were responding to people thinking that you were motivated by altruism—

That it's noblesse oblige?

Right. And you seemed to need to assert that that's not what motivates you, that your politics are for you.

Exactly. It is for me.

Let's talk about audience. It seems to me that you imagine a North American and British audience when you're writing.

I don't think so. I think I'm really writing for myself. I am both of those things, so I don't think I'm thinking of an audience that much. I try not to, actually, because I think you could really go bananas if you did that.

What gave me that impression is the sense, and maybe that's just because of my own subject position in reading your texts, that there's a way in which you're translating the Jamaican experience in the novels for an audience from outside Jamaica.

Well, I think as a political writer I want as many people to understand what I'm talking about as possible. But the discovery of the history, for example, in *Abeng,* that I go on at great length about, was my own discovery. It was for me that I was writing it.

What about in your choice of language? You've talked about your use of the patois. Your pattern seems to be to use so-called standard English for your narrator's voice and to use the patois in dialogue.

It depends on who's talking. When Jamaicans get together here, when we talk, we talk in patois, for the most part. Well, they talk in patois and I answer in it. The other day I met a Jamaican woman who is a professor at Eastern Connecticut State, and we immediately started talking in patois.

So that is part of your language?

Yes, it's a way of relating to each other as Jamaicans and not in the other language that we have to use to get by in the world. But I create in that other language as well. When you come from a polyglossal culture, which is what Jamaica is, you do speak in several tongues.

You talk about the homophobia in Jamaica. Do you see this as part of the colonial legacy?

Yes, I do. I have no idea why homophobia is so virulent there, but I think it must go back to slavery, the sexual use of black men by the slavemasters, perhaps.

We were talking earlier about the connection between the psychological and political in both **Abeng** *and* **No Telephone to Heaven.** *I find that political commitment doesn't come simply out of ideological belief but is always rooted in a psychological need. In Clare's case, her mother's denial of a close mother-daughter bond is a very important motivator. One of the things that concerns me as I teach* **Abeng** *and other anticolonialist, political-awakening novels, is that if the motivation for the protagonists comes so much out of their particular psychological formation, how do we use these texts to get students to think about the relevance of colonialist politics to their own lives?*

Well, that's tough. It's a very hard thing to do when you teach. The students really have to have compassion for what's going on around them. But I'll tell you something interesting. I was teaching the other day a marvelous novel called *Life with a Star,* by Jiri Weil. It's a novel about the Holocaust, set in Prague. It's one of the best books I've ever read, an absolutely superb novel. And the students said to me that they couldn't identify with the character because he lived in Czechoslovakia in the war, it was depressing, et cetera. But then we started to talk about what Irena Klepfisz calls "the Holocaust without smoke"—which is around us in Hartford, for example. How do you respond to homeless people on the streets? The star of the story is the yellow star. There's a scene where a group of people coming out of a restaurant look at the narrator but don't see him because he's become invisible to them. So we related that to the question, how do you respond to a homeless person? When you meet the person eye-to-eye, what do you say? It's just a matter of getting people to have compassion for other human beings, really. They should feel incomplete when they see somebody suffering like that. I think people are very self-protective, especially young people. It's hard to expect them to be anything else. I'm writing all this stuff from my thirties, and now forties, and they're just starting out in their lives, and they don't necessarily want to be reminded of all of this. They're brought up to deny it.

What I find disconcerting is the extent to which my students seem to feel that their psychological needs are best met by retaining the sorts of privileges they have.

Right, if that's what they've learned. It's hard to expect them to do otherwise, but you can't give up hope or else you'd go nuts.

Let's go back to **No Telephone to Heaven**: *whatever else we might say about its conclusion, it certainly highlights the difficulty of resisting neocolonialism. What do you see as the greatest challenges in that struggle, and where do you see positive opportunities for resistance?*

You caught me on a bad day. There are so many levels on which the struggle has to be waged. There's self-hatred, there's distrust of each other, there's the fact that whenever Jamaica—I'm speaking specifically of Jamaica—has taken a shot at revolutionary change, when Manley tried his socialist experiments, for example, it didn't last very long. When Bob Marley was coming up and getting a worldwide movement going—a kind of modern-day Negritude movement—he dies of cancer and he's thirty-five years old. We were the same age. And when Walter Rodney, the author of the stunning book *How Europe Underdeveloped Africa* gets killed, blown up. Grenada is invaded, Maurice Bishop is killed. It's like one step forward, seven steps back. It feels like the forces of the capitalist world, the colonialist world, are so ranged against movements of self-definition in the Caribbean that change is almost impossible at this point. The United States, with Grenada and Panama, has used foreign intervention as a way of trying to make America feel better about itself. That's what they do. With Castro in power, the last thing America wants is another socialist country off the American mainland. So I don't think we'll see any significant change, in my lifetime anyway. The other thing is the continuing diaspora. What happened in Jamaica in the seventies was that there was really a brain drain. The middle class left in droves because of Manley's socialist government. Instead of staying behind and trying to work to build up the country, they just left. They took their money and went to Miami. My family didn't leave, but many, many people we knew left.

So that was a period when you were in Jamaica?

Yes, it's the period of the party scene in *No Telephone to Heaven.* That party is almost true to the letter, though it's a conflation of many parties.

You first left Jamaica when you were three. Why did your parents leave at that point?

They left before. I came later, with an aunt. They left because there was no economic future for them, because it's an underdeveloped country and because they were light-skinned enough to pass. My parents went back to Jamaica in 1956—I was ten years old—and we lived there for several years. Then we came back here again because economically things weren't working out, and then after a period of

time we went back and forth more than once a year, to visit family.

So you were never quite as uprooted as Clare Savage.

No, not at all. Although the last time I was in Jamaica was 1975.

Why haven't you been back since then?

Partly because I'm gay, and I don't feel like I have a place there. I like writing from here; I like the view from here. I probably will go back someday, just to hang out or something.

Since 1975 is such a long time.

You know, it's not as long as it seems. I don't know that I would ever have written if I had lived there, and it's really the period when I've been writing that I haven't been there. So it's really not that long. I've been back to the Caribbean, just not to Jamaica.

So many exiled writers have said they couldn't write while they were in their native lands.

I think that's valid. James Baldwin, Salman Rushdie—there are a lot of us.

There's a history of books with black characters who were driven to murder. I'm thinking particularly of Native Son *and* The Street. *How do you see your character Christopher in relation to those novels?*

Christopher certainly relates to Bigger Thomas. *Native Son* had an enormous effect on me. What I wanted to show with Christopher is how a murderer is created, how somebody like Christopher is created, and how any chance that he has for self-respect or self-love is bashed, and his violent act is based in his self-loathing. When he asks to bury his grandmother and is brutally rebuffed, it's just too much for him. But he does brutalize the woman who works in the house who's the same color as he is far worse than he does the others, just like Bigger is much more brutal towards Bessie than he is towards the white woman. Bigger is motivated by self-hatred. He sees himself in Bessie. It's like when Cholly Breedlove rapes Pecola in Toni Morrison's *The Bluest Eye.* He sees himself as a little boy peeing in his pants when he goes to find his father.

This self-loathing turns Christopher, but there's still a spark of decency in him, which comes out when he witnesses the almshouse fire, which is based on a true event in Kingston. It happened during a political campaign in 1985, between Seaga and Manley. One of the political parties set fire to an almshouse and burned all these old women. It was on the front page of the *New York Times,* and I'll never forget it. About 180 old, poor women burned. And when Christopher witnesses that, he disclaims that fire as his. So there's still a decency about him. He knows what he did was wrong; he's internalized it into insanity.

The characterization of Christopher raises the same sorts of questions that Native Son *raises about the extent to which social circumstances determine individual development.*

Not just social circumstances. Well, I guess you could say it's all social circumstances, but I'm thinking for instance of Christopher's grandmother's attitude towards the preacher who tells him that Jesus is black. This description of Jesus is based on a contemporary description of Jesus. These characters are unable to love themselves because of the lives they have been allowed. They cannot believe that the Son of God—the figure they believe is the Son of God—would be black like them. They just think the preacher is crazy.

Christopher's name means "bearer of Christ." He's named that not just because of Christ, but also because of Christophe. I wanted to conflate in Brother Josephus's words Toussaint L'Ouverture and the Haitian revolution with Christ. But these people are unable to accept both black saviors. They are unable to accept themselves reflected in God, and therefore they are unable to accept their own liberation. So Christopher is stopped on every level of his being. One of the final blows is when he's passed on like goods to the woman in the country, who just tosses him aside when he becomes a man. He's just stripped away piece by piece.

In a sense, Christopher's and Clare's struggles are both about self-hatred.

Yes. They're very similar characters. He and she are the most important characters in the book, and Harry/Harriet is in the middle. Or maybe he's the apex of the triangle. He's the best of both: he's female and male, black and white, and he's managed to deal with it, managed to make a decision, to say "this is who I am. Even if I'm the only one in the world, this is who I am." But he's also been raped, and so he has a sense of gender oppression as well.

One of the things that connects your work with Irena Klepfisz's and Audre Lorde's is that, like them, you've given voice to so much anger, and that's been very helpful to a lot of readers.

That's true. I think the similarity between me and Irena, for example, since we're almost the same age, has to do with the fact that we're both children who came out of diaspora, and we both came to this country as children. I was thinking the other day that some of the people I feel close to—

not all—are people who don't have a country. They don't have the country of their birth. Irena I feel very close to, and it's really because of that shared situation, I think, and the fact that, although in different ways, we've each written a lot about what it's like to be a stateless person.

So you don't feel that any number of years of living in the U.S. will make this home?

No, not in the way it would be if I was a native-born American. It's just a different kind of being.

So that writing about America in **Free Enterprise** *has less to do with seeing yourself as American than with seeing the connections between the politics of different regions?*

Seeing the connections and then also writing through a protagonist—an American protagonist—Mary Ellen Pleasant, who's been written out of the history books. She funded John Brown's raid on Harper's Ferry. I'm writing through an American woman who was not seen as an American by mainstream America. Black Americans have never been wholeheartedly accepted as Americans in this country. So in a sense that's the kind of American I am.

Another thing that struck me about the relationship between Clare and Zoe, as well as between you and the real Zoe, as you described it in **"If I Could Write This in Fire, I Would Write This in Fire,"** *is that you're saying that there is no pure relational state that exists outside of social structures.*

They can't transcend it, even as girls.

Has the impossibility of transcending those differences been something that you've experienced throughout your life?

It's very difficult to talk about that. There have been times when I've felt very close to, say, a particular white person, and trusted them. It's hard to trust across racial lines; it really is. Occasionally—it hasn't happened that often, but because it's happened you're on your guard—you've given the trust and then the person uses a word or makes an assumption that is racist. You say that xyz is racism, and then they apologize, but the relationship is never the same. It can heal, but it's like going through life constantly being reminded that racism is the bottom line in the world in which we live. What W. E. B. Du Bois said about the problem of the twentieth century being the problem of the color line is true. And it just seems so idiotic to me. But as far as my relationship to other women of color, it's much less of a problem for me. I'm talking about African-American, American Indian, Latina women—we have had similar experiences in America.

So that those differences are perhaps erased in a different way in this environment than in Jamaica?

Right, because you've got class there. The separations between Clare and Zoe are really class-based. The class system is founded in race, but Clare would not make a racist assumption about Zoe. That just wouldn't be something she would do. But she would certainly make classist assumptions about Zoe and herself. When she takes the gun to shoot the wild pig, she's really taking power as a girl. It's a response to having read the article about the rape of another girl. She's taking power as a girl, but she's taking it through a male mode. She can't take it through a female mode because the power she's witnessed is always through a male mode. And Zoe then becomes a female in the situation. Then Clare, because of what she does, is removed from access to female power, which is embodied in the person of her grandmother, who shuns her, and her parents then send her to live with a white woman who's obsessed about race. So through this chain of events she loses access to various forms of real power, power which could be hers.

That white woman was incredibly horrible.

She was someone I knew. Both her and her sister Mrs. Stevens. The description of Mrs. Stevens in *Abeng* is almost an exact description of a woman I knew. The child she has when she's young I made up. She was a woman who was absolutely filthy. She would not wash. Finally, she got sick and they took her to the hospital and washed her. As soon as the water hit her skin she dropped dead. She had convinced herself she was unclean. Now I don't know where that came from. Also—and this is not in *Abeng*—she was a poet. The idea of a woman artist in her class—she was upper class—in the Caribbean was abhorrent. A woman simply wasn't an artist. I remember sitting with her on the verandah of that house, which was right on the Caribbean, and she would recite to me poetry that she had written. This was at the country house where they read the diary. So the whole time they were reading the diary out on the verandah, there's this "mad woman" over the wall. A poet. I don't have to have an imagination. All I have to do is record things. It's as if Bertha Rochester was next door, and this diary is connected up to writing and expression of oneself, which was then used to humiliate me, and she's a poet and look what's happened to her. So it's really an extraordinary little scenario.

How successful do you think the women's movement has been in dealing with white women's racism?

I think people have tried. I think an effort has been made. It seems to be something that's entered into the mainstream of feminism much more, and it's being taken seriously. One thing that I'd like to mention is an organization in the Caribbean, CAFRA, which has a newsletter. It's a feminist grassroots organization that works throughout the islands and is doing important organizing around conditions for working women, such as the minimum wage, and on violence against women, which is a huge problem in the Caribbean.

To what do you attribute the current popularity of writing by people of color?

I would first expand the category. In discussing this I would include, for example, somebody like Nadine Gordimer as a Third World writer, because she is an African after all, and I would include Patricia Grace, who's a Maori writer.

The most exciting writing that's going on right now is being done, for the most part, by people of color or Third World peoples, however you want to put it. We're able to be freer, more experimental because we're not faithful to Western forms as much as white, Western writers are. We have a different sense of time and space, and we have more access to a dream life. Some people may disagree with that, but that's what I think. The idea of literature in most white, Western European circles is as a discipline, and it's something that you're trained for, something that you fit yourself into as an artist. At least that's how I see it—that there is such a thing as *the* novel, such a thing as *the* short story. I think we are much more undisciplined, and therefore we have more access to our imaginations. That's a very prejudiced point of view, but that's how I see it.

Do you think that the positive reception this literature is receiving is purely on aesthetic as opposed to political grounds?

I think it's hard to turn it away because it's such good stuff. Take a novel like *Beloved*. Morrison said when she published it that she had no idea that anybody would read it because it touches on a subject that is so painful and so hidden. I've wondered, if it had been her first novel, would it have gotten the response that it got? She wrote it when she was established. But it's so beautifully written, how could it not be noticed? When I think of all the people who bought *Beloved*, I think, "What are they seeing when they read it? What do they get out of this book?" It's like people buying Stephen Hawking's *A Brief History of Time*. Probably a lot of people are limited—they can't accept the politics of *Beloved*, or even understand the point of view; they can't get it—but they can certainly appreciate Morrison's style, her writing, and, through that, her ideas may get to them on some level.

To take the example of Beloved, *I wonder about white readers' responses to a book that so powerfully "others" white people, such as through its use of the word "whitefolks."*

I think *Beloved* has had an enormous effect on literature. I'm writing a book about the slave trade. Caryl Phillips has just published a book on the slave trade called *Cambridge*, which

I just got and am dying to read. And I know about a couple of other writers of color who are writing books on the slave trade. I think *Beloved* has really opened it up to us. It's not a subject that was dealt with before. *Beloved* is an incredibly important book. Gordimer is interesting because she's not that experimental as a writer, although her latest book of short stories, *Jump,* is pretty wild. It's wonderful. Her politics are right there on the page.

They always call us Third World writers postmodern. That's one of the adjectives used. I remember at the Dia conference, a scholar from Pakistan, Homi Bhabha, got up and used the word "postcolonial" about the Third World, and Ama Ata Aidoo gave him hell. She said to call the Third World "postcolonial" is a sadistic joke. She used that exact expression, because there's nothing post about the colonialists.

Maria Helena Lima (essay date January 1993)

SOURCE: "Revolutionary Developments: Michelle Cliff's 'No Telephone to Heaven' and Merle Collins's 'Angel,'" in *Ariel,* Vol. 24, No. 1, January, 1993, pp. 35-56.

[*In the following essay, Lima compares and contrasts conventions of the postcolonial* Bildungsroman *that appear in Cliff's and Collins's novels, highlighting each writer's approach toward representation of revolutionary social transformation.*]

Michelle Cliff's *No Telephone to Heaven* (1987) and Merle Collins's *Angel* (1987), like many other postcolonial novels, indirectly parallel the formation of the young self to that of the developing nation. *No Telephone to Heaven,* the story of Clare Savage's development into revolutionary consciousness and her involvement in a symbolic act of revolution in Michael Manley's Jamaica, and *Angel,* a novel about a girl growing up during the people's revolutionary government of Grenada, share a similar authorial project—the possibility of revolutionary social transformation. When Cliff and Collins attempt to figure this transformation through the reconceptualization of the established genre of the *Bildungsroman,* however, they textualize their projects in significantly different ways. Through playing off the conventions of the novel against those of several other genres—history, the epistolary, allegory, autobiography, *testimonio*—Cliff and Collins expose the complexity of the contradictions within generic conventions.

The history of the *Bildungsroman,* from its beginnings in Germany to its development in England and adoption by commonwealth and, more recently, by postcolonial writers, has been one of adaptation and change, initially in thematic and then in formal terms. While genre does not in itself determine that a text must be read in a certain way, it brings with it a history of reading, a set of conventions and of specific aesthetic ideologies. The expectations engendered by the genre, as Catherine Belsey writes, can enter into a relation of tension and opposition with the project of the text: "The unconscious of the work (*not,* it must be noted, of the author) is constructed in the moment of its entry into literary form, in the gap between the ideological project and the specifically literary form." While contemporary postcolonial *Bildungsromane* do not break the conventions outright—they continue to ask the genre's old questions surrounding the relationship between experience, subjectivity, and social structures—they explore its possibilities, thereby expanding the genre. The novel of *Bildung* has been "chosen" in virtually all countries undergoing decolonization because it is the Western form of discourse that constitutes identity in terms of a relation to origin. The genre's survival might in itself mark the victory of the colonizer but its transformation in countries attempting decolonization offers provisional rewritings of origin and identity, rhetorical configurations that will undergo further change as the process of recovery continues.

Precisely because *Angel* and *No Telephone to Heaven* are written for different audiences, from distinct class perspectives and historical contexts, they tell very different stories about the possibility of real social transformation. Cliff's text is predominantly allegorical while Collins structures her novel on a predominantly historical figuration.

Postcolonial allegorical writing is engaged, according to Stephen Slemon, in a process of destabilizing and transforming fixed ideas of history. When history and literature come together, collectivity becomes the subject of narrative. As Edouard Glissant notes, the European novel's individualism is not for the Caribbean. Instead, he posits the "collective novel," the novel of the relationship of individual to collectivity, of individual to the Other, to help create a new nation and a new people, "liberated from the absolute demands of writing and in touch with a new audience of the spoken word."

The issue of language choice is thus central to postcolonial reconceptualizations and to any attempt at identifying an implied audience in the Caribbean context. What initially characterizes writing in the Caribbean is what George Steiner calls being "linguistically unhoused" for the writer must mediate between a "metropolitan" standard and the creole languages of her childhood and environment. Cliff's decision, then, to rely primarily on standard English and only cursorily to employ patois, not only marks the class/culture division between her narrator and the Jamaican characters who populate her fiction, but also signals the primary audience for whom the novel is written. Collins's choice of Grenadian creole, the language of the "subaltern" class, as the novel's language may also signify, among other purposes, her concern that the novel be accessible to those of that class who can read.

Angel, moreover, foregrounds the cautionary element inscribed in the original *Bildungsroman,* an aspect of the genre that is almost totally lost in the symbolism of *No Telephone to Heaven.* While *Angel* ultimately consists of a call to arms, *No Telephone to Heaven,* despite its critique of the People's National Party (PNP), does not want to bring Jamaicans together for another experiment in democratic socialism. In many ways my reading of Cliff's novel resonates with existing evaluations of Manley's government. Fitzroy Ambursley, one of Manley's critics, emphasizes the symbolism in the political philosophy of Jamaica's prime minister. While the first two years of the PNP government brought a general liberalization as well as some reforms—free secondary education, a literacy campaign, a partial land reform— the urban middle-class origins of the PNP became once again visible as most of the state institutions were placed under the control of representatives of the island's capitalist class.

When contrasted with *Angel,* Cliff's novel can be said to figure precisely this class privilege by reinforcing the split in the linguistic practices which separate the "educated" from the "less cultured" classes. If the language choice Cliff makes signals her intended audience, then, we might say that she addresses very educated Caribbeans, at home or in exile (like herself) and a North-American readership.

Cliff's implied audience is also familiar with the European tradition of the *Bildungsroman,* for Clare, like Jamaica Kincaid's Annie John, exists in dialogue with *Jane Eyre.* Like Jane Eyre, Clare is motherless; she is solitary and left to wander, having "no relations to speak of except [like Jane Eyre] an uncle across the water." Cliff, however, goes a step further than Kincaid and incorporates Bertha Mason into Clare's intertextual identity: "Captive. Ragout. Mixture. Confused. Jamaican. Caliban. Carib. Cannibal. Cimarron. All Bertha. All Clare."

Clare feels closer to "wild-maned Bertha." She remembers how her father was forever trying to tame her hair: "she refused it; he called her Medusa. Do you intend to turn men to stone, daughter?" Centered on the figure of Medusa is the disclosure of Clare's internalization of sexual and racial oppression, the extent to which she has been forced to deny both her (homo) sexuality and her Africanness. As Susan Bowers points out, Medusa's mythical image has functioned like a magnifying mirror to reflect and focus Western thought as it relates to women, including how women think about themselves. Rediscovering and remembering the vitality and dark power of the mythological figure of Medusa, that primary trope of female sexuality, is as important for Cliff as

Jamaica's revolutionary project itself. Attempting to trace the unconscious of the text, we might actually see these projects as related. By reworking the narratives that connect and separate mothers from daughters, moreover, Cliff's novel goes as far as to suggest that a return to a pre-oedipal, preverbal moment of origin can provide an instrument for binding the fragments of self.

Cliff posits Clare's urge to return to the island in essentialist terms, representing her homeland, the landscape of her identity, as female. The land is infused with the spirit and passion of Clare's grandmother and mother in a deeply personal, almost biological connection. In one of her mother's letters to her father, Kitty adds a postscript for Clare in which she expresses her hopes that someday Clare will make something of herself and be able to help her people. Kitty wants Clare never to forget who her people are: "Your responsibilities lie beyond me, beyond yourself. There is a space between who you are and who you will become. Fill it."

Clare's separation from her mother signals the rupture from the "African" and the collective in her, since Boy, Clare's father, counsels his daughter on invisibility and secrets and has "no visible problems with declaring himself white": "Self-effacement. Blending in. The uses of camouflage." Kitty leaves her daughter and her husband in the U.S. because she feels she *has* to return to her island, her "point of reference—the place which explained the world to her." Clare's loss of both mother and island clearly structure the novel, which is ultimately about her futile attempt at return and wholeness. There are many bits and pieces to Clare, Cliff writes: she is composed of fragments. Clare's journey back to Jamaica, she hopes, will be her restoration.

As soon as Clare finishes school in the U.S., she leaves for England, "with the logic of a creole. This was the mother-country. The country by whose grace her people existed in the first place." Her uncle writes to Clare to remind her that she has a chance to leave that narrow little island behind her. By "chance," Clare knows he means light skin. The fragmentation and isolation of the immigrant community in London, however, help shatter Clare's illusion of a shared heritage with the mother country. Yet, feeling only a little guilt, Clare uses her privilege to stay in Europe writing to her aunt and uncle, then living in Miami, that she is doing work for her degree on the continent, describing briefly the beauty of churches, managing to get more money from them in the process, as well as a letter extolling the tranquillity of the mainland after the turbulence of the island, caught as it was in riot, fire, burn.

Clare's inscription as Jamaican comes from an awareness of place that she initially tries to rationalize with her analysis of Aristotle's definition of *place* in the *Physics,* for which she is praised at the University: "Each thing exists in place.

Each thing is described by place." She immediately connects her feelings about place to her mother, who ties her loss of voice to the loss of home. The images Cliff creates to trace Clare's movement back to her homeland, however, are quite disturbing:

> The albino gorilla moving through the underbrush. Hiding from the poachers who would claim her and crush her in a packing crate against the darker ones . . . Make ashtrays of her hands, and a trophy of her head. She cowers in the bush fearing capture. . . . Not feeling much of anything, except a vague dread that she belongs nowhere. . . . She does not gather branches to braid into a nest. She moves. Emigrated, lone travel . . . Time passes. The longing for tribe surfaces—unmistakable. She is the woman who had reclaimed her grandmother's land.

Feelings of displacement characterize not only the exile but the postcolonial condition whose homelessness Cliff figures with images of absence of colour (the albino gorilla) instead of conferring her character a mestiza identity (and colour). "Gorilla" and "longing for tribe" convey the primitivism often associated with "African" and evoked in her own name. Clare's return to Jamaica also follows an almost biological urge: the island is female and the "albino" child is finally reunited with the lost mother. From a post-structuralist cultural feminist perspective, Cliff reifies "African," "female experience," and "woman." It is this essentialism which makes her project, the possibility of revolutionary social transformation, and its figuration ultimately incompatible.

As a crossroads character, Clare belongs at least in two worlds. Her first name, Cliff tells us, "stands for privilege, civilization, erasure, forgetting. She is not meant to curse, or rave, or be a critic of imperialism. She is meant to speak softly and keep her place." Her surname evokes the wildness that has been bleached from her skin. Cliff emphasizes how she uses the word *savage* to mock the master's meaning, "turning instead to a sense of non-Western values which are empowering and essential to survival and wholeness." As a colonized child, Clare understands that it is her bleached skin which is the source of her privilege and her power. A knowledge of her history, the past of her people, however, has been bleached from Clare's mind (the history Cliff attempts to recover with *Abeng*).

Whereas Walter Benjamin and Georg Lukács refer to the link between allegory and the annihilation of history, in Cliff, the allegorical serves to inscribe an alternative history as she makes clear how this female power originates in Nanny, the African warrior and Maroon leader who has been left out of most textbooks. At her most powerful, Cliff writes, the grandmother is the source of knowledge, magic, ancestors, stories, healing practices, and food. She assists at rites of passage, protects, and teaches.

When Clare recognizes, in a church graveyard in the town of Gravesend, yet another grandmother figure in Pocahontas, the daughter of Powhatan who was kidnapped by colonists, held against her will, forced to abandon the belief system of her people, and then taken to England in 1616 where she was displayed as a tame Indian, she begins a series of choices which will take her from England, the mother country, back to the country of her grandmothers: "She thought of her, her youth, her colour, her strangeness, her unbearable loneliness." The letters Clare receives from Harry/Harriet make her decide to return: "Jamaica needs her children . . . Manley is doing his best but people are leaving in droves—those who can." In another letter, Harry/Harriet tells her they "are supposed to be remembering, the grandmothers of our people. We are supposed to be remembering, through our hypocrisy, the 167 old women who burned up in a fire started by some bastard," a reference to the destitute women inmates who died in the Kingston Almshouse Fire.

The figure of the Maroon leader Nanny is also behind both Miss Mattie, Clare's grandmother, and the grandmother of Christopher, who inhabits the Dungle [the Kingston slums], and whose only power is the power to judge the worthiness or unworthiness of others. Against an identified "yard novel" tradition that represents what gives the community its identity, Cliff's Dungle does not draw people together, like the community in Orlando Patterson's *Children of Sisyphus* (1964), a novel that, according to Dell Lewis, inscribes a "psychological boundary: it is [the people's] beliefs which keep them together as a group to await something; and it also shows the element of hope they have." Lewis's idea of using the yard as a critical/aesthetic model relates directly to Africa (the transplant of the African compound to West Indian ground) and to Caribbean critics' "total roots-directed (re-)definition of ourselves." Cliff's novel figures the total breakdown of compound transplantation: we read *No Telephone to Heaven* as a tragically individualist tale whose protagonist does end her life "burned into the landscape of Jamaica, by gunfire." Through the character of Christopher, however, we can trace a counter-narrative of resistance that ultimately limits the significance of the comments, at the novel's closing, of the two whitemen, one British and one American:

> 'Jamaicans will do anything for a buck. . . . That brief shit with Manley was the exception. Oh, the poor followed him; the poor occasionally protest about prices, shortages, that kind of thing—' . . . 'Anyway, babe, about your fear, about revolution . . . the class system wouldn't permit. I mean, they're more English than the English in that regard.

At least, the ones on top are. The ones who call the shots.'

Although Cliff's revolutionary Jamaica falls short of a real "war zone," it is potentially more than the "stage set" Harry/Harriet believes the country to be. The truly revolutionary gesture lies in Christopher's "revenge" against Paul H.'s family, and the cautionary tale that it embodies if we read Christopher as Clare's alter ego. His childhood and "development" are marked by poverty and destitution. With the death of his grandmother, he "wandered the streets of the city, begging the tourists a few pence." As he grows up, Christopher's connections to other people, like his labour, are casual. In his loneliness, "he longed for his grandmother." It is when he asks his "master" for a little plot of land to give his grandmother a decent burial, and receives scorn instead, that something inside of him snaps.

Christopher remembers when Brother Josephus blessed him as "Christ-bearer" and told him of Toussaint, "dis Black man who carry Christ amongst de Black people of Haiti." Cliff's title, *No Telephone to Heaven,* suggests that Jamaicans should stop praying for those who have persecuted them: "Depression. Downpression. Oppression. Recession. Intercession. Commission. Omission. Missionaires. . . . Per'aps the line to heaven is one party line. But how could Massa God be their enemy?" They must "turn the damn thing upside down. Fight fire with fire." Christopher's killings have the force of a ritual. The narrator conveys an unstoppable urge in the character's movements and syncretic search:

> Cyaan tu'n back now. Capture the I in I. Then say Bless me Jah / Shango / Yemanja / Jehovah / Oshun / Jesus / Nanny / Marcus / Oshun. I am about to kill one of your creatures. Some of your children.

Whereas in *No Telephone to Heaven* the need for change is figured in the allegorical transformation of the island's terrain as "bush" takes over "garden" in Clare's grandmother's land, in *Angel* it is history itself that constitutes the novel's terrain. Collins's novel depicts the history of Grenada against and through the lives of her characters. The testimony of Collins's fiction is one of transformation in attitudes, ideas, and language. Her work is concerned with change—what enables it, what prevents it, why it is necessary.

Although some may perceive Collins's novel as old-fashioned realism, it is revolutionary in bringing together conventionally male and female spheres—public and private, personal and political—to chronicle the history of her country in the spectrum of creole languages available to her, and thus inscribes a "new" kind of self in her reconceptualization of the *Bildungsroman.*

To the individual novel of formation, Collins adds the collectivity of the *testimonio,* a literature of personal witness and involvement designed, according to John Beverly, to make the cause of these movements known to the outside world, to attract recruits, to reflect on the successes and/or failures of the struggle. Because *testimonio* is not so much concerned with the life of a "problematic hero" as with a problematic collective social situation, the narrator in *testimonio* speaks for, or in the name of, a community or group. In keeping with the predominant focus on the collective life of the community, characterization typically exemplifies modes of interdependence among community members. Concerned with continuity, *Angel* seeks to represent what gives the community its identity, what enables it to remain itself. Each individual *testimonio* then evokes an absent poliphony of other voices, other possible lives and experiences. A common formal variation on the classic first-person singular *testimonio* is the polyphonic *testimonio* made up of accounts by different participants in the same event. As a literary simulacrum of oral narrative, *testimonio* represents an affirmation of the individual subject, even of individual growth and transformation, but in connection with a group or class situation marked by marginalization, oppression, and struggle. Beverly dismissively contends that if it loses this connection, it ceases to be *testimonio* and becomes autobiography, that is, a "sort of documentary bildungsroman."

Collins transforms the *Bildungsroman* by incorporating into her novel elements of a polyphonic *testimonio,* to produce what could indeed be termed a documentary *Bildungsroman.* Rene Jara has discussed *testimonio*'s influence on other literary forms that become impregnated with what he considers a new combativity, "al mismo tiempo, acusacion y desafio," but he holds on to what ultimately is a false distinction: that between the novel and *testimonio.* For Jara, *testimonio*'s subject, more than in other discursive forms, must be historical reality itself. The difference Jara sees between the novel and *testimonio* is that while the novel's configuration implies an ending, *testimonios* are evidence for a history that still goes on.

Collins's *Angel* bridges some of the differences between the novel and *testimonio* through its powerful oral quality, for it achieves the effect of an ongoing conversation among characters. Collins creates a Grenadian creole which is ritualistic, proverbial, and metaphoric, embedding songs, poems, and proverbs which give the narrative a people's (not an individual's) perspective on events and communicate the complexity of their traditions. More important, like a *testimonio,* Collins's novel represents an affirmation of individual growth and transformation in connection with a group or class situation marked by struggle. The unifying feature of a testimony novel is its consciousness of a collective objective beyond the individual person. Collins becomes the living witness to a historical process, faithfully recreating both characters and society in a state of becoming.

The novel also achieves its documentary quality through its multiple narrative centres which convey sometimes overlapping, sometimes conflictual versions of self and history. *Angel* points to a social model of self, a self that exists in relationships, a self that is a product of all the discourses that the growing child incorporates as she develops. It is a more complex, less teleological model than the ideal of the European *Bildungsroman,* for there is no possibility (or desire) for an organic development. Collins's *Angel* focuses on the growth to political consciousness of three generations of Grenadian women and ultimately points to the children as the hope for change. Like Cliff, Collins implies that an understanding of her mother and grandmother is necessary for an understanding of her protagonist's development, which suggests interconnected rather than individual development.

With *Angel,* moreover, Collins reverses the erasure of the mother, and the daughterly act of "speaking for her," as Marianne Hirsch characterizes it, and enables both mother and daughter to speak for themselves as well as for and with one another. In the novels that Hirsch reads in *The Mother/ Daughter Plot,* it is the woman as *daughter* who occupies the centre of the reconstructed subjectivity while the woman as *mother* remains in the position of *other.* Collins writes in the voices of mothers as well as daughters by constructing *Angel* as a novel of *Bildung* for mother, for daughter, and for nation. The first section of the novel focuses more on Doodsie and her circle of family and friends, since Collins indeed adapts the conventions of individual development— of great expectations and lost illusions—to a communal model.

In *Angel,* three generations of women experience the changes that Grenada undergoes under Gairy's regime and the New Jewel Movement. "The Revolution has given me a theme," Collins tells us, "and has also developed a greater awareness of self and pride of being." The Revolution was also instrumental in validating the Creole language and affirming its power through popular culture. It effected a re-evaluation of the language and a reconceptualization of the curriculum which Grenadians initially resisted, as we see in the chapter that deals with the elections for the teachers' union, with secret campaigns "to ensure that Angel and those who shared her views did not get on to the executive."

Collins's novel explores the function of education, reading, and writing in nation-formation and decolonization. The Caribbean child's encounter with language through the colonial school drove a wedge between the "real" world she saw about her and the world of the school and its curriculum. While the reality of the colonizers' books is made to supplant the reality of the island, Collins traces the evolution of Angel's consciousness until she ultimately rejects the world the colonial school has created. Like Annie John, Angel devours Enid Blyton's adventures and the love stories her friends bring in. Angel's name is with time perceived as inadequate as she becomes darker, for in all books the children read "angels [are] white." Rather than concentrating on Sunday service, Angel thinks up all sorts of stories about faraway places: "In her mind, she went off sometimes by boat, sometimes by plane. . . . She never arrived anywhere in these daydreams; but she was often travelling." In Angel's case, however, the Revolution creates a discursive space in which she can posit herself as a subject in the new Grenada, and she is able to see through the "mist."

Only when she is very young does Angel feel sorry for herself and ashamed of her "unglamorous mother . . . who looked nothing like those of the pretty mothers in all the books, who never wore one of those frilly white aprons which made kitchen work look so inviting, whose kitchen looked nothing like the beautiful ones in books." Although initially Angel wishes herself transformed into one of the ladies in some of the love stories she reads—"long blonde hair flying in the unruly wind, blue eyes sparkling, laughing up at some dark-haired young man of indeterminate colour"— she grows to love black as beautiful and stops dreaming that "she was in fact really the child of some queen in a distant country, that she had been given a drug to change the colour of her skin." We see signs of future strength in the growing child when, for example, Angel wants to wake up her brother to help with the housework, but Doodsie tells her to let him sleep longer because he is a "man" whereas she is a "little girl." From Angel's feminist point of view, Doodsie submits too much to a patriarchal system of domination represented by her submission to her husband, whose betrayals she accepts.

We also perceive the changes in Angel, as she develops, in her reaction to the figures on her mother's wall. An image of Christ is initially in the family's living room but both Angel and her brother Simon want the Jesus pictures removed to the bedrooms. Auntie Ezra gives Doodsie an outline of the map of Grenada framed in mahogany that is placed next to the glass-covered words proclaiming Christ the Head of the House. Later on, however, when Angel thinks of the picture of "a white man wid a globe floatin aroun somewhere inside me," she feels sick. Angel's reaction to Leader's picture is almost as intense: "It upsetting enough having the man ruling the country and so many asses supportin him! But how you could have his picture up on the wall in you house?" When Angel returns from college in Jamaica, she brings a picture of a little rasta boy to put in her room, which her father objects to but does not say anything until Angel removes Leader's picture from the living-room. What gets figured through these changes in the images is the evolution in Angel's consciousness, from passively conforming to Christian values and wanting to be the "angel" in a Christmas play to rejecting this indoctrination with an iconography of revolution embodied in the rasta child.

The many different ways in which Collins conveys the evolution of both Angel's and Grenada's consciousness help create the documentary effect of the narrative—we get the truth from many angles of vision and through different channels—which makes the novel not only less teleological but more politically effective. Another evolutionary movement is figured in both the content and the form of the letters that the characters exchange throughout the novel. The epistolary validates creole as a written language, and the letters ultimately serve to represent the unity of the Caribbean peoples in diaspora. As they trace the characters' movement among islands and to the U.S., in search of better economic conditions, they ultimately help the reader to perceive them not only as an extended family, but as constituting a Caribbean community. The letters also allow Collins to articulate in the voice of the people the significance of the events that are occurring in the society: their own writing and interpretation of history, as in the first letter Doodsie writes to Ezra in Aruba, where she emphasizes their need for "a change but not in this way." Allan's letter to his friend Martin in St. Lucia shows Allan's and the Grenadian people's initial enthusiasm about Leader (Eric Gairy): "We want we own people to lead us. You should see him, black as me you know and talking big with the best in the land." Doodsie, however, cannot be fooled, and in more than one letter to Ezra she points out how "Leader just want everything for himself." In another letter, Doodsie complains that "The country is in a total mess," and Independence means only flag and anthem. Allan's letters from Wisconsin and Florida show the nature of migrant work and also point to other people from the Caribbean who are working in the States. We learn that Maurice Bishop is in power through Angel's letter to Simon in New York, where she tells him of "a revolution directed by radio," asking him to come home since "We need you for nation-building." Angel's former classmate from Jamaica writes to her to inquire whether she is "finding the answers we felt had to be found? Is it rewarding? Is it going somewhere?"

When Angel goes to the University of the West Indies in Jamaica, she is exposed to ideas such as Walter Rodney's call for Black Power and for a black class struggle, and she joins with other students to take an active role in the political transformation of the region. Collins fictionalizes the "Africa Night" held at Mary Seacole Hall (Mona Campus), in November, 1968, the first time that students were exposed in any serious way to African art, music, dress, poetry. The rhetoric of Black Power was appropriate to the Caribbean to the extent that it responded to a popular discontent with those black people who had managed to acquire economic resources or political power and had become, in Collins's figuration of Fanon's "black skin, white mask," like "roast breadfruit," black on the outside, but white on the inside.

Collins depicts the University, however, as a privileged space, an island which isolates the intellectual from the reality of most of the people living in Jamaica. The students start a group called "Search" to improve their "knowledge concerning the surrounding communities." Angel, Collins writes, maintained a "sort of detached interest," but gradually she remembers the knowledge of injustice that her grandmother and her mother passed on to her, and she is able to hear what Edward has to say:

> We have to live in the society and we live in a capitalist society. But we know it don benefit de majority and that we're on our way to reaping benefits that the women who come in to eat our left-overs are not likely to see. . . . It is because we see the unfairness that we would want to be involved in trying to change that even while we know it would mean individual losses for us . . . at least initially.

Collins challenges received images of history by telling it from multiple points of view. Her nested reconstruction of history can be found in inserted texts, like Sister Miona Spencer's poem. A member of the Literacy Programme, the Sister opens a zonal council meeting with a poem that recovers Grenada's history until that moment to celebrate the benefits that the Horizon government has brought to the people, and the year she refers to is 1951, the date Eric Gairy called for a general strike. Leader's rise to power comes at a time in Grenada when people came together yet one more time to try to stop being exploited by the big landowners:

> From all over the island, people walked, drove,
> rode to the city.
> Shouted. Laughed. Pulled one another along.
> "Make it! Make it, Papay-o! Is we day dat come!"

The novel actually opens with the burning of the De Lisle estate, an event which seems to be approved by all spectators. Maisie's humorous description of the burning cocoa as ungrateful children who do not acknowledge their own mother foreshadows, according to Carolyn Cooper, the theme of generational conflict that the novel develops later. The analogy also suggests the distortion of the organic relationship between the worker and the products of her labour. Because she is alienated from the fruits of her labour, the worker is forced to rebel:

> The lan coundn't be mine because I too black for one, an is white people that own lan because is them that did have slave in this country. If I was high brown I might ah have white background dat leave lan give me or I might ah be able to get big job, but it din work out so.

It is not only the call to Black Power, as Patrick Taylor notes, that ultimately underlies the revolutionary trajectory in the novel. The rhetoric of Black Nationalism gives way to the discourse of revolution as Horizon, which takes control of the state with the full support of the majority of the Grenadian population. The New Jewel Movement (an acronym for Joint Endeavor for Welfare, Education and Liberation) brings to light "the kind of talent that was there hidin all de time." The Party negotiates a socialism with an open plan until the crisis of October 1983 reveals that "truth" has solidified—that a universalized and closed narrative (encoded as Marxist-Leninism) has been imposed on the Party and the nation. The New Jewel Movement (Horizon) in Collins's textualization of history turns Marxism-Leninism against itself and the people.

The novel is so constructed that the line of the Party, assumed by Angel, is subverted by the interwoven comments of the family members who confront her. Faithful to the Party, Angel will not reveal what she knows about the crisis within. The Party will find its own solutions she repeats over and over. But from the community's point of view, the revolution is theirs, not that of the Party leaders. Carl, Angel's brother, accuses her of belonging to a "secret society." Rupert, once close to the Party, attacks its "ivory tower" elitism. He also tells Angel that "any Party dat in Mars while people on earth is not no party we want to know about anyway! Let it stay to ass in Mars!" This mode of representation foregrounds the fact that both fiction and history are discursive practices, subject to questions of authorship and authority: *whose* version of history ultimately prevails does make a difference.

The American myth of a liberated Grenada is another obvious target for demystification in the novel: "Is our country still, Carl. We wrong. We do real stupidness. But nobody don have a right to invade. We doesn invade dem when dey killin black people in their country." The American soldiers who invade the island act on the basis of a particular ideological conception which constructs the "other" as the communist enemy, black men as "boys," and women as "babes." Once the U.S. invasion occurs, a new contradiction appears: traumatized by the Party's dashing of her hopes, Doodsie thanks God for the intervention of the Americans thus succumbing to the new regime of terror. Angel, in contrast, picks up a gun to defend herself and her nation when the American troops land. As Angel's brother Rupert states, "people jump off one dream to go for a ride on another." There is no irony in Collins representation of the tragedy of the Revolution. Though "truth" is turned on its head, social transformation remains a historical possibility, a possibility underscored by the voices of the exploited black women.

Providing a site of resistance to narrative closure, the female voices in the novel have their own genealogy in relation to the independence movement and the critical response to that movement articulated in the Black Power and socialist move-

ments. But Angel's vision is not enough to maintain a critical distance from Party doctrine, whereas Doodsie knows better: "when ting just start all of us been speaking with one voice . . . Now mos people on same side again, saying leggo Chief, but now some of all you who fight wid us self sayin is because we stupid and we caan see de truth! . . . If a few of you see it an de res of us don see it, what you go do, tie us down? Is not so it is, Angel. Dat is not what we fight for. We moving together or if not, we jus not moving, ah suppose." If the novel presents unity from a woman's perspective, it does not exclude men. The words and actions of Angel's brothers help us see that it is not only from a female perspective that totalitarian structures can be recognized. It is in the very paradox of unity and fragmentation that the novel reaches history, as Taylor suggests, neither as utopia, nor as tragic failure, but as the hope and possibility of a new future.

Angel ends allegorically, with Doodsie warning her fowl to stay together so that the chicken-hawk cannot get any of them. Through the chicken-hawk metaphor a female authorial voice draws a moral from history: unity makes survival possible. Collins reiterates the idea of strength in people coming together that is first introduced with the hurricane: "Look how dis ting make us one, eh!" Later, she says: "We caan let one another sink. Is you, is me. We ha to hol one another up!" For Grenadians, Collins is saying, internal division allowed the U.S. invasion to temporarily end their revolution. Now it is time for the children "to fix that coop an keep the chickens inside." It is time for renewal (which the rain symbolizes), for Grenadian people to "fix" their country, to get rid of the "dirt" and to start again. The land, Collins tells us, "remains washed and waiting."

It is also significant that Angel returns to Grenada to perform a ritual wake. Although she feels "a little bit stupid" about what she is going to do, to light a candle and sing the song they always sang at wakes, with her good eye, in "her mind's eye," Angel sees that the spirits are sympathetic. As a communal form, the wake is a way for the living people to deal with the reality of death and the loss of a loved one. Angel sees the "figures circling the room," and she tells her Sunday school teacher, who has been dead for ten years, that the spirits are "either gone, or they sympathetic." The wake at the end of the novel functions as a symbol of past traditions which Angel must retain if she is to have an awareness of her community and her heritage. Angel is lighting a candle not only for the part of her self that was lost with the blinding of her left eye—the Angel that got carried away with party arrogance and detachment from the people they were supposed to be accountable to—but to all Grenadians who lost their lives trying to keep the Revolution alive.

In contrast to Cliff's apparent rendering of social transformation as a tragic impossibility, Collins's novel suggests that it is possible for Grenadians to come together again. Collins's historical novel recovers the discontinuities that Walter Benjamin refers to in his "Theses," allowing the oppressed to correct the distortions of official history. Cliff's more allegorical figuration of history, on the other hand, converts images of time into images of place, creating a dehumanized, almost paradoxically a historical space which ultimately removes the possibility of human agency. Although both writers are pursuing a common goal, to proceed beyond a deterministic view of history, their commitment to an emancipatory project cannot offer any guarantee that their narratives will indeed be liberatory. Collins's novel more than Michelle Cliff's functions as a call to arms because she emphasizes the notion that people are the agents of history through recreating their many voices. Both novels are intent on the destruction of boundaries and inventive in new ways of seeing. These novels of development are indeed central to nation-building since one of the functions of postcolonial writing is to turn a population characterized by differences of language, ethnicity, and religion, into a national unit to achieve some form of wholeness out of fragmentation.

Belinda Edmondson (essay date Winter 1993)

SOURCE: "Race, Privilege, and the Politics of (Re)Writing History, An Analysis of the Novels of Michelle Cliff," in *Callaloo,* Vol. 16, No. 1, Winter, 1993, pp. 180-91.

[*In the essay below, Edmondson examines the ways Cliff configures race, class, and gender distinctions in* Abeng *and* No Telephone to Heaven *to represent postcolonial West Indian identity.*]

Historicizing Race

The white creole occupies an ambiguous space in West Indian society. On the one hand she is the descendant of the colonizer: by virtue of her colour she is virtually guaranteed a position of relative power and privilege if she so chooses. Even if she does not choose, the creole is bound to her birthright by her race, since, as Albert Memmi observes, the colonial who does not accept the ideologies and privileges of the colonizer does not—*cannot*—effectively exist. Still, the white creole is in many ways culturally "black," or Afro-Caribbean: the Afrocentric dynamic permeates all classes and races of Anglophone Caribbean society regardless of its particular configurations within those groups. The creole is, in this sense, representative of both colonizer and colonized.

The question, then, of where the white creole writer locates herself in the West Indian intellectual community becomes of critical importance in evaluating whether her literature is to be read as an English novel of the tropics or a "Third World" narrative (and therefore backward, an anthropological document not destined to join the ranks of "real" literature). Whereas the novels of the first generation of white West Indian writers in the 19th and early 20th century, such as H. G. De Lisser, can for the most part be read as no more than extensions of European colonial ideology placed in exotic locations, the white West Indian writers of the pre- and post-independence era wrote, as did their non-white compatriots, with the intent of creating a regional cultural consciousness. The basis of this new consciousness was an Afro-Caribbean identity, and these texts are marked by their focus on the black poor and lower class as subject and the incorporation of the African-based patois into the narrative. Yet those writers did not examine their own status as "white," privileged West Indians even as they pursued an oppositional consciousness: in their uncritical acceptance of an Afrocentric-based discourse, they submerged—as did others of their generation—the implications of their race to the requirements of the genre, roundly criticizing the hypocrisies of the bourgeois mulatto and the arrogance of the white colonizer with the detachment assumed by someone who belongs to neither. Their unmediated acceptance of an Afrocentric-based definition of Caribbean culture arguably was in a sense as much a dissimulation as that of the previous era's wholesale acceptance of a Eurocentric-based definition. Even though it must be acknowledged that inasmuch as the West Indian concept of race is a fluid category such that a "white" creole may choose to designate himself as politically "black" if he so chooses (a proposition that sounds particularly absurd in the American or European context), yet it is only through the juxtaposition with his European heritage that the white creole achieves this fluid status.

Jean Rhys and Phyllis Shand Allfrey, white Dominican writers whose novels reflect the profoundly ambivalent relationship of white creole society to black West Indian society, have met with a peculiar critical resistance that questions their novels' fundamental "West Indianness." Kenneth Ramchand believes their works reveal the white creoles' "terrified consciousness" of the emergence of black power. Edward Brathwaite does not accept Rhys' *Wide Sargasso Sea* as an authentically West Indian novel in that it does not evince an Afrocentric outlook and dismisses Allfrey's *Orchid House* about a white West Indian family as a "brilliant but irrelevant novel in the West Indian context." According to Brathwaite, the white creole is fundamentally *incapable* of representing *genuine* (read black, "folk," politically revolutionary) West Indian society and their discourse reflects this. Even criticisms of Brathwaite's theory tend to accept its premise. For instance, though Evelyn O'Callaghan takes Brathwaite's formulations of "West Indianness" to task, her reasoning is that white creole writing represents an essential—if politically regrettable—part of the "creole continuum" which represents the different linguistic, social, and economic sectors of West Indian society, and thus cannot be separated from the West Indian literary tradition. She does not interrogate the assumption that the white creole's compromised *location* within the discourse necessarily dictates a compromised *consciousness*, with its inherent assumption that the empowering resistance properties of a West Indian text are to be found only in a narrative "blackness" which operates in direct relation to the writer's subject position.

In similar fashion the status of Michelle Cliff, a contemporary "Jamaica white" (a Jamaican of mostly white ancestry) West Indian woman writer who explicitly seeks to revalue black identity in her novels, is debated by West Indian feminists and intellectuals, many of whom feel that even as Cliff is described as a black feminist novelist in America (where she lives and writes) her novels are not truly part of an Afrocentric Caribbean discourse because her project as a feminist emanates from an American feminist sensibility and perhaps more importantly that her discovery of a black identity is a foreign fashion that she has appropriated. Yet I think it significant that it is white *women* in the West Indies who are questioning the terms of their ambivalent status and not the men; Elizabeth Nunez-Harrell observes that she has heard the working class blacks of Trinidad call white women—but never men—"whitey cockroach," and claims this is evidence of the blacks' perception that the white woman creole shares the status of the working class as a marginalized outcast. However, while certainly several feminist critics have used Fanon's model of colonialism to describe the relationship between male (colonizer) culture and female (colonized) status, and feminist scientist Sandra Harding has even suggested that the world views for white women and Africans converge, these do not begin to address the contradictions of white creole women, who are simultaneously both and neither. If we extend the binary logic of these genderized formulations, white creole women embody not simply both "First" and "Third" World sensibilities but also "male" (white, Euro-American) colonizing culture and "female" (black, post-colonial) colonized nature, a conflation of geo-political and gender categories that is highly suspect.

Thus, the problem of how to situate the white creole writer is further complicated when gender becomes an issue, as we have seen. The contemporary West Indian novel reflects a somewhat different sensibility than its predecessor: a significant percentage of today's West Indian writers are women, and they have recast the familiar project of articulating a national identify to reflect their specific experiences as women. Michelle Cliff's novels are critical to working out the problems of race and gender in this regard because they reflect her search for an Afrocentric identity through her matrilineal ancestry while attempting to come to terms with her father's lineage of planters and slave-owners; thus, the search for a black history/identity is intimately bound up with a la-

tent feminism as well as with a revolutionary social consciousness.

In this essay I shall explore how Cliff negotiates the dilemmas posed by race and class by exploring the convergences of personal and collective history in her largely autobiographical novel *Abeng* and its more fictive sequel, *No Telephone to Heaven.* She attempts to construct narratives that map the history of black, white, and mulatto Jamaica, mixing genres of narrative—historical, autobiographical, myth—to achieve a dialectical representation of the West Indian experience. I will discuss, first, how these novels extend and re-evaluate the preoccupations of Jean Rhys' *Wide Sargasso Sea,* her literary forebear, and second how in doing so her narrative experiments engage and attempt to transcend the twin poles of Naipaul's now-famous negation of West Indian history and Helen Tiffin's notion of the white creole identity as a double negation. Lastly, I will discuss the novels from the standpoint of Wilson Harris' dictum that the West Indian novel requires a revolutionary form which must transcend the traditional "novel of persuasion" in order to convey a revolutionary agenda.

(Re)writing Race

At the conclusion to her excellent study of Jean Rhys' fiction, Mary Lou Emery points out the extraordinary similarity between Antoinette's break with Tia in *Wide Sargasso Sea* and Clare Savage's dream in *Abeng,* both of which I have reproduced here:

> Then, not so far off, I saw Tia and her mother and I ran to her, for she was all that was left of my life as it had been. We had eaten the same food, slept side by side, bathed in the same river. As I ran, I thought, I will live with Tia and I will be like her. Not to leave Coulibri. Not to go. Not. When I was close I saw the jagged stone in her hand but I did not see her throw it. I did not feel it either, only something wet, running down my face. I looked at her and I saw her face crumple up as she began to cry. We stared at each other, blood on my face, tears on hers. It was as if I saw myself. Like in a looking glass.

Compare this to the conclusion of *Abeng*:

> That night Clare dreamed that she and Zoe were fist-fighting by the river in St. Elizabeth. That she picked up a stone and hit Zoe underneath the eye and a trickle of blood ran down her friend's face and onto the rock where she sat. The blood formed into a pool where the rock folded over on itself. And she went over to Zoe and told her she was sorry—making a compress of moss drenched in wa-

ter to soothe the cut. Then squeezing an aloe leaf to the wound. . . .

She was not ready to understand her dream. She had no idea that everyone we dream about we are.

Emery reads Cliff's rewriting of the scene as an extension of Rhys' anxieties about cultural marginality and an incipient formulation of a Third World women's tradition of writing and exile. Yet what is important about this scene is that Cliff does not simply repeat the doubling of black and white female identities but actually *reverses* the scene, so that "white" Clare Savage is the one who inflicts damage on black Zoe. If we consider this scene within the context of its literary history, Cliff is rewriting an *historical* relation of black and white West Indian women not only to link their cultural identities but to acknowledge the white woman's relation to power. That the scene is a dream highlights its status as part of a fictive (that is, literary) history as well as a real one; only an "unreal" medium can uncover the brutal power dynamics behind Clare's and Zoe's close friendship while allowing for future possibilities of healing. But Clare must first understand and acknowledge this unequal power dynamic before she can be (re)integrated with the society, with her history, and consequently her paradoxical identity. She comes to this understanding only in **Abeng's** sequel, **No Telephone to Heaven,** when Clare, after much soul-searching and a sojourn abroad, joins a group of black working-class guerrillas and participates in an attack on an American film crew. First, however, by having Clare read *Jane Eyre* Cliff shows Clare's direct relation to Antoinette Cosway, the madwoman in the attic of *Jane Eyre* who is the subject of *Wide Sargasso Sea:*

> The fiction tricked her. Drawn her in so that she became Jane. . . . No, she could not be Jane. . . . No, my girl, try Bertha. . . . Yes, Bertha was closer to the mark. Captive. Ragout. Mixture. Confused. Jamaican. Caliban. Carib. Cannibal. Cimarron. All Bertha. All Clare.

This passage is particularly important for the link it provides between Caliban and Bertha, the two gendered symbols of Caribbean independence and invisibility. Both inhere within the identity of Clare, who has been characterized as an epistemological paradox in the narrative. That the misnomer of Bertha—this is the name that Rochester forces onto Antoinette—is the name designated as "closer the mark" reminds us of the misnomer of "West Indies," and the struggle between the imposition of hegemonic history and uncoded reality which it embodies. The name represents a locus of struggle over identity, and we are guided to read Clare's name in this way. As the inheritor of her father's cultural and racial whiteness—her father has designated Clare to be the "white" child, to whom he shall impart the "gift" of Euro-

pean history and knowledge—Clare is the "masculine" daughter.

Yet whiteness, as a masculinized epistemology, and femaleness, which is aligned with blackness and historylessness, cannot be assimilated to each other. Clare's name points to this fundamental schism: "Clare" represents, obviously, the "light" of European ancestry, and yet Clare is named after a black woman who saves her mother's life—the sign of good, therefore, is black. "Savage" is an illustrious Jamaican name, and yet, as the name implies, it carries with it a barbaric history. Thus even *within* the paradox of the name are concealed paradoxes. The "Savage" reminds us of Caliban, and yet this is not to whom the name refers—Caliban/Black/Man and Bertha/White/Woman are reversed within Clare. As such, by the end of the narrative when Clare meets the mad white woman who had an affair with her black servant, we see the possibility of madness in Clare's future, the result of inexorable historical forces that cannot be assimilated into each other. This parallels Antoinette/Bertha's descent into madness at the conclusion of *Wide Sargasso Sea.*

The above passage also engenders within the reader a full realization that the site of dialogue is not simply with an ambivalent white creole tradition but also with the European literary canon itself, which freezes the colonized subject in an eternal relation of subject/object. Much scholarship has recently dealt with the feminist, anti-colonial critique contained in *Wide Sargasso Sea,* but, using the conflating logic referred to above, they tend to collapse the categories into one or the other.

As Emery points out, "feminist and Third World perspectives rarely combine in readings of Rhys' work. When they do, the resulting analysis usually depends upon a structural analogy between colonial hierarchies and sexual oppression that still positions the protagonist as a victim who lacks agency and offers little or no resistance." This can be said of most analyses of white creole women, . . . Furthermore, Emery notes, post-colonial and feminist scholars who both work on Rhys rarely converse with each other. (Even as feminist scholars are now utilizing postcolonial theories, the merging of discourses remains decidedly one-sided.) Again, this can be extended to the relations between post-colonial and feminist theory in general, and is, considering the suspicion under which feminist theory has been held in the "Third World," not surprising. The idea that feminist theory only utilizes the Third World as fodder to attain status within the elite Western theoretical discourses remains pervasive among Third World scholars.

(Re)Writing History

> . . . cruelty . . . resistance . . . grace. I'm not outside this history—it's a matter of recognition.

—No Telephone to Heaven

These, then, are the critical and historical frameworks that Cliff has inherited, and ones which she must reconcile in order to rewrite West Indian narrative to fit her peculiar position as both "white" and yet "Third World," "black" and yet "First World," feminist and yet post-colonialist. To achieve this she rewrites white creole history of privilege and collaboration to integrate it with the unwritten black and Amerindian histories of suffering and resistance; her texts attempt to dismantle notions of "official" history and the relation of that history to myth, myth to "real life," and "real life" to fiction by conflating Jamaican legends and myths with ancient and contemporary histories, autobiographical anecdotes and among all of these, intertwining Clare Savage's personal journey.

In *The Politics and Poetics of Transgression,* Stallybrass and White emphasize that to properly understand discourse one cannot separate it from its social space ("It is only when such related concepts as critical judgment, taste, authorship and writing are reconnected to their 'planes of emergence' as Foucault has called them, the social points at which such ideas surface, that they can be fully understood"). In returning Bertha Mason back to the West Indies where her "real" name is revealed, Rhys acknowledges that geo-political location is the crucial referent to "reading" Bertha, and by extension to making sense of West Indian discourse. Similarly, in *No Telephone to Heaven* Clare Savage returns to Jamaica after moving first to the United States and then to London, thereby retracing the "triangle" of the slave trade, only the other way around. Both of Cliff's novels reveal Clare Savage at different stages in her life, and yet the point is not to embody Clare as a character separate from her "plane of emergence" but rather to read that location through the conflicting and multiple identities that are Clare Savage: she is, as such, not a "character" in the traditional sense at all. Clare's final destination is not England and a descent into madness, but Jamaica and conscious resistance, though she, like Bertha, dies in the act of resisting.

Whereas Antoinette Cosway dreams of a location that is "somewhere else" to remove her from the Manichean world in which there is no psychic or social space for someone such as herself, Cliff seeks to *actualize* that location of "elsewhere" for Clare by creating within her novels a geo-political space of memory arising from Clare's slaveowner, slave, and Arawak ancestry. In this way she deconstructs the traditional historical chronological narrative, with its understanding that the "conclusion" allows us to elucidate the meaning of the history. In the Caribbean, whose "conclusion" was one of slavery, colonization and consequent "Third World" status, the historical narrative has functioned to contain or erase other histories by reading the region solely in

terms of how it served to construct the historical realities of Europe or America.

In *Resistance Literature* Barbara Harlowe notes that narratives of resistance must not only undo hegemonic recorded history, but they must also invent new forms of encoding resistance by inventing spaces of resistance. West Indian authors similarly emphasize the spatial aspect of narrative for West Indian literature; Wilson Harris suggests that the "authentic" West Indian novel uses the historical memory of the land, with its unknown past and infinite possibilities, to deconstruct the colonizer/colonized opposition, and thus upend the subject/object relation of European discourse to West Indian literature. Others, notably Alejandro Carpentier, have advocated magical realism as a way of recovering the "true" history of the region. But as Selwyn Cujoe observes, what they understand to be the "magical" properties of West Indian history—conquistadores, obeah, an extinct Amerindian culture—are in fact based on a *critical* understanding of reality, and that, as such, West Indian narrative should not be read as circular but rather as a spiral, not a repetition but rather an extension: what he terms a "critical realism." This is a useful concept for explicating Cliff's narrative in that Cliff explicitly seeks to *rewrite* and yet not to *repeat* history. In the following passage we hear the "official" history of Jamaica, resurrecting Naipaul's vision of West Indian History in *The Mimic Men* ("We pretended to be real . . . we mimic men of the New World" who are irretrievably "sunk in the taint of fantasy"), but infusing it with different meaning:

> These are the facts as I believe them. But as you no doubt are well aware, there are no facts in Jamaica. Not one single fact. Nothing to join us to the real. Facts move around you. Magic moves through you. This we have been taught. This fact that there are no facts. Wait. I can call up one fact. "The adamantine refusal of the slave-women to reproduce"—a historian report that. What of Gamesome, Lusty Ann, Counsellor's Cuba, Strumpet called Skulker—not racehorses, mi dear, women: barren. Four furious cool-dark sistren. Is nuh fact dat? Fact yes, but magic mek it so.

By blending the voice of the "official" history, which denies that there is a history, with the oral transmission of historical resistance encoded in the "magical" narrative of myth, the passage reveals historical representation in *discourse* to be the site of conflict, a point I will come back to later in this essay.

Unlike Rhys, whose novels reveal simultaneous attraction to and fear of Afro-Caribbean society and the consequent ambivalence which I have already discussed, Cliff understands that an understanding of black consciousness is crucial to resolving the complexities of being a white colonized subject, and more importantly is empowering not only to black people in the Caribbean, but to white people as well; her novels attempt to reclaim her African identity, which was "bred out" of her during her childhood in Jamaica. Jamaican sociologist and writer Erna Brodber observes of West Indian society, "[The literate] tended to see booklearning not simply as a tool for making a livelihood but as the ultimate truth. . . . The unlettered lowerclass, depending on the oral tradition for its information, was kept in touch with its past of Africa and slavery and with its African identity." The conflation of story and history in the West Indian context is therefore particularly important as a way of empowering the entire spectrum of people and providing a means for all to participate in the discourse of shaping a West Indian identity.

Cliff describes the process of coming to consciousness through writing in these terms:

> To write as a complete Caribbean woman . . . demands of us retracing the African part of ourselves, reclaiming as our own, and as our subject, a history sunk under the sea, or scattered as potash in the canefields, or gone to bush, or trapped in a class system notable for its rigidity and absolute dependence on color stratification. . . . It means finding the art forms of these of our ancestors and speaking in the patois forbidden us. . . . (**"A Journey Into Speech"**)

For the colonized West Indian, Europe had a history, Jamaica did not: the little history it did have consisted of a recitation of the skirmishes of the European imperial powers fought to determine who would own the territory. In colonial and much of post-colonial Jamaica, Jamaicans lived without knowledge of their past—they lived with absence. The unwritten history of Jamaica—the genocide of its inhabitants, the suffering of the black slaves, the cruelty of the white plantation owners—survived in myths. *Abeng's* odd blend of narrative techniques is an attempt to show how these historical events created the cultural duality that is the legacy of the creole. The narrative reflects that duality: it moves in abrupt staccato from historical facsimile to historical fiction to autobiography (in an essay she describes as factual events and people described in the novel, though the novel itself offers a disclaimer as to any similarities), and the choppy switching back and forth from genre to genre creates a restless tension in the narrative which is never resolved—or meant to be.

The novel traces the coming-to-consciousness of Clare Savage, a "Jamaica white" on the edge of adolescence, who becomes aware of her place in society through her relationships with various people: her autocratic Protestant white father,

descendant of Judge Savage who burned his hundred slaves on the eve of Emancipation in 1834, who teaches her to be proud of her white heritage; her mulatto, rural-born mother Kitty, who belongs to a "clap-hand" church and is "more comfortable speaking patois and walking through the bush"; her poor black friend Zoe, whose mother rents land from Clare's grandmother; and finally Miss Winifred, a white woman vilified and called mad by her family for falling in love with a black servant. Through these relationships Clare learns the parameters of her position in Jamaican society. When she tries to transcend those parameters retribution is swift: after Clare takes her grandmother's gun and accidentally shoots her bull, she is sent to live with Miss Beatrice who will teach her her "proper place" and not to "act like a boy." The white woman's enactment of a specific *gender* role, then, is a crucial link in maintaining class and power distinctions while simultaneously nurturing the vital contact with black culture. Her relationship with Zoe also is saturated with the imperatives of class, since it is only possible because Clare has the ability to move in and out of Zoe's world.

Still, the landscape of the country serves as a meeting place for these two children on opposite sides of the race divide:

> This was a friendship—a pairing of two girls—kept only on school vacations, and because of their games and make-believe might have seemed to some entirely removed from what was real in the girls' lives. Their lives of light and dark—which was the one overwhelming reality. *But this friendship also existed close to the earth, in a place where there were no electric lights, where water was sought from a natural source, where people walked barefoot more often than not.*

This landscape, then, does not simply contain an unwritten history but also contains the potential to heal that history.

Clare's love for Zoe is a manifestation of her more deeply rooted yearning for her mother's love and approval; her mother prefers her sister because she is darker and therefore closer to Kitty's black heritage, while Clare is considered to be her father's child. The narrative never really analyzes Kitty's perceptions of race, characterizing her simply as a woman who "loved darkness," is more comfortable "speaking patois and walking through the bush, and refers to Africa with 'reverence.'"

The ideological project in this arrangement is easy to see: Cliff is setting up a dichotomy in the white father/black mother parallel, so that Clare's search for a black identity becomes aligned with a woman-centered, incipiently feminist consciousness. This is borne out by Cliff's rewriting of the Jamaican myth of Nanny, a maroon fighter in the 1800s who was reputed to catch the bullets of redcoats between her buttocks; in *Abeng* she is transformed into Mma Alli, a lesbian obeah woman who teaches the slaves how to escape.

By recreating Nanny as a "woman-centered" figure Cliff is attempting to insert a wedge in the historical narrative of Jamaica which will revalue not simply a black experience but will also provide an empowering history for West Indian women. Similarly, she casts Kitty—and indeed all black women in this novel—as having a direct and unmediated linkage to a positive black history and consciousness. This contradicts the implicit logic of the narrative structure: it hopes to construct an historical identity from fragments and dislocations of identity, yet it leaves Clare as the sole embodiment of historical fragmentation without acknowledging that the imposition of colonial ideology and racial attitudes must have affected their relationship to black identity. Kitty, for instance, has, despite her desire to teach African history to poor black children, married a racist white man, yet her sense of black identity is never questioned in the interests of preserving the narrative's clear racial ideology (indeed, Kitty's explanation that she was pregnant and had no choice is meant to be interpreted as further evidence of the black woman's plight in Jamaica but rather smacks of an authorial "quick fix" to deal with such glaring ambiguity). Despite Clare's pivotal role, the power relations in this novel are structured in binary terms of a source of power (white men: Judge Savage and Boy Savage) and reactions to that power (black women: Mma Alli, Kitty). The logic of this arrangement dictates that were the oppressed (black women) to accede to power, the existing organization of class/race relations would be dismantled, an arrangement that does not acknowledge the diffusion of power in terms more complex than simply economic or racial.

Creating History, Creating Discourse

In *The Wretched of the Earth* Fanon declares that violence is an inevitable part of the decolonizing process, and much of West Indian writing acknowledges this potential for violent social upheaval. However, in the two most prominent West Indian novels dealing with revolutionary violence, Naipaul's *Guerrillas* and Lovelace's *The Dragon Can't Dance,* the revolution fails because of the internal incoherence of the protagonists. In *Dragon* rebellion leader Fisheye does not know what he is fighting for or indeed what he is fighting against, and in *Guerillas* Jimmy Ahmed seeks only to be a "real" hero, like the one he is writing about in his novel, whose "reality" is sustained in the fact that he is much admired—and feared—in England. Naipaul's novel is particularly important to our discussion of *No Telephone to Heaven* because it contains several thematic issues which are extended and rewritten in the latter.

In *Guerillas* a semi-retarded ghetto boy's murder of an En-glishwoman is constructed as the ultimate act of black violence run amok. It is violence that is the result of an existential crisis of identity, an identity which can only conceive itself on the other side of "reality": the revolution is revealed to be an empty contemporary cliché that masks this "truth." The depiction of revolution as symbol, as sign without connection to referent, echoes Naipaul's emphasis on the guerrilla's writing fantasy scenarios of revolt—the implication is that his rage, like his writing, is only given expression by romantic European liberal ideas, and consequently his violence, like his writing, can only be a caricature, an echo, or inversion of a European referent.

In what I shall read as a parallel scene to the above, Christopher (the garden boy in *No Telephone to Heaven*) murders his wealthy brown employers and their black maid because they refused to give him land to bury his grandmother, who had died some 13 years before. Christopher too is "mad" in one sense, but his "madness" becomes coherent in the historical context of the narrative, where the injustices of the past and present converge into a single act of "random" violence.

A doubling of this act occurs toward the conclusion of the novel when Clare Savage tells the leader of the guerrillas—a nameless black woman from a nameless country—that she is joining them because she needs to "mend" herself by burying her mother. Like Christopher, Clare's mother had died some time before. And, like Christopher's mother, Clare's mother is black, a significant element in the chronology of West Indian narrative where, as we have noted, the bodies which represent the site of dialogue have been those of white females. That these maternal bodies have been dead but not buried remind us of the invisibility of black women in the narration of West Indian oppositional discourse, as embodied by Caliban's mother, the absent Sycorax, who represents Caliban's past heritage of might and agency. Therefore, the attempt to "bury" the grand/mother becomes a metaphor for reconciling the "unburied"—that is, unrepresented, ghostly, "magical"—history of the people with the possibilities contained in the land, a fusion which requires violent rupture with present reality.

What the guerrillas understand, however, is that it is the power of *representation,* more so than the physical manifestations of poverty and privilege, which is the source of power. Significantly, it is the statue of Pocahontas which Clare encounters in England that hastens her return: in the symbol of Pocahontas is frozen the entire history of the New World, its violent resistance to European imperialism converted to acquiescent, feminine (I use the term deliberately) collaboration. The guerrillas' attack on an American film site would be the capstone of existential absurdity in a Naipaul novel. But even as the helicopters flying over the guerrillas' hiding places in the bush tell us that their mission has

failed, the novel ends with a burst of sounds—English, patois, bird sounds—which signify the unharnessed possibilities of discourse: the power to name, signify, create. These remain embedded in the landscape, future potential to reclaim representation.

No Telephone to Heaven builds upon ***Abeng*** by deconstructing the reductive gender/ race ideology in the former so that it is not solely white, male, European culture which is the focal point of conflict but language itself, wherein gender and geo-political categories are both created and fixed in memory. To attempt to imitate the "reality" of these categories thus becomes a futile project. In the final analysis, it is discourse which creates meaning; by creating an alternative "reality" in a narrative structure which both extends and engages West Indian and European representations, the text attempts not an imaginary nor an imitation universe but a new kind of reality.

Renée Hausmann Shea (review date Spring 1994)

SOURCE: A review of *Free Enterprise*, in *Belles Lettres*, Vol. 9, No. 3, Spring, 1994, pp. 32-4.

[*In the following review, Shea admires* Free Enterprise *for its woman-centered perspective on American slavery and the abolition movement.*]

Fire seems to be Michelle Cliff's element. The very title of an early autobiographical essay asserts **"If I Could Write This in Fire, I Would Write This in Fire,"** and she closes her earlier novel *No Telephone to Heaven* with an apocalyptic blaze. Yet, not until now, in her most recent work, the novel ***Free Enterprise,*** has she fully explored fire's properties: destruction, blending, clarification, and perhaps even rebirth. In this powerful novel, which centers on the fictional character Annie Christmas and the historical figure Mary Ellen Pleasant, Jamaican-born Cliff explains that she is continuing the work begun in Toni Morrison's *Beloved*—"remembering and reconstructing the past." Cliff calls *Beloved* a "watershed" for her and other writers, "the first modern novel to take on the subject of slavery in its deepest sense."

In an interview prior to a reading at Vertigo Books in Washington, D.C., Cliff explained that she became intrigued with Pleasant through a reference to this woman—who kept hotels in San Francisco and contributed $30,000 to finance John Brown's raid on Harper's Ferry—in Toni Cade Bambara's novel *The Salt Eaters.* According to Cliff, however, *Free Enterprise* began with the character of Annie, a Jamaican living in exile "who is in many ways standing for me." Her interest in Pleasant grew as the novel took shape until "she sort of came into the novel on her own," says Cliff.

"I've always been interested in the black woman resister, an Pleasant defeats every stereotype of an African-America woman in the 19th century: she was a successful business woman, an entrepreneur; she was always a revolutionary, and she never gave up the cause, even after the failure of the raid on Harper's Ferry." Pleasant wanted her grave carved with the simple statement, "She was a friend of John Brown," and Cliff herself made the pilgrimage to Napa, California, to witness the marble headstone bearing that testimony.

It is there that the fire began, a destructive fire that would sear away untruths and half-truths. An outraged Cliff recalls the response of a man working in the Napa Cemetery whom she asked for directions to Pleasant's grave, "Oh, you mean Mammy Pleasant?" "In the 1990s!" Cliff rails, "Mary Ellen Pleasant is still known by the name she detested," a name that symbolizes the "history" that remembers this extraordinary woman as a madam, voodoo queen, arsonist, and on and on rather than entrepreneur and revolutionary. In *Free Enterprise,* Cliff re-views history and invites her readers to participate in the process (in fact, she insists).

Annie and Mary Ellen are comrades whose relationship grows out of commitment to their common cause of liberation. In 1858, after both women hear Frances Ellen Watkins Harper speak on "The Education and the Elevation of the Colored Race," Annie accepts Mary Ellen's invitation to supper at a restaurant named the Free Enterprise. The richness of this phrase unfolds, as does the novel, and resonates long after. Ironically, free enterprise refers to the slave trade, which Cliff points out was the main industry in the country in the 19th century, as well as in the rest of the world. Says Cliff,

> Slavery wasn't just about the transportation of people; no, shipping companies were involved, insurance companies, people who provided salted fish for the slaves. It was an interlocking industry. To me it seemed the apotheosis of free enterprise, of capitalism. Also, Mary Ellen is an entrepreneur and believer in capitalism, and the enterprise that John Brown had in his heart was the enterprise of freedom—he and others; one engaged in an enterprise to free oneself and others. So the title has all of these different meanings. Then there's this little restaurant that's called Free Enterprise, which a man and his wife are trying to set up. This was meant to evoke things like the People's Grocery in Memphis, one of the first successful businesses owned by black people after the Civil War. You see, so many things are meant to ring a bell in people's minds about other things.

Free Enterprise opens with an epigram from Miles Davis, "I always listen for what I can leave out," which Cliff be-

lieves describes her fiction. "It's like wanting to leave out the main theme—things we all learned, like Lincoln freed the slaves, emancipation was handed to black people, slavery wasn't so terrible—to get to the more unusual music, the music that one hasn't heard yet." Cliff writes that "the official version is a cheat"; it has been "printed, bound, and gagged, resides in schools, libraries, the majority unconscious. Serves the common good. Does not cause trouble."

Cliff's fiery vision breaks down "the official version," but alternate versions emerge only through blendings and fusings that resemble Annie Christmas's decoration of the trees outside her house with various bottles, "ingredients from here, there, and everywhere." Cliff mixes myth and story, fact and fiction, madness and sanity, a range of time periods and even forms. "I can't stand the idea of the novel here, the history there, the biography there," she explains, "I can't see why these things can't be mixed. We have to bring our imagination to our history, because so much has been lost."

Mary Ellen Pleasant and John Brown are not the only historical figures in the work. Cliff includes the photographer Clover Adams and her cousin Alice Hooper. In their contact with Pleasant, Cliff intends her portrayal of these women to be "sympathetic."

> Part of my purpose in this novel is to show the problems of different lives of women in the 19th century, not just black women. Clover Adams is someone who intrigued me way back in the 1970s, when I was an art history student. My interest in her and Mary Ellen came together in this book. What I wanted to show was how the privilege of a woman of the upper class in this country, Brahmin Boston, pales beside the privilege of Mary Ellen as an activist. Clover Adams was more encumbered by her place in society than Mary Ellen was. Mary Ellen was able to transcend what was seen as her place by resisting. Unable to do that, Clover Adams committed suicide. I wanted her to stand for those women in the 19th century who were artists and who were passionate but were unable to practice their art or fuel their passion except in a very limited way, because of gender, class, and race.

> The thing that is available to these women is the cause of abolition. They're not able to engage in the feminist movement, for example, because they're too early for that historically. So, when Alice and Clover both say in different parts of the novel that they want to feel 'real,' meaning alive, the only time they can do that is during the Civil War, when they are able to leave their drawing rooms in Boston to work actively for the cause of abolition. When the war is over, they have no place to go because noth-

ing is available to them. So they both die. Alice Hooper died a sort of lingering mysterious illness when she was in her thirties, and Clover killed herself by drinking her own chemicals.

Malcolm X strides into this novel of 19th-century action, a "hologrammatical man" who is a waiter in the famous Parker House, "waiting on his time, when he would first be called Homeboy, then Detroit Red, then X." Cliff recalls her decision to bring him into her novel, some time before the Spike Lee movie came out, when she was writing the scene in that Boston restaurant: "Mary Ellen is in this very snazzy restaurant with dark paneling, pictures of Oliver Wendell Holmes and Emerson, and I remembered that Malcolm X had worked as a busboy there. It occurred to me that I could show him as a ghost of the future."

> What had happened was that I had driven across the country by myself when this novel was just a germ in my head in 1990. I stopped on the way back to California in the Omaha Black Museum on the weekend when Malcolm X would have been 60. I went into this beautiful museum—a neighborhood place, not funded or anything—and the people who ran it had done a terrific exhibit. I drove on to Grand Island, Nebraska, to the Pioneer Museum, where I asked about material on black Nebraskans. I was assured that there were no black people in Nebraska! So, that incident shows the whole thing I was writing about.

> I thought [about] what it was like for Malcolm X not to know somebody like Mary Ellen Pleasant ever existed; how would knowing about a female role in the earlier movement have changed what he might have done? When he says to her in *Free Enterprise,* 'Why didn't I know about you?' it's meant to be a very poignant statement, because he recognizes her as his ancestor.

In *Free Enterprise,* Cliff goes about setting some parts of the record straight. The outrage, anger, and occasional violence that burn through this novel lead to a clarification and reconstruction missing from her earlier works. Characters who have or find access to their own history survive and have something invaluable to pass on. A schoolmistress near the novel's close cautions her students about the fragility of books: "What they contain can easily be lost. We must become talking books; talk it on, like the Africans, children. Talk it on."

Whether in letters, dinner table conversations, heated debates, or interior monologues, characters in *Free Enterprise* "talk it on" to make connections. Through their own close friendship, kindred spirits Mary Ellen and Annie construct

and share a history that finally links life and death when Mary Ellen writes, "I bequeath to you the story of my life." Cliff, too, bequeaths history and story to her readers: "What I wanted to do in *Free Enterprise* is to show people, wherever we come from, whatever our backgrounds, what it has done to us not to know this history. Not to know that people like Mary Ellen Pleasant existed, that John Brown was not a crazy person but a decent human being. What has it done to lose that history? What unites all my books is the loss of history and my attempt to restore pieces of it for myself and the reader."

In *Free Enterprise,* Mary Ellen Pleasant wonders, "If bone structure is passed on, why not memory?" Why not indeed? In this latest novel, Michelle Cliff has written in fire, and memory is the phoenix.

Deborah McDowell (review date July 1994)

SOURCE: "Taking Liberties with History," in *Women's Review of Books,* Vol. XI, Nos. 10-11, July, 1994, pp. 32-3.

[*In the review below, McDowell considers the thematic relation between resistance and memory in* Free Enterprise, *focusing on multiple connotations of the novel's title.*]

"Who has ever heard of Annie Christmas, Mary Shadd Carey, Mary Ellen Pleasant?" asks the narrator of *Free Enterprise,* Michelle Cliff's third novel. All nineteenth-century comrades in the struggle for Black liberation, theirs, except perhaps for Carey's, are among the countless names "disappeared" from "official" accounts of resistance to slavery's domination.

Free Enterprise takes its inspiration from one such act of resistance: John Brown's famous raid on Harper's Ferry in October 1859. History has cast Brown as the lone and fearless warrior, the hero of folk songs and monuments, who first risked family, fortune and social standing, then martyred himself for the abolitionist cause. But in Cliff's novel, John Brown has a female collaborator, Mary Ellen Pleasant,

> Dedicated fighter . . . Mother of Freedom, Warrior and Entrepreneur, who some believed came back from the dead in nineteen and six to avenge her good name, and the loss of property she suffered at the hands of the fathers of San Francisco, who finally brought her down, charging she was a witch, casting spells with her one blue eye and her one black eye, poisoning the city water supply, wreaking havoc at the stock exchange, souring the milk of nursing mothers.

Mary Ellen's message—"The axe is laid at the foot of the tree. When the first blow is struck there will be more money to help"—is found on John Brown's body the night of the October raid. Though a fearless warrior, Mary Ellen does not act alone. At least a year before John Brown's raid, she meets Annie by chance in a Boston auditorium where Frances E. W. Harper is speaking on "The Education and Elevation of the Colored Race." They meet again later that evening in the back of a restaurant named Free Enterprise. There, in an act reminiscent of classic slave narratives, Mary Ellen gives Annie a new name, Annie Christmas, after the legendary figure of revolutionary times who was said to possess the physical power of John Henry. From the restaurant, they begin plotting a revolution before joining Brown's ill-fated raid. And after the raid is thwarted, they head south, armed with guns and passes forged by Mary Shadd Carey, founder of a Canadian school for refugee slaves.

Mary Ellen Pleasant, Mary Shadd Carey and Annie Christmas are three more names added to the pantheon of guerrillas Cliff has crafted and on whom she has conferred the legendary status that history denied. I think of the two revolutionaries from her first novel, *Abeng* (1984): Nanny, the sorceress, who could "catch a bullet between her buttocks," and Mma Alli, the "one-breasted warrior woman" who was "bred to fight." And then, in *No Telephone to Heaven* (1987), there is Clare, the light-skinned daughter of Jamaican landowners, who casts her lot with a band of freedom fighters marooned on an abandoned farm turned forest.

But *Free Enterprise* is not so much about "correcting" or adding names to the official story of John Brown's raid on Harper's Ferry, or, for that matter, about wanting "ownership of history," as Mary Ellen calls it, but rather about exploring what happens to the official record of one man's heroism when those formerly "in the silence" and the shadows emerge to tell their tales.

And there are tales aplenty here. Of Annie Christmas' cold-blooded murder of two white women on her way south to arm the slaves. Of her battle-fatigue and ultimate retreat to a leper colony on the banks of the Mississippi River following the aborted raid. Of Mary Ellen's later life as a successful California businesswoman who owns a string of hotels that cater to wealthy whites while doubling as safe havens for runaway slaves. Of maroons who kept each other company in hush harbors and hiding places. Of the murder of Captain James Cook by the "natives" he'd "discovered" on the Sandwich Islands in his great tropical sweep of the Pacific. Even of a Malcolm X-like figure who appears hologrammatically as a waiter in the dining room of the Parker House hotel.

But while there are multiple stories here there is little in the way of "Story," at least not according to the conventional laws of plot and character, cause and effect, probability, veri-similitude. Like all good post-modernists, Cliff frees herself from conventional narrative burdens, implicitly nodding to the truism that this age lacks the structure of story and must thus content itself with fragments of a narrative that can never be wholly written.

The novel boldly cuts back and forth in time and roams wildly and suggestively over territory that some might declare off limits. Cliff takes great liberties with a tissue of familiar historical and literary references that give the narrative the qualities and structure of a dream.

The richly evocative title—*Free Enterprise*—offers surprising twists and turns. While it refers, most obviously, to the material realm of money matters—free market, private property and profit margins—it refers perhaps most trenchantly to the free play of the imagination, to the dreamlike state that Cliff has entered to weave this tale in which fantasy and history are reflections of each other.

This strategy of telling is entirely consistent with the novel's implicit war on the notion of the all-seeing, all-knowing, "objective" eye of history. This attitude has become a convention unto itself, at least in academic circles: history is no longer to be revered or reposed in any single body. No, history must be seen as produced, co-produced and contested by all who have a stake in whatever story is being told. And it turns out that everyone in this novel has a stake in the story of slavery and its consequences, none more so than the band of "New World" guerrillas who populate its pages and their "New World" author who fights right alongside them.

Cliff's own stakes are plain to see. In stringing together this series of stories, she takes anything but a *laissez-faire, laissez-passer* approach to the business of telling the histories of resistance. The play of voices she orchestrates makes, at once, for the fertility and frustration of *Free Enterprise.* Allowing those "in the silence" to speak as co-producers and partners makes for a novel full of accounts that could never be incorporated into a single narrative frame with a shapely structure of beginning-middle-end. But the stories of these co-producers keep vanishing from the narrative almost as suddenly as they appear, scattering like the fugitive images of last night's dream.

They leave behind the lingering echoes of set pieces or speeches, illustrating this or that point about the philosophy of history and memory toward which Cliff has long been tending. For example, Clare Savage, the rebel of Cliff's *No Telephone to Heaven,* explains her investment in a "new sort of history" that complicates, if not brackets altogether, mundane concerns about proof and rules of evidence:

> [This history] involves me . . . the practice of rub-bing lime and *salt* in the backs of whipped slaves . . . the ambush tactics of Cudjoe . . . the promised flight of Alexander Bedward in rapture back to Africa . . . cruelty . . . resistance . . . grace. I'm not outside this history—it's a matter of recognition . . . memory . . . When I study Tom Cringle's silk cotton tree, I wonder about the fact that I have never been able to bear a necklace around my throat . . . not even a scarf.

This explanation calls to mind the concept of "rememory" in Toni Morrison's *Beloved.* As Sethe explains to Denver:

> I was talking about time. It's so hard for me to believe in it. Some things go. Pass on. Some things just stay. I used to think it was my rememory. . . . Some things you forget. Other things you never do. . . . Places, places are still there. If a house burns down, it's gone, but the place—the picture of it—stays, and not just in my rememory, but out there, in the world.

In confronting the nature of memory, *Free Enterprise,* in its most interesting moments, works off a similarly imagistic view that effectively nullifies forgetfulness. In one exchange, a character worries that "all we have are these stories, and they are endangered." She is reassured by another that "[o]nce something is spoken . . . it does not die. It . . . escape[s] into the cosmos, space," is "carried on the air."

Whatever we think is forgotten, then, actually lives in the timeless zone of the unconscious and the ether of the universe, capable of being retrieved or, as one of the voices in the novel puts it, passed down like "bone structure." This is one way of answering the question posed by the narrator of Gay Jones' novel, *Corregidora* (1975), with which *Free Enterprise* has much in common: "How could she bear witness to what she'd never lived?" It is also a way of resisting the domination of official historical dogma and its enslavement to "facts."

I worry, however, that Cliff's act of resistance is caught partly in domination's noose. Although the voices of those formerly "in the silence" rub against and stress the power of the official word, Cliff cannot finally let them have their say. In other words, they are silenced again by her compulsion to over-ponder her decision to be free of blind fidelity to time, space and ideas of the real. Story is sacrificed to philosophical meditation again and again in the novel and throughout Cliff's fiction. While these explanations contain their own value, interest and narrative appeal, they coexist in ungainly balance with the operations of the plot.

Cliff does not need to work so hard to justify her decision to attempt this free fantasia, moving backward and forward in time to form the points and counterpoints of history cum myth cum legend. When she frees herself of the compulsion to explain her decision to inhabit the "wild" and etherized zone, to rely upon the power of suggestion, of evocation, the result is a rich and strange layering of scenes and haunting suggestions that linger in the mind long after the book is done. This layering lends to the narrative a paradoxical quality of movement and stasis, of time going forward yet simultaneously standing still. For example, the story of the origins of the Mississippi River leper colony where "everyone was numbered" bears an eerie resemblance to descriptions of Nazi concentration camps and contemporary myths about the etiology of AIDS. And seen from yet another angle, the leper colony takes on the shapes (and sparks the fears) of the present-day "inner city" enclaved and encrypted from the "rest" of the world by the colonization of space and structure designed to quarantine the threat of "blackness," to prevent its spreading into "white."

The relation implied between the colonization of space and the values of the marketplace opens some intriguing questions in the novel. Cliff has obviously read and absorbed the heated debates in the abolitionist press about the links between free enterprise, based on property rights and ownership, and the ownership of slaves. To her credit, she has not written a morality play in which the wolf of free enterprise downs the lamb of political dissent. That Mary Ellen owns a string of hotels that cater to wealthy whites and secretly double as havens for runaway slaves indicates that wolf and lamb can and must lie down together.

While Cliff's John Brown wants to found a "communist African state as a Christo-utopia," believing that slaves were "better than capitalism, since we had been crucified by it," Mary Ellen will have no part of such idealism. She resists the idea that commerce is foreign to African heritage, countering that "In Africa, commerce came easily to us, there were no communist states." She then insists (does one hear Cliff's *sotto voce* support of "enterprise zones"?) that "the future of the African in this country . . . will only bear fruit if and when we get our own. Banks, schools, real estate, printing presses, newspapers, grocery stores . . . and partake fully in free enterprise."

I sense no irony in this passage. The novel seems committed to the idea that free enterprise affords the "freeing" enterprises of resistance, narrative and non-narrative alike. And yet, in the final instance, it offers dismal prospects for such liberation for people of African descent, since liberation depends on the ownership of capital and the means of production, and blacks lay claim to neither. As one character tells another. "We might as well give it up, our telling of the past. We own but a few of the presses. We wield no power in the mills that train the minds."

Michelle Cliff is certainly not the first to suggest that the industry of publishing and an industrialized academy are jointly employed and mutually complicit in the maintenance and manufacture of the status quo, including "official" stories and discourses from which all signs of wildness and resistance have been purged. But in invoking the publishing industry—one cog in the free market's vast and grinding machinery—she opens another string of vexing questions about the relation between domination and resistance, production and consumption, in the act of "representing history" in a free market economy.

> **Cliff does not need to work so hard to justify her decision to attempt this free fantasia, moving backward and forward in time to form the points and counterpoints of history cum myth cum legend. When she frees herself of the compulsion to explain her decision to inhabit the "wild" and etherized zone, to rely upon the power of suggestion, of evocation, the result is a rich and strange layering of scenes and haunting suggestions that linger in the mind long after the book is done.**
> *—Deborah McDowell*

Cliff has already anticipated her own problem, using a painting as a parable about publishing. Early in the novel, Alice Hooper, a rich New Englander on whom "the responsibility of capital" weights heavily, writes Mary Ellen to smooth over the commotion following the unveiling of "Slavers Throwing Overboard the Dead and Dying, Typhoon Coming On," a painting by one Joseph Mallord William Turner, bought for her as an investment by those who would free her of the disdainful task of "investment and planning." Expressing her regrets that too many New England fortunes "rest in the enterprise of slavery," she vows to try "as much as possible to separate [herself] from any profit which might . . . have been linked to the trade."

Writing to Annie two nights later, Mary Ellen expresses her revenge fantasy: "What if last night I'd emptied my mother's chambers into Mr. Turner's painting?" Then she goes on to lament again the "official version" of "John Brown's Raid on Harper's Ferry," adding that this is for "public consumption—in both senses of that word."

But if the "official version" is indeed written—or painted—for "public consumption," figured at once as degenerative disease and oppressive economic reality, how does *Free Enterprise* free itself from (and immunize itself against) this enterprise? That question assumes a special urgency in light of an apparently thriving trade market for fictionalizations of slavery. *Free Enterprise* invites comparison with a growing number of contemporary novels that challenge canned and synthetic narratives of slavery and refuse the lulling consolations of forgetfulness: Sherley Anne Williams' *Dessa Rose*, Toni Morrison's *Beloved*, Caryl Phillips' *Cambridge* and *Crossing the River* all come to mind. These books clearly do not constitute a chorus in unison or one quick to do the bidding of the literary establishment (whatever that might be). But the proliferation of such novels does indicate the willingness of a publishing industry to trade on slavery.

I'm reminded here of the question Gary Trudeau posed in his recent spoof on the newly-minted videos of Michael Milken's high-yield investment strategies: "Can history be bought?" Judging from publishers' lists, we could say that the history of representing slavery not only can be bought but is being bought—true to the nature and dictates of free enterprise. But at whose expense?

If, as Milan Kundera writes, the "struggle of [humans] against power is the struggle of memory against forgetting," and if the act of writing is part of that struggle, how can, how does, that writing remain free of the "official word" that publishing has some hand in manufacturing? *Free Enterprise* conjures up these messy material questions, but flings them—like the stories of resistance the novel beads together—outward on the winds, to melt like "all that is solid" into air.

Ramchandran Sethuraman (essay date Spring 1997)

SOURCE: "Evidence-cum-Witness: Subaltern History, Violence, and the (De)Formation of Nation in Michelle Cliff's *No Telephone to Heaven*," in *Modern Fiction Studies*, Vol. 43, No. 1, Spring, 1997, pp. 249-87.

[*In the following essay, Sethuraman offers an "ahistorical reading of the plot structure, character development, and stylistic nuances" of* No Telephone to Heaven *in terms of Cliff's "ambivalent double articulation" of the relation between psychyoanalytic and postcolonial cultural discourse.*]

"At a time when the *grands récits* of the West have been told and retold ad infinitum, when a certain postmodernism (Lyotard's) speaks of an 'end' to metanarratives and when Fukayama talks of an 'end of history', we must ask: precisely whose narrative and whose history is being declared at an 'end'? Dominant Europe may clearly have begun to deplete its strategic repertoire of stories, but Third World people, First World 'minorities'—women and gays and lesbians—have only begun to tell, and deconstruct, theirs." Ella Shohat

and Robert Stam's pointed question disrupting the diegetic hold of Western master narratives opens up a liminal space for Third World stories to be told whose possibilities we have barely begun to explore. But the massive project of an anticolonialist retelling and remapping, of enacting historical agency in the "slenderness of narrative" (Foucault's phrase), or as Homi Bhabha poignantly puts it, of "encounter[ing] a past that is your own country reterritorialized, even terrorized, by another" is bound to founder if we do not in our engagements with and resistance to Western hegemonic theories also unmask colonialism's demonic Other, namely, imperialism and its incestuous relationship with psychoanalysis. In this respect, the distressing problem is not so much the relation of postcolonial culture to psychoanalysis, since both are implicated in a long *durée* in and as history. What has not been adequately addressed, however, are the fundamental and constitutive elements of psychoanalysis itself, whose brutal colonial history is deeply grounded in and inseparable from its virulent racism. My interest lies in exploring the weighted valences on either side of the "and" between psychoanalysis and postcolonialism, whose pairing stages both a problematic link between the two disciplines that is yet to be theorized and also a temporal cut whereby one discourse undermines the totalizing tendency of the other.

In tracing psychoanalysis's discursive formation in relation to imperialism elsewhere, I argue that through the primacy of an elaborate machinery of visual relations, in particular the colonial gaze, psychoanalysis objectified, scripted, and racialized the exotic non-Western "people without history" for the prurient fascination of the masses in the West while masking and remaining obstinately silent about the racialized assumptions of its own ideological formations. By a perverse paradox, the transplantation of psychoanalysis onto alien soils also hybridized and fissured its praxis, producing the same ambivalence and destabilization of authority that occurred at the level of the state apparatus's interactions with indigenous peoples. If we are to rewrite history/narrative through the peculiar lens of the dispossessed/colonized, "not univocally but contrapuntally," in Said's sense of the term [in "Secular Interpretation"], "with a simultaneous awareness both of the metropolitan history that is narrated and of those other histories against which (and together with which) the dominant discourse acts," then we must enact a seismological shift in perspective, one that encompasses the painful disruption/eruption of history as trauma and trauma as history.

To rephrase Spivak, no writer more insistently says an "impossible 'no'" to structures of modernity, "which one critiques, yet inhabits intimately," than Michelle Cliff in *No Telephone to Heaven*. The back-and-forth migration of her protagonist from Jamaica to America to England and back again to Jamaica provides a frenetic frame to her novel that frustrates any attempt at a vantage point from which to gain mastery of the text. Refusing to cast the cultural debate in hackneyed binary oppositions—center versus margin, metropole versus colony, ruling class versus subaltern—Cliff's ambivalent double articulation on one level explodes the fixed boundaries of identity and difference. At the same time, the in-between space from which protagonists like Clare Savage enunciate poses the question, "Who am I in the transnational context?" Is Clare Jamaican or British or American? Is the process of hybridization always liberatory? What relationship exists between the freedom to travel that comes with race and class privilege and the perilous border crossings made by Mexicans to the United States? Like Toni Morrison, Cliff grapples with these and other issues by turning the colonial space, what Michel de Certeau has famously described as "the non-place from which all historiographical operation starts," into the "not-there," the site of other historical enunciations, of an "other" narrative of writing one's identity.

Cliff uses the ideological determinants of that preeminently Western genre, the novel—plot, character development, moral values, linear narrative—only to subvert its false claim to consistency and univocal meaning. As Cliff points out in her essay **"A Journey into Speech,"** "I alternate the King's English with *patois,* not only to show the class background of characters, but to show how Jamaicans operate within a split consciousness." Cliff's hybrid narrative, in which several genres meet, jostle, and collide, defies all attempts at categorization; fiction, poetry, lyric, multiple references to both Western and non-Western contexts, canonical and noncanonical texts are all combined and recontextualized to serve the author's artistic purpose. The narrative is partially filtered through the sporadic "rememoration" of Clare Savage—in a creative rewriting of the past as opposed to a simple reminiscing—as she is driven up the crest of the hill in a truck with her fellow revolutionaries. The truck emblazoned with the phrase "No Telephone to Heaven" is a prophetic embodiment of the way the revolutionaries will be excluded from the nation-state, as subalterns generally are from the socializing ends of the novel. Since Cliff's novel is deliberately episodic and fragmented, with several stories within stories, any attempt, as is the custom, to summarize the plot for the reader would be fraught with difficulties. One can partially and only imperfectly say at the outset that *No Telephone to Heaven* is about "not-there" place of the dispossessed within both the geopolitical context of Jamaica and a transnational framework.

No single character or image or voice constitutes the hub around which the other elements of *No Telephone to Heaven* rotate; instead, Cliff activates a melange of images in relation to a polyphony of voices. Disparate incidents across national boundaries—Jamaica, England, and America—are not only deeply connected but also inform, construct and deconstruct, and corrupt each other. Senselessly brutal or

bizarre passages—relating the Sunday School Bombing on 15 September 1963 that killed four school children in Georgia; or speaking of "dark women in saris cleaning the toilets at Heathrow"; or describing the "most beautiful beach on the island; the most secluded" owned by an "American absentee" landlord; or recounting the Triangle slave trade—are disjunctively syncopated.

In response to bipolar studies that principally emphasize the relationship of the mother country, England or France, with its colonies, Cliff redraws the political map to include the indispensable role played by American imperialism in the formation and perpetuation of the very same empire that existed at the turn of the century, besides performing on several colonial stages of her own. Lest we lose sight of America's pivotal role in the imperial project, W. J. T. Mitchell provides a timely reminder that "Americans are less disturbed by the idea of imperial decline than with the notion that the word 'empire' could ever apply to us." Similarly, the argument for the overlapping and disjunctive histories of Europe and America and "the rest" of the world is well made by Sandra Harding's *Whose Science? Whose Knowledge?* Building on the pioneering work of Walter Rodney's *How Europe Underdeveloped Africa,* Harding has this to say: "the history of Europe and the United States is African history also and . . . African history is also European and U.S. history."

In keeping with such a transnational cultural engendering and politics, for Caren Kaplan:

> Cliff articulates the boundaries between homelessness and origin, between exile and belonging. . . . A creole culture, Jamaica exists in many levels and time periods. Cliff moves through several of these identities. She rewrites her history to 'claim' an identity through her powers of story-telling and imagination. . . . This is a new terrain, a new location, in feminist poetics. Not a room of one's own, not a fully public or collective self, not a domestic realm—it is a space in the imagination which allows for the inside, the outside, and the liminal elements of inbetween.

For Françoise Lionnet, "[l]ike German writer Christa Wolf and Chinese-American writer Maxine Hong Kingston, Cliff uses postmodern fictional techniques that, in the words of Sidonie Smith, 'challenge the ideology of individualism and with it the ideology of gender.' . . . Cliff's strategy is to let the narrative show how authority is a construction of language, and how the multicultural subject is always the site of contradictions."

The multiple clashing genres that inform and "cut" across Cliff's text frustrate any reified one-to-one equation of mother/woman and the Jamaican nation-state. In fact, the eye of the British-American camera that is brought into play at the end of the novel, instead of functioning prosthetically as the "transcendent subject" for the viewer in Christian Metz's sense of the term, produces what Rey Chow has called "evidence-cum-witness" in a revolutionary refashioning of the elements of *testimonio* facilitating the transformation of the yardboy Christopher, enlisted as an actor in the film, from a savage "authentically" playing a role scripted for a Western audience into a forest god that comes to haunt and transform the very import of the novel. In other words, a facile, ahistorical reading of the plot structure, character development, and stylistic nuances of the novel performed from within what Richard Ohmann calls the "prophylactic view of literature" can only yield a dominant version of the story. But shimmering underneath the surface of the text lies another, more interesting tale that begs to be told.

Psychoanalysis and Postcolonial Subjectivity

Since Michelle Cliff works within and against the deleterious effects of visual politics in the construction of the subaltern, I wish first to examine how the gaze structures subjectivity within a neocolonial space. According to Lacan, the child's discordant reaction to its image—simultaneous attraction and aggression—is triggered by his conflictual perception of that image, which is unified and whole while the child himself lacks motor control. The child's entry into language positions the white male in possession of the symbolic while relegating the female outside it in a negative relation; men and women of color (which is not to ignore the complex gender and cultural differences between and within the two groups) are also jettisoned to the margins of the symbolic, to the limits of meaning and representation within Eurocentric traditions.

I wish to argue that what the child sees in the mirror is not simply an innocent, nonideological reflection but rather a complex image imbricated in the contradictory structures of social, historical, cultural, and political practices. In this regard, Abdul JanMohamed, fails to ask a crucial question: Are the emotive effects of the image in the mirror the same, for example, for an Afro-American or a Chicano or an Asian man or woman as they are for the white man? Or, for that matter, do men and women relate to the mirror stage within the space of the middle-class white bourgeois family (nuclear or single-parent) in the same way? The white man's reflection in the cultural mirror within psychoanalytical paradigms tells an altogether other story. We have to ask ourselves not only why the primacy of the visual in Freud's and Lacan's theories of ego formation and subjectivity, but also who sees whom, in what asymmetrical cultural, sexual, social, and gendered contexts? In the heart of civilization and its discontent there lies a disquieting tribulation. Just as the Lacanian mirror presents a false image of unity to the growing infant, the cultural mirror in my aberrant reading becomes the place in which the white, heterosexual male body is erased, providing, more crucially, for the liminal moment of the invisibility or silence of his race and ontological status. As Elizabeth Grosz has written, "[t]he evacuation of the male body is the condition required to create a space of reflection, of specul(ariz)ation from which it can look at itself from the outside." Deliberately keeping his own racial status undefined and abstract, and therefore invulnerable and superior, the white male, the "I/Eye" of the imperial subject, arrogates to himself the power, in Mary Louise Pratt's succinct words, to be the "monarch-of-all-I-survey," the inalienable right to see, to know, and to have commerce, in both senses of the term, with the land and the bodies of the subjected peoples.

Racial Theories and the Empire

What could more strikingly substantiate my thesis than the dialectics of race in Robert Knox's 1850 work *The Races of Men,* in which the racially unmarked Anglo-Saxon gains in racial superiority to the extent that the working-class Irish are denigrated? Robert Young's brilliant analysis of Knox's illustrations brings home the point: "Whereas the Irish Celts are portrayed as poor, over-fertile, their faces displaying negroid characteristics, there is no need to illustrate the Saxon type at all. Rather, Knox shows 'A Saxon House,' adding 'standing always apart, if possible, from all others': his stately mansion thus manages to suggest the fundamental class basis of the racial distinction, at the same time as implying the instinctive racial purity of the bourgeois Saxon." Set against the racial purity of the Anglo-Saxon, which is self-evident and therefore warrants no explanation, the Celtic race is depicted by Knox in a way that draws on stock stereotypes: the bodies are tightly compressed in a confined space; an adult male figure is seen in crumpled working-class clothes, his hair disheveled, his body slightly tilted to suggest a drunken stupor. The prominent portrayal of the men contrasts with the demure and lower position allotted to the women, who are dwarfed as a result. The woman in the foreground holding a baby has her back turned to a looking subject, while the other woman positioned close to the frame almost disappears into it. The two men wedged between the women blur any clear-cut alignment of the relationships among the sexes. The downcast glance of the woman away from the baby as the baby stares tangentially into blankness suggests that the baby's paternal identity is as much in question as is the morality of the figures in the frame. Reinforcing the motif of compromised morality, all the figures' glances are skewed and turned away from the judgmental gaze of the onlooker. Knox goes on in his book to claim that Irish misery cannot be attributed to English misrule but rather that "the source of all evil lies in *the race,* the Celtic race of Ireland. There is no getting over *historical facts.* Look at Wales, look at Caledonia; it is ever the same. The race *must* be forced from the *soil*; by fair means, if possible, still they must leave" (emphasis added).

Significantly enough, Knox's original version in his *Races of Men* illustrates "A Saxon House" twice, once on page 40 and again on page 56 with a slight alteration of the caption that carries significant meaning. The first caption reads, "A Saxon House; standing always apart, if possible, from all others"; the second reads, "An *Anglo*-Saxon house; it always, if possible, stands detached" (emphasis added). In the second version the foregrounding and inflection of the *Englishness* of the Saxon race is subtly insinuated with the prefix "Anglo." Interestingly, the word "race" in Knox's account applies only to the Irish, Welsh, and Scottish, but not to the Anglo-Saxon, a fact that raises a crucial question asked by Robert Young: "Did not Europe itself provide examples of successful hybrid races?" Young recognizes the twin forces of capitalism and colonialism in the establishment and legitimation of the slavery system, a system dating back to the "plantation" economies of the British colonies and the American South. However, Young's solely class-based account of the internal dissonance and racial tensions among the Anglo-Saxons, Irish, Welsh, and Scottish fails to acknowledge how the intertwined categories of race and class are imbricated in the fragile composition of Great Britain itself as a nation-state—at the very heights of its imperial dominance. Faced as Britain was with internecine struggles and racial divisions within and among the white races in the mid-nineteenth century, Her Majesty could not afford not to project a facade of national unity in order to maintain and vindicate the empire's show of force in the colonies.

It was against such "raceless chaos" that Matthew Arnold advanced his "theory of culture" in the widely acclaimed *Culture and Anarchy* and *On the Study of Celtic Literature,* works characterized by Young, despite Arnold's "claims for detachment," as "in fact fully immersed within the ideology of his time." Arnold becomes the perfect spokesman for an imperial culture at its apogee. As Young rightly observes, "Arnold leaves his reader in no doubt about how it [that culture] is manifested materially: [in its] institutions—Oxford University, the Established Church of England, the State." As in Knox's residential illustration of the invisibility of the Anglo-Saxon race behind the walls of stately, detached homes, in Arnold's depiction of race as culture we see the same disappearance of the racialized Anglo-Saxon body. Subsuming the older notion of "race as lineage" under what Young calls the newer "scientific notions of race as 'type,' as language, as mental difference, and above all as culture," Arnold can contain the threat from the imaginative and feminine Celtic culture and language by incorporating the latter within their more robust and virile English counterparts to produce a quintessentially English national spirit. Only Arnold's rhetoric of Englishness allows the disjunctive discourse of race to be circumscribed by notions of culture in

Britain while *lines of blood* remain the operative factor in the colonies. This double trope of race provided Britain with the ideological basis it needed for the project of civilizing so-called "restless natives," without endangering Great Britain's racial "purity" or its status as an imperial nation-state.

Lacan, Fanon, and Subaltern History/Agency

To clarify further the enmeshed relationship between colonialism, psychoanalysis, and empire, I wish to make another shift and read Fanon along with and against Lacan. Fanon's interpellation of the historical and social subject, in spite of its Lacanian leanings, never loses sight of the difference of race and class in the cultural formation of the colonial subject. What a black man sees in the mirror, writes Fanon in *Black Skin, White Masks,* is not a single but a conflictual double image that splits the subject and leads to a racialized struggle between the dominant values of light and darkness: "Moral consciousness implies a kind of cission, a fracture of consciousness into a bright part and an opposing black part. In order to achieve morality, it is essential that the black, the dark, the Negro vanish from consciousness. Hence a Negro is forever in combat with his own image." How is a colonized subject supposed to escape the self-destructive trap of the specular image? For Fanon a way out of the governing fiction is through a third term that is not "personal but social." Unlike Lacan, who sees the alterity and literariness of the symbolic exploding the myths of a unified, autonomous subject and the imaginary's fantasies of unity and resemblance, Fanon inserts differences of race and class into Lacan's symbolic narrative by exposing the internal hierarchies of inclusion and exclusion constituted by the very *processes of the symbolic.* Put another way, in the absence of social forms that would legitimize the subaltern's subjectivity and history, the oppressed people's struggle with sites of meaning requires, as it were, an "underground narrative of liberation," one "depicted . . . memorably," as Edward Said points out, in Fanon's *The Wretched of the Earth.*

In order to flesh out the "second," or other, narrative lodged within the multilayered ***No Telephone to Heaven,*** it is necessary to contextualize the politics of gaze in the novel. A case in point concerns the ghastly scene the reader explores along with Paul, an obsessively visual scene depicting the grisly murder of Paul's immediate family—his father, Charles, his mother, Evelyn, and his sister. Paul's visual appropriation of what has happened in his parents' house recalls the way the eye of the camera territorializes the body of a film scene. Paul is returning home after an all-night party at Buster Said's house. The Porsche he drives, his palatial home in the Stony Hills tucked away from the glaring, stark poverty of the shantytown dwellers on the outskirts of Kingston, the iron gate to ward off intruders, the Great Dane, and the swimming pool at the back of the house are sufficient indications of Paul's class, privilege, security, and sense of personal entitlement. As Paul enters through the iron gate, he is jolted by a series of surprises: "the dog hadn't barked when he approached"; "he called his name until his eyes met with Carlos' neck and Paul saw the thick red line of a wound from ear to ear. Machete"; "the dark, heavy mahogany door" to the house is ajar; his mother's almost always locked larder is also open wide; the kitchen floor is strewn with "salt, thyme, coffee, ginger root . . . all the ingredients of Jamaica were mixed together in this mess."

Disoriented as Paul is by this chaotic scene, nothing prepares him or the reader for what unfolds in his parents' bedroom. In the manner of a cinematic camera eye that controls, delimits, and ideologically positions not only what but, more important, how we see, Cliff introduces us to the chilling scene. Her lens, however, is split. Unlike the Godlike cinematic apparatus that stays hidden and even unobtrusive in Hollywood movies, completely immersing the audience in the seamless flow of the narrative unfolding on screen, Cliff's camera lens presents us with an ambivalent, "double" view. Paul surveys the scene:

> His father, it seemed to Paul, had put up no struggle. He lay on his back, naked and barehanded, his pajama top on the floor at least five yards away, his trousers not to be seen. His throat was cut like the dog's throat was cut and his penis was severed, so that it hung from his crotch as if on a thin string, dangling into the place between his open legs. How could he not defend himself? His wife? His eyes were closed—they told nothing.

Where Paul had previously sought to reaffirm his manhood through his identification with his father, in keeping with the Lacanian Law of the Father, he now finds himself emasculated by the sight of his father's severed penis. In the words of Kaja Silverman, "he is unable to align himself with the phallus because he is no longer able to believe in the *vraisemblable*." With the fictional power of the phallus taken away from him, Paul also loses the concomitant power to signify. His defense mechanism is to turn his disgust at his father's dereliction of the paternalistic duty to protect his wife into disgust for the feminized body that his father now symbolizes. Paradoxically, Paul eroticizes his father by writing on his body a feminine image—the horrifying empty space between his father's "open legs"—even as the scene compels a de-eroticized distance from the murdered body. It is in the disjunctive temporal gap between symbol and sign, in the gap between the phallus as the symbol of power in patriarchal culture and its ambivalent and unpredictable role in the scene to which we bear witness that we find what Homi Bhabha calls "another locus of inscription and intervention, another hybrid, inappropriate enunciative site, through that temporal split—or time-lag, . . . for the signifi-

cation of postcolonial agency." We will reach a better understanding of the local and historical struggles associated with subaltern agency a little later in the essay, when we go over the same scenes of massacre through the eyes of Christopher, the yard boy, and the perpetrator of the crimes.

Paul's next discovery, of his mother's dismembered body, again denies him the classic affirmation and disavowal of castration and difference that psychoanalysis perpetuates from a male perspective. It is a boy in Freud's account of sexual difference who sees the woman as castrated, as bearing a wound, and it is through the tropes of voyeurism and fetishism that males are able at once to acknowledge and to disavow castration by fantasizing the little girl as having a penis. The gift of speaking in one's culture and language exacts a heavy price of both men and women: the sacrifice, or castration, of one's being. Cliff frustrates Paul's desire to see castration not on his body but elsewhere, on his mother's body:

> Naked, as his father was naked, but with one arm across her eyes as if protecting herself from the eyes of others. Her Nature. . . . Afraid of her. Even his gentle touch to her cool face created chaos, as the back of her head sank deep into her pillow, widening the gap in her throat. His throat caught. He looked down at her, away from her neck, to where he had emerged twenty-five years before. The base of a rum bottle was caught between her legs. Wha'fe do? Terror at approaching this part of her. Have mercy. He pulled the bottle and saw that the neck was broken. Jagged. Blood poured from between her legs, catching in her fine curled hair. The flies swarmed anew as a new banquet lay before them. He felt a terrible shame.

The paralyzing distress for Paul pivots around his utter failure to shore up his sense of maleness, his power as doer and possessor of the gaze, in attempting to displace all that is passive, feminine, and the object rather than the subject of signification onto his mother. Paul's "gentle touch[ing]" of his mother's "cool face" is an act of fetishism that, in Laura Mulvey's words, "builds up the physical beauty of the object, transforming it into something satisfying in itself," while the gesture of pulling out the jagged rum bottle from between her legs is symptomatic of his voyeuristic side. Summarizing Mulvey's essay, E. Ann Kaplan writes, voyeurism, as in Paul's case, is "linked to disparagement, has a sadistic side, and is involved with pleasure through control or domination, and with punishing the woman (guilty for being castrated)."

Paul's hopes of finding his sister alive are also dashed: "Her legs were spread wide and she was bloodied. The gold bangle on her wrist glinted in the light. Beast, came into his spinning head." Paul's last discovery leads him "to the small room at the side of the garage" where the maid, Mavis, lives. In chilling detail Paul's gaze informs us that "her body was on the floor, slashed in a way none of his family had been slashed. The machete had been dug into her in so many ways, so many times, that Mavis' body became more red than brown. She had no more eyes."

In the cold, stringent account of Paul's naive desire to formulate Mavis's identity and history, we find Cliff's tracking of the two levels of history, one dominant and myopic, the other exploding at the subterranean level. Although Mavis had lived with Paul's family for the better part of her life, Paul still knows nothing of her history: "He did not know her surname, or the name of the place she had come from, . . . but there would be no canceled checks to reveal a surname, because Mavis was paid in cash each week, and each week his father complained to his mother about the amount . . . on top of the dresser was Mavis' Bible and her lime-green plastic purse. He opened the purse to find a couple of dollars and some change, nothing else . . . No papers. No birth certificate. No savings book, no insurance policy." Reading from the vantage point of a dominant discourse that does not simply reflect the appalling conditions of the poor but constitutes them through its material process of othering, Paul's literate mind is too illiterate to read the signs of the other narrative/history, invisible and yet writ large between the fault lines of his discourse.

In order to understand subaltern history, which cannot be bound in discourse or deciphered within the matrices of a dominant history that "tells the beads of sequential time like a rosary," we have to investigate the close links between trauma and history. Kaja Silverman writes that "trauma can best be understood as the rupture of an order which aspires to closure and systemic equilibrium by a force directed toward disruption and disintegration." Following Fredric Jameson's lead in *The Political Unconscious*, Silverman defines "history as a force capable of tearing a hole in the fabric of the dominant fiction, and so of disrupting its internal economy. In short, I will identify it with trauma."

The first blow that dislocates and ruptures the power relations of the dominant discourse is struck by none other than Christopher, the yard boy, with whom Paul has spent many a evening shooting birds. But apart from this veneer of camaraderie, differences of class and skin color (backra versus dark-skinned) set them a world apart. Christopher's history cannot be traced within the structures of the bourgeois culture, with the high premium it places on enlightenment, civility, rationality, and progress. He exists relentlessly to remind the bourgeois culture that he is a "hole in the (social) cell," as Hélène Cixous would put it. His formative years were spent in the "Dungle," where he lived with his grandmother; his makeshift house is a structure "crowned with sheets of zinc, [and] the places where the zinc rusted

filled with cardboard or newspaper or left to gape." "The Word was beyond him," since the social formation had assigned him the burden of living at the level of debasement and defilement. Christopher becomes, in the words of Sander L. Gilman, "the antithesis of European sexual mores and beauty," and his body symbolizes "the essential black, the lowest rung on the great chain of being, [which] is the Hottentot. The physical appearance of the Hottentot is, indeed, the central nineteenth-century icon for the sexual difference between the European and the black." Christopher's grandmother dies when he is only eight years old, leaving him orphaned and penniless. Even "De government men tek her body away fe bury dem say and leave him dere, never once asking if him have smaddy fe care fe him." Christopher becomes a wandering outcast who makes his bed in the cemetery and does casual yard work twice a week at Master Charles's home to stay alive. Beguiled by a retired police officer to think that he can retrieve the remains of his grandmother "thirteen Chrismus" after her death, Christopher arrives at Charles's house in the middle of the night, hoping "backra people could be soft around de Chrismus—dem who so mean the rest of the time" and grant his wish for a small plot of ground so that the restless "duppy" of his grandmother could now rest in peace.

Between Christopher's request for a small plot of land and his massacre of Charles's family with the machete lies the unfathomable chasm where the dominant and subaltern histories clash head on, shattering the acquiescence of the dispossessed to the settlers' appropriation of their homeland. Unlike Paul's controlling gaze, the white male gaze that is constituted by and in turn constitutes the paradigms of psychoanalysis, Christopher's "other" gaze functions in the manner of Chow's evidence-cum-witness to "supplement the identification of the native-as-image" with a simulation of the gaze that witnesses "the native's oppression prior to her becoming image." Entering the premises, however, Christopher's demeanor shows that the dichotomy and power relations between the master and the servant are still securely in place. Bruce Robbins notes in *The Servant's Hand* regarding Dickens's time that "the servants of life are themselves signs—signs of their master's status." In spite of the "ease given him by the rum," Christopher is "fearful" of the master. This fear of the backra-master evidences itself earlier in the text when Christopher is described as too "'fraid fe ask dem to stop de cyar, so him peepee 'pon himself. She [mistress] complain about de stink again an' about fe dem cyar seat." We encounter an undercurrent of deep anxiety regarding Charles's authority as master, masked skillfully, however, when this character refuses to grant Christopher's wish in the most acidic and acerbic tone that he can muster:

> "It cyaan wait till mornin'?" Harshness stayed in the man's voice. My God, there was a yardbwai in him bedroom. Askin' favor. Lord have mercy.

"Please, sah." Christopher was trembling. He looked down at his black rubber boot—his bare feet washed in sweat inside them.

In this discourse's performative enunciation of undecidability, what Foucault would characterize as "signs apparently *without* meaning and value—empty and excentric—in events that are outside the 'great events' of history," we see the emergence of a new Christopher, one who challenges our efforts to categorize him. The new Christopher is imaging rather than being imaged, signifying rather than being signified, enunciating rather than being enunciated; in the words of David Spurr, he is "neither one thing nor the other, neither civilized nor savage, but strangely without definition." Charles was looking forward to "a morning of golf at Constant Spring while his wife was at mass." Instead, Christopher, a man who has "no past" and "no future," strikes the blow that meets with "no resistance a-tall, a-tall" from Charles. Having done the same to Charles's wife and their daughter, Christopher punishes the maid, Mavis, "in a terrible way, exacting not just silence but obliteration, and he could not have said why. He cut her like an animal, torturing her body in a way he had not tortured theirs."

The question resonates through the novel: Why did Christopher wreak such havoc and wrath on Mavis's body, that of a sister who belongs to his own dispossessed class? The answer lies, ironically, in Mavis's hybrid identity, an identity spatially figured by her migration between the mistress's wealthy home and her own "small room" next to the garage on the premises, a migration symbolic of her mistress's position at the center and of her own subject position on the periphery. Having completely internalized her subordinate position in relation to her masters, Mavis is able to see things only from the masters' point of view: "'Wunna talk 'bout owe, bwai? Whatsoever wunna have, wunna owe to dem. Dem nuh rescue wunna?" It is Mavis as a contradictory threshold figure, her subject position rooted in subalternity but her discourse smacking of the masters, that Christopher must obliterate or else himself stand obliterated. As Christopher observes of this character, she was "in death, as in life, their faithful servant." Mavis's hybrid and hybridizing potential is what threatens Christopher and gives birth to his trauma. Trauma, as noted earlier, is another word for history—not for the dominant Hegelian History that imposes a unified vision but for the local bits and pieces of a history that "hurts" in Jameson's sense of the term and "can be apprehended only through its effects, and never directly as some reified force."

The effects of history are made disturbingly palpable and material in Cliff's novel's numbing violence. Mahatma Gandhi taps into the root cause of violence with his profound statement, made in another context, that poverty is a terrible violence against humanity. Is it gratuitous violence that Cliff recklessly subjects us to in going over the same heinous crimes from two different perspectives, or does the novel's violence serve another purpose? The question becomes all the more compelling in the light of Christopher's revisiting the dead bodies to obliterate them further with the jagged edges of the rum bottle.

Cliff provocatively speaks both within and against the socializing and civilizing ends of the novel and the nation-state in order to highlight the complex difficulties of speaking in one's own voice. Hers is a distinctive postcolonial style that does not ape that of the West while recognizing the colonized as deeply worked over by the processes of colonization. Christopher, in effect, says no to the oppressive socializing ends of a literary form that constructs him and his fellows in demeaning ways by unleashing another mode of narrative, another principle of organization, one that requires us to learn and cultivate a different mode of reading identity.

Whereas the novel's striking ocular motif fixes the Other as transparent, natural, and completely knowable to the penetrating gaze of the dominant subject, Cliff's counternarrative frustrates the desire to territorialize the Other by producing subaltern identity elsewhere. The interesting doubling of the gaze, those of Paul and Christopher, produces different valences at the level of language. Paul notices that his father's "eyes were closed—they told nothing"; his mother had "one arm across her eyes as if protecting herself from the eyes of others. Her nature"; Mavis "had no more eyes." On one level, the closed eyes of the victims at once acknowledge and disavow not only the otherness of Christopher but also his association with abjection, defilement, and filth. On another level, the closed eyes that say "nothing" also refuse to mirror and affirm the coded stable and proper bourgeois identity for Paul. Paul's retching and vomiting at the sight of his mother's body makes the domestic bourgeois space the very site of the filth that cannot be displaced elsewhere. Earlier on, Christopher's sheer fear of his new masters results in his "peepee 'pon himself" in their car, but now the fear is replaced by a defiant piss on their wall. The doubling of the scene produces an uncanny liminal effect, blurring the boundaries separating Paul from Christopher, bourgeois from subaltern, the pure from the contaminated.

Paul's failure to appropriate the "other" as History, his failure, in other words, to chronicle the lives of Mavis and Christopher with authority and certainty, is only one aspect of the larger problematics of the representation of subalterns in history and as history. Having "never been concerned with a mess in his life," since "he [Paul] and his surroundings have been tidied by darker people," Paul has no difficulty in presenting a myopic vision of Jamaica. As Clare Savage, who nonchalantly lets him "stick his cock into her" a day before Paul falls victim to Christopher's machete, observes, "He assumed, like so many of them, that Jamaica was the world; he said so. Not realizing, or willing to admit, that it was only one of the saddest pieces of the world." Cliff's archaeological excavation of the sedimented and multilayered histories of the neocolonial ruling class opens up a cultural future for postcolonial peoples by recasting the pertinent issues from a transnational, feminist, diasporic perspective. Her double articulation of the dominant ruling class has one resonance in Jamaica and quite another in England, the "motherland," or the United States, as the Savage family, who emigrate to the United States in the sixties, will painfully discover for themselves. It is through these figures— Boy Savage, who believes and lives out the advice he gives his daughter: "Self-effacement. Blending in"; Kitty, his wife, whose "point of reference—the place which explained the world to her—would always be her island"; Clare Savage, the elder of their two daughters, whose hybrid history is "composed of fragments"; and Harry/Harriet who plays havoc with the Western desire to classify and categorize individuals on the predictable grounds of race, class, and gender—that Cliff carries out a savage critique of the enabling and paralyzing effects of modernity on postcolonial societies.

The Politics of Location

I will begin with Kitty Savage, whose confidence in her dominant class position is shaken to the roots soon after the Savages arrive in Miami. Holding fast to his philosophy of remaining "invisible" in America, Boy Savage takes the "secondary roads" as he and Kitty travel to the home of relatives in New York, where they stay until Boy finds them a basement apartment in Brooklyn. Their trip marks Kitty's and Boy's two sharply contrasting styles of adapting to their new country. Whereas Boy Savage ignores the racist slogans dotting the route through Georgia, Kitty is quick to realize how unwelcome they are in the so-called land of immigrants. Next to an "abandoned NAACP office" the bold sign reads, "A MAN WAS LYNCHED YESTERDAY . . . 'Hello, America,' Kitty muttered to herself, after repeating the words on the sign for the family." Kitty's dominant status in Jamaica has no bearing on her shifting subject position in America, as is clear from the repeated discursive assaults on her being as a person of color: "RACIAL SELF-RESPECT IS NOT BIGOTRY, black ink on a white background promised, as if explaining the sign-post beside it: YOU ARE IN KLAN COUNTRY." The disturbing slogans function to reposition Kitty as a subject in demeaning ways that compel us to view the way subjects are interpellated in discourse not in the unitary fashion outlined by Althusser but in a way that acknowledges a heterogeneous semantic field where the inflections of subjectivity are multiple, conflictual, interchangeable, and often contradictory. Althusser's ideological apparatuses may well be used by the state to hail its citizen-

subjects, but the real sites of self-fashioning, of refashioning ethnicity, as Kitty's Brooklyn community exemplifies, are eccentrically local, made up of bits and pieces of life whose contours shape and are in their turn reshaped by cultural nuances introduced by new immigrant groups. For example, in one of her countless efforts to make a better living than she makes working in the laundry, Kitty interviews for a job at a bank. Before long the racist discourse of the manager constructs the lowly life to which she should aspire. Beginning with the question "'And where does that musical voice come from?'" the conversation turns more squarely to putting Kitty in her place: "'my wife and I have not had the pleasure of visiting your beautiful island, but we have heard all about it from our maid . . . ah, perhaps you know her . . . her name is Winsome.'" In the manager's discussion of race and ethnicity here, we have to bear in mind that these words themselves have to do with the social positioning of the other and are thus never free of relations of power and value. The manager's naive assumption that Kitty ought to know the maid Winsome bears two derogatory implications. First, the island is so small that one is bound to know all the inhabitants. Second, that Kitty herself is a maid and would therefore know her peers. Cornel West has suggested that the unity of racist discourse is a product of the "structure of modern discourse, . . . [of] the controlling metaphors, notions, categories and norms that shape the predominant conceptions of truth and knowledge in the modern West." Perhaps nothing exemplifies this better than the controlling metaphors that structure the bank manager's discourse. His parting shot to Kitty—"'there is a vacancy in our executive washroom. Perhaps your husband might be interested?'"— is a telling example of what "produces and promotes such an object [the white supremacy] of modern discourse."

If the controlling power of the gaze is the basis of Paul's racist discourse, the othering of Kitty revolves around the smell of her "curry," which the Brooklyn neighbors find offensive, since "smell, whilst, like touch, encoding revulsion, ha[s] a pervasive and invisible presence difficult to regulate." "Once, when the neighbors called about the smell of the curry, Kitty went out immediately and bought something called Air-Wick . . . which was supposed to remove all odors from the atmosphere. Instead, it seemed only to mask other smells, placing its own acridity over their sharpness or sweetness . . . and the smells of people." Her attempts to smother the smell with "Air-Wick" is an appropriate metaphor for Kitty's own divided life, a life that alternates between "straining to adjust to this place where she seemed to float, never to light" and the comforting familiarity of the "shopkeepers of Bedstuy," her "home away from home."

I now turn to the multiaccentual weight of racist discourse by shifting the critical study of its production from a national to a transnational theater in order to examine the metamorphosis of the Savages. Although they are largely the objects of racist slurs in America, the Savages themselves participate in a discriminatory discourse with regard to their own less fortunate underclass. The Savages not only draw clear boundaries separating their bourgeois identity from the lower-class identity of the maids who serve and wait on them but also draw upon their Caribbean heritage to distinguish themselves from the other ethnic groups, particularly from the Afro-Americans with whom they share more than a triangular slave history. Kitty seeks no one but Dorothy, for instance, her confidante and maid, to share her premonition that her mother, Mattie, is dead, a premonition that proves true when she receives the sad tidings from her brother the next day. Although "Kitty and Dorothy had wet the same bed when they were small," both children having been brought up by Mattie as if they were sisters, Kitty fails to share the actual loss of her mother with Dorothy. Reminded of her station in life, Dorothy can only react out of the mistress's earshot: "'Dem never change.'"

In a similar vein, Kitty's relation with her two Afro-American fellow workers is one of mutual suspicion: "Kitty and the women in the packing room—named Georgia and Virginia—spoke only from necessity. But when Kitty was in the outer office, not sitting between them, she could hear them chatting softly, laughing." Perhaps the history lesson of the divide-and-rule policy of the British Empire is not lost upon Mr. B., the white man who owns "White's Sanitary Laundry," as he draws the most purchase from suspicion and prejudice among minorities. Even before Kitty has an opportunity to confess to being the author of the supposedly offensive advice she had slipped in among the laundered clothes, Mr. B. had taken upon himself to fire the two Afro-Americans, who in his eyes can alone be the source of such duplicity and baseness. As Mr. B. says to Kitty, "'But, you know, that kind is just no good. Unstable. You know what I mean.'" The examples of racist discourse I have cited so far, taken from diverse sociopolitical and cultural groups, undermine and cut across fixed notions of race, class, and national origin. Put differently, the "controlling metaphors" of racist discourse have multifarious historical and cultural enunciations that take us beyond the binary ways in which, as Kwame Anthony Appiah asserts, "the margin is produced by the cultural dominant; Europe defining her sovereignty by insisting on the otherness of her colonies."

Having had no access to the power-knowledge axis, Christopher's manner of combating the racist discourse tattooed on his body is by way of the machete; the contraband notes on the subject of racial hatred that Kitty writes to her white clients and includes with their clean laundry offer a different way of disrupting the racist discourse that imprisons the minds of the colonized. Kitty Savage sets out to dismantle and negate systematically the association between black and evil, the notion of black bestiality as a metaphysical fact, as Fanon would say. Functioning initially within the demands and limits of white ideology, Kitty develops a persona, Mrs. White, the imaginary wife of an imaginary man, who at Mr. B.'s behest sends out wholesome advice to accompany the freshly laundered clothes. The word "sanitary" was "a keystone" to Mr. B., and the complementary image of an "older woman with gentle gray curls, pink skin," and "clear blue eyes" that was sent out with Mrs. White's advice served as a wholesome domestic image with which the normative white household could identify. Kitty's underground narrative soon changes everything, however. In her subversive messages to customers, Kitty performs what Gloria Anzaldúa calls "linguistic code-switching" in the face of censorious forces, "transforming silence with (an)other alphabet." The interesting point is Kitty's failure to provoke a response as long as the illusion of her whiteness is sustained among her invisible clientele. The eruption of race sends bourgeois narrative, which has failed to contain blackness, careening to a sudden death. "HELLO. MRS. WHITE IS DEAD. MY NAME IS MRS. BLACK. I KILLED HER." When Kitty gives up her job to return to Jamaica, no longer capable of feeling at "home with pretense" in America, she paradoxically serves the socializing ends of the bourgeois novel, which cannot be read or written as long as the recalcitrant voices of the silenced others are firmly lodged within its boundaries.

Neither Kitty's nativism nor Boy Savage's desire to become assimilated into white culture by way of his constant "streamlining for America" provides a cultural space from which to see Jamaica as being any different from its neocolonial shadow. Perhaps the hope for a cultural future comes from an unusual source: Clare Savage, "a light-skinned woman, daughter of landowners, native-born, slaves, emigres, Carib, English," who takes her place alongside déclassés "who easily could have hated her." Made up of "many bits and pieces," Clare's hybrid identity is itself mediated by a double structure. On the surface, Clare's colonial education in Jamaica and the freedom with which she has traveled, spending her formative years in America with her father before moving to England, her "mother country," to pursue a degree in Renaissance art, provide her with all the glaring signs of neocolonial privilege that we have seen elsewhere. They do not sit well with the idea that she might champion the cause and revolution of the underclass. However, a closer scrutiny of Clare's painful navigation of the straits of identity and history shows what R. Radhakrishnan would call "forms of self-consciencization," a practice of "self de- and re-identification, a deracinated consciousness." Cliff, in *Claiming an Identity They Taught Me to Despise,* makes a point that calls to mind the travails of Clare Savage. Cliff notes that "the question of my identity is partly a question of color: of my right to name myself. That is what I have felt all along." Although light-skinned, Clare faces discrimination and racism when her father places her in a school in New York. Mrs. Taylor, the principal, tells her father that "'foreign students begin a year behind so they [won't] get lost.'" She further adds that "'children from underdeveloped countries develop at a different rate than American children. Believe me, it's for the girl's own good.'" Mrs. Taylor stands by her decision in spite of Boy Savage's protest that his daughter is already well versed in Latin, French, and Greek. Troubled by Clare's hybrid racial identity, which fails to conform to biological topologies of "pure" race difference between whites and blacks, Mrs. Taylor makes a racist remark deriving straight from her incapacity to contain the inexorably shifting and multiple discourse of race. Referring to her spuriously scientific physician husband, Mrs. Taylor says to Boy Savage, "'He would call you White chocolate. . . . I mean, have you ever seen a child's expression when he finds a white chocolate bunny in his Easter basket? He simply doesn't understand . . . he thinks it strange. I do not want to be cruel, Mr. Savage, but we have no room for lies in our system. No place for in-betweens.'"

The racism Clare faces in England while studying for her master's degree is no better. During a seminar on the "hermetic tradition," the class as a whole hears "Chants. Shouts. Noise slamming against the glass of the well-appointed, high-ceilinged room. KAFFIRS! NIGGERS! WOGS! PAKIS! GET OUT! A banner—white bedsheet with black paint—went past. KEEP BRITAIN WHITE!" Vivienne Hogg-Hunter, a fellow student, commenting on the demonstration, has this to say to Clare at recess: "'I say, those nignogs are a witty lot.'" Clare in indignation turns to the woman and suggests softly, "'Why don't you go fuck yourself.'" The issue arises again when Liz, another fellow student, tries to separate Clare from the other blacks. "'I mean,'" says Liz, "'you are hardly the sort they were ranting on about.'" Although Clare uses shock to end the racist conversation, "'some of my ancestors were Caribs . . . cannibals,'" her comment cuts both ways and shows how Clare is implicated in the very outrage she also protests against. The context in which she speaks, in the library looking down and outside into the street, shows her three-way separation, by race, education, and class, from the working class.

Gendered Body as Nation and Nation as Gendered Body?

Divided by race, class, and nationality, Clare's fragmented identity is nowhere more excruciatingly written than on the surface of the body. She meets head on with the contradictions within her when she becomes pregnant with Bobby's baby. Because of Agent Orange, Bobby has a cancerous wound that drips yellowness "from a bright pink gap—no matter what Clare did." A facile reading would urge us to see Bobby's never-healing wound as a polyvalent metaphor not only for Clare's sterility after her miscarriage but also for the Jamaican land itself, particularly Clare's Nanny's land, which turns into a "ruinate." "Implicit in the metaphor of land-as-woman," Annette Kolodny explains in a work that

explores the exploitation of the American Western frontier [*The Lay of the Land*], "was both the regressive pull of maternal containment and the seductive invitation to sexual assertion," a statement that applies equally well to Jamaica. Cliff refuses to essentialize and equate the body of Clare with Jamaica as motherland/land-as-woman or vice versa. In fact, a reductive reading can draw close parallels between Jamaica's uncertainty and fragility as a nation-state and Clare's girlfriend, Harry/Harriet, a medical officer and formerly a nurse at Kingston Hospital and the mobilizing force behind the revolution. The central question to pose is whether Harry/Harriet, who is variously described by an "old woman, one who kenned Harriet's history," as "Mawu-Lisa, moon and sun, female-male deity of some of their [native] ancestors," is, like Clare, a metaphor for Jamaica. Is there an analogy between Jamaica's struggle to carve out an identity and Harry/Harriet's struggle to negotiate between the oppositional and split gendered identities designated by the names Harry and Harriet? Raped at ten by a white man in a "khaki uniform" in the service of "Her Majesty," Harry/Harriet refuses to blame her gender trouble on the white man's "brutishness": "'No, man, that t'ing didn't make me who I am. Didn't form me in all my complexity.'" Besides militating against the authority of biological determinism, Harry/Harriet reaffirms, to use the terms of Judith Butler's argument, that gender is not fundamentally an interior state but a performative act, that "gender is always a doing, though not a doing by a subject who might be said to preexist the deed." Harry/Harriet's narrative speaks against the facile gesture of allegorizing his/her fate, any more than Clare's miscarriage, as the fate of Jamaica. Cliff's heteroglot narrative does not tell a tale of narrow, individual angst, with all its attendant psychologizing and interiority; rather, it constitutes a polycentric world based on the plural *social discourse* of *the communitas*.

Cliff frustrates our easy coddling of what Paul Gilroy would call "ethnic insiderism" by shifting the focus of the novel from essentialized, fixed subject positions to multiple and even contradictory subject positions. However, in sharp contrast to some versions of postmodernism, Cliff's interest is not so much in uncritically orchestrating and celebrating access to multiple subjectivities as in exposing how subject positions in different geographical locations and historical moments produce and legitimate different social locations, different social discourses, and vice versa.

Indeed, to that very end Cliff elaborates how the wishes of subalterns must be stifled and exorcised in order to facilitate the production of ethical citizen-subjects whose desires are subordinated to the higher demands of the abstract "imagined community." In one of her last letters to Clare, Kitty Savage writes, "I hope some day you make something of yourself, and someday help your people . . . your responsibilities lie beyond me, beyond yourself. There is a space between who you are and who you will become. Fill it." This is precisely the in-between or interstitial space that becomes the locus for Clare's rewriting of her history from a postcolonial perspective. Armed with a burning desire to fill that gap Clare promptly returns to Jamaica. Unlike Harriet, who realizes that she "'cyaan live split'" and finally makes an ethical choice to live as Harriet and "'Harry be no more,'" Clare has a tougher road ahead of her before she can fulfill her mother's dream for her. While Harriet had been studying the "healing practices" both at the university and with "old women in the country, women who knew the properties of roots and leaves," Clare had been, as Harriet puts it, "'dragging her ass through parts unknown'" in Europe. The difficult task of "unthinking" the Eurocentric side of her education, an education that cannot help, in the fine formulation of Sandra Harding, but leave its "social fingerprints on the picture of the world," can only begin from the small steps that Clare takes to view the world not from the dominant perspective but by looking, in Harding's words, to "the lives of those who have been devalued, neglected, excluded from the center of the social order; . . . who provide perspectives from the other side of racial struggles; who enable a different perspective, one from everyday life; . . . and whose activities provide particularly illuminating understandings at this moment in history." Clare marks her homecoming with a pledge to educate schoolchildren about the "history of their . . . our homeland"; a history which can be found "underwater." Clare also realizes (and herein lies her process of deracination) that "the history I have learned . . . rather, recognized . . . since my return is something else. I know only that the loss, the forgetting . . . of resistance . . . of tenderness . . . is a terrible thing."

The Enthographer's Gaze, Hollywood Film, and Visual-Cultural Violence

Perhaps the key question to ask toward the end of Cliff's novel is why the insurgency that ought to be aimed against the neocolonial government is instead planned against a joint film company from Britain and the United States. Far from being facetious, the revolutionaries' proposed attack on the film crew strikes at the heart of the violence of visual culture, the ethnographer's violence of representing the other as History. Indeed, as the "contemporary heir of a more ancient visual medium: cartography," and I would add print capitalism, "the beginnings of cinema," in the apt words of Ella Shohat and Robert Stam, "coincided with the giddy heights of the imperial project, with an epoch where Europe held sway over vast tracts of alien territory and hosts of subjugated peoples." Michelle Cliff's strategic objective in depicting the methods of one mode of representation (film) within another (the novel) in her last chapter; appropriately titled "Film Noir," is not to mediate between the two genres as is common in classic Hollywood films but to use one to provide a "cut" or temporal break to bring the order of rep-

resentation of the other to crisis. Put differently, the jostling and colliding of the two genres in Cliff's narrative produces not familiarity or a naturalization of received social meanings but, entirely to the contrary, a defamiliarization that opens up a space for the production of antihegemonic new knowledges and new social locations.

Michelle Cliff does not begin this process by providing a neatly packaged summary of the film's plot. Instead, she takes the reader painstakingly through the nuts and bolts of the making of the film, unmasking the imperial modes of its production. Unlike James Clifford, for instance, who as "participant observer" practices an enlightened academic ethnography, the Eurocentric filmmakers don't even maintain a sanctimonious pretense of "gathering up" and memorializing the last vestiges of the valuable, and vanishing, primitive culture they are filming. Their objective, in other words, is not to problematize the representation of the scarce Coromantee people but to commodify them. A fancy Hollywood story line focuses on the romance of "Nanny, the Coromantee warrior," and Cudjoe, who rescues Nanny just in time from the monster played by Christopher, who is also called De Watchman after a reggae song that speaks of violent, revolutionary upheaval. Lost in this gross commercialization is the real history of the native Jamaican Nanny, "leader of the Windward Maroons, whom one book described as an old woman naked except for a necklace made from the teeth of whitemen—sent by the orishas to deliver her people." The English filmmaker does not shrink from blaspheming and distorting the indigenous story in his efforts to create the illusion of a French Mediterranean beach in Jamaica. But "all the black bums on the beach" stand in his way. His American counterpart, according to whom "'Jamaicans will do anything for a buck,'" clears them away with a little help from the almighty American Dollar. Having been warned by a traitor of the revolutionaries' planned attack, the British-American film crew are prepared to crush the insurgency. Clare Savage and Harriet, unaware of the traitor among them, lie in wait, "as silent as Maroons," for the ambush in a bitterbush as the shooting of the film begins.

In keeping with mainstream cinema's obsessive concern with establishing the "authenticity" of its narrative—a process that in fact serves to camouflage the inscription and production of stratified knowledge and absolute racial and cultural differences—the filmmakers choose not a seasoned actor but De Watchman, existing on the margins of society, to play the role of the savage: "'You look pretty good to me. Can you howl?'" asks the English director of the film. About the figure that De Watchman cut in a local rum shop the narrative has this to say: "[He was] draped in his split crocus sack, snake-haired. . . . The man's stench began to fill the tiny establishment, and the two white men edged back as far as they could." Furthering the desired goal to "make it real!" a woman whose racial identity is unknown but who nonetheless has been called upon in the past to play "any Black heroine, whether Sojourner Truth or Bessie Smith," is now commissioned to play the role of Nanny. In an equally stereotypical way, the role of Cudjoe goes to a "strapping man" who could well be a "former heavyweight or running back."

Despite the film crew's compulsive attention to caricatural details, things go horribly awry. What the Third World film producers and critics Kobena Mercer and Isaac Julien call "representation as a practice of depicting" (merely saturation with descriptive details) is interrupted and transformed by De Watchman's howl, a howl that goes beyond his assigned scripted role to become instead "representation as a practice of delegation" (which historicizes who speaks, how, and in what context). The instructions given to Christopher are easy enough, but at the performative and enunciative levels the filmmakers have no control over the tide of signification they unleash: "'Howl! Howl! I want you to bellow as loud as you can. Try to wake the dead . . . Remember, you're not human. Action!'"

We may recall Paul's controlling gaze whose reduction of the other-as-image was frustrated by what Rey Chow defines as a "form of evidence-cum-witness." Here once again, the eye/gaze of the camera captures a double signifying chain. Before Christopher's "bellows carrying into the darkening country" freeze into the image of a monster, the piercing howl activates the "simulation of the gaze" (in this case, the eye of the camera) that witnesses Christopher's "oppression prior to [his] becoming image"—and by extension that of all subalterns in Cliff's *No Telephone to Heaven.* The evidence-cum-witness shows for a brief moment the mythical transformation of Christopher into "the chaos of the forest god, until a new sound drowned him out." Subverting and transforming a series of oppositional binaries, something intervenes between symbol and sign, between Christopher as monster and Christopher as forest god, between representation as depiction and representation as delegation, between the genres of novel and film, between the Western visual violence of exoticizing the primitive and the counterviolence of the revolutionaries: it is the other narrative.

The double articulation of the gaze demonstrates the impossibility of cross-cultural translation, the failure of the dastardly process of reducing Christopher/De Watchman to the level of a monster. On a more interesting political level, the other narrative encountered here by the gaze—Christopher's transformation into forest god—cannot be read within the traditions of the Western novel as a form. Christopher the subaltern, at once an outcast/monster and a god, and Clare Savage the privileged landowner, an "outsider within" who painstakingly "reinvents herself as the Other," hail from two different and incompatible walks of life. They come together, however, in dying as they do in the fight for a more egalitarian and inclusive democratic society. Caught between rewriting a history that remains under water and wresting power for the people through revolutionary means, Clare and Christopher, like the rest of the makeshift insurrectionary army fall victim to counterrevolutionary gunfire in the "bitterbush." As David Lloyd in *Anomalous States* amply demonstrates, both Bakhtin's "heteroglossia" and Benedict Anderson's notion of the nation-state as an "imagined community" fall short of recognizing the bellicose voices of subalterns that "cannot be drawn into identity." Unleashed during the making of the Anglo-American film, those voices disrupt the internal diegesis of the narrative, leaving, in Lloyd's words, an "inassimilable residue that it can neither properly contain nor entirely exclude."

Such an intervention comes, in my view, from the maternal language—not an essentialized or mystified secret language, but a maternal discourse that constantly pokes holes in the symbolic structure of culture. At the liminal moment between life and death, when the itch for a positivistic definition of Jamaica is irretrievably lost in Cliff's shattering of the grammar of the Western novel, Clare hears that maternal language:

> Kitty-woo, kitty-woo, kitty-woo
> Whip-whip-whip-whip-whip-whip whip-whip-
>   whip-whip
> Back-raw, back-raw, back-raw, back-raw, back-raw
> She remembered language.
> Then it was gone.

The other narrative, suspended between Clare's life and death, has no subject (in the guise of an imperial I/Eye), no predicate, not even the comfort of a punctuating period allowing us to gather up and master the dispersed shards of meaning retroactively. Whichever way we read, nonetheless, whether within the privileged terms of the novel or within the unspeakable horror of the subaltern, that narrative has meaning all right. That meaning resides in an unspeakable horror that tenaciously clings to the body of the text like mushroom dust: it is history as trauma and trauma as history.

FURTHER READING

Criticism

Clarke, Roger. "Beneath the Mask." *New Statesman & Society* 3, No. 87 (9 February 1990): 36.
    Finds *Bodies of Water* "breathtakingly good," noting the stories's cinematic qualities.

Johnson, George. A review of *No Telephone to Heaven* by

Michelle Cliff. *New York Times Book Review* (19 March 1989): 32.

    Brief notice likening the novel's use of Jamaican slang to lyric poetry.

Levy, Francis. Review of *Abeng* by Michelle Cliff. *New York Times Book Review* (25 March 1984): 20.

    Detects "narrative inconsistencies" but concedes that Cliff's "pithy anecdotal descriptions . . . bring Jamaica's present and past to life."

Meade, Marion. Review of *Abeng* by Michelle Cliff. *Ms.* XIII, No. 1 (July 1984): 32.

    Succinctly summarizes the main themes of the novel, noting the "sophisticated and complex" meanings attached to shades of skin color in Jamaican culture.

Ratner, Rochelle. Review of *Claiming an Identity They Taught Me to Despise* by Michelle Cliff. *Library Journal* 106, No. 2 (15 January 1981): 151.

    Describes the organization and content of the "powerful" collection.

Spurling, John. "Shame about the Jackets." *Observer* (7 February 1988): 25.

    Concise outline of *No Telephone to Heaven,* commenting on its tone and style.

Additional coverage of Cliff's life and career is contained in the following sources published by Gale: *Black Literature Criticism Supplement; Black Writers,* **Vol. 2;** *Contemporary Authors,* **Vol. 116;** *Contemporary Authors New Revision Series,* **Vols. 39, 72;** *Dictionary of Literary Biography,* **Vol. 157.**

Louise Erdrich
1954-

American novelist, short story writer, poet, memoirist, children's fiction writer, and juvenile fiction writer.

The following entry presents an overview of Erdrich's career through 1996. For further information on her life and works, see *CLC*, Vols. 39 and 54.

INTRODUCTION

In her fiction and poetry, Erdrich draws upon her Chippewa heritage to examine complex familial and sexual relationships among midwestern Native Americans and their conflicts with white communities. Her eccentric characters attain mythic stature as they struggle to overcome isolation, abandonment, and exploitation. Jean Strouse has observed of Erdrich: "Her sure sense of the way people think and talk keeps it hard to remember she is making them all up, and her lithe, athletic prose makes wildly improbable events seem as natural as the weather."

Biographical Information

Erdrich was born in Little Falls, Minnesota, in 1954. Both of her parents, Ralph and Rita Erdrich, worked with the Bureau of Indian Affairs. Erdrich received her Bachelor's degree from Dartmouth College in 1976 and her Master's degree from Johns Hopkins University in 1977. In 1981 Erdrich married Michael Dorris, with whom she had six children (one of whom, Reynold Abel, died in 1991). A writer himself, Dorris frequently worked with Erdrich in developing stories until his death in 1997, and the two cowrote a novel, *The Crown of Columbus* (1991). Erdrich has taught poetry with the North Dakota State Arts Council and creative writing at Johns Hopkins University and has been a visiting fellow at Dartmouth College. Her fiction has garnered a Nelson Algren Award, a National Book Critics Circle Award, and a *Los Angeles Times* Book Award.

Major Works

Erdrich's first published volume, *Jacklight* (1984), is a collection of poems that garnered praise for infusing everyday situations with mythic qualities. Her first novel, *Love Medicine* (1984), for which she won the National Book Critics Circle Award, gathers fourteen interconnected stories related by seven different members of the Kashpaw and Lamartine families of the Turtle Mountain Chippewa community in North Dakota. In *The Beet Queen* (1986) Erdrich continued

her portrait of Turtle Mountain Chippewa but shifted her focus to the community outside the reservation. In *Tracks* (1988) a Chippewa elder and an abusive young female of white and Indian heritage relate the exploits of Fleur Pillager, a destructive yet magical woman who is an ancestor of several characters from *Love Medicine*. Characters from the first three novels recur in *The Bingo Palace* (1994) and *Tales of Burning Love* (1996), which again use multiple narrators and elements of magical realism to tell the stories of those living on and around the Turtle Mountain reservation. In 1993 Erdrich published an expanded edition of *Love Medicine*, adding different perspectives on the original story and dealing with different members of the families and those surrounding them. In *The Crown of Columbus* (1991) Erdrich and her husband Michael Dorris discuss historical inaccuracies in the story of Christopher Columbus and the impact of these inaccuracies on native peoples. In *The Blue Jay's Dance* (1995) Erdrich covered more personal ground, writing about the effect of motherhood on her work and her relation to the world around her.

Critical Reception

While some critics find Erdrich's use of multiple narrators and her return to the same characters in different novels to be unnecessarily confusing and her use of mythic allusions and elements of magical realism to be contrived, most applaud her unflinching portrayal of contemporary Native American life. Many commentators note that the large number of influential Indian women in her fiction and her exploration of the disparities between institutional and indigenous history cements her as one of the most important voices in contemporary Native American literature.

PRINCIPAL WORKS

Imagination (textbook) 1980
Jacklight (poetry) 1984
Love Medicine (novel) 1984; expanded edition, 1993
The Beet Queen (novel) 1986
Tracks (novel) 1988
Baptism of Desire (poetry) 1989
The Crown of Columbus [with Michael Dorris] (novel) 1991
The Bingo Palace (novel) 1994
The Blue Jay's Dance: A Birth Year (memoir) 1995
Tales of Burning Love (novel) 1996
Grandmother's Pigeon (children's fiction) 1996
The Antelope Wife: A Novel (novel) 1998
The Birchbark House (juvenile fiction) 1999

CRITICISM

Peter Stitt (review date Winter 1984)

SOURCE: Review of *Jacklight,* in *The Georgia Review,* Vol. XXXVIII, No. 4, Winter 1984, pp. 863-64.

[*In the following excerpt, Stitt examines the mythic patterns explored in* Jacklight.]

In *Jacklight,* her first book, Louise Erdrich arrives at an understanding of the modern world by discovering patterns within the experience she studies—mythic patterns derived from her own Native American background. The poems are narrative in structure, benefiting from a strong sense of both place and character. The poem **"Train,"** for example, expresses the sense of self which determines the speaker's progress through the world:

> Tunnels that the body strikes open in air.
> Bridges that shiver across
> every water I come to.
> And always the light

I was born with, driving everything before it.

The basic metaphor is technological, of course, and explained by the poem's title. But the underlying definition of self, the idea that calls up the metaphor in the first place, is the same notion that determines the plot of Ruth Bebe Hill's novel *Hanta-Yo.*

Mythic narrative, character, and setting—the building blocks of much good fiction—are of course not enough for the making of good poetry. At her best, Louise Erdrich combines these with an exciting sense of language to produce poems like **"Rugaroo"**—probably the best in the book. It opens with this arresting character sketch:

> He was the man who drank Vitalis
> and sat up all night
> with the mud puppies in the woodwork,
> with the lights on in every room,
> with the television, with the tap running,
> with the fan blowing, with the icebox
> sagged open, with the secondhand vacuum cleaner
> sucking air.
>
> . . . . .
>
> All night you could hear him in the woods
> coughing feathers.
> Next morning he sat across from you pouring
>   syrup
> down his jacket.
> His feet were the burnt stubs of brooms.

The images are pointed, striking, revealing both of personality and plot. The poem ends mythically, with this character being absorbed at his death into the surrounding environment. Thus the "you" of the poem, the sensibility most at issue here, will never be able to escape him:

> He was the man who couldn't sleep.
> He went down into the cellar
> And ate raw potatoes.
> He blew up with gas.
> And now he is the green light floating over the
>   slough.
> He is the one in the cattails at the edge of your
>   dream.
> He is the man who will not let you sleep.

In its liveliness, its way of investing the ordinary world with the magic of received mythology, the poem is typical of many in the book. Unfortunately, one whole section of the volume is given over to a sequence called "The Butcher's Wife," poems which are as literal in their declarations and imagery as they are prosaic in style. Except for this lapse, however, *Jacklight* is a striking and entertaining first book.

Russell Banks (review date 1 November 1986)

SOURCE: "Border Country," in *The Nation*, Vol. 243, No. 14, November 1, 1986, pp. 460-63.

[*In the following review, Banks asserts that* The Beet Queen, *in its best sections, rivals the novels of Charles Dickens in socially conscious storytelling.*]

The Beet Queen is a Dickensian story, an angry comedy about abandonment and survival, pluck and luck (ambition and coincidence), common sense and pretension, and wise children and foolish adults. The book is structured in an almost classical manner. It opens with a sudden, unpredictable disaster that tosses an ordered world into terrible disarray. It then follows the paths of the half-dozen affected lives through three generations of small triumphs and reversals, long digressions and quick returns, until at last, in a ceremonial event that reunites and reorders the scattered elements of the tale into symmetrical, benign relations, it circles back to where it began, with everything the same only different—which in classical comedy, as in Dickens, is almost always the point. It's a form that in the hands of lesser artists than Louise Erdrich often affirms the status quo and lends itself to sentimentality. When, however, the story is played against a view of history in which decent folks are victimized not by their dopey and amusing gullibility but by economic and social forces too powerful to overcome with wile or guile, then the story has a divine rage, and one sees the radical power of the old form renewed.

The story of *The Beet Queen* is the story of the entwined fates of three generations of women whose men orbit around them like distant planets, necessary to the system as a whole but taking all their heat and most of their momentum from the women at the center. The book is divided into sixteen chapters narrated by the main characters and covering four decades in the lives of Mary Adare, one of the most memorable women in recent American fiction; her beleaguered mother, Adelaide; her narcissistic cousin, Sita Kozka; her lifelong friend, the half-Chippewa Celestine James; and Celestine's daughter, Dot. There are three men of note—Mary's older brother Karl, who fathers Dot; Dot's godfather, Wallace Pfef; and Celestine's half brother Russell Kashpaw, a shattered war hero. There is also Omar, a barnstorming stunt pilot, who, in the opening chapter, flies off with Adelaide, permitting her to abandon her three children on the fairgrounds below. This is the desperate, sad act that initiates the tangled actions of the book.

Several minor characters from the author's first novel, *Love Medicine,* pop up in *The Beet Queen,* and the setting is essentially the same as in that book—the flat, sparsely populated farm country where eastern North Dakota turns into western Minnesota, the literal and figurative border country where Chippewa tribal lands and lives grind against the land and lives of small-time white farmers, who in turn are swallowed by agribusiness. Erdrich sets her fiction squarely in the tense zone where races, cultures, languages, technologies and classes clash and overlap. Like most good fiction writers, she lives year-round in border country.

The Beet Queen is the second of a projected quartet of books dealing with the same cluster of families and events. *Love Medicine,* widely praised for its energy, inventiveness and compassion, was focused more directly on the lives of the Indians, and might for that reason seem more explicitly political than its successor. Yet it's evident from *The Beet Queen* that Erdrich has quite as much compassion for the white inhabitants of the small town of Argus, North Dakota, and environs as for the Chippewas. Employing exquisite irony, she dramatizes the empty inner life of a small-town booster by letting him speak for himself:

> I'm Wallace Pfef. Chamber of commerce, Sugar Beet Promoters, Optimists, Knights of Columbus, park board, and other organizations too numerous to mention. In addition to supporting the B# Piano Club and managing the town swimming pool, I am the one who is bringing beets to the valley, beets that have yet to fail as a cash crop anywhere, beets that will make refined white sugar every bit as American as corn on the cob.
>
> There has been resistance to my proposition, and why not? Agronomists value cyclical regularities. They are suspicious of innovation, and my business is courting change. To woo them, I've become the friend to agricultural co-ops and visited each area farmer individually. I've drunk sloe gin and schnapps and nameless basement brews. In town I've joined up with a vengeance, for I know that within the fraternal order lies power. Eagles, Moose, Kiwanis, Elk. I need to belong. I've gained a hundred ears, pumped hands, exchanged secret passwords with my brothers. I've told them how beets are much more than a simple crop. They are the perfect marriage between nature and technology. Like crude oil, the beet needs refining, and that means Refinery. That spells local industry. Everyone benefits.

There is a Bruegel-like realism to *The Beet Queen*—crisply articulated details on the surface of figures and landscapes arranged as deliberately as a bowl of fruit—that affirms the presence of moral intent and suggests the immanence of moral truth. One attends to the story the way one attends to a Gothic fairy tale, full of sudden, unexpected turns and gory surprises. Indeed, there are a few too many allusions to fairy tales in the book, making one a little more conscious of the act of reading than one needs to be. This is not a self-reflexive tale and we ought not be distracted from the business at hand.

Briefly, the story begins when the respectable, married, bourgeois lover of the poor but beautiful, and pregnant, Adelaide Adare dies, abandoning her and their two children, Karl and Mary, to abject poverty (it's 1932, the worst of the Depression). Fleeing Argus for Minneapolis, where things only get worse, Adelaide takes her children to the fairgrounds one day and, as if on impulse, flies off with a barnstormer in his plane. Eleven-year-old Mary says, "Our longing buried us. We sank down on her bed and cried, wrapped in her quilt, clutching each other. When that was done, however, I acquired a brain of ice." It's her brain of ice that saves her and gets her back to Argus, where she is taken in by her aunt and uncle and gradually, after much suffering, makes a life for herself. Her brother Karl, a more fragile soul than she, ends up as a traveling salesman forever on the move. When he takes stock of his life he sounds like one of Sam Shepard's alienated Westerners:

> I sat there drinkless and coatless, my hat on, my keys dangling off a ring, until the sky turned orange and one by one the neon signs around the place flashed in bows and zippers. They were just moving figures. Nothing around me spoke. And as I sat there and the shadows gathered and the lizards scraped along the tiles, I made less and less sense, too, until I made none at all. I was part of the senseless landscape. A pulse, a strip, of light.
>
> I give nothing, take nothing, mean nothing, hold nothing.

Years pass quickly in this book. The chapters are alternately narrated by each of the main characters in a voice that belongs simultaneously to the character and to an impersonal, overseeing consciousness, so that the voices seem to blend, as in a chorus, without ever losing their remarkable individuality. Erdrich has been able to give each of her characters their own tone, diction, pitch and rhythm, without letting go of her own. The effect is to deprive the book of a single hero, one character against whom all the others are defined, and to replace it with something like a community. Although this was also true of **Love Medicine,** it is more successful in **The Beet Queen,** where the multiple voices are orchestrated more elegantly and the structure of the narrative is more rigorously formal. A number of recent books with similar ambitions come to mind—Carolyn Chute's *The Beans of Egypt, Maine,*

Joan Chase's *During the Reign of the Queen of Persia,* John Edgar Wideman's *Damballah,* for instance. It's as if these authors have chosen to eschew, on principle, a single central consciousness—an individualized sympathetic norm that, like the reader's consciousness, has found itself set in the center of a world gone wacky—and have instead attempted to make a family or a village or tribe, that is, a people, into the protagonist. They seem to be struggling to discover, or perhaps rediscover, a narrative form equal to a social and political vision radically different from the one we inherited from the modernists. Such books are proposing profound changes in the way we read fiction and, as a consequence, in how we see the world.

Louise Erdrich with Joseph Bruchac (interview date 1987)

SOURCE: "Whatever Is Really Yours," in *Survival This Way: Interviews with American Indian Poets,* Sun Tracks and the University of Arizona Press, 1987, pp. 73-86.

[*In the following interview, Erdrich discusses her process of writing and storytelling and emphasizes the importance of her heritage in her work.*]

It was a sunny day in New Hampshire when Louise Erdrich and her younger sister, Heidi Erdrich, a student in Creative Writing at Dartmouth, met me at the airport. We drove to the house her sister was subletting from Cleopatra Mathis, a poet and teacher at Dartmouth. Louise and I sat out on the back deck above a field where apple trees were swelling toward blossom, two horses moved lazily about their corral, and we could see the hills stretching off to the east. Louise is a striking woman, slender with long brown hair. She is surprisingly modest—even a bit shy—for one whose early accomplishments are so impressive: a powerful first book of poetry from a major publisher, a first novel which won critical acclaim, a National Book Critics Circle Prize, and the Los Angeles Times Book Prize in 1985. But as we spoke, her voice was clear and her convictions as strong as those of any of the complex white, Indian, and mixed-blood characters who populate her work and her memories.

[*Joseph Bruchac:*] *That poem* [*"***Indian Boarding School: The Runaways***"*] *is among the ones I like best of yours. It does two things I see as characteristic of your work—juxtaposes the two worlds and also hints at a natural unity which is broken yet hovering somewhere in the background. Why did you choose to read that particular poem?*

[Louise Erdrich:] It might be something as simple as that the rhythm is something I like. Probably I chose it because I've been thinking about it on the way over here because it's the one I knew by heart and it started me back on remembering when it was written and the place where I grew up.

I like the rhythm, but the subject matter, too, has a special meaning.

It does, even though I never ran away. I was too chicken, too docile as a kid, but lots of other kids did. This, though, is a particular type of running away. It's running home; it's not running away from home. The kids who are talking in this poem are children who've been removed from their homes, their cultures, by the Bureau of Indian Affairs or by any sort of residential school or church school. Many kinds of schools were set up to take Indian children away from their culture and parents and loved ones and re-acculturate them. So, it is about the hopelessness of a child in that kind of situation. There is no escape. The sheriff is always waiting at midrun to take you back. It's a refrain and it's certainly the way things were for a long time. I guess now that the boarding schools have finally started serving a positive purpose, the current Administration wants to cut them. They're finally schools that can take in children who have nowhere else to go. They do serve some purpose, but naturally they are threatened. It's just a damn shame.

It seems to me, too, to be a metaphor for the things that are happening with American Indian writing and culture in general. People have been dragged into the twentieth century, European/American culture and frame of mind and running away from that means running not away, but back.

Yes, running home. That's true. I have a very mixed background and *my* culture is certainly one that includes German and French and Chippewa. When I look back, running home might be going back to the butcher shop. I really don't control the subject matter, it just takes me. I believe that a poet or a fiction writer is something like a medium at a seance who lets the voices speak. Of course, a person has to study and develop technical expertise. But a writer can't control subject and background. If he or she is true to what's happening, the story will take over. It was, in fact, hard for me to do that when stories started being written that had to do with the Chippewa side of the family because I just didn't feel comfortable with it for a long time. I didn't know what to make of it being so strong. It took a while to be comfortable and just say, "I'm not going to fight it." **"Runaways"** is one of the first poems that came out of letting go and just letting my own background or dreams surface on the page.

In my own case, being of mixed ancestry, I'm sometimes surprised how strongly those voices speak from that small percentage of my ancestry which is American Indian. That seems to be true of many other mixed-blood writers of your age and my age, that for some reason that's the strongest and most insistent voice.

I think that's because that is the part of you that is culturally different. When you live in the mainstream and you know that you're not quite, not really there, you listen for a voice to direct you. I think, besides that, you also are a member of another nation. It gives you a strange feeling, this dual citizenship. So, in a way it isn't surprising that's so strong. As a kid I grew up not thinking twice about it, everybody knowing you were a mixed-blood in town. You would go to the reservation to visit sometimes and sometimes you'd go to your other family. It really was the kind of thing you just took for granted.

One reason I like **Jacklight** *so much is that it does deal with both sides of your family—the sections in the butcher shop are very real. They're no less strong than the sections which take place on the Turtle Mountain Reservation. When did you first begin to write, to write poetry or to write anything?*

Well, my Dad used to pay me. Ever so often he'd pay me a nickel for a story. So I started a long time ago. Both my Mom and Dad were encouraging, incredibly encouraging. I had that kind of childhood where I didn't feel art was something strange. I felt that it was good for you to do it. I kept it up little by little until I got out of college and decided, this great romantic urge, that I was going to be a writer no matter what it cost. I told myself I would sacrifice all to be a writer. I really didn't sacrifice a lot, though. (laughs) I took a lot of weird jobs which were good for the writing. I worked at anything I could get and just tried to keep going until I could support myself through writing or get some kind of grant. Just live off this or that as you go along. I think I turned out to be tremendously lucky. Once I married Michael, we began to work together on fiction. Then it began to be a full-time job. It's a great thing, a miracle for a writer to be able to just *write*.

That's something seldom talked about, those persons who enable you to be a writer. It's very hard when you're on your own to devote yourself completely to writing, even part-time.

Michael and I are truly collaborators in all aspects of writing and life. It's very hard to separate the writing and the family life and Michael and I as people. He's also a novelist and has just finished his first novel. It's called *A Yellow Raft in Blue Water* and it's in the voices of three women; a young girl, her mother, and the grandmother speak. Very beautiful—and unusual, intriguing, interesting for a man to write in women's voices. I think it is because he was raised only by women.

The male voices in **Love Medicine** *are very strong and legitimate. The book ends with a male voice.*

Yes. I don't know why that is, but they just seem to be. You don't choose this. It just comes and grabs and you have to follow it.

In one of your poems, "Turtle Mountain Reservation," I notice how strong your grandfather is, how strong his voice is. A storytelling voice, a voice connected to the past in such ways that some people may think him a little crazy—in the poem Ira thinks he is nuts. I wonder if that voice of your grandfather's has made you appreciate more and relate more to the voices of your male characters?

He's kind of a legend in our family. He is funny, he's charming, he's interesting. He, for many years, was a very strong figure in my life. I guess I idolized him. A very intelligent man. He was a Wobbly and worked up and down the wheat fields in North Dakota and Kansas. He saw a lot of the world. He did a lot of things in his life and was always very outspoken. Politically he was kind of a right-winger sometimes, people might say. I think he gave Tricia Nixon an Anishinabe name, for publicity. I always loved him and when you love someone you try to listen to them. Their voice then comes through.

His voice is a combination of voices, too. He can both be in the Bingo Parlor and then speaking old Chippewa words that no one but he remembers.

I think this is true of a lot of our older people. People who aren't familiar with Indians go out to visit and they can't believe that there's somebody sitting in a lawn chair who's an Indian. It's kind of incomprehensible that there's this ability to take in non-Indian culture and be comfortable in both worlds. I recently came from Manitoulin Island, a beautiful place. People are quite traditional and keep a lot of the old, particularly the very old crafts. There is a great quill-work revival. I don't know if you're familiar with the kind of quill-working done up in Ontario, but this is really the center for it. But people live, even there, incorporating any sort of non-Indian thing into their lives to live comfortably. That's one of the strengths of Indian culture, that you pick and choose and keep and discard. But it is sometimes hard because you want some of the security of the way things were. It's not as easy to find the old as it is to find the new.

In the poem "Whooping Cranes," legend-time and modern times come together, when an abandoned boy turns into a whooping crane. There's a sort of cross-fertilization of past and present in legend.

And natural history. The cranes cross over the Turtle Mountains on their way down to Aransas, Texas. We always used to hear how they'd see the cranes pass over. No more, though. I don't know if they still fly that way or not.

In some of Leslie Silko's work you see that mixing of times.

Someone may go out in a pickup truck and meet a figure out of myth.

Don't you, when you go on Indian land, feel that there's more possibility, that there is a whole other world besides the one you can see and that you're very close to it?

Very definitely. Crossing the border of a reservation is always entering another world, an older and more complicated world. How do you feel when you go back to Turtle Mountain?

I feel so comfortable. I really do. I even feel that way being in North Dakota. I really like that openness. But there's a kind of feeling at Turtle Mountain—I guess just *comfortable* is the word to describe it. There are also places there which are very mysterious to me. I don't know why. I feel they must have some significance. Turtle Mountain is an interesting place. It hasn't been continuously inhabited by the Turtle Mountain Band. It was one of those nice grassy, game-rich places that everybody wanted. So it was Sioux, it was Mitchiff, it was Chippewa. They are a soft, rolling group of hills, not very high, little hills—not like these (gestures toward mountains)—and there were parts that my grandfather would point out. The shapes were called this or that because they resembled a beaver or whatever kind of animal. He even incorporated the highways into the shapes because some of them got their tails cut off. (laughs) Even that people can deal with. Not always, though. There are many places that are certainly of religious significance that can never be restored or replaced, so I don't want to make light of it.

As in the Four Corners area.

Yes, I was thinking of Black Mesa. In the case of those hills at Turtle Mountain, there was that resilience because they were places which had a name, but not places—such as Black Mesa—much more vital to a culture and a religion. Catholicism is very important up there at Turtle Mountain. When you go up there, you go to Church! My grandfather has had a real mixture of old time and church religion—which is another way of incorporating. He would do pipe ceremonies for ordinations and things like that. He just had a grasp on both realities, in both religions.

I see that very much in your work. A lake may have a mythological being in it which still affects people's lives while the Catholic Church up on the hill is affecting them in a totally different way. Or you may have someone worrying about being drafted into the army at the same time he's trying to figure out how to make up love medicine—in a time when old ways of doing things have been forgotten. It seems similar, in a way, to Leslie Silko's Ceremony, where there is a need to make up new ceremonies because the old ones aren't working for the new problems, incorporating all kinds of things like phone books from different cities.

You may be right. I never thought about the similarity. This "love medicine" is all through the book, but it backfires on the boy who tries it out because he's kind of inept. It's funny what happens until it becomes tragic. But, if there is *any* ceremony which goes across the board and is practiced by lots and lots of tribal people, it is having a sense of humor about things and laughing. But that's not really what you're saying.

Maybe—maybe no.

Who knows? (laughs) Anyway, I don't deal much with religion except Catholicism. Although Ojibway traditional religion is flourishing, I don't feel comfortable discussing it. I guess I have my beefs about Catholicism. Although you never change once you're raised a Catholic—you've got that. You've got that symbolism, that guilt, you've got the whole works and you can't really change that. That's easy to talk about because you have to exorcise it somehow. That's why there's a lot of Catholicism in both books.

The second poem in **Jacklight** *is called "A Love Medicine."*

I was sort of making that poem up as a love medicine, as a sort of healing love poem. So, I suppose there are all kinds of love and ways to use poetry and that was what I tried to do with it.

There are several things I see in **Jacklight.** *One is an urge toward healing, a desire to ameliorate the pain, create something more balanced, even if it means facing difficult realities. Was that a conscious theme?*

I don't think any of it was very conscious. Poetry is a different process for me than writing fiction. Very little of what happens in poetry is conscious, it's a great surprise. I don't write poetry anymore. I've in some ways lost that ability. I've made my unconscious so conscious through repeated writing of stories that I don't seem to have this urge to let certain feelings build until they turn into a poem.

Another theme I see strongly in **Jacklight,** *and in all of your writing, is the theme of strong women who become more than what they seem to be. Transformations take place—in some cases, mythic transformations.*

That is true of women I have known. We are taught to present a demure face to the world and yet there is a kind of wild energy behind it in many women that *is* transformational energy, and not only transforming to them but to other people. When, in some of the poems, it takes the form of becoming an animal, that I feel is a symbolic transforma-

tion, the moment when a woman allows herself to act out of her own power. The one I'm thinking of is the bear poem.

That's a really wonderful four-part poem.

Oh, I'm so glad! But, you know, she's realizing her power. She's realizing she can say "No," which is something women are not taught to do, and that she can hit the sky like a truck if she wants. Yes, it's transformational. It goes through all of the work I've been doing lately. Part of it is having three daughters, I think, and having sisters. I have an urgent reason for thinking about women attuned to their power and their honest nature, not the socialized nature and the embarrassed nature and the nature that says, "I can't possibly accomplish this." Whatever happens to many young girls. It happens to boys, too. It happens to men, no question. In the book there are men—maybe not so much in the poetry, but in the fiction—like Lipsha, who begin to realize that they are truly strong and touch into their own strength. I think it's a process of knowing who you are. There's quest for one's own background in a lot of this work. It's hard not to realize what you're doing. And you say, "Funny thing, I have so many characters who are trying to search out their true background. What can this mean?" One of the characteristics of being a mixed-blood is searching. You look back and say, "Who am I from?" You must question. You must make certain choices. You're able to. And it's a blessing and it's a curse. All of our searches involve trying to discover where we are from.

It makes me think of Jim Welch's wonderful scene in Winter in the Blood *when that old man turns out to be his true grandfather.*

Oh yes, yes. Certainly.

In that same light, there's a similarity there with Leslie Silko, though I don't mean to imply that you've copied anything of hers.

No, no, that didn't even enter my head. She's working out of a whole different tribal background. She was a discovery for me in a particular way I don't think any other writer will ever be. I'm very attached to her work.

You don't write poetry now because you feel the conscious effort of writing prose makes it less available?

It sands away the unconscious. (laughs) You know, there's really not much down there. But what really sands away the unconscious is getting up in the middle of the night to rock your baby to sleep. When you live in isolation—I notice this whenever I leave—I dream poems. But when you get up at all hours feeding babies, you just don't have that kind of experience, you're just not able to let your unconscious work for you. However, I don't miss it. I'd rather have the kids than the tortured unconscious. Also, I have a very practical way of working. I just sit down and Michael works in one room and I work in the other and we just sit there as long as we can. I really have got more and more mundane about my work habits. There are times when I'm up at 4:30 and I feel like something extremely strange is about to happen— whether it's writing or not. Maybe I'm just crazy. But I sit down and, if something is there, it will be written. Usually, though, after the kids are taken care of, I try to write and very few poems come that way. Almost none. I maybe have three now since *Jacklight,* which I don't think I'll ever publish. Those poems now seem *so personal.* I just don't know if I can put them in a book again! (laughs)

I think you're tapping, though, the same sources for your prose that you've tapped for your poetry, even though the method may be different. I think the depth of experience, the types of metaphor, and the direction it goes are all on the same road.

I'm connected to the poems because you feel so protective toward your first outpourings. You want them to have some kind of continuity in their life. I think that is probably true. You can see the themes that were being worked with in *Jacklight* go on into the writing in other ways. The poem you mentioned, **"Family Reunion,"** turns into part of "Crown of Thorns" once it goes into the fiction. A lot of them do that. The next book, which is *The Beet Queen,* takes place in that sort of butcher shop world and incorporates people who are and are not in those poems. It's a very different book but also one which I think flows naturally out of both *Jacklight* and *Love Medicine.*

What years did you write the poems in **Jacklight***?*

All through '77 and '78. Then, once it was accepted to be published I wrote a few extra ones. I was so thrilled to be finally published. The manuscript went everywhere and I thought it would never be published. Then it was, and I was given this great boost. So I wrote some of the ones I really like, like the one about the bear and about living with Michael and the children, because I was so happy. I guess it was surprising. I thought I would live my whole life without being published and I wouldn't care, but as it turned out I was *really* happy.

When did you begin writing with Michael?

Once we were married. In '81. We began by just talking about the work, back and forth, reading it. He always—right at first before I got to know him—was the person I would go to with problems. I'd say, "Michael, should I get into teaching, should I quit writing? What should I do?" And he said to me, "Look, there's only one thing to do. Throw your-

self into your work. Don't take any more jobs." And I did it. I just tried what he said. (laughs) At times I found myself in some unpleasant monetary predicaments. But I've been lucky. I think it is because we started working together He had ideas for the whole structure of *Love Medicine* that became the book. We worked on it very intensely and closely, and I do the same with his work. We exchange this role of being the . . . there isn't even a word for it. We're collaborators, but we're also individual writers. One person sits down and writes the drafts. I sit down and write it by myself or he does, but there's so much more that bears on the crucial moment of writing. You know it, you've talked the plot over, you've discussed the characters. You've really come to some kind of an understanding that you wouldn't have done alone. I really think neither of us would write what we do unless we were together.

Didn't the genesis of **Love Medicine,** *"The World's Greatest Fisherman," come about that way. Michael saw the announcement of the Chicago Prize. . .*

Yes. Michael was flat on his back, sick, and he said, "Look, you've got to enter this! Get in there, write it!" And I did, brought it in and out to him, changed it around, together we finished it.

You have such a strong narrative line in all your work and stories seem so important to you, stories told by your characters in the poems, the stories of the poems themselves and then the structure of story in **Love Medicine,** *which is, in fact, many stories linked together. What is story to you?*

Everybody in my whole family is a storyteller, whether a liar or a storyteller (laughs)—whatever. When I think what's a story, I can hear somebody in my family, my Dad or my Mom or my Grandma, telling it. There's something particularly strong about *a told story.* You know your listener's right there, you've got to keep him hooked—or her. So, you use all those little lures: "And then . . .," "So the next day . . .," etc. There are some very nuts-and-bolts things about storytelling. It also is something you can't really put your finger on.

Why do you follow it? I know if there is a story. Then I just can't wait to get back to it and write it. Sometimes there isn't one, and I just don't want to sit down and force it. You must find that, too, because you tell a lot of stories.

Yes, there's something about a story that tells itself.

The story starts to take over if it is good. You begin telling, you get a bunch of situation characters, everything together, but if it's good, you let the story tell itself. You don't control the story.

Christopher Vecsey (review date 4 November 1988)

SOURCE: "Revenge of the Chippewa Witch," in *Commonweal,* Vol. CXV, No. 19, November 4, 1988, pp. 596-98.

[*In the following review, Vecsey dispels possible criticism of* Tracks *as stereotypical and improbable, instead positing that the novel's mythic elements bring American Indian history to life.*]

Tracks is Louise Erdrich's third novel of rural North Dakota. *Love Medicine* (1984) delineated a frayed line of Chippewa Indian lives in contemporary America. *The Beet Queen* (1986) portrayed a braid of their struggling, non-Indian neighbors of a generation or two ago. Both books were hung together by lyrical threads that highlighted and augmented the bleak and painful stuff of the stories wherein the lives of these peoples were intertwined. Both were masterworks.

Tracks brings the reader back to the early years of this century, 1912-1924, and it ties a knot of narrative around the previous novels. The style maintains the densely spiritual quality of her earlier work, resembling in some ways the "magical realism" of Gabriel García Márquez, and reveals some important history of the characters who people this rural world Ms. Erdrich is creating, or unraveling, before our eyes.

The narrative technique reveals the structure of the plot that in itself means to set forward the oppositional strands of twentieth-century Chippewa existence. Old Nanapush narrates half the chapters. Old Nanapush, named for the trickster-transformer of aboriginal Chippewa myth, upholder of the ancient, living traditions: the medicines, the hunting and trapping acumen, the land-related ethos, the familiar world view. Some might call him a liar like his namesake, but his lies and truths are tied and committed to ways that have served and survived the centuries' generations.

Pauline's chapters alternate with those of Nanapush. She is a half-breed. She lives for a time in the grubby Anglo town of Argus, away from the reservation. She returns, engages in lovemaking and love magic, receives or imagines a vision of the Virgin, gives birth, joins the convent, skins off her Indian ancestry, practices intense self-abnegation, and wages warfare against the Indian pagans who were formerly her associates, allies, and protectors. She, too, is called a liar; her lies and truths are tied and committed to a baroque and austere mission-house Catholicism.

Nanapush and Pauline engage in alternating narrative combat—his lies, her lies—as the white world inserts its roads into Indian lands, sinks its sawteeth into Indian timber, smothers Indian homes with layers of paper, and poisons Indian souls with printing ink. At the crux of this cultural biformity stands the Chippewa witch, Fleur, the mother of an auditor to whom Nanapush tells his version of the truth. Fleur stands against both worlds, Indian and white, cursing them each in turn, and working fabulous revenge when her times come. She gets no chance at narration, but her vision—as reported by the narrators (and the author)—disallows any romanticizing of either side.

A jaded reader might view the novel as yet another bipolarization of the age-old fight between whites and Indians, a dividing up of the North Dakota landscape into predictable factions. A reviewer might find some of the prose overwrought, and the two narrative voices indistinguishable in their cadences. A materialist might find the flights of Ms. Erdrich's fable too fantastic for suspension of disbelief. Yet readers will appreciate and applaud the vigor and inventiveness of the author in accurately displaying the passions and obsessions of these two opposing views of the world: Indian and white. Louise Erdrich is a Chippewa-German-American, and the world she is describing does more than resemble or evoke the environment and people in and around Turtle Mountain Reservation in North Dakota, where she grew up; it embodies it and brings it to life.

Thomas Matchie (essay date Summer 1989)

SOURCE: "*Love Medicine:* A Female *Moby Dick,*" in *The Midwest Quarterly,* Vol. XXX, No. 4, Summer, 1989, pp. 478-91.

[*In the following essay, Matchie outlines parallels between* Love Medicine *and Herman Melville's* Moby Dick.]

Published in 1984, *Love Medicine* is about a tribe of Indians living in North Dakota. Its author, Louise Erdrich, is part Chippewa and in the book returns to her prairie roots for her literary materials. Recently, Erdrich published another work entitled *Beet Queen,* also about the Red River Valley, and some of the same characters appear in both novels. *Love Medicine* is different from so much of Native American literature in that it is not polemic—there is no ax to grind, no major indictment of white society. It is simply a story about Indian life—its politics, humor, emptiness, and occasional triumphs. If Erdrich has a gift, it is the ability to capture the inner life and language of her people.

Since its publication, *Love Medicine* has won several national awards. Still, critics see in it a serious lack of unity—it was originally published as a series of short stories or vignettes. Also, some think it has little connection to authentic Indian values; students at the White Earth Indian Reservation in Minnesota identified more with *Giants in the Earth,* Rolvaag's epic novel about white immigrants on the Dakota prairie. My contention is just the opposite, that the book does function as a whole, though this may not be immediately evident, and that the author is highly aware of Indian history and tradition, which emerge in subtle ways, helping us to understand the mystery of existence, whatever our color or ethnic origin.

While reading the novel it may help, strangely enough, to keep in mind another novel, Herman Melville's *Moby-Dick.* These two works may seem far apart, one about the sea—"in landlessness alone lies the highest truth"—and the other about the Dakota prairie, the geographic center of North America. But one of Erdrich's characters, Nector Kashpah, sees himself as Ishmael—"call me Ishmael," he says, after escaping a particularly difficult situation. If one looks further into the matter, it becomes evident that there are many ways these two books are alike. First, they have similar episodic or disjointed structures. Then, the major characters in one story seem to draw upon those in the other. And through it all, the same motifs (e.g., water and fishing, wildness—particularly among the males, preoccupation with power as well as the importance of the heart, the alternating realities of life and death, concern with colors, especially white and red) appear again and again. Indeed, it may be that the truest unity and deepest values of *Love Medicine* come clear when juxtaposed with Melville's classic novel of the sea.

Love Medicine is different from so much of Native American literature in that it is not polemic—there is no ax to grind, no major indictment of white society. It is simply a story about Indian life—its politics, humor, emptiness, and occasional triumphs. If Erdrich has a gift, it is the ability to capture the inner life and language of her people.
—Thomas Matchie

In regard to structure, *Love Medicine* begins with a short account, told in third person, of the death of June Kashpah in 1981 in the boomtown of Williston, North Dakota. Then the novel proceeds with many short, seemingly unrelated episodes—some descriptive/narrative, some dramatic—told from multiple perspectives, but all about life on and off the reservation over a period of fifty years (1934-1984). Each vignette centers on shattered family life and the alienation of individuals. The parts may indeed seem dissimilar, unless one views them in an organic way, much as *Moby Dick* in 1850 represented a departure from the classic or three-part structure so common at that time. *Moby-Dick,* of course,

is about the disintegration of a ship, not only physically, but spiritually, for the purpose of the voyage and the unity of the crew collapse, all because of Ahab's preoccupation with one white whale. It begins with Ishmael's narrative, but then switches to everything from descriptions of the whaling industry, to poetic monologues, to dramatic episodes both comic and tragic. The parts, though different, are interposed erratically and often unexpectedly, but in the end they work together toward the whole. And that is how one must view *Love Medicine.*

In both cases the circle, so indigenous to Indian life, governs all, though in the case of the structure of *Love Medicine,* it takes fifty years to see it. *Moby Dick* starts with Ishmael's leaving New Bedford, contemplating many kinds of images of death (e.g., in the chapel, through Fr. Maple's sermon, in the Sprouter-Inn, in the prophecies of Elijah). Then, after the wreck of the *Pequod* (named after an extinct tribe of Indians), he surfaces in a circular vortex as he rises out of the chaos before coming home. In Erdrich's novel the action starts with June's death and then, after going back in time through a series of chaotic scenes dealing with Indian family life, circles back to the beginning when June's lost son Lipsha surfaces—rises psychologically and spiritually, not only to discover his real mother and family, but in his words to "cross the water, and bring her home."

Undoubtedly, Erdrich did not set out to write a book like *Moby-Dick,* but like Melville she writes about what she knows best—Indian life in this century—and like him she seeks through her characters the answers to some profound questions about human existence. It is in this context that she parallels in broad and general ways Melville's pattern of development, themes, characterizations, and motifs to create a virtual allegory of his work. In many ways her novel mirrors his, for her Dakota prairie can be as wild as his ocean typhoons, just as his sea can be as calm and dreamy as the Midwestern prairie. Indeed, as we shall see, the motif of wildness runs through the novel, but the character most directly exhibiting this quality is Nector Kashpah, who sees himself as reliving *Moby Dick.* Nector literally connects the various Indian families on the reservation; himself a Kashpah, he marries Marie Lazarre Morrissey, but never loses his passion for Lulu Lamartine, a promiscuous mother of a girl and at least nineteen boys, one of whom is Nector's.

Midway in the book Nector, a type of figure not uncommon in Melville because he is both comic and tragic, says:

> I kept thinking about the one book I read in high school . . . *Moby Dick,* the story of the great white whale. I knew that book inside and out. I'd even stolen a copy from school and taken it home in my suitcase. . . .

"You're always reading that book," my mother said once. "What is it?"

"The story of the great white whale."

She could not believe it. After a while, she said, "What do they got to wail about, those whites?"

I told her the whale was a fish as big as the church. She did not believe this either. Who would?

"Call me Ismael," I said sometimes, only to myself. For he survived the great white monster like I got out of the rich lady's picture [he'd been paid by a rich lady to disrobe for a painting she called "Plunge of the Brave"]. He let the water bounce his coffin to the top. In my life so far, I'd gone easy and come out on top, like him. But the river wasn't done with me yet. I floated through the calm sweet spots, but somewhere the river branched.

Here is where he falls headlong again for Lulu.

One of the ironies of the novel is that Nector is not really Ishmael at all, but more like Ahab, in that he is an irrational figure who thinks he can control all worlds—the Kashpahs and the Lamartines, his wife's and his lover's. A member of a most respected family and the chairman of the tribe, Nector becomes the victim of his sexual passions, falling for Marie as she escapes from the Sacred Heart Convent, but equally possessed with the beautiful and lascivious Lulu, into whose waters he continually sails to satisfy his fantasies. He finally concludes:

I try to think of anything but Lulu or Marie or my children. I think back to the mad captain in *Moby Dick* and how his leg was bit off. Perhaps I was wrong, about Ismael I mean, for now I see signs of the captain in myself.

In trying to burn a letter he's written to Lulu saying he is leaving Marie, he actually sets fire to Lulu's house—an event reminiscent of Ahab's burning masts in *Moby Dick*—before returning sheepishly to Marie. In the end he dies a pathetic old man, one who has literally lost his mind and has "to have his candy." He chokes to death on turkey hearts, the ironic symbol of his erotic needs and manipulative ways.

The Ishmael who discovers the real "love medicine" is Lipsha Morrissey, the bastard son of June Kashpah—the one who brings Nector the hearts. Like Melville's narrator, he is a wanderer who has to discover in painful ways the meaning of his universe and how he fits. He has to find that his true mother is June, who dies on her way home crossing the prairie. He has to find that his brother is King, his boyhood

tormentor, disrupted by the Vietnam War and as wild and torn as Nector. King is the real son of June and Gordie Kashpah. Gordie, the youngest child of Nector and Marie, is another wild character. Drunk, he goes berserk after the death of June; in a magnificent episode, he kills a deer (a wild animal akin in Erdrich's world to the whale), thinking it is June, and then returns to the convent to confess his deed, before ending in an open field "howling" as if he were "drowned."

But most of all Lipsha has to find that his father is the perennial criminal Gerry Nanapush, one of the older sons of Lulu Lamartine. His is another wild tale (narrated by Lipsha's counterpart Albertine Johnson) entitled "Scales," wherein he escapes from jail to visit in the tiny unit where they weigh trucks, Dot Adare, the woman who bears his child, before returning to his own (physical as well as mental) imprisonment. With this discovery late in the novel, Lipsha combines in his own person the larger symbolic family of the Chippewas. He does all this as a kind of innocent observer, like Ishmael, who only occasionally takes part in the action. But out of the death and destruction of his people he, unlike Nector-Ahab and his male counterparts, accepts the responsibility for his life and worth as he rises to the surface in the end. He is the one who truly "connects" all, for he completes the cycle begun by his mother whose spirit he now brings home.

If there is a parallel to Moby Dick in *Love Medicine,* it is June Kashpah. She dies early in the novel, but like the great white whale, her presence pervades the entire story and gives it depth. She is not there and yet there. Sometimes she even "comes alive," as when Gordie thinks the deer in his back seat, stunned and yet moving, is June herself. Initially having run away from Gordie, June is hungry and picked up in Williston by a stranger, whom she thinks is "different," but after falling from his truck, perishes walking across the cold white prairie as she "came home." In this early vignette, Erdrich captures the bleakness and boredom at the center of so much Indian life in this century. It is that dark side of life, the side which preoccupies Ahab in *Moby Dick,* something he equates through the white whale with a "inscrutable malice" behind the universe—a mask he wants to penetrate. Erdrich does not philosophize as much as Melville, but this concept of evil is a legitimate way of viewing the source of so many of the destructive aspects of Indian life depicted in *Love Medicine.* It is interesting that when June's inlaws—Gordie and Zelda and Aurelia—recall her life, one of the dominant incidents they remember is their trying to hang her, and her egging them on, like some kind of evil mind. *Love Medicine,* like *Moby Dick,* is a type of journey to penetrate the enticing but illusive mask that conceals the mystery of evil.

As the story unfolds, however, we discover a beautiful side

to June, much as Ishmael sees a mystifying and uplifting aspect to the white whale to counter Ahab's view. June has been raised by Eli, Nector's brother, the moral center of the novel, who lives in the woods and represents the old Indian past. At one point in the novel the irascible King insists that Eli have his hat, on which are the words the "World's Greatest Fisherman," for all agree Eli deserves it most. June is inevitably associated with Eli, with water, with fishing, with the good in the Kashpah history. All the Kashpah women admire June, as do her husband Gordie and son King, to whom she leaves money for a car. Like so many of the males, however, King's destructive wildness keeps him from being the responsible human being his mother wanted; this is left for Lipsha to achieve. June, then, is a driving force behind the Chippewa world, but the reader must pick between the beautiful and humanizing aspects of such a presence, and what Ishmael calls when reflecting upon the whiteness of the whale, "the all-color of atheism"—the possibility that behind the Indians' life patterns (which are now white patterns) is not much of anything at all.

There are, no doubt, significant differences even within the general likenesses of *Love Medicine* and *Moby Dick,* if only because Erdrich is a woman returning to the land and her people, rather than a man going to sea with a male crew. If Lipsha, for instance, is Ishmael, he only appears at the end to complete the circle. In the beginning his mentor and female counterpart, Albertine Johnson (perhaps the author's surrogate), returns to the reservation after and because of June's death. Albertine introduces us to the chief characters of the drama, much as Ishmael does when he boards the *Pequod,* telling us of the Knights and Squires, the chief mates and harpooners. But Albertine returns, not to the captain's quarters, but to the kitchen where her mother Zelda and aunt Aurelia, the daughters of Nector and Marie, are discussing June. Here we are first acquainted with the "familiness" of the Chippewas, and begin to know the characters—the Kashpahs, the Morrisseys, the Lamartines—whose stories stretch from 1934 to 1984, much as the characters on the *Pequod* evolve on the voyage to capture Moby Dick.

Good human relationships are important to both authors, and if Ishmael crosses cultures in making friends with the pagan harpooner Queequeg (who like Eli in *Love Medicine* is a kind of noble savage), Albertine is herself a half-breed, red and white, the daughter of Zelda and the "Swede." She suffers because of her double-nature, but her return, like Ishmael's setting out, comes from her uneasiness and is an effort to escape loneliness and build human bridges. Curiously enough, Albertine has her own chaotic history, and just as Ishmael may be an innocent observer, but is taken in by Ahab's powerful dark influence, so is Albertine taken in. As Erdrich's story circles back in time we find that Albertine in 1973 at fifteen tries to run away from the reservation. She

goes to Fargo, only to end up sleeping with Henry Lamartine Jr., one of Lulu's sons, on N. P. Avenue in the cheap Round Up Hotel. After making love, Albertine feels empty and wants to separate herself from him, whereupon he senses that she has "crossed a deep river and disappeared." In short, he needs her, and her horror pales beside his nightmare explosion. Like King, he has been damaged by the Vietnam War, and when he touches her the next day "weeping," she is now touched emotionally by the depth of their mutual loneliness.

In the beginning of the novel, however, Albertine returns to the reservation. Like Ishmael, she is not pure, but she has more distance than the others, having lived in a white woman's basement for some time away from home. Through her we meet Zelda and Aurelia. On the *Pequod* the chief mates, like Stubb and Flask, are skillful whalers, but not thinkers, and soon become extensions of Ahab's mind. The women of the reservation are also servants, but they are more free and happy people—like the harpooners in *Moby Dick* who dine in an atmosphere of merriment following their humorless captain's meal. These women don't fight the system, run by the males, but they are basic to its existence—giving birth to the children, planting and growing the food, cooking and baking for the men—like Gordie and King and Lipsha, who unconsciously quarrel over and destroy the newly baked pies. Among the Nanapushes, Gerry leaves prison temporarily to impregnate Dot, who is then left to raise and feed the child. These women may be treated like dogs, as Ahab treats Stubb, but they keep the whole operation afloat. They maintain the land, encourage their men, survive catastrophe. The *Pequod* is a commercial enterprise where under contract the mates and harpooners follow their mad leader without question. The women in *Love Medicine* are not paid, but they keep the family itself intact, in spite of the alcohol, the violence, the abuse and misuse of one another.

Albertine identifies with these women—their fun, their hopes, but also their fears and worry about the men. In one of the most powerful scenes in *Moby Dick,* Ishmael almost loses control of the ship as he gazes into the Try-Works (the red-hot pots of sperm oil), contemplating how intertwined are both the magnificent as well as the most hellish moments of life, even as the Catskill eagle flies high and yet at times swoops very low. Albertine-Ishmael, amid all the fighting and confusion, is worried about Lipsha and takes him for a walk in the fields, and gazing at the northern lights, she muses:

> I thought of June. She would be dancing if there
> was a dance hall in space. She would be dancing a
> two-step for wandering souls [like Lipsha]. Her long
> legs lifting and falling. Her laugh an ace. Her sweet
> perfume the way all grown-up women were sup-

posed to smell. Her amusement at both the bad and the good. Her defeat. Her reckless victory. Her sons.

So June, amid the high moments and the low, the bad and the good, gives substance to the Indians' quest for meaning. Lipsha will find himself in the end, but it is too early to know that now, and Albertine, his alter ego, can only hold his hand, and like Ishmael, try to keep the ship on course.

But the two female giants of *Love Medicine* are Marie Kashpah and Lulu Lamartine, and they take center stage as Albertine fades, just as Ismael gives way to more dramatic scores in *Moby Dick.* These two women are the Starbucks of the novel, for they buck the system—the government, church, or family—to keep their souls alive. Starbuck, of course, is Ahab's first mate who objects to Ahab's decision to take revenge on the white whale, but still decides "to obey, rebelling." Ahab fears Starbuck, but in a strange way respects him, comes to trust him with his life, and even confides in him shortly before his death. In Erdrich's work Marie will not be crushed. As a girl in the convent she outsmarts the grotesque Sister Leopolda, who tries to break her spirit, but to save face Leopolda must treat the stabbed hands of her underling as stigmata, and Marie emerges as Saint Marie, "Star of the Sea."

Escaping that world, she uses Nector Kashpah's advances to snare him into marriage, and then keeps him sober so he can run the tribe. She is close to Nector, as Starbuck is to Ahab, though she knows he plans to leave home for the amorous Lulu. But even here Marie uses his guilty feelings and fears to keep him in the house. Like the other women, Marie is a homemaker and protector; early in June's life she takes in the child, though Marie lets her follow her own desire to live with Eli in the woods. Overall, she resembles Starbuck. A wise realist, she is able to compromise without losing her identify in impossible situations which any moment may, like the sea, sweep one under.

Lulu, on the other hand, is the object of many men's desires. By Old Man Pillager, for instance, she has Gerry Nanapush, and she returns the advances of her suitor from St. Paul, Beverly Lamartine, who like Nector-Ahab pursues her for her body. These men are important to Lulu, for they fulfill her physical needs, but they never get the best of her. Though Nector is her favorite, she never lets him think that she is inferior to Marie. When as tribal chairman Nector informs her the government is taking her house, she stays put, even when it burns, till they furnish her with a new dwelling. Like Marie she has spunk and keeps her "starbuck" identity in spite of overwhelming odds. Like the other women, she is a good housekeeper, for her place is always neat and orderly. In the end Marie and Lulu come to know and respect each other at the Senior Citizens' home, where Nector's mind fades and he finally chokes to death. Here the two rivals come to feel for each other as women in a touching way—in Lulu's words "reflecting on the human heart." These two women, like Ahab and Starbuck, trust one another; in an awesome gesture Marie, removing the bandages from Lulu's eyes, enables her to cry again—something she has not done since childhood. Here the author employs water in another way as a kind of "love medicine" to generate new life. Together the two mourn Nector much as one might feel for Ahab, a proud but pathetic figure, as he continues (like most of Erdrich's men) his wild unrelenting pursuit until the end.

There are other major incidents in *Love Medicine* that pick up key threads in *Moby Dick,* like the close relationship between madness and wisdom. Both King Jr. and Henry Jr. are affected mentally by the Vietnam War to the point they become violent souls. Henry Jr., after a long drive with his brother Lyman, who cannot save him, drowns himself in his red convertible. In Melville's story, the castaway Pip loses his mind when Stubb will not save him from the sea, but he returns in his madness to offer sharp, bitter wisdom to Captain Ahab, and from him the captain accepts it. In Erdrich's world where one generation fails, the next seems to succeed, as when King Howard Kashpah Jr. (King and Lynette's young son), after all his father's rage, learns to write his name, Howard Kashpah, in school on a red paper heart. The marker label says "PERMANENT," and the teacher tells him "that means forever." So Howard in his Pip-like childish wisdom undercuts the adult world around him to establish his own identity as a human being. In this way Howard parallels the growth in Lipsha Morrisey, the other son of June.

Colors, especially red and white, are also crucial in both novels, for they are a part of the very texture. White and red seem to go back and forth in *Moby Dick,* as the red heat of the tri-pots lights up the *Pequod,* just as do the tapering white candles or mastheads struck by lightning. In one case Ishmael philosophizes on life, while in the other Ahab commits himself to death. In *Love Medicine* the Indian is, of course, the redman living in a white world. June in the beginning has on a red nylon vest when the stranger in a white jacket "plunged down against her" with a "great wide mouth," as though she were entering the whale itself. Then there is the red convertible in which Henry Jr. drowns; the mark of white society, this is the machine that spells freedom, but it cannot solve basic human problems where so many are held psychologically captive.

Finally, there is the red of the heart itself—a powerful symbol in both novels. On the *Pequod* Ahab, just before the fatal chase, talks to Starbuck about the importance of the heart, family, love. His words are touching, coming from a man bent on destruction: "I . . . do what in my own . . . natural heart, I durst not . . . dare," he says. In *Love Medicine* both Lipsha and Howard come to know the meaning of the heart—Lipsha through the turkey hearts which kill his Ahab-like grandfather, and Howard through the paper heart on which he writes his name. Lipsha says that love means forgiveness, that it is not magic, but a "true feeling." Later, when he discovers in a card game his true father and sees himself as part of the larger family, he says, "The jack of hearts is me." These awakenings give a kind of tragic joy to a story pervaded by so many deaths.

Love Medicine, then, is a book about the prairie that examines the wild, chaotic lives of several Indian families whose lives on the reservation have immersed them in a dark and often violent existence, one that the author seems to equate with Ahab. It is a world created by a white—shall we say malicious—intelligence, except that behind the scenes hovers an amazing human being, June Kashpah, whose life and recent death still give meaning and hope to its members. Albertine-Ishmael goes back to that world to experience again the rage dramatized by her grandfather Nector-Ahab, as well as other violent males. But she also discovers the values sustained by women like her mother, Zelda, and Aurelia and Dot Adare, but especially by Marie and Lulu, who in spite of the men and the systems and the power, give dignity and spirit to an otherwise hollow and violent world.

Out of the chaos emerges, through Howard and Lipsha, possible new worlds, just as June would have wished. Indeed, Lipsha-Ishmael begins to see the importance of love within all the families and in this way "brings June home" as he (to use Nector's words) lets "the water bounce his coffin to the top" in the end. *Love Medicine* is a novel about the land, but one which has so many parallels to *Moby Dick* that it draws tremendous power when placed beside Melville's classic novel about the sea.

Annie Finch (review date Summer 1990)

SOURCE: "Poets of Our Time," in *Belles Lettres,* Vol. 5, No. 4, Summer, 1990, pp. 30-31.

[*In the following excerpt, Finch praises most of* Baptism of Desire *but expresses reservations about the final section of the book, objecting to the comparative "ordinariness" of the poems there.*]

These three books of poetry [*Baptism of Desire* by Erdrich, *Green Age* by Alicia Suskin Ostriker, and *Toluca Street* by Maxine Scates], written by three women coming from very different places as poets at the beginning of the end of our century, make a revealing cross-section. Louise Erdrich, a successful novelist who has written only one other book of poems, presumably uses poetry to write in ways not possible with the novel form. Alicia Suskin Ostriker, well-established as a poet, uses this volume to continue ideas developed in

six other books of poems and three books of poetry criticism. Maxine Scates is new to the poetry scene; this first book of poems is published as the winner of an annual national poetry competition.

In the context of the wider poetry scene that these books reflect, Erdrich's *Baptism of Desire* is probably the most unusual and original of the three books. **"Hydra"** is typical, a poem full of private imagery and eclectic allusions, as in the following passage:

> Hour of the talk-show hostess.
> Hour of the wolf, of the tree service,
> of the worship of the god whose name adds
> to a single year. Abraxas, the perfect word.

It is not necessary for a reader to struggle through every bit of difficult meaning to find these poems rewarding. They are lush in imagery, fascinating in their suggestiveness, refreshing, often, in their very privacy. At times passages emerge from the obscure background with a startling clear immediacy that is all the more valuable by contrast. The final passage of the poem just quoted is such an instance:

> . . . Snake of hard hours, you are my poetry.
> According to God, your place is low,
> under Adam's heel, but as for me,
> a woman shaped from a secondary bone,
> who cares if you wrap my shoulders?
> Who cares if you whisper? Who cares
> if the fruit is luscious? Your place
> is at my ear.

This vivid invocation can speak intimately to almost every woman raised in a Judeo-Christian culture; the fact that Erdrich has arrived at this place through a sometimes tortuous path of private meanings makes it, in some ways, that much more marvelously universal. In some of the shorter poems, the difficulty can set a strange image in the mind like salt setting dye. **"The Kitchen Mandarins"** describes figures on china coming alive in the kitchen at night. It is a queer, disturbing poem that never quite settles down. It ends:

> Now they vanish among the branches in the
> teacups,
> the whips and rings.
> I know there will be no rest for me.
> No thimbleful of peace.

What are the whips and rings? Why a thimbleful? Nothing in the poem has indicated why there should be no rest for the speaker. But none of this matters; I am glad for these problems, which turn a potentially sentimental thought into a poem you can hold in your mind like a koan and never have to get the better of.

In the last section of the book, however, Erdrich sacrifices much of this strange power for the sake of more common effects. These poems, almost all rooted in a daily experience—a family going to sleep, a child in a basement—tend to rely on the images and stories themselves to create poignancy. The naturalistic language and free verse structure do little to charge or defamiliarize the described world. After the first four sections of the book, I found passages such as "The father pours the milk from his glass / into the cup of the child" (from **"The Glass and the Bowl"**) comparatively unmemorable.

Erdrich's unique strengths as a poet seem to be her gift for powerful incantatory rhythms and her ability to let strangenesses simply be. She can reach such singular places in her poetry that it is almost a shame to see her settling down, at the end of her book, to ordinariness—however well earned. But the reader, at least, has all the rest of the book with which to dream. . . .

James Ruppert (essay date Fall 1991)

SOURCE: "Mediation and Multiple Narrative in *Love Medicine*," in *North Dakota Quarterly*, Vol. 59, No. 4, Fall, 1991, pp. 229-41.

[*In the following essay, Ruppert explains the ways in which Erdrich allows readers of* Love Medicine, *both Native and non-Native American, to experience the Native perspective in the text.*]

Love Medicine is a dazzling, personal, intense novel of survivors who struggle to define their own identities and fates in a world of mystery and human frailty. In her writing, Louise Erdrich both protects and celebrates this world. To assume effectively the roles of protector and celebrant, Erdrich must mediate between two conceptual frameworks, white and Native. But as a contemporary Native American writer, she appreciates and utilizes both epistemological codes. Erdrich has at her disposal both Native American and white codes at any moment in the creation of the text. This dual vision allows her either to use one code to illuminate another, or to ignore one code and stay within another if she wishes. She can create value and meaning through a Native worldview or through a contemporary American worldview or both at the same time. Thus, her standpoint as a mediator is more complex and more open to a wide set of possibilities than authors positioned in only one culture or even authors perceived as merely standing between two cultures. She is capable of satisfying two audiences at once, commenting on two cultural systems from a position of deep understanding and knowledge. And perhaps more importantly, she can manipulate each audience so that it will experience the novel through the paths of understanding unique to each culture, thus assuring protection and continuance of a newly appreciated and experienced Native American epistemological reality.

Celebrating and protecting the stories of survivors can imply the creation of meaning in characters under the pressure of competing senses of identity. The cultural concepts of identity differ in Native American and white cultures. As Erdrich layers these identities in the text, the sets of cultural identities become visible through merging of epistemological codes which are used to create these identities. She harmoniously evokes the various story realities: each narrative grouping of the novel has the potential of being read as a psychological story and a social story (using the most common white senses of identity) or as a communal story and a mythical story (using Native American senses of identity) depending on the code and positioning of the perspective that Erdrich employs. Thus any section of the novel reveals multiple narratives embedded in the text. The mediational actions of the author serve to protect and celebrate culture by a continuing recreation of the multiple facets of identity through multiple narrative.

Mediation, as the central generative organizational principle, downplays mechanically plotted novel structure while encouraging multiple narratives. In this process the voices and ideas of a variety of culturally linked positions, a variety of identities, compete for readers' ears and thus their allegiance. This "struggle going on within discourse," as Bakhtin calls it, characterizes mediational texts, emphasizing their essential dialogic nature. For Erdrich, plot is far less important than the voices of her characters. She sets the oral tribal language against the half-breed language and the contemporary American language. Bakhtin, in his discussion of narrative discourse, clarifies the relationship of plot to languages when he writes:

> In a word, the novelistic plot serves to represent speaking persons and their ideological worlds. What is realized in the novel is the process of coming to know one's own language, coming to know one's own belief system in someone else's system. There takes place within the novel an ideological translation of another's language, and an overcoming of its otherness—an otherness that is only contingent, external and illusory.

The otherness is illusory in the successful mediational novel because the plot organizes the exposure of social languages and ideologies in such a way as to allow the reader into a new way of seeing and speaking about the world. For Erdrich, this new perspective is a dynamic one where the reader can understand a variety of perspectives on a Native and non-Native cultural spectrum. *Love Medicine* then becomes for the reader, what Bakhtin envisions, "The experience of a discourse, a world view, and an ideologically based act." Erdrich's goals include nothing less than ideological and epistemological transposition.

To illustrate her mediational positioning, consider the mode of Erdrich's discourse. She attempts to present an oral discourse in a written format. The importance of the oral tradition to Native American cultures is well known, and Erdrich's first-person narrators talk directly to the reader as if he or she were chatting over a kitchen table. They speculate, remember, complain, come to conclusions, and describe their actions; indeed, almost all the information, the meaning, the significance of the novel is developed through this homage to the most personal and least codified elements of a vital oral tradition. Oral tradition in this book defines the nature of all knowledge; for characters like Lipsha what they hear defines who they are.

Yet Erdrich's effort is structured by a set of highly Western novelistic conventions with contemporary parallels in experimental novels, semiotic poetry, and *cinema verité*. Erdrich never seems to be totally content with letting the characters speak solely for themselves. The author's presence is often felt both in the omniscient point of view and in the highly structured images which organize each section, especially those images which close each section. Robert Silberman has suggested that Native American writers, and especially Erdrich, in their attempts to move writing toward storytelling have been developing the "conventions of the oral," conventions every bit as necessary for generation of the text as the conventions of realism or naturalism. He identifies the use of a dramatic present tense and the occasional reference to the second-person pronoun, "you." But an examination of oral tradition would quickly add many more elements to the list. Erdrich's constant switching from past to present tense, her shifts from omniscient to first-person narration, her episodic structure, her use of dialect, and her use of foreshadowing and of flashbacks give an evocative rendition of a traditional storyteller's art. However, considering this expanded sense of the written conventions of the oral, it is clear that what we have is a novel, a Western structure, set with the task of recreating something of a Native oral tradition, a task it can never completely accomplish. Erdrich is using a very Western mode to arrive at a Native perspective and illuminating the conventions, significations, assumptions, and strengths of both as she does so. Obviously her goal is not to be a traditional storyteller, nor is it merely to add a sense of immediacy to her novel, but only by positioning the audience to accept a discourse with oral codes can she mediate and thus prepare both audiences for valuing Native ways of meaning and thereby Native cultures, which are the ultimate source of value in the novel.

Humorous examples of the stylistic and formal aspect of Erdrich's mediation in *Love Medicine* are found in Lipsha's malapropisms. Lipsha, who has taken some college classes, alternates, as Albertine tells us, between using "words I had to ask him the meaning of," and not making "the simplest sense." Lipsha's malapropisms, such as referring to "mental condensation" when he means concentration, or saying he was in a "laundry" when he means quandry, represent his oral appreciation of the learned diction more appropriate to writing. Yet Lipsha can also turn around and take a common current activity from the dominant culture to create a metaphor for an internal illumination at a moment when death surrounds him. Lipsha likens his revelations about himself and the world to a video game:

> You play those games never knowing what you see.
> When I fell into the dream alongside both of them
> I saw that the dominions I had defended myself
> from anciently was but delusions of the screen.
> Blips of light. And I was scot-free now, whistling
> through space.

His mediational style of expression reveals Erdrich's concern with every level of epistemological double-code embedding.

If one considers the larger goals of this mediational process, much of the richness of the text emerges. Central to a Chippewa worldview, and those of much of Native America, is a sense of the reciprocal nature of the relationships between man and the spiritual powers which activate the world. Man's actions in the natural world have spiritual repercussions. An Eskimo elder, worried about the actions of his people and the response of the spirit world, was quoted as saying, "No bears have come because there is no ice, and there is no ice because there is no wind, and there is no wind because we have offended the powers." The reciprocal relationship between man and nature and between man and the spirit world is also portrayed in *Love Medicine,* but in the novel it is manifest in the most immediate and personal manner; that is, in the gossip, the problems, and the survival of individuals as they interact with the universe in which they participate. Much Native American thought assumes that mental and physical phenomena are inseparable, and that thought and speech can deeply influence a world where no circumstance is accidental or free from personalized intent. As Paula Allen writes:

> It is reasonable that all literary forms should be interrelated, given the basic idea of the unity and relatedness of all the phenomena of life. Separation of parts into this or that category is not agreeable to American Indians, and the attempt to separate essentially unified phenomena results in distortion. . . . The purpose of a ceremony is to integrate: to fuse the individual with his or her fellows, the

community of people with that of the other kingdoms, and this larger communal group with the worlds beyond this one.

As a ceremonial philosophy, Native American thought unifies various levels of meaning which Western thought would separate. This unity of experience is what Joseph Epes Brown refers to as "A polysynthetic metaphysic of nature." Erdrich merges this Native sense of multiple levels of meaning for each physical act with a powerful belief in the mystery of events as they make manifest the sacred processes of the world, and this meaning informs all of *Love Medicine* (think of Nector and Marie on the path, or Bev and Lulu at the grave). Understanding slowly builds in the novel as people tell us more of their stories. Events take on spiritual, mythic, cultural, personal, and religious meanings for phenomena in which Western thought often would see only physical effects. Reciprocity between the various levels of existence ties the meanings together and helps Erdrich express a Chippewa worldview which appreciates a dynamic process of signification, or as Paula Allen so poetically puts it, a worldview which sees the "self as a moving event within a moving universe," a universe where "everything moves in dynamic equilibrium."

On the other hand, another clear goal of Erdrich is to present a complementary vision of individual will and history which is more psychologically based than communally oriented. The results of Nector's actions on those around him, the exploration of Marie through her relationship to the nun, Sister Leopolda, and King's vision of his life all suggest a psychological dimension which uses dominant-culture conceptual categories. Moreover, the novel itself clearly has a sociological agenda as illustrated by its treatment of economic development on the reservation, the influence of the white society, especially Christian religion, and the changes on the contemporary reservation such as old people living in an institution rather than with families. This use of both belief systems to illuminate each other supports Bakhtin's understanding of the novel's task, "coming to know one's own belief system in someone else's system."

As an illustration of the way these two cultural frameworks merge in the text, consider Henry Lamartine. From a white set of epistemological codes, he is clearly an example of the displaced soldier returning home; whatever meaning he holds for the text and the dominant culture could be seen in the commonplace insight that the experience of combat often destroys the soldier's sense of reality, making it difficult if not impossible to reintegrate himself into society. We know this by looking at the chronological series of events in his life, drawing a set of inferences based on causal reasoning. When he dies, we are not surprised since we have drawn a straight line from a shattering experience through his life to inevitable death. We've seen enough stories like this; it is a convention of the subject. Insights mount when the reader also considers that Henry's war was the Vietnam war with its political turmoil and disproportionately high number of minorities. White social and psychological codes give meaning to the events of his life, and the reader has an easy-to-read, satisfying text, complete with closure. When Lyman drives the red convertible into the river after Henry has drowned, the psychologically oriented reader sees suicide and a brother's desire to make a suicide look like an accident to save Henry's reputation.

Conversely, Henry's inability to resume normal life at home and his subsequent death can be seen as the result of actions out of harmony with the Chippewa sense of war, death, honor, and right thinking. As a draftee, Henry had no choice in his actions. He has not gone off to war with a vision which will give him power, nor has he danced the warrior's dance. The souls of his dead enemies will not rest. In the one military action we learn about, Henry is ordered to interrogate a dying woman who claims the bond of relationship with him. He is not prepared ritually for his departure for war, he breaks the bonds of relationship, and he is not purified of the spirits of dead enemies when he returns because his mother is afraid to take him to the old medicine man. At the end of the chapter, Henry's renewal of interest in his brother and the wild dance seem to undercut the possibility of psychologically motivated suicide. His one comment as he stands in the water, "My boots are filling up," does not have the purposeful ring of a suicide note. Perhaps his drowning performed in his unpurified state can be understood as a reciprocal response by the spiritual forces of the world around us to Henry's improper behavior, a water spirit's revenge. As the balance is set right again, Lyman's driving of the car into the river carries the weight of the custom of burying private personal possessions with the dead person. Each of the two perspectives I have mentioned has a certain level of completeness, yet the narrative's richness is revealed when each story, each narrative viewpoint on the meaning of the character Henry is seen in contrast to the other, and each complements and clarifies a different template of experience.

This use of one cultural code to illuminate the other is best shown in Erdrich's use of ghosts in *Love Medicine*. While ghosts are a very real part of the Chippewa worldview, when dealt with properly they do not often trouble the living. Anthropologist Ruth Landes observes: "The passage from life was considered tricky, beset with personified evils intent on murdering the wandering soul." But the proper instructions and recommendations delivered over a grave would assure the soul passage to the village of shadows. Conventional Western thought posits no existence to ghosts. While we allow them entrance into our world through literature, especially children's tales, ghosts are generally considered to be storytelling convention with no substance. So when Gordie sees June's ghost, Western epistemology is ready to posit no reality to the encounter, and we are encouraged to see this as a delusion brought on by alcohol and grief. That in his drunken frenzy Gordie should hit a deer and mistake it for June has no meaning other than the revelation of his psychological state of mind; we are not surprised that at the end of the encounter with Sister Mary Martin, he should end up running mad in the woods. However, in the traditional Chippewa worldview, the spirit world is the source of special insight and power. A dead wife returning to visit the husband who abused her is not unusual, especially if she is not buried in the appropriate manner; June's journey home at the time of her death is completed by her visit to Gordie. She visits Gordie because he has called her name and thus violated one of the most important prohibitions designed to keep the spirits of the dead on the trail to the spirit world. It is understandable that June would use a deer to aid her visit, as the spirits of animals are much closer to the world of the spirit than humans are. When Gordie clubs the deer with the tire iron, it is an action reminiscent of the times he hit June, and so his confession to the nun that he has killed June carries a ring of ironic truth and becomes more than the baseless ravings of a crazed drunk.

The psychological interpretation underlies and enriches the cultural one. Both stories' realities present valid worldviews and can stand alone to explain the meaning of the actions, yet each level of the text forces us to question exactly what we as readers believe. Can both be right? Can one be right and the other wrong? It seems clear that each reveals the strengths and weaknesses of the other code. An understanding of the psychological level clarifies the cultural framework; the cultural illuminates the psychological.

The return of Nector Kashpaw's ghost is even more mediational. Nector's sudden death leaves him without a chance to say good-bye to the two women he loves. Lipsha and Marie know that when ghosts return they have a "certain uneasy reason to come back." He visits Lulu, Lipsha, and Marie until he is admonished back to the spirit world by Lipsha. Nector's visit cannot be explained away as a drunken hallucination. Psychologically we can explain the presence of the ghost as being a figment of an imagination under the stress of grief. However, even by Western epistemological standards three independent visits observed by three independent observers come dangerously close to constituting corroborated reality. Yet the reality they tend to corroborate is one in which Western tradition places no credence. Lipsha comments on this philosophical and empirical paradox:

> Whether or not he had been there is not the point. She had *seen* him, and that meant anyone else could see him, too. Not only that but, as is usually the case with these here ghosts, he had a certain uneasy reason to come back. And of course Grandma Kashpaw had scanned it out.

This text perfectly conveys both attitudes toward the reality of ghosts and thus the validation of each worldview and epistemological framework. It can be read as saying that it doesn't matter if the ghost was real since it was real to Grandma in her altered psychological state. But Lipsha says that the point is if she saw him, others could see him. His comment also about the ghost's motivation shows that his belief in the existence of the spirit world and of ghosts is undisturbed. There is no question he was there because, of course, his spirit is still around, but the problem is that he can be seen, that he refuses to let go of this world. The ghost needs to be instructed as to what to do, and Lipsha's admonition parallels recorded Midewiwin orations to the dead. The thrust of all this is to take a Western issue of non-truth (non-reality) and treat it with the assumptions of Chippewa reality while layering psychological motivation and cultural act. Each code is used and illuminates the other. The end result of Erdrich's technique is that we are forced to look at the multiple meanings of an event.

Clearly, the two sets of cultural codes produce a doubling of narrative textures as distinct as the two audiences Erdrich tries to reach. Each audience is satisfied in many ways, but primarily by the developing sense of identity as the readers animate the emerging characters. The contemporary survivors which Erdrich creates are people for whom growth, becoming, and identity are vitally important ways to protect and celebrate individual and cultural values. Of course, inside of any cultural code one can search for identity with an inward looking eye or an outward looking eye, and as Bakhtin has concluded, every text has two voices, the personal and the social. Thus the reader can expect to find a social and a psychological story of identity in *Love Medicine*. Yet as we have seen, Western codes are but half of the narrative layers Erdrich has to work with in the creation of the development of any character. When considering Native American codes, one also finds two levels of identity, but these are different from Western codes of signification. Native cultures are often observed to avoid emphasis on psychological motivation, even in a form so personal as the autobiography. Instead, Erdrich uses Native American codes to develop characters with an inward looking sense of identity, one based on family and community where kinship defines who one is, and with an outward looking sense of narrative identity that places a person in the framework of the sacred processes of the universe where the distant past and the present merge in a continuing experience on a mythic plane. Consequently Erdrich and other contemporary Native American writers have available four distinct narrative layers in which to create a sense of identify: Psychological, social, communal, and mythic. For them, part of the ideological translation of which Bakhtin wrote is to let both audiences experience the variety of culturally framed definitions of identity. While not all layers need be present in the development of any text, these possibilities define the bounds through which mediation can be realized in the text—one's own belief system in someone else's. There takes place within the novel an ideological translation of another's language.

Think back again for a moment to Henry Lamartine. How does a reader define Lamartine's identity? Surely his identity can be defined socially when he is seen as a shell-shocked veteran unable to adjust to the world back home, but as I have suggested, the reader can also see him as a warrior haunted by the ghosts of his dead enemies which he cannot ritualistically exorcise. In this perspective, Henry is given a communal role, an identity based on his relation to the community and family as a young warrior and dutiful son. Each sense of identity satisfies its appropriate audience, but also because the reader holds both senses of identity as satisfactory, and the text validates both perspectives.

More central to the novel and more interesting are the stories which define Nector's identity. Nector comes from a family that is "respected as the last hereditary leaders of this tribe." His communal identity is set from the beginning, and much of his life is an attempt to live up to that identity, to understand it and grow into it. The Kashpaw sense of worth and Chippewa tradition constitute the essence of what Nector sees himself as. Socially he is the tribal chairman. While the dominant culture would assume that places him as the leader of his tribe, tribal custom does not give him that role unless he can live up to the traditional function of the leader, but Nector's psychological sense of identity undermines his social definition as leader in much the same way that his communal role as a Kashpaw supports it. As he says, "Chippewa politics was thorns in my jeans."

Psychologically, Nector sees himself as floating down a river complete with calm spots, rapids, and unexpected branchings. His sense of himself is that of a person being carried along by events, and he struggles to maintain control of the events of his life. Nector's retreat to apparent senility becomes a way that he can finally completely define himself in the midst of the river flow of emotions and the demands of politics. As Lulu says of him, "People said Nector Kashpaw had changed, but the truth was he'd just become more like himself than ever." Various layers of his identity created by the narrative are embedded in the text and held simultaneously by the reader. But while the communal, social, and psychological story is developed here, the mythic story is not.

Marie Lazarre has an identity defined by the community as one of those "dirty Lazarres." Despite her attempts to recreate her communal identity, the community has defined her role and position in its complex structure. This communal identity is contrasted to her psychological identity as molder of Nector, as defeater of Sister Leopolda, as woman defined by her kitchen and children. These two senses of identity complement each other while the social level remains mostly latent. As wife of the tribal chairman, her social position should be one of respect and leadership, but her communal identity as "a dirty Lazarre" is in contrast to it. As the wife left at home during a continuing extramarital relationship, her sense of a social identity is again undercut. As the woman who takes in lost children, she performs a social function which helps her clarify her sense of self on the psychological and communal level, but she is unable to allow this to help her develop a clearly defined social identity. Again the mythic story is not developed with this character.

Lulu Lamartine plays the communal role of the libertine. As a woman with eight boys and one girl by a variety of lovers, she is hated by the wives in the community and loved by their husbands. Though a disrupter of families, her family is vitally important to her. Her identity as libertine is contrasted by her psychological identity as consummate lover of beauty. After a grisly look at death in her early childhood, she comes to define herself as someone "in love with the whole world and all that lived in its rainy arms." What is viewed from the communal realm as irresponsible action is for Lulu an honest attempt to drink in the beauty and let it fill her up if only for a moment. Each sense of identity enriches the reader's understanding of the other and encourages the audiences to clarify their codes. Again, Erdrich has chosen not to develop the mythic or social story of this character.

In the character of Gerry Nanapush, Erdrich displays all four levels of narrative identity or story. On a social level Nanapush is the convict Indian turned political hero. As a member of the American Indian Movement, he is seen and sees himself as a social symbol to both the white and the Indian world, but he is also an individual who sees himself as a believer in justice, not laws. Psychologically he is presented as a loving husband and father. Nanapush is motivated by personal passions and definitions of self, yet on a larger plane, his actions recall the daring and rebellion of the trickster, Nanabosho, of Chippewa cultural identity while they add to his own idea of himself. Nanapush consciously takes on a mythic role and becomes a living embodiment of a trickster. His communal identity hinges on relationships as son of old man Pillager and Lulu Lamartine, lover of June Morrissey, and father to Lipsha Morrissey. As warrior against the social institutions of modern America, Nanapush presents the community an image through which it can project itself as successful and evasive, an unwilling warrior who is not destroyed by the spirit of dead enemies, however all-pervasive and overpowering they may be.

Lipsha Morrissey's character is, of course, the most obvious expression of the four stories of narrative identity. Socially, he is the outcast orphan with no clear parentage. He cares for the aged Nector and Marie out of gratitude and lethargy. His role as orphan/care-provider outlines a series of social relations which define him but against which he struggles. Psychologically his desire is to find himself a place in the family which coincides with the unique individual he senses he is. He sees himself as staying innocent and simple, but he wants to know about his roots and his background. As Lulu says, "'Well, *I* never thought you was odd. . . . Just troubled. You never knew who you were. . .'."

Communally, Lipsha is a healer, grandson of the powerful old shaman, Old Man Pillager. While his "touch" has been commonly acknowledged on the reservation, his identity as one of the tribe, with clear family ties and a useful function in the community, has not been. After he learns of this true parentage, he confusedly tries to join the army and become a warrior like his father, Gerry Nanapush, but it is not on the battlefields of the U.S. Army that he will fight, but on the battlefields of culture and community. He knows that he is defined by his family and communal position:

> Now as you know, as I have told you, I am sometimes blessed with the talent to touch the sick and heal their individual problems without even knowing what they are. I have some powers which, now that I think of it, was likely come down from Old Man Pillager. And then there is the newfound fact of insight I inherited from Lulu, as well as the familiar teachings of Grandma Kashpaw on visioning what comes to pass within a lump of tinfoil.

With his new realizations comes a new understanding of identity in a communal field.

But ultimately Lipsha is the son of trickster Nanapush. His mythic identity is linked to the tradition of the powerful trickster/transformer whose job it is to create the form of the world, to modify its contours in keeping with Earthmaker's plans. Lipsha's medicine trick with the turkey hearts proves to be an event which has the tragedy of a trickster's actions which backfire on him. But this is an event which is also in keeping with the Earthmaker's plan for all beings. By driving Gerry to freedom, Lipsha concludes a mythic tale which will live forever in Chippewa imagination. At the bridge, Lipsha delivers the trickster Nanapush/Nanabosho physically to Canada, but the communal level of identity provides unnoticed support when it is remembered that for many Midewiwin initiates the land of the dead is also called Nehnehbush's land and the passage from the physical world to the spirit world is made over a bridge. After Lipsha delivers Gerry back to the world of myth, he takes June's wandering soul in hand and prepares to lead her to her proper resting place as he did with Nector's soul. These actions show us that his identity will be defined communally as

something akin to a Midewiwin official, a healer, and mythically as a new reincarnation of Nehnehbush.

Lipsha has concluded that "Belonging was a matter of deciding to." This almost existential act unifies who he is on the psychological, social, communal, and mythic levels, and Lipsha becomes a complete human being—an experienced adult, a loving son, a healer, and a trickster/transformer. He feels all the threads of identity intertwining and blossoming:

> I felt expansion, as if the world was branching out
> in shoots and growing faster than the eye could see.
> I felt smallness, how the earth divided into bits and
> kept dividing. I felt the stars. I felt them roosting
> on my shoulders with his hand.

Feeling Nanapush's touch still on his shoulder, Lipsha is transformed in a moment of splendid mythic vision. Because he is a new complete human, he thinks of June Morrissey and is strong enough to bring her home, to help her, himself, and all of them complete a journey started long ago.

This cosmic unifying vision is the ultimate goal of mediation in contemporary Native American writing. As the text embeds the multiple narrative, it forces on the reader the same perspective that Lipsha experiences, a perspective from which an individual's perception is expanded and multiple connections are revealed. When readers are placed in this perceptual position, they begin to experience something of the Native American perception. Benjamin Whorf explains this perception of the world by reference to a cognitive linguistic realm inclusive of what English calls "present" and "future" as well as "subjective":

> The subjective or manifesting comprises all that we call future, BUT NOT MERELY THIS; it includes equally and indistinguishably all that we call mental—everything that appears or exists in the mind, or, as the Hopi would prefer to say, in the HEART, not only the heart of man, but the heart of animals, plants and things, and behind and within all the forms and appearances of nature in the heart of nature, and by implication and extension . . . in the very heart of the Cosmos itself.

From this perspective, events unfold on multiple layers of significance with multiple stories which clarify their connections. This is a worldview that Paula Allen described: the self as a moving event in a universe of dynamic equilibrium. Lipsha and the other characters of *Love Medicine* embrace the mystery of the world, but that mystery exists in a world and worldview where knowledge, meaning, truth, and signification already exist in a non-tangible realm which Benjamin Whorf called "manifesting" as opposed to the tangible realm where the processes of the world have already been realized as "manifested." The characters of *Love Medicine* perceive the world not as changing or progressing, but constantly in the process of becoming what it always was, but which we could not see; they see meaning in their lives and the world revealing itself, manifesting what has always been there much in the same way that meaning in Lipsha's life is the process of letting the forces at work in the world manifest themselves. Whorf saw the perception of a "manifesting" world as basic to the Native American worldview, a worldview where the universe is "the striving of purposeful desire, intelligent in character, toward manifestation." Robin Riddington clarifies Whorf's intentions and insights when he writes:

> Whorf's observations about Hopi time could apply equally well to many of the other native cultures of North America. . . . Although the Hopi have their own distinctive ceremonies and traditions, these arise out of a more general Indian thought world, which recognizes a timeless, vital or mythic principle in the universe.

In *Love Medicine,* Erdrich shifts the epistemological perspective of the reader so as to encourage a more Native American creation of meaning and knowledge, one which values the manifesting over the manifested.

Contemporary Native American writers adopt a mediational position through the use of multiple narrative, but their ultimate achievement is to shift the paradigm of our thought, to recharge Native readers and inspire non-Native readers with an appreciation of Native American epistemology and worldview. As the text opens its mysteries to the reader, the reader's perception expands beyond the boundaries of the text, and the universe reveals itself as timeless and mythic. In *Love Medicine,* Erdrich successfully accomplishes what Bakhtin described as the "ideological translation of another's language, and an overcoming of its otherness."

John S. Slack (essay date Summer 1993)

SOURCE: "The Comic Savior: The Dominance of the Trickster in Louise Erdrich's *Love Medicine,*" in *North Dakota Quarterly,* Vol. 61, No. 3, Summer, 1993, pp. 118-29.

[In the following essay, Slack contends that Love Medicine*'s loose structure as a novel is held tightly together by the recurring figure of the Trickster, represented by various characters.]*

One complaint occasionally directed at *Love Medicine* is that it is really not a novel but rather a collection of short stories bound together loosely by a common set of characters inhabiting successive stories. The arguments for its misnomer include the book's lack of either a central protagonist or a central conflict and its multi-narrational, and thus disjointed, narrative structure. However, this essay offers an argument in favor of *Love Medicine*'s "novelism," that is, at least as far as its possession of a central protagonist is concerned. As others, like Nora Barry and Mary Prescott, have suggested, it does have one: June (Morrisey) Kashpaw, whose disembodied spirit haunts or protects the lives of all the other main characters. However, I would further submit that, in this text, June is really the preeminent Chippewa woodland trickster figure, that wily, good/evil shape- and sex-changer, and as such, she embodies anagogically most of the central characters who people Erdrich's rich narrative.

In this sense, Erdrich's narrative is actually a retelling of some of the oral myth-tales of Naanabohzo the trickster, set in the medium of late 20th-century printed fiction. In other words, many of the stories in *Love Medicine* are related *to* and are a relating *of* the once verbally preserved cycle of Chippewa folk tales of the trickster. This reading of the text can help also to account for the novel's multiple narration as well as the sense of disjointedness some readers experience. Moreover, this reading firmly places Erdrich's text in league with those of another Chippewa writer, Gerald Vizenor, whose three books to date, but especially *Darkness in Saint Louis Bearheart* (1978), deal with a multiplicity of modern manifestations of the trickster figure.

Perhaps Erdrich and Vizenor, like the countless generations of Chippewa storytellers who spoke of the adventures and misadventures of their trickster figure, understand the one intrinsic value in all of them: the stories reveal that we all possess traits correlative to the trickster's. Robert F. Sayre briefly explores this human phenomenon:

> Let us start by admitting that we are all Tricksters as dumb and greedy as Wakdjunkaga [her/his Winnebago name]—have been and will remain—no matter how balanced and controlled we may ordinarily try to be in our waking, rational lives. We do and will leave rotting fish in the refrigerator, try to get something for nothing, soil underwear, masturbate, lust for [men]women on the beach, cut our own fingers and arms, and get fooled by squirrels in the attic and raccoons turning over our garbage cans.

Not unlike that of the original tales, Sayre's point is that humor and self-parody are elemental to a sane outlook on life. Indeed, according to Mac Linscott Ricketts, the trickster is the ultimate comic figure for humanity. Ricketts believes that by laughing at the tricks, boasts, and buffoonery of this clown, we are laughing at ourselves. He concludes that "[T]he myths of the trickster enabled the Indians to laugh off their failures . . . since they saw in the trickster how foolish man is, and how useless it is to take life too seriously."

Of course, most of the qualifications cited above are considered negative aspects of the trickster's "personality" as they are revealed in the original Chippewa myth cycles. Not only does s/he play tricks and get tricked, s/he is also a semi-divine, the offspring of a fisher-woman by the Great Spirit, or *manito,* who is known to the Chippewa as Misshepeshu. Moreover, Trickster, or Manabozho (also Naanabozho, Nanapush, Wenebojo, etc.), is the creator and namer of all the creatures of the world. Likewise, as Ron Messer indicates, Stith Thompson long ago proved that Longfellow's hero Hiawatha is really a one-sided, cleaned-up version of the Chippewa trickster-hero, Manabozho. In short, the trickster is both laughable fool and "comic savior," i.e., the preserver of the very human, humorous side of life.

Carl Jung, correlating the abilities of the trickster, shaman, and medicine man, suggests their "approximation" to a savior figure. This approximation, according to Jung, is a "confirmation of the mythological truth that the wounded wounder is the agent of healing, and the sufferer takes away suffering." Certainly, several of the traditional stories do give this aspect of acquiescence-in-adversity to Trickster. However, in my estimation, what makes this prankster more comical as a savior, and thus more prone to culture hero status, especially as s/he is manifested in the Chippewa myth cycles, is her/his inherently laughable high jinks and low (body) humor. According to Victor Turner, every manifestation of the trickster is "raw, undomesticated body and collective power, undefinable, uncontainable, and compounded equally of polymorphous libido and aggression." For, paradoxically, this comedic savior is just as often depicted as being endowed with a devilish wit and satanic demeanor.

This paradox is at the heart of Erdrich's *Love Medicine*—literally so. It is the trickster in this novel who provides the medicine that can heal all the damaged hearts (though in Lipsha's case he hilariously botches it); and it is the trickster manifested as con men, liars, cheats, wife beaters, and sadistic nuns who damages those hearts in the first place. As a result of this latter manifestation, Louise Flavin views *Love Medicine* as a negative depiction of life on a modern reservation. Such an observation is extremely lop-sided since there is about the book much reason to be hopeful. For instance, Nora Barry and Mary Prescott think Erdrich's novel envisions a changing culture—one that "draws upon the rich tradition of folklore and vision to offer characters a promising context for growth . . . ." The trickster, drawn from that tradition, is a survivor. And except for June, many of the young characters/tricksters in *Love Medicine,* like Lipsha, Gerry, Dot, Albertine, Lyman, and even Gordie, are definite survivors.

These and other characters provide the stories which make up the discoveries and mishaps that living brings and which Erdrich has utilized so that present and succeeding generations of her "listeners" can laugh at them and yet be forewarned. Perhaps, using the trickster stories as a teaching paradigm, Erdrich understands that her "love medicine" cannot always heal, but it can be a *written* prescription for health, both physical and spiritual. Like the trickster of the old folk tales, each of these new manifestations in *Love Medicine* acts heuristically but never didactically. Those who "hear" these accounts can either smile and take heed or plunge headlong into the abyss, as Nector appears to do in the painting done of him as a young brave.

The actual "accounts," if judged by chapter heads, number only fourteen; however, the first and last chapters each have four subdivisions and "The Good Tears" has two. Moreover, at least two of the other chapters have unnumbered breaks which divide them into two. Thus, by my estimation, there are as many as twenty-three possible trickster narratives in *Love Medicine.* The first of those accounts belongs significantly to June.

June, like the trickster that she is, is depicted as being always in flight, sensuous, erotic, and possessing a great physical hunger. In the only tale in which she acts physically, she gambles her sex for food and drink; however, unbeknownst to her, she plays her last hand with a white oil boom engineer before her planned return to the reservation. Instead, she is tricked by him, just as she is tricked by the weather, which she misjudges as an approaching, warm and mild, spring wind. As her niece Albertine observes, June was a plains Indian: "Even drunk she'd have known a storm was coming. She'd have known by the heaviness in the air, the smell of the clouds. She'd have gotten that animal sinking in her bones." June's demise, then, seems an enigma, until the cue comes (through the use of metaphor) from the narrator that this is some type of redemptive death. Erdrich seems to be implying that the trickster as savior has suffered for her people and now will be reborn in several new forms, both good and bad (and sometimes in combination), throughout the remainder of the novel.

June's two sons are perfect examples of good and bad reincarnations of the trickster. Although never actually acknowledged by her, Lipsha Morrissey is June's love child by Gerry Nanapush, the name-bearing Chippewa trickster figure in this novel. Believing himself abandoned and nearly drowned by a mother he never knew, Lipsha is raised by June's adoptive "mother" (really her aunt), Marie Kashpaw. He calls Marie "Grandma," which is significant since several versions of the traditional tales have Naanabozho raised by his grandmother, Nookoomis. Lipsha is Erdrich's most endearing example of a comic savior. His first-person accounts, including the story of the recovery of his past and his traditions which concludes the novel, are hilariously and heartwarmingly funny. However, as a savior of traditional ways, beliefs, and values, it is Lipsha who returns to the reservation (a somewhat typical modern tribal story-ending) after tricking his half-brother, King, out of his car.

King is the son of June by Gordie Kashpaw and perhaps the one truly "bad" and dislikeable manifestation of the trickster in *Love Medicine*; there is nothing of the culture hero in him. If Lipsha is more akin to divinity in his innocence, King is closer to the demonic in his guilt-ridden lowdown tricks. He steals the food from Lipsha's plate when they are growing up, teasing him that only real children can eat. He has also taken a potshot at his half-brother while out gopher-hunting together. King even tries to drown his own wife Lynette during a drunken binge, simply because she has fearfully taken his car keys. And in the penultimate scene between King, Lipsha, and Gerry, it is revealed that King did the truly despicable: he "sold out" a member of his own tribe.

Having been in the same prison as Gerry Nanapush, King gained Gerry's confidence and then betrayed him. In exchange for his own accelerated parole, he helped send Gerry to an Illinois maximum security prison. What makes King a trickster, however "unredeemable," is his affinity to that mythical character's unwavering ability to become entangled somehow in her/his own web of deceit. In his calculated betrayal of Gerry, according to Lipsha, King overlooked the sly capability of a true Nanapush to break out of any enclosure, including a federal prison: "No concrete shitbarn prison's built that can hold a Chippewa." Or, as Gerry's mother, Lulu, concurs when she "spills" the secret of Lipsha's paternity to him, while simultaneously revealing the hitherto unknown name of Gerry's own father, "There ain't a prison that can hold the son of Old Man Pillager, a Nanapush man. You should be proud that you're one."

One of the tales concerning Marie Kashpaw deals with a different type of enclosure: the convent located on the reservation. However, it too involves a kind of a breaking out; but what leads to Marie's breakout, the duel between two powerful tricksters, a sadistic nun and this foolishly wise fifteen-year-old, is very graphically described by Marie. However, it is important to note that, despite the graphic violence of the tale, this is a very funny story. Perhaps the humor is unsavory to some tastes because Erdrich is simultaneously taking a satirical swipe at Catholic fundamentalism. It seems to me that both these women confuse their trickster spirits with Satan. That confusion is due in part to Christianity's welding together of certain "negative" qualities of the trickster, confusion, disorder, cunning, and lustfulness, with the sin and pure evil incarnate in its Devil. Marie, an impressionable but gifted young woman, understands only that this presence is in her:

I stood out. Evil was a common thing I trusted. Before sleep sometimes he came and whispered conversation in the old language of the bush. I listened. He told me things he never told anyone but Indians. I listened to him, but I had confidence in Leopolda. She was the only one of the bunch he even noticed.

By inculcating her with tales of the devil, the school nuns have masked Marie's ability to unleash her own culture hero-tricksterhood. But by her misdirected zeal, Sister Leopolda ironically initiates Marie's cunning as a trickster. Marie plans to "steal" what the nun values most, Leopolda's eternal salvation, while winning her own place in heaven as a saint (culture hero). Leopolda, on the other hand, believes she can wrench evil from the girl, but ironically, she must employ the most drastic means to do it.

So she pours boiling hot water on Marie's back and bottom to burn out the devil. Then, in true trickster spirit, Marie tries to push the nun into an open baking oven; but the equally wily sister avoids this disaster and then stabs the girl in the hand and smashes her on the head with a poker, knocking her unconscious. These two tricksters are so cunning that the conclusion of this tale must be a draw. Marie momentarily gets her "sainthood" when she awakens: "For when I came around this was actually taking place. I was being worshiped. I had somehow gained the altar of a saint." However, the nun soon tricks Marie out of her glorification: "Leopolda had saved herself with her quick brain. She had witnessed a miracle. She had hid the fork. . . . And of course they believed her, because they never knew how Satan came and went . . . ." And as witnessed by a later tale, "Flesh and Blood," these two opposing types of tricksters even continue their power struggle a quarter of a century later.

Another kind of power struggle is to be found in Nector's stories, most of them lusty, gutsy tales truly worthy of a modern retelling of the Nanapush legends. One good indication of Nector Kashpaw's imminent trickster status is his twinhood. Almost every version of the Chippewa myth makes Naanabozho's birth a multiple one, sometimes triplets or quadruplets, but most often twins. As Hare, the trickster usually kills his brother, Wolf, who then wreaks havoc in the afterworld, thus setting up a dual domain. Likewise, Nector and Eli represent a dichotomy of sorts; the former is school-taught and city-wise, while the latter is unschooled but very knowledgeable about traditions and the ways of nature. "In this way, it is a good partnership," says Nector, referring to Eli's second sense for shooting geese and Nector's for selling the goods in town.

In one tale, with a pair of those geese strapped to his arms, Nector first encounters Marie the trickster, fresh from her duel with Leopolda. Nector, who lusts after Lulu Nanapush, feels nothing for this "skinny white girl, dirty Lazarre." Yet, when he tangles with her, he is tricked by her emerging feminine wiles, and takes her sexually, in plain view of the convent's inhabitants. Thus, unable to consummate his desire for Lulu, he sublimates this passion for a number of years, but in later "tales" he does have an affair with Lulu that ends with a disastrous fire set by the "Tricked-ster," Nector himself.

The mother of Gerry Nanapush and seven other sons all by different fathers, Lulu Lamartine is the fascinating subject of one story and the hilarious narrator of another. Indeed, she is another powerful female trickster figure and a comic savior to boot. Like her rival, Marie, Lulu has a huge heart; but while Marie takes in waifs, orphans, and abandoned children, Lulu takes in lost boys who pretend to be men. She is the preserver of passions as well as old traditions, both human and trickster. It is Lulu who teaches Lipsha to cheat at cards by marking them. Lulu must have also learned some tricks from her first lover Old Man Pillager. another disembodied trickster character, since "Old Man" is one of the proper names used in the Algonkian nation for the trickster. One of the funniest trickster narratives in the book is when Lulu is about to be forced out of her home by the tribal council; she turns the trick her way by appearing before them. There, she intimidates every man in the room into silence, for fear she will expose them in their sexual follies:

> Every one of them could see it in my face. They saw me clear. Before I'd move the Lamartine household I'd hit the tribe with a fistful of paternity suits that would make their heads spin.

Though her passion is more notorious than her compassion, Lulu is not amoral. When her third husband, Bev Lamartine, brother of her late husband and a minor evil incarnation of Trickster, reveals that he has "cheated" her, because he is still married to a woman in the Twin Cities, she sends him back there with her son, Gerry, to legalize their marriage by means of a divorce from Bev's first wife.

Gerry Nanapush, of course, epitomizes the most common and comical qualities of the trickster. Erdrich portrays him as elusive; in fact, he never gets a tale of his own, yet his presence, like June's, is all over the novel. Indeed, there is some innate affinity between these two tricksters; his memory of June, and not revenge, is what really motivates Gerry to seek out King at the end, according to Lipsha. But what Lipsha and all the other observers of Gerry marvel at most of all are his physical qualities. Those descriptions, while often deceptive and contradictory, make Gerry a prime example of the comic savior.

In describing his sense of humor, Albertine recalls the trial that put Gerry in jail in the first place. In a barroom brawl,

the trickster had used "reservation rules" and kicked a cowboy in the balls. In court, a doctor testified "in behalf of the cowboy's testicles" stating that he is possibly infertile. Gerry retorts that such a lasting effect seems impossible, since the bar was dark, his aim was bad, and his target extremely small. That seals Gerry's verdict, and, consequently, he spends half his life in jails, breaking out of them, or running away from those who wish to place him back in them. Albertine understands that all this particular trickster wants is to settle down, but the modern world will not allow it:

> So you see, it was difficult for Gerry, as an Indian, to retain *the natural good humor* of his ancestors in these modern circumstances. He tried though, and since he believed in justice, not laws, Gerry knew where he belonged—out of prison, in the bosom of his new family. (my emphasis)

A trickster with a family is not as uncharacteristic as it seems. According to Turner, later North American trickster myth cycles "describe the structuring of the trickster's life and activities: he marries, settles down, has children, obeys kinship, and affinal norms, etc."

Erdrich not only gives Gerry comical and familial features, but, as the storyteller, she also portrays him as a rebellious but peaceful savior, one who eventually gets culture hero status among the Chippewa. He is a great example of Ricketts' "trickster-fixer." Thinking of her renegade son, Lulu says, ". . . inspiring the Indian people, that was [Gerry's] life." Even more evocative is Lipsha's comments about his father's now-legendary abilities:

> . . . Gerry Nanapush, famous politicking hero, dangerous armed criminal, judo expert, escape artist, charismatic member of the American Indian Movement, and smoker of many pipes of kinnikinnick in the most radical groups.
>
> That was . . . Dad.

By connecting Gerry to radical politics, Lipsha identifies him as the persecuted promoter for drastic change; in short, he becomes a savior figure, one who must suffer for his people so that their cause may be heard. However, that does not keep Erdrich from surrounding Gerry's tales with downright good humor. In fact, the author allows Lipsha and his cousin Albertine to give her "listeners" an idea of the comically personable and extraordinarily physical qualities of this shape-changer.

Although a trickster herself, Albertine is definitely in awe of this great one. She seeks him out, knowing a bit of the legend surrounding Gerry: ". . . he was famous for leading a hunger strike at the state pen, as well as having been Henry Lamartine's brother and some kind of boyfriend to Aunt June . . . ." When she finds him (easy since he is so "large"), she and he have a friendly drink before Albertine is attacked by Dot Adare, Gerry's pregnant girlfriend. In true trickster style, when on the defensive, Albertine laughs in the face of her enemy. She is saved from utter annihilation by Dot when gigantic Gerry catches his girl "in midair and carried her, yelling, out the door."

Besides his ever-growing size and weight, Albertine is impressed with Gerry's androgynous features. As I have already indicated, tricksters can not only change shape, they can also switch genders. Albertine portrays Gerry as a giant mass with paradoxically delicate properties. His little fingers curl "like a woman's at tea" when he picks up his wife. In fact, his entire hands are "delicate and artistic," and he uses them "prettily." Albertine is so affected by his delicacy that she makes this odd comparison: "So many things Gerry did might remind you of the way that a beautiful courtesan, standing naked before a mirror, would touch herself—lovingly, conscious of her attractions." Juxtaposed in Albertine's mind with this femininity of Gerry is his absolute bulk, his leonine agility, and his incredible strength. He is a "mountain," "a hot-air balloon" who makes a "godlike leap" from a third-story hospital window, like "a fat rabbit disappearing down a hole." The allusion to Hare, whatever the waist size, is another signifier of the agility and potential ability of this elusive shape-changer.

At the conclusion of the novel, Lipsha witnesses yet another narrow escape by Gerry Nanapush. Only this time Lipsha, as trickster, is able to assist in his father's final flight. The instrument for that flight is King's Firebird (a car named for a Native American mythological bird), which Lipsha and Gerry wrest from the traitor in a symbolic, trickster-swindling poker game. In one version of the traditional tales, there is a climactic scene portraying a showdown between Naanabohzo and the Great Gambler, Gichi Nita Ataaged, in which trickster wins and the gambler dies. This modern re-enactment of that tale has King and Lipsha playing five-card stud using pieces of Lucky Charms cereal for chips before the arrival of Gerry. Gerry's "miraculous" appearance frightens King's family and increases his trickster-fixer status for Lipsha:

> The famous Chippewa who had songs written about him, whose face was on protest buttons, whose fate was argued over in courts of law, who sent press releases to the world, sat down . . . with his son and his cellmate . . . .

Of course, the game of cards is "won" with Lipsha's marked deck, which Gerry immediately recognizes as his mother-trickster's, Lulu's, special crimping system. Unlike the Great Gambler, King will not die, except symbolically in his son's eyes, who betrays his father's whereabouts when he mistakenly assumes that the police, in pursuit of Gerry, are after King.

In her first novel, *Love Medicine,* Louise Erdrich has managed to recount and thus recover for a "modern audience" some of the myths and traditional beliefs of the Chippewa. It seems to me that her polyglossic narrative technique is really the only way to tell anew the hilarious tales of the trickster; that is, by and through a variety of human faces and shapes who command some or all of the characteristics of this contemporary comic savior. In other words, storytellers have always had many voices, but *Love Medicine* reflects that multiplicity simply because a modern trickster narrative demands it. And June's presence begins and ends this narrative because, as the egg-eater, she spawns a progeny of tricksters (no matter how impossible genetically) which is constant only in its ability to be returned anew. Renewal, through laughter, is the prescription, and also the favorable prognosis, of *Love Medicine.*

Roberta Rubenstein (review date 14 November 1993)

SOURCE: "Louise Erdrich Revisits the Complex World of the Chippewa," in *Chicago Tribune Books,* November 14, 1993, pp. 3, 11.

[*In the following review, Rubenstein praises Erdrich's updated edition of* Love Medicine.]

Louise Erdrich is not the first author to return to a previously published work of fiction to amend it. The most well-known of such revisers, Henry James, published altered versions of his stories and novels—often accompanied by eloquent prefaces explaining the revisions—years after their original publication. Presumably, writers tinker with works already in print because events continue to develop and characters continue to pursue the lives their author has invented for them.

The latter seems especially true for Erdrich, whose first novel, *Love Medicine,* was originally published in 1984 and honored with the National Book Critics Circle Award that year. Returning readers, unlikely to have forgotten such vivid characters as Lipsha Morrissey and Lulu Lamartine, will relish the current expanded edition as a second visit to a familiar landscape.

The book is equally a feast for readers discovering Erdrich's richly realized world for the first time: several interrelated families of Turtle Mountain Chippewa Indians living in a community in North Dakota over a period of 50 years. Five new sections have been seamlessly spliced into the original narrative; each in some way extends the collective portrait of the community.

Using seven narrators from three families, *Love Medicine* is a collective history of the speakers' interwoven loves and hates, tangled passions and dreams, overlapping longing and grief. Through lyrical language, vivid characterizations and freshly minted images, the narrative masterfully sustains the illusion of oral stories. Although several are told by an omniscient narrator, most unfold through the distinctive voices of the characters themselves.

We hear the yearning voice of Nector Nanapush, who for nearly 20 years has struggled to reconcile his passionate feelings for two women, as he articulates his desire to "swim against the movement of time" and "pitch whoopee" again with the Lulu Lamartine of his (and her) youth.

The medley of narrative voices resembles the medley of colors in an Indian rug pattern: Each heightens the contrast and amplifies the design as a whole. Later in the narrative we see Nector through the eyes of his grandson, Lipsha Morrissey, whose uneducated diction is studded with lively perceptions as well as humorous malaprops. Lipsha, who has "the touch" (though he comes to doubt his medicinal powers), used to think a malpractice suit was "a color clothing quack doctors had to wear so you could tell them from the good ones."

In "The Island," one of the new sections, we get a glimpse of the rebellious and passionate Lulu Nanapush Lamartine as a young woman. Deserted by her mother in childhood, she returns to the reservation after running away and moves in with her uncle Nanapush and his stern wife, Rushes Bear.

Partly to disturb her aunt, Lulu visits an eccentric Indian much older than she who lives alone on an island. Her strange encounter with Moses Pillager, whom some believe is a windigo (spirit), evolves into her sexual initiation. When she becomes pregnant, she realizes that she needs "a midwife to guide (her), a mother."

The medley of narrative voices resembles the medley of colors in an Indian rug pattern: Each heightens the contrast and amplifies the design as a whole.
—*Roberta Rubenstein*

By the end of the winter on the island with Pillager, Lulu is rewarded for her odd vigil with a spirit message from her lost mother, who promises to aid her when the child—the

first of Lulu's eight children by several different fathers—is born. The tangled parentage of Lulu's sons forms a central part of the texture of *Love Medicine.*

Two other new sections appear near the end of the narrative. One movingly depicts the pain suffered by Marie Lazarre's son, Gordie, who cannot get past the death of his wife, and kills himself by swallowing Lysol.

Marie faces the irrevocability of her firstborn son's terrible death almost as if it were his birth. She recalls how "he had lain in her body in the tender fifteenth summer of her life. Now she could sense him gliding back and forth, faster, faster, like a fox chasing its own death down a hole. Forward, back, diving. She knew when he caught the rat. She felt the walls open. He connected, went right through with a blast like heat."

Another new section traces the misfortunes of Lyman Lamartine, Lulu's youngest son, as he tries to bring progress to the reservation. His "tomahawk factory" employs Chippewas to produce stereotypical Native American tourist souvenirs.

The venture deteriorates into comic chaos when the delicate balance of power that Lyman has attempted to maintain between his mother, Lulu and his father's widow, Marie Lazarre—the women who competed for the love of Nector Kashpaw, now deceased—collapses:

> After the fighting tapered off, those who were still in condition to do so, Nanapushes and Morrisseys and Lazarres alike, methodically demolished, scattered, smashed to bits, and carried off what was left of the factory. And as they did so, walking around me as if I were just another expensive and obsolete government-inspired mechanism, there was a kind of organized joy to it that I would recognize only many drinks later as the factory running backward.

In extending her characters' histories through the newly added sections, Erdrich satisfies our curiosity about the individuals she has brought to life. She convincingly conveys the complexity of their relationships as well as the tensions they feel as they ponder the meaning of poverty and despair and spiritual discovery and the sustaining strength of "love medicine."

Sidner Larson (essay date 1993)

SOURCE: "The Fragmentation of a Tribal People in Louise Erdrich's *Tracks*," in *American Indian Culture and Research Journal*, Vol. 17, No. 2, 1993, pp. 1-13.

[*In the following essay, Larson discusses Erdrich's depiction in* Tracks *of Native Americans' loss of land and cultural identity to white colonization.*]

Louise Erdrich's novel *Tracks* deals with the years between 1912 and 1919, when the North Dakota Chippewa, or Anishinabe, as they call themselves, were coping with the effects of the General Allotment Act of 1887, the purpose of which was to divide tribally allotted lands among individual Indians so that these Indians could leave their nomadic, communal cultures behind and become settled as farmers. After the Indian Allotment Act of 1904, each enrolled member of the Turtle Mountain Chippewa born before 1909 received one quarter section of land, with single members of the tribe receiving various lesser amounts depending on their age. This was part of the transformation of Indian land into Euro-American property; more significantly, as Mary Jane Schneider has noted in her book *North Dakota Indians,* allotment had the immediate effect of reducing the total acres of Indian land by 65 percent. *Tracks* is in part an autopsy of this process, whereby place becomes property, and an analysis of how the process affects innocent bystanders.

Mixed-blood Indian people occupy a marginal position in an already marginalized culture. In the case of the Turtle Mountain Chippewa, mixed blood has its origins in the historical influence of French and English fur traders on the tribe during the mid-eighteenth century. These traders obtained furs from the Chippewa, who received trade goods in return. This contact was more than economic, however, and resulted in intermarriage between French men and Chippewa women. Contact was encouraged by the fur companies as a means of keeping their men content, although most Frenchmen returned to Canada when the fur business declined. The children of these unions were called bois brulés, half-breeds, mixed-bloods, or Métis.

Another large influence on Indian people was the coming of European religions in the early 1800s. Julie Maristuen-Rodakowski, in her article "The Turtle Mountain Reservation in North Dakota," has pointed out that European religion came to the Chippewa in 1817, "when residents of the Red River Colony (Winnipeg) wrote to the Bishop of Quebec asking him to send religious leaders to minister to the Indians." Apparently, this resulted from negative aspects of the fur trade relationship, which brought abuse of alcohol by Indians and French and the abandonment of Indian women and mixed-blood children by Frenchmen. French Catholics responded by establishing schools and convents, accomplished at Turtle Mountain by Father Belcourt in 1885.

Erdrich points out serious problems associated with the coming of Catholicism. For example, in *Love Medicine,* Marie leaves a Catholic convent because of physical abuse.

Maristuen-Rodakowski states, "Marie later hears that the Sacred Heart Convent is a place for nuns that didn't get along anywhere else, and she finds some solace in that. So much for the ministering of the Roman Catholics, if this is true."

Louise Erdrich's assertion of abuse may seem controversial, but additional evidence of problems associated with Indian-Catholic relations exists in the writing of other Indian authors. An example is James Welch's *Winter in the Blood,* where the priest from Harlem, Montana, refuses to bury the narrator's grandmother in the family graveyard. The narrator says, "He never buried Indians in their family graveyards; instead, he made them come to him, to his church, his saints and holy water, his feuding eyes." Welch's passage in *Winter in the Blood* is similar to Louise Erdrich's reflection of negative aspects of Catholicism in *Tracks.* James Welch and I are cousins, and we both spent considerable time at our grandparents' ranch on the Fort Belknap Reservation. The perceptions of both Erdrich and Welch are authenticated for me by stories I remember our grandmother telling of drinking and sexual abuse of Gros Ventre females by priests at the St. Paul Mission at Hays, Montana, located at Fort Belknap.

The process by which European religion came to northern tribes such as the Anishinabe and Gros Ventre can be further explained by a passage from Sister M. Clare Hartmann's *The Significance of the Pipe to the Gros Ventres of Montana:*

> In 1840 Father De Smet was the first missionary to travel through the country in which the Gros Ventres and Assiniboines lived. Father Point (1846-47) and Father Giorda (1862), both Jesuits, visited them periodically. However, President Grant divided the missionary work with the Indians among various sects. Fort Belknap Reservation, the home of the Gros Ventres, was confined to the Methodists. As none of them ever came to take up their work, the Indians were befriended and taken over by the various Jesuit Fathers. In 1883 Father Eberschweiler came to Helena, Montana. On one of his visits to the Gros Ventres they asked for a resident missionary. In 1885 President Cleveland granted permission for the erection of a mission on the Fort Belknap Agency. Father Eberschweiler took up his abode at the agency.

The zeal with which various religious factions must have set about their work is reflected in President Grant's divvying up Indian Territory for them. The fact that the Gros Ventre's assigned ministers never showed up characterizes Gros Ventre luck at the time.

What makes this process so reminiscent of *Tracks* is the fact that the Gros Ventre asked for a resident missionary. They did this because they wished to escape the negative influence of soldiers stationed at Fort Assiniboine near present-day Havre, Montana. This is very similar to the Chippewa of *Tracks,* who are willing to embrace a new religion in return for help in escaping abuses brought to them by the fur traders.

Among the problems associated with Catholicism for Indian people were the ambivalence and tension that resulted when Indian people tried to live with both Native American and Roman Catholic religious beliefs. Knowledge of both was in some ways an advantage, but at other times it had a paralyzing effect resulting from contradictory systems. In "Reading between Worlds: Narrativity in the Fiction of Louise Erdrich," Catherine Rainwater states,

> In *Tracks,* Erdrich's two narrators likewise struggle with liminality in their efforts to leave behind early lives in favor of others they have chosen. Nanapush grows up Christian in a Jesuit school, but later chooses life in the woods and Chippewa tradition; the other narrator, Pauline, is a mixed-blood raised in the Native American tradition, but she wishes to be white and eventually becomes a fanatical nun, constantly at war with the "pagans" who had once been her relatives.

The fragmentation of Indian tribes can be seen as having been accomplished in a number of ways. The introduction of European diseases weakened the tribes sufficiently to make them vulnerable; after that happened, however, the influence of the English and French fur traders, the application of European religions, and political exploitation of mixed-blood people were considerable factors as well.

Intermarriage with fur traders, although generative in certain situations, was also very divisive in at least two powerful ways. Although Indian people were quite accepting of outsiders on some levels, especially as a way of making alliances they saw as advantageous, they still retained a homogeneity at the core of their kinship systems.

An example is research on mixed-bloods done by George Devereux in his book *Mohave Ethnopsychiatry.* Devereux points out that the Mojave have had a cultural fear of aliens, dictating avoidance of all close contact with other tribes and, even more, of intimate connections with alien races. The white race is considered the most dangerous because of its "acquisitiveness." Devereux goes on to say that "the three most intensive forms of physiological interactions—eating, cohabitation, and killing—and the most significant form of psychological interaction—discussing the knowledge ac-

quired in a dream—expose the Mojave to the dangers of foreign contamination."

Within this context, mixed-bloods are considered racially alien and therefore capable of causing full-blood Mojave Indians to contract "the foreign illness," or *Ahwe,* which the Mojave believe can cause death. As a result, mixed-blood infants were sometimes killed, or, if they were permitted to survive, their fate was harsh: They were rejected by their maternal kin and shunned by the rest of the tribe. Although this is perhaps more dramatic than examples of mixed-blood treatment found in *Tracks,* it does suggest foundations of Native American thought that are responsible for tribal organizations being quite strict with regard to identity.

Another example is the fact that mixed-bloods were considered peripheral to tribal government by traditional members. These traditional members were consistently opposed to giving up tribal land and to the process of assimilation into white culture. As a result, European administrators often turned to the mixed-blood population as a means of gaining enough support to obtain concessions; by proclaiming that mixed-bloods were to have a say in decision-making, white agents were often able to get their way.

In *Mixed Bloods and Tribal Dissolution: Charles Curtis and the Quest for Indian Identity,* William Unrau documents how Charles Curtis, a mixed-blood Kaw, supported assimilationist policies and allotment. Curtis, an attorney and politician, actually authored the 1898 Curtis Act, a precursor to the Allotment Act. Although Curtis envisioned the act as a great progressive measure, its ultimate result was tribal destruction for his people.

One of the ways this tribal destruction was accomplished was to give mixed-blood Kaws voting rights, which they subsequently exercised to overcome traditional views and facilitate allotment of Kaw lands. This exploitation of alienated mixed-bloods represents a primary tension in *Tracks*; it is part of the backdrop against which the characters live their chaotic and confused lives.

The book begins with Nanapush's reflections on the state of affairs among the Chippewa of 1912. In his winter count, he notes that the survivors of displacement and smallpox fought their way west to exile "in a storm of government papers," only to be stricken again, this time by tuberculosis. He considers the belief of some Anishinabe that the trouble is the result of dissatisfied spirits of the dead, then comes to his own conclusion: "Our trouble came from living, from liquor and the dollar bill. We stumbled toward the government bait, never looking down, never noticing how the land was snatched from under us at every step."

Although Nanapush aims toward present reality with his

statement, it is not because he is unaware of the influence of the past. He tells how Anishinabe dead can come to coax the living to go with them and how he and Fleur Pillager, a child he has rescued from the tuberculosis epidemic, nearly succumb to their urging. The dead feel it would be better to move on than to live amid the ruin of Indian culture, regarding the living as fools to do so. Nanapush replies,

> And we were. Starvation makes fools of anyone. In the past, some had sold their allotment land for one hundred poundweight of flour. Others, who were desperate to hold on, now urged that we get together and buy back our land, or at least pay a tax and refuse the lumbering money that would sweep the marks of our boundaries off the map like a pattern of straws. Many were determined not to allow the hired surveyors, or even our own people, to enter the deepest bush. They spoke of the guides Hat and Many Women, now dead, who had taken the government pay.

With this, Erdrich begins to make a more realistic statement about the seeming passivity of Indian people by personalizing their loss of land. Earlier, I said that what was significant about allotment was that it reduced Indian landholdings by 65 percent. What is even more significant, what goes without-saying too many times, is that, when the Indian people were coerced into giving up their land, it was at a time when they were literally at the point of starving to death in an environment that provided few alternative means of survival to the hunting culture that was destroyed.

The "bait" that Indian people stumbled toward was meager rations that would enable them to stay alive. Also implicit in the statement, however, is resistance, a determination by some to hold on to the land by the white way of paying money; others took action by calling on the ancient power once possessed by the Pillager Clan, "who knew the secret ways to cure or kill, until their art deserted them." Although some maneuver successfully to retain their land, they are forced to do so as individuals operating largely outside the tribal kinship system; the overall effect is one of further diminishment. What seems more empowering in the long run, though less profitable in the short term, is Nanapush's and Fleur's adherence to traditional ways.

Although Indian people were promised time and again that each land concession would be the last, whites continued to find means for further dispossession. In *Tracks,* although the Anishinabe have been given individual parcels of land by allotment, those parcels are still being taken away for failure to pay taxes. Nanapush complains about this, saying, "As you know, I was taught by the Jesuits. . . . I know about law. I know that 'trust' means they can't tax our parcels." What this means within the context of *Tracks* is that in spite of

the fact that the land was held in trust for Indians by the federal government, the states and others could step in and claim it under certain circumstances.

More specifically, Indian tribes are vulnerable to arguments based on legal doctrines such as statutes of limitation and adverse possession, doctrines that amount to a requirement of "use it or lose it" in various circumstances. During the twilight years from the 1880s to the 1960s, when they were virtually paralyzed by adversity, tribes often failed to exercise rights they would have had commensurate with federal recognition as separate but equal entities. These patterns of "nonuser," in legal parlance, or non-use by Indians, created powerful equities for governments and private landowners who ruled on or occupied lands more or less by default. It appears that the seizure of land for failure to pay property taxes referred to in *Tracks* stems from this, a practice finally struck down by the Supreme Court in the 1976 Minnesota case *Bryan v. Itasca County* (426 U. S. 373 [1976]).

In conjunction with this practice, land was apparently resold at auction after being seized. Nector Kashpaw, in a moment of realization, reiterates,

> If we don't pay they'll auction us off! Damien nodded, went on, ignoring Margaret's shocked poke at her knowledgeable son. Edgar Pukwan Jr. and the Agent control the choosing of the board who will decide who may bid on what foreclosed parcels and where.

Erdrich sets up the Morisseys as an example of those who have profited by buying allotments others have lost to taxes: "They were well-off people, mixed-bloods who profited from acquiring allotments that many old Chippewa did not know how to keep." Excluded from certain aspects of tribal society as they were, mixed-blood people clearly felt that some losses suffered by traditional people represented opportunities for them. In addition, consistent with the strong matriarchal strain in northern tribes, Bernadette Morrissey is the leader of the Morrisseys, and, as long as she is in charge, they prosper. Again, this is similar to James Welch's *Winter in the Blood,* where the narrator remarks, "We passed Emily Short's fields, which were the best in the valley. They had been leveled by a reclamation crew from the agency. Emily was on the tribal council." In *Tracks,* when Bernadette is faced with adversity, she reacts immediately: "In a week, with her cleanliness, her methodical handwriting, and her way with sums, she had found a way to save her land. In spite of the first consumptive signs in her lungs, Bernadette kept house for the Agent, reorganized his property records, and mailed debt announcements to every Indian in arrears." Bernadette is obviously a very capable individual; it is also clear, however, that her success is gained in large part at the expense of other Indian people.

Bernadette's success is limited in other ways as well. Like Teresa in *Winter in the Blood,* although she has won the battle to prosper individually, she is losing the war, in the sense that her family is in disarray. Her children, Clarence and Sophie, both marry no-account Lazarres and descend on her like a swarm of locusts, whereupon she leaves them on the farm and moves to town.

The significance of family for Indian people has been articulated by Janine Windy Boy-Pease in the 1985 Rattlesnake Productions film *Country Warriors: A Story of the Crow Tribe:* "But you know Crows measure wealth a little differently than non-Indians. . . . Wealth is measured by one's relatedness, one's family, and one's clan. To be alone, that would be abject poverty to a Crow." By isolating herself, Bernadette has allowed herself to become a shadow of property; as a consequence, she contributes to the colonization of the tribe and then, in turn, is colonized by her own children, who, without her guidance, fall into decadence.

On the other hand, Nanapush, representing the traditional Anishinabe, seeks to remain aligned with tribal tradition as much as possible. Although he is made to bend, he does not break, remaining perhaps the most empowered figure throughout the book:

> The Captain and then the lumber president, the Agent and at last many of our own, spoke long and hard about a cash agreement. But nothing changed my mind. I've seen too much go by—unturned grass below my feet, and overhead, the great white cranes flung south forever. I know this. Land is the only thing that lasts life to life. Money burns like tinder, flows off like water. And as for government promises, the wind is steadier. I am a holdout, like the Pillagers, although I told the Captain and the Agent what I thought of their papers in good English. I could have written my name, and much more too, in script. I had a Jesuit education in the halls of Saint John before I ran back to the woods and forgot all my prayers.

In fact, much of Nanapush's power derives from language. His entire narrative in *Tracks* is told in the form of a story to Lulu, his adopted daughter. This device is particularly striking to me, because it reminds me of my grandmother talking incessantly at me when I was very young. She made it a point to tell me in detail things one might think would be lost on a youngster. In order to get me to sit still for this, she resorted to things like making my grandfather saddle up a sawhorse in the kitchen so I would listen while she cooked and talked. I did not think much about it at the time, but I know the value of the stories now. Like Nanapush with Lulu, someone took the time to tell me who I am, and why, and that is valuable.

Nanapush emphasizes the value of storytelling throughout the book. He tells how he saved his own life during the smallpox epidemic by starting a story: "I fainted, lost breath, so that I could hardly keep moving my lips. But I did continue and recovered. I got well by talking. Death could not get a word in edgewise, grew discouraged, and traveled on." After he rescues Fleur and the spirits of the Pillagers come for them, it is talking that revives him again: "My voice rasped at first when I tried to speak, but then, oiled by strong tea, lard and bread, I was off and talking . . . I began to creak and roll. I gathered speed. I talked both languages in streams that ran alongside each other, over every rock, around every obstacle. The sound of my own voice convinced me I was alive."

Nanapush's verbal ability works on other levels as well. He sees himself as a talker and a hunter and as someone who can wound with jokes. This gives him a powerful tool to deal with things as they happen. He is a ladies' man who casts a verbal spell on Margaret Kashpaw after she comes to his cabin to upbraid him for giving her son love medicine to use on Fleur. He suggests to Margaret at one point that he finally may have lost his virility, and she replies, "As long as your voice works, the other will." There is a recognition of power in Margaret's statement as well as a wonderful evocation of what it can mean to be a person of age, knowledge, and experience.

This verbal power is shown to have negative possibilities as well. In "Narrativity in the Fiction of Louise Erdrich," Catherine Rainwater observes that Erdrich presents two distinct worldviews in *Tracks.* This is most vividly illustrated through the character of Pauline, who is a Puyat: "[T]he Puyats were known as a quiet family, with little to say. We were mixed-bloods, skinners in the clan for which the name was lost." This is the classic dilemma of the mixed-blood, people living between cultures and relegated to the lowly position of skinners, drudge work in the hierarchy of hunting society, so unimportant that the clan name has been forgotten.

Nanapush makes his feelings toward Pauline known early on:

> But I could not cast the Puyat from my mind. You might not remember what people I'm talking about, the skinners, of whom Pauline was the only trace of those who died and scattered. She was different from the Puyats I remembered, who were always an uncertain people, shy, never leaders in our dances and cures. She was, to my mind, an unknown mixture of ingredients, like pale bannock that sagged or hardened. We never knew what to call her, or where she fit or how to think when she was around. So we tried to ignore her, and that worked as long

as she was quiet. But she was different once her mouth opened and she started to wag her tongue. She was worse than a Nanapush, in fact. For while I was careful with my known facts, she was given to improving truth.

Pauline is indeed a handful, representing all the pain, rage, and frustration of a person forced to live in two different cultures while being rejected to a large degree by both. Early in the book, she pesters her father into sending her to Argus, where she intends to live as a white. Her past reappears almost immediately, however, in the form of Fleur Pillager, who shows up in Argus, is raped, then causes Argus to be leveled by a tornado. During the tornado, Pauline and her cousin Russell seek safety in an icehouse but are denied entrance by a group of white men already inside. Enraged, Pauline locks the men in from the outside, where all but one perish. Overwhelmed by guilt added to her existing identity crisis, Pauline becomes more and more aberrant.

In her confusion, Pauline wanders between white and Indian worlds. Initially, she assumes a role of keeper of the dead, then increasingly turns to religion. At the same time, she attempts to maintain contact on the reservation. Faced with the distance she has created between herself and the Indian people, however, she grows frustrated and destructive, becoming a caricature of the marginal person. Catherine Rainwater again observes,

> Despite her scorn for her Native American upbringing, Pauline (later to become Sister Leopolda) cannot quite escape her old way of construing experience . . . . She recounts the sufferings of St. John of the Cross, St. Catherine, St. Cecelia, and St. Blaise, and says with pride: "Predictable shapes, these martyrdoms. Mine took a different form."

This passage helps illuminate what can happen when cultural codes conflict. Pauline's interpretation of experience is presented as dual and irreconcilable; she is not allowed to privilege one religious code or to synthesize the two as a form of resolution. Instead, Pauline is placed in a permanent state of irresolution—she is crazy. The manifestations of her craziness, fueled by Catholicism, are clearly destructive, as Pauline gradually becomes more fanatic and embattled. In return for a crumb of recognition by Margaret, Pauline tells the story of what happened in Argus, information that Margaret solicits to use against her son's interest in Fleur Pillager. Warming to Eli and Fleur's sexual relationship, she tries to use Sophie Morrissey to get Eli for herself. When Nanapush tries to cure Fleur's waning powers in a sweat lodge ceremony, Pauline tries her best to interrupt by preaching Christianity.

Although Pauline's portrayal is not as attractive as others that

speak to the positive effects of mixed blood on the evolution of tribes, it is very effective in its detailed presentation of the tragic aspects of such a mixed-blood figure. And, indeed, it is true that for every admirable "cultural broker" created by forced acculturation, there are thousands of confused and broken Paulines thrown on the cultural scrap heap; it is important that their loss is not forgotten.

Nanapush has resisted assimilation to white culture to an amazing degree through words. He cajoles, teases, scolds, croons, and prays in ways to make a weasel think twice. In addition, he has followed another tribal tradition: He has taken three young people under his wing and taught them traditional ways. Eli has become a hunter able to survive in the woods, although he succumbs to capitalism and tries to find his way by getting a job. Fleur, also a competent hunter, embraces Nanapush's spirituality more fully, although she, too, is eventually beaten down by the loss of her child and the Pillager land at Matchimanito:

> She had failed too many times, both to rescue us and save her youngest child, who now slept in the branches of bitter oaks. Her dreams lied, her vision was obscured, her helper slept deep in the lake, and all her Argus money was long spent. Though she traveled through the bush with gunnysacks and her skinning knife, though she worked past her strength, tireless, and the rough shreds piled to our ankles and spilled across the floor, Fleur was a different person than the young woman I had known. She was hesitant in speaking, false in her gestures, anxious to cover her fear.

Although Fleur is finally beaten down, she becomes so only after having a powerful influence on all those around her. She demonstrates that there are different ways to live than liquor and the dollar bill and that there is dignity and even power in the way she has chosen. Even the fact of her demise is deeply moving: She hitches herself to a cart and leaves rather than stoop to live in a way she does not believe.

Eli and certainly Fleur are nothing to be ashamed of, but it is Lulu who proves to be Nanapush's ultimate triumph. With many of his traditional methods of resistance frustrated, Nanapush moves to Kashpaw land and takes up a position of leadership in the tribal council. From this position, he plays his remaining cards and is able to retrieve Lulu from boarding school.

Beset as Nanapush is from within and without, he unerringly turns to kinship ways to work his method of preservation, focusing on Lulu:

> You were the last to emerge. You stepped gravely

down, round-faced and alert, so tall we hardly knew to pick you out from the others. Your grin was ready and your look was sharp. You tossed your head like a pony, gathering scent. Your braids were cut, your hair in a thick ragged bowl, and your dress was a shabby and smoldering orange, a shameful color like a half-doused flame, visible for miles, that any child who tried to run away from the boarding school was forced to wear. The dress was tight, too small, straining across your shoulders. Your knees were scabbed from the punishment of scrubbing long sidewalks, and knobbed from kneeling hours on broomsticks. But your grin was bold as your mother's white with anger that vanished when you saw us waiting . . . .

With the return of Lulu, it is clear the saga of the Turtle Mountain Anishinabe is far from over. Nanapush's teaching has taken root, and, through this boisterous girl, tribal ways will not be forgotten. In *Tracks,* we are allowed to ponder lake monsters and ways of existence other than those of the white Anglo-Saxon Protestant; we are allowed to glimpse a part of the beginnings of a new people, the Métis; and we are told more about the dispossession of Indian people. In *Tracks,* however, the central image of earth, or loss of earth, proves to be only a vehicle for Erdrich's larger discussion of self, family, community, and place, a discussion that widens considerably in *Love Medicine.*

Julie Tharp (essay date 1993)

SOURCE: "Women's Community and Survival in the Novels of Louise Erdrich," in *Communication and Women's Friendships: Parallels and Intersections in Literature and Life,* edited by Janet Doubler Ward and JoAnna Stephens Mink, Bowling Green State University Popular Press, 1993, pp. 165-80.

[*In the following essay, Tharp discusses the destruction of Indian women's power and identity through Anglo colonization and demonstrates how Erdrich's explores this phenomenon in her fiction.*]

. . .The old women sit patiently in a circle, not speaking. Each set of eyes stares sharply into the air or the fire. Occasionally, a sigh is let loose from an open mouth. A Grandmother has a twitch in the corner of her eye. She rubs her nose, then smooths her hair.

The coffee is ready. Cups are brought from a wooden cupboard. Each woman is given the steaming brew. They blow on the swirling liquid, then slurp the drink into hungry mouths. It tastes good. Hot, dark, strong. A little bitter, but that is all to the good.

The women begin talking among themselves. They are together to perform a ceremony. Rituals of old women take time. There is no hurry.

This excerpt from Beth Brant's *Mohawk Trail* sheds light on the traditional women's community of her Native origins. Within the old traditions of the Longhouse, Brant finds a spirituality grounded within the Grandmothers' gathering to honor life, to honor one another as sources of life and healing. The women speak very little, but smile, laugh and sing, kiss and hug one another during the ritual. They need few words because the significance of their gathering is understood. She ends "Native Origin" with this: "The Grandmothers gather inside the Longhouse. They tend the fire." Female community signifies the life of the people, their survival in spirit as well as in body.

In *Mohawk Trail* this kind of community seems almost wholly a way of the past; Brant offers only one notable example of contemporary women's friendship, within a lesbian bar in Detroit, Michigan. The women there cling to one another as family because of legal and social difficulties in creating or maintaining other kinds of families. And, indeed, throughout Native American women's literature, the lack of women's gatherings like that depicted in Brant's "Native Origin" is conspicuous. Within the novels of Louise Erdrich, friendships between women are rare, much less formalized or ritualized. In *Love Medicine* the two powerful grandmothers, Lulu Nanapush Lamartine and Marie Lazarre Kashpaw, are intense rivals throughout most of the novel. In *Tracks* Pauline and Fleur are divided by their contrasting loyalties to assimilation and tradition. *The Beet Queen,* alternatively, narrates the friendship between Mary Adare and Celestine James, a friendship that can, however, only exist because of the women's particular circumstances. As Erdrich carefully points out in all of her novels, the circumstances that made life felicitous for her ancestors have been disrupted and distorted in contemporary Native culture. There are clear historical reasons for the shift from the powerful women's groups depicted in Brant's story to the isolated women in Erdrich's novels.

Paula Gunn Allen connects the dispersal and dissolution of women's communal power to the waning of Native power, saying:

. . .the shift from gynecentric-egalitarian and ritual-based systems to phallocentric, hierarchical systems is not accomplished in only one dimension. As LeJeune understood, the assault on the system of woman power requires the replacing of a peaceful, nonpunitive, nonauthoritarian social system wherein women wield power by making social life easy and gentle with one based on child terrorization, male dominance, and submission of women to male authority.

Allen locates four sites of change in the historical acculturation efforts of the federal government and of early missionaries: a change in religion that replaces female deities like White Buffalo Woman and Grandmother Spider with a male creator; a movement from egalitarian tribal government to hierarchical, male centered government; economic conversion from self-sufficiency to government dependency; and a shift from the clan system to the nuclear family system. The first change alters inner identity, cutting the individual loose from spiritual grounding within a matrifocal system and replacing that with the abstract notions of patriarchal dominance; individuals cease to recognize the "Grandmother powers that uphold and energize the universe." The movement from tribal to hierarchical government discredits women's political alliances in favor of one representative who needs to be male to interact with the federal government. The spiritual basis for tribal government is erased.

Converting from familial self-sufficiency to wage labor further increases the perceived power of the men, since they frequently earn the money to support the family, while women remain at home with the children. This movement intersects with the breakup of clan units (often matrilocal) and the subsequent isolation within nuclear families which Nancy Bonvillain argues "results in the isolation of women within small households, exacerbated by their husbands' absence from home. Work which previously had been shared between spouses today falls exclusively to women," and, Allen would add, to lone women rather than to groups of women laboring together. Marie Kashpaw, Lulu Lamartine and Zelda Kashpaw, for instance, all from *Love Medicine,* are depicted almost exclusively in their homes, often in their kitchens, husbands absent. Both the nuclear family household and wage labor isolate women from one another.

Acculturation to Anglo-American gender typing seems inevitable within these shifts. Citing both Patricia Albers and Paula Gunn Allen, Rebecca Tsosie argues that traditional Native gender roles were flexible and adaptive: "the ideal relationship between male and female [was] complementary and based on principles of individual autonomy and voluntary sharing. Because of this ethic, Albers claims that the concept of male 'dominance' was meaningless for the traditional Sioux." Molding the man into patriarch, however, and further dividing chores more strictly between men and women, replicates Anglo notions of gender as differential and hierarchical, notions that have, further, bred institutionalized control of women. Allen notes that battered wives and "women who have been raped by Indian men" are no longer

rare. Bonvillain's research concurs in this assessment and Erdrich illustrates it in *The Beet Queen* when Isabel Pillager marries a Sioux and moves to South Dakota:

> We hear she has died of beating, or in a car wreck, some way that's violent. But nothing else. We hear nothing from her husband, and if she had any children we never hear from them. Russell goes down there that weekend, but the funeral is long past. He comes home, telling me it's like she fell off the earth. There is no trace of her, no word.

Although Isabel is a powerful woman, niece of Fleur Pillager and foster mother to her siblings after the death of their mother, she too can be swallowed up by domestic violence and utterly forgotten within a culture that once honored strong women. King Kashpaw of *Love Medicine* beats his wife with astounding regularity, emulating mainstream Anglo notions of male gender, as Nora Barry and Mary Prescott point out in their article on Native American gender identity.

Because of reservation land allotments, women have been and often are geographically distant from one another. Rather than living in closely knit villages with an interdependent network of kin and friends, people live miles apart and gather occasionally. The very struggle to keep land often tore families and friends apart. Erdrich dramatizes this in *Tracks* when Margaret and Nector Kashpaw use all of the money saved to pay for Fleur Pillager's land allotment to instead pay for their own. Once close friends, Margaret and Fleur are wedged apart over the struggle for newly limited resources.

Within all three of Erdrich's novels heterosexuality either threatens to or does divide women. Pauline's sexual jealousy of Fleur keeps the women wary of one another and creates a vindictive streak within Pauline. Marie and Lulu cannot speak to one another as long as Nector lives. In *The Beet Queen* Erdrich deconstructs the heterosexual unions that disrupt female community. Neither Mary Adare nor Celestine James fits the stereotypical gender notions formulated within American popular culture and they, therefore, have a difficult time attracting men (not that they seem to care much). Mary at one point considers a relationship with Russell Kashpaw. She invites him to dinner with less than lustrous results:

> He looked at me for the first time that night. I'd drawn my eyebrows on for the evening in brown pencil. I'd carefully pinned my braids up and worn a black chiffon scarf to set off my one remarkable feature, yellow cat eyes, which did their best to coax him. But I don't know coaxing from a box lunch.

When Russell lets her know that he would be interested in

Sita Kozka (blond, thin and pretty), if anyone, and then later makes a joke of her touching him, Mary concludes: "I was cured, as though a fever had burned off. One thought was clear. I would never go out of my way for romance again. Romance would have to go out of its way for me." Because the experience is humiliating, from that point on Mary concentrates instead on her relationship with Celestine, one which affirms her "as is."

Celestine more obviously deconstructs the romantic ideology that influences both women when Karl Adare seduces her. It is quite possibly Celestine's non-stereotypical female beauty that attracts the bisexual Karl to her in the first place. She is taller than he and stronger; her face is "not pretty." Celestine evaluates the encounter through reference to the romance magazines she has read. (She "never had a mother to tell [her] what came next.") When Karl gives her a knife demonstration after their love-making, she ponders her expectations: "So, I think, this is what happens after the burning kiss, when the music roars. Imagine. The lovers are trapped together in a deserted mansion. His lips descend. She touches his magnificent thews. 'Cut anything,' he says. . . ." In a capitalist society the lover is ultimately a vendor looking for a quick sale. Karl does leave quickly, but he returns and this time Celestine asks him to leave: "In the love magazines when passion holds sway, men don't fall down and roll on the floor and lay there like dead. But Karl does that." Rather than boldly declaring his love and ravishing Celestine in the true fashion of the male hero, Karl passes out. Celestine's worldly assessment reveals both self-irony for having read the "love magazines" and a cynicism about popular culture versions of reality.

Months later she thinks, "Something in this all has made me realize that Karl has read as many books as I, and that his fantasies have always stopped before the woman came home worn out from cutting beef into steaks with an electric saw." Clearly the reason his fantasies and hers stopped short is because this reality defies the conventions of gender roles and romance. No heroine should be working as a butcher, and no hero should lie around the house all day. Celestine finds that heterosexual love does not live up to its reputation. It makes her feel like a "big, stupid heifer." It is further made unattractive to her because it comes between her and Mary, who "talks around [her], delivers messages through others. I even hear through one of the men that she says I've turned against her." Almost immediately after getting rid of Karl, Celestine calls to tell Mary.

When both women repudiate the expectations of romance and its attendant gender roles, they return with perhaps greater loyalty to their friendship and ultimately to themselves. In an interview with Joseph Bruchac, Erdrich speaks of writing for her daughters and sisters: "I have an urgent reason for thinking about women attuned to their power and

their honest nature, not the socialized nature and the embarrassed nature and the nature that says, 'I can't possibly accomplish this'." Neither obstinate, eccentric Mary nor fierce Celestine could be said to give up one ounce of their own power, except in their catering to Dot.

When Celestine gives birth to Dot, the two women find a mutual fixation. Mary continually tries to insinuate herself as a co-parent, although Celestine guards the right to herself. In the baby, Celestine finds a passion "even stronger than with Karl. She stole time to be with Dot as if they were lovers." For Mary, Dot is a small version of herself. The two women quarrel over parenting issues, even behave as jealous rivals, but ultimately act as co-parents to the child. They create a family. Toward the end of the novel when they are both aging, they behave like an old married couple, sleeping together at Sita's house, conspiring together, griping at each other and even reading each other's thoughts.

The two women can also be close to one another because of their economic self-sufficiency. Mary owns and runs the "House of Meats" and Celestine works there, enabling them to set their own timetables and living arrangements. They need not depend on men for money. Instead they hire men. They also work very hard, however, perhaps resembling Celestine's grandmothers in their butchering of animals and preparation of foods. The infant Dot is propped in a shopping cart instead of a cradleboard. Their work literally feeds the community.

Their kinship network, while geographically apart, is interdependent—Sita Kozka, Russell Kashpaw, Wallace Pfeff, Karl Adare, Mary, Celestine and Dot all comprise a clan of sorts that is notable in its tenuous connection to larger communities like the town of Argus or Turtle Mountain Reservation. Karl—a drifter—has no family whatsoever beyond this group. Sita would like to claim the beau monde of the Midwest (if that's not oxymoronic), as her community, but even a Minneapolis department store clerk snubs her. Wallace, entrepreneurial spirit of Argus, is marginalized by his sexuality. His bogus deceased fiancee is a secret that forever thwarts genuine interaction with the other townspeople. Russell, though canonized by the local museum for his war exploits, would not be welcome within one of the local families. He only returns to the reservation permanently as an invalid. These characters cannot or will not conform to community expectations of gender, ethnicity or sexuality. Within this marginalized group, the two female parents and their child form a core, a familial center from which to grow. Their dual mothering is attractive to the many characters who lack a mother themselves. The lone child of the many adults is their "dot" of hope for the future.

Erdrich, in the interview with Bruchac, poses a question shortly after her comment about women's power that provides a useful entry into this dilemma and that has everything to do with women's community within her three novels. She says, "There's a quest for one's own background in a lot of this work . . . All of our searches involve trying to discover where we are from." Although Erdrich does not specify here, background almost inevitably signifies "mother" for her characters. While many characters of *Love Medicine* and *Tracks* have lost their mothers through hardship or acculturation (I will say more on this later), the mothers of *The Beet Queen* are denied or renounced.

Both Karl and Mary renounce their mother for having left them stranded at the fairgrounds. Mary goes so far as to send word to her mother that her children starved to death. For Mary this solution seems plausible since she so readily plants herself within the new home in Argus. Karl, however, becomes completely unbalanced, helplessly relying upon any woman who will mother him as Fleur does when she finds him on the side of the railroad track and as Celestine does when she takes him in. He has no roots, only the branch he tears off the tree in Argus. Sita too renounces her own mother, identifying instead with her elusive aunt.

Mary and Celestine in fact first cement their friendship around their lack of parents. Asked about her mother and father, Mary responds, "They're dead," and Celestine answers, "Mine are dead too." Sita observes that suddenly the two girls seemed very much alike, with "a common sort of fierceness." The fierceness would seem to arise out of their motherless status. Forced to rely upon themselves, they develop an aggressive edge. In a sense, the two are grounded in their lack of a mother, perhaps the only coping strategy available to them and certainly better than Karl's strategy. Nonetheless, the ruling element of the novel is air, suggesting just how disconnected these characters are. Paula Gunn Allen develops the concept of grounding:

> Among the Keres, "context" and "matrix" are equivalent terms, and both refer to approximately the same thing as knowing your derivation and place. Failure to know your mother, that is, your position and its attendant traditions, history, and place in the scheme of things, is failure to remember your significance, your reality, your right relationship to earth and society. It is the same as being lost . . . not confined to Keres Indians; all American Indian Nations place great value on traditionalism.

Failure to know one's actual mother within Erdrich's novels is a metaphor for failure to grasp one's own significance within tribal traditions, within history. For women in particular, who lose all status within Anglo patriarchal traditions, it is a failure to embrace your own power. Celestine and Mary do not simply deny their mothers, however; they also create themselves in their own images of mother. Because Celestine did not know her mother well enough to carry on her traditions, and actually finds that her mother's heterosexual lifestyle does not suit her in any event, she becomes the mother she wanted. Mary rejects her distant self-centered mother and becomes an overprotective, indulgent mother. Both women are creating, from scratch, a family that can survive the harshness and sterility of Argus, North Dakota. Nevertheless, their lack of a women's tradition, of clan wisdom, leads to many mistakes in their mothering as Wallace Pfeff points out and as Celestine surmises.

In an article entitled "Adoptive Mothers and Thrown-Away Children in the Novels of Louise Erdrich," Hertha D. Wong describes in great detail the manner in which Erdrich develops complex mother/child relationships to dramatize the destruction of traditional family identities and the present need for maternal nurturance. That nurturance would not have been provided only by women in the past but rather by the entire tribe. Wong concludes that:

> Erdrich's novels, then, transcend easy categories of gender and ethnicity, reflect both Native American and Euroamerican influences, and extend Western notions of mothering. Mothering can indeed be a painful process of separation; it might be the necessarily insufficient dispensation of grace. But mothering can also be a communal responsibility for creating and maintaining personal identity.

Whatever Celestine and Mary's faults, they maintain Dot's identity, try to mother Sita and create a familial context for the men in their kinship network, men who are otherwise isolated. They take on the responsibility of mothering that the other characters either ignored or lost. Without each other, however, it is doubtful if the two women could even sustain that.

As Wong points out, Nanapush, in *Tracks,* is a nurturing figure in the tribal tradition of communal parenting, but his nurturing is put to harsh tests when he loses his entire family one by one, his land and ultimately his way of life. Although both lyrical novels, *Tracks* and *Love Medicine* are firmly situated within historical events. Julie Maristuen-Rodakowski confirms the historical accuracy of Erdrich's depiction of the Turtle Mountain Reservation in North Dakota and their rapid assimilation to American culture. Maristuen-Rodakowski notes in particular the strong bicultural nature of this reservation, bred as it is from both Ojibwa and French trapper/traders. She also maps out a genealogical chart of the characters, illustrating how central family is within these works, that the reader should even be capable of drawing a detailed chart, and suggesting that such a chart is necessary for comprehension of the families' complex interrelationships (Wong's article contains a less detailed genealogical chart). The almost obsessive concern with family origins within *Love Medicine* and *Tracks* seems in part to arise from the characterization and status accorded to each family—largely the Kashpaws, Nanapushes and Pillagers on the clearly Chippewa side and the Lamartines, Lazarres and Morrisseys on the more French, mixed blood side, the latter holding far less worth in most characters' eyes.

Another factor in this obsession is the mystery surrounding the parentage of many characters. Pauline, for example, hides her identity as Marie's mother after her liaisons with Napoleon Morissey result in the child's birth. Fleur is raped by three men, so literally does not know which man fathered Lulu. The destruction of Fleur's family leaves her orphaned; the removal of Lulu to a government boarding school divides her from her mother; because of Pauline's entrance into the Catholic order she leaves Marie with Sophie Lazarre. In *The Beet Queen* Adelaide Adare hides her children's father's identity until his death. For her, sexual license is not so much a choice made out of desire but rather one made out of economic necessity; her economic desperation leads to her abandonment of the children. Throughout all three novels families are both created and torn apart by economic, spiritual and social upheaval. Those same changes separate the women, who, together, could and eventually do resist their force.

The mothers of the two families most extensively portrayed within *Love Medicine* both obscure origin in their own ways, I would argue, because their own origins are problematic for them. Marie Lazarre Kashpaw raises, in addition to her own children, many stray and orphaned babies on the reservation, June Morrissey and Lipsha Morrissey to name two; to Lipsha she says only that his mother would have "drowned him in the slough" if she had not taken him in, a patent falsehood, as he learns later in the novel. Lulu Nanapush gives birth to eight sons and one daughter, all of different fathers and none fathered by the man she was married to the longest and whose name several bear. Both women redefine notions of the nuclear family. Marie's elastic household forms a kind of clan unit. In Lulu's many partners lies a deconstruction of the patriarchal family and Christian monogamy.

Nora Barry and Mary Prescott, in discussing the holistic vision of gender in *Love Medicine,* imply that Marie and Lulu act as facilitators to that holistic vision, Marie because she is "a blending of two complementary gender based traditions. Her life includes risk, transformation, householding, and medicine, as well as an integration of past and present." Speaking of Lulu, they write that she is "a worthy adversary because she is as effective at complementarity as Marie is. The two characters mirror one another in their role as mother, in their ability to take risks, in their way of blending past and present, and in their wielding of power in old age." Clearly it is because they resist gender bifurcation and emulate gender complementarity that they can become pow-

erful in their old age, speaking as Grandmothers of their clans. Still, while separate, they are unable to create an empowering matrix for these children.

In the role of Grandmother they are able to mediate various Anglo institutions. Marie rejects the "deadliness of the convent" in favor of life and Lulu remains mindful of the "conflict between old values and the influences of the white standard of economic success." One mother serves as a mediator between her people and white religious ideology, answering a call to the convent and just as quickly rejecting it when she confronts the violence of Sister Leopolda. The other mother mediates commodity culture, calling the "tomahawk" factory proposed to be built on the site of her house "dreamstuff."

Marie and Lulu also unite the two family groupings—Chippewa and French—the historical discord between which has eased Anglo appropriation of land. Marie seeks to deny the French/Catholic side and embrace traditional Native culture. Even so, her healing powers are associated with Catholicism. She is truly a sister of mercy in caring for orphaned children and in attending to Lulu. Even though that power is not exclusive of Native identity by any means, here it carries Catholic overtones. Lulu seeks to deny her Native/traditionalist mother and ignore her Nanapush/father's teachings and marries the French Lamartine. Ironically she is only a good Catholic in her fecundity. The fact that her boys all have different fathers reveals her innate attachment to her rebellious mother.

These two women, however, who have so much in common and could become powerful allies, can only come together after Nector dies, suggesting that heterosexuality as it has been influenced by Anglo culture takes priority over women's community and therefore divides women and dissipates tribal strength. Once the women have become fast friends Lipsha reports to Gerry Nanapush that Lulu had "started running things along with Grandma Kashpaw. I told him how she'd even testified for Chippewa claims and that people were starting to talk, now, about her knowledge as an old-time traditional." Women's friendship here signifies tradition and resistance to acculturation, but Lulu and Marie's friendship also reunites the characters with their own pasts, with their mothers, ultimately with their tribal past.

Tracks takes up the subject of displaced origins from early in the novel when Fleur conceives Lulu. The complexity is well expressed in Nanapush's decision to give Fleur Pillager's daughter his and his deceased daughter's names, not knowing what to tell Father Damien since the father was unknown:

> There were so many tales, so many possibilities, so many lies. The waters were so muddy I thought I'd

give them another stir. "Nanapush," I said. "And her name is Lulu."

The muddy waters originate with speculation, particularly about Fleur's relationship to the water monster in Lake Matchimanito. Like her mother, Lulu is stigmatized for her unconventional sexuality, but they both see through the hypocrisy of others. When the townspeople jeer Lulu at a town meeting, she offers to enlighten everyone as to the fathers of her children, an offer the people decline.

Lulu's "wild and secret ways" are an obvious legacy from her mother Fleur Pillager, one of the last two surviving Pillagers, a wild and powerful family living far back in the bush. The Pillagers know the ways to "cure and kill." Lulu rejects her mother—Nanapush's narrative is in part his attempt to explain Fleur's actions to Lulu—but in fact Lulu greatly resembles her mother in her ability to stand up to the current notions of "progress" and in her steadfast defense of erotic integrity in the face of community opposition. That Lulu should come to be in her old age a bearer of the old traditions marks at least a symbolic reconciliation with her mother.

The young mixed-blood Pauline Puyat, who seeks to punish her body in any way imaginable in the effort to drive out the devil, also seeks sexual experience before becoming a nun. Her rendezvous with Napoleon Morrissey results in an unwanted pregnancy. Pauline's efforts to keep the child from being born in order to kill both her and the infant force the midwife, Bernadette, to tie Pauline down and remove the baby with iron spoons used as forceps. The dual surprise of the novel is that Pauline becomes, at the end of the novel, Sister Leopolda; and the girl she gives birth to and names Marie is eventually raised by the soft-witted Sophie Lazarre. Rather than the offspring of a "drunken woman" and a "dirty Lazarre," Marie is the child of Pauline and Napoleon Morrissey. Marie obviously has no clue to Sister Leopolda's identity in *Love Medicine,* but Leopolda recognizes Marie at least up to the end of *Tracks.* Marie and Sister Leopolda's mutual obsession, which leads to Leopolda's sponsoring Marie at the convent, is ostensibly religious and caring. That Leopolda should lock Marie in closets, scald her with hot water, brain her with an iron pole and skewer her hand with a meat fork suggests that, like Lulu, Marie has a difficult relationship with her mother. In retaliation for the scalding, Marie attempts to push Leopolda into a huge oven. Nonetheless, from her experience with Sister Leopolda, Marie learns pity, a gift that enables her to help her husband back to her side and that leads her to reconcile with Lulu. (Marie's compulsion to visit the dying nun many years later ironically leads to a battle over the iron spoon that Leopolda habitually bangs on her metal bedstead.)

Lulu's mother is deeply harmed in obviously material ways by Anglo encroachment—her parents and siblings are decimated by disease, her land is lost and her forest leveled, she and her family are starved, killing her second child. Still Fleur Pillager maintains her will to fight, crushing the wagons of the loggers when they come to throw her off her land. To keep Lulu safe from these circumstances Fleur has sent her to a boarding school, an act for which Lulu cannot forgive Fleur. Pauline/Leopolda is deeply harmed in more obviously psychological ways. An odd person from the outset, Pauline desires to move with the times, assimilating rather than "living in the old ways" as Fleur does. One critic describes Pauline as a trickster figure, but Nanapush, himself a trickster, confesses to being completely baffled by the girl. In several places Erdrich seems to suggest that it is Pauline's unattractiveness that drives her outside of the community. She cannot marry and so must find an occupation. In a community that has accepted Anglo definitions of use, value and gender roles, a woman like Pauline can find no recourse.

Marie and Lulu's friendship closes the circle as the daughters of Pauline—who rejects mothering from a distorted allegiance to Anglo culture—and Fleur—who gives up mothering the child upon whom she dotes in order to fight for Native culture—come together in the effort to nurture one another. In putting "the tears in [Lulu's] eyes," Marie helps Lulu to finally feel pity for her mother. Together the women have reconciled their own and their mothers' dilemmas, Marie by taking the good from Leopolda's venom and Lulu by claiming her mother's protective spirit. In that relationship lies the potential for community transformation that Lipsha notes. Wong writes, "It remains for those left behind, the adoptive mothers and thrown-away youngsters, to reweave the broken strands of family, totem, and community into a harmonious wholeness."

The reconciliation takes place when Marie volunteers to help Lulu recover from cataract surgery. In the scene there is little dialogue and long periods in which the two women simply drink coffee and listen to music on the radio. Lulu thinks that "Too much might start the floodgates flowing and our moment would be lost. It was enough just to sit there without words." The women understand that with a gulf as wide as the one they must cross, words will only divide them further. The benign music on the radio, the "music" of Marie's voice, and the soft touch of her hand provide the healing communication necessary to their alliance.

For Lulu this meeting provides a revelation: "For the first time I saw exactly how another woman felt, and it gave me deep comfort, surprising. It gave me the knowledge that whatever had happened the night before, and in the past, would finally be over once my bandages came off." Marie indeed helps Lulu to "get [her] vision" as Lipsha testifies in the next chapter: "Insight. It was as though Lulu knew by looking at you what was the true barebones elements of your life. It wasn't like that before she had the operation on her eyes, but once the bandages came off she saw. She saw too clear for comfort." Having seen "how another woman felt" Lulu is now capable of seeing into everyone; she is given a "near-divine" power of vision. Through imagery, however, Erdrich reveals that this connection is not simply one of friendship. Lulu imagines Marie, caring for her eyes, swaying "down like a dim mountain, huge and blurred, the way a mother must look to her just born child."

In its coffee, contemplation and vision-seeking, this scene resembles the old women's ritual described at the outset and also depicted within Linda Hogan's short story "Meeting" about a contemporary women's ceremony:

> Mom was boiling coffee on the fire and serving it up. The women sipped it and warmed their palms over the fire. They were quiet but the lines of their faces spoke in the firelight, telling about stars that fell at night, the horses that died in the drought of 1930, and the pure and holy terror of gunshots fired into our houses. . . . Exhaustion had covered up all the mystery and beauty the women held inside. . . . I met myself that night and I walked in myself. I heard my own blood. I learned all secrets lie beneath even the straggliest of hair, and that in the long run of things dry skin and stiff backs don't mean as much as we give them credit for.

In the meeting between Marie and Lulu rest the seeds for a return to powerful female political alliances, for necessary friendship that will signify not just caring, but survival, and not just survival, but prosperity. Significantly, it is in the nursing home, a communal dwelling place that ends the women's previous geographical isolation, that Marie and Lulu come together. Neither is their friendship strained, however, by familial or spousal demands.

Clearly the community can never again be what it was previous to the events of *Tracks,* but its very survival is at stake with the outside forces of capitalism and Anglo-American social, governmental and religious systems tearing at its fabric. That survival cannot take place without some kind of cohesive resistance. Since the traditionalist male figures—Old Man Pillager and Eli Kashpaw—have retreated into the bush and silence, it is left to the women in the novels to somehow save the children. Even though for some of those children the mothers may only be a shadowy presence, Lulu's sons idolize her and Marie's clan quickly materializes en masse for family gatherings. The two women's mutual grandson, Lipsha, as an old people's child and a caregiver to the old ones on the reservation, holds forth promise for a more powerful male presence. Although the desperation of some Turtle Mountain Reservation characters depicted in *Tracks* and *Love Medicine* may seem greater

than of those characters living in Argus, the reservation also offers a portal to empowering traditions. Argus counts communal and personal strength only in dollar amounts.

Allen writes that in response to the "inhuman changes" wrought by Anglo colonization Indian women are trying to "reclaim their lives. Their power, their sense of direction and of self will soon be visible. It is the force of women who speak and work and write, and it is formidable." Female friendship enables the women in Erdrich's novels to recreate an empowering matrix that was frequently lost or disrupted through colonization and acculturation. In turn the women are strengthened in their capacity to act as leaders for ensuing generations.

Lawrence Thornton (review date 16 January 1994)

SOURCE: "Gambling with Their Heritage," in *New York Times Book Review,* January 16, 1994, p. 7.

[*In the following review, Thornton offers a positive appraisal of* The Bingo Palace *but expresses reservations about the novel's elements of magical realism.*]

One of the dominant motifs in the fiction of American Indian writers is the vision quest, whose goal is the integration of inner and outer being through knowledge gleaned from nature. Louise Erdrich has explored this territory in *Love Medicine, The Beet Queen* and *Tracks,* and she revisits it in her moving new novel, *The Bingo Palace.* Set, like the others, on the North Dakota plains, this latest book shows us a place where love, fate and chance are woven together like a braid, a world where daily life is enriched by a powerful spiritual presence.

Her story comes to us in the alternating voices of the inhabitants of the Chippewa reservation—the novel's chorus—and of Lipsha Morrissey, the central character, who is sometimes laconic, frequently passionate and, through painful experience, increasingly insightful. Presented in a counterpoint that is by turns colloquial and lyric, all these voices reveal how inescapably Lipsha's fate is inscribed within his heritage. To emphasize this connection, Ms. Erdrich begins and ends *The Bingo Palace* with the chorus, thus bracketing both Lipsha's good luck and his misadventures within a broader view of the world that binds the past to the present while looking uncertainly toward the future.

As the novel's title implies, gambling is a major force on the reservation; but while this may initially suggest that life there has been reduced to a game of chance, it soon becomes clear that luck, which means nothing in the world of contingency, is actually design in the realm of the spirits. Lipsha begins to learn this almost as soon as he returns to his people, quitting his job in a Fargo sugar beet factory where he has accumulated a covering of sweetness on his skin and clothes, a symbolic "seal of corrosion," separating him from his past. He has been frittering away his off hours in bars, "the tougher spots, the dealer hangouts and areas beneath the bridges where so much beyond the law gets passed hand to mouth." But when his grandmother Lulu Lamartine mails him a picture of his now-imprisoned father, Gerry Nanapush, copied from a post-office wanted poster, all this changes. Aware that the picture could foretell his own future, Lipsha goes home in search of an authentic life.

The community is "disgusted with the son of that wanted poster." Going back and forth to the city has, the chorus declares, "weakened and confused him and now he flails in a circle with his own tail in his teeth." But even though Lipsha has trouble written all over him, his uncle Lyman Lamartine offers him a job in his bingo parlor.

On his first night home, Lipsha attends the winter powwow, where he is undone by a beautiful dancer, Shawnee Ray Toose. An ambitious and kindhearted young woman intent upon winning prize money to pay for a college education, she has designed her own ceremonial "jingle dress," resplendent with beadwork and shining clackers. Struck by the elegance of her dancing, Lipsha is fascinated; his eyes "somehow stay hooked to Shawnee Ray."

The problem is that Shawnee Ray has had a child by Lyman; Lipsha's aunt Zelda Kashpaw has maneuvered them into an unofficial engagement and hopes that marriage will follow. What develops instead is a romantic rivalry between Lipsha and his uncle, which is complicated by the fact that Lyman soon becomes Lipsha's mentor, both in the world of business and that of the spirit. Even as he encourages Lipsha to invest his savings in a scheme to build a larger bingo palace on the shore of a sacred lake, Lyman takes his nephew to a healer who begins the process by which Lipsha will learn that the "bingo life" is an attraction that "has no staying power, no weight, no heart."

Ms. Erdrich's story of three decent people looking for love on a windblown prairie expands to accommodate supernatural events. The first occurs when Lipsha, wandering through the bingo parlor after hours, runs into the spirit of his dead mother, June Kashpaw, who is angry because his blue Firebird was paid for with her insurance money. In exchange for the car, June gives him a booklet of bingo tickets that will change his life.

Lipsha's magic tickets allow him to accumulate modest wealth, but he is still sick with desire. In search of love medicine to counter Lyman's hold on Shawnee Ray, he visits his great-grandmother Fleur Pillager. Their sweetly mysterious encounter loosens Lipsha's memories of his heritage and starts him on a journey toward the past. Helped by Lyman, he sets out on a spirit quest with the double motive of "getting the real old-time traditional religion" and impressing Shawnee Ray Toose.

This is a crucial turning point for Lipsha, who has misconstrued the effects of money and success. In its aftermath, he comes to understand that Lyman's scheme for the new bingo palace is leading everyone in the wrong direction: "Our reservation is not real estate, luck fades when sold."

Unfortunately, Ms. Erdrich's resolution of the conflict among Lipsha, Lyman and Shawnee Ray is subordinated to events that skew the novel's focus by turning Lipsha's quest into a wildly improbable madcap chase. For while June's appearance in the bingo parlor is a fine example of reality gracefully expanding to include the realm of the spirits, some of the novel's later ventures into magic realism seem contrived, merely artificial means of tying up strands of an overly complicated plot. Moreover, the delayed appearance of Lipsha's father, who has been little more than a mysterious presence from the opening chapter, only raises questions about this role rather than offering a satisfying resolution to an important strand in the narrative.

The Bingo Palace does, however, eventually return to its strengths, ending with a beautiful evocation of the spirit world. Part eulogy, part coda, the last few pages bind together the living and the dead in an elegiac choral voice. Here, as in most of the book, Ms. Erdrich's sympathy for her characters shines as luminously as Shawnee Ray's jingle dress. We leave this brightness aware of the complex pattern that links Lipsha, Fleur, Shawnee Ray and all the rest of the characters to both their community and their land.

Susan Meisenhelder (essay date January 1994)

SOURCE: "Race and Gender in Louise Erdrich's *The Beet Queen*," in *Ariel,* Vol. 25, No. 1, January, 1994, pp. 45-57.

[*In the following essay, Meisenhelder argues that Erdrich addresses problems of race and gender in her portrayals of white women and men of color in* The Beet Queen.]

To a number of reviewers and critics, Louise Erdrich's novel *The Beet Queen* is unusual in Native American literature because of its apparent silence on the issue of race. As Louis Owens has argued, the "excruciating quest for an Indian identity in late twentieth century American that haunts other fiction and poetry by Indian writers is simply not here." Certainly the most strident expression of this idea has been a review of the novel written by another Native American writer, Leslie Marmon Silko. Although she praises Erdrich's style, Silko attacks the novel for its failure to treat the social and political dimension of Native American concerns; the book, she argues, reduces society's problems to individual ones: "In this pristine world all misery, suffering, and loss are self-generated, just as conservative Republicans have been telling us for years." My purpose in this paper is to show that *The Beet Queen* docs in fact speak to questions of Native American identity in important ways. Far from being silent on sociopolitical concerns, Erdrich sustains an examination of the relationship between two crucial issues, race and gender, throughout the novel.

At first glance, gender seems the more sharply foregrounded theme in *The Beet Queen,* for Erdrich details through a number of characters the price both women and men pay for defying society's gender expectations. Mary, for instance, with her "blunt ways" and her smell "like white pepper from the sausage table" where she works as town butcher, throughout the novel remains loveless and childless, without a consort to match her fantasies. A woman of almost mythic spiritual proportions, she finds in modern American society no channel for her supernatural powers other than tarot cards and yarrow sticks. Similarly, Wallace (in many ways, the most maternal character in the book), comfortable in the traditional female role of midwife and host *extraordinaire* of children's birthday parties, must as a gay man in an intolerant society submerge his sexuality by masquerading as the grief-stricken lover of an unknown woman whose picture he displays.

> *The Beet Queen* does in fact speak to questions of Native American identity in important ways. Far from being silent on sociopolitical concerns, Erdrich sustains an examination of the relationship between two crucial issues, race and gender, throughout the novel.
> —*Susan Meisenhelder*

While Erdrich chronicles the toll that defiance of gender norms takes on these characters, she reserves the direst fate for two characters in the book who come closest to fulfilling social definitions of ideal male and female. In her treatment of the white woman, Sita, who bases her identity on physical beauty and marriage, and Russell, the Native American male who strives for success through football and military exploits, Erdrich both critiques white America's ideals of masculinity and femininity and suggests underlying similarities between racial and gender oppression in American society. By juxtaposing chapters focusing on Sita and Russell and thus highlighting symbolic parallels between their situations, she shows that, despite the racial gulf that separates

the two, they are similarly dehumanized, reduced to objects serving the interests of a society dominated by white males.

With marriage as her "dream," Sita, as a young woman, plans to move to Fargo and become a model in a department store:

> She imagined that she would also work behind the men's hat counter. There she would meet a young rising professional. They would marry. He would buy her a house near the county courthouse, on the street of railroad mansions not far from Island Park. Every winter she would walk down the hill to skate. She would wear powder blue tights and a short dress with puffs of rabbit fur at the sleeves, collar, and all around a flared hem that would lift as she twirled.

Unable to imagine an independent identity for herself and weary of the "determination" it takes to keep her twenty-two and a half-inch waist as she approaches thirty, she is convinced that the "only thing that would save [her], now, was to find the ideal husband." However, marriage and the traditional conception of femaleness she brings to it, in fact, destroy her. The threat to selfhood that marriage poses for Sita is foreshadowed even before her first wedding: although she is irritated that Jimmy calls her the names of his favourite desserts, she fails to see his increasing weight as evidence that she is being consumed. As the skating image of herself in her fantasy foreshadows, she remains a child (she likes to be called "girl" even as an older woman) in her relationship with both her husbands.

While Sita's story in isolation highlights gender oppression, Erdrich goes further to draw parallels between her fate and Russell's. Similarities between white treatment of women and Native Americans are starkly drawn in the description of Sita's first marriage. In Erdrich's telling revision of a theme from white folklore—the white woman's kidnapping and ravishment by "savage Indians," Sita is "kidnap[ped]" by the groom's male relatives as a joke. As this fact and Sita's stricken look of "surrender" imply, marriage represents, for Sita, not self-fulfilment but loss of autonomy. Erdrich further illustrates how marriage echoes the treatment of Native Americans when the men, uncertain where to leave her, finally, with a stroke of "genius," decide to dump her on the reservation, a grimly appropriate place to symbolize her fate. Like Russell, who is present in the bar where Sita takes refuge, and who later returns to the reservation after his usefulness as football star and war hero is exhausted, Sita is, as a woman, as imprisoned in the institution of marriage as he is, because of his race, on the reservation. Sita's degradation is unmistakable beneath the humor in the kidnapping scene—when wind turns her dress inside out and blows her through the door, she enters the bar not as a human being but as "a sudden explosion of white net, a rolling ball of it." As happens often, she loses her voice, reduced to "muffled and inhuman croaking."

For Russell, too, the success society offers involves self-destruction. Although with his picture in the papers as football star and his war medals in the state museum, he achieves masculine "success" beyond what he could expect as an Indian, Celestine, early in the novel, grimly forecasts the emptiness of that apparent achievement: "People say he is one Indian who won't go downhill in life but have success, and he does, later, depending on how you look at it." Ironically, for both Sita and Russell, the symbols of their status as ideal male and female—Sita's garnet necklace and Russell's war medals, which both wear with pride throughout the novel—are, in fact, stark emblems of their enslavement.

For both characters, the attempt to emulate the gender ideals of white culture results in profound dehumanization; in different ways (Sita as sex object and Russell as cannon fodder), both have social value only as bodies and receive approval only through physical sacrifice. The scene of Sita as a young girl bearing her new breasts in hopes of receiving affection and affirmation is reenacted throughout her life, first as she works as a model and later as she struggles to preserve her fragile physical beauty. This pivotal scene in Sita's life (she remembers it years later as she prepares to commit suicide) takes place, significantly, in a cemetery. Dancing on the graves after Celestine rejects her, Sita simultaneously enters the world of female sexuality and spiritual death. Russell's physical sacrifice is even more graphic: "getting shot apart is what [Russell] live[s] for all his life." Behind the accolade accorded him as "North Dakota's most-decorated hero" is, as his sister recognizes, a drama of objectification: "Now he must wait until some statehouse official scores the other veterans, counting up their wounds on a paper tablet, and figures out who gave away the most flesh".

Physical mutilation mirrors the psychic and emotional fragmentation both characters experience. After fighting in war after war, Russell becomes covered with "scars and stripes," Erdrich's satirical comment on his misplaced patriotism. "Mapp[ed]" like the land of his ancestors, he is exploited as a natural resource, his wounds "ridged like a gullied field," his body "plowed like a tractor gone haywire." Despite "heroic" efforts, like Russell, Sita becomes a physical wreck in seeking the perfect body; she "ends up looking stuffed and preserved." Both ultimately appear scarcely human. Just as Russell's face, which looks "all sewn together," seems freakish with its "claw marks, angry and long, even running past his temples and parting his hair crooked," Sita's face becomes "cavernous" and "wrinkled," distorted "into a Halloween mask, witchlike and gruesome."

The physical destruction and dehumanization both charac-

ters suffer is also paralleled in mental deterioration. The debilitating "nervous" disorders both endure—Sita's drug dependency and mental breakdown, Russell's alcoholism and stroke—reflect the spiritual deaths preceding their literal ones at the end of the novel (both are, in fact, described as "stiffs" and associated with death imagery throughout the novel). Further, both become paralyzed (Sita first emotionally and then later when injured). As both characters become increasingly debilitated, they lose their powers of self-expression: when they break out of the silence that often characterizes them, no one understands Sita's "jammed-up sentences" or Russell's "shattered vowels." Voiceless "puppets" and "robots," both characters remain dependent for their identities on external sources. Not surprisingly, Erdrich describes both as rootless—Sita is like a blossom on a tree, "the same frail kind of beauty that could be broken off a tree by any passing boy and discarded, cast away when the fragrance died" and Russell "like a tree half uprooted in a wind."

As creations of American society, both Sita and Russell symbolically inhabit a white male world with little space for females and Native Americans. Just as Russell winds up on the reservation created by whites, Sita spends her last days in the basement recreation room of her house, a distinctly male preserve filled with memorabilia signifying the personalities of her husbands—Jimmy's stereo equipment and beer lamps (one "a silhouette of a stagecoach pulled by horses and around a lit screen of mountains and desert cacti," another "of a canoe endlessly revolving in a blue lake") and Louis's short wave radio sets. In this room, a "monument to both of [her husbands] and to neither one," Sita sleeps on the pool table, a kind of centrepiece in this masculine world. As always, Sita misunderstands her position as a female in a male-dominated world. Having moved her possessions in, she has the illusion of ownership—"It is mine now"—and power, imagining "all that [she] could do by remote control":

> From here, I can turn on the television if I want. The face of the Morning Hostess might be flipping in a blur, but I can stabilize her with one twist. Headphones are at my elbow. I can push on the stereo power, the radio. I can listen to 8-track tapes, or, in silence, watch the brightly lit dials and barometers slide and flicker. I can operate the light control to dim or illuminate the imitation Tiffany overhead. I can turn on all of the beer lamps and watch them.

Sita is, despite her fantasies, merely another object in this world, more like a ruined piece of electronics equipment, with the "nerve connections" in her brain "short[ed] out," than an empowered human being. Just as she has mistaken marriage as the route to identity, she here confuses residence in a male world with meaningful power in it. Rather than becoming more alive in the home of her dreams, Sita resides in a house of death, a home with a lawn of grass like that in cemeteries in a town built on Indian burial grounds. Sita is spiritually buried there, "swathed in covers that have absorbed an earthen smell from the basement air." In more ways than one, Sita's death follows the shape of her life. Celestine and Mary find her dead outside her house, her body snagged on a broken branch and held up by her garnet necklace. She dies as frustrated as she has lived, her lips "set in exasperation, as if she had just been about to say something and found out her voice was snatched in death."

Parallels between Russell and Sita culminate in the parade, the piece of Americana that concludes the novel. Through a bizarre set of circumstances (Sita mistakenly enters the parade as a corpse), both Russell and she, icons of American masculinity and femininity, ride in the parade with the Beet Queen and her court. Significantly, both appear in the symbols of their gender aspirations—Sita in a white dress and her garnet necklace, with a "white leatherette purse in her lap"; Russell in his uniform with medals pinned in a "bright pattern over his heart" and a rifle in his lap. Both parade before the crowd as mindless, passive bodies, the dead Sita propped in Mary's truck (emblazoned with its name, House of Meats), and the paraplegic Russell propped up and strapped into a wheelchair. Just as Sita is buried in a male world, Russell ends up in a symbolically white one. Seemingly the centrepiece in this tribute to American military exploits, he is (as his physical condition starkly betrays) actually one of its victims. Like Sita, he is also buried on foreign turf, set on the float amidst a "field of graves . . . plastic grass and read poppies[,] [a] plain white cross . . . planted at his feet."

Although they are the ostensible objects of the town's admiration, it is bitterly ironic that no one notices Sita's death or Russell's near-deadly stroke during the procession. In fact, both characters—mute and completely immobilized—receive unqualified approval. The townspeople, for instance, assume Sita was "someone important, an alderwoman or the governor's wife," and her long-lost cousin thinks she looks better than ever. While Russell is amused that "the town he'd lived in and the members of the American Legion were solemnly saluting a dead Indian," Erdrich's message is much more serious. Just as Nector's experience with the movies in *Love Medicine* proves to him the white man's belief that "The only good Indian is a dead Indian," Russell's presence in the parade starkly demonstrates the dependency and spiritual death American society offers as success to Native Americans. In this episode, Erdrich develops this idea about racial oppression further to suggest that in white American culture, the only "good woman" is also lifeless.

At a time when the interrelations between race and gender concern many American women writers of colour, Erdrich, as a Native American herself, offers an interesting perspective on racial and gender oppression in *The Beet Queen* by uncovering similarities between the fates of white women and men of colour. Even though Sita consistently makes "fun of [Russell] for being an Indian, and he is always glad to see her taken down a notch," Erdrich suggests not only their unacknowledged affinities, but also their profound mistake in seeing one another as the enemy. Erdrich's novel is, however, not only the story of self-destruction for white women and Native American men. In the two female characters of Native American descent focussed on in the novel, Celestine and Dot, she offers a more positive alternative to the fates of Russell and Sita. Although Celestine and Dot are offered the same female roles that strangle Adelaide and Sita, both are able to forge more independent and powerful identities of their own.

Celestine, who could be Russell's twin "but for his scars," physically does not seem a candidate for Sita's fate. A big "six-footer," who is "not pretty" but "handsome like a man," she nevertheless has been imbued with the same myths about women's fulfillment. As she watches Sita play the coquette with a man, she wonders:

> Will I ever smile, flush, offer a tidbit of food? Are these things that Sita feels, these pleasures I have read about in books, the sort of feelings I might experience? It has never happened yet, although I've known men. Perhaps, I think, I'm too much like them, too strong or imposing when I square my shoulders, too eager to take control.

Although Celestine intuitively senses that female strength and traditional love relationships may be incompatible, she feels the lure of romance and, in her relationship with Karl, faces the same temptation to passivity and self-annihilation that Sita experiences in her marriages. While Erdrich injects substantial humour into her descriptions of the love affair between Karl and Celestine—their first passionate encounter takes place on the floor of the butcher shop, for instance—she finally depicts that relationship as a dangerous trap for Celestine.

At first, Celestine tries hard to play the female lover role as she has learned it should be played. Karl's initial sexual overtures make her think of "Sita testing vegetables. Now it seems as though something is happening to me. I turn around to look at Karl. His eyes are burning holes and he tries to look right through me if he can. This is, indeed, the way men behave in the world of romance." The fact that he is "slightly smaller than [Celestine], and also Mary's brother" are simply the first clues that the reality of sex and the myth of seduction do not match. Not only does Karl make his first moves before "the glances, the adoration, the many conversations [that Sita thinks] must happen" first, but the physical experience itself fails to match her expectations: "He steps in front of me and hugs me to himself, draws my face down to his face. I am supposed to taste a burning sweetness on his lips, but his mouth is hard as metal." Karl's unusual behaviour brings to light more discrepancies between reality and fantasy. When he turns abruptly from making love to displaying his knifewares, Celestine becomes increasingly aware of the absurdity of the myth: "So, I think, this is what happens after the burning kiss, when the music roars. Imagine. The lovers are trapped together in a deserted mansion. His lips descend. She touches his magnificent thews." As Karl keeps cutting pennies into perfect spirals, Celestine "decide[s] that I have now seen what love is about." She learns more about the banality of love when she returns to Karl late one night after work: "It is time, now, for Karl to break down with his confession that I am a slow-burning fuse in his loins. A hair trigger. I am a name he cannot silence. A dream that never burst." The conversation that follows is hardly so romantic:

> "Oh well . . ." he says.
> "What's that supposed to mean?" I ask.
> "Nothing."

It is not just Karl's inadequacy as a lover that troubles Celestine (although she notes that "In the love magazines, when passion holds sway, men don't fall down and roll on the floor and lay there like dead"). From the beginning she senses that female passivity is part of experience as scripted: "He is fighting me for the upper hand, straining down with all his might, but I am more than equal to his weight-lifting arms and thrashing legs. I could throw him to the side." Celestine knows her own strength but she "grow[s] curious" and initially suppresses her power. Although she stays for awhile to satisfy her curiosity, the relationship quickly "get[s] too predictable" for Celestine's taste. She gradually comes to see Karl's presence as an invasion: "I am tired of coming home to Karl's heavy breathing and even his touch has begun to oppress me." As she realizes, the problem is not Karl as an individual, but the spiritual drain involved in the kind of relationship they share:

> "It's not you," I tell him. "I don't want to get married. With you around I get no sleep. I'm tired all the time. All day I'm giving the wrong change and I don't have any dreams. I'm the kind of person that likes having dreams. Now I have to see you every morning when I wake up and I forget if I dreamed anything or even slept at all, because right away you're on me with your hot breath."

Aware that the relationship is dehumanizing—she feels like "some kind of animal. . .[a] big stupid heifer," Celestine rejects Karl's marriage proposal. Having arrived at a view similar to that of Mary who "look[s] on the married girls the way a wild dog might look through the window at tame ones, envying the regularity of their lives but also despising the low pleasure they get from the master's touch," Celestine refuses to become a slave for some measure of security. Thus, unlike Sita and Russell, who both remain rootless, Celestine emerges from the novel whole, "more solid than the tree Karl had embraced before he vanished."

Like her mother, Dot seems an unlikely character to follow in the footsteps of Adelaide or Sita. Even as a baby, prompt to use her voice in protest, she is not stereotypically feminine or passive:

> In her shopping-cart stroller she exercised to exhaustion, bouncing for hours to develop her leg muscles. She hated lying on her back and when put that way immediately flipped over to assume a wrestler's crouch. Sleep, which she resisted, did not come upon her gently but felled her in odd positions. Draped over the side of the cart or packed in its corner, she seemed to have fallen in battle. But it was only a momentary surrender. She woke, demanding food, and when set free exploded in an astonishing fast creep that took her across a room in seconds.

Appropriately cast in the school play as Joseph rather than Mary, Dot is a tough and fearless child. As she grows older and the pressures to conform grow stronger, she still remains far from the ideal middle-class female, her face "vivid in its rouge and orange cake," her hair "cut in a long shag that looked like a flattened mane," her feminine image destroyed by her "powerful" neck. Her dreams reflect her confusion about her identity. She alternatively imagines that

> She would live by the ocean like a movie star, or disappear like her Aunt Mary, who told Dot she'd hitched a boxcar. Dot would own a fried-chicken chain. She would drive trucks, bull-dozers, fly off forever like her grandmother Adelaide. She would travel the world and seek knowledge, or live up north on the reservation with her uncles Russell and Eli. She'd put the shot in the state track, from there to the Olympics.

As a young woman, Dot is at a crossroads in developing her sense of self. The role offered her at the end of the novel—that of Beet Queen—is, of course, a traditional female one involving objectification and circumscription of female strengths. Accepting that role would ally Dot with the other defeated females in the novel, Adelaide and Sita, a fact Celestine vaguely recognizes when she thinks of Dot on the stage as another of the "frothy confections . . . like magazine models or mannequins in store windows." However, like her mother, Dot breaks out of the constricting definition of female presented to her. Even dressed in her absurdly confining and immobilizing costume, Dot is "electric, tense with life"; she walks "bold with purpose," "her head lowered like a bull's." She frees herself by repeating—but with important differences—Adelaide's flight. Unlike Adelaide who wants to escape reality by flying into a romantic fantasy of female dependency on a man, Dot, "vault[ing] in [to the plane] without a hand up, or permission," embarks not on an unproductive escape but on a journey of independent self-definition. Writing her name, "Queen Wallacette" rather than "The Beet Queen" or even "Dot," she seeds the clouds with her new female identity. Her triumph is ultimately not simply a personal one or even a singularly female one, for it brings the rain that ends the symbolic social drought devastating the whole community. Further, the promise of renewal and fertility contained in this act has a specifically Native American referent. Native American spiritual revival is symbolically suggested in the descriptions of Russell, associated with the desiccated land throughout the novel and with thirst at its end (Dot is the only person to notice Russell's need for water during the parade). Dot's act not only offers a female rebirth but an Indian one as well; the rain she brings will symbolically revive Russell, the "lines in his face, deep and brown, jagged, running sideways . . . like the dry earth."

In important ways, Dot ends the novel not as an American beauty queen, but as a female power allied with traditional Native American ones. Erdrich has suggested this aspect of Dot's heritage much earlier in the novel, in a hauntingly beautiful image Erdrich has described as "the real heart of the book." As Celestine feeds the infant Dot late one night, she notices in the fine moonlit floss of her baby's hair, a tiny white spider making its nest.

> It was a delicate thing, close to transparent, with long sheer legs. It moved so quickly that it seemed to vibrate, throwing out invisible strings and catching them, weaving its own tensile strand. Celestine watched as it began to happen. A web was forming, a complicated house, that Celestine could not bring herself to destroy.

As Owens has suggested, Erdrich here offers a "fleeting sug-gestion of Spiderwoman's web of creation and connection" to suggest Dot's power. In *The Sacred Hoop: Recovering the Feminine in American Indian Traditions,* Paula Gunn Allen stresses the importance of this "quintessential spirit" who "weaves us together in a fabric of interconnection": "To her we owe our lives, and from her comes our ability to endure, regardless of the concerted assaults on our, on Her, being, for the past five hundred years of colonization." By rejecting white America's myths of femininity and tapping into more powerful Native American ones, Dot, like Erdrich, points the way toward more fruitful, independent gender and racial identities than those the society offers either Sita or Russell.

Nancy J. Peterson (essay date October 1994)

SOURCE: "History, Postmodernism, and Louise Erdrich's *Tracks,*" in *PMLA,* Vol. 109, No. 5, October, 1994, pp. 982-94.

[*In the following essay, Peterson presents a poststructuralist interpretation of* Tracks, *noting in particular the novel's treatment of history as potentially fictive and relative.*]

In a 1986 review of Louise Erdrich's second novel, *The Beet Queen,* Leslie Marmon Silko argues that Erdrich is more interested in the dazzling language and self-referentiality associated with postmodernism than in representing Native American oral traditions, communal experiences, or history. In Silko's view, the "self-referential writing" that Erdrich practices "has an ethereal clarity and shimmering beauty because no history or politics intrudes to muddy the well of pure necessity contained within language itself." Whether or not one agrees with Silko's characterization of postmodernism, with her criticism of *The Beet Queen* as apolitical and ahistorical, or with the implicit agenda that she proposes for Erdrich, it is true that reviewers of *Love Medicine* and *The Beet Queen,* the first two novels of Erdrich's recently completed tetralogy, tend to praise Erdrich's lyrical prose style and to applaud her subtle treatment of Native American issues. Erdrich's novel *Tracks,* published in 1988, almost seems to answer Silko's criticisms of *The Beet Queen* by overtly engaging political and historical issues. But writing such a novel did not come easily to Erdrich: she put the original 400-page manuscript for *Tracks* aside for ten years, and only after she had worked backward in time from *Love Medicine* to *The Beet Queen* did she take it up again and begin to link it to her already completed novels about contemporary generations of Chippewa and immigrant settlers in North Dakota. Erdrich's difficulty in fleshing out this historical saga is symptomatic of a crisis: the impossibility of writing traditional history in a postmodern, postrepresentational era. It seems epistemologically naive today to believe in the existence of a past to which a historian or novelist has unmediated access. Radicalized in the poststructuralist movement, language and linguistics have not only led to skepticism concerning access to the past but also instigated a debate about whether historical narratives can be objective representations or are (merely) subjective constructions of a researcher's and a culture's ideologies. Following Lacan, Saussure, and Althusser, prominent poststructuralists have without regret or nostalgia asserted the textuality of history—that there is no direct access to the past, only recourse to texts about the past. Even the facts of history are constructed in language, as Barthes observes: "It turns out that the only feature which distinguishes historical discourse from other kinds is a paradox: the 'fact' can only exist linguistically, as a term in a discourse, yet we behave as if it were a simple reproduction of something on another plane of existence altogether, some extra-structural 'reality'." Similarly deconstructing the linkage of history and the real, Derrida demonstrates in *Of Grammatology* the degree to which historicity is linked to writing: "Before being the object of a history—of an historical science—writing opens the field of history—of historical becoming." And elsewhere in *Of Grammatology,* Derrida makes the now famous pronouncement "there is nothing beyond the text," which indicates to some readers a radical ontological and epistemological skepticism that makes history pure fiction, with no referential link to events of the past. In the light of this cultural-intellectual trajectory, which radically destabilizes history, it is no wonder that Erdrich grappled with the difficulties and possibilities of telling a historical tale.

The crisis Erdrich confronts may also be viewed as an outgrowth of the Nietzschean view of history as a disease, an affliction, a burden. In *The Use and Abuse of History,* Nietzsche argues that historicizing is abusive when it overdetermines the present and future or when it leads to paralysis rather than action. Indeed, Erdrich's lengthy hiatus from working on *Tracks* might be read as a symptom of this Nietzschean paralysis; certainly Erdrich's comments about *Tracks* echo a Nietzschean anxiety regarding the weight of history: "I always felt this was a great burden, this novel." Extending Nietzsche's concerns about "an excess of history," Hayden White asserts in a chapter titled "The Burden of History" that "it is only by disenthralling human intelligence from the sense of history that *men* will be able to confront creatively the problems of the present" (emphasis added). Thus, as White suggests elsewhere, many historians and theorists have become interested in "getting out of history."

Getting out of history, however, is a strategy not available to those who have never been in it, as Diana Fuss observes. Fuss challenges White's position by arguing that "[s]ince women as historical subjects are rarely included in 'History' to begin with, the strong feminist interest in forging a new historicity that moves across and against 'his story' is not surprising." The same claim can be made on behalf of other groups that have been marginalized in traditional historical accounts—Native Americans, Asian Americans, African Americans, Latinos and Latinas, and so forth. Indeed, the burden of history is markedly different for writers from such groups since a lack of historical representations can be as burdensome as an excess. For writers such as Erdrich, a part-Chippewa woman, the history of America has often been exclusionary—a monologic narrative of male Anglo-American progress that constructs others as people without history.

Writing history (as historical novels and in other forms) has thus become one way for marginalized peoples to counter their invisibility. And yet at the very moment when they are writing their own accounts of the past, the possibility of writing history seems to have become passé.

In *The Politics of Postmodernism,* Linda Hutcheon offers a way to rework and renegotiate these contradictions. She argues that postmodern culture does not renounce historical representation altogether but questions its status:

> To say that the past is only *known* to us through textual traces is not . . . the same as saying that the past is only textual, as the semiotic idealism of some forms of poststructuralism seems to assert. This ontological reduction is not the point of postmodernism: past events existed empirically, but in epistemological terms we can only know them today through texts. Past events are given *meaning,* not *existence,* by their representation in history.

The distinction Hutcheon makes here between ontology and epistemology, between the past (event) and history (narrative), is crucial. To participate in the "ontological reduction" that Hutcheon speaks of is to question or even to deny that the Holocaust occurred—or the massacre at Wounded Knee or slavery or the internment of Japanese Americans during World War II and so on. To use poststructuralism to question the occurrence of these horrific events is to inflict further violence on the victims and survivors. And yet a historical position in postmodern culture necessitates the recognition that history is a text composed of competing and conflicting representations and meanings—a recognition that precludes any return to a naive belief in transparent historical representation or even in realism.

Writers like Erdrich thus face a vexing set of issues: unrepresented or misrepresented in traditional historical narratives, they write their own stories of the past only to discover that they must find a new way of making history, a way of "forging a new historicity," in Fuss's terms. Erdrich works toward a new historicity through the novel. Analyzing the need for literature to intervene in "the consequent, ongoing, as yet unresolved *crisis of history*" surrounding the Holocaust, Shoshana Felman and Dori Laub argue that "literature becomes a witness, and perhaps the only witness, to the crisis within history which precisely cannot be articulated, witnessed in the given categories of history itself." Similarly, Erdrich's historical novel, *Tracks,* enables readers to think through the issues and the stakes involved in the crisis of history surrounding Native Americans.

THE PAST AS REFERENCE POINT

Tracks poignantly portrays the history of the Turtle Mountain Chippewa's struggle to keep their land in the late nineteenth and early twentieth centuries. Throughout the novel, a tribal elder, Nanapush, tries to change the course of events so that the contestation over land tenure between the tribe and white settlers, which culminates in the battle over Fleur Pillager's land, will not destroy the tribe. Fleur, one of the few unassimilated full-bloods among the Anishinabeg (Chippewa), has been allotted a valuable tract of timber-filled land adjoining Matchimanito Lake. Although Nanapush does his best to retain Fleur's claim to the land, white lumber interests turn United States government policy to their advantage, and in the end, Fleur's land is lost.

Tracks opens with an elegiac description of the plight of the Chippewa at the turn of the century. Nanapush, one of the novel's first-person narrators, tells Lulu, Fleur's daughter, the history of their people. I quote and analyze the passage at length because it serves as a microcosm of Erdrich's method throughout the novel.

> We started dying before the snow, and like the snow, we continued to fall. It was surprising there were so many of us left to die. For those who survived the spotted sickness from the south, our long fight west to Nadouissioux land where we signed the treaty, and then a wind from the east, bringing exile in a storm of government papers, what descended from the north in 1912 seemed impossible.

> By then, we thought disaster must surely have spent its force, that disease must have claimed all of the Anishinabe that the earth could hold and bury.

> But the earth is limitless and so is luck and so were our people once. Granddaughter, you are the child of the invisible, the ones who disappeared when, along with the first bitter punishments of early winter, a new sickness swept down. The consumption, it was called by young Father Damien, who came in that year to replace the priest who succumbed to the same devastation as his flock. This disease was different from the pox and fever, for it came on slow. The outcome, however, was just as certain. Whole families of your relatives lay ill and helpless in its breath. On the reservation, where we were forced close together, the clans dwindled. Our tribe unraveled like a coarse rope, frayed at either end as the old and new among us were taken. My own family was wiped out one by one, leaving only Nanapush. And after, although I had lived no more than fifty winters, I was considered an old man. I'd seen enough to be one. In the years I'd passed, I saw more change than in a hundred upon a hundred before.

> My girl, I saw the passing of times you will never know.

> I guided the last buffalo hunt. I saw the last bear shot. I trapped the last beaver with a pelt of more than two years' growth. I spoke aloud the words of the government treaty, and refused to sign the settlement papers that would take away our woods and lake. I axed the last birch that was older than I, and I saved the last Pillager.

Erdrich's writing lays tracks here for a revisionist history and a new historicity. Nanapush's speech is revisionist because it defamiliarizes the popular narrative of American history as progress by showing the costs of that "progress" to native peoples. His speech to Lulu presents an alternative narrative of certain past events—epidemics ("the spotted sickness," "consumption") and "government papers" (various federal treaties and legislative acts)—that led to hardship and death for members of the tribe. Indeed, academic history "documents" the "fact" that Nanapush's historical account corresponds to past events: academic accounts report that North Dakota was afflicted with outbreaks of smallpox from 1869 to 1870 and of tuberculosis from 1891 to 1901. In fact, European diseases such as smallpox, measles, and tuberculosis are said to have been more deadly to native populations across the country than Indian-white warfare was.

But Erdrich's work moves beyond documentation. Such historical "facts" do not fully acknowledge the horror of depopulation and genocide, a horror that is marked in the opening passage by the shift from "we" (the people) in the first paragraph to "I" (the only surviving witness) in the last. The problem of relating the past in the form of history is further addressed in that passage when Nanapush instructs Lulu on the limits of his own narrative: "My girl, I saw the passing of times you will never know." Without denying the referentiality or importance of his historical narrative, Nanapush acknowledges that the real (or "what really happened") is that which Lulu "will never know"—in other words, the complexity of the past exceeds his (and anyone else's) ability to re-present it fully. Nonetheless, Nanapush insists on telling this history to Lulu, for only by creating his own narrative can he empower her.

The question of power and empowerment is central: Erdrich's novel focuses not only on the limits of documentary history but also on its politics. "Documents originate among the powerful ones, the conquerors," writes Simone Weil, a French Jew exiled to London during World War II. "History, therefore, is nothing but a compilation of the depositions made by assassins with respect to their victims and themselves." Indeed, a documentary history of Native America would necessarily be based on treaties, legislative acts, and other documents written or commissioned in the name of the United States government and subsequently (ab)used to take land from indigenous peoples. The history of treaty making and treaty breaking with Native Americans demonstrates that such documents are not autonomous, objective, or transparent statements but texts open to interpretation by whoever is in power.

Since traditional written history, based on documents, is another kind of violence inflicted on oppressed peoples, *Tracks* features oral history. The opening of the novel uses oral storytelling markers: the narrator does not name himself, as he would not in a traditional face-to-face storytelling situation, nor is the addressee named except to designate her relationship to the narrator ("Granddaughter"); the last two paragraphs quoted above contain a rhetorical pattern typically associated with orality, repetition with variations ("I guided," "I saw," "I trapped"). Other oral markers signify Erdrich's rejection of the language of documents: Nanapush refers to "the spotted sickness," not to smallpox or measles; he uses traditional oral tribal names (Nadouissioux, Anishinabe) rather than anglicized textual ones (Sioux, Chippewa); he speaks of "a storm of government papers" instead of naming specific documents affecting the tribe. The turn to oral history in *Tracks* signals the need for indigenous peoples to tell their own stories and their own histories.

But the evocation of the oral in a written text implicates this counterhistory in the historical narrative that it seeks to displace. *Tracks* renders a history of Anishinabe dispossession that moves within and against an academic account of this history. Indeed, the need to know history as it is constructed both orally and textually is indicated by the contextual phrases that begin each chapter: first a date, including the designation of season(s) and year(s), then a phrase in Anishinabe followed by an English translation. This information establishes two competing and contradictory frames of reference: one associated with orality, a seasonal or cyclic approach to history, a precontact culture; the other linked with textuality, a linear or progressive approach to history, a postcontact culture. Erdrich creates a history of dispossession that moves between these frames, that is enmeshed in the academic narrative of dates and of causes and effects concerning the loss of land. Indeed, only by knowing this narrative can the reader attach any significance to the fact that chapter 1 begins in 1912.

The academic historical narrative that Erdrich uses and resists typically begins with the reservation period: the United States government initially disrupted tribal ways of life by establishing reservations so that the tribes were confined within strict boundaries while white settlers claimed more territory. Then the Dawes Allotment Act of 1887 codified a turn in government policy, making it relatively easy to divide up land formerly held communally on reservations and to allot it to individual Indians. The point of allotment was to convert tribes such as the Chippewa from a communal hunting and gathering organization to a capitalistic, individualistic agricultural economy. The allotted tracts were to be held in trust for twenty-five years (according to the original plan), during which time the owners would be encouraged to profit from the lands (by farming, selling timber rights, and so on) but would not be required to pay property taxes. The goal was to use the trust period to assimilate the Indians into the "white man's" way of life so that they would become productive capitalists, capable of assuming the responsibilities of landholding—such as paying taxes—without further governmental intervention. But in 1906 Congress passed the Burke Act, which allowed the commissioner of Indian affairs to shorten the twenty-five-year trust period for "competent" Indians. Under this act, those deemed competent were issued a fee patent rather than a trust patent; they could therefore sell or lease—or lose—their allotments. Then in a 1917 "Declaration of Policy," Commissioner of Indian Affairs Cato Sells announced that all Indians with more than one-half white blood would be defined as competent and thus would be made United States citizens and that they would be granted fee patents for their allotments. Although the professed original intent of allotment was to maintain Indian land ownership, the policy had the opposite effect: "before allotment 139 million acres were held in trust for Indians. In 1934 when allotment was officially repealed, only 48 million acres of land were left and many Indians were without land." Some Indians lost their allotments because they could not pay the taxes after the trust period ended; others were conned into selling their allotments at prices well below the land's value; still others used their allotments as security to buy goods on credit or to get loans and then lost the land after failing to repay the debts.

By opening in 1912 and proceeding through the disastrous consequences of Sells's 1917 declaration, *Tracks* dramatizes the tenuousness of land tenure for Native Americans. Although Nanapush tells Father Damien, "I know about law. I know that 'trust' means they can't tax our parcels," the map Father Damien brings along—with its seemingly innocuous little squares of pink, green, yellow—shows that the agent's office is busy calculating who will be unable to pay. As Fleur, Nanapush, Eli, Nector, and Margaret work to raise money to pay their taxes, native traditions are forced into a new economic context: the Pillager-Kashpaw family gathers and sells cranberry bark, just as Turtle Mountain women sold herbs and roots to raise money, while Eli traps and sells hides, activities that Turtle Mountain men had to engage in. These efforts raise just enough money. But when Margaret and Nector go to pay the taxes, they are told that they have enough only to pay the taxes on their own tract. No doubt Fleur's land is too valuable to be left to Indian ownership; the lumber is worth too much for the encroaching capitalists to leave it unharvested. As Nanapush recognizes, the late-payment fine levied by the agent is probably illegal, yet greed and desire divide the Anishinabeg, turning some, such as Bernadette Morrissey and Edgar Pukwan Junior, into "government Indians," while prompting others—Margaret and Nector—to look out for themselves at the expense of communal values.

Erdrich's novel takes up (corresponds to) a turning point in the history of Anglo-Indian land conflicts. But the absence of names for the dates, acts, and other specifics attached to this kind of history displaces this narrative, even as it is invoked. That is, the tension and conflict at the heart of *Tracks* come into focus only when readers have some knowledge of the Dawes Allotment Act of 1887, but the text does not refer to the act directly. The documentary history of dispossession that the novel uses and resists functions as an absent presence; the text acknowledges the way in which this historical script has impinged on the Anishinabeg but opposes allowing this history to function as the only story that can be told.

Moreover, by refusing to participate in such documentation, Erdrich's novel refocuses attention on the emotional and cultural repercussions that the loss of land entails. In one of the final events of the novel, the trees on Fleur's tract are razed. Fleur does not communicate the trauma of this event; she is not a narrator in the novel, though she is a central character (perhaps *the* central character). Instead, the razing of the trees accrues import through its link to two earlier episodes: Fleur's rape by the butchermen of Argus, North Dakota, after her victory at poker and Margaret's "rape" by Clarence Morrissey and Boy Lazarre, who shave her head out of vengeance. In all three incidents, a nexus of forces—capitalism, sexism, violence—causes irreparable loss. Fleur has ways to redress these wrongs: she causes the tornado in Argus that maims and kills the butchermen, she reduces Boy Lazarre's speech to babbling because of his voyeurism, and she asks the manitou of Matchimanito Lake to drown men who cross her. But her powers cannot ward off the whites and government Indians greedy for land, money, and power. The novel portrays Fleur's loss in this sociocultural war as tragic: it is because traditional Anishinabeg like Fleur and Nanapush are dispossessed and because Native American clans and tribes are consequently fragmented that the tracks of Native American history and culture are so difficult to discern. At the end of the novel Fleur is said to walk "without leaving tracks," a foreboding development since she is described by Pauline as "the hinge" between the Chippewa people and their manitous and by Nanapush as "the funnel of our history." And yet, Fleur's disappearance and tracklessness at the end of the novel function as a present absence—her absence becomes a haunting presence in the narrative, signifying the need for a reconceptualization of history, for a new historicity that both refers to the past and makes a space for what can never be known of it.

HISTORY AS STORY

Tracks dramatizes the problematic nature of historical narrative, which cannot give voice to the (precontact) past directly—a notion figured in the character of Fleur—but which mediates that past in language and narrative. The novel works toward an understanding of history not as an objective narrative but as a story constructed of personal and ideological interests. Arising from this insight is a vexing theoretical issue: If history is just a story, how is it possible (or is it possible at all) to discriminate between one account of the past and other accounts?

The postmodern novel, which Hutcheon terms "historiographic metafiction," characteristically foregrounds the fictionality of history. E. L. Doctorow exemplifies this position in his essay "False Documents," where he argues that there is no difference between history and fiction, that both are narratives constructing the only world that can be known. Erdrich's work resists absolute groundlessness or relativity by contrasting the two narrators who construct the story of *Tracks*.

The second narrator—in addition to Nanapush—is Pauline, an orphaned young woman who is trying to make sense of the beginnings of sexual desire and her alienation from both the tribe and Anglo society. She eventually resolves this psychic tension by becoming a nun, but only after becoming pregnant, trying to force a miscarriage, and then forgetting about the illegitimate baby after it is delivered. Ignoring her part-Chippewa ancestry, she declares herself to be "wholly white" in order to become a nun. Pauline's narrative voice reproduces a phenomenon Bell Hooks describes in *Black Looks:* "Too many red and black people live in a state of forgetfulness, embracing a colonized mind so that they can better assimilate into the white world." Indeed, Pauline embraces Catholicism to repress her sexual desire and her connection to tribal culture; but the perverseness of this repression becomes apparent when she begins masochistically punishing herself for being unworthy.

Because of different identities and allegiances, Nanapush and Pauline narrate contrasting interpretations of the historical moment that unfolds in *Tracks*. Nanapush's elegiac historical saga runs contrapuntally with Pauline's assimilationist version, which interprets the Anglo settling of America as progress. Whereas Nanapush sees the allotment policy and the concomitant conversion of the Anishinabeg from hunters and trappers to farmers as the cause of starvation, poverty, and land loss, Pauline suggests that "many old Chippewa did not know how to keep"—that is, to farm—their allotments and therefore deserved to lose them. In addition, while Nanapush views the destruction of Anishinabe society and culture as tragic, Pauline sees it in terms of Christian millennialism:

[A] surveyor's crew arrived at the turnoff to Matchimanito in a rattling truck, and set to measuring. Surely that was the work of Christ's hand. I see farther, anticipate more than I've heard. The land will be sold and divided. Fleur's cabin will tumble into the ground and be covered by leaves. The place will be haunted I suppose, but no one will have ears sharp enough to hear the Pillagers' low voices, or the vision clear to see their still shadows. The trembling old fools with their conjuring tricks will die off and the young, like Lulu and Nector, return from the government schools blinded and deafened.

Although part Chippewa, Pauline justifies the maneuvers of Christian and governmental authorities to dispossess the people of their land and culture. By teaching at Saint Catherine's Pauline becomes one of the agents that blind and deafen children to their native culture and language. In contrast, Nanapush rescues Lulu from boarding school and its inevitable racism. This difference in perspective is also reflected in Pauline's eagerness to be renamed and reborn as Leopolda—a name given to her by white Christian authorities—in contrast to Nanapush's refusal to reveal his name to those authorities. Pauline recognizes that indoctrination into white culture is a kind of mutilation—her students will be "blinded" and "deafened" as she herself has been—but she sees this development as inevitable. The white Christian capitalists will win the cultural-epistemological war, in Pauline's view, and she will side with the victor.

Erdrich's novel holds Nanapush's and Pauline's antithetical views in tension, showing point of view to be inherent to any historical narrative. Moreover, these conflicting stories and visions reflect a tribal vision of the world that allows for competing truths and, according to Paula Gunn Allen, for gender balance rather than gender oppression. Because historical events caused intact tribes and bands like the Turtle Mountain Chippewa to become split at the root, Nanapush's and Pauline's points of view are both necessary to provide an "indigenous" account of what happens in *Tracks*.

Pauline's and Nanapush's narratives also correspond to the need to comprehend both textual and oral history. Nanapush tells the story to Lulu, but Pauline addresses no one in particular and thus implicitly addresses a reader, not a listener. The lack of an immediate audience also signifies Pauline's distance from oral tribal culture. But Nanapush himself cannot maintain an exclusively oral perspective. At one level he participates in the construction of a binary opposition that measures the distance between his narrative and Pauline's: oral "tribal" values in contrast to textual "Anglo" values. In the novel, an Anglo-American worldview is figured in terms of money and writing, systems that historically have been alien to the Anishinabeg and that Nanapush believes pose a threat to the tribe:

I've seen too much go by—unturned grass below my feet, and overhead, the great white cranes flung south forever. I know this. Land is the only thing that lasts life to life. Money burns like tinder, flows off like water. And as for government promises, the wind is steadier.

Nanapush sees that money is an unstable system of value: for white capitalists, it is the measure of progress, but for his people, "[d]ollar bills cause the memory to vanish." Moreover, the white settlers prefer documents, written words, to fix their meaning, whereas the Anishinabeg rely on spoken words, oral promises, to wield power. Nanapush alone foresees that the white man's written promises are texts that are open to endless interpretation and reinterpretation:

[O]nce the bureaucrats sink their barbed pens into the lives of Indians, the paper starts flying, a blizzard of legal forms, a waste of ink by the gallon, a correspondence to which there is no end or reason. That's when I began to see what we were becoming, and the years have borne me out: a tribe of file cabinets and triplicates, a tribe of single-space documents, directives, policy. A tribe of pressed trees. A tribe of chicken-scratch that can be scattered by a wind, diminished to ashes by one struck match.

Nanapush deconstructs the West's reverence for the written word as the stabilizer of meaning and tradition.

And yet Erdrich's novel points out that conserving Anishinabe history and worldview is not by itself a successful political strategy for withstanding the threat of colonialism. Nanapush recognizes that paper must be fought with paper, in contrast to Fleur, who trusts in tradition to prevent her land from being taken—"She said the paper had no bearing or sense, as no one would be reckless enough to try collecting for land where Pillagers were buried." Paradoxically, Nanapush's ability to adapt to these new conditions comes in part from his traditional namesake: the Chippewa trickster Naanabozho. In fact, episodes in the story of Naanabozho parallel episodes in Nanapush's story. Both share the ability to come back to life after death or near death; both are noted for their keen ability to track people; both avenge wrongs committed on family members; both are powerful storytellers.

Most significant, perhaps, is that both Nanapush and Naanabozho are tricksters who are sometimes tricked by others. Once duped, however, both adopt the techniques of the oppressor to even the score and to balance the distribution of power. For instance, when under-water spirits (manitous) kill his nephew, Naanabozho finds and wounds them, but they escape. He tracks them, however, and tricks the old woman who is doctoring them into divulging not only where the manitous are but also how to get past the guards and kill the manitous. He then kills the woman and skins her; putting on her skin, he disguises himself as the oppressor. His tactics succeed, and he avenges his nephew's death. Like Naanabozho, Nanapush assumes the guise of the oppressor to defuse the oppressor's power. For example, Nanapush allows Father Damien to write a letter recommending Nanapush as a tribal leader. In making this concession, Nanapush does not leave behind his earlier (traditional) skepticism concerning the written word; rather, he increasingly realizes that it is politically necessary for him not to stay outside the system of written discourse but to use the technology against itself. In fact, he becomes a bureaucrat and uses the "authority" of the written word to save Lulu from exile at boarding school. Producing the birth certificate filed by Father Damien, which names Nanapush as Lulu's father, Nanapush gains the power to call Lulu home. Ironically, Lulu's birth certificate—recognized as an authentic document by white authorities—is a lie, for Nanapush is not her biological father. And yet in a tribal view Nanapush is certainly Lulu's spiritual father, the one who mentors her and teachers her the old ways. Thus, the piece of paper— both fiction and fact—becomes a clever tool for saving Lulu from assimilation.

The final paragraph of *Tracks,* describing Lulu's return from school, thus strikes a note of cautions optimism. As Lulu emerges from "the rattling green [government] vehicle," she bears the marks of her encounter with Anglo-American authority: hair shorn, knees scarred from attempts to make her docile, attired in the shameful "smouldering orange" of a runaway, Lulu at first seems alien to Nanapush and Margaret. As they watch, however, Lulu's prim, school-taught walk becomes a leap, and her face is electrified with Fleur's bold grin and white-hot anger. Marked by her encounter with the shapers of mainstream American history, Lulu is only "half-doused" and will carry forward a trace of Anishinabe history and myth.

Nanapush's negotiation between the old ways and the exigencies of the present is the significant legacy he leaves to Lulu. He recognizes that it is no longer possible to rely solely on the oral tradition to pass down narratives of the past. To do so would be to end up like Fleur, the funnel of oral history silenced by white encroachment and by writing itself. As pure Indian, Fleur is a near-mythic figure—a source of inspiration for Lulu, but one that seems beyond emulation. (And this is perhaps why Fleur does not have a direct voice in the narrative.) Pauline, Fleur's opposite, does not offer Lulu a model either, for Pauline's assimilation into the dominant culture results in a voice that echoes hegemonic history. Moreover, by forgetting the past and radically rewriting her own identity and experience, Pauline signifies history as pure fiction with no referential value whatsoever—a position that Erdrich's work ultimately rejects. By contrast, the link between Lulu and Nanapush, which the novel affirms, signifies a kind of history writing and history telling that neither relinquishes nor oversimplifies its referential debt to the past, that is grounded in tradition and ready to adapt to (post)modern conditions.

Both Nanapush's and Pauline's narratives suggest that history is not objective and impartial, as traditional documentary historians assert. It is always constructed in the interests of a particular party or ideology. In his critique of documentary history, Dominick LaCapra asks historians to acknowledge that they are in "dialogic interchange with the past," that is, that they rewrite the past in part out of presentist interests. What interests, then, resonate in Erdrich's late-twentieth-century reconstruction of Native American history? In part, Erdrich's work seems to be a reaction to the excesses of poststructuralism and postmodernism, which attempt to reject the referential function of language and narrative. Thomas M. Kavanagh suggests in *The Limits of Theory* that the unrecognized need for theory to "master" its object means that "the real itself" has become "at best irrelevant"—because of its complexity and unpredictability. Similarly, Susan Stanford Friedman argues for a complex reactivation of certain terms poststructuralism has rendered "taboo," such as *the author, agency, identity,* and *reference.* Erdrich participates in this revisionary project by renegotiating the postmodern crisis of history. The new historicity that *Tracks* inscribes is neither a simple return to historical realism nor a passive acceptance of postmodern historical fictionality. *Tracks* takes up the crucial issue of the referentiality of historical narrative in a postmodern epoch and creates the possibility for a new historicity by and for Native Americans to emerge.

Sue Halpern (review date 16 April 1995)

SOURCE: "Mother's Day," in *New York Time Book Review,* April 16, 1995, p. 14.

[*In the following review, Halpern praises* The Blue Jay's Dance *for its realistic portrayal of early motherhood.*]

I recently saw an ad for an instructional CD-ROM on "parenting, prenatal to preschool" whose contents I could only imagine: sage advice from professionals and video clips of children whose exemplary behavior—so different from one's own child's—sells the sequel. Louise Erdrich's first book of nonfiction, *The Blue Jay's Dance: A Birth Year,* which is about being a parent, is nothing like that. Aside from a few recipes (lemon meringue pie, fennel and chicory salad, anise apples) and bits of painfully gained wisdom (when dealing with a screaming, colicky baby, "I use my most soothing tone of voice to call her names. The tone helps her, the words help me"), the book is delightfully impractical. It is a narrative, not a manual.

Ms. Erdrich is not only a successful novelist; she is a successful novelist who is also the mother of young children. In the past she shielded her family life from public scrutiny—allowing the press to interview her only away from her New Hampshire home, for instance, and purposefully declining to talk about her life there. Her marriage to the writer Michael Dorris was well known, and so was the fact that Ms. Erdrich and Mr. Dorris had six children, three of them adopted. The oldest of these, Abel, who died in 1991 after being hit by a car, was the subject of Mr. Dorris's harrowing book about fetal alcohol syndrome, *The Broken Cord.*

Ms. Erdrich's reticence to invite the news media into her kitchen was so unusual that it fanned a small mystery about her. "How does she do it with all those kids?" people—especially women, especially women with babies—asked one another as the novels *Love Medicine, The Beet Queen, Tracks, The Bingo Palace* and *The Crown of Columbus* (co-written with Mr. Dorris) were published to critical acclaim.

The Blue Jay's Dance might be expected to answer that question. "I finished this book for our daughters because I hope these pages will claim for them and for others, too, what it is to be a parent—an experience shattering, ridiculous, earthbound, deeply warm, rich, profound," she writes in the introduction. That said, she then steps back. "The baby described is a combination of our three babies whom I nursed and cared for in a series of writing offices. I do not name our children, and if I refer to them obliquely sometimes, I hope that readers will forgive. After all, these words will one day add to our daughters' memories, which are really theirs alone."

It is a hard task, writing a book that attempts to be public and private at the same time, to tell all in essence and not in fact; the writer's ambivalence is always apparent. In this case, though, Ms. Erdrich's ambivalence inspires trust. After all, she is protecting her children not only from our prurience but from her own, and this alone suggests that she is the kind of mother whose story should be told. But then she doesn't tell it, not directly. Instead she tells what her story has taught her, and what she was thinking about, seeing and feeling, while it was unfolding.

Ms. Erdrich writes lovingly of the woods around her house and the child she carries with her on her walks, and about the blue jays and ducks and woodchucks they encounter there. The book is a ramble, and sometimes the reader is tempted to stray from Ms. Erdrich—when she celebrates her husband's thick hair, for instance, or when she chronicles all the adventures of the neighborhood cats. But no matter

where she is roaming, and what she is writing about, she is observant, tender and honest. And she is not afraid to write about the mind-numbing 3 A.M. despair of new motherhood, just as she is not given to forgetting that her beloved cats have claws. Of one's offspring, she says: "We cannot choose who our children are, or what they will be—by nature they inspire a helpless love, wholly delicious, also capable of delivering startling pain."

This is not an original insight, but then having babies and raising them is not exactly new, either. What makes *The Blue Jay's Dance* worth reading is that it quietly places a mother's love and nurturance amid her love for the natural world and suggests, passage by passage, how right that placement is. When the birth year is over, and Ms. Erdrich hands her young daughter over to a baby sitter in order to be able to continue doing her other creative work, we glimpse the mechanics of her writing life. But it is in the months before that, as Ms. Erdrich sits in her office stroking her baby with one hand and holding a pen with the other, that we begin to understand how connected, and how necessary, the left hand is to the right.

Mark Childress (review date 12 May 1996)

SOURCE: "A Gathering of Widows," in *New York Times,* May 12, 1996, p. 10.

[*In the following review, Childress praises Erdrich's storytelling and characterization in* Tales of Burning Love.]

Louise Erdrich is attracted by the miraculous possibilities of love. Romantic love, religious ecstasy, the strange mixture of devotion and misunderstanding that runs through families—all are steeped together. The result is a rich and fragrant infusion.

Tales of Burning Love is her sixth novel (including *The Crown of Columbus,* written with her husband, Michael Dorris). The publisher says this book "extends the boundaries of her literary vision," but any reader familiar with *Love Medicine* and *The Beet Queen* will recognize the characters and settings. Once again we are firmly placed in the bleakly beautiful landscape surrounding Argus, N.D. Once again many of the characters are Native Americans with a fading connection to the reservation, confused Roman Catholics on the lookout for miracles, lonely women searching for that thing called love.

In this case, the male component of that thing is Jack Mauser, a lapsed Chippewa who marries five times in 13 years—four times for love and once as a result of booze, painkillers and a horrible toothache. The story opens in 1981 with that toothache, which has put Jack into such a state that he takes up with the first woman he sees in the Rigger Bar. The attending clergyman is on the next bar stool. The wedding rings are the pop-tops from two cans of beer.

When his new bride wanders out drunkenly into a blizzard, Jack—who can't quite remember her name—lets her go. After the blizzard has lifted, she is found frozen against a fence post, "her hair loaded with melting stars. No one had touched her yet. Her face was complex in its expectations. A fist of air punched Jack to earth and he knelt before her with his hands outstretched."

The guilt of that moment will haunt Jack through each of his subsequent liaisons. He's an impulse marrier, operating on the "if at first you don't succeed" principle, trying and failing, then trying again. Unlike Elizabeth Taylor, though, Jack seems to get luckier as his marital career goes along.

Wife No. 2 is Eleanor, a writer and teacher, a quivering bundle of erotic emotion and neurotic opinion. The third is Candice, a blond and beautiful dentist: "With her stiff pink-white mask covering the lower half of her face, she was a mysterious priestess." Fourth in the line is Marlis, a blunt-spoken, dreamy-eyed vixen in the Ally Sheedy, mature-beyond-her-years mode. Jack's last wife is solid, responsible Dot, an accountant at his failing construction company, as brusque and unfancy as her name.

Jack Mauser is the thread binding these women's stories. Each of them has loved him in a different way, and each of their marriages to him has failed for its own reasons. At first, the structure of *Tales of Burning Love* seems as shaggy and chaotic as something from Chaucer. The stories pop up seemingly at random, overlapping, circling back and forth through time and crossing one another in ways that are often ingenious and only occasionally confusing.

Soon enough, though, Ms. Erdrich skillfully gathers up all these threads. Jack touches bottom. His half-completed subdivision is a failure. Drunk and alone in his unpaid-for dream house, he allows a small fire to blaze out of control when he realizes that his death—or, at least, the appearance of his death—could be a major problem solver. "Things were falling into place," he realizes, "great things, huge problems over which he had had no control now were being solved precisely because he had relinquished control and God had smiled a big hot smile on him."

God plays a major offstage role in this plot. The four Mauser widows come together the night of Jack's funeral, which also happens to be the night of another ferocious blizzard. The women become trapped in Jack's red Explorer in the middle of a snow-blasted nowhere. Shivering, munching stale candy, they spend the whole night in the car, sharing the stories of how they fell in love with Jack and why they broke up with him. The aptly named Explorer becomes "a confessional."

"Rule one," Dot proposes. "No shutting up until dawn. Rule two. Tell a true story. Rule three. The story has to be about you. Something that you've never told another soul, a story that would scorch paper, heat up the air!"

This sequence is the comic centerpiece of the novel. By the time they're all together, we know these women well, and their stories bump together to strike real comic sparks. One wife is in a post-Jack spin, having lost her job after an embarrassing sexual misadventure and gone to live in a convent, where she is studying a nun she suspects of sainthood. Two of the wives have fallen in love with each other and are caring for Jack's infant son. The remaining wife is just plain disgusted with Jack, suspecting that he married her so she couldn't be forced to testify against him.

What these women discover is that loving Jack Mauser has changed their lives in very particular ways. "It isn't entirely farfetched to say that we each married a different man," Eleanor observes. "No one of us has a quarrel with any woman in this car. No more so than if we'd all had different husbands."

They discover that one of them loved Jack more than the others—still loves him, in fact—and although it would spoil the surprise to give her away, this discovery infuses the latter parts of the novel with great poignance and charm. Miracles and possibilities come together here to produce a kind of earthly magic that is more potent than magic realism. No one emerges from the Explorer unchanged. Ms. Erdrich's saints are nearly as lively as her sinners, and that's a real achievement.

If I have a quibble with this story, it's with the man at the heart of it. Jack's wives are vivid and fully realized, and Jack is too—as long as he's at center stage. Whenever he's out of sight, though, he doesn't seem as interesting as the women who loved him. I wanted them to stop trying to explain their attraction to him and tell us more about themselves. Most of all, I wanted to hear more of Louise Erdrich's constantly inventive prose, as when she describes the surprised sound made by a gut-shot deer: "A wild laugh like a little girl on a Halloween street, running."

Verlyn Klinkenborg (review date 16 June 1996)

SOURCE: "A Gulliver Shipwrecked on a Coast of Women," in *Los Angeles Time Book Review,* June 16, 1996, pp. 3, 13.

[*In the following review, Klinkenborg praises* Tales of Burning Love *and conjectures that the book signals a fundamental change in Erdrich's writing.*]

There has always been something fervent about Louise Erdrich's fiction. Her characters seem to burn with consciousness and desire in a difficult landscape, a place where isolation and hard weather and poverty clarify the nature of longing. The life she sets loose in her novels is so incendiary that it can only be contained, so it seems, within a shape that is nearly symbolic in purpose. If Erdrich were writing for a different time, her novels would be about saints' lives—narratives in which pain is also joy and death is transfiguration. There is about each of them something exemplary, in the cautioning sense of that word.

Tales of Burning Love is Erdrich's sixth novel, not counting *The Crown of Columbus,* which was written with her husband, Michael Dorris. Erdrich has an extraordinary ability to grant her characters parole—allowing them to move from one novel to the next—without ever seeming repetitive or calculating.

Tales of Burning Love, a comic, expansive book, begins with the same story of doomed courtship that opens *Love Medicine,* Erdrich's first novel, except that it is told through a different set of eyes. That story ends with June Kashpaw dying in an Easter snowstorm. In *Love Medicine,* June's death haunts everyone. But in *Tales of Burning Love,* her death haunts only Jack Mauser, the man who married her under a false name and who watched her flee, after a few hours of marriage, from their motel room into the thickening storm.

Mauser is a Gulliver shipwrecked on a coast of women. He has had— although he isn't sure what tense to use when he thinks about it—five wives: the snowbound June; Eleanor Schlick, a lapsed academic; Candice Pantamounty, an aseptic dentist; Marlis Cook, a saloon singer and blackjack dealer; and Dot Nanapush, an employee at his construction firm and a recurring character in Erdrich's earlier novels.

So many marriages to such vital women is a puzzle to everyone. In *Tales,* it happens that four of Jack's five ex-wives end up trapped together in a car all night long during a freak blizzard, returning home from a bar in Argus, N.D. (The car also contains, disguised as a hitchhiker in the rear cargo compartment, Dot's first, and undivorced, husband, Gerry Nanapush, who has escaped from prison.)

To keep themselves awake and thus alive, the Mauser wives try to solve the puzzle of Jack's marriages and to absolve themselves, as it were, of each other's presence. "The real question is this," says Eleanor. ". . . If he was so ultra-normal, so banal, so pathetically male, why did any of us agree to marry him?"

Jack is puzzled, too. Here is how he describes himself to Eleanor when they were arguing about getting married. "I'm just this guy. . . . I'm from North Dakota dirt farmers, Indians, a railroad executive, big-shot and little-shot people." Mauser has all the masculine virtues except the love of dogs, and he has kept a kind of native wildness long beyond the onset of what passes in most men for maturity. He is a maker, good with tools and machines, good with what Eleanor calls his "kind hands."

But what singled him out for each of these women was his patent need. In him, they recognize an absence they can accommodate. When he met June, Jack believed that "by climbing into her body, he would exist." As Marlis, his fourth wife, says, "I had no intention of even going out with Jack, but he was starving for it."

It, of course, is not just sex, though this is a deeply, almost reverently sexual novel. It is completion, absolution, forgetfulness and memory all at once. *Tales of Burning Love,* like all of Erdrich's novels, is a book about recovering from the belief that you can stand alone.

Only one person manages a kind of self-sufficiency in this novel, and that is the ferocious, desperate nun, Sister Leopolda, who lives in a convent just outside Argus and is the subject of Eleanor's research. Sister Leopolda's words measure the metaphysical dimensions of Erdrich's erotic world. When Eleanor speaks with Sister Leopolda just before her death, the nun tells her there is "No relief to love, no end, no wave, no fall, only a continual ascension."

When Eleanor finds herself blown at last through the great Argus blizzard, Sister Leopolda returns to her in a vision. "Love is brutalizing," the nun says, "a raw force, frail as blossoms, tough as catgut wire. Lost, found, sprinkled with the wild sweet oils, love changes and is immutable. . . . You want abiding rightness, an assurance of your course. You will not find all that in a man. No, that imaginary conviction is a cross that will break his back."

Tales of Burning Love is a more garrulous book than any Erdrich has written in the past, again excepting *The Crown of Columbus.* It occupies a different space, so to speak, within the same landscape as her other novels. And it hinges upon a different kind of necessity—not the self-enclosed fate one feels on the reservation but a kind of open, almost forgiving sense of possibility, which carries its own kind of compromises, the ones associated with the boom economy that is engulfing the town of Argus: sloppiness, haste, sterility, blandness.

Though Erdrich again conjures with the past in *Tales of Burning Love,* this book marks a shift in her career, a shift that is suggested rather than fulfilled. Argus is familiar to her readers, and so are many of the names here: Kashpaw, Nanapush, Lamartine. But there is new country coming into Erdrich's sight, and this novel is her first welcoming account of it.

Julie Barak (essay date Fall 1996)

SOURCE: "Blurs, Blends, Berdaches: Gender Mixing in the Novels of Louise Erdrich," in *Studies in American Indian Literatures,* Vol. 8, No. 3, Fall 1996, pp. 49-62.

[*In the following essay, Barak discusses Erdrich's use of gender mixing in the Indian tradition of the figures of the berdache and the trickster.*]

> We have come to the edge of the woods,
> out of brown grass where we slept, unseen,
> out of leaves creaked shut, out of our hiding.
> We have come here too long.
>
> It is their turn now,
> their turn to follow us. Listen,
> they put down their equipment.
> It is useless in the tall brush.
> And now they take the first steps, not knowing
> how deep the woods are and lightless,
> How deep the woods are.

Erdrich, "Jacklight"

In an interview with Jan George shortly after the publication of her first book of poems, *Jacklight,* Louise Erdrich comments on the title poem, explaining that "Jacklighting and hunting are both strong metaphors for me of sexual and love relations between men and women. In the male tradition, men are the hunters and women are their prey, but in the poem 'Jacklight,' I am trying to say something like this: If our relationships are going to be human, . . . men have to follow women into the woods and women likewise. There must be an exchange, a transformation, a power shared between them." "Living in empty country," she says, "the woods to me have always been a place of mystery, shelter. That's where we have to go to find each other."

Erdrich and her husband and collaborator, Michael Dorris, have apparently found each other in that woods. Their many publishing successes in recent years are proof of the strength of their writing relationship, anyway. Both of them describe that writing relationship as a sensual/sexual union. Erdrich explains to Kay Bonetti in a 1988 interview how she and Dorris collaborate: "Michael and I plunge into each other's work with very little ceremony. We plot together, we dream up our characters together, we do everything together, except write the actual drafts, although even the writing is subject to one another's deepest desires." Erdrich describes their joint efforts as "co-conceiving" and says that she feels "more and more that we're seeing out of the same set of eyes . . . we think each other's thoughts, truly, so it is very much like having one vision." Dorris experiences their relationship in much the same way, noting that "when writing about both male and female characters it is a distinct advantage to have an absolutely trusted and equitable input from someone of the other gender who shares the same vision, almost as an opposite-gender version of yourself."

At one point, early in their collaborating lives, Erdrich and Dorris did join together to publish under a pseudonym, Milou North. The name and their collaborative efforts under it were an experiment, they explain in a 1987 interview with Hertha D. Wong, one that they enjoyed for "the romance of it." They thought it established a sense of mystery for their readers—"You really think that's probably a female, but you don't know." Through their play with authorial gender and the gender blending of their authorial selves in their shared labor they create the exchange and transformation Erdrich sees as necessary in gendered relationships.

Just as they played with their readers' expectations of authorial gender in the creation of that pseudonym, in their collaborative plotting they play with their characters' genders in the discovery stages of their novels. Dorris tells Wong how the character of Rayona in *A Yellow Raft in Blue Water* evolved during a long car trip he and Erdrich took together:

> When we left New Hampshire the book was about a young boy who was coping with his mother's death, and by the time we reached Minnesota it was about a young girl whose mother lives. Since then it has expanded into three parts. One of which is in the mother's voice, and the next in *her* mother's voice. All of that really evolved out of changing the main character from a male to a female. Louise, I think, proposed that originally. It was hard to think of. It's like sending somebody to Sweden for a sex change operation, but it just worked better.

Erdrich and Dorris play with gender roles and boundaries in other ways, too. Where Rayona's gender is, finally, decided and firm, even though they experimented with it in the early stages of the novel, several characters in their work, especially those in the tetralogy published under Erdrich's name—*Love Medicine, Tracks, The Beet Queen,* and *The Bingo Palace*—are "gender-mixed" characters who are described either as exhibiting or in some way acting out opposite sex role mannerisms or behaviors. In developing this line of thought in what follows I will focus almost entirely on the tetralogy and cite these works as Erdrich's. The importance of Dorris's contributions should not be slighted or forgotten, however.

Erdrich develops a fluidity of gender identities in her characters by recreating a gender role available to her through her Native American background—that of the berdache, a powerful figure in many precontact aboriginal societies in North America. In "The North American Berdache" Charles Callender and Lee M. Kochems define the berdache as a "person, usually [but not exclusively] male, who was anatomically normal but assumed the dress, occupations and behavior of the other sex to effect a change in their gender status. This shift was not complete; rather, it was a movement toward a somewhat intermediate status that combined social attributes of males and females."

It is important to note that because many berdaches participated in cross-dressing it was often assumed that berdaches were all homosexual. However, Callender and Kochems believe that this "frequent equation with homosexuality distorts the sexual aspects of berdachehood," and they have found that though berdaches and their spouses or partners were the most consistent participants in homosexual behavior, "their orientations could be bisexual or heterosexual." Several other scholars support Callender and Kochems in this conclusion. Harriet Whitehead, in "The Bow and the Burden Strap: A New Look at Institutionalized Homosexuality in Native North America," asserts that "there is no evidence that homosexual behavior as such was used as a reason for promoting reclassification of an individual to the gender-crossed status. In contradistinction to occupational and clothing choice, cross-sex erotic choice is never mentioned as one of the indicators of the budding berdache." Of female berdaches, or manly-hearted women, Midnight Sun, in "Sex/Gender Systems in Native North America," writes that the role was "only associated with gender status and not cross-dressing or lesbianism."

Many North American tribes attributed a special status to berdaches and recognized them as especially valuable members of the community. Economically, berdaches were a boon to the community because they performed so many tasks so well. Callender and Kochems note that "[m]ale berdaches are consistently described as exceptionally skilled in women's work, while female berdaches showed a similar pattern of excelling in male activities, with hunting most often cited." The berdaches' ability to perform both roles, however, is what made them special to the community. A significant element in the prosperity of a household inhabited by a berdache "rested on the intermediate nature of their gender status, allowing them to combine activities proper to men and to women and maximize their economic opportunities."

Along with their economic success, berdaches were thought to possess many other talents or assets. James Thayer Steel, in "The Berdache of the Northern Plains: A Socioreligious Perspective," details the most common of these. They were often called upon to give children names in naming ceremonies and they were thought to have a special talent in educating children that accompanied a reputation for intelligence. They were seen as match-makers or "love-talkers" because of their ability to move easily between men and women. Moreover, they were reputed to have extremely active sex lives. Many berdaches had reputations as healers, especially good with love medicines, but also with childbirth, insanity, and wounds. Berdaches often oversaw funeral rites. They were thought to be blessed with both a lucky and a long life.

The female berdache is more commonly referred to by anthropologists as a manly-hearted woman. Oscar Lewis, in "Manly-Hearted Women Among the North Piegan," details the qualities that distinguish manly-hearted women from their sisters, noting that aggressiveness, independence, ambition, boldness, and a pronounced sexuality, as well as wealth and maturity, are among her common characteristics. Like the male berdaches, manly-hearted women excel in both men's and women's work. They also often practice medicine. Lewis notes that in contrast to the quiet demeanor of other women, manly-hearted women "do not hesitate to make speeches in crowds, they joke and tease and express opinions and disagreements, just as though they were men. They are often avoided because of their sharp tongues and readiness to defend themselves from criticism by exposing others to ridicule and humiliation." Moreover, manly-hearted women are reputed to be *ikitaki,*—passionate women, and their sexual unconventionalities are the subject of much gossip." A woman becomes known as manly-hearted when she "can equal men in their own skills, in personal wealth, in the manipulation of property, in sexual prowess, and in religious participation, [and] break away from the verbalized restrictions applied to [her] sex."

Thayer points out that berdaches were both respected and ridiculed among their people, noting that the berdache "tended to be a marginal figure among the tribal groups of the Plains, but at the same time had a clearly recognized status and clearly defined talents." Because they received the call to become a berdache in a vision they were thought of as holy or special. "However," continues Thayer, "there was also a profound ambivalence towards this figure. On the one hand, his ritual and ceremonial power were highly regarded and his womanly talents highly praised, but because of his awesome vision and exotic life, the berdache also had a feared and avoided place in social relations." Because of their "in-between" status, berdaches in many tribes were treated, not just for a ceremonial moment but for all of their lives, like initiands in rites of passage ceremonies; they were freed from the restrictions of the usual, feared and respected for the powers granted them by their difference.

Many of Erdrich's characters fit, partially or completely, the definition of the berdache detailed above. Some do not, however, and these exceptions are telling in their own ways. A prime example of the disaster of mono-genderedness is Russell Kashpaw in *The Beet Queen.* Russell is a man—through and through. He was a high school football player, a volunteer for service in and a decorated veteran of three wars, who fell in love with the most stereotypically feminine of all of Erdrich's women, Sita Kozka. He suffers from a series of strokes and heart attacks which leave him completely paralyzed. When he is "displayed" in his uniform with all his medals in the Argus Beet Queen parade, many of the spectators believe that he's "stuffed." Suffering in the same way that Russell does are King, Henry Jr., and Gordie of *Love Medicine* whom Nora Barry and Mary Prescott describe in "The Triumph of the Brave: *Love Medicine*'s Holistic Vision" as "doomed, but only because they are fixed upon their inabilities to measure up to the demands of traditional masculine ritual, and because they are unable to imagine anything else for themselves."

Some of her male characters are gender-mixed but unable to accept that mix gracefully; they struggle to find a way to live comfortably within it. This was common to many berdaches. They received their call to berdachehood in a vision, but they could refuse to pay heed to that vision, choosing instead to walk a safer, more conventional line. Ignoring a vision, however, often creates difficulties. Wallace Pfef, for example, in *The Beet Queen,* is aware of his homosexuality, but denies it to his community. Instead, he buys a picture of a pretty young girl at a farm auction and displays it in a prominent place in his living room. He creates a story for the townspeople about their love and her tragic death so that he won't be expected to court or marry any of the women in the community. Like the berdache, Wallace is good at making money. He is also good at both men's and women's tasks. Along with being a prominent citizen in Argus and a sharp businessman, he decorates his new home tastefully and cooks delicious meals, for both his adopted niece, Dot, and for his sometime lover, Karl Adare. He is present at Dot's birth, helping Celestine Jones in any way he can, and in this way is responsible for her naming: Dot's legal name is Wallacette.

Wallace's lover, Karl Adare, is another good example of a gender-mixed character who is uncomfortable with his vision. He is bisexual; he has affairs with both Wallace and Celestine Jones. Descriptions of him in the novel hover between the masculine and the feminine. He, too, has good luck with jobs and money, though he never amasses as much wealth as Wallace. Karl is a wanderer, never settling down long enough to create a niche for himself in any community.

He's scared of love—searching constantly for the love his mother took away from him when she flew off into the afternoon sky with Omar the stunt pilot. Hans Bak observes that Karl "harbor[s] both masculine and feminine elements . . . [and] hovers uneasily in-between, unable to reconcile both sides into a balanced whole, incapable of finding rest or rootedness in either homosexual or heterosexual love, but always vulnerable to the danger of plunging into an underlying void."

Several other male characters in the novels are more comfortably gender-mixed and take on feminine tasks in the tradition of the berdache. Eli Kashpaw, for example, an expert hunter in *Love Medicine,* adopts June and cares for her. Barry and Prescott point out that "besides sharing with her his knowledge of the woods, he mothers her in a way she can trust." They continue: "Eli's behavior is unorthodox and encourages gossip because in his relationship with June he demonstrates complementary male and female ritual." He also acts as a healer later, in *The Beet Queen,* when he takes in and cares for his half-brother Russell after his strokes paralyze him.

Old man Nanapush, in *Tracks,* the "prequel" to *Love Medicine,* like many berdaches is a healer. His care saves Fleur from death when consumption is raging on the reservation. When Lulu's feet are frozen, he thaws them for her. As he sings a "cure song" to calm her as the blood pours back into her feet, he thinks,

> Many times in my life, as my children were born, I
> wondered what it was like to be a woman, able to
> invent a human from the extra materials of her own
> body. In the terrible times, the evils I do not speak
> of, when the earth swallowed back all it had given
> me to love, I gave birth in loss. I was like a woman
> in my suffering, but my children were all delivered
> into death. It was contrary, backward, but now I had
> a chance to put things into a proper order.

When Fleur leaves the reservation after losing her land, Nanapush becomes Lulu's guardian, raising her as his own. He is also adept at love medicines, as berdaches often are, providing Eli with the medicine he needs to win Fleur. And, like many berdaches, he is sexually attractive and active, even into his eighties when he takes up with Margaret Kashpaw.

Many of Erdrich's female characters are berdaches or manly-hearted women too, though there are, as with the male characters, exceptions. The tragicomic life of Sita Kozka in *The Beet Queen,* like Russell Kashpaw's in that same novel, serves as an example of the perils of mono-genderedness. June, in *Love Medicine,* functions much like Karl Adare and Wallace Pfef do in *The Beet Queen.* She is called to be and trained in berdache ways, but is unable to accept her intermediate or mixed-gendered status. She has been taught to hunt by Eli; in many ways she is his "son," even dressing like Eli when she is younger. But she refuses this role in life and seeks out feminine, traditional women's roles. Through the course of her life she fails as a beautician, a secretary, and a waitress. She also fails at motherhood, abandoning two sons. Like Wallace and Karl she resists the call of her vision and is tortured by her refusal to answer it. June is one of those who can't be comfortable in accepting a gender mix inside herself.

Pauline in *Tracks* is, perhaps, another. As is common to many berdache, one of her occupations is overseeing funeral rites. Physically, she is described in both male and female terms. William Gleason, in "'Her Laugh an Ace:' The Function of Humor in Louise Erdrich's *Love Medicine*," says that Pauline's passion is the "repressed rage of latent lesbianism," citing Leopolda's vicious scolding of Marie followed by her sensuous rubbing of liniment in "slow wide circle[s] into Marie's naked back," to support his assertion. Julie Tharp, in "Women's Community and Survival in the Novels of Louise Erdrich," claims, on the contrary, that Pauline's heterosexuality, her jealousy of Fleur's relationship with Eli, "keeps the women wary of one another and creates a vindictive streak within Pauline." Whatever her sexual preference, however, Pauline is definitely a tortured soul in terms of her sexuality, who finally chooses the chastity of the nunnery over sexual relationships with either men or women.

Mary Adare and Celestine James in *The Beet Queen* are both manly-hearted women. Both of them are economically independent, choosing to remain single and to support themselves, rather than marry. Marie Kashpaw, in *Love Medicine*, is a manly-hearted woman, too. She has raised herself up economically and socially by marrying Nector Kashpaw and she has, as many manly-hearted women do, made him into the man he is in the community. Lulu Nanapush is another. Lulu is well-known for her sexual promiscuity. She is bold about her sexual history, though, and like the manly-hearted woman she is unafraid to boast about her exploits. In *Love Medicine*, she hears people whispering "bitch" and "All those Lamartine sons by different fathers" behind her back during a tribal meeting. As a manly-hearted woman, she speaks up. "'I'll name all of them,' I offered in a very soft voice. 'The fathers . . . I'll point them out for you right here'."

However, Fleur is the quintessential berdache or manly-hearted woman. She is a good hunter, better than most men on the reservation. She is big and strong, capable of lifting sides of beef and pork by herself and of hauling her cart of odds and ends for sale throughout the community. She has great luck in cards, winning enough in her stay in Argus to pay taxes on her land for two or three years and, years later,

winning her land back in a game of cards with Jewett Parker Tatro, the former Indian agent who had acquired her land in her absence. She lives alone, until Eli falls in love with her and comes to join her. Then their sexual exploits give the reservation plenty to talk about. She is also a healer, collecting medicines and distributing them. She saves Marie's life in childbirth. Lipsha goes to Fleur for love medicine in *The Bingo Palace*. Like many berdaches she is both feared and respected for her powers in her community.

I've detailed descriptions of only a few of the berdache characters in Erdrich's work. Lyman Lamartine, Gerry Nanapush, and Lipsha Morrisey also possess berdache characteristics. Shawnee Ray and her sisters, Mary Fred and Tammy, Zelda Kashpaw, Dot Adare, and Rushes Bear are among the women characters whom one could consider to be manly-hearted. Erdrich's reasons for blurring and blending gender borders in so many of her characters can, perhaps, be understood by comparing it to the other transformational or border-crossing characters in Native American myth.

In "Why Bears are Good to Think and Theory Doesn't Have to Be Murder: Transformation and Oral Tradition in Louise Erdrich's *Tracks*," Joni Adamson Clarke discusses the bear's importance to Chippewa myth. Bears were considered "quasi-human in anatomy, erect carriage, a cradling of young with the forearms, enjoyment of sweets and liquors, manner of drinking liquid, shows of intelligence, and inclination to moderate behavior despite great physical strength. . . . Moreover, a bear's life cycle, moving from hibernation in winter to reemergence in the spring, made him seem at once a symbol of both life and death." Clarke claims that "by thinking or 'playing' with the bear's human-like qualities and seasonal cycle, formerly sharp borders—like those between animal and human, life and death—fade and 'novelty emerges from unprecedented combinations of familiar elements'." Mixed-gender characters in Erdrich's fiction are "good to think" in this same way because, "as Judith Butler points out in her discussion of the subversion of gendered identity, 'perpetual displacement constitutes a fluidity of identities that suggests an openness to resignification and recontextualization'."

Erdrich's texts promote an openness to "resignification and recontextualization" not only by blurring gender boundaries but also by blurring other boundaries. Many of her characters are, for example, ethnically mixed and their genealogies and family relationships are hard to trace. Moreover, Erdrich blurs narrative lines in her fiction, fracturing her story line by employing many different narrative voices. Other critics have observed how Erdrich's work crosses genre boundaries and have attributed her power as a story teller to that aspect of her writing. Ann Rayson, in "Shifting Identity in the Work of Louise Erdrich and Michael Dorris," cites a review of their jointly-authored novel, *The Crown of Columbus*, in which the reviewer claims it is "a very mixed bag" that "tries on too many costumes—domestic comedy, paperback thriller, novel of character, love story—and finally decides that, unable to make up its mind, it will simply wear them all at once." Rayson believes that "[i]n this artistic synthesis lies the power of Louis Erdrich and Michael Dorris and the challenge to critics who would seek a clear female or ethnic voice to legitimize theories of feminist and Native American literature."

Geoffrey Galt Harpham, in *On the Grotesque: Strategies of Contradiction in Art and Literature,* observes that "genre, genus, and genitals are linked in language as in our subconscious." Erdrich's blurring of all three in her fiction creates a grotesque art that "threatens the notion of a center by implying coherencies just out of reach, metaphors or analogies just beyond our grasp. . . . Looking at ourselves looking at the grotesque, we can observe our own projections, catching ourselves, as it were, in the act of perception." Erdrich's play along the boundary lines of genre, genus, and genitals acts in exactly this way in her novels. In her play with gender borders, in particular, she is attempting to break down her reader's notions of traditional gender roles by creating, over and over again, characters who cross over and through traditional gender definitions, who cannot be classified, who refuse to fit the traditional mold.

There is a connection, obviously, between the berdache figure and the figure of the trickster. Many critics have decoded Erdrich's characters as tricksters. The name of one of the main characters in *Tracks* is Nanapush, one of the linguistic variants of the name of the Chippewa trickster. This name is shared by two other characters in the text: Lulu Nanapush, his adopted daughter, and her son Gerry Nanapush. Several other characters in the novel inherit trickster traits from her or her son, most notably another of her sons, Lyman Lamartine, and Gerry's son, Lipsha Morrisey. Gerry's sometime lover, June Morrisey, as well as Mary Adare and her brother Karl, from *The Beet Queen,* have also been identified convincingly as trickster figures in recent criticism. The question to deal with here is not whether these characters are tricksters (there is certainly no lack of evidence to support that assertion) but rather how the blurred gender traits of so many of Erdrich's characters fit into the trickster motif.

In "A Tolerated Margin of Mess: The Trickster and His Tales Reconsidered," Barbara Babcock-Abrahams discusses the ambivalence of the trickster's character, labeling such characters "dialogic phenomena." She believes that "the ambivalence and the contradictions with which Trickster's tales abound are not proof, as Radin and others imply, of an incapacity to differentiate true from false, good from evil, beneficence from malevolence. Rather, they *express the generative situation of ambivalence and contradictions* that

are the very basis of culture" (italics mine). Furthermore, she asserts that "the mediating figure of Trickster does not represent a regression to a primal, undifferentiated unity *but is created in response to a present and constant perception of opposition*" (italics mine). The plethora of mixed-gendered tricksters in Erdrich is her literary response to the present and constant perception of opposition in her life and in the lives of her characters. The fact that so many of her characters are mixed-gendered tricksters leads to the conclusion that one of the most threatening aspects of contemporary life in America is its insistence on strictly bifurcated gendered behavior.

Like so many of Erdrich's characters the trickster figure often crosses over gender borders. In one story in the Winnebago trickster cycle, for example, the trickster decides to find a home for himself one cold winter by disguising himself as a woman using an elk's liver and kidneys to create a false vulva. He presents himself to the chief of a nearby village, is accepted into the family, marries the chief's son and bears three sons. Later, while being teased by his mother-in-law, he loses his false vulva; his identity is discovered and he is forced to flee. Trickster's gender switching in this story functions in quite the same way that bears function in Ojibway/Anishinabe myth; trickster's crossing over encourages an openness to a fluidity of identities that can lead to resignification and recontextualization of traditional binary relationships.

Many definitions of trickster label him or her as a liminal figure, living on the edges of the worlds of animal and human, physical and spiritual, male and female. Like trickster, many of Erdrich's characters live in-between worlds—and not just gender worlds. Fleur, for example, is often thought of by others and depicted in their stories as a bear-woman, a fish-woman, a spirit-woman. We are told very emphatically several times in Nanapush's story that he lives at a crossroads in the town. He is also one of the only survivors from "before the white people," crossing the borders between the old and the new ways. Gerry Nanapush is both a hero and a villain. Lipsha's return to the reservation after a long absence is described in all sorts of "in-between" ways: "He slid through the crowd during the *middle* of an *Intertribal* song. We saw him *edge* against the wall to watch the whirling dancers, and immediately we had to notice that *there was no place the boy could fit*" (*Bingo Palace,* italics mine).

Victor Turner points out in "Betwixt and Between: Liminal Period" that "in liminal situations, neophytes are sometimes treated or symbolically represented as being neither male nor female. Alternatively, they may be symbolically assigned characteristics of both sexes, irrespective of their biological sex." Turner believes that the grotesqueness and the monstrosity that such gender negation or blurring imply are not aimed so much at terrorizing or bemusing neophytes into submission or out of their wits as at making them vividly and rapidly aware of what may be called the "factors" of their culture. . . . Elements are withdrawn from their usual setting and combined with one another in a totally unique configuration, startling neophytes [and I believe other participants, too, observers or readers for example] into thinking about objects, persons, relationships and features of their environment they have hitherto taken for granted.

As liminal figures, berdaches and tricksters serve this same purpose in Erdrich's fiction, working between worlds to raise questions about accepted patterns of thought and action.

When Lipsha returns to the reservation at the beginning of *The Bingo Palace,* people are confused, not only about where he fits in but also about what sort of person he is. The description of who he is *not* emphasizes his mixed genderedness and his status as a liminal figure.

> He was not a tribal council honcho, not a powwow organizer, not a medic in the cop's car in the parking lot, no one we would trust with our life. He was not a member of the drum group, not a singer, not a candy-bar seller. Not a little old Cree lady with a scarf tied under her chin, a thin pocketbook in her lap, and a wax cup of coke, not one of us. He was not a fancy dancer with a mirror on his head and bobbing porcupine-hair roach, not a traditional, not a shawl girl whose parents beaded her from head to foot. He was not our grandfather, either, with the face like clean old-time chewed leather, who prayed over the microphone, head bowed. He was not even one of those gathered at the soda machines outside the doors, the ones who wouldn't go into the warm and grassy air because of being drunk or too much in love or just bashful. He was not the Chippewa with rings pierced in her nose or the old aunt with water dripping through her fingers or the announcer with a ragged face and a drift of plumes on his indoor hat.

He is not male or female, not old or young, not in or out of the tribe. "He was none of these, only Lipsha, come home."

What Lipsha's reappearance and his antics do for the community is to help them revise their thinking about themselves as individuals and their goals as a community; his actions are a catalyst in the community's re-visioning experience. He is a "combination" character, a berdache figure, whose strength comes from his special role in the community and from the ways he is "mixed." Turner believes that "during the liminal period, neophytes are alternately forced and encouraged to think about their society, their cosmos, and the powers that generate and sustain them. Liminality may be partly described as a stage of reflection." It creates an unsettled situation in which "there is a promiscuous intermingling and juxtaposing of the categories of event, experience, and knowledge, with a pedagogic intention." Lipsha certainly learns his lesson in *The Bingo Palace,* and there is great hope at the end of the novel that, as the person in whom much of the community is joined, he will be able to share it with them.

Robert Pelton believes that "the trickster is not an archetypal idea, but a symbolic pattern that includes a wide range of individual figures." He calls trickster "a sort of inspired handyman, tacking together the bits and pieces of experience until they become what they are—a web of many-layered meaning." According to Pelton, the trickster represents the human race "individually and communally seizing the fragments of his experience and *discovering* in them an order sacred by its very wholeness." Hence, "the trickster discloses the radically human character of the whole cosmos," while at the same time "he shows the holiness of ordinary life." In many ways, Erdrich entreats her readers to join the carnival of her text in this role of "inspired handyman," to join together the pieces of her narrative strategies, genre crossings, and gender blurrings to create their own quilt of a text. The reader becomes the trickster, responsible for making the pieces fit for herself and for those for whom she interprets the text.

In *Love Medicine,* Lipsha begins "to see how instantly the ground can shift you thought was solid. You see how all the everyday things you counted on was just a dream you had been having by which you run your whole life." This is the message that readers of Erdrich's fiction begin to see, too. Her narrative strategies impress the reader with the idea that neither individual nor collective points of view are reliable or consistent. Her play with the berdache role nudges the reader toward seeing that this is also true of hegemonic gender expectations. Every kind of firm belief, in fact, becomes suspect. Everything is a puzzle, there is no one "true" way to solve it, the pieces never fit together in only one way. Nothing can be assumed, everything has gestaltic possibilities, the facts keep rotating gyroscopically, offering everchanging possibilities. Just as Shawnee Ray puts together a ribbon shirt for Lipsha at the end of *The Bingo Palace* from "brown, calico, blue, cream, salmon trim—fitting the collar to the shoulders, figuring out the way she would join the ribbons at the yoke . . . [piecing in] scraps of other projects—turquoise, black and yellow satin," so the reader must put together a new view of gender roles and possibilities and of other generally held truths.

In the last chapter of *The Bingo Palace,* Fleur packs her sled with her ancestors' bones and takes them with her on her journey into death, trading her life for the life of her great-grandson, Lipsha. She doesn't leave them for good, however. Bear and berdache, she keeps them asking essential questions about themselves and their lives. Often in the night they hear her "bear laugh" as she watches them through the panes of window glass:

> yet, no matter how we strain to decipher the sound it never quite makes sense, never relieves our certainty or our suspicion that there is more to be told, more than we know, more than can be caught in the sieve of our thinking . . . and all night our lesser hearts beat to the sound of the spirit's drum, through those anxious hours when we call our lives to question.

Thomas Matchie (essay date Fall 1996)

SOURCE: "Louise Erdrich's 'Scarlet Letter': Literary Continuity in *Tales of Burning Love*," in *North Dakota Quarterly,* Vol. 63, No. 4, Fall, 1996, pp. 113-23.

[*In the following essay, Matchie discusses similarities between* Tales of Burning Love *and Nathaniel Hawthorne's* The Scarlet Letter.]

In an address on National Public Radio, Amy Tan said she would rather be recognized as an American author than classified among multi-cultural writers as Chinese American. Perhaps for some the same might be said of Louise Erdrich, "the foremost practitioner of Native American fiction." She is most often represented as a mixed-blood, and much of the critical analysis of her fiction centers around her use of Chippewa mythology as a key to illusive meaning in her novels. It is also true, however, that Erdrich is an ardent student of American literary history and culture. One has only to look for references to Melville's *Moby-Dick* in *Love Medicine* (1984), Flannery O'Connor's notion of the Christian grotesque permeating *Tracks* (1988), or Lipsha's language and naiveté resembling those of Huckleberry Finn in *The Bingo Palace* (1994). And I would like to suggest that her latest novel, *Tales of Burning Love* (1996), is her contemporary answer—or parallel—to the classic American romantic love novel, *The Scarlet Letter.*

Those familiar with Hawthorne's plot know that Hester Prynne goes through many stages, manifesting in different contexts various "selves." There is the past self with her husband, Roger Chillingworth, a physician for whom she feels "no love" and leaves behind in Europe. Next, there is her past secret self with the minister, Arthur Dimmesdale, including a sexual act she later claims had "a consecration of its own." Ironically, though some would brand her with a "hot

iron" for her "sin," she emerges as a kind of saint, an image of "sinless motherhood." A third tragic self is the Hester who promises Chillingworth she will keep his identity "secret," while he pursues his destructive vengeance on Dimmesdale. Still, another more assertive self surfaces in the forest with her pastor. After confessing her "deception," she throws off the scarlet letter and confronts Arthur directly with the "weight of misery" that this society has laid on him. Her honest talk of love and freedom (their leaving together for Europe) triggers in him a radical change—a "revolution" of "thought and feeling" that borders on the comical. But Hester's most pervasive self is the practical role she plays in public. In spite of either man or her own "shame," her sewing and other service causes the townspeople to "love her," and in this context she outlasts the other major characters in the novel. All things considered, there are at least five different postures (selves) that Hester takes toward reality in Hawthorne's Puritan love story.

Tales of Burning Love is a contemporary romance set in "the beautiful bleak landscape" in and near Fargo, North Dakota. It depicts not one but five "sharp portraits" of women with "fully individualized voices," all married to but one man, Jack Mauser, a mixed up, mixed-blood construction engineer. Neither religious like Dimmesdale, nor scientific as is Chillingworth, Jack is Erdrich's rendition of the modern (rather than a Puritan) male—one who has unfortunately buried "the Ojibwa part" of himself. But it is through him, or the relationships of the women to him, that Erdrich explores such Hawthorne-like themes as the mystery of love between the sexes, the inner and outer worlds through which it is manifested, the dubious connection of sexuality to religion, and how various types of personalities enter into and affect a marriage or lovers' union. In fact, if one takes these women separately, they might be seen as Hester's different selves relating to "a man," in this case, Jack, as well as to the public. Less moralistic and more humorous than Hawthorne, in *Tales* Erdrich may have written her "funniest, sexiest, most optimistic" novel. But she is every bit as much the romantic as Hawthorne, filling her plot with images of nature, particularly sunshine and snow, but especially fire, to accompany each of the wives' distinctive, "burning" tales of love.

Jack's first wife is June Morrissey. In *Love Medicine* and *Bingo Palace,* and now in *Tales,* June jumps from a truck near Williston in 1981 to get away from its drunken driver, apparently after meeting him in a bar only hours before. We now know from *Tales* that that man was Jack Mauser, and that he and June were united in a "one-night marriage." The episode is important, not only because June's presence permeates at least three of Erdrich's novels, but because it exemplifies a particular kind of love, one not far removed from that characterizing the marriage of Hester Prynne and Roger Chillingworth. That, too, happened in the past. Never feigning love, she fled to America apparently to escape her relationship with a cold old man; in Erdrich's novel, June had jumped from the pickup and walked away to her death. Roger pursues Hester anyway; and in *Tales* we learn later that Jack thinks regretfully of his botched sexual affair with June. Later, having burned down his house and faked his own death, he comes to the rescue of his mourning ex-wives caught in the snowstorm in which each has been telling her tale of love. On the way he imagines June "wearing a wedding dress" and "bringing him home." Though some see Jack as simply "a loser," Michael Lee says Jack's other marriages represent a long-time effort to "recapture the love" he had for June, one (unlike Chillingworth's) that is finally fulfilled in Eleanor.

The woman in *Tales* most concerned, even preoccupied, with sex is Eleanor Schlick, Jack's second wife. As with Hester, Eleanor has a curious sexual past, ironically coupled with a "saintly" present. Nobody in the Puritan community shares Hester's private life, for the object of her love remains "a riddle," and of him Hester "refuseth to speak." As time goes on, however, Hester emerges as a virtual saint, in spite of the Puritan authorities and the people's initial scorn. In her "Divine Maternity" she walks among them as the mother of Pearl and sews garments for the rich and poor as a virtual New Testament model. Stubbs says Hawthorne represents her as a "madonna of Renaissance art" that contrasts with the rigid Puritan code. Others speak of a "spiritual greatness" that transcends her own weakness, the Puritan society, and Hawthorne himself. This is not to say that Hester is a saint, any more than it is true or likely that she and Arthur will get together as lovers, for their motives—which Crews says are "inaccessible to the conscious will"—are different. It only suggests that Hester's protecting the identity of her lover—who does not share her transcendental vision—is in itself a sacrifice of self that is the stuff of saints rather than sinners.

In *Tales* Erdrich in turn juxtaposes Eleanor's sexual past with the present in the context of sainthood, though her method is different, often comic. A novelist whose "eye for sensual detail is impeccable," she even shares with the reader graphic aspects of Eleanor's former erotic life, including intimate thoughts she remembers from her diary:

> He turns me on my back carefully and kneels, his thighs just under my hips. . . . He comes into me, comes again, quietly and emotionally, looking into my eyes. "You're the one," he says . . . and we keep going, fuck ourselves stupid. . . .

We also know a great deal more about Eleanor's past than we do Hester's. Specifically, her mother, Anna, was rejected by her father, Lawrence Schlick, a noted funeral director in Fargo, over a past sexual affair between Anna and Jack Mauser. Strangely enough, Eleanor herself then had an affair with Jack and faked being pregnant as a way of getting her parents back together. She even dressed like a kind of "passive martyr," or "Holy Mary"—a virtual parody of Hawthorne's representation of Hester. After leaving Jack, Eleanor went into teaching, but that didn't allay her "sexual need." Fired for seducing a student, she is now nourishing her spiritual life at a convent retreat house in Argus, north of Fargo, while doing research on the first potential mixed-blood saint, Sister Leopolda—whose own story appears in *Tracks* and *Love Medicine.* It is in this context that the spiritual dimension of Eleanor's love life comes into play.

While walking in the convent garden with the saintly nun, whose own prayer is ironically "a tale of burning love," Eleanor has a "miraculous" experience connected to her past sexual life. Jack, an engineer, catapults over the convent wall in a backhoe bucket at midnight to visit his ex-wife. In a hilarious episode, including "lightning" and thunder, Eleanor and Sister Leopolda (quite ignorant of what is really happening) end up "worshipping" Jack wrapped in a cloak standing on a pedestal being prepared for a statue of the Virgin Mary. If the whole affair seems like another comic version of something sacred, it also mirrors in a mythic way the union of all great lovers—from the Greek Leda (the name Jack and Eleanor hoped to give their baby) to Hawthorne's own Hester and Dimmesdale. In each case a dubious sexual union, symbolically if not really, seems to have the blessing of the gods.

After Leopolda expires, Eleanor and Jack meet inside the convent where they continue to discuss their love, often realized in secret, but which they have never been able to make work in marriage, any more than have Hester and Dimmesdale. In Jack and Eleanor's case, though they truly loved each other, "fury burned through" their love; "we fought over how we couldn't fight," she says, so she left him—went home to mother, entered college, even flew overseas. In speaking of Hester and Dimmesdale, Hawthorne himself claims that love and hate are often very close; and the same might be said of Eleanor and Jack. Unlike Hawthorne's lovers, however, these two eventually do get together. Late in the novel, after the snowstorm in which she walked away from the Ford Explorer stuck on the airport road in Fargo, Eleanor imagines that the saintly Leopolda appeared and "saved her life"—a life which eventually involves her return to the arms of Jack. Dave Wood notes that the novel, the author's "most sensual," ends with sex on a religiously symbolic staircase, testifying once again to the close relationship in Erdrich (as in Hawthorne) of sexuality and religion.

Jack's third wife is Candice Pantamounty, D.D.S., a dentist, "A professional!" Blonde, beautiful, and "brisk," she is interested in her own career and dependent on nobody. Free, but self-absorbed, her only companion is her dog, Pepperboy. Candy represents that part of Hester that relates to Roger Chillingworth after he comes to America. Hester, too, is free, for no individual or system—not Roger or the Puritan hierarchy—can touch her being. But then something happens. Chillingworth, who has no "household fire" in his heart, commits Hester to secrecy about his identity, whereupon he becomes Arthur's "medical advisor," a role he uses to undercut the man he suspects to be Hester's lover. His approach, motivated by revenge, and done with scientific precision, hits at the "heart's entire substance." In this way Chillingworth destroys Dimmesdale's chance at a full human relationship with Hester, and likewise Hester's with Dimmesdale.

In *Tales,* a similar pattern occurs. After a hysterectomy, Candy (a scientific type herself) enjoys frequent sexual episodes with men, for there is no risk of pregnancy. An old classmate of Jack's, she meets him again through a dental appointment, has sex with him, and goes hunting with him along with her dog; then they are married. What kills the marriage is Jack's abuse of Pepperboy. After being bitten, he hits and eventually kills the dog, not realizing what that does to Candy. He thinks it is accidental, "a goddamn freak occurrence," but she loses respect for one who misuses "helpless things." Hester's tragic flaw is that, in effect, she permits Chillingworth to tantalize her loved one, Dimmesdale, and only realizes it too late. It is that self of Hester's that Candy represents in *Tales*—the part that allows another's abuse of someone or something one loves, and indirectly undercuts a burning love of one's own. Candy is more conscious than Hester of what is going on; in *Tales* it is Jack who doesn't make the connection, but in either case the abuse drives the woman closer to her real lover—in Hester's case Dimmesdale, in Candy's another wife of Jack's, Marlis, who is pregnant with the child Candy would love, but can never have.

Marlis Cook is Jack's fourth wife. She has no Native blood (like June or Dot—Jack's fifth wife), no intellectual/spiritual bent (like Eleanor), no professional expertise (like Candy). She is simply a black-jack dealer at the B & B Bar—a pastime familiar to Erdrich—who meets Jack by accident. Quickly she gets "a thing" for him, and becomes pregnant—the only one of the wives to do so. His reaction, however, is to abuse her—"twisted my arm. . . . Shoved me. Hit me," she says. What distinguishes Marlis, however, is the direct way she responds. She treats Jack like none of the others; she not only tells but also shows him what he is like. Marlis is that side of Hester who, when the opportunity comes, speaks directly to Dimmesdale about their relationship. It happens midway in the book when they go into the forest together. Here, in letting down her hair and throwing off the letter A, she shows him what it would take to transcend his Puritan rules, to be free, to share her spirit.

Sandeen calls this show of passion the "most moving" part of the book—a time when love itself transcends sin, guilt, shame, hypocrisy. And Hawthorne accompanies the event with a "burst of sunshine" in the sky. For Fogel the sun is a natural symbol, "real and indispensable," that is connected with love and never controlled by human law.

In Marlis' tale, she meets Jack quite by accident. She is knocked out after touching an electrical cable and Jack revives her. Later, he again "Dutch-rubs" her paralyzed face, giving her new (physical) life. Grateful, she marries him. "I love you so deep," she says. "Love me back." But he doesn't. In fact, he doesn't stop manhandling her, psychologically or physically—criticizing her makeup as well as twisting, hitting, and shoving her when he learns about the baby. In one way "childlike," but in another "mature-beyond-her-years," Marlis finally concludes: *"What the hell do you know about being a woman?"* She is much like Hester who through her language and gestures gives Dimmesdale a lesson in being a human being, not a product of a religious system.

Marlis' method, however, is unique. She and Jack are in a motel where she wraps him in duct tape while he is sleeping. When he is powerless, she pierces his ears, plucks his eyebrows, waxes and shaves his legs, and forces him to put on high heels in order to demonstrate what a woman has to go through. Her tactic is a bit different from Hester's with Dimmesdale—external rather than internal—but as with Hester it works, at least temporarily. In the woods Dimmesdale is elated and dances back to town, a new man, determined to become "wholly the lover and flee from all his obligations to the community." In *Tales* Jack is furious with Marlis, but he gets the point. Later, when Marlis wants to make love, he sees that her action was not a personal vendetta. "I'm using you," she says, and now he responds differently to the "taste" of her hair. Late in the novel, Jack, amid "snow" and "sun," comes to understand and accept many people he had heretofore neglected. He develops a new fire for John, Jr.—"a baby's indignant spoiling squawl of hunger," as well as "a piercing love" for a statue that looked like his mother, June, Eleanor, "All the women he'd ever loved." Though all this may be the result of a religious experience, much of the credit goes to Marlis. Like Hester, she is a good teacher because she is honest, personal, and direct, though in a modern, violent way that is as shocking as Hawthorne's more subtle psychological approach a century and a half ago.

When *Tales of Burning Love* opens, Jack is married to his fifth wife, Dot—the young arrogant girl in *Beet Queen* married in *Love Medicine* to Gerry Nanapush, now in and out of prison. Like Candice, an old high school acquaintance of Jack's, Dot is still impulsive, marrying Jack on a dare. If Hester's needle makes her a valuable part of the community, Dot's "accounting skills" save Jack's business, making her more a "business associate" than his wife; they even "make love with efficiency." Like Hester, Dot is "loyal" to her mate, and if people love Hester because she makes garments for everybody from Pearl to the Governor, Dot (who also knits) is the most practical among the wives. After Jack's mock funeral—he burns his house as a way of avoiding bankruptcy—Dot insists on seeing and handling Jack's ashes (which don't really exist), pays the funeral bills because she is Jack's latest wife, and drives the others to the B & B Bar in West Fargo to get Marlis' vote on what to do with what is left of Jack. In Hawthorne's novel, Hester is the one character, says Baym, "truly concerned with society and human relations"; Dot performs a similar mission in *Tales*. Less passionate than the other wives, she is the self who functions best in public.

Though the community "cannot do without Hester," says Sandeen, she still feels like a "pariah." In Erdrich's novel, Dot is also the loner in the group; June is dead, Eleanor is the object of Jack's passion; Candy and Marlis have each other—Candy having helped deliver Marlis' baby in the absence of Jack, and the two are together as lovers in the back seat of the Explorer during the storm. Never really divorced, Dot's "first love" is Gerry, but he is gone, or appears only periodically; in *Tales* he is the hitchhiker who joins the four women in the red Explorer where, "alive in the wrecked cold" after surviving a plane crash, he appears and "sealed her mouth with his."

But such moments are rare for Dot. More significant is that she capitalizes on her distance from Jack. In her alienated state, Hester cultivates a special knowledge of "the hidden sins" in others, the "unsunned snow" that contrasts with her own "burning shame." Dot does something equivalent. Unlike the intuitive Hester, she is aggressive, inquisitive, and brash, but this is her way of exposing others. Initially, she gets Jack to admit that she is "the goddamn fifth" of his wives, and almost stabs him with her knitting needle. "I don't know you from shit," she says, while exposing his secret past with Eleanor. Often the mouthpiece of Erdrich's "pungent and smart" dialogue, Dot abhors superficial talk. At the funeral when Eleanor says Candice looks happy, Dot (a former classmate of Candy's) replies, "Scum floats." Finally, it is Dot who sets the rules for each wife to tell her tale while marooned in the north Fargo blizzard. The least romantic of the wives, Dot is the firebird who sets ablaze the others' secret lives.

Though fond of Jack, Dot finally sees him as her "burnt hope," which is Hester's ultimate view of Dimmesdale. Recovering in the hospital after the storm, it is Dot's mother Celestine, not Jack, who comes to her side. Erdrich seems to use Dot to assert, not sex or romance, but the extended family so important to Native Americans. "Solid, responsible . . . brusque," Dot reserves her most genuine affection for

Gerry, and a big priority in her life is to raise Shawn, whom she views as simply "my part of the deal." Real life, after the romance is over, is Dot Nanapush's role, much as it finally becomes Hester Prynne's, who continues to mother Pearl while serving others after her lover is gone.

So that is Erdrich's story—the five faces of Hester, so to speak, as reflected in the five wives of Jack Mauser. If Hester has a past marriage that has failed, causing her to flee across the sea, that is June Morrissey setting out in the snow near Williston in 1981. If Hester has had a secret life, where the passionate and sexual are intertwined with the spiritual and the saintly, that is Eleanor as she works out her relation to Jack in the convent garden in Argus in 1996, and later (after a vision of Leopolda) in the passionate scene on the stairs with Jack which ends the book. If Hester errs by allowing her estranged husband, now in America, to torture her new lover to the point of death, that is Candice, who is not able to sustain her relationship with Jack because he physically abuses her Pepperboy. If Hester needs to speak directly to her beloved and so takes him to the woods, where her words temporarily free the man from his rigidities, that is Marlis who ties up Jack and literally shows him what it feels like to be a woman. And if Hester must still maintain a public face, in spite of all her inner worlds, that is Dot, the "live-in accountant" of Jack Mauser, for whom personal love is not so important as the daily companionship of a man, the love of her family, and the knowledge that she can makes things work.

There is an irony in *Tales* that may also be a modern comment on *The Scarlet Letter,* as Erdrich like Hawthorne focuses on her favorite themes, "the salvation of love" through "the power of narrative." In *Tales,* two of the women, Candy and Marlis, struggle with each other. Candy, who would like a child, fawns on Marlis' baby—the baby she cannot have. If Jack has a problem with the pregnancy, Candy calls it "a treasure," and it is she, not Jack, who helps in the delivery room. Though at first Marlis resists Candy's concern and affection, eventually their struggle—an important factor in both Hawthorne and Erdrich—brings them together where their "first kiss tells everything." Finally, in the back of the Explorer in the snowstorm, they make love, having come to understand and accept each other as women—something Jack cannot seem to accomplish. For the author it is "an intimacy that rivals any lover's union." This love affair serves as a foil for Hawthorne's portrayal of the relationship of Chillingworth and Dimmesdale—a story of revenge, hatred, and manipulation that destroys both men. It involves a different type of dispute, but the implication is that men have to control, whereas women's struggles lead to self-sacrifice and love. It is another kind of tale of burning love—sinful and scandalous, perhaps, in the eyes of many, but also respectful and caring, much like that between Hester and Dimmesdale in *The Scarlet Letter.*

The Scarlet Letter is a romantic novel that represents a landmark in the history of psychological love. Though deprecated by Hawthorne's critics at the time, the novel made a much deeper impression than his other works. One of the reasons, says Cotton, is that "the symbolic" is different from "the real." Hester may have violated the Sixth Commandment, but she emerges as a free spirit who has integrated her sexual life into her being and now, Dimmesdale notwithstanding, lives a rather Christ-like life in public. She has faults, however, as does he, and because of them, the story is tragic—a conflict between religious repression and sexuality. What lives on in the reader, however, is a less-than-rigid notion of sexual love and its relation to holiness. Baym says that society's coming to love Hester shows its willingness to "make room for the human heart and its private needs." And Sandeen claims that in her public life she "bears the burden of man's affective nature, including outlawed passion," which the Puritan society tries to suppress "but cannot do without." For these critics, *The Scarlet Letter* is, above all, a love story wherein the heroine transcends her culture.

In *Tales of Burning Love,* Louise Erdrich uses *The Scarlet Letter* mythologically to paint a rather complex picture of love in a post-Christian era. Jack Mauser may be a flawed human being; toward the end he is still dealing with Lyman Lemartine, the money-driven entrepreneur "planning for a casino" whose devious ways are developed in *The Bingo Palace.* But Jack is convincing as a modern male, a "satisfying multi-dimensional character." A less-than-successful engineer, he is greedy, he drinks too much, he is egocentric, but he likes and needs women in many ways. June is a fellow mixed-blood Chippewa with whom, even in her fragmented life, he momentarily identifies and ever after pursues her spirit. Dot, too, is connected to the reservation, a steady companion more than a lover, but still there, a crucial part of his work-a-day life. Jack's abusive side surfaces in his relationship with Candy, and it takes Marlis to teach him something about feeling with a woman. It may be in response to her that he ultimately comes to appreciate other human beings—their son, his own mother, all his wives.

In the end, however, Eleanor is his real Hester Prynne, the one for whom his love smolders throughout *Tales* and finally bursts into flame. Lee says she represents "the passionate reversal" of his "sexual failure" with June. In contrast to Hawthorne, Erdrich makes sexuality, religion, and nature work together, so the ending is not tragic. Early on, Eleanor says:

> Her love for Jack was still alive, disguised as everything. It ached pulled from the ground, it drew the air for her chest, sat of her head like bricks, closed across her lips like the wings of a moth.

Later, in contrast to *The Scarlet Letter* in which Hester departs for the forest after her lover's death, Erdrich in *Tales* actually brings "the forest" to bear on Eleanor and Jack; they consummate their love at the top of a stairs while outside "spears of grass rustled in their sheaths." If Erdrich is a "master of the heightened intimate moment," that skill comes through such lyrical passages.

One of those coincidences in the novel that perhaps "stretch credulity" is a miracle that sets up the finale—a phenomenon, says Max, Erdrich is "not afraid of involving" in her plots. Having survived the falling statue of a "stone woman"—a mysterious event testifying to the sainthood of Eleanor's idol, Sister Leopolda—we are told he "felt an unbearable heat of emotion, a jet of fear and joy." So both Jack and Eleanor experience epiphanies that change their lives and bring them together sexually, with the stairs adding spiritual significance to their passion. Moreover, says Lee, the images surrounding the encounter suggest a Chippewa-like identification with the earth that Jack had suppressed.

That may be, but the seasons, too, are ever changing and unpredictable. Jack is still a modern male, a businessman, "charming, preening," and "self-destructive." None of these women satisfy him completely, nor does he them. Eleanor says at one time that maybe "we each married a different man," as though it is Jack who has the different selves. Sister Leopolda tells Eleanor in her vision, "You and your sisters are blind women touching the vast body of the elephant, each describing the oddness beneath the surface of your hands." If that is so, then it may be that any one woman, given her needs, must go through five individuals to find one good man. In *The Scarlet Letter,* Hester's love remains tragically unfulfilled, though symbolically she transcends her loss. Erdrich's love story ends with Eleanor's passionate fulfillment. But it borders on tragedy that her counterparts must find other ways to keep the fire of love burning in a contemporary world, less Puritan but more complex than Hawthorne had ever imagined.

Susan Castillo (essay date Winter 1996)

SOURCE: "Women Aging into Power: Fictional Representations of Power and Authority in Louise Erdrich's Female Characters," in *Studies in American Indian Literatures*, Vol. 8, No. 4, Winter, 1996, pp. 13-20.

[*In the following essay, Castillo examines issues of women and power in Erdrich's novels.*]

Some years ago, when I was casting around for a topic for my Ph.D. thesis, I was struck, as I read so-called canonical authors, by the number of female protagonists in American literature who come to unsavory or untimely ends. Heroines, particularly those who challenge prevailing social and cultural norms, are all too prone to every sort of disaster: they are either condemned to social ostracism (as is the case with Hester Prynne in Nathaniel Hawthorne's *The Scarlet Letter* or Sister Carrie in the novel by the same name by Theodore Dreiser) or die in ways which are more or less aesthetically appealing (as is the case with Hawthorne's Zenobia in *The Blithedale Romance,* Henry James's heroine Daisy Miller, Kate Chopin's Edna Pontellier, and so very many others).

In our own century, however, it is curious that female protagonists who actually manage not only to survive but actually to prevail and even prosper can be found in significant numbers in popular fiction and in fiction by so-called "ethnic" or minority writers. Perhaps for this reason, I have found novels by Native American women particularly attractive. When I began to read Leslie Silko's *Ceremony,* for example, I was fascinated by the roles attributed to women. The narrative is focused through a female deity, Ts'its'tsi'nako, Spider Woman, weaver of ideas and source of discursive authority. The women in the novel own land and work magic, and it is they who are largely responsible for the cure of Tayo, the male protagonist. In novels by other Native American women writers, we can encounter similar portrayals of Indian women as figures of strength and power. Some of the most fascinating examples of this phenomenon can be found in the texts of Chippewa writer Louise Erdrich.

The subject of women and the exercise of power has been, as one might expect, the source of intense polemic. In the anthology *Women, Culture and Society,* anthropologist Michelle Zimbalist Rosaldo has come to some insights which I feel can be useful not only for the field of anthropology but also for the analysis of representations of gender roles. Rosaldo, drawing on the work of Max Weber and M. G. Smith, distinguishes between the concepts of *power* and *authority.* In this perspective, power is "the ability to act effectively on persons or things to make or secure favorable decisions which are not of right allocated to the individuals or their roles." Authority, on the other hand, is socially validated and implies a hierarchical chain of command and control. In this view, women have always exercised considerable power (particularly in the domestic realm), while men have retained authority, which is a culturally legitimated phenomenon. Among many Native American groups, women in traditional narratives are accorded both power and authority. However, in contemporary America, when Native American women are marginalized by traditional patriarchal structures not only because they are women but also because they are Native American, it is often the case that the texts they produce will portray women of power, though not necessarily of authority. It should also be noted, nonetheless, that in recent years increasing numbers of female characters who exercise both power and authority have begun to emerge in Native American fictional narratives.

Within the corpus of Louise Erdrich's fiction, two female characters have always held a particular fascination for me: Marie Lazarre and Zelda Kashpaw. Like most of Erdrich's characters, both Marie and Zelda are complex, often maddening, full of contradictions, and above all eminently real.

Marie's childhood is the antithesis of a Norman Rockwell-style Anglo-American idyll. She is the illegitimate daughter of Pauline Puyat, who appears in Erdrich's novel ***Tracks*** as a member of a family of "mixed bloods, skinners in the clan for which the name was lost." Pauline is an immensely powerful (though not authoritative) figure, though she uses her power toward negative and often self-destructive ends as she struggles to become assimilated into so-called mainstream America. She becomes pregnant by Napoleon Morrissey, described as belonging to a family of mixed-bloods who had profited from acquiring allotments that more traditional Chippewas had not known how to hold on to. Marie, the product of their union (if such it can be called), is delivered with spoons instead of forceps. After her birth, Pauline leaves her to be raised by her grandmother Bernardette Morissey and then enters a convent as Sister Leopolda. Marie ends up living in the woods with her Lazarre relatives, who have a reputation for being dishonest, dirty, and indolent.

Marie, however, is anything but a typical Lazarre. She is a bewildering mixture of toughness and compassion, of tenderness and astringent candor. Perhaps inevitably, she enters her mother's convent. There Pauline/Leopolda, who is totally deranged but nonetheless radiates a certain dark power, terrorizes the unsuspecting Marie by claiming that the devil is within her and, finally, by pouring boiling water into her ear in an effort to exorcize evil. Marie, despite her apparent docility, is no weakling either and retaliates by attempting to push Leopolda into a bread oven in an episode that reminds one of Hansel and Gretel, who end up cooking the Wicked Witch. Leopolda's wrath is terrible to behold, but Marie is not cowed:

> She was fearfully silent. She whirled. Her veil had cutting edges. She had the poker in one hand. In the other she held that long sharp fork she used to tap the delicate crusts of loaves. Her face turned upside down on her shoulders. Her face turned blue. But saints are used to miracles. I felt no trace of fear.
>
> If I was going to be lost, let the diamonds cut! Let her eat ground glass!
>
> "Bitch of Jesus Christ!" I shouted. "Kneel and beg! Lick the floor!"
>
> That was when she stabbed me through the hand

with the fork, then look the poker up alongside my head, and knocked me out.

Needless to say, this is hardly an idyllic vision of the mother-daughter relationship. The surreal imagery of Pauline with blue inverted face, holding aloft the fork and poker as she whirls like a demented dervish, is one of immense tragicomic impact. Erdrich describes her as an adolescent made of "angles and sharp edges, a girl of bent tin," and the description still holds true of her as an adult. But Marie is her mother's child in many ways, and she has inherited Pauline's courage as well as her power, though fortunately not her insanity. This enables her to stand up to what would often seem a mad or profoundly unjust reality. Though "mainstream" society would dismiss both Pauline and Marie as persons without authority, as merely an addled nun and an insignificant half-breed girl, both are powerful and disturbing characters who stay vivid in the reader's mind.

As one might expect, Marie ends up fleeing from the convent. In doing so, she literally crashes into Nector Kashpaw. Nector, who describes her as "the youngest daughter of a family of horse-thieving drunks," is convinced she has robbed a pillowcase from the convent, and thus stops her in order to recover the stolen goods. Marie, after calling him "you damn Indian" and telling him "You stink to hell!," kicks him as hard as she can. But after this most unpromising beginning, she and Nector marry. Nector is an amiable weakling, a man who is clever and charming (all too charming, as things turn out, especially to the sexy widow Lulu Nanapush). He plaintively expresses his feelings for Marie (and indeed for Lulu) in the following terms: "Her taste was bitter. I craved the difference after all those years of easy sweetness. But I still had a taste for candy. I could never have enough of both . . . ." He is prone to indolence and to a certain tendency to drink more than is good for him. Marie decides to use her *power,* however, to propel Nector into a position of *authority:*

> I had plans, and there was no use him trying to get out of them. I'd known from the beginning I had married a man with brains. But the brains wouldn't matter unless I kept him from the bottle. He would pour them down the drain, where his liquor went, unless I stopped the holes, wore him out, dragged him back each time he drank, and tied him to the bed with strong ropes.

> I had decided I was going to make him into something big on the reservation.

Indeed she does: Nector ends up as tribal chairman. Significantly, though Marie is by far the stronger figure of the two, she does not aspire to a position of authority on her own behalf.

Marie's daughter Zelda, when she appears in the novel *Love Medicine,* is similar to her mother and grandmother Leopolda in that she is fascinated by the all-female world of the convent, a realm in which women exercise both power *and* authority. In one unforgettable scene, Marie takes Zelda up to the convent to meet Sister Leopolda. Marie flaunts her respectability and social clout on the reservation before Leopolda. Regarding Nector's position as tribal chairman, she states baldly, "He is what he is because I made him." We can paraphrase the words "because I made him" in two ways: because she has literally forced him to achieve the chairmanship, and also because he is very much her creation. Leopolda reacts by diving under the bed for an iron spoon (as we recall, Marie had been delivered by two iron spoons) and then making a fearful racket on the iron bars of her bed. Marie wants desperately to wrest the spoon, the emblem of power, from her:

> I wanted that spoon because it was a hell-claw welded smooth. . . . *It had power.* It was like her soul boiled down and poured in a mold and hardened. . . . Every time I held the spoon handle I'd know that she was nothing but a ghost, a black wind. . . . I would get that spoon. (emphasis added)

In the end, though she struggles with Leopolda for the spoon, Marie is overcome by the force of her own compassion. She has perceived that Leopolda's power is the power of death, of negativity.

When they return home, Zelda finds a note on the kitchen table which reveals her father's plans to leave Marie for the seductive Lulu Nanapush. Marie is stunned. She reacts by stripping the wax from the kitchen floor. Symbolically, she has been brought to her knees by love for Nector and by her own insecurities. But suddenly Marie seems to realize that she is a person in her own right. Power, after all, lies within us, while authority is conferred by others, and Marie does not need the reflected authority of Nector's position to exercise her own power:

> But I was not going under, even if he left me. . . . I would not care if Lulu Lamartine ended up the wife of the chairman of the Chippewa Tribe. I'd still be Marie. Marie. Star of the Sea! I'd shine when they stripped off the wax.

Zelda, rather than entering the convent as she had wished to earlier, ends up getting pregnant by a man called Swede Johnson from the nearby boot camp, who promptly goes AWOL for good. Her only comment in later years is to state drily, "Learnt my lesson. . . . Never marry a Swedish is my rule." Later, her daughter Albertine tells us, she remarries. Her second (Swedish?) husband's name is Bjornson, and she lives with him in an aqua-and-silver trailer on the reservation. Albertine mentions her "rough gray face." Zelda and Albertine get on each other's nerves: Zelda asks her daughter about possible Catholic boyfriends and is horrified that Albertine might wish to be what she calls, in terms which remind one of Fifties films about secretaries with long painted fingernails, a Career Girl. Albertine is furious at her mother for not telling her about her Aunt June's death, but she eventually goes home to visit, saying, "I wasn't crazy about the thought of seeing her, but our relationship was like a file we sharpened on, and necessary in that way."

In Erdrich's next novel, **The Bingo Palace,** Zelda reappears. Lipsha Morrissey describes her in the following terms:

> Zelda is the author of grit-jawed charity on the reservation, the instigator of good works that always get chalked up to her credit. . . . Zelda was once called raven-haired and never forgot, so on special occasions her hair, which truly is an amazing natural feature, still sweeps its fierce wing down the middle of her back. She wears her grandmother Rushes Bear's skinning knife at her strong hip, and she touches the beaded sheath now, as if to invoke her ancestor.

Clearly, Zelda is not a woman to be trifled with. Despite her criticism of Albertine, she has developed a career of her own, working in the Tribal Office. There she uses her authority to enroll her grandson Redford as a full-blood member of the tribe and manages to obtain WIC food to feed him. In her middle age, her passive/aggressive tendencies are even more accentuated, and she attempts to control others through her relentless goodness. Lipsha Morrissey, who has been raised to consider her his aunt, describes her as a medium stout woman in a heavy black velvet, beaded dress and adds, "When women age into their power, no wind can upset them, no hand turn aside their knowledge; no fact can deflect their point of view."

Lipsha has reasons to fear his aunt's intervention: he is vying with his slick cousin Lyman Lamartine (the son of Nector and Lulu Nanapush and father of Redford) for the affections of Shawnee Ray Toose, the daughter of Zelda's old flame Xavier. Thus, in the convoluted web of relationships on the reservation, Zelda is what Lipsha calls Lyman's "under-the-table half sister," and Zelda does what she can to further Lyman's courtship of Shawnee Ray. Lipsha is aware that he is up against a formidable adversary, and when Zelda comes to visit the bingo palace owned by Lyman where Lipsha is a waiter, he decides to get her drunk by spiking her tonic water with increasing amounts of gin. His purpose in doing so is ostensibly to mellow her up a bit. But this, predictably, backfires:

My motive is good—to make Shawnee Ray's life a

little easier, for once the slight amounts of alcohol start having their effect, Zelda's basic niceness is free to shine forth. Right and left, she always forgives the multitude. . . . No matter how bad things get, on those nights when Zelda stays long enough, there is eventually the flooding appeasement of her smile. It is like having a household saint.

But you have to light a candle, make a sacrifice.

. . . . .

I like my aunt, even though I find it difficult to keep from getting run over by her unseen intentions.

Eighteen-wheeler trucks. Semis, fully loaded, with a belly dump. You never know what is coming at you when Zelda takes the road.

Here in one brief sequence Zelda is compared to a queen nodding right and left to an adoring crowd, to a martyred saint, and—perhaps most accurately—to an eighteen-wheeler truck, in metaphors that convey a volatile mix of regal self-possession, relentless virtue, and power which will flatten you if you get in its way, as Lipsha soon finds out. She begins by telling her nephew "a tale of burning love," a phrase redolent of Presleyian thwarted romance and Fifties 45 rpm records. It is the story of her rejection of her boyfriend Xavier Toose because of her wish to marry a white man who would carry her away to a Doris Day life in the city. Xavier stood outside in the snow waiting for her to say that she loved him and ended up nearly freezing to death. As a result, he lost his fingers to frostbite. Zelda then reveals to Lipsha that June, his mother, had tried to kill him as a baby by throwing him into a creek in a gunnysack weighted down with stones.

Zelda, curiously enough, has some characteristics in common with her nephew: both are persons of immense power but not a great deal of socially validated authority. Also, throughout her life Zelda shows a certain coldness of the heart, a fear of love and vulnerability; she literally freezes Xavier out. Lipsha, an androgynous character who is often feminine (though not effeminate) in his behavior, is also cold at heart. Though he is obsessed by his love for Shawnee Ray, he thinks only of himself, causing her to cry out, "You got the medicine, Lipsha. But you don't got the love." As Shawnee Ray knows intuitively, power (in Lipsha's case, the power to work magic) only succeeds if it is not used for selfish ends, while mere authority (as exemplified by Lyman) is contingent upon the vagaries of individual destinies and the twists and turns of history.

In the dramatic final scenes of the novel, both Lipsha and his aunt manage to overcome the cold they have felt all their lives. Zelda finally swallows her pride and summons up the courage to go to her old lover Xavier Toose. As she approaches, she literally thaws out: "Zelda's face bloomed toward his as though his features gave out warmth." Paradoxically, her new-found vulnerability is not weakening but empowering: "Light dashed itself upon Zelda, but she wasn't shaken. Her hands floated off the steering wheel and gestured, but she wasn't helpless."

Lipsha, in a parallel process, seems to experience the same discovery of the power of gentleness. At the end of the novel, as he lies trapped in a stolen car with a small baby during a blizzard, he recalls his parents:

> I think about my father and my mother, about how they have already taught me about the cold so I don't have to be afraid of it. And yet, this baby doesn't know. Cold sinks in, there to stay. And people, they'll leave you, sure. . . .

My father taught me his last lesson in those hours, in that night. He and my mother, June, have always been inside of me, dark and shining, their absence about the size of a coin, something I have touched against and slipped. And when that happens, I call out in my bewilderment—*"What is this?"*—and the thing I never knew until now it was a piece of thin ice they had put there.

But Lipsha, though he could attempt to escape on his own, refuses to abandon the baby to freeze to death. At the novel's end, it is unclear whether Lipsha has survived the blizzard or not. It is more than possible, however, that he and Zelda will surface once again in further novels by Erdrich, perhaps to exemplify the enormous force that is derived from the blurring of gender stereotypes and from the emergence of new concepts regarding the exercise of power and authority by men and women alike.

Additional coverage of Erdrich's life and career is available in the following sources published by Gale: *Authors and Artists for Young Adults,* **Vol. 10;** *Bestsellers,* **1989: 1;** *Contemporary Authors,* **Vol. 114;** *Contemporary Authors New Revision Series,* **Vols. 41, 62;** *Contemporary Literary Criticism,* **Vols. 39, 54;** *DISCovering Authors Modules:* **Multicultural, Novelists, Popular Fiction and Genre Authors;** *Dictionary of Literary Biography,* **Vols. 152, 175;** *Major Twentieth-Century Writers;* *Native North American Literature;* *Something about the Author,* **Vol. 94.**

Krzysztof Kieslowski
1941-1996

Polish filmmaker.

The following entry presents an overview of Kieslowski's career through 1998.

INTRODUCTION

Kieslowski was a widely acclaimed and respected Polish film director known for works which dealt with labor- and industrial-related subjects. Although his films have important political implications for Poland, he did not fit in with either hard-line Communists or political dissidents. Eventually Kieslowski turned his attention to more universal social themes which garnered him international attention.

Biographical Information

Kieslowski was born in Poland in 1941. During World War II, the Kieslowski family relocated several times. After the war, his father contracted tuberculosis and spent time in a sanitarium before finally succumbing to the disease while Kieslowski was still a boy. His father's death had a profound effect on his life; the impact the dead have on the living became a prevalent theme in many of his films. Kieslowski's childhood was bleak. His mother was forced to work at a series of clerical jobs to support the family, and Kieslowski himself suffered from lung disease. Kieslowski's original interest was in stage direction, but he decided to attend film school to prepare himself for his career as a stage director. He applied to the prestigious Lodz School of Cinema and Theatre and completed his cinematic studies in 1969. Despite the political themes of his films, Kieslowski had very little involvement in politics, with the exception of a small role in a student uprising over the deportation of Jews from Poland in 1968. After graduation from Lodz, he began making documentaries about life behind state propaganda. Television feature films depicting bleak lives in oppressive states such as *Podziammne przajscie* (*Pedestrian Subway*; 1973) and *Personel* (*Subsidiaries*; 1973) established his reputation as a daring, provocative filmmaker. He became disenchanted with documentaries when he realized his footage could be used by the authorities against his subjects, and turned instead to feature films. Kieslowski was never prohibited from making films in Poland, but the Polish government frequently stopped or limited distribution. Kieslowski retired from filmmaking after making the trilogy *Trois Couleurs* (*Three Colors*; 1993-94), saying he had lost the patience it required to be a director. He died of heart failure in 1996.

Major Works

Many of Kieslowski's films deal with the struggle between inner reality and social reality. *Amator* (*Camera Buff;* 1979) is the story of a worker turned amateur video cameraman. After buying a video camera to record milestones in his baby's life, the protagonist becomes fascinated with capturing life on film. *Przypadek* (*Blind Chance;* 1981) concerns the arbitrary nature of life. Kieslowski relates three different versions of a young man's life based on whether or not he catches a train to Warsaw. In one scenario he catches the train and becomes a Party activist, in another he misses the train and becomes a dissident, and in the last he stays home and becomes a politically neutral family man. *Bez Konca* (*No End,* 1984) focuses on a human rights lawyer who dies just before he is scheduled to defend a Solidarity activist. The film examines events following his death, his wife's subsequent suicide, and the activist's plight after an unscrupulous lawyer takes over the case. The film has religious undertones and contrasts the personal and the political. *Dekalog* (*Decalogue,* 1988) is a series of ten short films based on the Ten Commandments. The films deal with ordinary people struggling with everyday moral choices. They are tied together by a recurring character, an angelic figure who acts as a silent witness to the action of the films. *La Double Vie de Véronique (The Double Life of Veronique;* 1991) follows two women as they lead parallel lives in Warsaw and Paris. They each affect the other's life without ever meeting. *Three Colors* is a critically acclaimed trilogy of films named after a color symbolizing a different theme; *Blue* (1993) representing liberty, *White* (1994) representing equality, and *Red* (1994) representing fraternity.

Critical Reception

Kieslowski's work has generally garnered critical praise. *Amator* won first prize at the Moscow film festival in 1979 without the judges realizing that it was an indictment of Socialist governments. The final installment in the trilogy *The Three Colors: Red,* was favored to win a Prize at the Cannes Film Festival in 1995, but lost to Quentin Tarantino's *Pulp Fiction.* Critics note Kieslowski as a ruthless editor and praise his precisely filmed scenes and attention to minute detail. Phil Cavendish said of *Decalogue,* "There has been some pretty brutal pruning between the conception and final product, much of which created the economy and precision for which the films have been so highly praised." Many reviewers refer to Kieslowski as a humanist because of his interest in the individual, his sympathy for his characters, and his refusal to judge his characters. Christopher Garbowski states, "All things considered, few contemporary directors can match him in allowing the viewer to enter the protagonist's realm of vision and thus sharing his or her *I.*" Commentators are divided on the use of political themes in Kieslowski's films. Some assert that Kieslowski abandoned the political realm with *Decalogue,* but others feel that even his films focusing on individuals have political undertones. Some reviewers who believe Kieslowski left politics behind find his later works diminished. Geoffrey Macnab stated, "Perhaps Kieslowski is, as his supporters so ardently proclaim, the most important film-maker in Europe; but his blithe abandonment of social issues and retreat into a remote, mystical realm where personal experience is all that matters, do not augur well for the future." Kieslowski's move from the Polish to the international film scene prompted recognition of the universal themes in his work and made him an international success. Marilynne S. Mason remarks, "Starting out as an innovative, intellectual documentary filmmaker, Polish director Krzysztof Kieslowski evolved into one of the great artists of the contemporary European cinema."

*PRINCIPAL WORKS

Z miasta Lodzi [*From the City of Lodz*] (documentary film) 1968
Fabryka [*Factory*] (documentary film) 1971

Podstawy BHP w kopalni miedzi [*The Principles of Safety and Hygiene in a Copper Mine*] (documentary film) 1972
Przejscie podziemne [with Ireneusz Iredynski; *Pedestrian Subway*] (documentary film) 1973
Personel [*Personnel*] (documentary film) 1975
Spokoj [*Calm Before the Storm*; also known as *Peace*] (film) 1976
Siedem kobiet w roznym wieku [*Seven Women of Different Ages*] (documentary film) 1978
Amator [*Camera Buff*] (film) 1979
Przypadek [*Blind Chance*] (film) 1982
Bez konca [with Krzysztof Piesiewicz; *No End*] (film) 1985
†*Dekalog* [with Piesiewicz; *Decalogue;* also know as *The Ten Commamandments*] (film) 1988
‡*Kroti film o zabijaniu* [with Piesiewicz; *A Short Film about Killing*] (film) 1988
‡*Kroti film o milosci* [with Piesiewicz; *A Short Film about Love*] (film) 1988 .
Podwojne zycie Weroniki [with Piesiewicz; *The Double Life of Veronique*] (film) 1991
***Trzy kolory: Niebieski* [with Piesiewicz; *Blue*] (film) 1993
***Trzy kolory: Czerwony* [with Piesiewicz; *Red*] (film) 1994
***Trzy kolory: Bialy* [with Piesiewicz; *White*] (film) 1994

*Kieslowski wrote and directed all the films listed here; bracketed information refers to screenwriting credit only.
†This television mini-series consisted of ten short films: *Dekalog 1* [*I Am the Lord Thy God*]; *Dekalog 2* [*Thou Shalt Not Take the Name of the Lord Thy God in Vain*]; *Dekalog 3* [*Honor the Sabbath Day*]; *Dekalog 4* [*Honor Thy Father and Thy Mother*]; *Dekalog 5* [*Thou Shalt Not Kill*]; *Dekalog 6* [*Thou Shalt Not Commit Adultery*]; *Dekalog 7* [*Thou Shalt Not Steal*]; *Dekalog 8* [*Thou Shalt Not Bear False Witness*]; *Dekalog 9* [*Thou Shalt Not Covet Thy Neighbor's Wife*]; *Dekalog 10* [*Thou Shalt Not Covet Thy Neighbor's Goods*].
‡These films are expanded versions of *Dekalog 5* [*Thou Shalt Not Kill*], and *Dekalog 6* [*Thou Shalt Not Commit Adultery*], respectively.
**These films are collectively refered to as the *Three Colors* trilogy.

CRITICISM

Krzysztof Kieslowski with Gustaw Moszcz (interview date Spring 1981)

SOURCE: "Frozen Assets: Interviews on Polish Cinema," in *Sight and Sound,* Vol. 50, No. 2, Spring, 1981, pp. 86-91.

[*In the following excerpt, Kieslowski discusses the impact of political changes on the film industry in Poland and how politics have affected his own work.*]

Living in Poland now is to participate in momentous events which are, at the time of writing (January 1981), still in turmoil, although not quite the chaotic mess that the Soviet bloc media would have the West believe. The independent trade organisation (*union* is not an adequate term to describe a network of combined worker and intellectual groups which now conservatively account for ten million people) Solidarity exerts a discipline over its affiliated sub-sections which gives a coherent structure and aim to a nation which has progressively declined in moral hope and social cohesion since the first defeat of working class aspiration to democratic representation in 1956.

Since that year (the events of which are given as major reference points in Wajda's *Man of Marble*), there have been three further clashes with state power—in 1968, 1970 and 1976. The last date saw the formation of several dissident groups, notably KOR, which formed a new pattern of close links between intellectual opposition and working class frustration with severe economic depression. With the toppling of Gierek from power in late summer 1980 the way has been opened for cautious pressure to be exerted on the new régime.

The dilemma of the Soviet Union concerning the growth in strength and organisational intelligence of Solidarity, has been to calculate the cost of a military intervention versus toleration of a more profoundly democratic and widely supported opposition group than even the wildest liberal in Prague '68 could have dreamt possible. Unlike any other post-war social development in Europe, the intellectual repression and material hardship in post-'56 Poland has thrown up that revolutionary rarity—an organisation in which the intelligentsia and the working class have concurrent aims and a unity of practice to achieve those aims. It is impossible to know how long this may last.

As David Robinson pointed out in the last issue of *Sight and Sound,* the function of Polish cinema in the last decade had come to be that of a public moralist, albeit frequently silenced and hindered. Part of the demands of Solidarity are the unearthing of figures of known corruption. The much vaunted purge of the Polish CP has in fact been a fairly cosmetic device, with only Gierek, his central committee clique, and various senior functionaries around the regional administrative centres losing their posts. The previous head of Polish TV and radio, Szczepanski, has been found guilty of multi-million dollar corruption (amongst other things), and has been placed in an asylum as being unfit to plead, though he has asked for an open hearing. The feeling among Solidarity members is that Szczepanski is being silenced for fear that he will incriminate other senior and middle level party officials. In Zanussi's latest film there appears the character of the man 'who can arrange everything'—the whole of *Contract* stands as a bitter indictment of the degeneration of social mores in a nation which Zanussi describes as having a ruling élite made up of 'consumption oriented middle-class people who have a lack of respect towards the people, which is a rightist attitude.'

Arguably, the strength of Polish cinema derives paradoxically from the moral debilitation and economic collapse that the country has suffered. Film-makers in Poland simply have a wealth of genuine complaints and extreme problems to focus on, both in actually trying to produce cinema and in their ordinary existence. The best of them have been engaged in a subtle guerrilla campaign to speak clearly and pointedly about their own society. It's impossible to imagine a Polish *Star Wars,* not simply because of the limitation of finances but precisely since there are more urgent human issues to give voice to. This doesn't mean there are no sterile Polish films being made, nor should we mistake the major talents of Wajda, Zanussi and Kieslowski for representations of an iceberg of submerged artistic creativity and moral acerbity— the largely unseen bulk of production unfortunately really is cold, heavy and uninteresting. A crucial article by Boleslaw Sulik in the Winter 1980 issue of *Survey* makes this only too clear:

> In past years one of the really damaging weaknesses of Polish cinema has been the amount of dead wood it was carrying. Over fifty per cent of practising directors have failed to prove their worth in either artistic or commercial terms. Out of eighty feature films completed in the period 1975-78, forty have failed in distribution to recover more than two-fifths of production costs, and sixteen have been seen by less than 100,000 people—an extraordinary statistic. And with one or two exceptions the commercial failure of such films was not caused by artistic experimentation . . . dozens of demonstrably untalented people continue to plan films and occasionally make them, ostensibly because the socialist economy guarantees employment to all graduates from the State Film School in Lodz. The deeper, underlying reason is that there is no political danger in making dull, uninspiring films. At times of tension . . . any film that catches the mood of the time and communicates well with its Polish audience is politically disturbing to the ruling party. A recourse to pliant mediocrity becomes a more attractive option than ambitious attempts to comment truthfully on the social realities of the day.

But despite the mass of dull literary adaptations and trivial costume dramas churned out from the various Film Units, there are several people in Polish production, not only the known figures of Wajda and Zanussi (though their lead is tremendously important, not least because they possess international reputations which encourage other cinema workers to take stands on issues), who are working towards a revitalisation of the industry under the impetus of Solidarity's determination. There has been a real opening up within Polish film and TV in the last few months of 1980, with many previously banned films being shown on TV and new productions being started which could previously have been only fantasies. A film which uses material shot in the Gdansk Lenin shipyards, *Robotnicy '80* (*Workers '80*), has toured widely, and Solidarity is pursuing the demand for codification and relaxation of censorship, as agreed by the Government in the signed document which settled the summer 1980 strikes. An important aim of the Polish Film-Makers' Association is to take control of the distribution of finances for the industry. Whether either of these will actually be realised is still an open question—if successfully evolved they will have controversial consequences for the state's control not only of cinema but of cultural practice generally.

In an effort to obtain a first-hand view of developments in Polish cinema, I conducted a series of interviews with people involved in production of some of the important recent films. Three of these interviews are given here in an edited version. The first is with Krystyna Janda, the young actress who had leading roles in Wajda's *Conductor* and *Man of Marble* and is currently working on his sequel to the latter, *Man of Iron.* Interviewed with her in November 1980 was Edward Klosinski, director of photography on all Wajda's recent films except *Conductor*—a notable exception considering that film's rather inferior technical achievement. The final interview is with Krzysztof Kieslowski, who at forty is probably Poland's leading documentarist, and as a feature director can be classed with both Wajda and Zanussi. Kieslowski is perhaps best known in Britain for **Camera Buff,** shown at the 1979 London festival. Kieslowski is a deputy chairman of the Polish Film-Makers' Association (Wajda is president) and also teaches at the new film school in Katowice, along with Zanussi.

The demoralisation of the cinema industry in Poland broke with the formation of Solidarity—all three interviewees are members, along with Wajda and Zanussi. The flurry of activity they are at present involved in is not only a sign of renewed vitality in the industry, but also stems from bitter memories of previous periods of liberalisation which eventually degenerated into the familiar patterns of enforced silence and censor-hacked films. Their willingness to talk now in such frank terms is born both of courage and the desire to seize the opportunity to speak while the present liberalisation lasts.

The experience of official disfavour extends across all lev-

els of the Polish industry. Zanussi lost his teaching post at the Lodz State Film School in the 70s for having 'intolerable' ideas. He was told they were 'incompatible with the instrumental nature of film art.' At the main entrance to the Lodz school there is a large notice which declares 'Film is the most important of all the arts—Lenin', and this simplistic approach to the industry has dominated Polish cinema since the war. Its more remarkable products have emerged despite the state's close ties with cinema. Often this interference has taken the form of very trivial control. In interview, Zanussi commented that, 'Our ex-leader's wife often expressed her opinions concerning TV programmes and films, and this influenced the careers of some actors, whom she liked and disliked, because some . . . cowards tried to follow her choices. It happened. I don't blame her for having opinions, but the middle functionaries who were so eager to fulfil her desires.'

But there is no determination by Polish film-makers to return to free enterprise production. Their criticism is not of the system but its practical defects. As Zanussi says, in a remark which most in the industry would echo, 'I'm happy that culture and especially film is subsidised by the state, it should be, but I'm also happy that I don't depend on this subsidy alone, because if my films make money (which they do) that gives me more freedom. I don't want to feel gratitude.'

Polish cinema, which Zanussi described to me as 'the strongest bastion of social criticism in Poland in the last few years,' has laboured under the state's demand to present Utopian rhetoric about contemporary social life, nostalgic costume epics, and lugubrious reminders of Resistance heroism. Given the quantity of talent the industry currently possesses, the liberalisation could unleash a volume of new productions which will be fascinating and less allusive than has previously been the case. . . .

My films are always observations of a man in a situation which forces him to make a choice to define his standpoint. It is always an attempt at considering which is right, objective reality or the character who works against that reality.
—*Krzysztof Kieslowski*

[*Moszcz:*] *What are you working on at the moment?*

[Kieslowski:] I'm finishing a script for a new film, called *Chance.* Three different fates of the same man are presented, three possible lives for the same person. In one he is a party activist, in another an opposition activist, and in the third he is just a man fulfilling his ordinary human obligations, as a doctor. Each course depends on a chance, in the contingent sense that our lives now may be changed completely by whether we turn right or left when we leave this hotel today.

The film argues that a person is as if destined to behave in a certain way regardless of circumstances—it's a dispute between freedom and necessity. The character in the film finds three different fates but essentially remains the same. If it were a film about a corrupt bastard he would be that throughout the three lives, and if about an honest man (as he in fact will be) then he will remain honest in all three incarnations, in spite of the fact that he is nominally on different sides of the barricade.

Is there a constant thread running through your films?

My films are always observations of a man in a situation which forces him to make a choice to define his standpoint. It is always an attempt at considering which is right, objective reality or the character who works against that reality. I'm convinced that as individuals—and I'm concerned with individuals in my films—we always find ourselves opposed to reality. In my films I present two models of life. The private inner one, self-realisation, and objectively existing reality, social conditions and relations. These use different languages which cannot be reconciled and a conflict is therefore inevitable.

Does this bring you into conflict with the 'objective reality' presented in the programme of the Polish state?

It's a natural consequence of my views. I do not participate in anything which doesn't agree with my outlook on the world. This is not the case though with many writers, journalists and directors in Poland and elsewhere in the Eastern bloc.

An immediate effect of this is that none of my documentaries has ever been sold abroad and some are stopped from being screened in Poland. This is no heroism on my part, because the most essential thing for me is to *register* a given event or situation. Of course it's pleasant to see crowded cinemas, to show films at festivals and be given awards, but this is additional, not essential.

I automatically place myself in the position of making films which are stored and not shown for years, sometimes never. The scripts are usually accepted, I was never actually denied the right to *make* any of my films. Perhaps I'm clever at writing screenplays which pass a qualifying committee, but with finished products the case is different.

It may seem strange that I have received so many festival prizes, but the point is that, having been shown and praised

at festivals abroad, the films are then withdrawn from distribution, over which of course I have no control. This is analogous to the situation of many writers who, as we say, 'wrote for the desk drawer', who created work which they knew in advance could not be made generally available. But with me there is a slight difference—film costs an awful lot of money. I often have doubts about making yet another film which will be just a frozen investment.

How many films have been stopped in this fashion? Quite a number at different periods. But distribution, as I said, is not an essential measure of success for me. I would like them to be exploited but it's no tragedy if they are not. Not that I don't believe that some of them are very important social documents at given moments. One such, *Spokoj* (*Peace*), was made four years ago but shown on TV only in October of '80. Even though it was delayed, and lost some of its critical edge in the process, I still think the most important thing was done, which was to register on film the story of a man who had a minimum programme for his life, and was not allowed to realise even this small aim because he was entangled in dirty business against his own will.

Do you manage to have much contact with cinema outside the Soviet bloc?

I did a lot of travelling but it didn't give me much in the professional line. I have many superficial contacts abroad, but social rather than professional. When I'm abroad I'm interested in the same things as in Poland—finding out human desires, views, ideas, discovering everyday situations. I rarely see the films when I go to festivals—in all my journeys I saw perhaps three I really wanted to. Particularly Tarkovsky's *Mirror*. I myself value most those films which join fictional with documentary elements. I have, as it were, participated in the development of a new sub-genre in Polish film, which draws from the documentary approach and techniques.

What would be your conception of the ideal relationship between state and film industry in Poland?

What we are postulating is that the industry should have the opportunity of recording whatever phenomena it wants without hindrance from the state. We want the power of decision, under the assumption that we are more representative of this nation than the authorities. This is the aim of all artistic groups in Poland, control over finance, distribution, a codification of the censorship. It's an obvious goal. Naturally I'm a member of Solidarity, as are the majority of working people.

But I'd like to warn you against the exaggeration of censorship as a problem. It isn't the worst thing of our system. Far worse is the state's arbitrary limitation of human thinking to certain chosen subjects. Censorship applied the directives resulting from that policy. We need to beware of slipping into that situation again under the new authorities.

The real harm was not what censorship prevented but all those things which were not even thought of as possible because people were discouraged from creative thinking and practice. There was a whole system of silence in communication, from the Ministry of Culture right down to the humblest local village authorities.

As a documentarist, many of your films deal with the total demoralisation of social life in Poland, which only recently has become possible to discuss publicly. How do you explain this degeneration?

The theory of our system is very good but unfortunately it happened that in practice it has been very different, has actually never been put into practice. Demoralisation is not limited only to the authorities; it originated there but has spread in widening circles.

The corruption spread through the way in which the theory was realised. In many instances people have lost the ability of clearly distinguishing right and wrong, and the tragedy of this country is that what is wrong has become good, or at least unimportant, unworthy of notice. In the film industry I could point to many people who have taken an easier route just because it makes it more comfortable to live and work. It doesn't necessarily bring great material benefits. In film one is particularly exposed to pressure from the authorities because they consider film an important instrument of propaganda.

What was considered convenient for those who held power was regarded as good for the nation and the state. Which obviously is not always true. It was not so much that money dominated, or censorship ruled, or that people were flung into jail unjustly—human *dignity* was ignored. In acting against the interest of the people the régime acted against its own interests. But they have never understood this simple truth and don't seem to now. It seems they never will, not until we live to see democratically elected governments. Theoretically our system should give us more artistic freedom than in Britain. In practice . . . well, it looks different.

This lack of respect explains the strength of the new movement, which is national, not merely based in the working class. Wajda put it very well when he said that people could not agree to being called *robol* [In a footnote, Moszcz defines this as a contemptuous term for a worker]. The agitation in Poland now is not for luxury consumer goods. One of my recent films, *Talking Heads,* is a short in which I ask two questions of people aged from about two to a hundred—'Who are you?' and 'What do you want?' The answer to the second question is *not* a new car, more money, a washing machine, or whatever, but generally *freedom* and *justice*. And this explains, partly, the popularity, which is immense, of any new film from the West. In such films we often get two treats in one parcel—a representation of a mode of life we have not achieved, materially, but also the sight of the film-makers making critical judgments about that mode of life, unabridged, which chance we haven't achieved either.

What is your view of Solidarity's chance of surviving as a real centre of broad alternatives to the current régime?

Having an independent union is probably the best result that could have been hoped for. I do not see any danger of its becoming bureaucratic with time. The danger lies *outside* the organisation—it may be crushed or outmanoeuvred or split. I am afraid that if the authorities act wisely and cautiously they may gradually eliminate Solidarity. Certainly the events which brought Solidarity into being are crucial, but I cannot say whether the final result of a game is more important than the game itself, especially if the predicted loser turns out to be the winner. If the result is bad it means a war. If good then the changes will be incomparably further reaching than in Prague '68. This cannot dissolve into nothing.

Paul Coates (essay date 1990)

SOURCE: "Exile and Identity: Kieslowski and His Contemporaries," in *Before the Wall Came Down: Soviet and East European Filmmakers Working in the West,* edited by Graham Petrie and Ruth Dwyer, University Press of America, 1990, pp. 103-14.

[*In the following essay, Coates discusses the cohesiveness of Kieslowski's work and the fusion of Eastern and Western influences in his films.*]

How the West was Won is the title of the East European producer's unrealized dream film: a horn of plenty discharging hard currency into the coffers of its debt-ridden country of origin. At a time when hopeful speculation is resurrecting the specter of Central Europe, however, it may be worthwhile asking just where the West is. As a purely Utopian image in the East European consciousness, it may be located across the Atlantic; as a place of relative material well-being one may visit and work in, it may—for the Polish actor or actress—go by the provisional name of Hungary. (Or—if one is Wajda or Zanussi—West Germany or France.) Does the West exist wherever a Westerner is present? Such questions are prompted by the problematic nature of borders, which are far more prone to shift at the behest of the world market than their apparent post-Yalta fixity would lead one to suspect. As the world economy becomes increasingly tight-knit, it is ever harder to determine just where the East and West lie. The growing frequency of co-productions—of equal interest to Western companies seeking to trim budgets by using non-unionized labour, and to Eastern countries needing hard currency to service their debts—blurs the borders. As borders become increasingly mobile, however, it may be salutary to remember that there may well be something that resists the law of exchange. One might be tempted to term that thing identity, were it not that in one of its senses the word itself embodies the notion of exchange. The ambiguous designator of both individual selfhood and its loss, the word "identity" may in fact be a linchpin in the workings of ideology—a key term in a Marxist version of the Freudian lexicon of primal words—as it seduces one into the system by implying that one can both conform and remain oneself, become identical and retain identity. As an increasingly identical economic totality subsumes into itself all individual identities, it may be preferable to speak of the individual as non-identity vis-à-vis the false whole. It will be the thesis of this paper that such a position of non-identity is occupied virtually uniquely in Poland by the work of Krzysztof Kieslowski.

A certain stereotype exists concerning Polish directors: the daring ones either leave for the West, or visit it periodically to escape the native chill. The stereotype derives from the careers of Polanski, Skolimowski and Borowczyk, frozen out of Polish cinema by the stultifying cultural policy of the early sixties; from those of Wajda and Zanussi, with their intermittent excursions to the West; and from that of more recent figures, such as Agnieszka Holland, whose *To Kill a Priest*—a fictionalization of the murder of Father Jerzy Popieluszko—could hardly have been filmed in Poland itself. (Though one should note here that the film's silence concerning the State televising of portions of the murderers' trial pretends that official reference to such events is impossible in Poland thereby simplifying the country's contradiction-laden reality.) It is assumed that sooner or later the director of integrity will be compelled to go into exile, re-enacting the primal drama of a Mickiewicz or a Milosz—or, at the very least, to do some work abroad. And should one come home, it will only be to do a co-production. The problematic nature of these options can be gauged through brief consideration of two films: Zanussi's *Year of the Quiet Sun* (*Rok spokojnego slonca*) and Agnieszka Holland's recent *To Kill a Priest*.

The Year of the Quiet Sun, Zanussi's first Polish-language film in several years, was a co-production in form (the co-sponsors were companies in Berlin and New York) and in content also: like Wajda's near-contemporaneous *A Love in Germany,* it reflects on war-time relations between Poles and non-Poles, forty years after the end of World War Two. It is a strangely willed and yet half-hearted film. The mixture of Scott Wilson's nervously lachrymose intensity in the role of Norman, the American ex-POW, and the mannered, head-tossing spinsterly stoicism of Maja Komorowska's Emilia, is a tragedy of errors, with the man too self-doubting to press his claims and the woman too intent on remaining pure in the sight of her own conscience to wish to be saved, but the details of their relationship never quite ring true. There is a clear, almost banal reason for this: Zanussi never really solves the problem of how the two communicate across the language barrier. He is too sophisticated to invoke love's telepathy or animal magic, but their complete linguistic incompatibility and the evident uselessness of their interpreters render it hard to guess how they built up a rapport. The film tends to be both flat and cryptic, particularly in Norman's memories of his humiliation as a POW. Even the fine closing vision, showing an ideal encounter in which the two dance in an American desert dreamland, is uncanny in tone, and somehow self-frustrating. The dance motion seems too fast, with an air of nightmare, and it is eerie that the camera should concentrate so on the dust at their feet and then lose them in the distance of the longshot. The sequence is placed further offkey by the fact that *Stagecoach,* whose Monument Valley setting it employs, had earlier been mentioned as the favorite film of Emilia's *mother.* (There may be an implication here that Emilia's identification with her mother is so deep that it even pervades her dreams.) The film's tragedy irritates, because it feels forced: Emilia is unable to escape to the West because she has insufficient funds to smuggle both herself and her mother out—knowledge of which causes the mother to induce her own death to allow Emilia to leave with the love of her life. Could not Emilia have explained the necessity to Norman, before her mother offered her the present of death she then refuses to accept? When Zanussi allows her to tell Norman that there can be happiness even in suffering he hints at a masochism whose aetiology he refuses to probe further. And when Zapasiewicz, as a brutal black marketeer turned Party member, warns Emilia that she won't be able to leave without official permission, his petty viciousness is cloaked in the inappropriate ominousness of Fate in a Hardy novel: *diabolus ex machina.* The film's vision of the nobility of sacrifice is clouded by one's doubts regarding its necessity. One is almost tempted to conclude that repeated work in foreign languages had dulled Zanussi's sense (threatened in any case by his preoccupation with near-autistic protagonists) of the mechanics of human interaction.

To Kill a Priest opens with an image whose resonance raises one's expectations of the film to follow. A mundane activity becomes a powerful metaphor: using a coin, a hand scrapes a hole in the frost on the inside window of a bus; the young scout holding it—already an insider in Polish society—peers out at the scene that has been revealed, a group of people marching with Solidarity banners. Holland's image rejects the metaphor that would speak of a 'thaw' in the frost of People's Poland; the freeze continues, though it can be punctured at points by scraping back the ice. A thaw would embrace society as a whole, but the disparity between the uniformed scouts inside and the motley of Solidarity outside indicates that the hope for change is far from universal. The theme of partial visibility intriguingly—and probably inadvertently, for the two directors were working independently of one another—echoes the central device of Kieslowski's *Short Film About Killing* (*Krotki film o zabijaniu*). Unfortunately, little in the subsequent film matches the promise of this opening moment. There is probably only one other moment of similar suggestivity, when Stefan—the Interior Ministry spy assigned to the turbulent priest, whose seeming impunity galls him—slows down a videotape of the priest addressing the faithful. He can only control the man's reflection in an image, not his reality; and as the priest's voice slows down into a prehistoric, subverbal roar, its sound evokes the would-be controller's nightmarish sense that he is failing to make any progress, as well as suggesting that the two men will meet on an atavistic plane of sheer suffering.

Holland's film is, of course, an international production based on the murder by Polish State officials of the awkward pro-Solidarity priest, Father Jerzy Popieluszko. The original event, which took place late in 1984, precipitated a lightning investigation and the unprecedented spectacle in the Eastern bloc (and perhaps anywhere) of the televised trial of the three guilty secret policemen. Like Kieslowski in *A Short Film About Killing,* Holland omits their trial; though where Kieslowski does so on aesthetic grounds, omitting the inessential, Holland's grounds seem to be more ideological: it would complicate her simplified image of how the Polish state works. It is in fact only to the extent to which it removes itself from the story of Popieluszko himself (here called Father Alek) that the film is interesting. Frustratingly, it prompts one to speculate on the work that might have been had Holland made more of the license created by fictionalization, rather than engaging in a two-dimensional hagiography spiced up with banal hints of "human interest" (a girl floats around Alek, who manfully resists seduction). The treatment is not the TV movie it could so easily have become, though there are moments that come dangerously close, such as the clumsily-staged sequence showing the imposition of martial law, where the dialogue is wooden and improbable. The film is tantalizing in its failure to realize its possibilities, such as the potential for irony built into the parallel plots: the encounters between Stefan and Alek and their respective political superiors could have been pointedly contrasted presentations of each as a martyr to his cause, with Stefan the more consistent communist, and Alek the better Christian, than his superior. Most of the squandered possibilities concern Stefan: the playing of Ed Harris suggests that he could have been the center of an hallucinatory, *Conformist*-like evocation of the political heart of darkness. Holland's inability to shift the film's center of gravity to Stefan is an artistic miscalculation. One applauds the film's

courage even as one recognizes that having one's heart in the right place is no guarantee of a masterpiece. And even the film's most interesting aspect—the image of Stefan as a self hating inquisitor, a figure from Bertolucci or Scorsese—is vitiated by its function as revenge fantasy: no one loves Communists, who are all either paranoid or insane, Holland argues. (Stefan's wife hysterically demands of him why "they", the Solidarity activists who supposedly threaten his life, cannot simply be locked up.) The film reaches a nadir of tendentiousness in the names it gives to the dogs Stefan and Alek keep: "Pope" in the former case, and "Spy" in the latter. What is more, Holland's hagiography is tainted by an ambiguity that brings it to the verge of two-facedness: Alek has no answer to the soldier facing execution for training his guns on his superiors, and who is critical of the utility of the non-violence the priest preaches and practices; the criticism is reiterated at the end by Alek's chauffeur, who says that although Alek could forgive, "we" cannot. If Alek's non-violence is not to be emulated, the film is simply pretending that he is its hero—perhaps half-reluctantly hitching a ride on a religious bandwagon that may at present be the strongest alternative to the Polish state, but whose final destination is very different from Holland's.

The preceding examples (which could be augmented with many others) begin to help one understand why Kieslowski's work has a cohesiveness lacking even in the oeuvres of a Wajda or a Zanussi. If every artwork is, in Adorno's words, an "urteiloses Urteil", then those of Kieslowski pass judgement on those of his contemporaries; a judgement, one hastens to add, which the director himself would never extend to the *persons* of Wajda or Zanussi. With admirable acumen and tenacity, Kieslowski has grasped and exploited the change in the rules governing cultural production in Poland: one may still need to use one's wits to slip radical work past the censor—as was the case with *A Short Film About Killing,* smuggled through behind the protective shield of a clutch of films based on the Decalogue—but the current desperation of the authorities for any sign of participation in the public sphere has blunted the censor's scissors. In this changed climate, however, it is no longer sufficient to make the allusive critical gestures that served a purpose in the past; in order to avoid co-optation, one's gesture must be as dark and radical as that of *A Short Film About Killing.*

The preceding remarks may seem to be underpinned by a form of nativism: the implicit thesis may seem to be that only the Polish director who resists the blandishments of the West can be truly significant. Framed in these terms, the thesis recalls compromised nationalist traditions of rejection of "the cosmopolitan". It would be a disservice to Kieslowski, however, to allow my remarks to be taken thus: the director of *No End* is in fact one of the most cosmopolitan and intellectually sophisticated directors at work anywhere in the world. Where Wajda has succumbed to academic frenzy, and the early Zanussi's passion for the crystalline has become somewhat theoretical and bloodless, Kieslowski offers fiercely conceived structures that embody the haunting possibility of a recovery of the lost intellectual legacy of the late sixties. Profound immersion in the particular has enabled him to distill the image of the universal; the most Polish of directors is thus the most Western. Certain of Kieslowski's works reinvent the passionate, unstable mixture of politics and auto-analysis that characterized the early Bertolucci. In particular, **Blind Chance** (*Przypadek*) fuses preoccupations usually polarized between "East" and "West".

Blind Chance marries a "Western" preoccupation with the effects of the death of the father—with the sense of arbitrariness that afflicts choice in a world emptied of paternal prototypes—to an "Eastern" reluctance to renounce humanism by invoking such psychoanalytic scenarios as the Oedipal one. Arbitrariness dictates the very form of the film, which gives three different versions of a crucial period in the life of one young man, Wit Dlugosz. Each version begins like a dream, with the young man running to catch the Lodz-Warsaw train. In the first version he succeeds, and becomes a Party activist with a bad conscience; in the second, he fails and become a dissident; and in the third his failure causes him to stay at home, marry, become a trainee doctor, and die in an aircraft explosion (the failure to reach Warsaw is interpreted as the equivalent of remaining in the antechamber of political awareness). In each case the decision to leave for Warsaw follows the death of the father, whose earlier wish that his son become a doctor loses its binding force. "Nic nie musisz" ("you don't have to do anything"), the dying father tells his son through a telephone that seems also to relay a voice from the interior. The bereaved son requests a leave of absence from the medical academy's dean, and seeks an alternative to the paternally-prescribed path. The father's death thus frees both son and film from necessity— this particular linkage of form and theme being one of the features that recalls the early work of Bertolucci, particularly *The Conformist,* whose simultaneously exuberant and deranged formal play is soul-murder of Godard, Bertolucci's cinematic father. Stylistically the first section is the most arresting, beginning with images presented as rapidly and laconically as at the start of *Pierrot le Fou,* and then modulating into a Tarkovskian adherence to the line of "real time": no time is edited out of any of the sequences in this section. The second version is edited more conventionally, highlighting the "key" moments in a scene—those that advance the dramatic conception—and omitting all else. The final version is edited most conventionally of all, virtually in the no-nonsense manner of a TV movie, with point-of-view shots, shot/reverse-shot, and so on. Asked whether or not any one of the three versions should be privileged as "the true one", Kieslowski has stated—with sibylline cunning— that it should be the last one, because it is the most conventional. It is clear, however, that the conventional is of no

great interest to Kieslowski: this section is brief and brisk, and its protagonist is blown up in the end. The almost disdainful destruction of the protagonist suggests that Kieslowski feels that Filip Mosz, the hero of **Camera Buff** (**Amator**), was wrong to choose peace and mediocrity rather than follow the pull of filmmaking to Warsaw. One suspects that in fact Kieslowski prefers the first version, given his stated admiration for Tarkovsky's long takes and the amount of thought that has gone into this section. If the final section *is* to be privileged, it is rather for a reason Kieslowski did not mention when I discussed the film with him: because it allows one to place the film's first image, which shows a man screaming "Nie". We recognize him as Wit on the plane, following the first small explosion in the fuselage, and anticipating the fatal second one. The final section is privileged in that it confronts its protagonist with death.

In each section figures who played major roles earlier on are recast in minor functions. The Communist old believer, an influential substitute father in section one, becomes a passer-by later on; the priest of section two is glimpsed incidentally at the airport in section three, about to lead the group excursion to France from which the authorities had debarred Wit in that earlier "life". In all three sections, however, Wit is "the same" person. He is always preoccupied with the degree of coincidence in people's lives (it is as if he suspected that the life he is leading is merely an accidental variant of an alternative ranged alongside it): he drops to his knees and clutches his forehead in moments of crisis (in version A— after the secret police car has sped away with his girlfriend; in B—when a fellow-conspirator demands the return of the key to the secret printing shop the militia have discovered; and in C—when his girlfriend announces her pregnancy). The film is profoundly subversive of ideas of destiny; fate belongs in the mythical world of the fathers, whose ending precipitates one into the new world of fortuity. In the process it subverts the black-and-white notions of character that are so prevalent in a Polish ideology which deems one either one of "us" (a martyr) or one of "them" (a traitor). In each of his first two lives Wit is the victim of these stereotypes: in the first his girlfriend ostracizes him after her release from custody, assuming that he used his pull as a Party member to secure her freedom; and in the second a colleague assumes that his non-arrest when his conspiratorial cell was breached indicates complicity with the authorities. One can just as easily land on one side of the party line as on the other. The film's subversiveness extends into a doubt of memory, in the manner of Resnais: the first section shows us a boy bidding Wit farewell before going up a hill to a VW; in the second section we learn the boy's name, Daniel (he is the brother of a girl with whom Wit has an affair), and discover that the goodbye preceded Daniel's departure for Denmark. And yet he says there was no automobile on the scene. His words confirm the fact that the farewell with the car was part of a different life, but they disturb one by extending the principle of arbitrariness into the distant past. As they suggest that memory is creative, they question the cinematic dictum that seeing is believing.

The first time we see Witold he is a child, reflected in a mirror, doing homework; his father says he makes a certain figure as his dead mother did. The presentation of the protagonist as a mirror image is typical of the openings of Kieslowski's recent works: it is thus that Antek first appears, reflected in a bookcase, in *No End,* whilst in *A Short Film About Killing* Jacek is first seen mirrored in the glass covering the *Wetherby* poster in the new section of the Old Town. The films thus begin by reminding us that what we are seeing is not reality but an image; that the true life is perpetually displaced. The life we live is governed by coincidence (one translation of the title "Przypadek")—rather as coincidence carries the taxi-driver (as he bypasses two sets of potential passengers) to his encounter with Jacek. There is no Platonic form of the true life; neither—equally importantly—is there any such archetypical form of the false life as Bertolucci offers in *The Conformist,* with its pat explanatory primal scene. All Kieslowski's work appears to be about the effects of the loss of the prototype; and the theme may be fueled by autobiographical forces, since Kieslowski lost his father when still young. The loss of compelling reasons why one should do one thing rather than another may also be an argument against leaving the country, that is—against a potentially *irrevocable* choice (the desire to return after having crossed a border is found in double form at the beginning of *No End,* in Tomek's return to Poland and in Antek's return as a ghost; one may even see it in the title). By staying in Poland one haunts the grave of a father one lost rather than killed. The Pole does not define himself through Oedipal parricide, for the father is not perceived as the locus of power: power lies elsewhere, with the true rulers who pretend merely to be brothers, ever-ready to provide "fraternal aid". One does not kill the father, for his murder has been carried out by the alien powers. (And in *Blind Chance* even the mother has been killed in a sense by Poland's alien order: she dies giving birth to Wit during the Poznan protests of 1956, and a recurrent memory flash shows a man being dragged across a floor, leaving a trail of blood—as if this bloody dragging forth is Witold's birth.) This is surely the key difference between a Kieslowski and a Bertolucci (in other words, between the East European and the West European director); it is a difference that severely threatens the likelihood of any East European producing his or her most valuable work in the West. For the Pole the father is castrated, powerless, the dead father of *Blind Chance* or *Man of Iron;* and so when Wajda casts the same actor as both father and son, it is to underline their fundamental spiritual identity, not—as in Bertolucci's *Spider's Stratagem*— as a metaphor for Oedipal or mimetic rivalry between them. (*The Spider's Stratagem,* incidentally, demonstrates that despite Girard's polemical opposition to Freud, mimetic de-

sire is quite compatible with Oedipal desire, and may even be one of its forms.) Hence the dynamics of East European cinema are not—like those of the West—linked to the Oedipal triangle. The East European director who comes to the West may deal with father-son relations, but it will be on the understanding that the father is more helpless than tyrannical (see, for instance, Szabó's *Father* or Skolimowski's *The Lightship* and *Success is the Best Revenge*). And it is this sense that power lies elsewhere that renders East European cinema so bewitchingly accurate a mirror of our era— the era so often described as postmodern—since the crumbling of nationality before the pressure of the empire of the world economy defines power as something that continually relocates itself on the far side of continually displaced borders. The knowledge that the cause of the effects we feel is perennially absent pervades Kieslowski's work (one never learns why Jacek kills the taxi-driver). Its base in Poland gives it a deeper consciousness of exile than is available to the exile who thinks there is a homeland.

Krzysztof Kieslowski with Phil Cavendish (interview date Summer 1990)

SOURCE; "Kieslowski's *Decalogue,*" in *Sight and Sound,* Vol. 59, No. 3, Summer, 1990, pp. 162-65.

[*In the following interview, Kieslowski discusses the development and filming of his series of films,* Decalogue.]

With his latest films based on the Decalogue, the Polish director Krzysztof Kieslowski seems to have pulled off two difficult feats in one stroke. Not only has the ten-part series established him as a world-class talent, but it has also aroused a new interest in the Ten Commandments.

Certainly, the critics who first saw the cycle at the Venice festival last year were as eager to praise as they were frantic to discover the relevant commandments (an Italian communist was caught by Kieslowski himself reduced to ringing the Vatican at three o'clock in the morning from a public phone booth). Since then, success has followed success: *A Short Film About Killing* (Decalogue Five) voted Best European Film of 1988; Part Six, *A Short Film About Love,* described as 'perfection' by one reviewer, and the whole cycle given wide publicity and a primetime BBC2 Sunday slot after its launch on 6 May in Britain.

With twenty years in film behind him, Kieslowski is mildly bemused by this response. In a wry moment, loyally chain-smoking Polish cigarettes, he will put it down to snobbery, the 'fad for things from the East' which has swept through Western Europe in recent months. But this is the deliberate modesty of someone who still considers himself a 'provincial' film-maker and for whom, at the age of 49, fame has come relatively late in life. It is also a little unfair to accuse critics of modish pretence, since many know his previous work and have acclaimed it accordingly. They have simply recognised the fact that the *Decalogue* is a series of stunning, compelling and extremely well-made films from a director at the height of his creative powers.

Undoubtedly it is surprising that anyone should have taken on the Ten Commandments at all, bearing in mind their awesome dimensions, least of all Kieslowski himself, a self-confessed agnostic. Ethical dilemmas have always intrigued him, it is true, but his reputation had been based solidly on films of a strong political bent. What could be more different than the *Decalogue,* these tightly honed homages to ordinary people struggling with everyday moral choices, with their exclusive focus on the personal? How could it be that a supremely Polish director has made ten films in the mid-1980s which deliberately ignore the realities of the time and concentrate their energy on a wide range of dramas, but all lying well outside the political domain?

His evolution has been gradual, partially reflecting the needs of the public, but also developing an internal creative momentum of its own. He started life in documentaries, believing with many of his contemporaries who graduated from the Lodz Film School in the late 1960s, that the genre could 'describe the world'. Films like *Lodz—The Town, The Factory, Standards of Safety and Hygiene in a Copper Mine* and *Workers '71* are fascinated with the details of life concealed behind a wall of official propaganda.

He later became dissatisfied with the limitations of documentary, finding that 'the closer the camera gets to its human object, the more that human object seems to disappear before the camera.' He transferred his interests into the realm of features. Films such as *Camera Buff,* the comic story of a worker turned amateur video-cameraman who starts to see the problems of film-making when he clashes with the official version of reality, placed him squarely in the 'Moral Anxiety' school of directors of the time. These were films very much concerned with the moral compromises demanded by the System, as well as the discrepancy between the official version and reality itself. By the early 80s, however, Kieslowski's interests can be seen moving away from films whose characters tend to represent defined social groups and whose scope seems narrowly political. *Blind Chance,* for instance, made mostly in 1981 but set in the immediate pre-Solidarity months, still confronts the world of politics, but with an additional twist—Fate. A young medical student decides to take time off from his studies to think about his life after the death of his father. He sprints to catch a train as it leaves a station and, at this point, the narrative splits three ways, each taking him into a different social milieu. One road takes him into the Party, another into the opposition, the third

leaves him politically neutral, seeking a 'quiet life.' The film is a tribute to the importance Kieslowski attaches to the element of hazard in people's lives, and would no doubt have raised a few eyebrows in Poland had it not been banned for several years.

With his next film, he evolves further. *No End* is set at the height of martial law, yet while the tone is typical of the gloom, despondency and sense of terrible defeat prevalent at the time, Kieslowski ignored the superficial symbols of 1982: tanks, riot police, etc. It is a quiet film and for the first time a strong personal narrative and metaphysical element creep into his work.

A human-rights lawyer, who appears in the first scene to explain perfunctorily that he died three days ago, had been due to defend a Solidarity activist arrested for organising a strike after martial law. The case is taken over after his death by an older lawyer who is keen to plea-bargain a morally dubious deal with the authorities. The activist, under pressure from his family and buckling under the weight of the lawyer's matter-of-fact philosophy, succumbs. However, placed alongside this moral tragedy is the terrible despair of the dead lawyer's wife, who eventually decides to commit suicide. For her, the drama being played out in the political arena is overshadowed totally by the loss of her husband.

No End was seen as a deeply religious film, and rightly so: much of the style and 'feel' of it is but a short step away from the *Decalogue.* Significantly, it was the first film co-scripted with Krzysztof Piesiewicz, a lawyer by training and one of the prosecutors in the Popieluszko trial of 1984. The two men met in 1982 while Kieslowski was trying with official permission to make a documentary about political trials. Piesiewicz was the first to notice that the cameras were unnerving the judges, causing them to suspend sentence, and started booking the documentary-maker for his clients. It was Piesiewicz, described affectionately by Kieslowski as 'a man of extraordinary sensitivity who has a lot of time on his hands and therefore probably does too much thinking', who later suggested taking on the Ten Commandments.

'*No End* had a terrible reception in Poland,' Kieslowski remembers. 'The authorities hated it, the opposition criticised the pessimism in the film, and the church objected to the suicide and the fact that the leading actress was filmed several times without a bra and once without her underwear. I bumped into Piesiewicz on the street by chance. We were both depressed. It was raining. I had lost a glove. Then he suddenly turned to me and said: "Someone should make a film about the Decalogue. You should do it."

'People ask me all the time why we decided to go ahead with it—obviously it was a terrible idea! But the truth is I simply don't know and neither does he. Maybe there was something tangible in the air. We were living in difficult times and everything in Poland was in a colossal mess. No one really knew what was right and wrong any more or why we even carried on living. We thought maybe it was worthwhile going back to the simplest, most basic, most elementary principles of how to lead one's life.'

The script, which he co-wrote with Piesiewicz in the cramped kitchen of his Warsaw apartment, took twelve months to complete. From the very beginning, they were appalled by the enormity of what they had taken on. There were no models they could turn to and the project was bound to arouse animosity in a Catholic country like Poland, where the Commandments were held with deep orthodox reverence.

They spent much time reading up as much as possible about the Old and New Testaments, as well as several commentaries on the Commandments themselves, before deciding to dispense with the information altogether. They were not setting out to be priests and wanted to avoid didacticism. In any case, for Kieslowski, who once said he would rather read a book than go to the cinema, other authors were perhaps more significant. Dostoevski, Mann, Kafka and Camus are the four names he is reluctantly prepared to list when asked the awful question as to his influences.

Gradually, a concept began to emerge: ten films which they would offer to Polish television as a series. They ignored political parables, since Kieslowski was 'bored' with politics by then and recognised that the public was disillusioned and had collapsed into a general state of apathy. Developing his earlier interest in hazard, he decided that the camera should seem to pick its subjects at random. The original concept was to show a stadium in which the camera would alight on one face out of thousands, but he and Piesiewicz eventually opted for a Warsaw housing estate, the epitome of everything urban and contemporary. The characters would be ordinary people, some of whom would appear fleetingly even in the films in which they were not the leading protagonists, in order to create a kind of unity and pathos.

The films are also held together as a unity by a mysterious young man who appears at crucial moments. He has been dubbed the 'silent witness' and appears symbolically in the first frames of *Decalogue One,* warming his hands by a fire near the small lake where the young son of the scientist drowns, and actually looking straight into the camera for a few seconds. His expression is uncanny, a combination of disapproval and disappointment. He was only written into the original screenplay at a late stage and his presence in all but two of the cycle has prompted speculation as to who he is supposed to represent: an Angel of Fate, God, Kieslowski himself?

'No, it is not me—I don't really know who he is. For a long time, I felt there was something missing in the scripts. Then one day I happened to be watching the film of a colleague along with an old Polish writer. We all thought the film was pretty mediocre, but the writer said he liked it and particularly liked the scene in a cemetery where a man dressed in black appeared. No one else had seen that man. The director told him he didn't exist. "But I saw him," said the writer. One week later, he had died. I suddenly understood what was missing in the films—an element of mystery, something elusive and inexplicable .

There are many such moments: omens, mirrored situations, repeated gestures, the twists and turns of the plots which constantly shift expectations and sympathies, demanding recognition of the tricks fate plays in life. The characters are placed deliberately in extreme situations, but Kieslowski avoids both moralising about their dilemmas and banality. While a dispassionate observer (he has been accused in the past of a certain coldness and himself once admitted that 'all my films are made as if under glass'), in *Decalogue* he reserves sympathy for everyone. He agrees that his position is essentially that of the humanist.

'I know it is very unfashionable these days, but I do believe in Humanity. I believe in Right and Wrong, although it is difficult to talk about black or white in the times in which we live. But I think one is definitely better than the other and I do believe that people want to choose Right—it is just that sometimes they are unable to do so.'

This conflict, or tension, is at the heart of his modern-day stories. Although the Commandments are only the springboard from which he focuses themes of love, death, redemption and solitude, they are nevertheless relevant. It is important to know which film is based on which commandment, and generally they follow the sequence as given in Chapter 20 of Exodus. Some, however, may be more confusing than others.

Decalogue Two, for example, is from the Commandment 'thou shalt not take the name of the Lord thy God in vain.' Although it does touch on the issue of abortion, the film is largely about the surgeon in the hospital who is reluctant to 'play God' and not only predict the death of his patient but also decide the fate of an unborn child. There has also been much head-scratching over *Decalogue Six,* the series version of *A Short Film About Love,* but it is, according to the director, loosely based on 'thou shalt not commit adultery'. Thus *Decalogue Nine,* which seems a more obvious candidate for the adultery theme, becomes 'thou shalt not covet thy neighbour's wife'.

There is a fair quota of deaths and a tangible sense of hopelessness in the films, which many have remarked upon. But despite labelling himself a 'professional pessimist', Kieslowski refuses to accept that the films are in any way bleak. 'The films don't exactly have a "happy ending", but they do end well,' he says. Even *A Short Film About Killing?* 'Yes, even that one. I think that the lawyer who is shown weeping at the end of the film has learnt something. He has understood that it is necessary to find some kind of "way".'

What this 'way' might be is never made explicit. True to his agnosticism, Kieslowski is reluctant to speculate about the existence of a higher deity, but will admit that several characters speak lines with which he would be happy to concur. One example is the scene in the first film between the young boy and his Catholic aunt (a scene, incidentally, not in the original screenplay), when he asks her who God is. She embraces him and asks him what he feels. 'Love,' he says. 'Exactly,' she replies. 'That is where He is.' Another is when the professor of ethics in *Decalogue Eight* is asked who it is who judges human actions. She answers: 'He, who is. He, who is in all of us. I don't go to church and never use the word "God". But you can live with Belief without using the word.'

Remarkably, the actual filming took less than twelve months, but the cycle was not shot in numerical sequence. *A Short Film About Killing* came first because a deal had been struck for two of the series to be turned into feature-length versions and this was the one Kieslowski said he most wanted to direct. After that, the series was shot according to the availability of cameramen and locations. On some occasions, this could involve takes for three films on the same day if the same location on the housing estate was used in more than one film. Only one serious interruption occurred: everyone on set, including the stuntmen, was so disturbed by the execution scene in *Decalogue Five* that Kieslowski decided to stop filming and resumed only the next day. 'It was only eleven o'clock in the morning, but everyone had gone weak at the knees, including myself. Although we all knew it was not for real, the sight was simply unbearable.'

Taking into consideration the fact that ten different cameramen were used, the films are also remarkable for their stylistic unity. Apparently, this was accidental. Always ready to dispel any notion of the omnipotent director, Kieslowski insists that he gave his photographers absolute freedom to do as they liked. It was cameraman Slawomir Idziak's idea, for example, to use the filters in *A Short Film About Killing*—in all, an astonishing 600 were required. Many have commented on the consistent play of light and dark in the series, but on this point the director is prepared only to have a little joke at his cameramen's expense: 'I really did tell them they could do what they liked. If they wanted to use one kind of lighting, I said okay. If they wanted to use the rails, I said fine. In fact, the whole thing became a sort of competition. And what happens? All the films look the same.'

If he gave the cast and cameramen a certain amount of freedom, arguing that style and tone were obvious from the screenplays, the same cannot be said of the editing. There has been some pretty brutal pruning between the conception and final product, much of which created the economy and precision for which the films have been so highly praised. Several scripted sequences were drastically rearranged or simply cut. *Decalogue One,* for example, contains a long scene in which Krzysztof, the scientist, asks his computer why his son had to die: the final version shows the screen with only the words 'I am ready'—a terrible irony bearing in mind Krzysztof's unpreparedness for death. Kieslowski himself is critical of young directors who are so attached to their work that they cannot bear to cut anything at all. He, in stark contrast, even purged the silent witness from *Decalogue Seven* because the pictures shot were 'no good'.

One paradox is that the *Decalogue* is quite likely to strike more of a chord with Western viewers than in Poland. The ratings there were not bad—twelve million watched the first, which rose to fifteen million for the last—although, ironically, an opinion poll commissioned not long after revealed that seventy per cent of Poles did not know what the Decalogue was, and twenty per cent thought it was something to do with the Olympics. Part of the reason for this general indifference, one suspects, is psychological. By the time the series was shown on Polish television early this year, the population had other things to concentrate its mind on, most of them economic or political. Many no doubt considered the Ten Commandments a luxury they could perhaps ill afford.

The other commodity the country cannot afford, alas, is films: the cinema industry is virtually bankrupt and the government is withdrawing its subsidies to the various studios. Kieslowski is reluctant to trail around with a begging bowl while there are two hundred directors desperate for money and work. Fortunately, he is one of the lucky few who can trade their talent and reputation in exchange for foreign funding. His next project is being financed by a French production company and is a love story, in which he hopes to cast American actress Andie McDowell in a leading role. Cowritten with Piesiewicz, it allegedly has a 'good ending', even a 'happy ending'. This, in Kieslowski-speak, means one of the heroines dies and the other lives on.

It would seem as if he has come to the end of the road as far as Poland is concerned. Although still living in Warsaw and working to help reorganise the cinema industry, he openly admits to not understanding what the public want from him there. The *Decalogue* could therefore well be the last film he will make in Poland altogether.

He is not being forced to work abroad: it is his personal choice and reflects his creative interests. He is now more interested in the West, where he says people may be more lonely than in the East, but has developed nevertheless a convenient argument to justify this decision: 'It is not important where you put your camera, but why you put it where you do. It is a particularly elegant theory because I know I am probably never going to work in Poland again.'

Michael Tarantino (review date December 1990)

SOURCE: "The Cave," in *Art Forum,* Vol. XXIV, No. 4, December, 1990, pp. 22-3.

[*In the following review, Tarantino discusses Kieslowski's use of character, setting, and plot in* Decalogue.]

Krzysztof Kieslowski's **The Decalogue,** 1988, is a series of investigations into the question of choice, both esthetic and moral. The director and his scriptwriter, Krzysztof Piesiewicz, based this series of ten one-hour television dramas on the Ten Commandments. (Two of the films, **A Short Film about Killing** and **A Short Film about Love,** have been expanded to feature length for cinema release.) The works have a number of constants: each is based on one of the commandments, some more directly than others. Each takes place in a bunkerlike apartment complex in Warsaw. And characters reappear from one film to another, sometimes as protagonists, sometimes merely as figures glimpsed in elevators or hallways.

Decalogue 1: Thou Shalt Worship One God, undermines the notions of certainty and blind acceptance called for in the commandment. The protagonist, Krzysztof, is a college professor of linguistics who is as scientific in his private life as in his profession. The first scene finds his 11-year-old son, Pavel—Krzysztof is a single parent—solving a child's riddle by putting the variables on his computer. (The boy can even lock the door and turn the water on with a computer program.) When Pavel asks his father if it is safe to go skating on a local pond, the two feed weather data into the computer to calculate the thickness and safety of the ice. Convinced, Krzysztof gives his permission. Eventually we realize that the boy has drowned. Krzysztof goes to pray at an altar put up at the site of the accident, where his grief turns to rage and he overturns the altar, wax flowing down the toppled Madonna's face like tears. Kieslowski has begun his examination of the commandments with a depiction of a crisis of belief.

Returning in each film to the same characters and location, Kieslowski balances our growing familiarity with these people and their surroundings against an inability to predict the outcome of their encounters. "I wanted to work for the television public, which is a little bit special," he has said. "I wanted them to recognize these people, that they would get used to them every Sunday afternoon. I knew that it would not be a serial that the public waited for with all the members of their family each week. There would be different characters. But I wanted it to at least resemble a series: to limit ourselves to a certain area, to certain buildings." This area, "the least unsightly of all the new apartment blocks in Warsaw," is a real and recognizable place to the Polish public, but proves to contain an infinite number of surprising narratives.

Kieslowski consistently presents images and sounds only in part, to be explained later on. Often, these mysteries turn out to be crucial to our understanding of the story. In **Decalogue 7,** we hear a child screaming as the camera pans over the concrete apartment block during the opening credits. We hear the screams again as the movie continues, but we are unable to locate their source. Finally, Kieslowski shows us Ania, a young girl waking after a nightmare that has become a normal part of her life. Her scream, an attempt to exit the dream, reflects her real situation: a child raised by her maternal grandmother, she is eventually "kidnapped" by her mother. Stolen in turn by both women, she is the victim of their maneuvers, and her cry is the moral center of the film.

More foreshadowing of this kind occurs in the opening scenes of **Decalogues 4** and **8.** In the former, a man douses a young girl with water as a practical joke. As the soaked nightgown outlines her body, he pauses for a moment in the doorway, staring at her. Eventually we realize that she is his daughter, and that the scene predicts the incestuous conflict to come. In **Decalogue 8** we find an image of two people, one a child, walking at night, visible only by their clasped hands. Later we learn that this walk took place in 1943: a young Jewish girl was fleeing the Nazis. Her return to Poland, 35 years later, is the subject of Kieslowski's film.

The director's use of the foreshadowing strategy plays into the understanding of realism in these films. Unraveling in a Balzac-like world of revolving characters and interlocking stories bound by the confines of geography and class, they are far from what used to be called kitchen-sink realism or "slice of life." The coincidences that punctuate each story are explicitly acknowledged. For every time we recognize someone from another installment, for every time we feel we have put together a piece of the overall puzzle, other elements are less easily assimilated: the character who appears in different guises and professions throughout the series, the emphasis on spilled liquids, unexplained phones ringing. Visual and aural tropes are repeated in rhythmic, almost mathematical patterns, revealing a firm sense of construction and determinacy. To Kieslowski, encounters are never the result of chance.

"For me," says Kieslowski, "this is a film on the conflict between the wish to understand the world and the impossibility of doing just that." His skepticism about the possibility of an ordered view of the world results in a work about order. The director has a background in documentary work, but his style conjures memories of Ingmar Bergman and Alfred Hitchcock, making *The Decalogue* a curious hybrid that reflects, albeit indirectly, the current transitional period in Polish politics. Yet though there is no escaping the fact that these characters are Polish and that their conflicts take place in the social context of the late '80s, specific references to contemporary Polish history are few. Instead, suspense arises from how the characters will resolve their moral dilemmas. The only certainty is the absence of the kind of fixed moral center the Ten Commandments claim to provide.

For Kieslowski, in fact, the commandments represent a code of behavior to be rigorously questioned. The commandment "Thou shalt not kill" is duplicitously applied by a society that condones capital punishment. "Thou shalt not steal" can apply to emotions as well as to possessions. "Thou shalt worship one God" may turn destructive when dogmatically applied. If it can be related to the current state of Poland and other countries in Eastern Europe, *The Decalogue* stands as testimony against any system that incorporates a monolithic interpretation of belief. Says Kieslowski, "When I hear the word 'moral,' I want to get out of the room."

The viewer of *The Decalogue* moves between recognition and ignorance. In a 1989 interview, Kieslowski remarked, "I established . . . a sort of game with the spectators. I said to them 'Decalogue 1.' They look at the film and then want to know which commandment it refers to. They begin to review the commandments. Whether they want to or not, they have to perform a kind of intellectual labor." That labor can be hard: "The term which best defines the relationship of each of the films with the Ten Commandments would be 'pretext.'" The connections that the viewer must make may develop in any number of directions. What is important is that the work is done. But in the game between director and viewer, Kieslowski can also deploy a certain sense of inexorability: in *Decalogue 5,* for example, in which a young man kills a taxi driver and is in turn executed by the state, one senses the ending from the first shot of a rat lying in the gutter.

The two concluding episodes are perhaps the most illustrative of the director's approach. The ninth film—touching on the Ninth Commandment, "Thou shalt not covet thy neighbor's wife"—deals with a husband, Romek, who finds out his wife is having an affair. The tone ranges between Hitchcockian dread, as in the scene where Romek finds a postcard from the lover and reads it in the apartment-building lobby as a dog howls in the background, and subtle irony, as when we see that the card is an image of the pope mugging for the camera. The film contains perhaps the most unnerving episode of the series: Romek is hiding in a closet, waiting for his wife to receive her lover. The scene is shot from his vantage point, using the door of the closet as a framing device that divides the two spaces. At one point, however, Ania turns around, looks directly at her husband (at the camera, at the spectator), walks toward him and confronts him. As in the closet scene in David Lynch's *Blue Velvet,* 1986, it is the spectator who is implicated in this sequence for his or her voyeuristic distance.

Decalogue 10, arising from the commandment "Thou shalt not covet thy neighbor's goods," is perhaps the lightest in tone. It is the tale of two brothers who inherit their father's stamp collection. At first they want to sell it, but then become obsessed by a search for a particular issue to complete the set. In the end, after a series of plot twists and turns that takes the film into a Dostoyevskian maze of paranoia and coincidence, they spot three characters from previous, quite separate encounters, all meeting in the street. This apparently coincidental yet exceedingly unlikely combination of people can be read as both an offer of narrative closure—a way of explaining what has happened—or as a demystification of narrative, for it is unlikely that these characters could have engendered a plot to match the brothers' suspicions. The scene also provides the key to Kieslowski's project, in which "plot," in its double sense of mystery and explication, is stretched in any number of ways. For the director, once the bonds of history and practice are broken, the possibilities of reinterpretation begin to emerge. Recognition goes hand in hand with revision.

Dan Millar (essay date January 1993)

SOURCE: "A Great Polish Film-Maker: Krzysztof Kieslowski," in *The Durham University Journal,* Vol. LXXXV, No. 1, January, 1993, pp. 131-35.

[*In the following essay, Millar praises Kieslowski's* Dekalog *and* La Double Vie de Véronique *as examples of Kieslowski's greatness as a filmmaker.*]

Krzysztof Kieslowski is not interested in Sin. In fact, he is not a 'theological' director at all, even though he is best known for his TV series *Dekalog* (*The Ten Commandments*) and its spin-off cinema films, *A Short Film about Killing* (i.e. the fifth commandment, Catholic numbering) and *A Short Film about Love* (sixth commandment), both 1988. But then who is a theological director? John Ford, with his Irish Catholic sentiments and Protestant hymns? Obviously not. The austere Robert Bresson? Bresson wisely cut out the theological verbiage when filming Bernanos' *Diary of a Country Priest,* keeping the drama—and the diary itself. (Bernanos' late *Mouchette* gave him less resistance a decade and a half later.) No, blasphemous Buñuel is the only convincing candidate—he used to read medieval theology for fun.

The films of Graham Greene's novels and stories (since Greene hid his real theological interests beneath a veil of convert's pseudo-theology) manage to lose the real stuff, keeping if anything only the pseudo; though there is a sense of evil in *The Comedians* (thanks to Lillian Gish) and a dash of other-worldly mystery in *The End of the Affair.* (*The Quiet American* is only political, and certainly not Greene's left politics; *The Fallen Idol* eschews ambiguity, to its own detriment, telling us: 'Adultery is good for you!')

No, Krzysztof Kieslowski, along with his Christian-rather-than-Catholic writing partner, ex-lawyer Krzysztof Piesiewicz, is a philosophical director, if that does not sound even more off-putting. Worse yet, an old-fashioned (comparatively speaking) moral philosopher—Cambridge University called its philosophy tripos by the imposing title, 'Moral Sciences', so perhaps Kieslowski could aptly be called a moral scientist. Certainly people who imagine that philosophers discuss values and concepts are nearly a century out of date: philosophers discuss the impossibility of discussing concepts.

Kieslowski takes a well-known moral code—well, not that well known, since the Faber edition of the scripts gives the wrong (Protestant) version, numbering from 3 to 9 the commandments that are 2 to 8 in the Catholic (and, in English, Douay-based) version that Polish ex-Catholics like the agnostic Kieslowski and his free-thinking co-writer actually know . . . As I was saying, a known code that was not seriously challenged before the rise of collectivist Fascism and Red Fascism, i.e. Communism (pink Fascism is more fashionable in the West these days). Kieslowski, who does not acknowledge collectivism's challenges, subjects this code to testing, questioning, close examination in terms of values, judgements, ethics—one of his characters, in *8,* is herself a professor of ethics who discusses abstract principles in the context of brief stories such as supply the basic plotlines for these short films: 'Once upon a time, our time, in this Warsaw housing estate of bleak apartment blocks and chill winds, there was a man who . . .' or, better yet, 'a woman who . . .'

The stories they tell are 'little' stories only in the sense of involving few people, often two or three, not in lacking a larger moral dimension. Apparently throwaway ones like *3—Remember that thou keep holy the Sabbath day* (actually Christmas Eve) and *10—Thou shalt not covet thy neighbour's goods,* still involve a complex of family responsibilities and moral ties, their real subject. In *10,* the only

comedy, two brothers are divided by a stamp collection, left to them jointly by their remote, difficult father, a political prisoner for seven years too; but in the end they are reunited by its loss, after at first suspecting each other. Each section or film (there are recurring characters on the fringes, including a young man known as The Angel) expresses a word or concept, as the following selected list indicates:

1—Thou shalt not have strange gods before me . . . The maths prof, Krzysztof, loves reason, rationality, the materialistic: yet he discovers emotion when his young son, Pawel, is found drowned through skating on ice that ought to have been safe. The new American computer said it was all right, not having full data. In the script, the power station emptied hot water into the lake; but in the film the cause of the accident remains mysterious. Krzysztof attacks an altar to revenge himself in the god he does not believe to exist: irrationality is a strange god, too, but very popular in the world.

2—Thou shalt not take the name of the Lord thy God in vain. The consultant surgeon does not want to play god in asserting or denying that his patient, Andrzej, is or is not dying of cancer—he is very seriously ill, though. But another potential life hangs in the balance: Dorota, Andrzej's wife is pregnant by another man, now estranged and never as much loved as Andrzej himself. Dorota is considering an abortion; but it is pointless if Andrzej dies. She might as well have someone to love and live for, the baby. (Maybe she might be reconciled with the father, it is just hinted.) The consultant, in finally telling her that Andrzej is as good as dead, half-lies, since he knows the X-rays are ambiguous, maybe positive. Having lost his whole family in one night during the war, he hates to think of termination; the abortion is cancelled (nowadays Dorota would find the greatest difficulty in booking an abortion at all in Poland). Following a miraculous recovery, infertile Andrzej has no difficulty in taking a second miracle in his stride: 'We're going to have a baby.' The consultant says: 'I am pleased, Mr. Geller, very pleased.'

3—Remember that thou keep holy the Sabbath day. For Jews, the Sabbath was a family feast, so Christmas Eve is substituted. Taxi-driver Janusz plays Father Christmas to his hard-pressed wife and children Antos and Kasia. Ewa, an old flame, then drags him off on a wild goose chase around the city, pretending to look for the husband who remarried and settled in Kráków years before. The cab damaged, Janusz has to pretend it was stolen to get it back. He promises his wife he will not see Ewa again. The choice between the roles of Father and Lover has to be and is made once and for all. Ewa is isolated:

> [Janusz + wife]
> [ex-husband + new wife]

Ewa

[Antos + Kasia]
[2 children]

The grouping is symmetrical and she has no chance with either. The Family, the Sabbath, Christmas: these are the values that strive against the anarchy of love, with its late-night *tristesse* and morning regrets, another kind of hangover. (Interestingly, alcohol plays no serious role in any of the films; evidently Kieslowski and Piesiewicz do not eavesdrop much at confessionals.)

5—A Short Film about Killing (85 minutes, i.e. half an hour longer than the TV version). The young lay-about Jacek, depressed because his sister was killed in an accident for which he was partly responsible years before, fails to grow up and plans a clumsy murder of an old taxi driver, an obnoxious oaf but still a human being of sorts. Jacek fails to strangle him but bashes his head in with a rock. A young lawyer, newly qualified (newly a father too), defends him and pleads for his life, but with no success. The ritual is clumsily performed, with even Jacek embarrassed at the amateurishness of it all. However, he ends up duly hanged, and his excreta fall correctly into the pan beneath the gallows. The lawyer is upset, but everyone says he did his best; next time he will be less involved.

6—Thou shalt not commit adultery or *A Short Film about Love.* The longer film ends sooner, as I shall explain: the film version is therefore more ambiguous, since we do not know how Tomek will survive his suicide attempt and hospital recovery. Tomek, a teenage post office clerk, commits adultery in his heart and masturbation in his penis by spying on Magda, a thirty-something textile designer with a casually promiscuous lifestyle and a sour, discontented look after all her 'freedom' (even in ten superbly acted films, which do not seem 'acted' at all but are subtly stylised nonetheless, both Grazyna Szapalowska and, as Tomek, Olaf Lubaszenko, have to be mentioned as stand-outs; she can be glimpsed on the cover of the printed scripts, he cannot). Having been initiated by the son of his landlady, now on national service, he has gone one better than an old pair of binoculars and stolen a very phallic telescope (sometimes a cigar is not just a cigar, Dr Freud). He times his meals round her sex life. Finally he takes her out for a coffee, and tells her he loves her, but cannot translate this into desire, let alone action. She leads him on and he comes too soon; that's Love, she tells him, a physical spasm. He cuts his wrists, spends time in hospital. She repents, talks to the landlady (who disapproves, naturally, of Tomek's choice). In the TV version, he finally emerges 'cured'; he no longer peeps or thinks he loves her—she is just one more almost middle-aged woman who wears her skirts too short. That's Love, that was.

7—Thou shalt not steal. A schoolgirl has a baby but her head teacher is also her mother and takes over the child. Six years later (as the film begins), the girl Majka, no longer a child herself, decides that Ania is her daughter, not her mother's and 'steals' her back, running away in a hopeless and disorganised fashion to nowhere and nothing, actually at first to her old lover, once a promising young teacher, now a maker of kids' stuffed toy animals. The pair of runaways, Majka and Ania, are soon caught, without much help from the police. Ewa, the mother, loves Ania better than her real daughter and hardly tries to conceal it. She has Ania back but Majka runs away again at once on the train—they were waiting overnight in a station. Perhaps she will kill herself, or just disappear and never come back, or go abroad . . . She will end up a loser anyhow, sad and waifish, unlike her robust little daughter.

8—Thou shalt not bear false witness against thy neighbour. This is the only one of the series grounded in exclusively Polish experience of the War, anti-Semitism, patriotism (right-wing) v. Communism (Soviet-orientated) and so on. An ethics professor, Zofia, meets her American translator, Elzbieta, who turns out to be a little Jewish girl whom she refused to help during the War, on grounds of religious conscience. She had originally agreed to act as a fictitious godparent or witness to the child's Christian baptism; a priest had also agreed to pretend to have baptised the girl. Instead their refusal is really based on information, obtained by Zofia's late husband (he had died in a communist prison) through his work in army counter-intelligence, that the couple who were subsequently to hide the girl were Gestapo agents. The man, a tailor, had then been cleared of suspicion just in time (unlike the British film, *Orders to Kill,* for instance, in which the order of execution is countermanded too late), only to end up in the same prison cell as Zofia's husband, though he had survived and been released. By sheer good luck the girl had also survived anyway, and now forgives Zofia: she had herself been a 'false witness' of what had occurred, which as a child she had seen without understanding. She meets the tailor who would have sheltered her; but he refuses point-blank to discuss the War. Zofia then tells the priest the good news, forty-odd years late. During the complicated confusions of the War and occupation, 'everyone has his reasons', in the much-quoted phrase of Renoir (or 'Everyone is right') and the difficulty lies in seeing the whole picture. Actually, the film is about bearing false witness FOR your neighbour (or not), since it is quite normal, at least with ex-documentarist Kieslowski and ex-lawyer Piesiewicz, to think by opposites and contradictions.

9—Thou shalt not covet thy neighbour's wife. In this story of adultery, the emphasis is less on the adulterous couple than on the cuckolded husband, who covets his own wife (medically, the writers are off-target in that *libido* declines with waning powers; but on the more important distinction between sex and love, they are right). Since Roman is impotent rather than, like Andrzej, terminally ill (or not), the treatment is slightly more comic, though in a dark mode. Having spied on his wife and apparently seen her ending an adulterous affair, he decides on suicide when her ex-lover follows her to a ski resort to which she has gone for a few days on her own. As Roman is ineffectual as well as technically impotent, his attempt is half-hearted and he survives. Even when treating their characters with a touch of cruelty, Kieslowski and Piesiewicz invariably regard them with affection. Unlike, say, Ruth Rendell/Barbara Vine, who uses her antipathy and contempt to sometimes brilliant effect, e.g. in *A Fatal Inversion.*

Kieslowski maintains that all the *Dekalog* films have 'happy' endings; but this can hardly be true of *1*—the drowned son; *5*—the hanged teenager (though opinions may differ); or *7*—the lost daughter, i.e. Majka (not Ania, who is briefly lost only during the hour the film lasts). Also questionable are *3*—the barely surviving marriage; and *6*—in either version, especially the TV one, where Tomek seems emptied of life and love, while Magda is hardly ready for a new start (the point of the film version may be to leave her future more open and even promising: maybe she can rediscover Love). *10* might seem dark enough as comedy goes, with its sinister stamp dealers, half-mad guard dog, heavy metal bars (possibly reminding Artur of his musical style as a struggling 'rock star'), and atmosphere of mutual mistrust, but in fact it is funny. Though the brothers lose the collection (stolen) and Jerzy loses a kidney—ironically swapped to make up a now missing set—they rediscover each other and their belief in one another.

To sum up, what do these words analysed really amount to? GOD: NAME OF THE LORD: HONOUR: FAMILY: SABBATH: FATHER: (NOT) KILL: LOVE: (NOT) STEAL: (TRUE) WITNESS: COVET: WIFE: GOODS: BROTHER: EQUAL. Is this enough for a 'philosophy' or basis for 'doing philosophy'? One could be cruelly reductive, and say it is just a code for a Christian society in a socialist (rather than red fascist) context; and therefore already too dated by events to be still relevant.

However, the films shared the FIPRESCI (International critics') prize at Venice in 1989, and in 1991 Irène Jacob won Best Actress at Cannes for her dual role in *La Double Vie de Véronique.* So presumably the critics, or their representatives, saw more than just humanistic worth in the films: not superhuman values, but a visual style of distinction, based naturally on the counterpoint of the rigid horizontals and verticals of those grim blocks of flats (so surprisingly middle-class in occupation) and the diagonals at which the camera is so consistently and naturally placed—solving the riddle of why all the films (with the obvious exception of *Killing*) really look much alike, despite the involvement of so many cameramen and directors of photography, and certainly like the fully realised work of one director with a distinct vision. The vision is not really oblique, but seems so because lack of hypocrisy is itself embarrassing, raising too many questions: 'We didn't want to adopt the tone of those who praise or condemn, handing out a reward here for the doing of Good and a punishment there for the doing of Evil. Rather, we wished to say: "We know no more than you. But maybe it is worth investigating the unknown, if only because the very feeling of not knowing is a painful one!"' So says Kieslowski in spring 1990, after preparing the scripts for publication. Having instanced the theme of capital punishment in *Killing,* he adds: 'We endeavoured to construct the plot of this film so that the viewer would leave the film with the same questions in mind which we had asked ourselves when the screenplay was only an empty page fed into the typewriter.' The Brechtian notion of forcing the audience to question rather than accept is implicit here; and in this instance so is the Brechtian conviction of having access to the correct answer already. But the example is untypical of Kieslowski, if typical of Brecht, an author of much more rigid opinions, not necessarily self consistent.

Cinematic style is a combination of sound and vision, obviously. Even to non-Polish speakers, the terse, often tense quality of the dialogue exchanges, particularly between a man and a woman, is evident as much as the angle of framing; the brisk rhythm of cutting, always in tune with what we want to know next; the subtly stylised acting which appears so naturalistic that we are slightly surprised to recognise a well-known star face (Krystyna Janda; Daniel Olbrychski). There is also the command of narrative, of telling the story, that no great film-maker, however apparently casual or even slow, ever really loses; the fine, unbroken thread of attention to a particular world that may be quite strange to us but is wholly convincing while the movie runs (Kieslowski is an artist but he is not arty).

The same tight, sympathetic style informs the first (Polish) half-hour of *Véronique;* the French hour, set in Clermont-Ferrand and Paris, is slightly less secure. Kieslowski's sense of milieu falters slightly, becomes vaguer, despite such brilliant episodes as the chase on foot through the streets of Paris (Véronique on the run from her future lover, a distinctly fey childrens' author and puppet manipulator—you could do better, Véronique, with your looks and your forceful personality or—dare anyone say it now?—greatness of soul, we can't help thinking). Maybe the double-soul theme, regrettably artificial when spelt out, was intended to make this point about moral scale, as is having a larger budget and a fancier shooting style, travel shots ad lib. Kieslowski remains, though, a very physical, sensual maker of films: there is no overt sex in *The Ten Commandments,* not really in *Love* itself, where it is left to our imagination. There are a few brief sex scenes in *Véronique* but by current standards they are very mild (and why not? It is too easy to be vulgar nowadays).

Poland has not produced a great film-maker since Andrzej Wajda, the latter part of whose career was bizarrely mixed in quality (*Zanussi* never really made it, especially not with British audiences). Though he is now 45, Kieslowski has only just begun as a world-class director. It is too easy to think of eight or nine hours of television as the equivalent of a month's episodes of *Neighbours*. Yet Jean Vigo's reputation is secure on hardly more than a third of that as a lifetime's work. Our own documentarist, Humphrey Jennings, took a decade and a half, his entire career to clock up some 500 minutes of film (Kieslowski himself began as a documentarist out of film school in Lodz). *Dekalog* is a major achievement by any standards; and *Véronique* shows promise of more to come.

During the 1980s, Hollywood has stood still or gone backwards. Fringe countries—Sweden, Poland, China, Australia and New Zealand; but not in general Britain, France or Italy—have turned out the vintage wines of the movies. With the ten TV films and two cinema versions, Kieslowski has presented us with a whole case of the best. Let us be grateful; appreciate; above all, enjoy.

Geoffrey Macnab (review date November 1993)

SOURCE: A review of *Trois Couleurs: Bleu* (*Three Colors: Blue*), in *Sight and Sound*, Vol. 3, No. 11, November, 1993, pp. 54-5.

[*In the following review, Macnab asserts, "Perhaps Kieslowski is, as his supporters so ardently proclaim, the most important film-maker in Europe; but his blithe abandonment of social issues and retreat into a remote, mystical realm where personal experience is all that matters [in his* Trois Couleurs: Bleu], *do not augur well for the future.*"]

[In Kieslowski's *Trois Couleurs: Bleu,*] Julie, a young French woman, loses her husband and child when the family car careens out of control on a remote country lane and crashes into a tree. Badly injured in the accident, she tries to commit suicide on waking up in a hospital bed, but her attempt is thwarted by a vigilant nurse.

At the time of his death, Julie's husband Patrice, a famous composer, had been working on a piece of music to be performed simultaneously by 12 different orchestras in all the EC capitals. While Julie is convalescing in the hospital, a journalist visits her, asking if she will finish the piece herself, and enquiring whether the rumour is true that she wrote all of Patrice's music; Julie refuses to answer. Discharged

from the hospital, she returns to the family château, sorts through her belongings, and instructs her lawyer to sell everything. She even destroys Patrice's remaining work. After spending one night with Olivier, a composer friend, she tells him to forget about her. Hiring an anonymous apartment in Paris, she tries to build a new life, away from her past acquaintances and music. She makes occasional visits to her elderly mother, who is living in a nursing home. Otherwise, her time is spent in a daze, as she swims, potters round her flat and grieves. Her one new friend is her neighbour Sandrine, a prostitute whom the other neighbours want to evict. Julie refuses to sign their petition, and Sandrine is allowed to stay.

One night, she receives a call from Sandrine, who had been performing in a striptease joint, and had spotted her father in the audience. As she is consoling Sandrine at the club, she notices her own photo is on television, in a programme about Patrice. Interviewed by the journalist who harassed Patrice in the hospital, Olivier admits he has been commissioned to finish the piece. Julie is amazed that any of the score has survived, and alarmed by pictures showing Patrice with another woman. She searches out Olivier and offers to help him. She also quizzes him about the "other women" and learns that he had been unfaithful for years. Julie tracks down Patrice's mistress, a successful lawyer, eventually confronting her in a restaurant cloakroom. The mistress claims Patrice loved her. Julie accepts this, but is shocked to discover the lawyer is pregnant with Patrice's baby.

Having completed the score, Julie offers it to Olivier. He refuses to accept it, saying he can't take credit for her work. Julie resumes her relationship with him. Learning the château has not yet been sold, she moves back in herself, and begins to make provisions for the lawyer's baby. The lawyer is not surprised by her decision, saying Patrice had always emphasised she was an honourable woman.

After the privations endured by the saints and sinners of Kieslowski's Polish *Dekalog,* where moral choices had to be balanced against political and economic necessity, and where austerity was the watchword, life—at least in material terms—has become very much easier for the protagonists of *Trois Couleurs: Bleu.* The first part of a trilogy, with each film taking as its starting point one of the shades of the tricolour, *Bleu*'s ostensible theme is liberty (equality and fraternity, white and red, are to be its sequels).

It is not freedom of choice or expression that concerns the director here, but a rather more abstract notion of individual freedom. Although the picture is nominally inspired by one of the great revolutionary symbols, Kieslowski and his scriptwriter Krzysztof Piesiewicz are singularly uninterested in invoking the spirits of Danton and Robespierre. Their 'unpolitical,' almost Proustian project is to consider how far individuals are able to detach themselves from family, memory and material objects, the very things which give most lives a definition.

The film is seen entirely from the perspective of a recently bereaved woman who, in her grief, tries to sever all links with the past. Our first sight of her, a huge close-up of the side of her face, emphasises this is to be her story. Slowly, she flickers into consciousness. Refracted on her iris as she lies in her hospital bed is the image of the doctor, telling her she has lost her husband and child in the car crash. We are seeing through her eye.

What has been described as Kieslowski's "luminous, numinous and ominous" visual style is much in evidence. As in *The Double Life of Véronique,* reasonably familiar landscapes—French countryside, Parisian city scenes—are given an eerie, uncanny quality. Fields are draped in mist, streets are labyrinthine, and there is the same vertiginous sense of time distorted. It is never really clear whether the story takes place over days, weeks or months. Any narrative progression is haphazard, occurring through chance or coincidence. In a cafe, Julie just happens to hear a street busker playing snatches of her husband's last, uncompleted work on his flute. She just happens to catch a glimpse of herself on television. She just happens to find out about her husband's mistress.

The only common thread linking these random events is music. There are frequent, highly stylised moments of near-epiphany when the action freezes as Julie experiences some pang of involuntary memory, and the music blasts out on the soundtrack. At first, she seems overly obsessed with the myth of her husband's genius, and there is a danger the film will become bogged down in a ponderous elegy for the dead composer. But *Bleu* is not so much about celebrating the 'great' man as exercising him. It turns out that Patrice was far from the model figure she remembers; and there are constant hints that he didn't actually write the music himself. Perhaps Julie was the composer all along. Perhaps, indeed, Kieslowski is taking a sly dig at the whole cult of the auteur.

Arguably, *Bleu* follows more in the tradition of the French New Wave than of its director's Polish-based work. In particular, it echoes Godard's *Vivre sa vie,* in which Anna Karina was similarly cast adrift in the big city landscape. Not only do Binoche and Karina look remarkably alike, with identical haircuts and the same, mournful stare, but both pictures portray women struggling to live their own lives in a world where men pull the strings. And both directors seem intoxicated by their stars. Like Godard with Karina, Kieslowski risks aestheticising Julie's sense of isolation. With its swirling classical music, sumptuous production values and *la belle* Binoche at its core, there are moments when the movie seems like an upmarket brandy commercial. But

it is rescued from the dead end of art-house chic by a riveting central performance and the director's always idiosyncratic eye for detail. Kieslowski manages to convey Julie's grief most effectively through almost throwaway images. She stares in morbid fascination at a rat tending its litter; her gaze seizes on countless little objects, many of them, predictably enough, blue: under her scrutiny, these take on immense, totemic significance. Although the film veers toward the melancholy, there are moments of mordant humour, notably when we discover Patrice's dying words were nothing more profound than the punch-line to a stale joke.

In the end, *Bleu* seems anti-climactic. Julie comes in from the cold, resumes her relationship with her irritating lover, who has been pursuing her round the city like a droopy St. Bernard dog. She completes her husband's score for him and makes provisions for his mistress's child. Yet, banal as this all is, the film finishes with a flourish. The music, so far heard only in staccato fragments, is finally played in full as the camera pans from Julie and her boyfriend, encased like ornaments behind a glass screen, across a series of *tableaux vivants* of the main characters featured in the film—among them Julie's elderly mother and the wide-eyed boy who witnessed the accident. It's a glorious moment, and one which testifies to Kieslowski's ability to startle us with his formal virtuosity, even as his narrative crumbles round him.

Perhaps Kieslowski is, as his supporters so ardently proclaim, the most important film-maker in Europe; but his blithe abandonment of social issues and retreat into a remote, mystical realm where personal experience is all that matters, do not augur well for the future.

Marilynne S. Mason (review date 25 March 1994)

SOURCE: "Through the Lense of a Polish Filmmaker," in *The Christian Science Monitor,* March 25, 1994, p. 15.

[*In the following review, Mason recommends* Kieslowski on Kieslowski "*for film buffs, students, or anyone interested in the cultural history of Eastern Europe.*"]

Starting out as an innovative, intellectual documentary filmmaker, Polish director Krzysztof Kieslowski evolved into one of the great artists of the contemporary European cinema.

Kieslowski gained international prominence with his *Decalogue,* a series of 10 films based on the Ten Commandments made for Polish television. His *The Double Life of Véronique* made in France with French actors catapulted him to critical acclaim. *Three Colours* is a new series of films based on the colors of the French flag—blue, white, and red—symbolic of liberty, equality, fraternity. The first of these films, *Blue,* is an elegant, fully realized work of art—a mysterious investigation of the inner life of its heroine and a meditation on the nature of liberty.

Kieslowski is frequently cryptic in his responses to journalists, refusing to respond to questions about the meaning of a particular film. But in the fascinating new book, *Kieslowski on Kieslowski,* he reveals a little more of himself, and while his pessimism sometimes surfaces in odd, self-deprecating ways, the artist's warmth trickles through, too. The book is compiled from a series of interviews that the filmmaker had with Danusia Stok, who also edited the work.

Having attended Lodz Film School, Kieslowski later became a founding member of the Cinema of Moral Anxiety (1974-1980), a partnership that turned into lasting friendships with filmmakers who would later find international fame—Agnieszka Holland, Andrzej Wajda, Edek Zebrowski, and Krzysztof Zanussi. The Cinema of Moral Anxiety concerned itself with difficult moral issues affecting Poland—issues that were often socio-political.

But Kieslowski is not a political filmmaker. His brief involvement with politics, notably including a student uprising over the deportation of Jews from Poland in 1968, ended with the painful realization that he had done no good and that the compromises he made were being paid for by others. At one point, the police tried to frame him, claiming he had sold sensitive tape recordings to Radio Free Europe. They gave up the investigation. Later, during an episode of martial law in 1981, he obtained permission to film trials of dissidents. The camera had an unexpected impact on the proceedings: Judges did not want to appear ruthless, and sentences were light or dismissed altogether.

But in his documentaries, he was often able to slip reality by the censors. "There was a necessity, a need . . . to describe the world. The Communist world had described how it should be and not how it really was."

Later, when he came to make *Decalogue,* he searched for ways to express the spirit behind the Mosaic law, reexamining the meaning of right and wrong. He even took up the meaning of sin—an unusual choice for a contemporary filmmaker. But what comes out of his musings is a profound sense of the importance of life and of individual action.

Throughout the book, Kieslowski's practical observations about filmmaking suggest a concern for young filmmakers, an acute mind, a somewhat sad disposition, and a profound skepticism that nevertheless cracks open in the face of art, revealing a man capable of brilliant insight and poetic vision. The language is sometimes halting because the book is based on interviews, so redundancies, skipping about in

time, digressions, and all the problems associated with translation are here. Yet it is an engrossing read for film buffs, students, or anyone interested in the cultural history of Eastern Europe.

Philip Kemp (review date May 1994)

SOURCE: "Slightly Excited," in *Sight and Sound,* Vol. 4, No. 5, May, 1994, p. 35.

[*In the following review, Kemp asserts that more can be learned of Kieslowski from watching his films than from the book* Kieslowski on Kieslowski.]

Faber's 'Directors on Themselves' series, of which some half-dozen volumes have so far appeared, suffers from two inbuilt drawbacks. The obvious one is that some directors don't have anything interesting to say about their own films, in which case—as with David Thompson's valiant editing job on Barry Levinson—the sound of some fairly desperate barrel-scraping can be heard. The other is that, even given an articulate and perceptive subject, there's often a curiously airless feel to the books: the need for some keen critical sidewinds, for windows to open up an alternative vista or two, makes itself insidiously felt.

Such ventilation can be achieved by turning the book into an extended dialogue between film-maker and critic, as Philip French did with his excellent *Malle on Malle.* Danusia Stok likewise bases her book on long interviews with the director, but she has cut out her own questions, stitching what remains into a seamless Kieslowski monologue that traces his life chronologically. In addition, Stock tells us, excerpts from articles written by Kieslowski for a Swiss magazine have been "worked into the text"—a phrase which arouses the same twinge of misgiving as when one spots chunks of feature film footage spliced unannounced into a documentary.

Still, the result reads fluently—Stok has done a fine job of translating Kieslowski's Polish into idiomatic English without losing his personal tone of voice. So it's not her fault if, for most of its length, this book makes pretty dispiriting reading. That Kieslowski should recall the early years of his career with scant nostalgia is hardly surprising. He gives a bleak account of the subterfuges, compromises and petty betrayals required of anyone trying to survive as a filmmaker in Communist Poland.

But the experience, far from generating any stubborn sense of inner worth, seems to have cast a pall of disillusion over everything including himself ("I was too lazy or too stupid or both to change profession"), the business of directing ("very costly, very tiring, and gives very little satisfaction"), and film in general ("a much more primitive medium than literature"). Wearily he writes off political activity of any shade, along with his own once-hopeful generation ("We are all lost"), Poland as a whole and indeed most of the human race, concluding that he will probably never direct movies again. It's strange to realise that when these interviews were taped, Kieslowski was barely 50.

Now and again the prevailing gloom is tempered by wicked black humour, as in his memories of film school at Lódz, a city where industrial accidents were so common that the students played spot-the-mutilated: one limb missing scored one point, two missing two points, all four ten points. (The aim was to amass 15 points by breakfast.) And Kieslowski's account of his childhood yields intriguing pointers to the source of certain recurrent themes, such as the influence of the dead over the living (*No End, Decalogue 4, The Double Life of Véronique, Three Colours: Blue*): "My father was more important to me than my mother because he died so young." That casual "because" would repay further investigation.

It comes as a relief when the clouds start to lift some two thirds of the way through, at about the point where Kieslowski embarks on his *Decalogue* project. From here on he even guardedly confesses to liking things about his job: he gains pleasure from working with actors and cinematographers, and from the editing process—though typically he gets a masochistic kick from throwing out good scenes. Editing, in fact, is his favourite part of film-making, eliciting the nearest we are likely to get to Kieslowskian rapture: "Slightly excited, I await the results of every action on the cutting table."

Despite Kieslowski's seeming frankness, it is hard to avoid a sense that he's holding out on us, adopting the pose of the incurably pessimistic Pole to discourage anyone from digging deeper. At one point he virtually admits as much: "I'll never tell you about the time I suffered most; nor will I tell anybody." His stated motivations as a filmmaker don't give much away, either. "You make films to give people something, to transport them somewhere else." "If I have a goal, then it's to escape from literalism."

The evidence that there is rather more to Kieslowski than this lies in the films themselves—haunting, idiosyncratic and elusive. Sombre too, certainly; but (as with Bresson) capable at their darkest of giving vent to a sudden impulse of ecstasy—as in *Véronique,* when after Veronika's death in mid-concert the camera soars joyously skywards like a soul released. "Things are very rarely said straight out in my films," Kieslowski warns us. No doubt; but it's there—rather than in Stok's book, for all its merits—that insights into this enigmatic director can be found.

Krzysztof Kieslowski with Tony Rayns (interview date June 1994)

SOURCE: "Glowing in the Dark," in *Sight and Sound,* Vol. 4, No. 6, June, 1994, pp. 8-10.

[*In the following interview, Kieslowski discusses influences on his filmmaking, including themes, financing, and the political situation in Poland.*]

Hong Kong: 25 March—Dinner at the Pacific Club with Krzysztof Kieslowski, hosted by Golden Harvest, the local distributor of the *Three Colours* trilogy. Kieslowski is in town for the Hong Kong Film Festival (which opens with *Blue* and closes with *White*) and has spent the day giving interviews to promote the upcoming releases of the films. His producer Marin Karmitz, the ex-radical who runs the Paris production/distribution company MK2, has faxed ahead with precise instructions for prospective interviewers: "No stupid questions."

Kieslowski's left forearm is in plaster ("A skiing accident—my first vacation in three years, and this happened on the second day"), but he is in high spirits. He is flying on to Tokyo next, and dinner-table talk about Japan prompts him to tell a very funny story about his first visit to the country years ago. His over-solicitous hosts, he recalls, kept asking him what he wanted to do in Japan, and he finally came up with two absurd requests to keep them quiet. But they took him seriously, and so he found himself roaring out of Tokyo on the latest 750cc Honda motorcycle . . . and then taken on a mysterious three-day trip into the mountains which climaxed with a fleeting glimpse of Emperor Hirohito.

It doesn't surprise me that a Japanese PR person didn't grasp Kieslowski's irony, but the anecdote raises larger questions about his distinctive tone of voice. Irony was, of course, a key weapon in the armoury of all East European intellectuals in the communist years, and ironic quips come as easily to Kieslowski as one-liners do to Bill Murray. But how much of the current critical backlash against the director is founded on a mishearing of his tone of voice?

That question came to a head at the Berlin Film Festival in February, when Kieslowski gave a press conference on *White* that shocked many hacks present by its apparent sarcasm and cynicism. He also announced that he has no plans to make more films after the trilogy. The Berlin audience had no trouble with *White* itself (it polled high in the local newspaper surveys), but journalists—some of whom booed the announcement of Kieslowski's Best Director prize—seemed to feel either shortchanged by the film's 'lightweight' tone or outraged by the man's insistence that he has had enough of working as a film director.

Berlin: 15 February—*White* premieres in the festival, and turns out to be the trilogy's scherzo: a black comedy about an unconsummated Polish-French marriage, a messy divorce and a problematic sexual-emotional reunion. The storyline intersects only very briefly with that of *Blue* (we now see that it was Zbigniew Zamachowski and Julie Delpy's divorce hearing that Juliette Binoche nearly barged into when she went to the Paris courthouse to look for her late husband's mistress), but both films climax with extremely emotive love scenes in which the protagonists overcome their mindsets and surrender to their hearts. The humour springs less from the tribulations of the central couple than from the accompanying picture of Poland in the 90s: a country of swindlers, strong-arm men and criminals where it is possible to buy anything at all, including a fresh Russian corpse.

Two days after the screening, the PR people working for MK2 allow me 45 minutes with Kieslowski. Much of what he tells me echoes and amplifies his succinct answers at the press conference; as I transcribe the interview, I am several times struck by the thought that it would be easy to misunderstand these words, to hear them as bitter or arrogant. I can only say they didn't sound like that at the time; the problem is that level of irony again. Kieslowski speaks better-than-viable English, but this interview was given in Polish and simultaneously interpreted in both directions by an unnamed translator. The whole thing was conducted at amazing speed, partly because of the time constraints and partly because that's the way Kieslowski thinks.

Two brief caveats. First, this is not a complete transcript of the interview but an edited selection from it. Second, this was conducted, before I saw either *Red*, which provides a new perspective on the trilogy as a whole, or Danusia Stok's excellent book *Kieslowski on Kieslowski,* which is a fascinating counterpoint to a viewing of the man's films and clarifies his reasons for wanting to retire from film-making.

[Rayns:] Why a trilogy? Why isn't one film enough?

[Kieslowski:] Because it makes everything more interesting. Differing points of view are inherently more interesting than one point of view. Since I don't have any answers but do know how to pose questions, it suits me to leave the door open to varying possibilities. I realised this some years ago. I don't want to pose as a relativist, because I'm not one, but I have to admit that there's an element of relativism in play here.

Is **White** *in some sense a parody of the other films in the trilogy, in the way that* **Decalogue 10** *parodied aspects of that series?*

You could see it that way. But I think *Red* is different in tone. It's hard to put a handle on it.

Isn't the 'liberté-égalité-fraternité' theme a pretext, just as the Ten Commandments were for **Decalogue?**

Yes, exclusively that.

So you don't lie awake at night worrying about such themes?

No, but I did spend a lot of time thinking about them.

How seriously do you discuss these things with your co-writer Krzysztof Piesiewicz?

We crack a lot of jokes. We talk about cars, about women. The conclusion we came to about equality is that nobody really wants it. Karol in *White* doesn't want equality, he wants to be *better* than others.

Did anyone pressure you to make the three parts of the trilogy in different countries?

No, I did it this way because I wanted to. The issues these films raise are deeply rooted in European traditions, so it was natural to spread them around Europe. The production company helped us decide where to shoot, but nobody forced us.

This isn't a case like **The Double Life of Véronique,** *where there's a material relationship between the financing and the structure of the story?*

Actually, that film didn't need to be a co-production between Poland and France. You could imagine it done with one girl living in Krakow and the other in Gdansk. I didn't frame the story of *Véronique* that way because of the financial background to the production; the subject itself was something close to my heart.

But the way you finally made the film did reflect the financing?

For sure. But this trilogy is a rather different case. I don't think these storylines are as original as the one in *Véronique,* and anyway, these are mainly French films.

You have a strong sense of humour, but there isn't much evidence of it in serious films like **Véronique** *and* **Blue.**

It's true that I have a certain sense of . . . irony. Sometimes you have to laugh, but I think it's worth trying to be serious from time to time. It's difficult to do both at the same time, but I hope that *White* strikes the odd lyrical note. For example, the character, Mikolaj, who wants to die—he's kind of serious.

What's the song Karol plays on the comb in the Métro?

A pre-war Polish song, every Pole knows it. It's stupid and sentimental; we sing it when we drink. It goes: "This is our last Sunday, tomorrow we part forever . . ." We become very sentimental when we drink.

White *offers a fairly scathing picture of post-communist Poland.*

Only in the background. But yes, that's the way it is now—unfortunately.

You still live in Poland?

Yes. I see it with a certain bitterness. I'm not against Polish entrepreneurialism, but people now care for nothing but money. I don't know what happened to us.

Do people in Poland resent the fact that you're working abroad?

Patriots do, yes. Normal people, I hope don't.

Who are these patriots? Do they have any power?

Nationalists, fascists, call them what you like. They're a crazy minority, but they shout loudly enough to be heard. They have newspapers, and access to television.

Last year in Poland, I found a widespread desire to come to terms with the past—for example, the treatment of the Jews. But the election result suggested a nostalgia for the 'security' of the communist period . . .

What you say is evident, but I don't think it's just. For me, it wasn't that the Left won, it was that the Right lost. That's not the same thing. There's no nostalgia for the Left. After 45 years of being told what was good and what was bad, Polish people have had enough of it. They don't want someone else telling them the same story, even if the meanings are reversed. What happened was that they threw out the Right and the Church.

Do you see a way forward for Poland?

I think we have to die first, all of us. Eventually there will be new people with new ideas. It's not just a generational change, it's a matter of changing a way of thinking that has been inculcated for 45 years. I can't see it taking less than two generations. Decades of Marxist education have left Poland unable to think in normal human terms. We can only think in terms of Left and Right.

You've said you won't make any more films. So how come I've seen the outline for a film you've written for the BFI's 'Century of Cinema' series?

That's just a short film for television. I promised to do it some time ago, so it's just a matter of fulfilling a promise. But the financial side of it hasn't been sorted out yet; I hope they won't find the money, so I won't be obliged to do it.

Why do you want to stop making films?

I don't have enough patience for it any more. I didn't realise it, but it suddenly dawned on me: I've run out of patience. And patience is a fundamental requirement in this line of work.

Does the situation in Poland have anything to do with it?

No, I've just become old. I want to live normally. I've had no normal life for the past 20 years, and I want to go back to having one.

Are you rich? Don't you need to work?

Not that rich, but I don't need many things. I have enough to live . . . peacefully.

How will you fill your days?

There are many books I haven't read. Or books that I've read four times and want to read three times more.

You'll be missed.

Don't worry, someone else will come along.

Liberty, equality and fraternity may well have been the starting points for Kieslowski and Piesiewicz's thinking about *Three Colours*, but this is finally a trilogy about love in the 90s.
—*Tony Rayns*

London: 8 May—*Red* closes the *Three Colours* trilogy—and Kieslowski's career as a director—on a magisterial note of wish-fulfilment. Each of the film's four main characters is a distinct centre of interest with her or his own narrative orbit; and these orbits intersect only occasionally and sometimes in surprising ways. But one of them, the retired judge played by Jean-Louis Trintignant, sees himself as a silent and embittered god. Emotionally wounded by a faithless lover and morally shaken by episodes in his courtroom, he has retreated from society to live alone and eavesdrop on his neighbours' phone conversations, exultantly monitoring the messes they, too, are making of their lives.

His stance is changed by the accidental arrival in his life of the young model Valentine (Irène Jacob): he moves from passive observation to intervention. He is too old to romance her himself, and so (thanks to a mystical transference that could only have come from the director of *The Double Life of Véronique*) he lines her up with a younger surrogate of himself, a young man he has never met but who is busy reliving the judge's own youthful experiences. In other words, the judge starts playing god in an active sense, manipulating lives and relationships. Kieslowski knows as well as you or I that this is also what a film director does. The closing scene of *Red* amounts to a brilliant synthesis of the judge's handiwork and the director's vision. And since it's a scene that involves the protagonists of *Blue* and *White,* it also brings the entire trilogy to a tremulous but emotionally satisfying conclusion. Not bad for a filmmaker who says he has trouble with endings.

Liberty, equality and fraternity may well have been the starting points for Kieslowski and Piesiewicz's thinking about *Three Colours,* but this is finally a trilogy about love in the 90s. It's not giving much away to say that all three films quicken in pace as they move towards climaxes in which the characters discover in themselves an unsuspected capacity for reciprocating intense feelings. In all three cases, this involves putting behind them earlier relationships that they believed at the time to be happy and fulfilling. For Julie in *Blue,* it means accepting that her idyllic marriage was a sham, acknowledging her own role in co-writing her late husband's music and opening herself to the sincere affections of Olivier. For Karol and Dominique in *White,* it means outgrowing the whirlwind excitement of their hasty marriage—seen in ironic, slow-motion flashbacks—and realising that their attempts to destroy each other were actually declarations of love. And for Valentine in *Red,* it means splitting from her jealous, absent boyfriend and embracing the possibilities revealed to her by the judge. Of the three, Valentine's future seems the least secure, since circumstances have only just thrown her together with Auguste, the young man who is perhaps the judge's younger self. But everything is in place to push her into the new relationship: the judge's design, Kieslowski's story structure, and the audience's will.

The trilogy is also, of course, about colour: about blue as the colour of remembering and melancholy, about white as the colour of weddings and orgasms, about red as the colour of jeeps and emergency rescue services. That's a jokey way of saying that Kieslowski integrates his colour motifs into the social and psychological fabric of his storylines, making connections and finessing moods. This relates to other visual strategies in the trilogy: the recurring play of light on Julie's face in *Blue,* the four fades to black at moments when time stands still in *Blue,* the cuts from light to darkness in *White,* the disquieting tracking shots (disquieting because not tied to anybody's point of view, even when they initially seem to be) in *Red.* These and Kieslowski's other formal strategies are hardly avant-garde, and audiences (if not critics) clearly have no trouble reading them, but they are arresting enough to give the trilogy a creative energy missing from most other mainstream film-making these days.

Two years ago, introducing an Edward Yang retrospective in a film festival catalogue, I wrote: "Imagine a kind of film-making that's truly in tune with the ways you think and relate to other people. A deeply humane kind of film-making, but free from 'humanist' lies and sentimental evasions. Not a dry, 'realistic' kind of film-making, but one in which all the imaginative and creative efforts have gone into understanding the way we are. A kind of film-making as sensitive to silence as to speech, and alert to the kind of meanings we prefer to hide away. To my knowledge, only two directors in the world are currently making films like that. One is Krzysztof Kieslowski in Poland. The other is Edward Yang in Taiwan."

When I wrote that, I had no idea that Kieslowski was interested in Yang's work (he is, and asked me about it over dinner in Hong Kong), or that the *Three Colours* trilogy would move into and take over the territory mapped out by Yang in *The Terroriser*—that inexplicable terrain where the aleatory becomes objective chance and lives intersect as if fulfilling some higher design. Neither director is at all religious in the orthodox sense, but Kieslowski is no doubt the more 'spiritual' of the two: the more willing to privilege moments of sixth-sense intuition and the more receptive to ideas such as the existence of the soul and parallel lives. But both men are perfectly in tune with the patterns, issues, tics and tropes, of modern life, and Kieslowski's ultimate achievement in *Three Colours* is to have pinpointed the mood of Europe in the 90s. Of course, he is right that another critical darling will soon come along to replace him. But who else is going to do for Europe what Edward Yang is doing for Asia?

Dave Kehr (essay date November-December 1994)

SOURCE: "To Save the World: Kieslowski's *Three Colors* Trilogy," in *Film Comment,* Vol. 30, No. 6, November-December, 1994, pp. 10, 12-13, 15-18, 20.

[*In the following essay, Kehr traces the movement from isolation and solitude to acceptance of community and interdependence in Kieslowski's* Three Colors.]

When *Red,* the concluding episode in Krzysztof Kieslowski's *Three Colors* trilogy, was screened at this May's Cannes Film Festival, the 53-year-old Polish filmmaker took the opportunity to announce his retirement. He now had enough money to keep himself in cigarettes, he told a group of American journalists through an interpreter, and rather than subject himself to the strain and bother of making films, he would prefer to sit quietly in a room by himself and smoke. Perhaps he would watch a little television, but never, never would he go to the movies.

Like most of Kieslowski's public statements, his proclamation of retirement should be taken with a grain of salt. He has long hidden his creative passions behind a mask of sardonic detachment—as did Alfred Hitchcock, a director with whom Kieslowski's career intersects in a number of interesting ways. But while it's hard to imagine an artist of Kieslowski's gifts retiring at the height of his powers, there is something in the image he uses that rings true. Retired or not, Kieslowski will always be that solitary smoker, an artist who sits at a reflective remove from mankind, contemplating the paradoxes and savoring the ironies of human existence.

It's an unusual position for a maker of movies—the most gregarious of mediums, the one art form that is both created and consumed in the midst of crowds—yet Kieslowski is devoted to solitude as a subject and isolation as a point of view. As a Pole, born in 1941 in an occupied country, Kieslowski comes from an entire history of separation and exclusion. Caught between Russia and Germany, Poland is the traditional battleground between East and West, belonging fully to neither tradition, neither culture. Under Communism, Kieslowski was too much of a quirky individualist to please the Party, and too much of a moody defeatist to please the firebrands of Solidarity. Even now, he is a reluctant capitalist, protesting the "economic censorship" of the West, while preserving a distinct nostalgia for the state subsidized film industry of the past, free of box-office constraints.

In the 1979 *Camera Buff,* the first of Kieslowski's films to attract international attention, a factory worker (Jerzy Stuhr) buys an 8mm camera to film his new baby, but soon begins shooting his family, friends, and workplace. Eventually, he finds that his elevated position as a dispassionate recorder of reality has set him fatally apart from others, costing him his job and his wife. In *No End,* made in 1984 during the darkest days of martial law, the widow (Grazyna Szapolowksa) of a Solidarity lawyer tries to find a place for herself in a world that has lost all value and meaning.

A Short Film About Killing ('88, an expansion of part of the TV series *The Decalogue*) is centered on an alienated, virtually wordless young man (Miroslaw Baka) who murders a taxi driver and is himself killed by the Polish state. In *A Short Film About Love* (also from *The Decalogue*), a postal clerk (Olf Lubaszenko) falls in love with a woman he knows only through his telescope. *The Double Life of Véronique* ('91, the first of Kieslowski's films financed with Western money) tells of two identical young women (Iréne Jacob, in both roles) who lead parallel lives in Paris

and Warsaw; they affect each other's lives in mysterious ways but never meet.

Each of the ten stories in *The Decalogue,* Kieslowski's massive television series based on the Ten Commandments, takes place in or passes through the same housing project in Warsaw. Though the characters occasionally cross one another's paths, they never come together in a significant way, never realize how much they have in common with the others, how closely intertwined their lives, in fact, are.

The *Three Colors* trilogy—*Blue* (first shown at the Venice Film Festival in September '93), *White* (premièred at the Berlin Film Festival in February '94), and *Red* (shown in Cannes, in May '94)—also takes isolation as its subject, though this time Kieslowski is able to move to another level. Taken as a whole—which is the only way the three, closely intertwined episodes should be taken—the trilogy charts a movement from a deep sense of solitude to an understanding and acceptance of community, to a sense of shared values and mutual interdependence. *Three Colors* is an epic of reconciliation, in which fragmented parts come together to make a whole, just as the three colors of the title create the French flag, and the three films in the series constitute one continuous gesture.

The structure of the trilogy follows the traditional pattern of the three-act play: and opening statement of themes and images (*Blue*), a reversal of those themes (*White*), and finally a synthesis and resolution (*Red*) that moves the themes to a different level. In spite of Kieslowski's declarations, the three films play best in the sequence in which they were written, filmed, and premièred; they contain an infinite number of inner correspondences, some playful and some quite essential.

In *Blue,* a chic Parisian woman, Julie (Juliette Binoche), loses her young daughter Anna and her husband Patrice (Claude Denton), a celebrated composer, in a car accident. Determined to forget the past and start a new life without emotional attachments, she takes an apartment in a working-class neighborhood and tries to loses herself in the anonymous life of the city. But she is drawn irresistibly into the lives of others: first by Olivier (Benoit Regent), her husband's assistant, who wants her help in completing his final score; next by Lucille (Charlotte Véry), a prostitute who is in danger of being expelled from Julie's building; then by Sandrine (Florence Pernel), a lawyer whom Julie discovers was her husband's lover, and who is carrying his child.

White begins in Paris, where Karol Karol (Zbigniew Zamachowski), a hard-working Polish hairdresser, is being sued for divorce by his cold-blooded French wife, Dominique (Julie Delpy). Having lost his wife, his shop and his self-respect, Karol takes to playing Polish folk songs on a comb in the subway, until he is rescued by a fellow Pole, Mikolaj (Janusz Gajos), a professional bridge player who smuggles him back to Warsaw in a trunk. Once back in the modest home he shares with his brother Jurek (Jerzy Stuhr), Karol vows never to be humiliated again, and sets about amassing a fortune in Warsaw's unscrupulous new currency and real estate markets. To lure Dominique back to Poland, he fakes his own death, then frames her for his murder. But when he sees her in prison, he realizes that he still loves her; she sees him and begins to cry.

The action of *Red* takes place in Geneva, where Valentine (Irène Jacob), a student and part-time model, has come to an impasse with her fiancé, off on an eternally extended voyage. Driving through the city at night, she accidentally strikes a German shepherd with her car, and, after a visit to the animal hospital, takes the wounded dog to its owner, a retired judge (Jean-Louis Trintignant) who lives in misanthropic isolation in a suburban house. Valentine is horrified to discover the judge's hobby—listening in to the phone conversations of his neighbors—but becomes fascinated by this man who is apparently able to live without love. Meanwhile, a young law student, Auguste (Jean-Pierre Lorit), continually crosses Valentine's path; he is in the process of discovering the infidelity of his fiancée, Karin (Frédérique Feder), while studying for his exams, an episode that precisely mirrors a decisive moment in the judge's past, forty years before. In desperation, Valentine takes the ferry to England, hoping to confront her elusive lover; Auguste is on the same ship, which encounters a violent storm and sinks. Watching television, the judge sees the faces of the six individuals who (along with an unknown ship's waiter) have survived the disaster: they are Julie and Olivier, Dominique and Karol, and Valentine and Auguste.

Three Colors was co-written by Krzysztof Piesiewicz, Kieslowski's collaborator on *The Decalogue,* and a lawyer formerly active in the opposition to martial law. Says Kieslowski: "Blue, white, red: liberty, equality, fraternity. It was Piesio's idea that having tried to film *The Decalogue,* why shouldn't we try liberty, equality, and fraternity? Why not try to make a film where the commanding dictums of *The Decalogue* are understood in a wider context? . . . The West has implemented these three concepts on political or social plane, but its an entirely different matter on the personal plane. And that's why we thought of these films."

In *Blue,* liberty becomes a tragic notion. Julie is free because she has been violently separated from her past and from her family. With no emotional ties, and wealthy enough to do what she wants, she steps off into a void. Kieslowski returns several times to the tomblike image of a huge, deserted indoor swimming pool, where Julie goes to wear herself out and neutralize her senses. At the same time, there are moments of penetratingly sharp, physical pain, as when Julie, returning from her perfunctory lovemaking session with Olivier, scrapes her knuckles along a wall. Pain is its own escape from pain, intense feeling is the same as no feeling.

Blue is a film of an intense subjectivity, where the camera sometimes occupies the body of the actor (Julie, lying in her hospital bed after the accident, sees the world at an angle) and even swoons when the character does (the periodic fades to black, which represent sudden, unwelcome recoveries of memory for Julie). Cinematographer Slawomir Idziak, whom Kieslowski calls upon for his most expressionistic work (*A Short Film About Killing, The Double Life of Véronique*), shoots with a depth of field so shallow, a focus so precise, that his lens can barely hold a single, small object in clear view. The cut glass hanging that Julie takes from her husband's studio, or the metallic candy wrapper that her daughter held in the wind just before the accident—these and other emotionally charged objects are allowed to dissolve into shapeless impressions and free-floating clouds of color (blue, of course), hanging over Julie's world like strange spiritual effusions.

The sound mix of the early part of the film renders the dialogue almost inaudible, with only the sudden, sharp passages of music—from the deceased husband's unfinished concerto—cutting through the perceptual fog, involuntary memories that bring back all that Julie has tried to forget. Time stops, and becomes meaningless: it's impossible to know how many days, weeks, or months the action occupies, when there are no external events to mark their passing. Julie is intrigued, though just barely, by a flute player she sees in the street. At first he is playing for coins (anticipating Karol's occupation in *White*); later he is seen descending from a limousine; still later, found lying unconscious. Another story is unfolding alongside her, though its episodes seem out of order, scrambled, unaccountable.

Julie's journey back from this frightening, too perfect freedom begins when Lucille, the prostitute, forces her way into Julie's apartment, where she notices the blue chandelier—she had one, too, she says, suggesting to Julie that there are tragedies other than hers in the world. (Lucille's trauma, though it is never dramatized, seems to be linked to her father. He shows up at the sordid Pigalle nightclub where she dances nude, in a scene that looks forward to *Red,* when the judge attends Valentine's fashion show.) Julie's discovery of sympathy for Lucille is her first opening to the world. The tight framing relaxes, swelling to the possibility of a two-shot that allows Julie and Lucille, two lonely souls, to share the same image.

Like the deceased lawyer in *No End,* Julie's husband has left some unfinished business behind—a concerto to honor the unification of Europe—which it is left to the widow to complete. Julie may, in fact, be the actual author of her husband's music (a possibility Kieslowski leaves tantalizingly open), but she is certainly his most gifted interpreter, bringing the dead score back to life after Olivier nearly buries it with a trite orchestration. And she participates in another resurrection when she shares in the birth of Sandrine's baby, giving the child full rights to the father's name and property. When the unification concert is finally heard, it occasions an extraordinary burst of imagery—a collective epiphany, in which Kieslowski's camera pans through space, catching each of the characters who has been involved in Julie's tale (including the farm boy who ran to the scene of the accident, and Julie's stern, silent mother, played by Emmanuelle Riva of *Hiroshima, Mon Amour*) as it sweeps along in one continuous movement, ending with the unborn baby outlined in the blue waves of an ultrasound image.

Blue takes place in a Paris that could only be imagined by an Eastern outsider (Julie lives an improbably chic life for the widow of a contemporary composer of serious music). *White* takes place in an insider's Warsaw, a city that reeks of failure, betrayal, and disillusionment. Kieslowski says it all in the visual comparison between Karol's handsome hairdressing salon on a grand boulevard in Paris and the tacky storefront on a muddy back street in Warsaw to which the defeated Karol returns. (Karol's goodhearted brother has tried to brighten it up with a flickering electric sign, explaining, "We're part of the West, now.")

In Paris, there is voluptuous sorrow, leisurely pain; in Poland, there is a kind of frenetic, financial slapstick, a primitive market economy as grotesquely speeded up as the action in a Keystone short. ("For *White*," Kieslowski says in the press kit, "I named the hero Karol—Charlie in Polish—as a tribute to Chaplin.") Rejected by the West, and betrayed by his Western wife (Julie Delpy, whose coldness for once is perfectly used, and perfectly transferred to the porcelain bust Karol brings back from Paris as a motivating souvenir), Karol is reduced to a state of comic impotence. Kieslowski's clear metaphor for a county of no use to anyone.

The theme of *White,* then, is equality—as reflected in Karol's grim determination to become more equal than anyone else. The whiteness of *White*—snow, subway tiles, sheets, statuary—suggests an emptiness that is also a new beginning, a void that might be filled. And so, the film's emphasis on mock resurrections: Karol unexpectedly climbing from the coffinlike trunk in which he has been smuggled back into Poland; Mikolaj's revival in the subway, when he realizes that Karol has shot him with a blank; and the elaborate scheme (including the purchase of a Russian corpse) that produces Karol's return from the dead for Julie, a resurrection that includes his sexual powers (Dominique's orgasm is accompanied by a fade to white). And white is finally the color of marriage, which haunts Karol in his flashbacks to

his wedding day, and which gracefully recurs at the end of the film, when Karol and Dominique see each other through the bars of the prison where she has been sent, and she signifies, with a gesture of her ring finger, her willingness to remarry the man who has so completely, and so perversely, devoted his life to her.

In discussing *The Double Life of Véronique,* Kieslowski makes a distinction between the "synthetic" narrative style of the first, Polish half of the film—by which he means a narrative that goes from episode to episode, covering a year or so of the heroine's life in half an hour of screen time—and the "analytic" style of the French part, which focuses on Véronique's state of mind as reflected in the nonnarrative elements of the mise-en-scène: camera placement, color, and so on.

The same distinction applies to the French and Polish components of *Three Colors:* Julie lives in a subjective, inwardly focused, visually oriented environment, Karol in an objective, aggressive, action-oriented world. *White* was photographed by Edward Klosinski, a cameraman who worked previously with Kieslowski only on the second episode of *The Decalogue,* but who has done extensive work for Andrzej Wajda (including *Man of Marble* and *Man of Iron*). And *White* does have the visual sweep and social orientation of a Wajda film—wide framing, eye-level camera placement, a number of characters interacting in a shot, in a way that creates a subtle sense of theater. *White* is the most public of the three films, the most overtly political, the most readily accessible.

If *Blue* is psychological drama and *White* is social comedy, *Red* is something else again—an exchange between two characters that is at once emotional, philosophical, and symbolic. With *Red,* Kieslowski takes a step toward a thematic abstraction, and a concentration on entirely cinematic means of expression, that occurs no place else in his work. To find anything like it, it's necessary to go back to Griffith's *Intolerance,* with its grand vision of historical synthesis, played out in the pure and beautiful mechanics of montage.

The final chapter in this trilogy of isolation is set in the most isolated of countries, studiously neutral Switzerland, and more specifically in Geneva, a city of coolness and suspicion, of lonely, individual houses (as Kieslowski films them) clinging to a vertiginous hillside.

Red begins with an image of mechanical process, as does *Blue* (the undercarriage of an automobile, leaking brake fluid) and *White* (the trunk containing Karol, bumping along an airport conveyor belt). In *Red,* through a breathless rush of forward movement, we follow an electronic impulse as it travels from a telephone in England, through a snarl of switches and wires under the sea, and surfaces in a Geneva telephone exchange, where it encounters a flashing red busy signal.

Red is the most insistent of Kieslowski's three colors, the color of blood, danger, embarrassment, violence, and love. It fills the screen in the first few minutes of *Red*—a red signal, a red car, a red awning, a red blanket, a red jacket, a red stoplight. As in *Blue,* the action is set in motion by a car accident, though this time it is not fatal, and the victim is a dog—Rita, a sad eyed German shepherd. Valentine (played by *Véronique's* Iréne Jacob, here enjoying her third life) takes the bandaged animal to its owner, who callously refuses it.

Kieslowski's films, like Hitchcock's, are full of watchers, from the politically naïve camera buff who doesn't know what he's seeing to the young man in *A Short Film About Love* who spies on the sexually active woman living across the courtyard. But there are also those watchers who come from someplace else, such as the ghost of the lawyer in *No End,* who stays near his wife but is unable to help her, and the mysterious young man who appears in eight of the ten episodes of *The Decalogue,* balefully looking on from a perch in the background. "I don't know who he is—just a guy who comes and watches," Kieslowski says, "He watches us, our lives. He's not very pleased with us. He comes, he watches, and walks on."

The Judge, played by Jean-Louis Trintignant in a fierce, bitter, tremendously moving valedictory performance, is clearly one of these figures, though if he has any supernatural powers, he himself seems to be unaware of them. And yet, there is the strange affinity he has for light: One conversation with Valentine is illuminated by a sunburst and another, nighttime visit by a bulb that burns out and is swiftly replaced.

The Judge, compulsively eavesdropping on his neighbors' telephone conversations through his home stereo system, knows everything but does nothing. Valentine is appalled by his voyeurism, but finds herself unable to denounce him. In a neighboring house, a good, Swiss *père de famille* is having a conversation with his male lover on the upstairs phone; when Valentine runs next door to warn him that the judge is listening, she finds a loving wife whose complacency she cannot break and (far more disturbingly) a little girl listening in, with no visible reaction, on the downstairs line.

This shared knowledge creates a powerful bond between Valentine and the Judge; Kieslowski films them in densely composed, space-collapsing two-shots that seem to press them together, in a clutter of doorways and window frames, into some special, private dimension. Within the heart of the city, they are living a life above life, Valentine as she waits for her lover to return, the Judge as he waits to die. Theirs is a shared isolation, and within it, something important passes between them—a sense of fraternity, perhaps.

In each of the three films of the trilogy, a betrayal leads to a sense of larger understanding. In *Blue,* Julie's discovery of her husband's infidelity allows her to forgive him and recover him, in the form of Sandrine's child; in *White,* Dominique's sexual athletics with her unseen lover cause Karol, who has been spying on them through an open window, to finally renounce his claims, and set about the process of reinventing himself.

There are two stories of betrayal in *Red,* though they are both the same story. As she moves through Geneva, Valentine is constantly crossing paths with Auguste, the young law student who lives in an apartment across from hers. His story becomes *Red's* subplot, as Kieslowski weaves in glimpses of his life as a student, preparing for the big exam that will qualify him to be a judge, and his relationship with Karin, a young woman who operates a personalized weather service out of her apartment. Auguste passes his exam, thanks to a trick of fate (a book he dropped fell open to the exact answer he needed for the test the next day), but Karin has fallen out of love with him. She has a new friend, a sailor, and as Auguste peeps through yet another window, he sees them having sex.

Later, as the Judge sits in an empty theater, trying to account for the emptiness of his life to Valentine, he tells the same story, down to the same magical detail of the book. It happened to him, and it is happening again: Auguste is the Judge as a young man, with the opportunity of living his life over again. If Valentine, in her freshness and openness, has come too late for the tired old man, she has come just in time to rescue the younger. They will find themselves on the same ferry to England, caught in the same storm—a circumstance that the Judge has arranged.

It seems all but impossible to account for the emotional impact of the last two reels of *Red,* an impact that reaches far beyond the narrative events depicted. One has the sense of an immense formal structure, one that extends not only across the three films of the trilogy but back to the beginnings of Kieslowski's career, coming to a moment of crisis and resolution. Throughout the trilogy, Kieslowski uses quick, enigmatic flash-forwards (such as the shots of Dominique entering an unknown hotel room in *White*) to give a fatefulness to the proceedings. Whether or not we consciously register these images (and many people do not), they create a feeling of resonance and fulfillment when they recur in the course of the narrative (it's the room Dominique checks into when Karol succeeds in luring her back to Warsaw). Through these moments, Kieslowski makes it seem as if the entire work were moving toward a single point of convergence, toward one grand climax. It's the narrative equivalent of a planetary alignment.

Some of the elements are purely whimsical, such as the shared taste of the trilogy's characters for the symphonic works of Van der Brudenmajer, the fictional musician invented by Kieslowski and his greatly gifted composer, Zbigniew Preisner, for *The Double Life of Véronique*. Other of the repeated elements carry a tremendous moral weight, acquired over time: a tiny, bent old woman, first glimpsed by Weronika hobbling down a street in Poland and later by Véronique in Paris, reappears in *Blue,* struggling to deposit a glass bottle in the too-high opening of a recycling bin. Wrapped up in her own grief, Julie doesn't notice her, but when she reappears to Karol (as a man this time? the image is ambiguous), he watches her and smiles a rather cruel smile, as if her problems were only a comic distraction from his. Only when the old woman turns up in Geneva is there an act of recognition and intervention. Valentine, as she leaves the theater near the end of *Red,* sees the old woman struggling and stops to help her, reaching up to drop the bottle in its slot. In a sense, that single, simple act of kindness is the climax of the entire trilogy, the gesture that saves the world.

One shouldn't be surprised to find Biblical allusions in the work of a man who has filmed the Ten Commandments; they are in the background of *Three Colors,* but they are there— the references to Mary, the *mater dolorosa* whose iconographic color is blue, in Julie's story; the mock resurrections that accompany Karol Karol on his journey. *Red* has its roots in the Old Testament, with its prickly, cranky, jealous God who keeps close tabs on his creations, judging them harshly and sending down rains and floods when they fail to perform to His expectations.

Trintignant is that Old Testament God, but a pathetically diminished one, whose power extends to light bulbs but not lightning, and whose apparent control over the winds and seas may be explained by the fact that he knows a good number to call for a personalized weather forecast. He may not be a god at all, but merely a man who takes himself for one—like filmmakers do, when they create their little worlds and send their characters scurrying through them. Trintignant invests the Judge with much of Kieslowski's own flinty contrariness, and it isn't hard to imagine the solitary smoker of Kieslowski's retirement occupying a house just like the judge's, sitting just as quietly amid the clutter of a lifetime.

"Who are you?" asks Valentine during the conversation in the theater, and his answer—"a retired judge"—marks the moment of recognition. The empty theater, where Valentine has just performed in a celestial fashion show (the flashbulbs providing more miniature thunderbolts), has a cathedral-like stillness and grandeur; a storm suddenly blows up outside and Valentine rushes to shut the windows against the rain. The camerawork in this scene, as in much of *Red,* is defined by the emphatic crane work of cinematographer Piotr Sobocinksi; the sudden, rapid shifts in point of view, from high to low and low to high, mirror the film's continuous movement between a cosmic overview and the tiniest of personal details.

The defining characteristic of Kieslowski's style may be this double vision, the ability to balance an immense, rigid, carefully worked out formal structure with an improvisational openness to nuances of feeling. If everything in *Three Colors* feels predestined, from the dominant hues of every scene to the ritual recurrence of objects, characters, and situations, Kieslowski's attentiveness to his actors allows him to preserve a sense of spontaneity and surprise. He allows himself to be influenced and astonished by the contributions of his performers (one feels his great respect for the work of Binoche and Trintignant, and his fatherly affection for the more limited work of Irène Jacob), thus establishing a protected reserve of chance and free will within the sleek predetermination of his narrative.

There is no more beautiful example of Kieslowski's balance of structure and spontaneity than the climax of *Red,* in which the immense image of Valentine that has brooded over Geneva since the film's beginning—a huge banner advertising, of all things, Hollywood brand chewing gum—is revealed to be a precise prophecy of a singular event. All of the streams and rivers of *Three Colors* suddenly run together at this moment, with an irresistible plastic and emotional force. Three films that seemed to have been carefully distinguished by tone, content and appearance turn out to be the same film, telling the same story of alienation overcome, loneliness dissolved in human warmth, isolation subsumed by a sense of infinite interdependence.

Both *Blue* and *White* end with tight closeups of their protagonists. Julie stands at a window, crying for the first time since her husband's death, but as the blue light of dawn becomes to come up, a smile plays at the corners of her mouth. Karol cries as he watches Dominique, behind a barred window, mime out her offer to remarry him if he can get her out of prison; then he smiles, too.

At the end of *Red,* the Judge looks out his window, toward the storm that has just passed; there's a tear in his eye, though his face is otherwise expressionless. But then there is another shot—the banner image of Valentine, now recreated in real life like a promise fulfilled, a covenant kept. The judge is the first of the trilogy's characters to see someone beyond himself; for Kieslowski, all the hope for the world resides in that fact.

Jonathan Rosenbaum (essay date 16 December 1994)

SOURCE: "Seen and Unseen Encounters: Kieslowski's *Red*," in *Chicago Reader*, December 16, 1994, pp. 47-53.

[*In the following essay, Rosenbaum discusses the possibility of resurrection in Kieslowski's* Three Colors *trilogy, especially* Red.]

A film of mystical correspondences, *Red* triumphantly concludes and summarizes Krzysztof Kieslowski's *Three Colors* trilogy by contriving to tell us three stories about three separate characters all at once; yet it does this with such effortless musical grace that we may not even be aware of it at first. Two of the characters, both of them students, are neighbors in Geneva who never meet—a model named Valentine (Irene Jacob) and a law student named Auguste (Jean-Pierre Lorit)—and the third is a retired judge (Jean-Louis Trintignant) who lives in a Geneva suburb and whom Valentine meets quite by chance, when she accidentally runs over his German shepherd.

Eventually we discover that Auguste and the retired judge are younger and older versions of the same man (neither of *them* meets, either). Another set of correspondences is provided when, in separate scenes, Valentine and the judge are able to divine important facts about each other: he correctly guesses that she has a younger brother driven to drug addiction by the discovery that his mother's husband is not his real father; she correctly guesses that he was once betrayed by someone he loved—which also happens to Auguste during the course of the film.

With so many different instances of chance, telepathy, and prophecy in *Red,* one's credulity is constantly being challenged, but not to the point where the film itself ever threatens to crumble. The coexistence of the real and the everyday, on the one hand, and the mysterious and the miraculous, on the other, is one of the movie's givens, and much of what is beautiful in Kieslowski's style stems from its moment-by-moment charting of that charmed coexistence as he cuts or pans or tracks or cranes between his three characters, interweaving and dovetailing their separate lives and daily movements.

What emerges is not a "realistic" world in any ordinary sense, yet it is a fully and densely realized one, and one that has more insight into the world we all live in than conventional Hollywood wish fulfillments, which are no less fanciful in their details. Even the recurring uses of the color red—which seems to be found rather than planted in the various Geneva locations—impress us less as fantasy or invention than as one person's way of seeing the world, alert to all the feelings and conditions that are generally associated with that color in human interactions: passion, jealousy, pain, injury, fear, embarrassment, love.

Perhaps one reason why we can accept the strange congruences of Kieslowski's world even when our rational responses reject them is that the city of Geneva itself and its customary channels of communication and connection help to bring them about. Streets, cars, windows, posters, newspapers, radios, TVs, and, most of all, telephones become the vehicles of these casual conjunctions and gorgeous everyday miracles, which suggest that these channels *could* bring all of us together in ways that we never suspected, even if they usually don't. Valentine has a jealous boyfriend living in England, and Auguste's girlfriend in her flat operates a telephone weather report service periodically used by the judge. All five of these characters constantly rely on telephones as conduits out of their isolation, even if they more often only confirm their loneliness. The remarkable opening sequence traces the phone lines between Valentine and her boyfriend across the English channel, red wires and all. It's the first of Kieslowski's many dry and mordant Polish jokes: at the end of this epic journey, the call hits a busy signal.

When the judge is brought to court after confessing to a crime, Valentine learns about it in the newspaper, and when Valentine makes an appearance at a fashion show, the judge learns about it the same way. Even if Valentine and Auguste never meet, their apartment windows repeatedly frame each other's activities in the streets below. The huge poster advertising chewing gum that we see Valentine posing for is eventually unfurled on a busy intersection; soon afterward, she returns to her flat and finds the lock to the front door jammed with chewing gum, most likely as a result of this poster. It is a car accident that causes Valentine to come into contact with the judge, and it is a busy intersection where Auguste drops his law books while crossing the street; one book falls open to a page that contains the answer to a key question on the law exam he is about to take, a chance occurrence that also happened to the judge many years before.

In the November-December 1994 *Film Comment,* Dave Kehr—in the best critical account of *Three Colors* that I've read, pointedly titled "To Save the World"—compares this complex juxtaposition to the cutting between different stories and historical periods in D. W. Griffith's *Intolerance,* seeing it mainly in terms of parallel editing. Yet if one concentrates instead on spatial proximities—the proximities between Valentine and Auguste on the same street or in the same neighborhood, or even the proximities between Valentine and the judge, conversing and interacting in their three pivotal scenes together—one may also be reminded of Jacques Tati's *Playtime.* But neither reference point, which concentrates, respectively, on temporal and spatial continuities, comes close to fully accounting for the intricate web of interconnectedness and the poem of rhyming destinies that Kieslowski finds between three lonely urban individuals, a vision that is at once ecstatic and despairing, tragic and utopian.

This universe of interconnectedness is bounded at one end by total obliviousness (Valentine and Auguste are strangers to each other in the same neighborhood) and at the other by obsessive, gloating attention: the judge spends much of his time listening to his neighbors' phone calls. When Valentine's horrified discovery of his snooping persuades him to blow his cover, making the neighbors aware of his eavesdropping, many retaliate by throwing rocks through his window. Between that obliviousness and that obsessive attention loom utopian possibilities of communal urban life as well as the essential and debilitating isolation of all these people, and Kieslowski plays on these dialectical registers as if on a master keyboard; the subject of his music is nothing less than human possibility in the contemporary world.

Apart from a few obvious exceptions, masterpieces take a while to impose themselves and be recognized as masterpieces. People often prefer to forget this, but excitement about the first features of Godard, Truffaut, and Resnais in the late 50s and early 60s was not universally shared, nor were their meanings fully apparent the first time around, even to critics. A lot of proselytizing, discussion, and debate had to take place before they began to take on the status of classics. The same process took place with Bergman, Antonioni, and Fellini; long before these and other filmmakers became canonized and then vulgarized by imitation in American movies (by directors ranging from Woody Allen to Bob Fosse to Paul Mazursky) they were still regarded as controversial and problematic artists, and in some respects they remain so even today—which is why the most recent works of all three, all made many years ago, have yet to be released in this country. (Bergman's *Fanny and Alexander* is a six-hour film made for Swedish TV, and the version shown in the United States is 105 minutes shorter than the original; Antonioni's *Identification of a Woman* and Fellini's *The Voice of the Moon* have never been released here in any form.) Nowadays most critics, lulled by the outsized studio ad campaigns and eager for the currency that comes with instant recognition, tend to be much lazier than they used to be about grappling with more difficult and innovative pictures, and many go out of their way to avoid them entirely. Many of the most important new names in international cinema are missing from the just-published third edition of David Thomson's *A Biographical Dictionary of the Cinema*, and the same is partially true for the posthumously completed second edition of Ephraim Katz's *Film Encyclopedia*, thereby ratifying the relative inertia of critics happy to stick mainly or exclusively with Hollywood merchandise.

Even after three viewings, *Red* remains an exquisitely mys-

terious object to me—an experience that has grown in beauty and density each time I've seen it, without ever convincing me for a minute that I've perceived all of its meanings and riches. The same could be said for *Three Colors* as a whole, which has been playing in Chicago in installments since last winter. I'd say *White* seems the weakest of the three and *Blue* the second best, but this comes from seeing them as separate movies; it's possible that after seeing all three in sequence, I might view all of them somewhat differently.

Another school of thought, and one that's a great deal more prevalent, says that movies should blow their wad—put up or shut up—the first time around, even (or especially) if you're a film critic. If this school of thought has a dean, it would be Pauline Kael, and if it has a curriculum, the required movie of the moment would surely be *Pulp Fiction*. Kael, of course, retired four years ago, but that doesn't mean that her gospel of instant response and unretractable opinion isn't fully in force in today's marketplace; given the planned obsolescence of our culture as a whole, and the preference for light entertainment over any other aesthetic activity, it could hardly be otherwise. In fact, if you turn to the testimony of David Denby, one of Kael's oldest disciples, writing recently in *New York,* you might conclude that Kieslowski—"an artificer, perhaps, but not an artist"—isn't fit to polish Quentin Tarantino's boots:

> With *Red*, Kieslowski has completed the trilogy that began earlier with *Blue* and *White,* and it would be wonderful to announce that the three films amounted to a major work. (They've been hailed as such in Europe and in some quarters in America.) Unfortunately, it's not so; and, if I'm not mistaken, there's an element of dismay and put-on lurking in the praise. One senses an illusion close to cracking—the dissolution of a set of assumptions that animates a half-dozen film festivals a year. The truth is, the European cinema has lost its authority. It's not that there aren't good films every year. Of course there are (and there may be other good ones we don't see). But great films are not being made—not the way they were each year in the 50s and 60s—and much of what we see here of French, German, Italian, and Eastern European movies seems feeble or imitative or cultured in a trancelike way that means little to us. A nihilistic pop masterpiece like *Pulp Fiction* blows away European movies even faster than it does most American movies. For good or ill, American movies are eating the world market, and until new economic conditions emerge for the film business on the Continent, we may have to do without major European directors.

Given such sentiments, it's small wonder that Kieslowski recently announced his retirement from filmmaking. Assuming that it's possible to distinguish between economics and aesthetics in the above directive (a frequent problem in writing of this kind), Denby's authority here rests on a form of telepathy and prophecy that goes well beyond Kieslowski's. Like Kael before him, Denby is notorious for avoiding film festivals (making it impossible to determine which half-dozen he could be thinking of), so his conclusion that "great films are not being made" necessarily rests on a faith in the critical acumen of U.S. distributors bordering on religious—not to mention an implied reverence for European cinema in the early 50s that I for one would like to see him justify. Of course he's perfectly entitled to regard *Three Colors* as a failure; what I object to is his presumption of expertise regarding world cinema in general.

In fact, Denby's entire paragraph reeks of the kind of unearned (albeit confident) authority that legislates our entire film culture at the moment. The way he can write that Kieslowski's trilogy has been hailed as a major work "in Europe and in some quarters in America" automatically implies that Europe is unified and uniform in praising *Three Colors* whereas America is not—the sort of assumption one can make only if one doesn't go to the trouble of checking the facts. A few French critics, for instance, scornfully speak about Kieslowski's "cinema of Esperanto." Moreover, Denby's divvying up of "the world market" between America and Europe excludes the rest of the world as immaterial when it might be argued that a key difference between contemporary film culture and that of the 50s and 60s is the emergence of major filmmakers in Africa, the Middle East, and the Chinese-speaking world—not "major" in the sense of Tarantino or Spielberg but "major" in at least the same ballpark as Ozu, Mizoguchi, or Satyajit Ray—and major inroads made by Chinese commercial films in the world market as well. And is "cultured in a trancelike way" supposed to refer only to *Red* and not to *Pulp Fiction?* Kieslowski has Valentine tell her boyfriend on the phone how much she liked *Dead Poets Society.* Is this pop reference "blown away" by the equally adoring references to McDonald's Quarter Pounders in *Pulp Fiction?*

The words in Denby's paragraph that most reflect Kael's influence are the first-person plural pronouns—the royal "we" and "us" in the phrases "that means little to us" and "we may have to do without major European directors." Both support a fundamental cleavage between foreigners and Americans, creating an imaginary rift between foreign and American sensibilities that not even personal pronouns can cross. Perhaps foreigners who regard *Pulp Fiction* as "their" movie—not to the exclusion of Americans, but in concert with them—are provisionally tolerated in this form of tribalism. But Americans who feel the same way about *Red* (and I'm far from being the only one) become automatically and irrevocably excluded from the discussion; the very notion of a *shared* tradition or experience between Americans and non-

Americans is deemed inadmissible by definition, unless a popular American export happens to be at stake. In more ways than one, the xenophobic underpinnings of cold war rhetoric live on (even if multicorporate property rights now commonly take the place of politics), and the growing consequences of this enforced isolation are not pretty to contemplate. If anything or anyone has "lost its authority," this is the part of the critical establishment that continues to pass judgment on films it hasn't seen—unless what Denby means by authority is something that comes out of a cash register or sprays bullets.

Born in Warsaw in 1941, Kieslowski is nine years younger than Godard and seven years younger than Truffaut would be if he were alive, but he still can be regarded as a member of their generation, for better and for worse. Though he has described himself as not very religious, and though his main collaborator, Krzysztof Piesiewicz, who has cowritten every Kieslowski film for the past ten years, describes himself as Christian rather than Catholic, the thematic treatment of fate and the worshipful attitude toward young women as Madonna figures in Kieslowski's films both reflect the preoccupations of a Catholic sensibility that can also be traced through the films of Godard and Truffaut (among other French New Wave filmmakers) as well as those of Rossellini and Hitchcock, two of their key mentors.

In this respect, at least, his films are old-fashioned, and *Red* is no exception. Valentine is viewed throughout in idealistic and sexist terms, as Denby (among others) has pointed out, and the same could be said of Juliette Binoche in *Blue* and Julie Delpy in *White* (though in the latter case, the idealization is complicated by betrayal and treachery, as it often is in Godard's early features). All these women are treated as mythical and transcendental figures, though in some respects the major male characters are mythologized as well—the dead composer-husband in *Blue,* the Chaplinesque fall guy (Zbigniew Zamachowski) in *White,* the retired judge as a caustic, embittered seer in *Red.* As powerfully and beautifully embodied by Trintignant, this last character may represent the weightiest mythological presence in any Kieslowski film to date.

On the other hand, Kieslowski's sardonic and absurdist Polish wit infuses his films with a kind of harsh irony that is quite distinct from anything found in the French New Wave. As suggested earlier, *Red* abounds in poker-faced Polish jokes, from the scene of the German shepherd escaping from Valentine into a church service to Valentine hitting the jackpot in a slot machine in her neighborhood café, which leads a bystander to comment that it's a sign of bad luck. Much later, the row of winning red cherries gets framed in the foreground of a shot while one of the characters passes outside the café in the background, not so much a joke as a reminder of the earlier one. Like so much of Kieslowski's style and

vision, his wit tends to be more interrogative than declarative, which may cause some difficulties for viewers accustomed to Hollywood platitudes. The kind of cinema more interested in posing questions than in answering them—the cinema of Stroheim, Preminger, Rossellini, Cassavetes, Rivette, and Kieslowski, among others—is always bound to encounter resistance from viewers who go to movies in search of certainties, and who often settle for half-truths or outright lies as a consequence. To interrogate the world is to inaugurate a search that continues after the movie's over, implying a lack of closure that most commercial movies shun like the plague.

The difficulties of judging, of loving, of trusting are central to the lives of all the leading characters in *Three Colors,* and if the burnt-out case of the judge comes to stand in some ways for all of them, this is largely because, like the heroine of *Blue* and the hero of *White,* his identity is chiefly formed by a life already lived—and shattered. Whether or not he has experienced a genuine resurrection by the end of *Red* remains an open question, but there is little doubt that he has glimpsed the possibility of one, much as Julie (Binoche) and Karol (Zamachowski) have before him. Throughout *Three Colors,* Kieslowski's style has been devoted to discovering, exploring, and allowing us to glimpse this possibility. Judging by *Red,* the more we allow ourselves to experience his style, the more hopeful that possibility becomes.

Christopher Garbowski (essay date 1995)

SOURCE: "Kieslowski's Seeing I/Eye," in *The Polish Review,* Vol. XL, No. 1, 1995, pp. 53-60.

[*In the following essay, Garbowski discusses Kieslowski's use of point of view in his films.*]

There is a scene in *Bleu* [*Blue*], the opening film of Krzysztof Kieslowski's trilogy *Trois couleurs* [*Three Colors*], which shows the director's mastery of unspoken dialogue with the viewer. The film's heroine Julie is sitting on a Parisian park bench facing the street. Following a whiteout, we see a bent elderly lady on the sidewalk slowly walking toward a bin with a plastic bottle in hand. She can barely reach the opening in order to dispose of the bottle. The viewer has been cued previously by the "blue-outs" that the white-out has to do with the three colours of the trilogy.

The problem dealt with in this vignette is "equality," or rather lack of it. On the one hand, we have the young woman basking in the sun who in spite of her tragedy has the future before her; on the other, the elderly woman who is nearing the end of her life. Even the time in which the latter was born

seems wrong: her generation suffered from much poorer nutrition as evidenced in her case by her stunted growth. The present time also mistreats this older woman in many subtle ways; contemporary ergonomists have not bothered to take her size into account when placing the holes in the garbage disposal containers. Yet the same sun shines on both women and treats them with the same warmth; at some level, unfathomable to us, they are equal.

This scene shows how even in his current works the Polish director is influenced by his beginnings as a documentary filmmaker. The viewer is asked to look carefully at insignificant people. The documentary eye aims in its own way to achieve a similar effect that the director has worked on in his films since *Przypadek* [*Coincidence*]. In this 1980 film, characters from one part are met as anonymous passersby in another part; hence the viewer is invited to contemplate how someone unknown to you might be experiencing a drama of profound dimensions. With his concern for the seemingly anonymous person, even the simple passerby becomes a potential protagonist for Kieslowski. The director seems to be saying this movie could just as well be about him or her.

Does the eye always tell the truth though? In one of the early sequences of *Coincidence,* Witek watches his friend Daniel leaving up a hill. When they meet again after many years they reminisce about their parting. Witek mentions having seen a car on top of the hill (the viewer also saw this car); his friend denies that any car was there.

The question raised by these sequences is more than just the subjectivity of sight. Since the narration followed one protagonist's perception and not the other, the problem of film art's reflexivity is alluded to. This is somewhat reminiscent of that other documentarist-cum-narrative filmmaker, Antonioni, and his films such as *Blow-Up.* Paul Coates notices when studying Kieslowski's films that:

> The presentation of the protagonist as a mirror image is typical of the openings of Kieslowski's recent works: it is thus that Antek first appears, reflected in a book case in *No End* (In *Dekalog piec* [*Decalogue Five*], the lawyer character appears reflected in the mirror while he is readying himself for his final bar exam—C. G.) [. . .] The films thus begin by reminding us that what we see is not reality, but an image; that the true life is perpetually displaced.

Another symbol of reflexivity is Tomek's telescope in *Dekalog szesc;* [*Decalogue Six*] through which we look at Magda and share the former's voyeurism; the viewer is thus reminded of the voyeuristic nature of the cinematic experience. Kieslowski, however, may be pointing out something else as well. Charles Eidsvik interprets the director's intent in this way:

> Unlike films (such as *Peeping Tom* or *Rear Window*) in which there is something perverse about voyeurism, in Kieslowski's world the urge to watch is at least a result of the desire to share another's life, and a potential preliminary to making closer contact.

Eidsvik goes as far as to say the director's works "have little interest in reflexivity; his films are about people, not about movies."

In both interpretations there is an element of truth. Much like a number of contemporary filmmakers, Kieslowski does give indication through many recurrent symbols in his films that this is a cinematic experience. His philosophy seems to be, however, that one cannot plumb reality without taking into account the *fact* of art, especially when this is the tool by which the analysis is being undertaken. Otherwise the realism rings false.

Dekalog cztery [*Decalogue Four*] is a good illustration of this problem. Anka, the heroine of this episode, finds herself in somewhat of a quandary. Her conscience will not permit her to open a letter she has found, since that would be going against her father's will. There has been extant tension between father and daughter for a number of years and something must be done to resolve this. Anka intuits the contents of the letter and makes her mind up to confront her father. She herself is an acting student and decides to pretend that she opened the letter and even goes as far as forging the unopened letter. Thus this Anka who confronts her father becomes an "actress" playing a role. Her "art" is effective because at a deeper level her father wants to resolve the problem as well. This daughter "protagonist" becomes real to him because she speaks a truth he was in some ways not fully conscious of, nor was he brave enough to deal with the problem openly.

Not just the viewer is asked to look carefully at the world and others; in fact, it would seem that an important attribute of Kieslowski protagonists is their ability to see. Ewa of *Dekalog trzy* [*Decalogue Three*] observes a young boy who continually runs away from what is apparently a hospital on Christmas Eve and identifies very closely with his efforts. Julie in *Blue* converses with people in a cafe and looks toward a musician/vagrant(!) in the square. This characteristic of the director's characters can be seen right from his first short television fiction film *Przejscie podziemne* [*Pedestrian Subway*], where the two protagonists eye the denizens of a subterranean habitat in Warsaw from behind a peephole-like tear in a sheet of paper. Protagonists are often given the sensitivity Kieslowski acquired as a documentary film-maker and thus sight is elevated to major component of their makeup.

Another aspect of the protagonist's sight must first be broached on theoretical terms. There is a point at which the film protagonist's body could be said to transcend the actor: when the spectator is cued that what he is observing is an optical point of view of a not visible character. This is impossible in any other art form. In the theater, if the spectator is in the right position, it is possible to see more or less what the protagonist does, but from a considerably different angle, plus the actor is visible at the same time. These point of view shots are most effective when they are worked into the film narrative in such a way that our empathy for the protagonist allows us to understand what they are feeling at the time. The hero's "window on the world" becomes his "mirror of the soul."

In *Decalogue Four,* after a dramatic night where the heroine has confronted her father with her doubts as to their "biological" relationship, she wakes up to find him gone. Finally we see her at the window looking out frantically. The window is several stories up in a high-rise apartment building. In the next shot we look through Anka's eyes at a man walking off in the distance—it is her father. We feel her uncertainty: her father has been known to escape from difficult situations—is he running away now?

At times this inner body of the protagonist is almost palpable. In *Dekalog dziewiec* [*Decalogue Nine*], for example, we have a number of contrasting moods from a single protagonist's point of view. It is not hard to guess what the hero of the episode feels when the surgeon general asks Roman to help him pour some black market gasoline from a canister into his car. Roman has recently discovered that his impotency is permanent. When he helps implant the nozzle of the canister into the gas tank, the obsessed Roman sees a potent phallus which contrasts with his flaccid one. Yet toward the end of the episode, a point of view shot for the same protagonist yields a different gamut of emotions. The husband and wife have come up with a pragmatic solution for their marital crisis, they will adopt a girl. Roman contentedly boils some milk in his apartment's kitchen. We see his face looking out the window. The camera focuses many stories lower to a girl playing with her doll. Roman's dreams of a sedate family life for the viewer watching this scene are almost tangible.

The most dramatic case of this subjective way of seeing is when two characters are opposite each other in a shot/reverse-shot sequence, the camera occupying the place of one and then the other of the characters.

Jean-Pierre Oudart finds such cases disturbing and believes the viewer is "uneasy" when the camera is in such a position. Irrespective of the author's complex theory of *suture,* part of the reason for this "uneasiness" must be the unusual position the spectator is placed in. The typical shot/reverse-shot situation involving two characters gives the viewer the screen just behind the shoulders of one of the characters (or some other visible feature), and then switches to a similarly landmarked view behind the second character with a more or less frontal portrait of the opposite character. With both characters in view, the spectator has a feeling of security; he or she is an arbitrator that gets a good look at both "points of view." In the optical point of view shot/reverse-shot the placement is subjectively reversed. For one thing, we "share" the now invisible character's view in a peculiar way. The character in front of the spectator as a rule does not look toward the camera (i.e. "us," plus the off-screen character), but rather slightly to the left or right of us. Thus the spectator has the feeling of the off-screen character being slightly behind his or her shoulder; this can be just a little discomforting. Small wonder this sequence is one of the least used in traditional (e.g. early Hollywood) cinematography.

What is of further interest here is a certain "privilege" the viewer can be said to gain and its relationship to the protagonist. This may be made clearer with the assistance of certain reflections of the early Bakhtin. In his essay *Author and Hero in Aesthetic Activity,* Mikhail Bakhtin first examined the essential place of the protagonist in art. It was here that he claimed that the body of the protagonist is essential in organizing the axiological space of the work of art. While reflecting on aspects of the mind/world split, Bakhtin utilized a metaphor that is relevant to our concerns.

It can be reasonably stated that no two bodies occupy the same space at the same time. Thus what the person across from the other sees is different; even moving closer together their line of vision cannot be identical. For instance, one can see the other's back which is impossible for the first person and vice versa. In terms of you and I, we both have an "excess of seeing" in relation to each other. This is vital because, according to Bakhtin:

> Ethical and aesthetic objectification requires a powerful *point d'appui* outside itself; it requires some genuine source of real strength out of which I would be capable of seeing myself as another.

Returning to the metaphor of sight, there is no way of gaining this excess of seeing by one's self. Even with the help of a mirror the self seen is not fully identified with and is evaluated "not for ourselves, but *for* others and *through* others." For example, the above mentioned lawyer protagonist was examining his appearance to please his examiners to be.

Only the other, by sharing his surplus of seeing can fully complete us. Thus Bakhtin posits an invisible internal self

and a visible external one. In the relationship between I and the other sharing our surplus of seeing, a dialogic space is created. Two fragmentary visions are "sutured" together one might say.

In the shot/reverse-shot with the optical point of view of the characters film comes closest to creating such dialogic space. Whereas in film, as opposed to the novel, we do not have the internal body's most effective presence, i.e. thought or internal speech, the internal body of the protagonist's most physical trace is sight. And this sight is most dramatically cued by the reciprocating look of another character or protagonist. The spectator is brought into this spatial dialogue as well: sharing by proxy the internal body of first one and then the next character by seeing what they see.

In *Coincidence,* Kieslowski's second-last film before the *Decalogue* series, there is a scene in which the protagonist Witek converses with Werner, an older Communist he has met on a train. This part of the film is dominated by long travelling takes, such as the camera following Witek into the kitchen and then back into the main room. And so the shot/reverse-shot sequence of their conversation is also somewhat slower than is usual in films, heightening the intimacy of their dialogue. Yet only Werner is given an inner body and we see Witek through his eyes, i.e. during a key shot/reverse-shot sequence in Werner's apartment, we see Witek through Werner's eyes (Werner off screen) while in the reverse shot we are looking over Witek's shoulder. The major protagonist is constantly in our sight, as if under a microscope. Why is this the case? The reasons for a director's choices can only be inferred, but I would like to point out a few considerations.

Coincidence is a film in which Kieslowski explores the responsibility people have towards others. The director is fascinated by the territory between optimism and pessimism. The film shows three possible scenarios of a single protagonist's life; each differing diametrically. Although circumstance would seem to be a dominating factor in why the protagonist lives out one scenario and not another, there is another consideration which plays a determining role. At a crucial point Witek is at a disoriented stage of his life; his influential father has just died, necessitating him to make his own choices. Because of chance, the protagonist meets a different person in each case. This person has a decisive influence on which path Witek takes after meeting him or her.

One of these influential people happens to be Werner. He is a Communist by conviction, but he has been sorely disillusioned by the practice of the Communist State. Werner is himself a little undecided at this juncture, but he has an edge over Witek in experience and he has an authentic, if tarnished, dream. This edge over his younger interlocutor is partly expressed in vision: in the shot sequence we have examined Witek is visually bared before the older man.

Later in the film Werner's friend Adam gives Witek an application form to the Communist party. Witek asks Werner what he should do; he is not asking much, merely for advice. This he does not receive from Werner, the latter gives him the evasive answer: "Do whatever you want." Ultimately, of course, we are responsible for our own decisions, but the director seems to imply that none the less we do have a responsibility to do what we can for others. Werner had influenced his young friend a great deal and had indirectly led him to a certain predicament, but he was unwilling to tell him one way or another, or even more fully share his doubts.

In a way, through sharing this surplus of vision with Werner, the viewer is also implied in this responsibility toward the protagonist. During an interview regarding the *Decalogue* series, Kieslowski said that the main message he tried to impart was that the viewer become more sensitized to the people around him. In the I-Other relationship, the Witek type of protagonist is the profound "other," he is exposed before us and we are asked how we would respond to him.

A build-up of dialogic space in *Decalog jeden [Decalogue One]* is likewise instructive. The sequences that deal with the main characters primarily involve Krzysztof, the father, and Pawel, the son, or the latter with Irena, his aunt; the father also appears briefly with the sister. There is an intimate relationship between the father and son. The traditional over-the-shoulder point of view shot/reverse-shot is rarely used. But neither is the optical point of view version as such. The spectator is given oblique points of view of the son (father not visible), with something approaching optical points-of-view of the father. In this case it is a major character that has the surplus of seeing. But the eye-line is different: the son is looking up at his father, it is a questioning look.

The dialogic shots are similar in the scenes with the boy and his aunt, only here a situation does develop with almost equal optical point of view exchanges. This is an interesting sequence, when the boy and aunt maneuver into a two-shot establishing frame they are almost touching, then there follow several optical point of view exchanges and the distance between them is physically increased without any narrational clue of them having moved away from each other. The reason seems obviously the technical requirement of at least minimal distance for the shot/reverse-shot exchanges, which is made up for artistically by the emotional closeness of such shots.

Finally, after exploring the dialogic potential of the shot/reverse-shot sequence in the confrontation of protagonists and characters, let us not forget that it is at one level simply a compositional device in the film narrative. Perhaps the "ideal" dialogic sequence would be of one hundred and eighty degree shots with the characters equally framed; this is rarely the case. More typical is the exchange in *Dekalog osiem [Decalogue Eight]*: Zofia and Elizabeth face each other in the former's apartment after a dramatic evening. Zofia is quite submissive, she has successfully broken through the barrier between them erected by an ignoble incident in their mutual past and now they are communicating. The exchange is quite tender. To show that she is submitting herself totally to Elizabeth's judgement, Zofia is exposed in a stirring series of close-ups while the latter is framed from the bust up, looking just slightly down at her. This artistic device best externalizes the protagonists' relationship. Can it be called dialogic, though, with such intervention on the part of the director?

What is beyond question, however, is that such a shot sequence can best be used by filmmakers who genuinely believe in their protagonists and that the latter really have something worthwhile to communicate to each other and thus to the viewer. Significantly, directors such as Antonioni that have virtually abandoned this shot sequence typically dwell on the alienation of their protagonists.

The vision we infer to a protagonist organizes the aesthetic persona in a manner that is not possible in the novel, adding another dimension to its realism. If we accept Bakhtin's analysis of the protagonists in Dostoevsky, it is in the realm of ideas where we find the most potent organizing factor for the literary work of art. Ideas explore the verbal aspect of thought and allow us to quite effectively enter the inner body of the protagonist. Is the verbal component of thought the only one worth exploring though? There is also a strong nonverbal, or "preverbal" aspect of thought that, although it does not escape linguistic description, certainly loses substantially by it. And at this juncture vision is a much stronger medium for evoking such "thought."

This brings us back to Kieslowski. All things considered, few contemporary directors can match him in allowing the viewer to enter the protagonist's realm of vision and thus sharing his or her *I*.

Janina Falkowska (essay date Winter 1995)

SOURCE: "'The Political' in the Films of Andrzej Wajda and Krzysztof Kieslowski," in *Cinema Journal*, Vol. 34, No. 2, Winter, 1995, pp. 37-50.

[*In the following essay, Falkowska compares and contrasts the presentation of and audience reaction to the political content in Andrzej Wajda's* Man of Iron *and Kieslowski's* Without End *and* A Short Film about Killing.]

Films of Polish directors are frequently called political or are said to reveal political content. This essay constitutes an introductory proposal for a new project exploring issues which I have been working on for some time. The project deals with the questions of politics in Eastern European film and how they manifest themselves in works by Polish film directors. For the purposes of this study, I have chosen to focus on Andrzej Wajda's *Man of Iron* along with Krzysztof Kieslowski's *Without End* and *A Short Film about Killing,* works which can be considered representative of the Polish political film.

Before concentrating on the films of the two directors, I would like to devote some attention to the very concept "political," which, in general, is being applied indiscriminately to all levels of film analysis. On the one hand, film theoreticians describe films as "political" or as implying and revealing political content. On the other hand, analysts of the formal aspects of film talk about political film form or about films made "politically."

In relation to film, then, the very word "political" gets used in several senses on two different levels of analysis: one of the senses applies the term to film interpretation in general and the other to a particular grouping of films. On one level, the concept "political" pertains to the process of interpreting any film, and, on another level, the political defines films which form a polyphonic heterogeneous patchwork which includes social problem films, resistance films, revolutionary films, ideological films, and so on labeled according to the researcher's methodology, intention, and focus. Generally speaking, the two domains in which political appears in relation to film can thus be identified as political film criticism and political film, the category. In the interpretive sense, the term "political" is sometimes used to refer to a radical, new approach to an analysis of any film. The word "political" is applied to any film interpretation which differs from the established interpretive norms of its time. On the one hand, political denotes contestation and revolt against the given and the existing, but on the other hand, the term indicates a strong declaration of new critical values as opposed to old ones.

Within the context of film interpretation, radically political (or "resistant") readings and poststructuralist readings illustrate the way in which the term "political" gets used. These film readings are considered political from different epistemological perspectives: the first meaning of political signals a radically different interpretation of the film *content* while the second refers to a description of a radically different film *form.*

The term "political," when used to refer to the interpretation of film content, is often employed in the context of "seeing films politically." The politically radical theory which advocates this approach postulates that every film comprises certain ideological values not necessarily detected by an ordinary spectator. What is represented as visible in the dominant discourse is in fact made *seeable* by the arbitration of the dominant ideology that postulates one and only one meaning for it. For instance, Mas'ud Zavarzadeh, a practitioner of a politically radical interpretation of films, demonstrates how aesthetic notions obscure the ideological effects produced by viewing films, particularly the production of the spectator as the subject of social class. In this sense, films are read not as aesthetic acts but as modes of cultural exchange that form (desired) social subjectivities. Films, even the most trivial films, constitute political spaces that contest or naturalize the primacy of those subjectivities necessary to the status quo and suppress or privilege oppositional ones. Zavarzadeh states that a dominant ideology circulates in every film and helps to establish an epistemological relation between the spectator (the subject) and the world. In this approach, the viewer's interest is not so much in the film's aesthetics but in its politics: why do these films mean what they are supposed to mean in a particular cultural and historical context?

A similar political struggle is clearly evident in a political reading of a film often called the "ethical," to emphasize the self-fashioning autonomy of the subject. It concentrates on the resistance of the subject as agent rather than on the dominance of prevailing social arrangements. This political reading resistance, in Foucault's words, is situated everywhere in all the activities of producing and viewing film, from the aesthetic counterforces within the filmic text itself to the refusal of the spectator to support the subject positions offered by the film. This position has been especially strongly postulated in establishing the site of the cinematic pleasure, particularly in works dealing with the theory of the desire of the spectator and its role in the formation of the subject. Radical theorists, such as Laura Mulvey, who in the well-known article "Visual Pleasure and Narrative Cinema" theorized cinematic pleasure from the feminist point of view, have posited the patriarchal cinema as a political apparatus through which the female body is subjugated and fetishized as the object of a pleasureful male "gaze." The term "political" in this sense refers to the political strategy in which the functioning of desire is evoked for emancipatory practices: to critique the oppressive practices of mainstream cinema.

These examples of a political, interpretive analysis of film have to be dissociated from the notion of the political put forth by poststructuralism concerning the interpretation of film's structure. The poststructuralist sense of political refers to the film's discursive self-awareness, "a self-reflexivity that renders the 'meaning' of a text an 'undecidable' and contingent effect of the rhetorical tensions between containment and excess." In poststructuralist film theory, ideology is a synonym for unproblematized *representation* and has very little to do with the radical notion of politics as diverse semantic practices serving class interests. In this reading, deconstructing the logic of representation is interpreted as being political. For instance, the films in which the continuity editing that marks the classic Hollywood film is subverted (so that the material discontinuity of the film is displayed as a means for showing the arbitrary connection of the signifier with the signified) are considered to be made politically, without necessarily displaying a political content by challenging or supporting the status quo in society. In this understanding of the notion political, avant-garde and experimental films can be considered political because they subvert or transform the classical film form.

The concepts of opposition to and resistance, in addition to a strong statement in favor of new values, lie at the basis of the concept political when it is applied to films with explicitly political subject matter. In a film which reveals political content or, in other words, which presents the political discourse explicitly, the dominant ideology may be challenged, but it may also be reinforced. In opposition films, the dominant ideology is confronted more or less openly, its postulates are questioned, and the wrongdoing of the ruling class is exposed. In propaganda films, which reinforce the dominant ideology, however, the currently dominant ideology or new emerging ideologies are presented in a positive light, openly praised and venerated. John Grierson's classic definition, "Propaganda is the art of public persuasion," does justice to the concept of propaganda but also explains its political power.

In this basic conceptualizing of the political in reference to films having political content, one must add a further category of political film. The entry of films under this heading would depend entirely upon an audience's disposition toward them. The film may be considered political not because a politically important historical event is presented on the screen but because the audience decides that the whole film or some of its aspects should be interpreted as political. In this case the political enunciative power of a film lies specifically in the discursive relationship with the spectator. In contrast to a psychoanalytical interpretation of enunciation, according to which it is the film discourse which speaks the film, in the political enunciation it is the audience which speaks the film and not the film itself.

In the case of films interpreted as political by the audience, the concept "political" seems to be an empty vessel which is filled with semantic substance by audiences at a particular time of film viewing. The act of negotiating the film's

meaning becomes a continual process of accommodating and rejecting different ideological positions presented and not a process of instruction. The film does not inform the audience about how to make sense of the global reality of the culture—how to fit together the details of reality to compose a coherent model of relations through which, as radical politics suggests, an all-encompassing picture of the real emerges. The word "political" in this context is understood within its historical and material grounding—within what Bakhtin referred to as "the power of the word to mean." This power evolves from concrete situational and ideological contexts, that is, from a position of enunciation that reflects time, place, and ideological values.

Especially in Eastern Europe, where the ideological positions, political situations, and a whole sociohistorical position of viewing changes every five or six years with new historical developments, the evaluation of any film as politically important depends greatly on the context of viewing. As the discussion of Wajda's and Kieslowski's films will show, such an interactive understanding of political will have to inform my discussion of the three films. In all of them, a specific relationship is established between the film's message and the audience. My analysis will show how this relationship is played out and how the concept "political" is revealed in different contexts of interpretation. It appears that the films are political by virtue of the fact that they provoke a multiplicity of reactions on the part of the audience. The audience reacts to various aspects of the political discourse more or less explicitly presented in the films and engages in its own discursive practice, which either criticizes the two directors or approves of their presentations.

Up until the beginning of the nineties both film directors, Andrzej Wajda and Krzysztof Kieslowski, presented to the public a picture of Polish political dilemmas and controversies. Their creative productions serve not only as good material for deliberations concerning the concept "political" in film analysis but also as examples of two different film aesthetics employed to facilitate the depiction of political discourse on the screen. Although both directors produced their films at approximately the same time and the films depicted the reality and the struggles of the Polish society, their films differ considerably in their aesthetic impact and the "temperature" of the events presented on the screen. Wajda presents a passionate, excessively emotional and extroverted aspect of the political debate, while Kieslowski functions almost as Wajda's alter ego. Although Kieslowski's films contain powerful political statements, they are more subdued in their aesthetics, more intellectualized, and more serene than those of his countryman. The two directors differ significantly in the way they interact with the audience: Wajda functions more as a provocateur and instigator of a political dialogue with the public, while Kieslowski paints aesthetically refined, touching pictures of human suffering which affect the audience at a more subliminal level than Wajda's films.

The three films I am going to discuss in this essay, Andrzej Wajda's *Man of Iron* and two films by Krzysztof Kieslowski, *Without End* and *A Short Film about Killing,* are examples of different interpretations of political on the screen. Wajda's *Man of Iron* presents an open declaration of a political message directed straight at the spectator, proclaimed by the film protagonists in front of the camera, while Kieslowski's *Without End* and *A Short Film about Killing* convey a political message hidden between the lines.

Making its presence felt in the works of both directors is the dominant ideology of socialism. The films in question debate the intentions of this system of values whether through indirect references or an open challenge of it. This fact places the films within the problematic characteristic of almost all films produced in Eastern Europe. In these films, the socialist ideology is present either as a set of values within which the protagonists of the film function, as in the films of social security in the sixties in Poland, during the period of economical stabilization under Gomulka; or as a point of reference in the films of the Polish school called "the films of moral concern" in the seventies. In these films, the socialist ideology is present, with its theoretical love for humans and their work and a belief in democracy and equal distribution of goods among citizens, but it is simultaneously undermined by the undercurrent of opposition present either in a particularly grim cinematography, a strange solution to the plot, or other means detected by intelligent spectators. Although describing simple events of no specific political importance, the films can be read as subversive statements, undermining the dominant ideology through the method of presentation. Despite an official ban on subversive messages, powerful oppositional statements are present in the form of Aesopian tales, which the Eastern European spectator deciphers with utmost delight.

Andrzej Wajda's *Man of Iron* (produced in 1981) deals with the famous 1980 strike in the Gdansk shipyard which brought about the collapse of the socialist system in Poland. Maciek Tomczyk organizes this strike with the moral support of Agnieszka, his wife and political ally. The film's story begins at the moment of the historic strike at the shipyard. A journalist from Warsaw, Winkiel, is sent to Gdansk to produce a broadcast on the strike leader. Winkiel gathers the necessary information from a series of conversations he carries out with Maciek's friends and his wife. In the process of gathering information on Maciek, Winkiel, initially in the film representing the authorities, becomes more and more involved in the lives of Maciek and the members of the opposition movement. Finally, Winkiel changes his political position and joins the striking workers. The strike ends with victory. However, Winkiel is rebuffed by the workers and leaves the shipyard disappointed and dejected. On leaving the shipyard he encounters Badecki, the security official, who tells him that the agreement between the workers and the government which ended the walkout is not valid.

Andrew Sarris's words bluntly summarize the political films of Andrzej Wajda: "it is almost invariably People against Them." In this sense of the political film, *Man of Iron* openly criticizes the government for its totalitarian practices, denounces the society for its act of consent to such practices, and sympathizes with the opponents of the dictatorship. Two aspects of the political are manifest in Wajda's film: the film presents the opposition to those in power and also propagates the ideology of the victims in an aggressive way. When incorporating into his film documentary footage, Wajda does not limit himself to that taken during the strike in August 1980. He also includes the footage taken during previous famous antigovernment demonstrations in 1970. All this documentary material is then interlaced with passionate monologues of the protagonists relating the portentous events.

The overtly propagandist presentation of the political discourse in Wajda's film is opposed by a subdued film of Krzysztof Kieslowski. Wajda's passionate *Man of Iron* may be placed in direct contrast with Kieslowski's *Without End,* in which the struggle of the opposition members against the forces of providence is depicted as hopeless. In this film, a lawyer-cum-underground Solidarity activist dies in unexplained circumstances, leaving behind unfinished business and unsolved mysteries. His beautiful wife, played by Grazyna Szapolowska, the femme fatale of the Polish cinema, tries to unravel the mysteries of her husband's life. Through his notes and contacts she gets in touch with the members of the opposition movements and begins to take part in the political life of Poland, a life which had not previously interested her. She joins the activities of the underground Solidarity movement, although she sees its hopelessness in the context of the martial law in which they function. Moreover, the opposition activists prove to be a constant and painful reminder of her beloved husband. Finally, after several unsuccessful attempts to begin a new life with other men, she decides to join her husband in heaven (or hell?) and commits suicide.

Without End, not surprisingly, was severely criticized in Poland for its inexcusable presentation of the discourse of opposition in the context of the discourse of death with an ambiguous religious undertone. The revolutionary Poles detested this negative, philosophical picture reflecting on their powerlessness and, in general, on the pointlessness of any political effort. In this film, Kieslowski paints a grim cinematic picture in which the political discourse merges with the discourse of love and despair. The religious aura enveloping the whole film does not predispose the spectator to engage in a polemic with the protagonists on the screen; instead, it wraps him or her in a blanket of sadness expressed in the film by the overall color palette. Most scenes are shot in dark interiors, and in the scenes where the ghost of the dead husband appears to his wife, Kieslowski employs a blue filter, which adds to the scene's mysterious quality. The political discourse in *Without End* exists as the cause of the husband's death and is accepted as an omnipresent power affecting the most intimate aspects of human life.

At the time of its release Kieslowski's artistic statement was perceived as political in that in those volatile times, only a year after martial law ended, it dared question the sense of the political struggle. The audience felt betrayed and rejected. In the grim conditions of martial law, the audience needed a kind of unambiguous art which *zagrzewala ich do walki* (could warm them up to the fight) and offered some hope. This highly symbolic film, in which the ghost of the dead lawyer accompanies the living like a romantic phantom, could never have been received well at that time. *Without End* was attacked both by the official press such as *Trybuna Ludu* and by the underground Solidarity press, which did not identify with the message the film presented. In fact, Kieslowski produced an apolitical film about martial law which reflected his own personal experience. The filmmaker observes the reality of martial law as one who at the time of its imposition has already left the country. Like Zyro, the deceased lawyer, he sympathetically watches the desperate efforts of those who stay and try to fight till the bitter end.

The film seems to question the relevance of that revolutionary effort which finally brought about the implementation of martial law. The sense of *Without End* is clear from Kieslowski's statement at one of the filmmakers' meetings in the eighties, at which he said, "We have never been able to agree with the implementation of the martial law but we have had to live with it, unfortunately." Kieslowski bluntly shows the time of martial law as a time of the degeneration of moral ideals, a time of despair and ethical compromises. The film is about lowering one's head in the context of history. As the worker, Artur Barcis, accused of organizing an illegal strike during martial law, proudly lowers his head after hearing the verdict, so Polish society was supposed to accept the fate of martial law with calm respect. At the time this subdued reaction reflected the feelings of a major part of the Polish society, which treated the Polish revolution with a great dose of scepticism.

The film provoked a number of critical comments. For instance, respected film critic Tadeusz Sobolewski in *Gazeta Wyborcza* rhetorically asks, "What was this whole mourning for? After all, the Polish nation won this war." The answer is problematic. The Polish society won the war with the political system by showing the world that the socialist structure had been totally discredited and that the masses wanted change. It did not win the war on the psychological plane, as martial law brought about a state of common suffering for the whole nation. In this context the film was considered political not only because the content of the film clearly refers to revolutionary events but because the way in which these events were presented provoked highly critical comments. Kieslowski literally asked the depressed audience to accept their own state of depression as inevitable. The director did not create a revolutionary fairy tale on the screen, as Wajda did in *Man of Iron*; instead, he showed life as it is, something which the highly politicized Polish audiences could not accept at all.

A similar picture of powerlessness and despair is painted by Kieslowski in his shocking *A Short Film about Killing* in which a young hoodlum brutally kills a taxi driver. (He based the story on a real event.) Quickly arrested, the boy is then condemned to death by hanging. The state apparatus kills the young boy in a similarly brutal and inhuman way. The final scene of the boy's state execution is presented in detail as gruesome as that of the taxi-driver's murder. Lit with white, blaring light, the execution scene is depicted with scientific precision. The boy's hanging takes ten minutes of screen time. The apparatus of state murder—rope, trapdoor, lever, plastic tray (to catch the evidence of panic)—is more cruelly methodical than the boy's own killing tools (rope, iron bar, bare hands) and, argues Kieslowski, less forgivable. By beginning the film with a brutal murder and ending it with an equally brutal execution, Kieslowski has clearly established a framework in which the overpowering system may be seen operating behind every action of its subjects.

The film, this time painted in yellow, brown, and gray hues (thanks to yellow filters put on the camera lens by Kieslowski's favorite cameraman, Slawomir Idziak), presents the hopelessness of everyday existence for those representatives of the lower levels of society for whom the act of killing is the only way to get coveted goods—the car, the money, and the hope for a better life. The young hoodlum, Jacek, a boy from the provinces, comes to Warsaw to get a job. Due to his lack of a proper education and proper accent, his decent and promising qualities go unnoticed. The film creates an atmosphere of such despair and meaninglessness of life in Poland that the act of killing is a logical consequence of the images preceding it. The audience associates the grim reality seen from the point of view of the young hoodlum with the reality of contemporary Poland. The film director criticizes the system, which, in principle, was supposed to offer all people an equal chance but in reality differentiates between the poor and the rich, those from the provinces and those from the city. Consequently, the system reaps what it has sown: incurable monsters who have to be eliminated.

A Short Film about Killing is an example of an Aesopian tale which produces such a politically strong picture of contemporary Poland that, although the film diegesis does not directly address political events themselves, the film is unanimously interpreted as an important political statement. As Paul Coates states in *Sight and Sound*, Kieslowski presents several reasons why Jacek commits his hideous crime. One of the reasons is that the boy wants to have a car. There are other reasons, however, on a symbolic level, which Coates summarizes as

> the search by means of a murder, for which one knows the penalty is hanging, for a form of suicide that will not preclude burial in consecrated ground alongside one's beloved sister; the country boy's need to assert himself in the city; youth's revenge on age. . . . Equally significant, however, is his [Kieslowski's] sombre insistence on the typicality of the crime in contemporary Poland in the process of becoming hell.

Unlike Wajda, whose films express an enthusiasm for revolutionary effort, Kieslowski presents a more realistic depiction of the despair and hopelessness of life in a socialistic Poland. Kieslowski seems to say that there is only a small group of activists ready for revolutionary action. The majority of people in Poland, however, consists of such young hoodlums who cannot find a future for themselves in a socialist country.

The film is interpreted as political in another sense of the word as well. It presents in all its brutal lucidity an extremely volatile issue of capital punishment. As two prominent Polish legal journalists, Wanda Falkowska and Barbara Seidler, note in their comments on the film, Poland is one of seven countries in which the death penalty is readily implemented in all kinds of cases. (Other countries that until 1988 eagerly exercised capital punishment were Thailand, Ruanda-Urundi, Sri Lanka, the Philippines, Jamaica, and South Korea.) Moreover, the death sentence is still widely supported by the mostly Catholic Polish audience. Statistics in 1988 showed that 60 percent of Poles supported implementation of capital punishment. In presenting the act of the boy's hanging by the state as an act of murder, not much different in its meticulous brutality from the murder committed by Jacek himself, Kieslowski questions the moral value of the death sentence. The Polish spectators did not like putting an equal sign between a murder committed by an individual and a murder committed by the state and considered the film a controversial contribution to the debate on the issue. Here, Kieslowski did not oppose the dominant ideology of the socialist state but the ideology of any state which sanctions capital punishment. The film was considered highly political because a painful and controversial issue was presented in such a way

that it questioned the moral integrity of both the spectators and the state apparatus.

When compared to the highly sophisticated fables of Krzysztof Kieslowski, Wajda's political films look blatantly straightforward, bordering on the naive in addressing the gut feelings of the spectators. *Man of Iron* in this context is an example of an openly oppositional film in which the dominant ideology is confronted in a straightforward manner, even aggressively: its postulates are questioned and the wrongdoings of the ruling class are exposed. The same film, however, is also an example of a propaganda film in which the newly emerging ideology of the Solidarity movement is presented in a positive light, openly praised and venerated. Especially striking in the manifestation of the political in Wajda's *Man of Iron* is a blatant use of propaganda techniques. In order to contravene the ideology of the dominating, Wajda presents a counter-ideology, that of the dominated, which he conspicuously dresses in propagandist garb. In this way, *Man of Iron* becomes political in a propagandistic sense in that it communicates the set of values established and sanctioned by the ideology of the dominated. The rival ideology is not necessarily different from the dominant ideology in its principles, but it stresses the idealistic components of the former. While the propagandistic elements severely criticize the negative phenomena in the dominating's execution of power, they openly praise the positive elements of the dominated yet also unwittingly illustrate their growing power as expressed in the form of various prohibitions that the strike committee imposed on the citizens of Gdansk (among others, a ban on alcohol). The new power of the dominated is clearly present in the spectacular documentary shots of masses of workers which function as an ominous sign of future tragedies. Wajda uses every possible cinematic trick to reinforce the perlocutionary power of his film. The most obvious elements of propaganda—the glorification of the victims of the political system; the condemnation of the authorities; the revival of mythical or religious beliefs; the superseding of reality; the direct address to the audience; and the black and white characterization of the protagonists—are overtly used by Wajda to convince the viewer of the legitimacy of the dominated's claims.

In Kieslowski's films, on the other hand, the dominant ideology is sadly commented upon, alluded to, or treated as a cursed background for the tragedies of life—murder in *A Short Film about Killing* and suicide in *Without End*. The careful construction of these films points to the underlying cause of the life conditions of contemporary Poles and the tragic consequences of the realities of the socialist system. Kieslowski's political messages are even more subversive than Wajda's blatant monological imposition. In fact, with the creation of *A Short Film about Killing* Kieslowski established himself as a more powerful political filmmaker than Wajda, in whose film everything seemed to be conspicuously concocted to serve one propagandistic purpose.

There is one moment in *Man of Iron,* however, which jeopardizes the uniformity of Wajda's presentation. Winkiel, the journalist, through whom the film diegesis is presented, is himself a highly questionable character. The choice of Winkiel as the central protagonist of the film functions as a bitter reminder that Wajda himself was funded by the regime the opposition movement was trying to discredit. The circumstances in which Winkiel finds himself depicts the worst-case scenario for an author whose power of enunciation depends completely on the whims of the regime. Winkiel's subjugation to the regime also signifies the nightmare situation for film directors like Wajda whose presentation of events could go only as far as the authorities allowed it. Although the film seems openly provocative, it still does not show the most dramatic aspects of the strike. Wajda was careful not to alienate the authorities because the release of his film still depended on those in power. Consequently, not everything was shown in this influential political film. In this sense, the film was made in a political way to avoid the intervention of censorship.

In *Man of Iron,* Wajda seems to position himself diegetically in the place of Winkiel, as Wajda himself came to Gdansk only at the very end of the strike, and, although he did not actively support it, he witnessed the event with sympathy and understanding. His ardent depiction of the strike in Gdansk reflects his passionate feelings about the events but also his ambivalence concerning his own participation. The director watched closely but did not join the strike, hoping that within the basic structures of socialism the political and economic situation could be benignly reformed. However, as a sympathizer of Solidarity he suffered greatly after its defeat. While martial law lasted in Poland (December 1981 to July 1983) he was not only attacked by the government and the official press but was also forced to resign as president of the Polish Film Union and as the director of the film unit he had led.

In Wajda's haste to produce *Man of Iron,* his critics detected a self-serving motive: to achieve success at the forthcoming Cannes Film Festival. Their predictions that it would win the prize were right—both the Cannes audiences and the Cannes judges were stunned by the film's openness in the presentation of historical and social facts. Thanks to the film's fame, Wajda could count on the future support of the Polish sponsors of his films. He also knew that due to the sensationalist aspect of his work the Polish audience would be inclined to view his film both as a work of art and as a premonition or warning of things to come, specifically the growing threat to the freedom of the Polish artist.

In *Man of Iron,* the political discourse functions as the here

and now to both the narrative and the enigmatic position of Wajda as both film director and participant in the political events. Although apparently monological (in the sense of Wajda's imposed voice in the creation of the global message of the film), *Man of Iron* depicts Wajda's inner tensions concerning the role of the artist at important moments in history, the function of the media, and the position of the political activist in the formation of history. A political discussion of Wajda's film can thus be undertaken at many levels. The film functions as the director's exposé, on the one hand, but, on the other, as a presentation of events which, as a text, involuntarily enters a dialogical relation with the public. Everything about this film is questioned by the public: Wajda's intentions, his version of events, his suspicious manipulation of the documentary material, his haste in film production. All these elements, of text and reception of text, contribute to the understanding or misunderstanding of the political intentions of the film director.

At the time of the first screening of the film, the Polish audience felt overwhelmed by the directness of the film's address, literally submerged in the excess of ideology. Yet it also accepted the film enthusiastically as a reflection of its own feelings and as support for the revolutionary cause. The response of the audience we can call political for the following reasons: in supporting the film, the audience expressed its backing of the new and growing power of the dominated (the opposition movement in Poland at the peak of the political activity of Solidarity was estimated at ten million members and supporters) and it also reflected its deep hatred of the dominating. However, a smaller section of the audience doubted the intentions of the filmmaker and was suspicious of Wajda's haste in production and his blatantly negative presentation of the authorities whom he had served for so many years.

In each case, the audience engaged in a different discursive practice: from scepticism to overt enthusiasm, the response was politically charged in the context of the historical year 1980 in Eastern Europe. After all, the strike signified an imminent shift of power in Poland, the doubting of which was considered politically reactionary and smelled of cowardice. Alternately, unequivocal support for the movement in 1980 was politically dangerous because the dominating still held considerable power, as the introduction of martial law in December 1981 would demonstrate.

Wajda's films treat the political discourse as a nucleus around which the cinematic web is woven more or less carefully. The spectators are not left immobile in their seats but are provoked to take active part in the negotiation of the political meanings which are exposed on the screen. In Kieslowski's films, in contrast, the spectator is submerged in sadness and despair. The political discourse is introduced as the fatalistic power behind the events on the screen and is not passionately negotiated with the emotional force rendered in Wajda's films. In their interpretation of Kieslowski's films, the audiences engaged in a discursive practice different from that of the films by Wajda. While *Without End* was perceived as an apolitical depiction of very political events and, subsequently, the director was criticized for his lack of involvement in the revolutionary movement, *A Short Film about Killing* was interpreted entirely within the context of the political situation of Poland. This discursive practice situated the film within the political discourse, although the film's diegesis did not explicitly refer to such. There is a partial truth in the perspective of each director. Some Poles—the intelligentsia, political activists, and so on—would have identified with the activist political discourse of Wajda's films; many others would see the despair of their lives represented in the films of Kieslowski.

Finally, a word on the film form. None of the films presented here can be treated as representative of political filmmaking in its formal sense. Eastern European film, especially popular feature film, very rarely advocates a politically radical (in the sense of the politics of representation) film form. Indeed, it seldom differs formally from the classical norm. That the message is transmitted via the film is more important than the method of transmission. An average Eastern European spectator wants to identify with the protagonist on the screen without any formalist diversions and thus disregards formal experiments performed for art's sake. Separate studies, however, are required on the Eastern European avant-garde, which has always existed in the form of short, experimental films but, because of poor distribution in the cinemas, has been honored at special events only. These films are produced for a sophisticated intelligentsia who indulge in the films' formal delights and relish the subversive political messages hidden amidst the distractions of formal experimentation.

The three films I have presented in the essay do not display any politically revolutionary means of expression. All three have a conventional narrative line which carries the plot safely to the film's end without the narrative disruptions characteristic of the films of the French New Wave, for instance. Kieslowski's films are entirely fictional melodramas, referring to the political events of the eighties, while Wajda's film, although a collage of forms, tells a story of Maciek, the Solidarity hero. We might argue here that despite its conventional, melodramatic line, Wajda tries to make *Man of Iron* revolutionary in its formal aspect as well. The film combines elements of the conventional feature film and staged docudrama with documentary footage. It contains both the staged presentation of political events (for instance, the signing of the famous Gdansk Agreement in August 1980) and documentary footage of the mass held during the Gdansk strike, as well as staged interviews with many political personae (for instance, Anna Walentynowicz, whose dismissal

from the shipyard, among others, triggered the Gdansk strike). However, all these formal devices reinforce only the global message of *Man of Iron* and constitute its powerful propagandistic element. The formal manipulations were severely criticized by the Polish press, who saw in them a lack of consistency in the film's construction. The film was neither a good story nor a careful document of the events. Many of the staged "historical" facts were later criticized by the Polish press, who demanded from the director a journalistic scrupulousness and precision in the presentation and disregarded the necessity for consistency of cinematic diegesis and for the aesthetic compactness of the cinematic image. Various formalist devices, such as staged interviews with historical personae and footage coming from another film about the Gdansk strike (*Robotnicy* by Zajaczkowski and Chodakowski), were treated not as a revolutionary formalist device but as a trick, the purpose of which was to manipulate the audience on the emotional level. These devices were monologically imposed onto the unwitting spectator, who reacted emotionally to the film's poetic function but with disbelief to its referential function.

Although openly political in its discrediting of the dominant ideology and advocating of new ideologies, Wajda's film was perceived in a surprisingly sceptical way by a more critical Polish public. An audience used to the *jouissance* of Aesopian tales was disappointed by the open condemnation of the authorities in *Man of Iron,* which resembled kicking a man when he's down and had nothing to do with a constructive criticism. In the situation of an open revolt and an imminent change of political system in Poland, such an ambivalent reaction on the part of the audience was considered political in still another way. It signaled a feeling of distrust toward the director and scepticism in accepting new ideologies which use the same old Socialist realism techniques to discredit their opponents.

To recapitulate: it is the audience which creates multiple senses of political in these three films. Despite the fact that Andrzej Wajda's film incorporates openly propagandistic means in order to promote the ideology of the dominated and his *Man of Iron* attacks the spectator by imposing its authorial message in a dictatorial way, the audience sceptically accepts this monological intrusion. The film is considered an important political statement mainly because it dares to present portentous historical facts of the strike without any stylistic obfuscations. On the other hand, Krzysztof Kieslowski's *Without End* proposes a comparatively less enthusiastic interpretation of the oppositional activities, thus stimulating a highly critical reaction on the part of the members of the movement and those members of society at large who supported it. However, due to the psychological depth in the presentation of historical realities of martial law, the film is considered a significant political statement which provokes multiple reactions in the audience. Finally, *A Short Film about Killing* is an Aesopian tale which metaphorically refers to the desperate state that the Polish society is in. The film's grimness and despair more powerfully comment on the social reality than do any overt statements of Wajda's revolutionary heroes.

Georgia Brown (essay date May 1996)

SOURCE: "Auteur Tricolore," in *Art Forum*, Vol. XXXIV, No. 9, May, 1996, pp. 21, 118.

[*In the following essay, Brown traces Kieslowski's career from documentaries to feature films and analyzes the director's relationship to Poland.*]

When Krzysztof Kieslowski retired from cinema at 52 "to sit on a bench in Poland," Cannes reporters seemed almost more shocked at the Poland part. (Why, when he could be sitting in Paris?) Two years later he left us wondering why anyone with his resources would have heart surgery in Warsaw. Few in the West understood the man's ferocious Polish complex. Because he came to the attention of most film audiences only in the final phase of his career, while working in France, we barely grasped the extraordinary integrity of his life or his project, and even critics who praised the four French coproductions—*The Double Life of Véronique* and the *Three Colors* trilogy—groped to put these intimate domestic dramas in context. Arriving the same year (1994) as *Pulp Fiction, Red* was even attacked as fraudulent. I doubt that anyone familiar with the director's entire career would make such a charge.

Kieslowski was born into World War II Poland. The German occupation launched the Kieslowski family on a series of relocations. After the war, his father, suffering from TB, moved from sanitarium to sanitarium while his mother supported the family by taking clerical jobs in nearby villages. Krzysztof himself had "bad lungs" and was often sent to "*preventoria*" for kids. He read. His sensibility, it's clear in retrospect, was formed in pity and grief, and showed an inclination, a melancholic tilt, toward death.

He always represented himself as an accidental rather than a born filmmaker, claiming that the only reason he persevered in his application to the famed Lodz Film School— three tries in three years—was the look on his mother's face when he failed. "I don't know whether she was crying or whether it was the rain," he said. It was an image he would re-create in film more than once.

In school he gravitated to documentary, a subversive genre in a country where citizens were forbidden to acknowledge the absurdity of daily reality. He and his friends were interested not in dramas of noble sacrifice but in the possibilities of neighborliness, decency, kindness toward the elderly. They wanted to help Poles bear their lives.

A passion for pattern and linkage is evident early on in his work. From the titles of his documentaries, it seems that he was compiling an encyclopedia of the city: *The Tram, The Office, Factory, Bricklayer, Hospital, Station*. . . . In his 15-minute *Talking Heads,* he posed three questions to 79 Poles ages 7 to 100: When were you born? What are you? What would you like most? In *Seven Days a Week,* the segments from Monday to Saturday show slices of six different lives. On Sunday we find the six people sitting around a dinner table, members of the same family.

But documentary had a catch. After filming a woman through her pregnancy to the birth of a daughter (*First Love*), he began work on a sequel, with plans to follow the newborn to adulthood and her own pregnancy. Early on, though, he began to fear that anything he filmed could be used against the family, and he terminated the project. (Since his only child was born around the same time, this aborted documentary, a sort of crypto-*Véronique,* would have traced the life of his daughter's double or proxy.)

One day, after filming in a train station (*Station*), Kieslowski had his footage confiscated by the police. He found out later that a girl had murdered her mother and hidden the body parts in one of the station's lockers. Filming live, he realized, risked turning him into a police informer (compare this to democracies, where citizens vie to capture wrongdoing on camera). He quit making documentaries.

Despair for the genre informs the marvelous *Camera Buff,* a densely packed inquiry into filmmaking under communism. A factory worker named Filip (Jerzy Stuhr) buys a primitive 8-millimeter camera to record the life of his newborn daughter—"month after month," he promises—but he quickly grows infatuated with filming everything around him, including his workplace. (There he shoots, clumsily, a documentary about a dwarf coworker that Kieslowski himself had once planned to make.) When his amateur movie wins a prize, Filip becomes, touchingly, and much to his wife's dismay, an obsessive cineaste.

Initially encouraging, factory authorities inform him that only some of reality is fit for public viewing. His wife walks out, taking his daughter; a mentor loses his job. A hero to some, Filip feels like a goat. Alone at the end, he turns the camera on himself and begins telling the story of his daughter's birth—the opening of the movie we're watching. As a form of artistic suicide, there's much here that reflects Kieslowski's own deep-seated frustrations with cinema.

Camera Buff offers other glimpses of Kieslowski to come:

the fairy light playing around the infant's eyes, a portentous broken mirror, red- and blue-lighted sections of film, as well as a narrative that wheels around on itself. Fifteen years later in *Red* (a story that has an analogue in the past), several of the lines spoken by Irène Jacob (in the role of the model Valentine) directly echo statements by Filip's wife. Coincidentally, the daughter in *Camera Buff* is named Irene.

The 1981 *Blind Chance* could have been titled *Triple Life of Witek:* to dramatize his ideas about fate—that destiny chooses us—Kieslowski imagines three alternate futures for a young man racing after a train. In parallel scenarios Witek becomes a party official, an opposition leader, and an apolitical family man. As in *Véronique,* the "purest" character dies suddenly. In *No End,* a young lawyer appears to his wife as a ghost, allowing Kieslowski to extend his exploration of alternate worlds to the afterlife—here, an escape from the official lies of martial law.

With its ten episodes based on the Commandments, the made-for-TV *Decalogue* is both a metaphysical soap opera and an immensely entertaining grammar of morals. Inhabitants of the same Warsaw housing project suffer various losses: loved ones, potency, a small fortune, life as it had been. In the eighth installment—the one that breaks the series' domestic frame—a visitor from America arrives with preconceptions about wartime guilt and little appreciation for the degree to which history has put Poles in ethical danger. "What a strange country this is," she observes once she begins to grasp the maze of secrets she's wandered into.

Véronique, Blue, White, and *Red* could almost be set in one *Mitteleuropa* apartment complex—with *Véronique* called *Yellow* after its dominant filter. (*Véronique* leaps to *Blue* when the actor playing Véronique's nurturing father becomes the doctor who tends Juliette Binoche's Julie as she awakes from her coma). The four films have many rhyming elements and refer to earlier works, including the unfinished attempt to follow the life of a girl from birth to adolescence. (Kieslowski's concerned, fatherly portraits of young women coincide with his daughter's coming of age.) But while these later dramatic films retain strong elements of his early documentary work—the grounding in daily ritual, family, work, and a social world encompassing old and young—more and more Kieslowski seems summoned by beauty.

As a way of interrogating the lives and counterlives of his characters, Kieslowski and longtime screenplay collaborator Krzysztof Piesiewicz continued to develop their tantalizing system of signs (like the pulsating telephone signals that stand for heartbeats in *Red*). But he added new devices—shifting light, myriad reflections, wild camera angles, music, amplified sound—to work directly on viewers' emotions. This ecstatic style exposed him to the scorn of those resistant to the spell. And I do mean spell. Watching

Véronique recently, I noticed that my limbs were heavy; I'd entered a kind of trance and was transfixed, impaled by light. It's possible to feel tears on your face and wonder if it's raining.

Back in documentary days Kieslowski picked up a nickname, "Ornithologist," for the quality of his attention. A patient spy, he watched for the soul to light and begin building its nest. In *Blue,* in order to show what Juliette Binoche was seeing, he had to superimpose an image over the actress' pupil. By the time he made *White,* he'd found a 200-millimeter lens strong enough to view the passing world in Julie Delpy's eye.

Geoffrey Macnab and Chris Darke (essay date May 1996)

SOURCE: "Working with Kieslowski," in *Sight and Sound,* Vol. 6, No. 5, May, 1996, pp. 16, 18.

[*In the following essay, Macnab and Darke talk to three former colleagues of Kieslowski about working with the director.*]

We were in the same school. Krzysztof was one year ahead of me. We didn't really work at school together because the system was to team up directors with cameramen who were one year up. It was incredibly difficult to get into Lodz film school. Exactly like Krzysztof, I applied three times before I was accepted. There were at least 25 candidates for each place. And usually half the places were taken up by people who had some kind of leverage, sons of ministers or whatever. It was very fashionable to be in the film school. There were a lot of people posing as filmmakers. I first really met Krzysztof just after school, when I went to work in the documentary film studio in Warsaw.

I met him on a professional basis because he was doing the film, *Factory.* I was assigned to the cameraman photographing the film. It was very instructive. This cameraman was very peculiar. He was working as if he was a wildlife photographer but looking for people instead of animals—he was just hunting for faces. He and Krzysztof were incredibly good at observing people. Krzysztof, even then, was somebody with a very specific idea.

Documentaries then were quite different from what we regard as documentaries nowadays. There was more structure. Rather than go with the camera and see what happens, we were taught to come with some specific idea. Krzysztof was very good at it. He was very influenced by the pre-war English documentary makers, such as John Grierson and Robert Flaherty, who were totally different, but had this very strong visual style. He was fascinated by the English new wave. Lindsay Anderson for instance. Although Ken Loach was a communist, Krzysztof loved his films. He wouldn't say anything good about any other communist, but he really loved Loach's films. I suppose because they were so truthful. I remember we saw *Kes* together, and he was totally shattered by it; that you can get something so powerful and truthful from the little boy who obviously was not an actor.

Krzysztof learned to be ruthless with material. He would throw scenes away if they didn't ring true with the main thrust of the film. On the documentary *Workers '71,* we shot in the region of 25:1, which even by western standards is enormous, and he was chopping into that like crazy. It was the biggest exercise in documentary filmmaking I've ever been involved in. We had seven crews, a helicopter, and we were shooting an enormous amount of stuff. Except for that one film, he never overshot. He would have an idea of the film's structure from quite early on. In the later films, the numerical ideas of *Dekalog* or *Three Colours,* you can see this was just as important to him. He liked to place things in some natural order of the world.

Why did we make documentaries? Well, when we came out of school, we couldn't get into features. They were so stiff and so clogged with the older generation. Krzysztof didn't want to make features anyway. We were living in a place that was full of lies and there was a need for us to create a way of describing the world. I remember talking to Krzysztof many times and he would insist that the world which is not properly described doesn't really exist. That was his main premise—just to see that little world we were living in and to quite honestly describe it. All the films we made then were trying to describe little places, little societies. Except perhaps *Workers '71,* which was trying to create some kind of panorama. And it failed. It was just too big and there was too much politics entailed. It wasn't scripted at all. It was an attempt at getting the temperature of the country, which was quite impossible to do. It was not long after the big riots, the change of government.

The authorities saw it as an opportunity for propaganda. They thought this young group of filmmakers would be easy to manipulate. They were quite wrong. We'd go to all the big factories and interview all the people that were involved in the strikes and try to gauge what was behind all this unrest.

We discovered that most of the strikes were stage managed, but we couldn't put that in the film. In all the strike committees, there were people who were not genuine workers. That was a major disillusionment. We thought those strikes were a wonderful thing—that something was happening with the country. But it was just politics, such a dirty game. By the time the film was finished and edited, that whole period of liberal tolerance was ended. They turned the screw back.

Suddenly what would have been allowed three months ago was considered way too open-minded. By this time, the new regime was very firm and set in its way. The authorities took all the controversial scenes out and put more music into it, and more optimistic commentary. Obviously Krzysztof didn't want to be associated with it at all. We all took our names off it. It was disillusioning, but as a filming exercise it was great.

As I said, this was Krzysztof's only film on such a scale. Afterwards, he worked on a much smaller scale. All the other films, when I look at the titles—*Factory, Refrain, Night Porter, Station*—described a tiny little place which was somehow a symbol of the society. And you're confined to observing an enclosed space. And he just used to describe it, to see what the relationships were. He had a couple of very good assistants and researchers. He would research a film for a long time. He would meet me well in advance of shooting. He would visit locations time and time again. He believed in getting a very close relationship with his subjects. The crew would meet them too. So when we arrived to shoot, everybody would just be like friends.

Often, he would do the sound recording before shooting. He felt that this was a very intimate activity. You don't have all the paraphernalia of the filmmaking lamps, cameras and all that circus. People are more liable to tell you private things. He would just sit there for hours and hours. He was very good at listening to people. He had this rare quality, like a father-confessor. People would tell him things. He was able to listen in a way that was not provocative and yet encouraged people to say things. He tried to be honest, and people sensed that in a way. He would never impose himself on people.

Take *From a Night Porter's Point of View,* for example. Krzysztof came across a memoir of some porter from a factory. He was one of those little men who has a tiny bit of power, but uses it in a very aggressive way. The original night porter lost all his teeth, and you can't film somebody with synched sound when they don't have any teeth because that would be like taking the piss out of them. You wouldn't understand anything. The challenge was to find somebody exactly like this man, not easy. We found another three similar nightwatchmen, as outspoken, with more or less the same fascist views, and eventually chose one.

Krzysztof did something which is probably a bit unorthodox, even nowadays—he structured the main thrust of the film around the sound. We filmed the film almost to the playback. Before we did the scenes, we knew more or less what voice-over would be used. Usually you shoot something first and then put the voice-over on it later. We wanted to do this film a little bit more like a feature than the earlier documentaries. It worked beautifully. I even tried lighting devices that you'd only use in features. I was using a very long lens for some of the time. When you're working on a long lens, you have to get your focuses and pre-set some things which you're really not supposed to do in documentary. That film certainly looks a little more stylised than the rest. But, in a way, it is stronger because of that. This was probably his most successful documentary.

Nobody wanted to show it, of course. It was saying so much about the totalitarian society and the attitudes of people who create the basis for such a society, like this little porter. After two or three years, the authorities exhibited it in the deepest suburbs of Warsaw. It was about 20 minutes long. These documentaries were always meant as the first programme, they were always attached to some kind of main feature in the cinema. They paired *From a Night Porter's Point Of View* with some Mongolian film. Now who would go to a Mongolian film in Warsaw? For the authorities, that was a way of saying we give it a censorship visa, but let's hope nobody will see it anyway so it will be forgotten. But they were absolutely wrong. There was only one tram going to this suburb, but the cinema in the middle of nowhere would be packed day after day. And people would leave before the main feature, before the Mongolian film started.

Funnily enough, Krzysztof became very friendly with this little porter. Obviously, the porter was ridiculed in the film and made into this stereotype of the cynical, aggressive Nazi-like thinking. But privately they became very friendly. Krzysztof even hired the porter as an extra in two of his feature films because he liked him and he liked his face. (Unless somebody was heavily disloyal to him or very obviously bad in some way, he basically liked people. He was very humanist.)

Personnel was a more personal film for him. He'd worked as a theatrical trainee and knew the backstage environment very well. But at this time in his career, he was very inexperienced as a feature film director. He was fascinated by the actors. At the same time, he was scared about actually directing them. But by then he knew a lot about making documentary films. So he decided to bring real people into the film. It was about the people who sew and cut things, the tailors and costume designers. So he used real workers. Although it was supposedly his first feature, it was still to some extent like documentary. All the people in that workshop were real workers and he'd create situations round them.

I had this camera operator who was very good at hand-held work. The film was probably 80 percent hand-held. That was very unusual at the time, especially for a television film, but because Krzysztof had this idea of a documentary look, he wanted hand-held camera, even in quite static situations. He was determined to make the camera alive rather than just to

immure it on legs. He would be standing next to the camera operator and he would nudge him, push him a little bit. And this guy would say, "What the fuck are you doing to me?" And Krzysztof would say, "Calm down, I'm just making you move a little." We had a couple of disagreements about that. "Let the operator do it," I'd protest. And he would say, "No, at this moment, I just feel the camera should shake." And the operator couldn't say anything because he was recording sound—so Kieslowski would just shake the operator himself.

Angela Pope (essay date August 1996)

SOURCE: "In Memory," in *Sight and Sound,* Vol. 6, No. 8, August, 1996, p. 69.

[*In the following essay, Pope asserts that Kieslowski's* Three Colors: Blue *"tells how, as they say, life goes on, and while you are alive you have no choice but to be part of it."*]

We were there to choose Best Picture: David Leland, Harry Hook, Sally Hibbin, Mike Figgis, Simon Relph and me. Stephen Frears was late. When he finally arrived, it was quite an entry. "BAFTA owes me £7.50," he bellowed, slinging a seat stub across the table at Chairman Relph. "I paid . . . *paid* to see *Forrest Gump.*" The message was clear; no one disagreed. *Forrest Gump* was no Best Picture.

One film disposed of. That left three others: *Four Weddings and a Funeral, Pulp Fiction* and *Three Colours: Red.* No contest, to my mind. Wonderfully enjoyable though the other two were, the prize had to go to *Three Colours: Red.* Kieslowski was so masterfully in control of his resources: the script, actors, design, composition and music merging seamlessly to portray his unique moral and human landscape. A truly great film. I thought, that spoke to the heart and mind.

But there was a powerful lobby for *Pulp Fiction* and even more formidable for *Four Weddings and a Funeral.* The argument went something like this. "This is a terrific achievement." (No quibble with that.) "It's really tough to get a good looking, slick and enjoyable film out of the British industry, because we're not sufficiently practised. Mike Newell should get the gong for managing to do just that." Thus one of the great masters of contemporary cinema was passed over in favour of true Brit grit. Ah well . . .

Watching *Red* again for the jury I felt that Kieslowski was talking straight to me. It's a trick he has and I don't know how he does it. The characters are not remotely like me, their everyday dilemmas are not mine, but, in some fundamental way, I am at one with them. The film creeps into your innards and touches something deep within, something beyond reason, and sometimes profoundly hidden.

Of the films in the *Three Colours* trilogy I most admired *Red*. *White* made me laugh a lot, but *Blue* was overwhelming. I had reason to find it so. You remember the story: Julie (Juliette Binoche) survives a car accident. Her husband, a composer, and her small child are killed. She cannot take her own life, so she decides to free herself from pain by disconnecting from the past. *Three Colours: Blue* is, loosely, the Liberty part of the trilogy. Julie leaves her home, sells her possessions. She won't indulge in memory, she simply decides to blot it out.

My husband died of leukaemia not long before I first saw *Three Colours: Blue*. Before there had been an 18 month rollercoaster of hope and despair. Then, suddenly, it was over. He was gone. I didn't sell up, move out, move on. Nor did I try to blot out the past. I didn't need to because I couldn't remember it, though I tried hard enough. I wore his clothes, read the books he read, tried to speak as he spoke, think as he had thought. None of it worked; the memories stayed stubbornly erased. (Much later they would come back, without my summoning, and with startling ferocity.)

That was in private. In public it was business as usual and I worked obsessively. Life was a pageant watched through a window. I couldn't touch it, smell it or join it. I was outside the human race and, in an odd way, content to keep it that way. But nothing stays the same. Suddenly, when least expected, a feeling would come from somewhere: loneliness, fear, bitterness, anger. Awful feelings, but feelings, and through them, reluctantly, you know you're back in the business of living.

This is the story of *Three Colours: Blue;* different in detail to my own but essentially the same. It tells how, as they say, life goes on, and while you are alive you have no choice but to be part of it. Kieslowski tells his story with great delicacy, often through small, mundane incidents. In the middle of the night, Julie accidentally locks herself out of her flat. Dressed only in a T-shirt she waits in a dark, empty stairwell. Downstairs a hooker, Lucille, discreetly takes in a customer. Unseen, Julie watches. She finds mice in her flat, a mother and babies. They terrify her, but she can't kill them. A boy who witnessed her car accident goes to great lengths to find Julie. He wants to return a necklace he found at the scene of the accident. It reminds Julie of her husband and that he was telling a joke when they spun off the road. In remembering, she laughs. She discovers her husband had had a lover and that the woman is pregnant with his child. It brings an awful wave of jealousy. Olivier, a composer, is trying to complete her husband's last work and she's furious. "It isn't fair, it isn't right," she yells. But she decides to work

with him, bringing the music to life. Feelings, connections, emotions; Julie cannot avoid them. No one can.

In the final breathtaking moments of *Three Colours: Blue* Kieslowski constructs a montage of the people in Julie's life. We see the man who loves her, the boy who wears her necklace, her senile mother who barely knows her, the hooker who has reached out to her. On an ultrasound picture we see her husband's unborn child and on the soundtrack we hear, for the first time, great stretches of the concerto he was working on when he died. It is set to St. Paul's Epistle to the Corinthians (I, 13):

> Though I speak with the tongues of angels, but have not love, I speak as a hollow brass. Though I have the gift of prophesy and understand all mysteries and all knowledge, if I have not love, I am nothing. . . . Love is patient, love is kind, it bears all things. Love never fails, for prophesies shall fail, tongues shall cease, knowledge shall whither away. . . . These three, faith, hope and love shall abide. But the greatest of these is love.

Julie knows this is true. Kieslowski knew too. His work is shot through with an understanding of it and, without moralising or preaching, he asks us to know. I think he is saying that without it we cannot be truly free or alive.

Paul Coates (essay date Winter 1996-97)

SOURCE: "The Sense of an Ending: Reflections on Kieslowski's Trilogy," in *Film Quarterly*, Vol. 50, No. 2, Winter, 1996-97, pp. 19-26.

[*In the following essay, Coates analyzes the misconceptions revolving around Kieslowski's films.*]

Krzysztof Kieslowski's films have long resisted categorization. For the author of this piece, such Polish features as *Camera Buff, Blind Chance,* and *No End* had a paradoxical, teasing ability to be political without endorsing political melodramas, without dissipating the air of reality by dividing Polish society into angelic dissidents and demonic Party members, as the New Wave Polish poet and essayist Adam Zagajewski complained most Solidarity sympathizers did. This ability took them beyond "the cinema of moral unrest," a term that was nevertheless piquantly apposite for his work. Even *The Scar,* his 1976 debut feature so often termed "political," seemed rather to fuse politics with a fascinated tragic character study of a manager's fatal flaw—his urge to fix lives. The slightly misshapen quality of the film's screenplay surely reflects its groping beyond ready-made schemas of understanding. Pungently independent, corrosive of such schemas, Kieslowski's works almost court misunderstanding.

Subsequent screenplays may have been more polished, but the misunderstandings have lingered, and not just in Poland; in 1994, Tony Rayns wondered "how much of the current critical backlash against the director is founded on a mishearing of his tone of voice?" One is tempted to argue that the fame of the "late" Kieslowski films—the adjective justified by his proclaimed retirement after **Red**—is the one Rilke deemed a sum of misconceptions. But if "mystery" is a keyword in the film-maker's own discourse about his films, a full understanding may not be feasible. A film about the three watchwords of the French Revolution may look political, but billing it *"Three Colours"* pulls the flag over politics, draping them with idiosyncrasy. And while these co-productions' gloss might seemingly make them more "French" than "Polish," and disconcert admirers of the "grittier" early Kieslowski, may not gloss itself be a form of the separating glass obsessively shattered from one film to another? If *Three Colours* offers a deeply personal take on political aspiration, perhaps only equally personal reflections can even hope to begin to do it justice. Where understanding proves elusive, analysis may be condemned—or freed—to be essayistic. Such at least is the suspicion animating this piece, the ruminations of a quondam Polonist and student of Polish politics who now teaches film.

Alain Resnais once remarked puckishly that of the basic senses to which cinema appeals—sight and sound—sound matters more, for it is easier to shut one's eyes than to stop up one's ears. When Julie, the protagonist of **Blue,** loses her husband Patrice and her child in a car crash, all she wants to do is close out the world. She arranges to sell her house, first summons then rejects the love of her husband's friend Olivier, moves to an apartment, moves again when Olivier locates her, refuses interviews, and seeks to destroy her husband's last score—which is probably also her own, since rumor deemed her the writer of his music. (The question of whether or not she really was could become an irritant, but fortunately is not obtrusive: Kieslowski's approach reverses that of the eager reporter, and the vagueness finally does not seem to matter.) "You won't miss me," she tells Olivier, leaving too abruptly for him to get dressed and follow. Julie's shattering is imaged in that of the hospital window breaking, as if spontaneously, after the doctor announces her bereavement. His tiny reflection in her large pupil as she regains consciousness is no mannerist conceit, but indicates how small and distant the world now is in her eyes. The breaking glass may have metaphorical force, but the next moment recalls Kieslowski's stated distaste for metaphor: a cut shows that Julie has shattered a window to distract a nurse, gain access to the pharmacy, and take an overdose. She crams the pills in her mouth but cannot swallow.

Again and again in **Blue,** Julie closes her eyes, retreating to an inwardness of music as reflections play around her blue-lit face, outward manifestations of her otherworldliness. Again and again, however, noise jolts her into the world. Indeed, at times the film seems to have been scored more by John Cage than Zbigniew Preisner. Noise is the offscreen, the invisible, the danger Julie wants to shut out, the racket as a street brawl safely watched from her apartment window percolates up the frenzied beating on her door ending in the swish of something (someone?) being dragged away. Noise is the squeaking of the mice that terrified her in childhood and are back again now, in the room next door. It is the aftershock of the car crash to which she reacts with melancholic mourning, her conflicting urges to shatter and preserve the self—to let violence do its worst and yet find protection—issuing in the compromise formations of symptomatic wounding of a body part (scraping her hand along a wall), symbolic self-destruction (watching a garbage van chew over the last score), or burying oneself alive. In *Touching the Rock,* his remarkable autobiographical account of descent into blindness, John Hull—a Religious Education Professor who lost his sight in 1983—argues that sound "has absence built into it as its counterfoil, whereas sight does not. Sound is always bringing us into the presence of nothingness." Viewed thus, Julie's periodic entries into pure sound are dips into nothingness, like her recurrent plunges into water, and the uncannily silent images of the bungee jumpers on the TV set at her mother's nursing home are transformations of Julie herself, leaping into the abyss yet always stopping just short of death. Channeling the violence, Julie herself becomes abrupt, intransigent; a would-be interviewer says she has become rude. "Now I have only one thing to do: nothing," she tells her mother. But though she immerses herself repeatedly in the blindness mythologically linked to music, she always opens her eyes. Shutting noise out risks shutting oneself out of life, a metaphorical implication rendered image—as if by dreamwork—when she opens the door in the silence after the staircase fracas, asks if anyone's there, then hears the draught slam her own door, condemning her to a night on the landing. The antithesis of nothingness is, of course, love. Hence in the passage from 1 Corinthians 13 set to music by Patrice/Julie, nothingness summons forth love, its opposite, in the verse that states "If I have not charity, I am nothing." The antithesis is at the film's heart, though Kieslowski's penchant for "asymmetrical composition," noted by the Polish critic Tadeusz Szyma, reserves its explicit formulation for the end.

Kieslowski's film sensitizes us to sound, tempts us to watch with eyes closed, but for all the identification with Julie's numbness, in the end it shows her wakening from a trance. What wakes her has the rudeness of noise, of all awakenings; as the great 19th-century Polish poet Cyprian Norwid remarked in his essay "Silence," a sleeper cannot be woken gently. For Kieslowski, as for Norwid, silence is *a part of speech.* Julie's awakening comes when she learns of Patrice's infidelity, the illusoriness of her supposed happiness. Is it significant that the episode's keyword—*liberté*—becomes visible at this point, as she visits the Palais de Justice where Patrice's lover works? Negatively free initially, nothing left to lose, Julie sees freedom reconjugated into liberty to love, the lifting of mourning. She may flirt with death one last time, plunging into the cool blue swimming pool and remaining underwater, but in the end she comes up again, coughing. (Blue may be the color of day for night—of the night of so much of the film's early part—but it is only the cousin of darkness, not darkness itself.) After that plunge, however, she will go to Olivier as the music heard only in snatches up to this point flowers majestically around images that are a roll call of the film's characters. Even when down, seemingly out, music can sustain one, as it had the busker who—in one of the film's jokier moments—is dropped off at the street side by a patron's limousine. It may be unfortunate that Zbigniew Preisner's slightly conventional score does not quite rise to the occasion, its lack of the plangency achieved in *The Double Life of Veronique* rendering somewhat coy the reference to Van Den Budenmeyer (his pseudonym), but it is perhaps fitting that sound finally takes a back seat to the images magnificently scrolling across the dark, across the mind of Julie, with whom we end. She can open her eyes again: the worst is over.

The humor present only intermittently in *Blue* has full play in the mordant *White.* The two films' moods intersect as tangentially as its characters, Julie peeking for a moment into the courtroom—and into the trilogy's future—as Karol, the film's unhero, pleads his case against divorce. But if in *Blue* a joke can accompany death—Julie's husband repeating its punch line as he expires—perhaps humor needs to be taken more seriously. *White* does so. Karol Karol—the name a homage to Chaplin, Kieslowski says—a hairdresser divorced and rendered penniless (and impotent) by his French wife Dominique, returns to Poland, amasses a fortune by upstaging land speculators, then lures Dominique there with a report of his death and the bait of a rich legacy. Once in Poland she is accused of Karol's murder and incarcerated, as helpless before the law as Karol had been in France: *égalité*—which means getting even—has been achieved. The end shows us Karol, a tangible unperson, peering through binoculars at Dominique's cell window as she pantomimes—among other things—the placement of a ring on her finger.

Just as each section of *The Decalogue* activates several of the Ten Commandments, so each portion of *Three Colours* arguably revolves around more than one of the hallowed revolutionary watchwords, dramatizing both its own ostensible keyword and—in undertones—those of the other sections. *Liberté,* tragically achieved through loss of husband and child, has *égalité* as one subtext (Julie may have composed her husband's scores) and *fraternité* as another (to be exact—sisterhood, particularly with the prostitute whom Julie befriends). In *White,* meanwhile, Karol achieves the absolute *liberté* of the corpse and benefits from the Polish *fraternité* that abets his plot.

Initially devastated by his divorce, Karol busks in the Métro, playing on his comb the hit—"It is the Last Sunday"—that romanticized suicide for interwar Poles. The song enables a passerby to recognize a compatriot. There is *fraternité* as well as *égalité.* Recognition may be prompted by something we do not yet know: Karol's new friend, Mikolaj, is himself suicidal. Mikolaj smuggles Karol back to Poland in his suitcase (a bumpy ride, since thieves abduct Karol and are angry to find the anticipated loot a mere battered Pole with a two-franc piece in his pocket); wishing to spare his family's feelings by masking his suicide, he offers Karol a fee to kill him. Down in a subway again—the then-incomplete Warsaw one—Karol fires a blank, giving his friend the second life that so obsesses Kieslowski. "Firing blanks" could indeed be deemed the film's leitmotif. Mikolaj nevertheless presses the killing fee on Karol and helps found the business Karol wills to Dominique after feigning his own death. (Since each step eastwards increases deprivation—a theme to which I will return—a Russian corpse simulates the dead Karol.) At last the Pole has an object desirable to Westerners: capital. After Karol's mock funeral, Dominique finds him in her hotel bed, but the next morning he slips out; a complex conspiracy instigated by Karol has incriminated her in his death, and police burst in. The *égalité* Karol achieves is the effective revenge that precludes further retaliation. Although a single plan executes his desires for revenge upon and recovery of Dominique, the final tableau of him smiling through tears at her prison window is paralyzed by the fact that those desires clash. The ending's *égalité* is stalemate. Kieslowski's own description of it as happy may seem ironic, but its enigmatic art-cinema openness is nevertheless the loophole through which Dominique will escape to appear still alive, outside Poland, at the close of *Red.*

White is the only "Polish" film in Kieslowski's trilogy. Read allegorically, it dramatizes Polish fears of exclusion from Europe (fears that ramify into ones of "a second Yalta"), and thus posits and taps a ghostly persistence of the "Aesopian" reading habit once so widespread among Polish filmgoers, adept at decoding the parables directors used to outwit the censor. Is Kieslowski counting on the habit's persistence or not? Is he even counting on its persistence in the same form as Karol, officially dead but impotently present? While addressing a Western audience, *White* simultaneously summons up a more Polish hermeneutic too: with its double audience, it has a double life. One should not be surprised at its reverse echo of the asymmetrical structure of *The Double Life of Veronique* (this time moving from France to Poland). The hinted links between Karol's impotence and his presence on foreign soil may partly explain the opening's apparent anxiety to return home. Its image of a suitcase trundling along the conveyor belt is Hitchcockian, the inscrutable lengthy focus on something apparently innocent merely intimating its duplicity. Certainly Karol is more formidable once in Poland. He still carries scissors (not just the plaintive comb of his busking), the would-be thieves note, as he lunges at them. Working as a bodyguard in Warsaw, he tells his boss he does women's hair. "Is that all?" comes the leering reply. And consummation is achieved in a Warsaw hotel: as Karol lies in Dominique's bed and her hand extends towards him, the iconography of resurrection has sexual, not religious, resonance.

If *White* is to be read allegorically, its referent—wittingly or not—may include Kieslowski himself. Particularly interesting in its correlation of exclusion and cinema-going is the ending's echo of *A Short Film About Love.* In *White,* unlike *Blue,* the references to earlier Kieslowski motifs are not fitful but focused tellingly in the finale. Karol holding binoculars reincarnates both Tomek, the adolescent fixated on Magda in the opposite apartment block, and Magda herself, training her gaze on Tomek's window later on to discover his fate. Meanwhile, the prison and the question of Dominique's sentence for murder recall its companion piece, *A Short Film About Killing.* (For good measure, Karol, the ghost in his own life, resembles the dead protagonist of *No End.*) Tomek's erotic exclusion conjugates into that of the Pole before a Europe none too eager to grant admission. He is surely also the Polish artist. But where modern production conditions so restrict authorial "freedom" as to render it more and more the hunger-artist's ingenuity in creating legroom within chains, directors educated under Eastern Europe's political censorship may be well placed to thrive. All the same, Kieslowski's own freedom—like Karol's—may be the phantom of liberty. "Universalization," be it the deliberate de-Polonization of much of *The Decalogue,* or—as in *Three Colours*—the use of predominantly French themes, stars, and locales, is the price of access to the European co-production money the impoverished Polish film industry so desperately needs. Intentionally or not, *White* gains force by allegorizing Kieslowski's own possible fears and feelings about working in the West. And may not its final braiding together of multiple auto-allusions also connote a directorial sense of exclusion from oneself—from the moment at which one worked most unself-consciously—that is perhaps the final transformation of the motif of the double life in Kieslowski's oeuvre? Could systematic auto-reference be the antechamber of retirement? Allegorical readers may see Karol's vanishing, his life-in-death, as prefiguring that of the maker whose initials he shares, and take Kieslowski's avowal that the trilogy is his last work all the more seriously. (Alas, there is no longer any chance that this sentence—written before Kieslowski's death—might be proven false.)

The dominant color of *White* is less assertively present than that of *Blue*—perhaps because white itself (the anti-color of impotence because of its association with absence) is less obtrusive. It is most haunting in the agonized, lyrical flashbacks of the white wedding, which surely recurs as the fetishized moment before trauma: in court we learned that the problem followed the marriage. Karol's own appearance in the final version of the flashback is too little, too late. With the wit of metaphysical poetry, the idea of whiteness even generates an interlinguistic pun: commissioned to kill Mikolaj, Karol fires a bullet French terms *blanc.* Over and above its metaphorical reference to Karol's condition, the moment parodies the falsity of cinematic death. For all the shocked and delectable Pekinpah slow motion, it is not real, as the erstwhile documentarist well knows. The thought may well reflect Kieslowski's view of his own work. Ever more virtuoso variations on past themes dent reality less and less.

In *White* Karol, Kieslowski himself, and the spectator become homologous. Karol's impotence may be that of the Pole confronting locked European doors, his snipped credit card a severed lifeline, but even if the artist passes through them it is, like Karol, as a ghost, and he too may weep in the end as he smiles at his plot's success. And there is surely a third figure excluded here too: the viewer. Kieslowski is acutely conscious of the situation of the spectator marginalized by film's fantasy of never-ending exclusion, the impossibility of ever entering the filmic space (something whose psychoanalytic decipherment in terms of the ever-unattainable parent is sanctioned by the filmmaker's motif of frustrated love across generations). Dominique's prison window is a cinema screen. Moreover—as several critics have noted—the exquisite, strangely beguiling ending is not fully readable; there is no way of guessing what will happen next. It may haunt us just as much as it does Karol.

In *Red* a fashion model, Valentine, runs over a German shepherd dog she then returns to its owner, a retired judge engaged in illicit electronic eavesdropping. Their conversations culminate in his admission of the betrayal in love that started him eavesdropping (surely jealousy's obsession with the hidden, the bolting too late of the door of inattention). Meanwhile, Auguste, a law student whose experiences match the judge's with near-mystical precision, also suffers betrayal. At the film's end he is rescued from a ferry disaster, as is Valentine, inviting one to speculate that the judge may somehow have united them. *Red* sums up *Three Colours* by numbering the trilogy's other protagonists among the seven survivors.

As haunting as the ending of *White, Red*'s ending may be the best starting point for reflection. Like several other Kieslowski works, these films may seem to exist almost entirely for their final moments' iconic condensations of earlier themes. They become increasingly complex, gaining density and mass, until yielding the last image whose weight stuns their movement. Here it is one of Valentine, her hair sea-drenched, caught in a freeze frame against the red of an anorak, and it recalls her earlier pose in—of all things!—a chewing gum poster, one the photographer elicited by asking her to look sorrowful. Here the sorrow of mere image becomes that of the disaster's reality. It resurrects, and redeems from commodification, the poster taken down just before the storm that seems to have swept Europe. (Only here do we discover Valentine's full name, in a TV report; the moment of naming is a turning point, followed by silence.) The two images are brought to rhyme by the camera's delving into a freeze frame of Valentine beside Auguste. The moment's pregnancy suggests that he will be the one beside her when she wakes and smiles in 40 years' time, as foretold in the judge's dream. The camera's subsequent zeroing in on Valentine identifies with the judge's look, reminding us of his exclusion and her status as the girl he never met. Excising the more fortunate Auguste emphasizes the judge's exclusion from a *promesse du bonheur* whose distant glow warms him nevertheless. After all, Auguste too is now a judge, and his life has echoed the other's—with their dropped law books falling open at the right page before an exam, their lucklessness in love. Happiness achieved through one's double may be more than vicarious.

The finale's doubling and double, bittersweet perspective is fitting, for in it the scales of justice—of the law that haunts Kieslowski—achieve the balance permitting closure, the filmmaker's own Prospero-like retirement. The balance also encompasses the contrasting voices of the judge and Valentine which embodies Kieslowski's own split monologue. The judge may be retired, but Valentine switches off her answering machine, desiring peace, that Kieslowski keyword. The judge's final retreat from surveillance echoes Kieslowski's own two withdrawals—from documentary in the early 80s, from feature-making a decade later. The deepening dialogues between Valentine and the judge finally excavate the bedrock of his suffering during the storm after the fashion show, though its lightning had flickered already in the flashbulbs around the catwalk. Valentine guesses his trauma as he had guessed hers. When the judge mentions seeing his girlfriend's treachery in a mirror, a crash on the sound track catapults us into the past—the auditory, disembodied realm he inhabits—as mentally he shatters the reflection. Broken glass, that crucial Kieslowski motif, connotes unpredictability, catastrophe, the cost of relationship. Once the judge has confessed his eavesdropping, barrages of stones assail his windowpanes. Valentine's hand on the departing judge's car window imprints both the desire for relationship and its impossibility.

Red ends, much as it began, on an image of red. Like *Blue* and *White,* its references to its key color cluster most densely around the opening, with red proliferating in cars, café awnings, chairs, and so on. Where the "Polish" Kieslowski might have headlined each part by key concept, highlight-

ing key colors instead may seem more attractive to a self-consciously "post-ideological" era. Paradoxically, however, it hampers entry to the film. Mindful of the title, one cannot help noting the carrier of the keynote color rather than the whole image in which it appears, and even when the color's almost showy initial multiplication thins out, instance can still irritate. This is, I think, deliberate. Like the judge, Kieslowski will not be easy of access: the virtuosity is a smoke screen, apparent accessibility concealing deeper reserve. It is like Valentine's advertising poster, which finally metamorphoses into something deeply private, a transformation eased by its removal from the public domain, its taking down. And so, as the film deepens, dwelling increasingly within the judge's home, the key color might be said to shift to brown. Here, as in *A Short Film About Killing,* the privilege accorded red is that of the visible young female, but there is also the alternative brown world—the "brown study"—the judge inhabits, and as relationships deepen it sinks into near-total darkness. The recurrent single color seems to represent distraction, and imply that the links between characters are merely coincidental (Kieslowski underlines his disinterest in politics by refusing to connect red with the Communism that pollutes it for many Poles).

And what of the keyword of *Red, fraternité?* An early image shows Valentine so moved by her brother's image in an article on drugs that she touches it, as she later does the judge's car window, seeking to nullify distance, make media mediate. At 15, her brother Marc had learned he was not his father's son. What devastated him broadened her definition of family: strangers can be brothers. "You can't live your brother's life for him," the judge says, the apparent truism echoing Cain's truculent demand. Valentine, however, *is* her brother's keeper (Biblical morality deepens and gives substance to the revolutionary one). She tells the judge, "People aren't bad . . . they may be weak sometimes." Kieslowski may be partly of the judge's party and ironize her status as "a breath of fresh air"—"a touch of freshness," after all, is her gum poster's slogan—but she really does function as such, and can also be ironic, asking the judge who said he wanted nothing if he's still breathing. Valentine wants to act, to grasp what needs to be done. For the judge, however, her very being is action: she need only be. Since being is breathing, one need only breathe to find freshness enter in.

In *The Decalogue,* a young man materialized repeatedly at crucial moments in the protagonists' lives. Many critics have likened him to an angel. If he is, he is a recording one. Is the judge his older incarnation—the impotent angel unable to alter the lives he tracks? Is his impotence perhaps mocked by his suggested status of demiurge changing lives by flipping a coin? His drifting across sound waves can recall the angels of *Wings of Desire.* But for Kieslowski, unlike Wenders, the helpless recording angel does not enter humanity, but confronts it in the one who intervenes—Valentine, who picks up the dog she has run over, visits the judge after his trial for eavesdropping, and thinks of Auguste's flat battery when obliviousness to anything but his betrayal causes him to leave his lights on. If the recurrent hunched pensioner seeking to drop a bottle in a recycling bin had seemed a mannerism earlier in the trilogy, repetition with a difference justifies the image: Valentine helps insert the bottle, and its smashing is noise as musical reprise. One long film moving toward a finale, *Three Colours* cannot be judged prematurely, however much the distribution mechanisms that permit viewing of only one or two parts court misunderstanding. And if the recurrence of Van Den Budenmeyer can irritate, Kieslowski's own reprises are fully justified, and nowhere more so than in the last image's long-resounding final chord.

Ruth and Archie Perlmutter (essay date Winter 1996-97)

SOURCE: "A Testament to Krzysztof Kieslowski," in *Film Criticism*, Vol. XXI, No. 2, Winter, 1996-97, pp. 59-61.

[*In the following essay, the Perlmutters discuss the bio-documentary on Kieslowski's life,* Krzysztof Kieslowski—I'm So-So *by Krzysztof Wierzbicki.*]

Very much like a fortuitous event in one of his own movies, Krzysztof Kieslowski, the renowned director, consented to be in a bio-documentary shortly before his death. *Krzysztof Kieslowski—I'm So-So* was made in Denmark by Krzysztof Wierzbicki, who had worked with Kieslowski as his assistant director on *The Scar* and *Camera Buff*.

Equally fortuitous was Wierzbicki's decision to start the film with a group of professionals analyzing aspects of Kieslowski's personality. Their explanations are like eerie premonitions of Kieslowski's sudden death during heart surgery a few months after the film was shot. A cardiologist held up a set of x-rays and suggested that circulatory problems were inevitable judging from the patient's drinking habits, chain-smoking, and pressured life. As if already a memorial, a graphologist delineated the filmmaker's fine aesthetic sense, while a clairvoyant, acknowledging Kieslowski's telekinetic propensities, remarked on his ability to portray the inner lives of several people at once. Another professional added that the director sometimes seemed to assume the role of God—a provocative suggestion in the light of the problems Kieslowskian characters have with authority.

From then on, *I'm So-So* alternates Kieslowski's direct-to-camera interviews with sequences from his films, including early ones that have never been shown here (*Talking Heads* and *The Calm*). We learn that Kieslowski was always uncomfortable as a filmmaker, that indeed, he decided to make films in order to equip himself for his first love, stage direction, and that although he failed the entry exam to the prestigious film school at Lodz three times, he was tenacious and determined to pass, as a matter of pride.

Throughout the film, Wierzbicki intersperses motifs, musical strains, ideas from his mentor's film. Seated in a shanty near a lake in Poland (to which he had retired from filmmaking a few months earlier), Kieslowski explains that his early documentary films attempted to capture the emptiness of the grey, sad world of Poland under socialism through depiction of claustrophobic "micro-worlds"—the school, the factory, and the office. Yet, despite a professed ambivalence about his homeland (delineated in his writings as well as his films), Kieslowski admits that he always wants to return because he feels like a stranger abroad. In fact, in a funny sequence, he describes his dislike for the self-congratulatory tone of Americans abroad who always respond that they feel "extremely well"—while he can only say "I'm so-so" (the title of the film).

The documentary continues with Kieslowski agonizing about how his early films were manipulated for propaganda purposes. He states that when people told the truth in front of the camera, it was used against them. He deplores how he was forced to re-edit *The Calm* (which was not shown for three years) because it included images of workers on strike (a communist taboo). He was proud that despite official revision, the film sustained an intangible sense of freedom (he called it "a kind of metaphysical secret") and sprinkled his remarks with observations about his primary concerns—the necessity to describe and identify the world and the difficulty of filming real death ("Is one not entitled to die alone?"). Another time, he modestly yet mischievously asks and answers, "What do I want?—Calmness," and poignantly, "Who am I?—Just a retired film director." From time to time, he would repeat stories already told in *Kieslowski on Kieslowski* (his book of reflections) about people who had telekinetic experiences similar to those depicted in *The Double Life of Veronique,* 1991. One woman, astonished that her own experiences paralleled the coincidences in the film, asked him how he could have known her so well.

A discussion of *Camera Buff* disclosed how much the scenes of the protagonist overexposing his film and turning the camera on himself reflected Kieslowski's own angst as he discovered the power of the camera and the fact that it can be used destructively in spite of the best intentions. For all those who scan his films for autobiographical information, Kieslowski wryly revealed that although he will not tell where or why, he has often turned the camera on himself in his movies (as a non-intervening observer, like the ubiquitous angel of *The Decalogue?*). At any rate, "secrets" are very important to Kieslowski, and he is most satisfied when notions about God and afterlife are left unanswered. At one point, he states, "Not knowing is my business."

Interviewed at the Montreal Film Festival, Wierzbicki explained that Kieslowski not only approved the idea of bringing in experts to describe his idiosyncratic personality but also really got enthusiastic about the idea of being a main character, a "hero" in a film. In fact, Wierzbicki relates that he was feeling very insecure the first day of shooting, even though he had worked with Kieslowski since the early days. "Kieslowski was so much more able than anybody else—with angles, lighting, tonality." But the nervousness quickly disappeared when Kieslowski walked in with a series of costumes—different jackets and shirts—and stated, "I'm a hired man. Do what you wish with me."

Wierzbicki went on to tell the ironic story of the triumph of *Camera Buff* at the Moscow Film Festival the year it was made. Already known in Poland as a critic of the system, Kieslowski was usually given minimal resources and an innocuous story line. When *Camera Buff* was completed, it was considered harmless enough to send to the Soviet Union. Much to the surprise and chagrin of the authorities, Kieslowski was called back on the final day of the festival because he was about to be awarded the grand prize. He arrived to discover that the Russian officials had opposed the vote (considering the film subversive), but the head of the jury (from Germany) had put up a fuss and threatened to resign. A compromise was reached with the prize split three ways in order to minimize Kieslowski's victory.

In hushed tones, Wierzbicki described to us how no one was prepared for the shock of Kieslowski's death. He had gone into the heart operation as if it were a visit to the dentist and was actually annoyed that he could not try out a new car he had just bought.

An eloquent funeral oration was given by Professor Trishner, a well-known liberal priest, who ended his eulogy with: "Poland didn't understand Kieslowski? Was that the real Poland? No—Poland is here, and it understands him."

Despite his announcement the year before he died that he would retire from filmmaking, Kieslowski had already composed a treatment for a new trilogy, called *Heaven, Hell,* and *Purgatory.* Unfortunately, for the world of cineastes and Kieslowski devotees, *Blue, White,* and *Red* was followed by a tragic "Black." Kieslowski had handed down his "Ten Commandments," explored humans' highest aspirations in the *Tricolors,* and dared to postulate immanent spiritual forces in an alien world. He was finally recalled by that spirituality—possibly back into his own camera.

All the more reason now to value the magical camera that was turned on him by this tender documentation of his reflections, wry witticisms, and rare, exceptional persona . . . As was his life, his death was unpredictable.

Annette Insdorf (essay date March-April 1997)

SOURCE: "An Affectionate Look at Krzysztof Kieslowski's *Three Colors,*" in *Film Comment,* Vol. 33, No. 2, March-April, 1997, pp. 46-8.

[*In the following essay, Insdorf asserts that* "White *illustrates how Kieslowski is a cinematic 'poet,' a Polish artist whose rich audiovisual vocabulary expresses a profound vision of human fallibility, as well as transcendence.*"]

Three Colors: White is one of Krzysztof Kieslowski's deceptively simplest films. Of the trilogy, it has received the least critical attention, overshadowed by *Blue* and *Red.* But *White* illustrates how Kieslowski is a cinematic "poet," a Polish artist whose rich audiovisual vocabulary expresses a profound vision of human fallibility, as well as transcendence. Ironic but tender, his style includes haunting images that suggest spiritual forces at work in the perceptual world. Co-written with Krzysztof Piesewicz, *White* is the second part of the trilogy, which Kieslowski said derives from the colors of the French flag—the concepts of liberty, equality, and fraternity. *White,* for which he won the Best Director Prize at the Berlin Film Festival, corresponds to equality—but in the ironic sense of "getting even," or revenge. Of all three films, it is the lightest and most humorous because of its picaresque quality; nevertheless, the tone is that of very dark comedy.

Karol Karol (Zbigniew Zamachowski)—whose name literally means Charlie Charlie—loses everything in a Paris courtroom: his French wife Dominique (Julie Delpy) divorces him for not consummating their marriage. The hapless hairdresser—now bereft of home, beauty salon (which they shared), car, and credit cards—is befriended in a métro by a fellow Pole, Nikolaj (Janusz Gajos); the latter, well-to-do and world-weary, agrees to smuggle Karol back to Poland in a trunk. Upon arriving in Warsaw, the oversize valise is stolen and Karol emerges from it to find angry thieves; they beat him, throwing him down a garbage heap from which he glimpses "home, at last." His brother Jurek (Jerzy Stuhr) is delighted to have him back, but Karol is not content to remain in their hair salon. In the newly capitalist Poland, he cleverly scrambles to entrepreneurial success, aided by Nikolaj. His aim—to get Dominique back, and to get back at Dominique—is realized when he stages his own death. She arrives for the funeral, only to be visited by a very live—and sexually potent—Karol. The long-delayed consummation of their marriage is followed by his disappearance and her arrest for his "murder." The film ends with Karol secretly visiting her in prison. Each is now clearly in love with the other, but trapped in his scheme.

Kieslowski tells his story through recurring images, both visual and aural. White is the color of an innocence that characterizes Karol at the film's opening; when he later runs elatedly on a frozen pond with Nikolaj—who says he feels like a child again—white is virgin ice. From the beginning, white is associated with the flapping and cooing of birds on the soundtrack, especially pigeons. A slow-motion flashback to the wedding of Karol and Dominique shows, from the groom's point of view, her white veil as they approach the church door where pigeons are cooing.

We hear the same sound when he later sees the bust of a woman in a window, white like Dominique's alabaster skin; it is repeated when Karol cries out her name at night with the bust in the foreground. (This icon of female beauty is smashed by the airport thieves, but Karol lovingly puts it back together again—as he will do with his image of Dominique.) The sound of the bird returns with the flashback of the veil, and then the screen goes to white after they kiss in front of the pigeons. The use of white—the color of unconsummated marriage—is particularly ironic when Dominique finally has an orgasm with Karol and the screen goes to a whiteout with her screams of pleasure. By the end she is a caged bird.

But in the present tense of the film, the first thing a pigeon does is to defecate on Karol, comically foreshadowing his imminent victimization in the Paris courtroom. When we later see a bird—quite incongruously—in the métro, or flying in the warehouse where Karol buys a Russian corpse, the humor is dark indeed. Kieslowski's particularly Polish sensibility balances irony and affection for a character moving into capitalist experience (as in his *Decalogue 10,* where Zamachowski and Stuhr play brothers trying to make a fortune from their dead father's stamp collection).

Stuart Klawans's perceptive review in *The Nation* of *Three Colors: Red* adds to an understanding of Kieslowski's imagery; he describes how at the start of *White* "its color literally falls out of the sky onto the protagonist . . . in the form of a pigeon dropping; and from there on, Karol keeps getting whited out in emphatically material fashion, whether on the snowy streets of Warsaw or between the sheets with his estranged wife." One could say that he is definitively whited out when he stages his own death; however, Karol is paradoxically making his mark.

Kieslowski's ironic tone is equally present in, and a product of, other cinematic elements, including music, casting, and direction of actors, and visual style. Broke and homeless in the Paris métro, Karol plays on his comb "The Last Sunday," a popular Polish wartime song; the melody is what draws Nikolaj to him. After they get spacious new offices in Poland, Karol plays the song on a comb again, reminding Nikolaj how far they have come.

In a larger sense, the original score by Zbigniew Preisner is narrative rather than ornamental. Whereas he composed a symphony for *Blue* and a bolero for *Red,* he created a tango for *White.* This Argentine musical form is appropriate to Kieslowski's pattern; the tango is simultaneously lyrical, playful, and deliberate—like Karol's scheme.

The tango music begins after Karol has returned to Poland, and it accompanies his intricate planning. As anyone who has ever essayed an Argentine tango knows, the man is in control; even if the high-heeled, swirling-skirted woman is the one who does the flashy steps, she can move only to the extent that the man's hand—quietly but insistently controlling the bottom center of her back—allows her to. As Karol becomes increasingly self-confident via his wealth, he manipulates Dominique in an elaborate—if long-distance—dance. (And, like a good poem, the tango can express romantic longing through formal constraints.)

Kieslowski's casting and direction of actors are as supple as the tango form. Zamachowski's Karol, true to his name, is a Chaplinesque figure who strikes back resourcefully. Delpy's Dominique is in charge on French soil, but vulnerable once in Poland. Although Kieslowski considered Julie Delpy for *The Double Life of Véronique* (the part finally went to Irène Jacob), her distinctive French quality makes her more appropriate to *White.* (Delpy's fair skin is beautifully photographed by Edward Klosinski, whose credits range from Andrzej Wajda's *Man of Marble* to Krzysztof Zanussi's *Camouflage.*)

The visual style of *White* is as playful as Preisner's tango. The opening credits are over a trunk arriving at an airport—a mysterious image that will turn out to be the way that Karol is smuggled, passportless, to Poland. The flashforward is used again in brief shots of Dominique entering a hotel room while we hear Karol's breathing: these prefigure her arrival in Warsaw. Flashforwards embody a predetermined universe; what will happen later is already "printed" on film, so things cannot but transpire as they do.

The understated irony typical of Kieslowski continues when Karol says "home at last" after being dumped by the thieves. Home is a Warsaw about which the director remarked, "The political and economic upheavals taking place in Poland, the result of years spent under an ultimately rejected system, had created a picturesque and photogenic muddle. It's possible to buy anything in Warsaw today: a tank, a kilo of uranium, houses whose owners have disappeared, forged passports, stolen cars, a birth certificate, a real or fake university diploma. This is the world in which our simple story unfolds."

It is a world in which religion has little function. Despite the traditional importance of the church in Poland, **White** shows it as "useful" only in two senses: When Karol has succeeded in outwitting the gangsters for whom he works, he combs his hair in the reflection from a religious painting. And when the gangsters realize they have been duped and try to kill him, Karol foils them with the declaration that his will leaves everything to the church. They are forced to buy back from him the land he purchased.

Kieslowski's irony includes the fact that Karol returns to Poland, the opposite of his fellow Eastern Europeans leaving for the West. As the director put it, "In Poland we say, 'Everyone wants to be more equal than everyone else.' It's practically a proverb. And it shows that equality is impossible: it's contradictory to human nature. Hence, the failure of Communism. But it's a pretty word, and every effort must be made to help bring equality about . . . keeping in mind that we won't achieve it."

Despite the clarity of his images, there is an ambiguity throughout Kieslowski's work: the piercing intelligence he brings to the screen is refreshingly free of didacticism. He called himself an artisan or craftsman rather than an artist because "artists have the answers. I pose questions." He offers the concreteness of details, but with metaphysical weight—like a two-franc coin that seems to stick to Karol's palm.

When asked what he was trying to capture with closeups, the director said, "Perhaps the soul. In any case, a truth which I myself haven't found. Maybe time that flies and can never be caught." This comment leads to the end of the film, in which the camera—representing Karol's point of view in the prison courtyard—moves into a closeup of Dominique's face behind bars. The camera "removes" the bars via a zoom shot, so that the image of her shifts from imprisoning to liberating. Her hands play out a little scene—no, she doesn't want to escape from prison; she will stay so that they can remarry—as tears roll down Karol's face. Kieslowski called it a happy ending because they both realize they love each other: "Would you rather for the story to finish with him in Warsaw and her in Paris, with both of them free but not in love?" he asked.

The context of the trilogy provides support for the director's atypical optimism. The final sequence of **Red,** a ferry accident, reunites the major characters of all three turns. Like a miniature Noah's ark, a lifeboat carries from the accident a pair of lovers from **Blue,** a pair from **Red,** as well as Karol and Dominique. She presumably got out of prison, and returned with renewed love to her ex-husband. **Red** culminates

in reconciliation even if **White** ends in limbo, with Karol just as trapped as Dominique: equality indeed.

But this is perhaps the point of departure from which the relationship can finally work. Karol, who is impotent in Paris (invoking on a political level Eastern Europe's impotence in the West), must die and resurrect himself in Poland for the relationship to resume. (Kieslowski needed the economic support of French-based Marin Karmitz to produce the trilogy, while the producer needed the director's art—an added East-West symbiosis.) Death and resurrection figure prominently in **White,** beginning with Nikolaj's disconcerting offer to Karol: he knows a man who wants to kill himself but is unable to, and will pay someone to shoot him. Karol accepts, arrives in the designated place, and finds that the suicidal target is none other than Nikolaj—who pays him and insists that he fulfill the mission. Karol shoots him. But he has used a blank, and when Nikolaj opens his eyes, Karol asks if he is sure that he still wants to go through with it. Having almost died is enough. The two go out drinking instead.

Karol, too, stages his own death; but as with Nikolaj, it is deceptive, and death turns out not to be the answer. Both "die" to be reborn; each gets a second chance—a theme that permeates the trilogy. In **Blue,** the heroine (Juliette Binoche) loses her husband and child in a car crash; death is the point of departure for a woman who, by the end of the film, has earned her own second chance at life.

In **Red,** the opening credit sequence consists of someone dialing a phone number (which the camera follows in an exhilarating physical trajectory as Kieslowski enters the filaments of phone cables, conveying the technological path of the human spirit); the line is busy. "Redial"—which could serve as the subtitle of Kieslowski's oeuvre—enables the call to be placed again; this time contact is made.

The story of **Red** gives the character of the aged judge (Jean-Louis Trintignant) a second chance by Valentine (Irène Jacob) to be human; at the end of the trilogy, she too is given a second chance—whether by fate, God, or the judge-as-magician—to escape the ferry disaster and be "reborn" together with a younger version of the judge. When the film was completed, Kieslowski stated that he was exhausted and would make no more movies after **Red:** was he staging his own professional death in order to be born again?

As we approach the millennium, **Three Colors** seems a timely work: at the end of a century riddled with mistakes, Kieslowski's characters enact an ultimately compassionate scenario. Karol and Dominique, for example, will get another opportunity to love each other—now that they are "equal" after mutual emotional violence. In this regard, the symmetry of the director's images—including variations on white, pigeons, male gaze, song-on-comb, telephones, and faked death—nourishes the notion of second chances: repetition becomes accumulation, with a prior mistake as a base for successful action.

At the beginning, Karol stares up at Dominique's Paris window; unable to bear the sight of a man's silhouette next to hers, he phones her hysterically. At the end, he stares up silently at her window in the Warsaw prison. The second time, Dominique returns his gaze—and with love. Having overcome language barriers, their communication is wordless (in a scene that calls back to silent movies). Separated in space, they are nevertheless united by Kieslowski's expressive technique—a poetic blend of camera placement, movement, editing, music, and vision.

Ruth Perlmutter (essay date Winter 1997-98)

SOURCE: "Testament of the Father: Kieslowski's *The Decalogue*," in *Film Criticism*, Vol. XXII, No. 2, Winter, 1997-98, pp. 51-65.

[*In the following essay, Perlmutter asserts, "Although glimmers of hope and oxymoronic moments of a kind of desperate joy temper the suffering throughout the ten films [of Kieslowski's* The Decalogue], *their message is clear—the Ten Commandments exist in our consciousness but are most often beyond our realization.*"]

The Decalogue marks an important midpoint in Krzysztof Kieslowski's career. As a kind of serialized melodrama, it consolidates his move from documentary to fiction after he first explored the disadvantages of the documentary form (the "truth-telling" genre) in his early fiction film, *Camera Buff*. The ten episodes are also building-blocks for the four feature films—*The Double Life of Veronique* and *Blue, White* and *Red*—that follow. Similar narrative situations are fleshed out; character types and visual forms persist as thematic moral connotations deepen.

Although with *The Decalogue*, Kieslowski ostensibly abandoned political issues for more universal moral concerns, in a Kieslowski film, the personal cannot be severed from the political. The struggles of his characters with identity, career options and parental responsibilities, emanate from Kieslowski's ambivalence towards his own repressive "father"-land, which seems to hover in judgment over his Polish characters like a vengeful Old Testament patriarch.

In *The Decalogue*, Kieslowski intensifies forms and metaphors that relate to basic issues, like the attempt to "save" family and children from dangers that range from human pride and petty rivalries to deep moral corruption. He calls

attention to these concerns with a ubiquitous angel-like figure who haunts the various segments. Functioning as a silent witness to their futile efforts at liberation and self-realization, the "angel" underscores the tremendous emotional cost to Kieslowski's morally confused characters in their desire to change life patterns.

Since the Polish filmmaker's untimely death, his films more than ever seem like ghost stories—not the horror film variety, of course, but the visionary kind, as in the works of Tarkovsky and Wenders. Kieslowski's ghosts are spiritual and cinematic emanations of some internalized moral conscience that grows in proportion to his sadness about Poland and human powerlessness. In his corporeal absence, Kieslowski has now begun to function as an authorial ghost whose phantom presence inhabits his cinema.

In his early fiction films—*Camera Buff, Blind Chance,* and *No End*—Kieslowski's protagonists try to escape the entrapment of their highly-charged politicized world, but they pay a heavy price. At the end of *Camera Buff*, Filip, a budding documentary filmmaker, abandons family and job and turns his camera on himself, subsumed by his new occupation. Determined to film in a society rife with moral ambiguities and hidden political agendas, knowing that freedom can be exercised at the expense of others, Filip chooses to record his interior life rather than risk the possibility that his work might be modified and used in the interest of the state. His life and philosophy become the material for his creative work when, symbolically, in his final reflexive gesture, he passes through his "looking glass," and, like Alice-in-Wonderland, enters his own dream world.

The search for self-realization that leads Filip to his painful abandonment of documentary filmmaking parallels Kieslowski's own dissatisfaction with state manipulation of this so-called objective genre. With fiction as his new mode, the Polish filmmaker could critique the government by implication as he probed sub-surface reality (sex, death, internal feelings) not accessible to the documentary form.

Although in Kieslowski's early fiction films after *Camera Buff*, his characters become increasingly resentful of political intervention and the wretched state of affairs in Poland under socialism, they also feel victimized by the vagaries of chance and coincidence. His next film, *Blind Chance,* is about absent or misguided "fathers" and personal goals that conflict with state or familial responsibilities. A cynical film about the capricious outcome of human choices, *Blind Chance* follows a medical student named Witek through three alternative stories and three different compromises, all of which end with his inability to escape from Poland. In the various segments, Witek succumbs to political and peer pressure, waffles on moral responsibilities, agonizes over his uneasy relationship with his father, and finally, when he chooses an ostensibly neutral apolitical career, he is nevertheless frustrated by "blind chance." For all his protestations of freedom of choice and attempts to evade political machinations and oedipal duties, Witek is trapped in a world ruled by expediency, human frailty, father substitutes, and in the end, death.

Despite the clumsy handling of the three-part sections, *Blind Chance* represents the beginnings of Kieslowski's commitment to a form of serial narrative that poses what-if questions about life-style choices. The film's strength comes from the suggestion that despite its denial of a traditional single-line story, the protagonist is still essentially trapped—because he has been shaped by a common environment within an oppressive system (specifically, Poland under socialism).

Most of Kieslowski's characters are severely constrained in their efforts to adopt alternative life-styles. Filip renounced all social ties to gain a pyrrhic independence. *Blind Chance* gave its hero three chances to get out of Poland. Rather than accept tyranny, the female protagonist of Kieslowski's next film, *No End,* "chooses" suicide to join the ghost of her dead husband, a betrayed Solidarity lawyer. A lugubrious tonality throughout the film expresses the unbearable heaviness of living in Poland. With a musical score that is like a lament, the film is a jeremiad about the state as the punitive "father" of a country racked by purges, rigged trials, and growing anomie. Fundamentally renouncing state-controlled "professionalism" (the form of socialism in Poland under martial law), *No End* suggests that the only "happy ending" (the film's original ironic title) is to join the virtuous departed souls. They are all around us, Kieslowski claimed, as spectral reminders of our unexamined moral obligations. For all the denials and rejections that pervade *Camera Buff* and *Blind Chance,* none equal the harsh indictment of Poland under martial law in *No End.* With human action both base and fruitless, the only recourse for the morally pure in Kieslowski's homeland, lies in departure—in death.

Given Kieslowski's history of translating the malaise and frustration of aspirations in post-communist Poland into stories of oedipal and other patrimonial conflicts, it seems fitting that his last Polish project, *The Decalogue,* is loosely based on the ultimate patriarchal proscriptions, the ten "Thou shalt nots" of the Old Testament. Kieslowski himself has described the films as "cries of alarm," warnings of bleakness and evil in a country cut adrift from autocratic socialism and without re-established moral standards.

Born out of Kieslowski's desire to focus on decent people faced with "essentially fundamental, human and humanistic questions," the ten one-hour films were apparently designed as apolitical melodramas. Made for Polish television, they use strategies of multiple characters acting out typical TV-soap situations, like family problems and issues of distress or disaster, that take place in a single locale. Yet they refrain from the high production values, glamorous stars, and romantic notions about heroism common to mainstream narratives.

The ten sections of these fables unfold in a minimal Warsaw housing project where neighbors live in an atmosphere of anonymity and occasional hostility. Moving within a wide range of human weakness, from vanity to murder, almost every character prevaricates, some steal, while others engage in adultery or voyeurism. Generally in states of anxiety or anguish, they find themselves on paths that lead to terrible self-reckoning. Questions about parenting (from adoption to incest) are present in almost every segment, as are biblical allusions to the sins of the fathers and attempts to love one's neighbor. Often, more than one injunction is inferred in a particular segment, and at times, the same characters, motifs, and moral questions reappear in other sections.

These connections are reinforced by parodic counterpoints or reversals among the segments. The first two stories, for example, are both concerned with characters who attempt to defy commandments one and three: playing God as a form of blasphemy, they rely on their belief in the certainty of human reason. In *Decalogue 1,* an intellectual convinced of scientific infallibility makes an erroneous prediction and loses his only son; in *Decalogue 2,* a doctor who has lost his own world (his family during the war), gives what turns out to be a false prognosis (that a patient will die) in order to "save" an unborn child.

These first two parts of *The Decalogue* pose unresolved or ambiguous questions that thread the entire series—about parental responsibilities and "saving" children from potential disasters. In *Decalogue 3,* an illicit love affair threatens to spoil a family gathering on Christmas day, but paternal duty prevails. After a night riddled with schemes, lies, and betrayals by an ex-mistress, the protagonist returns to his home and rejects a romantic liaison in favor of family and fidelity. *Decalogue 4* is an enigmatic rendering of the fifth commandment to honor one's parents. Although it is unclear whether a sealed letter is opened which may state that the man who reared the protagonist is not her real father, the letter serves a salutory function. It gives both characters a chance to strike a balance between an unanswered biological question and a shared emotional history as father and daughter.

Decalogue 5, which relentlessly explores the commandment against killing, including capital punishment, is concerned with a young murderer, alienated from societal connections and made brutish by urban inhumanity and an indifferent state bureaucracy. As in so many of Kieslowski's works, the patriarchy, both familial and socio-political, is held accountable for tragic consequences.

In another reversal of similarities between two sequences, *Decalogue 6* also centers on a callow youth who suffers from a lack of familial or cultural sustenance, but instead of becoming a killer, he turns against himself after multiple infractions—stealing, eavesdropping, and lying. In *Decalogue 7,* about two mothers who battle over the possession of a child they share, a shameful teen-age pregnancy, abduction, and Solomonic questions about the nature of "true" parenting are couched in a nexus of lovelessness that has passed on from one generation to another.

With the commandment against bearing false witness as its basis, *Decalogue 8* concerns a professor of ethics who, ironically, is confronted with a moral decision she made during the Holocaust that could have doomed a Jewish child. *Decalogue 8* directly questions the dictates of conscience and personal responsibility when faced with the possibility of "saving" a life, especially that of a child.

Like *Decalogue 6, Decalogue 9* is also about lying, voyeuristic eavesdropping, sexual jealousy, and attempted suicide. Unlike *Decalogue 6,* however, this sequence ends on a positive note with a decision to adopt a child and an affirmation of the strength of love, marriage, and family.

With wry wit (echoed again in *White*), *Decalogue 10* parodies the idea of the sins of the fathers. Two brothers left with their father's legacy of a valuable stamp collection are plagued by cheating, robbery, and betrayal until they realize that their filial attachment is their real inheritance. The ironic tonality of *Decalogue 10* illuminates how much Kieslowski shares the special Eastern European comic sensibility born of human myopia and impotence.

Together with the team that collaborated with him from *No End* through *The Tricolors* (*Blue, White, Red*), Kieslowski created his own brand of visionary-moral realism. Luminous images, filtered plays of light, mesmeric music, and frequent use of parallels and premonitions combine to transmute prosaic life into lyrical meditations on the fragility of existence. In Kieslowski's metaphoric cinema, mysterious occurrences erupt like poltergeists responding to a world in disarray, as in *Decalogue 1,* where an ink bottle spills without cause and a computer starts up on its own. His is a discomfiting style that conveys both the unexplained immanence behind the surface of objective experience and the malaise of his sympathetic but morally weak characters.

Although nine different cameramen worked on *The Decalogue,* the entire series shares a consistency of tone, texture, and hallucinatory cinematic rhetoric. Characters are usually plunged in semi-darkness and observed across courtyards or along dingy corridors. They see and are seen only partially. Separated by framed devices (doors, windows, mirrors, louvers) and connected by a series of visual skewers, they meet and interact, grope towards each other in a tapestry of coincidence, subliminal communication, and unspoken need.

Habitual crossovers of intersecting characters and coincidental encounters become weighty, mysterious signifiers. Protagonists in one series turn up as minor characters in another. In *Decalogue 5,* the dying man and his wife, who play prominent roles in *Decalogue 2,* are waiting for a cab, as if anxiously en route to the hospital, and they are treated rudely by the taxicab driver. Certain motifs recur across sequences: candles and altars in *Decalogue 1* and *8* act as ironic icons of revelation; milk as a symbol of purity and, when spilt, a metaphor for lack of nurturing, reappears in *Decalogue 1, 4, 6;* in almost every segment, characters make bets or play games of chance as if believing they can control their own destinies. Suggesting the hostility bred by a repressive society, each section has its share of antagonistic or indifferent people. Sometimes a single banal moment in one episode takes on added meaning in another. When the father in *Decalogue 4* has unwillingly admitted his sexual attraction to his adopted daughter, he picks up a toy bear, which reminds him of his paternal role. The toy turns up again in *Decalogue 7,* where the little girl's real father turns out to be a maker of toy bears, while the segment as a whole is concerned with the difficult distinction between a biological and a surrogate parent.

In almost every sequence, bizarre metaphoric moments punctuate the overall somberness and become satirical reminders of human folly and moral ambivalence. In *Decalogue 3,* a melodramatic situation is interrupted when the harassed couple enter the vast space of a railroad station late at night and discover a female guard skate-boarding along the empty corridors. In *Decalogue 8,* after an elderly ethics professor has been forced to confront her failure to fulfill a past promise, she meets a contortionist, who invites her to mimic his wild flexibility. The physical distortions echo the casuistic manipulation of her moral values when faced with the opportunity to save a child.

Despite all the common elements, however, each episode of *The Decalogue* has its own individual thematic and formal emphasis. In *Decalogue 5,* green filters exaggerate the already yellowed, dingy urban setting. Almost all ancillary characters are dyspeptic and inhospitable, creating an atmosphere for the alienation of the sociopathic killer. Motifs of thrown or suspended objects foreshadow the detailed and dramatic execution by hanging. In the first shots, a wet rag is carelessly thrown down from a window above as a sign of the indifference of the residents; the disturbed protagonist chases away the pigeons of a complaining old woman; he watches a violent gang attack, then hurls rocks at cars from an overhead trestle; later, expressing repressed frustration, he plays with the cord that becomes the murder weapon.

Like an ironic talisman of brutality by state, individual, or even the crass murdered taxidriver, a miniature severed head with a grotesque smile hangs ominously from the rearview mirror of the victim's taxicab.

In *Decalogue 6,* reflexive doublings, optical devices and distancing camera views evoke the voyeurist theme of *Rear Window.* Maternal issues are elaborated in *Decalogue 7* by continuous references to children. The segment opens with the sounds of a crying child being soothed by a surrogate mother. Later, after a school play, her real mother, still a child herself, abducts her own daughter and takes her to the home of her child's father, a toymaker, where the little girl lies ensconced against his stuffed bears. In *Decalogue 9,* associative editing creates foreboding connections. As in F. W. Murnau's *Nosferatu* and Jean Vigo's *L'Atalante,* the couple seems to respond to each other telekinetically—at a distance. The wife awakens with a start just as her husband has a biking accident. Other ominous warnings are made by cuts to an unanswered telephone or by the repetition of the parallel white lines of two different highways—as her bus speeds home and he bikes towards disaster.

Starting with a shot of dead fish in an aquarium and a coffin thrusting towards us, *Decalogue 10* is filled with images of entrapment. Alarms, locks, nailed-down windows, and a ferocious watchdog represent the extraordinary measures taken by the two brothers, heirs to their dead father's valuable stamp collection. The punk rock song (from the group called "City Death") that begins and ends the episode adds a satirical note of defiance against all the commandments ("Everything belongs to you," so kill, steal, covet, etc.), and ultimately, against all "fathers."

This modern version of the Cain and Abel story, as well as its lesson about the malevolence of materialism, brings *The Decalogue* back full cycle to *Decalogue 1,* the segment most heavily invested with Biblical imagery and the eternal conflict between man and God. Structured like a fundamentalist tract that invokes both Testaments, *Decalogue 1* moves the main character along the path from transgression (the breaking of the first commandment due to idolatrous worship of science and reason) to punishment (the carrying out of an Abraham/Isaac sacrifice), then anger, and finally, to a kind of desperate understanding and acceptance. In frustration and pain, the protagonist overturns an altar of lit candles and watches the wax run down the face of a Byzantine icon, matching his own tears. Then he kneels and out of a wooden trough lifts up a luminous frozen disc, a lens of milky glass like his blurred vision and tragic enlightenment. In despair, he presses the wafer to his face, as an act of acquiescence to the "Host."

This stuff of transmutation, miracle, and revelation play counterpoint to the protagonist's belief in the certainty of human reason. Nowhere is his hubris more poignantly revealed than in the sequence where he delivers a lecture on the computer as a linguistic intelligence that will one day be capable of an act of choice. Meanwhile, the boy, a spectator in the back of the auditorium, manipulates a slide projector that creates a parallactic view of his father's image. It is as if the boy, already sensitized to spiritual matters (by the absence of his mother, the piety of his aunt, and his foreboding experience of finding a dead dog), perceives his adored father within the frame of human limitations. The child thereby puts into question the father's prognostication that a machine will someday be capable of judgment. The notion of the fallibility of human reason is embedded in the projector's partial field of vision, while the rectangular screens of the computer and television mock myopic reality. Meanwhile, the juxtaposition of gazes between the boy and the dismantling shots of his father is crosscut with the recurring image of a strange witness to the father's tragic transgression. Seated beside his campfire, this non-intervening "angel" turns to look off-screen, as if towards impending exterior forces. With the interpolation of luminous substances and cinematic references, Kieslowski synthesizes presence and absence, matter and spirit, real and illusion. All the signs coalesce to warn of the danger inherent in human pretension to the role of creator. The commandment to believe in the ineffable is pervasive in a multitude of metaphors: the primordial elements (fire, ice, water), the use of liquid substances to suggest the miraculous (a cracked milk bottle, spilt ink, melting wax that forms tears on a religious icon), the Godlike eye of a self-generating computer, and the presence of a strange witness who appears and vanishes at crucial moments. The injunction of the second commandment against the graven image is reinforced by the haunting subliminal image of the absent boy on the pernicious TV screen.

The Decalogue, Kieslowski's last Polish production, sums up a number of his central concerns. Its brooding, crepuscular tonality is in keeping with the desperate world of its characters, isolated in the misguided belief that they can direct their own lives. Writing about the feature films that extended *Decalogue 5* and *6,* Charles Eidsvik indicates how they reflect Kieslowski's despair about his "moribund land" and suggests that in such an alienating country, murder in *Decalogue 5* provides a way of escape, while voyeurism in *Decalogue 6* represents a pathetic means of trying to connect with others.

As if it were possible to control their fates, even change their country, history, and their very bodies, Kieslowski's characters make bets, play games of chance, and attempt to strike moral bargains. The thematic notion that human experience is unpredictable and devoid of wished-for alternatives is reinforced by consistent narrative strategies. Kieslowski's propensity for serial (or omnibus) narration is energized by his revision of traditional angel movie yearnings to rectify old mistakes.

Seriality as a form of narrative provides a canvas that allows for changes in character and complexity rather than the simplicity of a central consciousness with only one outcome within a discrete film. Since so many of Kieslowski's multiple characters, especially in the Polish films, usually end up only partially achieving their dreams or a second chance, serial narration also demonstrates the tenet that it is impossible to change character or role. It is as if the absent creator has tried every device to help his characters alter their life plans, yet, ultimately, they can never totally escape—themselves, destiny, or their author.

Filip, in *Camera Buff,* discovers that living a life according to movies and outside of conventional societal traps results in a bittersweet solipsism. In *Blind Chance,* the protagonist tries three alternatives, all of which end up demonstrating a lack of moral certainty, either within institutions or privately. In *No End,* death is paradoxically the only hope for a better life.

In *The Decalogue,* a group of characters living within a single realm blindly and ineffectually grope for guidelines, only to discover that the universe is really ruled by indifferent chance. Their moral confusion is further exploited by the non-diegetic presence of an apparent "angel," who, contrary to most of the benevolent spirits of traditional angel movies, does not intervene or offer flawed characters a second lease on life.

A persistent presence, the angel-like "young man" (as Kieslowski refers to him throughout the script), is mute and outside the diegetic events. Though sometimes noticed, he barely makes eye contact and has little interaction with the other characters. Yet in each segment he has some symbolic significance, since he appears in different guises, crops up at critical moments, and often serves as either counterpoint or catalyst for the actions of the protagonists. In *Decalogue 1,* in startling contrast to the professor's highly structured life-style, he is a homeless person, sitting outdoors near the fateful frozen lake beside a makeshift campfire. Once, as if in anticipation of the imminent tragedy, he appears to wipe away a tear, and for a fleeting moment, the professor connects the "angel's" disappearance from his accustomed post with the horrifying premonition of his son's accident.

In *Decalogue 2,* the mysterious stranger is a hospital technician who appears twice in sequences that concern important moral decisions. He walks by just as the doctor is absorbing dire information about his patient and reappears when the adulterous wife tells her critically ill husband that she loves him. In *Decalogue 3,* the "young man's" trolley almost collides with the taxi of the protagonist who is hell-bent on an obsessive, ultimately questionable mercy trip.

The "angel" turns up again in *Decalogue 4* rowing a kayak at the moment when the young daughter appears to decide not to open a fateful letter. In fact, in a series of crosscuts as he nears her on shore, she seems to return his gaze, while an assertive musical accompaniment suggests the possibility that he may be an almost telekinetic restraining influence. The music resumes later, just as the "young man," carrying his kayak, passes by at the episode's moment of "truth." The daughter has convinced her assumed father (whom she had accused of lying) that she too had lied about opening the letter, and they return to their original familial relationship.

In *Decalogue 5,* the "young man" is a land surveyor who crosses the path of the fateful murder vehicle and seems to shake his head in a disapproving "no." As if subliminally warned, the prospective murderer shrinks back into the shadows, but only for an instant, since he subsequently commits the heinous act. The "young man" is seen again during the trial seated next to an older woman in tears (who could be the murderer's mother) and just before the idealistic attorney learns that he has a newborn son. Thus, the "angel" is present at a paradoxical moment, where a reminder of the defendant's blighted childhood and imminent death is counterpointed by signs of birth and hope.

The intersection of encounters in *Decalogue 6* occurs at two highly charged moments. Happily returning from his first meeting with the woman on whom he had spied from a distance, Tomek bumps into the "angel" and says "sorry." They pass each other again just after the young woman, in mockery of Tomek's naiveté, has induced him to premature ejaculation. Thus, the "angel" is present at both self-awareness and disillusionment. He reappears in *Decalogue 8* as one of the students in an ethics class when difficult moral questions are discussed. The editing choices at that moment—a series of shots between him and the ethics professor—suggests that he functions as a conscience for the contentious issues exemplified throughout the series. In *Decalogue 9,* he is a biker who impassively observes the attempted suicide of the frustrated husband.

This puzzling non-diegetic presence provokes contemplation. Is the figure some allegorical reminder that filial relations as well as ambivalent choices can fail when commandments are broken? Is he a witness, a foreboding of accountability? to the characters? to ourselves? And from whom? And would intervention alter the outcome of choice? Are film spectators guilty of eavesdropping, like Kieslowski's voyeurs—Tomek in *Decalogue 6,* the impotent husband in *Decalogue 9*—and therefore, are they already dimly aware of the angel as an omnipresent witness to their own transgressions?

In his silence, marginality, and non-intervention, the angel-like figure suggests that there is neither easy solution nor metaphysical release in Kieslowski's world of characters who try to navigate some moral field out of the trivia of their daily existence and symbiotic interdependencies. On their own, within shifting perspectives, glimmers of regret, and crises of consciousness, they can only divine that they might have loved better or acted with more humility and courage. Ultimately, the young man may be a narrative connective to a shared, dimly remembered origin of sin, abandonment, and obsession that binds us in a universal fate, the tragi-comic human condition of corporeality.

Now that Kieslowski is dead, the ephemeral and yet visible presence of the angel of *The Decalogue* takes on an even more ghostly meaning, especially in the light of a documentary made just before his death, Krzysztof Wierzbicki's *I'm So-So . . . A Film On Krzysztof Kieslowski.* At one point in the bio-film, Kieslowski wryly reveals that, although he will not tell where or why, he has often secretly turned the camera on himself in his films.

Whether or not this intensely spiritually aware "agnostic mystic" (as he describes himself) has consciously inserted himself, Kieslowski's characters are haunted surrogates for his cinematic "passion"—a quasi-religious mission to use the camera as an ethical conscience that will surmount conformity and external repression in a world eroded by compromise and self-delusion. His commitment to a transcendent cinema is expressed in magical realist forms and metaphors: oblique angles, refractive light, repeated images of water and other liquid substances, atmospheric effects, things that move as if on their own, distorted "mirror" shots, and "bliss" images (like prismatic effects and radiant emanations) that seem to light his characters from within and convey a sense of weightlessness.

If, as Kieslowski claims, filmmakers really make only one film all their lives, then the most indelible image of his career is the ghost lurking behind the screen, hiding inside the camera lens, and hovering over Poland, urging us to reverse the decline of freedom and morality and to reestablish a spiritual world that will find compassion for the powerless and the perplexed.

Although the ten character studies of frailty or hubris serve as pretexts for displaying the futility of political or social action in Poland, they are also a fertile setting for Kieslowski's preoccupation with the tenuous balances among pragmatism, desire, freedom, and the relationship between man and God. According to Kieslowski, God may be the "absolute judge" who exacts obedience, but he is also absent and therefore remains only an "ideal reality" or "point of reference," against which we inevitably resist, rebel—and sin. For Kieslowski as for Kafka, guilt is presumed, sin inevitable, questions have no certain answers, and the knowledge of universal laws exists without the lawgiver. In a sense, the Ten Commandments were handed down *because* of God's absence, and we live with both the freedom and the dread of disobedience. In Kieslowski's brand of emotional nihilism, we may think of ourselves as free agents, but we are really governed by irresistible passions and biological imperatives. Even without the threat of punishment by the state, human nature, according to Kieslowski, cannot readily follow its own principles of moral behavior. Although glimmers of hope and oxymoronic moments of a kind of desperate joy temper the suffering throughout the ten films, their message is clear—the Ten Commandments exist in our consciousness but are most often beyond our realization.

FURTHER READING

Criticism

Combs, Richard. "The Game-Player of Lodz." *Times Literary Supplement,* No. 4782 (25 November 1994): 16-17.
> Discusses Kieslowki's career and asserts that "many of Kieslowski's artistic decisions amount to, not escapism exactly, but an almost pedantic need to define himself, to insist on not being where he doesn't want to be, on not serving a purpose he doesn't want to serve."

Iordanova, Dina. Review of *Kieslowski on Kieslowski,* by Krzysztof Kieslowski. *Slavic Review* 54, No. 1 (Spring 1995): 168-69.
> Lauds *Kieslowski on Kieslowski* for "reflect[ing] the important presence of the director in humanity's discourse in these times of uncertainty and anxiety."

Romney, Jonathan. Review of *La Double Vie de Véronique,* by Krzysztof Kieslowski. *Sight and Sound* 1, No. 11 (March 1992): 42-3.
> Discusses the complexity and paradoxes of Kieslowski's *La Double Vie de Véronique.*

Additional coverage of Kieslowski's life and career is contained in the following sources published by Gale: *Contemporary Authors,* Vols. 147, 151.

Elmore Leonard
1925-

American novelist.

The following entry presents an overview of Leonard's career through 1997. For further information on his life and works, see *CLC,* Volumes 28, 34, and 71.

INTRODUCTION

The author of such best-selling novels as *Stick* (1983) and *Get Shorty* (1990) Leonard has been lauded as one of the finest contemporary crime writers in the United States. His gritty accounts of urban life feature the exploits of lower-class characters trying to make fast money and are often set in the locales of southern Florida and Detroit. Although he began writing during the 1950s, Leonard did not receive widespread attention until the 1980s. Since then he has enjoyed a broad and loyal readership. The film adaptations of his novels, including *Mr. Majestyk* (1974), *Fifty-two Pickup* (1974), *Stick,* and *Get Shorty,* have further enhanced his popularity. Biographer David Geherin noted: "Leonard's fiction represents a major achievement in crime writing. . . . In their artistry, originality, and impact, Leonard's novels deserve a permanent place beside those of [Dashiell] Hammett and [Raymond] Chandler on the shelf marked simply Outstanding American Fiction."

Biographical Information

Leonard was born in New Orleans and grew up in Detroit. During the 1950s, while working as an advertising copywriter, he began writing western stories for pulp magazines and eventually published several western novels, of which *Hombre* (1961) is the best known. Also during this period he sold the film rights to his western short stories "3:10 to Yuma" and "The Tall T," thus beginning a long and lucrative relationship with the Hollywood film industry. By the early 1960s, however, public interest in westerns had waned, and Leonard turned to writing mystery and suspense novels, the first of which, *The Big Bounce,* was rejected eighty-four times before being published in 1969. Discouraged by this apparent lack of interest in his suspense fiction, Leonard returned to writing westerns but abandoned the genre again after the film rights to *The Big Bounce* sold for $50,000. He published several crime novels in the years that followed, including *Fifty-two Pickup, Cat Chaser* (1982), and *Unknown Man, No. 89* (1977), but did not achieve major success until the publication of *Stick* in 1983. Favorable reviews by respected critics in the *New York Times* and the *Washington Post* fueled interest in *Stick,* and in 1985 the novel

was made into a film directed by and starring Burt Reynolds. Although Leonard disavowed the film, citing Reynolds's refusal to remain faithful to the plot and tone of the original work, it solidified his status as a talented and bankable crime writer.

Major Works

Critic Michael Kernan has observed that the typical Leonard novel is distinguished by "guns, a killing or two or three, fights and chases and sex. Tight, clean prose, ear-perfect whip-smart dialogue. And just beneath the surface, an acute sense of the ridiculous." Many of these elements can be seen in *Glitz* (1985). In this work, Miami cop Vincent Mora travels to Puerto Rico to recover from a bullet wound and meets Teddy Magyk, a murderer and rapist whom he once put in prison. Their cat-and-mouse chase leads them to Atlantic City, where they tangle with mobsters and drug dealers before their final confrontation. Leonard's other works incorporate variations of the elements praised in *Stick,* namely memorable characters, sharp dialogue, and suspenseful plot. *Bandits* (1987) follows the adventures of Jack Delaney, an ex-hotel thief who is persuaded by an ex-nun to steal five million dollars from a Contra leader in order to help the Sandinistas in Nicaragua. In *Touch* (1987), a former seminarian who heals the sick and exhibits stigmata tries to free himself from the influence of con men and unscrupulous religious leaders who want to exploit his powers; this novel was adapted for film in 1996. *Killshot* (1989) revolves around a working-class couple who, after witnessing a murder, must elude a hit-man and a psychopath. *Get Shorty,* which served as the basis for the highly successful 1995 film starring John Travolta and Danny Devito, centers on Chili Palmer, a small-time hoodlum who becomes involved with movie producers, actors, and the mafia. The protagonist of *Maximum Bob* (1991) is Bob Gibbs, a bigoted judge known for his tough prison sentences; throughout the course of the narrative, he becomes the target of several assassins. *Rum Punch* (1992) which was adapted for the 1997 film *Jackie Brown* directed by Quentin Tarantino, concerns a group of criminals attempting to smuggle money into the United States; the characters include Florida gunrunner Ordell Robbie, ex-con Louis Gara, and flight attendant Jackie Burke. In *Pronto* (1993), small-time criminal Harry Arno flees to the Italian Riviera to escape threats from both the FBI and the Miami syndicate; a U.S. Marshal, Raylan Givens, pursues Arno and tries to prevent his murder at the hands of the mob. Both Arno and Givens reappear in Leonard's next novel, *Riding the Rap* (1995), in which the former character is held hostage by seasoned gambler Warren "Chip" Ganz and his accomplice, Louis Lewis. In *Out of Sight* (1996), which was adapted for a film starring George Clooney, Leonard departs somewhat from his traditional plotlines and presents a narrative driven in large part by a love affair between the two main characters, bankrobber Jack Foley and U.S. Marshal Karen Sisco. In *Cuba Libre* (1998), which is set just before the Spanish American War, Leonard combines elements of his western and crime novels. The narrative includes such characters as cowboy Ben Tyler, who robs banks at which the people who owe him money hold accounts; Tyler moves on to exporting horses to Cuba with businessman Charlie Burke, and both men become acquainted with their buyer, the dangerous Roland Boudreaux. *Be Cool* (1999) marks the return of *Get Shorty*'s Chili Palmer, who again seeks box office success, this time directing sometimes perilous events in his own life and the lives of others in order to establish the best plot for his screenplay.

Critical Reception

While he is often compared to crime writers Ross Macdonald, Chandler, and Hammett, Leonard acknowledges Ernest Hemingway, John Steinbeck, and John O'Hara as his literary influences. The lean prose style of these authors is evident in such works as *Killshot, Touch,* and *Glitz.* Leonard has been praised particularly for his ability to capture the nuances and rhythms of conversation. *Time* magazine called Leonard "Dickens from Detroit" because of his strong character portrayals and realistic dialogue. Minimizing narration and description, Leonard allows his characters' conversations to tell the story. Of Leonard's writing technique, Diane K. Shah observed: "There appears to be no narrator at all: as if a bunch of honest, hard-working guys and a parade of deadbeats had run into each other in Detroit or South Florida and begun talking; as if, by chance, this Elmore Leonard, lurking in the shadows, had turned on his tape recorder, getting it all."

PRINCIPAL WORKS

The Bounty Hunters (novel) 1953

The Law at Randado (novel) 1954

Escape from 5 Shadows (novel) 1956

Last Stand at Saber River (novel) 1957; also published as *Lawless River,* 1959; and *Stand in the Saber,* 1960

Hombre (novel) 1961

The Big Bounce (novel) 1969; revised edition, 1989

The Moonshine War (novel) 1969

The Moonshine War (screenplay) 1970

Valdez Is Coming (novel) 1970

Forty Lashes Less One (novel) 1972

Joe Kidd (screenplay) 1972

Fifty-two Pickup (novel) 1974

Mr. Majestyk (novel) 1974

Mr. Majestyk (screenplay) 1974

Swag (novel) 1976; also published as *Ryan's Rules,* 1976

The Hunted (novel) 1977

Unknown Man, No. 89 (novel) 1977

The Switch (novel) 1978

Gunsights (novel) 1979

City Primeval: High Noon in Detroit (novel) 1980

High Noon, Part 2: The Return of Will Kane (screenplay) 1980

Gold Coast (novel) 1980; revised edition, 1985

Split Images (novel) 1981

Cat Chaser (novel) 1982

LaBrava (novel) 1983

Stick (novel) 1983

Glitz (novel) 1985

Stick [with Joseph C. Stinson] (screenplay) 1985

52 Pick-Up [with John Steppling] (screenplay) 1986

Bandits (novel) 1987

*The Rosary Murders [with Fred Walton] (screenplay) 1987

Touch (novel) 1987

Desperado (screenplay) 1988

Freaky Deaky (novel) 1988

Cat Chaser [with Joe Borrelli] (screenplay) 1989

Killshot (novel) 1989

*Based on the novel by William X. Kienzle.

CRITICISM

Jefferson Morley (review date 25 March 1985)

SOURCE: "Middle Class Hustlers," in *New Republic,* Vol. 192, No. 2, March 25, 1985, pp. 38-40.

[*In the following review, Morley offers a mixed assessment of* Glitz.]

You've heard about Elmore Leonard—probably sometime in the last ten days. After a long career of writing pulp Westerns and crime novels, he's hit it big with *Glitz.* The book, which follows Miami detective Vincent Mora to Atlantic City as he looks for the killer of a dumb, young Puerto Rican prostitute named Iris whom he once had a crush on, has made the Book of the Month Club and is said to be on its way to Hollywood. But the excitement isn't just hype. The critical measure of Leonard is also routinely high. His dialogue is edgy, hip, inarticulate; his plot twists are unnerving; his characters are as familiar and surprising as a new friend.

So why am I going to say bad things about him? Mainly to try and help preserve his reputation. The swell of critical praise for Leonard's last several books has grown into a mighty tsunami of raves for *Glitz.* Leonard is this year's model of the sudden literary celebrity lifted from obscurity, a regular William Kennedy or Martin Cruz Smith or John Kennedy Toole. I happen to think Leonard's writing is both more fun and more evocative of American life, of its hustle, glamour, ugliness, and yearning, than any of the above. But what's best about him is getting lost in, well, in the glitz.

The hint of social observation in the title indicates why *Glitz* is a slight disappointment. Detective Mora walks into the Atlantic City scene trying to figure out who threw Iris off the 18th-floor balcony of a new condominium, and soon realizes he's got to find an old enemy, a psychopathic rapist named Teddy Magyk. The title has announced that this book is about the world of 24-hour gambling, hundred dollar bills, complimentary suites, and just-flew-in-from-Dallas types,

and, in a vivid and exciting way, it is. But this self-consciousness diffuses the duel of Magyk and Mora. In his previous novels Leonard never let the bright lights get in our eyes.

It is the utter lack of self-consciousness that makes Leonard's earlier books so authentic. He does not tint his evocation of the American scene with affection or contempt or even self-importance. He just gives it to you: an inner-city liquor store, a sprawling suburb, a divorcée's home, a hotel bar, a Miami tourist motel. He captures American life precisely because he doesn't belabor it. He makes it astonishingly real by acting like it is simply a great setting for a crime story.

And it is. Typically Leonard throws us in with some middle-class Americans who, by dumb luck or criminal calculation, are within reach of their main chance—and who are wondering how to grab it. What makes us enjoy these characters is not so much how they do wrong as how their scams fit into the background of their ordinary middle-class lives. In *Swag* (1976) Frank Ryan, ex-car salesman, and Ernest J. Stickley, hot-wire artist, go into the armed robbery business in suburban Detroit. They quarrel, they talk up the bored women sunbathing around the pool of the apartment complex where they live. They throw parties, vacuum the Doritos out of the carpet in the morning, and stash their cash in a box of Oxydol under the kitchen sink. Stick's got a crush on a neighbor who he thinks turns tricks on the side, but he winds up in bed with Arlene, one of the sunbathers who is smart enough to let him think he made the first move. So what's he supposed to do when they fall in love and she lets it slip that she knows how he pays the rent?

Leonard doesn't take this world where everyone is inventing themselves any more seriously than the people who live in it. (Ryan tells the girls by the pool that he and Stickley are consultants in the business of "sales motivation.") He just sits back and enjoys the whirl of people moving in from somewhere else, looking for a chance to get down, figuring out how to move up, or just going along for the ride.

Stickley, who drifted to Detroit from Oklahoma, resurfaces in Miami as the title character of *Stick* (1983). He wants to go straight but winds up a chauffeur for Barry Stam, a self-made dope lawyer with vanity plates on his Mercedes that read "BS-1." Barry likes to talk as if he graduated from a Liberty City street corner instead of from Wake Forest Law. His investment adviser is a pretty, preppy Wall Street liberal with a brother who pitched for the Red Sox. She enjoys the danger of rubbing shoulders with the lowlife, and toys with the idea of making Stick her personal rehabilitation project. Meanwhile, out in the parking lot of Barry's country club, the black chauffeurs trade stock tips overheard from the white folks talking in the back seat. It's the free-for-all of American life.

Leonard is too interested in the flaws in his characters and in the details of the world they live in to be classed with three-chord crime hacks like John D. MacDonald and George V. Higgins. His company, for better or worse, is Bobbie Ann Mason and John Updike. The restlessness, the insecurities, the private resentments, the quiet ambitions, the best-laid plans that Mason and Updike evoke are all there in Leonard—and often with less posturing. When a Bobbie Ann Mason character opens the refrigerator and sees a ham, it is bathed in the soft florescent glow of the Iowa Writer's Workshop and we're supposed to hear the bell of Meaning go ting-a-ling. When Stick goes to the fridge for a Stroh's, it's because he's thirsty.

Leonard's chief flaw is that no matter where he drives you, you still go through familiar intersections. The trouble isn't that he relies on a prototypical hero. There's no harm in knowing that the central character of a Leonard book is likely to be a shrewd operator with a yearning for a good woman (or two). He'll be decent, divorced, smart, and, once in a while, a son of a bitch. In the same way it's not bothersome that he's likely to live or be from Detroit. But I find it a little distracting when the mechanics of plot and character recur from book to book.

This kind of perfunctory writing compounds the self-consciousness of *Glitz.* In *Stick* Ernest J. has a memorable yet deflating evening in the successive company of a *Playboy*-type knockout, an unhappily married woman, and the working girl of his dreams. The situation is faintly echoed in *Glitz,* where the same three types wind up awkwardly face-to-face in Mora's hotel room. Mora also has exactly the same instantaneous rapport with the married woman in this trio as the hero of *Cat Chaser* (1982) has with the wife of an exiled Latin torturer. Both women have self-made, stolid, dense husbands, and both first meet the hero in connection with a nubile prostitute whom the hero has befriended. These recycled devices drag *Glitz* to a flat conclusion. Toward the end, you get the sneaking suspicion Mora's just cruising Leonard country in search of a plot twist.

So let's leave well enough alone. Leonard's books are a revelation precisely because he is such a self-effacing writer, because he makes his point by never making any points. He deserves his success. But if he were a character in his own books, someone would be pulling a fast one on him right about now—just when he thinks he's got it made. Keep your eye on the ball, Elmore.

Roger Kaplan (review date May 1985)

SOURCE: "Hard Guys and Heroes," in *Commentary,* Vol. 79, No. 5, May, 1985, pp. 64, 66-7.

[*In the following excerpt, Kaplan provides a mixed review of* Glitz, *and compares and contrasts Leonard's novels with works by author Ross Thomas, whose novel is also reviewed.*]

After eighteen novels written over the course of three decades, Elmore Leonard, who lives and writes in a suburb north of Detroit, has made it big with *Glitz,* a novel about a policeman, a psychopathic criminal, two beautiful women, and Atlantic City gangsters. His previous books were paperback originals, but this one is near the top of the hard-cover best-seller list, it is a book-club selection, and it is receiving favorable reviews just about everywhere, except where it is getting raves.

Less spectacular is the success of Ross Thomas, a resident of Malibu, California, whose twentieth novel (including five written under the pseudonym Oliver Bleeck), *Briarpatch,* also is winning its author many new readers. In recent years Thomas has begun to surface from what might be called the obscure glory of a devoted cult following, and each of his last few books has been a contender for best-sellerdom, attracting increasingly widespread, and favorable, reviews.

Although both Leonard and Thomas deserve the recognition, if not necessarily the uncritical adulation, they are receiving, neither new novel is truly representative of its author's best work. *Glitz* is mediocre by the standards Leonard set in his brutal documentary novels of 1970's Detroit, when the city acquired its reputation as a case-study of urban failure and the murder capital of the nation; *Briarpatch* is driven by Thomas's characteristically mordant wit and romantic sorrowfulness, but it lacks the exuberant verve and zany inventiveness of his better work.

A crime writer is perennially faced with a choice between, on the one hand, circling around and around a carefully plotted mystery (*à la* Raymond Chandler) and, on the other hand, painstakingly describing the overlapping zones of the criminal-justice system and the underworld (*à la* Dashiell Hammett). This, in fact, is one obvious point of contrast in the work of Leonard and Thomas. But important as this is, it is as nothing compared with the writer's choice of how to portray the criminal environment itself. A mystery can always be solved; why a man gets involved in one and what he discovers there about himself and others is what is interesting. That many Americans have found this a fascinating subject for stories about themselves and their cities is itself an important key to our national culture.

The culture of crime certainly fascinates Elmore Leonard; his interest in the ordinary details of the lives of the people who inhabit that culture is what has led to comparisons of him with Dickens and (by none other than George Will) Anthony Trollope. Dickensian, Leonard's novels certainly are not; their range is much too narrow. Entertaining, however, they are. *Glitz*, true to its title, is filled with razzle-dazzle motion, jarring dialogue, amusingly frightful characters. (Leonard may have mellowed a bit; in his earlier Detroit novels the characters are invariably appalling.)

The hero of *Glitz* is Lieutenant Vincent Mora of Miami. Almost always in Leonard's novels the good man is a police officer, and Mora is both a good guy and an excellent detective. But he has a small problem. In the strictest self-defense (in fact his restraint caused him to be wounded), Mora killed an armed robber and it bothers him (it is his first killing). While he is convalescing in Puerto Rico, a pathological criminal named Teddy Magyk, whom Mora had sent to jail for several years, appears, determined to seek revenge. So at the very time that Mora needs to be on his most agile toes, he is both physically and psychologically distracted. The question is, basically, who will be faster on the draw?

The answer is not surprising and it should not be. Psychotic killers do not defeat the law in Elmore Leonard. The only question is how Lt. Mora will deal with his problem.

As with all Leonard's books, there is no real plot (though in this one he indulges in some uncharacteristically incredible twists), attempts at humor are rare, the conversation is notable for its vulgarity, and the characters are detestable to the point of caricature. The climax is more or less inevitable as soon as the key characters are defined. There are no sudden reversals at the end. The simplest way of defining the underlying thesis of *Glitz*, as of all Elmore Leonard's work, is to say that it proves a man's got to do what he's got to do.

Leonard's portraits of the worst kinds of human wrecks, particularly the eighteen-to-thirty-year-old hard-core recidivists who, according to police statistics, commit most of the violent urban crime, are done with a documentary realism that is, unquestionably, shocking, but that also corresponds to much of the evidence about the fate that has befallen large parts of some of our cities. Leonard's popularity, at any rate, has increased as the Hobbesian view of society that his novels project has gained adherents. Even Detroit's extremely liberal mayor, Coleman Young, who is black, and who won his office by running against the police, is now trying to increase the size of the force and is demanding strict security in the schools, enforceable by searches. And it is interesting that the one Leonard criminal who is likable, Ernest Stickley (in the Detroit novel *Swag* [1976] and the Florida novel *Stick* [1983]), is pitted against the kinds of psychopaths normally taken care of without much due process by Leonard lawmen, and that Stickley takes care of them the same way they do.

Leonard is a realist in the background, one might say, and a melodramatist in the foreground. (Earlier in his career his heroes were Arizona gunslingers, and his *Hombre* of 1961—with a gunslinger in the role of a Christ-figure—was named one of the best Westerns of all time.) Certainly he does not mistake the utter grimness of his cityscapes for a portrait of the way we live. The moral dilemmas are not drawn as sharply as they are, for example, in Dashiell Hammett, not because Leonard fails to see them but because most of his criminals inhabit an underworld where such issues would have no meaning. The cops therefore can hardly waste time fretting over them. . . .

Leonard's tales correspond to an abiding view of their society that Americans have expressed through their crime fiction: the streets are dangerous, but there are men strong enough to make them at least a little bit less so. Thomas's novels express a sensibility at once more anachronistic and more contemporary, the distrust of government and its ruthlessly corrupting influence. That both authors are popular today really should not surprise us.

Thomas D'Evelyn (review date 28 January 1987)

SOURCE: "Canned Politics and Lovely Rascals," in *Christian Science Monitor*, January 28, 1987, p. 19.

[*In the following mixed review of* Bandits, *D'Evelyn asserts that the novel does not live up to Leonard's abilities as a "master craftsman" of crime novels.*]

Elmore Leonard is everywhere. After 24 novels, salty-bearded, high-domed, he squints out at us affably from behind his big specs—a blue-collar, wiry version of Mr. Magoo. He's a media star.

> **Leonard is a master craftsman. He specializes in local color (Detroit, Florida's Gold Coast, Atlantic City, New Orleans), patterns of sloppy but undeniably American speech, a Hemingwayesque use of negative space (what he leaves out the reader spontaneously fills in), and brutal, very *macho* fun and games.**
> **—*Thomas D'Evelyn***

Since his early days as a writer of Westerns (his oldest fans continue to prefer them to his crime novels), Leonard's reputation has grown steadily. It took years to crest with *Glitz* (1984). With his newest book, *Bandits*, the wave has broken, and Leonard has definitely arrived.

Leonard is a master craftsman. He specializes in local color (Detroit, Florida's Gold Coast, Atlantic City, New Orleans), patterns of sloppy but undeniably American speech, a Hemingwayesque use of negative space (what he leaves out the reader spontaneously fills in), and brutal, very *macho* fun and games.

Up till now, the beat of Leonard's crime novels has been true to the heart of the crime story, its generic hero. As an outsider with a heart of gold, or at least a sense of simple human justice, the crime or suspense hero makes the mystery novel a version of romance.

In *Bandits,* the internal tensions of the genre—between the axes of good and bad and right and wrong, between realism and romance—become obvious. Among other things, *Bandits* is a series of stories told by aging ex-cons. Some of the stories are vintage Leonard: beautifully proportioned and paced, often bawdy (Leonard's language is said to offend his own mother).

Jack Delaney is the ostensible hero of *Bandits.* He's recently rehabilitated, having served time for hotel robbery, what he calls his "trade." He's had other jobs: He's been a male model; he's hauled organ pipes; and now he works for his brother-in-law at Mullen & Sons, Funeral Directors, the family business.

Or does until, moved by his hatred for the business and a new attractive proposition, he quits to return to his criminal trade to help the real hero, or affective center, of the story, Lucy Nichols, an ex-Franciscan nun just back from Nicaragua, where she cared for lepers. There she witnessed the brutal murder of civilians and indeed some of her patients at the hands of the villain of the story, the contra leader Col. Dagoberto Godoy.

Armed with a letter from President Ronald Reagan, Colonel Godoy (notice the pun in his name) has come up to New Orleans to raise funds for the contras. The letter from Reagan allows Leonard to show off his ability to imitate voices: "He writes like he talks," Jack says of Reagan when he reads the letter.

The comic-strip colonel is balanced by a classic Leonard character, Franklin de Dios (his name an echo of the colonel's), a Miskito Indian who works as a hit man for the colonel but whose profound hatred for the Sandinistas goes back to their genocide of his people.

In *Bandits,* Elmore Leonard's fabled sense of comic timing has an extra dimension: He's timed the novel to rhyme with the headlines!

The plot of *Bandits* is straight out of Robin Hood. Inspired by Lucy, Jack calls together two other ex-cons. Together they plot to steal from the colonel the funds he has raised from the likes of Lucy's father, a conservative oil man.

Just back from special versions of hell—prison and Nicaragua—Jack Delaney and Lucy Nichols are as committed to self-discovery as they are to the cause of justice. For them, politics is a part of a bigger whole; Lucy and Jack are not ideologues. And in *Bandits,* beyond Politics, lies Romance.

Note the big *R*.

Item: Although Jack sleeps with two women in the book, his old flame Helene, and Lucy, that's all they do, sleep. In *Bandits,* we're talking salvation, or the search-for-the-true-self, not sex.

Item: As a child Lucy fell in love with St. Francis. Now, looking at Jack Delaney, she thinks of him again.

Item: Lucy is a smart dresser (some pair they make: Jack was once a model), but her change of habit isn't restricted to Calvin Kleins. She claims her taste for clothes comes out of magazines.

She says, "It's only a cover, Jack, while I change into something else."

"You don't mean clothes."

"No, it's more like changing your skin, your identity."

"Are we talking about another mystical experience?"

"I don't know."

"What do you think you're going to turn into?"

"I don't know that either."

The flatness of this dialogue is a virtual parody of Leonard. Through the sometimes violent, often outrageously funny pages of *Bandits,* Jack and Lucy chart each other's changes.

In the end, though, we're not surprised when Jack goes back to his old girlfriend and Lucy returns to Nicaragua. The novel ends on a somewhat knowing note of dubiety.

So much for Romance!

I prefer Crime. I prefer *Stick* or *Glitz.* A good crime hero—say Stick, of Leonard's novel by that name—is what he is, an all-too-human "simple soul." When I read Crime, I'm invited to become simple, too. But Lucy, not Jack, is the hero of *Bandits,* and when she talks, I don't believe her. As for Jack, he's a sentimental version of the "simple soul"; not even James Garner could make him believable.

No, *Bandits,* with its canned politics and beautiful rascals—always excepting the lovingly portrayed Franklin de Dios—feels like a TV movie. I've come to expect more—or is it less?—from Elmore Leonard.

Glenn Most (essay date Spring 1987)

SOURCE: "Elmore Leonard: Splitting Images," in *Western Humanities Review,* Vol. XLI, No. 1, Spring, 1987, pp. 78-86.

[*In the following essay, Most examines Leonard's use of language and conventions of narrative and plot to illuminate the moral views of his readers.*]

Towards the beginning of Elmore Leonard's *Split Images,* a rather odd thing happens. A multi-millionaire named Robbie Daniels has shot and killed a Haitian refugee who has broken into his house in Palm Beach. This, unfortunately, seems not to be odd at all, at least not in Leonard's world. What is odd is what happens next. Gary Hammond, the young squad-car officer who questions Daniels, asks him whether the woman accompanying him had entered the house together with him, and the millionaire replies, "Yeah, but when I realized someone had broken in, the way the place was tossed, I told Miss Nolan, stay in the foyer and don't move." "The squad-car officer paused," continues the narrator. "One of Mr. Daniels's words surprised him, bothered him a little." We wonder: which word? why? Leonard does not tell us, and we must read on, hoping that this tiny perplexity will at some point be resolved.

This perplexity is in fact the only mystery at the beginning of this novel—which is surprising, considering that the first sentence announces a murder has been committed and that a conventional murder mystery would be devoted to solving the question of who had done it. That question is not in dispute here—no one doubts that the millionaire shot the Haitian—but it will turn out that the circumstances are less clear than we might have thought. The millionaire claims he shot the burglar while the latter threatened to attack him with a machete; the Haitian, before dying, says that he was unarmed and that the millionaire ordered him to approach and shot him in cold blood. Faced by these competing versions, we are likely to respond the same way as the patrolman's superior, Walter Kouza, does when Gary Hammond discusses the case with him: of course the Haitian tells it differently; we would expect him to. What could be more

natural, Kouza thinks, then that a starved and vicious Caribbean should break into a house and try to kill its owner with a savage native weapon? What could be more absurd than that a wealthy American businessman should shoot a man in cold blood? When the opposing versions are estimated according to the calculus of social probabilities, the choice of the likelier one seems easy. But that calculus is founded upon stereotypes and prejudices: how true are they? how confident can we be that our clear sense of the differences between a Haitian and a millionaire is not radically defective? Gary Hammond, the squad-car officer, has been bothered by something, and we are about to find out by what. His dialogue with his stolid superior continues:

> Gary Hammond was patient. He was going to say what was bothering him.
>
> "He said something to me, Mr. Daniels. He said he come in—he realized somebody was there from the way the place was tossed."
>
> "Yeah? . . ."
>
> "He used the word *tossed.*"
>
> "So?"
>
> "I don't know, it seemed weird. Like he used the word all the time, Mr. Daniels."
>
> The detective said, "He say it was going down when he got home? How about, he looked at the guy but couldn't make him? TV—all that kind of shit come out of TV. They get to be household words. *Tossed,* for Christ sake."

What had bothered the squad-car officer had been a linguistic anomaly, a stylistic break he was sure he had observed in the millionaire's speech: he would not have expected a rich and presumably well-educated white man to use a word from underworld slang like "tossed." To his hypersensitive ears, the anomaly was odd enough to suggest that this millionaire might not be everything he seemed to be: that in other words the stereotyped contrast between millionaire and Haitian might not correspond to the realities of this particular situation. So too, a few pages earlier, Gary Hammond had been talking with the Haitian's widow in the hospital while they waited for him to die:

> She said, "I go home tonight and fetch a white chicken and kill it."
>
> Gary said, "Yeah? Why you gonna do that?"
>
> The woman said, "Because I'm hungry. I don't eat nothing today coming here."

Gary said, "Oh."

Why does Gary ask her what she intends to do with the white chicken? Elmore Leonard does not tell us: but there can be no doubt that Gary imagines she intends to perform some weird Voodoo ritual requiring the use of a chicken, and of a white chicken at that. But her answer repudiates his unintentionally racist fantasy and indicates merely that she is a human being just as he is, one who suffers hunger and eats chickens. True, she may speak a little oddly and she may kill her chickens herself rather than purchasing them frozen in a supermarket: yet the point of the dialogue is that she is not as different from him as Gary had thought. But not only as Gary had thought: as we had thought too. For Leonard is careful not to hint at Gary's fantasy of a Haitian Voodoo ritual by even a single word: we readers must supply such a fantasy ourselves in order to make his question intelligible.

Thus Leonard has tricked us into injecting our own racial stereotypes into our reading of the novel and has shown us at the same time how unfounded they really are. But if the Haitian is not so different from the policeman, and the millionaire uses the language of criminals, what remains of the calculus of social probabilities upon which we had based our estimation of the competing versions of the circumstances of the Haitian's death? Kouza rejects the patrolman's intuition, arguing that mass culture has blurred linguistic boundaries, and by implication social ones: yet he does not realize that his own argument destroys his foundation for instinctively preferring to believe the millionaire. Eventually he will pay for this error when, near the end of the novel, Robbie, the millionaire psychopath who dreams of committing murder on television and who had shot the Haitian in fact only for target practice, kills him too. Gary Hammond, on the other hand, suspects that Robbie, like many Elmore Leonard characters, has been so influenced by popular culture that he has begun to enact the violent fantasies he had been consuming. Gary will turn out to be right in his suspicions: but his being right will do no good at all, it will neither prevent murders nor solve murders, but remain as a sad and sterile wisdom.

This dialogue between the patrolman and the millionaire is a curious encounter. It brings together symmetrically a member of the upper classes who descends to the language of the underworld, and an ordinary street cop who momentarily rises to the height of a considerable stylistic sensitivity—yet it brings them together without purpose or consequence, and allows them first to intersect at a moment of truth in which the criminal cannot help but betray himself and one policeman cannot help but understand, and then to drift on as though that moment had never happened. Such intense and futile intersections define the fictional space of Elmore Leonard's novels.

II

The elements of that space are familiar from the crime novels of many other authors. The characters that populate it are a Hobbesian congeries of clever or unscrupulous egotists on the one hand and stupid or cautious ones on the other. The best that strangers can hope for from one another in this world is distrust; the likeliest is malice. Altruism is unknown, self-interest is taken for granted, greed is the most common motive. People's actions veer between coercive force and manipulative shrewdness; their lives are stretched taut between fantasies of whose implausibility they are not quite unaware and are punctuated by the exclamation point of violent sudden death. The large and colorful cast of secondary figures is drawn from the extremes rather than the center of economic and social life, and primarily serves to furnish spectators and victims for a central duel, which pits against one another a man who kills and a man who, often (but not always) with the blessing or at least the connivance of the state, kills men who kill. Women can enter this terrain, but—a generic weakness in Leonard's style and moral vision—almost always as victims. If they become the object of lust, that is only another form of the attempted exercise of power: true love is as rare in these novels as true friendship, and as surely doomed.

But if the elements in this narrative space are all familiar, its structure and boundary are in fact quite different from those of most other novels: an Elmore Leonard novel resembles nothing else in the world except another Elmore Leonard novel (and conversely, any one Elmore Leonard novel bears far too strong a resemblance to most other Elmore Leonard novels). There are especially three distinguishing features in these novels:

First, from the side of the detective figure, it is remarkable that there is almost never any process of detection. We readers generally know from the very beginning who the murderer is, and often the detective figure finds out soon after, but he is always prevented from arresting or killing his man at once. What prolongs his pursuit, and thereby gives the novel its necessary length, is generally not a process of investigation, with the careful gathering and sifting of evidence, and the drawing and testing of tentative conclusions, but rather a frustrating combination of legal procedural constraints that are often portrayed as arbitrary, and the killer's own animal wiliness and absurd good luck. By and large, there are no clues in an Elmore Leonard novel.

Second, from the side of the killer, it is striking how frequently Leonard's criminals are straightforward psychopaths, borderline or full-fledged homicidal maniacs who kill simply for fun or for the most immediate forms of greed or revenge. This is a remarkable fact, one that cannot simply be explained as social realism. Rather, the phenomenon of the psychopathic killer is best seen as related to another oddity in these novels, the almost total absence in them of the family. For the detective to be familyless, typically a divorced or widowed male, was of course traditional in the crime novel: this was thought to ensure his incorruptibility and the single-mindedness of his dedication to solving the mystery. But on the other hand, the crime itself, at least from Aeschylus through Ross Macdonald, always found its most fertile matrix in the prolonged tensions and covert violence of the ordinary nuclear family. In Leonard, not only is the detective figure usually a bachelor: so too is the murderer, and his victims are most often people he hardly knows. The result is that both of the central characters operate for the most part as detached and isolated individuals, free-floating agents. They are monads with guns.

Finally, and most importantly, in the absence of both the rational necessity of an investigative process and the biological necessity of a family context, what ends up organizing the plot of an Elmore Leonard novel is largely chance. The characteristic form of these novels is not detection but pursuit. But it is a particular type of pursuit. There are for example few if any one-sided chase scenes, with the policeman hot on the heels of the fleeing malefactor, of the sort loved by the movies and television. Instead, the pursuit is always mutual: the man who kills and the man who kills killers circle around one another, hovering, waiting for the chance to strike, and hope that their attack will be so overwhelmingly forceful and so unpredictably timed that it will kill the other even though he has been anticipating and planning for it from the beginning. This means that an intimate bond links the two figures in this central duel, one expressed in Leonard's fondness for heroes who have served time in prison or for plots which show the two males competing for a single female. But it also means that the narrative sequence of these novels becomes a broken temporality, one rationalized by no redeeming progress towards a goal. Without a telos, Leonard's novels could go on forever: what breaks them off and provides a conclusion is almost always a fluke of chance, and these endings are almost always flamboyantly artificial, deliberately unsatisfying. Thus Robbie, the lunatic millionaire of **Split Images,** possesses an enormous gun collection; but the only reason another policeman (not Gary Hammond) can succeed in the end in pinning a murder on him is that, with unaccountable stupidity, Robbie happens to use the same gun on two different victims. Or consider **City Primeval:** here the policeman has been tracking the psychopath Clement for the whole novel and finding himself blocked constantly by legal constraints and bad luck; at the end, there is a showdown between the two in which the policeman shoots the murderer when the latter reaches for—a can opener. Even when the novel is about to close with an apparent success for that character who has least alienated our sympathies, Leonard is careful to add a bitterly ironic twist. The title character in **LaBrava,** who has knowingly fallen

in love with an aging actress because of the seductive roles in mystery films he had seen her play in when they were young, helps her to pull off a murderous swindle for which she finally has the chance to write her own script: of course, she ends as the big winner, and he is left saying the curtain line she had always had to mouth, the patsy's "Swell." The title character in **Stick** kills and is almost killed for revenge and seventy-three thousand dollars—just enough, he learns on the novel's last page, to cover exactly the back payments on his alimony.

How can such novels be structured before their off-key endings? During their course, this broken temporality is articulated above all by Leonard's most important innovation in the mystery genre: the irony produced by constantly shifting the point of view from which the story is told. Leonard never employs first-person narration; but his use of the limited third-person point of view is extraordinarily sophisticated. Any chapter in an Elmore Leonard novel can be narrated from the perspective of any character: even a murder victim, as in the second chapter of **Glitz,** can furnish the viewpoint from which the story of his death is told. But, as we might expect, the viewpoints Leonard prefers are those of the detective and the murderer, and for most of their course his novels oscillate uncannily between the one and the other. It cannot be over-stressed how innovative this technique is within the mystery genre. For in the traditional mystery novel, the author's control over an unvarying and sovereign viewpoint, whether it was first- or third-person, had guaranteed the closure and the intelligibility of his story. Of course, there had been rare exceptions of a shift in narrative viewpoint—one thinks of Agatha Christie's *Murder of Roger Ackroyd* or *Ten Little Indians*—but these were unrepeatable experiments in wit designed to confirm the code they momentarily violated. In terms of the history of the genre, Leonard's shifting viewpoints conflate the use of the first-person from the viewpoint of the detective, common in the whole tradition of Hammett, Chandler, and Macdonald, with the use of the first-person from the viewpoint of the schizophrenic murderer, a specialty of Patricia Highsmith. Many readers find such Highsmith novels as *This Sweet Sickness* or the Ripley tales disturbing, for one cannot be told a story from a certain perspective without at least conceiving of the possibility of the legitimacy of that perspective, and many of us feel uncomfortable sharing, even if only in part and only in a fiction, the goals and desires of a homicidal maniac. The choice of a narrative perspective is never merely a technical, but rather always also a moral question, and Leonard's use of point of view is in fact more radical, and more disturbing, even than Highsmith's. For the consistency of Highsmith's perspective means that it can be rejected *in toto:* even if we read her novel to the end, we have long since concluded that the restrictiveness of the point of view from which the story is being told is part of the very sickness of the schizophrenic who is telling it: his expression in fact aids our therapy. But in Elmore Leonard's society, both evil and good have become equally respectable alternative points of view from which a story can be told. How can we bestow our sympathy upon the hero from whose perspective one chapter is narrated and then withhold our sympathy from the psychopath whose viewpoint shapes the next one?

III

With obsessive frequency, the murderous gunshot in these novels is accompanied by the sound of shattering glass. *Glitz* begins and ends when Vincent is shot as he carries mostly liquid groceries: the first time, "Hearty Burgundy, prune juice and spaghetti sauce. This time chablis, J & B Scotch, Puerto Rican rum and a family-size bottle of Coca-Cola." Both times the bottles fall and shatter and he collapses wounded into a pile of broken glass. Clement performs his first murder in *City Primeval* by shooting a judge through a windshield, "the windshield taking on a frosted look with the hard, clear hammer of the evenly spaced gunshots, until a chunk fell out of the windshield." So too, the bullets Robbie shoots into Curtis for practice in a garage in the middle of *Split Images* shatter an automobile's windshield and those he fires when he kills Chichi towards the end of the novel make a bottle on the side-table shatter and several windowpanes in the French door explode. In *Unknown Man No. 89,* Virgil's shotgun blast kills Lonnie, "making a terrible noise and shattering a full-length mirror, wiping it from the wall . . . ." In *Gold Coast,* Ed Grossi watches his own death in the splitting images of a shattered mirror:

> In his mind, in that moment, Grossi heard Vivian saying, "You're getting old," and his own voice saying, "Oh my God," and heard the heavy muffled gunshot hard against him, jabbing him, and saw in the mirror blood coming out of his shirtfront and on the mirror itself, his blood sprayed there as from a nozzle, seeing it in the same moment the sunburst pattern of lines exploded on the glass, his image there, his image gone.

And, in perhaps the most striking instance of all, in *52 Pick-Up,* Bobby goes out of his way, for no apparent reason, to shoot his accomplice Leo through a plate glass window. He has been talking with Leo in the latter's nude-model studio, and could have killed him there at any moment, easily, privately, and safely. Instead,

> Bobby steered Leo over to the desk and gently, with his hand on his shoulders, sat him down. . . . Bobby walked away from the desk to the front door counting one, two, three, four and a half steps. He opened the door, gave Leo a nod and a little smile and walked outside. . . . Glancing at the street, at the few

cars going by but not studying them or worrying about them, he walked back to the front door of the model studio, counted one, two, three, four and a half steps past it, stopped, faced the black-painted plate glass in front of the D in NUDE MODELS, raised the revolver belt-high and fired it at the glass, getting the heavy report and a hundred and twenty square feet of shattering glass and the D disappearing in front of him, gone, all at the same time.

Why does the bullet that kills break glass so often in Leonard's novels? We might think of explaining this as a dramatic device which provides a striking acoustic accompaniment to the sound of the gunshot, or as a visual effect underlining the power of the shot more forcefully than its impact on the human body alone could show, or even as an ironic moral emblem suggesting the brittleness and insubstantiality of the lives of so many of the characters in these novels. Such explanations may well capture part of the point of this motif; but there is another aspect to it I would like to suggest in conclusion here.

For the nineteenth-century realistic novel, the most traditional image for describing the relationship between the author and the society he depicted was glass. Whether the novelist was described as looking out from a corner window upon the crowds passing below him on the street, or as holding up a mirror to society, or as walking on the city's sidewalks carrying a mirror, his contact with society was not direct but was mediated by a pane of glass. On the one hand, of course, the barrier imposed by this medium implied the aesthetic distance which was necessary if the novelist was to be understood as providing us, not with reality itself, but rather with some version of or comment upon it—from Plato onwards, the looking-glass is a recurrent feature in theories which emphasize the artwork as a mere image of real things. But on the other hand, the logic of this metaphor enforced a correlation between the sovereignty of the author's point of view, and the unity of the society he represented: for just as only one man, the author, stood before the window or held the mirror, so too all of the events and circumstances he saw, however disparate and unconnected they might have seemed to be on their own, became inextricably linked to one another by forming part of the single image visible in and through the glass. By their shared presence within the frame of the looking-glass, two events which the merest chance might have juxtaposed in reality seemed to enter into mysterious connection with one another: suddenly, they became parts of a whole, communicating by subterranean channels which were all the more potent the harder their traces were to discern. Thus, in the traditional realistic novel, the narrator's unfailing control over point of view entailed the dream of an ultimately unitary society, and the novel's mission became inevitably that of uncovering hidden connections.

This was the formula the classic detective novel had not only followed with bland fidelity, but indeed had exaggerated and perfected. Yet while the detective novel did so, for many decades it was being left behind by developments in other kinds of novels. While the detective novel continued to provide its readers with unitary viewpoints, organic societies, and the investigation of the traces of hidden links, the high novel had for most of this century been exposing these very conceptions to searching criticism. How could one retain faith in the unitary viewpoint after Joyce, or in an organic society after Dos Passos, or in the full discoverability of hidden links after Conrad? Measured against the novels of early twentieth-century modernism, let alone against those of more recent movements like the French New Novel, detective stories could come to seem increasingly artificial and distant from the very social realities they often purported to analyze.

In recent years, there have been numerous attempts to reform the detective-novel genre from above by such high-culture authors as Robbe-Grillet, Butor, and Borges. Elmore Leonard's novels may represent the most successful attempt so far to transform it from below: another first step in such a transformation must be a shattering of the traditional looking-glass of realistic fiction. For on the one hand, once popular culture has permeated so fully in all domains of social behavior that the border between image and reality becomes irremediably blurred, the glass which had always prevented the novel from actually becoming reality and kept it instead a merely aesthetic artifact must inevitably break down: if Robby in *Split Images* has read so many detective novels and seen so many murders on television that the language of crime has seeped into his vocabulary and his dream has become that of starring in the videotape of a murder he really commits, if Jean Shaw in *LaBrava* stages the heist she had always been prevented from pulling off in her films and uses for that purpose a man who has fallen in love with her because of her movie roles as a dangerous, manipulative temptress, then reality is imitating art and we can no longer confidently draw the line between what is fiction and what is truth. And on the other hand, Leonard's jaggedly shifting narrative perspectives, his sense of the sheer chance and blind arbitrariness of social encounters, and his repudiation of classical investigation and detection as modes of acquiring knowledge, cooperate not only to provide a sustained critique of the conventions of the traditional murder mystery, but also to create thrillers whose texture and rhythms are closer to the lives we are led, by television and the other mass media, to believe we actually lead. The evident popularity of his novels is the best evidence for his success.

But there is, or should be, a price for this success. For the glass that had separated the traditional novel from reality had also protected its reader from full moral complicity in the evil it had represented. But both of the innovations I have just mentioned converge in a single profoundly disquieting question: why do we read Leonard's novels? If the line between popular culture and social reality can become blurred beyond recognition, and if we can share, even if only intermittently, the perspectives and goals of a psychopathic killer, then what are the possibilities for evil within ourselves that are responding to Leonard's narratives and what forms might their response one day take? What reason do we have to believe that our own capacity for evil will be, not exacerbated, but purged by these novels? This is, I would suggest, the glass that the bullets in Elmore Leonard are really aimed at: the looking-glass of the reader's moral complacency. Leonard shatters that glass: its fragments give us splitting images of ourselves.

Thomas R. Edwards (review date 13 August 1987)

SOURCE: "Indictments," in *New York Review of Books,* Vol. XXXIV, No. 13, August 13, 1987, pp. 50-1.

[*In the following excerpt, Edwards provides a largely positive assessment of* Bandits.]

Even those who don't care for crime fiction may like what Elmore Leonard makes of it, especially his way of representing common or low American voices. Consider this splendid speech in *Bandits,* by an old but still lively Louisiana bank robber banished by his relatives to a shabby nursing home:

> "My boy wanted me to stay with them, I mean live there," Cullen said. "It was Mary Jo was the problem. She'd been thinking about having a nervous breakdown ever since [her daughter] Joellen run off to Muscle Shoals to become a recording artist. . . . See, Mary Jo, all she knows how to do is keep house. She don't watch TV, she either waxes furniture or makes cookies or sews on buttons. I said to Tommy Junior, 'What's she do, tear 'em off so she can sew 'em back on?' I got a picture in my mind of that woman biting thread. First day I'm there, I look around, I don't see any ashtrays. There's one, but it's got buttons in it. I go to use it, Mary Jo says, 'That is not an ashtray. We don't have ashtrays in this house.' I ask her, well, how about a coffee can lid I could use? She says if I'm gonna smoke I have to do it in the backyard. Not in the front. She was afraid the neighbors might see me and then she'd have to introduce me. 'Oh, this is Tommy's dad. He's been in the can the last twenty-seven years.' See, it's bad enough Joellen takes off with this guy says he's gonna make her a record star. Mary Jo sees *me* sleeping in her little girl's bedroom with the stuffed animals and Barbie and Ken and she can't

handle it, even sewing on buttons all day. She keeps sticking her finger with the fucking needle and it's my fault. So I have to leave. . . ."

It looks easy—just suppress some conjunctions and relative pronouns, start a few sentences with "See," throw in an occasional defective verb tense or down-home locution, and life leaps at you off the page. But as in the "realistic" speech in Dickens or Joyce or Hemingway, it takes art to show Cullen's knack for ironic mimicry ("become a recording artist" must be how Joellen, or Mary Jo, put it—Cullen himself later just says "record star"), the folkish shrewdness in a phrase like "thinking about having a nervous breakdown," his malicious imagining of Mary Jo's regal prissiness ("We don't have ashtrays in this house") collapsing into "been in the can," a verbal betrayal by the lawless indecorum she so badly wants kept outside. Cullen knows that her obsessive sewing is material for comedy, and he understands, quite unforgivingly, that it comes from her powerlessness to "handle" the rest of her disappointing life.

In **Bandits** Leonard directs his artful renditions of common reality toward a more difficult subject than realistic crime fiction usually takes on, the entrance of national nightmares into domestic dreams of money and personal freedom. In New Orleans Jack Delaney, an erstwhile clothing salesman, amateur fashion model, hotel jewel thief, and convict, now works in his brother-in-law's funeral home. Nearing forty, educated by the Jesuits, at Tulane (for a year), and in Angola Penitentiary, Jack is no fool on his own turf, but he is not very knowing about the larger world outside it; "I'm not good at environment," he cheerfully confesses, "I'm weak in those areas." But that world intrudes on his all the same, in the person of Lucy Nichols, a young ex-nun just returned from Nicaragua. Lucy has given up the Sisters of Saint Francis but not her concern for good works, and she persuades Jack to help her save a young Nicaraguan beauty queen, Amelita Soza, whose brutal former lover, once a friend of Somoza and now a *contra* commander, seeks to kill her for (he frantically supposes) infecting him with leprosy.

Jack hasn't kept up with the news from Central America, and his idea of religious sisterhood leans heavily on old Deborah Kerr movies and Sally Field playing the Flying Nun. But Lucy is attractive enough, and his present life dull enough, to induce him to help protect Amelita as well as to relieve Colonel Dagoberto ("Bertie") Godoy of the large sums he has raised from rich right-wing Americans to aid the *contras*. Half the loot is to go to Jack and the gang he recruits for the project, but he's also pleased that Lucy will take the rest to Nicaragua to help repair the harm Godoy and his ilk have done.

Leonard writes neatly and convincingly about most of the people in **Bandits:** the tough, monstrous, finally frivolous Godoy; his enigmatic Miskito Indian hit man, Franklin de Dios, who likes to ask, "How you doing?" but kills men as other men kill flies; Delaney's buddy Roy Hicks, an ex-cop and ex-con whose nerve and ruthlessness scare even his friends; Jack Delaney himself, whose amiable, boyish recklessness isn't big on idealistic causes but who knows that scheming and fighting for people you like is more fun than doing it just for money. Lucy and her well-connected oilman father, who thinks of contributing to Godoy's secret arms fund but decides it's too risky an investment, seem flatter and more familiar; but one would not say this about the redneck gun dealer in Gulfport who dismisses the Klan as a "bunch of negative thinkers" because they don't see that "commonism" is the real menace, or Jack's old girlfriend Helene, who finds the techniques of embalming fascinating and decides to make it her profession. As for Ronald Reagan, it would be hard to improve on his testimonial letter to Godoy ("To assist you in delivering your message of freedom to all my good friends in Louisiana, I have written to each one personally to verify your credentials as a true representative of the Nicaraguan people, and to help affirm your determination to win a big one for democracy").

Godoy aims, however, not at winning a big one for democracy but at securing a lot of big ones for himself and his druglord pals in Florida; he has no intention of delivering the money to the *contras*. It's a touch that recent news makes plausible, but it leads to a difficulty in **Bandits** that Leonard's other books don't have. In them he deals sympathetically with people who are, or have been, criminals at least in some technical way, or with policemen whose occupational closeness to crime makes the line between good guys and bad guys sometimes hard to see. His is the familiar but still intriguing premise that, since hardly anyone is innocent in the old-fashioned sense, we are all potentially free to make a life with some new but authentic claim to value, a value based not on learned rules but on impulsive acts that will henceforth define us. The bad people in his books don't accept this freedom, and they must pay the price, usually a grim one. But those who accept it may survive and even profit, though (old rules do die hard) usually not by getting rich. In the end Jack Delaney gives Lucy not half but all the *contra* money, though he still has Godoy's new $60,000 Mercedes to sell off, and he isn't sure he won't keep the proceeds.

Leonard has sometimes used politics for fictional background—*Cat Chaser,* for instance, recalls the American intervention in the Dominican Republic in 1965—but the moral implications of public policy in **Bandits** press much harder than before on personal behavior. Godoy's people are not just bad characters, Detroit street hoods or Miami dope runners; they are agents of a social and political malaise that the author, to his credit, wants us to be seriously anxious about. Private guilt is not disabling in itself; Jack Delaney has stolen before and is ready, if not exactly eager, to steal again, especially for what he can consider a good cause. The danger for him isn't guilt but going back to jail. Lucy Nichols is a nun who has always been on the right side, against her rich, complacent parents as well as ogres like Godoy; she has trouble thinking that stealing from Godoy is a crime, even if committed in the company of a thug like Roy Hicks, who seems as vicious as Godoy himself. But Jack and Lucy increasingly have to ask themselves if ends justify means, and even Hicks is puzzled when he learns that Godoy has the protection of certain local and federal authorities: "I want to know what side we're supposed to be on," he tells Jack, "the good guys or the bad guys." He's willing to be either, but it helps to know.

Godoy's gunman probably gets closer than anyone else to the heart of the puzzle: "Franklin de Dios was wondering if he was certain about the sides. If there were more than two sides. If he was on the side he thought he was on or on a different side. He was getting a feeling, more and more, that he was alone." (Franklin's eventual decision that he is in fact alone and will not kill for anyone but himself is what makes things come out more or less justly for the others.) And the experienced reader of Leonard's stories may also be doing some wondering. The book has proposed views of Godoy that don't mesh: does he stand for a political nightmare in which the American government and private wealth conspire to support an odious public intention, or is he just a brutal crook like those in Leonard's other novels, serving no intention save his own greed and *machismo*?

The latter view suits the genre Leonard has perfected; to side, as we do, with Jack and Lucy is only to prefer nominal lawlessness, in otherwise likeable people, to the real and ugly thing, and that seems no problem. But the moralizing political view, in which Leonard has invested so much effort and feeling, is harder to accept, even for a reader who suspects that the real *contras* are largely a pretext for corrupting conspiracies like the one the book describes. A real Godoy might of course combine both views, but Leonard's kind of novel hasn't enough room for such complexity. *Bandits* is not as efficient and coherent as Leonard's best books, like *LaBrava, Stick,* and *Split Images*; but readers who care as much about what is happening in the political underworld as about crime books may feel glad that he wrote it.

Cyra McFadden (review date 8 May 1988)

SOURCE: "Weirdos on the Barricades," in *New York Times,* May 8, 1988, section 7, p. 7.

[*The following is McFadden's commendatory review of* Freaky Deaky.]

How dearly Elmore Leonard loves a scam, a con, a slippery scheme. How fond he is of the schemer, especially the schemer who thinks big. What a master criminal Mr. Leonard would make if he got tired of writing thrillers and changed professions. The plot of *Freaky Deaky* races along, constantly changing course and doubling back on itself, like a cunning fox in front of the hounds.

The setting is contemporary Detroit. The cast of characters includes a recycled Black Panther turned man Friday to a millionaire, a pair of student revolutionaries left over from the 1960's, assorted narcotics dealers and kneecappers, and Chris Mankowski. A straight-arrow cop no one will ever nickname Lucky, he's already in trouble with the novel's opening sentence: "Chris Mankowski's last day on the job, two in the afternoon, two hours to go, he got a call to dispose of a bomb."

After six years on the bomb squad, nagged into it by his girlfriend, Chris has requested a transfer. Now "a guy by the name of Booker, a twenty-five-year-old super-dude twice-convicted felon," is sitting in a green leather wing chair with several sticks of dynamite planted in the cushion. Along with Chris, who's always puzzling over its shifting boundaries, we've entered Elmore Leonard's ethical and moral "gray area."

Booker's life, arguably, isn't worth saving. Chris should attempt to disarm the bomb anyway, even if he gets blown to bits. He makes what most of us would agree is the right decision, one a reviewer shouldn't reveal. Let's simply leave it that Mr. Leonard's spectacular 26th novel starts out with a bang.

Tricky stuff, dynamite, as we soon learn from Skip Gibbs, "a thirty-eight-year-old kid" originally from Indiana, who still uses such Midwestern locutions as "I like to died." Skip is a demolitions expert for movie companies these days. That's after serving a long prison sentence for blowing up a Federal building, back in the time when blowing up Government buildings was a political act. Alas, the forces of law and order didn't see it that way. Neither does Skip, any longer. "Sweet-heart," he tells Robin Abbott, his fellow street fighter and assistant bomber of long ago, "that whole show back then was a put-on. You gonna tell me we were trying to change the world?. . . Where's everybody now? We've come clear around to the other side, joined the establishment."

"Some have," Robin observes grimly. Having served time for the same bombing, she's had eight years to figure out who blew their cover after she and Skip got arrested, jumped bail and went underground. Their betrayer must have been Mark Ricks, fellow student radical turned theatrical producer, or Mark's brother Woodrow (Woody) Ricks, a physically repulsive specimen known even in his college days as "the Poor Soul." The Poor Soul inherited $50 million from his mother. Robin wants to redistribute the wealth.

Brother Mark ended up with pocket change, relatively speaking; he wants a chunk of Woody too. So does Donnell, former Black Panther and self-appointed houseman to "Mr. Woody" who keeps his boss in a booze-and-drug-sodden stupor. In fact, so many people want a piece of Woody, a hilarious and awful grotesque, that the line winds all the way around the block. Even Chris ends up in the particular gray area where Woody's money exerts its magnetic pull, as does Ginger, the red-haired actress who replaces the nag as Chris's girlfriend.

He's not a great deal better off. It's understandable that Chris's father thinks that his son should try dressing better and maybe changing his after-shave.

In short order the stage of *Freaky Deaky* is crowded with as many rogues as *The Beggar's Opera,* from Juicy Mouth, a black hit man with a gray tongue as big as the sole of a shoe, to Skip and Robin, once again a dynamic duo. Fortunately for Chris and for Woody, the world's weirdest person, the lot of them aren't any longer on brains than they are on scruples.

"All these ones here," a cop named Wendell says to Chris about Juicy Mouth and retinue, "they got their game going, living on the edge. . . . We get a feel for that kind of action, huh? Know when to step outside, so to speak, let them do their own kind of freaky deaky. You remember that sexy dance? . . . Man, we had people shooting each other over it."

Wendell could be talking about Elmore Leonard, who steps back from his characters just enough to marvel at their gyrations, as everyone tries to shake down everyone else. He's got a feel for their kind of action. His ear is the best in the business. No one writes better or funnier dialogue, whether the speaker is stoned-out Woody, joylessly intoning "Boy-oh-boy," or Donnell trying to strike a deal with Juicy Mouth:

> "You out of work, you out of finances. I have a man for you needs to be vamped on. Tell me what you charge to bust his leg. . . ." "Yeah, I'll bust his legs good. Just one.
>
> "I'll give you a deal for the same price. I'll put him away." "Juicy?"
>
> "I'll take him out someplace. . . . Nobody ever see him again."
>
> "Juicy? How much just for the one leg?"

Robert Sandels (essay date Winter 1989)

SOURCE: "Common Criminals and Ordinary Heroes," in *Armchair Detective,* Vol. 22, No. 1, Winter, 1989, pp. 14-20.

[*In the following essay, Sandels surveys Leonard's crime novels and reveals how the author departs from and provides commentary on traditional crime story formulas; Sandels also delineates standard themes and elements of plot and character found in these works.*]

Elmore Leonard's crime novels have much of the flavor of his earlier Westerns. In *City Primeval*(1980), subtitled **High Noon in Detroit,** a police detective, Raymond Cruz, and a killer, Clement Mansell, face each other in a classic Western shoot-out. The shoot-out which ends *Glitz* (1985) is almost identical to the one which ends Leonard's 1979 Western novel *Gunsights.* The tone of his Westerns of the 1960s and 1970s conformed to the social criticisms of the day. Blacks, Indians, and Mexicans instead of WASPs were often the protagonists, and they looked deceptively harmless on the outside. On the inside, they were tough and resourceful, as their enemies soon found out. Leonard shattered other aspects of the traditional Western formula by allowing his heroes to shoot at men carrying white flags of truce and to kill the horse because it was easier to hit than the rider. In **Gunsights,** the wife of the hero interrupts the walk-down between her husband and a nasty antagonist by hauling out a rifle and shooting the man off his feet. Leonard infuses many of his contemporary crime novels with elements of the Western formula, but it is his own version, not the traditional one, which we see.

Many of the protagonists in Leonard's contemporary crime novels have the same kind of Mexican names and looks that decorated his Western heroes. Raymond Cruz in *City Primeval* even wears a big mustache that makes him look "old-timey," like "someone in an old tintype photo." From time to time, he and Clement reflect on how, in an earlier time, "we might have settled this between us."

Leonard also adds elements of the police procedural to his three crime novels that feature police protagonists. (*City Primeval, Split Images,* and *Glitz* have police heroes. Two others have protagonists with some quasi-legal past: *Unknown Man #89* and *LaBrava.*) There is the procedural's obligatory introduction of the officers of the homicide team. They have interesting personalities. They talk of bullet "frags" and exit wounds. But good police work does not make much difference, and justice remains elusive.

Having employed two of the most enduring fictional approaches to the pursuit of justice—the frontier's direct confrontation of good and evil and modern, scientific criminal detection—Leonard turns both into farce. His police novels become almost a parody of the police procedural because none of the procedures is going to convict anybody. In *City Primeval,* some friends of a murder victim—Albanians in dark suits—provide a model for effective procedure: they go to Clement's apartment building, pull out their guns, and fire away at him on a public street. When the leader of this tribe of innocents asks homicide detective Raymond Cruz, "If you know he kills people, why do you let him?" Raymond has no answer. But, later on, he too goes to the Clement apartment, pulls out his gun, and starts shooting, though not before permitting Clement to go for his can-opener sharpened to a knife-point.

Leonard raises here the disturbing and timeless question of vigilante justice. This theme is amplified in *Split Images,* wherein an amateur assassin kills out of a warped sense of justice. His accomplice, an ex-cop, once killed out of frustration at the law's protection of "the guilty." When everybody kills for reasons of justice, which they themselves provide, where exactly is the contest of good and evil being carried out?

As Leonard avoids rational resolution of crime, he also makes simple frontier justice practically impossible by immersing it in contemporary jurisprudential difficulties. After presenting crime and criminals in their rawest, frontier-like simplicity, he withholds the satisfying final scene of heroic retribution. In the one novel in which he allows that scene to take place—handgun against can-opener—it is in the form of burlesque. He creates situations in which an intensely personal combat goes on between good men and bad but in which the simple opposites of the Western formula are present in form only. The contest of good and evil takes shape in the narrative as a contest between delusion and reality.

It is among the rich that Leonard locates the source of much of this delusion. Loathing for the rich and powerful, a belief that their corrupting influence lies at the root of social problems, is one of the founding assumptions of the hardboiled tradition, stretching back to the 1920s. It serves as a form of class struggle in that tradition shaped by writers of a generally liberal and proletarian political outlook such as Daly, Hammett, and Chandler. Their tough-guy heroes could work among the rich like beekeepers, insulated by their professional hardness, self-denial, and weary *weltschmerz.* But, in Leonard's hands, the tough-guy motif takes on a decidedly aesthetic quality. His heroes adopt a kind of everyday, pedestrian simplicity of style. They offer realistic sensibilities in opposition to the posturing and self-delusion of those around them.

Leonard's rich thrash about in a frenzy of acquisition. It is their primary form of aesthetic expression, a game in which the object is the scorekeeping. Eventually, a point is reached at which their lives become "irrelevant," having "nothing to do with reality." Worse, their wealth weighs heavily on the susceptible who try to emulate them. Angela Nolan, a writer making a study of the rich of Palm Beach, tells police detective Bryan Hurd in *Split Images* about her poor schnook of a father who drives around Palm Beach in his Cadillac, talking about real estate and "trying to sound rich. But he doesn't know how." That's what's wrong with the rich, she says: "The rich people make their lives look so goddamn good we all bust our ass trying to get the same thing." Evil appears in Leonard's crime novels as that mysterious force which makes criminals out of petty men with hopelessly wrong ideas about who they are and how the world really works.

An inventory of the criminal characters pursued in Leonard's books shows that they are almost never the great masterminds of the perverted American success myth. General de Boya, the butcher of the Dominican Republic in *Cat Chaser* (1982), Francis X. Perez, the sinister con man of *Unknown Man #89* (1977), and Nestor Soto, the ruthless drug czar of *Stick* (1983), are men of elegant strategies who have a firm grasp of how things are done, and nobody is trying very hard to bring them to justice. It is generally the lesser men, the obscure psychopaths and small-time hustlers with harebrained schemes and no chance of a long life, who are confronted by Leonard's heroes. His books remain this side of reality by respecting the criminal hierarchy. Exiled Latin American generals living in mansions in Florida are not normally hauled before police magistrates. They live too close to our fantasy of the American Dream. Leonard's heroes do not labor to rid the earth of evil but to cart away the nuisances.

George Moran in *Cat Chaser* faces down General de Boya but only to take his wife away from him. Can he help it that she brings along a suitcase full of the general's money? In *Stick,* Ernest Stickley only wants some money that a minor drug dealer owes him, and so he goes, hat in hand, to Nestor Soto, the master drug trafficker, to seek permission to poach on his territory. *Stick* is a crime comedy of class and manners—a kind of *Upstairs, Downstairs* of South Florida financial hustling, in which Ernest Stickley lives in the chauffeur's garage apartment while learning how to fit himself into the game going on in the Big House. Leonard has made a specialty of writing about men and women who take what is coming to them, perhaps win a point of honor, but leave justice to a higher authority.

One of the characters in *LaBrava* refers to the cockroaches in the walls and basement of an old Miami Beach hotel who labor mightily to hold the place up. Like those indispensable insects, Leonard's better class of criminals are taken to be part of the foundation, so ingrained that removal could bring the edifice down. There are, then, limits to how much justice one seeks in this world.

What remains to struggle with Leonard's heroes are the small-time nobodies of crime. It is not the mobsters or international drug magnates in Atlantic City on whom police detective Vincent Mora concentrates in *Glitz,* but the murder of an obscure casino "hostess" by Teddy Magyk, one of Leonard's most interesting sociopathic creations. He is a petty criminal so ignorant and befuddled that he can never translate his criminal willingness into the glitz of Atlantic City and has to wheedle gas money from his old mom in order to go out and kill people for slot-machine quarters. Nobody expects to get rid of the cockroaches in the basement, but we do expect them to keep their troops out of the living room.

Typically, the objects of pursuit are like Teddy or like Richard Nobles in *LaBrava* or Roland Crowe in *Gold Coast* (1980)—swamp thugs who have only recently emerged from the Everglades or the bayou to heave their reptilian bulk about on dry land and to look in condos and carpeted offices for prey. They are sometimes menacing Colombians or Cuban "boat-lifters" from Mariel who run amok in the free enterprise of an endless con game. In the end, they have little to show for their efforts. Teddy Magyk is shot in the back by a casino lounge singer who has never held a gun in her hand and in the front by the very man he has been stalking. Richard Nobles is manipulated and murdered by the very same actress he has expected to take for all she is worth. Clement Mansell is shot at by Albanians, locked in a safe and left to die, and finally murdered by a policeman. Even the likable Frank and Ernest, the methodical, fun-loving holdup men of *Swag* (1973), cannot seem to keep to their ten commandments for stick-ups and soon go to prison. In *LaBrava,* Richard Nobles' schemes for making illegal money are comically pathetic. His idea of extortion is to walk into a hotel lobby and threaten to "dump" in the hotel pool if the proprietor does not pay protection money.

Nobles and his ilk are not great criminal success stories. They cannot understand why Joe LaBrava or Vincent Mora is after them. They imagine themselves to be immune, just as the Nestor Sotos and General de Boyas are. Teddy Magyk really thinks he is magic. He does not need to plan anything because everything is supposed to work for him.

The criminal is linked through his own delusions to the man he stalks. There is something about the man that challenges the criminal's self-image. Leonard often represents these contrasts in his characters' perceptions of reality by images on film. Teddy Magyk takes pictures of Mora, but they do not tell Teddy why he has to kill him. Robbie Daniels, in *Split Images,* makes a murder video which is supposed to validate his crime. While Joe LaBrava, a professional pho-

tographer, is out trying to make a living recording the world of the "barefaced fact" in Miami Beach, Jean Shaw, an ex-movie queen from the days of *film noir,* is watching her old movies to get inspiration for the day's intrigues. Joe cannot tell when she is real and when she is just using such movie lines from the 1940s as "I need you Joe."

The Vincent Mora who shows up in the photographs that Teddy takes of him is not an imposing person. Leonard's heroes never are. They are like the melon farmer in *Mr. Majestyk* (1974). On the outside, he is just a melon farmer with a Polish name and no money. Inside, he is tough and clever. When a professional hit man, Frank Renda, accidentally encounters him, Renda cannot figure him out but knows he has to kill him for what Renda thinks is arrogance.

> He couldn't get the melon grower out of his head; he wanted to hit him so bad, and he wasn't sure why. Not because the guy had belted him a couple of times; though that could be reason enough. No, it was the way he pulled that cheap cool shit and acted like he couldn't be bought.

Teddy wants to kill Mora for much the same reason. It is not simply revenge for having sent him to prison. It has something to do with what Teddy sees in Mora's eyes—a look which he has to eradicate. It is a look, Teddy thinks, that is not exactly of hate—"it was more a look of knowing something."

Teddy does not say exactly what the thing is, but Mora's personal style provides a clue. Like many other Leonard heroes, Mora is utterly straight. His professional hardness is modified by humor and perspective. He values unaffected speech and simple dress, he values truth, frankness, and love. He is not a man to take at face value the absurd posturing of a Teddy Magyk. Teddy does not see reflected in Mora's eyes the person whom Teddy imagines himself to be but rather the reflection of a "poor wimp who thought he was magic and couldn't be scared." Teddy has substituted for the real world the norms of his own fantasies. That is why he cannot figure out Mora's look—the way Mora can see into his head and know that he is a vicious jerk. "Guy thinks he knows more about you than you do," Teddy thinks: "Like he can look into your head and see things that make him want to blow your head right off." As Mora leaves a liquor store with a bag in his arms, Teddy steps up to shoot him. "I want to be looking in your eyes as I pull the trigger," Teddy says. His obsession with that look is what gives Linda Moon enough time to creep up and shoot him in the back. Delusions, then, can be fatal things.

This tension between the illusions of the criminal and the utter straightness of the hero provides the dramatic formula for nearly all of Leonard's crime novels. It binds the two characters together with an affinity that explains their compulsive fascination with each other, the one following his illusions and the other wondering, as Joe LaBrava does, how they "get so sure of themselves . . . without knowing anything."

The chief function of a Leonard hero seems to be to try and bring a little reality into people's lives. He is a kind of psychiatric device operating in the world of the badly deluded. He spreads a gospel of healthy straightness, and sense as well, to other characters who, though they may not be indictable, still share something of the killer's delusionary diseases.

Virtually all major characters in *Glitz* can be categorized by how far they have sunk into the fog of delusions that afflict Teddy Magyk and by how likely they are to be saved by Mora. Jackie Garbo, the casino manager, talks incessantly about big deals and is always wrong. He has no idea how to deal with women, how to avoid the police, or how to claim the loyalty of his employees. When Mora comes to warn him against laundering money for drug dealers through the casino tables, Jackie assumes that Mora is a cop on the take and has him beaten and thrown out by his bodyguard. La Donna Padgett, a former Miss Oklahoma and Jackie's mistress, thinks that Jackie has everything figured out and spends her life drying up in a desert of inattention.

As he proceeds, Mora attracts straight people such as Jackie's bodyguard, DeLeon Johnson, who can see Mora's cool professionalism. "You way, *way* ahead of me, ahead of Jackie, ahead of everybody," DeLeon tells Mora:

> All this hip shit. You understand what I mean? The casino business, all this razzle-dazzle. All the people thinking they know everything. Now you, I see you go about quietly doing your business. I know I been exposed to Jackie too long.

There is about all this—about the very language of DeLeon's speech, for example—a concern for something of value in the past now lost or buried. Leonard's books are often set in places where rapid social change has smothered older values: Atlantic City casinos, the Detroit of the rust belt and South Miami Beach—a museum of art deco tawdriness. In such places, one can glimpse a past more abandoned than outlived and now given over to coke dealers and swamp thugs who accompany the forces of change. They do not have any nostalgia; they are looking for the main chance.

Robbie Daniels, the playboy assassin of *Split Images,* laments the liquidation of his Detroit nuts-and-bolts factory— a casualty in the Japanese automobile offensive. And, not without some tenuous connection, he practices his murder techniques on a hapless Haitian refugee wandering onto his Palm Beach estate. Robbie is no ordinary murderer. He is in training for his first assault on the forces bringing the country down. His enemies include Yassir Arafat and the PLO *fedayeen,* Carlos the Venezuelan terrorist, and the Baader-Meinhof gang. But for starters he will shoot Chichi, a local womanizer and drug dealer.

Robbie's accomplice, a cynical ex-cop named Walter Kouza, clings to his Polish working-class sentiment for the old neighborhood in Detroit and, apparently, to some of its older values. Killing the bad guys on Robbie's list who are terrorists or drug dealers is one thing, but he will take "no parts of shooting broads," he tells Robbie Daniels. When Robbie later kills a woman who has witnessed the shooting of Chichi, Walter drops the video equipment with which he has been recording the event for Robbie and flees to Detroit. He flees not as a fugitive but as a man going home. Like DeLeon Johnson, an Ethiopian who never entirely left his tribal past, Walter Kouza is still rooted somewhere in his ethnicity. The detective hero finds him without much trouble in a Detroit tavern, measuring the precipitate decline of the West by the fact that only one Frank Sinatra record can be found on the jukebox amidst incomprehensible music by groups called The Ants and The Infections. "The In*fect*ions, for Christ sake. What's going on? Look—picture of the broad over there on the wall?" Pointing to a poster of David Bowie, Kouza asks, "Who knows who she is?" He remembers a time when everybody worked at Dodge Main, when the Japanese "were still making birthday-novelties and toys that fell apart."

Here, nostalgia indicates a condition of personal disconnectedness, of characters sailing rudderless into moral oblivion. When Frank Sinatra is displaced, so is Walter Kouza. Leonard's salvageable people have somehow or other preserved their links with the reliable values more carefully than has Walter Kouza. Leonard's "best people" have that personal style which denotes goodness. They talk right, "without buttering words to slip past emotions." They are "into real life."

Walter and Robbie have looked at their situations and each in his own way has tried to answer the question of who is to blame for the social decay which they perceive all around them, and each takes action according to his imperfect analysis. Like many other Leonard characters, Walter and Robbie are embodiments of prevailing notions of "how one should live," "how one should get ahead," and "who is to blame." The criminal's delusion is like a disease, the toxic consequences of too much change. Imperfectly understood historical and social changes set loose ever new criminal viruses. People such as Walter Kouza and Robbie Daniels, Ernest Stickley and DeLeon Johnson either survive because of the strength of their connections with older values or they go down.

Somewhere among the forces of change that have con-founded Walter Kouza is Leonard's answer to the question which his heroes so often ask: "How do they get so sure of themselves?"

Marc Baldwin (essay date Spring-Summer 1990)

SOURCE: "The Convention of Crime and the Reading of Signs in Elmore Leonard's *Glitz*," in *Clues*, Vol. 11, No. 1, Spring-Summer, 1990, pp. 85-93.

[*In the following essay, Baldwin illustrates Leonard's use of symbols and unique approach to conventions of crime fiction and societal norms in* Glitz.]

In the beginning of **Glitz,** one of Elmore Leonard's finest crime novels, Vincent Mora, a Miami Beach cop, is shot by a mugger he subsequently kills. In the end, Vincent is shot by Teddy Magyck, a psychopathic rapist and murderer whom Vincent had arrested and sent to prison seven years before. Teddy, having sworn revenge, stalks Vincent throughout the book, only to fail thanks to Vincent's girl friend, Linda Moon. Linda shoots Teddy before he can finish Vincent off. Vincent lives, Teddy dies.

Within this frame Leonard represents an underworld in search of itself, a Great Wrong Place (as W. H. Auden said of Raymond Chandler's novels) where the difference be-tween the good, the bad, and the marginal is how they read and react to the signs of society and language. The roles people play are as unstable as the characters themselves. Leonard explores the subjectivity with which people assign value to the conventional trappings of society, such as power, money, and appearances. The significance of these conven-tions shifts along with the alternating narrative perspectives which Leonard employs. Throughout the novel, the conven-tions and signs are as contingent as the contexts which de-termine their meaning. Characters and the signifiers which define them derive meaning extrinsically, through their dif-ference.

In their quest for a stable identity, the self-reflexive charac-ters (Vincent and Linda), are aware of the roles in which so-ciety has cast them, and thus wrestle constantly with the questions of seeming and being, what is and what is not re-ality. Ultimately, Vincent, the cop-in-doubt, must engage Teddy, the psycho-killer, in a duty dance, a hermeneutic cir-cling around each other, if you will, wherein cop and crimi-nal share ever alternating roles of author/reader, at once creating and interpreting each other's thoughts and actions. And though Leonard effects a closure of sorts with Teddy's eventual demise, it is a closure only of one criminal's spree. The cop knows no great peace, experiences no transcendent

triumph. The Great Wrong Place thrives obliviously on. Crime's unsolvable underworld survives.

At the novel's outset, after he's shot, Vince mulls over his reactions and concludes that he hadn't handled it right. He'd been carrying groceries and didn't want to drop them to go for his gun. And he was over-confident, cocky and casual. He'd misread the signs, gotten shot, and only then dropped to the pavement, got his gun and shot back.

"'I didn't scare him enough,' Vincent said." Fear is one of the weapons of both cops and criminals. It's a currency which signifies action throughout Leonard's books: you give someone fear, they give you money, truth, whatever you want. Vincent learns early on in **Glitz** the significance of fear.

Not your average, stereotypical cop: Vincent didn't want to shoot the guy. He'd never killed anyone before. His part-ner, Torres, tries to comfort him by saying: "'How do you know when you've scared him enough or you have to shoot him to save your own life?'" That is the difference for Vincent, that split second moment in which he has to read the criminal's eyes and movements and interpret infallibly the intentions of a stranger holding the ultimate sign of death, a gun pointed right at him. In the ambiguity of the moment, Vincent failed to instill fear in the criminal and so was shot and forced to kill. It made him self-reflexive; the killing sig-nified the death of his own innocence.

The gun, of course, is a transcendental signifier, empower-ing the criminal intent, effecting whatever meaning its wielder desires. The gun speaks its own language, one whose ideology presumes that might makes right. To the criminal, society's laws and codes of behavior are empty constructs, mere public conventions meant to frustrate the self-serving desires which a gun readily grants. Like a magic wand, the gun is waved and the wish is granted. Almost a passive act, gun toting substitutes for communication and negotiation, and reifies everyone else into others and obstacles, mere ob-jects in possession of the signifying desire, money. The criminal becomes the gun: it is his voice, his authority, the manifestation of his subjected state. He is his desire, and through the force of fear and its power to obliterate language, his gun creates whatever meaning its author intends. For the lawless, the gun is language. For the lawful cop, however, the creation of a corpse "made him think about his own life."

One difference between criminals and the rest of us is their use of guns, force, and other illegal means to obtain money. They operate outside the language of society. In Elmore Leonard's novels, the criminals and their victims have in common their blind pursuit of money. The victims, however, are generally innocent, i.e., they don't speak with guns. Vincent was innocent, got shot, and quickly abandoned his innocence to save his own life. With this new discomforting foreign language of guns, Vincent traveled for recuperation from his wounds to the comforting, not-so-foreign island of Puerto Rico.

We next see him there through the narrative perspective of a local taxi driver named Isidro. But that takes a few pages. First, we listen to Isidro delighting in his good fortune at having found the perfect fare: "Mr. Tourist, every taxi driver's dream." To Isidro, Teddy, the book's psychopathic killer, is an innocent, stereotypical tourist. This unwary, unsuspecting character is the first of several innocent people who misread the signs, judge Teddy harmless because that's what he seems, and thus are doomed to be his victims. Isidro thinks Teddy's his "prize" because he tips him well and even reveals his money belt. "He trusts me," Isidro told his wife. His wife warned him to be careful but Isidro saw no reason to listen to her: he was blinded by Teddy's money.

On the third day in Puerto Rico, with "his tourist wandering about taking pictures," Isidro stood on the beach and recognized a beautiful prostitute talking to "a man with a cane." The prostitute's name, Isidro remembered, was Iris, and she had her standards. She'd told Isidro she would only go with "men who stay at the Hilton, the Condado Beach, the DuPont Plaza, and the Holiday Inn." Presumably, those hotels insure respectable types.

Isidro moved close enough to overhear Vincent and Iris converse. In response to Vincent railing about people being trapped by the convention of wanting only a tan from their two week vacations, Iris said: "'I was born with a tan, I got a tan wherever I go. What's that? I want to be where people *are* [italics Leonard's], where they doing things, not where they go for a week.'" Iris seems to perceive some difference between people really being somewhere and someone, yet she denies that she's a prostitute, saying that she only does it with certain men and, as Isidro explains to Teddy later, she isn't paid.

> "You leave a gift."
> "What kind of a gift?"
> "Well, you could leave money, is okay."
> "Then what's the difference?"
> "One is payment," Isidro said. "The other, is for her to buy her own gift. Save the man the trouble."

Teddy knows there's no difference; but for the law's sake and the woman's pride, money signifies a gift not a payment. Unfortunately, everything is not simply what you call it.

In Isidro's case, he failed to make the correct call on Teddy. He misidentified the subject of Teddy's attentions and it cost him his life. When he sees the pictures Teddy has taken of Vincent and Iris, Isidro thinks Iris is the subject. Blinded by his desire for money and the belief that Teddy is a typical

tourist just secretly photographing a pretty girl, Isidro mistakes the subject of Teddy's pictures and so displaces himself into an adversarial position with Teddy. Thinking it will please Teddy, Isidro picks up the pictures and delivers them to him. Suspecting that Isidro and Vincent have been spying on him and are somehow trying to trick him, Teddy kills Isidro.

After visiting Iris and paying her for sex (she was irritable and unwilling before seeing the money), Teddy waits for and confronts Vincent outside his hotel. Their first meeting since the courtroom when Teddy was sentenced, Vincent doesn't recognize him and refers in his narrative to Teddy as the tourist. But unlike Isidro who couldn't see beneath Teddy's slick surface, Vincent quickly makes Teddy for a criminal. "'You know why I don't recognize you?'" "'Why?' the tourist said." "'Because all you shifty ex-con assholes look alike,' Vincent said."

Rather than remain in the dark without a name to attach to the face, Vincent calls his cop buddy back home with the license plate number of Teddy's rental car. The numbers reveal the name. Meanwhile, Vincent's concern for Iris—she announced she was taking a job as a hostess in Atlantic City—leads him to visit the man who hired her. At Tommy Donovan's house, Vincent talks to Nancy, his wife, about what a hostess does. He finds out that hostess is another name for prostitute. But it's her choice, says Nancy. "'Whatever the girl does, it's still her choice.'"

Vincent had tried to warn Iris against going: "'You're gonna be a comp . . . like the champagne, a gift.'" As Isidro had explained to Teddy, for gifts Iris prostitutes herself. Now she's the gift. Her first night in Atlantic City, at Tommy's casino, she sits with Jackie Garbo, Tommy's manager, and lets him run his hand up the inside of her thighs. She "hoped a casino manager was an important guy." That would make it okay. Two weeks later she was dead. To lure Vincent to Atlantic City, Teddy killed Iris. He pushed her from a penthouse balcony to the street eighteen floors below.

When Vincent gets the word, he goes to Atlantic City just as Teddy had planned. But he can't recognize her "coloring book face." Dead, Iris no longer looks like herself. Teddy created a big difference in her appearance. Later in the book, Leonard slowly, in pieces, reveals the events and details of Iris's fall from the top through the narrative perspectives of several who were there before Teddy did the deed.

The most central of those new characters, Linda Moon, meets Vincent in the funeral home and tells him that all Iris ever talked about was clothes. Linda, too, was recruited by Tommy to play piano in Atlantic City. But once she arrived, Jackie turned her into a stereotype, forcing her to front a Latin band. "'I wear an orange outfit with ruffles.'" Isidro couldn't see Teddy under the conventional tourist and Iris couldn't see herself as an unconventional whore. Linda, aware of the conventions, endures and survives them with wit and irony. Those who read the signifiers only one way, who can't see them for what they are, can't survive.

Linda tells Vincent that Iris was up in the condo's penthouse entertaining high rollers after hours. As a variation on the lucky lady convention, "'He made her take her clothes off, because he said a naked girl brought him good luck. He'd rub the dice in her pubic hair.'" That's the gamble Iris took. Vincent knew that "It was only money. What this town was all about, money. Nothing else."

Linda hates her role but must play it for money. The money makes her compromise her talents, at least for the time being. The band which she fronts plays standard rock songs with a Latin flare. Vincent had to listen hard to recognize Michael Jackson's "Beat It" and look twice to recognize Linda. "Linda said, 'Cute, uh? Jesus.' 'You look different. I'll say that.' 'I have to wear this goddamn Chiquita Banana outfit four straight sets. No costume change.'" After work, she always changes into herself: a person who defies types. "Everytime he saw her she looked different."

Meanwhile, Vincent conducts his investigation into Iris's death. Since he has no idea at this point that Teddy was responsible, the reader may observe his methods of interpreting the crime. By questioning the condominium's security guard, he finds out that there were two seemingly different people involved: the night before Iris's murder, the guard had accepted a bribe to allow someone else to watch the door for a while, and on the night of the murder, a strange, sub shop delivery boy gave the guard a spare steak sub to allow him inside.

Without jurisdiction in Atlantic City, Vince is a cop out of context, different than himself, and thus able to operate differently. He threatens the guard and gets several names of people who were there, including Jackie and the substitute doorman: Ricky Catalina, Ricky the Sicky, a big-time hit man.

Improvising all the way, Vincent kidnaps Ricky, accuses him of botching the job on Iris and tells him that Frank (another known crime boss) put the contract out on him. Ricky believes him. And then Vincent says:

> "Frank wants it done, you know, according to custom. I guess set an example. So I gotta ask you something."
> "The fuck're you talking about?"
> "My question is, do I cut your dick off and stick it in your mouth before I shoot you—"
> "Hey—hey, listen to me a minute, no shit—"

"Or do I shoot you and then cut your dick off? I always wondered. . ."

Having fun playing with conventions, playing the hit man with the hit man, Vincent listens to Ricky and pretends to make a deal. Ricky will pay him $10,000 the next day to forget about the contract with Frank.

Before that gets resolved, however, we have to backtrack in this deliciously layered story to Nancy's narrative. Up in her Eye-in-the-Sky—an elaborate system of surveillance cameras and network of catwalks above the see-through mirrored glass ceiling of the entire casino—Nancy (who really runs the show) finds out from one of her employees that Tommy and Jackie are allowing Benavides (a Columbian drug dealer and the gambler whom we found out from Linda was given Iris as a comp) to use the casino to "launder" his money. "'That's a word,'" says Tommy. A signifier better left unsaid. "'. . . we have to be objective. By that I mean this business is about money, and all money looks alike.'" Money is the object; nothing personal, no other subject should be considered where money is concerned.

Shortly after this, Nancy comps Vincent to a suite when he shows her the $12,000 in cash that he found in the trunk of Ricky's Cadillac. The money so impresses her, she takes him up to her Eye-in-the-Sky and seduces him. Leonard has fun playing with conventions here. As they kiss, the jackpot bells go off on the casino floor below them. At the same time, we see Teddy hitting on his latest victim, an innocent old lady for whom those jackpot bells tolled. She couldn't see through his flattery, trusts him when he tells her he'll show her the best slot machines in town, leaves with him, and ends up raped and strangled under the boardwalk. When Vincent later hears of the dead woman, the modus operandi signifies the criminal: Teddy's name pops into his mind and he knows who killed Iris.

Vincent then kidnaps Teddy, and in an elaborate scheme of blackmail, borrows Jackie's jet to fly him to Puerto Rico and turn him over to the police for Isidro's murder. When the police have to let him go for lack of evidence, Vincent picks up Isidro's wife and tails Teddy to a restaurant where they confront him. Although others are skeptics, Vincent believes in Isidro's wife's prophetic capabilities. When she lays her eyes on Teddy, she says: "'Is the one kill my husband.'" Teddy laughs it off, of course, but when Vincent shows him the urn full of Iris' cremated remains, Teddy is momentarily shaken. However, Isidro's wife says that "'No police can catch him,'" and Teddy grins. Vincent asks Isidro's wife what she sees for Teddy's future and she says it's hard to see him. "'Now you see me,' Teddy said, 'now you don't.'" Teddy believes his own hype, the magic of his name. Vincent wonders about it too: "Who was Teddy? You couldn't say Teddy was Teddy."

In the climactic scene, Teddy waits outside Vincent and Linda's hotel room, spying up at their lit second floor balcony. Leonard tightens the circle now, cutting perspectives rapidly back and forth from Vincent to Teddy to Linda. When Vincent goes out for groceries without his gun, momentarily forgetting the language, dropping his guard, Teddy follows him across the street to the store. Linda, peering out the hotel window spies Teddy waiting for Vincent. Fittingly—for Teddy always victimizes the unsuspecting, the innocent—she grabs the gun and rushes out just in time to shoot Teddy in the back as he is demanding that Vincent look him in the eye before pulling the trigger. The bullet passes through Teddy and into Vincent as Teddy's body crashes into him. The groceries smashed between them, Teddy fires his gun several times as they stagger, Vincent pushing Teddy off before he falls to the ground. Linda drops down and gives Vincent the gun as Teddy turns to fire again. "'Drop it,'" said Vincent but Teddy didn't. "So Vincent shot him. Put one dead center through Teddy's solar plexus and killed the poor wimp who thought he was magic and couldn't be scared."

In Elmore Leonard's world where criminals have no moral direction or philosophical basis for their actions, and laws have little hope of being enforced, the cop—especially if he's not actively a cop—may, for the greater good, play the criminal's game. The difference between greater and lesser crimes and conventions resides in motivation: the criminal acts unconsciously only for himself, the cop acts consciously on behalf of others.

Linda Stewart (review date 29 July 1990)

SOURCE: "Hollywood's Left Twisting in the Plot," in *Chicago Tribune,* July 29, 1990, section 14, p. 6.

[In the following review, Stewart praises Get Shorty.*]*

If writing well is the best revenge, Elmore Leonard just merrily evened a lot of scores. *Get Shorty* gets Hollywood right where it lives and the joke is so funny, so infinitely tricky, so perfectly synchronized on so many levels that it's apt to make you spin.

Leonard, who has written more than 15 screenplays (8 of them produced) and has had most of his 28 novels "under option," has an eminently reasonable cause to want revenge. Hollywood doesn't simply shoot Leonard's novels, it slowly, very painfully tortures them to death.

Of course, the only authentic Hollywood novel is a comedy of manners—atrocious manners, where people are likely to eat their own hearts out with the wrong fork, or backstab each other with the wrong knife. It's this sensibility that

Leonard brings to town, encased in a framework that's pure Pirandello and still pure Leonard.

> **If writing well is the best revenge, Elmore Leonard just merrily evened a lot of scores. *Get Shorty* gets Hollywood right where it lives and the joke is so funny, so infinitely tricky, so perfectly synchronized on so many levels that it's apt to make you spin.**
> **—*Linda Stewart***

But before you spend not inconsiderable money on a book, you, like Hollywood, want to know what it's about. The answer is "Don't ask."

Leonard makes it entirely impossible to answer that question. The novel has a plot, but it's not about the plot, it's all about the ways people plot. How they plot out a screenplay; how they plot their own lives, and how the two get hilariously and wackily confused.

Start with the hero, Chili Palmer. He's Leonard's prototypical good guy/bad guy—Miami loan shark and part time collector for Vegas casinos. Chili (Chapter One) is going after a gambler—a local dry cleaner who'd skipped, owing money, but a funny thing happened. The plane he was skipping on crashed in the Everglades and the guy wasn't on it. He was listed as on it, his luggage was on it, his wife called the airline and told them he was on it, and the wife got $300,000. Here's another funny thing: The guy skipped town again—this time forever—with the money, not the wife.

And here comes the topper: By page 41, Chili has trailed the guy to Hollywood and is trying to sell what actually happened in the first 40 pages as a movie idea to an out-of-luck producer named Harry Zimm, head of ZigZag Productions. And a couple of pages later, Harry's rewriting Chili's story. Rewriting Chili's life.

What happens after that becomes as lunatic and byzantine as Hollywood itself. In fact it's got an atmosphere of *Boy Meets Girl* meets *To Die in L.A.*

Harry's main investors are a couple of guys who run a limousine service plus coke operation. These are not guys to mess with but Harry's messed around. He's lost their investment playing blackjack in Vegas, and the guys are getting mad. So Harry forms an uneasy partnership with Chili to keep them off his back.

Meanwhile, Harry's got a whole other deal—a screenplay that's sure to be his ticket out of slime. And not only that, he's got some "definite interest" from the star. What he has to get now is half a million dollars, a studio's backing, a meeting with the star, and the dealers off his back.

These four quests form the heart of *Get Shorty*—not exactly knightly, but not exactly not. Grails, like comedy and love, are where you find them and Chili finds them all.

Some of the jokes are broadsides, and some are one-liners (the character who's "seen better film on teeth") and some are very subtle. If it's true, as William Goldman says, that "nobody knows anything," it's also true in Hollywood that everybody knows everything, and especially that everybody knows how to write.

"You asking me," the drug dealer comments indignantly, "do I know how to write down words on a piece of paper? That's what you do, man, you put down one word after the other as it comes in your head. It isn't like having to learn how to play the piano, like you have to learn notes."

Another of the subtler joys of *Get Shorty* is watching Leonard make fun of himself. If Hollywood has told him that his heroes are occasionally too much observers—that they don't "make it happen," that they don't set the action—then here he revels in hero-as-observer, not only in the plot about Chili Goes Hollywood but also in the several scripts-within-the-plot.

Don't get me wrong, *Get Shorty* is not a surrealistic novel. It's a good rootin'-tootin' Elmore Leonard adventure, with the usual suspects, the locker full of money, the wheelers, the dealers, the crazies, and the girl.

But if I were rewriting it, here's what I'd do. . . .

Charles Champlin (review date 29 July 1990)

SOURCE: "Leonard Cocks a Snook at Hollywood," in *Los Angeles Times Book Review,* July 29, 1990, p. 9.

[*In the following review, Champlin offers a favorable assessment of* Get Shorty.]

Long before he earned his present eminence for his swift and sharp-tongued contemporary mysteries, Elmore Leonard knew Hollywood and Hollywood knew him, initially as a writer of Westerns. Among the movies based on his novels were *The Moonshine War* and *Mr. Majestyk* (both of which he also scripted), the Martin Ritt/Paul Newman *Hombre, Valdez Is Coming* and *3:10 to Yuma.*

Leonard's impressions of Hollywood from the early '60s forward were evidently indelible and amused, and he has drawn upon them for his new novel, *Get Shorty,* a book that Raymond Chandler and Nathanael West might have written if they had decided to join forces (an engrossing idea if there ever was one).

Goodness does not abound in *Get Shorty*; it seldom does in Leonard's work. Hardly anyone, including his protagonist Chili Palmer, is without sin. Chili is a loan shark, previously operating out of Miami. He is a collector whose main weapon is a steely glare that melts the most obstinate defaulters.

There are deadlier operatives than Chili, plus other lowlifes and a couple of film stars with large but unsupportable opinions of themselves. Yet with all potential for explosive nastiness, Leonard's tone by his standards is rather mellow, although at no sacrifice in interest or suspense.

His strength has always been in the vividness of his characters and the unpredictability of their interactions, with the narrative constructed primarily of colloquial speech. This is especially true in *Get Shorty,* a satirical portrait of what might pass as second-level or possibly third-level Hollywood: significantly below the solemn majesty and abundant funding of the majors but with the really big time so tantalizingly near you can sniff the expensive colognes and the coke.

Leonard's pleasing conceit is that a man with a background in loan-sharking for a crime family, a streetwise cat accustomed to raising hob with law and order generally, is ideally suited to become a writer-producer abounding in stories and equipped with the muscle to sustain his point of view when he takes a meeting.

Get Shorty is not without violence, which includes a smash finale high in the Hollywood Hills. But it is at heart a portrait of the community, less angry than *Day of the Locust* but not less devastating in its tour of the industry's soiled follies and the gaminess beneath the grandeurs.

The plot is customarily intricate. Chili has come to Las Vegas in pursuit of a deadbeat who has fled with the proceeds of a faked death. For a Vegas pal, while he continues to seek the deadbeat, Chili agrees to collect a quarter-mil gambling debt from a small-time producer named Harry Zimm. Zimm is trying to move up from horror films. He is romancing Karen, a sometime horror queen, and trying to put together a package with an arrogant but short-brained stud star called Michael Weir. Chili moves in with, or on, this little family.

Leonard's recall isn't totally perfect—Chasen's doesn't do lunch, for example—but his ears, eyes and recall are so nearly perfect as makes no matter.

"Here, wherever you look it's something different," Chili says. "Like Times Square. I think the movie business is the same way. There aren't any rules—you know, anybody saying this's how you have to do it. What're movies about? They're all different—except the ones that're just like other movies that made money. . . . The movie business, you can do anything you want because there's nobody in charge."

The villain, Bo Catlett, explains to Chili the simple matter of doing a script: "You have the idea and you put down what you want to say. Then you get somebody to add in the commas where they belong, if you aren't positive yourself. Maybe fix up the spelling where you have some tricky words. There people do that for you. Some, I've even seen scripts where I *know* words weren't spelled right and there was hardly any commas in it. So I don't think it's too important. You come to the last page and you write 'Fade out' and that's the end, you're done."

"Then what do I need you for?" Chili asks him.

There is nothing like knowing the territory.

Nora Ephron (review of 29 July 1990)

SOURCE: "The Shylock Is the Good Guy," in *New York Times,* July 29, 1990, section 7, p. 1.

[*Ephron is a novelist and screenwriter whose works include* When Harry Met Sally *and* Heartburn. *In the following review, she commends* Get Shorty.]

I am an Elmore Leonard fan. I tell you this primarily so you will understand that I would never, ever, under any circumstances read a review of a new Elmore Leonard book. I am not even sure what I'm doing writing one, except that it gave me the opportunity to read the new Elmore Leonard before anyone else.

Anyway, this one's about Hollywood, about the movie business, it's about how everyone out there wants to write a movie, and if you're an Elmore Leonard fan what you probably want to know is, is it as good as *LaBrava.* No, it's not, but what is? So then you want to know, is it better than the last one, which I forget the name of. And the answer is yes, it's better. But I should make clear where I'm coming from: even the not-great Elmore Leonards are redeemed by great, punchy, pitch-perfect Elmore Leonard dialogue and great Elmore Leonard sentences, long looping twisting strings of words that turn around and back up and go the other way, managing somehow (but how?) to avoid all the accouterments of punctuation like colons, semicolons and parentheses.

Get Shorty begins in Miami, with the theft of a leather jacket from a restaurant checkroom. This guy named Chili Palmer puts his leather jacket in a checkroom and this other guy named Ray Bones walks off with it, for which Chili Palmer shoots him in the scalp, for which Ray Bones never forgives him. Twelve years later, Ray Bones ends up as capo of Chili Palmer's shylocking operation, and he forces Chili to go west to collect a debt from a dry cleaner named Leo who died in a plane crash but didn't really. This is the kind of stuff I can't stand reading in reviews, but I haven't told you anything that ruins the plot. I haven't even told you anything you couldn't find out in the first chapter of the book.

But here's the point (and here, also, is the point where you should probably stop reading this review if you have any intention of reading the book): Chili Palmer ends up in Hollywood, and within a day or two he's working on a movie with Harry Zimm of ZigZag Productions. ("Zig for the maniac, escaped lunatic and dope-crazed biker pictures," Harry explains. "Zag for the ones featuring mutations fed on nuclear waste, your slime people, your seven-foot rats, your maggots the size of submarines.") Actually, Chili ends up working on two movies: one of them already written but, like all movie scripts, in desperate need of a major male star and a new ending; the other the story of a guy who comes to Los Angeles to collect a debt from a dry cleaner named Leo who died in a plane crash but didn't really.

Elmore Leonard is justly praised for integrating physical setting with plot (I often recommend *Stick* to friends planning to visit Miami), but in *Get Shorty* what he's working with is not the physical setting of Hollywood but the psychological one. In fact, Mr. Leonard doesn't know Los Angeles physically in the way he knows Miami and Detroit, but he understands it perfectly. He understands that in Hollywood nothing is wasted: every love affair, every divorce, every criminal act has a shot at being, at the very least, a pitch and, at the very most, a major motion picture. Chili moves through Hollywood, tracking down Leo and then outwitting Ray Bones, but his real-life adventure is just prelude to the point, which is getting a movie made from it. And the most pleasurable parts of *Get Shorty* are the sections where Chili, having lived through it, pitches his story to the Hollywood people he meets, only to be told that it's not good enough.

"'You know why it doesn't work?' Harry said. 'I mean even before I find out you don't know how it ends. There's nobody to sympathize with. Who's the good guy? You don't have one.' "Chili said, 'The shylock's the good guy.'. . . "Harry said, 'You kidding me? The shylock's the heavy in this. . . . You don't have a good guy, you don't have a girl . . . a female lead . . . you have a first act, you're partway into the second.'

"Chili said to him, 'I guess I better tell you about my coat getting ripped off and this guy named Ray Bones I shot one time and wants to pay me back.'

"Harry said, 'Jesus Christ.' He said, 'Yeah, I think you better.'"

By the time the book ends, Chili's movie has a second and third act, a female lead who used to scream at slime people in Harry Zimm's movies, and Chili is as close to being a good guy as he can possibly be and still be the protagonist of an Elmore Leonard novel. It would be easy to assume that what Mr. Leonard is saying here is that con men are right at home in the movie business; but it seems to me he's making an even wittier point, which is that even tough guys want to be in pictures.

One last thing about Elmore Leonard books: there's always some moment in them where you don't understand something. O.K., let's be honest: where I don't understand something. I'm going along just fine and then, suddenly, I don't quite know what's happening or how we got to South Miami Beach or who the guy in the wheelchair is, something. This book I finished without having a moment like that. I understood every single word of it. I had to pay close attention when I got to the locker scene at the airport, because it's tricky what happens in it, but I got it, I understood it, I admired it. Then I closed the book and realized I had no idea what the title meant. Days passed as I hoped the meaning of the title would rise up and smack into me. I even read the book a second time. Finally, I broke down and called the publisher, who explained the title. And it's obvious. I mean, once you hear it, it's obvious. But I hope they fix it someday, in the place where they fix all broken book titles: Hollywood.

Barry Gifford (review date 28 July 1991)

SOURCE: "The Alligator Rings Twice," in *New York Times*, July 28, 1991.

[*In the following review, Gifford applauds* Maximum Bob, *and calls Leonard "the greatest living writer of crime fiction."*]

Elmore (Dutch) Leonard confirms with this, [*Maximum Bob*,] his 29th novel, his right to a prominent place in the American *noir* writers' hall of fame, along with Charles Willeford, Dan J. Marlowe, Jim Thompson, the Elliott Chaze of *Black Wings Has My Angel* and John D. MacDonald. The other Dutch Leonard, Emil, who was a pretty fair right-handed pitcher with the Brooklyn Dodgers, Washington Senators, Philadelphia Phillies and Chicago Cubs, and from whom Elmore appropriated his nickname, won 20 games in a season only once. This Dutch has accomplished the feat in his own ball park a solid baker's dozen times or more, which is a monster of a career, better than Emil's. (Emil, in the end, won only 10 games more than he lost.)

Nobody I've ever read sets up pace, mood and sound better than Elmore Leonard. Listen:

> Music was coming out of hidden speakers and the go-go whore was moving to it on the terrazzo floor, looking around bug-eyed like she'd died and gone to whore heaven. "Mumbo on down the hall," Elvin said. He followed her cute butt sliding side to side in a little skirt that barely covered it, no backs to her high heels clicking on the marble. She wasn't too bad looking for a crackhead junkie. Had her G-string on under the skirt to give Dr. Tommy a show.

Maximum Bob is the story of a crackpot cracker judge in Palm Beach County, Florida, who resembles the actor Harry Dean Stanton and who acts like the Hanging Magistrate, Roy Bean. He is saddled with a space-cadet wife named Leanne, who comes complete with a second personality, a 12-year-old black girl named Wanda Grace, with a Butterfly McQueen voice, who lived 135 years ago; the judge is dying to get rid of both of them. And there are more than a few uglies on the prowl who are partial toward seeing Circuit Court Judge Bob Isom Gibbs become bloated gator gruel in the 'Glades. Maximum Bob's appellation comes, of course, from his habit of hitting an offender with the full sentence provided by law.

Elmore Leonard writes in a manner calculated to keep the reader leaning. A. I. (Buzz) Bezzerides, the author of *They Drive by Night* and *Thieves' Market,* once told me how he explained to the director Robert Aldrich, during the filming of the *noir* classic *Kiss Me Deadly* (for which Mr. Bezzerides had written the screenplay), the way to shoot a scene in which a man is thrown over the side of a cliff. It was better not to show the guy going over, he said, but instead to show only the men doing the job, and then keep the camera on them as they watch the victim fall. This, he said, will make the viewers lean forward in their seats, as if they might catch a glimpse of the flier. Mr. Leonard knows how the body looks when it lands, too.

Maximum Bob Gibbs, who fancies himself a lady's man, has his eye on a cute young probation officer named Kathy Diaz Baker. He tries hard to set her up, but she won't tumble. This low-rent Crowe family keeps getting in the way, especially Dale Junior and his ex-con Uncle Elvin, an A-No. 1 Bad Dude fresh out of the Florida State Prison at Starke. (Dale Senior has one leg—the other was lost to gangrene following a gator bite—and his broken jaw has been wired shut.) Bob put them away, now they're trying to put Bob away.

Also there's a smooth cop Kathy likes, Gary Hammond, who gets in between, and a dumpsterful of weird dudes like Dr. Tommy Vasco, a crack addict-dermatologist who spends his days sunbathing; his cross-dressing man Friday, Hector; and Earlene, the go-go whore, who can't catch any kind of break.

Florida has long been an ideal setting for fiction that features nefarious goings-on. Being the wealthiest state in the Deep South, it attracts a steady supply of transients, mostly from Alabama and Georgia, including a fair share of fugitives. I grew up there, shooting at water moccasins in the swamps with my Sears .22-caliber rifle, working construction and laying sewer pipe alongside a goodly number of men short on history and long on mean. Once on a job building roads in Cocoa Beach, when I was 15 years old, a couple of lawmen pulled up to the construction site in their beige-and-white, got out and went up to an old boy I'd got to like pretty well and hauled him right off the steamroller he was driving without bothering to cut the ignition. Turned out he was a former sheriff wanted in Georgia for child molestation. He grinned and gave me the victory sign with his right hand as the law stuffed him into the back seat. Elmore Leonard, a Michigan resident, does the place justice.

Maximum Bob hires Dicky Campau, a swamp-punk frog-gigger with a large, nasty-mouthed wife named Inez, to scare off Leanne by bringing an alligator to the house. See, when Bob's wife was a mermaid at Weeki Wachee Springs, a gator swam into the middle of her act and freaked her out, so maybe, the judge thinks, a repeat will make her run now and take Wanda Grace with her. Only it doesn't, not really. I mean, everything backfires, to the max.

Elmore Leonard is the greatest living writer of crime fiction. Find a body does it better, you call me. Hear?

Joseph Hynes (essay date Winter 1991)

SOURCE: "'High Noon in Detroit': Elmore Leonard's Career," in *Journal of Popular Culture,* Vol. 25, No. 3, Winter, 1991, pp. 181-87.

[*In the following essay, Hynes surveys Leonard's career, noting various qualities unique to the author's works.*]

Elmore Leonard is perhaps as popular as a writer can hope to be. After twenty-eight novels his inventiveness seems as inexhaustible as that of Dickens, to whom he has been favorably compared. Nevertheless, despite his turning out a book every year or two, and despite the predictably favorable reviews he earns and the high esteem in which he is held by his peers, Leonard tends to be critically regarded as a lesser achiever, one whose works fall into journalistic compartments labeled "Westerns" or "Criminal Proceedings" or "Annals of Crime" rather than simply "Fiction." Moreover, this is the case even though Leonard has never been interested in mystery stories, "whodunnits," or detective fiction.

Leonard has not been known to complain about his ranking or about the calibre of his reception. Indeed, he seems to be so busy turning out his books that he would have little time for taking on the critics. Furthermore, his public comments suggest that he's having a wonderful time doing what he's doing, the implication being that status within the universal authorial pantheon is hardly one of his concerns.

My purpose is certainly not to try placing Leonard's achievement definitively, but to focus on a few characteristics of his writing that may serve as the basis of a longer and more detailed analysis. In my opinion it is important to attempt such a study for the same reason or reasons that it is important to explode the distinction that Graham Greene makes between what he calls his "entertainments" and his "novels," or what may be meant or implied as the difference between "popular" and "serious" writing. In short, it's good to know what we're reading and what we're talking about. Given the limitations of this presentation, I will focus on five books, although I will refer to others as well. The five, ranging in locale from western to modern rural to urban, are *The Big Bounce* (1969), *Forty Lashes Less One* (1972), *Gunsights* (1979), *City Primeval: High Noon in Detroit* (1980), and *Bandits* (1987). Although these titles cover only the most recent twenty years, I think my comments are also true of the earlier period of Leonard's career, roughly 1953 to 1968.

To begin, then, we should note that Leonard creates labyrinthine situations, the complexities of which keep the action either just beyond the law or alternating between the fringes of that law and the less defined area beyond formal codes. He is concerned not only about criminals, who take their chances by breaking laws, but also about non-criminal men and women—sometimes cops or ex-cops—whose predicaments and temperaments dictate that they finesse or blast their way to resolutions that may or may not qualify as strictly legal. A Leonard plot regularly builds a situation or a set of situations that carry implications for society but that society ignores, misunderstands, bungles, or cannot handle on its own (legal) terms.

For instance, Jack Ryan in *The Big Bounce* has served time for breaking and entering, is currently drifting from one seasonal unskilled job to another, and finds himself tempted to cooperate with Nancy Hayes in her plan to steal a 50,000 payroll. When he realizes that she is using him and indeed planned to kill him just for kicks (the "big bounce" of the title), he turns her over to the police for killing someone else by mistake. Ryan doesn't articulate his motivation, but the action makes clear that he sees Nancy as a menace and a spoiled rotter, and also that he has been impressed by the unpretentious friendliness of his employer, Mr. Majestyk, who proffers beer and a Detroit Tigers game on television, as well as a job. Ryan is also ashamed of himself for mistaking the intentions of a summer renter who wants not in the least to be sexually assaulted but only to have her stuck window loosened, as she tells him. In short, his experiences tempt him back into theft and then pull him into an underplayed decency—both because Nancy Hayes is a very unpredictable and dangerous pain in the ass and because goodness has its own attractions.

All of this could cost Ryan something, for Nancy may be able to implicate him—an ex-convict—in the plan to steal that payroll. Ryan of course knows this risk and accepts it. The point is that although his temptations and decisions are the sort that could have an effect on others—such as the cucumber-pickers who are to be paid from the $50,000—Ryan chooses to turn Nancy in not because he has any fondness for law and order in the absolute or as represented by the police, but because a handful of understated events have awakened his sense of decency. He seems more disgusted by his association with Nancy than he is worried about how she could send him back to prison. He's doing what he sees to be right, not particularly easy or convenient; and he's doing it without analyzing or discussing or taking credit for it. Moreover, he's doing it as he does everything, on the outskirts of the law.

This brings us more directly to another important feature of Leonard's books—the loner status of his protagonists. Even when they operate in a tight group, as in *Gunsights,* where Kate and Dana Moon and Brendan Early contrive to defeat the villainous Phil Sundeen, the trio operate on murkily complex motives not specified or understood fully by themselves or the reader. Early is a perennial sophomoric, lady-killing opportunist. Dana Moon is quieter and less self-assured. Kate, whose bullet is likely the one that finished Sundeen, sees both Early and Moon as little boys who need her touch to show them the importance of acting to preserve life, marriage, family, and home. Kate disregards for the most part the complications of who works for the government or the mining interests or the army or the sheriff, and of whose investments stand to lose or gain should Sundeen win. All she knows is that she cannot stand around waiting for the law or for her two colleagues to agree to halt Sundeen. She stops him literally dead, beating even her husband to the draw. Comically, Early misses the whole showdown. In short, each of the "good guys" is privately motivated even though they would normally be seen as banded together against the "bad guy."

It is worth noting, too, that these three are joined by some blacks and resident Arizona Indians. Leonard is an equal opportunity writer, one whose women characters evolve from being extreme instances of gold-diggers, tramps, or sainted virgins (see, for instance, *The Big Bounce, Escape from Five Shadows, Forty Lashes Less One, Hombre*) to heavier and more complex involvement in the action as well as to richer and more ambiguous characterization—as in *52 Pick-Up, Mr. Majestyk, The Switch, Gold Coast, City Primeval, Stick, LaBrava, Glitz, Bandits,* and *Killshot.* In much the same way, Indians and Mexicans are typically put-upon collectively in the Westerns, but in the city can be deadly gunmen—like any other person of whatever ethnic origin—as in *Killshot.* Blacks, too, gravitate from being somewhat improbable victims in the Westerns to being just part of the racial sprawl in urban novels, where they may be good or bad, cops or not, and mixed of motive like others. Instances of this increasingly all-around character fullness include Karen DiCilia in *Gold Coast,* Linda Moon and DeLeon Johnson in *Glitz,* Margaret Dawson in *The Switch,* Armand Degas and Carmen Colson in *Killshot,* Donnell Lewis in *Freaky Deaky,* and Lucy Nichols and Franklin de Dios in *Bandits.* Perhaps the richest case of the minorities' acting outside the law to achieve justice is that of *Forty Lashes Less One,* where two convicts—Raymond San Carlos (Apache) and Harold Jackson (black)—collaborate with the warden to kill a number of outlaws and escaped convicts who have mistreated them, to return to prison the boss of the prisoners' syndicate and his doxy, and then to head south for the freedom offered by Mexico.

Leonard's protagonists, then, whether men or women, minorities or not, tend to operate alone as a rule, or at least without formal substantial assistance from the law. This persistent trait helps to solidify Leonard's comment that he thinks himself influenced not so much by the likes of Raymond Chandler as by movies such as *The Plainsman, My Darling Clementine,* and *Red River,* and especially by Hemingway's *For Whom the Bell Tolls.* The situations in which Leonard places his protagonists accentuate the inefficiency or incompetence or ignorance or crookedness or obstructiveness or indifference of sheriff or police force (that is, of Western or urban lawkeepers) and the consequent need for individuals to prove their personal mettle.

Pragmatism thus becomes the inevitable rule, as for so much thinking and writing from Henry James and Mark Twain, through Hemingway, to our day. Indeed, pragmatism would seem the inevitable code of those for whom absolutes no longer signify but upon whom moral relativism nevertheless makes demands. Henry James's Lambert Strether fashions his own moral code as he proceeds, as does Huck Finn. Hemingway's Jack Brennan, the central figure of "Fifty Grand," which Grantland Rice called the best sportswriting he had ever read, could well be the model for any Leonard story, whatever its locale. It will be recalled that Jack has been an honest fighter and a real welterweight champ, but one who is aging and tightfisted and who wants to fight only once more, pocket his purse, and retire to the bosom of his wife and children. As a realist, and after conferring with gamblers, Jack bets his savings on his formidable young opponent, Jimmy Walcott. In the eleventh round, when Jack is honestly losing, Walcott belts him in the crotch. Jack sees in a painful flash that everyone else has double-crossed him and has bet on Jack to win by default. If that should happen, all the others—the opponent's camp and the gamblers— would grab a fortune in view of the odds against Jack, and Jack would lose everything. Jack thus has no choice but to wave off the referee, who is about to award the fight to Jack on a foul, and to hold himself physically together long enough to deliver two truly crippling groin shots of his own. Jack thus loses the fight, beats his betrayers (who had declined to bring him into the deal presumably because of his renowned integrity), and earns the fortune for which he had gambled. All of this goes on outside the law, but anything shady on Jack's part appears almost saintly in comparison to the traitorous behavior of everyone else. The pragmatic loner thus follows his own code and wins.

Any pragmatist forsakes absolute principle, as in the film *High Noon,* wherein the Quaker wife gives up her absolutist non-violent principle in order to kill the man who is about to kill her husband. Almost any Leonard story could be regarded implicitly as a variation on *High Noon,* even as *High Noon* is a variation on *The Ambassadors* and *Huckleberry Finn.* Indeed, Leonard's *City Primeval: High Noon in Detroit* may be regarded as an archetype of his entire output and, in some ways, of the whole history of pragmatic fiction.

In *City Primeval,* Raymond Cruz is an unorthodox police lieutenant who, like Elmore Leonard, vividly remembers Gregory Peck's cool outfacing of the bad guy in *The Gunfighter.* Like the gunfighter played by Peck, Raymond works with the law when its resources enable him to fight criminals, but commonly finds it necessary and useful to go outside that law in order to bring about justice. He finds police routine sometimes pragmatically cumbersome or counterproductive, although his goals and those of the police department are ultimately the same. For example, legal loopholes and other such codified niceties enabled Clement Mansell to defeat the law on an earlier occasion, and seem about to enable him to do so again. It is only when Mansell beats up his liberal lawyer, Carolyn Wilder, that she begins to see his true character and the legal frustrations of Raymond Cruz, who genuinely wants justice served and Mansell nailed. Like the Quaker wife of *High Noon,* Carolyn thereafter cooperates with anything Cruz wants to do in order to stop Mansell and protect everyone from him. In the Western-style showdown that Cruz's code forces on him instead of allowing Mansell to starve to death in a sealed room reminiscent of the cell in Poe's "Cask of Amontillado," Cruz remembers the facedown between Peck's gunfighter and his opponent

and blasts Mansell rather than allow himself to be duped. The method is unorthodox and will doubtless not be literally transcribed in the police report. On the other hand, Mansell, a monstrous murderer, is removed, justice (if not the statutory code) is served, and society is better off.

Something of this same independence appears again in *Bandits,* where three fringe-dwellers—an ex-cop and two ex-convicts, including Jack Delaney, the protagonist—steal two million dollars from Reagan-supported fundraising Nicaraguan *contras.* The three men intend to give half of the money to Lucy Nichols, an ex-nun, to rebuild a hospital destroyed by *contra* forces. In the end, Lucy and Jack agree that half should go to Franklin de Dios, a Miskito who actually procures the money and who has been tricked into doing the *contras'* will by the argument that the *contras'* struggle is synonymous with the Miskito struggle. Jack agrees that Lucy should have the other million for her hospital. This leaves the three original bandits in the cold, but the book, which is about Jack's maturing, shows this outcome as right.

How might we move from those particulars and sum up Leonard's ideal pragmatic protagonist? He or she is smart and imaginative, capable of seeing complexities of a situation and likely consequences of various kinds of action, willing to do what is necessary to win, irrespective of how closely choices conform to codified law. Moreover, in Leonard's books the protagonist's purposes are shown to be morally better than alternatives presented, with the result that the reader is on the protagonist's side. The protagonist may have to work alone to gain his or her ends, but even when the protagonist works with others, his or her motivation is personal rather than primarily social. Perhaps most importantly, the Leonard pragmatist earns the right to an individualistic motivation by virtue of a commitment to pay for success. It is usual for the protagonist to risk imprisonment or death because he or she believes in the chosen action and accepts responsibility for it. Jack Delaney's consciousness of his personal lukewarm motivation, for instance, prompts him to accede to Lucy's reasoning that the two million should be given to those willing to die for it rather than to him and his cronies, who are only after the loot. Finally, nothing assures victory for Leonard's protagonists. Usually they and their positions are winners, but sometimes they may die (as in *Hombre*) or emerge chastened and wiser (as in *Bandits*), having contributed to furthering the good cause. That is, Leonard tends to favor comic structures, but sometimes writes ironies.

In the long run, what makes these central figures tick? What spurs them on? Sometimes they may appear to be moved by selfishness or by a cynical despair in the face of overwhelming moral evil. Undoubtedly Leonard is aware of original sin and its effects. But his protagonists never despair. On the contrary, like Hemingway and James, Leonard is a romantic who believes in free will to some extent. At heart he believes in the possibility and desirability of achieving good ends, although he is profoundly skeptical of doing so through channels. More specifically, despite Leonard's obvious sense what we've all eaten of the apple, he also believes that isolated, ordinary individuals, like his protagonists, can surmount their own weaknesses and criminal records in order to do right. Because such people can show up not only in detective fiction but anywhere, it matters not whether they do their work in the Arizona Territory or Detroit: Mr. Smith goes to Washington while Natty Bumppo saves the wilds.

The loner in these books adopts a solitariness that enables him or her to *avoid* despair and cynicism and that in fact describes true commitment to an ideal. Reaching for success on these terms is risky because one is alone and because society at large cannot be expected to sympathize or even understand. But Leonard's main figures know of no other way to avoid despair and social disillusionment or to attain results that are morally good for society whether or not society agrees on that or even knows what has happened. I find it impossible to regard these books as only "popular," if "popular" is meant as the opposite of "serious." Leonard has a crisp delivery, a splendid ear, and a great sense of humor, but these attributes should not lull us into forgetting that he is always driven by a vision of our social milieu, of the human condition, and of the good. His central figures are tough because they are usually understatedly aware of risking a great deal, even their lives, responsibly. Typically, they would never make such a gong-smashing assertion about themselves. But they don't attend such conferences as this.

Christopher Lehmann-Haupt (review date 23 July 1992)

SOURCE: "Books of the Times; How to Make a Fast Buck without Really Dying," in *New York Times,* July 23, 1992.

[*In the following excerpt, Lehmann-Haupt offers a favorable review of* Rum Punch.]

Once again, as in Elmore Leonard's previous novel *Maximum Bob,* the pivotal character in *Rum Punch,* Mr. Leonard's 30th work of fiction, is a woman. This suggests that the author of such crime thrillers as *Stick, LaBrava* and *Glitz* is intent on continuing down his path away from stories starring macho men compelled to seduce every woman who falls in their way.

And this time the experiment works, because unlike Kathy Diaz Baker in *Maximum Bob,* Jackie Burke in *Rum Punch* is surrounded by a strong supporting cast involved in an intricately compelling plot.

Jackie is an aging, attractive flight attendant who has been reduced to working for a Caribbean airline and doesn't relish a future of offering passengers complimentary rum punch. To build her retirement fund, she has taken up smuggling large quantities of cash into Miami for an illegal arms dealer named Ordell Robbie. Unfortunately, someone has tattled to the Federal authorities trying to build a case against Robbie, and she is arrested. She has the unpleasant choice of either serving time in prison or snitching on a violent man who does not suffer stool pigeons gladly.

Ever resourceful, Jackie sees in her dilemma the opportunity to extract an enormous cash rip-off. With the help of her bail bondsman, Max Cherry (his calling card announces, "Gentlemen prefer bonds"), who is excited by her willingness to take risks, she sets a trap to win the cheese that all of the mice are after.

The only possible drawback to *Rum Punch* is that the reader is asked to believe that no one is hurt, not even the taxpayer, when profits from illegal arms trading fall into other than the Government's hands, a debatable premise at best. But by the time this moral conundrum is crystallized in *Rum Punch,* we are too caught up in the exciting climax to worry about it seriously.

There is a character in *Rum Punch* who likes to commit armed robbery just because it makes him feel good. This is about as deep as Mr. Leonard ever gets into the psychology of his hoodlums. . . .

Ann Arensberg (review date 16 August 1992)

SOURCE: "Elmore Leonard for Beginners," in *New York Times,* Vol. 97, August 16, 1992, p. 13.

[*In the following review, Arensberg provides a highly commendatory assessment of* Rum Punch.]

I didn't know it was possible to be as good as Elmore Leonard. As a devout—or, more truthfully, addicted—reader of British whodunits, I had sampled hard-boiled crime novels when my source of supply had temporarily dried up and I needed something to steady my nerves, see me through a plane ride or a sleepless night. Since I've only now dipped into Elmore Leonard, I must admit, as a mystery buff, to having been half literate.

When I stepped over the border from Christie-Sayers country into Leonard territory, as it is depicted in *Rum Punch,* I was disoriented at first. The subtropical scenery, mostly exteriors, was colorful. The lighting was bright, so different from the muted backgrounds, mostly interiors, of English writers, or from the chiaroscuro of Raymond Chandler and Ross Macdonald, whose characters also inhabit a hot climate. The glare of the south Florida sun had a demoralizing effect, shining down on the lawful and the lawless alike, obliterating the class differences that are basic to the harmonious, structured society of the British detective story.

The formal detective novel, called the "thriller of manners" by the critic George Grella, is an elitist enterprise, dedicated to preserving both the moral and the social order. We as readers identify with the detective hero in his search for a solution that will repair the crack created by the crime. "We" are good and "they"—the perpetrators—are bad. As soon as the killer is caught, our anxieties are appeased. We are no longer threatened by him or in danger of becoming like him.

In *Rum Punch,* of course, Elmore Leonard stands this classic dichotomy on its head. We good people are in danger because he refuses to keep us insulated from the criminal element. He gives the bad guys too wide a range of interesting traits and recognizable passions.

Ordell Robbie, the light-skinned black gun dealer who propels the plot, is an ex-convict making it big for the first time. He is also flashy, funny, intuitive, resilient and likable, entertaining company unless he sees you as an obstacle to his plans. Louis Gara, a dark-skinned white man, plays a kind of pitiable Sancho Panza, cowed by the prison system, his reflexes slower than they used to be, putty in Ordell's hands. Elmore Leonard seats us right up close, putting us on the stage while the actors are performing, so we are forced to respond to his villains fully, with a confusing mixture of attraction and repulsion, instead of remaining safely separate from them.

In the world of traditional detective fiction, notions of right and wrong square with what we learned in church (with a margin for psychopathology, as in P.D. James and Elizabeth Daly). In Mr. Leonard's book, morality is situational, choice permeated by circumstance—as ambiguous as Ordell's and Louis's racial identities are at first glance. The forces of virtue are less than compelling. Representing the good guys are two cops, Faron Tyler and Ray Nicolet, overambitious, one step south of corruption; and a burned-out bail bondsman in his 50's, Max Cherry, who meets Ordell when he bails out one of the gun dealer's enforcers.

Max has carried indecision to the limit. The insurance company that backs his business has been taken over by mob interests. He knows he should pull out, but shilly-shallies. Separated from his wife of 27 years, he keeps putting off divorce. All he has left by way of integrity is his eroding professionalism. Ordell sums up Max's situation, tells him he's "dealing with scum . . . and trying to act respectable."

Max is roused out of his lethargy by Jackie Burke, a still-attractive veteran flight attendant, who has been carrying Ordell's payoff money from the Bahamas. If he joins in her scheme to keep the money for themselves, he will have displayed some courage, at least by his own lights, for the first time in years.

Outpacing the classic hard-boiled novel, leaving the British detective novel in the dust, Elmore Leonard has compressed *Rum Punch* into almost pure drama, as close to playwriting as novel writing can get (and get away with). Mr. Leonard never tells you; he shows you. The story is all action, a scam within a scam: Ordell outfoxing Jackie and the cops; Jackie and Max duping the cops and Ordell.

> **Outpacing the classic hard-boiled novel, leaving the British detective novel in the dust, Elmore Leonard has compressed *Rum Punch* into almost pure drama, as close to playwriting as novel writing can get (and get away with).**
> —*Ann Arensberg*

His style is the absence of style, stripped of fancy baggage (social philosophy, abnormal psychology, beautiful diction)—the absence, as far as it's possible, of an authorial ego. He puts his ego in the service of his characters and their stories, and by doing so strikes a blow for that most radical of notions: that no one human being is better than any other, that there is no "other."

Being a new reader of Elmore Leonard, I believe I have a distinct advantage over his longtime fans. I have 29 more novels to look forward to. They have only *Rum Punch.*

Teresa Carpenter (review date 17 October 1993)

SOURCE: "Crime/Mystery; On the Lam in Rapallo," in *New York Times,* Vol. 98, October 17, 1993, p. 39.

[*In the following review, Carpenter offers a mixed assessment of* Pronto.]

Somewhere along the line, it became fashionable to discuss Elmore Leonard in terms formerly reserved for the likes of Flaubert, an excess of flattery that must certainly cause the man embarrassment. Mr. Leonard writes crime fiction. It is not so important that his books make insightful observations on contemporary culture—which they often do—or whether they contain sharply drawn portraits of characters on the fringe of society—which they invariably do. The bottom line is, are they fun?

Pronto, the author's 31st novel, is fun—relatively speaking. It doesn't have the bite of *Get Shorty* or the full-tilt looniness of *Maximum Bob.* But there is a payoff in Opus 31, and that is the glee with which Mr. Leonard sends up the mob.

Pronto tracks the misadventures of Harry Arno, a small-time operator who runs a sports book for the Miami syndicate. Federal investigators try to pressure him to rat on his boss, Jimmy Cap, by planting a rumor that he is skimming. As, of course, he is. Squeezed by both sides, Harry takes his nest egg and flees to Rapallo, a harbor town on the Italian Riviera. Why Rapallo? Harry, it turns out, was stationed there during World War II. It was the first, and last, place he ever killed anyone, and so the locale holds nostalgic associations. He also has a curious fascination with a onetime Rapallo resident, Ezra Pound, whose poetry he does not understand. The bookie leases a villa, intending to pass himself off as a member of the landed gentry, when his enchanted April is spoiled by the arrival of pursuers.

First on the scene is Raylan Givens, a United States marshal whom Harry has twice given the slip. Raylan is a raw-boned good ol' boy who stands out like Wyatt Earp on the Via Veneto. He has come partly to vindicate himself, but also because he likes Harry and wants to protect him from two thugs—Jimmy Cap's personal emissary, Nicky Testa, and an Italian hit man named Tommy (the Zip) Bitonti.

The American Testa and the Sicilian Bitonti are supposedly on the same side, but as they hail from opposite sides of the Atlantic, their ideas on how to do business are worlds apart. The Zip looks on Nicky, and indeed all New World Mafiosi, as colonials gone soft on tofu and Evian water. Nicky, for his part, disdains Bitonti as an old-timey guy. The Zip is, in fact, an anachronism who fancies that he looks like Frank Costello and goes to great lengths to protect the crease in his trousers. Both hoods are so preoccupied with primping that it seems little wonder the bosses in South Beach are losing ground to the Colombians.

When the fortunes of Raylan Givens, Nicky Testa, Tommy Bitonti and Harry Arno converge in Rapallo, the question becomes who, in the heat of a showdown, has the nerve to pull the trigger. By now Mr. Leonard's fans know full well that the nicest guy is not always the quickest draw.

What is missing here is the flavor and feel of Italy, an omission made all the more peculiar in light of Mr. Leonard's demonstrated ability to evoke the flavor of American cities like Detroit and Miami. About all we get is a view of Rapallo's Via Veneto from Harry's table at the Gran Caffe

Rapallo and descriptions from Givens's recently purchased guidebook. Mr. Leonard does provide us with a vivid rendering of Harry's villa, a crumbling mustard-yellow estate with loads of atmosphere. It is also wet and drafty, considerations that should give pause to anyone planning to rent during the off-season.

Plotting is not always Mr. Leonard's strong suit, and the narrative tends to unravel when the Government inexplicably loses interest in Jimmy Cap and drops its pursuit of Harry, forcing Givens to pursue the bookie on his own time. By then, however, the author has managed to hook us on characters who are dangerous despite themselves and unpredictably hilarious. (A crew boss muses upon the verb "to whack": "You know, you didn't hear that word so much till I read John Gotti uses it all the time.")

Wise guys, maybe. Bright guys, no. Elmore Leonard has captured them perfectly, a culture of vainglorious goons who have had their heyday. And this is how it ends—not with a bang, but a simper.

Dick Lochte (review date 24 October 1993)

SOURCE: "When Honor and Justice Were Things To Be Cherished," in *Los Angeles Times Book Review,* October 24, 1993, p. 8.

[*The following is Lochte's laudatory review of* Pronto.]

Elmore Leonard begins his 31st novel [*Pronto*] with a Miami bookmaker, Harry Arno, about to tell his girlfriend Joyce his biggest secret. But she already knows it: When he was stationed in Rapallo, Italy, during WWII, he shot a deserter. The joke, and the setup for the novel, is that Harry doesn't realize that he has talked about his "secret" often—whenever he's had too much to drink. And when the FBI, out of perversity, puts him on the spot with Mafia boss "Jimmy Cap" Capotorto, forcing Harry to hop it to his special Italian hideaway, everybody knows where he is.

Maybe not everybody. But Raylan Givens, the U.S. marshal responsible for keeping track of Harry, knows. And so does Tommy Bitonti, a.k.a. Tommy Bucks or the Zip, a hit man of the old Sicilian school who believes that the new Mafiosi, Jimmy Cap included, are a bunch of wusses. The stage is thus set, admirably, for another of the author's stylish, darkly funny confrontations between a laid back but quirky professional, Givens, and a street-smart but equally quirky sociopath, the Zip. The fact that Harry, the man they're determined to help and harm, respectively, is a selfish, insensitive, essentially worthless lout does nothing to alter the intensity of their dedication.

It's a mistake to categorize Leonard's novels as mysteries or thrillers. Murderers are not announced in their final chapters, secrets are not revealed, the fates of nations do not hang on their outcome. They are tales of heroes and villains engaged in mortal and moral struggle. What distinguishes them is Leonard's ability to create characters, conversations and situations that are as natural and convincing as they are unique. He seems to know the hustlers, con men, killers and especially the good guys firsthand, and he passes along this knowledge in an understated way that suggests we readers are his equals in awareness.

Here, for example, is Raylan Givens explaining himself to Nicky Pesta, a Miami punk whom the Zip has sent to kill him:

> "Mr. Zip . . . offered me money—did he mention that to you?—30 million lire, which sounds like a lot more'n it is, if I'd go away and quit bothering you people. To me, that was an insult. Not the amount, you understand, but that he'd entertain the idea I might take it. A man like him thinking everybody has a price. Well, there was a time he could've had me for $15 a day—hell, less than that—when I was a boy working in the coal mines. Anybody ever asked what was my price, that would've been it, 15 a day. I've worked deep mines, wildcat mines, I've worked for strip operators, and I've set out over a year on strike and seen company gun thugs shoot up the houses of miners that spoke out. They killed an uncle of mine was living with us, my mother's brother, and they killed a friend of mine I played football with in high school. This was in a coal camp town called Evarts in Harlan County, Kentucky, near to 20 years ago. You understand what I'm saying? Even before I entered the Marshals Service and trained to be a dead shot, I'd seen people kill one another and learned to be ready in case I saw a bad situation coming toward me. . . . In other words, if I see you've come to do me harm, I'll shoot you through the heart before you can clear your weapon. Do we have an understanding here?"

It should be noted that Leonard began his career as an author with yarns about cowpokes and villains. His 1981 contemporary police novel, *City Primeval*, was constructed very much like a Western, complete with shootout in the street; and in case the point was not made, it carried the subtitle *High Noon in Detroit*. This new book, with its thoughtful, mild-mannered lawman protagonist looking a bit silly and out of place in Italy wearing his Dallas special Stetson (think Joel McCrea in his prime), is another of his wild West/urban crime melds. It mixes the romantic notions of the past, when honor and justice and a woman's love were things to be cherished, with Leonard's particularly adroit insight into the harsh realities and tensions of today. The mixture works beautifully.

Martin Amis (review date 14 May 1995)

SOURCE: "Junk Souls," in *New York Times*, Vol. 100, May 14, 1995, p. 7.

[*In the following favorable review of* Riding the Rap, *Amis applauds Leonard's characteristic style of narrative and dialogue.*]

Let us attempt to narrow it down. Elmore Leonard is a literary genius who writes re-readable thrillers. He belongs, then, not to the mainstream but to the genres (before he wrote thrillers, he wrote westerns). Whereas genre fiction, on the whole, heavily relies on plot, mainstream fiction, famously, has only about a dozen plots to recombinate (boy meets girl, good beats bad and so on). But Mr. Leonard has only one plot. All his thrillers are Pardoner's Tales, in which Death roams the land—usually Miami and Detroit—disguised as money.

Nevertheless, Mr. Leonard possesses gifts—of ear and eye, of timing and phrasing—that even the most indolent and snobbish masters of the mainstream must vigorously covet. And the question is: How does he allow these gifts play, in his efficient, unpretentious and (delightfully) similar yarns about semiliterate hustlers, mobsters, go-go dancers, cocktail waitresses, loan sharks, bounty hunters, blackmailers and crime syndicate executioners? My answer may sound reducive, but here goes: The essence of Elmore is to be found in his use of the present participle.

What this means, in effect, is that he has discovered a way of slowing down and suspending the English sentence—or let's say the American sentence, because Mr. Leonard is as American as jazz. Instead of writing "Warren Ganz III lived up in Manalapan, Palm Beach County," Mr. Leonard writes, "Warren Ganz III, living up in Manalapan, Palm Beach County." He writes, "Bobby saying," and then opens quotes. He writes, "Dawn saying," and then opens quotes. We are not in the imperfect tense (Dawn was saying) or the present (Dawn says) or the historic present (Dawn said). We are in a kind of marijuana tense (Dawn saying), creamy, wandering, weak-verbed. Such sentences seem to open up a lag in time, through which Mr. Leonard easily slides, gaining entry to his players' hidden minds. He doesn't just show you what these people say and do. He shows you where they breathe.

Mr. Leonard is as American as jazz, and jazz is in origin a naive form. Yet Mr. Leonard is no Louis Armstrong. He can do melody, but he is also as harshly sophisticated as late Coleman Hawkins. He understands the post-modern world—the world of wised-up rabble and zero authenticity. His characters are equipped not with obligingly suggestive childhoods or case histories, but with a cranial jukebox of situation comedies and talk shows and advertising jingles, their dreams and dreads all mediated and secondhand. They are not lost souls or deal souls. Terrible and pitiable (and often downright endearing), they are simply junk souls: quarter-pounders, with cheese.

In *Riding the Rap,* Chip Ganz, aging pretty boy, parasite and predator, plans to commit the crime of the century. Not this century: the next. His crime will be a new crime. "Burning herb," "maintaining on reefer," the marijuana-sotted Chip has picked up various odds and ends about the hostages in Beirut—"seen them on TV when they were released, read a book one of them wrote." His idea is to take rich Miamians hostage. "You talking about kidnapping?" asks his associate, Louis Lewis. No. You don't demand a ransom. You don't call his family. You wait, and then you ask the victim how much his life is worth.

"Starting out, Chip had pictured a damp basement full of spiders and roaches crawling around, pipes dripping, his hostages huddled against the wall in chains. He wanted it to be as bad as any of the places in Beirut he'd read about."

"He told Louis and Louis said, 'Where we gonna find a basement in Florida?'"

So the malefactors have to catch as catch can. The hostage they take is not a politician or a diplomat; he is a mob bookie called Harry Arno. The muscle they hire is not a Shia terrorist but a Puerto Rican debt collector called Bobby Deogracias. The dungeon they use is not a fetid cellar but a spare bedroom in an oceanfront residence in Palm Beach owned by Chip's mother. The diet they put their hostage on consists not of bread and water but of frozen dinners and Jell-O. "Louis said the Shia fixed their hostages rice . . . but no doubt would have given them TV dinners if they had any."

Of course the scheme unravels into a peculiarly American chaos. Crime, Mr. Leonard insistently informs us, is always half-baked, and always goes off half-cocked. Death (or life, behind bars) comes in the form of the fast buck, or its promise. Ranged against these seedy blunderers is United States Marshal Raylan Givens (a welcome carry-over, like Harry Arno, from Mr. Leonard's previous novel, *Pronto*). Raylan is perhaps the cleanest character in the entire oeuvre, dead straight and "all business," a genuine enforcer, unlike the gray-area skip tracers and writ servers who, in Mr. Leonard's work, usually represent the law-and-order industry. Raylan isn't post-modern, he is an anachronism from out of town.

And he is fascinating, because he shows you what Mr. Leonard actually holds dear—the values he can summon in a different kind of prose, in different American rhythms, those of Robert Frost, or even Mark Twain:

> "He could cut official corners to call a man out . . . but couldn't walk in a man's house unless invited, or else with a warrant and bust down the door.

> "It was the way he was raised, to have good manners . . . back when they were living in a coal camp and the miners struck Duke Power: Raylan walking a picket line most of the year, his dad in the house dying of black lung, and company gun thugs came looking for Raylan's uncle. . . They came across the street, five of them, a couple with pick handles, and up the walk to where his mother stood on the porch. . . . The gun thugs said they wanted to speak to her brother. . . . She told them, 'You don't walk in a person's home 'less you're invited. Even you people must believe that. You have homes, don't you? Wives and mothers keeping house?' . . . They shoved her aside and hit Raylan with the pick handles to put him down. . . .

> "Her words hadn't stopped them. No, what they did was stick in Raylan's mind—her words, her quiet tone of voice—and stop him, more than 20 years later, from breaking into this man's house."

I first read *Riding the Rap* in mid-January. In mid-March I read it again. The reviewer curling up with the present participle. Re-reading Elmore Leonard in the morning, and saying it was work. The experience, like the book, was wicked and irresistible. This was post-modern decadence. This was bliss.

Robert Worth (review date 18 August 1995)

SOURCE: "Plumbing the Shallows," in *Commonweal,* August 18, 1995, pp. 24-5.

[The following is Worth's positive review of Riding the Rap.]

Elmore Leonard has been writing great crime fiction for years with the same cozy formulas, the same cast of South Florida rednecks and drug-runners and gamblers and cops and abused ex-wives. So it has been a little strange to see his profile rise abruptly in the past year, with highbrow critical praise, a big Hollywood film, even an appearance in the *New Yorker.* One has to wonder sometimes whether all this attention is going to his head, making him too self-conscious. It has happened before: Dashiell Hammett never wrote a good line after Hollywood discovered him. But these fears are groundless. *Riding the Rap* is as good as anything Leonard has ever written.

As much as any contemporary fiction writer, Elmore Leonard has discovered a style of his own. His books consist mostly of dialogue, and even the descriptions sound like someone talking: clipped, fragmentary, familiar. It is the voice of someone looking in the rearview mirror, describing what he sees on a two-way radio. Definite articles drop out, as do adjectives and pronouns; everything occurs in a rolling, improvised present tense. Verbs give way to the participle: "Bobby watching the fortuneteller standing next to Harry in the recliner, the fortuneteller looking this way now, brushing her long hair from her face with the tips of her fingers, looking this way right at Bobby—Bobby sure of it, the woman calm, still looking this way. . . ." This style can be hard to follow at first, because the point of view drifts between characters, like a cloud of exhaled smoke, without ever seeming to settle on anyone in particular.

Leonard's brilliance consists in having matched his style to his subject perfectly. These are not characters who would bloom into life in the hands of a more sophisticated writer. They are complete, because they are shallow. Their lives are rootless, transient, a blur of violence and get-rich schemes and failed relationships. Yet they are comic, because they do not dream of anything better than the next heist. They reinvent themselves all the time, using whatever materials come along. Louis Lewis, for instance, one of the bad guys in *Riding the Rap,* "was originally from the Bahamas . . . he could sound Bahamian if he wanted to, but preferred being African-American and worked at it. A popular variation, he tried an Islamic name, Ibrahim Abu Aziz, till Chip started calling him Honest Ib and then Boo for Abu and Louis decided that was enough of that shit."

Leonard's characters live through TV and the movies. In *Riding the Rap* an aging gambler named Warren "Chip" Ganz has decided to make money by kidnapping people and forcing them to come up with a way to make the payments. Only he wants it to be exactly like the hostage crisis in Lebanon, which he saw on TV. He wants a basement, "full of spiders and roaches crawling around, pipes dripping, his hostages huddled against the wall in chains. . . . he told Louis and Louis said, 'Where we gonna find a basement in Florida?'" Their first hostage is Harry Arno, who spent Leonard's last novel (*Pronto*) being chased by Italian gangsters. This time he is left blindfolded in an upstairs room at Chip's place, while the bad guys sit around downstairs channel-surfing between Harry (on the house video-surveillance system) and "Oprah." The video system monitors the driveway too, so the main action of the novel becomes (for Chip and Louis) a TV show. When U.S.

Marshall Raylan Givens arrives at the house looking for Harry, they recognize his "outdoor good-guy look" from the cowboy shows they've seen. And when the inevitable showdown comes, Louis can't get over the correspondence. "We like in the movies, huh?"

Raylan, no TV junkie, models himself on the real thing, the handlebar-mustached sheriffs of the old Western frontier. Like most Leonard heroes, he is fortyish and tough, having struggled up from poverty and a bad marriage. Unlike the bad guys, he retains some connection with his past, though he doesn't like to talk about it. Born in an Appalachian mining town, he still remembers vividly the day when company thugs broke into his mother's house to get to his uncle, a striker. And now, without a warrant but knowing that Harry is held hostage in Chip's house, he remembers how his mother told those company men that you do not walk into a house uninvited: "Her words hadn't stopped them. No, what they did was stick in Raylan's mind—her words, her quiet tone of voice—and stop *him,* more than twenty years later, from breaking into this man's house."

Raylan also struggles to justify his calling to his girlfriend Joyce, who cannot forgive him for having shot two mobsters back in *Pronto.* Raylan is no philosopher, but his stalwart fatalism redeems the black comedy of crime that is all around him. Transporting a violent redneck to prison, he tells him: "What you'll have to do now is ride the rap, as they say. It's all anybody has to do."

> **Reading Leonard is in fact a little like watching a film, though no filmmaker has yet matched his pacing or reproduced his laconic humor on screen. And the dialogue might wilt in the mouths of actors.**
> —*Robert Worth*

This stoic acceptance of a world of violence, alternating with an ironic, TV-borne detachment from it, is the baseline of Leonard's sensibility. There is something profoundly cheering about it, because it seems to bring a frightening world closer without lessening its glamour. In this respect Leonard is kin to *Pulp Fiction* filmmaker Quentin Tarantino, who gets a nice allusive compliment in the first few pages of *Riding the Rap.* Reading Leonard is in fact a little like watching a film, though no filmmaker has yet matched his pacing or reproduced his laconic humor on screen. And the dialogue might wilt in the mouths of actors. It is tempting to say that no one writes as authentically as Leonard, but I have no idea whether people in South Florida talk like that. What really matters is that after reading one of his novels I want to talk the way Elmore Leonard's people do.

Frank J. Prial (essay date 15 February 1996)

SOURCE: "It's No Crime To Talk Softly," in *New York Times Biographical Service,* February 15, 1996, pp. 298-300.

[*In the following essay, Prial surveys Leonard's life and career, and includes commentary by the author on his works and personal experiences.*]

Birmingham, Mich.

There's a tendency in this country to confuse appearance with reality. It's like that when you meet Elmore Leonard.

He writes these tough-guy books like *Get Shorty, Riding the Rap, LaBrava* and *Stick.* They are loaded with taut dialogue, violence and marvelous characters, inept low-lifes out to score big.

But Mr. Leonard himself? A pussycat. With his innocent-looking eyes and scraggly beard, he comes down somewhere between an El Greco saint and a saintly George Carlin. An Elmore Leonard character he's not. He doesn't lurk in Miami bars or prowl Detroit's meaner streets. He doesn't consort with confidence men, retired strippers or people who deal in controlled substances.

Someone suggests a stroll through a tough Detroit neighborhood, a Leonard milieu. He looks out from his elegant two-story house at his tennis court and pool and pushes home the point again that he writes about those places, for Pete's sake, he doesn't hang out in them. And all those hoods, hookers and hustlers in his books? He makes them up. He is not even a gun nut.

What he is is a writer, and a fine one by common consent. He does what good writers do: he sits at a desk all day and wrestles with words. He has written 33 books and numerous screenplays.

The only thing tough about him is his nickname, Dutch, a moniker favored by gangsters of another era and given to him in his school days.

It was a quiet time recently in the Leonard home in this affluent Detroit suburb. *Riding the Rap,* which was published last year, was doing well. His newest thriller, *Out of Sight,* which is due out in July, had just been finished and was already sold to Universal Studios.

And Mr. Leonard, 70, said that MGM-United Artists has been hinting about another book on Chili Palmer, the hero, sort of, in *Get Shorty,* the screen version of which is doing handsomely at the box office but which was snubbed, along with its star, John Travolta, when the Academy Award nominations were announced on Tuesday.

Mr. Leonard, 70, is the father of 5 and the grandfather of 10. He is quiet-spoken, laconic, actually, and easygoing and completely open. Oh, and quite rich.

"I am what you call an overnight success," he said with heavy sarcasm, "after writing almost anonymously for 30 years." *LaBrava,* his novel published in 1983, was his first book to gain wide public acclaim. *Glitz,* published two years later, insured his reputation as one of the best, if not the best, writer of crime fiction.

Reviewing *Riding the Rap* in *The New York Times* last May, Martin Amis defined Mr. Leonard as a genre writer rather than a mainstream novelist. But, Mr. Amis wrote, he "possesses gifts—of ear and eye, of timing and phrasing—that even the most indolent and snobbish masters of the mainstream must vigorously covet."

Born in New Orleans in 1925, Mr. Leonard moved around as a child while his father scouted locations for General Motors dealerships. The family arrived in Detroit when he was 9 and he has lived there, or here in its tony suburbs, ever since.

After serving in the Navy and graduating from the University of Detroit, he joined an advertising agency, Campbell-Ewald, where he wrote—what else in Detroit?—Chevrolet ads. In the morning, before going to work, he wrote western stories.

"I always wanted to write," he said. "My first effort was in the fifth grade: a one-act play based on *All Quiet on the Western Front,* which had just been serialized in *The Detroit Times.* A guy is hooked on the barbed wire; someone has to crawl out and get him. That was it. Our audience was the Mother Superior."

His first commercial success was a western story published in 1951 in *Argosy,* a men's magazine. "Westerns were big in the 50's," Mr. Leonard recalled. "*The Saturday Evening Post, Colliers,* all the big magazines published westerns. If you didn't make it there, you went to books like *Argosy.* Then came the pulps—Dime Western, Zane Grey, Ten-Story Western—at 2 cents a word."

A 4,500-word short story called **"3:10 To Yuma"** brought in $90 from one pulp. Columbia Pictures bought it for $4,000, but the magazine's publisher exercised a contractual right to take 25 percent. "I learned then to read the fine print," he said.

The Bounty Hunters, his first novel, appeared in 1953, followed by four others during the next eight years. When *Hombre* appeared in 1961, he quit his copywriting job. Bad timing.

"The market for westerns was running dry," he said. "There were 30 westerns on TV each week; why read them? I was married, had five kids and a new house. So I did industrial films, ad copy, anything, until 20th Century Fox finally bought *Hombre* in 1967 for $10,000."

His next book, *The Big Bounce,* in 1969, was his first try at a crime theme. As one critic said later: "Elmore Leonard was finally in Elmore Leonard territory."

From then on, a new book has appeared almost every year. Hollywood also beckoned, and he found himself commuting from Detroit to turn his books and those of others into screenplays. Most of his scripts never made it to the screen, but the money was good and he continued to write novels back home in Michigan.

In 1977, his life underwent some drastic changes. On Jan. 21, with a final Scotch and ginger ale—and the help of Alcoholics Anonymous—he ended 35 years of drinking. Also that year, his marriage of 25 years ended in divorce. He married again in 1979, but his second wife died of cancer in 1993. Six months later he met Christine Kent, a gardener working on his lawn; she also taught French at the University of Detroit. They were married two months later.

A Leonard book runs to about 300 pages. "I write the first 100 pretty fast," he said. "Then I slow up to think out where I'm going. I take a hard look at my characters. Do they work? Are they believable? If they can't talk, I drop them, or I give them new roles.

"Names are terribly important. I spend forever coming up with names. Sometimes a character doesn't work until I change his name. In *Bandits,* Frank Matusi didn't work. I changed him to Jack Delaney and suddenly he opened up.

"At the same time, I try to avoid continuous characters like Raylan Givens and Harry Arno" (who appear in *Pronto* and *Riding the Rap*). "If a studio buys a book, it owns the character," he continued. "MGM got Chili Palmer when they bought *Get Shorty.*"

Just as musicians say Vivaldi wrote the same concerto 400 times, some critics argue that each Leonard novel is much the same as the last, that only the names change. "It's true, I guess," he said. "They are often the same guys and I change the name.

"But then, I don't plot things out. I put these guys in the story, but I have no idea what they're going to do. Some-times major characters go and minor guys become more important.

"Sometimes, on tour, people say to me, 'Too bad that so and so bought it. He was interesting.' So I give him a brother, and put him in the next book."

Endings, Mr. Leonard insists, are no problem. "There are all kinds of way to end," he said. "Remember, there are no puzzles in my books; I don't write mysteries."

It takes Mr. Leonard about six months to write a book. A writing day is 9:30 A.M. to 6 P.M. "I try for five pages," he said. "On an odd day, I might get eight or nine."

He writes in longhand on unlined yellow paper, usually three paragraphs. "I have the paper made up for me, usually 50 boxes at a time," he said. He transcribes the paragraphs with a typewriter, cutting and tightening the few lines he's done. No word processor. "With one of them, you just shift material around," he said. "My way, you get to rework every word."

The ideas for an Elmore Leonard book come from Elmore Leonard. So does much of the detail. A character in *Bandits* is a mortician. "I researched embalming," he said. "I visited a mortuary, went out and picked up a suicide victim, went through the whole thing." He was delighted to discover that the embalming fluid was called PermaGlo. "Those are the touches I love," he said.

He also employs a full-time researcher, Gregg Sutter, who ranges the country for him, digging out bizarre people and arcane facts. "I wanted to do a bail bondsman," Mr. Leonard said, "so I asked Gregg to find me one. He talked to half a dozen and found a good one. Then I went to talk to the guy."

Dialogue is different: he gets it firsthand. No researcher. Like many writers, Mr. Leonard is a listener. When he hears peculiarities of speech on the street, on television, he writes them down.

His own reading is eclectic. "I read four or five books a week," he said, but almost nothing in the crime field. "I read John D. McDonald in the early 1950's and said, 'This is what I should be doing.'

"My heros are John O'Hara and Steinbeck and Hemingway," he continued. "I studied Hemingway. I loved the white space on the pages. It meant there was plenty of dialogue to move the story along.

"I was fascinated by the structure of his books, but I didn't share his attitudes and that's what shapes your style. He had no sense of humor."

Few of his friends are writers and he has little interest in literary circles. "They sit around all day talking about writing instead of doing it," he said.

Occasionally he is asked to talk to writing students. "It's kind of sad," he said. "They have their pads out and their pens, and they're ready to hear the secret, to write it down. There isn't any secret. You sit down and you start and that's it."

Ed McBain (review date 25 August 1996)

SOURCE: "A Love Story (With True Grit)," in *Los Angeles Times Book Review,* August 25, 1996, p. 3.

[*In the following review, McBain provides a primarily favorable assessment of* Out of Sight.]

The irony of it is surely not wasted on Elmore Leonard, himself a master of irony.

After years of indifferent Hollywood movies based on his novels, after decades of having his own screenplays abused, misused or merely trashed, Leonard writes a payback novel sending up Tinseltown's denizens and guess what happens? It becomes a hit movie! So now the jacket of his new book blatantly advertises "a novel by the author of *Get Shorty.*" This after more than 30 other novels, almost all of which were far superior to *Get Shorty.* It is to laugh.

Having at last been "discovered" by the moon pitchers, Leonard perversely survives the temptation to go Hollywood by delivering a new novel that is eminently filmable. *Out of Sight,* however, is a rarity in the Leonard canon: It is a genuine love story. True, there have been boy-girl plots in many of his previous books, but these were always subservient to the convoluted bad guy-good guy machinations of the main story. Here, the love story is the novel's engine, and—wouldn't you know it?—its principals are a bad guy and a good guy.

The bad guy is 47-year-old Jack Foley, who's robbed more banks than he can remember and who's done far too much time in prisons hither and yon, one of which he's escaping from as the story begins. The good "guy" is a 29-year-old deputy U.S. marshal named Karen Sisco, who has a penchant for shotguns and short skirts. Serving process at the prison—a con has filed a civil rights suit because he doesn't like macaroni and cheese—Karen finds herself in the middle of the break and subsequently in the trunk of the getaway car with Jack. (Don't be tempted into thinking this is "meeting cute." Oh, no. This is simply the way boy meets girl on Leonard's turf.) Neither Karen nor Jack can help wondering what might have happened if they were people other than

who they are, meeting under different circumstances. Whether they will, in fact, meet again, and whether their diametrically opposed occupations will stand in the way of true love become in Leonard's telling the stuff of high romance and taut suspense.

He knows better, though, than to leave an entire novel in the shaky hands of a pair of accidental lovers. So he peoples the book with his usual mix of good guys acting tough and bad guys sounding soft; he introduces a trio of heavies intent on a home invasion that will yield treasures broadly hinted at by a talkative con to a fellow prisoner. These truly frightening robbers from hell make every other crook in the novel seem saintly by comparison. "Was worse than you imagined it, wasn't it?" a woman comments. "Baby, you with the bad boys now." Watching Leonard as he skillfully transports Jack and Karen into the orbit of these monsters is one of the novel's many pleasures.

Another joy is the way Leonard integrates facts and convinces us that he knows everything about anything, as in, "two guys doing laps side by side around the field, counterclockwise, the way inmates always circled a yard here and in every prison Foley had ever heard of." Who would know that "counterclockwise" stuff except someone who's served time himself—which Leonard very definitely has not. I think. Or listen to this: "He told them he'd spot the car a customer wanted and use a slim-jim or lemon-pop to get in, a slaphammer to yank the ignition, a side-kick to extract steering column locks and usually liquid nitrogen to freeze the alarm system." Exactly. What else? And then there are moments that have nothing to do with research.

"Buddy was about to jimmy the door when he saw a woman coming from Winn-Dixie, middle-aged, wearing pearls and high heels in the afternoon."

That's Leonard himself, observing and zeroing in on the single telling detail, adding "in the afternoon" almost as an afterthought. Oh, how sly.

Sometimes—perhaps because he knows he can write people talking the way no one else on Earth can—Leonard relies too heavily on pages and pages of dialogue, sounding a bit like George V. Higgins on a roll. Sometimes, too many of the people in *Out of Sight* sound like too many of the people in some of his other books, chatting about favorite movie scenes, sipping Diet Pepsi, relating in ways that are often superficial. The ending, too, screams for something stronger, something more painfully operatic. But for the most part, Leonard is on target, and when he hits the bull's-eye, he hits it cleanly.

It's no surprise that *Out of Sight* will be made into a motion picture by the same people who gave us *Get Shorty.*

Neither is it surprising that Quentin Tarantino, whose *Pulp Fiction* was a fine pastiche of Leonard's style, has bought the rights to four of his novels. This is merely as it should be in Elmoreleonardland.

Ralph Lombreglia (review date 8 September 1996)

SOURCE: "Mr. Wrong," in *New York Times*, September 8, 1996.

[*In the following review, Lombreglia faults* Out of Sight *as unrealistic.*]

The oldest unsolved mystery on the books, human love, is the case to crack in *Out of Sight,* Elmore Leonard's new novel, in which the cop is a lady with a gift for meeting Mr. Wrong and the robber is a guy who just might have been, in a different life, Mr. Right. It begins auspiciously with a prison break, a group of convicts tunneling out of the medium-security Florida pen where Jack Foley, a career bank robber, is doing time after his third major fall.

On first glance, Foley seems to be the classic crime-fiction hard guy, "a celebrity hard-timer" who gives talks in prison on how to stay alive. "If you saw it coming, hit first with something heavy. Foley's choice, a foot or so of lead pipe, never a shank, a shank was crude, sneaky, it put you in the same class as the thugs and hogs. No, what you wanted to do was lay the pipe across the guy's jaw, and if you had time break his hands with it." Yet you notice the personal ethics—situation ethics, to be sure, but more than you'll get later from a couple of truly bad guys in this book.

In fact, Foley wouldn't be in jail at all except that he messed up while robbing a bank to compensate his former wife for their rotten marriage. Now he emerges from a mucky hole into freedom to find Karen Sisco, a beautiful blond Federal marshal, pointing a shotgun in his face. Moments earlier, Karen had two other escapees in her sights, but she didn't shoot. She doesn't shoot this time either, and is overpowered by Foley and his accomplice, Buddy, a man who will later say of Foley, "You might've been a good cop." They put Karen in the trunk, Foley gets in with her, and the car takes off.

And here, for this reader at least, *Out of Sight* slides off the road into an Everglades of incredibility. For in order to accept the main action of the rest of the novel, we must now accept that both kidnapped and kidnapper—a female Federal law-enforcement officer and the man who has robbed more banks than anyone in the F.B.I.'s computer—experience in the trunk of a moving car a conversational intimacy that leaves them helplessly infatuated with each other, even

as Karen Sisco conceals a .38-caliber pistol between her legs. It's a bizarrely relocated movie "cute meet," and the busy scribes of Hollywood should be stealing pages from Elmore Leonard's book, not the other way around.

There is simply no way that these two people could have a calm, increasingly tender exchange on topics ranging from the details of Clyde Barrow's death to their mutual admiration of Faye Dunaway's sexually charged repartee with her leading men in several movies, *Bonnie and Clyde* among them. The strange physical intimacy of the scene is ignored altogether. Unreal bits of drama can certainly work in fiction, but not as the concrete slab upon which one erects a compelling crime novel.

If you step back from *Out of Sight,* you see that its serious flaws stem from ambition. The novel wants to portray complex characters who aren't simply good or bad. It yearns to embody the idea that cops and criminals can be profoundly similar people. And, of course, Mr. Leonard is too talented and experienced to produce a book devoid of his well-known charms. I admire, as always, the way he pulls the old cards from his sleeves and shuffles them a new way—the perfectly sketched minor characters, the flash-photographed locations, the blown chances and near-misses and lucky guesses—and deals out the scenes and the fates. He has a page-to-page delivery that any fiction writer could study. After Karen escapes her captors, and she and Foley begin their recollision course, there are moments so good they made me sad that I wasn't more emotionally invested in the story.

But in the end, Karen Sisco and Jack Foley are bundles of contradictions impossible to resolve into believable human beings. They seem to be constantly going in and out of character. It would be nice to say that they are pulled out of their personalities by the profound influence of each other, but first you'd have to accept that a career outlaw and a Federal officer would have such tenuous grasps on their own identities.

I think most readers, regardless of the height of their brows, are willing to believe in the great long shot of utterly irrational, unexpected love in unlikely circumstances—love that could destroy your life, or save it, or both. But it's only a possibility, and a slight one at that. Writers have to make it real.

Alec Wilkinson (essay date 30 September 1996)

SOURCE: "Elmore's Legs," in *New Yorker,* Vol. LXXII, No. 29, September 30, 1996, pp. 43-7.

[*In the following essay, Wilkinson presents Leonard's re-*

searcher, Greg Sutter, and traces Sutter's various experiences while gathering background material for Leonard's works.]

Elmore Leonard, the writer of sleek and authentic novels about criminals, such as **Stick** and **Get Shorty,** has never much enjoyed doing research. His earliest books were written in the fifties and involve cowboys and bandits. Leonard has spent most of his life in Detroit. To describe a mountain or a canyon or a butte, he consulted one issue or another of the magazine *Arizona Highways.* After the market for westerns disappeared, in the sixties, he relied on a newspaper reporter he knew who covered crime. "I don't like to research," he says. "I like to write." Nevertheless, for the last fifteen years, what verisimilitude in his novels is not the result of his imagination is the result of legwork. Not his legs.

Leonard's legman is named Gregg Sutter. He lives mostly in Hollywood, Florida, a popular destination for tourists from Quebec. Sutter came to Florida four years ago from Michigan, to do research for Leonard, and he likes it well enough, although sometimes he feels rootless there, he says, and he still has Michigan plates on his car. He lives along the beach, where two-story, flat-roofed motels alternate with apartment buildings that look like file cabinets. He has a one-bedroom apartment, filled with a lot of books and hi-fi and video and computer equipment. When he gets up in the morning, he stands his bed against a wall to make more room.

Sutter is forty-five. He is tall and large-boned, he has shaggy dark hair and small features, he stoops a little, and he has a shuffly walk. He frequently tucks his chin down and to one side and looks back at you with eyes askance, a form of shyness. His manner is somewhat measuring and aloof. "I'm very charming when it comes to librarians," he says, "but I don't have any charm otherwise."

Sutter's name occasionally appears in newspaper and magazine stories about Leonard, usually because Leonard has mentioned it. A friend of mine noticed it and suggested I call him. When I asked Sutter what he was working on, he said that when Leonard finished **Out of Sight,** his newest and thirty-third novel, which recently arrived in bookstores, he had intended to write about the fashion industry. Leonard—whom Sutter referred to as Dutch—expected the book to include the Mafia and he sent Sutter to New York last February to look around.

"I walked the fashion district for a few days and took the usual assortment of photos," Sutter said. "Dutch is very visual. I do a lot of panoramas—picture, picture, picture, then tape them together. I went to the New York Public Library and ran the clips for Mob stuff, but it turned out they had a lot less to do with the industry now than they had even ten years ago. Then I got the call from Dutch: 'It's getting to be too much like work. We're doing the Spanish-American War.' Meaning that in one day I'm going from reading fashion-retailing guides and talking to better-dress guys in the Graybar Building to the Span-Am War and bandits and insurgents and runaway slaves and race riots, and thinking, Hey, this is all right."

I asked Sutter if I might come and see him and maybe visit some of the places he had been to with Leonard and meet some of the people who had figured in his research, and he said sure. I stayed in a Holiday Inn next door to his building. Some highlights: In Palm Beach, we drove down a sand road through trees along the border of the golf course at the Breakers Hotel and looked at the greens Sutter had drawn on a map for Leonard to use in plotting the kidnapping of a wealthy guy in his recent novel **Riding the Rap.** We drove up Worth Avenue, where Sutter once made a videotape at a rally of Klansmen and Nazis and bikers because he thought that such an event in such a place contained sufficient irony to make it interesting to Leonard. *Rum Punch* begins, "Sunday morning, Ordell took Louis to the white-power demonstration in downtown Palm Beach." We sat in a courtroom in West Palm Beach presided over by Judge Marvin Mounts, Jr., the outline of whose life suggested to Leonard the title character Judge Bob Gibbs in **Maximum Bob.**

Sometimes while driving we listened to the tape of an interview Sutter conducted with a man who had escaped from more prisons in Florida than anyone else. **Out of Sight** revolves mainly around a convict named Jack Foley and an ex-convict named Buddy. As the book opens, Foley is engaged in breaking out of the Glades Correctional Institution, in Belle Glade, Florida. Leonard modelled the prison break on an escape made from Glades in 1995 by Cuban prisoners, who dug a tunnel under the prison fence. Leonard decided that Foley would lure a prison guard into the prison chapel, jump him for his clothes and hat, then follow the Cubans through the tunnel, and that Buddy would be waiting by arrangement with a car in the prison parking lot. When the Cubans leave the tunnel, they are chased and shot at, and two are killed. Dressed as a guard, Foley walks.

That a con might remain in possession of his nerves during a prison break was suggested to Leonard by listening to the tape. "You're getting ready to escape and you're scared," the guy said. "Your adrenaline's flowing, and you can reach a point where you're too scared to move. You're immobile. When people romance breaking out of prison, man, they don't romance *that.* To move you got to master your terror. How do you do it? The way to control your emotions is to act. You *act* cool, you going to *be* cool. I *walk* to the fence— I don't run and crash and frantically climb that fence. I walk up like my attitude is 'Fuck it, man. Ain't no big thing.' And when I come down the other side, I don't haul ass and run, either. That's *panic.* Soon as I hit the ground, I walk off. Man, I *stroll.* And, when you hit those woods, Hallelujah, God damn, that's a wonderful feeling."

In January of 1981, Leonard needed someone to read newspaper files and he thought of Sutter, who had called him a year and a half earlier. Sutter and a friend had been trying to start a magazine called *Noir* and wanted an interview with Leonard for their first issue. At the time Sutter got Leonard's phone call, he was working on the final assembly line at a car factory—an experience he hopes he may someday make part of a novel—"a Nathanael West on the line," he says. Sutter's own ambitions as a novelist he is content to defer. "I may not yet be successful as a writer, but I am successful as Elmore Leonard's literary researcher," he says. "I'm like someone who leads an archeological dig, then turns the findings over to someone who knows what they mean. Where I get satisfaction is in knowing that these stray bits I collect will be used in making something large and original and valuable."

Except inadvertently, he does not supply Leonard with material for characters. "He makes the bad guys up," Sutter says. The response that Sutter works hard to produce in Leonard is delight. Sutter values Leonard's allowing him to pursue what he intuitively feels will be interesting, and he doubts whether he could work happily for any other writer— certainly not for one who would simply give him lists of material to retrieve. Devotion, above all, is what Sutter feels for Leonard. "Life being a series of tests of loyalty, some of which I have already failed, I am here for the long run," he says. "If Dutch ever had a reversal of fortune, I would be there." The only disappointment I have heard Sutter express was after I mentioned how pleased I had been by a scene in *Out of Sight.* Sutter said, "I envy people who get to read him and have all the thrills. By the time the books are finished, I'm too familiar with the story."

For *Rum Punch,* Leonard asked Sutter to find a bail bondsman who would explain how bonds were written. Using a newsletter given to him by Judge Mounts, Sutter found Mike Sandy, a half-Lebanese, half-Sicilian former teacher. Sandy has an office across the street from the West Palm Beach courthouse with a sign on the door that says "Private." I asked him, as Sutter once had, about writing bonds, and that led to a description of the anxieties involved in a bondsman's life.

"Here's what happened to a bondsman in Miami," he said. "For years, one of his clients was a Colombian who brought him cases. We'll say the Colombian's name is Pedro Lopez. Very reliable. Suppose the bond is two hundred and fifty thousand. Lopez brings two hundred and fifty thousand, counts it out, then counts out the twenty-five-thousand-dollar premium for the bondsman. No collateral, no complica-

tions, cash business. Arrives with boxes and chests of money, like it was the Captain Kidd days.

"One day, an individual Lopez has paid for doesn't show up in court. Lopez comes into the bondsman's office, says, 'We don't want you to pay this bond,' and picks up his money. A few days later, Pedro Lopez is found floating in the bay off Key Biscayne. The bondsman gets a phone call from someone saying, 'Pedro has fallen on a serious accident, please be at such-and-such a bar at eleven tonight.' The bondsman's concerned. He's *innocent*—he's done nothing out of line that he can think of—but these people are Colombians. He shows up at the bar, with his brother. Why his brother? I don't know. The bartender greets him by name. The bondsman's lived all his life in Miami—he's never seen this guy, he's never been to this bar—but the guy knows his name. True story. Bartender points to a table in the corner and tells the bondsman and his brother to wait. Bar's dark.

"Time passes, music plays, maybe some people come and go. Eventually, three Colombians walk in and join the brothers at the table. One man talks, another interprets, and the third says nothing at all. Third guy has a mustache. The one talking tells the bondsman that Mr. Lopez developed a problem the other night, he fell on a power saw. In his apartment. Bondsman nods. He's listening closely. He's sweating a little. He's thinking, Why am I here? 'But before he fell on the power saw,' the man says, 'he told us that you returned only a hundred and fifty thousand of the two-hundred-and-fifty-thousand-dollar bond.'

"When the bondsman hears this—which isn't true—he doesn't say, 'He's lying,' he doesn't say, 'There's been some mistake,' he doesn't say, 'I don't know what you're talking about.' He stands up and says, 'An hour. We'll make some calls. My brother will wait here, and I'll be back in an hour with the money.'

"The Colombian says, 'No, no, sit down. We want you to know that after Mr. Lopez fell on the power saw we found the money. That's not why we called you here.' Bondsman sits down. The Colombian says, 'We asked you to meet us so that we could demonstrate the faith we have in you by introducing the man you and Mr. Lopez have been working for.' They'd brought the heavy-weight, you see. Show of confidence. The man talking points to the third man at the table, who hasn't said a word and never does: Pablo Escobar. True story."

Chronology: Sutter was born in Detroit, in 1951. The hospital was later torn down to make way for a Cadillac plant. He went to Catholic grade school, and in 1969 he went to Oakland University, in Rochester, Michigan, thirty miles north. "My first major was behavioral science, which I still don't know what it is," he says. "Then I fell into film history. I thought of myself as a cine-Marxist—sit around the apartment and talk about the Revolution and watch movies. I wrote about Cuban revolutionary posters and Nazi cinema, and got a degree in history, never thinking about what I would do the day after I graduated."

Before Sutter went to work for Leonard, he held a series of obscure jobs: among other things, he did publicity for the Women's Symphony of Detroit; he was the editor of the *Grapevine Gazette,* the house organ of the Detroit Metropolitan Bar Owners Association ("Sad little stories about bar owners and liquor-commission violations," he says); he and some friends started a magazine called *Artbeat,* which folded after four issues, when it ran out of money; and in November of 1975 he got a job at Norman Levy Associates, an industrial liquidator. "We'd go into a shop, such as a lathe shop," he says, "assign a book value to everything, scrub the machines with kerosene to make them shiny, repaint the lettering, and send in a photographer with an assistant to wave sheets behind the machines to give the picture an opaque background for the auction catalogue."

In August of 1977, Sutter got a job on the assembly line at the Oldsmobile factory in Lansing. "It was exciting in some ways," he says. "I loved the harsh, nervous sound of hundreds of air drills working at once, like gunfire, and the big, ocean-liner-like procession of the line, but it was also my life going down the drain. For a while, I was an extra man—meaning I didn't have a specific task—and they had me unload boxcars of tire rims, or prime the engine and do transmission-fluid top-off, because they were disgusting jobs and you came home smelling of diesel fuel and transmission fluid. Or I wrote the job number with a grease pencil on the sides of tires as they came by, or I was on air cleaner, which I liked especially, because I had a table for my stock where I could set up a novel. I'd get several air cleaners ahead and try to read two pages before a car was in front of me again. Working air cleaner is when I got really interested in hardboiled fiction—Woolrich, Chandler, Cain, pulps, all the tough-guy writers of the thirties. I read Elmore Leonard then—*Fifty-two Pickup* when it came out in paperback, and because it was about Detroit it deeply addressed a feeling I had of being stuck in a permanent backwater. Here was someone writing about streets that had always seemed inconsequential and overlooked by everyone else, and suddenly they weren't. I read everything of his I could find. All his books about Detroit had something in them that elated me, even if it was just the description of a Near East Side bungalow with a Blessed Virgin birdbath in the back yard. In the summer of 1979, I looked up Elmore Leonard in the phone book and called him."

Sutter said that he was flying to Detroit to meet Leonard to go over material for *Cuba Libre,* the book on the Spanish-American War, and he agreed to take me with him. He picked me up at my hotel, and on our way to the airport we stopped at a used-book store called John K. King, so I could look for some old Leonard books and Sutter could see if he could find anything on Cuba. He didn't expect to—he had been to King's a few days before—but he wandered into a back room and came out with two copies of Volume I of a book called *Our Islands and Their People.* It was published in 1899 and was the size of an atlas, and it had a lot of photographs of things such as sugar plantations and boats in Havana Harbor. Sutter bought a copy for himself and one for Leonard. While he stood at the counter waiting to pay for them, he said, "If it was between me and another guy for this book, there would be blood."

Leonard lives in a suburb north of Detroit. As we drove through the town's leafy streets, Sutter paused in front of a red brick house and said that Leonard had lived in it until eight years ago, and then he turned onto a street of much larger houses and said, "See if you can pick out where he lives now." I pointed to a château-looking place with a big rug of a lawn and awnings on one side, and was surprised when he turned on to its circular driveway.

The door was answered by Leonard—a small-framed man, in a T-shirt and jeans, with gray hair and narrow shoulders, wiry and slightly stooped. We sat in his big living room. I asked how the Spanish-American War book was going, and he replied, "I'm on page nine." He said that the novel begins with a saddle bum shipping horses from Galveston, Texas, who arrives in Havana Harbor two days after the Maine has blown up and sees the buzzards cruising the sailors' corpses and wonders what has happened. "The dialogue is different," Leonard said. "I can't swing with it yet, and I don't know what obscenities they used."

I asked if Sutter's work had ever changed the course of a book, and Leonard said, "Not exactly, but one time I was interested in getting some background on Porfirio Rubirosa, a Dominican playboy, because I had a character like that in **Split Images,** in 1982, so Gregg got me a magazine that had a piece about Trujillo's daughter, who was married to Porfirio. I was reading that, and here was a picture of a squad of Marines walking down a street in Santo Domingo, and I thought, That's my next book—one of these guys goes back fifteen or sixteen years later to walk his perimeter and meets this girl sniper who shot him. That became **Cat Chaser.**"

While I was still writing that down in my notebook, Sutter laid *Our Islands and Their People* on a coffee table and said, "Look what I got." Leonard leaned forward in his chair and rested his elbows on his knees and said, "Oh, my God! Oh! Look at this!" He turned each page slowly and sometimes shook his head. Sutter sat beside him, smiling slightly. It was clear that he drew pleasure from Leonard's proximity. When Leonard had examined about half of the book's pages, he leaned back and said, "This book, I can't believe it. A *picture* book of the period." He looked at Sutter and said, "This is all I need—I don't know how you found it—I can get everything I need out of this."

Sutter slumped and let out his breath. "Don't say that," he said. "That's the last thing I want to hear."

Annie Gottlieb (review date 21 October 1996)

SOURCE: A review of *Out of Sight,* in *Nation,* Vol. 263, No. 12, October 21, 1996, p. 33.

[*In the following review, Gottlieb responds negatively to* Out of Sight.]

> To put spoken language into writing is a mere trick. And I found it—nobody else. Making spoken words go in literature isn't stenography: you have to change the sentences and rhythms somehow, to distort them—to use an artifice, so that when you read a book, it's as though someone is actually speaking to you. The same thing happens as with a stick plunged into water. If you want it to look straight you have to break it slightly—or bend it. . . . When you put one end in, a normally straight stick looks bent—and the same with language. On the page, the liveliest dialogue taken down word for word seems flat, complicated, heavy. . . . To reproduce the effect of spontaneous spoken life on the page, you have to bend language in every way—in its rhythm and cadence, in its words.

That isn't Elmore Leonard boasting. It's Louis-Ferdinand Celine, the literary genius (better remembered, alas, as a political moron) who smashed the formal architecture of French grammar to liberate the lowlife vox populi of Paris on the page. But Leonard himself might be forgiven for wondering, "When did I say that?" For there could be no better description of his own "trick," the sleight of style that lifts his crime novels above the genre. In a word, it's street: the savor and savvy, slyness and swagger of the talk that's talked on street corners and in bars, at taped-off crime scenes and in prison yards.

On first reading, Leonard seems simply to have recorded, with the fidelity of digital audiotape, the "spontaneous spoken life" of thieves, thugs, hustlers and the world-weary, wised-up pros who stalk them. But look again and you spot the broken stick, the language bent "in every way" so it sounds more real than real. As short a sentence as "The fuck you talking about?" is trademark Leonard. It's a matter of omission and elision, skipping the inessentials and cutting

to the chase, as the mind does in its darting pursuit of satisfaction and its game of tag with the truth. Or, as Miles Davis put it, "I always listen to what I can leave out."

> **On first reading, Leonard seems simply to have recorded, with the fidelity of digital audiotape, the "spontaneous spoken life" of thieves, thugs, hustlers and the world-weary, wised-up pros who stalk them.**
> **—Annie Gottlieb**

The Miles connection is not accidental. Celine knew that what he was really making was music—he called his distortion of language "a little harmonic tour de force"—and the music Leonard makes is Celine's favorite, jazz. Just look at him in Annie Leibovitz's classic portrait: dressed all in black like a fifties hipster, a little Olivetti on his knees, playing keyboard. Jazz, like Leonard's writing, can be enjoyed naively, as popular entertainment, while aficionados savor its subtle wit and artistry. And jazz (especially saxophone, that voice straight from the belly) often sounds like talk stripped of words, laying bare its emotional and psychosocial essence, whether it's the hilarity and hyperbole of a bunch of guys hanging out or the warm nostalgia of inner reverie (for of course we talk to ourselves, too). The psychological acuity of jazz, its grasp of the full range of human scams and sorrows, gives voice to the wisdom of the street. Elmore Leonard knows how to fit words back to that music without muffling it, as words so often do.

So accurate and so smart is the man's ear that one imagines it mapped over most of his cortex, crowding out the other senses. Nearly all the information in Leonard's novels comes through the auditory channel, but he makes that channel carry it with wonderful economy and clarity, like fiber-optic cable. We never see a character except by eavesdropping on another's thoughts, with the result that we learn something about both: "She liked his type, his rough-cut bony features, big hands. . . . Big hands, big schlong" adds a simultaneous stroke (no double entendred) to the portraits of ex-con Louis Gara and sexual sponger Melanie in *Rum Punch.* Each of Leonard's memorable characters exists as a distinctive speaking and thinking voice, leitmotif and cadence, yet these creatures made of sound take on such flesh for us that we miss them after we close the book's back door.

When these characters interact, they jam, a couple of cops or a cop and a crook playing off each other's riffs like veteran jazzmen, old friends or rivals. Leonard's "bad guys" tend to solo compulsively, blowing gaudy flights of self-display and self-delusion that will prove their downfall, but are redeemed by inimitable style. His "good guys" listen with the acuity of hunters and the unerring good taste that for

Leonard is the same as true morality. (In this he is a fifties hipster, hewing to the aesthetic and ethic of understated authenticity that was then called "cool.") Like all hunters, Leonard's law enforcers and bail bondsmen are a little bit in love with their prey; they can shoot or shackle a perp and still be entertained by him or her. But their ear for narcissistic pretension and kitsch is merciless. "Tillman wasn't her type," Karen Sisco, 29-year-old U.S. marshal and heroine of [*Out of Sight,*] Leonard's new novel, muses about an ex-boyfriend. "It was the little annoying things about him, like saying 'Ciao' instead of so long or see you later, or the way he called her 'lady' and it made her think of Kenny Rogers." A fine romance in a Leonard book often begins when a man and woman recognize each other by what they don't say (see, for instance, *Touch*)—cool glades of understatement in the midst of the tropical clamor of egos.

So an alarm bell went off when the love story at the heart of *Out of Sight* began with a lengthy conversation—in the trunk of a car. Veteran bank robber Jack Foley, ripe for a midlife crisis (yes, crooks have them too), crawls out of a prison escape tunnel moments after Karen Sisco drives up to the Florida prison on routine marshal business. Jack and his waiting partner deal with this glitch by stashing Karen in the trunk of the getaway car—and Jack climbs in with her! Covered with stinking tunnel muck, he cradles her spoon-style while she hides her .38 between her thighs. And they talk. Coolly and rather normally, for pages and miles, while Jack's hand wanders more in wonder than lechery. He's one of Leonard's "good bad guys," you see, those basically decent, nonviolent individuals who, through moral laziness, drift into the criminal life and can't get out. It's a class of people toward whom the author is sympathetic, but ultimately as unforgiving as life itself: They've made their choice, and it's one that ends badly.

Love across the fine line that separates cops and robbers is a compelling subject, but our belief in Jack and Karen's growing obsession with each other—after she gets away—pivots on the plausibility and magic of that conversation in the car trunk. And this reader just doesn't buy it. I don't care how tough and nervy a girl is, or how innately gallant her abductor; locked in a dark car trunk in the arms of a freshly escaped convict, she's going to feel fear and revulsion. She's not going to launch into a conversation so casually chatty that the reader has to work at remembering they're in the trunk. (That's why this scene will work better in the movie—a first clue to what's wrong with this book.) The weird normality of the talk is what's supposed to make it so unforgettable; instead, it's just unbelievable. And so *Out of Sight* gets off on a badly wrong note.

Worse yet, what do they talk about? Movies! Now, I hate those dinner parties where people talk about movies they've seen instead of their own experiences. Although I am sadly sure that in reality bank robbers, too, now talk about movies and fancy themselves Brando or Bogart characters, I read writers like Leonard for the illusion (isn't it ironic) that I'm meeting people who still have real experiences, outside the womb of the multiplex and the home entertainment center. "Quoting" movies delivers a prefab emotional effect; if our best writers start doing it, who's going to provide us with memorable moments minted from life? It's depressing to watch Leonard fall into this pomo echo chamber, quoting Hollywood's crush on itself.

Out of Sight has been pre-sold to the movies, to the same team that made *Get Shorty*. Is that why Karen Sisco is so generic? All we know about her looks is that she's slim and blond; about her character, that she's brave. The most interesting thing about her is her father, a semi-retired P.I. in golf duds who, in one breath, worries when his little girl will get married and, in the next, gives her hard-ass professional advice. Leonard has never been very good at young people; he's just not very interested in them—he's a bard of experience, not of innocence. But Hollywood needs sexy young heroines, so let the starlet fill in the blanks.

Then there's Jack Foley: Supposedly from Louisiana, he displays a puzzling lack of regional speech or savor—puzzling, that is, until you realize that where he really comes from is the movies: *Bonnie and Clyde, Three Days of the Condor*. (Bogart in *The Treasure of the Sierra Madre* lurks in this novel's subconscious, but isn't mentioned.) That's even where he learned to fire a Beretta, "for Christ sake." At the very end, we learn we've been inside Jack's maudlin movie all along, and we get dumped out of it as unceremoniously as he does. It's as if Leonard said, "See? I've been putting you on with this movie stuff." Well, thank God—but the last two pages of the book is too late to find that out.

Aficionados of Leonard's books-as-jazz will bitch. Where's the music? Confined mostly to walk-on characters: We don't hear nearly enough of the abused Moselle (back from *Freaky Deaky*), whose voice is as dire and fatalistic as Billie Holiday's, or the wisecracking Adele, Jack's 40ish ex and an out-of-work magician's assistant. To be sure, this book has lines: "I never forget anyone I've cuffed and shackled," Karen says, and a minor character responds to a sign in a boxing gym: "NO PAIN NO GAIN. No shit." But Leonard shows an uncharacteristic—and uncool—tendency to nudge us in the ribs. When Jack goes in to rob a bank and picks up a brochure saying "LOOKING FOR MONEY? YOU'VE COME TO THE RIGHT PLACE," it's very funny. It's not funny when, two pages later,

> Foley handed him the brochure he'd taken and Buddy smiled, "'Looking for money? You've come to the right place.' They got that right. It's like they're asking for it."

And the heart sinks when someone inevitably says, "You know what she said. . .? 'I never forget anybody I've cuffed and shackled.'"

Out of Sight feels like time out, like the band's on break and a tinny tape is playing. Maybe Leonard is. . . tired, and it's easier to write one straight for the movies—let the director do the casting, pick the soundtrack—than to do that painstaking Ellingtonian orchestration Celine called "torture. . .the hardest job in the world." Or maybe he's tired, finally, of the self-justifying jive of bad guys—for those in this book aren't remotely entertaining, just stupid and for frightening. Maybe Jack Foley speaks for his creator when he says the sounds have gone sour:

> watching Maurice duck and weave, telling how crafty he'd been in the ring; listening to White Boy's dumb remarks and the annoying way he laughed; listening to Kenneth speaking a language that seemed all hip-hop sounds, rhythmic, but making hardly any sense; Foley listening to sociopaths offering their credentials, misfits trying not to sound like losers. . . . Buddy mak[ing] quiet comments that were meant to zing but fell flat, the same old same old, that stand-up talk you heard in the yard, but nobody here bothering to listen, busy thinking of what they'd say next. All us tough guys, Foley thought.

What's the remedy for this Unterweltschmerz? A change of scene? The world of stage magic could be a promising venue for a Leonard novel; he obviously respects its tricks and relishes its lore. (It's not so far from *Pronto* to Presto.) Or just a rest? Hollywood has its hands full with Leonard's backlist, and his hard-core fans don't need a book a year. We'd rather wait for the real stuff. When the craving hits, we'll just re-read the old ones. (My mate reads them over and over, the same way he listens to his Erroll Garner and Basic CDs.) For another book as good as *Glitz* or *Killshot* or *Rum Punch,* we'd wait as long and loyally as we wait for Thomas Harris's sequel to *The Silence of the Lambs.*

William Fiennes (review date 27 April 1997)

SOURCE: "She Keeps a Pistol, Leg Irons, Handcuffs and a Shotgun. Now THAT'S Girl Power," in *Observer,* April 27, 1997, p. 16.

[*In the following review, Fiennes offers a mixed assessment of* Out of Sight.]

Forty-eight-year-old Jack Foley is in prison for robbing more banks 'than anyone in the computer', has an ex-wife in Mi-

ami working as an assistant to a magician called Emil the Amazing, and remains supernaturally attractive to beautiful young women of far greater prospects than he. Foley is, in other words, an Elmore Leonard hero: another low-grade Florida criminal, hard-boiled but soft-centred, with the familiar Leonard pathology of 'wanting to be a good guy' and the familiar Leonard cool of a con who breaks out of prison just in time to watch the Super Bowl. *Out of Sight* is Leonard's thirty-third novel, and it's business as usual.

Foley is picked up outside the prison walls by his old partner, Buddy, and an aspiring hotshot called Glenn 'Studs' Michaels. But he had not reckoned on the arrival of US Marshal Karen Sisco, the latest in Leonard's long line of sassy professional women (often known as 'broads') who invariably wind up in bed with his protagonist. Even her father— a private investigator, naturally—describes Karen as 'the tough babe'. She smokes. She wears medium heels and black Chanel suits. And in the trunk of her car, she keeps a pistol, a ballistic vest, several sets of handcuffs and leg irons, an expandable baton, a can of Mace and a Remington pump-action shotgun. Karen seems to have got the hang of the whole empowerment thing.

You can see why Quentin Tarantino loves Elmore Leonard. He is about to start filming Leonard's novel *Rum Punch,* but no movie has yet caught the nimble, hipster's rhythm his fleet pages require. Leonard's novels read like screenplays-in-waiting, and film, not literature, is the tradition they repeatedly acknowledge.
—*William Fiennes*

The tough babe gets mixed up in the escape and soon finds herself locked in the trunk of Buddy's car with Foley. The two of them do the obvious thing in such circumstances, which is to discuss the films of Faye Dunaway. After the convicts have ditched Karen, Foley can't get her out of his head. She's a little smitten, too, taken in by the nonchalant charm of a thief who, before asking the cashier to hand over the money, would say something such as: 'I sure like your hair, Irene. Is that the latest style?' Or, 'Mmmmm, your perfume sure smells nice. What's it called?'

Foley and Buddy head for Miami. Karen is determined to bring them in. Glenn heads for Detroit to meet Maurice 'Snoopy' Miller and rob the home of Wall Street scammer Richard 'Dick the Ripper' Ripley. Leonard fans will by now be experiencing a certain amount of *déjà vu.* He has experimented in the past (as in 1987's *Touch,* an eerie account of a faith healer), but *Out of Sight* is generic Leonard, strictly on home turf. It's another tale of minor-league crooks set against a backdrop of Miami kitsch: Buddy's 'imitation Danish sofa'; the 'pastel-coloured apartment hotels'; Foley dressed up as a tourist in 'a color-coordinated orange and bright ocher beach outfit' and dark socks with his leather sandals.

Leonard's romanticism has always coexisted uneasily with some truly nasty violence. Here, Foley's affair with Karen is pure male fantasy, perilously close to schmaltz. But Maurice's brother Kenneth, 'wired on crystal meth', is a serial rapist and murderer whose acts are too brutal for Leonard's characteristic rosy glow. Leonard loves guns, but he makes light of what guns do, indulging instead a fetishist's enthusiasm for their associated terminology: MAC-10, Ruger .22, Beretta nine, .38 Smith snub-nose and—heaven!—an entire Swat team armed with MP-5 submachine guns.

You can see why Quentin Tarantino loves Elmore Leonard. He is about to start filming Leonard's novel ***Rum Punch,*** but no movie has yet caught the nimble, hipster's rhythm his fleet pages require. Leonard's novels read like screenplays-in-waiting, and film, not literature, is the tradition they repeatedly acknowledge. *Out of Sight* alludes not only to Faye Dunaway, but to *Stranger than Paradise,* Steve McQueen prison pictures, Woody Allen's *Take the Money and Run, Repo Man, Kiss Me Deadly* and *Pulp Fiction.*

Film may be able to capture Leonard's heists, weapons and smart lines (Karen's father: 'I always liked nuns. They're so clean. They never seem to sweat.') But it won't catch the zero-gravity float of his third-person narration, which drifts in and out of the characters' interior monologues, as if to pick up the tempo of their thinking. And for all his movie sensibility, Leonard's novels are full of a chanced-upon verbal lyricism, like the names of the card tricks Adele can do—'The Hindu shuffle, overhand shuffle, the doubt lift, the glide. . .'—or the hard, consonantal music of Cadillac, Pontiac, Buick. *Out of Sight* is remarkable for its lavish automobile taxonomy: blue Chevy Caprice, white Cadillac Sedan De Ville Concours, '89 Olds Cutlass Supreme in faded maroon, '94 Lincoln Town Car, Chrysler Newport. No writer alive has such colourful, evocative traffic.

It's been fashionable to make big claims for Leonard ('One of the best novelists of any genre, high or low'), as if these books have the vast empathy, perception and inventiveness of, say, Saul Bellow. *Out of Sight* is a novel Leonard's written several times before under different titles, such as 1984's *Stick,* the story of a fortysomething ex-bank robber with a good heart who's just out of prison and romances an extremely desirable young stockbroker (and tough babe) called Kyle.

You don't read it so much as breathe it in, like a gas. And the memory of it evaporates almost the instant you lay it down, even such prize moments as Buddy and Foley visiting the Jewish Recycling Centre to buy warm coats for the Detroit freeze, Foley choosing a navy blue double-breaster. 'A slim cut, not at all boxy, like the coat was wearing him.' But it's a lot of fun while it lasts.

FURTHER READING

Criticism

Callendar, Newgate. "Criminals At Large." *New York Times Book Review* (4 April 1976): 34.
    Favorable review of *52 Pick-up,* which Callendar calls "one of the best of the year."

Carver, Robert. "Old Sparky." *New Statesman & Society* 4, No. 172 (11 October 1991): 25.
    Applauds *Maximum Bob,* characterizing it as "a brilliant, funny, hugely enjoyable black comedy."

Stuewe, Paul. "Of Some Import." *Quill & Quire* 56, No. 8 (August 1990): 25.
    Primarily favorable review of *Get Shorty.*

Additional coverage of Leonard's life and career is contained in the following sources published by Gale: *Authors and Artists for Young Adults,* **Vol. 22;** *Authors in the News,* **Vol. 1;** *Bestsellers,* **89, Issue 1; 90, Issue 4;** *Contemporary Authors,* **Vols. 81-84;** *Contemporary Authors New Revision Series,* **Vols. 12, 28, 53, and 76;** *Dictionary of Literary Biography,* **Vol. 173;** *DISCovering Authors Modules: Popular Fiction and Genre Authors; Major Twentieth-Century Writers.*

Gary Snyder
1930-

(Full name Gary Sherman Snyder) American poet, essayist, and translator.

The following entry presents an overview of Snyder's career through 1998. For further information on his life and works, see *CLC,* Volumes 1, 2, 5, 9, and 32.

INTRODUCTION

Known for his writing and philosophies on environmental subjects, Snyder is considered one of the most important American poets of his generation. Throughout his career, he has been at the forefront of American literary and cultural developments such as the Beat movement of the 1950s, the popularization of Oriental thought and religion in the 1960s, and the growth of environmental consciousness. Despite his association with these popular movements, critics note that he has pursued his own agendas without concern for his popularity. His poetry, which fuses Oriental and Native American myth with a strong and personal connection between man and nature, has been compared with the work of Walt Whitman, Ezra Pound, and William Carlos Williams. Snyder is the recipient of several literary honors and awards, including a Pulitzer Prize for poetry for *Turtle Island* (1974).

Biographical Information

Snyder was born on May 8, 1930 and was raised on small farms in Washington and Oregon. His family was poor, but freethinking, advocating socialism and atheism, thus encouraging Snyder to question the dominant culture. Throughout his life he has held jobs as a logger, merchant marine, fire lookout and United States Forest Service trail crew worker. He earned undergraduate degrees in literature and anthropology at Reed College, where he pursued his interest in Native American Culture. Snyder began graduate work at the University of Indiana before transferring to the University of California at Berkeley, where he pursued his emerging interest in Buddhism and Asian languages. Between 1953 and 1956, Snyder became involved with the Beatnik movement in Northern California, writing poetry and attending the famous reading of Allen Ginsberg's "Howl." He was featured in Jack Kerouac's book *The Dharma Bums*. Just as the beatnik movement was gaining national attention, Snyder moved to Japan where he studied Zen Buddhism. He remained in Japan until the late 1960s when he returned to the United States. He and his third wife and two sons made their home on a farm he called Kitkitdizze, on the San Juan Ridge of the Sierra Nevada Mountains. He continues to live there, writing poetry and essays on environmentalism, both subjects he teaches at the University of California at Davis.

Major Works

Snyder's writing reveals an appreciation for the hard work of rural life and the nearness it affords with nature. His work also focuses on an interest in the spiritual link between primitive cultures and nature, and contains a deep sense of involvement with humanity. In his poetry and his nonfiction writing, Snyder has advocated a close association and a mutual respect between humans and the natural world. He has emphasized the interconnectedness of life, using and manipulating Native American folklore, Asian myths, and Buddhist thought, creating an unique blend of Eastern and Western philosophies. Snyder's first collection of poetry, *Riprap* (1959), is largely based on his experiences as a manual laborer; the title itself is taken from a term which designates the laying of stones to create a horse trail in the mountains. *Myths and Texts* (1960), his next collection, is a long highly allusive lyrical poem divided into three sections:

"Logging," "Hunting," and "Burning." This poem is considered to be among his best work. *The Back Country* (1967), divided into five sections—"The Far West," "The Far East," "Kali," "Back," and translations of work by the Japanese poet Miyazawa Kenji—reveals the influence of East and West on both the style and content of Snyder's poetry. Building on his success and years of study, Snyder achieved greater public acclaim with the Pulitzer Prize winning *Turtle Island*, an intensive contemplation of his life and its connection with the Sierra Nevada landscape. The title is an allegory to North America and in it he extends the metaphor of his life in California to human existence in American and the world. In *Axe Handles* (1983) he focuses on domesticity and his relationship with his family. After more than forty years of work, Snyder completed and published *Mountains and Rivers without End* in 1996. In addition, Snyder has published numerous collections of essays, articles and speeches about the environment, Native American and Asian mythology, and his life experiences.

Critical Reception

Scholars acknowledge Snyder's profound influence on the development of American poetry in the postwar period. Critics note that from Beat to mystic to bioregional poetry, Snyder has shaped both content and form. Critics have lauded Snyder's blending of Western and Eastern philosophies; his imaginative use of Native American and Asian mythology; his unique and evocative treatment of landscape; his competent handling of sound, phrasing, and rhythm; and the sureness of his imagery. Consistently, throughout his career, scholars have noted his importance in "reimaging the landscape," or, the conceptualizing of new ways in which to interpret nature and man's relationship to it. Thomas J. Lyon argues that Snyder's' success comes from eliminating the distance between man and nature in his writing, in keeping his poetry direct. And Christopher Benfey calls him ". . . the unofficial poet laureate of the environmentalist movement." However, reviewers agree that the quality of Snyder's' work is uneven. They state that, while individual poems in his other collections are outstanding, only *Myths & Texts* is consistently and collectively successful. In addition, critics have become dissatisfied with Snyder's increasing focus on environmental-political issues in his poetry. Scholars such as David A. Carpenter argue that the poetic has suffered at the hand of the political. Despite these shortfalls, commentators agree that Snyder's reputation as an unique, pathbreaking poet remains strong.

PRINCIPAL WORKS

Riprap (poetry) 1959
Myths & Texts (poetry) 1960
Riprap & Cold Mountain Poems (poetry) 1965

The Back Country (poetry) 1968
Earth House Hold: Technical Notes and Queries for Fellow Dharma Revolutionaries (essays) 1970
Regrading Wave (poetry) 1972
Turtle Island (poetry) 1974
Axe Handles (poetry) 1983
Left Out in the Rain: New Poems 1947-1985 (poetry) 1986
No Nature: New and Selected Poems (poetry) 1992
A Place in Space: Ethics, Aesthetics, and Watersheds (prose) 1995
Mountains and Rivers without End (poetry) 1996

CRITICISM

Thomas J. Lyon (essay date Spring 1970)

SOURCE: "The Ecological Vision of Gary Snyder," in *Kansas Quarterly*, Vol. 2, No. 2, Spring, 1970, pp. 117-24.

[*In the following essay, Lyon places Snyder's work at the forefront of the new naturalist movement.*]

There are some positive signs—more than straws in the wind—that a significant number of Western minds are forsaking the progress-domination theory inherent in the political view which has ruled and conquered for so long, in favor of a more relaxed and open way with the world founded on ecological sensitivity. The political mind, based ultimately on bossmanship in theology and bent on converting world matter into exclusively human use with efficient if violent technology, seems to be giving way to a gentler feeling of mutuality. We are coming, many think, to a great verge: Pisces then, now Aquarius . . . or Vico's fourth stage in cyclical history, returning to awe of the supernatural . . . or Yeats's "Second Coming." Whatever it is called, the apparently dawning age seems not to give its allegiance to hierarchies of dominance and power, nor to profane Growthmanship, but to a steady-state interdependence with all the world, its trees, rocks, rivers, and animals. The enormous expansion and deepening of the conservation movement, the new interest in the ecological sciences, and the wide search for cooperative, sacral, communal forms are all evidence that we seem to be trying to raise our sights to a holy vision of the world as a unity.

The eternal dream of the peaceable kingdom, if it can be called a dream now and not the only sane hope for survival—escape from the self-doom of ecological sin—is also emerging as a force in contemporary writing. Not as outright prophecy, Jeremiad, or prescription, but as theme growing from massive contact with natural particulars—viz., Ginsberg's important "Wales Visitation"—this kind of writing gives promise of transcending conventional romanticism to the same degree that Wordsworthian ecstasy transcended the rational optimism that went before it.

The literature of the new ecology has apparent roots in Romantic writing, certainly, as well as in Oriental thinking and in the contemporary subculture's opening of the "doors of perception" to the realization of endless interrelatedness. But perhaps the most important roots—direct apprehension of wild nature and perception of the primitive reference point in human (Indian) terms—are not so obvious, and it is here that the student of Western American literature can draw on the traditions of his regional field for insights.

Before the West had produced a great writer on its own ground, Henry David Thoreau had mapped it out as the great mother-center of wilderness and the place to learn ecological truth—"The West of which I speak is but another name for the Wild; and what I have been preparing to say is, that in Wildness is the preservation of the World"—and most of the best Western writers from later years have lived on Thoreau's map. John Muir, Robinson Jeffers, Walter Van Tilburg Clark, and Frank Waters, just to name four, have built on direct experience of elemental and often violent Western nature, working toward a post-humanist, post-technological world-view in which man fits into natural patterns rather than simply following his greed into the city of ecological imbalance and poisoning. This is not really to be wondered at; nature in the West has been primary, sometimes even overwhelming. It is not, except for the tourist industry, leisure-time beauty; garden-variety, escapist romantics have not grown well here. Jeffers wrote of the California coast as "crying out for tragedy," speaking of the great forms and space and immense changes in sea and sky that became his poetic world; one of the dimensions of his total work is the tragedy of Western civilization's drive to render the wild world tame . . . leaving finally only "introverted man," "taken up / Like a maniac with self love." Jeffers said he stood "west of the west"; his "Inhumanism" is nothing more shocking than the ecological vision looking back on the strictly "humanist" westward movement of plunder and destruction.

The limitations of White/Western thought have also been limned, for serious Western writers, by the presence of the Indian, who lasted long enough in the West to be the model of primitive ecology and religious responsibility to earth. But the critique has not been simple-minded. Frank Waters, to name perhaps the deepest student of the Indian among writers, has long been recommending a supra-rational, supra-emotional synthesis between cultures, making finally an ecologically responsible civilization and psychically whole persons; the Western writer's ability to take the Indian seriously has resulted in real trailbreaking.

It may be—I almost believe it—that the West's great contribution to American culture will be in codifying and directing the natural drive toward ecological thought: a flowering of regional literature into literally world-wide attention and relevance. Now, after all this prologue, I come to my subject, the poet Gary Snyder, for as Snyder begins to emerge as an important force in the ideas and art of America, he shows signs of embodying the Western ecological vision in a culturally viable form. His writing is popular, certainly, and as I hope to show, it is valid in deeper, permanent ways.

The first thing that strikes one about Snyder's poetry is the terse, phrase-light and article-light diction, the sense of direct *thing*-ness. In common with most of the poetic generation that has rebelled against the formulaic Eliot rhetoric and intellectual abstraction, Snyder writes a solid line, but the special quality in his diction, the personal voice, lies in his knowledgeable selection of objects. They are things he has worked with and felt the grain of, and thus known better than good-sounding "poet's" catalogs:

> Rucksack braced on a board,
>   lashed tight on back.
> sleeping bags, map case, tied on the
> gas tank
> sunglasses, tennis shoes, your long tan
> in shorts
> north on the west side of Lake Biwa
> Fukui highway still being built,
>   crankcase bangd on rocks—
>   pusht to the very edge by a
>   blinded truck
> I saw the sea below beside my knee:
> you hung on and never knew how close.

Experience is not elaborately prepared for, in the Snyder poetics, just handed over: "Woke once in the night, pissed, / checkt the coming winter's stars / built up the fire" opens a poem and puts the reader in the mountains without any pastoral-tradition framing. This is the "near view" of the Sierra that John Muir wanted so much and knew that conventional art didn't give. Snyder's open directness moves toward solving one of Muir's and other transcendentalists' great dilemmas: how to talk about things, especially wild ones, without harming their integrity by language; how to preserve and communicate sauciness without falling into an arch aesthetic distance between subject and object, a romantic decoration that destroys the very wholeness, which is wildness, one loved and wanted to convey somehow. The thin line of poetic truth between overstatement and private code requires first of all respect for things, letting them stand free instead of being marshaled into line for a mental performance. Snyder apparently recognizes the lover's paradox in writing ("each man kills the thing he loves"), and turns back on his own mind with good humor:

> foxtail pine with a

clipped curve-back cluster of tight
   five-needle bunches
  the rough red bark scale
and jigsaw pieces sloughed off
    scattered on the ground.
—what am I doing saying "foxtail pine"?

The comment might be on alliteration and rolling rhythm, as well as on the general deceit of naming: the poem moves beyond nature love to a focus on relation, among Snyder and his poem and the tree, and the ironic mode of the final question enters dimensions of richness quite beyond simple appreciation, if such a thing is simple. The openness of Snyder's seemingly casual presentation of objects, then, should not be mistaken for naïvete. The freshness of youth in his perceptions seems to be the result of having passed through a midstage of poeticizing and returned to the primal, simultaneous brotherhood-in-separateness of all objects. This is the wild world which Thoreau intuitively saw great poetry aiming at. Leaving it in integrity requires only pointing, and here Snyder's long Zen training provides the exact discipline needed. But the poet can also bring himself in and show the paradoxical nature of knowledge (and the poignant human consciousness of separateness) by levels of irony. So we have Snyder writing,

When
Snow melts back
    from the trees
Bare branches   knobbed pine twigs
    hot sun on wet flowers
Green shoots of huckleberry
Breaking through the snow.

on the one hand, and

A clear, attentive mind
Has no meaning but that
Which sees is truly seen.
No one loves rock, yet we are here.

on the other. The inclusiveness resulting is literally "part" and "parcel" of the ecological vision. Tingeing the Zen core with irony, though it is far from his only technique, is one of Snyder's singular contributions to modern poetry, a byproduct of the connection he has knitted in his life between East and West. In a sense, Snyder is moving westward in the way that Whitman meant for us to do, the total effect of his final synthesis being, to use one of his essay titles, a **"Passage to More than India."**

Snyder shows his naturalness and American-West roots most obviously in his colloquial, object-laden language, but another and perhaps more important consonance with the wilderness world can be felt in his verse rhythms. "I've just recently come to realize that the rhythms of my poems follow the rhythms of the physical work I'm doing and the life I'm leading at any given time," he wrote in 1959, and many of his poems are tuned so closely to muscular and breath paces that they seem quite as spontaneous as his analysis implies. A bit of **"Riprap,"** which grew out of building trails on slick granite in the Sierra, will illustrate this:

Lay down these words
Before your mind like rocks,
    placed solid, by hands
In choice of place, set
Before the body of the mind
    in space and time:
Solidity of bark, leaf, or wall
    riprap of things:
Cobble of milky way,
    straying planets,
These poems, people,
    lost ponies with
Dragging saddles—
    and rocky sure-foot trails.

There are some fine rhythms starting from non-human wilderness, too, where the birds and other animals seem almost to have written the poem by themselves.

Birds in a whirl, drift to the rooftops
Kite dip, swing to the seabank fogroll
. . . .
The whole sky whips in the wind
Vaux Swifts
Flying before the storm
Arcing close hear sharp wing-whistle
Sickle-bird

Snyder flirts with meter and with internal rhyme and alliteration, clearly, but the forming principle is not external. He once described formal poetry as "the game of inventing an abstract structure and then finding things in experience which can be forced into it," identifying this kind of writing with the rationalistic philosophy-culture of the West—of civilization—and then stated his preference for wilderness: "the swallow's dip and swoop, 'without east or west.'" The basic direction of his prosody is that of his image-selection: to go beyond the midstage to the consciously primitive, where there is no "east or west." Since we are both an unconscious, animal process and a conscious intellect, Snyder's poetics can be seen as an attempt at continuous self-transcendence, a leading through ego-borders into the wild. Self, ego, is at work in nature-love, as it is more obviously in nature-hate, as it is also in cultural typologies and forms for poetry. The ultimate meanings in Snyder's poetry, deeply revolutionary meanings in the sense of consciousness-changers, putting man in a different place from where he thought he was all these years, can be sensed very clearly in his formal poetics alone. His work is therefore organic rather than contrived, and although this can be said of many contemporary poets and indeed marks the fundamental direction of modern American poetry, the special virtue in Snyder's work is that he has created or allowed to develop a form that grows so rightly out of *wild* things, and which leads the reader uncannily ahead to a wild point of view. This is the technique of the ecological sense which goes past both the primitive and primiti*vism,* into something else, in certain poems the ecstatic ecology of wholeness. Then to keep the sense of mind—"all the junk that goes with being human," as Snyder wrote once—alive along with the transparent eyeball, is art. Snyder's best poems, in my opinion, are the ones that move through these levels of apprehension, keeping the whole thing alive and total, finally conveying the great molecular interrelatedness, yet not as a static "thing," not even as a "poem," sweated out, but with the rhythmic feel of the unworded wild truth. **"Wave,"** a recent poem, simultaneously perceives, creates, and leaps over form in this way:

> Grooving clam shell,
>   streakt through marble,
>   sweeping down ponderosa pine
>   bark-scale
>   rip-cut tree grain
>   sand-dunes, lava
>   flow
>
> Wave   wife.
> woman—wyfman—
> "veiled; vibrating; vague"
> sawtooth ranges pulsing;
>   veins on the back of the hand.
>
> Fork out: birdsfoot-alluvium
>   wash
>   great dunes rolling
> Each inch rippld, every grain a wave.
>
> Leaning against sand cornices til they
>   blow away
>   —wind, shake
>   stiff thorns of cholla, ocotillo
>   sometimes I get stuck in thickets—
>
> Ah, trembling spreading radiating   wyf
>   racing zebra
>   catch me and fling me wide
> To the dancing grain of things
>   of my mind!

The solidity in Snyder's writing, which is often commented on, results from the fact that his ideas, like the verse rhythms, flow from close attention to wilderness, unmediated percep-

tion of grain and wave. The total structure appears in startling systematic clarity, once one gets used to the point of view. Thing/rhythm/idea, over and over, so that the meanings are inextricable from the settings. The contrasting point of view, where there is always the anthropocentric splitting which prevents things from expressing completely their innate rhythms, and which keeps things from entering our heads in fullness, should immediately be more familiar in our unpoetic culture. We tend to mark everything according to its vulnerability. But this grasping approach seals itself off from authentic experience by refusing the integrity or self-nature of things: rocks, trees, people . . . anything. This integrity is what is meant by wildness; according to Snyder, it takes a consciously primitive sensibility to know it and respect it, that is, one not overlaid with the programmed covetousness our culture seems to demand. Poets have to deal from authentic experience in order to communicate the wild truth of the matter, which is, Snyder holds, "at deep levels common to all who listen." He describes the moment of connection between feeling and making, in **Earth House Hold:**

> The phenomenal world experienced at certain pitches is totally living, exciting, mysterious, filling one with a trembling awe, leaving one grateful and humble. The wonder of the mystery returns direct to one's own senses and consciousness: inside and outside, the voice breathes, "Ah!"

So far, our culture has managed to include this untamed poetic mind as a kind of occasional delight or relief, thus blotting up its power. As Herbert Marcuse and many others since *One-Dimensional Man* have commented, it has been the peculiar strength of the instrumental, technological culture to be able to make tame commodities out of potentially revolutionary states of consciousness. The taming of the mind has kept even pace with the taming of the outer wilderness; conventional-romantic nostalgia is a good example of the parallelism I am suggesting. It is perfectly powerless to regain its lost paradise, its noble savage or gentle woods-bowers, because its civilized formulations are only half real. There have been writers from Blake onward, to be sure, who have seen that we stand to lose immensely by conquering the world; but very few—Thoreau, Jeffers, Snyder, perhaps alone—have made the connection between outer and inner wilderness, and have dared to suggest that a primitive mind can understand it most clearly. The direct link between the two sides of wild integrity is the ground of the ecological values. Perceiving the link enables one to stand with and among, yet retaining and developing the consciousness of membership—or the ironies of mental separateness. Either way, this sort of perception calls into question the major assumptions of Western civilization. By going beyond both technohumanist instrumentalism and cutely impotent romanticism, this approach builds a whole new mind. "Poets," Snyder writes, "as few others, must live close to the world that primitive men are in . . . " and poetry itself, in this world, becomes "an ecological survival technique."

The solidity in Snyder's writing, which is often commented on, results from the fact that his ideas, like the verse rhythms, flow from close attention to wilderness, unmediated perception of grain and wave. The total structure appears in startling systematic clarity, once one gets used to the point of view.
                                    —*Thomas J. Lyon*

It is perhaps expectable that Snyder contrasts the primitive/poetic mind with the world of "nationalism, warfare, heavy industry and consumership," which are "already outdated and useless," but what is not so expectable is that he has developed a forthrightly revolutionary system of ideas on his poetic perceptions. With the exceptions again of Thoreau, and possibly. Jeffers, most of our wilderness poets have been rather passive regretters of the destruction closing in on them. But Snyder speaks, almost millenially, of healing. There are ways to the ecological mind, and they can be shown; people are more ready than ever. "The traditional cultures are in any case doomed, and rather than cling to their good aspects hopelessly it should be remembered that whatever is or ever was in any other culture can be reconstructed from the unconscious [our inner side of the vast pool of wilderness], through meditation. In fact, it is my own view that the coming revolution will close the circle and link us in many ways with the most creative aspect of our archaic past."

It might be argued that this progressivism, reversed as it is, shows Snyder's American heritage. In an outward, ideological sense, yes; but the core of it is the ecological understanding, the primitive (primal) sense of things. In turn, the chief ingredients of the ecological understanding seem to me to be Snyder's American West wilderness experience—he has worked as a logger, fire lookout, and trail crew-man, and has backpacked and climbed extensively in California, Oregon, and Washington, working on the actual skills of primitive ecology and developing close ties to several Indian tribes—on the one side, and his formal, disciplined study of Buddhism on the other, beginning in 1956 in Kyoto.

Although it is somewhat tempting to read Snyder's going to the Zen temple in Kyoto as a resolution for tensions generated during 1952-56, when he worked part of the time as a tool of the anthropocentric culture (as a logger), and when he came to the end of conventional graduate-school climbing, I think Snyder's intellectual history is not a simple move from West to East. On the early end, he had been disenchanted with Christianity since childhood. "Animals don't have souls," he had been told as a child; making the connection between this pronouncement and the general Western ethos had been his intellectual work for years before 1956. This, along with positive motivations, resulted in a kind of textual Buddhism, especially when Snyder became reasonably expert in Chinese while at Berkeley, and one can see the going to Kyoto as merely putting theory into practice. On the other end, after the Zen training, Snyder has repeatedly shown his independence of traditional structures. His Buddhism is not programmatic. "Institutional Buddhism has been conspicuously ready to accept or ignore the inequalities and tyrannies of whatever political system it found itself under," he wrote in 1961, showing that left-anarchist, IWW ideas from working in the logging industry were not abandoned in favor of quietism. And the wild, original reference point, the special Snyder flavor, is shown in comments like this one from *Earth House Hold:*

> The Far Eastern love of nature has become fear of nature: gardens and pine trees are tormented and controlled. Chinese nature poets were too often retired bureaucrats living on two or three acres trimmed by hired gardeners. The professional nature-aesthetes of modern Japan, tea-teachers and flower-arrangers, are amazed to hear that only a century ago dozens of species of birds passed through Kyoto where today only swallows and sparrows can be seen: and the aesthetes can scarcely distinguish those.

My point is that Snyder has not been susceptible to either gross cultural influences or temporary currents, but has always seemed to measure things according to a primal standard of wild ecology. The basic materials of this he learned in the West. The Buddhist training has been extremely important, I do not doubt, and the steeping in Oriental writing, particularly Chinese poetry, has helped Snyder as a poet; but I am suggesting that he is now into something like a world-relevant fusion, a planetary consciousness, both in ideas and techniques. Berkeley Professor Thomas Parkinson writes, "He has effectively done something that for an individual is extremely difficult: he has created a new culture, and I think this may very well be the case. At the least, Snyder has provided the articulation, both in his poems and now in *Earth House Hold,* that can shape the generalized, inchoate desire for an ecological life.

As a cultural figure, his durability is evidenced by his fame having outlasted all three of the major movements in the American West since World War II—the Beat Generation, the Zen interest of the 50's, and the Hippies of the 60's. The strong points of these currents—creative alienation from robotlife, purified mind, and gentle community, respectively—had been present in Snyder's work from the start, and his steady focus on wilderness clarity helped him avoid the well-publicized pitfalls along the way. Thus he has always seemed ahead of the times, which is essential for a popular American bard-seer. Another, more fundamental requirement for such a figure is that his work, thought, and life be of a piece; as I hope I have shown, it is almost inevitable that this be true of the ecological vision. In our accelerating re-examination of civilization in the light of enduring perceptions and longings, it is not too much to suggest that Gary Snyder's insights can be extremely valuable.

Herbert Leibowitz (review date 23 March 1975)

SOURCE: "Ecologies of the Finite and the Infinite," in *New York Times Book Review,* March 23, 1975, p. 2.

[*In the following review of* Turtle Island, *Leibowitz argues that Snyder has failed to adequately transform stray thoughts into powerful poetry.*]

When Walt Whitman advised his countrymen in 1871 to book passage to India he was not dreaming of extending the American empire to Asia, though he was enough of a chauvinist to view the restless migration to the Pacific complacently. Before the Civil War, American mercantile interests, New Englanders prominent among them, had discovered the lucrative China trade. Thoreau had carried the "Bhagavad-Gita" in his bag to Walden Pond, and Emerson's Transcendentalism had taken much from Hindu, Buddhist and other Oriental philosophies. For Whitman, as for Emerson and Thoreau, the allure of the East was that it was not tainted by the allegedly worn out forms and methods of Europe. The enterprising American artist might draw on new sources of inspiration, uncover new-old versions of the self, acquire a new lingo of spiritual ecstasy and enlightenment.

This fascination with Oriental script and scripture ("the elder religions," Whitman called them) continued unabated into the 20th century. By his own testimony, Pound's stumbling on Ernest Fenollosa's work with the Chinese ideogram decisively changed Pound's thinking about—and writing of—poems. And even William Carlos Williams, that stubborn champion of local idiom, remarked in 1950 that poets living in West Coast cities, facing the Orient, had the grand opportunity of "crossing cultures," of being less confined by the "debased precedent" of Europe than their Atlantic or inland peers.

It should come as no surprise, then, that Allen Ginsberg chants hare krishnas, mantras, and oms at his poetry readings or that Gary Snyder, having spent several years in a Zen monastery in Japan, should look to the East for literary and religious models. For both poets, the West, with its crazed technology and its stress on the exploitative ego, is a threat to the "planetary biological welfare." The East, by contrast, schools the will to go beyond the acquisitive self and to concentrate on "the power within."

> **"The ideas of a poet should be noble and simple," Snyder quotes the Chinese poet Tu Fu. It is an accurate motto of his purposes in *Turtle Island*, his seventh book.**
> **—Herbert Leibowitz**

"The ideas of a poet should be noble and simple," Snyder quotes the Chinese poet Tu Fu. It is an accurate motto of his purposes in *Turtle Island,* his seventh book. Like Thoreau, he wants a "broad margin" to his life and believes that "a man is rich in proportion to the number of things which he can afford to let alone." The virtues of simplicity are the lesson he has learned from Chinese and Japanese poetry.

Snyder's poems fall roughly into three categories: lyrical precepts (prayers, spells, charms) designed to instill an "ecological conscience" so that we will respect the otherness of nature, frequently personified as the tender, generative mother, and use her wisely. (Linked with these poems are a group that register his disgust at the heedless wasters, interlopers and marauders, the suburban developers for whom if you treat nature right, "it will make a billion board feet a year.") Several poems celebrate domesticity and the family, the poet as doting father and husband bestowing benedictions on his wife and sons. By far the largest segment of his work records quiet moments when he observes the "whoosh of birds," cloud movements, a volcanic crater, the coyote's wail, the Douglas fir or a red leaf. These imagistic poems employ a spare notation.

Snyder's subjects are often appealing: walks, mountains, children, the skinning of a deer, love-making, communion with friends on a camping trip—all the ceremonies of innocence. But the poems themselves are thin, scattered, forgettable, their rhythmical pulse sluggish, as in **"Pine Tree Tops,"** a standard Snyder poem:

> in the blue night
> frost haze, the sky glows
> with the moon
> pine tree tops
> bend snow-blue, fade
> into sky, frost, starlight.
> the creak of boots.
> rabbit tracks, deer tracks,
> *what do we know.*

The reader feels he is watching home movies, leafing through snapshots of an exotic trip. What stays afterwards are silhouettes of experience: a bare breasted woman stooping to pick a shell while her children play nearby, or this:

> my friend broke open a dried coyote
> scat
> removed a ground squirrel tooth
> pierced it, hung it
> from the gold ring
> *in his ear*

Despite a few lovely poems—**"The Egg," "Straight-Creek-Great Burn,"** and **"The Hudsonian Curlew"**—*Turtle Island* is flat, humorless and uneventful. (Snyder's prose is vigorous and persuasive.) The poems are also oddly egotistical. Any random scrap jotted into a journal, the miscellaneous thoughts and images that are the seeds of shaped poems and that most poets discard, are transferred into the poems without the imagination's critical intervention. *Turtle Island* is a textbook example of the limits of Imagism.

I am reluctant to mention these doubts since as the bulldozers stand poised to despoil the wilderness by strip-mining the West for the sake of more dreck and civilized trumpery. Snyder's sane housekeeping principles desperately need to become Government and corporate policy. He is on the side of the gods. But as Snyder remarks, "Poetry is the vehicle of the mystery of voice," and the voice of *Turtle Island,* for all its sincerity and moral urgency, lacks that mystery and "inspired use of language" we call style. . . .

Lee Bartlett (essay date Spring 1983)

SOURCE: "Gary Snyder's Han-Shan," in *Sagetreib*, Vol. 2, No. 1, Spring, 1983, pp. 105-110.

[In the following essay, Bartlett discusses Snyder's translations of the works of seventh-century Buddhist poet Han-shan.]

Kenneth Rexroth, whose fourteen books of translations include many poems from the Chinese, has argued recently that Chinese poetry probably began to influence a few English speaking writers when *Three Hundred Poems of T'ang* was translated into French free verse in the mid-19th Century. Certainly the English translations of early sinologist Herbert A. Giles, collected in his *Gems of Chinese Literature,* marked in their archaic and doggerel renderings no advance in verse, as Giles' short reworking of Wei Ying-Wu's "Spring Joys" makes evident:

> When freshlets cease in early spring

> and the river dwindles low,
> I take my staff and wander
>> by the banks where the wild flowers
> grow.
> I watch the willow-catkins
>> wildly whirled on every side;
> I watch the falling peach-bloom
>> lightly floating down the tide.

Non-readers of French, Rexroth continues, of course had to wait until the turn of the century for first Arthur Waley's translations, then Ezra Pound's (and he finds the work of both Waley and Pound in this area lacking, as it gives the appearance that Chinese poetry is "as dependent on quantitative rhythms as on accentual"). Still, the effect of Chinese poetry (and [Ernest Francisco] Fenollosa's theoretical substructure, "The Chinese Written Character as a Medium for Poetry") on verse in English was of course profound, entering "the American and to a much less degree, English poetic consciousness at exactly the right moment to purge the rhetoric and moralizing of 19th Century Romantic poetry and even more moralistic, preachy poetry of the 90's." Pretty much across the board—from Imagism to Objectivism, from H. D. to Oppen—its influence was felt.

Gary Snyder dates his own interest in Chinese art from about the time he was "eleven or twelve":

> I went into the Chinese room at the Seattle art museum and saw Chinese landscape paintings; they blew my mind. My shock of recognition was very simple: "It looks just like the Cascades." The waterfalls, the pines, the clouds, the mist looked a lot like the northwest United States. The Chinese had an eye for the world that I saw as real. In the next room were the English and European landscapes, and they meant nothing. It was no great lesson except for an instantaneous, deep respect for something in Chinese culture that always stuck in my mind and that I would come back to again years later.

In fact, years later, he did. While an undergraduate anthropology major at Reed College, he discovered both Waley's and Pound's translations, Confucius, the *Tao Te Ching,* and many works of Chinese and Indian Buddhist literature. While Snyder admits that he valued Pound highly "as a teacher in poetic technology" (this influence can be seen most readily in *Myths & Texts*), his own interest in Chinese poetry came as much from inspiration of the *figure* of the Chinese "hermit poet / nature poet" as from an interest in technique.

Snyder's first "collection" of poems to see print actually appeared a year before *Riprap,* when in 1958 in its sixth issue *Evergreen Review* published his translations from the 7th

Century Chinese poet Han-shan, along with a short introduction and a few notes on the text. Snyder discovered Han-shan while doing graduate work in the Department of Oriental Languages at the University of California at Berkeley in the fall of 1955. He had been taking seminars in Chinese poetry, and had done a few translations of T'ang poems, when his interest in Buddhism in particular prompted him to ask Professor Ch'en Shih-hsiang to direct him in a tutorial on a Chinese Buddhist poet. Dr. Shin-hsiang suggested Han-shan, whose work at that time had been rendered into English only sparsely (Arthur Waley's "27 Poems by Han-shan" had appeared in *Encounter* in 1954). Snyder remembers that his teacher was "not a Buddhist, as indeed all contemporary Chinese intellectuals are not Buddhist, and I think he had a certain amount of anti-Buddhist feeling as all contemporary Chinese do," but that the Han-shan project changed his mind a bit, "partly in seeing the excitement with which I put it into English; it made him see the possible freshness in it as before he had seen it as a kind of stale set of ideas."

Snyder's first "collection" of poems to see print actually appeared a year before *Riprap*, when in 1958 in its sixth issue *Evergreen Review* published his translations from the 7th Century Chinese poet Han-shan, along with a short introduction and a few notes on the text.
—*Lee Bartlett*

We know almost nothing of the facts of Han-shan's life, save that he was a reclusive poet who lived during the T'ang Dynasty. Lu-ch'iu Yin, an official of the Dynasty, wrote a short preface to Han-shan's three hundred-plus poems, in which he explained that he caught sight of the poet (and his friend Shih-te) only once:

> I saw two men standing in front of the stove warming themselves and laughing loudly. I bowed to them, whereupon the two raised their voices in chorus and began to hoot at me. The joined hands and, shrieking with laughter, called out to me, "Blabbermouth, blabbermouth Feng-kan! You wouldn't know the Buddha Amitabha if you saw him! What do you mean by bowing to us?"

And the two strange men ran off and disappeared into the mountains. According to Lu-ch'iu Yin, he then organized a group of monks to collect Han-shan's poems, which the poet had written on "trees and rocks or the walls of the houses and offices in the nearby village." It is this collection of poems we have come to call "Cold Mountain," after the vivid mountain landscape Han-shan describes. But as Arthur

Waley has noted, Cold Mountain is more than a place—it is also a state of mind. "It is on this conception," Waley wrote in his introduction, "as well as on that of the 'hidden treasure,' the Buddha who is to be sought not somewhere outside us, but 'at home' in the heart, that the mysticism of the poem is based."

Snyder was certainly familiar with Waley's translations, and he was obviously drawn to Han-shan's work as both a circumstance of place and a state of mind. Snyder's short preface to his translations presents Han-shan as a kind of archetypal Beat wanderer and holy man, a "mountain man in an Old Chinese line of ragged hermits," not unlike Jack Kerouac's sense of Snyder himself in *The Dharma Bums*. In fact, Snyder carries the identification even further, as he feels his own experience in the mountains of the northwest helped him capture the ethos of the originals in a way other translators could not:

> I was able to do fresh, accurate translations of Han-shan because I was able to envision Han-shan's world because I had much experience in the mountains and there are many images in Han-shan which are directly images of mountain scenery and mountain terrain and mountain weather that if a person had not felt those himself physically he would not be able to get the same feel into the translation—it would be more abstract. I think that was part of the success of those translations—a meeting of sensations.

By "accurate translations" Snyder does not mean, of course, literal ones, but rather "imitations" in Robert Lowell's sense—to "keep something equivalent to the fire and the finish" of the originals. Pound's *Cathay* and "The Seafarer" really established the modern idea of translation for American poets, that is the privileging of sense or tone over literal accuracy. If the translator proceeds as a scientist, Ben Belitt argues, if "a simplistic semantics and a misguided analogy with scientific method" leads him "to identify the truth of a poem substantially with its 'words' and its 'intent,'" "he will end up with a "science fiction of translation." Rather, he must give a "pulse to his language," must "make a poet's demands on the emerging English rather than a pedant's or a proctor in" some Intermediate Original. The point is that when a literal translation has been accomplished, the translator's real work then begins.

Thus Snyder's translations of Han-shan (like Lowell's *Imitations* and Robert Bly's more recent renderings from Rilke) attempt to bring over the experience of the poems as poems into English. In a letter to the linguist Dell Hymes, Snyder explains his method of translation with explicit reference to his versions from the Chinese. "I get the verbal meaning into mind as clearly as I can," he writes, but then make an enormous effort of visualization, to "see" what the poem says, nonlinguistically, like a movie in my mind, and to feel it. If I can do this (and much of the time the poem eludes this effort) then I write the scene down in English. It is not a translation of the words, it is the same poem in a different language, allowing for the peculiar distortions of my own vision—but keeping it straight as possible. If I can do this to a poem the translation is uniformly successful, and is generally well received by scholars and critics. If I can't do this, I can still translate the words, and it may be well received, but it doesn't feel like it should.

In addition to capturing the ethos of the original, then, this notion of translation also means that the English poem becomes—in its language, its imagery, and, even to an extent, its rhythm—finally as much a product of Snyder's poetic imagination as of Han-shan's. And indeed as readers when we study the versions of Pound, Lowell, Snyder, Bly, Kinnell, and other poets, we look to those poems to tell us as much about the interests, influences, and techniques of the translator-poets as anything else.

While there is not quite the same sense of compression or ellipsis in Snyder's versions of Han-shan's poems as in a poem like "Praise for Sick Women," still the poems are obviously of a piece with Snyder's other early work; in fact, in 1969 he collected the early books together as *Riprap & Cold Mountain Poems* (San Francisco: Four Seasons Foundation), as if to signify a unity of style and subject between his early original poems and the translations. Certainly it is difficult to detect much difference between **"Mid-August on Sourdough Mountain Lookout"** (the lead poem in *Riprap*) and, for example, "I settled at Cold Mountain long ago" (number 7 of the sequence). The language of both poems is simple and direct, and in each we encounter a similar situation—the poet in seclusion, and his exhilaration in nature.

Perhaps an even more interesting exercise is to set one of Snyder's translations alongside one of Waley's. In 1954, Waley published the following reworking of a Han-shan poem as "XVI" in his *Encounter series:*

> The people of the world when they see Han-shan
> All regard him as not in his right mind.
> His appearance, they say, is far from being
>   attractive
> Tied up as he is in bits of tattered cloth.
> "What we say, he cannot understand;
> What he says, we do not say."
> You who spend all your time in coming and going,
> Why not try for once coming to the Han-shan?

In his collection, Snyder translated the same poem as the last in the sequence, "24":

> When men see Han-shan
> They all say he's crazy
> And not much to look at—
> Dressed in rags and hides.
> They don't get what I say
> & I don't talk their language.
> All I can say to those I meet:
> "Try and make it to Cold Mountain."

Compared to Herbert Giles' "Spring Joys," Waley's translation is certainly less stilted; his language seems almost casual in tone. Yet beside Snyder's version, Waley's is more wordy and privileges the "poetic." Snyder has obviously tried to strip the poem to its bare essentials ("people of the world" becomes "men"; "not in his right mind" becomes "crazy"), and to give Han-shan not only a language that approximates speech, but a truly contemporary language. Where "What we say, he cannot understand; / What he says, we do not say" still retains a hint of a certain traditional poetic resonance, Snyder transforms the lines to everyman speaking: "They don't get what I say / & I don't talk their language."

In an interview, Snyder's close friend Lew Welch explained,

> Poi-Chui was a very great poet that used to have a peasant lady who was illiterate yet very smart. She ran a garden down the road and he would go and engage her in conversation. And then he would dump the poem on her and if she didn't recognize that he had just said a poem, he figured that he had written it right. If she had gone "huh?" or something, if it seemed awkward to her or wrong, somehow ungraceful, then Poi-Chui would go back and fix it. He tested his stuff against a lady who had never read a poem in her life and never wanted to. That's a standard, and that's the way I feel about that standard.

And Snyder would, I think, agree. Of course Poi-Chui's peasant lady would not have chased Waley down the street with a trowel, as his language is fairly idiomatic; but we can be sure that on hearing Snyder's poem, she wouldn't have even looked up from her weeding, for the language is purely contemporary, purely conversational.

Additionally, Snyder's translation seems to tie the importance of the wilderness more closely to one's psychological state. As I mentioned earlier, Waley's notion of Cold Mountain is that it is "not somewhere outside us, but 'at home' in the heart." Thus in the last line of his version of the poem, travellers are admonished to "try for once coming to the Han-shan," that is, the Buddha inside themselves. There is no distinction made between place ("Cold Mountain") and poet (Han-shan). Snyder would have no quarrel with this identification, and it is one both evident in his own poem and central to Zen thought. Yet in his translation, the poet seems more directly part of the natural world. Where Waley's Hanshan wears "bits of tattered cloth," Snyder's is "dressed in rags *and hides*" (italics mine), which thus links him more explicitly with the animal realm. And more important, Snyder's rendering of the last line underscores a crucial separation between individual and environment as the poet advises passers-by to "try and make it to Cold Mountain." As in the **Riprap** poems, it is only when an individual has placed himself back in nature that he can properly look into himself and hope to find some sort of understanding and psychic quiet.

Katsunori Yamazato (essay date Summer 1983)

SOURCE: "A Note on Japanese Allusions in Gary Snyder's Poetry," in *Western American Literature,* Vol. 18, No. 2, Summer, 1983, pp. 143-48.

[*In the essay below, Yamazato traces Snyder's use of Japanese folktales and culture in his poetry.*]

Recent criticism of the poetry of Gary Snyder has focused on the poet's use of allusions. While Buddhist and Chinese allusions have gradually been identified and explicated, the equally important Japanese allusions in Snyder's poetry have attracted little attention. Reflecting the poet's Japanese years (1956-1968), these allusions range widely over such subjects as classical Japanese literature, folklore, religion, and the Japanese way of life in general. The allusions to the Japanese subjects indeed are so varied that a coherent discussion of them would require a much longer study than the present one. Instead of attempting an exhaustive discussion of Snyder's Japanese allusions, then, I would like to narrow my focus and discuss a few representative examples.

In poem 4 in the "Logging" section in **Myths & Texts**, Snyder alludes to a Noh play, *Takasago,* written by Zeami (or Seami) Motokiyo (1363-1443). Snyder juxtaposes the allusion to the play with scenes from "logging," the mindless destruction of nature the poet has witnessed at the early stage of his poetic career:

> Pines, under pines,
>   Seami Motokiyo
>   The Doer stamps his foot.
>   A thousand board-feet
>   Bucked, skidded, loaded—
>   (Takasago, Ise) float in a mill pond;

> A thousand years dancing
> Flies in the saw kerf.

The first three lines in the passage cited allude to the stage setting and the author of *Takasago.* In the Noh play, two pine trees appear on the stage, symbolizing both prosperity and longevity. "The Doer" (or the principal actor: *shite* in Japanese) is the spirit of one of the pine trees who in the shape of an old man engages in a conversation with a travelling priest. The characteristic Noh movement of the Doer ("The Doer stamps his foot") triggers an ironic shift to the next three lines, a metonymic representation of the destruction of nature. The embedded flashback to Takasago and Ise suggests that even the sacred pine trees at these places are not totally free from the destructive attitude toward nature. "A thousand years dancing" alludes to the celebrated longevity of the pine tree at Takasago:

> Among them all, this pine
> Surpasses all other trees,
> Attired in the princely robe
> Of green of [a] thousand autumns,
> Timeless fresh forever.
> By Shiko a court rank
> Bestowed, the superb tree,
> Overseas and in the land alike
> By all is loved and admired.

Takasago ends with the pine god's dance, *kamimai,* which gives blessing to the land; and the whole play is usually construed as a hymn to the sacred pines which are the symbols of prosperity and longevity. Instead of celebrating nature, however, Snyder shows us its destruction in our time: "A thousand years dancing / Flies in the saw kerf." The dramatic vision in *Takasago* presents a harmonious interaction between the gods of the sacred pine trees and the travellers, and, needless to say, the world view that informs Zeami's dramatic vision forms a sharp contrast with that of the Judaeo-Christian tradition which Snyder regards as responsible for nurturing the destructive attitude toward nature depicted especially in the "Logging" section of **Myths & Texts**.

Poem 4 in the "Logging" section is the first poem in which Snyder extensively alludes to Japanese subjects, but it is typical of the kind of Japanese materials and world view which attracted Snyder's attention at the early stage of his poetic career. As is implied in the poet's allusion to Zeami's play, Snyder has always been interested in obliterating the line which differentiates between man and nature. An allusion to a Japanese folktale entered in his early journal is another example: "Sparrows entertained me singing and dancing, I've never had such a good time as today." The allusion is to "The Tongue-Cut Sparrow," a famous Japanese folktale which has been frequently translated into English. The tale tells of a kind-hearted old man who helps a sparrow after its tongue is cut by his greedy and cruel wife. The old man eventually visits the sparrow's home built of bamboo, and the "tongue-cut" sparrow and his fellows entertain the old man with food, drink, and the sparrow dance. The tale has a didactic ending, but Snyder seems more interested in the attitude toward nature expressed in the tale than its didactic import. The quotation in the journal highlights the joyful interaction between man and nature; it is not the cruelty of the wife that catches Snyder's attention but the subsequent harmony of man and bird.

"Kyoto Born in Spring Song" in *Regarding Wave* is a poem in which Snyder's profound veneration for nature's buddhahood is expressed. Man and nature coexist harmoniously in this poetic cosmos. By calling those born in spring "children" and "babies," man and animal alike, the poet obliterates the differentiating line.

The first stanza presents an ambiguity as to the identity of the "Beautiful little children":

> Beautiful little children
> found in melons,
> in bamboo,
> in a "strangely glowing warbler egg"
> a perfect baby girl—

As we read through line 4, we feel that the speaker in the poem perhaps is speaking of "wild babies" (1. 30) rather than "human" babies. Yet the diction in line 5, "a perfect baby girl," is ambiguous enough to call our attention to the identities of the "children." Who and what are they? The ambiguity is uniquely Snyderian, and it arises from the poet's use of three ancient Japanese folktales.

"Melons" in line 2 cited above alludes to "Urikohime," a tale of a girl who is found inside a melon. (*Uri* in Japanese means melon). The tale has recently been retold by Yanagita Kunio, a renowned Japanese folklorist whose works Snyder read during the Japanese years. A quotation from the opening passage of the tale will help us see clearly Snyder's allusion to this tale:

> Long ago there was an old man and an old woman. The old man went to the mountains to cut wood and the old woman went to the river to wash clothes.

> One day when the old woman went washing as usual at the river, a melon came floating down the stream. She picked it up and took it home to divide with the old man. When she cut it open, a very beautiful little girl was born. Because she was born from a melon, they named her Urikohime or Princess Melon. Little by little she grew up and at last she was a good daughter who wove at the loom day after day.

The "bamboo" in Snyder's line 3 alludes to one of the most famous Japanese folktales, "Kaguyahime," which tells of a beautiful tiny girl discovered inside a bamboo. The tale seems to have been Snyder's favorite, and he also alludes to it in **"Foxtail Pine"** in *The Back Country*: "baby girl born from the split crotch / of a plum / daughter of the moon—". "A plum" is apparently Snyder's creative adaptation of "Kaguyahime," and like Kaguyahime Snyder's "baby girl" is a "daughter of the moon." Line 4 of **"Kyoto Born in Spring Song"** alludes to "Uguisuhime," *uguisu* meaning a bush warbler. "Uguisuhime" is a variant of "Kaguyahime," and there is little difference in plot between the two tales. Again a quotation from Yanagita will illuminate Snyder's allusion to the tale:

> Long, long ago there was an old man in Sugaru province. He made his way in life by going into the mountains to cut bamboo and making it into all kinds of trays and things which he sold. In old books he is called *Takctori-no-Okina* and *Mizukuri-no-Okina.*

> This *Mizukuri-no-Okina* went into a bamboo grove one day, and there he found *an especially radiant egg in a nightingale's nest* [italics mine]. When he carried it home carefully and set it down, it broke open by itself. From inside there was born a very tiny, lovely princess. Because she was born from a nightingale's egg, the old man named her Uguisuhime or Princess Nightingale. He brought her up as his own child.

We can perhaps appreciate the poem without knowing the folktales alluded to in the first stanza of the poem, but Snyder's vision of the inseparability of man and nature will be seen more vividly when we learn the identities of the "Beautiful little children." For the children in the folktales and Snyder's poem, there is no differentiating line between man and nature.

"Kyoto Born in Spring Song" expresses Snyder's profound Buddhist vision of life:

> O sing born in spring
> the weavers swallows babies in Nishijin
>   nests below the eaves
>
>   glinting mothers wings
>   swoop to the sound of looms
>   and three fat babies
>   with three human mothers
> every morning doing laundry
>   "good
>   morning how's your baby?"
> Tomoharu, Itsuko, and Kenji—

"Nishijin" district in Kyoto is well known for textile fabrics it produces; one can actually hear "the sound of looms" as he walks through the district. In the passage cited above, Snyder emphasizes the harmonious coexistence of man and nature. The juxtaposition of the sentient beings in "the weavers swallows babies in Nishijin" (significantly without commas) and the internal rhymes resounding in the whole passage cited above subtly suggest the harmony achieved in spring.

When discussing Snyder it is almost a cliché to quote passages from scholars of Zen Buddhism to support or clarify one's argument, but the following statement nevertheless clearly illustrates the basic Zen Buddhist notion of nature which has informed Snyder's Japanese allusions: " . . . Nature not as an object to conquer and turn wantonly to our human service, but as a fellow being, who is destined like ourselves for Buddahood."

Patrick D. Murphy (essay date Winter 1985)

SOURCE: "Mythic and Fantastic: Gary Snyder's 'Mountains and Rivers without End,'" in *Extrapolation*, Vol. 26, No. 4, Winter, 1985, pp. 290-99.

[*In the following essay, Murphy analyzes Snyders' poem "Mountains and Rivers without End" in terms of Tzetvan Todorov's theories on the fantastic.*]

Critics of the Fantastic tend to ignore poetry, overlooking poems from the mainstream of poetic tradition and dismissing, usually as facile, poetry appearing in science fiction and fantasy magazines. Serious work has been and is being done in the area of fantasy-oriented poetry, but this work rarely receives critical attention as Fantastic literature or as poetry using fantastic techniques for its effects. I do not claim that modern poets are turning to the Fantastic in some marked degree, but I do claim that they use the Fantastic, particularly mythic fantasy, for their artistic purposes and that such elements deserve serious critical attention. One reason that relatively little use of the Fantastic appears in current American poetry is that contemporary poetry still remains to some extent within a turning away from narrative forms. Some poets, such as Robinson Jeffers, who did manage to cling to narrative forms through the first half of the century certainly used the Fantastic, in its broad generic sense. After the war, Ginsberg's nightmares also produced some narrative fantasy, while other Beats used fantasy to express spiritual moments beyond rational description and invoked myth to enlighten readers to principles drawn from Taoism, Tantrism, Hinduism, and Buddhism.

Gary Snyder was part of the Beat movement as well as be-

ing influenced by Jeffers and such major figures as Lawrence and Pound. He was also influenced, through anthropological studies, by native American kiva rituals, shamanism, and myths which he saw linked with Eastern mystical philosophy. This mixture encouraged him to see religious visions and mythic fantasies as spiritual forces in a modern world without philosophical grounding. From primitivism, Snyder begins to see the poem as shaman chant, power vision, and healing prayer. From Zen Buddhism and its Hindu precursors, he begins to see poetry as harmonious sacred song and köan training. Focusing on Zen philosophy, Snyder has come to emphasize not Eastern teleology but the presence of the world, its *tathata,* or suchness, in which life is a wandering path through which one travels breaking down illusions and opening the mind to *satori,* the instant of spiritual enlightenment when the ego drops away and the individual recognizes the interdependence of the spiritual energy pathways of the universe. Snyder's poetry from the first has expressed his developing philosophical system and his belief that America needs a new guiding myth as the foundation for creating a new culture based on harmony rather than conflict with the universal life flow.

> Snyder's "Mountains and Rivers without End," a long sequential poem on which he is still working, provides the most striking example of his efforts in this direction of opening the reader's mind to the possibility of spiritual enlightenment and his use of mythic fantasy and fantastic hesitation to achieve that purpose.
> —*Patrick D. Murphy*

Snyder's **"Mountains and Rivers without End,"** a long sequential poem on which he is still working, provides the most striking example of his efforts in this direction of opening the reader's mind to the possibility of spiritual enlightenment and his use of mythic fantasy and fantastic hesitation to achieve that purpose. Snyder draws deeply on Hindu-Buddhist and native American mythology to present his spiritual vision. Without the uses of mythic fantasy and dream narratives, a number of these poem sequences could not have been written. Narrating instances of inward vision, Snyder wields myth and fantasy in an effort to replicate moments of religious revelation; attempting to describe experiences beyond rational consciousness, he draws the reader into fantasy episodes which produce feelings of spiritual immanence and emotive response to the ineffable—"epiphanies" of enlightenment. He attempts through these to inculcate in readers a new consciousness opening a way for modern man to reestablish himself in balance with Earth.

Before turning to a brief close reading, it is necessary first to discuss some aspects of Tzetvan Todorov's definition of the fantastic. In *The Fantastic,* Todorov defines the heart of his genre as an event occurring which cannot be explained by the laws of the world familiar to the reader and/or the character." The reader must opt for one of two possibilities: he is a victim of an illusion with a rational explanation, in which case the world remains as he knows it; or, the event is real, in which case the world does not remain as he knows it, but a new reality opens up which functions by laws unknown to him. He argues: "The fantastic occupies the duration of this uncertainty. Once we choose one answer or the other, we leave the fantastic for a neighboring genre, the uncanny or the marvelous. The fantastic is that hesitation experienced by a person who knows only the laws of nature, confronting an apparently supernatural event." I believe that such hesitation occurs not only in fiction but also in poetry. Poets use techniques of the Fantastic, in the broad generic sense, including those of the fantastic, as Todorov narrowly defines the term. A complication exists, though, in poetry which Todorov uses to dismiss it entirely from the fantastic genre. He states:

> If as we read a text we reject all representation, considering each sentence as a pure semantic combination, the fantastic *could not appear:* for the fantastic requires, it will be recalled, a reaction to events as they occur in the world evoked. For this reason, the fantastic can subsist only within fiction; poetry cannot be fantastic.

Yet, earlier in his book Todorov admitted: "Poetry too includes certain representative elements, and fiction properties which render the text opaque, intransitive." To the degree that it does this, Jeffers' "The Double Axe" and Dorn's *Slinger* being two twentieth-century examples, poetry can also present an event which requires the reader to choose between a logical explanation and a supernatural one, and fantastic hesitation may appear in the process of that choosing, as it does in Snyder's **"Mountains and Rivers without End."** Not surprisingly, such a hesitation may be of far shorter duration in a poem than in a novel, but nevertheless it occurs. In poetry, however, the hesitation may result from three possibilities rather than two, the third being that the strange event is neither natural nor supernatural, but is solely a figurative device not intended to be representational. Though Todorov devotes some attention to categorizing the fantastic as exclusively fictive prose, his arguments leave room in which to introduce certain modern poems.

Besides the opacity of poetic narrative, Todorov's discussion of Freud can also be turned to use for criticism of poetry. Todorov states: "According to Freud, the sense of the uncanny is linked to the appearance of an image which originates in the childhood of the individual or the race." Taken a step further, one can argue that through the functioning of the collective unconscious the invocation of myths and archetypes in poems transports the reader toward the uncanny and then beyond it into a period of fantastic hesitation. The reader wonders whether the character's mythic dream or spiritual vision is a psychologically reducible event and thus merely uncanny, or if the character's experience occurs in a truly spiritual realm in which the myth reveals itself as truth. The latter suggests that the reader himself could enter such a realm. In this case, the reader passes from hesitation into the marvelous when myth-turned-truth reveals universal laws and causes which function beyond the scope of man's familiar world. This occurs whether or not the laws validate the mythic characters associated with them or if, instead, the myths serve solely to reveal the laws themselves.

In poems in which myth is not merely alluded to but integral to the story, the reader will have difficulty from the outset in ascribing this use of myth to the figurative and thereby avoid any hesitation, quite simply because people recognize that dreams are real, and the dimensions of myth and dream frequently overlap. Deciding to which reality the myths belong may cause hesitation: the reality of the native American kiva with its smoke hole to the world above, the reality of the shaman with the power of animal spirits, or the reality of the world in which dreams are representations of a collective unconscious residing within and struggling up out of an interior psyche. In other words, the myths belong to a series of imaginary beliefs based on religious idealism and are, therefore, marvelous, that is supernatural; or, the myths belong to the natural processes of the human mind and are, therefore, uncanny, arising from physical rather than spiritual origins. Todorov's dismissal of poetry from his study of the fantastic (based on linguistic theories of poetic language as essentially non-narrative and self-referential), if critics were to heed it, would deny them valuable insights into the experience of the reader encountering the use of the Fantastic in poetry.

Todorov's chapter "Themes of the Self" provides an opening for a particular kind of poetry: mythic fantasy and spiritual vision, poetry which Snyder writes. Todorov claims: "Pan-determinism signifies that the limit between the physical and the mental, between matter and spirit, between word and thing, ceases to be impervious"; "The physical world and the spiritual world interpenetrate; their fundamental categories are modified as a result." Such an interpenetration stands as a fundamental starting point for shamanist and Hindu-Buddhist beliefs, beliefs which Snyder poetically demonstrates in **"Mountains and Rivers without End."**

In **"Bubbs Creek Haircut,"** the opening poem of the sequence, Snyder begins with a first-person narrator preparing for a journey. The first stanza seems straightforward enough. The narrator gets a haircut in preparation for entering the mountains and it turns out the barber has been where the narrator intends to go. But in the next stanza, reality unravels a bit in the Goodwill Store. Discarded items are described as having lives of their own, and the proprietor is referred to as "The Master of the limbo drag-legged," invoking the mythic image of a limping god. A mood is established indicating that this journey represents a crucial quest to resolve some unstated crisis.

The next few stanzas begin the actual journey and initiate a process of interweaving memories and present events in a collapsing of time and space, a process foreshadowed in the Goodwill Store and begun in earnest with the memories of an earlier haircut and a past friendship. Attachments are being dropped away by the narrator in the same way that he sheds his hair—the implication that the haircut was a preparatory rite is here reinforced, it being akin to the shaving of Buddhist monks' heads at the beginning of their training in imitation of Guatama Buddha. Quickly the narrator brings the reader to a different land:

> a half-iced over lake, twelve thousand feet
> its sterile boulder bank
> but filled with leaping trout:
> reflections wobble in the
> mingling circles always spreading out
> the crazy web of wavelets makes sense
> seen from high above.
> the realm of fallen rock
> a deva world of sorts—

The narrator warns the reader that he has reached a world of spirits in which the laws of the city no longer apply. Not only is it named a "deva world," but also the web formed by spreading circles implies the net of universal energy which is symbolized by water in Hindu mythology. There water symbolizes both the continuous flow of energy and the vastness of the cosmic ocean in which one may lose individual consciousness. The lake and its flowing waters are both representational and symbolic, but whether they are symbolic of a supernatural truth or only a semantic abstraction remains unresolved at this point.

The next section of the poem casts the reader into the midst of a strange meditation, first referring back to the Goodwill proprietor as "King of Hell" and then moving into a celebration of the dance of "moon breast Parvati," who is both Shiva's consort and an earth goddess figure. The real world of the lake and its life-brimming water has become a mythic fantasy world—what Manlove might term a metaphoric fantasy—of Hindu gods celebrating the belief that all things have their "deva" nature, or spiritual essence, and that all these natures interpenetrate. The Goodwill proprietor is "King of Hell" because he seeks to chain the items in the store to lives solely limited to the uses of man. The reader can interpret this episode as a figurative series of allusions,

a dream vision, a hallucination, or a religious experience. Before he can really decide, the narrator returns to descriptions of a seemingly normal world, memories again of other trips and friends reinforcing the poem's representational character; but this ends with a revealing parenthetical: "on Whitney hair on end / hail stinging bare legs in the blast of wind / but yodel off the summit echoes clean." The narrator has undergone a spiritual experience involving purification. Hunt comments: "One has the feeling that Maya's mirror of illusion has been wiped clean in the moment of interpenetrating conjunction with the Nature Goddess." The poem then moves into its conclusion:

> all this came after:
> Purity of the mountains and goodwills.
> The diamond drill of racing icemelt waters
> and bumming trucks and watching
> Buildings raze
> the garbage acres burning at the Bay
> the girl who was the skid-row
> Cripple's daughter—

All that the reader has been told came after the haircut. This statement claims that all that has been told has really occurred. "Purity of the mountains and goodwills" suggests a link between his purification and the realization of inter-dependence of all things in life, the wilderness and the cities, man and artifacts, rock and water, gods and world. The "diamond drill" reinforces the spiritual vision as true experience and as a source of purification because it is an oblique reference to the "Diamond Sutra," a key Buddhist text. There the Buddha teaches that "a body-form is not a body-form" and that "all that has form is illusory." The real is the energy flow represented by the water in which the ego may be dissolved, while the unreal is the appearance of material forms whereby the ego defines itself. Hunt explains the conclusion in this way:

> If we perceive a universe of objects, with identity, solidity, and a fixed nature, we only continue to delude ourselves and our consciousness will remain willful and ego-centered. If, however, we see the ever-changing, interconnecting, fleeting character of things we will at least recognize the universe for what it really is: a mirage, or, as Zimmer puts it, "Mäyä-maya, 'of the stuff of Mäyä.'"

What then is the reader's response to this strange, rapturous story? After the narrator looks into the lake he sings a celebration of the flowing waters of Parvati's dance, enacting the continuous energizing of the universe with its cosmic contradiction of the endless life-death cycle represented by a half-frozen lake with sterile banks but filled with living trout. Is he in the realm of figurative poetic discourse, and so should interpret the poem as merely metaphor for an invigorating weekend in the mountains; is he in the realm of the uncanny and so should interpret the spiritual visions and feelings of purification as neurotic guilt displacement; or, is he in the realm of the marvelous and so should interpret the spiritual vision as relating a new set of universal laws by which the world operates? As Todorov summarizes themes of the self: "We may further characterize these themes by saying that they essentially concern the structuring of the relations between man and the world. We are, in Freudian terms, within the *perception-consciousness* system." The narrator would say that we are in the system of the Buddha, in which one can recognize the *tathata* (suchness) of the world, that mind is matter, matter mind, and the distinction between object and subject an illusion of Western logocentrism.

"Bubbs Creek Haircut" opens up to the reader a new way of perceiving the world around him, suggesting a different set of laws from the one by which he normally operates. The poem does not seek to convert, but rather to surprise the reader, causing him to hesitate and reassess his perceptions. He will thereby become more open to different perceptions of reality continuously unfolded throughout **"Mountains and Rivers without End."** Depending on his resolution of hesitation, the reader will either accept or reject this new world he is offered.

"Journeys," another poem in the sequence, takes the reader through several worlds, both to break down his normal channels of rational thought and to tap into his unconscious through archetypes and myths. This poem begins with the narrative "I" again, but Part One is a dream sequence. There a bird becomes a woman who leads the narrator on a subterranean journey through a maze. When he is about to lose his way she gives him a slice of apple and he awakes. Evidently a dream, but whether a figurative one or a real one experienced by an autobiographical narrator remains unclear as the literary and the symbolic mix with the narrative representation because of the heavy presence of archetypal material.

Parts Two and Three, with no indication of being dreams, describe the narrator as travelling with others in a strange land. As primitive hunters they reach a plateau where they flee the sun in awe of its power while shooting arrows at it. Again archetypes and myths appear: ancient hunters enter northwestern America; they attempt to shoot the sun; they view it as another being, perhaps a god. The story can also be interpreted as primitive ritual for gaining power and knowledge. The reader may not hesitate here, but quickly conclude that such a story is purely figurative. Still, the mythic archetypes have affected him and his sureness of decision making. The following two parts of the poem narrate experiences in the familiar world and their quotidian reality calls into question the extraordinary reality of the previous

parts. Perhaps the primitive ritual is a memory resurrected from the collective unconscious of the race or handed down through oral tradition, such as stories found in native American legend. If so, it is no longer simply figurative or self-referential in this poem. Instead, it becomes the written record of a historical event and a testimony to the diachronic continuity of human community identity.

The reader of the poem is probably confused at this point. Part Six heightens the confusion. The narrator describes a journey through high mountains, ending "now I have come to the LOWLANDS." Nothing, though, is done to resolve the confusion over whether or not the earlier sections of the poem are all dreams retold. Perhaps they are different forms of the mind: dreams, archetypal images, oral history, and personal memories—all forms of mental experiences of the world, but experiences in which time and space are twisted around and shifted back and forth through the activity of the psyche.

The last three parts of the poem are crucial to unravelling the mystery that tends to make the reader suspend judgment until the poem's end. Section Seven returns to a dream format, an archetypal one, again with an underground maze. It is destroyed city, an urban nightmare:

> Movies going, men milling round the posters
> in shreds
> the movies always running
> —we all head in here somewhere;
> —years just looking for the bathrooms.
> Huge and filthy, with strange-shaped toilets full of
> shit.
> Dried shit all around, smeared across the walls of
> the
> adjoining rooms,
> and a vast hat rack.

Surely a Freudian nightmare, but one that contains the modern-day equivalent of oral legend and primitive myth, the cinema. Here the narrator is alone, but the distinction between figurative language and real dream remains unclear.

Section Eight returns to a narrative of a bus ride, a world of daylight and friends, but the distinction between dream narratives and travel narratives has blurred—both are journeys. The reader may become suspicious of seemingly simple descriptions. In the final section the narrator is also travelling with a friend; it begins: "We were following a long river into the mountains." The spiritual components are present: water as energy and mountains as form. It starts out like the preceding travel narrative, but then:

> Ko grabbed me and pulled me over the cliff—both
> of us falling. I hit and I was dead. I saw my body

for a while, then it was gone. Ko was there too. We were at the bottom of the gorge. We started drifting up the canyon, "This is the way to the back country."

The reader must decide, not only for the final section but also for the poem as a whole, whether or not it is another dream, a figurative device of self-referential language, or a spiritual vision of a reality in which "all form is illusory."

Placement of the narrator's fall and death at the end of the poem becomes comprehensible if interpreted as an experience of sudden enlightenment, similar to that in **"Bubbs Creek Haircut."** Zen, as well as shamanism, would be able to explain what has died, as well as to agree with the accuracy of the claim, "I saw my body for a while, then it was gone." The narrator has shed his ego and with it his sense of body as separate from the rest of the world. The object and subject interpenetrate, and as they do, each disappears; the body dies as the spirit awakes.

There is more here than Zen symbolism, though, as suggested by the poem's final phrase. That is to say, the poem cannot be reduced to an explication of symbols merely to detect a religious doctrine as a literary source. It needs to be read as one always reads Fantastic literature the first time through: in terms of the psychological and emotional elements of the reader's response. Within that framework major questions suddenly arise at poem's end: where does this back country lie? Have all these journeys occurred within a spiritual back country hidden by the illusion of form which Western thought teaches as the only reality? Are spiritual visions symbolic or real?

The power and success of Snyder's mythic fantasies reside in the immediacy with which this final question confronts the reader. In the end, whether he opts for psychological interpretations of the poems, placing them in the uncanny; considers them attempts to render in inadequate language a spiritual experience, placing them in the marvelous; or, consigns all of the journeys to figurative language, he is confronted by the need to resolve any hesitation. He must decide if spiritual visions are real. If so, then do the worlds of shamanism and Zen offer laws by which the universe functions beyond those known to Western man's familiar world? Some might argue that by referring to the texts as mythic fantasies I have already resolved this question, since myths are fictions designed to interpret something a culture does not understand. The opposite is the case. One does not have to believe in Parvati or Satan to be affected by myths and dream archetypes to the point of questioning his own theory of how the world works. If those myths have proven unsatisfactory, perhaps new myths are needed to bring man closer to the source of life's mystery.

In my own case, Snyder has produced a hesitation still resonating. While I reject the old myths, I am not sure that invalidates their purpose; new myths may be needed to open up a spiritual realm in which, as Todorov observes, there is the "effacement of the limit between subject and object." Snyder's **"Mountains and Rivers without End"** undertakes what Todorov terms a theme of vision: "The 'themes of vision' are based on a breakdown of the limit between psychic and physical," a task undertaken by all myth, and one at which Snyder succeeds. Snyder's wielding of the mythic and fantastic demonstrates the existence of a genre category in poetry which Todorov attempts to reserve for prose, a category with farther-reaching critical application than his structural and historical strictures would originally admit.

Woody Rehanek (essay date Fall 1987)

SOURCE: "The Shaman Songs of Gary Snyder," in *North Dakota Quarterly,* Vol. 55, No. 4, Fall, 1987, pp. 162-69.

[*In the essay below, Rehanek focuses on* Axe Handles *and considers Snyders' philosophy of the interconnections between man and nature.*]

> Shamanism relates to the most archaic of human religious practices . . . It informs the fundamental lore of the planet, that is to say, all of the worldwide body of folktale that we all share. The folk motifs of Native America are scattered all across Europe and Asia. We are all in the same boat, stemming from ten to thirteen thousand years back in the Pleistocene. We are all sharing the same information and the same religious disciplines. It is to the credit of some peoples, like the Native North Americans, that they kept it going longer, and I think they were right. We must all work to help them keep their lands and cultures together.

Axe Handles is Gary Snyder's first book of poetry since the emergence of Pulitzer Prize-winning *Turtle Island* eight years ago. Here we see an elaboration and expansion of themes which have run like tributaries through the mainstream of his body of work. *Axe Handles* is grounded in essentials—knowing our local watershed, how we relate to the earth/Mother Gaia and to each other. He brings to bear craftsmanship, precision, and tradition as a master carpenter knows the woods, tools, and designs of his craft.

Like transparent overlays in a medical textbook, where circulatory, respiratory, and digestive systems overlap the skeleton and musculature to form a coherent whole, Gary Snyder's themes overlap layer on layer, taking us from upper Paleolithic times to the bioregional future. Central is the concept of basic "human-ness" being formed 40,000 years ago: "Our human experience and all our cultures have not been formed within the context of civilization in cities or large numbers of people. Our self—biophysically, biopsychically, as an animal of great complexity—was already well formed and shaped by the experience of bands of people living in relatively small populations in a world in which there was lots of company: other life forms, such as whales, birds, animals." This unconventional interpretation of history opens doors to a rich body of analogies, parallels, and correlations which are woven through the simple/complex fabric of his work.

Gary Snyder was raised on his father's small dairy farm in Kitsap County, Washington, "on the edge of logging country." His father "was a smart man, a very handy man, but he only knew about 15 different trees and after that he was lost. I wanted more precision; I wanted to look deeper into the underbrush." Young Gary went to work in the woods, logging and manning fire lookouts in the Skagit country.

Like transparent overlays in a medical textbook, where circulatory, respiratory, and digestive systems overlap the skeleton and musculature to form a coherent whole, Gary Snyder's themes overlap layer on layer, taking us from upper Paleolithic times to the bioregional future.
—*Woody Rehanek*

He developed a dry, precise, descriptive journal form which is excerpted in *Earth House Hold.* Add to this a degree in anthropology at Reed College in Portland, mix with the leavening of Buddhist/Hindu studies, sift in several years of Zen Buddhist discipline in Japan. Add a stout dash of San Francisco poetry readings in lofts and livingrooms during the Fifties, plus the famous public poetry forum where "Beat" poetry sprouted as a media event. Spice with homesteading on San Juan Ridge near the South Fork of the Yuba River in the Sierra Nevada foothills. Preheat in an atmosphere of poetry readings, zazen (sitting meditation), and beating the planet drum for Mother Gaia long before it came into vogue, and you have the beginnings, the basic loaf, the elemental staff of Gary Snyder's life.

He has lived on San Juan Ridge for a decade, deepening his "sense of place," of belonging to the land. Both *Turtle Island* and *Axe Handles* probe the richness of family/community/watershed interface. The poems are distilled from direct experience, allowed to simmer and percolate as fragments in card files, then synthesized and polished into finished form. Like the high, almost imperceptible whang! of an axe

as it splits woodgrain, these poems hum with the authenticity of direct experience.

In the Australian interior desert, which by some peculiarity of the language is called the *Outback,* aboriginal peoples literally "sing the land." That is, the entire myth/lore of the race is embodied in songs which are sung while walking. You would learn who did what and where, the great epics of your people. You would also, in learning the songs, be learning a specific *map* of the terrain: where a hidden spring can be dug for, a cache of food, a shrine, a power spot, a clump of herbs, perhaps a stand of white gum trees among the mulga bush and mallee scrub, a red kangaroo run, perentie lizard abode, a roost for galah birds, a wild fig tree.

So in "singing the land" you would be learning precise information about the physical landscape while simultaneously exploring what Alan McGlashan calls "the savage and beautiful country" of the mind. You would, in short, be singing both internal and external terrains synchronously: the epics of your people and the physical contours of the land.

"Singing the land," then, is a very exalted and sophisticated means of orally transmitting an entire cultural matrix. In **"Uluru Wild Fig Song,"** Gary Snyder tells of

clacking the boomerang beat,
   a long walk
  singing the land.

As he describes the desert, you can feel the sacred, arid land open up before you. The poem's prime symbol is a wild fig tree, a natural shrine which still feeds its people. Gary Snyder expands this theme in *Coevolution Quarterly* No. 39, an article titled, **"Good, Wild, Sacred."** The history of natural shrines in Australian aborigine, Japanese Ainu, Paleolithic European, and contemporary American contexts is sketched. He also gives five ways to visualize your local watershed (Ainu "iworu":field) as teacher.

An African tribe calls the written language "word-trapping." Gary Snyder's work forms an important cross-cultural link between oral tradition ("singing the land") and written tradition ("word-trapping"). We'll probe how the poet, in Snyder's view, aspires to healing in his songs in the ancient function of shaman/brujo/medicine man/healer. Ultimately, it's in the singing of healing songs, songs which enlarge and refine the listener's vision, that Gary Snyder brings to fruition the deep and complex array of connections in his works.

Besides forming a cross-cultural link between oral and written traditions, his work forms parallel bonds between Oriental thought (especially Tibetan and Zen Buddhism) and Western culture (cowboys seen as priests of protein-conversion), between human and nonhuman realms (in a Corn

Maiden Dance, the dancer becomes the corn), between local people rooted in a sense of place and the interlocking global village (as in the poem, **"For All"**), and between upper Paleolithic modes of perception and possible bioregional scenarios of the future (**"What's Meant by 'Here'"**).

Gary Snyder stands as human spokesman for Mother Gaia, a living Being. He links macrocosm and microcosm, reaching across time/space continuums for old and new affinities, rooting out a 40,000 year continuity in human culture, a much longer and deeper range than is generally accepted by historians. His symbol for this range is embodied in the term "loops."

The 71 poems in *Axe Handles* are structurally divided into three sections: "Loops," "Little Songs for Gaia," and "Nets."

The Japanese word *bushi* or *fushi* means "a whorl in the grain . . . like a knot in a board." They are also ". . . specific turbulence patterns of the energy flow that manifest themselves temporarily as discrete items, playing specific roles and then flowing back in again." *Loops,* in other words: whorls, knots. The 25 poems in this section loop back to the upper Paleolithic era, in time. They probe unadorned human nature, without its civilized accoutrements: "the fertility of the soil, the magic of animals, the power-vision in solitude, the terrifying initiation and rebirth, the love and ecstasy of the dance, the common work of the tribe."

"The out-of-time function of poetry is to return us to our own true original nature at this instant forever." It loops us back to Original Mind, **"The Back Country,"** the intersection of one's inner nature and Mother Nature, and beyond the wilderness of the unconscious to the eternal Now. Gary Snyder likens Original Mind to "the old image of the mirror without any dust on it. . . ."

"I think that poetry is a social and traditional art that is linked to its past and particularly its language, that *loops* and draws on its past and that serves as a vehicle for contact with the depths of our own unconscious"

Gary Snyder demonstrates through his poetry that this looping is indeed rich ground. Take the title poem, **"Axe Handles."** It is the simple story of making an axe handle with his son, Kai. They use an axe to carve a new handle, and the poet recalls both Ezra Pound and Chinese poet Lu Ji in a work entitled *Wen Fu* (4th c. A.D.) saying that "the pattern is near" when doing this. He then draws an analogy that *he* is an axe and his son an *axe handle,* and that his son will become the axe, passing culture on down the line. This analogy describes very precisely the transmission of culture on several levels at once—by showing, by being the model, and by being the tool that carves the new. Like a Zen riddle, it grows on you!

In the second poem, **"For/From Lew,"** the dead poet Lew Welch urges Snyder to "teach the children about the cycles. The life cycles. . . . " Again, we loop back to early man and the pure perception (minus thought/word/static) of Original Mind. In **"True Night,"** the poet graphically describes himself waking and chasing two young racoons into the night where he is transformed: "I am all alive to the night." An ancient experience—men have been chasing animals from their firesides since time immemorial. The poet loops back to a satori-like state of transcendence and union with the night.

> **The poems are distilled from direct experience, allowed to simmer and percolate as fragments in card files, then synthesized and polished into finished form. Like the high, almost imperceptible whang! of an axe as it splits woodgrain, these poems hum with the authenticity of direct experience.**
>
> **—*Woody Rehanek***

"So Old—" provides another loop/link, describing a local creek, its canyons and a town perched on a slope; spending "a good day, we know one more part of our watershed." This is a vital and recurring theme in his work—"this bioregional ethic," developing "a sense of place," of belonging to the local ecosystem, of knowing the drainage, the lay of the land, soil, plants and animals, winds, clouds, myriad microclimates, shrines—just as Australian aborigines know these things in "singing the land," or native American Indians in their songs and rituals, myths and lore. "By being in place, we get the largest sense of community. We learn that community is of spiritual benefit and of health for everyone, that ongoing working relationships and shared concerns, music, poetry, and stories all evolve into the shared practice of a set of values, visions, and quests. That's what the spiritual path really is."

The poem **"Soy Sauce"** suggests another kind of loop: man identifying with, representing, and finally *becoming* a totem animal. This experience transcends intellectual rapport and becomes a total affinity with the nonhuman. Gary Snyder is helping friends build their house when he notices the smell of aged soy sauce on a windowframe. He's told that deer lick the frames at night; the framewood came from a giant redwood soy sauce tank in San Jose. The smell kindles a richness of association in the poet's memory—days past in Japan! It also transforms him into a voice for the nonhuman, as he puts himself in place of the deer licking windowframes.

A vital aspect of shamanism is this ability to become one with the animal: "The practice of shamanism in itself has at its very center a teaching from the nonhuman, not a teaching from an Indian medicine man, or a Buddhist Master. The question of culture does not enter into it. It's a naked experience that some people have out there in the woods."

The ancient theme of honoring one's ancestors surfaces in **"At the Ibaru Family Tomb."** A sense of continuity between past and future is established in **"Eastward Across Texas":** in Snyder, Texas, the poet speaks ironically about being remembered by the future. The timeloop is enlarged to include both distant past and future, ranging from ancient ancestors to future descendants.

"Working on the '58 Willys Pickup" deals with time parallels between Gary Snyder's own life and objects from his surroundings. The year the truck was made, he was studying sutras in Kyoto; he gathers sawdust from a mill abandoned about the time he was born. He hauls gravel from old placer diggings and reads about old Chinese farmers of the past. We begin to sense time, not as a linear sequence of moments, but as an ever-present reservoir, a reservoir which can be tapped for depth and richness of meaning as a vehicle for entering the eternal Now.

Gaia—Earth Mother—is a living Being, "alive to her very recesses," to quote Don Juan. These short songs are further explorations of nature and provide a voice for nonhuman realms. The poems illustrate Snyder's adherence to describing the "flat, concrete surface of 'things,' without bringing anything of imagination or intellect to bear on it." The images are spare taut and dry, almost "flat"; their bare-bones leanness is intended, and the analogies here work quite well in their elegant and voluntary simplicity.

Gary Snyder concerns himself with *what is,* thereby linking himself with certain Western Romantic traditions hearkening back to Wordsworth. "I don't invent things out of my head unless it is an actual experience—like seeking a bear in a dream, this is a true mode of seeing a bear." This focus on what is directly perceived, without attaching excess baggage to it, creates a purity of perception in his work which is very rare, undoubtedly aided by 30 years of zazen. Poems range from the dry and prosaic (**"Dead doe lying in the rain"**) to the ethereal (**"As the crickets' soft autumn hum"**).

"Little Songs . . ." displays Snyder's virtuosity with the precision of language. *Precision* is a key word in his talks and interviews; one of his functions as poet is to hone and sharpen the meanings of words, to refine and distill the language so that nuance and subtlety are matters of shades of meaning without vagueness. "In the flow of linguistic utterance . . . the poem or the song manifests itself as a special concentration of the capacities of the language and rises up into its own shape." He also follows the trajectories of *seed*

syllables of language in his work, i.e., magical constructs such as OM or HUM which originate from Sanskrit but are not used in language except in special contexts. Etymology, the origin and historical development of words—their semantic derivation and evolution—is an integral part of his poetry. *Regarding Wave* and *Turtle Island* are particularly rich in word origin/derivations.

"Nets" is the third part of *Axe Handles.* The word "net" derives from Indo-European *ned,* to bind or tie; from the Germanic *natilo,* nettles or hemp plants; and from the Latin *nodus,* a knot, node, or nodule. This part of *Axe Handles* deals with networks, connections, the organic web of life— all in the specific context of poems as healing/shaman songs. In *Earth House Hold* Gary Snyder speaks of "the glittering nets of language." He also describes Indra's net in Hindu cosmology—"the vast jewelled net" where each of us shines as a node illumined by the pure light of Brahma.

The four parts of "Nets" are roughly equivalent to four layers of healing songs defined in "Poetry, Community & Climax," the final chapter of *The Real Work.* "That specialized variety of poetry which is the most sophisticated . . . is the 'healing songs' type . . . The poet as healer is asserting several layers of larger realms of wholeness." Oneness with nature is the first level of the healing song. **"Walked Two Days in Snow, Then It Cleared for Five"** paints the appearance and habits of seven animals without naming them (except for a hawk). In **"Three Deer One Coyote Running in the Snow,"** he observes how animal activity becomes transcribed into snowtracks. These poems are a sturdy lesson in conciseness, precision, and compressed language. "Here the poet is a voice for the nonhuman, for the natural world."

Another layer of healing songs "asserts a level of humanity with other people outside your own group." Here, the poet extends his range of songs to embrace rodeos, his work on the California Arts Council, & Governor Jerry Brown. **"What Have I Learned,"** like the poem **"Axe Handles,"** deals with cultural transmission, "passing it on." These poems constitute a conscious "biopoetic beginning of a new level of poetry and myth. That's the beginning for this age, the age of knowing the planet as one ecosystem, our own little watershed, a community of people and beings, a place to sing and meditate, a place to pick berries, a place to be picked in."

In the third layer of healing songs, "the poet as myth/handler/healer is also speaking as a voice for another place, the deep unconscious, and working toward integration of interior unknown realms of mind with present moment immediate self-interest consciousness." **"Uluru Wild Fig Song"** becomes a haunting lyric which echoes with graphic intensity and associative richness because it touches long-standing veins in our unconscious. **"Dillingham, Alaska, the**

Willow Tree Bar" presents the dark side of the unconscious mind (and of civilization) where men are engaged in "the pain/of the work/of wrecking the world."

A crescendo is reached in the fourth level of healing songs. Here the poems deal with a condition/state of mind called climax. "The communities of creatures in forests, ponds, oceans or grasslands seem to tend toward a condition called climax, 'virgin forest'—many species, old bones, lots of rotten leaves, complex energy pathways, woodpeckers living in snags, & conies harvesting tiny piles of grass. This condition has considerable stability and holds much energy in its web—energy that in simpler systems (a field of weeds just after a bulldozer) is lost back into the sky or down the drain. All of evolution may have been as much shaped by this pull toward climax as it has by simple competition between individuals or species." Gary Snyder also defines climax as a state of mind: "When we deepen or enrich ourselves, looking within, understanding ourselves, we come closer to being like a climax system."

It is in the singing of healing songs—songs which enlarge and refine the listener's vision—that Gary Snyder brings to fruition the deep and complex array of connections in his works.

This is the shaman song in full bloom—healing songs encoded with all the intricacies, density and diversity of a climax forest. Because we're dealing with layers, they can be superimposed on each other like transparencies, each level adding a dimension of richness and complexity. "**Money Goes Upstream**" evokes the poet's power to be indoors, yet directly experience a sunlit weedpatch outside the window. "**Old Rotting Treetrunk Down**," like "**On Top**" in "Loops," sings a resonant song of compost, turnover, decay. "**Old Woman Nature**" is a humorous litany centered around bones. In "**The Canyon Wren**," a bird song is heard above the roaring rapids as men run the Stanislaus River. The canyon wren's song represents the healing quality of all song, its power "to purify our ears." In "**For All**," the poet celebrates a September morn with a "singing inside/creek music, heart music" and pledges allegiance to the soil of Turtle Island, our continent.

If we be true to the spirit of challenge and the web of life, perhaps we can sing such songs. Perhaps we can live such songs. Perhaps we can seek out a condition of climax in our hearts and minds, seeking simultaneously to heal the earth and the "savage and beautiful country" within ourselves.

Tom Lavazzi (essay date July-August 1989)

SOURCE: "Pattern of Flux: The 'Torsion Form' in Gary Snyder's Poetry," in *The American Poetry Review*, Vol. 18, No. 4, July-August, 1989, pp. 41-7.

[*In the essay below, Lavazzi documents the connection between Snyder's cosmology and his poetic structure.*]

> It would be best to consider this a continuing "revolution of consciousness" which will be won not by guns but by seizing the key images, myths, archetypes, eschatologies, and ecstasies so that life won't seem worth living unless one is on the transforming energy's side.

Snyder's view of social reform is the inevitable consequence of a poetics that pushes beyond the margins of the page and asserts itself as a psychosocial mode of existence. To change a culture is not to overthrow its social-political institutions, but to change its mind, its world view. The dialogue among text, self, and the world—both the public world and the nonhuman, other world of nature—permeates Snyder's poetry. Poetry becomes a means of expanding the consciousness, of mentally channeling us into the "transforming energy" and exploding our field of awareness in order to make such a "revolution of consciousness"—which is also a revolution of spirit—possible.

One way this expanded, "liminal consciousness," as Charles Molesworth phrases it, "this in-between awareness" is achieved is through an image-symbol nexus that mobilizes an intricate network of relationships, blending sexual, ecological, spiritual, and social concerns. The touchstone image is a spiral, whorl, or knot. Its distancing effect as a figure of speech is lessened, if not eliminated, by incorporating it in the poems as a verbal (twisting, turning, folding writhing, whirling, swooping, curving, circling, intertwining, tangling), as an object (seashell, animal horn, tree trunk, nebula, wave, sex organ), and sometimes by embedding it in the structure of an entire poem. Thus the spiral is more than a "symbol" of unity, of a sexual/ecological/spiritual complex—it is a re-presentation, a reenactment of it. As "torsion form," to borrow Jerome Rothenberg's term, or vector, the spiral functions as energy graph, mapping forces both in the external world and the unconscious. Because of this, it is continually transforming; the symbol-making hand of the poet is kept in the background, allowing free play of the archetypal motion to find its own forms in any given situation.

The poems, then, not only accept their referentiality, as Robert Kern points out, but are actual means, as seed syllables in chants are means, of breaking ego boundaries and imaginatively penetrating to the sources of being. The poems are not "imitations" of the things presented, but linguistic interpretations of and interpenetrations with them. "Nature's way and mind's way rhyme," says Hugh Kenner, speaking of the relationship between nature and language structure. By refusing to view the poem from a modernist, new-critical perspective as autonomous art object, Snyder establishes the poem as the only available voice for the things or states of being presented. The subject and object become, in this sense, one, and the poem exchanges beings with the objects it encounters. Charles Altieri points out that a major achievement of Snyder's poetry is its "development of an ontological function for aesthetic structure." The poems create a mind space where the "other" and "self" meet to conceive the whole.

As **"The Bath"** demonstrates, an important step in getting beyond the self, beyond the boundaries of the ego, is becoming aware of the body—not as an entity or personal identity, but as an outgrowth or branch of a larger continuum. Though the poem begins familiarly and straightforwardly, the speaker "washing Kai in the sauna," toward the end of the first stanza, we get a taste of what is to come: the speaker is "washing-tickling out the scrotum, little anus," Kai's "penis curving up and getting hard," the sexual contact producing a spontaneous delight in Kai who begins "laughing and jumping, flinging arms around." From the start, the boundary-breaching, destabilizing verbals are there, embedded in the poem: "curve," "curving," and "flinging" in stanza one and, in later stanzas, "winding," "turning," "flow," "curling," and "boiling." When Masa enters, in the second stanza, the sexual joy deepens; the poem becomes slippery, lubricous, and begins its graceful acrobatics. Snyder reaches out to "cup" Masa's "curving vulva from behind," and the contact sends a current of awareness through him, a mute, pre-verbal message: the vulva becomes "a hand of grail" (not "like" one—the identification is immediate and actual), which evokes the visionary image of a

> . . . *turning double-mirror world of*
> *wombs in wombs, in rings,*
> *that start in music,*
> *is this our body?*

Snyder's contact with the sexual organ brings him to a greater comprehension, a deeper awareness of the essential forces, essential rhythms of life. The real-world vulva appears to be in motion, "curving," and is collocated with the more abstract "turning" image; both are expressed as verbals, as participle phrases, to stress ongoingness and their interrelatedness as diverse expressions of the same energy. "Double-mirror" suggests the reflection of a reflection, the elusiveness of identity as it is gradually dematerialized in the poem. As soon as Snyder makes physical contact with the vulva, the poem drops away from its narrative structure and the syntax begins to leap. In the line "a soapy tickle a hand of grail," for example, white space, a thought/breath pause, forms the only bridge between the juxtapositions of pure sense imagery and more metaphoric (and ultimately visionary) modes of perception/expression. The vulva feels

like an indistinct braille, but its sound double, "grail," is what appears on the page. The seen and felt guide the speaker's quest into the trans-sensual and ultimately unsayable. As soon as the sense/mind juncture is achieved, the poem's imagery implodes, penetrating into the heart of creation, the generative life force. Visually, the image "wombs in wombs, in rings" shifts almost instantaneously from representational to abstract, with only a brief caesura between, while phonically the end of the line "rings," concretely and percusively, into the next line—an undefined music, rhythm, and sound, which must carry on where language, even as stripped of particular literal context as these last images are, cannot go. As Snyder says in **"Poetry and the Primitive,"** the poet is always "steering a course between crystal clouds of utterly incommunicable nonverbal states—and the gleaming daggers and glittering nets of language."

At the end of the second stanza, the mind leaps once again, this time back to the immediate context of self/body, but with an expanded consciousness of the latter's significance. It is not just the speaker's body but "our" body; not just the personal body—his, his wife's, his child's, all naked, close, and touching—but the human body; not the body as biological entity, but as a "way": It has brought him, imaginatively, to "the gates of awe," the brink of creation; it is formally inevitable, then, that "this our body" becomes the refrain line for the poem, a touchstone for the interconnectedness of the personal/familiar, physical/sexual, and spiritual/visionary that the poem's imagery and movement enact.

Snyder's poetry is full of such sudden plunges. At any moment, the omission of a connective, the creation of a white space, the break of a line, plummet us or send us imaginatively soaring into bottomless, boundless, timeless being. In **"Song of the Slip,"** for example, the first line, "SLEPT," in bold type, resounds with a Jungian suggestion of sleep/unconscious as a medium for slipping beyond the self; from the start, we are propelled into a world of dream time and dreamscape. The second line, "folded in girls," interweaves the masculine self with the feminine other and necessitates the ritualistic "feeling their folds":

> **SLEPT**
>
> *folded in girls*
> *feeling their folds; whorls;*
> *the lips, leafs,*
> *of the curling soft-sliding*
> *serpent-sleep dream.*
>
> *roaring and faring*
> *to beach high on the dark shoal*
> *seed-prow*
> *moves in and makes home in the whole.*

As in **"The Bath,"** contact with the sexual organ precipitates syntactical and imaginative leaps: After a brief internal caesura following "folds"—the semicolon, which is also a connective—we are hurled into relationship with an abstract, essential motion-form, "whorls." The collage technique and pared down syntax eliminate grammatical lapses between the two images, and "folds" speaks directly to "whorls." Starting off on that note, the poem is a hop-scotch integration of body, nature and the unconscious—"lips, leafs,/curling soft-sliding/serpent-sleep dreams." The fold-whorl-curl-serpent image cluster cross-syntactically transports us "roaring and faring" into the depths of the collective unconscious, and the phallic seed-prow speeds us the rest of the way onto the "dark shoal" of origins, the life force itself. The poem's closing line slips back out of the unconscious and integrates it with the conscious by resolving the fragmented activity of nouns and verbals—objects in motion—into the key concept of wholeness.

Ontologically, Snyder's poetry presents patterns and figures of flux. In **"Re-inhabitation,"** Snyder defines men as "composite beings whose sole identifying feature is a particular form or structure changing constantly in time." As **"The Bath"** and **"The Song of the Slip"** show, this sense of participating in a larger continuum, of acknowledging our relationship to a being much greater than the ego-centered self in its particular historical pocket, can be explored both in the realms of the visionary and of the everyday. Often, as in **"The Bath,"** the diurnal is a way into the former realm; in **"Night,"** however, the sense of the vastness of being is latent in images that, though highly resonant, remain in the daily realm. In all three poems, sex is both symbol of and key to the merging of self with what lies beyond. In **"Night,"** the sleeping lovers lying with "Twined legs" and "hair all tangled together" unconsciously mimic what Wilhelm Reich called "orgonomic functional thinking . . . frozen motion": form as movement, which was often expressed, for Reich, in the "basic form" of the "sexual embrace." In the poem, this interlocked state is only temporary; the sum is soon "hitting the shades"; a record has been left "soundlessly spinning," suggesting that beneath any particular melody or tune, beneath any formalized musical expression, is the essential mandala rhythm of movement and change, combinations and recombinations, like legs crossed and recrossed as lovers turn in sleep. The music stops, but the movement, the rhythm continues. The voice of the poem, which slips out of the individual consciousness of the sleeping poet-lover, holds both images in mind—the intertwined bodies and the spinning record—and threads through the whole scene and series of events (the night of lovemaking, the house left in disarray, the first strands of morning light), pushing toward a larger synthesis: the knowledge that we are only temporary gatherings of energy (the sex/love continuum is only one of its manifestations) and that at every moment we are part of a larger entity that flows through us and that we ultimately flow back into.

The interdependency of the sexual and spiritual and the comprehension of sex as a "way," a path toward an enlightened, holistic consciousness is more obviously the theme of **"Song of the Tangle"**:

> Two thigh hills hold us at the fork
>> round mount center
>
> we sit all folded
> on the dusty planed planks of a shrine
> drinking top class sake that was left
>> for the god.
>
>> calm tree halls
>> the sun past the summit
>> heat sunk through the vines,
>>> twisted sasa
>
>> cicada singing,
>>> swirling in the tangle
>
> the tangle of the thigh
>
>> the brush
>> through which we push

Bob Steuding claims that the poem describes the meditative/erotic "yab-yum," a type of Tibetan "sitting coitus," and points to the importance of love, for Snyder, as "an act of communion" and of worship. Quoting Snyder: "'To follow the ancient path in company with a lover means both must have practiced the lonely yogas and wanderings, and then seek the center of the individual-body and group-body mandala; dedicating their two bodies to the whole network'" (**"Dharma Queries"**). As in **"The Bath,"** image and structure actualize the poem's ontological stance. The nature/sex nexus is established in the first line "Two thigh hills. . . ." "High" (height of the natural object; spiritual elevation) is contained in "thigh"—literally and as a ghost rhyme—and the hills "hold" the "us," the poet and his presumably feminine companion, establishing a sympathetic connection among them. The nature/sex/enlightenment formula is completed by the second line, physically centered below the first to visually suggest the poem's imagistic and spiritual center—the Buddhist shrine. The poet and his companion sit "all folded" before the shrine, sharing food that was meant "for the god." Though ego-centered consciousness is left behind almost from the start, imbibing the food of the god (which is also a product of nature) is, ritualistically, the jumping off point: in the rest of the poem, the identity of the human worshippers, the "we" of the poem, is merged with nature; the shrine becomes the scene of ritualistic self-annihilation. As in **"The Bath,"** the poem opens with a relatively stable situation, clearly locating the speaker and his companion in time and space. In the third stanza, however, human identity begins to dissolve into the surrounding sounds and motions, only partially resurfacing in the "we" of the last line. Structurally, this merging of self and other is emphasized by indenting and aligning key images—the shrine, the worshippers, and the images of nature (trees, sun, vines, cicadas, and brush). But worship, here, is not a matter of bowing before icons; no image of Buddha is mentioned; in fact, the worshippers are the Buddha, and the interpenetration of god-worshippers-nature is established not only imaginatively, but biologically, through eating, thus weaving an ecological strand into the nexus.

The cicada's song, the sound center of the poem, whirls together the sexual, spiritual, and biological; it is the undifferentiated voice, the seed syllable expressing an undefinable, illimitable wholeness. The song of the tangle is at once a physical and an imaginative interpenetration, both sexual intercourse and metaphysical quest—"the brush/ through which we push."

Buddhism, especially Tantrism, is a strong current in Snyder's aesthetic. Tantrism provides a path out of "ego-driven anxieties" and into the diversity of life. The key is tensionless harmony, being able to see all aspects of life—suffering and joy, birth and death—as part of the whole network, of the fabric of life. Altieri claims that the purpose of the dialectic in Snyder's poetry is to "reduce tension by affirming the opposites' need for one another"; they mutually support each other to present a dynamic, holistic moment of consciousness, like wind eddies stirring up leaf fall on a bright, clear fall day: they just happen together; the day is not less bright because dead leaves swirl at our feet, but we should be aware of them.

> *Delight is the innocent joy arising*
> *with the perception and realization of*
> *the wonderful, empty, intricate,*
> *inter-penetrating,*
> *mutually-embracing, shining*
> *single world beyond all discrimination*
> *of opposites*

("On 'As for Poets'")

Clarity in Snyder's poems often reveals darkness: darkness=depth, both geologically—into the earth's evolutionary past—and psychologically—into the "wilderness" of the unconscious. Tantrism's emphasis on comprehending birth and death, or the "womb tomb" as Snyder refers to it, means that, aesthetically, the "poet holds the dark and the light in the mind, together" (**"The Real Work"**). The enlightened dialectic moment irradiates several of Snyder's best

poems, kindling a warm hum in the imagination of a reader as the energies are released through syntactic fluidity, image collocations and collage structuring. The poems are reifications, Metonymic whirlpools; by responding to the poem, the thing on the page, we also respond to the inspired, intense mind-in-action it presents.

In **"Rainbow Body,"** dark and light are imagistically presented without conflict, and the lack of "ego interference" (Snyder's term)—the mind's transparency—is achieved through the poem's dialectical structure and through a voice that originates in nature and the unconscious and only temporarily locates itself in the personal "we." For Snyder, the "real work" of mankind today is to "uncover the inner structure and actual boundaries of the mind," which requires a certain amount of boundary breaking: "We all live within skin, ego, society, and species boundaries" (**"Poetry and the Primitive"**). **"Rainbow Body"** jostles our sense of self in just such a deconstructive way. "The goal of revolution is transformation."

The poem opens with night sounds and images. A "wall of twanging shadow," not a man-made wall but a nature-made one of "bamboo thickets," is alive, in all its "dark joints and leaves," with the chanting of cicadas. The imagery is free floating; the voice is not connected to a particular speaker; it is not until the third stanza that a "we" half surfaces—they "half-wake" and then flow quickly back into the natural imagery. In Altieri's words, "the role of the lyrical ego or creative synthetic imagination" is lessened "by treating place as the poet and the human writer as (merely) an attentive mediator." In the second stanza, the voice takes on the ancientness of a volcano "rumbling down wind"; as "ash and steam" rise from the volcano to mix with "salt clouds" that brush its summit, an illusion of "breathing the Milky Way" is produced. But who or what is breathing? The night, the volcano, or the voice? The syntax, stripped of all personal and relative pronouns, simultaneously makes all three possible; the confusion is functional, carrying the imagistic effect beyond optical illusion to a mind/body interchange of being—voice = breath = steam and ash rising from the rumbling gut of a millennia-old geological formation = an astrophysical rhythm:.

> *Salt clouds skim the volcano*
> *mixed with ash and steam*
> *rumbles downwind*
> *from the night gleam*
> *summit, near Algol,*
> *breathing the Milky Way.*

The Milky Way is comprehended in the breath/thought of a single line; as the vision's scope and the voice's range expand, the lines work their way back out to the margins of the page. The effect of interrelatedness, of seamless bonding is heightened as the stanza's imagery merges into the final touchstone image of the torsion form, this time a galactic whorl of stars.

In the third stanza the volcano's voice, now become a chant, a "great drone / in the throat of the hill," joins with an almost ritualistic beat—"The waves drum." The aural image cluster of cicadas-volcano-waves unites the natural surroundings into a single, pulsing rhythm, empty of human speech and significance. The movement of the poem corresponds to natural cycles, so the rhythm of night/day rolls the dark imagery over into light as the poet and his wife wake "in the east light/fresh." The dark/light structure of the poem, then, evolves naturally. The fourth stanza is filled with light, clarity, and identification with the nonhuman. The human couple literally flow into nature as they "swim out through a path in the coral"—not a human but a sea made path:

> & into the land of the sea-people:
> rainbows under the foam of the breakers
> > surge and streaming
> > > from the southern beach.
> > the lips, where you float
> > clear, wave
> > with the subtle currents
> > sea-tangle tendrils
> outward roil of lava. . . .

The ocean has "lips," suggesting a sexual/biological exchange of being, as if the humans were being swallowed or, by osmosis, ingested by the nonhuman. The sixth line isolates the words "clear, wave," feeding the concept of enlightenment into that of wave forms. In Snyder's poetry, waves, to use Sherman Paul's phrase, express "contours of feeling." Paul calls the wave Snyder's "Ur phenomenon"; it is the "current of the universal being." The syntactical collocation of "clear" and "wave" makes the ocean a medium, a natural analogue to meditation. In **"Tanker Notes,"** Snyder describes the mind as a "clear spring—it reflects all things and feeds all things but is itself transparent"; it is "the hidden water underground." To enter the ocean is to enter an other world, a world simultaneously of nature and the unconscious, a world of "subtle currents" and "sea-tangles," of mergings and flowings and transformations that deny stasis and categorical definition and alter the nature of perception.

Through the daylight clarity of water, which acts like a lens for the empty consciousness, the dark is still evident, but the "outward roil of lava," solidified evidence of the island's cataclysmic origins, is not exaggerated or dramatized as a symbol of "evil." It is simply there, part of the seascape. Of course it is a reminder of the temporariness of any state of being, of the great earth processes that precede and outlast all life, of the inevitability and naturalness of change. But the image itself diffuses any "moral" we might try to attach

to it. As Molesworth puts it, "Snyder's unconscious is amoral, or premoral, and the laws of identity and contrariety do not apply to it." The lava is cool and solid; it has a still life; it is a "frozen motion" melding a geologically remote past with the present into a single living instant, "into the eternal now of geological time" (**"The Incredible Survival of Coyote"**). And "roil," as a motion, speaks to tangling sea grasses and to the continual spiral breakings of waves into billions of tiny stars.

In **"Rainbow Body,"** opposing categories of animate and inanimate, human and nonhuman, alive and dead cannot be applied with certainty. The language of the last two lines of stanza four, pared down to naming and essential movements and modifiers, brings us face to face—almost lip to lip—with a "cobalt speckled curling / mouth of a shako clam." The meeting is matter of fact—no attempt to evaluate or interpret or turn the clam into symbol—and yet the clam's relevance to the poem and to Snyder's aesthetic is apparent in the unconscious gesture of its body's evolution, the biologically determined "curling" of the mouth, the sign of its interrelatedness. The entire poem performs like a living, breathing organism; throats, lips, and mouths suggest an internalizing process that ranges from a single clam of a particular species to the entire galaxy. The "bamboo thickets," the "sea-tangle tendrils," the "roil of lava"—all are involved and all carry, in the very nature of their structure, the sign and sense of the whole.

In the poem's last stanza, the poet and his wife enjoy a simple meal of "melon and steamed sweet potato / from this ground." Though the image, like the action it describes, is simple, it comes in the wake of the knowledge mimed by the previous image clusters. The emphasis of the stanza is on human involvement, on man's place and responsibility in this vast body of being. Here the human couple live quietly and cooperatively with the land: "We hoed and fished— / grubbing out bamboo runners. . . ." And now, relaxed and nourished, they "nap in the bamboo thicket / eyes closed, / dazzled ears." The poem's emotional ambiguity, however, is not resolved but sustained in the closing stanza; flowing naturally out of the event of napping, the last two lines drop off into darkness and thoughtless profundity, keyed to the indecipherable sounds of the surf, inevitably involving the poem's final, peaceful moment with the bulk of its pluralistic image structure.

The final stanza is fulfilling in two ways. First, it realizes the non-dualistic awareness of Tantrism and Mahayana Buddhism's emphasis not just on zazen (meditation), but also on active involvement in the world. Second, Snyder tells us in **"Re-inhabitation"** that "knowing who and where [we are] are intimately linked." The plants, animals, and geology of a region are the "ground of our own mind" (**"The East West Interview"**); maintaining contact with our bio-energy sources, the food we intake and transform, helps keep us sane and in touch with our own bodies, and through them with the body of nature. The goals of Buddhism and ecology unite in the manual labor and relinquishment of consciousness of the last stanza; the poem is not brought to a closure but cadenced, keeping its dialectic ever open.

In **"Re-inhabitation,"** Snyder describes a satellite photo of the earth as showing "the whole blue orb with spirals and whorls of cloud," and paraphrases Stewart Brand in calling this photograph a "landmark of human consciousness." The clouds tell us: one world, one nature. In **"Poetry and the Primitive,"** Snyder quotes from the Brihadaranyaka Upanishad: "'Now this Self is the state of being of all contingent beings.'" Buddhism merged with ecology means our own bodies and minds are also the body and "mind" of nature. The connection with the primitive is clear. The shaman poet, or "poet as healer . . . is asserting several layers of larger realms of wholeness" (**"Poetry, Community & Climax"**). They include identifying with nature, integrating the unconscious and conscious, and identifying with the "other" outside our group—humanity at large. "This is the kind of healing that makes whole, heals by making whole." From the primitive perspective there is, literally, no separation between *man* and *nature*. In *Black Elk Speaks,* according to Snyder, Black Elk describes all living things as "individualized turbulence patterns," temporary interruptions and shapings of a universal energy flow (**"Knots in the Grain"**); this "primitive" ontological theory is directly relevant to Snyder's aesthetic: "I like to think of poetry as that . . . as the knot of the turbulence, whorl. . ." and "the poem or the song manifests itself as a special concentration of the capacities of the language and rises up into its own shape." Snyder also compares the structure, the phenomenon of his poems to "bushi or fushi" (Japanese words for song) "which means a whorl in the grain . . . an intensification of the flow [of energy] at a certain point that creates a turbulence of its own which then as now sends out an energy of its own, but then the flow continues again." The torsion form, as knot, whorl, spiral, or more generically as "turbulence pattern," with its origins in Buddhism, ecology, and primitive ontology, means to Snyder what the gyre meant to Yeats: it is a key image, a pivotal point for his entire aesthetic. Buckminster Fuller's definition of man as a knot of metabolic processes—processes that occur everywhere in nature and come together in a certain way and for a certain period of time to compose the biological entity called "man"—may be another intellectual source for the ecological twist in the spiral. At any rate, the concatenation of biology, ecology, Buddhism, and the primitive in Snyder's aesthetic is evident. In **"Poetry and the Primitive,"** Snyder says:

> The Australian aborigines live in a world of ongoing recurrence—comradeship with the landscape and continual exchanges of being and form and po-

sition; every person, animals, forces, all are related via a web of reincarnation—or rather, they are "interborn." It may well be that rebirth (or interbirth, for we are actually mutually creating each other and all things while living) is the objective fact of existence which we have not yet brought into conscious knowledge and practice.

> It is clear that the empirically observable interconnectedness of nature is but a corner of the vast "jewelled net" which moves from without to within. The spiral (think of nebulae) and spiral conch (vulva/womb) is a symbol of the Great Goddess. It is charming to note that physical properties of spiral conches approximate the Indian notion of the world-creating dance, "expanding form" . . . "each whorl or part of a whorl [quoting D'Arcy Thompson] . . . constitutes a gnomon to the whole previously existing structure."

"Comradeship with the landscape" is not just a "primitive" feeling—it is an ecological principle; "jewelled net" is a Buddhist image of interconnectedness ("om mani padma [jewel in the lotus] hum"). The language and imagery of the above passage fuse the three perspectives, all of which stress the same fundamental values—unself-consciousness, transformation, totality, and self-fulfillment through absence of self. And, as several of Snyder's poems demonstrate, sexual contact with the male or female "other" is a way of penetrating into the life-generating secrets of the "jewelled net," of immersing the self in the universal flow of transforming energy. For Western culture, as Snyder points out in **"Poetry and the Primitive,"** woman became the dominant symbol of nature and "The Other," intertwining notions of the "Muse" with "Romantic Love" and making the lovers' bed "the sole place to enact dances and ritual dramas that link primitive people to their geology and the Milky Way." Thus the telescoping of vulva/womb into spiral conch: the former is a means of self-expansion through physical penetration, and the latter is not merely a symbol but a physical product of the "world-creating" forces, a living torsion form. Each whorl of the conch grows out of the previous to form the whole, just as we develop as individuals from former selves; as present cultures evolve out of previous ones; as the spiritual world blossoms out of the physical; and just as all physical objects—human and nonhuman, animate and inanimate—enter into and become each other (are "interborn"), physiologically and spiritually, by slipping into and reemerging from the transforming stream of energy through growth, death, or intense meditative/ imaginative effort.

To Snyder, the primitive, biology, and ecology are, like Buddhism, not simply sources for poetic imagery. They stratify an aesthetic program that can deepen our consciousness of the range and responsibilities of the self. This is fundamental revolution:

> The biological-ecological sciences have been laying out (implicitly) a spiritual dimension. We must find our way to seeing the mineral cycles, the water cycles, air cycles, nutrient cycles, as sacramental—and we must incorporate that insight into our own personal spiritual quest and integrate it with all the wisdom teachings we have received from the nearest past. The expression of it is simple: gratitude to it all, taking responsibility for your own acts; keeping contact with the sources of the energy that flow into your own life (i.e., dirt, water, flesh). (**"Re-inhabitation"**)

And in **"Poetry and the Primitive"**:

> The primitive world view, far-out scientific knowledge and the poetic imagination are related forces which may help if not to save the world or humanity, at least to save the Redwoods.

The artist, then, though not a "moralist" in conventional, Judeo-Christian terms, has an ethical responsibility. He delves "into personal depths for nutrients hidden there" and gives them "back to the community. The community and its poetry are not two" (**"Poetry, Community & Climax"**). Art puts us back in the mainstream. It does this through looping—from present to past and back again, from conscious to unconscious and back again, from self to other and back again. Art is the "recycling of neglected inner potential . . . an assimilator of unfelt experience, perception, sensation, and memory for the whole society."

The interdependency and moral value of science, the primitive, and the poetic imagination are clearly presented in **"Toward Climax."** Within ninety-eight lines, the poem takes us on a journey from life's elemental beginnings—"salt seas, mountains, deserts"—to the present (late 1960s)—"Forestry. 'How / Many people / Were harvested / In VietNam?'" From pre-human beginnings we quickly pass through a state of pre-verbal, unself-conscious, physical oneness with the environment; we then move on to the beginnings of language and an awareness of our difference from, but also kinship with nature and our effects on nature ("big herds dwindle / —did we kill them?") and, consequently, the need for ritual to preserve unity and fertility; nature-worshipping rituals lose their potency, however, (we "lose dream-time") as agriculture and city-building—the beginnings of modern civilization—take over; "Reason" and law further bracket our perceptions and only in the present do we begin to remember ancient knowledge, to respiritualize nature, to internalize natural phenomena as a mode of consciousness. The irony of this poem's final section is intensified by the depth of human life, history, and prehistory; the "unfelt experience" and "sense-detritus," behind it.

The imagery of the first stanza is pre-human—a heterogeneous rhythm of "Cell mandala," "nerve network," and primate body parts. Man evolves in the second stanza and the next few stanzas are a collage of interactions and identifications with nature:

> *scavenge, gather, rise up on rear legs.*
> *running—grasping—hand and eye;*
> *hunting.*
> *. . . . .*
> *Bison, bear   skimmed and split;*
> *   opening animals chests and bellies, skulls,*
> *   bodies just like ours—*
> *pictures in caves.*

Then, man begins to learn more about his world: he learns plants; he learns how to "send sound off the mouth and lips" to form a language that unites "inner structures," the subconscious, with the "daily world"; through language he becomes "kin to grubs and trees and wolves"; he learns to "dance and sing," to celebrate his world, and to go "'beyond'" into myth and dream-time. Then, with the beginnings of agricultural society, he begins to think about getting "better off"; he begins to "make lists" and to "forget wild plants, their virtues / lose dream-time." He turns his back on nature and becomes self-involved—"get safer, tighter, wrapped in, / winding smaller, spreading wider"—the counter motion / image of the outward evolving, looping, all-encompassing torsion form. He starts laying out towns, draining swamp lands and, in the poem's second section, making laws, but eventually, in section three, discovers that "science walks in beauty." Biology and ecology try to reconnect us with our environment:

> *nets are many knots.*
> *. . . . .*
> *maturity, stop and think, draw on the mind's*
> *stored richness. memory, dream, half-digested*
> *image of your life.*

The knot, as torsion form, as Buckminster Fuller describes it, is a design of intersecting forces or energies. From this perspective, it is not one specific thing—a double coil of rope; it can also be a plant transforming solar energy into oxygen, the intertwined bodies and passions of two lovers, the merging of conscious and unconscious, or loops of time—in this poem, the intersecting loops of pre-history and the present. The abbreviated, elliptical syntax of the poem collages essential traits from various geological/evolutionary periods to enact great time leaps within a few inches on the page:

fins   legs   wings—
teeth, all-purpose little early mammal molars.
primate flat-foot.
. . . .
catch fire, move on.
eurasia tundra reindeer herds
sewn hide clothing, mammoth-rib-framework tent.
. . . .
squash blossom in the garbage heap.
    start farming.
cows won't stay away, start herding.

The syntactical compression creates an effect of poetic density and diversity analogous to the mental and geological pressure of the poem's ecological, time-warping, and ultimately moral vision.

As we have seen, the torsion form in Gary Snyder's poems, as symbol/energy graph, whirls together Buddhist, ecological, and primitive perspectives, and not just for artistic effect. The polysemous texture of the poetry is a vital expression of the density and diversity of consciousness, and a sense of moral responsibility follows in the wake of such an expanded awareness. In Snyder's poetics, too, the perspectives are fused so thoroughly that the sense of the whole of his aesthetic program can be adequately expressed only through a hyphenated word group: "jeweled-net-interpenetration-ecological-systems-emptiness-consciousness" (**"Re-inhabitation"**). Seven individual words here function as a unit; no word can be extracted without altering the meaning of the whole. The hyphenated word group is perhaps the only semantic unit in modern English that approaches the indefinableness of the seed syllable, the "om" of Buddhism, the "wha, wha, wha" of Raven and Magpie in a Hopi ritual (**"Through the Smoke Hole"**) or, as Gen, Snyder's young son, put it (**"The Bath"**):

   Bao! Bao! Bao! Bao! Bao!

R. J. Schork (essay date Summer 1990)

SOURCE: "Echoes of Eliot in Snyder's 'A Stone Garden,'" in *Journal of Modern Literature*, Vol. 17, No. 1, Summer, 1990, pp. 172-77.

[*In the following essay, Schork speculates on the influence of T. S. Eliot's poem "Preludes" on Snyder's "A Stone Garden."*]

When Gary Snyder in a 1954 letter to Kenneth Rexroth utterly dismissed the imitators of T.S. Eliot and Ezra Pound, he indicated his lack of respect for poets who derive from the Modernist Masters:

Very well: high compression, complexity, linguistic involutions are all virtues in poetry—but in the hands of the mediocre, just so much frillery. Which disposes of the imitators of Ezra & Eliot.

Samuel Johnson said that no man became great by imitation, and Snyder doubts that such a poet can even be good. It is surprising, then, to find Snyder himself closely tracking Eliot's "Preludes" in **"A Stone Garden,"** imitating its four-part structure and echoing specific phrases. Published in Snyder's collection *Riprap & Cold Mountain Poems* (1959), **"A Stone Garden"** encounters Eliot's pessimism but weaves in Japanese materials to suggest alternatives to Eliot's decline of the West. As a variation on Eliot's poem, **"A Stone Garden"** demonstrates that Snyder did not merely ignore his High Modernist predecessor—it is often supposed that the "Beat" poets merely ignored tradition—but, instead, that he considered Eliot's achievement and answered him poem for poem.

Both poets close their first sections with images of suffering animals, but Snyder reverses the significance of Eliot's animal image. For Eliot, the animal incarnation satirizes the limitations of human spirituality, whereas Snyder's bear-self is an implicit criticism of anthropocentrism, the worldview in which man is central in the universe.

—*R. J. Schork*

Both poems are divided into four sections, and in the first section of each poem an energetic vision of the street gives way to a depressed reality in which, in "Preludes," "morning comes to consciousness." The tones differ markedly: Eliot's vision, with its windblown garbage and stale beer, expresses Swiftian disgust:

   And now a gusty shower wraps
   The grimy scraps
   Of withered leaves about your feet. . .

In contrast, **"A Stone Garden"** registers sounds of good work, bright sun, and worthy materials:

   Stone-cutter's chisel and a whanging saw,
   Leafy sunshine rustling on a man
   Chipping a foot-square rough hinoki beam. . .

Eliot's pessimism in the close of his first section takes the form of ironic epiphany, for, after the energetic stirrings,

   A lonely cab-horse steams and stamps.

And then the lighting of the lamps.

That "lamps"—all the enlightenment that Eliot's street will receive—rhymes with "stamps" underscores the poet's belief that spiritual yearnings will fail for those trapped within bestial natures; again, Eliot resembles Swift in his emphasis on the painful limitations of the flesh.

Snyder's poem follows Eliot's with the substitution of a bear for Eliot's cabhorse:

> And I that night prowled Tokyo like a bear
> Tracking the human future
> Of intelligence and despair.

Both poets close their first sections with images of suffering animals, but Snyder reverses the significance of Eliot's animal image. For Eliot, the animal incarnation satirizes the limitations of human spirituality, whereas Snyder's bear-self is an implicit criticism of anthropocentrism, the worldview in which man is central in the universe. As in Faulkner's short story "The Bear," Snyder's bear tracks human arrogance from the periphery. In turning away from man-as-the-center, Snyder works in the tradition of Robinson Jeffers' "Inhumanism." Poets such as Snyder and Jeffers contrast the Mind of Europe as discussed in Eliot's "Tradition and the Individual Talent" with the Mind of Nature as witnessed by the non-human.

Echoes of Eliot intensify in the second section of **"A Stone Garden."** The water scattered "on the dusty morning street" recalls similar images from "Preludes." Eliot's image points to a civilization literally being run into the muddied ground, but Snyder's image retains hope. The Japanese children, contrasting in their youth to Eliot's old women, are responsible stewards of their world:

> Little black-haired bobcut children
> Scatter water on the dusty morning street—.

The second section of **"A Stone Garden"** reverses the image concluding the second section of "Preludes." Eliot's stanza proceeds through images of hangover and ennui to an ironic epiphany in which hands (cut off, like "muddy feet," from bodies) grudgingly negotiate with sunlight:

> One thinks of all the hands
> That are raising dingy shades
> In a thousand furnished rooms.

Eliot funnels the sordidness and disappointments of human life into a *Noh*-like gesture. His image of a dreary morning-after becomes, in Snyder's poem, an image which expresses compassionate acceptance of the aging process:

> Seeing in open doors and screens
> The thousand postures of all human fond
> Touches and gestures, glidings, nude,
> The oldest and nakedest women more the
> sweet. . . .

In Eliot's poem, thousands of others are trapped in dingy lives; in Snyder's poem, the thousand gestures signify human warmth and contact. These women, "more the sweet," ripen with age. Snyder reverses the significance of Eliot's image in order to include Eliot's subject matter (aging, decline), while rejecting Eliot's conclusions about that subject matter.

The Japanese prostitutes differ sharply from Eliot's women. They appear in Snyder's poem as people with levels of feeling rather than merely as indices to cultural degradation. The fact that women scavenge for fuel signals, for Eliot, a spiritually bankrupt universe—"The worlds revolve like ancient women / Gathering fuel in vacant lots." Snyder takes issue with Eliot's cosmology:

> And saw there first old withered breasts
> Without an inward wail of sorrow and dismay
> Because impermanence and destructiveness of
> time
> In truth means only, lovely women age—.

By expressing cheerful acceptance through the Japanese women, the poem leaves pessimism behind. The Japanese context, evoking the Buddhist tenet that we must value all aspects of existence, becomes especially significant in Snyder's poem, in which even the leveled cities from World War II continue to express the fullness of existence:

> The cities rise and fall and rise again
> From storm and quake and fire and bomb,
> The glittering smelly ricefields bloom,
> And all that growing up and burning down
> Hangs in the void a little knot of sound.

The void which Snyder refers to is surely an Eastern Buddhist void rather than, say, the Western Existentialist void of Sartre's *Nausea.* As the lines on fires, storms, and falling cities show, it is possible to see Ground Zero as a prelude to growth.

The "little knot of sound" looks forward to Snyder's third section, which is filled with human music, birds, and "The noise of living families," but little if anything that can be traced to T.S. Eliot. Instead, Snyder replaces Eliot's images of psychological breakdown with images of imaginative creation. The musical voice of this section stands in contrast to the bed-ridden visionary of Eliot's poem, who

. . . clasped the yellow soles of feet
in the palms of both soiled hands.

Eliot's lines, again, show the degraded search for spirituality in "soles," whereas the lines in Snyder's third section express no such frustration:

Grope and stutter for the words, invent a tune,
In any tongue, this moment one time true
Be wine or blood or rhythm drives it through—.

Snyder's lines, in counterpoint to Eliot's, have a Yeatsian ring as Snyder moves increasingly towards a philosophy of acceptance. Rather than being clothes upon a stick or a projector of sordid images, a man should sing and louder sing.

No reader quickly forgets the strikingly divided consciousness that Eliot captures in the two final stanzas of "Preludes," wherein the hopeful "I am moved by fancies" is followed by the spiteful peroration, "Wipe your hand across your mouth, and laugh." Eliot presents us with a tense confrontation between the hunger for spiritual fulfillment and its worldly denial. The poem leaves to the reader the corollary that this is our tension.

In the fourth section of **"A Stone Garden,"** however, we are given no verbal echoes, no sordid images or "vision of the street / As the street hardly understands." Snyder denies Eliot's grim dualitics, and so he leaves behind the divided Mind of Europe for the mind, especially the aesthetic sensibility, of Japan. Still, non-dualism is an elusive quality: it is important to note that he establishes Eliot as a Western model against whom he may react. Snyder's "emptiness" imagery escapes the dualistic morality of "Preludes," but, at the same time, his Eastern non-dualism defines itself against Eliot's (Western) experience of modern emptiness. Or, one might argue, Snyder's poem complements rather than opposes Eliot's: **"A Stone Garden"** shapes presumably useless materials such as those found in Eliot's grimy streets into a poetic equivalent of the Japanese stone garden.

"A Stone Garden" begins Snyder's lifelong dialogue with Eliot. *Myths and Texts* (1960) is, with its cycles of waste and rejuvenation, an answer to *The Wasteland* (1922), and in *The Real Work* (1980) Snyder gives his mature appreciation of Eliot:

What's really fun about Eliot is his intelligence and his highly selective and charming use of Occidental symbols which point you in a certain direction. . . . Eliot is a ritualist, a very elegant ritualist of key Occidental myth-symbols with considerable grasp of what they were about.

In this interview Snyder goes on to say that *Four Quartets*

is his favorite work by Eliot, and readers of Snyder may anticipate the completion of *Mountains and Rivers Without End* to see how Snyder responds, in poetic terms, to Eliot as a "very elegant ritualist."

Bill McKibben (review date 11 April 1991)

SOURCE: "The Mountain Hedonist," in *New York Review of Books,* Vol. 38, No. 7, April 11, 1991, pp. 29-31, 34.

[*In the following review of* The Practice of the Wild, *McKibben argues that Snyder believes as environmentalists we must bridge our estrangement from nature.*]

We talk in a lazy shorthand when we speak about "the environment" and "the environmental movement" as if there were a single, obvious program for the planet's protection. But the environmental movement is far broader and more diverse than any of the "progressive" campaigns that preceded it, since no single policy can deal with problems as diverse in scale and scope as the greenhouse effect and the extinction of the spotted owl, the pollution along Louisiana's Cancer Alley and the destruction of the tropical rain forests. No one expects economists to put together programs, or even philosophies, that simultaneously increase the market share of Remington razors and redress the global balance of trade. Yet the environment is a far more complex subject than the economy.

One of the pressing questions raised by Gary Snyder's new collection of essays, *The Practice of the Wild,* is: How much room for nature is there in the environmental movement? In the Earth Day speeches last spring there was little talk about trees or animals or wilderness; the discussion largely centered on air pollution, on solid waste, on global threats like ozone destruction. The concerns expressed were mostly for ourselves, and for future generations of our species, and even those who talked about such problems as the preservation of the rain forest tended to focus on the great supply of drugs that might be found among its plants, or its calming effect on climatic oscillations. The mainstream of the environmental movement tends to look pragmatically at the problems we face, and to try to fix them technologically or with the least possible change in the way we live, in the belief, rightly, that this is the best way to make a difference quickly.

Another, smaller, band of environmentalists, however, is still inspired by Thoreau and by the work that John Muir, Aldo Leopold, and other naturalists have left behind. Though not generally opposed to the pragmatists (indeed they are often in coalition with them), these environmentalists tend to think that environmental problems are much more deeply rooted in our ways of life, in our thinking, and in our estrangement from nature. This is the tradition to which the new book by the poet Gary Snyder—his best prose work so far—makes an impressive contribution. Whether Snyder, who lives in the California woods, can help the problem of the ozone layer is a question to which I'll return.

His publisher claims that Snyder is a "counterculture hero," and in a way this description is accurate. The model for Japhy Ryder in Kerouac's *Dharma Bums,* Snyder read his poem **"The Berry Feast"** at San Francisco's Six Gallery the night that Allen Ginsberg first read "Howl," an event that is often said to have launched the Beat movement. Snyder soon after left for Japan where he spent much of the Sixties meditating in a Zen monastery. He returned to San Francisco in time to act as host, with Ginsberg, of 1967's First Great Human Be-In in Golden Gate Park. For all that, though, in his life and writing he has scrupulously avoided alienated rebellion and claims of saccharine bliss, seeking instead to be in touch with his immediate surroundings.

The Practice of the Wild draws its strength from the theme that unites Snyder's odd life—his love for and understanding of the mountains, woods, and native peoples of the northern half of the Pacific Coast. Born in 1930, he grew up on a farm near Puget Sound, and for the last twenty years he has lived in a house he built for himself "on the western slope of the northern Sierra Nevada, in the Yuba River watershed, north of the south fork at the three-thousand-foot elevation, in a community of black oak, incense cedar, madrone, Douglas fir, and Ponderosa pine." He has, at various times, cut down the trees of this region, climbed its highest peaks, built Park Service trails across its ridges, watched from fire towers for signs of its smoke. Because of his daily physical contact with this world—he lives beyond the power lines, past the place where the oil truck goes—he has never succumbed to the strain of dippy environmentalism that is endemic in parts of California. "It is not enough," he writes, "just to 'love nature' or to want to be in harmony with Gaia.' Our relation to the actual world takes place in a *place,* and it must be grounded in information and experience." Place is a given of his poetry (on occasion he will even tell us its longitude and latitude). Consider **"So Old—"** from the collection *Axe Handles:*

> Oregon Creek reaches far back
>   into the hills.
> Burned over twice, the pines are
>   returning again.
> Old roads twist deep into the
>   canyons,
>   hours from one ridge to the next
> The new road goes straight on the
>   side of the mountain,
>   high, and with curves ironed out.
> A single hawk flies leisurely up,

> disturbed by our truck
> Down the middle fork-south fork
>   opening,
>   fog silver gleams in the valley.
> Camptonville houses are old and
>   small,
>   a sunny perch on a ridge,
> Was it gold or logs brought people
>   to this spot?
>   a teenage mother with her baby
>   stands by a pickup.
> A stuffed life-size doll of a Santa
>   Claus
>   climbs over the porch-rail.
> Our old truck too, slow down the
>   street,
>   out of the past—
> It's all so old—the hawk, the
>   houses, the trucks,
>   the view of the fog—
> Midwinter late sun flashes through
>   hilltops and trees
>   a good day, we know one more
>   part of our watershed. . . .

Snyder has emerged as perhaps the most eloquent American champion of what is called "bioregionalism," the idea that political boundaries should reflect the land we live on, and that decisions within those boundaries should respect that land. Alaska and Mexico, he writes, meet "somewhere on the north coast of California, where Canada jay and Sitka spruce lace together with manzanita and blue oak." If you follow the Douglas fir region, where Snyder started his life and where he has returned, you know "what your agriculture might be, how steep the pitch of your roof, what raincoats you'd need." The fir trees outlive "the boundary of a larger natural region that runs across three states and one international border." Everyone lives in a region, defined by its trees and rainfalls and climate and the movement of animals, by the effects of "cirrus clouds to leaf mold," Snyder wrote fifteen years ago in *The Old Ways.* To address our ecological crises, therefore,

> a worldwide purification of mind is called for: the exercise of seeing the surface of the planet for what it is—by nature. With this kind of consciousness people turn up at hearings and in front of trucks and bulldozers to defend the land of trees. Showing solidarity with a region! What an odd idea at first. Bioregionalism is the entry of place into the dialectic of history.

A problem with this vision is that, in practice, it only sometimes holds. When the US Forest Service holds its hearings about logging in Grants Pass, Oregon, many local people turn out to argue for the destruction of old-growth forests, driving there in trucks that carry signs that say "Save a Job— Kill a Spotted Owl." Snyder recognizes this limitation, I think. He recognizes that it's not simply our boundaries that must be changed but our desires as well, since they drive the economy that is destroying the wilderness. The possibilities for this radical change of heart, as radical as any religious conversion or the change in our souls that Martin Luther King sought, dominate *The Practice of the Wild:*

> Native Americans to be sure have a prior claim to the term native. But as they love this land they will welcome the conversion of the millions of immigrant psyches into fellow "Native Americans." For the non-Native American to become at home on this continent, he or she must be *born again* in this hemisphere, on this continent. . . .

Snyder has spent much of his life studying Native American culture. His undergraduate thesis, at Reed College in 1951, was on a Haida Indian version of a nearly universal myth about a swan that changes into a woman and is loved by a man, who then loses her. In the thesis, which was published nearly thirty years later, in 1979, he discusses literature based on myth and ritual, with the priest-shaman-storyteller-writer as the central figure.

This scholarly interest has long since grown into something more urgent. *The Practice of the Wild* includes a marvelous essay about a folktale of a woman who wedded a bear: her brothers kill the bear and she kills them. "That was a very long time ago. After that time," he writes, "human beings had good relations with bears. . . . Bears and people have shared the berryfields and salmon streams without much trouble summer after summer." But this period

> is over now. The bears are being killed, the humans are everywhere, and the green world is being unraveled and shredded and burned by the spreading of a gray world that seems to have no end. If it weren't for a few old people from the time before, we wouldn't even know this tale.

Snyder's experience—his feel for his region, the skills that make him at home in the outdoors, the humility and discipline of his Buddhism, the tribal sense of his hippie past and present—unite in this goal: to teach people to live in an easy harmony with the land, much as the Indians once did.

One feature of Native American life that is absent from our time, Snyder says, is physical contact with the world we live on, especially physical work. "If there is any one thing that's unhealthy in America," he told an interviewer in 1977, "it's that it is a whole civilization trying to get out of work." There is, he insisted, "a triple alienation when you try to avoid work: first, you're trying to get energy sources. . . to do it for you; second, you no longer know what your body can do, where your food or water come from; third, you lose the capacity to discover the unity of mind and body via your work." Snyder has the pride of a self-sufficient man. Only once in all the interviews with him that I've read does he turn prickly, and that is when an interviewer suggests that he no longer did physical work. "I not only built my own house, I do everything around it continually. I'm farming all the time: cutting six cords of firewood for the winter, planting fruit trees, putting in fencing, taking care of the chickens."

But Snyder does not believe that hard work is good because it helps you to get ahead, or because it prepares you for "the real world" or teaches you the value of a dollar. It is important for just the opposite reason: it brings us down from the soft clouds of whatever modern life we're leading, and back into contact with the world that every other generation of human beings has ever known, and that is the source of our instinct, our myth, our art. "That's the real work: to make the world as real as it is, and to find ourselves as real as we are in it."

Snyder's conception of work as a sacrament closely resembles the ideas of the Kentucky farmer and essayist Wendell Berry (*Axe Handles* includes an affectionate poem about Berry, his wife, Tanya, and a fox). But if Berry is a half-Amish, Jeffersonian farmer. Snyder is a latter-day hunter-gatherer. Largely, I think, their differences have to do with climate and geography. With wise stewardship Berry's rich Kentucky soil can bear crops in abundance; Snyder can grow beans, but

> the tendency of that whole area is to go into forest; old farms are abandoned and are turning back into woods. Consequently, nowadays any of us who think about any gardening or farming think about it in very limited terms as something which is possible in special areas but not desirable in the region as a whole (since the region produces a great deal of life without human interference, enough life to support human beings in small numbers, in reasonable numbers).

This support traditionally came in part from eating the flesh of dead creatures. In later times these deaths have been removed to slaughterhouses, and their flesh wrapped in plastic and made into a commodity. Or the killing has been circumvented by vegetarianism, which is more or less what you might expect an aging hippie to advocate. Snyder, a lifelong archer, has considered the complicated fact that the civilizations that lived in closest harmony with their natural surroundings spent many of their working hours in pursuit of fish and game. The position he arrives at is morally more ambiguous than either that of many animal rights activists or that of the Beef Industry Council (whose egregious current slogan is "Real Food for Real People"). "Other beings (the instructors from the old ways tell us) do not mind being killed and eaten as food, but they expect us to say please, and thank you, and they hate to see themselves wasted," he writes. "There is no death that is not somebody's food, no life that is not somebody's death." But instead of taking this as a sign that "the universe is fundamentally flawed," we should participate in the web as a sacrament.

> The archaic religion is to kill god and eat him. Or her. The shimmering food-chain, the food-web, is the scary, beautiful condition of the biosphere. Subsistence people live without excuses. The blood is on your own hand as you divide the liver from the gallbladder. A subsistence economy is a sacramental economy because it has faced up to one of the critical problems of life and death—the taking of life for food.

This is not a prosaic argument about biological determinism. Just the opposite.

> If we do eat meat, it is the life, the bounce, the swish, of a great alert being with keen ears and lovely eyes, with foursquare feet and a huge beating heart that we eat, let us not deceive ourselves.

In practice his view would mean not eating meat you hadn't raised yourself or seen raised, without cruelty; it would mean hunting, if you hunted, with a solemnity not found in most American sportsmen: it would mean welcoming other predators back to the woods, instead of fighting (as hunters across America have fought) against wolves and coyotes and other competition: it would mean singing for your supper. In older times, in older legends, Snyder says, animals

> liked the human people and enjoyed being near them for their funny ways. . . They still wanted to be seen by people, to surprise them sometimes, even to be caught or killed by them, so they might go inside their houses and hear their music.

It would mean, finally, admitting that you too are an animal, and even welcoming your eventual inclusion in the food chain. "We are all edible. And if we are not devoured quickly, we are big enough (like the old down trees) to provide a long slow meal to the smaller critters."

What sort of animal are we exactly? "What sucks *our* lineage into form?" We are larger than a wolf, smaller than an elk . . . not such huge figures in the landscape. . . . Berries, acorns, grass-seeds, apples, and yams all call for dextrous

creatures something like us to come forward." But it's not pure function. If we are

> here for any good purpose at all (other than collating texts, running rivers, and learning the stars), I suspect it is to entertain the rest of nature. A going of sexy primate clowns. All the little critters creep in close to listen when human beings are in a good mood and willing to play some tunes.

We are wild creatures, not in some metaphorical sense, but quite literally.

> The involuntary quick turn of the head at a shout, the vertigo of looking off a precipice, the heart-in-the-throat in a moment of danger, the catch of the breath, the quiet moments relaxing, staring, reflecting—all universal responses of this mammal body. They can be seen throughout the class [of animals].

And the danger in denying this, besides the destruction of the planet, is that we'll miss out on certain pleasures that are our due as animals. "The truly experienced person, the refined person, *delights in the ordinary,*" just as animals delight in sun, softness, warmth, exercise, the commonplaces of their day. Once, working on a trail crew in Yosemite, Snyder tried to spend each day with his mind engaged in Milton, whom he was reading at night.

> Finally, I gave up trying to carry on an intellectually interior life separate from work, and I said the hell with it. I'll just work. And instead of losing something, I got something much greater. By just working I found myself being completely there, having the whole mountain inside of me, and finally having a whole language inside of me that became one with the rocks and the trees.

The evidence that he found such a language is in ***Riprap,*** the book of poems that grew out of that summer job. The seamlessness of observation in **"Water"** accounts for its power.

> Pressure of sun on the rockslide
> Whirled me in a dizzy hop-and-
> step descent,
> Pool of pebbles buzzed in a Juni-
> per shadow,
> Tiny tongue of a this-year rattle-
> snake flicked,
> I leaped, laughing for little boul-
> der-colored coil—
> Pounded by heat raced down the
> slabs to the creek
> Deep tumbling under arching

walls and stuck
Whole head and shoulders in the
 water:
Stretched full on cobble—ears
 roaring
Eyes open aching from the cold
 and faced a trout.

Searching for delight, Snyder does not ignore sex and drugs and loud music. He is part mountain hedonist, a wine jug hooked on his forefinger and resting on a muscled arm. But instead of treating them as commodities for private consumption, he wants to see them as part of a community's activity. "In South India," he writes in *Practice of the Wild,*

> the adolescents are charged with keeping parrots out of the ripening crops. The birdchasing work is known as an occasion for trysting. The dancer sings and strolls forward and back through the gardens, waving a stick, startling up flocks of birds. . . . The crops, the soil, the parrots, the work, the dance, and young love all come together.

This is both less and more enlightenment than most of those at The Great Human Be-In imagined, I think. "In our present over-speeded and somewhat abnormal historical situation, the long stability of traditional peasant culture of primitive hunting and gathering cultures seems maybe dull," he told an interviewer once.

> What looks like dull centuries of simple cultures are intense meditations on one level in which inner discoveries are gradually being made. When we steer toward living harmoniously and righteously on the earth, we're also steering toward a condition of long-term stability in which the excitement, the glamour will not be in technology and changing fads. But it will be in a steady enactment and reenactment of basic psychological inner spiritual dramas.

This is, more or less, the kind of community he's found, and helped to create, in the northern Sierras, where there are "a friendly number of people, diverse as they are, who have a lot of the same spirit," and who expect their descendants will be in place together there for "the next two or three thousand years."

Though he would no doubt live as he does even if the air and sea and land were not despoiled, Snyder constantly returns in his writing to the need to save not just the wilderness but also the human environment. His 1974 collection of poems, *Turtle Island,* for instance, includes **"Four Changes,"** an "environmental manifesto" that begins (with an uncharacteristically tired image), "Man is but a part of

the fabric of life—dependent on the whole fabric for his very existence." *The Practice of the Wild* contains many references to overpopulation, atmospheric change, the ozone layer, and so on. The question arises, even if you grant (as I do) the beauty of his vision and life: Is it also useful as a response to our environmental woes?

The answer depends on how you conceive the problem of pollution. We are used to thinking of pollution as something gone wrong—a factory with a primitive smokestack or water filter, a badly tuned car without the latest control equipment, a drunken sea captain in a single-hulled ship. If these are the enemies, then neither Thoreau nor Snyder has much to say about dealing with them. All that is needed is somewhat better management and technology, and much better regulation of greed. But there is an emerging, quite different category of pollution, which is caused by things working essentially as they should, but on much too large a scale. The expansion of humans into the few remaining wilderness areas is such a case, of course, but not the only one. Consider the exhaust pipe of a car, for instance. Out of it pours carbon monoxide, a deadly pollutant, which a better-designed, better-tuned engine will all but eliminate. But carbon dioxide, the source of the greenhouse effect, pours out of the exhaust too, and the engine can't be redesigned to reduce it. It is an inevitable byproduct of fossil fuel combustion. Perhaps we'll develop hydrogen cars instead, or perhaps we'll learn to drive less, and change our lives.

Much of the environmental damage scientists anticipate is of the same sort, the result not of technical flaws but of too many people whose material standard of living is too high. If you subscribe to that diagnosis, and especially if you give weight to the fortunes of other species, then how you live matters. Snyder's views on how one might live a simpler life begin to sound more practical, as "realistic" as recycling and smokestack scrubbing. One can then forgive him his occasional excesses (his earlier prose, though not the more controlled and mature *Practice of the Wild,* makes semiparanoid reference to "liquid metal fast-breeder reactors" as harbingers of the police state, and so on) and agree on the urgency and the sad precision of his central view:

> Creatures who have traveled with us through the ages are now apparently doomed as their habitat— and the old habitat of humans—falls before the slow-motion explosion of expanding world economies. If the lad or lass is among us who knows where the great heart of this Growth-Monster is hidden, let them please tell us where to shoot the arrow that will slow it down. And if the secret heart stays secret and our work is made no easier, I for one will keep working for wildness day by day.

We can't all live the way Snyder does, of course, not in this crowded generation. He remarkably overstated the situation in his earlier book, *Earth House Hold* (1969). He wrote that "industrial society appears to be finished," but everyone can learn from his notion of responsible work: walking, not riding; composting or recycling, not throwing things out. Even in the middle of the city, everyone can practice his fellowship with other species. In the first place, wilderness is everywhere: "ineradicable populations of fungi, moss, mold, yeasts, and such . . . deer mice on the back porch, deer bounding across the freeway, pigeons in the park, spiders in the corner." But if you want something a little grander, an outpouring of letters to Washington on behalf of Oregon's spotted owl is a decent equivalent of the Native American's personal identification with one creature or another.

Everyone, except the poor, can consciously lower his or her standard of living. And most important, everyone can try to find pleasure not so much in the acquisition of things, but in the body, in friendship, in dance and music, in an effort to create a community. We can start to make deep changes now, and someday, generations hence, if we haven't already gone too far, we might slowly subside into some equilibrium with the earth. I have no illusion that we will do these things in great numbers, but this is an interesting moment when the long-held aesthetic arguments for a simpler life are suddenly being seen to coincide neatly with the hard-headed calculations of the atmospheric chemists. Snyder is among the first to sense this conjunction.

I read *The Practice of the Wild* this summer while traveling through the Buryat region of Siberia on the banks of Lake Baikal. The Buryat people, ancestors of many Native American peoples who came across the land bridge when it still linked the continents, are shamanistic in practice to this day. We were greeted, healed, blessed by any number of shamans whose authority, though lessened, has outlasted that of the various commissars. But, like Snyder, the Buryats are also Buddhists, converted by the flow of that idea north from Mongolia. It is a syncretic and relaxed Buddhism, co-existing happily with what went before. We came to a holy place on the shore of Lake Baikal (even the Communist officials call this vast freshwater sea "sacred Baikal"), and found a Buddhist monk chanting a long prayer. When he was done I asked for a translation, and it turned out he was reciting the name of every tributary and mountain that surrounds the lake. That world may be slowly dying, but Snyder's life and work show that it may be slowly reviving too.

Julia Martin (essay date Fall 1991)

SOURCE: "Speaking for the Green of the Leaf: Gary Snyder Writes Nature's Literature," in *CEA Critic*, Vol. 54, No. 1, Fall, 1991, pp. 98-109.

[*In the following excerpt, Martin explores Snyder's environmental writings and the ways in which Snyder challenges the dominant Western discourse.*]

. . . As early as 1969 and even before, Snyder described what he considered to be the repressive thrust of the dominant Western culture in terms of sexual politics, identifying its origins within the "patriarchal, patrilineal family." In attacking this value system, his poetry becomes polemical and angry. Whereas much of Snyder's work is characterized by its attention to minute particulars, his most overtly political writing depends to some extent on generalization and caricature. Like some radical feminist rhetoric, his critique of the dominant discourse is strategically useful, if somewhat reactive and philosophically dubious. Here is a characteristic example from the poem **"Mother Earth: Her Whales:"**

> How can the head-heavy power-hungry politic
> scientist
> Government two-world Capitalist-Imperialist
> Third-world Communist paper-shuffling male
> non-farmer jet-set bureaucrats
> Speak for the green of the leaf? Speak for the soil?

The invective is sharp, the attack directed toward an agency that is clearly androcentric. Earlier in the same poem, the familiar oppositions are reversed in a similar way. Human beings become Other, robot-like; nature is alive and sentient:

> The living actual people of the jungle
> sold and tortured
> And a robot in a suit who peddles a delusion
> called "Brazil"
> can speak for *them*?

If the dominant discourse (and economic and political practice) has no language for "the green of the leaf," for Snyder this lack is due in part to a religious model that tends to give primacy to the transcendental Word, effectively silencing Other voices. Although in recent years there has been some critique of this silencing from within the Church, the mainstream Judaeo-Christian world view has, historically, assumed that a feminized "nature" is something from which we are (or should be) distinct: "Man" names the animals, keeps the land. Snyder describes this attempt to raise man above his (sic) environment, somewhat rhetorically, as follows: "men are seen working out their ultimate destinies (paradise? perdition?) with planet earth as the stage for their drama—trees and animals mere props, nature a vast supply depot." Several early poems (for example in *Myths & Texts*) identify in this system of values the origins of the present ecological crisis. In *Turtle Island,* the conflation of nature and "the feminine" that the paradigm implies appears in the poem **"Front Lines."** The effect is a strong polemic against capitalist America's acquisitive devastation of the wilderness: "Landseekers, lookers, they say / To the land / Spread your legs." Later in the poem, the metaphor of rape is extended in the depiction of a disgustingly destructive bulldozer ("grinding and slobbering / sideslipping and belching on top of / the skinned-up bodies of still-live bushes") in the pay of "a man from town."

As these extracts suggest, Snyder reads the patriarchal construction of nature as feminine Other as being linked to the idea that nature is something hostile and dangerous, and adversary. The corollary is the view that the "natural" desires (particularly sexual) are fallen and dangerous: "To make 'human nature' suspect is also to make Nature—the Wilderness—The adversary." In an early poem, **"Logging 15,"** Snyder identifies the repression this involves as follows:

> Men who hire men to cut groves
> Kill snakes, build cities, pave fields
> Believe in god, but can't
> Believe their own senses
>   Let alone Guatama. Let them lie.

The view that one is "above nature" implies that one can't afford to believe the senses. This attitude is seen here to be symptomatic of a culture that has denigrated the value of the senses in favor of the bliss of a supra naturalistic heaven, where all experience is incorporeal. A poem called **"The Call of the Wild,"** for example, examines the connotations of "wildness" for a culture founded in dualistic metaphysics. The poem describes "a war against earth" that corresponds to a war against (or repression of) the "natural" self. Ironically, certain members of the so-called counterculture (dreaming of India, of "forever blissful sexless highs") are shown to be as alienated from wild systems as is the dominant (specifically American) culture that they superficially oppose. The outcome of the transcendental metaphysics that they share is horrible destruction, launched from a position that is, like that of all sky gods, high above the earth. Once airborne, the Americans never come down

> for they found
> the ground
> is pro-Communist. And dirty.
> And the insects side with the Vet Cong

Once having enlisted the mentality that identifies the Other as enemy, any destruction can be sanctioned:

> So they bomb and they bomb
> Day after day, across the planet
>   blinding sparrows
>   breaking the ear-drums of owls
>   splintering trunks of cherries
>   twining and looping
>   deer intestines

in the shaken, dusty, rocks.

In an early essay, Snyder refers to a marginal tradition that has existed alongside the dominant, historically antifeminist, religion of Jehovah. Much of the poetry seeks to revive the subversive potential of this counter-tradition, which celebrates "woman as nature the field for experiencing the universe as sacramental." To speak of "woman" and "nature" in this way means to identify with that which the dominant culture constructs as Other. This reversal of value has historical analogues in, for example, the black consciousness movement, and it corresponds closely with those women writers who, as Julia Kristeva puts it, seek to "give a language to the intrasubjective and corporeal experiences left mute by culture in the past." In Snyder's case, this involves giving expression to the "voice from the wilderness, my constituency." Two important features are the use of metaphors of descent and a revaluation of the quotidian.

Like many women writers (I think of Adrienne Rich, Susan Griffin, Margaret Atwood), Snyder often uses metaphors of descent to indicate an attempt to recover what has been drowned, buried, marginalized, and silenced by the dominant discourse. The metaphor works at several levels, as the poem **"Anasazi,"** a description of an imaginative descent into Native America's so-called primitive past, illustrates. The speaker's reconstruction of the social system of the Anasazi reveals mysteries inherent in their daily activities: growing, watching, giving birth. The close spiritual identification with nature that this involves contrasts strongly with the supranaturalistic emphasis of patriarchal monotheism. In an experience of shamanistic identification, the human person is drenched and absorbed in the nonhuman. The gods are encountered through descent into the material, rather than through spiritual transcendence:

> sinking deeper and deeper in earth
> up to your hips in Gods
>   your head all turned to eagle-down
>   and lightning for knees and elbows
> your eyes full of pollen
>   the smell of bats
>   the flavor of sandstone
>   grit on the tongue
>   women
>   birthing
> at the foot of ladders in the dark.

In this account, the speaker's immersion in the holy involves a progressive absorption into the maternal earth. Engaging the "lower" part of the body ("hips" rather than heart or mind), this experience is sensual—physical—as much as it is spiritual or mental. Descending deep enough into the ground reveals the continued presence of women who are giving birth. Their place in the "dark" reinforces the effect of "down" and "earth," contrasting strongly with the "light," "ascent," and "sky" of patriarchal religion. Similarly, in foregrounding women's labor, in identifying it as being, precisely in its physicality, simultaneously a spiritual experience, the poem reverses the dominant view of both "woman" and bodily functions. Syntactically, the use of indefinite participles suggests that this is not an isolated moment on history's timeline. Instead, such sacramental experience is part of a continuous process, and therefore always accessible.

To emphasize descent in this way implies for Snyder an orientation that is repeated in numerous other poems about wilderness, women, bodies, animals, and the so-called primitive. In proposing an alternative to the tendency in patriarchal monotheism to stress transcendence of the material world, such poetry recalls traditions that model this very world as being sacramental. One consequence of this emphasis is a revaluation of what Adrienne Rich has called "the enormity of the simplest things," those unobtrusive, hidden, everyday activities that facilitate the progress of the dominant culture. In place of a focus on achieving spiritual transcendence of material limits, the poetry repeatedly proposes the importance of mindful attention to ordinary daily activities. Many of the poems therefore celebrate activities that are often viewed as either trivial, or mundane, or insignificant: doing housework, eating and preparing food, gardening, making love, caring for children, looking at animals and plants, fixing machinery.

This view of the quotidian is partly informed by Snyder's involvement with Zen Buddhism, a discipline stressing attention to simple particulars—no activity is intrinsically more valuable than another, and all activities are interconnected. But for Snyder, as for many feminist writers, to write poetry celebrating ordinary activities is also a political choice. If patriarchal discourse silences not only woman and nature but also the sort of work habitually done by women and subject peoples, then it becomes important to assert the value of such silenced work.

To foreground and defend marginalized Other in the ways I have described may be a necessary response to exploitative mastery. But for Snyder, as Buddhist and ecologist, such reversal of value is useful only to the extent that it makes possible a conceptual model not founded in binary oppositions. The function of Snyder's treatment of "nature" and "woman" is, paradoxically, to approach such a model.

As I noted at the beginning, what we call "nature" is, from an ecological viewpoint, not an aggregate of competing, autonomous entities but a cybernetic system in which organism and environment are interdependent. To see this relation in terms of binary oppositions (Self-Other, Nature-Culture) is to misinterpret the necessary exchange of information and energy between constituent participants. In representing this understanding of the natural ecosystem, Snyder's poetry from the period under discussion draws metaphors from those versions of goddess mythology and Buddhism that emphasize the arbitrariness of binary dichotomies. For example, the Buddhist term *Prajan-paramita* denotes wisdom that has gone beyond all dualisms. But it is also, simultaneously, the name of a goddess. Paradoxical symbolism of this kind is particularly clear in Snyder's account of the goddesses Gaia ("the great biosphere being") and Vak ("the Voice through all"). In each case, the use of the goddess as metaphor of ecological interdependence suggests a basis for a nonbinary conceptual model.

Snyder uses "Gaia" to refer to the planetary ecosystem, the biosphere, the whole earth. This allusion to the primal earth mother suggests a view of "nature" as interdependent system. In *Axe Handles,* one of the **"Little Songs for Gaia"** describes it as follows:

> ah, this slow-paced
> system of systems, whirling and turning
> a five-thousand-year span
>   about all that a human can figure,
> grasshopper man in his car driving through.

Like a Chinese landscape painting in which human beings are depicted as diminutive figures in a vast natural environment, the poem provides a setting for (and so defamiliarizes) the impact of human agency. In contrast to the hawk's free flight, the insectlike "man in his car" follows a linear track through "nature" as though he is separable from it. But his point of view, which foregrounds the human in opposition to the environment and limits history to five thousand "civilized" years, is qualified by the rest of the poem. By attending to the world that his view marginalizes, the poem evokes an image of the whole biosphere, Gaia, that ancient "system of systems," within whose rhythmic "whirling and turning" each individual is necessarily a participant.

Snyder frequently uses the related metaphors of the net, the woven fabric or web, and the family to evoke this view of the biosphere. Like Mary Daly in *Gyn/Ecology,* Snyder associates the traditionally feminine activity of weaving this network of correspondences with a mother goddess, specifically **"Mother Gaia."** Appropriately, then, in place of the nuclear family as isolated unit, the speaker is located as a member of the family of all beings. The poem **"On San Gabriel Ridges"** is a characteristic example. Seeing the designs of twigs and seeds that have impressed themselves on his skin, the speaker recognizes his participation in the fabric of interconnection. Old friends and lovers, children, squirrel, and fox are all woven in its pattern, and the present moment is similarly informed by the past, to which it is still connected:

O loves of long ago
    hello again.
and all of us together
with all our other loves and children
twining and knotting through each other—
intricate, chaotic, done.

Family relationships are shown to be part of the same process that links squirrel and fox in the food chain:

woven
into the dark.
squirrel hairs,
squirrel bones crunched
tight and dry in scats of
fox.

The poem suggests that the life of each is, often quite literally, bound up with that of the others—dissolved, rotten, and reconstituted in a new form. This evidence of the food chain is, then, for Snyder probably the clearest sign of our interdependence in the "family" of Gaia, and many poems deal with this exchange of energies, what he calls "eating each other." Here, as before, the metaphors work to subvert the habitual view of the individual (self, family, class, nation, gender, species) as something separable from the environment.

In *Regarding Wave,* the goddess Vak is the focusing metaphor for a similar perception of the interdependence of self and ecosystem. Looking at the texture of the phenomenal world, the speaker finds that all things (including himself) are wave-patterned, various expressions of an energy he calls "a shimmering bell / through all." As Vak, or "Voice," this omnipresent energy is metaphorically depicted as a lover. But, as with the image of Gaia as mother, the feminine symbolism refers to the ecosystem as a whole rather than to something outside of and separate from the self. The poems **"Wave"** and **"Regarding Wave"** convey the role (simultaneously observer and participant) that this concept implies for the speaker.

If the dominant discourse cannot speak for "the green of the leaf," then Snyder's work seeks a language for what has been silenced. In response to the dualistic model that structures experience in terms of binary oppositions, and so legitimizes the repression and exploitation of the Other, this poetry offers a view of the universe as an interpenetrating network of correspondences. By foregrounding what the dominant culture has marginalized, much of Snyder's writing finds in a metaphorically feminized ecosystem a model of interconnection and relationship that attempts to resist binary division and the exploitation such division implies. Snyder's view, which he has called "a spiritual ecology," is not dependent on belief in a metaphysical "other realm." Instead,

it is based on the observation that individual and environment are interdependent, that social formations and psychic relations are inextricable.

Of course, there are contradictions. First, there is the problem any oppositional discourse has in attempting to "talk back": One's own voice takes shape as another text, to be encoded as yet another part of the dominant discourse. Partly for this reason, Zen Buddhist texts characteristically avoid assertions of belief, seeking rather, through paradoxical and illogical expression, to disrupt the sequential, dualistic thinking encoded in language. Julia Kristeva argues similarly that "Once it is represented, even by the form of a woman, the 'truth' of the unconscious passes into the symbolic order," and the Tao Te Ching opens with the words, "The Way which can be spoken is not the Way." And yet we must go on speaking.

A second problem concerns Snyder's tendency to caricature the Western tradition, his consequent identification with its repressed Other, and his use of a gendered image (a goddess) as metaphor for a nondualistic view. Does this not involve a mere reversal of the current model, generating an inverted image of the combatted power, preparing the way for another pattern of dominance, another totalizing ideology? If the simultaneous exploitation of women and the natural biosphere has derived ideological support from the supposed association between "woman" and "nature," is the attempt to renew this association in the metaphors of Gaia and Vak not harmful and regressive? Why use an anthropomorphic metaphor anyway, when its purpose is to evoke a world in which humans are only part of the picture?

For Snyder as Zen poet, all such metaphors, like any linguistic articulation of a nondualistic perspective, are provisional and tentative. Any given metaphor can be valuable as long as it is strategically useful and emotionally compelling. When I interviewed Snyder in 1988, he conceded that gendered metaphors for nature are potentially problematic and suggested that Gaia was "a theatrical device" to be used only "as long as it plays" (**"Coyote-Mind"**). In his recent contributions to nature's literature, the network of interdependence is evoked in descriptions of what he calls "the wild." There is little mention of goddesses.

It should be clear that my reading of Snyder's position is generally sympathetic. I make my own position explicit because no reading is neutral. Our situation demands that readers, writers, and teachers of literature engage with issues that concern us deeply. From deconstruction and Buddhist teaching, we know about the relativity of all propositions of belief and the fiction of a grounding truth, a transcendental signified. And yet, in these uncertain times, there are some things we can be sure of: The earth is one system, and our lives are interdependent; we live in a suffering world, and there is nowhere else to go. Whatever else may be said, the planetary biosphere, "nature" if you like, is the ground of all our meanings. Snyder calls it "our only sacred spot":

> This small blue-green planet is the only one with comfortable temperatures, good air and water, a wealth of animals and plants, for millions (or quadrillions) of miles. A little waterhole in Vast Space, a nesting place, a place of singing and practice, a place of dreaming. It's on the verge of being totally trashed—there's a slow way and a fast way. We are all natives here, and this is our only sacred spot. We must know that we've been jumped, and fight like a raccoon in a pack of hounds, for our own and all other lives. (**"Wild"**)

Certainly, neither textual revolution nor engaged criticism can substitute for social and political transformation. For Snyder, writing poetry is only part of a much wider practice. Poems can't feed the hungry or heal the ozone layer or liberate women or bring justice in South Africa. But sometimes they can disturb our old opinions, enter our dreams, and help us to find new words.

Katsunori Yamazato (essay date 1991)

SOURCE: "How to Be in This Crisis: Gary Snyder's Cross-Cultural Vision in *Turtle Island*," in *Critical Essays on Gary Snyder*, edited by Patrick D. Murphy, G. K. Hall & Co., 1991, pp. 230-47.

[*In the following essay, Yamazato discusses the way in which Snyder's unique interpretation of Buddhism shapes his poetry.*]

For Gary Snyder, Buddhism was and is not merely a system of faith and worship; as he succinctly summarizes, "Buddhism is about existence." Buddhism teaches one how to be in this "impermanent" world, and this is one of the aspects of Buddhism that Snyder especially deepened and solidified during his Japanese years (1956-68). Despite persistent skepticism toward traditional, institutionalized Buddhism, he gained valuable insights into its strengths and weaknesses during his stay in Japan, and these insights grew into an ontological vision. "How to be" is the central question that Snyder asks and tries to answer throughout *Turtle Island,* as in **"What Happened Here Before"**:

> *now,*
>
> we sit here near the diggings
> in the forest, by our fire, and watch
> the moon and planets and the shooting stars—

my sons ask, who are we?
drying apples picked from homestead trees
drying berries, curing meat,
shooting arrows at a bale of straw.

military jets head northeast, roaring, every dawn.

my sons ask, who are they?

> WE SHALL SEE
> WHO KNOWS
> HOW TO BE

Bluejay screeches from a pine.

As he states in his essay **"Energy is Eternal Delight,"** the question of "how to be" is closely related to his vision of an alternative culture: "The return to marginal farmland on the part of longhairs is not some nostalgic replay of the nineteenth century. Here is a generation of white people finally ready to learn from the Elders. How to live on the continent as though our children, and on down, for many ages, will still be here (not on the moon). Loving and protecting this soil, these trees, these wolves. Natives of Turtle Island." In 1970, two years after his return from Japan, Snyder and his family moved to Kitkitdizze—a name he gave the wild land that he bought in 1967. They were joined by others settling roots on the San Juan Ridge, Nevada City, California, and a community began to emerge, a group of people determined to live as "natives of Turtle Island," seeking ways of "how to be." The answer to his sons' question, "who are we?" cannot be separated from the answer to the question of "how to be," and one of many things that makes Gary Snyder a distinguished poet and thinker is that he seeks answers to this perennial compound question by actually experimenting in the heart of Turtle Island, Snyder's mythic, alternative name for North America. He rejects an easy answer, for the question is based on his quest for an alternative culture. In the heart of Turtle Island, he has tested his conviction that "Buddhism is about existence," and Buddhism has been effective in finding an answer to his radical question.

To understand fully Snyder's cross-cultural vision in *Turtle Island* we need to explore the Buddhist elements that pervade the book. Among the teachings of Buddhist sects that he studied in Japan, Zen Buddhism naturally constitutes his basic attitude, as he suggested in a 1979 interview. In that interview, Snyder laughs away conventional and stereotypic images of Zen Buddhism, and the laughter is indicative of the depth and sophistication that he attained during his rigorous training at the Daitoku-ji in Kyoto. Zen became fundamental for the poet—a way of seeing and working through life—and as such, it manifests itself in such unlikely places as **"Why Log Truck Drivers Rise Earlier Than Students of Zen."** At this point, Zen has become so fundamentally embodied in his works that it is difficult to pinpoint particular "Zen aspects" in the poems collected in *Turtle Island*—as difficult, in fact, as isolating water from the cells of a plant. Zen has become the basis of Snyder's everyday life.

Moreover, it is dangerous to discuss *Turtle Island* and other works written after the poet's return to the United States solely in terms of Zen, for Snyder also studied and incorporated teachings of other Buddhist schools in Japan, bringing these into play in his work. In *Turtle Island,* he uses some teachings of other Buddhist sects in his attempt at a "cross-fertilization of ecological thought with Buddhist ideas of interpenetration." Since the Buddhist ideas that Snyder drew on to "cross-fertilize" with ecological ideas have received little critical analysis, a discussion of the Buddhist concept of interpenetration, a key metaphor in *Turtle Island,* is well in order.

Buddhism holds that every being in this universe is interrelated. According to Junjiro Takakusu, "The universe is not homocentric; it is a co-creation of all beings." In the Buddhist universe, nothing can exist separately from other beings, and "everything is inevitably created out of more than two causes." This is called "Dependent Production or Chain of Causation," or, in Japanese, *engisetsu,* and, as Takakusu explains it: "From the existence of *this, that* becomes: from the happening of *this, that* happens. From the non-existence of *this, that* does not happen. Everything in the universe is mutually related, and, as Takakusu succinctly puts it, "all is . . . a product of interdependence."

In Buddhism, there are two ways of explaining the universe. Seen in terms of time, all things contained in the universe are depicted as "impermanent"; but in terms of space, the things in the universe become "interrelated." Snyder occasionally refers to the impermanence of life in this world, yet we should note that he tends increasingly to emphasize the spatial aspect in Buddhism, that is, the interpenetration of all things.

The theory of causation or the idea of universal interpenetration has been developed by various schools of Buddhism. Among these, the Kegon school, which upholds the Avatamsaka sutra, is said to have developed the idea of interpenetration to its climax. The idea of interpenetration, according to D. T. Suzuki, is "the ruling topic of the sutra," and the central image in the sutra is "the world of all realities or practical facts interwoven or identified in perfect harmony." This word is called, in Japanese, *jijimuge-hokkai,* and the sutra introduces "Indra's net" to illustrate the magnificent image of interpenetration. As Takakusu puts it, it is "a net decorated with bright stone on each knot of the mesh," and the jewels reflect each other endlessly, reflecting "the real facts of the world" mutually interpenetrating. Interpenetration is the fundamental insight of the Avatamsaka sutra,

and, by using the image of "Indra's net," the sutra illustrates, in D. T. Suzuki's words, a "perfect network of mutual relations."

From the beginning of his career, Snyder has repeatedly referred to the Avatamsaka sutra and its key image. In **"Lookout's Journal,"** for instance, he writes: "—shifting of light & cloud, perfection of chaos, magnificent *jijimu-ge* / interlacing interaction." In **"Buddhism and the Coming Revolution,"** an essay first published in 1961, he points out that "Avatamsaka (Kegon) Buddhist philosophy sees the world as a vast interrelated network in which all objects and creatures are necessary and illuminated." And in **"Poetry and the Primitive"** an essay later published in *Earth House Hold,* Snyder sketches the idea of interpenetration in a more elaborate context, foreshadowing its full development in *Turtle Island:* ". . . every person, animals, forces, all are related via a web of reincarnation—or rather, they are 'interborn.' It may well be that rebirth (or interbirth, for we are actually mutually creating each other and all things while living) is the objective fact of existence which we have not yet brought into conscious knowledge and practice. "It is clear that the empirically observable interconnectedness of nature is but a corner of the vast 'jewelled net' which moves from without to within."

Continuing in the same vein in a 1973 interview given in New York, Snyder refers again to the fundamental Buddhist idea of interpenetration: "I find it always exciting to me, beautiful, to experience the interdependencies of things, the complex webs and networks by which everything moves, which I think are the most beautiful awarenesses that we can have of ourselves and of our planet." In his lecture, **"Reinhabitation,"** delivered at the Reinhabitation Conference held at San Juan Ridge County School in August of 1976, Snyder continues: "The Avatamsaka ('Flower Wreath') jewelled-net-interpenetration-ecological-systems-emptiness-consciousness tells us, no self-realization without the Whole Self, and the whole self is the whole thing." Even a cursory survey of the poet's references to the nets and webs imagery in the Avatamsaka sutra tells us that Snyder gradually developed and incorporated the key image of this sutra into his own system. We also notice how the idea of interpenetration becomes deepened, refined, and finally solidified as a vital element in the poet's consciousness—as seen in the growth of his ontological vision.

Buddhism and ecology "cross-fertilize" each other well. Coined by the German biologist Ernest Haeckel in 1869, the term *ecology* has since gained a wide popularity only a century later, and its key concept has been a common assumption of nature-conscious people in the second half of the twentieth century: "All units of the ecosystem are mutually dependent. This is a good point to keep in mind when we are tempted to extol the importance of some group of organisms in which we happen to be especially interested." Humankind is "a part of 'complex' biological cycles" dependent on the food web of eating and being eaten. Snyder was well aware of this key concept of ecology in his early stage, as in **"Japan First Time Around,"** in which he sketches the link in the chain: "salts—diatoms—copepods—herring—fishermen—us. eating."

It is clear, then, that Snyder in Japan deeply realized that Buddhism and ecology shared a vision of the world in terms of the interrelatedness of all beings. The former is a picture of a spiritual world caught in the Eastern religious vision, and the latter a model of the natural world presented by the rational thinking of Western science. During his first sojourn in Japan (1956-57), he discovered the connection between Zen and the Avatamsaka teachings: "So, Zen being founded on Avatamsaka, and the net-network of things," and three short months later, the shared imagery of the Avatamsaka sutra and the principles of ecology were fused in his mind: "Indra's net is not merely two-dimensional. . . .—two days contemplating ecology, foodchains and sex."

Science, for Snyder, does not "murder to dissect." Ecology with its ethical and spiritual dimension is "divine," and he writes that "science walks in beauty" (**"Toward Climax"**). Unlike many visionaries, he does not reject rational thought, and he is attempting to fuse science and religious teachings to create a guiding principle by which to live on Turtle Island. This is a daring new American synthesis, perhaps not feasible in the vision of traditional Buddhists, as Snyder himself is aware: "Traditional orthodox Buddhists are not concerned with building new cultures any more than they are interested in natural religion or girls. Poets must try to get them together—playing a funny kind of role, today, as pivotman, between the upheavals of culture-change and the persistence of the Single Eye of Knowledge. In Snyder's continuing synthesis, ecology helps him see his position clearly and concretely in exploring the heart of Turtle Island, and his life there is given a spiritual depth by his acute awareness of the interrelated existence of all beings in the universe. As I shall show, this double structure serves as the basis for most poems in *Turtle Island*.

Further, the Mahayana belief in *bussho,* which teaches that all beings are endowed with "Buddha-nature" (the inherent capacity to become a Buddha), demands—along with ecology—that people treat other beings responsibly. The human, in Snyder's words, is "an animal that was brought into being on this biosphere by these processes of sun and water and leaf." Endowed with "Buddha-nature," other beings demand a radically different treatment. Snyder writes that "as the most highly developed tool-using animal, [people] must recognize that the unknown evolutionary destinies of other life forms are to be respected, and act as gentle steward of the earth's community of being" (**"Four Changes"**). Thus,

the insights from the Avatamsaka sutra and other Buddhist teachings merged with an ecological consciousness, to become a guiding principle in living on Turtle Island.

This guiding principle, moreover, involves an attempt to restore "life" to other beings that modern civilization has tended to regard as "dead matter." In his criticism of modern civilization, Snyder writes that "at the root of the problem where our civilization goes wrong is the mistaken belief that nature is something less than authentic, that nature is not as alive as man is, or as intelligent, that in a sense it is dead, and that animals are of so low an order of intelligence and feeling, we need not take their feelings into account" (**"The Wilderness"**). Writing in **"Four Changes,"** he goes further, aiming at "transforming" a civilization that he has long found destructive: "We have it within our deepest powers not only to change our 'selves' but to change our culture. If man is to remain on earth he must transform the five-millennia-long urbanizing civilization tradition into a new ecologically-sensitive harmony-oriented wild-minded scientific-spiritual culture." His quest in Japan reaches a climax here, and we understand that his is a vision that, by combining East and West, deeply urges the reader to reconsider the validity of traditional cultural paradigms.

To support and guide one's behavior by a religious vision provided by Buddhism, and to be deeply aware of the ecological reality of Turtle Island, and to learn at the same time from the Native American cultures, all these have offered parts of the answer for the poet's question of "how to be." The poems in *Turtle Island* reflect Snyder's exploratory life and his pursuit of the perennial question in the heart of the mythic American land. The Buddhist concept of interpenetration, "cross-fertilized" with classical Western ecology, runs beneath the poems collected in *Turtle Island* and enriches the poetic world depicted there. Solidified in the poet's consciousness during his years in Japan, the Buddhist-ecological matrix manifests itself in various modes in his poems. Some poems in *Turtle Island* are candidly satiric and political, and Snyder's attack on problems inherent in modern civilization is based on his conviction of the interrelatedness of all beings. In **"Front Lines,"** for instance, the poet depicts the destructiveness in contemporary society. When rain continues and the log trucks are unable to work, "The trees breathe." But the destruction of nature continues: "Every pulse of the rot at the heart / In the sick fat veins of Amerika / Pushes the edge up closer—." A bulldozer is "grinding and slobbering / Sideslipping and belching on top of / The skinned-up bodies of still-live bushes." The trees and bushes, depicted thus, are not just dead matter. For Snyder, they share "Buddha-nature" with human beings, all belonging to "the great community of living creatures," and their lives must equally be respected (**"Four Changes"**). Yet, for the greediness of "a man / From town," trees are suffocated and bushes are destroyed.

Snyder's attitude is not merely that of "a nature lover"; he is indicting a civilization, devoid of sensibility of and respect for other life forms, mindlessly engulfed in its own destructiveness. He goes a step further. As he concludes, we perceive clearly that the interplay of Mahayana Buddhism and his ecological consciousness implies, perhaps even demands, social activism:

> Behind is a forest that goes to the Arctic
> And a desert that still belongs to the Piute
> And here we must draw
> Our line

The poet's criticism of a destructive civilization and his compassion for "all other members of the life-network" are sometimes expressed as "spells" against destructive forces, incantations that will arrest and convert negative energy (**"Four Changes"**). **"Spel against Demons"** (first printed in *The Fudo Trilogy,* 1973) is a poem that attempts to exorcise the demonic forces inside the civilization by introducing a powerful figure from Buddhism, "ACHALA the Immovable" (Fudomyo-o, in Japanese). *Fudomyo-o* is a deity that belongs to the *Shingon* school (also known as *Mikkyo;* literally, the secret teachings), a branch of Mahayana Buddhism in Japan. The *Shingon* teachings are said to have originated in second-century India, and, after transmission to China, were systematized in Japan by the Japanese Buddhist Priest Kukai (774-835). According to Shōkō Watanabe, *Fudomyo-o in Shingon* is regarded as an incarnation of the Mahavairocana Buddha or the Great Sun Buddha, whom Snyder also refers to in **"On 'As for Poets.'"** Originally a Hindu deity, *Fudomyo-o* became an object of popular worship in Japan after its incorporation into the *Shingon* teachings.

Shingon or *Mikkyo* comes into the poet's work through his interest in the *Shugendo* (or *Yamabushi*) tradition in Japan (*Yamabushi* is a Japanese term for those priests who discipline themselves in the mountains). *Shugendo* originally was a nature-worship religion that borrowed its theoretical basis from *Shingon; Fudomyo-o,* a deity originally belonging to *Shingon,* also became a powerful deity for the *Shugendo* tradition. Snyder's penchant for the tradition manifested itself earlier in his essay, **"Anyone with *Yama-bushi* Tendencies,"** printed in *Zen Notes* in 1954. His interest in the tradition persisted throughout the Japanese years, and he did a pilgrimage to Mt. ōmine, a sacred mountain for the *Yamabushi* tradition, and was initiated as a *Yamabushi* ("a mountain priest") in 1961.

In **"Spel against Demons,"** the poet introduces *Fudōmyō-ō,* hoping to exorcise "demonic energies" in society:

> Down with demonic killers who mouth revolutionary

slogans and muddy the flow of change, may they
> be
> Bound by the Noose, and Instructed by the
> Diamond
> Sword of ACHALA the Immovable, Lord of
> Wisdom, Lord
> of Heat, who is squint-eyed and whose face is
> terrible
> with bare fangs, who wears on his crown a garland
> of
> severed heads, clad in a tiger skin, he who turns
> Wrath to Purified Accomplishment,
>
> whose powers are of lava
> of magma, of deep rock strata, of gunpowder,
> and the Sun.
>
> He who saves tortured intelligent demons and
> filth-eating
> hungry ghosts, his spel is,

> NAMAH SAMANTAH VAJRANĄM CHANDA
> MAHAROSHANA
> SPHATAYA HUM TRAKA HAM MAM

As we see above, *Fudomyo-o* (*Fudo* meaning "Immovable" in Japanese) always holds a sharp sword in his right hand, which subdues devils or evil spirits. The rope, "the Noose," held in the diety's left hand, is used to capture, bind, and lead evil spirits into enlightenment. The facial expression of the deity is fierce and contorted with bare fangs, and his halo is aflame. According to Watanabe, the word *achala* originally means "something immovable, that is, "mountain," and hence it also represents "nature in general." The mantra, "his spel," that Snyder quotes, is called *jikunoshu* in Japanese, and it is the most famous among the mantras attributed to *Fudomyo-o.*

"Spel against Demons" clearly shows that Snyder's studies in Buddhism enlarged beyond Zen, and in the comic and now-famous **"Smokey the Bear Sutra"** (not included in **Turtle Island**), he again incorporates *Fudomyo-o*'s mantra, comfortable enough in his Buddhist work to be at once playful and serious:

> Wrathful but Calm, Austere but Comic, Smokey
> the Bear will
> illuminate those who would help him; but for
> those who
> would hinder or slander him,
>
> HE WILL PUT THEM OUT.
>
> Thus his great Mantra:
> Namah samanta vajranam chanda maharoshana

Sphataya hum traka ham mam

"I DEDICATE MYSELF TO THE UNIVERSAL DIAMOND BE THIS RAGING FURY DESTROYED"

"**Smokey the Bear**" unfolds with a discourse given "about 150 million years ago" by "the Great Sun Buddha," in which the Buddha predicts he will enter a new form in America of the future "to cure the world of loveless knowledge that seeks with blind hunger; and mindless rage eating food that will not fill it. "The Great Sun Buddha then reveals himself "in his true form of SMOKEY THE BEAR." A *Fudo* figure, Smokey the Bear holds a shovel in his right paw "that digs to the truth beneath appearances; cuts the roots of useless attachments, and flings damp sand on the fires of greed and war." The left paw, continuing the *Shingon* symbology, is "in the Mudra of Comradely Display—indicating that all creatures have the full right to live to their limits and that deer, rabbits, chipmunks, snakes, dandelions, and lizards all grow in the realm of Dharma." Thus, for the poet, Smokey the Bear is an American incarnation of *Fudomyo-o,* an earlier incarnation of the Great Sun Buddha. "**Smokey the Bear Sutra**" is both a spell against destructive forces and an invocation for, among others, "the age of harmony of man and nature." The "official" image of Smokey the Bear is transformed, and, in Snyder's alternative vision, becomes a guardian deity, protecting not only the oppressed human beings but also the interpenetrating beings from "a civilization that claims to save but only destroys."

While *Turtle Island* introduces a strong political and satirical tone to Snyder's work, it contains compassionate and sometimes elegiac elements as well. "**The Uses of Light,**" for example, extends his compassion for other beings to include inanimate "stones," and, contrary to its surface simplicity, reflects a deeper harmony:

> It warms my bones
>   say the stones
>
> I take it into me and grow
> Say the trees
> Leaves above
> Roots below
>
> A vast vague white
> Draws me out of the night
> Says the moth in his flight—
>
> Some things I smell
> Some things I hear
> And I see things move
> Says the deer—

> A high tower
> on a wide plain.
> If you climb up
> One floor
> You'll see a thousand miles more.

As the source of energy in the solar system, the sun draws out various reactions from the beings in the poem, and the second stanza is fundamentally ecological. The solar light is pervasive in the world, giving each being energy to live by. But how do people react to this world of light? Unlike other beings given only a limited sight (or no sight, as in the cases of "the stones" and "the trees"), humans climb "a high tower" of vision and wisdom. Their awareness of the idea of interpenetration renders them compassionate, not exploitative, toward other beings—sentient and nonsentient—and the poet implicitly advises readers to use their superior sight both for a harmonious whole and for their function as a "gentle steward of the earth's community of beings." People need "to always look one step farther along" to gain a deeper and clearer vision for "the life-network"— an attitude that Snyder sharpened during his rigorous training in Zen in Japan.

"**The Uses of Light**" also reflects Snyder's respects for the "Buddha-nature" in other beings, and, in this context, the "light" takes on a spiritual dimension. The principal Buddha in the Avatamsaka sutra is Vairocana (the Sun Buddha), who is depicted in that sutra as the center of the universe. Takakusu explains both the causation theory and the world depicted in the Avatamsaka sutra: "The causation theories particular to this school mean general interdependence, universal relativity, causes and effects being interwoven everywhere. Thus it makes from the beginning one perfect whole without any single independent thing—all comprehensive *mandala* (circle) and the Cycle of Permanent Waves illumined throughout by the great Sun-Buddha (Vairocana)."

Thus, at a deeper level, "stones," "trees" "moth," "deer," and people in this world are all interrelated and constitute a harmonious whole while *illumined* by the spiritual light that emanates from the Sun Buddha. The stanzaic arrangement gives the impression that both the sentient and nonsentient beings depicted are separate and independent, and yet one must say that the spiritual light pervades the space between the stanzas, connecting at a deeper level humans and other beings into "one perfect whole."

"**Light**"—spiritual and ecological—is one of the dominant images in *Turtle Island,* and another poem, "**Two Fawns That Didn't See the Light This Spring,**" shares a spiritual dimension with "**The Uses of Light.**" The poem consists of two anecdotes told by the poet's friends. First, "a friend in a tipi in the / Northern Rockies" hunting whitetail shoots by mistake a doe carrying a fawn. The friend is not wasteful, and he expiates his mistake by performing a "ritual": "He cured the meat without / salt; sliced it following the grain." The second anecdote is told by a woman in the Northern Sierra. She hits a doe with her car, and the poet's friends perform an impromptu "ritual" of death and birth. Butchering the doe, they discover a fawn:

> "—about so long—
> so tiny—but all formed and right.
> It had spots. And the little
> hooves were soft and white."

In Snyder's Buddhist-ecological vision, to be born permeated with "light" is basically joyful; we do not "wawl and cry" coming into this world. As he suggests in the Buddhist detachment in **"Night Heron,"** the joy of birth and death arises from the fact that one becomes interrelated with and serviceable to other beings in the network illumined by the spiritual-ecological "light":

> the joy of all the beings
> is in being
> older and tougher and eaten
> up.

In **"Two Fawns That Didn't See the Light This Spring,"** Snyder expresses his controlled sorrow for the two fawns that missed being part of the joyful, interdependent world permeated by the "light" that emanates from one compassionate Buddha. Snyder does not explicitly lament, and yet his sorrow and sense of loss take on an elegiac tone.

"The Hudsonian Curlew" is one of the most successful poems in *Turtle Island* in depicting interdependency between humans and other animals. It involves "killing" birds, but is an affirmative poem based on the poet's idea of the Buddhist-ecological interpenetration of beings in this world. What we see in the poem is the ritual of the food web, of eating and being eaten. The eating has a spiritual significance arising from Snyder's veneration for the life of other beings.

The poem unfolds with an image of "the Mandala of Birds." Amid the gathering of various birds, the human being is simply another animal engaged in hunting for food:

> we
> gather driftwood for firewood
> for camping
> get four shells to serve up steamed snail.

The hunters then shoot two curlews, and the poet dwells on the concrete preparation of the birds for eating. It is a long passage, but the whole is worth quoting:

> The down

> i pluck from the
> neck of the curlew
> eddies and whirls at my knees
> in the twilight wind
> from sea.
> kneeling in sand
>
> warm in the hand.
>
> *"Do you want to do it right? I'll tell you."*
> he tells me.
> at the edge of the water on the stones.
> a transverse cut just below the sternum
> the forefinger and middle finger
>   forced in and up, following the
>   curve of the ribcage.
> then fingers arched, drawn slowly down and back,
> forcing all the insides up and out,
> toward the palm and heel of the hand.
> firm organs, well-placed, hot.
> save the liver;
> finally scouring back, toward the vent, the last of
> the
>   large intestine.
>
> the insides string out, begin to wave, in the
> lapping
>   waters of the bay.
> the bird has no features, head, or feet;
>   he is empty inside.
> the rich body muscle that he moved by, the wing-
> beating
>   muscle
> anchored to the blade-like high breast bone,
> is what you eat.

The "i" in this poem is drastically different from the dwarfed, passive "i" seen, for instance, in the works of e. e. cummings. Snyder's humble but joyfully monistic "i" is aware of his place in the interpenetrating web, and the "i" recognizes the potentialities of other beings and their "Buddha-nature." This perhaps is a radically new "i" in modern poetry written in English. The traditional, "anthropocentric" modern "I" cannot assert its superiority in the world of this poem, and gratitude, not guilt or aggressiveness, is the central attitude in this food web of eating and being eaten. Moreover, the minute and concrete depiction of the preparation and cooking of the bird, combined with the poet's neatness, accuracy, and reverential attitude—"kneeling in sand"—in the process suggests a spiritual depth; depicted thus, eating finally becomes a joyful ritual of the food web. In **"Japan First Time Around,"** the poet asks: "just where am I in this foodchain?" This is 1956, and Snyder, in a sense, disciplined himself in Japan to find an answer for this ontological question. By combining Buddhism and ecology (and perhaps through a Native American model for bunting), he found an answer for the question, offering it to his reader.

As I mentioned earlier, Zen is pervasive in *Turtle Island,* and, in addition to the underlying Kegon (Avatamsaka) philosophy, we detect an unmistakable Zen attitude in this poem. It reflects the poet's ritualistic neatness and attention to small details sharpened in his Zen training; as Snyder records in **"Japan First Time Around,"** "the Zen Master's presence is to help one keep attention undivided." Further, the Zen attitude is reflected in the central act of this poem, that is, eating. As Snyder points out in *The Wooden Fish* (a manual of Zen that Snyder and Kanetsuki Gutetsu, a Japanese colleague, compiled), "Eating is a sacrament in Zen training. No other aspect of ordinary human daily life is treated with quite such formality or reverence in the Sodo la training hall for monks]." That eating is a sacrament is also evidenced in the verses that monks recite before meals. I quote below a representative verse from *The Wooden Fish:*

> First, let us reflect on your own work, let
> us see whence this comes;

> Secondly, let us reflect how imperfect our
> virtue is, whether we deserve this offerings [sic].

> Thirdly, what is most essential is to hold
> our minds in control and be detached from
> the various faults, greed, etc.

> Fourthly, that this is taken as medicinal
> to keep our bodies in good health;

> Fifthly, in order to accomplish the task of
> enlightenment we accept this food.

This verse is called, in Japanese, *Shokuji gokan* ("The Five Reflections"), and it clearly shows the Zen attitude toward eating. Although the passage quoted from **"The Hudsonian Curlew"** does not show metaphysical elaboration, its reverential and sacramental attitude toward the birds is convincing and renders the poem one of the most successful in *Turtle Island.*

Since the Buddhist-ecological interpenetration is best rendered concretely and specifically, a number of poems focus on home life at Kitkitdizze. These poems directly reflect the poet's earliest exploration of the literal land and a quest for its mythical element, essential parts of his attempt to establish a sense of place, and—ultimately—to find answers for the question of "how to be." To develop a sense of place means to live as a native of the land, not as a sojourner, and the life of the land at the same time is a quest for a vision of a new, alternative culture as it flowers.

Snyder's life at Kitkitdizze as reflected in *Turtle Island* is exploratory; he wants to know accurately where he is, and, as he states in a 1974 lecture, it is "a work to be done," and essentially "the old American quest . . . for an identity." He had envisioned such a life during his long sojourn in Japan—he bought the land in 1967, a year before his permanent return—and, with his vision for an alternative culture, his life at Kitkitdizze reflects the work of exploration in the forest of North America.

"The Wild Mushroom," for instance, shows the poet exploring the forest at Kitkitdizze. He and his son Kai go mushrooming with "A basket and a trowel / And a book with all the rules," and the father gives the following instruction:

> Don't ever eat Boletus
> If the tube-mouths they are red
> Stay away from the Amanitas
> Or brother you are dead.

These instructions are directed not only to his son but also to the reader and the poet himself, and thus, mushrooming is a way of knowing Turtle Island. This exploration is full of joy, and the poem becomes a praise for the interpenetrating web, acknowledging the identity of a mushroom family that, "Shining through the woodland gloom," coexists with the poet's family in this place in North America.

The exploration of Turtle Island continues, bringing in the process the poet and his family closer to the land. **"The Bath"** depicts the love and harmony in the family, and the poem ultimately becomes a praise for our body and the earth on which we live, perhaps Snyder's most ecstatic vision of harmony. We see the family settling deeper into the land, and the familial harmony depicted in the simple act of bathing reflects the larger web of beings:

> Clean, and rinsed, and sweating more, we stretch
> out on the redwood benches hearts all beating
> Quiet to the simmer of the stove,
> the scent of cedar
> And then turn over,
> murmuring gossip of the grasses,
> talking firewood,
> Wondering how Gen's napping, how to bring him
> in
> soon wash him too—
> These boys who love their mother
> Who loves men, who passes on
> her sons to other women;

> The cloud across the sky. The windy pines.
> the trickle gurgle in the swampy meadow

> *this is our body*

Fire inside and boiling water on the stove
We sigh and slide ourselves down from the
    benches
    Wrap the babies, step outside,

black night & all the stars.

Instead of depicting a tension between human and nature, the passage arrests and asserts a harmonious moment in which every being in this cosmos contributes tenderly to sustain each other. The sky, winds, trees, waters, grasses, animals, children, men, and women are the members of "great / earth / sangha" (**"O Waters."**) The poem implies an answer for the question of "how to be," and the poet affirms, laughing with his family on "the Great Earth," the life that he and his family are creating on Turtle Island.

The knowledge gained in living everyday life on the land and the spiritual attitudes that underlie such a life must be transmitted, as Snyder in **"Energy Is Eternal Delight"** implies, to community, to society, and to posterity as a legacy if one is to continue fruitfully to live in a place as a native of it. In this sense, Snyder increasingly becomes a "teacher" in his poetry and essays; his is not only one person's vision but is directed to humanity at large. By his reverential and attentive attitude toward nature, and by actually living close to a devastated territory—an aftermath of hydraulic gold mining and logging—he seeks a way of healing it, which in turn teaches his reader and audience how to live in this world of ecological crisis.

In **"Pine Tree Tops,"** Snyder depicts the interpenetrating natural world that is almost mythic and sacred beyond people's meager knowledge:

    in the blue night
    frost haze, the sky glows
    with the moon
    pine tree tops
    bend snow-blue, fade
    into sky, frost, starlight.
    the creak of boots.
    rabbit tracks, deer tracks,
    what do we know.

The beauty of the interpenetrating nature that the poet captures this night is awesome, and he characteristically avoids asserting his presence in the world—a typical Snyder poem that places "human tracks" next to "rabbit tracks" and "deer tracks." The last line is almost an ecstatic statement, telling the reader that dissecting, dichotomizing knowledge is unnecessary and that this holistic nocturnal beauty arising from the interpenetration of all beings is just enough.

Continuing in the same vein, in **"By Frazier Creek Falls,"**

Snyder shows that people are not separate from nature, that finally "We are it":

    This living flowing land
    is all there is, forever

    We *are* it
    it sings through us—

    We could live on this Earth
    without clothes or tools!

Earlier in his career, Snyder referred to Japanese literature to show human inseparability from nature; by this stage of his development, however, such literary allusions are no longer necessary. He finds new values through his direct contact with the interpenetrating land on Turtle Island, and those values are offered, along with his discoveries, to the reader, to the larger society, and to posterity. Thus, the merging of Buddhism and ecology has become an essential element in Snyder's exploratory poems on Turtle Island, and, beyond enriching the poetic world, these poems are didactic, directing poet and reader to answers for the question of "how to be."

Snyder believes that, in its anthropocentric view of the world, modern industrial civilization—East and West—has tended to ignore the lives of other beings that coexist with humanity. From this general tendency, it has earned the ecological crisis that we witness today. *Turtle Island* offers the reader not only a sense of "how to be" in a world with just such an ecological crisis but also, in Charles Molesworth's words, "a new sense of what it means to be human." Gary Snyder blends the insights gained in his cross-cultural quest in Japan and Western traditions (including the indigenous American cultures) to create a vision that transcends the mythic American land. By creating the myth of Turtle Island and unfolding it to the reader in his poetry and prose, he urges the reader to reconsider the validity of the old myths on which modern civilization is based. His cross-cultural quest begun in the mid-1950s thus results in a new ontological vision.

Michael Strickland (review date Summer 1992)

SOURCE: Review of *The Practice of the Wild*, in *The Georgia Review*, Vol. XLVI, No. 2, Summer, 1992, pp. 382-83.

[*In the following review, Strickland praises Snyder's wisdom and attention to craftsmanship in the essays from* The Practice of the Wild.]

Reading the essays in *The Practice of the Wild* one can almost see Gary Snyder, the new-age hunter-gatherer so en-amored of "good tools" and "high quality information," pecking away at his Macintosh computer (to which he has written a celebratory poem)—the consummate Zen crafts-man of words. None of the 1960's rhetoric sometimes found in his earlier essays is here, only eloquence and an "ecol-ogy of language." Whether the subject is the history of com-munal lands and the development of wilderness areas, or the implications of an imposed Western-culture curriculum for the education of twenty-first-century Alaskan Inupiaq chil-dren, Snyder's tone is always careful and driven by a pin-point focus of thought. Such focus was already there in the earlier work, with its even-handed weighing of alternatives in favor of "the old ways," but what makes his new collec-tion of essays so riveting is its exquisite craftsmanship and new maturity in style.

The Practice of the Wild offers a series of deeply entwined discourses on geography, ecology, history, ecofeminism, lin-guistics, and Native American culture. In the tradition of Montaigne and Thoreau, Snyder refuses to follow a prescrip-tive formula; instead, we are invited to follow the conscious-ness of the author as he explores his subject, to participate in learning rather than observe a performance. This is the essay as meditation, what William Covino calls "the art of wondering."

> **Snyder's tone is always careful and driven by a pinpoint focus of thought. Such focus was already there in the earlier work, with its even-handed weighing of alternatives in favor of "the old ways," but what makes his new collection of essays so riveting is its exquisite craftsmanship and new maturity in style.**
> **—Michael Strickland**

One of Snyder's most effective devices is the personal an-ecdote, which he uses throughout these essays as metaphor—rather like the discursive Zen koan. One of my favorites has Snyder standing with a climbing partner on the peak of a glacier, observing the vast beauty of the wilderness around them, and the partner saying, "You mean there's a senator for all this?" Such are the gemstones of these essays, scat-tered throughout, as when we are reminded that we too are wild: "Our bodies are wild. The involuntary quick turn of the head at a shout, the vertigo at looking off a precipice, the heart in the throat in a moment of danger . . . all univer-sal responses of this mammalian body. They can be seen throughout the class."

Snyder has been one of our most ardent spokespersons for the bioregionalism movement, and he describes himself as

"foremost a person of the Yuba River country in the Sierra Nevada of northern California." Bioregionalism is the con-cept that political borders should not be arbitrarily imposed, but should reflect natural boundaries of geography, flora, and fauna. For instance, the Douglas fir is the definitive flora of Snyder's "Shasta bioregion" of Northern California and the Pacific Northwest. As he points out, "[t]he presence of this tree signifies a rainfall and a temperature range and will in-dicate what your agriculture might be, how steep the pitch of your roof, what raincoats you'd need."

To understand one's bioregion in Snyder's terms is to know "the spirit of a place." At a conference of Native American leaders and activists, Snyder hears a Crow elder say, "You know, I think if people stay somewhere long enough—even white people—the spirits will begin to speak to them. . . . [T]he spirits and the old powers aren't lost, they just need people to be around long enough and the spirits will begin to influence them."

Critics have sometimes complained about a surface simplic-ity in Snyder's work, particularly in his poetry. Yet what *seems* to be simplicity is nearly always the reflection and in-fluence of his Zen and Native American roots. There is a deep wellspring of wisdom and tradition that runs through-out his writing and urges us to "make a world-scale 'Natu-ral Contract' with the oceans, the air, the birds in the sky." Any serious consideration of Snyder's work, whether criti-cal text or classroom study, now must include ***The Practice of the Wild.***

Richard Tillinghast (review date 27 December 1992)

SOURCE: "Chants and Chainsaws," in *New York Times Book Review,* December 27, 1992, p. 2.

[*In the following excerpt, Tillinghast praises* No Nature *for uniting a lifetime of Snyder's work.*]

Only in our age could a poem have been written that gives an account of life in California's Sierra Nevada from the per-spective of 300 million years of natural and human history. And only Gary Snyder, with a command of geology, anthro-pology and evolutionary biology unmatched among contem-porary poets, could have written that poem, **"What Happened Here Before."**

"First a sea: soft sands, muds, and marls," the poem begins, "loading, compressing, heating, crumpling." Then 220 mil-lion years along the evolutionary trail, "warm quiet centu-ries of rains." There is an understated majesty about the ease with which Mr. Snyder puts the present into perspective. He sketches the life of California Indians: *And human people came with basket hats and nets winter-houses underground yew bows painted green, feasts and dances for the boys* and *girls songs and stories in the smoky dark.*

And when the European settlers appear in search of gold, their life is evoked with a quick brushstroke: "horses, apple-orchards, card-games, / pistol-shooting, churches, county jail."

Mr. Snyder writes in an allusive journal-entry style that owes something to Ezra Pound's later poetry, and he also follows in the lineage of Pound as the type of self-taught, extramural American scholar who follows his own compass into uncharted territory. Born in San Francisco in 1930 to working-class parents, Mr. Snyder grew up in Oregon. He worked as a logger and laborer, then manned a Forest Service lookout tower and worked on a trail-building crew in the Sierras, where he developed a love for wilderness that would later lead him into environmental politics. Somewhere along the line he found time to graduate from Reed College and to study Oriental languages at the University of California, Berkeley.

In the 1950's, he shipped out as a merchant seaman and then sojourned for 10 years in Japan, where he lived in a Buddhist monastery and learned the practice of Zen before Zen became a household word in the United States. He made a pilgrimage to the Indian subcontinent with Allen Ginsberg and others. Jack Kerouac wrote a fictional portrait of him as Japhy Ryder in the novel *The Dharma Bums.* Mr. Snyder has had the knack of anticipating trends such as environmentalism, Eastern spirituality and communal living that have later become influential in the culture at large.

Having participated in the Six Gallery reading in San Francisco that marked the first public impact of the Beat Generation as a literary phenomenon, Mr. Snyder had the staying power to play an important role in the 60's counterculture, when the environment became a political issue at the time of the People's Park demonstrations in Berkeley. His essay **"Why Tribe"** was influential among commune dwellers. He may have been the first American poet to use the word "ecology": the title of his book of prose writings **Earth House Hold** is a free rendering into plain English of what was then an unfamiliar word.

Longtime readers of Gary Snyder's poetry will have on their shelves his classic New Directions paperbacks with their austere black-and-white covers, their pages dogeared and stained from hard traveling on the overland trek to India and Nepal, rained on during camping trips to Yosemite. His new book, **No Nature,** brings together a generous sampling of the poetry and allows one to read it as one consistent lifetime's work.

Work is something this poet, who has combined a number of jobs, most of them outdoors, with his studies and his writing, evokes uncommonly well. In his poems we hear the sound of "a ringing tire iron / dropped on the pavement" and the "whang of a saw / brusht on limbs" (from **"Some Good Things to Be Said for the Iron Age"**). In **"What You Should Know to Be a Poet,"** he praises "work, long dry hours of dull work swallowed and accepted / and livd with and finally lovd." Technology, particularly old technology, fascinates him. Here, in its entirety, is **"Removing the Plate of the Pump on the Hydraulic System of the Backhoe"**: *Through mud, fouled nuts, black grime it opens, a gleam of spotless steel machined-fit perfect swirl of intake and output relentless clarity at the heart of work.*

At the same time, no one has written so forcefully against urban sprawl, pollution and mechanization, the "thousands / and thousands of cars / driving men to work." Somehow he has managed to stay outside what used to be called the System and to remain a free man. . . .

David Barber (review date June 1997)

SOURCE: Review of *No Nature,* in *Poetry* (Chicago), Vol. 164, No. 3, June, 1997, pp. 167-71.

[*In the following review of* No Nature, *Barber argues that Snyder's work has lost an element of vitality and urgency.*]

With the appearance of **Riprap** in 1959, Gary Snyder added contour and credence to the emerging claims of a Pound-Williams line of descent in midcentury American poetry, a poetics of open forms and seemingly limitless prescriptive dictums. Snyder's poems looked the part and fit the bill: they were "fields of action," they were "composed in the sequence of the musical phrase," they had a sinewy, backcountry specificity that seemed manifestly in the spirit of "no ideas but in things." They were also suggestibly radical in outlook and orientation, informed by ecology, anthropology, and regional folklore, responsive to the gravitational pull of what would later be coined the "Pacific Rim," altogether aloof to the anxieties of influence afflicting so many metrically baptized poets of Snyder's generation.

In hindsight it's easier to see that the "poetics of the new American poetry," as one widely noted anthology called it, was more of a loose amalgamation of experimental energies and polemical attitudes than any kind of true school or unified crusade. What's clearer too is that Snyder's most enduring work stands some considerable distance apart from these much-documented countercultural agitations and affiliations. Alone among his cohort, Snyder staked himself to a prosody of disciplined contemplative acuity and distilled perceptual awareness, a poetry of mindfulness rather than intellect, a tradition of Asian quietism and concision, craft so well-tempered and translucent that it borders on artlessness:

> Down valley a smoke haze
> Three days heat, after five days rain
> Pitch glows on the fir-cones
> Across rocks and meadows
> Swarms of new flies .
>
> I cannot remember the things I once read
> A few friends, but they are in cities.
> Drinking cold snow-water from a tin cup
> Looking down for miles
> Through high still air.

"Mid-August at Sourdough Mountain Lookout"

What made this poem original and disarming—genuinely radical, even—in the late '50s remains largely undiminished: lines governed by pulse and cadence as opposed to regular stresses, phrasing that's at once telegraphic and meticulously scored, emotion and significance entrusted to the inner workings of rhythm, measure, and syntax rather than given over to the self-dramatizing dynamics of tone, style, or "voice." Here on the opening page of *No Nature,* we can see that Snyder has already advanced well beyond an ideogramic method a la Pound, has already transformed technique into temperament. Nor is this limpid mastery mainly a paradigmatic instance of an "Oriental" manner smoothly assumed. The form and demeanor may point us to Far Eastern models of thought and expression, but the ear that parses this poem's measure is cannily attuned to the grain of English, to the patterns and tolerances of sound that run beneath the surface of the poet's native tongue. It's the same knowing counter-balance that's evident in a later Snyder poem that's rightfully become a favorite anthology piece, **"Pine Tree Tops"**:

> in the blue night
> frost haze, the sky glows
> with the moon
> pine tree tops
> bend snow-bluè, fade
> into sky, frost, starlight.
> the creak of boots.
> rabbit tracks, deer tracks,
> what do we know.

Snyder's seductive offhandedness has had many imitators, but he really has no peer when it comes to this spare mode of spacious utterance. Part of the secret lies in how coolly Snyder sheds the overfamiliar first-person singular that dominates the vast share of American lyric poetry: in effacing himself to the point where all that remains is "the creak of boots," he also liberates himself from a vision of the natural world overshadowed by the Egotistical Sublime of the English Romantics. The linguistic torque of "bend snow-blue, fade / into sky" is worth a fortnight of "craft" workshops; the vernacular inscrutability of those closing three lines epitomizes the comingling of naturalism and mysticism that has been one of Snyder's most singular contributions to the poetic sensibility of his day.

Snyder has also excelled through the years at writing a quite different kind of meditative poem, so-called poems of "process" in which the rhythmic and verbal cast aims at embodying not charged stillness but the apprehended experience of recurrence and flux. The conception is clearly an outgrowth of Snyder's deep and abiding immersion in Buddhism and his preoccupation with what he refers to in one essay as "the mythological present," but in practice these philosophical trappings are neither as abstruse or ethereal as a generalized description makes them sound. On the contrary, this attention to the interconnectedness of matter and spirit has prompted Snyder to write a handful of stirring homages to human labor and rugged toil—celebrations of "Wedge and sledge, peavey and maul / little axe, canteen, piggyback can / of saw-mix gas and oil for the chain, / knapsack of files and goggles and rags" (**"Getting in the Wood"**) or of the arduous chore of stowing away **"Hay for the Horses"**: "With winch and ropes and hooks / We stacked the bales up clean / To splintery redwood rafters / High in the dark . . . / Itch of haydust in the / sweaty shirt and shoes." These poems help remind us that Snyder has never been a "nature poet" in the conventional sense of the term, any more than he's presumed to be a Zen master or a modern shaman. Few contemporary poets have written with such authentic incisiveness about the particulars of work and the rhythms of subsistence, and done so without succumbing to class-rooted righteousness or rural nostalgia.

Snyder's most realized work holds up so well precisely because its intrinsic precepts stem from sources and traditions other than the strictly literary. It's also earned Snyder a wider readership and broader cultural relevance than most serious poets ever come close to mustering, especially those who deliberately swim clear of the mainstream. *No Nature* suggests, however, that all this has been something of a mixed blessing: the vigor and output of Snyder's poetry has clearly been on the wane over the last 20 years, even as his social and ethical insights have gained stronger currency. Combing through these forty-odd years of work, one is struck by how even the more obscure and diffuse efforts from his early to mid career—the totemic, incantatory sequences from *Myths and Texts,* the oracular songs and Japanese settings of *Regarding Wave*—exude an urgency and restlessness that's all but dissolved in the poems Snyder's published since his Pulitzer-winning 1974 collection *Turtle Island.* The younger Snyder wouldn't have abided the looseness, not to mention the unexamined sentiment, of the opening lines from **"For All"** ("Ah to be alive / on a mid-September morn / fording a stream / barefoot") and would have found a way to keep the truths articulated in a poem like **"Axe Handles"** from shading off into truisms: "And I see: Pound was an axe, / Chen was an axe, I am an axe / And my son a handle, soon / To be shaping again, model / And tool, craft of culture, / How we go on." The poet who was formerly adept at elucidating intimations now seems to be content with simply espousing positions.

It would be churlish to point out that the younger Snyder also wasn't university professor, a member of the American Academy of Arts and Letters, or an official California poet laureate (so named during the tenure of former governor Jerry Brown, who makes suitably offbeat appearances in a couple of Snyder's later poems here). Only avowed detractors will want to claim that worldly success has softened the man or left him overly fond of playing the sage. The best of Snyder's newer poems are leavened with a humor and self-deprecation that some readers may find a refreshing departure from the hermetic portentousness that runs through his best-known books; a mildness and crinkle-eyed autumnal serenity has replaced the old avid thirst for enlightenment. In **"The Sweat"** he says as much: "Older is smarter and more tasty. / Minds tough and funny—many lovers— / At the end of days of talking / Science, writing, values, spirit, politics, poems—." And while it's true that Snyder's mellowness is often indistinguishable from an easiness, an absence of animating drive, it also strengthens one's conviction that he's resisted the temptation from the beginning to write programmatically or to fall back on the tried-and-true for the sake of generating material. Snyder's essential poems would make for a far more slender volume than the bulky assemblage in *No Nature,* yet they would more than clinch the case that Snyder ranks among the small company of figures who have vitally altered the way American poetry moves and breathes.

Christopher Benfey (review date 24 March 1997)

SOURCE: "The Critter Poet," in *The New Republic,* Vol. 216, No. 12, March 24, 1997, pp. 38-42.

[*In the following review, Benfey reconsiders Snyder's career from the 1950s to the present.*]

Gary Snyder was a character in a novel before he published his own first book. In Jack Kerouac's *The Dharma Bums,* that vivid account of the birth of the San Francisco Poetry Renaissance and the Beat movement, there is a biographi-

cal sketch of Japhy Ryder, "the number one Dharma Bum of them all":

> Japhy Ryder was a kid from eastern Oregon brought up in a log cabin deep in the woods with his father and mother and sister, from the beginning a woods boy, an axman, farmer, interested in animals and Indian lore so that when he finally got to college by hook or crook he was already well equipped for his early studies in anthropology and later in Indian myth and in the actual texts of Indian mythology. Finally he learned Chinese and Japanese and became an Oriental scholar and discovered the greatest Dharma Bums of them all, the Zen Lunatics of China and Japan. At the same time, being a Northwest boy with idealistic tendencies, he got interested in oldfashioned I.W.W. anarchism and learned to play the guitar and sing old worker songs to go with his Indian songs and general folksong interests.

This is the beginning of the Snyder myth. For all I know, and for all that I can glean from Snyder's autobiographical writings, it is entirely true.

What makes *The Dharma Bums* a pleasure to read, forty years after its publication, is the way Kerouac, in the guise of his ordinary-Joe narrator, undercuts Japhy Ryder's humorless, self-satisfied ethos. Ray, the writer's stand-in, walks into Japhy's shack, and there is Japhy "sitting cross-legged on a Paisley pillow on a straw mat, with his spectacles on, making him look old and scholarly and wise, with book on lap and the little tin teapot and porcelain cup steaming at his side. He looked up very peacefully, saw who it was, said, 'Ray come in,' and bent his eyes again to the script." "What you doing?" "Translating Han Shan's great poem called 'Cold Mountain' written a thousand years ago some of it scribbled on the sides of cliffs hundreds of miles away from any other living beings." "Wow." Japhy proceeds to teach Ray all about Asian poetry and culture, including the proper way to have sex. When Ray walks in on Japhy, in the lotus position, making meditative love ("*yabyum*") to a woman called Princess, Japhy explains that "This is what they do in the temples of Tibet. It's a holy ceremony, it's done just like this in front of chanting priests. People pray and recite Om Mani Pahdme Hum, which means Amen the Thunderbolt in the Dark Void. I'm the thunderbolt and Princess is the dark void, you see."

A part of Gary Snyder's considerable prestige in the small world of American poetry is owed to the impression that he has put in the time and done the work: graduate study in anthropology at Berkeley; summers on lookout duty in national forests and parks ("The prolonged stay in mountain huts . . . gave me my first opportunity to seriously sit cross-legged"); ten years in Japan, mainly in the 1960s, doing Zen and studying Japanese aesthetics; his current roughhewn life with his family on a hundred acres in the Sierra foothills, with a teaching appointment in English and ecology at the University of California at Davis. All this experience has gone into Snyder's poetry, the best of which manages to suppress his didactic side.

Snyder at his most moving is an elegiac poet, mourning the loss of forests, "critters" (as he calls animals), lovers, places. Snyder at his most annoying is the pedantic guv on the Paisley pillow who says, "I'm the thunderbolt and Princess is the dark void, you see." To those of us in whose early intellectual lives Snyder was a significant chapter, a return to his work after long absence can have its own embarrassments. When I was 17, spending a year in Japan, Snyder's *The Back Country* (1968) was one of the books that I carried everywhere with me. My favorite poem in it, which I still know by heart, was **"December at Yase,"** the last of the **"Four Poems for Robin."** It begins:

> You said, that October,
> In the tall dry grass by the orchard
> When you chose to be free,
> "Again someday, maybe ten years."
>
> After college I saw you
> One time. You were strange.
> And I was obsessed with a plan.

Ten years and more go by, in which the poet considers trying to win the woman's love back. "I didn't. / I thought I must make it alone. I / Have done that." The poem concludes:

> Only in dream, like this dawn,
> Does the grave, awed intensity
> Of our young love
> Return to my mind, to my flesh.
>
> We had what the others
> All crave and seek for;
> We left it behind at nineteen.
>
> I feel ancient, as though I had
> Lived many lives.
> And may never now know
> If I am a fool
> Or have done what my
> karma demands.

I can't say whether this poem is any good. It's too close to me, and it too perfectly captures some of my own feelings from those days. I can see now how the poem uses little clumps of Imagist detail, drawn from Pound's translations from the Chinese: "in the tall dry grass by the orchard," and

how the enjambment is rather arch: "After college I saw you / One time." But, even when I was young, I knew that those last two lines about karma were a disaster. (They're crossed out in my battered copy of the book.) What they show is that Snyder, as he looks back on his early obsession "with a plan," still subscribes to one, a higher one, which he now calls "karma." All the uncertainty and the wistfulness and the delicacy of the rest of the poem is caught in the harsh headlights of "what my karma demands."

Something similar happens toward the end of what may be Snyder's best and most enduring poem, **"I Went into the Maverick Bar"** (from *Turtle Island,* 1974):

> I went into the Maverick Bar
> In Farmington, New Mexico.
> And drank double shots of bourbon
>   backed with beer.
> My long hair was tucked up under a cap
> I'd left the earning in the car.
> Two cowboys did horseplay
>   by the pool tables,
> A waitress asked us
>   where are you from?
> a country-and-western band began to play
> "We don't smoke Marijuana in Muskokie"
> And with the next song,
>   a couple began to dance.
> They held each other like in High School
>   dances in the fifties;
> I recalled when I worked in the woods
>   and the bars of Madras,
>   Oregon.
> That short-haired joy and
>   roughness—America—
>   your stupidity.
> I could almost love you
>   again.
> We left—onto the freeway
>   shoulders—under the
>   tough old stars—
> In the shadow of bluffs
>   I came back to myself,
> To the real work, to
>   "What is to be done."

Snyder's pleasure in being able to "pass" for a macho man is nicely rendered here, and the temptations of that life are palpable in the poem. But the rejection of "that short-haired joy and roughness" is too pat in those final two lines. One wishes this guy weren't quite so certain about the nature of the "real work," a favorite phrase of Snyder's. The revolutionary readiness of Lenin's old phrase, "what is to be done," sends a chain-saw through all that romance in the bar. Snyder knows that the dancing couples are part of the problem, and that he has the solutions. He's like the wistful revolutionary who muses, "What a beautiful church. I was baptized here. Too bad I have to blow it up."

Prescriptions for "the real work" and lists of "what is to be done" dominate Snyder's prose, much of which is collected in *A Place in Space*. On reducing world population, for example:

> Try to correct traditional cultural attitudes that tend to force women into childbearing; remove income-tax deductions for more than two children above a specified income level, and scale it so that lower income families are forced to be careful, too.... Explore other social structures and marriage forms, such as group marriage and polyandrous marriage, which provide family life but many less children.

The decisive verbs here are "correct" and "force." Correct those wrongheaded cultural attitudes and force those poor families to be careful.

In recent years, Snyder has become a popular speaker on the Green circuit. He is the unofficial poet laureate of the environmentalist movement. A few years ago, he exhorted the graduating class of Reed College, his alma mater: "Let's go on into the twenty-first century lean, mean, and green." (No quibble with lean and green, but why mean?) In his recent prose, Snyder is particularly attentive to the link between "endangered cultures and species." He insists that "the destruction of cultural diversity goes hand in hand with ecological destruction." So he's a strong proponent of ethnopoetics, "the study of the poetries and poetics of nonliterary peoples," which he compares to "some field of zoology that is studying disappearing species."

But, while Snyder loves nonliterary poetry, he seems to have little fondness for the literary kind, especially if it comes from the West. As he sees it, Western poetry is dominated by "the Judeo-Christian-Cartesian view of nature (by which complex views all developed nations excuse themselves for their drastically destructive treatment of the landscape)." That's quite a three-headed monster, the Cerberus of Western culture, but I don't see what critters have to fear from it. Why should Jews or Christians or Descartes be held as prime suspects in crimes of ecological disaster? I'm sure Snyder has in mind some vague notion of a sinister "dualism," as against the "holistic" conceptions of nature and humanity presumably found everywhere else on the globe. He evidently assumes that such arguments and objections no longer need to be spelled out.

Snyder's prose is laced with American Indian sayings and Zen proverbs and Chinese epigrams, but he almost never quotes a "Western" poet. In a talk on **"Unnatural Writing,"**

he does pause to take a swipe at two lines by Howard Nemerov: "Civilization, mirrored in language, is the garden where relations grow," wrote Nemerov, "outside the garden is the wild abyss." While Nemerov may be, as Snyder patronizingly calls him, "a good poet and a decent man," he is, judging from these lines, an enemy of nature, and in need of correction:

> The unexamined assumptions here are fascinating. They are, at worst, crystallizations of the erroneous views that enable the developed world to displace Third and Fourth World peoples and over-exploit nature globally. Nemerov here proposes that language is somehow implicitly civilized or civilizing, that civilization is orderly, that intrahuman relations are the pinnacle of experience (as though all of us, and all life on the planet, were not interrelated), and that "wild" means "abyssal," disorderly, and chaotic.

Poor Nemerov, displacer of Third and Fourth World peoples, all because he suggested that language is better equipped for gardens than for wilderness. But even Whitman, whom one might have expected to garner some praise from Snyder, is chastised for his errors of thought, in a talk that Snyder delivered in Spain on the hundredth anniversary of Whitman's death:

> Whitman is unexcelled in his attribution of a kind of divinity to ordinary (white) men and women. However, the respect and authenticity he gives to human beings is not extended to nonhuman creatures.

But is this true? Here's the fourteenth section of "Song of Myself" (1891-92):

> The wild gander leads his flock through the
>   cool night,
> *Ya-honk* he says, and sounds it down to me
>   like an invitation,
> The pert may suppose it meaningless,
>   but I listening close,
> Find its purpose and place up there toward
>   the wintry sky.

This is the Whitman who said, "I think I could turn and live with animals. . . . They do not sweat and whine about their condition, They do not lie awake in the dark and weep for their sins"; the Whitman who said, when his tread scared the wood-drake and the wood-duck, "I believe in those wing'd purposes"; who said, "And the look of the bay mare shames silliness out of me."

But Snyder has not been reading *Leaves of Grass*. His dismissal of Whitman, it turns out, is based on a cursory reading of *Democratic Vistas,* in which, according to Snyder, "we miss the presence of people of color, of Native Americans, of wilderness, or even the plain landscape." Well, then, one feels like shouting at Snyder, why don't you read Whitman's damn poetry, in which you will find all these things, and in richer and more convincing profusion than in any other American poet of his time or after?

Snyder's prose is too often chastising, moralizing, didactic. His best essay by far is called **"Crawling,"** a three-page description of what it feels like to navigate on one's stomach through the Sierra underbrush:

> No way to travel off the trail but to dive in: down on your hands and knees on the crunchy manzanita leaf cover and crawl around between the trunks. Leather work gloves, a tight-fitting hat, long-sleeved denim work jacket, and old Filson tin pants make a proper crawler's outfit. Along the ridge a ways, and then down a steep slope through the brush, belly-sliding on snow and leaves like an otter—you get limber at it. . . . To go where bears, deer, raccoons, foxes—all our other neighbors—go, you have to be willing to crawl.

This is fresh and exhilarating. It reads like a poet's prose. "You can *smell* the fall mushrooms when crawling." There are perhaps a dozen pages like this in *A Place in Space.*

Already in that Berkeley shack, on April 8, 1956, Snyder had begun *Mountains and Rivers Without End,* a title that—as sections were published across forty years—came to seem predictive. Now Snyder has declared the poem finished, and published it in a handsome volume, with the twelfth-century Chinese scroll painting that inspired it reproduced on the endpapers. He has appended a helpful essay on the making of the poem, as well as explanatory notes and a publication record of where the many parts of the long poem first appeared.

Do the many sections of *Mountains and Rivers* comprise a single long poem? If so, it's a pretty loose and baggy one. The guiding metaphor of the structure of the poem is the gradual unfolding of the painted scroll, with the reading and viewing eye following the progress of a journey through a landscape of mountains and rivers. The book opens with a masterly description—in the tradition of ekphrasis, or writing inspired by a painting—of the painting in the Cleveland Museum of Art that serves as Snyder's muse.

> Rider and walker cross a bridge
> above a frothy braided torrent
> that descends from a flurry of roofs
>   like flowers
> temples tucked between cliffs,

a side trail goes there. . . .

Snyder doesn't ignore the seals and the writings at the end of the scroll, added by owners and connoisseurs. One of these jottings says: ". . . Most people can get along with the noise of dogs and chickens; / Everybody cheerful in these peaceful times. / But I—why are my tastes so odd? I love the company of streams and boulders." It's clear that Snyder conceives of his poem as another such tribute, added to the scroll by a poet-connoisseur many centuries later.

Mountains and Rivers is best read as a sort of autobiographical journey in verse and verbal collage. Some of the earliest written sections have a distinctly period feel, with Bob Dylan rhymes—"Fat man in a Chevrolet / wants to go back to L.A."—and hitchhiking lyricism—"Caught a ride the only car come by / at seven in the morning / chewing froze salami / riding with a passed-out L.A. whore / glove compartment full of booze, / the driver a rider, / nobody cowboy, / sometime hood, / Like me picked up to drive / & drive the blues away. / We drank to Portland / and we treated that girl good." The more recently written sections arise from Snyder's current preoccupations with species loss and "cultural genocide." To my ear, the most rewarding passages are those in which Snyder imagines a world of wild nature beneath the structures of civilization, as in **"Walking the New York Bedrock / Alive in the Sea of Information"**:

> Squalls
> From the steps leading down to the subway.
> Blue-chested runner, a female,
>   on car streets,
> Red lights block traffic but she like the
> Beam of a streetlight in the whine of
>   the Skilsaw,
> She runs right through.
> A cross street leads toward a river
> North goes to the woods
> South takes you fishing
> Peregrines nest at the thirty-fifth floor. . .

Snyder's populist take on the "cliffdwellers" in their high-rises reads like something out of an updated Dreiser: "Towers, up there the / Clean crisp white dress white skin / women and men / who occupy sunnier niches, / Higher up on the layered stratigraphy cliffs, get / More photosynthesis, flow by more ostracods, / get more sushi, / Gather more flesh, have delightful / Cascading laughs. . . ." But when Snyder attempts to merge entirely with the world of "nature," his poetry can descend into bathos, as in his sub-Whitmanian love song to a river, **"The Flowing"** (1974): "The root of me / hardens and lifts to you, / thick flowing river, / my skin shivers. I quit / making this poem." Better the pithy, no-ideas-but-in-things observations of **"Old Woodrat's Stinky House"**: "A venerable desert woodrat nest of twigs and shreds / plastered down with ambered urine / a family house in use eight thousand years."

Snyder discerns a tension between the mountains and rivers of his title, between "the tough spirit of willed self-discipline and the generous and loving spirit of concern for all beings." There is a similar split in Snyder as well. His less savory side is the disciplined commissar of "what is to be done," with his endless lists of "corrections," and his self-satisfied certainty that he is living the good life while most of us are going to the dogs. But the Snyder I treasure is the wry and grizzled wilderness dweller, generously at ease in both the garden and the wild, who can cheerfully admit: "My wife Carole and I are now using computers, the writer's equivalent of a nice little chainsaw," and then add, "Chainsaws and computers increase both macho productivity and nerdy stress." That sounds to me like the Snyder who goes into the Maverick Bar and feels at home there, and can almost love America's stupidity.

FURTHER READING

Criticism

Burt, Stephen. A Review of *Mountains and Rivers Without End,* by Gary Snyder. *Yale Review* 85, No. 3 (July 1987): 150-54.
> Mixed review of *Mountains and Rivers Without End.*

Carpenter, David A. "Gary Snyder's Inhumanism, from *Riprap* to *Axe Handles.*" *South Dakota Review* 26, No. 1 (Spring 1988): 110-38.
> Argues that Snyder has allowed political messages to overshadow the creative voice of his poetry.

Costello, Bonnie. "The Soil and Man's Intelligence: Three Contemporary Landscape Poets." *Contemporary Literature* 30, No. 3 (Fall 1989): 412-33.
> Explores the varying conceptualizations of landscape in the poetry of A. R. Ammons, Charles Wright, and Snyder.

Denney, Reuel. "The Portable Pagoda: Asia and America in the Work of Gary Snyder." In *Asian and Western Writers in Dialogue: New Cultural Identities,* pp. 115-36, edited by Guy Amirthanayagam. London: Macmillan Press, 1982.
> Considers the American and Asian influences on Snyder's poetry.

Duane, Daniel. "A Poem, 40 Years Long." *New York Times Magazine* (6 October 1996): 62.
> Reviews *Mountains and Rivers Without End* and explains the collection's forty-year history.

Howard, Richard. "Three Found Poets." *Poetry* CXXVI, No. 6 (September 1975): 346-51.
> Praises the style and themes of the poetry in *Turtle Island.*

Howes, Victor. "Poets on Different Borders." *Christian Science Monitor* (29 May 1968): 11.
> Reviews *The Back Country* and describes Snyder's poetry as plain and spare.

Klien, Michael. "Stay Together, Learn the Flowers, Go Light." *The Kenyon Review* XVI, No. 1 (Winter 1994): 198-205.
> Reviews *No Nature* and compares Snyder's earlier and more recent poetry.

Lavazzi, Tom. "Pattern of Flux: Sex, Buddhism, and Ecology in Gary Snyder's Poetry." *Sagetrieb* 8, Nos. 1-2 (Spring-Fall 1989): 41-68.
> Considers the unique methods Snyder employs to evoke his subject matter.

Leed, Jacob. "Gary Snyder: An Unpublished Preface." *Journal of Modern Literature* 13, No. 1 (March 1986): 177-79.
> Considers Snyder's work as a translator of Japanese poetry.

Martin, Julia. "The Pattern Which Connects: Metaphor in Gary Snyder's Later Poetry." *Western American Literature* 22, No. 2 (Summer 1987): 99-123.
> Argues that Snyder employs metaphor to address the interconnectedness of life.

McNally, Dennis. "Prophets on the Burning Shore: Jack Kerouac, Gary Snyder, and San Francisco." In *A Literary History of the American West,* pp. 482-95. Fort Worth: Texas Christian University Press, 1987.
> Compares the life and works of Snyder and Jack Kerouac.

Murphy, Patrick D. "Penance or Perception: Spirituality and Land in the Poetry of Gary Snyder and Wendell Berry." In *Earthly Words: Essays on Contemporary American Nature and Environmental Writers,* pp. 237-49, edited by John Cooley. Ann Arbor: University of Michigan Press, 1994.
> Considers the work of Wendell Berry and Snyder in the context of the Judeo-Christian tradition.

Murphy, Patrick D. "Two Different Paths in the Quest for Place: Gary Snyder and Wendell Berry." *American Poetry* 2, No. 1 (Fall 1984): 60-8.
> Explores the similarities and differences in the environmental thinking of Wendell Berry and Snyder.

Nichols, William. "Environmentalism and the Legitimacy of Hope." *The Kenyon Review* XVIII, Nos. 3-4 (Summer-Fall 1996): 206-13.

> Places Snyder's *A Place in Space* in the context of other contemporary environmental writing.

Parkinson, Thomas. "The Poetry of Gary Snyder." In *American Writing Today*, pp. 376-87, edited by Richard Kostelanetz. Troy, New York: Whitston Publishing Company, 1991.

> Considers Snyder's use of prosody, meter, and rhythm.

Schultz, Robert and David Wyatt. "Gary Snyder and the Curve of Return." *Virginia Quarterly Review* 62, No. 4 (Autumn 1986): 681-94.

> Considers the recurring themes in Snyder's works.

Additional coverage of Snyder's life and career is contained in the following sources published by Gale: *Contemporary Authors*, Vols. 17-20 [rev. ed.]; *Contemporary Authors New Revision Series*, Vols. 30, 60; *Dictionary of Literary Biography*, Vols. 5, 16, 165; *DISCovering Authors Modules*; and *Poetry Criticism*, Vol. 21.

Amy Tan

1952-

(Full name Amy Ruth Tan) Chinese American novelist.

The following entry presents an overview of Tan's career through 1996. For further information on her life and works, see *CLC,* Volume 59.

INTRODUCTION

Amy Tan gained immediate popularity and garnered high praise from critics with her first novel, *The Joy Luck Club* (1989). The novel explores the unique situation of the Asian-American immigrant, but has universal appeal in its expression of the conflict inherent in mother-daughter relationships. Tan's next two novels were also both popular and highly acclaimed.

Biographical Information

Tan's father, John Tan, an engineer and Baptist minister, immigrated to the United States from China in 1947. Her mother, Daisy, came to the United States from China in 1949, leaving behind three daughters from a previous marriage. Tan was born in Oakland, California, in 1952, and given the Chinese name En-Mai (Blessing of America). Throughout her childhood, Tan's mother told her stories about her Chinese heritage, and she uses these stories in her fiction to emphasize the importance of the act of storytelling. Tan lost both her older brother Peter and her father to brain cancer in the late 1960s. After their deaths, her mother decided to move the rest of the family to Europe in order to escape what she felt to be the evil of their diseased house in California. Tan rebelled while in Europe and was arrested when only sixteen years old. When her family returned to the United States, she entered Linfield College in Oregon, where she intended to study medicine, but decided to pursue a degree in English. Tan transferred to San Jose State University, where she earned her bachelor of arts degree in 1973. In 1974 she married Lou DiMattei and received her master's degree in English and linguistics. Tan enrolled in the doctoral program at the University of California Berkeley, but withdrew from the program in 1976 after the murder of her best friend. From 1976 to 1981 she worked as a language-development specialist for disabled children. She edited a medical journal and worked as a technical writer during the 1980s. Her first novel, *The Joy Luck Club,* brought her instant acclaim and rose quickly on the *New York Times* best-seller list. She followed her initial success with a second critically acclaimed novel, *The Kitchen God's Wife* (1991).

Major Works

Through sixteen interconnected stories told by four immigrants from China and their four American-born daughters, *The Joy Luck Club* illuminates the nature of mother-daughter relationships in both cultures. The theme of Tan's novel focuses on the impact of past generations on the present. The structure, in which the daughters' eight stories are enveloped by those of the mothers, implies that the older generation may hold a key to resolving the problems of the young. *The Kitchen God's Wife* again tackles mother-daughter relationships, but this time Tan limits herself to one family and the relationship between Winnie Louie and her daughter Pearl. The relationship between Winnie Louie and Pearl is strained because of the secrets they keep from each other. It is only when they reveal their secrets that they establish a connection. *The Moon Lady* (1992) is a children's story based on an episode from *The Joy Luck Club* which is derived from a Chinese legend. In *The Hundred Secret Senses* (1995), Tan focuses on the relationship between two sisters: Olivia, an American-born daughter of a Chinese father, and Kwan; her older Chinese-born sister from her father's previous marriage. The conflict in this novel arises from Kwan's mystical belief in ghosts and previous lives and Olivia's pragmatic attachment to the concrete and the real.

Critical Reception

Praising Tan's storytelling abilities, commentators note that the chapters of *The Joy Luck Club* could stand on their own as short stories. Merle Rubin asserted, "Each story is a gem, complete in itself. Yet each is further enhanced by its relationship (direct or indirect) with the others." Tan is often compared to Maxine Hong Kingston in her presentation of the Asian immigrant's experience in America. Criticism leveled against Tan includes the implausibility of *The Hundred Secret Senses,* particularly the physical evidence of Kwan's previous life; and reviewers question the authenticity of Tan's descriptions of Chinese life in her novels, even though others cite her particularization of Chinese culture as one of her greatest talents. Helen Yglesias stated that "it is through vivid minutiae that Tan more often exercises her particular charm." Reviewers consistently laud Tan's gift as a storyteller and the compelling nature of her narratives. Elgy Gillespie stated, "Once again I found myself reading Amy Tan all night, unable to put the story down until I knew what happened in the end, sniffling when I got to the sad bits . . . and finally going to sleep at dawn with the conviction that Tan had provided an education for the heart."

PRINCIPAL WORKS

The Joy Luck Club (novel) 1989
The Kitchen God's Wife (novel) 1991
The Moon Lady (children's literature) 1992
The Joy Luck Club [with Ronald Bass] (screenplay) 1993
The Chinese Siamese Cat (children's literature) 1994
The Hundred Secret Senses (novel) 1995

CRITICISM

Merle Rubin (review date 21 April 1989)

SOURCE: "Chinese-American 'Bridge' Club," in *Christian Science Monitor,* Vol. 81, No. 102, April 21, 1989, p. 13.

[*In the following review, Rubin asserts, "In Tan's hands, these linked stories [of* The Joy Luck Club]—*diverse as they are—fit almost magically into a powerfully coherent novel."*]

Amy Tan's first novel, *The Joy Luck Club,* is a touching, funny, sad, insightful, and artfully constructed group portrait of four mother-daughter relationships that endure not only

a generation gap, but the more unbridgeable gap between two cultures.

The Joy Luck Club is an informal "institution" started by Suyuan Woo upon her arrival in San Francisco in 1949. Suyuan finds three other Chinese immigrant women to play mah jongg, cook and consume special foods, tell stories, gossip, invest in stocks, and plan for joy and luck. In the years that follow, the club links the four families, enabling them to pool resources and keeping them in touch with their past as they take on the challenges of adjusting to a new country.

Nearly 40 years after the first meeting, as the novel opens, Suyuan Woo has died and her place at the mah jongg table is assumed by her 36-year-old daughter, Jing-mei. Like many another American-born child of immigrants, Jing-mei has little understanding of her mother's values or the world that shaped them, although recently, the general interest in ethnicity has prompted her to revive her Chinese name, "Jing-mei," in preference to the American "June May," and has made her more curious about her roots.

When her Joy Luck "aunties" (Lindo Jong, An-mei Hsu, and Ying-ying St. Clair) offer Jing-mei a trip to China to meet her long-lost half sisters, whom Suyuan was forced to abandon as infants while fleeing war-torn Guilin, the "aunties" (now edging into their 70s) urge Jing-mei to tell her half sisters the story of the mother they never knew. The trouble is, Jing-mei feels she never really knew her mother, either—a feeling shared by the other Joy Luck daughters: Waverly Jong, Rose Hsu Jordan, and Lena St. Clair. The daughters' difficulty in comprehending their mothers is echoed by the mothers' frustration at not being able to pass on the benefits of their accumulated wisdom and experience.

> **Amy Tan's first novel, *The Joy Luck Club,* is a touching, funny, sad, insightful, and artfully constructed group portrait of four mother-daughter relationships that endure not only a generation gap, but the more unbridgeable gap between two cultures.**
> **—Merle Rubin**

The 16 linked stories that make up this novel fill in both sides of the gap: four sections of four stories each, told by seven voices. In the first section, "Feathers from a Thousand *Li* Away," we hear the voices of the four mothers (with the exception of the late Suyuan Woo, whose story is told by Jing-mei), each with a memorable, even shocking, tale of life in China. The next two sections contain stories by the four daughters: recollections of mother-dominated childhoods under the rubric "The Twenty-Six Malignant Gates" (a Chinese book spelling out the various hazards—26 of them—awaiting hapless infants) and accounts of adult life under the heading "American Translation." In the fourth section, "Queen Mother of the Western Skies," the mothers speak again, this time about their lives in America and their daughters, and in the closing story, Jing-mei goes to China to meet her half sisters.

Each story is a gem, complete in itself. Yet each is further enhanced by its relationship (direct or indirect) with the others. The range is remarkable: The author deftly captures the neurotic comedy of contemporary life styles and the scarring tragedies of the hidden Chinese past.

It's amazing how much plot, character, drama, and atmosphere are crammed into these short (15-page) narratives: the comic warfare of mothers competing over whose daughter is the most talented; the bitter experiences of a Chinese concubine; the ingenuity of a Chinese girl faced with the *fait accompli* of an arranged marriage; the courage of a mother struggling to cope with the loss of a child. By the time we are through, we—and Jing-mei—fully appreciate the determination and pathos of the mothers' efforts to mold their daughters' characters, as well as the daughters' inevitable reactions.

As a testament of Chinese-American life, **The Joy Luck Club** may well be compared to Maxine Hong Kingston's *China Men* and *The Woman Warrior.* Like them, it makes exceptionally good use of short stories to present the many strands of an intricate cultural tapestry. Tan's style is warmer and less austere than Kingston's, and her subject matter offers a more direct emotional appeal to the reader.

In Tan's hands, these linked stories—diverse as they are—fit almost magically into a powerfully coherent novel, whose winning combination of ingredients—immigrant experience, mother-daughter ties, Pacific Rim culture—make it a book with the "good luck" to be in the right place at the right time. This first novel is a featured alternate of two major book clubs and is being serialized in four magazines. It also happens to be a novel that deserves its fortune.

Scarlet Cheng (review date Summer 1989)

SOURCE: "Your Mother is in Your Bones," in *Belles Lettres,* Vol. 4, No. 4, Summer, 1989, p. 12.

[*In the following review, Cheng praises Tan's* The Joy Luck Club *for its accessibility and vision.*]

With clarity of voice and lucidity of vision, Amy Tan's delightful first novel, **The Joy Luck Club,** reveals to us that

for all life's contradictions and tragedies, the true path of existence is convergence.

This is a hard faith to hold when modern life seems so cacophonous, so divisive. But it is key for immigrants to this country who must try to adjust to the new world without being swallowed up by it, who must raise children whose first impulse is to reject their cultural heritage. The frustration is especially deep for those immigrants cut off from their homeland, as were the Chinese who fled from the extremist politics and social upheaval of postwar China.

Tan's book revolves around four such immigrant women and their daughters, each chapter unfolding in the first-person voice of one of them. Some begin their tale far back in China, a world of traditions both suffocating and embracing; some start here in the United States, where the plethora of choices sometimes leads to making the wrong one. All are beautifully interwoven with legend and memory, archetype and longing. Like Maxine Hong Kingston's brilliant *The Woman Warrior,* published more than a decade ago, these tales blend the mythical and the mundane, and the endings are often astonishing connections of the two.

The mothers meet in California shortly after World War II and form a mah jong quartet, the Joy Luck Club. Even under hard-pressed financial and social conditions, they sit down regularly to play at the noisy game of tiles, to eat delicacies, and to "say stories." The daughters are born in the Chinese ghettos of California, growing up ashamed of their un-mainstream backgrounds and eccentric mothers.

With the mothers and daughters split by historical, geographic, and cultural experience, misunderstandings and cross purposes abound. As the novel begins, Jing-mei "June" Woo, the central "I" of the novel, sits down with mixed emotions to the Joy Luck Club table. She is taking the place of her mother, who has recently died, and must overcome her lifelong view of the club as a "shameful Chinese custom, like the secret gatherings of the Ku Klux Klan or the tom-tom dances of TV Indians preparing for war."

Unexpectedly, the three "aunties" reveal that her mother's first two children—daughters left behind in China—are alive. They give her the mission of returning to China to tell them about their mother. June protests that she did not really know her. "Not know your own mother?" one auntie cries out. "How can you say? Your mother is in your bones!"

Conversations with the "aunties" remind June of painful distances: "My mother and I never really understood one another. We translated each other's meanings and I seemed to hear less than what was said, while my mother heard more."

Language itself has been a major gap. When June's mother

once tried to explain the difference between Jewish mah jong and Chinese mah jong, June's puzzlement led her to think, "These kinds of explanations made me feel my mother and I spoke two different languages, which we did. I talked to her in English, she answered back in Chinese." The two languages are literal, as well as figurative, because even in English the mothers speak with the cadence and the mindset of the Chinese. While they frequently mangle idioms—"college drop-off" for college drop-out and "so-so security" for social security—these inadvertent neologisms are uncannily apt, as are the mothers' twisted observations of American life.

Tan also demonstrates that a fundamental faith in invisible forces pervades traditional Chinese culture and that this, too, divides the first and second generations. For example, Waverly Jong is taught the "art of invisible strength" at the age of six by her mother. When Waverly launches on an unexpected career as a junior chess champion, her mother proudly shepherds her around, dispensing folksy advice like, "It is just tricks. You blow from the North, South, East, and West. The other person becomes confused. They don't know which way to run."

But being modern and increasingly cocky with her success, Waverly resents what she feels to be her mother's misplaced credit taking. One day she tells her mother off on a Chinatown street, and this, incredibly, is the beginning of the end of her prodigious career. Too late, "I realized my mother knew more tricks than I had thought."

Amy Tan has managed to express the sense and sensibility of being Chinese in a remarkably accessible way, while remaining uncompromisingly true to her own experience, her own vision. Each chapter has a self-contained quality—several were published individually in magazines—and is a marvel unto itself. However, they are tied together so adroitly in the end that your mind burns long afterward, and the book's dedication to Tan's mother and "the memory of her mother" returns to haunt you: "You asked me once what I would remember. This, and much more."

Robb Forman Dew (review date 16 June 1991)

SOURCE: "Pangs of an Abandoned Child," in *New York Times Book Review,* June 16, 1991, p. 9.

[*In the following review, Forman Dew points out a few problems with Tan's* The Kitchen God's Wife, *but concludes that the novel is "in the end, greatly satisfying."*]

Within the peculiar construction of Amy Tan's second novel is a harrowing, compelling and at times bitterly humorous

tale in which an entire world unfolds in a Tolstoyan tide of event and detail. No doubt it was daunting to attempt a second book in the wake of the enormous success of *The Joy Luck Club,* but none of Ms. Tan's fans will be disappointed. *The Kitchen God's Wife* is a more ambitious effort and, in the end, greatly satisfying.

The novel gets off to a slow start, but Ms. Tan eventually relates the story of Jiang Weili (Weiwei) from the time she was 6 years old in the China of 1925 through the present, in which she is Winnie Louie, the widowed matriarch of an extended Chinese family living in San Francisco. It is unfortunate that we first encounter her through the eyes of her 40-year-old daughter, Pearl, because Winnie seems disappointingly stereotypical. She is full of dour aphorisms, is preternaturally cranky and so intrusive that Pearl has kept secret for seven years the fact that she is afflicted with multiple sclerosis.

Perhaps it is Ms. Tan's intention to present us with a formulaic character and then slowly reveal to us our own misconceptions. But I believe she was searching for a subtle way to pose a philosophical question. I think she faced the problem of how to tell the amazing tale she needed to tell and persuade us to ponder it apart from being merely entertained by it. In the long run, she succeeds in this remarkable book, even though her method is initially awkward and sometimes downright unbelievable.

It turns out that it is not only Pearl who has been hiding a crucial truth for so many years. Winnie also has harbored secrets that, for various reasons, she finally feels compelled to relate to her daughter. The method of this revelation, however, is labored. Winnie persuades her daughter to visit one afternoon, serves her a bowl of soup, a cup of tea, and for the next three hundred pages or so relates the story of her life while Pearl sits at her mother's kitchen table.

Amy Tan manages to get away with this, although it is irritating each time she insists on bringing us back from Winnie's mesmerizing tale. Whenever Winnie halts her narrative to ask her daughter some question whose answer we only infer—Pearl does not speak—Ms. Tan challenges our suspension of disbelief. But never mind. These occasional intrusions are momentary and, indeed, it is very nearly hypnotic to be submerged in the convoluted story of the life of Jiang Weili.

Her mother abandoned her under mysterious circumstances when Weiwei was 6; she was sent away from her father's prosperous, communal household in Shanghai to live with her paternal uncle's family in the countryside. Over 60 years later Winnie Louie still suffers the pangs of the abandoned child she once was: "For many years, my mother was the source of funny and bad stories, terrible secrets and romantic tales. . . . I felt so bad to hear them. And yet I could not stop myself from listening. I wanted to know how it could be that my mother left me, never telling me why. . . . Now I no longer know which story is the truth. . . . They are all the same, all true, all false. So much pain in every one." And so, too, is the reader persuaded that all is true, all is false, as the tale unwinds.

Her mother's disappearance is the first of many losses, humiliations and sorrows so great that it is only Weiwei's exasperated humor and her tone of harsh certainty—a kind of bossiness—that maintains credulity. In 1937, when she was 18, she made what she had hoped would be a marriage that would change her luck, that would remove her from a household in which she was treated kindly, but certainly not cherished. Her marriage to the dashing young pilot Wen Fu, however, was disastrous almost from the first day. Her desperation first to comprehend and then to escape the brutality and degradation of this union shapes the rest of her story, which carries through World War II in China to Weiwei's second marriage and eventual immigration to the United States.

As Weiwei's story encompasses the deaths of her first three children and the further disintegration of her first husband's boorish and finally psychotic personality, we begin to understand that this is a chronicle not only of a woman's victimization, but of the unwitting conspiracy within society to ignore and therefore perpetuate the condition. There are still, unfortunately, many contemporary parallels. Ms. Tan also manages, even within often tragic circumstances, to illuminate the nobility of friendship and the necessity of humor.

But the major question posed by the investigation of the life of Jiang Weili/Weiwei/Winnie is how much our circumstance is fated and how much is shaped by individual choice, or if, in fact, fate and individual choice are even entirely separate things. This idea is like an undercurrent throughout Winnie's tale, and I wish Ms. Tan had not underscored her point by making the equation between the horrors that befell Winnie and the disease that has befallen her daughter. This is not to say that multiple sclerosis is less terrible a deprivation of autonomy, but Jiang Weili was trapped in a time and culture that all but precluded individual choice in her case; her daughter has been stripped of a degree of individual choice by her disease. The problem, however, is that the consequences the two women endure are simply not equally horrific, and Pearl's real despair and fear, when she finally confides in her mother, is diminished in our minds when we inevitably make the comparison.

I would rather not have had to deal with this problem when talking about *The Kitchen God's Wife.* I would rather say something to the reader much like what I said to my children in their early teens when I urged them to press on

through *War and Peace:* "It's not important the first time around to worry about the names, the war or the peace; just read it to see what happens." That's what I want to convey. Don't worry about the obstacle of the framework of this novel, simply give yourself over to the world Ms. Tan creates for you. It's the story she tells that really matters.

Elgy Gillespie (review date Summer 1991)

SOURCE: "Amy, Angst, and the Second Novel," in *San Francisco Review of Books,* Vol. 16, No. 1, Summer, 1991, pp. 33-4.

[*In the following review, Gillespie discusses the problem of a second novel and asserts that Tan's* The Kitchen God's Wife *is both different from her first novel and successful in its own right.*]

Granted, she has her reasons. When Amy Tan wrote amusingly and tellingly about "Angst and the Second Novel" in a recent *Publishers Weekly,* she was so sympatico about the frightening game of fiction that it seemed unfair to those who usually call the shots around here: the reviewers. In essence, our Amy defanged all her potential critics, silencing us with the sheer weight of her apprehension, guilt-tripping them in advance.

The Second Novel, she said, is always compared to the first, specially if the first was an unexpected runaway success; and the First Hit Novel is the curse from which few best-selling authors can ever recover: "It's like the kid brother sticking his tongue out going *nyah-nyah-nyah.*" And critics are always worse when the First Novel was really big—like Tan's best-selling *The Joy Luck Club.*

"With the first," Tan continues, "they put you on this great big pedestal. But by the time The Second Book comes around, you realize you're not sitting on a pedestal at all. It's one of those collapsible chairs above a tank of water at the county fair." After that, to slap *The Kitchen God's Wife* would be brutish. But there would be a scintilla of resentment attached to any praise—for how can a reviewer experience the new book adequately and objectively after the neurosis cited by Tan? And, since this book *is* more about mothers and daughters—a particular Chinese mother called Winnie in Shanghai during the forties and her life story and her feelings towards her daughters—we may be forgiven for reacting with skepticism to Tan's assertion that this book is no replay.

Whatsamatta, Amy? Tired of being appreciated so highly, suspicious that overvaunting praise must come before a fall? Listen up: this is show biz, sister, and you *can* take your reviews right on the chin. Playwright Brendan Behan used to say that critics were mere eunuchs, willing to carp and destroy because of their naked envy; they knew what was being done but could not do it themselves. In the end, though, Behan would have been a eunuch himself without those castrated critics.

Maybe the reason for Tan's Second Book nerves is because this time she did it without a safety net, so to speak. She has been writing by herself instead of taking each new chapter to her weekly writing class, as she did with *Joy Luck*. Both are dedicated to her writing-class teacher, Molly Giles, and her peers in the class were certainly also a major influence on the first book. After three false starts, with exhortations to make Chinese customs more accessible, to stop starting sentences with "And . . . ," as well as to iron out inconsistencies, Tan delivered her firstborn to agent Sandra Dijkstra.

But this one came into the world *sans* those extra midwives. "You can say this," reported Molly Giles, when I asked about her influence on Tan's progress as a writer, "She has gone out on her own now and that's the way it should be. That's the aim of the writing class. To help a writer go out on their own." Tan still holds the classes in her house every week, but is very often away on reading or speaking engagements at schools and libraries of one kind or another, the kind of gigs that swell your fans and disarm any critics and which are necessary for writers now.

The Kitchen God's Wife begins as Pearl-ah, a young Chinese-American woman at a big family reunion, starts to tease out the relationships between her relatives from Chinatown and the Avenues, only to discover that her mother, Winnie, had several children before Pearl was born. We then abandon the story of Pearl and her mother's second family and go back to where Winnie's story begins, in the first person. As the third wife of a rich Shanghai merchant, Winnie's mother is a melancholy figure right up to her sudden and unexplained death. Married off young to the evil and vicious Wen-Fu, Winnie endures the loss of her children and her husband's infidelities and abuse during the upheaval of the Japanese invasion. Her life as Wen-Fu's wretched victim is ended by the arrival of the Allies, when she meets Pearl's -father, loses him again when she is jailed, and is finally swept away to San Francisco. It is a story with a believably happy ending, for Winnie is delivered from her torturer and reunited with her American love.

The raves have already started for *The Kitchen God's Wife* ("A ravishing, vivid, graceful, and unforgettable tale of womanhood, endurance and love, lit by gentle humor and the healing aspect of truth. Stock up. Amy Tan's admirers are growing into a voracious legion," said *American Librarian*). But Tan may have a point about critics and the Second Book.

Like others, I took up *The Joy Luck Club* somewhat skeptically, unable to believe a blockbuster that had hogged the top of the *New York Times Book Review* best-sellers list could be anything other than a schlockbuster. But if I felt that tinge of resentment about Tan's *The Kitchen God's Wife* I soon forgot it, just as the slight condescension I had felt towards its predecessor vanished the moment I forgot the best-seller charts and began to read. It is indeed possible to pull off a second novel as good as (and perhaps better than) the first. It is also quite possible for a best-seller to be an estimable piece of writing as well as a ripping read, something I only came to credit quite recently. Once again I found myself reading Amy Tan all night, unable to put the story down until I knew what happened in the end, sniffling when I got to the sad bits (specially the loss of Yiku and Danru, Winnie's first babies) and finally going to sleep at dawn with the conviction that Tan had provided an education for the heart.

There is a poem by the Irishman Derek Mahon called "In a Disused Shed in County Wexford," in which a man who stumbles upon trays of forgotten mushrooms growing unseen in the darkness compares them to the lost victims of history and to "magi, moonmen, lost people of Treblinka." Millions of lives lived in obscurity, oceans of pain and suffering, are recalled by their sad round white faces glowing in the blackness of the forgotten. Tan's second book is further testimony to the endurance of the human spirit, to the many privations and humiliations borne by the unseen and unheard victims— particularly those who were female—in China's recent history.

> **If anything, *The Kitchen God's Wife* is a more satisfying book than its predecessor. It deals with the same themes, but more profoundly and sensitively, and its linear structure allows puzzles to be unraveled and truths to unfurl along the way.**
> **—Elgy Gillespie**

You may have seen *The Last Emperor,* you may have read *Empire of the Sun,* and you may have a notion that you know the tiniest bit about what happened in Harbin and Tientsin and Shanghai in the forties, Tienanmen in the eighties. But after reading this book, you will see how little you knew about the forgotten millions whose homes you may one day snap as a tourist, and their brave but often futile efforts to survive and carry on. In Mahon's words, "You with your light meter and your relaxed itinerary / Let not our naive labors have been in vain!"

If anything, *The Kitchen God's Wife* is a more satisfying book than its predecessor. It deals with the same themes, but more profoundly and sensitively, and its linear structure allows puzzles to be unraveled and truths to unfurl along the way. Its characterization is sometimes exaggerated and comic, but its dialogue is so natural that the people practically stand beside you. There are some splendidly cinematic scenes—the meeting of Winnie and her Chinese-American true love, Jimmy Louie, for instance, in a crowded, drunken dance-hall, where she is confronted with two hideous sights: her own vicious and jealous husband who abuses her in front of everyone, and a shamed Chinese wife who is being passed along from soldier to soldier like an unstrung puppet.

As a backdrop, of course, we learn more about the nature of arranged marriages in Chinese societies and also about the kind of inter-wifely accommodation arranged by second or third wives and their offspring. It is like being invited into a dusty room full of castoffs, and being given a chance to re-apprehend them in their former richness. We get to understand how this society worked, and we understand how, why, and from where Chinese-American society evolved. All this is the most important job of fiction, of course; and since Chinese women lived lives not just of forgotten obscurity, but of hermetically sealed oblivion, Tan is handing us a key with no price tag and letting us open the brass-bolted door.

Despite some superficial similarities between *The Joy Luck Club,* with its mother-daughter mah jong-style symmetry, and *The Kitchen God's Wife,* with its deepened mother-daughter dynamic, the new novel bears out Tan's claim that it is different. It is at once simpler and truer; the voice firm, unalloyed. Tan's army of sisterly defenders have nothing to fear.

Penelope Fitzgerald (review date 11 July 1991)

SOURCE: "Luck Dispensers," in *London Review of Books,* Vol. 13, No. 13, July 11, 1991, p. 19.

[*In the following review, Fitzgerald states that it is the attitude of the older generation that distinguishes Tan's* The Kitchen God's Wife.]

Amy Tan was born in San Francisco soon after her parents emigrated from Communist China. A few years ago she joined a Writers' Circle, which told her, as Writers' Circles always do, to write what she had seen herself. She wrote about what she had seen herself and what she hadn't—her own experience and her mother's. She produced a long, complex and seductive narrative, *The Joy Luck Club,* which was one of the best-sellers of 1989. The Joy Luck Club itself is a group of young wives, stuck in Kweilin during the Japanese invasion, who keep up their spirits by playing mah jong with paper money which has become worthless. All four of

them escape to California, and one of them, as an old woman, wants to tell her Americanised daughter, who has 'swallowed more Coca Colas than sorrows', what happened to them, then and afterwards. But the story at best will be no more than a fragment of the whole memory—like a single feather from a swan that has flown.

In *The Kitchen God's Wife* Amy Tan returns to more or less the same material, seen in a more comic but at the same time a sadder light. The Kitchen God, surely one of the most irritating minor deities ever conceived, was once a rich farmer called Zhang, with a kind and patient wife. But he chased her out of the house, spent all his substance on another woman and reduced himself to beggary. Nearly at death's door, he was carried into the kitchen of a charitable lady who took pity on the unfortunate. *Ay-ya!* The lady was none other than his wife! Ashamed, Zhang tried to hide in the fireplace, and was burned to ashes. But when he reached the other world, the Jade Emperor rewarded him, because he had admitted his fault, by making him the Kitchen God and entrusting him with the task of watching over human behaviour and deciding who deserved good luck, who bad. He must always be placated, therefore, with gifts of cigarettes, tea and whisky.

No problem in buying a porcelain image of Zhang at any good China Trading Company. It is impossible, of course, to get a statue of his wife. She is not an Immortal, although she tried with her tears to put out the fire that burned Zhang. Time and history may bring her into her own, though if she were to be translated, she would be the goddess, not of independence, but of consolation and compassion.

As a writer, and a second-generation immigrant, Amy Tan wants to provide a fair hearing for the past, the present and the future. The novel is told from the viewpoint of Winnie Louie, formerly Jyang Weili. At the beginning and end we hear the voice of her daughter, Pearl. Winnie's oldest friend, Helen—once Hulan—who followed Winnie to America, has decided (quite mistakenly) that she must soon leave this world, and in order to free herself from the burden of lies, proposes to tell everyone the never-referred-to story of their earlier life. Fear and embarrassment drive Winnie to do the telling herself. 'I will call Pearl long, long distance. Cost doesn't matter, I will say . . . And then I will start to tell her, not what happened, but why it happened, how it could not be any other way.'

It could not be any other way, not only because of human weakness and 'the mistakes that are mine', but because of the universal rule of luck. Chance determines your birth, luck decides your life, although it can be deflected at any moment by an unhappy word. 'According to my mother, *nothing* is an accident,' thinks Pearl. 'She's like a Chinese version of Freud or worse.' Winnie's luck has been bad. Her mother deserted her father and she was brought up on an island upriver from Shanghai by an uncle and his two wives, Old Aunt and New Aunt. She is married off to Wen Fu, a brute for whom no excuses are made. 'He would roll me over, unbend my arm, unbend my legs as if I were a folding chair.' It is a feudal marriage and her in-laws measure her worth by her husband's belch. In 1937, when the Japanese invade, Wen Fu begins training as a pilot in Hanchow with the three hundred-strong Chinese Air Force. But his unit, with their wives, have to retreat across the mountains, first to Chungking, then to Kunming. In 1949 Winnie makes her way to Shanghai, only five days before the Communist flags go up over the city. Her little son dies of a rat-borne plague, she is arrested for deserting her husband, and after a year in jail begins the painful process of bribing her way out of China. At the last moment, Wen Fu turns up, rapes her and threatens to tear up her visa. But the Luck Dispensers cause her old friend Helen to come into the room at that moment, and between them they are able to down Wen Fu.

Evidently this could make, and does make, a long, large, engrossing, colourful, comforting, first-and-second-generation saga—comforting because Winnie marries a Baptist minister and later opens the Ding Ho flower shop in San Francisco. You expect, and get, heroic mothers, bewildered sons-in-law, bizarre relations, crowded weddings, open-casket funerals where the generations join battle, and a confusion of cultures—what to keep, what to throw away. When Helen turns out her purse she finds two short candles, her American naturalisation papers in a plastic case, her old Chinese passport, one small motel soap, knee-high nylons, 'her *pochai* stomach pills, her potion for coughs, her tiger-bone pads for aches, her good-luck Goddess of Mercy charm if her other remedies do not work'. Corresponding to this mix-up are the beguiling variations of spoken English. (Timothy Mo has said that his Hongkong novel, *An Insular Possession,* is essentially about language.) Amy Tan indicates particularly well the differences between Chinese speaking Chinese to each other, Chinese speaking fluent American and broken Chinese and Chinese speaking a version of the 'funny English' which has been the novelist's standby ever since Defoe created it for Man Friday.

What gives *The Kitchen God's Wife* its distinction is the refreshingly sweet-sour and practical attitude of the older generation.
—Penelope Fitzgerald

What gives *The Kitchen God's Wife* its distinction is the refreshingly sweet-sour and practical attitude of the older generation. Winnie admires her preacher husband, but she feels she ought to have got him to take a different job, because

swallowing other people's troubles has changed his own luck. She herself finds forgiveness difficult. 'When Jesus suffered, everyone worshipped him. Nobody worshipped me for living with Wen Fu.' On the subject of Communism, she says she would have joined the Party if it was the best way out of her marriage. 'If I had had to change the whole world to change my own life, I would have done that.' Helen is her friend, but they tell each other lies and exasperate each other. It's true that Pearl perceives that the lies are a form of loyalty, 'a devotion beyond anything that ever can be spoken, anything that I will ever understand'. But there is no way for Winnie to express it, or even what she feels for her daughter.

In this tale of survival the future should rest with Pearl. She is the traditional carrier-on. But Pearl also has a secret to tell: she is in the early stages of multiple sclerosis. At the end of the book Helen and Winnie are preparing to take her on a visit to China, a journey of memory and forgetting and, they believe, of miraculous healing—all at cut-price through a Chinatown travel agency. But we are not encouraged to think that Pearl will be cured.

Helen Yglesias (review date September 1991)

SOURCE: "The Second Time Around," in *Women's Review of Books,* Vol. VIII, No. 12, September, 1991, pp. 1, 3.

[*In the following review, Yglesias delineates the reasons that Tan's* The Kitchen God's Wife *may surpass the success of her* The Joy Luck Club.]

Amy Tan is an immensely popular writer. Her first novel, *The Joy Luck Club,* was a knockout success, and her second is well on its way to equal, if not surpass, it. The readers who loved the first will surely love the second, since both tell the same story—and this time around Tan has executed the work better in conception, in design, in detail and in sheer pleasure for the reader.

If this sounds like criticism in the guise of praise, it is not. Amy Tan commands an intriguing style which, along with her highly special subject matter, makes for a unique contribution to contemporary writing. *The Joy Luck Club* introduced her as a young novelist; more or less inevitably, what she had to say was not entirely successfully done the first time. It is to our advantage that she returned to her powerful material for another try.

Amy Tan herself comments that things Chinese are fashionable these days, and some part of her extraordinary success is due to its chic aspect, if only in the most surface way. (Note *The New Yorker*'s recent two-part article on Chinatown, much of whose opening up of this closed society was undone by its emphasis on the area as the center of a new Mafia, reinforcing the image of Chinatown as a sinister place.) Chic or not, our contemporary interest in Chinese-American society is a corrective to former attitudes of vilification at worst, and abysmal neglect at best.

Even more blatantly than prejudice towards blacks, Native Americans, Latins, Jews and gays, ignorance of the culture and humanity of Asians has given anti-Asian racism a special twist. "Orientals" have been cast as quintessentially *other,* giving Westerners leave to ascribe villainy to everything about them, beginning with the shape of their eyes and extending to their religion and the mysteries of their enclosed private lives. Everybody of my generation hides memories of anti-Chinese chants, shouted as we raced past the local Chinese laundry. In entertainment, we have parlayed our ignorance into a mish-mash of comic-strip mythology in which Chinese women, when they aren't helpless victims of murderous males, yellow or white, are campy villains, Dragon Ladies all.

There isn't a single Chinese laundry in either one of Amy Tan's novels, and no Dragon Ladies. Tan rescued the Chinese-American woman from numbing distortion in *The Joy Luck Club,* but the central gimmick of that book's design was finally limiting. In 1949, four Chinese women in San Francisco form a club to play mah-jong, invest in stocks, eat dim sum and remind one another of their pasts in China, neatly combining basic elements of Chinese life—gambling, money, eating, ancestral power and community. Tan told the mothers' stories as well as those of their four daughters, revealing the tension that is engendered in any mother-daughter relationship, but especially between first-generation American daughters and their immigrant mothers. This shaping presented the reader with eight separate protagonists, a spread too thin and too confusing to be truly successful.

In *The Kitchen God's Wife,* without sacrificing a social breadth we cherish as readers, Tan hews closely to one woman's story. Once again a mother and daughter exchange secrets. In speaking her bitterness, the mother's tale evokes an entire female generation's excruciating trials. Almost all of us are immigrants or daughters and granddaughters of immigrants, and our identification with the story Amy Tan tells is the source of the powerful sway she exerts on us as readers. Because I am Jewish, I find the parallels with the Jewish immigrant ordeals most moving, but perhaps readers of all backgrounds feel a similar identification. To paraphrase Gertrude Stein, the immigrant experience is the immigrant experience is the immigrant experience, and the violent shocks of dislocation were, and are, common to all.

Back in 1976 when I published *Family Feeling,* which attempted to do the daughter-and-immigrant-mother syndrome as fiction, one reviewer (Bell Gale Chevigny in the pages of *The Nation*) recognized the intent and commented on its placing a woman at the center of this experience of dislocation. Anzia Yezierska had done her bit earlier in the century in a highly idiosyncratic manner, and later Kate Simon added her compellingly beautiful memoirs; but overall in the chronicle of the Jewish migration, women writers have performed against a background of powerful males already dominating, and distorting, the tale. It's interesting that in the Chinese-American rush of truth, women writers predominate.

The power of literature over sociology lies in particularization, and it is in its details *The Kitchen God's Wife* excels. Hooked to the legend of the kitchen god, a weak, selfish and thoughtless man saved from damnation by the virtue and good sense of his wife, who of course never becomes a god herself, the thrust of the book is made plain—perhaps too obviously. The novel hardly needs the legend to sustain its clear intent to elevate the kitchen god's wife to her rightful place in history. But, nothing lost, it enhances the book with a striking title.

Amy Tan is gifted with a quirky style, a broad historical sense, and great energy as a story-teller. Winnie's life is recounted backwards, from her present existence in contemporary San Francisco to her beginnings in the old China before the Second World War, for the understanding of her daughter Pearl, a Chinese-American speech and language clinician married for fifteen years to a non-Chinese physician. The young couple and their little children are very much the American middle-class family wrapped up in the interests consistent with their status—except for the exotic ingredient of Pearl's Chinese family, and the terrible note struck by her affliction with multiple sclerosis.

Pearl is keeping this diagnosis a secret from her mother, just as her mother has kept fundamental information secret from her. The novel is the working out of these mysteries between the two. On the surface, Winnie's ways are more irritating than mysterious to the daughter, who arrogantly assigns herself a critical perspective on her mother's life. But with the full account of that life, Pearl comes to know—as does the reader—not only an identifiable and deeply moving woman who engages our full sympathies, but also the cruel mores, the male domination and the rigid class structures of the society that distorted the child her mother was into the seemingly crabbed old woman she appears to be.

History is also set straight, Winnie reminding her daughter that World War Two began for the Chinese when Japan invaded China. The account of forced flight from the advancing Japanese is powerful story-telling, but it is through vivid minutiae that Tan more often exercises her particular charm. Some anecdotes, done with astonishing mastery in Winnie's voice, are complete diversions within themselves, encompassing no more than a couple of paragraphs.

> . . . like that girl I once knew in Shanghai, the schoolmate who went to the same Christian school as me. She came from a rich family like mine. She was almost as pretty as me. Around the same time I married my first husband, she had a wedding contract to a rich banking family. But after the summer, her face became marked forever with smallpox, and that contract disappeared. I pitied that girl because she had lost her face two ways.
>
> Many years later I met her again . . . in Fresno. She was married to an American Chinese man who owned a grocery store, selling soda pop, potato chips, cigarettes, everything at high prices. That's how I met her again, at the checkout counter. I was buying ice cream on a stick. She cried "Sister, sister, remember me!" But she didn't give me a discount. After I paid her, she told me how her husband was honest, very kind, very nice and as she said this, she pushed her many jade bracelets up her arm so they would fall back down and clink together like rich music. She was smiling so big all her pock marks looked like the happy dimples she now wore.

Tan weaves trivia into rich and illuminating character portrayal, treasures that literally appear on every page. Here is Winnie describing her closest friend, Hulan, and in the mirror image, herself:

> Hulan could not be called pretty, even if you judged her with an old-fashioned eye. She was plump, but not in that classical way as a peach whose pink skin is nearly bursting with sweetness. Her plumpness was round and overflowing in uneven spots, more like a steamed dumpling with too much filling leaking out of the sides. She had thick ankles and large hands, and feet as broad as boat paddles. While she had cut her hair in a popular Western style—parted deep on one side like this, combed back smooth, and curled halfway down—she had applied the curling sticks to her hair unevenly. So here it was lumpy, there it was flat. And she had no sense of fashion, none at all. One day I saw her wearing a Western-style flowery dress on top of a yellow Chinese dress that hung down like a too long slip. On top of this she wore a sweater she had knit, with the sleeves too short. She looked just like laundry hung out to dry.
>
> . . . When we washed together every evening, she sat on the stool with her legs wide open like this, scrubbing herself vigorously—her breasts, under her arms, under her legs, between her legs, her backside, the crease of her bottom—until her skin was covered with red streaks, And then she would get on her hands and knees, just like a dog, and naked like that, she would dip her hair into the basin of cloudy hot water left over from her bath.
>
> I was embarrassed for her—and for myself, knowing this was the way I appeared to my husband every night. I tried not to look at her. I would pretend to be busy washing myself, my thin arms folded in front of my breasts, one large cloth over my lap, while I used another cloth to wash what was underneath without showing any obvious motions. But I could not stop myself from watching Hulan.

Another of Tan's strengths lies in her evocation of large positive emotions without descending into sentimentality, though she can come very close to the edge. Winnie describes herself during her first marriage, still in wartime China, horrified by her bullying husband, attracted to another, gentler man: "I was a married woman, yet I had never felt love from a man, or for a man. And that night I almost did. I felt the danger, that this was how you love someone, one person letting out fears, the other drawing closer to soothe the pain. And then more would pour out, everything that has been hidden, more and more—sorrow, shame, loneliness, all the old aches, so much released until you overflowed with joy to be rid of it, until it was too late to stop this new joy from taking over your heart."

If the novel goes on a little too long and the final resolution is perhaps too pat, a little unlike life as we know it in its wrapped-up gratifications, these very elements add to the satisfactions it gives us. Like Winnie, we end mellow but still sharp: "Now help me light three sticks of incense. The smoke will take our wishes to heaven. Of course it's only superstition, just for fun. But see how fast the smoke rises—oh, even faster when we laugh, lifting our hopes, higher and higher."

Scarlet Cheng (review date Fall 1991)

SOURCE: "Amy Tan Redux," in *Belles Lettres,* Vol. 7, No. 1, Fall, 1991, pp. 15, 19.

[*In the following review, Cheng lauds Tan's* The Kitchen God's Wife *stating, "The ending, with its extraordinary convergence of all that has gone on before, is a marvel."*]

Yes, it's true: Amy Tan has done it again—with searing clarity of vision she has spun a tale that lyrically weaves past and present, myth and memory. And she has written a true novel this time, one sustained story that lasts all of some four hundred pages.

For the many who read her first book, *The Joy Luck Club,* the second opens on familiar territory—Pearl is the grown daughter of a very Chinese mother, Winnie, who speaks English with the snappy cadence and salty metaphors of her native tongue and whose way of thinking—of linking the visible and the invisible worlds—has come with her across the Pacific to the San Francisco Bay Area.

While Winnie still lives in Chinatown, Pearl is living fifty miles outside the city with a Caucasian husband and two Americanized little girls. They come together for a cousin's engagement dinner and for an aunt's funeral. Each has been guarding a secret: Pearl has multiple sclerosis; Winnie a checkered past she tried to leave behind in China.

But meddlesome Aunt Helen takes it on herself to set the record straight. When she nags Pearl to reveal her illness, Pearl protests that she does not want to worry her mother.

> "This is her right to worry," says Aunt Helen. "She is your mother."
>
> "But she shouldn't have to worry about something that isn't really a problem."
>
> "That's why you should tell her now. No more problem after that."
>
> "But then she'll wonder why we kept this a secret from her. She'll think it's worse than it is."
>
> "Maybe she has some secrets too." She smiles, then laughs at what must be a private joke. "Your mother, oh yes, plenty of secrets!"

Winnie does have plenty of secrets, and revealing them takes most of the book. While both mother and daughter learn to share what has been locked deep inside, this is really Winnie's story. She tells of the turns of fate she suffered in a China that was attempting to modernize but was still fundamentally feudal and often brutal to women.

First Winnie (Weili in her other life) conjures up the romantic memory of her own mother, the first of the moderns of Chinese society to have unbound feet. "When my mother was eight years old," Winnie recalls, "her feet were already unbound, and some people say that's why she ran wild." Her mother received an education, which some later called "bad." But Winnie says, "If you were to ask me, what happened to my mother was not a bad education but bad fate. Her education only made her unhappy thinking about it—that no matter how much she changed her life, she could not change the world that surrounded her."

Her bad fate was to fall in love with one man but be forced to marry another. Then one day she mysteriously disappears, and her young daughter is dispatched to be raised by relatives on a remote island. Weili grows up dreaming for her disgraced fate to change. When she gets matched to the dashing young Wen Fu, a man from a well-to-do family, she believes that it has. But as soon as she is married, her in-laws make off with her immense dowry, and her groom turns out to be a selfish brute whose behavior gets progressively worse.

As one of the first pilots for the Chinese Air Force, Wen Fu is transferred from training camp to military base and finally to Kunming, the Kuomingtang stronghold towards the end of the war. Weili naturally moved with him, trying to maintain the semblance of home, preparing special meals and treats purchased with the dowry money that was, fortunately, banked in her own name.

In such ways Weili and her friend Hulan, both alternately foolish and valiant, seek happiness even as the world around them is collapsing. Tan captures beautifully this helter-skelter period in China, when many lived on the run, never knowing how long they would be in one place—or one piece, as the Japanese battered cities with aerial raids.

It seems that Weili endures one humiliation, only to have greater sorrow come to crush her. She is physically beaten, her babies die, and more, much more. Yet this woman grows less foolish, more resilient, until she finds the courage to grasp her own happiness.

The ending, with its extraordinary convergence of all that has gone on before, is a marvel.

At a recent appearance in Washington, D.C., Amy Tan said, "I always find that it's necessary to write with some reader in mind, and for me, that someone is always my mother." In a haunting way, she has also successfully taken on her mother's voice in *The Kitchen God's Wife*—or, at least, the voice of someone of her mother's generation who lived through the tumultuous period of history her mother did. In addition to this remarkable mediumship, Tan displays superb storytelling—spinning personae and situations that are credible and compelling. But more, she has the courage to share heartfelt sorrow and grief, to acknowledge human imperfection and fate's ambiguities. Tan shows us that a life can encompass all that—grief, imperfection, ambiguity—and still add up to triumph, a triumph of the spirit, of the human soul to endure, to show compassion, and to hold fast to dreams.

Walter Shear (essay date Spring 1993)

SOURCE: "Generational Differences and the Diaspora in *The Joy Luck Club*," in *Critique,* Spring, 1993, pp. 193-99.

[In the following essay, Shear analyzes the mother-daughter relationship in Tan's The Joy Luck Club.*]*

Orville Schell's review of **The Joy Luck Club** for the *New York Times* emphasizes that those millions of Chinese who were part of the diaspora of World War II and the fighting that resulted in the triumph of the Communists were subsequently cut off from the mainland and after 1949 left to fend for themselves culturally. Though Schell is struck by the way this book renders the vulnerability of these Chinese women in America, the novel's structure in fact succeeds in manifesting not merely the individual psychic tragedies of those caught up in this history, but the enormous agony of a culture enmeshed in a transforming crisis. What each person's story conveys is the terror of a vulnerable human consciousness torn and rent in a culture's contortions; and although, like other Chinese-American books, this novel articulates "the urge to find a usable past," it is made up of a series of intense encounters in a kind of cultural lost and found.

The structure that presents this two-fold impression recalls works such as Sherwood Anderson's *Winesburg, Ohio,* Ernest Hemingway's *In Our Time,* and William Faulkner's *The Unvanquished,* books that feature distinct, individual narratives but that as a group simultaneously dramatize the panorama of a critical transition in cultural values. In **The Joy Luck Club** Tan organizes her material in terms of a generational contrast by segregating stories of mothers and their daughters. The separate story sections are divided into four parts with mother figures telling two stories, mostly concerned with their past in pre-1949 China, and their daughters telling two stories, one about growing up and one about a current family situation. The exception to this pattern is Jing-mei Woo, the daughter of the founder of the Joy Luck Club, who narrates a story in each of the four sections and who adds additional continuity by narrating the first and last section. Though all these people, for the most part, know one another, few of the stories involve contacts with anyone outside the immediate family group. While the daughters' stories usually involve their mothers, the mothers' stories tend to feature a distinct life, involving rather rigid family experiences in old China and their current relationship to their American daughters. By using the perspectives of both mothers and daughters, Tan initially seems to solve what Linda Hunt, examining Maxine Hong Kingston, describes as a basic problem for a Chinese-American woman: "being simultaneously insider (a person who identifies strongly with her cultural group) and outsider (deviant and rebel against that tradition), she cannot figure out from which perspective to speak."

Nevertheless, just as in *The Woman Warrior,* the communication barrier here is a double one, that between generations and that created by the waning influence of an older culture and the burgeoning presence of another. Jing-mei announces in the first section: "My mother and I never really understood one another. We translated each other's meanings and I seemed to hear less than what was said, while my mother heard more." Generally, the daughters tend to perceive cultural blanks, the absence of clear and definite answers to the problems of family, whereas the mothers tend to fill in too much, often to provide those kinds of cultural answers and principles that seem to empower them to make strong domestic demands on their daughters. Thus, as in *Woman Warrior,* the object of "confrontation" for a daughter is often the mother, "the source of authority for her and the most single powerful influence from China."

The mothers tend to depict themselves as, in a broad sense, students learning about the social realities around them and using their experiences to come to conclusions about essential forms of character strength and weakness. For example, one of the mothers, An-mei Hsu, seems to see in her own mother's suicide how to use the world for her own advantage. She not only traces how her mother makes the Chinese cultural beliefs work for her—"suicide is the only way a woman can escape marriage and gain revenge, to come back as a ghost and scatter tea leaves and good fortune"—but also she realizes almost immediately the acute significance of the words of her mother who tells her "she [the mother] would rather kill her own weak spirit so she could give me a stronger one."

Ying-ying St. Clair claims, "I have always known a thing before it happens." Her daughter tends to confirm at least an ironic version of her mother's acquired powers by adding, "She sees only bad things that affect our family." In at least one case the mother's knowledge is a gift passed to the daughter: Waverly Jong opens her story by claiming, "I was six when my mother taught me the art of invisible strength. It was a strategy for winning arguments, respect from others, and eventually, though none of us knew it at the time, chess games." In the last case the knowledge apparently blossoms from the mother's folk saying, "Bite back your tongue," and although Waverly regards it as a secret of her success in chess, she herself is finally a victim of her mother's more authoritarian deployment of the tactic, as it suddenly takes the form of simply ignoring her.

As the last interaction demonstrates, there is nearly always some tension in the exchange between mother and daughter, between old China and the new American environment. Most often the focus is either on a mother, who figures out her world, or on the daughters, who seem caught in a sophisticated cultural trap, knowing possibilities rather than answers, puzzling over the realities that seem to be surrounding them and trying to find their place in what seems an ambivalent world. Strangely, given the common problems presented, there is little concern with peer communication among the daughters. Jing-mei explains, "Even though Lena and I are still friends, we have grown naturally cautious about telling each other too much. Still, what little we say to one another often comes back in another guise. It's the same old game, everybody talking in circles." This difficulty in communication may simply be a consequence of living in what Schell describes as an "upwardly mobile, design-conscious, divorce-prone" world, but it also tends to convey a basic lack of cultural confidence on the part of daughters and thus a sense of their being thrown back into the families they have grown up in for explanations, validations, and identity reinforcement and definition.

Again, in the tradition of *The Woman Warrior,* **The Joy Luck Club** explores the subtle, perhaps never completely understood, influence of culture on those just beginning to live it. The mother-daughter tensions are both the articulation of the women's movement and the means of specifying the distinctness of Chinese and Chinese-American culture. As in *Woman Warrior,* behind the overt culture is odd intuition of a ghost presence, at times a sense of madness waiting at the edge of existence. It is an unseen terror that runs through both the distinct social spectrum experienced by the mothers in China and the lack of such social definition in the daughters' lives. In this context the Joy Luck Club itself is the determination to hope in the face of constantly altering social situations and continually shifting rules. The club is formed during the Japanese invasion of China, created by Jing-mei's mother as a deliberate defiance of the darkness of current events. With a mixture of desperation and frivolity, she and a group of friends meet, eat, laugh, tell stories, and play mah jong. She reasons, "we could hope to be lucky. That hope was our only joy." "It's not that we had no heart or eyes for pain. We were all afraid. We all had our miseries. But to despair was to wish back for something already lost. Or to prolong what was already unbearable."

It is the old China experience that manifests most definitely the enormous weight of fate in the lives of the characters. On the one hand, the constrictive burden is due to the position of women in that society. An-mei seems to regard the woman's role as an inescapable fate: "I was raised the Chinese way; I was taught to desire nothing, to swallow other people's misery, to eat my own bitterness. And even though I taught my daughter the opposite, still she came out the same way. . . . she was born a girl. And I was born to my mother and I was born a girl. All of us are like stairs, one step after another, going up and down, but all going the same way." Another mother, Lindo Jong, is the victim of a marriage arranged when she was only a child. In her struggle to extricate herself from the situation, she does not blame her family who made such arrangements but the society, the town

where she grew up, a place she claims is frozen in custom at a time when the rest of China was beginning to change. Although the old culture places the family at its heart, as the experience of the women in this revolutionary situation demonstrates, its attitude toward women begins in the more fluid modern world to tear away at this fundamental unit, making the difficulty of mother-daughter bonding a crucial problem for the culture as a whole.

Ying-ying St. Clair blames herself more than her circumstances, but it is her early social circumstances that structure the experience that so haunts her and cripples her psychically. Situated higher in the social scale of old China than the other members of the club, she seems to fall as a child into a subconscious state from which she never fully recovers, a state that in the social context may stand as a paradigm for individual nightmare in a fragmenting culture. Hers is an episode with a fantasy/folk flavor and a motif of dreaming, which seems to represent a naive, open but mechanical relationship to culture—opposed to a vital reciprocity of being. Ying-ying (the childhood nickname here may be intended to suggest the regressive nature of her trauma) describes her adventures on a boat cruise during the Moon festival, which in her account becomes a symbolic episode, a psychological drifting from the fundamental reality of family. While everyone else sleeps, the little Ying-ying watches in fascination as some boys use a bird with a metal ring around its neck to catch fish. The bird serves its purpose, catching the fish but being unable to swallow them, its social function thus symbolically dependent on an intensely personal, intensely perverse individual frustration.

Finally the boys leave, but Ying-ying stays, "as if caught in a good dream," to watch "a sullen woman" clean fish and cut off the heads of chickens and turtles. As she begins to come back to self-consciousness, she notices that her fine party clothes are covered with the mess of these deaths—"spots of bloods, flecks of fish scales, bits of feather and mud." In the strangeness of her panic, she tries to cover the spots by painting her clothes with the turtle's blood. When her Amah appears, the servant is angry and strips off her clothes, using words that the child has never heard but from which she catches the sense of evil and, significantly, the threat of rejection by her mother. Left in her underwear, Ying-ying is alone at the boat's edge, suddenly looking at the moon, wanting to tell the Moon Lady her "secret wish." At this key moment in her young life, she falls into the water and is about to be drowned when miraculously she finds herself in a net with a heap of squirming fish. The fishing people who have saved her are of a class known to her, but a group from which she has previously been shielded. After some initial insensitive jokes about catching her, they attempt to restore her to her family group by hailing a floating pavilion to tell those aboard they have found the lost child. Instead of the family appearing to reclaim her, Ying-ying sees only strangers and a little girl who shouts, "That's not me. . . . I'm here. I didn't fall in the water."

What seems a bizarre, comically irrelevant mistake is the most revealing and shocking moment of the story, for it is as if her conscious self has suddenly appeared to deny her, to cast her permanently adrift in a life among strangers. To some degree this acute psychic sense of and fear of being abandoned by the family is a basic reality for all the mothers in this book, each of whose stories involve a fundamental separation from family, an ultimate wedge of circumstances between mother and child.

Though Ying-ying is finally restored to her family, the shock of separation has become too intense a reality. She tries to explain, "even though I was found—later that night after Amah, Baba, Uncle, and the others shouted for me along the waterway—I never believed my family found the same girl." Her self-accusations at the beginning of this story become a miniature autobiography: "For all these years I kept my mouth closed so selfish desires would not fall out. And because I remained quiet for so long now my daughter does not hear me. . . . I kept my true nature hidden. . . . " Later she accuses herself of becoming a ghost: "I willingly gave up my *chi,* the spirit that caused me so much pain." She fears that this abandonment of self has in some way been passed on to her daughter. "Now," she announces to herself, "I must tell my daughter everything. That she is the daughter of a ghost. She has no *chi.* This is my greatest shame. How can I leave this world without leaving her my spirit?" Her first narrative ends with her trapped in the legendary world of old China, still a child but with all the terrible insight into her later life: "I also remember what I asked the Moon Lady so long ago. I wished to be found."

The *chi* that she refers to may be impossible to render wholly into English, but it involves a fundamental self-respect, a desire to excel, a willingness to stand up for one's self and one's family, to demonstrate something to others. It may well be a quality that the daughters in the book lack, or that they possess in insufficient amounts. Veronica Wang states, "In the traditional Chinese society, women were expected to behave silently with submission but act heroically with strength. They were both sub-women and super-women." Possibly those cultural expectations, although almost totally erased in American culture, could still survive in residual roles when validated by a concept such as *chi.*

Whereas the major problem for the older generation had been the struggle against fate, the younger generation perceives their essential difficulty to involve the making of choices. The problem, as Rose Hsu Jordan defines it, is that America offers too many choices, "so much to think about, so much to decide. Each decision meant a turn in another direction." Like their mothers, many of the daughters are

moving out or thinking of moving out, of family relationships, but such moves involve decisions about divorce, about whether their marriages are working out, about whether their husbands or future husbands fit into their lives.

One group of stories concerning the daughters features the struggle for maturity, a rather typical generational tension with the mothers. Perhaps surprisingly, the older women are for the most part not portrayed as pushing their daughters into an outmoded or inappropriate set of values and traditions, but they do insist on a basic cultural formulation. Lindo Jong's comments express a typical attitude: "I wanted my children to have the best combination: American circumstances and Chinese character." This sounds a note of compromise, but in reply to her daughter's declaration, "I'm my own person," she thinks, "How can she be her own person? When did I give her up?"

Curiously, in two instances, the generational tensions appear to have their origins in what seems a very American ambition. Waverly feels that her mother leeches off her chess achievements with an appropriating pride, and Jing-mei feels her mother, inspired by a competition with Waverly's mother as well as the belief that in America you could be anything you wanted, pushes her beyond her abilities, at least beyond her desires. The familiar cry "You want me to be someone that I'm not!" accelerates to "I wish I wasn't your daughter. I wish you weren't my mother." and finally to "I wish I'd never been born! . . . I wish I were dead! Like them." The "them" are the other daughters her mother had been forced to abandon in China. This story of Jing-mei moves toward the kind of muted conclusion typical of most of the daughter stories: "unlike my mother, I did not believe I could be anything I wanted to be, I could only be me." There is the sense that this "me" lacks some vital centering, the cultural force that would provide its *chi.*

In the context of cultural analysis, the happiness of the conclusion seems only partially earned by what has preceded it. And the fact that the return and the reunion with the two half-sisters reflect almost exactly the author's own experience suggests that there may be more than a little biographical intrusion here. Ultimately, however, the book's final cultural argument seems to be that there is always a possibility for the isolated "me" to return home. At one time Jing-mei notes, "in a crowd of Caucasians, two Chinese people are already like family." As she makes the return trip to China in the last story, she feels she is at last becoming Chinese. What she discovers in her reunion with her Chinese half-sisters, in her father's story of her mother's separation from these children and from the mother's first husband, and in the photograph of her and her sisters is a renewed sense of her dead mother. The mother's living presence in them is the feeling Jing-mei has been searching for, the feeling of belonging in her family and of being at last in the larger family of China. In this case the feeling of cultural wholeness grows out of and seems dependent on a sense of family togetherness, but the return to the mainland certainly suggests a larger symbolic possibility, one, however, that must still cope with the actual barriers of geography, politics, and cultural distinctness.

In contrast to the treatments of generational differences in earlier books such as *Fifth Chinese Daughter,* both Maxine Hong Kingston and Amy Tan are empowered by current feminist ideas in their examinations of the Chinese-American woman's dilemma. In both *The Woman Warrior* and *The Joy Luck Club,* much of the focus springs out of the mother-daughter relationships and the way the diaspora has created a total contrast in the experiences of mother and daughter. Kingston's influential book tends to sort out the problems of a single "I" persona and is thus sharper in its dramatizations of the varied identity strands of a single individual, whereas Tan's multiplicity of first person narratives establishes a broader canvas with more feeling of fictional detachment between the reader and "I" and creates a voice for both generations. Both these authors testify to a rupture in the historical Chinese family unit as a result of the diaspora, but both seem to believe in a cultural healing. However, as her conclusion suggests, Tan seems to place more emphasis on the Chinese identity as the healing factor. Although perspectives are difficult to come by with contemporary work, the ability of both Kingston and Tan to render the experience of a culture through vividly dramatic individual narratives provides a sound basis for what seems to be a developing tradition of Chinese-American women's writing.

Stephen Souris (essay date Summer 1994)

SOURCE: "'Only Two Kinds of Daughters': Inter Monologue Dialogicity in *The Joy Luck Club,*" in *MELUS,* Vol. 19, No. 2, Summer, 1994, pp. 99-124.

[*In the following essay, Souris applies Wolfgang Iser's theory concerning multiple-narrator novels to Tan's* The Joy Luck Club.]

Amy Tan has said that she never intended *The Joy Luck Club* to be a novel. Instead, she thought of it as a collection of stories. But she did plan on having the stories cohere around a central theme, and she did plan the prefaces from the start, although they were written last. More importantly, her collection of first-person monologues participates in and contributes to a tradition of multiple monologue narratives. Since the precedent-setting experiments of Woolf and Faulkner—*The Waves, The Sound and the Fury, As I Lay Dying, Absalom, Absalom!*—a number of interesting novels written in the decentered, multiple monologue mode have

been published. Louise Erdrich's *Tracks,* Peter Matthiessen's *Killing Mister Watson,* Louis Auchincloss's *The House of the Prophet,* and Kaye Gibbons's *A Virtuous Woman* are just a few of the contemporary examples of this compelling genre.

> **Because of its decentered, multi-perspectival form, *The Joy Luck Club* invites analysis from critical perspectives that theorize and valorize fragmented, discontinuous texts and the possibilities of connection across segments.**
> **—Stephen Souris**

Because of its decentered, multi-perspectival form, *The Joy Luck Club* invites analysis from critical perspectives that theorize and valorize fragmented, discontinuous texts and the possibilities of connection across segments. Mikhail Bakhtin may come to mind first because of his emphasis on and celebration of texts flaunting a diversity of fully valid and autonomous voices with relativistic and centrifugal consequences as well as counter-centrifugal tendencies such as the active intermingling of perspectives within single consciousnesses (what I call "intra-monologue dialogicity"). Tan's "novel" offers a heteroglot collection of very different, fully valid voices each presented from its own perspective, with relativistic and centrifugal implications. Moreover, its unique theme—mothers from China and their American-born daughters struggling to understand each other—allows for a rich array of dialogized perspectives within single utterances: the Chinese, the American, and the Chinese-American, all three of which can be discerned, to varying degrees, in the monologues.

My concern in this essay, however, will not be with the counter-centrifugal phenomenon of "intra-monologue dialogicity." Rather, it will be with what I call "inter-monologue dialogicity," or the potential for active intermingling of perspectives across utterances, with the site of the dialogicity located in the reader's experience of the narrative. Although Bakhtin has some provocative things to say about the dialogic potential of textual segments set side by side and even hints at the role a reader would have to play in establishing that dialogicity, his theory does not fully allow for a reader's moment-by-moment processing of a text. Wolfgang Iser picks up where Bakhtin leaves off regarding the counter-centrifugal dialogicity that can be said to exist between textual elements in a multiple narrator novel. It is with his narrative model that I propose to uncover and articulate the dialogic potential across monologues in *The Joy Luck Club.*

Iser's phenomenologically rigorous model of the act of reading is ideally suited to the pursuit and articulation of inter-monologue dialogicity in narratives modeled more or less after *The Sound and the Fury, As I Lay Dying,* or *The Waves.* Although *The Act of Reading* is a classic text in the reader-response school, a brief summary of the main points of Iser's theory will establish the context for my analysis of the potentially interacting structures of *The Joy Luck Club.*

Like other reader-response critics, Iser emphasizes the active involvement of the reader in the creation of meaning. For Iser, reading is a "dynamic happening" and is the product of a "dyadic interaction" between text and reader. "Meaning is an effect to be experienced," he asserts; it does not inhere in a literary work independent of the reading experience. For Iser, "literary texts initiate 'performances' of meaning rather than actually formulating meanings themselves." Meaning for Iser is "text-guided though reader-produced." What a reader encounters in processing a text are "instructions for the production of the signified."

Iser's emphasis on the reader's active involvement with the text does not allow for the extreme subjectivism that Norman Holland and David Bleich allow for in their theories. As such, Iser's model is relatively conservative because it insists that all concretizations be "intersubjectively" valid: "The subjective processing of a text is generally still accessible to third parties, i.e., available for intersubjective analysis." Indeed, the reason for restricting the creative activity of the reader is to allow for observations that can be agreed upon across subjectivities: "One task of a theory of aesthetic response is to facilitate intersubjective discussion of individual interpretations." To that end, Iser distinguishes between "meaning" and "significance": "meaning" is what all readers who are properly following the "instructions for the production of the signified" should arrive at; "significance" concerns how a particular reader might apply that meaning to his or her own life. But the emphasis in Iser's model is always with the processing of textual elements rather than the production of a detachable message, as he indicates by asserting that "what is important to readers, critics, and authors alike is what literature does and not what it means."

In calling for an "erotica of art" (following Sontag), and in inviting the reader to "climb aboard" the text, Iser emphasizes the moment-by-moment experience of what a text "does" to the reader. He refers to the reader's "wandering viewpoint" because of this emphasis on the temporal experience of a text. "The wandering viewpoint," he argues, "divides the text up into interacting structures, and these give rise to a grouping activity that is fundamental to the grasping of a text." These interactive structures are conceptually apprehended as a gestalt. Any perspective of the moment—or "theme," in his terminology—is apprehended against the backdrop of a previous "theme," which becomes the "horizon." For Iser, responding to the textual prompts as "instruc-

tions for the production of the signified" amounts to actively recalling previous moments and allowing them to enter into significant combinations with present moments. Or, since his model allows for readers rereading, any present moment can be creatively paired up with a moment one remembers will be encountered later in the text. Constantly creating fore-ground/background *Gestalten,* an Iserian reader's experience of a text is very three dimensional. But each theme/horizon concretization is temporary and may have to be modified as other *Gestalten* are experienced. Iser expresses this complex concept thusly: "The structure of theme and horizon constitutes the vital link between text and reader . . . because it actively involves the reader in the process of synthesizing an assembly of constantly shifting viewpoints, which not only modify one another, but also influence past and future syntheses in the reading process." Iser illustrates the concept of constantly modifying one's concretizations by comparing the reading experience to a cybernetic feedback loop. Because of this experiential emphasis, he can assert that "the text can never be grasped as a whole, only as a series of changing viewpoints, each one restricted in itself and so necessitating further perspectives."

"Gaps" or "blanks" (*Unbestimmtsheitsstellen*) provide the impetus for the creation of a theme/horizon gestalt by inviting the reader to respond to an interruption in the flow or exposition with a meaning-creating pairing. "Wherever there is an abrupt juxtaposition of segments there must automatically be a blank," he argues, "breaking the expected order of the text." Iserian gaps have been explained as "conceptual spaces" between textual elements that allow for reader ideation. According to Iser, "Gaps are bound to open up, and offer a free play of interpretation for the specific way in which the various views can be connected with one another. These gaps give the reader a chance to build his own bridges." But gaps do not really allow for "free play"; the reader must engage in "intersubjectively" valid concretizations: "The structured blanks of the text stimulate the process of ideation to be performed by the reader on terms set by the text. The concept of *Unbestimmtsheitsstellen,* or gaps, is Iser's central trope for figuring the active reader involvement required by the reading experience.

The final concept to summarize before applying Iser's phenomenologically precise model of the reading process to Tan's *Joy Luck Club* is negativity. For Iser, the depiction of anything unattractive or deformed automatically causes the reader to imagine a positive counterbalance. This is another kind of gap, then: deformity creates a space in which the active reader compensates for the unattractive depiction with the imagining of a more positive situation or character.

Iser's unusual sensitivity to the moment-by-moment construction of the text by a reader makes his theory especially relevant to fragmented texts. Indeed, he "valorizes the discontinuous work" that is full of gaps. This can be seen in his comments on *Ulysses, The Sound and the Fury,* and Humphrey Clinker in *The Implied Reader* and *The Act of Reading.*

Reading *The Joy Luck Club* in the context of Iser's elaborately worked out theory and his remarks on fragmented, multi-perspectival texts require paying attention to the way in which a reader's moment-by-moment processing of the text confers a centripetal coherence upon a potentially chaotic, centrifugal collection. We need to ask how the discontinuous nature of the narrative (the gaps between sections, in particular) impels the reader to establish *Gestalten* that are multiple, constantly shifting, and thematically suggestive. We need to look for ways in which initial constructions of foreground/background configurations have to be revised as additional text is encountered. And we need to ask where the line can be drawn between responses that are "intersubjectively" valid and those that range beyond what can be agreed upon intersubjectively.

The segmented presentation of *The Joy Luck Club* allows for many combinational possibilities. I will present some of the most salient *Gestalten*; other foreground/background paintings will, no doubt, suggest themselves based on the examples I offer.

One way *Gestalten* can be created is through juxtapositions of contiguous and non-contiguous monologues. With contiguously placed utterances that "speak to" each other, the side-by-side placement of monologues with common denominators, or, to use Bakhtin's term, "semantic convergence," constitutes an overt invitation to the reader to explore the dialogic potential between the monologues. In these cases, the gap between the sections, which always invites a reflective pause, ensures that a rereading reader will make the connection (although the reader still deserves credit for making the connection).

The first cluster of four monologues provides us with some examples of meaningful juxtapositions, both contiguous and non-contiguous.

In the opening monologue of the novel, Jing-mei (June) offers comments on both Ying-ying and An-mei that color our attitude toward those two. Of Ying-ying, she says that the aunt "seems to shrink even more every time I see her." A few pages later, she adds to this unflattering picture by reporting what her mother thought of Ying-ying. "'Oh, I have a story,' says Auntie Ying loudly, startling everybody. Auntie Ying has always been the weird auntie, someone lost in her own world. My mother used to say, 'Auntie Ying is not hard of hearing. She is hard of listening.'"

A few monologues later, we meet Ying-ying from her own point of view. Her account of the traumatic experience of falling off her family's boat and, more generally, growing up in a wealthy family without much contact with her mother, sets up a meaningful gestalt with Jing-mei's comments. On first reading, June's unappreciative comments prejudice us against Ying-ying as the "weird" one; when we read her own account of her childhood and pair that with Jing-mei's words, we realize Jing-mei's account is reductive. On the outside she may appear to be shrinking, and she may appear "hard of listening" on the inside she has a story to tell that helps explain why she is the way she is. The experience of this gestalt, which shifts depending on one's position in the text (June's words as foreground, Ying-ying's monologue as background, or the latter's monologue as foreground, and June's unappreciative words as background), points out to the reader that greater understanding can lead to greater appreciation and tolerance.

June also comments on An-mei in an unappreciative manner, reporting what her mother has said of An-mei. This allows for the establishment of another theme/horizon configuration.

> "She's not stupid," said my mother on one occasion, "but she has no spine. . . ."
>
> "Auntie An-mei runs this way and that," said my mother, "and she doesn't know why."
>
> As I watch Auntie An-mei, I see a short bent woman in her seventies, with a heavy bosom and thin, shapeless legs. She has the flattened soft fingertips of an old woman.

When we meet An-mei in "Scar," immediately after June's opening monologue, we realize that her childhood helps explain why she appears to have no spine. Her moving account of her painful separation from her mother and the traumatic circumstances resulting in her throat scar establishes a context for her apparent spinelessness; it adds to the outer appearance of weakness a story that makes the reductive labeling inadequate to the human reality. This juxtaposition would be interesting even if An-mei herself said she did not have spine: the theme/horizon juxtaposition would make for a poignant realization in the reader's mind of the subjective, limited nature of understanding, with An-mei's terrible childhood, on the one hand, helping to explain why she behaves the way she does, and the unsympathetic, reductive pigeonholing by Suyuan, on the other, typifying the overly reductive manner in which we often sum people up.

The theme/horizon gestalt produced and experienced by the reader following the textual prompts is further enhanced, however, when it is remembered that An-mei thinks she herself does have spine, and that her daughter Rose is the one who is weak. Rose tells us in "Without Wood": "My mother once told me why I was so confused all the time. She said I was without wood. Born without wood so that I listened to too many people. She knew this, because once she had almost become this way." June's mother, Suyuan, who was a bold woman, may have thought that An-mei lacked spine; An-mei, who is proud of having stood up for herself after her mother died, thinks that her daughter lacks "wood": what results is a vivid realization in the mind of the reader who is alert to the potential dialogicity between textual segments that some things are entirely relative.

Another kind of inter-monologue dialogicity in the first cluster of four monologues consists of a triptych of personality difference the monologues of An-mei, Lindo, and Ying-ying. At the center of this trio of self-portraits is a remarkably bold and strong individual who managed to extract herself from a repressive situation cleverly and diplomatically so that everyone benefited. Lindo's resourcefulness and boldness is framed by two portraits of passivity and weakness: An-mei and Ying-ying are victims of their childhood circumstances. As we move from An-mei's "Scar" to Lindo's "Red Candle," we are impressed with the very different responses to repressive circumstances; as we move from Lindo's "Red Candle" to Ying-ying's "Moon Lady" we return to the perspective of a victim. One specific gestalt the reader is invited to create between Lindo's "Red Candle" to Ying-ying's "Moon Lady" revolves around the "semantic convergence" (using Bakhtin's phrase) of losing and finding oneself. Lindo tells us that she discovered her inner power through an epiphany:

> I asked myself, What is true about a person? Would I change in the same way the river changes color but still be the same person? And then I saw the curtains blowing wildly, and outside rain was falling harder, causing everyone to scurry and shout. I smiled. And then I realized it was the first time I could see the power of the wind. I couldn't see the wind itself, but I could see it carried the water that filled the rivers and shaped the countryside. It caused men to yelp and dance.
>
> I wiped my eyes and looked in the mirror. I was surprised at what I saw. I had on a beautiful red dress, but what I saw was even more valuable. I was strong. I was pure. I had genuine thoughts inside that no one could see, that no one could ever take away from me. I was like the wind.
>
> I threw my head back and smiled proudly to myself. And then I draped the large embroidered red scarf over my face and covered these thoughts up. But underneath the scarf I still knew who I was. I made a promise to myself: I would always remem-

ber my parents' wishes, but I would never forget myself.

This remarkable passage about self-discovery and self-assertion in the midst of repression can be set in dialogue with the concluding passage in Ying-ying's monologue following Lindo's, where Ying-ying tells us that the most important moment of her childhood was when she lost herself:

> Now that I am old, moving every year closer to the end of my life, I . . . feel closer to the beginning. And I remember everything that happened that day [the day she fell into the water] because it has happened many times in my life. The same innocence, trust, and restlessness, the wonder, fear, and loneliness. How I lost myself.
>
> I remember all these things. And tonight, on the fifteenth day of the eighth moon, I also remember what I asked the Moon Lady so long ago. I wished to be found.

These contiguously placed monologues with a common denominator of finding or losing one's self enter into a dialogicity of difference with the reader as the agent and site of the dialogicity. The result is to enhance the range of personalities offered: the mothers, for all their similarities, are indeed very different, as comparisons such as the one just made establish. Tan succeeds in achieving a truly diverse and heteroglot range of mothers's perspectives in *The Joy Luck Club*.

Another example of a counter-centrifugal gestalt the reader is invited to create from contiguously placed monologues consists of a pairing of Lena's worries in "Rice Husband" with Waverly's worries in "Four Directions." In this third quartet of monologues, both Lena and Waverly express frustration over their meddlesome mothers. In "Rice Husband," Lena is apprehensive about her mother's visit, fearing that her mother will perceive that her relationship with Harold is flawed. Ying-ying has an unusual ability to sense trouble and even predict calamity.

> During our brief tour of the house, she's already found the flaws. . . . And it annoys me that all she sees are the bad parts. But then I look around and everything she's said is true. And this convinces me she can see what else is going on, between Harold and me. She knows what is going to happen to us.

Knowing that there is something wrong with the rigid policy she and Harold follow of sharing all costs equally, she is afraid her mother will confront her with a truth she does not want to admit. Waverly, on the other hand, is worried that her mother will poison her relationship with Rich the way

Lindo poisoned her marriage with her previous husband, Marvin. Lindo had effectively ruined the gift of a fur coat Rich had given Waverly: "Looking at the coat in the mirror, I couldn't fend off the strength of her will anymore, her ability to make me see black where there was once white, white where there was once black. The coat looked shabby, an imitation of romance." Lindo has destroyed something that Waverly took pleasure in. Likewise, she is apprehensive that Lindo will undermine her love for Rich.

> I already knew what she would do, how she would be quiet at first. Then she would say a word about something small, something she had noticed, and then another word, and another, each one flung out like a little piece of sand, one from this direction, another from behind, more and more, until his looks, his character, his soul would have eroded away. And even if I recognized her strategy, her sneak attack, I was afraid that some unseen speck of truth would fly into my eye, blur what I was seeing and transform him from the divine man I thought he was into someone quite mundane, mortally wounded with tiresome habits and irritating imperfections.

Whereas Ying-ying will confront Lena with something Lena should deal with, Lindo will insidiously undermine the love Waverly has for Richard, thus poisoning her relationship. The gestalt that the text invites the reader to create from these contiguously placed monologues counters the centrifugal tendency of this decentered text by setting into an aesthetically meaningful dialogue these two very different kinds of apprehension. This linkage across monologues works to point out the difference between the two daughters—thus enhancing the heteroglot nature of the multi-voiced narrative even as it creates coherence across fragments through the essential similarity.

In Bakhtinian terms, we might think of Lena's and Waverly's apprehensions as entering into a dialogic relationship of similarity. Bakhtin points out in *Problems of Dostoevsky's Poetics* that there can be a dialogicity between two speakers uttering the same words—"Life is good"—depending on the particular nuances each gives to the utterance from embodied and distinct reference points. Simple disagreement can be less dialogic than agreement, he points out. We might say that Lena declares, "Mothers are meddlesome," and that Waverly concurs with "Mothers are meddlesome"; the reader is the agent and the site of the dialogic engagement of these two essentially similar, yet very different, complaints.

My final example of counter-centrifugal *Gestalten* created from contiguously placed monologues is the triptych of three mothers in the final cluster. An-mei's "Magpies," Ying-ying's "Waiting Between the Trees," and Lindo's "Double Face"

all present the reader with a mother who wants desperately to reach out and establish a connection with her daughter—in spite of the disagreements and conflicts. Each mother hopes to establish a closer relationship by telling her a story. And each mother is shown with a story to tell. Each mother offers the second installment of her life story: An-mei tells what it was like living with her mother as Fourth Wife; Ying-ying describes her marriage in China, the murder of her child, and her marriage to her current husband; and Lindo tells about how she left China and came to the United States. In each case, however, it appears that the actual communication does not occur. Tan's multiple monologue novel seems to participate in the convention of having speakers speak into the void—or to the reader as audience. No actual communication between mothers and daughters occurs. Presented with these three monologues, the reader is invited to establish the connection between them. The dialogicity of similarity in this gestalt, where each theme of the moment can be set against one or both of the other monologues as the horizon, is a powerfully persuasive method of arguing on behalf of the mothers. No narrative voice need announce that mothers should be listened to; the narrative makes the reader poignantly aware of the distance between each mother and daughter by showing the unbridged gap between them and the potential for sharing and communication that is only partially realized. This triptych of well-meaning mothers who want to pass on something to their daughters is another example of how there can be dialogic potential between similar utterances (as in "Life is good," "Life is good") in a multiple narrator novel, with the reader's consciousness as the site of the inter-monologue dialogicity.

So far, my discussion of the counter-centrifugal *Gestalten* created by the reader has focused on the pairing of "themes" (Iser's term for perspectives of the moment) that are already presented by the narrative in a relationship through simple contiguous juxtaposition. It is also possible to consider *Gestalten* that a reader's wandering viewpoint might create from "themes" that are not already set side-by-side. These juxtapositions might be called conceptual rather than contiguous (although even with side-by-side placement, the resulting gestalt must be a creation in the reader's mind and thus conceptual).

The pairings possible with monologues from Lena and Ying-ying are examples of the interesting *Gestalten* creatable from non-contiguous monologues. We might take Lena's "The Voice from the Wall" as a starting point. Her perspective on her mother is entirely unappreciative here; she has no understanding or sympathy—and how could she, since Ying-ying's past is never talked about ("My mother never talked about her life in China, but my father said he saved her from a terrible life there, some tragedy she could not speak about."). She presents her mother as psychologically imbalanced. She thinks of her mother as a "Displaced Person," using a photograph taken after the scared woman was released from Angel Island Immigration Station to represent her personality:

> In this picture you can see why my mother looks displaced. She is clutching a large clam-shaped bag, as though someone might steal this from her as well if she is less watchful. She has on an ankle-length Chinese dress. . . . In this outfit she looks as if she were neither coming from nor going to some-place. . . .
>
> My mother often looked this way, waiting for something to happen, wearing this scared look. Only later she lost the struggle to keep her eyes open.

We realize that Ying-ying's troubled mental state must have impinged negatively on Lena as she grew up, and we sympathize with her for that. But as readers who are privileged to know the inner thoughts of every character, we can balance off that perspective with what we know from Ying-ying's "Moon Lady" monologue, where we learn about the childhood trauma that has clearly affected her personality. And from "The Voice from the Wall," we can look forward, as well, and set Lena's frustration with her mother's aberrational personality against "Waiting Between the Trees": in this moving monologue, Ying-ying reveals a side of herself that Lena would be surprised to learn about. The Ying-ying we meet here is completely unknown to her daughter.

> So I will tell Lena of my shame. That I was rich and pretty. I was too good for any one man. That I became abandoned goods. I will tell her that at eighteen the prettiness drained from my cheeks. That I thought of throwing myself in the lake like the other ladies of shame. And I will tell her of the baby I killed because I came to hate this man so much.
>
> I took this baby from my womb before it could be born. This was not a bad thing to do in China back then, to kill a baby before it is born. But even then, I thought it was bad, because my body flowed with terrible revenge as the juices of this man's firstborn son poured from me.
>
> When the nurses asked what they should do with the lifeless baby, I hurled a newspaper at them and said to wrap it like a fish and throw it in the lake. My daughter thinks I do not know what it means to not want a baby.
>
> When my daughter looks at me, she sees a small old lady. That is because she sees only with her outside eyes. She has no *chuming,* no inside knowing

of things. If she had chuming, she would see a tiger lady. And she would have careful fear.

This set of *Gestalten*—"Voices" and "Moon Lady," "Voices" and "Waiting"—points out the relativity theme that this multiple narrator novel, like many, proposes. The very structure and narrative mode of the novel suggest that we appreciate the subjective nature of perception there is in Lena's thinking of her mother as a Displaced Person and Ying-ying's thinking of herself as a "Tiger Woman." However, **The Joy Luck Club** differs from other radically decentered multiple narrator novels such as *As I Lay Dying* and, more recently, Auchincloss's *The House of the Prophet* or Matthiessen's *Killing Mister Watson*—in that it does not insist on absolute epistemological relativism. The reader who actively pairs momentary "themes" realizes that there is more to Ying-ying than Lena's "Displaced Person" label allows for; the reader senses the potential for dialogue between mother and daughter that fails to take place.

This repeated failure for mother and daughter to enter into meaningful exchange is effectively represented through another Lena/Ying-ying gestalt: the pairing of Lena's "Rice Husband" monologue with Ying-ying's "Waiting Between the Trees." In "Waiting," Ying-ying is apparently about to cause the unstable table to fall, sending the vase crashing to the floor. She hopes to attract her daughter's attention and get her to come into the room where Ying-ying can talk to her. Ying-ying clearly wants to use it as the occasion to tell Lena everything she has wanted to tell her and to pass on her *chi* to her daughter. But in "Rice Husband," five monologues prior to "Waiting," the vase has already crashed to the floor and mother and daughter have already had their moment together. From what Lena reports in "Rice Husband," nothing came of the encounter. Tan's use of the unstable table as a common denominator across the two monologues constitutes an effective exercise in triangulation, a common technique in multiple narrator novels to demonstrate (usually) the subjective nature of perception.

Another example of triangulation that prompts the reader to create a gestalt pairing two monologues that have a common denominator occurs with An-mei's "Magpies" and Rose's "Without Wood." The common denominator inviting a pairing of the monologues is Rose's psychiatrist. This gestalt is an especially interesting one for the novel because of the way it foregrounds the distance between the traditionally minded Chinese mother living in the United States and the American-born daughter who has embraced many American ways. From the American perspective, it is normal and even stylish for Rose to see a psychiatrist; from the Chinese perspective, seeing a psychiatrist is incomprehensible; indeed, An-mei might even regard it as bringing shame upon the family. An-mei's "Magpies" begins and ends with her complete dismissal of the idea of seeing a psychiatrist; she does not approve of Rose's seeing one. But this conceptual gestalt—"Without Wood" and "Magpies" on the issue of seeing a psychiatrist—is more interesting than just the representation of complete lack of understanding on the part of mother and daughter. Rose actually does stop seeing her shrink—and she's better off because of it. She stops talking to other people as well, which her mother recommended. After a prolonged period of isolation and sleep—three days—she emerges defiant, ready to take on Ted. She thus relies on her own inner strength and faces up to Ted, which is just what her mother wanted her to do. However, she reaches this point on her own, not by simply listening to her mother (her mother's alternative to seeing a psychiatrist is the daughter simply listening to the mother's advice). And confronting Ted seems to have unleashed a realization at a deeper, psychic level about the abusive nature of her mother, as well. In her dream, her mother is planting weeds in her garden that are running wild.

Another example of how non-contiguous "themes" can be set into a gestalt through the active memory and conceptual pairing activity of an Iserian reader is the linkage of the moments of self-assertion throughout the novel. This involves a series of linkages, with several possible pairings, or even one mega-gestalt. Rose's self-assertion in "Without Wood" can be linked up with June's in "Two Kinds," An-mei's in "Magpies" (where her self-assertion after the death of her mother is described), and Lindo's in "The Red Candle" (where she describes the epiphany that led her to her ruse, as previously discussed). Here we have another example of the dialogic potential of similar utterances: each of these women has had to assert herself in the face of some kind of oppression; in spite of their differences, they are united on this theme, but each has a different nuance to give to the statement, "I have had to assert myself."

Another way in which *The Joy Luck Club* invites through its discontinuous form the creative work of a reader pairing segments into order—conferring *Gestalten* in response to textual prompt—is with the four prefaces. They serve, much like the interludes in *The Waves,* as a universalizing backdrop against which to see the particularized monologues. Each monologue can be set against the preface, and each cluster can be taken as an Iserian "theme" set against the "horizon" of the respective preface. The prefaces also help the reader pick up on what Tan calls the "emotional curve" of each "quartet."

The prelude to Part One, "Feathers From a Thousand Li Away," presents in fable-like form a nameless Chinese woman who emigrated to America with hopes that she'd have a daughter who would lead a better life than was possible for a woman in China. The Chinese woman is full of good intentions and hopes for that daughter. But her relationship with her daughter is characterized by distance and lack of communication. The following four monologues reveal mothers who bemoan the distance to their daughters but who had good intentions. This prefatory piece, then, helps us organize the four very different opening monologues around that "emotional curve," which serves as a horizon against which the monologues can be apprehended.

The preface to Part Two, "The Twenty-Six Malignant Gates," helps organize the way we think about the daughters's monologues in that section by suggesting that Chinese mothers can be overbearing in their attempts to protect and control their daughters, and that this will result in rebelliousness on the part of their daughters, as well as misfortune. This brief fable-like anecdote manages to encapsulate the dynamics of the monologues that follow and helps us organize the disparate elements of those monologues around the implied criticism of overprotective, overbearing mothers. If the first preface prepares us to be sympathetic towards the mothers, this second preface prepares us to be sympathetic towards the daughters as we read each monologue against that preface as a backdrop.

The preface to Part Three, "American Translation," also enters into a dialogic relationship with the monologues of that section through the gestalt-producing activity of the reader. Introducing another round of daughters's monologues, it presents us with a mother who appears to be overbearing in her desire for a grandchild. She insists that her daughter mount a mirror on the wall for good luck. The mother sees her grandchild in the mirror; the daughter sees only "her own reflection looking back at her." Tan seems to be suggesting with this the theme of conflicting perspectives and the struggle between daughters and mothers—a theme that is seen in the monologues that follow. Mothers see one thing; daughters see something entirely different. But the metaphor here is actually relevant only to the daughters's perspective: it suggests that mothers project their own subjective preferences upon what they see whereas daughters see objectively, which is itself a distorted notion. From the mothers's perspective, they see clearly and daughters distort reality. Because this preface is designed to make us sympathetic to the daughters, it is slanted towards them; the "emotional curve" is with the daughters.

A dialogic relationship also exists between the final fable-like preface and the final four monologues when the gestalt-creating capacity of the reader is called upon. The preface gives shape to the monologues that follow by presenting a mother who has a grandchild and who is treated sympathetically: she is self-critical and hopeful for her daughter, wishing that her daughter can learn "how to lose [her] innocence but not her hope." Very sympathetic to the mother, this preface prepares us to organize the monologues we are about to encounter in a manner that is sympathetic to the mothers.

Reading each monologue in this cluster against the backdrop of the fourth preface helps establish the thematic point.

The *Gestalten* the reader creates from the four prefatory pieces thus confer considerable order upon what might at first appear to be a dizzying display of very different personalities, even with the common denominator of Chinese mothers and Chinese-American daughters. Like *The Waves*, *The Joy Luck Club* sets monologues against third-person interludes that function by suggesting a universal backdrop to the series of individualized voices; unlike *The Waves*, however, which uses nature as the universal backdrop, *The Joy Luck Club* prefaces use nameless human figures and abstract situations to suggest general truths.

Although the narrative invites the reader to establish all sorts of specific pairings between contiguous and non-contiguous monologues, the fundamental *Gestalten*, of course, consist of pairings of mothers collectively and daughters collectively. The daughters complaining about their mothers can be gathered together as one gestalt, with each daughter set against another daughter or the rest of the daughters. Presenting the daughters together in the middle two quartets encourages this kind of pairing. The mothers complaining about their daughters can be gathered together as well, with each complaining mother set against any other or the group. The narrative's most basic gestalt is that of mothers apprehended against the backdrop of daughters, or daughters apprehended against the backdrop of mothers. Among the daughters and among the mothers there is a dialogicity of sameness that consists of a fundamental similarity with individual nuances.

The narrative steers the reader, however, towards a particular kind of gestalt consisting of mothers's and daughters's perspectives; we have more than just an array of different perspectives with combinational possibilities among them. The daughters's positions, however understandable and valid, are enclosed and framed by the mothers's positions; however unreasonable or narrow-minded the mothers may seem in their attempts to impose their wills on their daughters, the narrative's structure, which invites the reader to apprehend the daughters against the backdrop of mothers, gives the mothers the upper hand in the argument. The three mothers presented before Jing-mei's closing monologue acquire a critical mass; their voices add up to an overwhelming appeal to respect the life experience and wishes of the mothers. Amy Ling's observation that the book "more often takes a sympathetic stand toward the mother" is a sound assessment because of the shape Tan gives the collection by allowing the mothers to have the final say.

The reader's processing of the four quartets over time necessitates changing initial assessments and thus illustrates Iser's concept of reading as a feedback loop requiring the revision of *Gestalten*. The Iserian reader's primary activity and response consists of creatively pairing different sections or moments into meaningful *Gestalten* and then revising initial constructions when new material is encountered. The clustering of monologues into quartets tempts the reader into certain judgments that must be revised as more of the text is encountered (upon an initial reading): the first cluster biases us towards the parents; the second and third clusters make us more sympathetic to the daughters; the final cluster ensures that the mothers get the upper hand in the debate, even though the daughters are given a very full hearing. The various foreground/background conceptual structures (and *Gestalten* from contiguously placed monologues are conceptual as well as *Gestalten* from non-contiguous monologues) can be created during an initial reading, or upon re-reading (which allows one to reach forward as well as backwards from any present moment of reading).

Iser's concept of negativity, another kind of "gap," also applies to *The Joy Luck Club*. The reader is poignantly aware of the potential for greater communication and understanding, but only in the reader's mind is the dialogicity between positions uncovered and experienced. The mothers and daughters are speaking into a void, not to each other (I read the occasional use of the second person in some of the monologues as an aside to an imagined audience, not an actual audience). Thus the narrative form and the thematic point complement each other. The result of this depiction of failed communication is that the reader, through the process of "negativity," is motivated to imagine a healthier response. Although the narrative provides a solution to the dilemma in the final chapter, the reader's experience before the final chapter of the failure to communicate ensures that the reader will be motivated to avoid such incommunicative relationships in his or her own life.

At this point I would like to address the issue of closure in *The Joy Luck Club*. Although depicting in the final chapter an answer to the problem of non-communication demonstrated up to the ending may seem like the perfect way for Tan to conclude, I have had difficulty accepting what seemed to me to be an overly sentimental and facile resolution. I would like to present my initial assessment of this issue and then attempt to move beyond that resisting response with a more accepting reading of the ending. My purpose in presenting my own experience with the issue of closure in *The Joy Luck Club* is to foreground various issues that I believe are important for an understanding of Tan's book.

In my 1992 study of contemporary American multiple narrator novels, I summed up my discomfort with June's novel-ending monologue thusly:

> My sense, when viewing *The Joy Luck Club* in the context of other multiple narrator novels, is that the

book is at odds with itself. The various monologues of mothers and daughters, monologues that foreground difference—indeed, that flaunt discrepancy, conflict and relativism—set in motion a centrifugality that cannot so easily be overcome. The happy ending . . . [is] not true to the heteroglot diversity actually revealed throughout the text. . . . In my experience of *The Joy Luck Club,* the Suyuan/Jing-mei reconciliation is not convincing, and there clearly is no final reconciliation between all the mothers and daughters. Thus, as I see it, the attempt to reign in the heteroglossia does not do justice to the resonating diversity; that diversity actually eludes subduing through the kind of reductive thematic reading [that the ending invites].

I then pointed out the similarity between my observation about closure in *The Joy Luck Club* and Dale Bauer's comment about the novels she analyzes in her *Feminist Dialogics.* In Bauer's Bakhtin-inspired uncovering of repressed heteroglossia, she observes that "while the plot resolutions give closure to the novels, the dialogue resists that closure." I continued my attempt to articulate my discomfort with the ending by arguing that the process Iser terms "negativity" is sufficient to make the thematic point without a heavy-handed ending.

> The reader's sense of the poignancy inherent in a situation where mothers and daughters do not communicate as fully as they might in itself implies a remedy, in itself motivates the reader to imagine a solution—one that would accommodate the needs of both mothers and daughters. . . . *The Joy Luck Club* interferes with the imagined affirmation by prodding the reader too much. It is one thing to show Waverly, at the close of "Four Directions," attempting to impose an artificial, superficial pleasantness on her deeply problematic relationship with her mother by thinking about taking her mother with her on her honeymoon that reveals an interesting split within this particular consciousness; it is another matter to have Tan . . . [impose] a superficial sense of harmony at the end of the book that does not do justice to the actual diversity and conflict between the covers. The collection of stories is full of moral potential without the heavy-handed ending simply through its presentation of multiple voices, artistically organized.

My having been immersed in Bakhtin, Iser, and Faulkner at the time contributed to my lack of appreciation for the way this novel ends. Bakhtin's take on the novel as a genre is one that privileges the flaunting of diverse perspectives that, while dialogized, are never resolved into harmonious agreement or simple synthesis. His insistence on "unfinalizability"

led me to privilege open-ended multiple narrator novels over those with strong closure. Iser's model led me to privilege texts that allow the reader to establish the thematic point without having it boldly announced. And my reading of Faulkner's own multiple narrator novels likewise biased me. *As I Lay Dying,* for example, while providing a sense of ending, flaunts diversity and discrepancy across subjectivities; it revels in the diverse viewpoints and the isolated personalities. *The Sound and the Fury,* too, while offering closure, resists its own ending and the thematic answer it provides (through Dilsey) to the problem of the solipsistic ego epitomized by the Quentin and Jason monologues. Faulkner, as I read him, is more interested in the poetic potential of pathology than in offering any thematic proposition about life.

My effort to rethink my initial response to the strong sense of closure in *The Joy Luck Club* involves a number of considerations based on feedback about this response from other scholars and my own students.

One of those considerations is gender. The "sentimental" ending of the novel may simply evoke different responses from male and female readers. With the kind of psychodynamic model of personality development that feminists like Nancy Chodorow offer (c.f. *The Reproduction of Mothering*), it is possible to argue that women, who are more oriented to bonding and relationships than men (men emphasize separation and autonomy instead, according to this theory), are less likely to resist Tan's ending. My experience teaching the novel in an all-female classroom at Texas Woman's University was enlightening because no one found the ending to be sentimental or false. . . .

Perhaps the most useful approach to the issue of closure in *The Joy Luck Club* is a culturally grounded one. When Tan's contribution to the multiple narrator sub-genre is considered in the context of Asian values, the desire for an ending that brings the resonating diversity and conflicting positions to a tidy close is entirely understandable.

A culturally nuanced reading of the novel might begin with the fundamental orientation toward the group rather than the individual in Asian cultures generally, as stated in the following passage taken from the classic reference book cited earlier of Asian culture for American therapists whose client population includes Asian Americans:

> American society has tended toward the ideals of the self-sufficient, self-reliant individual who is the master of his or her fate and chooses his or her own destiny. High value is placed on the ability to stand on your own two feet, or pull yourself up by your own bootstraps, or do your own thing. In contrast, Asian philosophies tend toward an acknowledgment that individuals become what they are because of

the efforts of many things and many people. They are the products of their relationship to nature and other people. Thus, heavy emphasis is placed on the nature of the relationship among people, generally with the aim of maintaining harmony through proper conduct and attitudes.

This general orientation toward the group is manifested in the emphasis on respecting and serving one's parents, not resisting them. "The greatest obligation of East Asians," according to McGoldrick and her colleagues, "is to their parents, who have brought them into the world and have cared for them when they were helpless. The debt that is owed can never be truly repaid; and no matter what parents may do the child is still obligated to give respect and obedience"—an attitude that can be traced back to Confucius.

> **Although *The Joy Luck Club* gives equal time to the position of daughters who resist or resent a domineering mother, an American reader is less likely to grant those mothers their due without understanding that Asian mothers normally behave in a more heavy-handed manner than their American counterparts.**
> **—Stephen Souris**

Another aspect of Asian cultures generally (East Asian in this particular case) that is pertinent to a culturally nuanced response to *The Joy Luck Club* has to do with shaming. McGoldrick and her co-authors explain that in these cultures, "shame and shaming are the mechanisms that traditionally help reinforce societal expectations and proper behavior." Vacc and his colleagues explain more specifically that "control of the children [in Chinese and Japanese families] is maintained by fostering feelings of shame and guilt." Without knowing this, it is more likely that the shaming behavior some of the mothers of *The Joy Luck Club* engage in to control their children will result in a reading that blames those mothers for inappropriate behavior. As a consequence of the misunderstanding, such a reader would not grant those mothers the sympathy for which they qualify.

Yet another aspect of Asian culture that contributes to a sensitive reading of Tan's novel is the close relationship between a mother and her children in Asian countries. McGoldrick and her co-authors explain it thusly:

> The traditional role of the mother must also be understood and respected within the context of her role expectations within the family. Issues involving the children reflect upon her self-esteem as a mother. We must remember that in the traditional family, the children are primarily her responsibility, as well as her resource for the future. Frequently, issues around perceived dependence of children and over-protection of the mother are raised by American therapists who are unfamiliar with traditional family dynamics of Asian families. Therapists do not always understand that within the family mutual interdependence is stressed and expected. This is not to say that individuation does not occur or is not promoted, but it is constantly tinged with the subconscious knowledge of the relationships and obligations between the individual and other family members.

Although *The Joy Luck Club* gives equal time to the position of daughters who resist or resent a domineering mother, an American reader is less likely to grant those mothers their due without understanding that Asian mothers normally behave in a more heavy-handed manner than their American counterparts.

The final point I wish to make about Asian cultures that contributes to a balanced response to both the mothers and the daughters in *The Joy Luck Club* is that Asian families in America tend to place extraordinary emphasis on the importance of education for their children. Vacc and his co-authors explain it thusly:

> The pressure to succeed academically among Asians is very strong. From early childhood, outstanding achievement is emphasized because it is a source of pride for the entire family. . . . Reflecting the emphasis on education is the finding that college enrollment rates for Chinese and Japanese between the ages of 18 and 24 and the percentage completing college is higher than for any other group in the United States. Parental expectations for achievement can be an additional stress factor in young Asian-Americans.

This information is important for a sensitive response to both Jing-mei and Suyuan, who calls her daughter a "college drop-off." It is in the context of explaining her dropping out of college that Jing-mei tells us: "My mother and I never really understood one another. We translated each other's meanings and I seemed to hear less than what was said, while my mother heard more."

With this background information in mind, it is easier to understand the thematic readings of Tan's novel that do not focus on the differences between mothers and the differences between daughters as much as upon the similarities. In this culture-specific context, Tan's attempt to rein in the reverberating heteroglossia has a compelling logic.

The readings of **The Joy Luck Club** offered by Amy Ling and Elaine Kim are undertaken within this context. They emphasize the mother/daughter gestalt discussed earlier and the importance of the broader dynamic between mothers and daughters that this gestalt suggests; Ling and Kim are not as focused on individual personalities as a reader coming from Faulkner, Bakhtin, and Iser would be. Ling argues that "though the mothers all have different names and individual stories, they seem interchangeable in that the role of mother supersedes all other roles and is performed with the utmost seriousness and determination. All the mothers in **The Joy Luck Club** are strong, powerful women." Kim likewise argues that "one of the triumphs of the book is that it is easy to lose track of the individual women's voices: the reader might turn distractedly to the table of contents, trying to pair the mothers and daughters or to differentiate among them, only to discover the point that none of this matters in the least." Ling's reading privileges the mothers's perspectives and argues that the narrative endorses their position more than the daughters's resisting positions. Her reading of the novel is that it "more often takes a sympathetic stand toward the mothers's. Ling further argues that in spite of the battles described, the daughters eventually acquiesce: "The daughters' battles for independence from powerful commanding mothers is fierce, but eventually, as in [*The Woman Warrior*], a reconciliation is reached. The daughters realize that the mothers have always had the daughters' own best interests at heart." Ling has no problem with Jing-mei's "act of filial obedience" closing the narrative. Her concluding remarks clearly indicate her acceptance of the ending as a perfectly appropriate one; she does not resist the narrative's attempt to counterbalance the conflicting voices with its ending. "[The novel] ends on a note of resolution and reconciliation. The struggles, the battles, are over, and when the dust settles what was formerly considered a hated bondage is revealed to be a cherished bond." Thematizing the novel, she interprets its message thusly

> To be truly mature, to achieve a balance in the between-world condition then . . . one cannot cling solely to the new American ways and reject the old Chinese ways, for that is the way of the child. One must reconcile the two and make one's peace with the old. If the old ways cannot be incorporated into the new life, if they do not "mix" as Lindo Jong put it, then they must nonetheless be respected and preserved in the pictures on one's walls, in the memories in one's head, in the stories that one writes down.

Bonnie TuSmith, in her recent study of the importance of community in American ethnic literatures, *All My Relatives*, offers a reading of the battling positions of the narrative that also privileges the mothers's perspective. She interprets the passage describing the Polaroid shot of the three sisters as follows: "This composite image of three daughters who, together, make up one mother reflects the novel's communal subtext, which works as a counterpoint to the textual surface of individualistic strife between mothers and daughters." More specifically, she suggests that the narrative argues against the daughters's individualistic voices and for the establishment of harmony with the mothers:

> The novel opens with Jing-Mei's assuming her mother's role at the mahjongg table of the Joy Luck Club. Her "substitute" role is recalled in the conclusion when she is in China and taking her mother's place once again. This literary frame alone suggests that, although the mother-daughter power struggle appears individualistic on the surface, there is a different message embedded in the text.

The culturally based, heavily thematic readings that TuSmith and Ling offer thus emphasize the overall *Gestalten* of mothers set against daughters and daughters set against mothers with a nod towards the position of the mothers. Ling emphasizes the importance of the daughters respecting and acknowledging the position of the mothers; TuSmith offers a more complex surface versus deep structure analysis that sees the conflicting perspectives as merely a surface phenomenon and the difference-transcending communalism as a more fundamental underlying impulse.

Although my own earlier reading was not sufficiently cognizant of cultural factors—such as the emphasis in Chinese-American cultures on group and family orientation, respect for parents, shaming by parents for control of children, dependent relationships, and education of children—a reading of **The Joy Luck Club** that fully accounts for its complexity perhaps requires taking a middle-ground position: the narrative, with its overall structure (framing) and thematic conclusion, suggests resolution and reconciliation, but the actual collection of voices cannot with complete accuracy be reduced to a thematic reading. If one imagines Tan writing with her mother looking on (and from what she has said about her relationship with her mother, this seems accurate), there should be no surprise that the novel argues for something while at the same time resisting it through the very presentation of a heteroglot array of individual voices.

In either case, a Bakhtin-inspired and Iser-based reading of **The Joy Luck Club** is possible and contributes to a moment-by-moment uncovering and articulation of the counter-centrifugal dialogicity in the collection of monologues. An Iserian reading locates the various points of difference and agreement across monologues and establishes the connections between them. As Bakhtin suggests, the dialogicity can be of agreement as well as disagreement; to use his example, "Life is good" and "Life is good" can resonate through slightly different accents given to the basic proposition.

"Mothers are oppressive" and "Mothers are oppressive"—or "daughters should show respect" and "daughters should show respect"—can likewise resonate across monologues by having a different accentuation with each speaker.

Whether or not one agrees that the novel genuinely achieves a resolution and reconciliation (that might be an objective "meaning" versus subjective "significance" issue, in Iserian terms), an Iscrian reading focuses on the moment-by-moment experience of the dialogicity of difference and agreement across monologues. On a first reading, during a rereading, or standing back after reading and selectively meditating on the assemblage, there are several ways the segments enter into a dialogic relationship through the active agency of the reader responding in a controlled way to textual prompts. Meaningful connections can be established between contiguous monologues, non-contiguous monologues, moments within monologues or entire monologues, prefaces and post-preface monologues, and quartets (such as the mothers's quartets framing the daughters's quartets). We might say that the fundamental Iserian gap in this text is the conceptual space between daughters and mothers, between one generation and the other. The primary objective "meaning" that obtains at the site of the dialogicity—the reader's consciousness—is one of unrealized potential. That, in itself, argues, through Iserian negativity, for children and parents to try to listen better and communicate more. By writing a multiple narrator novel with an argumentative edge to it —a thematic thrust that extends beyond an assertion of the relativity of perception—Tan makes a distinct contribution to the genre of the multiple first-person monologue novel.

Judith Caesar (essay date Fall 1994-1995)

SOURCE: "Patriarchy, Imperialism, and Knowledge in *The Kitchen God's Wife*," in *North Dakota Quarterly*, Vol. 62, No. 4, Fall, 1994-1995, pp. 164-74.

[*In the following essay, Caesar states, "By making us question the validity of American knowledge and the 'otherness' of what Americans consider foreign* [in The Kitchen God's Wife], *Amy Tan has helped to enlarge the American narrative."*]

If, as Jean-Francois Lyotard says, a "master narrative" is required to legitimate artistic expression, for the past thirty years the legitimizing narrative of mainstream American literary realism has been the quest for personal fulfillment. The increasingly stagnant, if not outright polluted, mainstream has produced novel after novel concerning the mid-life crises (and sometimes accompanying marital infidelities) of self-centered American men, with even the once rich Jewish and Southern literary traditions now given over to nov-

els like Bernard Malamud's *Dubin's Lives,* Walker Percy's *The Second Coming,* and Reynolds Price's *Blue Calhoun,* all concerning a middle-aged (and in the first two instances, wealthy) white man's discontent. All are a far cry from the writers' earlier ethical and philosophical concerns. The consideration of the reflective person's stance toward questions of political and social justice, central to the 19th- and early 20th-century novel from Charles Dickens' *Bleak House* to Ernest Hemingway's *For Whom the Bell Tolls,* seems to have become limited to experimental postmodern novels (E. L. Doctorow's *Ragtime,* Thomas Pynchon's *Vineland*) and to the kinds of essays on domestic politics, international affairs, and human rights that appear in *The New Yorker, Harpers',* and *The Nation.* Worse, American literary realism's concentration on the purely personal has led to a delegitimation of other experience, namely, the experience of introspective and articulate people who have lived lives devastated by social and political forces outside their control. These people are relegated to inarticulate images on the television screen—in Sarajevo, in Somalia, in the Middle East, in Thailand, and in China. These people, then, whose real stories and histories remain untold to the American public, become less "real" than many of the characters who populate American literary fiction.

In this context, it is very significant that the supposedly "popular" novels of minority American women—Alice Walker, Toni Morrison, Maxine Hong Kingston, Louise Erdrich, and now Amy Tan—seem to be reaching a larger audience than much mainstream literary realism. In part, this is because all five can create such an engaging and often witty surface and because all seem to deal with the popular topics of TV talk shows: spouse abuse, recovering from divorce, finding one's roots, etc. And of course all are hyphenated Americans of some sort, a fact which engages the curiosity of readers who do not share the writers' backgrounds. (Chicana and Native American writers like Sandra Cisneros and Leslie Silko, who use more experimental techniques and deal with a wider range of subject matter, have yet to reach the Waldenbooks reader.)

Yet Tan, for one, does much more than articulate popular media issues. She causes us to question the very basis of how we know what we know. She creates her own narrative by seeming to affirm popular American assumptions in the formula of the popular novel and then undermining that very narrative in a complex political allegory that questions the basic American (indeed Western) concepts of truth and rationality.

In keeping with this subtly deceptive plan, *The Kitchen God's Wife* seems at first like a lively but somewhat clichéd popular novel, a modern pseudo-feminist retelling of the folklore story of the abused wife (patient Griselda in the West, the kitchen god's wife in the East) who wins her husband's love by passing all his tests or his remorse by her generosity of spirit. What makes it modern is that the abused wife is angry at her ill treatment and seemingly "finds herself" in that anger. The women, moreover, are the "good guys" while the men seem quite unrelievedly evil, with the exception of the male rescuer. It seems, in short, to be a type of formula novel which provides women readers with clear heroines, heroes, and villains, all without disrupting the Gothic romance's illusion of rescue by "the right man." Jiang Weili, the narrator of the central three-fourths of the novel, endures the most horrifying abuse from her brutal husband, Wen Fu, while traditional Chinese society not only fails to intervene but colludes in her victimization. The only twist seems to be that instead of winning her husband's love, Weili is rescued by a handsome prince, in this case, Jimmy Louie, a Chinese-American soldier who marries her and takes her back to the United States. In fact, one can see the novel as a rather smug indictment of the misery of women in traditional Chinese society in contrast to American society's enlightened feminism. Moreover, the story that frames the story, that of Jiang Weili's daughter Pearl and her relationship with her mother, seems like yet another story about returning to one's roots to discover some less complicated identity. In short, there seems little here to challenge conventional American thinking.

Yet nothing in the novel is as it seems. Certainly, in the beginning, nothing is as it seems to Weili's American-born daughter Pearl, who narrates the opening chapters of the novel and embodies the American sensibility in all its directness and in all its limitations. Like well-meaning Americans in China, Pearl makes cultural gaffes in dealing with the older Chinese-American community and even with her mother because she doesn't seem to understand the differences between outer display and actual feeling or the realm of implied meanings that are so much a part of Chinese tradition. Thus, at the funeral of elderly Grand Auntie Du which opens the novel, Pearl sees a group of sobbing women in threadbare padded jackets and takes them for recent immigrants from China, Grand Auntie Du's "real friends," when in fact they are Vietnamese professional mourners. Worse, with all the confidence of American pop psychology, Pearl advises her mother to speak frankly to her contemporary, Auntie Helen, about her feelings that Auntie Helen should be sharing more in Grand Auntie Du's care. Pearl says,

> "Why don't you just tell Auntie Helen how you feel and stop complaining?" This is what Phil [Pearl's Anglo husband] had suggested I say, a perfectly reasonable way to get my mother to realize what was making her miserable so she could finally take positive action.

Of course, Pearl doesn't realize that her mother is quietly boasting to Pearl about her own dutifulness and implying that more could be expected of Pearl as well. Thus, Pearl is shocked when her mother is so profoundly offended that she will barely speak to her for a month.

She knows her mother as Winnie Louie, her American name, her kindly but often inexplicably crotchety mother to whom she is bound by sometimes tiresome traditions that don't seem to apply to other Americans. She doesn't realize until the end of the novel that her mother is also Jiang Weili, a woman brought up in China who has survived both a disastrous marriage and the invasion and occupation of her country by a brutal enemy army. And because she doesn't know who her mother is, Pearl also doesn't know that she herself is not the daughter of the kindly Jimmy Louie but of Wen Fu, the brutal first husband. This is but one of the novel's pattern of multiple and mistaken identities that suggests the ambiguity of all knowledge and the incompleteness of the official (legitimate) narrative.

In particular, the novel explores the incompleteness of the American narrative, an incompleteness that comes from a refusal to see the validity of the knowledge of other cultures or of the experiences of people who are not Americans. Pearl, with her confident American knowledge of the way things are, her faulty Mandarin, and her imperviousness to implied meanings, misses much of what is going on beneath the surface, although she is sensitive enough sometimes to realize that there are some things she doesn't understand: ". . . apparently, there's a lot I don't know about my mother and Auntie Helen," she thinks at one point. Since the bulk of the novel is Weili's story, it would seem that one of the purposes of having Pearl as the initial narrator is not only to contrast the American sensibility with the Chinese, but to alert the American reader to the subtext beneath Jiang Weili's story as well. Although the reader would first identify with the American, Pearl, it is very clear that Pearl doesn't know all that needs to be known.

Weili's story is also much more than it would first seem to an American reader. Most obviously, Jiang Weili's is the story of a progressively more violent and degrading marriage set against the backdrop of the Japanese invasion of China. Weili is married off to a man of a socially "suitable" family, although both her father and her aunts and uncles clearly have a sense of the man's flawed character. Because they know something of his deceptiveness, if not his outright cruelty, they marry Weili to him and not her favored cousin, nicknamed Peanut, who had wanted to marry her. Wen Fu proves to be a sexual sadist who delights in humiliation games, a liar who uses his dead brother's diplomas to become an officer in the Nationalist air force (another confused identity), and a coward who manages to save his own life throughout the war by deserting his fellow pilots whenever they encounter Japanese aircraft. Because of Wen Fu's social position, however, no one acknowledges any of these failings.

As the war continues and the Nationalist army flees from Shanghai to Nanjing and finally to Kunming, so Wen Fu degenerates. He refuses to leave a card game to get a doctor for his sick daughter, and then he publicly blames Weili when the child dies. He brings a concubine into the house and then discards her when she becomes pregnant. He forces Weili to "admit" publicly to being a prostitute, despite her very obvious fidelity. He is the enemy of whatever is life-affirming and generous (Weili's maternal responses to save her child, her sisterly desire to help the ignorant concubine) disguised as patriarchal morality. Throughout all of this abuse, no one interferes; in fact, when Weili tries to run away from Wen Fu, her friends Hulan (later Helen) and Auntie Du tell him her hiding place. The increasing viciousness of Wen Fu parallels the increasing closeness of the Japanese army, so that by the time Weili has run away and been brought back to a still more degraded life, the Japanese are bombing Kunming.

The parallel between the victimization of Weili and the Japanese conquest of China is further emphasized by the fact that old Jiang, Weili's father, has collaborated with the Japanese, betraying his country in the same way he betrayed his daughter. His pattern of ineffectual resistance and subsequent capitulation, moreover, continues throughout the novel. He throws a teacup against a priceless painting to show that he would rather destroy China's heritage than betray it—and then accedes to Japanese demands; in Shanghai, when both he and Weili are Wen Fu's victims, he gives Weili the money with which to leave Wen Fu—and then is too ill to help her when Wen Fu accuses her of theft and has her imprisoned.

Even at this level of the political allegory, however, there is little in equating Chinese patriarchy with Japanese expansionism and imperialism that would discomfort or challenge an American reader. It is still "those people" who have done these terrible things, not "us." Yet it is not so comforting if one carries the political allegory to its logical conclusions. Weili's victimization couldn't have taken place if Chinese society had not condoned it to such an extent that even her best friends didn't want to blemish their reputations by helping her escape—at least until the very end of the novel, when they try to get her out of jail (ineffectually, it turns out) by saying that they had witnessed her divorce. These friends, who later join her in the United States, are not all that different from the United States itself, which, as Tan points out, helped to keep the Japanese war machine running by supplying the Japanese with oil and scrap metal all through the 1930s and later helped China only after the United States itself was under attack. Hulan thinks that she freed Weili through her second husband's influence with the Nationalist government; in fact, it is Weili's cousin Peanut, now a

communist cadre who runs a shelter for abused wives, who gets Weili out of prison because Nationalist officials in charge of Weili's case fear reprisals from the communists. If Weili is China, then it is a communist who helps to liberate her, although the liberation is far from complete.

Moreover, if we interpret the novel as a fairly literal political allegory, there is yet another disturbing implication. Wen Fu is never punished. When Weili finally gets word of his death, she learns that he has died an old man, surrounded by his family and respected by his community—the very definition of a righteous man's proper death in Chinese tradition. In contrast, Weili's good husband Jimmy Louie dies relatively young and in great pain, seemingly denied by Pearl, the daughter whom he raised. The pain and prematurity of Jimmy's death is one reason it so haunts Weili. Weili, furthermore, is eking out a living in a foreign country (America), widowed and at least, as the book opens, culturally estranged from her children. One could see this as paralleling the fact that all the former imperial powers—Japan among them—are both more prosperous and more respected than their former victims. To cite the most literal sort of example, the Western media tends to blame the human rights abuses and the political unrest in China and the rest of the former colonial world on the ideological systems that ejected the colonial powers, not on the after-effects of imperialism itself. And the crimes of imperialism did go unpunished. The war crimes trials after World War II focused on the Japanese abuse of western POWs, not on the Japanese imprisonment and massacre of millions of Chinese civilians.

> **One reason for Tan's equation of imperialism and patriarchy is essentially rhetorical. It is easier for an American audience to sympathize with the victims of patriarchy than with the victims of imperialism. Many American women have been the victims of patriarchy, after all, while very few have been the victims of imperialism.**
>
> —*Judith Caesar*

One reason for Tan's equation of imperialism and patriarchy is essentially rhetorical. It is easier for an American audience to sympathize with the victims of patriarchy than with the victims of imperialism. Many American women have been the victims of patriarchy, after all, while very few have been the victims of imperialism. We have not had our country invaded and occupied by a foreign army or had laws imposed on us by people who didn't know our language or culture—except, of course, for Native Americans. The type of suffering Weili endures, moreover, is primarily emotional and psychological rather than physical. She is humiliated and exploited; she cannot even complain about her plight. But she is not being starved, beaten, or tortured at a time when millions of her countrymen (and women) were, as Weili herself points out. Weili's suffering is that of a middle-class woman married to a bully. An American reader can identify with this, at least to some degree; and once one has done this, one can begin to get a sense of the type of suffering that Tan suggests only metaphorically or seemingly incidentally—the Nanjing massacre, for instance. Then other events fit into place. Weili and Wen Fu's children die, one the direct victim of Wen Fu's neglect, two the indirect victims of the Japanese. Tan's presentation helps to legitimize a narrative of suffering otherwise so far outside the American experience that it could seem beyond our capacity for empathy.

But there are more complex philosophical reasons for linking imperialism and patriarchy. For one thing, they both shape the "legitimate" printed narratives of Weili's story. To the Shanghai press covering Weili's case, Wen Fu is a war hero whose wife has been seduced and corrupted by a lecherous American. In this patriarchal narrative, Weili wants to escape Wen Fu not because she has been abused, but because she is "crazy for American sex." This is as true as the printed leaflets the Japanese drop on Nanjing, explaining that civilians will not be harmed.

Behind these official narratives is the assumption that some people's suffering is more significant than other people's sufferings. The Chinese historian Szuma Chien once ironically remarked that some deaths are as heavy as Mount Tai, while others are lighter than a feather—that is, in official versions of events. Thus, the honor of men is more important than the dignity of women, and the deaths of ordinary Chinese simply aren't important at all. This assumption isn't merely Oriental, moreover, since it underlies the current American narrative that the personal emotional crisis of an American is the only suffering interesting enough to write about. The official narratives are used to ignore or justify the sufferings of the powerless.

Consequently, all the official facts in Tan's novel are questionable. Weili's divorce is officially valid when Wen Fu holds a gun to her head and makes her sign the paper, but it can be made invalid by her ex-husband's tearing up the paper. What is a divorce and what does it mean under those circumstances? Weili can be "officially" a thief for taking the gold her father gave her, and then later be "officially" innocent when her imprisonment is termed an "error of the court." Even Pearl's official American knowledge that World War II began with the bombing of Pearl Harbor is questionable, since, as Weili points out, it began for China with the Japanese invasion of Manchuria. (Or did it begin even earlier, with the German concession of the Shantung peninsula to the Japanese?) The Western narrative is at best an incomplete truth. When does a divorce or a war begin or end?

The narrative structure of the novel also suggests the problematic nature of truth. As Edward Said has pointed out in *Culture and Imperialism,* the narrative structure of the classic 19th-century realistic novel, with its omniscient narrator or reliable first-person narrator, helped to underscore the idea of an authoritative and "correct" version of events. Despite the polyphonic narrations of the high modernist novel, the 20th-century popular novel has generally preserved the 19th-century technique, as has much of contemporary literary realism. The modernist novel, moreover, focuses on the psychological and philosophical implications of competing narratives (*Mrs. Dalloway, As I Lay Dying,* etc.), not on their political implication. Much contemporary fiction thus tends to confirm the value of Americanness over foreignness, a kind of contemporary imperialism. (Think, for example, of Cormac McCarthy's National Book Award-winning *All the Pretty Horses* in which the good guys are all American men and the bad guys either Mexican or female. Consider how different it would be if any of the Mexican or women characters gave their version of events.) In contrast, Tan has two narrators and three versions of events—Pearl's, Weili's, and Hulan's, all of which seem credible in some respects.

While Tan's use of a polyphonic narrative is significant in itself, perhaps more significant is who speaks. Through much of the novel, after all, it is an elderly Chinese immigrant whose syntax and word choice reflect the patterns of Chinese-accented English, a speech pattern marginalized and mocked by contemporary mainstream American society. Tan helps to give this voice a validity and dignity in the same way that Walker and Morrison have helped to legitimize African American speech. She has made the sufferings of those who speak in this voice "as heavy as Mount Tai."

The details of the novel confirm both the validity of these Chinese women's experience and the subjective nature of truth. What Hulan remembers is different from what Weili remembers, yet Hulan's insights are given sudden credibility when she tells Pearl, "You know how she [Weili] is, very hard to thank. . . ," and we realize how very true this is of both Weili and Pearl. Just as Pearl rejects her "cousin" Mary's comforting casseroles when Mary learns of Pearl's illness, Weili would indeed be repelled by the idea of being indebted to Hulan in any way. We also realize the extent to which Hulan's behavior, which Weili had interpreted as simply contrary and obstructive, was well intended. What is interesting here is that in personal relationships, unlike political ones, conflicting versions of the truth are not necessarily divisive, since neither version is used as a means of control or suppression. Thus even the quarrels between Winnie (once Weili) and Helen (once Hulan) are not precisely quarrels at all. Pearl observes,

> I watch them continue to argue, although perhaps

it is not arguing. They are remembering together, dreaming together.

Tan also contradicts this idea of a rational Western truth through the pattern of double and shifting identities of her characters and by her clear indications that the commonly accepted criteria for determining identity are sometimes irrelevant. Tan shows a world of multiple and contradictory truths, truth as a series of Chinese boxes, not a unitary truth to be "discovered" in the Western sense. Tan's is not even a Western "postmodernist" truth of multiple linear narratives, but of contradictory truths and partial truths intermixed in layers of meaning. Through the contradictions in Winnie's (Weili's) character, we see that a complete person can be both large-spirited and petty, loving and distant. Indeed, self-knowledge consists of acknowledging these seemingly contradictory traits. At one point Weili tells Pearl,

> I have told you about the early days of my marriage so you can understand why I became strong and weak at the same time. Maybe according to your American mind, you cannot be both, that would be a contradiction. But according to my life, I had to be both.

The simultaneous existence of these opposites is indeed very different from what our American minds tell us is rational, and thus it calls into question the validity of that rationality.

Moreover, none of the characters is precisely what they seem, even concerning the most common determiner of identity, family relationships. Consider, for instance, the ways in which the characters seem to be related but aren't. Pearl calls Hulan "auntie" and thinks of Hulan's children Bao-Bao and Mary as her cousins. Indeed, Winnie and Helen, with all their feuding and tenderness, act like sisters. And Pearl is as exasperated and yet connected to the "cousins" as she would be with any blood relative, a relationship Tan underscores by using them as foils to Pearl. Pearl has believed the "official version" that Helen is the widow of Winnie's younger brother, but she learns very early in her mother's story that Helen is "merely" a person she has known ever since her youth.

Thus it is not surprising that Pearl's discovery of her parentage, her "real identity" does not have the significance the episode's placement in the novel would seem to grant it. Finally, the great climatic revelation that Wen Fu is Pearl's "real" father seems to be irrelevant after all. It is the pattern formed by all the revelations leading up to it that is important. That Jimmy Louie is Pearl's "real" father is simply one more item in the list of things that seems true, isn't true, and finally is in a larger sense as true as any of the novel's other ambiguous truths. And on the level of character, it doesn't matter either. Pearl is not at all like Wen Fu, as Winnie points

out. Ancestry and blood relationship finally do not matter very much—a very non-Chinese idea in a very non-American narrative.

Meaning and truth exist in layers, and what is true on the surface is contradicted by another truth underneath, which is in turn contradicted by a third layer. And all are "true." We see this kind of paradox even in the names of minor characters. Pearl's cousin Roger is named Bao-Bao, "precious baby," because his parents were so happy to finally have a child, but the nickname sticks as he grows up because it becomes a sarcastic description of his superficial and immature behavior. The only one of the Chinese-American characters to have a Chinese name, he speaks like a cartoon of an American and gets married and divorced as carelessly as a character in a Woody Allen comedy. Is it then because he is so American that he is so superficial? In fact, in his self-centeredness and sexual inconstancy, he seems like a comic and relatively benign version of Wen Fu. He's a beloved precious baby who has become a spoiled precious baby whose faults are equally American and Chinese.

In this context, it is not surprising that nationality doesn't matter very much in determining the identity of both Weili and Pearl either. It merely determines their modes of expression. Pearl is very much an American version of Weili. Like Weili, she is a concerned and loving mother, she faces difficulties (her multiple sclerosis, for example) with such stoicism that she cuts herself off from both her husband and her mother, she is witty and critical, and she is willing to let things be understood without spelling them out. Yet in her manners and beliefs, she is an American. When, at the end, she accepts her mother's herbal cures and the offering to Lady Sorrowfree, she does so as an acceptance of her mother's solicitude, not her beliefs. She hasn't found a "Chinese identity" in the way the characters in *Song of Solomon* and *The Color Purple* find an African identity; instead she has found a closer relationship with her mother and an insight into the seemingly conflicting layers of reality in the world around her, beginning with the multiple identities of her mother and the Chinese "relatives" whom she thought she knew. Personal identity, like both personal and political truth, is many-layered and elusive, something accepted rather than discovered.

Under the outward layer of a highly readable popular novel, Tan has written an extremely complex postmodern literary novel that challenges the dominant narratives of contemporary American society, particularly our ideas of who matters and who does not, of whose version is "true" and whose is not, and indeed of how one can find what is true. Through the voices of characters like Weili and Hulan, Tan presents a world in which complex and intelligent people must find a way of accommodating hostile political and social forces against which they are powerless to rebel—a type of suffering from which most American readers have been sheltered. Thus, Tan verifies the reality of a world outside the American experience as nevertheless part of the human experience and questions the sense of entitlement and cultural superiority that allows Americans to dismiss the sufferings of foreigners. This sense of entitlement, the idea that "our" deaths are as heavy as Mount Tai and "their" deaths are light as feathers underlies the callousness of all imperial narratives—the novels of contemporary America, as well as narratives of the Imperial China of which Szuma Chien wrote and of patriarchal China and Imperial Japan, of which Jiang Weili speaks. By making us question the validity of American knowledge and the "otherness" of what Americans consider foreign, Amy Tan has helped to enlarge the American narrative.

Bonnie Braendlin (essay date 1995)

SOURCE: "Mother/Daughter Dialog(ic)s in, around and about Amy Tan's *The Joy Luck Club,*" in *Private Voices, Public Lives: Women Speak on the Literary Life,* edited by Nancy Owen Nelson, University of North Texas Press, 1995, pp. 111-24.

[*In the following excerpt, Braendlin analyzes how the women's liberation movement has affected mother-daughter relationships, specifically focusing on the mother-daughter dialogics in Tan's* The Joy Luck Club.]

In the 1970s I became, almost simultaneously, a feminist teacher/critic and the mother of a daughter. While analyzing novels emerging from the Women's Liberation Movement, where daughters struggle to free themselves from enslaving ideologies of wife/motherhood, I tended to identify with the daughters and to deplore the maternal machinations of fictional mothers, often characterized as little more than co-opted wives in cahoots with domineering fathers to coerce rebellious daughters into traditional wife/mother roles. As a mother of a daughter in an era when feminism was demanding a place for women in male-dominated culture, I often felt the conflicts among my perceived duty to socialize her toward survival and success in a masculine world, my determination not to replicate my own mother, and my desire to be my own woman and to let my daughter be hers. And just as often my daughter seemed caught between her need for parental direction and her desire for independence. . . .

Antagonisms between mothers and daughters in U.S. history and literature became particularly acute during and after the 1970s, when the women's movement—advocating equality in a man's world—defined subjectivity in masculinist terms that privileged independence, self-sufficiency, and autonomy

at the expense of traditional "feminine" relational values of nurturing and caring. Because these values had been embodied in an ideology of motherhood defined and dominated for years by patriarchal males, daughters of the liberation movement viewed them as outdated restrictions foisted upon them by their retrograde mothers. Defining themselves in ways formerly allowed only to men, "liberated" daughters wanted to usurp the traditional son's position, to move out of the home and into the workplace, to climb the ladder of success. . . .

Conflicts between mothers of one generation and daughters of another are inscribed in numerous texts of the liberation era, for instance Rita Mae Brown's *Rubyfruit Jungle,* Alice Walker's *Meridian,* Lisa Alther's *Kinflicks,* Margaret Atwood's *Lady Oracle,* and Maxine Hong Kingston's *The Woman Warrior,* all published in the early to mid-seventies. In *Kinflicks,* independence for the daughter necessitates both divorce and rejection of her own child, and her mother's abrogation of maternal control. The novel represents maternal self-sacrifice as a fatal blood disease, implying that mothers must die in order for daughters to live. Hong Kingston's fictionalized autobiography also portrays the mother-daughter relationship as antagonistic and obstructive to female development, but she at least spares the mother, and at the end her "Song for a Barbarian Reed Pipe" unites autonomy, nurturing, and artistry, albeit in a fantasy of utopian female solidarity. . . .

In the eras following the women's liberation movement, we daughters of the seventies have become disillusioned with and conscious of our own co-option in masculinist ideologies and our efforts to replicate our fathers at the expense of maternal values; we've begun to identify with the mothers we had formerly rejected, thus complicating what formerly seemed to be a simple daughter versus mother conflict. Women can now, if they wish, be nurturing without being servile and can encourage men to care about others, protect and nourish relationships. In both fictional and critical texts, moreover, we are moving from antagonistic dialectic arguments—which were often (among critics and between mothers and daughters) really monovocal power plays—to more polyvocal, more dialogic, forms of spoken and written communication.

Dialogism, according to Mikhail Bakhtin, is the constant interaction among meanings expressed in spoken or written communication, insuring that no word, ideology, or discourse is privileged or remains privileged, even when it is supported by some kind of authority. In life, the development of individual subjectivity (personhood or self) occurs in the context of one's social and cultural languages (discourses); during the development process, when adolescents and young adults are encouraged—or coerced—into internalizing the discourses of their elders, conflicts arise because the new generation also resists becoming the old. But while individuation is the process by which a society indoctrinates its young into its value systems, it also creates a space for defiance of tradition and of choice among other, competing ideologies. Resistance to and re-evaluation of old values, coupled with new choices, introduce new voices into society; thus as the young grow up into adulthood, becoming modified versions of their parents, they promote and insure sociocultural change (if not, necessarily, progress). In the novel, Bakhtin suggests, the interaction among discourses appears as dialogues among characters, between an author and the characters, between readers and texts, and among various ideologies that permeate a work, linking text and contexts. Literary characters may be read as representing various subject positions, beliefs and behavior patterns that shift and change as the characters act and react within their fictional milieu. And we as readers interpret literature in the context of our own lives; who we are—our cultural, social, political, and psychological selves—guides our reading. Those selves, of course, change over time, modifying the way we read.

As my daughter grows up, I am changing as a mother, becoming less concerned about guiding her development and more willing to appreciate her as a fellow adult, a young woman who struggles to make her own decisions, to become the person she wants to be, while retaining something of her parents' values and mores. She, I can tell, vacillates between resistance to becoming like me and a desire to emulate those qualities in me she admires. And my reading of literature continues to be guided by my own experiences as a daughter/mother and also by my study of contemporary feminist theory. Increasingly, feminist authors, theorists and critics—as we wrestle with issues of gender, race, and class, of history, ideologies, and aesthetics—are calling into question binary oppositions such as culture/nature, male/female, and mother/daughter. Cultural feminist theorists are redefining these putatively "natural" oppositions as socially constructed and thus dependent upon consensus for their continued existence and also open to modifications. Not only have I changed as a reader and critic since the 1970s, but women-authored novels have changed as well, reflecting the increased diversity of American culture and the literary scene, as formerly marginalized and silenced women and ethnic groups voice their perspectives. Published in 1989, Amy Tan's *The Joy Luck Club* both imitates and revises works like *Kinflicks* and *The Woman Warrior,* which antedate it by some fifteen years. Tan's novel depicts the socialization of young women as a dialogical process in which the mother/daughter opposition becomes more complicated, with mothers and daughters still antagonistic, but also more accepting of the similarities between generations. Instead of one daughter confronting one mother, Tan creates four mothers (three living and one deceased) and four daughters—contemporary young women caught in the marriage/motherhood discourse

of western bourgeois capitalism. In conflict with their mothers, who embody marital/maternal ideologies of old China, the daughters express their desire for individuality and independence, often entailing divorces from marriages that entrap them in "other-defined" roles. While their mothers object to these separations and appear to coerce their daughters into remaining in marital "enslavement," their own stories of their early lives in China reveal a female desire for self-definition and resistance that transcends generations, closing generational gaps. And, unlike earlier novels where the daughters' stories predominated, even to the extent of eclipsing the mothers' autobiographies, *The Joy Luck Club* foregrounds the mothers as characters and narrators who tell their own stories. . . .

The mother-daughter dialog(ic)s of Tan's novel inscribe various discourses, both traditional (for example, patriarchal ownership of women, the sacredness of motherhood) and resistant (as in the desire for independence and selfhood). These are not exclusively expressed by either the mothers or the daughters; although communication between the two is hindered by differences in language and social orientation, both mothers and daughters share inherited beliefs about wife/mother roles that empower and disempower women. Both are in conflict over simultaneous desires to comply with and to resist society's demands and definitions of women. And although the mothers feel compelled to persuade their daughters to accept prescribed marital and maternal duties, they too resist total compliance with demands made by these roles. Some readers of *The Joy Luck Club* complain that its ending, with daughters reunited with one another and with the spirit of the dead mother, is too easy, too simplistic, too utopian in light of the continued conflictual relationships between "real" mothers and daughters. As a feminist mother in the nineties, I read the ending of the novel, where Jing-Mei Woo holds her long-lost Chinese sisters in an embrace, as a resurrection and vindication of their dead mother, who longed to reunite her daughters, and as a rewriting of earlier novels where lone daughters repudiated their mothers' desires. Like *Kinflicks,* Tan's novel kills off a mother, but then replicates her in her daughter, creating a matrilinear genealogy of resemblances less utopian than that in *The Woman Warrior.* It can also be argued that closure in Tan's novel applies an Eastern philosophy of "both/and" to a Western predicament of either (daughter)/or (mother).

What I want to do in the remainder of this essay is to change the format to reflect the multiplicities of mother/daughter relationships and feminist readings of them in literature. As a feminist critic I object to the authoritarian word of the "fathers," the master scholars who appropriate knowledge, possess it, and (often reluctantly) give it over to their chosen initiates. Thus, instead of insisting upon a position as a mother who replicates the fathers by preaching the authoritative interpretation of a novel, I want to open my text to multiple voices and invite you as readers to interact with them, to participate in a dialog(ic) that "concerns the relations among persons articulating their ideas in response to one another, discovering their mutual affinities and oppositions, their provocations to reply, their desires to hear more, or their wishes to change the subject."

What follows is a scenario I have created as a dramatized pastiche of *The Joy Luck Club.* Imagine the table around which three of Tan's mothers and one daughter gather to play mah jong and to socialize the daughter into the mother role. Just as Tan increases the number of voices and hence complicates the socialization process by interpolating the stories of other mothers, grandmothers, and daughters, so I wish to complicate (but also illuminate) the issue of mother/daughter relations by gathering together around the table several women for a discussion, mixing in postmodern fashion textual figures and "real" people. I as moderator work to unify the group and focus the discussion, in much the same way as a mother might attempt to orchestrate a dining-table conversation (like Mrs. Ramsay in Virginia Woolf's *To the Lighthouse,* for example) or as a novelist, according to Bakhtin, tries to orchestrate the "Tower of Babel mixing of languages," the "heteroglot voices among which [her] own voice must also sound" in her text.

By illuminating subtleties in the mother/daughter binary opposition, this polyvocal conversation suggests ways in which mothers and daughters may exchange and sometimes change their (and our) ideological positions and thus encourage a better understanding of one another's views. This dialog(ic) inescapably reinscribes but also defies the opposition—socially and textually constructed in the liberation era—through interchange of ideas and identities among women who both adhere to and resist traditional roles, who agree and disagree, exchanging roles and positions so "that [binary] oppositions are only apparent, that the alleged polarities inhabit each other." In the women's discussion, differences may not be resolved, but emerging similarities among the women call into question the divisive mother/daughter dichotomy that plagues intergenerational relationships.

My scenario opens Tan's text to a contextual dialogue that resists the closure of any one interpretation; in the end, there will be no resolution to the discussion or to the generational conflict. But I hope that through the exchanges and in the gaps and interstices between them, meanings will be made and interpretation enhanced by the participants, including you as reader. Here you may participate in the dialogue as one does in any conversation where speakers anticipate answers and exchange ideas, constructing meaning in the process; you are invited not to be "a person who passively understands but . . . one who actively answers and reacts,"

offering either "resistance or support," but in either case "enriching the discourse."

Gloria Shen (essay date 1995)

SOURCE: "Born of a Stranger: Mother-Daughter Relationships and Storytelling in Amy Tan's *The Joy Luck Club,*" in *International Women's Writing: New Landscapes of Identity,* edited by Anne E. Brown and Marjanne Goozé, Greenwood Press, 1995, pp. 233-44.

[*In the following essay, Shen discusses the importance of storytelling to the mother-daughter bond in Tan's The Joy Luck Club.*]

Amy Tan's first work, *The Joy Luck Club,* is a challenge to the novel as a "narrative paradigm" in several ways: form, narrative structure, and narrative techniques. It is not a novel in the sense that only one story, "his story" is presented; it is a work of sixteen "her stories." The stories are "presented" not by one single third-person narrator either from her particular perspective or from the various "points of view" of the characters. These are narrative techniques conventionally associated with the novel of the nineteenth and twentieth centuries. The book is divided into four main sections; the stories are told from the viewpoints of four Chinese mothers and their Chinese American daughters. The only exception is Suyuan Woo, who, having recently died, speaks not for herself but through her daughter, Jing-mei. The daughter tells her mother's stories as she takes her mother's place at the mahjong table and on the fateful trip to China. The stories, "told" by the three mothers and four daughters at different times and in different settings, resemble fragments of stories collected by a sociologist and randomly put together, rather than carefully constructed narratives set in a deliberate order by an author. In other words, *The Joy Luck Club* employs an unusual narrative strategy. In this chapter, I explore the connection between the narrative strategy employed in *The Joy Luck Club* and the relationships between the Chinese mothers and their American-born daughters.

In *The Joy Luck Club,* important themes are repeated in the stories like musical leitmotifs and presented from slightly different angles in order to give the reader a continuous sense of life as well as a full understanding of the significance of each event. The unique structure of *The Joy Luck Club* allows the unconnected fragments of life, revealed from different but somewhat overlapping perspectives by all the "reliable" narrators, to unfold into a meaningful, continuous whole so that the persistent tensions and powerful bonds between mother and daughter, between generations, may be illuminated through a montage effect on the reader.

The traditional novel as a "narrative paradigm" entails a set of rules that bestow legitimacy upon certain narrative forms and preclude certain other forms. Jameson expounds the notion of "narrative paradigm" by claiming that the "forms" of the novel as the "inherited narrative paradigms" are: "the raw material on which the novel works, transforming their 'telling' into its 'showing,' estranging commonplaces against the freshness of some unexpected 'real,' foregrounding convention itself as that through which readers have hitherto received their notions of events, psychology, experience, space, and time." The "inherited narrative paradigms" determine rules of the game and illustrate how they are to be applied. The rules define what has the right to be said and done in the culture in question. Oral narrative forms, such as popular stories, myths, legends, and tales, are thus viewed as belonging to a "savage, primitive, underdeveloped, backward, alienated" mentality, composed of opinions, prejudice, ignorance and ideology. As Lyotard notes, oral narrative forms have been deemed fit for women and children only and have not been rightly considered as appropriate or competent forms to be subsumed under the category of the novel. As a Western-conceived notion, the "narrative paradigm" of the novel thus excludes various minority subnarrative traditions, including women's. Structurally, *The Joy Luck Club* is an interesting example because it rejects artificial unity and espouses the fragmentary, one of the main features of postmodernism.

The dissolution of unity in the traditional novel, best manifested in the "fragmentation" of the work, serves to highlight different themes that evolve around the mother-daughter relationship. *The Joy Luck Club* is divided into four sections, each of which consists of four stories. Each of the four sections of the book begins with a prologue, a brief narrative illustrative of the theme of that section. The Joy Luck Club is a monthly mahjong gathering to which the generation of the Chinese mothers has belonged for decades and with which the generation of the American daughters has grown up. Like four Chinese boxes, the complexity of the narrative structure is revealed through stories told within stories by the mothers to the daughters. In this manner, Tan directly puts forward the views, feelings, emotions, and thoughts of her characters, stressing the mixture of action, consciousness, and subconsciousness. In the chapter "Without Wood," a daughter tells about a dream she once had as a child that reveals subconsciously the daughter's strong desire to resist the clutching influence of the mother on her. In this dream, the daughter finds herself in a playground filled with rows of sandboxes. In each sandbox there is a doll. Haunted by the feeling that her mother knows exactly which doll she will pick, the daughter deliberately chooses a different one. When the mother orders the guardian of the gate to the dreamworld to stop her, the little girl becomes so frightened that she remains frozen in place.

Tan's storytelling technique reveals the complexity of the dark, invisible mind of cultural consciousness and subconsciousness best portrayed by the stories within stories. In *The Joy Luck Club*, Tan moves with swiftness and ease from one story to another, from one symbol or image to another. In a sense, *The Joy Luck Club* can be properly called a collection of intricate and haunting memories couched in carefully wrought stories. Tan has purposely externalized the eight characters' mental world by allowing each of them to tell her own story in a deceptively simple manner, thus allowing the reader to plunge into the mind of the characters. The motives, desires, pains, pleasures, and concerns of the characters are thereby effectively dramatized. This particular writing strategy allows Tan to transcend the conventional novelistic dichotomy of preferred "showing" and undesirable "telling." The stories thus tell us a great deal about individual characters, their reaction to each other, and their activities together. Because the stories are all told in the mothers' and the daughters' own voices, we are spared the pressing question with which the reader of a conventional novel is constantly bombarded with: Am I dealing with a "reliable" or "unreliable" narrator? While immersed in particular and individual perspectives, the reader of *The Joy Luck Club* also confronts the more general and lasting concerns of many generations. Unlike Maxine Hong Kingston's *The Woman Warrior,* which relates the life experience of one woman and concentrates on one single family, the stories in *The Joy Luck Club,* with its characters and circumstances skillfully interwoven, presents a continuous whole more meaningful than the sum of its parts.

In *The Joy Luck Club*, Tan probes the problematic mother-daughter relationship in sixteen separate stories spanning two generations of eight women. Though the eight characters are divided into four families, the book itself is concerned more with an unmistakable bifurcation along generational lines: mothers, whose stories all took place in China, and daughters, whose stories deal with their lives in America. Though the mothers all have different names and individual stories, they seem interchangeable in that they all have similar personalities—strong, determined, and endowed with mysterious power—and that they all show similar concerns about their daughters' welfare. As a result, the mothers are possessively trying to hold onto their daughters, and the daughters are battling to get away from their mothers. The four mothers and four daughters are different, but their differences remain insignificant as the action of the novel is focused on the persistent tensions and powerful bonds between them.

Tan's characters are seen in both detail and outline. The first-person testimonies allow the reader to examine each of the characters closely and to develop a sense of empathy with each of them; but, at the same time, the testimonies reveal a pattern, particularly in the way the mothers and daughters relate to one another. The purpose of this treatment is obvious: to portray the mother and daughter relationship as both typical and universal.

In Tan's novel, The Joy Luck Club is a bridge uniting both space and time. The Joy Luck Club connects the sixteen intricately interlocking stories and helps to reveal and explain the infinite range and complexity of mother-daughter relationships. Within the narrative, it joins two continents and unites the experiences of the mothers and the daughters. The American daughters are alien to Chinese culture as much as they are to their mother's uncanny, Chinese ways of thinking. To the daughters, cultural and ethnic identity is possible only when they can fully identify themselves with their mothers through their maturation into womanhood. The sharing of cultural experiences between mothers and daughters through the device of storytelling transforms structurally isolated monologues into meaningful dialogues between mother and mother, daughter and daughter, and, more important, mother and daughter and coalesces the sixteen monologues into a coherent whole. While the mother and daughter relationships are unique in the ethnic context of Tan's novel, they also have a universal aspect. Indeed, all women share this experience, regardless of time and space. An-mei Hsu is puzzled by both the specific and universal qualities of the mother-daughter relationship. Raised traditionally, she was taught to swallow her desires, her bitterness, and the misery of others. Rejecting her upbringing, she tries to instill in her daughter a strong sense of self. Unfortunately, her daughter is a passive individual. An-mei Hsu is thus convinced that regardless of their respective upbringing, mothers and daughters are somehow condemned to being similar: "And even though I taught my daughter the opposite, still she came out the same way! Maybe it is because she was born to me and she was born a girl. And I was born to my mother and I was born a girl. All of us are like stairs, one step after another, going up and down, but all going the same way."

Through her structural experiments with the elements of fiction and her storytelling device, and with the testimonial mode of characterization, Tan has pushed her novel beyond the merely conventional practice of the novel (to mimic the convention of the appearance of life, as done by many traditional novelists). Instead, she tries to do away with "his story" and present "her life" from the perspectives of the individual women characters in the form of loosely connected monologues. These monologues serve to translate as faithfully as possible the intricate relationship that can exist between a mother and her daughter.

Tan's extensive use of symbols and images creates a mood of expression that reveals and explains the infinite range and complexity of these mother-daughter relationships. Each of the four sections of **The Joy Luck Club** begins with a prologue, defining the theme of that section while disclosing certain aspects of the problem in the mother-daughter rela-

tionship. The first prologue contains a cluster of images that highlight the nature of this relationship in the book and summarize the whole novel. This prologue centers around an old woman who remembers that, while still in Shanghai, she bought a swan for a small sum. The swan, according to the vendor, was once a duck who had managed to stretch his neck in the hope of becoming a goose. On the boat sailing to America, the old woman swore to the swan that she would one day have a daughter whom no one would look down upon, for she would speak only perfect English. In order for this daughter to know her mother's meaning, she would give her the swan.

However, upon arriving in America, the swan is confiscated, and the old woman is left with only one of the swan's feathers. This feather is far too insignificant for her to convince anyone, least of all her daughter, how beautiful the swan was. Furthermore, the daughter she had hoped for has become an unsympathetic "stranger" who does not even speak her language. The prologue thus ends on a poignant note. Indeed, year after year, the mother waits for the moment when she would be able to tell her daughter in perfect American English that the feather is far from worthless, for it symbolizes all of her "good intentions."

The prologue sets the tone and the reasons for the tensions and conflicts in the mother-daughter relationship. The "swan" and the "old woman" who sailed across the ocean together, "stretching their necks toward America," are an emblem of the four mothers who came to the United States, hoping to give their daughters a better life than the one they had in China. The "good intentions" are clearly stated. But the mother, left with an almost worthless feather, is condemned to wait patiently many years until the daughter is finally mature enough to come back to her, to appreciate her, and to reconstruct the beautiful swan from the feather. The swan is therefore emblematic of both the mother's new life in America and, more important, her past one in China, an experience the mother wants to communicate to her daughter. However, only a mature daughter, who has overcome the psychological and cultural gap separating her from her mother is capable of coming to terms with this experience.

The mother-daughter relationship is the central issue and focal point in the dialogues between the mothers and daughters in Tan's book. The novel traces the psychological development of the American daughter and her final acceptance of the Chinese mother and what the Chinese mother stands for. Jing-mei Woo, who replaces her recently deceased mother at the mahjong table, is the first to tell a story on behalf of her mother; she is also the very last daughter to recount her own story. It is interesting to note that when she is asked by her three "aunts" to go to China in order to fulfill her mother's long-cherished wish to meet her lost twin babies, Jing-mei shocks and upsets them with her confused yet honest remark that she would not know what to tell her sisters because she did not really know her mother: "What will I say? What can I tell them about my mother?"

The mothers are all frightened by this response. Indeed, they sense in it the confusion of their own daughters. In Jing-mei, they recognize their own daughters, all as ignorant and as unmindful of the truths and hopes their mothers brought over with them from China. Ironically, the accomplishment of the mother's dream for her daughter, a dream that entailed her physical removal from the motherland, results in multifarious problems in the relationship with her daughter.

In Tan's novel, the Chinese mothers are all strong-willed, persistent, hard to please, and overly critical. They often make their presence and their goodwill look like outrageous impositions rather than tacit influences. When, for example, Jing-mei Woo describes her mother's New Year crab dinner, we learn that, although she does not like this dish, she is obliged to eat it since her refusal to do so would constitute a rejection of her mother's love. The food and the advice offered by the mothers are hard to refuse not only because they are a symbol of love but also because they tend to carry the full weight of maternal authority. That is why Waverly Jong is convinced that telling one's mother to be quiet would be tantamount to committing suicide. In another example, Waverly tries to make her mother accept her American boyfriend by showing her a fur coat that he has given her as a token of his love. Totally dejected by her mother's antagonism toward her boyfriend, whom the mother does not consider good enough for her daughter, Waverly Jong feels distressed at not being able to shake off her mother's clutching influence. When she looks once again at the coat her mother has just finished criticizing, she becomes convinced that it is, indeed, shabby.

The mother's wish for the daughter to live a better life than the one she had back in China is revealed in the conversation between the Chinese woman and her swan on her journey to America in the novel's first prologue. Ironically, this wish becomes the very source of the conflicts and tensions in their relationship. This is made perfectly clear by Jing-mei Woo when she half-jokingly, half-remorsefully recalls her ever-agonizing childhood, a period during which her mother unsuccessfully attempts to transform her into a child prodigy. In order to prepare Jing-mei for a future that she hopes will be brilliant, Suyuan Woo nightly submits Jing-mei to a series of tests while forcing her to listen to countless stories about amazing children. Mother and daughter finally settle on Jing-mei's becoming a concert pianist, and Jing-mei begins to take piano lessons from Mr. Old Chong, a retired piano teacher who happens to be deaf. As a result, the daughter manages to get away with playing more or less competently while her teacher conducts an imaginary piece of music in his head.

Another daughter, Rose Hsu Jordon, is married to a "foreigner" who wishes to divorce her. Her mother, An-mei Hsu, urges her to speak up in the hope of saving her marriage. She does this by juxtaposing the Chinese way with the American way. The Chinese way consists of not expressing one's desires, not speaking up, and not making choices. The American way consists of exercising choices and speaking up for oneself. An-mei Hsu raised Rose in the American way. She hoped that this would allow her daughter to lead a better life than the one she had in China. Indeed, in China people had no choice. Since they could not speak up, they were forced to accept whatever fate befell them. An-mei Hsu reminds Rose that by not speaking up, she "can lose her chance forever."

The frustration that Waverly's mother, Lindo Jong, feels is shared by all the mothers. This frustration is best summarized in her painful and poignant confession during the course of which she accuses herself of being responsible for the way Waverly has turned out. Her sense of responsibility stems from the fact that she is the one who wanted Waverly to have the best of both worlds, and it leads her to openly berate herself for not being able to foresee that her daughter's American circumstances would not necessarily mix well with her Chinese reality.

The alienation between mother and daughter often stems either from a lack of understanding or from various forms of miscommunication. While the daughters, all born in America, entirely adapt to the customs and language of the new land, the immigrant mothers still hold onto those of China. All the mothers feel their daughters' impatience when they speak Chinese and are convinced that their daughters think they are stupid when they attempt to communicate with them in broken English. If Jing-mei is initially reluctant to carry out her mother's long-cherished wish to be reunited with her two lost sisters, it is mainly because she believes that she and her mother have never understood one another. The language barrier that existed between them was such that both mother and daughter imperfectly translated each other's words and meanings.

In a tragicomic incident that exemplifies the futile attempt to bridge the mother-daughter gap, Lindo Jong is proudly speaking to her daughter about Taiyuan, her birthplace. Waverly mistakes Taiyuan for Taiwan and is subsequently visibly irritated when her mother loudly corrects her. The daughter's unintentional mistake, combined with the mother's anger, destroys their attempt to communicate. Consequently, they are both plunged, once again, into a steely silence. In another example of Tan's lightness of touch straining with ambivalence, Lena St. Clair defines her mother as a "displaced person" who has difficulties expressing herself in English. Born in Wushi, near Shanghai, she speaks Mandarin and only a little English. Lena's father, who spoke only a few canned Chinese expressions, always insisted that his wife learn English. Unable to express herself clearly in English, she communicates through gestures and looks and sometimes in a broken English punctuated by hesitations and frustration. Her husband thus feels justified in putting words in her mouth.

The mothers' inability to speak perfect American English has multiple ramifications. For one thing, as they themselves have not lived in a foreign country, the daughters are left with the false impression that their mothers are not intelligent. As a result, the daughters often feel justified in believing that their mothers have nothing worthwhile to say. Furthermore, when mother and daughter share neither the same realm of experience and knowledge nor the same concerns, their differences are not marked by a slip of the tongue or the lack of linguistic adroitness or even by a generational gap, but rather by a deep geographical and cultural cleft. When the mother talks about American ways, the daughter is willing to listen; when the mother shows her Chinese ways, the daughter ignores her. The mother is thus unable to teach her daughter the Chinese ways of obeying parents, of listening to the mother's mind, of hiding her thoughts, of knowing her own worth without becoming vain, and, most important of understanding why "Chinese thinking is best."

The gulf between the Old World and the New, between Chinese mother and American daughter, is exacerbated by the ethnic and racial biases against the Chinese that the young daughter has to deal with on a regular basis. A conversation between Waverly and her mother, Lindo Jong, shows that even as a young child, the daughter is fully aware of the hurtful effect these prejudices have had on the Chinese mother, who has not adjusted well to the life and customs of the new land. One night, while Lindo Jong is brushing her daughter's hair, Waverly, who has overheard a boy in her class discuss Chinese torture, wickedly asks her the following question: "Ma, what is Chinese torture?" Visibly disturbed by this question, Lindo Jong sharply nicks her daughter's skull with a hairpin. She then softly but proudly answers that Chinese people are proficient in many areas. They "do business, do medicine, do painting . . . do torture. Best torture."

While the Chinese mother seems able readily to shrug off the detrimental influence of ethnic and racial biases, she cannot help but feel the effect of them upon her daughter. Lindo Jong is unable to overcome the painful reality that sets her apart from her daughter. She is ashamed because she knows that the daughter she is so proud of is ashamed of her and of her Chinese ways. The constantly growing cleavage of ethnic and national identity drives the daughter to make persistent efforts to Americanize herself in order to lessen her mother's commanding influence.

The daughters' battles for autonomy and independence from powerful imposing mothers are relentless, and the confrontations between mothers and daughters are fierce. In the chapter "Without Wood," daughter Rose Hsu Jordan describes the decision she made as a child in her dream to pick a different doll from the one her mother expected her to choose. Another daughter, Jing-mei, adopts a self-defensive strategy against her mother's expectation that she be a child prodigy by disappointing her whenever she can. She does this by getting average grades, by not becoming class president, by not being accepted into Stanford University, and finally by dropping out of college. By consistently failing her mother, Jing-mei manages to assert her own will.

The struggle between mother and daughter is equally ferocious. It often takes the form of psychological warfare between the two. Waverly Jong, a child prodigy chess player, envisages this struggle as a chess game in which her mother is transformed into a fierce opponent whose eyes are reduced to "two angry black slits." The struggle is also expressed in physical and verbal fights. When, for example, the daughter Lena St. Clair overhears a mother and daughter who live next door shouting and fighting, she is not overly surprised when she learns from the daughter that both of them "do this kind of stuff all the time."

This type of painful and dramatic confrontation also characterizes the relationship between Jing-mei Woo and her mother, Suyuan. Following a rather violent physical fight, Jing-mei Woo accuses her mother of wanting her to be someone she is not. Suyuan responds to this accusation by telling her that only two types of daughters exist: obedient daughters and disobedient daughters. Following this pronouncement, the daughter screams that she wishes that she was not her mother's daughter. When Suyuan reminds her that this is something that cannot be changed, Jing-mei utters the worst possible thing that a Chinese daughter could ever say to her mother: "Then I wish I'd never been born! I wish I were dead! Like them." This "them" refers to the twin babies whom her mother was forced to abandon in China while attempting to escape the invading Japanese troops. Before Jing-mei realizes what a mindless thing she has just said, Suyuan, badly hurt, falls silent, backs out of the room, and like a small leaf in the wind, appears "thin, brittle, lifeless."

In spite of the daughters' successful resistance and rejection of their influence, the mothers valiantly refuse to give up. After having tried many different strategies throughout their lives, the mothers finally discover that storytelling is the best way to reach the hearts and minds of their daughters. Realizing that sharing her past with her daughter might be the last and only trump card she has in order to "save" her daughter, Ying-ying St. Clair decides to give it a try. Her decision, nevertheless, reflects her awareness of the nature of the clash—the daughter's lack of ethnic and cultural identity, which Ying-ying is convinced will lead to her daughter's unhappiness. By telling her past to a daughter who has spent all of her life trying to slip away from her, Ying-ying St. Clair hopes to reclaim her, "to penetrate her skin and pull her to where she can be saved." Jing-mei Woo's dying mother also realizes that her daughter's problem similarly stems from her refusal to embrace her Chinese roots. Indeed, before her trip to China, Jing-mei relentlessly denies her Chinese heritage. On the train to China from Hong Kong, Jing-mei finally comes to terms with her true identity. Reflecting on her past, she admits to feeling different. Furthermore, she is now prepared to concede: "[M]y mother was right. I am becoming Chinese."

The device of storytelling by women to women is employed extensively throughout the novel as a means to achieve various ends. For instance, it is the means by which Lindo Jong is physically set free. As a young girl, Lindo managed to get out of an arranged marriage. She accomplished this feat by inventing stories about her husband's ancestor's wish for him to marry a servant girl. The mothers also resort to storytelling when trying to impart daily truths and knowledge to the daughters. Through storytelling, they hope to help their daughters rise above negative circumstances or simply avoid unknown dangers. Waverly Jong remembers her mother's telling her a story about a girl who carelessly ran into a street and was subsequently killed by a taxi. Lena St. Clair remembers the story her mother made up about a young woman who fell in love with an irresponsible man and had a baby out of wedlock. After her mother's maid tells the child An-mei Hsu about the rape that led to her mother's shameful position as the third concubine of a wealthy man, An-mei Hsu realizes that she is now better able to grasp the meaning of many of the things that previously escaped her. For the mother, Ying-ying St. Clair, telling her daughter about her past is a tangible proof of her love. In sharing her past with her daughter, she hopes to counter the fact that her daughter has no *chi,* no spirit. Lena's lack of *chi* is Ying-ying's greatest shame, and her stories become a means by which she hopes to help her submissive daughter regain her "tiger spirit."

Telling Lena about her past is absolutely necessary because both mother and daughter are "tigers" and both are "lost . . . unseen and not seeing, unheard and not hearing." By learning about her mother's past, Lena becomes better equipped to fight back and restore her happiness (marital happiness, in her case) in much the same way her mother did in the course of her own life. For Ying-ying St. Clair, who has already waited far too long to tell Lena her story, storytelling is also a positive experience since it allows her to find herself, to remember that long ago she "wished to be found."

Through the sharing of personal experiences, a reconcilia-tion between mothers and daughters is reached. The daughters realize that their mothers have always had their best interests at heart. Echoing the old woman and the swan in the first prologue at the beginning of the novel, mother Lindo Jong explains her feelings most poignantly: "I wanted everything for you to be better. I wanted you to have the best circumstances, the best character. I didn't want you to regret anything." Because their own lives in China had been circumscribed by social and parental constraints that invariably led to pain, humiliation, and tragedy, the mothers all came to America to give their daughters a better life. However, daughters must first understand the real circumstances surrounding their mothers: how they arrived in their new country, how they married, how hard they tried to hold onto their Chinese roots. Once they have understood this, the daughters are better able to understand why they themselves are the way they are. Ultimately, this understanding will also lead them to finally appreciate their mothers. The mothers try very hard to leave an imprint of themselves on their daughters through various means. For the mother Lindo Jong, names carry a symbolic significance. She tells her daughter that the reason she named her Waverly is that, when she gave birth to her, they lived on a street with the same name. In naming her thus, she was convinced that her daughter would feel that she belonged on that street and that when it would come time for her to leave home, she would take with her a "piece" of her mother. While Waverly is left with a "piece" of her mother in her name, An-mei Hsu inherits from her mother a ring of watery blue sapphire, and Jing-mei receives a necklace with a jade pendant from hers. These pieces of jewelry are also symbolic of their mothers' continued presence in their lives. However, the daughters' acceptance of, and identification with, their mothers does not take place until all of them come into contact with their mothers' past through stories. Thus, after her mother's death, when she sets foot on Chinese land for the first time in her life, Jing-mei learns about her mother's long-cherished wish. Also during this trip, she discovers the meaning of her mother's name as well as the meaning of her own name: her mother's, Suyuan, means "Long-cherished Wish," and hers, Jing-mei, means "Younger Sister of Pure Essence." After learning the hidden meanings of these names, Jing-mei is full of remorse: "I think about this. My mother's long-cherished wish. Me, the younger sister who was supposed to be the essence of the others. I feed myself with the old grief, wondering how disappointed my mother must have been."

The sharing of cultural experience between mother and daughter through the device of storytelling transforms the naive, self-protective daughters, who try hard to move away from, or surpass, their ethnic roots, into the mature daughters who are appreciative of their mother's Chinese ways. Through storytelling, the daughters come to accept their mothers' and their own race and are willing to seek their ethnic and cultural roots. Jing-mei goes to China and reunites with her twin sisters. Waverly and her American husband go to China together with her mother and spend their honeymoon there.

With a new consciousness, the mature daughter sees her mother in a new light. As Waverly Jong puts it: "[I]n the brief instant that I had peered over the barriers I could finally see what was really there: an old woman, a wok for her armor, a knitting needle for her sword, getting a little crabby as she waited patiently for her daughter to invite her in." The daughter's defiance turns out to be baseless, and the "scheming ways" of the mother who seemed relentless in her pursuit of her daughter's weakest spots prove to be unfounded. After her mother's death, Jing-mei Woo also realizes, for the first time, that Schumann's music, which as a child she had played at a fateful recital, is in fact, composed of two parts: "Pleading Child" and "Perfectly Contented." Interestingly, it is the former piece that she played so poorly. While in mourning for her mother, Jing-mei also comes to the realization that she has always been biased by a one-sided view of life and by a poor opinion of her mother. When she plays the two pieces of music together, she suddenly understands that they are "two halves of the same song." Schumann's music thus serves as a metaphor used by Tan to highlight the relationship between mother and daughter. This relationship encompasses, like Schumann's music, two phases of the human experience. At times, these phases may appear to be contradictory, but, in fact, they are really two natural and complementary stages of life. Tan thus seems to imply that a complete and holistic experience of life requires an understanding and an acceptance of both phases.

The novel ends with the arrival of Jing-mei Woo in China, the "motherland," where the three sisters are reunited and where Jing-mei finally accepts her Chinese identity. Jing-mei had to leave the West and travel all the way to China before she was able to realize that both her mother and China are in her blood. Only when she has reached maturity is she able to close the geographical gap and come to terms with her ethnic, cultural, and racial background. In doing so, she transcends the psychological gap that had alienated her from her mother and from herself. When the struggles and battles are over, when the daughter is mature enough to be able to accept the mother and identify with what she stood for, what was formerly considered a hateful bondage is revealed to be a cherished bond.

Sau-Ling Cynthia Wong (essay date 1995)

SOURCE: "'Sugar Sisterhood': Situating the Amy Tan Phenomenon," in *The Ethnic Canon: Histories, Institutions, and Interventions,* edited by David Palumbo-Liu, University of Minnesota Press, 1995, pp. 174-210.

[*In the following essay, Wong analyzes the anthropological aspects of Tan's novels* The Joy Luck Club *and* The Kitchen God's Wife *and their place in literary tradition.*]

The sensational success of Amy Tan's first novel, *The Joy Luck Club,* is the stuff of publishing legend. Before the shrewd eye of agent Sandra Dijkstra spotted a potential winner, Tan was entirely unknown to the literary world. But lavish advance praise—the dust jacket of the hardcover edition bears enthusiastic blurbs by Alice Walker, Alice Hoffman, and Louise Erdrich—and postpublication rave reviews instantly propelled *The Joy Luck Club* onto the *New York Times* best-seller list, where it stayed for nine months. The hardcover edition was reprinted twenty-seven times and sold 275,000 copies; frenzied bidding by corporate publishers pushed the price for paperback rights from a floor of $100,000 to an astonishing $1.2 million. *The Joy Luck Club* was a finalist for the National Book Award and the National Book Critics Circle Award, and a recipient of the 1990 Bay Area Book Reviewers Award for Fiction.

Tan's second novel, *The Kitchen God's Wife,* has not duplicated *Joy Luck's* blockbuster success. However, it too is a highly acclaimed best-seller, with most reviewers declaring it as good as, if not better than, its predecessor. The $4 million advance that Putnam reputedly paid on it has apparently been money well spent. The Amy Tan phenomenon continues its momentum with a new children's book, *The Moon Lady,* spun off from an episode in *The Joy Luck Club;* a third novel in the works; and a film adaptation of *The Joy Luck Club* made by noted Chinese American director Wayne Wang.

Like Maxine Hong Kingston's *Woman Warrior, The Joy Luck Club* is a crossover hit by a female ethnic writer; it also straddles the worlds of "mass" literature and "respectable" literature, stocking the shelves of airport newsstands as well as university bookstores, generating coffee table conversations as well as conference papers. Tan's stellar status in the publishing world, further assured by *The Kitchen God's Wife,* causes one to wonder: wherein does the enormous appeal of her fiction lie?

To say that book buyers and readers are simply responding to Tan's good writing—briskly paced, easy to follow, by turns poignant and hilarious—is to give a naive and decontextualized, if partially true, answer. It goes without saying that the history of literary reputations abounds with instances of "good" writing belatedly recognized, or else of "bad" writing amply rewarded in the marketplace. (Without getting into a general disquisition on the social construction of taste, I use the "good"/"bad" distinction here to refer to either a disjuncture between academic/critical opinion and popular success, or else a revision of judgment over time.) To narrow the consideration to contemporaneous Asian

American Women's writing alone, the year *The Joy Luck Club* appeared also saw the polished novelistic debut of another young writer, Cynthia Kadohata (*The Floating World*), as well as new books by two established figures: Kingston's *Tripmaster Monkey: His Fake Book* and Bharati Mukherjee's *Jasmine*. All three works show remarkable artistry and garnered strong reviews, but none became a commercial triumph. That elusive element, "timing" or "luck," usually summoned to explain cases of overnight celebrity, must be restored to historicity: What is it about the subject matter of *The Joy Luck Club* and its treatment that somehow "clicked" with the times? What prompts Tan's following to come back loyally to *The Kitchen God's Wife?* Where is her fiction positioned in the multiple discourses that make up American writing? What discursive traditions does it participate in, and to what ideological effect, to create Tan's trademark fictional world and a niche market?

One of the most obvious reasons for the success of *The Joy Luck Club* and *The Kitchen God's Wife* is the centrality of the mother-daughter relationship in these books. This subject matter places them squarely in a tradition of matrilineal discourse that has, as a part of the feminist movement, been gathering momentum in the United States over the last ten to fifteen years.
—Sau-Ling Cynthia Wong

Tan has often been presented in the media as a meteoric individual talent, bursting full-blown from obscurity onto the literary scene. She has even been implicitly credited with single-handedly ushering in an Asian American literary renaissance, even though Tan herself takes pains to point out that many of the writers of the 1991 "wave" named by the mainstream media (David Wong Louie, David Mura, Gish Jen, Gus Lee, Laurence Yep, Frank Chin) had been writing and publishing before—some, like Chin and Yep, long, long before—she became known, and that they represent very different, unique voices. The media account of Tan's singularity, based on tacit meritocratic assumptions and a late twentieth-century variation on the myth of the original romantic artist, obscures the role of politics in the making (and breaking) of Asian American and other ethnic minority writers. Demythologizing this kind of portrayal, this essay situates the appeal of Amy Tan's fiction in its sociohistorical context and analyzes the discursive demands and contradictions experienced by Chinese American (and to some degree other Asian American) writers at this juncture in American history.

Feminist/Matrilineal Discourse and China Mama's Revenge

One of the most obvious reasons for the success of *The Joy Luck Club* and *The Kitchen God's Wife* is the centrality of the mother-daughter relationship in these books. This subject matter places them squarely in a tradition of matrilineal discourse that has, as a part of the feminist movement, been gathering momentum in the United States over the last ten to fifteen years. In 1976, Adrienne Rich wrote that the "cathexis between mother and daughter—essential, distorted, misused—is the great unwritten story." In 1984, Tillie Olsen was still able to lament, "Most of what has been, is, between mothers, daughters, and in motherhood, daughterhood, has never been recorded." But a scant five years later, as Mickey Pearlman notes, the profusion of creative writing as well as social-science scholarship on the "linked lives" of mothers and daughters had become overwhelming.

That the success of Amy Tan's fiction is a product of, and testimony to, the strength of the feminist movement is easy to see. Both her books capture the contradictions that have been identified as characteristic of the "literature of matrilineage" in Nan Bauer Maglin's simple but convenient schema:

> 1. the recognition by the daughter that her voice is not entirely her own;
>
> 2. the importance of trying to really see one's mother in spite of or beyond the blindness and skewed vision that growing up together causes;
>
> 3. the amazement and humility about the strength of our mothers;
>
> 4. the need to recite one's matrilineage, to find a ritual to both get back there and preserve it;
>
> 5. and still, the anger and despair about the pain and the silence borne and handed on from mother to daughter.

Any number of pithy quotations from *The Joy Luck Club* and *The Kitchen God's Wife* can be culled to illustrate these interconnected themes. What is harder to determine than Tan's place in American matrilineal discourse is the reason why her fiction has so conspicuously eclipsed works by Euro-American writers on similar subject matter, as Kingston's *Woman Warrior* did over a decade ago. The white feminist reading public appears to have an unusually keen appetite for mother-daughter stories by and about people of color. In particular, as one British reviewer wryly observes from across the Atlantic, "Whether by a quirk of literary fate or because it is their psychological destiny, Chinese American women seem to have won the world rights to the mother/daughter relationship." Why? Why this privileging of Chinese American mothers and daughters in literature while no equivalent is forthcoming in the realm of, say, employment opportunities or provision of child care?

I suggest it is neither literary fate nor psychological destiny that has conferred favored status on the Chinese American mother-daughter relationship, but rather a convergence of ethnic group-specific literary tradition and ideological needs by the white-dominated readership—including the feminist readership—for the Other's presence as both mirror and differentiator.

Contrary to popular belief, Kingston did not invent Chinese American matrilineal discourse, and Tan, creating something of an accessible *"Woman Warrior* without tears" in **Joy Luck,** is not so much revisiting Kingston territory as sharing a concern long of interest to many other Chinese American women writers. Antecedents for Kingston's strong Chinese women can be found in the female-centered household in Su ling Wong and Earl Cressy's little-known collaborative autobiography, *Daughter of Confucius.* Even propatriarchal Chinese American autobiographies from the pre-1965 period, such as Helena Kuo's *I've Come a Long Way* and Jade Snow Wong's *Fifth Chinese Daughter,* like *Daughter of Confucius,* show occasional inruptions of matrilineal consciousness, as in Kuo's anecdote of mother-daughter complicity in novel reading, or Jade Snow Wong's descriptions of hours spent with her grandmother and mother learning about Chinese customs—at once mother-daughter bonding and induction into the woman's submissive role in the culture. That is to say, even earlier male-identified Chinese American women writers are, at some level, aware of the precariousness of their place in a patriarchal society—an awareness also reflected in the virtually obligatory opening explanations of how they come to receive a decent education, thanks to generous fathers willing to mitigate prevailing gender norms. Chinese American interest in matrilineage continues in the post-1965 period; examples range from Chuang Hua's recurrent image of the majestic matriarch in *Crossings* (again in spite of an overt obsession with the father's approval); to Alice P. Lin's combined ethnic/matrilineal root-seeking journey in *Grandmother Has No Name*; to the fiction of younger writers like Sarah Lau, Wen-Wen C. Wang, and Fae Myenne Ng, who, like Kingston, explore their bond with immigrant mothers simultaneously tough and vulnerable.

Chinese American preoccupation with the mother-daughter bond can be further situated in a broader Asian American discourse of matrilineage, both pre- and post-*Woman Warrior.* Hisaye Yamamoto's classics, "Seventeen Syllables" and "Yoneko's Earthquake," predate *The Woman Warrior* by over two decades; apparent inspiration for "The Handkerchief" and "Songs My Mother Taught Me" by Wakako Yamauchi, Yamamoto's literary disciple; these stories depict the ambivalent and largely unspoken emotional exchanges between un-

happily married mothers and daughters on the verge of womanhood, in ways again reminiscent of Maglin's schema. Despite the protagonists' expressed yearning for the father's love, the presence of abrasive, abusive, but irrepressibly vigorous grandmothers is indelible in Burmese American Wendy Law-Yone's *Coffin Tree* as well as Japanese American Cynthia Kadohata's *Floating World;* the grandmother/matriarch figure, coupled again with an absent mother, resurfaces in Singaporean American writer Fiona Cheong's *Scent of the Gods.* The resilient spirit of female ancestors embodied in the Vietnamese legend of the woman warrior, along with the support of living women relatives, is lovingly recalled in Le Ly Hayslip's account of her life during and after the Vietnam War, *When Heaven and Earth Changed Places.* Merle Woo's "Letter to Ma" articulates a radical, lesbian perspective on Asian American mother-daughter relationships. Ronyoung Kim's *Clay Walls* chronicles the strong ties between a Korean immigrant woman and her daughter. Short fiction such as South Asian Appachana's and Dhillon's, and Japanese American Sasaki's, continue the exploration of matrilineage. If we broaden the Asian-American canon to include Asian Canadian works, then Joy Kogawa's *Obasan* offers a distinctly matrilineal text, in which themes like the search for the absent mother, surrogate motherhood (or maternalistic aunthood), silence breaking, and rituals of reclamation are woven into an account of the uprooting of Japanese Canadians during the Second World War. More recently, South-Indian Canadian writer Mara Rachna's *Of Customs and Excise* places the story of the "immigrant daughter's revolt" in a multigenerational, postcolonial global context to deepen one's understanding of matrilineage.

This quick survey of the literature of matrilineage in the Chinese-American and Asian-American traditions is meant to contextualize Tan's work more precisely: to dispel the notion that her fiction is simply riding on the coattails of white feminism, tapping directly into "universal" concerns from the vantage point of individual insight. Even if there had been no white buyers of **The Joy Luck Club** and **The Kitchen God's Wife,** there would still have been a readership for these books among Asian American women, many of whom are hungry for validation of their own experiences as daughters of immigrant mothers.

Identifying a matrilineal Asian American tradition is important in terms of not only racial politics within feminism, but also gender politics within cultural nationalism. The kind of rehabilitation of Asian American literary patrilineage undertaken by the *Aiiieeeee* group, essential as it is, is attained at the expense of the female perspective. In the influential Introduction to *Aiiieeeee!* the numerical superiority of Asian American women writers is categorically denounced as a sign of the literature's emasculation by white society, while not one living Chinese American woman writer is included in *The Big Aiiieeeee!* the sequel to the first anthology. Frank

Chin's *Year of the Dragon,* a play about a disintegrating Chinatown family in the 1960s, is emblematic of this suppression of the woman's voice. In addition to a scatterbrained American-born mother humming inherent snatches of song, the play features China Mama, the patriarch's first wife left in China because of immigration restrictions and suddenly transported to San Francisco to assuage the dying man's cultural and familial guilt. This *gum sahn paw* (Cantonese for "Gold Mountain wife") is portrayed as totally devoid of subjectivity: a recalcitrant, alien presence unceremoniously deposited in the Eng family's living room, mute except for sporadic attempts to communicate with the children in gibberish-like Cantonese. In Chin's play, the old immigrant woman from China is just a convenient symbol, not a human being with decades' worth of experiences and grievances to recount. In this context, *The Joy Luck Club* and *The Kitchen God's Wife* are China Mama's revenge: the Joy Luck aunties get not only their own voices back but equal time with their American offspring. And when Winnie in *The Kitchen God's Wife* holds forth about her past, she is allowed to do so endlessly, for more than 330 pages, until her daughter Pearl nearly falls off the chair from surprise at revealed secrets, and we the readers from sheer fatigue.

It is vital to recognize the Asian American discursive context for Amy Tan's fiction, but the Asian American readership for matrilineal discourse is simply not large enough to support the kind of sales that Tan's fiction has enjoyed. Today's book-buying readers of literature are predominantly white and female. The question thus remains: what do these readers—some with conscious feminist leanings, some without—find so engrossing in Tan's stories of the mother-daughter bond?

"Sugar Sisterhood": The Persistent Allure of Orientalism

This brings me to the odd-sounding title of this essay, "Sugar Sisterhood," derived from the phrase "sugar sister" used by Winnie in *The Kitchen God's Wife.* Winnie is explaining to Pearl, her English-speaking daughter, her closeness to cousin Peanut. Peanut has found a face-saving way to reveal that she has given up Wen Fu, a charming, wealthy, but as it turns out abusive, young man, for Winnie to marry; the emotionally orphaned Winnie is grateful for Peanut's generosity:

> And that's how we came to be as close as sisters once again for the rest of the time I had left with my family. In fact, from that day forward, until I was married, we called each other *tang jie,* "sugar sis-ter," the friendly way to refer to a girl cousin.

Tang jie, again presented with the "sugar sister" translation for Pearl's benefit, is repeated in a later scene, when Winnie and Peanut are temporarily reunited. The phrase "sugar sister" is an egregious mistranslation based on Amy Tan's con-fusing two Chinese homophones, while the accompanying explanation of how the two young women come to address each other by that term betrays a profound ignorance of the Chinese kinship system. What is most remarkable about this passage is its very existence: that Amy Tan has seen fit to include and elaborate on such a "gratuitous" detail—gratuitous in the sense of not functioning to advance the plot or deepen the characterization, of which more later—on something of which she has little knowledge. Furthermore, this putative clarification issues from the mouth of Winnie, a native Chinese-speaker born and raised in China for whom it should be impossible to make such mistakes.

I use the term "sugar sisterhood," then, to designate the kind of readership Amy Tan has acquired, especially among white women, through acts of cultural interpreting and cultural empathy that appear to possess the authority of authenticity but are often products of the American-born writer's own heavily mediated understanding of things Chinese. By examining the "sugar sister" solecism and related uses of Chinese or Chinese-seeming details, by analyzing the stylistic features and narratological design in both of Tan's works, and by uncovering the culturalist reading practices that such novelistic elements encourage, I argue that the "Amy Tan phenomenon" must ultimately be situated in quasi-ethnographic, Orientalist discourse. Occasional anti-Orientalist statements made by the characters, and the opportunities for anticulturalist interpretation provided by Tan's keen observations of Chinese American life, do not negate my assessment. In fact, they are functional in that they enable Orientalism to emerge in a form palatable to middle-class American readers of the 1980s. Specifically, for the feminist audience, the Chinese American mother/daughter dyad in *The Joy Luck Club* and *The Kitchen God's Wife* allegorizes a Third World/First World encounter that allows mainstream American feminism to construct itself in a flattering, because depoliticized, manner—an outcome unlikely to be delivered by mother-daughter stories penned by writers from Euro-American traditions.

Since the "sugar sister" phrase provides the entering wedge for my thesis, I will dwell a moment longer on its significance. Besides the confusion of two different characters for *tang,* there are several other implausibilities in this passage. The term *tang jie* does exist and can be used in the relationship between Winnie and Peanut. (Peanut is the daughter of the younger brother of Winnie's father.) But *tang jie* is a descriptive label and a term of address defined stringently by one's position in a patrilineal system of blood ties; it is not, as Tan suggests, a friendly term of endearment, to be assumed at will when two girl cousins feel close to each other. Moreover, in the thoroughly hierarchical, age-conscious Chinese kinship system, *jie,* or "older sister," is always complemented by *mei,* or "younger sister": two women cannot simultaneously be the *jie*—not even in "courtesy" situations where blood ties are not involved, such as *xuejie/xuemei* (fellow students) or *qijie/qimei* ("sworn sisters") relationships.

In citing the "sugar sister" passage, I am not practicing an idle and mean-spirited "Gotcha!" school of criticism. Something larger is at issue: what is sought is a more precise determination of Tan's stance toward her audience(s) and the types of discourses her works participate in, leading to a clearer understanding of her popularity. To readers who protest that Tan is just writing fiction, I concede that a phrase like "sugar sister" does little to detract from her overall achievements as a writer—from the page-turning narrative drive of her novels, or the general contours of Winnie's vivid character. Given this, the question arises, then, of what function is served by this kind of detail—a romanized Chinese phrase with an appositive explanation, tossed off as an aside by a Chinese-speaking character to her English-dominant daughter—or other similar details of language and custom, minimally warranted by the immediate narrative context but providing occasions for elucidating an exotic Chinese culture.

A list can easily be compiled of such highly dubious or downright erroneous details: Lindo Jong's first husband in Taiyuan is described as yanking off her red veil at the wedding ceremony—a suspiciously Western practice, since traditionally the bride's red veil is removed only in the privacy of the wedding chamber, before the consummation of the marriage; in Ying-ying St. Clair's childhood reminiscences, the customs that are allegedly part of Moon Festival celebrations—burning the Five Evils and eating *zong zi*—actually belong to the *Duanwu* or "Dragon-Boat" Festival on the fifth day of the fifth lunar month; the operatic version of the Moon Lady-Hou Yi story witnessed by Ying-ying includes a detail from another legend about another festival—the annual meeting of two star-crossed lovers on the seventh night of the seventh month; the mother-in-law's rebuke to the young bride Lindo, "*Shemma bende ren!*" rendered in English as "What kind of fool are you!" sounds like a concoction by some first-year Chinese student and necessitates a quiet emendation by the Chinese translator of *The Joy Luck Club*; the warning Rose Hsu Jordan remembers from her mother, shortly before her younger brother's drowning, likewise sounds gratingly unidiomatic in Chinese—"*Dangsying tamende shenti*," translated by Tan as "Watch out for their bodies"; except for the first one, the characters used for the Chinese version of McDonald's name, *mai dong lou*, are not what Lindo Jong says they are, "wheat," "east," and "building"; in *The Kitchen God's Wife*, the Chinese pilots allegedly give General Chennault a good Chinese name, *shan*, "lightning," and *nao*, "noisy," but his name actually has a well-known standard Chinese translation, *Chen Naide*. The list goes on.

The function of such insertions of "Chinese" cultural pres-

ence is worth investigating not only because a history of controversy exists in Asian American cultural politics concerning issues of authenticity, but also because Tan's books have been showered with praise precisely for their *details*.

Detail and Myth

The Joy Luck Club is repeatedly applauded by reviewers for the specificity of its descriptions—entire "richly textured worlds" evoked by details "each . . . more haunting and unforgettable than the one before." The book is called "dazzling because of the *worlds* it gives us"; the word "tapestry" is used to describe this effect of intricacy and richness. This view of Tan's distinctive gift is carried over to reviews of *The Kitchen God's Wife*: "The power of literature over sociology lies in particularization, and it is in details that *The Kitchen God's Wife* excels"; "it is through vivid minutiae that Tan more often exercises her particular charm"; "what fascinates in *The Kitchen God's Wife* is not only the insistent storytelling, but the details of Chinese life and tradition"; *The Kitchen God's Wife*'s "convincing detail" is said to give her fiction "the ring of truth," and Dew urges her readers to give themselves over to Tan's "Tolstoyan tide of event and detail."

This emphasis on details as a main source of Tan's appeal is intriguing because it coexists with a seemingly opposite type of commendation: that details do *not* matter that much in *The Joy Luck Club,* and to a lesser extent *The Kitchen God's Wife,* since they are lyrical, mythical, dreamlike: "full of magic," "rich in magic and mystery." Of Tan's second book, Perrick writes, "There is something dizzyingly elemental about Tan's storytelling; it melds the rich simplicities of fairytales with a delicate lyrical style." Fairy tales, we may note, are "generic" stories stripped of historical particulars, and lyricism is generally associated with moments of inwardness set apart from the realm of quotidian social facts.

The Joy Luck Club draws comparisons with myth even more readily. One reviewer calls it "almost mythic in structure, like the hypnotic tales of the legendary Scheherazade." In the eyes of some readers, the lack of differentiation between the rapidly alternating narrative voices in *Joy Luck,* far from betraying a limited artistic repertoire, is in fact an asset: the mark of universal appeal to women or a more capacious sensibility. Orville Schell, who wrote a widely quoted glowing review of *The Joy Luck Club,* acknowledges that the book's segmented structure, with its abrupt transitions in time and space, may be confusing, but argues that "these *recherches* to old China are so beautifully written that one should just allow oneself to be borne along as if in a dream." Juxtaposed with the daughters' "upwardly mobile, design-conscious, divorce-prone and Americanized world," the mothers' vanished world in China seems "more fantastic and dreamlike than real," a product of "memory" and "revery"—and herein, Schell seems to suggest, lies its peculiar charm.

Is there any necessary incompatibility between these two views of Tan's fiction, one lauding her mastery of details, the other deeming them relatively inconsequential in its overall effect? Not at all, if one takes into account another recurrent theme in reviews of the two novels: their value as anthropological documents, giving the non-Chinese reader access to an enigmatic culture. A review of **The Kitchen God's Wife** finds it a convenient lesson in Chinese history and sociology:

> As a backdrop . . . we learn more about the nature of arranged marriages in Chinese societies and also about the kind of inter-wifely accommodation arranged by second or third wives and their offspring. It is like being invited into a dusty room full of castoffs, and being given a chance to reapprehend them in their former richness. We get to understand how, why, and from where Chinese-American society evolved. . . . Tan is handing us a key with no price tag and letting us open the brass-bolted door.

In view of the inaccurate cultural details we have seen, this coupling of Tan's fiction with anthropological discourse, which carries with it implicit claims of credibility and factual verifiability, may be ironic. But the issue is not so much how Tan has failed as a cultural guide; it is, rather, the text- and reception-oriented question of how and why the American reading public has responded so eagerly to her writings as faithful chronicles of things Chinese. Tan's fiction has apparently been able to hold in colloidal suspension two essential ingredients of quasi-ethnographic Orientalist discourse on China and the Chinese, which both have a long genealogy in this country. These ingredients are "temporal distancing" and "authenticity marking." Tan's ability to somehow keep both details and "nondetails," as it were, in busy circulation allows readers with culturalist propensities—that is to say, a large proportion of the American reading public—to recognize the genre and respond accordingly, with enthusiastic purchases as well as a pleasurable mixture of respect and voyeurism, admiration and condescension, humility and self-congratulation.

Temporal Distancing and Other "Othering Maneuvers"

Johannes Fabian, in his *Time and the Other: How Anthropology Makes Its Object,* suggests that "temporal distancing" is a means of constructing the Other widely employed in ethnographic discourse. He proposes the term "Typological Time" to refer to a use of time "almost totally divested of its vectorial, physical connotations": "instead of being a measure of movement, it may appear as a quality of states" presumably "unequally distributed among human populations

of this world." The concept of Typological Time produces familiar distinctions attributed to human societies such as preliterate versus literate, traditional versus modern, peasant versus industrial, the term with which the anthropologist identifies himself/herself invariably being the privileged one. The contrast between some such binary states—traditional versus modern, superstitious versus secular, elemental versus materialistic, communal enmeshment versus anomie—is, we may note, precisely what **The Joy Luck Club** and **The Kitchen God's Wife** are engaged in exploring.

Whereas the ethnographer relies on the temporalized protocols of the "field method" to achieve Othering—field notes in the past tense, subsequent generalizations about the culture in the "ethnographic present" tense—Tan's two novels effect it through a number of narratological and stylistic means. (Whether Tan consciously employed them is another matter: *means* here refers not to goal-oriented artistic choices but an after-the-fact reconstruction of how the reader is affected.) Chief among these is the way the stories about old China are "framed" by reference to the present time of America. In **The Joy Luck Club,** except for the short chapter entitled "Scars," all the mothers' narratives open with some kind of time signature in the United States of the 1980s, in the form of a silent addressing of the daughter as "you" or some mention of "my daughter" in her present predicament. In **The Kitchen God's Wife,** of course, Winnie's entire tale is framed by the "now" of Pearl's dealings with her mother in connection with cousin Bao Bao's wedding and Grand Aunt Du's funeral; periodically, too, within what amounts to a lengthy monologue, Winnie supplies answers to queries (unrecorded), rhetorical questions, proleptic allusions, and philosophical musings for the benefit of her daughter.

The temporal distancing that makes possible the Othering of the Chinese mothers does not consist in locating their stories in elapsed time—after all, the daughters too tell about their childhood. Instead, it works through a subtle but insistent positioning of everything in the mothers' lives to a watershed event: arrival in the United States. Like using the arrival of the white man to demarcate two modes of being, the later one redeeming the earlier from cyclical repetition as a matter of inevitable "progress," this practice bears the unmistakable traces of a hegemonic cultural vantage point vis-à-vis a "backward" Third World. The Typological Time in both novels revolves around an unstated aporetic split between the static, ritual-permeated, mythical Time of a China past, where individuals' lives are deprived of choice, shaped by tradition and buffeted by inexorable "natural" circumstances (in terms of which even wars are described), and the unfolding, enlightened, rational, secular Time of contemporary America, where one can exercise decision making and control over one's life and where learning from the past is possible. The mothers, who are portrayed as fixated on old hurts and secrets and obsessed with cultural transmission in the form of aphorisms, and whose transformation in America from young refugees to stolid matrons is never delineated, belong to the mythical time so beloved of many a non-Chinese reader.

The Othering accomplished by temporal distancing is augmented by the stylistic uniformity of the Joy Luck mothers' voices when recounting their lives in China, which has the effect of constructing the Third World women's experiences as interchangeable and predictably constrained, because so overwhelmingly determined by culture. As Renato Rosaldo observes, "social analysts commonly speak . . . as if 'we' have psychology and 'they' have culture." The *content* of one set of stories is no doubt distinguishable from the next, but the *manner* of presentation is not. In *The Kitchen God's Wife,* despite Tan's claim of a new departure, her stylistic range can hardly be said to be noticeably extended, and Winnie's voice inevitably recalls Lindo Jong's or An-mei Hsu's.

Both *The Joy Luck Club* and *The Kitchen God's Wife* contrast a "low- resolution" picture of the mothers' lives in China with descriptions of high material specificity or informational density in the daughters' sections. The American-born and -bred daughters—whose world Tan shares—are able to *name* things in their world to a high degree of topical and local precision: a scroll-length calendar from the Bank of Canton hangs on Auntie Hsu's wall; candy is not just candy but See's Nuts and Chews or M&M's; Shoshana's outing is to not just any science museum but to the Exploratorium; the trendy restaurants Rose dreams of asking Ted to go to are Cafe Majestic and Rosalie's. In contrast, the items in the mothers' stories are much more "generic": the fish in the Fen River are not identified; the variety of lanterns at the Moon Festival is not differentiated; the bicycle on which An-mei Hsu's little brother rides has no brand name.

This lack of elaboration cannot be explained away as merely a realistic mirroring of the mothers' memory lapses. In the minds of many older people, recollections of remote childhood events often surpass, in clarity and specificity, those of more proximate occurrences. And young children are not nearly as oblivious to culturally meaningful distinctions as retrospective idealization makes them out to be. Finally, while the consumer orientation of present-day American society may partly account for the profusion of named objects in the daughters' narratives, it would be ignorant and condescending to attribute a preindustrial simplicity to the mothers' China. Whether uneven distribution of authorial knowledge about the two worlds is a factor in the textural fluctuation in the novels, or whether Tan is consciously manipulating the degree of resolution, remains an open, perhaps unanswerable, question. However, from the point of

view of reception analysis, the leveling of descriptive details in the "Chinese" segments is an important source of pleasure for white readers, who accept and appreciate it as a "mythic" treatment of a remote but fascinating China.

Markers of Authenticity: "The Oriental Effect"

Are the reviewers simply misguided then when they laud Tan's "convincing details"? Not at all. The details are there, but their nature and function are probably not what a "commonsense" view would make them out to be: evidence of referential accuracy, of the author's familiarity with the "real" China. Rather, they act as gestures to the "mainstream" readers that the author is familiar with the kind of culturally mediated discourse they have enjoyed, as well as qualified to give them what they expect. I call these details "markers of authenticity," whose function is to create an "Oriental effect" by signaling a reassuring affinity between the given work and American preconceptions of what the Orient is/should be.

The term "Oriental effect" borrows from "the reality effect" posited by Roland Barthes. In an essay of that name, Barthes investigates the function of apparently "useless" descriptive details in realist fiction—details that are "scandalous (from the point of view of structure)" or "allied with a kind of narrative *luxury,*" lacking "predictive" power for plot advancement, and salvageable only as a cumulative indicator of "characterization or atmosphere." Citing epideictic discourse in classical rhetoric, in which "plausibility [is] not referential, but overtly discursive"—"it [is] the rules of the discourse genre which laid down the law"—Barthes goes on to argue that in the modern aesthetic of *vraisemblance,* the function of apparently superfluous details is to announce "*we are the real*" and produce a "reality effect." "It is the category of the 'real,' and not its various contents, which is being signified." Extending Barthes's analysis, I argue that, in both *The Joy Luck Club* and *The Kitchen God's Wife,* there are many details whose existence cannot be justified on structural or informational grounds, but whose function seems to be to announce "We are Oriental" to the "mainstream" reader. These are the details for which reviewers have praised Tan. Marking the discourse as "authentic," but in a discursive rather than referential dimension, they are in a sense immune to revelations that "real" Chinese cultural practices are otherwise.

An important class of such details is made up of romanized words of limited, at times nonexistent, utility in structural or informational terms. Their usage ranges from "redundant" romanization (such as the appearance of *pai* in the same sentence where the standard English name for mahjong pieces, *tiles,* also appears; or adding "bad *pichi*" to "bad temper," when the latter is a perfectly serviceable equivalent of the Chinese term); to correct renditions of Chinese based on a sophisticated knowledge of the language and culture (such as the clever pun on Suyuan's name); to plausible and justifiable uses of Chinese for concepts without full English equivalents (such as *shou* for filial piety), or for representing the Americanized daughters' cultural gropings (as when Rose remembers the term *hulihudu* during her postdivorce disorientation). Errors of the "sugar sister" type, like the ones listed earlier in this essay, actually constitute only a small percentage of Tan's handling of Chinese matters. But whether "gratuitously" deployed or not, whether informed or not, the very insertion of italicized words in a page of roman type, or of explanatory asides about what the Chinese do and think in a story, is a signal that the author has adopted a certain stance toward the audience. She is in effect inviting trust in her as a knowledgeable cultural insider and a competent guide familiar with the rules of the genre in question: quasi ethnography about the Orient.

We can extend the concept of authenticity marking to a peculiar variety of prose Amy Tan has developed, which has the effect of announcing "Chineseness" in the speakers. The preponderance of short, choppy sentences and the frequent omission of sentence subjects are oft-used conventions whereby the Chinese can be recognized as Other. In addition to these, Tan employs subtle, minute dislocations of English syntax and vocabulary—jolting the language out of whack just enough—to create an impression of translation from the Chinese even where no translation has taken place. For example, in Ying-Ying's recollections of her childhood trauma at the Moon Festival, an old woman's complaint about her swollen foot takes this form: "Both inside and outside have a sour painful feeling." This is neither an idiomatic English sentence nor a direct English equivalent of an idiomatic Chinese sentence; it cannot be attributed to Ying-Ying's poor command of English, for the mothers' laborious, grammatically mangled, often malapropic English appears only in "real life," that is, when they are in the United States, speaking with their daughters. Elsewhere, when telling their own stories, they are given a different kind of English, fluent if simple, by Tan's own avowal designed to better articulate their subjectivities, do full justice to their native intelligence, and restore them to the dignity they deserve. This cause is decidedly not well served by such slight linguistic skewings, which in the American popular imagination have been associated with the "comic," pidginized "Asian English" found in Anglo-American writing on Asians. However, reading exactly like the kind of quaint, circumlocutious literal translations, or purported literal translations, in the tradition of self-Orientalizing texts, they indicate the comforting presence of cultural mediation to the "mainstream" reader. Thus it is not surprising to find white reviewers like Miner and Schell praising the *authenticity* of the immigrant women's diction. This valorized "Oriental effect" exists independent of Tan's sincerity in wanting to give

voice to first-generation Chinese women, which we have no cause to doubt.

If, as Todorov maintains in *The Poetics of Prose,* verisimilitude in literature is less a relation with "reality" than "what most people believe to be reality—in other words, with public opinion," and with "the particular rules of [a] genre," then the reviewers' satisfaction with Tan's details is entirely consistent with their assessment of *The Joy Luck Club* and *The Kitchen God's Wife* as "mythic" or "lyrical." Tan's details may lack referential precision, but what shapes the reviewers' expectations is verisimilitude in Todorov's second and third senses. The reviewers' dual emphases—on a timeless mythic realm and on presumably authentic details—are ultimately Orientalist in spirit. It is a certain image of what China must be like ("public opinion"—here defined, of course, as the opinion of the "mainstream") and familiarity with a certain type of writing about China ("rules of the genre") that have influenced their estimation of Tan's fiction. Paradoxical as it may seem, an author with more direct historical knowledge about China than Amy Tan may well be *less* successful in convincing the American reading public of the "truthfulness" of her picture, since, in such a case, the element of cultural mediation would be correspondingly weaker.

Counter-Orientalist Gestures

It is fair to say that gestures of cultural mediation are an important component in Amy Tan's novels and are responsible, in no small part, for their popularity. But it is also fair to say that the variety of Orientalism informing *The Joy Luck Club* and *The Kitchen God's Wife* is far from simple-minded or unproblematized. It is not the knowingly exploitative misrepresentation described by Peanut in *The Kitchen God's Wife:*

> They sell *Chinese* garbage to the foreigners, especially people from America and England. . . . They sell anything that is broken, or strange, or forbidden. . . . The broken things they call Ming Dynasty. The strange things they say are Ching Dynasty. And the forbidden things—they say they are forbidden, no need to hide that. (italics in original)

After all, Tan, born in racially heterogeneous Oakland, California, in 1952 (albeit in a predominantly white neighborhood), grew up in the 1960s; however peripherally or obliquely, her works cannot but bear traces of the ethnic consciousness movement of that era. These traces range from relatively inconsequential information about the characters or satirical observations on ethnic chic (and its cousin, prole chic), to the pervasive, if often implicit, presence of the vocabulary and concepts of identity politics in *The Joy Luck Club*—what does it mean to be Chinese? to be an ethnic minority? to be American? The white middle-class book-reading and book-buying public of the post-civil rights era, likewise touched, has learned to enjoy its exotica flavored by the rhetoric of pluralism and an awareness of domestic and global interethnic connectedness. An unself-consciously ingratiating invitation to the cultural sightseer, such as the tourist brochure-style, zoom-in description of San Francisco Chinatown in the opening paragraph of Jade Snow Wong's *Fifth Chinese Daughter,* has a decidedly old-fashioned ring to it and no longer carries the persuasiveness it once possessed. Indeed, this type of writing is no longer produced by any Asian American writers of note. A credible cultural middleman for the contemporary "mainstream" reader needs to demonstrate, in addition to access to an authentic originary culture (or the appearance thereof), some sophistication regarding the limitations of monologism.

On this score Amy Tan fits the bill well. Again, whether by design or not, she manages to balance on a knife edge of ambiguity, producing texts in which Orientalist and counter-Orientalist interpretive possibilities jostle each other, sometimes within the same speech or scene. The complex, unstable interplay of these possibilities makes for a larger readership than that enjoyed by a text with a consistently articulated, readily identifiable ideological perspective. The nonintellectual consumer of Orientalism can find much in *The Joy Luck Club* and *The Kitchen God's Wife* to satisfy her curiosity about China and Chinatown; at the same time, subversions of naive voyeurism can be detected by the reader attuned to questions of cultural production.

Contending Interpretative Possibilities

That Tan's works have a little bit of something for everyone can be illustrated by a few examples from *The Joy Luck Club.* (*The Kitchen God's Wife,* which is fashioned from the same range of elements as its predecessor but contours them differently, will be discussed at greater length in a later section.) Waverly Jong's first chapter, "Rules of the Game," contains a portrayal of the young Chinatown girl as hit-and-run cultural guerrilla: to get back at a Caucasian tourist who poses her with roast ducks, Waverly tries to gross him out with the disinformation that a recommended restaurant serves "guts and duck's feet and octopus gizzards." An anti-Orientalist impulse animates this incident; in Tan's account of daily routines among bakeries, sandlots, and alleyways, one recognizes a desire to demystify the tourist mecca and evoke a sense of Chinatown as home, not spectacle. However, this effect is undermined by what appears to be a retroactive exoticizing reading of an everyday detail: Waverly, now seeming to have adopted the tourist's mentality, recalls that her meals used to begin "with a soup full of mysterious things I didn't want to know the names of." Furthermore, the chapter opens with language highly reminiscent of fortune cookie wisdom, Charlie Chan aphorisms, and the kind

of Taoist precepts scattered throughout Lin Yutang's *Chinatown Family:*

> I was six when my mother taught me the art of invisible strength. . . . [S]he said, "Wise guy, he not go against wind. In Chinese we say, Come back from South, blow with wind—poom!—North will follow. Strongest wind cannot be seen." . . . My mother imparted her daily truths so she could help my older brothers and me rise above our circumstances.

At times, the characters in *The Joy Luck Club* articulate a historicized understanding of their situation and an awareness of the perils of essentializing ethnicity. For example, as her marriage deteriorates, Lena St. Clair begins to appreciate the advice of her friend Rose, herself a disappointed divorcée:

> "At first I thought it was because I was raised with all this Chinese humility," Rose said. "Or that maybe it was because when you're Chinese you're supposed to accept everything, flow with the Tao and not make waves. But my therapist said, Why do you blame your culture, your ethnicity? And I remembered reading an article about baby boomers, how we expect the best and when we get it we worry that maybe we should have expected more, because it's all diminishing returns after a certain age."

Coexisting with such insights into Chinese American exigencies, and indeed outnumbering them, are statements encouraging a culturalist view of Chinese American life. Much is made of the so-called Chinese horoscope with the twelve animal signs: Ying-Ying St. Clair emphasizes the mystical, quasi-genetic cultural transmission from her "tiger lady" self to her "tiger girl" daughter, while Waverly Jong attributes her conflicts with her mother to incompatible horoscope signs, horse and rabbit.

Given the mutually subverting and qualifying copresence of contradictory tendencies in *The Joy Luck Club*—Orientalist, culturalist, essentialist, and ahistorical on the one hand, and counter-Orientalist, anticulturalist, constructionist, and historicist on the other—the same narrative detail may yield widely divergent readings. Lindo Jong's mother, in response to her daughter's mock-innocent question about "Chinese torture," answers, "Chinese people do many things. . . . Chinese people do business, do medicine, do painting. Not lazy like American people. We do torture. Best torture." How is this statement, delivered "simply," to be read? Is it a straightforward expression of the mother's ethnocultural pride? Or is it an ironic gesture of exasperation at, and resistance against, the daughter's early induction into hegemonic discourse? Has she already seen through the daughter's "wickedness" in transforming a personal irritation and minor filial rebellion into an ideological struggle? (If so, then even the mother's air of matter-of-factness is suspect; Waverly could have been simply insensible of her parodic inflection.)

The reader's quandary parallels Jing-mei Woo's puzzlement in the face of her mother's explanation about Jewish versus Chinese mah jong: "Jewish mah jong, they watch only for their own tile, play only with their eyes. . . . Chinese mah jong, you must play using your head, very tricky." For all intents and purposes, Mrs. Woo could be just describing the difference between novice and expert playing—in which case the scene affords an intriguing glimpse of culturalism in action: the mother mobilizing ethnicity xenophobically to reinforce the exclusivity of her cultural authority. But if, like Jing-mei, one is brought up on reified ethnic categories and has an emotional investment in believing the speaker's cultural knowledgeability, the purported insider's explication might leave one in a curious state of suspended judgment (which could be mistaken for cultural sensitivity and respect for the mysteries of the Other's life).

The temptation to galvanize this uncertainty into a definite interpretation is strong, and, given the current voguishness of multiculturalist rhetoric, the safest course for the befuddled non-Chinese reader might be to take the fictional "insider" speaker at face value. This spells the ultimate, if circuitously achieved, victory of Orientalist readings at the expense of other approaches. A handful of scholars of Asian American literature have argued emphatically against a one-dimensional view of *The Joy Luck Club* as a tale of intergenerational cultural confrontation and resolution. Melani McAlister, for example, has provided compelling evidence that socioeconomic class is as much a factor as culture in the mother-daughter conflicts in *The Joy Luck Club*—that, in fact, "cultural difference" can function as a less volatile or more admissible surrogate term for class anxieties. When the yuppie daughters are embarrassed by their mother's color-mismatched outfits or "un-American" restaurant manners, McAlister observes, they are consumed by the fear of being déclassé, even though they may, in all sincerity, be experiencing their distancing from the mothers *in terms of cultural conflict.* Like McAlister, Lisa Lowe, as part of a larger theoretical project on the "heterogeneity, hybridity, and multiplicity" of Asian American identity, has warned against reductionist readings of *The Joy Luck Club* that leave out class concerns. Nevertheless, voices such as McAlister's or Lowe's, already a minority in the academy, are unlikely to reach the "airport newsstand" readership of Tan's works.

Furthermore, McAlister's thesis that culturalist readings of *The Joy Luck Club* are *mis*readings—implying that a class-informed reading is somehow closer to Tan's intentions—

may itself be a simplification. It is true that, as McAlister points out, when reviewer Orville Schell poses the Americanized daughters against the Joy Luck mothers wearing "funny Chinese dresses with stiff stand-up collars and blooming branches of embroidered silk sewn over their breasts," he is betraying a binarist mind-set. (The Joy Luck mothers have been wearing slacks, print blouses, and sturdy walking shoes for years. "Tonight, there is no mystery.") Schell's telescoping of historical moments—the late 1940s and the late 1980s—freezes the mothers at their moment of immigration, absolutizes the foreign-American distinction, and reproduces the American myth that intergenerational strife is the inevitable price of assimilation. To that extent, one is justified in speaking of a *mis*reading. However, in another sense, Schell is not "wrong," for *The Joy Luck Club,* as we have seen, is filled with features that would amply support the spirit if not the letter of his reading. The ending of the novel itself offers a powerful essentialist proposition: despite much wavering throughout the crisscrossing narratives, "family" and "blood" eventually triumph over history. When Jing-mei travels to China to meet her long-lost half sisters, she discovers "what part of [her] is Chinese" and is able to "let [it] go." This ostensible reconciliation presupposes the reality of a self-alienating ethnic malaise (without considering how it could be an ideological construction in the service of monoculturalism), then locates redemption in origin, thus in effect nullifying or at least discounting the "American" temporality of the Chinese American experience.

The Joy Luck Club is not a misunderstood, co-opted ethnic text that has been unfortunately obscured by a culturalist haze and awaits recuperation through class- or gender-based readings. To suggest so risks explaining away the persistence of Orientalism as a matter of the individual reader's ignorance, inattention, or misguidedness. It is more defensible to characterize *The Joy Luck Club* as a multidimensional cultural product, one whose many ideological layerings, reflections, and refractions are aligned, for a broad cross section of the American reading public, with the contending needs and projections of the times. The book's popular success—and the "Amy Tan phenomenon" in general—cannot be fully understood apart from its *equivocation* vis-à-vis issues of culture and identity, allowing a profusion of interpretive claims to be made with seemingly equal cogency.

The "Declaritive Modality" and Its Implications

Many of the issues raised in the foregoing discussion of how to "read" Amy Tan recall the controversy surrounding Maxine Hong Kingston's *Woman Warrior.* Some Chinese American critics have accused Kingston of distorting traditional myths and cultural practices to capitalize on the Orientalist inclinations of the white reader. Indeed, *The Woman Warrior,* like its successor *The Joy Luck Club,* has excited many reviewers who single out its picturesque details about old China for praise. The tacit assumption, as Kingston notes in an exasperated complaint about many of her so-called admirers, is that the author's Chinese blood is a natural and sufficient guarantor of reliable knowledge; thus the questions Kingston raises in the book about the very cultural ignorance and confusion of the American-born Chinese are casually brushed aside. The question of Kingston's possible complicity in her own misreading is too vast to examine here; her relationship to Orientalism cannot be summed up in a few sentences. And in a way, any ethnic writer who takes on the issue of stereotyping is caught in a bind: like the man in the Zen parable who holds on to a tree branch with his teeth and is asked the way by a straying passer-by, he is lost whatever he does. If he opens his mouth to give the "right" answer, he falls and gets hurt; but if he keeps silent he only deepens the surrounding confusion. How does one protest a problem without mentioning it? But in mentioning it, does one not risk multiplying its visibility and potency, through reiteration if nothing else? Generalization aside, confining ourselves to *The Woman Warrior* and *The Joy Luck Club,* we may note a crucial difference between the two works: in modality of presentation.

According to Elliott Butler-Evans, *The Woman Warrior* is distinguished by an "interrogative modality"—it ceaselessly deconstructs its own narrative authority and overtly thematizes the epistemological difficulties of the American-born Chinese. Its governing rhetorical trope is the palinode, or the taking back of what is said. In other words, despite the first-person form, the narrator/protagonist lays no claim to referential advantage: the negotiations of her consciousness are foregrounded. In Naomi Schor's terms, she is an *interpretant* (interpreting character; as opposed to the interpreter, or interpreting critic/reader of the book), constantly aware of the hazards of under- or overreading, yet unable to refrain from trying to wrest cultural meanings from bewildering details. Through the interpretant, the author Kingston "is trying to tell the interpreter something *about* interpretation." In contrast, *The Joy Luck Club* is epistemologically unproblematized—in Butler-Evans's view, its narrative modality is "declarative." The mothers' narratives about their Chinese life are displayed as immediate, coming directly from the source, and, for that reason, are valorized as correctives to the daughters' unenlightened or biased outlook. The intervention of a narrating consciousness is thus erased. This is what creates the space for equivocation about culture and identity: one is never entirely sure when a reinsertion of this mediation is necessary, and whether attribution of a Chinese American cast to such mediation is justified. Whereas the conflation of Chinese and Chinese American is explored in *The Woman Warrior* as a perilous legacy of Orientalism—the need to sort out the conflation defines the narrator/protagonist's lifelong act of self-creation—it is never actively interrogated in *The Joy Luck Club.*

The "declarative modality" of *The Joy Luck Club* is arguably appropriate for the project of giving voice to the immigrant mothers. Of course, this project is not the only one inferable from Tan's first novel. The "four-by-four" structure of the work—four sections each with four chapters, so that, except for the deceased Mrs. Woo (whose story is told through Jing-mei), each mother-daughter set gets to speak twice—allows the alternating accounts to resonate with, balance out, and qualify each other. The daughters' worlds, if depicted as flawed by greed and small-mindedness, are at least fleshed out enough to be counterpoised against the mothers'. Despite the compromised nature of the voice Tan assigns to the mothers, with its many Orientalist stylistic maneuvers, the narrative design does not draw overwhelming attention to the issue of the voice's truthfulness.

The Valorization of Origin

Yet a question remains, one whose ramifications do not become fully evident until *The Kitchen God's Wife.* Unlike *The Woman Warrior,* whose narrator/protagonist has to outgrow the illusion that talking to mother will resolve cultural disorientation and crystallize truth, *The Joy Luck Club,* while posing subjectivities "declaratively" against each other, does not push the relativistic implications of this move to their limit. The ending of *The Joy Luck Club,* as well as the tentative dramas of mother-daughter reconciliation within the body chapters, suggest there is indeed a locus of truth, and that locus is origin. The daughter's task is to break through the obfuscation caused by her American nativity and upbringing. Certainly there is poignancy in the picture of the mother whose voice is not heard by her daughter:

> Because I remained quiet for so long now my daughter does not hear me. She sits by her fancy swimming pool and hears only her Sony Walkman, her cordless phone, her big, important husband asking her why they have charcoal and no lighter fluid.

But there is also an asymmetry in the poignancy of this isolation *à deux:* the burden is on the daughter to educate herself into truth, to put aside her fears and needs, so that she can see her mother for what she is. The China trip—planned by Waverly, actually undertaken by Jing-mei—is in some ways an extended trope for this embrace of origin. Origin stays put, long-suffering but autotelic, awaiting rediscovery and homage.

But if there is a privileging of origin—which, in the context of Tan's books, means privileging China and the Chinese (whether "native" or diasporic)—does it not run counter to the colonialist tenor of Orientalism?

This question becomes even more pertinent when we examine *The Kitchen God's Wife,* in which both the "declarative modality" of narration and the valorization of the mother's life in China are far more pronounced than in *The Joy Luck Club.* The broad shape of characters and story types from the first novel is preserved—the assimilated, upwardly mobile daughter married to a white husband and living in the suburbs; the immigrant mother in Chinatown with a thing or two to teach her daughter about life; sufferings in China recounted; secrets revealed, old grievances banished, blood ties reaffirmed. But much more explicitly than in *The Joy Luck Club,* the daughter's role is ancillary. The staggered framework has given way to a sandwiching of the mother's tale, which forms the bulk of the novel, between two thin slices of the daughter's life. The daughter's presence, its countervailing function almost reduced to irrelevance, is now little more than a conduit for the True Word from mother, a pretext for Winnie's outpouring.

What is accomplished by this accordion-like redistribution of narrative and thematic priorities? Judging from the way they concentrate on Winnie, most reviewers of *The Kitchen God's Wife* would probably answer "Not much." Humphreys considers Pearl's opening segment merely a "long prologue" making for a "late start" of the "central story," which gathers "energy and momentum" only when Winnie begins speaking. Dew bemoans the novel's "slow start," and Howe feels that whenever Pearl and her husband appear the novel "bogs down." To these critics, Pearl's presence might be the result of an artistic miscalculation, a nuisance one has to get past to reach the good stuff, or else a residue from the successful formula of *The Joy Luck Club.* Yet in the context of repackaging Orientalism—considered again as de facto impact on the reader—this apparently awkward or primitive narrative convention in fact serves useful functions for *The Joy Luck Club* and especially for *The Kitchen God's Wife.*

The Americanized Daughter's Functions

The Americanized daughter, who needs to be enlightened on things Chinese, serves as a convenient, unobtrusive stand-in for the mainstream reading public. White readers, their voyeurism concealed and their curiosity indulged by "naturalized" explanations, are thus relieved of possible historical guilt, free to enjoy Chinese life as a depoliticized spectacle. In such a spectacle, the interesting localness of nomenclature and custom overshadows larger historical issues. The "sugar sister" statement, besides being a "marker of authenticity" establishing the author's credentials, is thus also a cultural demonstration addressed simultaneously to the Americanized daughter and the mainstream American reader, overtly in one case, covertly in the other. Working in much the same way are Winnie's asides about linguistic trivia, such as her remarks on the formulaic expression *yi wan* (ten thousand) ("That is what Chinese people always say . . . always an exaggeration"), or the distinction between *syin ke* (literally, "heart liver"), a Chinese term of endearment, and En-

glish *gizzard.* The phrase *taonan* elicits the following from Winnie:

> This word, *taonan?* Oh, there is no American word
> I can think of that means the same thing. But in Chinese, we have lots of words to describe all kinds
> of trouble.

The English language can hardly be guilty of lacking words for "all kinds of trouble"—a quick flip through Roget's Thesaurus would show that readily. What Winnie gives Pearl is not empirically grounded contrast but the kind of cultural tidbits Orientalist readers enjoy—decontextualized, overgeneralized, speculative, and confirmative of essential difference.

In the larger scheme of China on display, the propositional content of any specific comparison is relatively immaterial. At times the United States seems to come out ahead, portrayed as institutionally more advanced, such as when Lindo Jong of *The Joy Luck Club* speaks of flood damage: "You couldn't go to an insurance company back then and say, Somebody did this damage, pay me a million dollars." At other times commonality seems to be stressed, such as when Lindo compares herself to an American wife on a TV detergent commercial in terms of eagerness to please the husband. What matters more is that, by setting up the Americanized daughter as the one to whom Chinese life has to be explained, while at the same time endowing the mother with ancestral wisdom born of the sheer vastness of her life experiences, the edge is taken off the suffering of the Chinese people (in particular, Chinese women). The enormity of Chinese suffering is now made safe for literary consumption. As Rey Chow remarks of what she calls the "King Kong syndrome," the "Third World," as the "site of the 'raw' material that is 'monstrosity,' is produced for the surplus-value of spectacle, entertainment, and spiritual enrichment for the 'First World.'"

This is the process that enables *Newsweek* reviewer Pico Iyer to apply an adjective like *glamorous* to Winnie in *The Kitchen God's Wife:* "the dowdy, pinchpenny old woman has a past more glamorous than any fairy-tale, and more sad." The American-born daughters and the readers they stand in for, from the secure distance of their material privilege, can glamorize suffering as ennobling. They can have their cake and eat it too, constructing the Chinese woman—as a type of Third World woman—in such a way that their own fundamental superiority vis-à-vis the foreigner, the immigrant, is not threatened. The Third World woman is simultaneously simpleminded and crafty, transparent and unfathomable, capable of surviving unspeakable victimization but vulnerable in the modern world. She may be strong and resourceful in privation—a suitable inspiration for those grown soft from the good life—but ultimately she still needs the validation and protection of the West (in the form of immigration, a white husband, or, in the case of Winnie, Jimmy Louie—an American-born Chinese who speaks perfect English, dances, wears an American uniform, and has God on his side). Superficially, to concede that women such as Winnie, Lindo Jong, even Ying-Ying St. Clair could hold the key to truth and be teachers to the Westernized or Western woman may seem a sign of humility before the Third World. But such a concession does not really threaten the Western(ized) woman's image of herself as "secular, liberated, and having control of their own lives." Rather, the mothers' repeated message to the daughters is that the latter have frittered away their chance to enjoy what women in the West take for granted—freedom, choice, material plenty. The harrowing accounts of arranged marriages, sadistic mothers-in-law, sexual humiliation, floods and famines, bombings and dead babies, government corruption, technological backwardness, and other assorted bane for the Third World woman are meant to bolster, not undermine, the incontrovertible desirability attributed to the Western(ized) woman's station. (The exaltation of origin is not incompatible with this message, for it removes the Chinese American's proper arena of struggle from material and political concerns in the United States, relocating in privatized psychology and dehistoricized geography.) In fact, to those readers with feminist sympathies, the books' emphasis on sexist oppression as the basis for cross-cultural, cross-generational female bonding invites a facile sense of solidarity. A reassuring projection of universal Woman obscures the role of the West in causing the very historical catastrophes from which Tan's mothers so gladly escape.

Judging from the frequency with which *The Joy Luck Club* has been anthologized and adopted for courses during the brief period since its publication, and the way Amy Tan has been chosen to perform the Asian American spokeswoman/figurehead function once assigned to Maxine Hong Kingston, Tan currently occupies a place of substantial honor in the "mainstream" literary canon.
—*Sau-Ling Cynthia Wong*

In setting tales of personal tribulation against a Chinese historical backdrop, the mothers' chapters in *The Joy Luck Club* and Winnie's recitation in *The Kitchen God's Wife* overlap the discursive space occupied by a proliferating number of English-language works in which the upheavals of "recent"—meaning post-Western contact (Fabian's Typological Time is again at work here)—Chinese history are used as a foil for personal dramas, often those of women from prominent, Westernized families, or women marrying

prominent white Americans. Constituting a subgenre that might be called "the Chinese *Gone with the Wind*," these works are billed sometimes as memoirs (of varying degrees of fictionalization), sometimes as historical fiction. Virtually all involve a multigenerational family saga interwoven with violent historical events (the "Boxer Rebellion," the Republican Revolution, the Nationalist-Communist Civil War, the Cultural Revolution, the Tiananmen Square massacre), as well as a culminating personal odyssey across the ocean to the West, signaling final "arrival" in both a physical and an ideological sense. From these works of epic sweep about China in turmoil, American readers can derive the concomitant satisfaction of self-congratulation and limited self-flagellation: "Thank heavens we natives of the democratic First World don't have to go through that kind of suffering; but then again, we miss out on the opportunity to build character and we lose touch with the really important things in life—Roots, Culture, Tradition, History, War, Human Evil." So the equation is balanced after all.

The "Psychospiritual Plantation System" in the Reagan Era

Thus the daughters' presence in the narratological apparatus of *The Joy Luck Club* and *The Kitchen God's Wife* serves another vital purpose: it tempers the novels' critique of Reagan-era rapacity and hedonism, rendering it temporarily chastening but ultimately undemanding. After listening with appropriate awe, empathy, and "culture envy" to her mother, the daughter returns to yuppiedom (to which Chinese Americans have been allowed qualified access) and continues to enjoy the fruits of assimilation. In the same manner, the "sugar sisterhood" among Tan's readership returns edified from the cathartic literary excursion, but its core of historical innocence remains undisturbed.

A kind of "psychospiritual plantation system"—a stratified world of privileged whites and colored servers/caregivers—is at work in Amy Tan's novels as well as films from roughly the same period such as Bruce Beresford's *Driving Miss Daisy,* Woody Allen's *Alice,* and Jerry Zucker's *Ghost.* All these products of popular culture make indictments against the shallow, acquisitive, image-conscious (read "middle- and upper-middle-class white") world of wealth and institutional power by putting selected members of this world in physical and/or emotional crisis, and by engineering their education/rescue by a person of color. Tan's mothers, the African American chauffeur in *Driving Miss Daisy,* the Chinese herbalist in *Alice,* and the African American medium in *Ghost* all surpass their uptight, disaffected protégés in vitality, vividness of personality, instinctual wisdom, integration of self, cultural richness, interpersonal connection, and directness of contact with elemental presences (love, death, spirituality). At the same time, these Third World healers, like loyal Black slaves of the past, are remarkably devoid of individual ambition and content with a modest piece of the American pie. If, like the frugal Joy Luck mothers or the flamboyant small-time crook in *Ghost,* they value money, that interest has an almost childlike forthrightness to it, dissociated from the "rational" pursuit of status that is the forte of their overcerebral, impeccably schooled charges. In short, the world is neatly stratified into those who have wealth and power but no soul, and those who have soul but neither wealth nor power. The latter group nurtures the former but is not interested in displacing or replacing it.

What Renato Rosaldo says of the discipline of anthropology is a good gloss on "psychospiritual plantation" discourse:

> Social analysts . . . often assert that subordinate groups have an authentic culture at the same time that they mock their own upper-middle-class professional culture. In this view, subordinate groups speak in vibrant, fluent ways, but upper-middle-class people talk like anemic academics. Yet analysts rarely allow the ratio of class and culture to include power. Thus they conceal the ratio's darker side: the more power one has, the less culture one enjoys, and the more culture one has, the less power one wields.

Both *The Joy Luck Club* and *The Kitchen God's Wife* tacitly subscribe to a worldview in which the inverse relationship between political power and cultural visibility is deemed natural. Despite its chatty, upbeat tone and inspirational effectiveness, Tan's fiction, too, has a darker side.

Conclusion

Judging from the frequency with which *The Joy Luck Club* has been anthologized and adopted for courses during the brief period since its publication, and the way Amy Tan has been chosen to perform the Asian American spokeswoman/figurehead function once assigned to Maxine Hong Kingston, Tan currently occupies a place of substantial honor in the "mainstream" literary canon. The movement for curricular diversification in the academy has created a demand for fairly accessible ethnic works of a multiculturalist, preferably also feminist, bent, and *The Joy Luck Club,* whatever its other complexities, fits the bill well. Tan's place in the Asian-American canon is less clear: there has been some academic interest in *The Joy Luck Club* (less so for *The Kitchen God's Wife*), but hardly comparable in amount and intensity to what *The Woman Warrior* generated. Only time will tell what the staying power of the "Amy Tan phenomenon" is.

The fortunes of once-popular, now overlooked cultural interpreters in Chinese American literary history, such as Lin

Yutang and Jade Snow Wong, suggest that cultural mediation of the Orient for the "mainstream" readership requires continual repackaging to remain in sync with changing times and resultant shifts in ideological needs. It will be interesting to see whether Tan will be superseded by another "flavor of the month," and if so, when, how, and to what degree. Unlike Lin Yutang's and Jade Snow Wong's, Amy Tan's books appeared *after* the Asian American consciousness movement, at a time when Asian American cultural production is burgeoning, Asian American literary studies has been instituted as a force (albeit still a weak one) in cultural politics, and Asian American critics are busily engaged in defining a canon dissociated as much as possible from Orientalist concerns, through teaching, practical criticism, and other professional activities if not conscious, explicit theorizing. Although there is obviously no end point in the canon-formation process, there are already signs that the "Asian American" canon, the one arising from contestations within the community, differs considerably from the one shaped by the publishing industry and the critical establishment. It would be intriguing to study how these two canons are related and how they act upon each other.

Whatever the future holds, the extent of Amy Tan's sensational success becomes somewhat more comprehensible when we see her works as standing at the confluence of a large number of discursive traditions, each carrying its own history as well as ideological and formal demands: "mainstream" feminist writing; Asian American matrilineal literature; quasi ethnography about the Orient; Chinese American "tour-guiding" works; post-civil rights ethnic soul-searching; the "Chinese *Gone with the Wind*" genre; multiculturalist rhetoric; and Reagan-era critiques of materialism—to name only those touched on in this essay. (The literature of immigration and Americanization is an obvious tradition that has been omitted in this discussion; the literature of New Age self-healing might be another.) This heteroglossic situation, where discourses press against each other, generating now synergy, now conflict, is what makes possible the intriguing equivocation in *The Joy Luck Club* and *The Kitchen God's Wife* and allows readers of differing persuasions to see what they expect (or desire) in the texts.

Claire Messud (review date 29 October 1995)

SOURCE: "Ghost Story," in *New York Times Book Review,* October 29, 1995, p. 11.

[*In the following review, Messud praises the characterization of Kwan in Tan's* The Hundred Secret Senses, *but says that the novel fails to convince.*]

The tremendous success of Amy Tan's two previous novels, *The Joy Luck Club* and *The Kitchen God's Wife,* lay in her capacity to evoke, vividly and with subtle humor, the cultural dislocation of America's Chinese community. She has conjured the tortuous lives of an older generation of women whose fate brought them from China to this country, as well as the frustration and fascination of their American-born daughters. It is not surprising, then, that in her latest book, *The Hundred Secret Senses,* she should offer an apparent reworking of this theme.

However, rather than focusing again on the mother-daughter bond, Ms. Tan has shifted her attention slightly, choosing this time an exploration of sisterhood. Olivia Bishop, a commercial photographer, is the novel's primary narrator. She is the child of an irresponsible American mother and a Chinese father who died when Olivia was almost 4. Kwan, her half sister, is 12 years her senior, the product of their father's first marriage in China; she appeared in Olivia's life when Olivia was still a small child. Theirs is not, from the younger sister's perspective, an easy relationship: Kwan is eccentric, naive and annoying. She "believes she has yin eyes," Olivia tells us. "She sees those who have died and now dwell in the World of Yin." She also holds conversations with these ghosts, a habit that landed her in a mental institution not long after her arrival in America.

Now in her late 30's, Olivia—priggish, cynical and wholly American in her perspective—has never ceased to be embarrassed by her sister's behavior, and to be consumed with guilt for that embarrassment. "She's like an orphan cat, kneading on my heart," she says of Kwan. "She's been this way all my life, peeling me oranges, buying me candy, admiring my report cards. . . . Yet I've done nothing to endear myself to her. . . . I can't remember how many times I've lied to get out of seeing her."

Despite all this, Kwan remains fiercely loyal to her recalcitrant sister. She is intent on reuniting Olivia with her estranged husband, Simon, and luring the pair to China, to her native village of Changmian. But her most ambitious goal is a spiritual one: to encourage her sister to acknowledge the reality of the World of Yin and the truth of reincarnation. Thus the novel is threaded with a second narrative, Kwan's story of her fate in a former life, when she was a one-eyed servant girl named Nunumu in the employ of a group of Western missionaries in Changmian in the 1860's, and specifically of Nunumu's friendship with Miss Nelly Banner, an American with a complicated love life and a tragic destiny.

Eventually, it becomes clear that Kwan's fidelity to Olivia and Nunumu's to Miss Banner are not unconnected: the past lives on in the present. Thanks to a handy assignment from a travel magazine, Olivia, Simon and Kwan are able to go to Changmian. And as their visit is transformed into its own bittersweet tragedy, Olivia abandons her cynicism and em-

braces, with rather sticky sentimentality, Kwan's faith in the shadow world of the secret senses. At the novel's conclusion, Olivia gushes: "The world is not a place but the vastness of the soul. And the soul is nothing more than love, limitless, endless, all that moves us toward knowing what is true. . . . And believing in ghosts—that's believing that love never dies."

The dislocation Ms. Tan exposes here is not so much between the Chinese and the American experience—although Olivia initially assumes it to be so—as between a mystical and a pragmatic world view. (Upon her arrival in China, Olivia discovers that while Kwan's friends there may be more tolerant of her communion with the spirits, they don't necessarily believe in it.) In appealing to Olivia's—and the reader's—unacknowledged mystical urges, Ms. Tan taps a rich but risky source: our relationship to the dead is also a measure of our connection to life itself, and Kwan's belief in eternal cosmic renewal is enticing.

The difficulty arises from Ms. Tan's determination to make actual the links between past and present lives. In the face of physical evidence, Olivia comes to believe not only in the spiritual truth of Kwan's visions but in their literal truth: hence her cringe-making exclamations about love, the soul and ghosts. To accept the novel as anything more than a mildly entertaining and slightly ridiculous ghost story, the reader must also make this demanding leap of faith, turning a blind eye to rash improbabilities and a host of loose ends. For this reader, at least, that leap was not possible. Even Olivia's conversion fails to convince.

Nonetheless, Kwan, in particular, is a memorable creation. Of her belief in the World of Yin there can be no doubt. She emerges as a character at once innocent and wise, the relative Olivia both suffers and relies upon. Kwan gently forces Olivia to face the worst in herself and, in so doing, to find her strengths. We could all do with such a sister.

Penelope Mesic (review date 5 November 1995)

SOURCE: "Sisterly Bonds," in *Chicago Tribune Books,* November 5, 1995, pp. 1, 11.

[*In the following review, Mesic praises Tan's* The Hundred Secret Senses *stating, "She provides what is most irresistible in popular fiction: a feeling of abundance, an account so circumstantial, powerful and ingenious that it seems the story could go on forever."*]

Down in Birmingham, Alabama, under a sign that says Ollie's, there's a circular stainless-steel structure like a just-landed flying saucer. It seats 400 and is always full. Only two things are served there, barbecue and pie. Clearly, Ollie, whoever he was, realized that no third thing could ever be as good and quit while he was ahead. It may seem that this has nothing to do with Amy Tan's latest novel, *The Hundred Secret Senses,* which is about two Chinese half-sisters, but there is a marked similarity. The novel is like Ollie's in combining three qualities almost never found together: popularity, authenticity and excellence. And like that wonderful restaurant, this book is going to pull a crowd that includes both sophisticates and the simple-hearted, not by being bland but by offering sharp flavors—the prose equivalent of vinegar, pepper and wood smoke.

Tan's novel shows us a pair of women whose peculiarities, whose resentments, whose tactless truth telling, odd beliefs, jokes and quirks and annoyances, give them a pretty much universal appeal. One sister, the narrator Olivia, grows up Chinese-American in San Francisco. The other, Kwan, comes from mainland China in her late teens to join her father's second family.

Waiting at the airport, the family expects a timid, scrawny waif, but Kwan is "like a strange old lady, short and chubby . . . her broad brown face flanked by two thick braids." "Anything but shy," Olivia tells us, Kwan "bellowed, 'Hall-oo! Hall-oo!' Still hooting and laughing she jumped and squealed the way our new dog did whenever we let him out of the garage."

The description brilliantly captures Kwan's lack of self-consciousness, her eagerness. And it suggests, too, Olivia's cruel distaste for a loud and clumsy interloper.

Throughout Olivia's childhood, a pattern persists. Kwan is humble, tender, always striving to please Olivia. But Olivia, much younger, is resentful at having to share her mother's love; resentful that her older half sister takes her mother's place in caring for her; resentful that Kwan, ignorant of American ways, appears to "come from Mars."

We see the nature of their relationship perfectly expressed when Olivia recalls seizing the shining length of Kwan's beautiful hair. "I'd grab her mane and yank it like the reins of a mule, shouting, 'Giddyap, Kwan, say hee-haw!'" Years later, their attitudes are still the same. Kwan invites her sister to dinner, Olivia refuses. Kwan persists. "Feel sick?" "No." "You want me come over, bring you orange? I have extra, good price, six for one dollar." "Really, I'm fine."

The elder is unfailingly loyal, blind to insult, generous. When Olivia can't restrain her irritation and says something unforgivable, Kwan of course forgives her. Even more irritating, Olivia realizes, is the fact that after such an outburst, "The wound Kwan bears heals itself instantly. Whereas I feel guilt forever."

These are characters more than plausible. They have all the awful, wonderful vitality of fact. As Tan structures the narrative, the reader is drawn in, feeling the sympathy for Kwan her sister withholds. Even so, readers are far more likely to identify with the grudging Olivia.

Kwan is in almost every way a very ordinary woman, no one it would be the fulfillment of a fantasy to identify with. She's unstylish, scarcely educated, a tireless advice-giver and boringly down to earth in her preoccupation with family, ailments and bargains ("Guess how much I don't pay!" she cries triumphantly). Nevertheless, it is in exactly such humble vessels that mysteries are contained, and Kwan possesses some uncanny abilities.

Chief among them is her power to see and hear yin spirits, or ghosts. The wonderful thing about Tan's novel as ghost story is that in a kind of mental jujitsu, Tan makes us take her ghosts seriously precisely because she makes no apparent effort to convince us that these visitors are particularly spooky or, indeed, real.

Kwan herself takes their visits for granted. In trying, for example, to convince Olivia they should journey to China to set the spirit of their dead father to rest, Kwan's arguments are not metaphysical but comically practical. "Virgie can cook for Georgie, and Georgie can take care of your dog, no need to pay anyone."

Olivia does her best to regard Kwan as crazy. "Kwan is wacky, even by Chinese standards, even by San Francisco standards. A lot of what she says and does would strain the credulity of most people who are not on anti-psychotic drugs or living on a cult farm." But Tan's shrewd abstention from the usual brooding, mysterious atmosphere of the spirit world makes Kwan's ghosts, with their vigorous bickering about marriage, food and money, particularly convincing.

What gradually emerges from dreamlike passages set 100 years ago in China, during the fierce struggles between bandits and foreign traders in the opium wars, is that two of the spirits Kwan listens to are previous incarnations of Olivia and Kwan. The older sister's determination to serve the younger, her humility and her love arise directly from the experiences of a former life.

Eventually, after much prodding by Kwan, the two women pay their visit to China, taking with them Simon, the ex-husband for whom Olivia feels a lingering tenderness. If there is anyone who seems faint and improbable, it is this male character. The world of the book is a woman's world. Men are flickering presences, like candle flames invisible in daylight.

The China they visit is real enough modern China, where

pursuit of a fast buck is rapidly supplanting Maoist doctrine and villages previously kept quaint by poverty are losing their looks to modern conveniences. But their family's town is largely unchanged, familiar to Olivia because of all the stories Kwan has told her. And yet there's no chance to drown in its loveliness. The first words out of Kwan's mouth, when, gasping, she catches sight of a beloved childhood friend, are, "Fat! You've grown unbelievably fat!"

Beneath this banter lie the tragedy of a childhood accident, the bloodshed of the opium wars and the discovery of a few battered 19th-century objects that give substance to Kwan's stories. Increasingly the narrative reverts to a century back. Kwan's mental visits to the past are as credible and as vivid as the present. For example, when the Kwan of a former life is trying to escape a Manchu raiding party and pulls clothes off a line before she departs, she thinks of "all the terrible things that happened during the time the laundry had changed from wet to dry."

In such details there is the effortless mix of invention and reliance on reality that makes Tan's fiction so engrossing— a kind of consistency of action that suggests one could ask anything about a character and Tan could answer. She provides what is most irresistible in popular fiction: a feeling of abundance, an account so circumstantial, powerful and ingenious that it seems the story could go on forever.

Donna Nurse (review date 6 November 1995)

SOURCE: A review of *The Hundred Secret Senses,* in *Maclean's,* Vol. 108, No. 45, November 6, 1995, p. 85.

[*In the following review, Nurse asserts, "Kwan's dreams comprise the most skillfully realized sections of* [The Hundred Secret Senses], *mingling elements of gothic romance and folktale with historical chronicle."*]

In Amy Tan's earlier novels, **The Joy Luck Club** and **The Kitchen God's Wife,** individual personal histories powerfully influence future family dynamics. Even though traditional Chinese superstitions about luck and fate shape both stories, neither work strays far from the realistic mode. In Tan's latest novel, however, ghosts replace memories as the link between past and present. With **The Hundred Secret Senses,** Tan ventures into the realm of spirits and reincarnation through her favorite character type: a Chinese-American woman who is ill at ease with her racial makeup. Olivia Bishop, a 38-year-old commercial photographer, feels that her life is devoid of meaningful ties. She still longs for the attention of a neglectful mother who was too busy seeking husbands to meet her daughter's needs. Olivia has recently separated from her husband, Simon Bishop, with whom she

shares a small freelance business, and whom she accuses of providing her with nothing but "emotional scraps."

> With *The Hundred Secret Senses,* Tan ventures into the realm of spirits and reincarnation through her favorite character type: a Chinese-American woman who is ill at ease with her racial makeup.
>
> —*Donna Nurse*

Olivia was born to a Chinese father and an American mother. She has spent all of her life in California, but she lacks satisfying attachments to either American or Chinese tradition. Her adoring half-sister, Kwan, tries to introduce her to the richness of her Chinese heritage. But from childhood, Olivia has felt mostly embarrassment about and contempt for Kwan, who is 12 years her senior and was born and raised in China. Olivia resents the way Kwan's foreign attitudes and beliefs uncomfortably highlight her own racial differences. She especially loathes hearing Kwan speak of her "yin" eyes, which she invokes with her "hundred secret senses" in order to see and communicate with spirits. Nevertheless, Kwan's ghost-filled visions eventually invade Olivia's psyche. Olivia complains that her half-sister has "planted her imagination into mine."

Kwan's dreams comprise the most skillfully realized sections of the novel, mingling elements of gothic romance and folktale with historical chronicle. Tan summons remote landscapes and lifetimes with incomparable ease. According to Kwan, the dreams reveal her former life as a one-eyed maiden named Nunumu who lived with foreign missionaries in China during the mid-19th century. The book is utterly mesmerizing when Kwan recites the events surrounding the opium trade and the rule of the Manchus.

Tan moves back and forth between Kwan's past life experiences and Olivia's story. Unfortunately, after Kwan's dream passages, Olivia's speeches often strike a discordantly mundane note. Even so, Olivia's story contains several memorable episodes, many of which involve hilarious cultural clashes between the two sisters. Tan also displays a talent for pointing out the absurdities of exuberant Americanism: she describes how Olivia's mother once won "a county fair prize for growing a deformed potato that had the profile of Jimmy Durante."

The two stories come together after Simon and Olivia travel to China on a final joint assignment, bringing along Kwan as an interpreter. In Asia, Olivia's desires and Kwan's ghosts progress towards a startling climax. In **The Hundred Secret Senses,** the spirit world proclaims the existence of a collective, living past. And, in a way, for Tan, storytelling accomplishes the same end. It helps forge a shared mythology and creates a sense of belonging to a past and a people.

M. Marie Booth Foster (essay date 1996)

SOURCE: "Voice, Mind, Self: Mother-Daughter Relationships in Amy Tan's *The Joy Luck Club* and *The Kitchen God's Wife,*" in *Women of Color: Mother-Daughter Relationships in 20th-Century Literature,* edited by Elizabeth Brown-Guillory, University of Texas Press, 1996, pp. 208-27.

[*In the following essay, Booth Foster discusses the importance of daughters listening to their mothers' voices in order to discover their own voices in Tan's* The Joy Luck Club.]

In *The Joy Luck Club* and *The Kitchen God's Wife,* Amy Tan uses stories from her own history and myth to explore the voices of mothers and daughters of Chinese ancestry. Each woman tells a story indicative of the uniqueness of her voice. Mary Field Belensky, in *Women's Ways of Knowing,* argues that voice is "more than an academic shorthand for a person's point of view. . . . it is a metaphor that can apply to many aspects of women's experience and development. . . . Women repeatedly used the metaphor of voice to depict their intellectual and ethical development; . . . the development of a sense of voice, mind, and self were intricately intertwined." In Tan's fiction, the daughters' sense of self is intricately linked to an ability to speak and be heard by their mothers. Similarly, the mothers experience growth as they broaden communication lines with their daughters. Tan's women are very much like the women Belensky portrays in *Women's Ways of Knowing:* "In describing their lives, women commonly talked about voice and silence: 'speaking up,' 'speaking out,' 'being silenced,' 'not being heard,' 'really listening,' 'really talking,' 'words as weapons,' 'feeling deaf and dumb,' 'having no words,' 'saying what you mean,' 'listening to be heard.'" Until Tan's women connect as mothers and daughters, they experience strong feelings of isolation, a sense of disenfranchisement and fragmentation. These feelings often are a result of male domination, as Margery Wolf and Roxanne Witke describe in *Women in Chinese Society.*

A photo that is in part a pictorial history of Tan's foremothers is the inspiration for many of her portrayals of women. Tan writes in "Lost Lives of Women" of a picture of her mother, grandmother, aunts, cousins:

> When I first saw this photo as a child, I thought it was exotic and remote, of a faraway time and place, with people who had no connection to my American life. Look at their bound feet! Look at that funny lady with the plucked forehead. The solemn little girl was in fact, my mother. And leaning against the rock is my grandmother, Jing mei. . . . This is also a picture of secrets and tragedies. . . . This is the picture I see when I write. These are the secrets I was supposed to keep. These are the women who never let me forget why stories need to be told.

In her remembrances, Tan presents Chinese American women who are forging identities beyond the pictures of concubinage and bound feet, women encountering new dragons, many of which are derived from being "hyphenated" American females. She views mother-daughter relationships in the same vein as Kathie Carlson, who argues, "This relationship is the birthplace of a woman's ego identity, her sense of security in the world, her feelings about herself, her body and other women. From her mother, a woman receives her first impression of how to be a woman."

The Joy Luck Club and *The Kitchen God's Wife* are studies in balance—balancing hyphenation and the roles of daughter, wife, mother, sister, career woman. In achieving balance, voice is important: in order to achieve voice, hyphenated women must engage in self-exploration, recognition and appreciation of their culture(s), and they must know their histories. The quest for voice becomes an archetypal journey for all of the women. The mothers come to the United States and have to adapt to a new culture, to redefine voice and self. The daughters' journeys become rites of passage; before they can find voice or define self they must acknowledge the history and myth of their mothers—"her-stories" of life in China, passage to the United States, and assimilation. And each must come to grips with being her mother's daughter.

The Joy Luck Club is a series of stories by and about narrators whose lives are interconnected as a result of friendship and membership in the Joy Luck Club: Suyuan and Jing-mei Woo, An-mei Hsu and Rose Hsu Jordan, Lindo and Waverly Jong, and Ying-ying and Lena St. Clair. The stories illuminate the multiplicity of experiences of Chinese women who are struggling to fashion a voice for themselves in a culture where women are conditioned to be silent. The stories are narrated by seven of the eight women in the group—four daughters and three mothers; one mother has recently died of a cerebral aneurysm. Jing-mei, nicknamed June, must be her mother's voice. The book is divided into four sections: Feathers from a Thousand Li Away, The Twenty-six Malignant Gates, American Translation, and Queen Mother of the Western Skies. Each chapter is prefaced with an introductory thematic tale or myth, all of which tend to stress the advice given by mothers.

Tan tells her mother's stories, the secret ones she began to tell after the death of Tan's father and brother in *The Kitchen God's Wife.* Patti Doten notes that Tan's mother told stories of her marriage to another man in China and of three daughters left behind when she came to the United States in 1949, a story that is in part remembered in *The Joy Luck Club* with An-mei's saga. In *The Kitchen God's Wife,* a mother and daughter, Winnie Louie and Pearl Louie Brandt, share their stories, revealing the secrets that hide mind and self—and history—and veil and mask their voices. Winnie Louie's tale is of the loss of her mother as a young girl, marriage to a sadistic man who sexually abused her, children stillborn or dying young, a patriarchal society that allowed little room for escape from domestic violence (especially against the backdrop of war), and her flight to America and the love of a "good man." Daughter Pearl Louie Brandt's secrets include her pain upon the loss of her father and the unpredictable disease, multiple sclerosis, that inhibits her body and her life.

Tan's characters are of necessity storytellers and even historians, empowered by relating what they know about their beginnings and the insufficiencies of their present lives. Storytelling—relating memories—allows for review, analysis, and sometimes understanding of ancestry and thus themselves. The storytelling, however, is inundated with ambivalences and contradictions which, as Suzanna Danuta Walters argues, often take the form of blame in mother-daughter relationships.

Voice balances—or imbalances—voice as Chinese American mothers and daughters narrate their sagas. Because both mothers and daughters share the telling, the biases of a singular point of view are alleviated. Marianne Hirsch writes, "The story of female development, both in fiction and theory, needs to be written in the voice of mothers as well as in that of daughters. . . . Only in combining both voices, in finding a double voice that would yield a multiple female consciousness, can we begin to envision ways to live 'life afresh.'" Tan's fiction presents ambivalences and contradictions in the complicated interactions of mothers' and daughters' voices.

Regardless of how much the daughters try to deny it, it is through their mothers that they find their voice, their mind, their selfhood. Voice finds its form in the process of interaction, even if that interaction is conflict. "Recognition by the daughter that her voice is not entirely her own" comes in time and with experiences (one of the five interconnecting themes referred to by Nan Bauer Maglin in *The Literature of Matrilineage* as a recurring theme in such literature). The experiences in review perhaps allow the daughters to know just how much they are dependent upon their mothers in their journey to voice. The mothers do not let them forget their own importance as the daughters attempt to achieve self-importance.

As Jing-mei "June" Woo tells her story and that of her deceased mother, the importance of the mother and daughter voices resonating, growing out of and being strengthened by each other, is apparent in her state of confusion and lack of direction and success. Perhaps her name is symbolic of her confusion: she is the only daughter with both a Chinese and an American name. As she recalls life with her mother, Jing-mei/June relates that she is constantly told by her mother, Suyuan Woo, that she does not try and therefore cannot achieve success. June's journey to voice and balance requires self-discovery—which must begin with knowing her mother. June has to use memories as a guide instead of her mother, whose tale she tells and whose saga she must complete. She must meet the ending to the tale of life in China and daughters left behind that her mother has told her over and over again, a story that she thought was a dark fairy tale.

The dark tale is of a previous life that includes a husband and daughters. Suyuan's first husband, an officer with the Kuomintang, takes her to Kweilin, a place she has dreamed of visiting. It has become a war refuge, no longer idyllic. Suyuan Woo and three other officers' wives start the Joy Luck Club to take their minds off the terrible smells of too many people in the city and the screams of humans and animals in pain. They attempt to raise their spirits with mah jong, jokes, and food.

Warned of impending danger, June's mother leaves the city with her two babies and her most valuable possessions. On the road to Chungking, she abandons first the wheelbarrow in which she has been carrying her babies and her goods, then more goods. Finally, her body weakened by fatigue and dysentery, she leaves the babies with jewelry to provide for them until they can be brought to her family. America does not make Suyuan forget the daughters she left as she fled. June Woo secretly views her mother's story as a fairy tale because the ending always changed. Perhaps herein lies the cause of their conflict: neither mother nor daughter listens to be heard, so each complains of not being heard. June Woo's disinterest and lack of knowledge of her mother's history exacerbate her own voicelessness, her lack of wholeness.

At a mah jong table where, appropriately, June takes her mother's place, she is requested by her mother's friends to go to China and meet the daughters of her mother. Thus her journey to voice continues and begins: it is a journey started at birth, but it is only now that she starts to recognize that she needs to know about her mother in order to achieve self-knowledge. She is to tell her sisters about their mother. The mothers' worst fears are realized when June asks what she can possibly tell her mother's daughters. The mothers see their daughters in June's response, daughters who get irritated when their mothers speak in Chinese or explain things in broken English.

Although it startles her mother's friends, June's question is a valid one for a daughter whose relationship with her mother was defined by distance that developed slowly and grew. According to June, she and her mother never understood each other. She says they translated each other's meanings: she seemed to hear less than what was said, and her mother heard more. It is a complaint leveled by mothers and daughters throughout *The Joy Luck Club* and later in *The Kitchen God's Wife*. Both women want to be heard, but do not listen to be heard. They must come to understand that a voice is not a voice unless there is someone there to hear it.

Jing-mei is no longer sitting at the mah jong table but is en route to China when she summons up memories of her mother that will empower her to tell the daughters her mother's story. In the title story and in the short story "A Pair of Tickets," she occupies her mother's place in the storytelling, much as she occupies it at the mah jong table, and she is concerned with the responsibilities left by her mother. In her own stories, "Two Kinds" and "Best Quality," she is concerned with her selves: Jing-mei and June— the Chinese and the American, her mother's expectations and her belief in herself. Her stories are quest stories, described by Susan Koppelman in *Between Mothers and Daughters* as "a daughter's search for understanding" of her mother and herself. As June makes soup for her father, she sees the stray cat that she thought her mother had killed, since she had not seen it for some time. She makes motions to scare the cat and then recognizes the motions as her mother's; the cat reacts to her just as he had to her mother. She is reminded that she is her mother's daughter.

According to Judith Arcana in *Our Mothers' Daughters*, "we hold the belief that mothers love their daughters by definition and we fear any signal from our own mother that this love, which includes acceptance, affection, admiration and approval, does not exist or is incomplete." It does not matter to Jing-mei that she is not her mother's only disappointment (she says her mother always seemed displeased with everyone). Jing-mei recalls that something was not in balance and that something always needed improving for her mother. The friends do not seem to care; with all of her faults, she is their friend. Perhaps it is a "daughter's" expectations that June uses to judge her mother. Suyuan tells the rebellious June that she can be the best at anything as she attempts to mold her child into a piano-playing prodigy. She tells June she's not the best because she's not trying. After the request by the Joy Luck Club mothers, June, in really listening to the voice of her mother as reserved in her memory, discovers that she might have been able to demonstrate ability had she tried: "for unlike my mother I did not believe I could be anything I wanted to be, I could only be me." But she does not recognize that the "me" is the one who has made every attempt to escape development. The pendant her late mother gave her is symbolic. It was given

to her as her life's importance. The latter part of the message is in Chinese, the voice of wisdom versus the provider of American circumstances.

In archetypal journeys, there is always a god or goddess who supports the "traveler" along his or her way. In *The Kitchen God's Wife*, Lady Sorrowfree is created by Winnie Louie, mother of Pearl, when the Kitchen God is determined by her to be an unfit god for her daughter's altar, inherited from an adopted aunt. The Kitchen God is unfit primarily because he became a god despite his mistreatment of his good wife. A porcelain figurine is taken from a storeroom where she has been placed as a "mistake" and is made into a goddess for Pearl, Lady Sorrowfree. Note Winnie's celebration of Lady Sorrowfree:

> I heard she once had many hardships in her life. . . . But her smile is genuine, wise, and innocent at the same time. And her hand, see how she just raised it. That means she is about to speak, or maybe she is telling you to speak. She is ready to listen. She understands English. You should tell her everything. . . . But sometimes, when you are afraid, you can talk to her. She will listen. She will wash away everything sad with her tears. She will use her stick to chase away everything bad. See her name: Lady Sorrowfree, happiness winning over bitterness, no regrets in this world.

Perhaps Tan's mothers want to be like Lady Sorrowfree; they are in a sense goddesses whose altars their daughters are invited to come to for nurturance, compassion, empathy, inspiration, and direction. They are driven by the feeling of need to support those daughters, to give to them "the swan" brought from China—symbolic of their her-stories and wisdom, and the advantages of America, like the mother in the preface to the first round of stories. In the tale, all that is left of the mother's swan that she has brought from China after it is taken by customs officials is one feather; the mother wants to tell her daughter that the feather may look worthless, but it comes from her homeland and carries with it all good intentions. But she waits to tell her in perfect English, in essence keeping secrets. The mothers think that everything is possible for the daughters if the mothers will it. The daughters may come willingly to the altar or may rebelliously deny the sagacity of their mothers.

The mothers struggle to tell their daughters the consequences of not listening to them. The mother in the tale prefacing the section "Twenty-six Malignant Gates" tells her daughter not to ride her bike around the corner where she cannot see her because she will fall down and cry. The daughter questions how her mother knows, and she tells her that it is written in the book *Twenty-six Malignant Gates* that evil things can happen when a child goes outside the protection of the house. The daughter wants evidence, but her mother tells her that it is written in Chinese. When her mother does not tell her all twenty-six of the Malignant Gates, the girl runs out of the house and around the corner and falls, the consequence of not listening to her mother. Rebellion causes conflict—a conflict Lady Sorrowfree would not have to endure. June Woo and Waverly Jong seem to be daughters who thrive on the conflict that results from rebellion and sometimes even the need to win their mother's approval. June trudges off every day to piano lessons taught by an old man who is hard of hearing. Defying her mother, she learns very little, as she reveals at a piano recital to which her mother has invited all of her friends. June notes the blank look on her mother's face that says she has lost everything. Waverly wins at chess, which pleases her mother, but out of defiance she stops playing until she discovers that she really enjoyed her mother's approval. As an adult she wants her mother to approve of the man who will be her second husband; mother and daughter assume the positions of chess players.

Tan's mothers frequently preach that children are to make their mothers proud so that they can brag about them to other mothers. The mothers engage in fierce competition with each other. Suyuan Woo brags about her daughter even after June's poorly performed piano recital. All of the mothers find fault with their daughters, but this is something revealed to the daughters, not to the community.

Much as Lindo Jong credits herself with daughter Waverly's ability to play chess, she blames herself for Waverly's faults as a person and assumes failures in raising her daughter: "It is my fault she is this way—selfish. I wanted my children to have the best combination: American circumstances and Chinese character. How could I know these things do not mix?" Waverly knows how American circumstances work, but Lindo can't teach her about Chinese character: "How to obey parents and listen to your mother's mind. How not to show your own thoughts, to put your feelings behind your face so you can take advantage of hidden opportunities. . . . Why Chinese thinking is best." What she gets is a daughter who wants to be Chinese because it is fashionable, a daughter who likes to speak back and question what she says, and a daughter to whom promises mean nothing. Nonetheless, she is a daughter of whom Lindo is proud.

Lindo Jong is cunning, shrewd, resourceful; Waverly Jong is her mother's daughter. Waverly manages to irritate her mother when she resists parental guidance. Judith Arcana posits that "some daughters spend all or most of their energy trying futilely to be as different from their mothers as possible in behavior, appearance, relations with friends, lovers, children, husbands." Waverly is a strategist in getting her brother to teach her to play chess, in winning at chess, in gaining her mother's forgiveness when she is rude and getting her mother's acceptance of the man she plans to

marry. Lindo proudly reminds Waverly that she has inherited her ability to win from her.

In literature that focuses on mother/daughter relationships, feminists see "context—historical time and social and cultural group" as important. Lindo relates in "The Red Candle" that she once sacrificed her life to keep her parents' promise; she married as arranged. Chinese tradition permits Lindo's parents to give her to Huang Tai for her son—to determine her fate—but Lindo takes control of her destiny. On the day of her wedding, as she prepares for the ceremony, she schemes her way out of the planned marriage and into America, where "nobody says you have to keep the circumstances somebody else gives to you."

It takes determination to achieve voice and selfhood, to take control of one's mind and one's life from another, making one's self heard, overcoming silence. Lindo does not resign herself to her circumstances in China. Waverly reveals that she learns some of her strategies from her mother: "I was six when my mother taught me the art of invisible strength. It was a strategy for winning arguments, respect from others, and eventually, though neither of us knew it at the time, chess games." Therein lies Lindo's contribution to her daughter's voice.

Lindo uses the same brand of ingenuity to play a life chess game with and to teach her daughter. Adrienne Rich writes in *Of Woman Born:* "Probably there is nothing in human nature more resonant with charges than the flow of energy between two biologically alike bodies, one which has lain in amniotic bliss inside the other, one which has labored to give birth to the other. The materials are there for the deepest mutuality and the most painful estrangement." Lindo has to contend with a headstrong daughter: "'Finish your coffee,' I told her yesterday. 'Don't throw your blessings away.' 'Don't be old-fashioned, Ma,' she told me, finishing her coffee down the sink. 'I'm my own person.' And I think, how can she be her own person? When did I give her up?"

Waverly is champion of the chess game, but she is no match for her mother in a life chess game. She knows her chances of winning in a contest against her mother, who taught her to be strong like the wind. Waverly learns during the "chess years" that her mother was a champion strategist. Though she is a tax attorney able to bully even the Internal Revenue Service, she fears the wrath of her mother if she is told to mind her business: "Well, I don't know if it's explicitly stated in the law, but you can't ever tell a Chinese mother to shut up. You could be charged as an accessory to your own murder." What Waverly perceives as an impending battle for her mother's approval of her fiancé is nothing more than the opportunity for her mother and her to communicate with each other. She strategically plans to win her mother's approval of her fiancé, Rick, just as if she is playing a game of chess.

She is afraid to tell her mother that they are going to be married because she is afraid that her mother will not approve. The conversation ends with her recognition that her mother also needs to be heard and with her mother's unstated approval of her fiancé. Waverly Jong recognizes her mother's strategies in their verbal jousts, but she also recognizes that, just like her, her mother is in search of something. What she sees is an old woman waiting to be invited into her daughter's life. Like the other mothers, Lindo views herself as standing outside her daughter's life—a most undesirable place.

Sometimes Tan's mothers find it necessary to intrude in order to teach the daughters to save themselves; they criticize, manage, and manipulate with an iron fist. An-mei Hsu and Ying-ying St. Clair play this role. "My mother once told me why I was so confused all the time," says Rose Hsu during her first story, "Without Wood." "She said that I was without wood. Born without wood so that I listened to too many people. She knew this because she had almost become this way." Suyuan Woo tells June Woo that such weaknesses are present in the mother, An-mei Hsu: "Each person is made of five elements. . . . Too little wood and you bend too quickly to listen to other people's ideas, unable to stand on your own. This was like my Auntie An-mei." Rose's mother tells her that she must stand tall and listen to her mother standing next to her. If she bends to listen to strangers, she'll grow weak and be destroyed. Rose Hsu is in the process of divorce from a husband who has labeled her indecisive and useless as a marriage partner. She is guilty of allowing her husband to mold her. He does not want her to be a partner in family decisions until he makes a mistake in his practice as a plastic surgeon. Then he complains that she is unable to make decisions: he is dissatisfied with his creation. Finding it difficult to accept divorce, she confusedly runs to her friends and a psychiatrist seeking guidance.

Over and over again her mother tells her to count on a mother because a mother is best and knows what is inside of her daughter. "A psyche-atricks will only make you hulihudu, make you heimongmong." The psychiatrist leaves her confused, as her mother predicts. She becomes even more confused as she tells each of her friends and her psychiatrist a different story. Her mother advises her to stand up to her husband, to speak up. She assumes the role of Lady Sorrowfree. When Rose does as her mother advises, she notices that her husband seems scared and confused. She stands up to him and forces him to retreat. She is her mother's daughter. She listens to her mother and finds her voice—herself.

Like the other mothers, An-mei demonstrates some of the qualities of "Lady Sorrowfree." An-mei is concerned that her daughter sees herself as having no options. A psychologist's explanation is "to the extent that women perceive themselves as having no choice, they correspondingly excuse themselves from the responsibility that decision entails." An-mei was "raised the Chinese way": "I was taught to desire nothing, to swallow other people's misery, to eat my own bitterness." She uses the tale of the magpies to indicate that one can either make the choice to be in charge of one's life or continue to let others be in control. For thousands of years magpies came to the fields of a group of peasants just after they had sown their seeds and watered them with their tears. The magpies ate the seeds and drank the tears. Then one day the peasants decided to end their suffering and silence. They clapped their hands and banged sticks together, making noise that startled and confused the magpies. This continued for days until the magpies died of hunger and exhaustion from waiting for the noise to stop so that they could land and eat. The sounds from the hands and sticks were their voices. Her daughter should face her tormentor.

An-mei tells stories of her pain, a pain she does not wish her daughter to endure. Memory is, in part, voices calling out to her, reminding her of what she has endured and of a relationship wished for: "it was her voice that confused me," "a familiar sound from a forgotten dream," "she cried with a wailing voice," "voices praising," "voices murmuring," "my mother's voice went away." The voices of her mothers confused her. She was a young girl in need of a mother's clear voice that would strengthen her circumstances and her context. The voices remind her, in "Scar," of wounds that heal but leave their imprint and of the importance of taking control out of the hands of those who have the ability to devour their victims, as in the story "Magpies." A scar resulting from a severe burn from a pot of boiling soup reminds her of when her mother was considered a ghost: her mother was dead to her family because she became a rich merchant's concubine. With time the scar "became pale and shiny and I had no memory of my mother. That is the way it is with a wound. The wound begins to close in on itself, to protect what is hurting so much. And once it is closed, you no longer see what is underneath, what started the pain." It is also the way of persons attempting to assimilate—the wounds of getting to America, the wounds of hyphenation, close in on themselves and then it is difficult to see where it all began.

An-mei remembers the scar and the pain when her mother returns to her grandmother Poppo's deathbed. Upon the death of Poppo, she leaves with her mother, who shortly afterward commits suicide. Poppo tells An-mei that when a person loses face, it's like dropping a necklace down a well: the only way you can get it back is to jump in after it. From her mother An-mei learns that tears cannot wash away sorrows; they only feed someone else's joy. Her mother tells her to swallow her own tears.

An-mei knows strength and she knows forgetting. Perhaps that is why her daughter tells the story of her loss. It is Rose

Hsu who tells the story of her brother's drowning and her mother's faith that he would be found. She refuses to believe that he is dead; without any driving lessons, she steers the car to the ocean side to search once more for him. After her son Bing's death, An-mei places the Bible that she has always carried to the First Chinese Baptist Church under a short table leg as a way of correcting the imbalances of life. She gives her daughter advice on how to correct imbalances in her life. The tale prefacing the section "Queen of the Western Skies" is also a fitting message for Rose Hsu. A woman playing with her granddaughter wonders at the baby's happiness and laughter, remembering that she was once carefree before she shed her innocence and began to look critically and suspiciously at everything. She asks the babbling child if it is Syi Wang, Queen Mother of the Western Skies, come back to provide her with some answers: "Then you must teach my daughter this same lesson. How to lose your innocence but not your hope. How to laugh forever."

Like all the other daughters, Lena must recognize and respect the characteristics of Lady Sorrowfree that are inherent in her mother, Ying-ying. Ying-ying describes her daughter as being devoid of wisdom. Lena laughs at her mother when she says "arty-tecky" (architecture) to her sister-in-law. Ying-ying admits that she should have slapped Lena more as a child for disrespect. Though Ying-ying serves as Lena's goddess, Lena initially does not view her mother as capable of advice on balance. Ying-ying's telling of her story is very important to seeing her in a true mothering role; her daughter's first story makes one think that the mother is mentally unbalanced.

Evelyn Reed in *Woman's Evolution* writes: "A mother's victimization does not merely humiliate her, it mutilates her daughter who watches her for clues as to what it means to be a woman. Like the traditional foot-bound Chinese woman, she passes on her affliction. The mother's self-hatred and low expectations are binding rags for the psyche of the daughter." Ying-ying, whose name means "Clear Reflection," becomes a ghost. As a young girl she liked to unbraid her hair and wear it loose. She recalls a scolding from her mother, who once told her that she was like the lady ghosts at the bottom of the lake. Her daughter is unaware of her mother's previous marriage to a man in China twenty years before Lena's birth. Ying-ying falls in love with him because he strokes her cheek and tells her that she has tiger eyes, that they gather fire in the day and shine golden at night. Her husband opts to run off with another woman during her pregnancy, and she aborts the baby because she has come to hate her husband with a passion. Ying-ying tells Lena that she was born a tiger in a year when babies were dying and because she was strong she survived. After ten years of reclusive living with cousins in the country, she goes to the city to live and work. There she meets Lena's father, an American she marries after being courted for four years, and con-

tinues to be a ghost. Ying-ying says that she willingly gave up her spirit.

In Ying-ying's first story, "The Moon Lady," when she sees her daughter lounging by the pool she realizes that they are lost, invisible creatures. Neither, at this point, recognizes the importance of "listening harder to the silence beneath their voices." Their being lost reminds her of the family outing to Tai Lake as a child, when she falls into the lake, is rescued, and is put on shore only to discover that the moon lady she has been anxiously awaiting to tell her secret wish is male. The experience is so traumatic that she forgets her wish. Now that she is old and is watching her daughter, she remembers that she had wished to be found. And now she wishes for her daughter to be found—to find herself.

Lena, as a young girl, sees her mother being devoured by her fears until she becomes a ghost. Ying-ying believes that she is already a ghost. She does not want her daughter to become a ghost like her, "an unseen spirit." Ying-ying begins life carefree. She is loved almost to a fault by her mother and her nursemaid, Amah. She is spoiled by her family's riches and wasteful. When she unties her hair and floats through the house, her mother tells her that she resembles the "lady ghosts . . . ladies who drowned in shame and floated in living people's houses with their hair undone to show everlasting despair." She knows despair when the north wind that she thinks has blown her luck chills her heart by blowing her first husband past her to other women.

Lena, Ying-ying's daughter, is a partner in a marriage where she has a voice in the rules; but when the game is played, she loses her turn many times. Carolyn See argues that "in the name of feminism and right thinking, this husband is taking Lena for every cent she's got, but she's so demoralized, so 'out of balance' in the Chinese sense, that she can't do a thing about it." In the introductory anecdote to the section "American Translation," a mother warns her daughter that she cannot put mirrors at the foot of the bed because all of her marriage happiness will bounce back and tumble the opposite way. Her mother takes from her bag a mirror that she plans to give the daughter as a wedding gift so that it faces the other mirror. The mirrors then reflect the happiness of the daughter. Lena's mother, as does Rose's mother, provides her with the mirror to balance her happiness; the mirror is a mother's advice or wisdom. It is Lena's mother's credo that a woman is out of balance if something goes against her nature. She does not want to be like her mother, but her mother foresees that she too will become a ghost; her husband will transform her according to his desires. Ying-ying recalls that she became "Betty" and was given a new date of birth by a husband who never learned to speak her language. Her review of her own story makes her know that she must influence her daughter's "story" that is in the making. Lena sees herself with her husband in the midst of problems so deep that she can't see where the bottom is. In the guise of a functional relationship is a dysfunctional one. Her mother predicts that the house will break into pieces. When a too-large vase on a too-weak table crashes to the floor, Lena admits that she knew it would happen. Her mother asks her why she did not take steps to keep the house from falling, meaning her marriage as well as the vase.

The goddess role becomes all important to Ying-ying as she becomes more determined to prevent her daughter from becoming a ghost. She fights the daughter that she has raised, "watching from another shore" and "accept[ing] her American ways." After she uses the sharp pain of what she knows to "penetrate [her] daughter's tough skin and cut the tiger spirit loose," she waits for her to come into the room, like a tiger waiting between the trees, and pounces. Ying-ying wins the fight and gives her daughter her spirit, "because this is the way a mother loves her daughter." Lady Sorrowfree helps her "charge" achieve voice.

Tan's women with their American husbands attempt often without knowing it to balance East and West, the past and the future of their lives. A level of transcendence is apparent in the storytelling, as it is in *The Kitchen God's Wife*. Mothers and daughters must gain from the storytelling in order to have healthy relationships with each other.
—*M. Marie Booth Foster*

From the daughter with too much water, to the mother and daughter with too much wood, to the tiger ghosts and just plain ghosts, to the chess queens, Tan's women in *The Joy Luck Club* find themselves capable of forging their own identities, moving beyond passivity to assertiveness—speaking up. They are a piece of the portrait that represents Amy Tan's family history—her own story included; they are, in composite, her family's secrets and tragedies. Tan is unlike some Asian American writers who have had to try to piece together and sort out the meaning of the past from shreds of stories overheard or faded photographs. As in her stories, her mother tells her the stories and explains the photographs. Bell Gale Chevigny writes that "women writing about other women will symbolically reflect their internalized relations with their mothers and in some measure re-create them." From Tan's own accounts, her interaction with her mother is reflected in her fiction.

Tan's women with their American husbands attempt often without knowing it to balance East and West, the past and the future of their lives. A level of transcendence is apparent in the storytelling, as it is in *The Kitchen God's Wife*.

Mothers and daughters must gain from the storytelling in order to have healthy relationships with each other.

In *The Kitchen God's Wife,* Winnie Louie and her daughter Pearl Louie Brandt are both keepers of secrets that accent the distance that characterizes their relationship. Pearl thinks after a trip to her mother's home: "Mile after mile, all of it familiar, yet not this distance that separates us, me from my mother." She is unsure of how this distance was created. Winnie says of their relationship: "That is how she is. That is how I am. Always careful to be polite, always trying not to bump into each other, just like strangers." When their secrets begin to weigh down their friends who have known them for years, who threaten to tell each of the other's secrets, Winnie Louie decides that it is time for revelation. The process of the revelation is ritual: "recitation of the relationship between mother and daughter," "assessment of the relationship," and "the projection of the future into the relationship." At the same time revelation is a journey to voice, the voice that they must have with each other. Again, voice is a metaphor for speaking up, being heard, listening to be heard. No longer will stories begin as Pearl's does: "Whenever my mother talks to me, she begins the conversation as if we were already in the middle of an argument." That they argue or are in conflict is not problematic; it is the "talks to" that should be replaced with "talks with." As much as Pearl needs to know her mother's secrets, Winnie Louie needs to tell them in order to build a relationship that is nurturing for both mother and daughter.

Pearl's secret is multiple sclerosis. At first she does not tell her mother because she fears her mother's theories on her illness. What becomes her secret is the anger she feels toward her father, the inner turmoil that began with his dying and death. Sometimes the mother's voice drowns the voice of the daughter as she attempts to control or explain every aspect of the daughter's existence. "If I had not lost my mother so young, I would not have listened to Old Aunt," says Winnie Louie as she begins her story. These might also be the words of her daughter, though Pearl's loss of mother was not a physical loss. The opportunity for the resonating of mother and daughter voices seems to be the difference between balance and imbalance. American circumstances are to be blamed for the distance; the need to keep secrets grows out of the perceived necessity of assimilation and clean slates. Because her mother was not there, Winnie "listened to Old Aunt." Winnie Louie's dark secret begins with her mother, who disappeared without telling her why; she still awaits some appearance by her mother to explain. Her mother's story is also hers: an arranged marriage—in her mother's case, to curb her rebelliousness; realization that she has a lesser place in marriage than purported; and a daughter as the single lasting joy derived from the marriage. The difference is that Winnie's mother escaped, to be heard from no more.

Winnie's family abides by all of the customs in giving her hand in marriage to Wen Fu: "Getting married in those days was like buying real estate. Here you see a house you want to live in, you find a real estate agent. Back in China, you saw a rich family with a daughter, you found a go-between who knew how to make a good business deal." Winnie tells her daughter, "If asked how I felt when they told me I would marry Wen Fu, I can only say this: It was like being told I had won a big prize. And it was also like being told my head was going to be chopped off. Something between those two feelings." Winnie experiences very little mercy in her marriage to the monstrous Wen Fu.

> In *The Kitchen God's Wife,* **Winnie Louie and her daughter Pearl Louie Brandt are both keepers of secrets that accent the distance that characterizes their relationship.**
> —*M. Marie Booth Foster*

Wen Fu serves as an officer in the Chinese army, so during World War II they move about China with other air force officers and their wives. Throughout the marriage, Winnie knows abuse and witnesses the death of her babies. She tries to free herself from the tyranny of the marriage, but her husband enjoys abusing her too much to let her go. Her story is a long one, a lifetime of sorrow, death, marriage, imprisonment, lost children, lost friends and family. Jimmie Louie saves her life by helping her to escape Wen Fu and to come to the United States. She loves Jimmie Louie and marries him. The darkest part of her secret she reveals to Pearl almost nonchalantly: Pearl is the daughter of the tyrant Wen Fu.

The daughter asks her mother: "Tell me again . . . why you had to keep it a secret." The mother answers: "Because then you would know. . . . You would know how weak I was. You would think I was a bad mother." Winnie's actions and response are not unexpected. She is every mother who wants her daughter to think of her as having lived a blemish-free existence. She is every mother who forgets that her daughter is living life and knows blemishes. Secrets revealed, the women begin to talk. No longer does Winnie have to think that the year her second husband, Jimmie Louie, died was "when everyone stopped listening to me." Pearl knows her mother's story and can respect her more, not less, for her endurance. She is then able to see a woman molded by her experiences and her secrets—a woman who has lived with two lives. With the tiptoeing around ended, the distance dissipates. By sharing their secrets, they help each other to achieve voice. The gift of Lady Sorrowfree is symbolic of their bonding; this goddess has all of the characteristics of the nurturing, caring, listening mother. Her imperfections lie

in her creation; experiences make her. She has none of the characteristics of the Kitchen God.

The story of the Kitchen God and his wife angers Winnie Louie; she looks at the god as a bad man who was rewarded for admitting that he was a bad man. As the story goes, a wealthy farmer, Zhang, who had a good wife who saw to it that his farm flourished, brought home a pretty woman and made his wife cook for her. The pretty woman ran his wife off without any objection from the farmer. She helped him use up all of his riches foolishly and left him a beggar. He was discovered hungry and suffering by a servant who took him home to care for him. When he saw his wife, whose home it was, he attempted to hide in the kitchen fireplace; his wife could not save him. The Jade Emperor, because Zhang admitted he was wrong, made him Kitchen God with the duty to watch over people's behavior. Winnie tells Pearl that people give generously to the Kitchen God to keep him happy in the hopes that he will give a good report to the Jade Emperor. Winnie thinks that he is not the god for her daughter. How can one trust a god who would cheat on his wife? How can he be a good judge of behavior? The wife is the good one. She finds another god for her daughter's altar, Lady Sorrowfree. After all, she has already given her a father.

Even as Winnie tells her story, one senses that the women are unaware of the strength of the bond between them that partly originates in the biological connection and partly in their womanness. Storytelling/revealing secrets gives both of them the opportunity for review; Winnie Louie tells Pearl that she has taught her lessons with love, that she has combined all of the love that she had for the three she lost during the war and all of those that she did not allow to be born and has given it to Pearl. She speaks of her desire "to believe in something good," her lost hope and innocence: "So I let those other babies die. In my heart I was being kind. . . . I was a young woman then. I had no more hope left, no trust, no innocence." In telling her story, she does not ask for sympathy or forgiveness; she simply wants to be free of the pain that "comes from keeping everything inside, waiting until it is too late."

Perhaps this goddess, Lady Sorrowfree, to whom they burn incense will cause them never to forget the importance of voice and listening. On the heels of listening there is balance as both Winnie and Pearl tell their secrets and are brought closer by them. East and West, mother and daughter, are bonded for the better. Arcana notes that "mother/ daughter sisterhood is the consciousness we must seek to make this basic woman bond loving and fruitful, powerful and deep. . . ." It ensures that women do not smother each other and squelch the voice of the other or cause each other to retreat into silence.

In exploring the problems of mother-daughter voices in relationships, Tan unveils some of the problems of biculturalism—of Chinese ancestry and American circumstances. She presents daughters who do not know their mothers' "importance" and thus cannot know their own; most seem never to have been told or even cared to hear their mothers' history. Until they do, they can never achieve voice. They assimilate; they marry American men and put on American faces. They adapt. In the meantime, their mothers sit like Lady Sorrowfree on her altar, waiting to listen. The daughters' journeys to voice are completed only after they come to the altars of their Chinese mothers.

Ruth Pavey (review date 16 February 1996)

SOURCE: A review of *The Hundred Secret Senses,* in *New Statesman & Society,* Vol. 9, No. 390, p. 38.

[*In the following review, Pavey considers Tan's unifying device in* The Hundred Secret Senses *unconvincing, but asserts that, "this does not detract from the great appeal of her character, Kwan (who combines saintly good humour with wit, practicality and guile), or the enjoyable liveliness of her style."*]

Kwan, the co-heroine of *The Hundred Secret Senses,* has yin eyes, second sight. At least she thinks she has, which is why she talks of relating to ghosts as an everyday experience. There is nothing fey about Kwan. Having spent the first 18 years of her life in rural China, she takes uncomplainingly to being uprooted to join her dead father's new family in San Francisco. But how is her much younger half-sister to accommodate Kwan's hotline to the past? From the first sentence of this novel, Amy Tan sets up a tension between Kwan's Chinese-born certainties and the distancing ironies of Olivia's San Francisco inheritance.

To begin with, Olivia, or Libby-ah, has a firm grip on the narration, which begins when she is already well over 30 and married to Simon. There seems little chance of her, or the reader, getting caught by Kwan's fancies. It is not long, however, before Kwan muscles in. She takes us back to a former life, in 1864, when she was a servant to an English missionary, Miss Banner, at the time of the Taiping rebellion. For the reader this is initially fine, a good story into which we dip. But for Libby-ah herself, Kwan's stories have always represented a strain—a long childhood of traction away from her own reality, back to the culture her father left.

Not only does Olivia have Kwan's past, or pasts, to put into

the balance of her brittle, first-generation American life. There is another ghost. Before meeting her, Simon was in love with a girl who died young. Elsie, adopted by Mormon parents, had been convinced she was really Elza, of Polish-Jewish descent. Her unquiet presence has always disturbed Olivia's marriage.

By halfway through the novel, when Kwan, Olivia and Simon set off for China, there are already more than enough spirits clamouring to be put to rest. At this point, the strain Libby-ah has always felt about Kwan's unusual gifts starts to affect the reader. Apprehensions of a detour to Auschwitz prove unfounded, but it becomes clear that we too are being asked to accept the possibility that Kwan was indeed the servant girl and Olivia was Miss Banner. Like Kwan in the caves of Guilin, the last part of this story gets a little lost before returning to a favourite theme of Tan's: hope for the future, embodied in the relationship between mother and daughter.

As a device for meshing several different periods into one fiction, yin eyes may not be as convincing as the straightforward use Tan made of memory in *The Kitchen God's Wife.* But this does not detract from the great appeal of her character, Kwan (who combines saintly good humour with wit, practicality and guile), or the enjoyable liveliness of her style.

In a thoughtful book about being an orphan, the American writer Eileen Simpson observes that most Americans are more or less orphans, immigrants missing their past. The persistent themes of Amy Tan's novels seem to bear that out. In this one alone there are at least six orphans, and hardly anyone leading a settled, secure life.

FURTHER READING

Criticism

Greenlaw, Lavinia. A review of *The Hundred Secret Senses,* in *Times Literary Supplement* 4846 (16 February 1996): 22.
> A review in which Greenlaw concludes that "*The Hundred Secret Senses* is fast-paced but ultimately aimless."

Houston, Marsha. "Women and the Language of Race and Ethnicity." *Women and Language* XVIII, No. 1 (Spring 1995): 1-7.
> Houston traces the importance of multiple languages in Tan's *The Joy Luck Club* and Maxine Hong Kingston's *The Woman Warrior.*

> **Additional coverage of Tan's life and career is contained in the following sources published by Gale:** *Authors and Artists for Young Adults, Vol. 9; Bestsellers, Vol. 89:3; Contemporary Authors, Vol. 136; Contemporary Authors New Revision Series, Vol. 54; Dictionary of Literary Biography, Vol. 173; DISCovering Authors Modules: Multicultural Authors, Novelists, and Popular Fiction and Genre Authors;* **and** *Something about the Author Autobiography Series, Vol. 75.*

☐ Contemporary Literary Criticism

Indexes

Literary Criticism Series
Cumulative Author Index
Cumulative Topic Index
Cumulative Nationality Index
Title Index, Volume 120

How to Use This Index

The main references

Camus, Albert
1913-1960 . . . . . . .CLC 1, 2, 4, 9, 11,
14, 32, 69; DA; DAB; DAC; DAM
DRAM, MST, NOV; DC2; SSC 9;
WLC

list all author entries in the following Gale Literary Criticism series:

BLC = *Black Literature Criticism*
BLCS = *Black Literature Criticism Supplement*
CLC = *Contemporary Literary Criticism*
CLR = *Children's Literature Review*
CMLC = *Classical and Medieval Literature Criticism*
DA = *DISCovering Authors*
DAB = *DISCovering Authors: British*
DAC = *DISCovering Authors: Canadian*
DAM = *DISCovering Authors Modules*
  DRAM = *dramatists;* *MST* = *most-studied*
  authors; *MULT* = *multicultural authors;* *NOV* =
  novelists; *POET* = *poets;* *POP* = *popular/genre*
  writers; *DC* = *Drama Criticism*
HLC = *Hispanic Literature Criticism*
LC = *Literature Criticism from 1400 to 1800*
NCLC = *Nineteenth-Century Literature Criticism*
PC = *Poetry Criticism*
SSC = *Short Story Criticism*
TCLC = *Twentieth-Century Literary Criticism*
WLC = *World Literature Criticism, 1500 to the Present*
WLCS = *World Literature Criticism Supplement*

The cross-references

See also CA 89-92; DLB 72; MTCW

list all author entries in the following Gale biographical and literary sources:

AAYA = *Authors & Artists for Young Adults*
AITN = *Authors in the News*
BEST = *Bestsellers*
BW = *Black Writers*
CA = *Contemporary Authors*
CAAS = *Contemporary Authors Autobiography Series*
CABS = *Contemporary Authors Bibliographical Series*
CANR = *Contemporary Authors New Revision Series*
CAP = *Contemporary Authors Permanent Series*
CDALB = *Concise Dictionary of American Literary Biography*
CDBLB = *Concise Dictionary of British Literary Biography*

DLB = *Dictionary of Literary Biography*
DLBD = *Dictionary of Literary Biography Documentary Series*
DLBY = *Dictionary of Literary Biography Yearbook*
HW = *Hispanic Writers*
JRDA = *Junior DISCovering Authors*
MAICYA = *Major Authors and Illustrators for Children and Young Adults*
MTCW = *Major 20th-Century Writers*
NNAL = *Native North American Literature*
SAAS = *Something about the Author Autobiography Series*
SATA = *Something about the Author*
YABC = *Yesterday's Authors of Books for Children*

See also DLB 151, 172
Andrews, Cicily Fairfield
See West, Rebecca
Andrews, Elton V.
See Pohl, Frederik
Andreyev, Leonid (Nikolaevich) 1871-1919
TCLC 3
See also CA 104
Andric, Ivo 1892-1975 .... **CLC 8**
See also CA 81-84; 57-60; CANR 43, 60; DLB
147; MTCW 1
Androvar
See Prado (Calvo), Pedro
Angelique, Pierre
See Bataille, Georges
Angell, Roger 1920- .... **CLC 26**
See also CA 57-60; CANR 13, 44, 70; DLB 171,
185
Angelou, Maya 1928-CLC 12, 35, 64, 77; BLC
1; DA; DAB; DAC; DAM MST, MULT,
POET, POP; WLCS
See also AAYA 7, 20; BW 2, 3; CA 65-68;
CANR 19, 42, 65; CDALBS; CLR 53; DLB
38; MTCW 1, 2; SATA 49
Anna Comnena 1083-1153 .... **CMLC 25**
Annensky, Innokenty (Fyodorovich) 1856-1909
TCLC 14
See also CA 110; 155
Annunzio, Gabriele d'
See D'Annunzio, Gabriele
Anodos
See Coleridge, Mary E(lizabeth)
Anon, Charles Robert
See Pessoa, Fernando (Antonio Nogueira)
Anouilh, Jean (Marie Lucien Pierre) 1910-1987
CLC 1, 3, 8, 13, 40, 50; DAM DRAM; DC
8
See also CA 17-20R; 123; CANR 32; MTCW
1, 2
Anthony, Florence
See Ai
Anthony, John
See Ciardi, John (Anthony)
Anthony, Peter
See Shaffer, Anthony (Joshua); Shaffer, Peter
(Levin)
Anthony, Piers 1934- .... **CLC 35; DAM POP**
See also AAYA 11; CA 21-24R; CANR 28, 56,
73; DLB 8; MTCW 1, 2; SAAS 22; SATA 84
Anthony, Susan B(rownell) 1916-1991 T C L C
84
See also CA 89-92; 134
Antoine, Marc
See Proust, (Valentin-Louis-George-Eugene-)
Marcel
Antoninus, Brother
See Everson, William (Oliver)
Antonioni, Michelangelo 1912- .... **CLC 20**
See also CA 73-76; CANR 45, 77
Antschel, Paul 1920-1970
See Celan, Paul
See also CA 85-88; CANR 33, 61; MTCW 1
Anwar, Chairil 1922-1949 .... **TCLC 22**
See also CA 121
Apess, William 1798-1839(?)NCLC 73; DAM
MULT
See also DLB 175; NNAL
Apollinaire, Guillaume 1880-1918TCLC 3, 8,
51; DAM POET; PC 7
See also Kostrowitzki, Wilhelm Apollinaris de
See also CA 152; MTCW 1
Appelfeld, Aharon 1932- .... **CLC 23, 47**
See also CA 112; 133

Apple, Max (Isaac) 1941- .... **CLC 9, 33**
See also CA 81-84; CANR 19, 54; DLB 130
Appleman, Philip (Dean) 1926- .... **CLC 51**
See also CA 13-16R; CAAS 18; CANR 6, 29,
56
Appleton, Lawrence
See Lovecraft, H(oward) P(hillips)
Apteryx
See Eliot, T(homas) S(tearns)
Apuleius, (Lucius Madaurensis) 125(?)-175(?)
CMLC 1
See also DLB 211
Aquin, Hubert 1929-1977 .... **CLC 15**
See also CA 105; DLB 53
Aquinas, Thomas 1224(?)-1274 ..... **CMLC 33**
See also DLB 115
Aragon, Louis 1897-1982.. **CLC 3, 22; DAM
NOV, POET**
See also CA 69-72; 108; CANR 28, 71; DLB
72; MTCW 1, 2
Arany, Janos 1817-1882 .... **NCLC 34**
Aranyos, Kakay
See Mikszath, Kalman
Arbuthnot, John 1667-1735 .... **LC 1**
See also DLB 101
Archer, Herbert Winslow
See Mencken, H(enry) L(ouis)
Archer, Jeffrey (Howard) 1940- ..... **CLC 28;
DAM POP**
See also AAYA 16; BEST 89:3; CA 77-80;
CANR 22, 52; INT CANR-22
Archer, Jules 1915- .... **CLC 12**
See also CA 9-12R; CANR 6, 69; SAAS 5;
SATA 4, 85
Archer, Lee
See Ellison, Harlan (Jay)
Arden, John 1930-CLC 6, 13, 15; DAM DRAM
See also CA 13-16R; CAAS 4; CANR 31, 65,
67; DLB 13; MTCW 1
Arenas, Reinaldo 1943-1990 . **CLC 41; DAM
MULT; HLC**
See also CA 124; 128; 133; CANR 73; DLB
145; HW 1; MTCW 1
Arendt, Hannah 1906-1975 .... **CLC 66, 98**
See also CA 17-20R; 61-64; CANR 26, 60;
MTCW 1, 2
Aretino, Pietro 1492-1556 .... **LC 12**
Arghezi, Tudor 1880-1967 .... **CLC 80**
See also Theodorescu, Ion N.
See also CA 167
Arguedas, Jose Maria 1911-1969CLC 10, 18;
HLCS 1
See also CA 89-92; CANR 73; DLB 113; HW 1
Argueta, Manlio 1936- .... **CLC 31**
See also CA 131; CANR 73; DLB 145; HW 1
Ariosto, Ludovico 1474-1533 .... **LC 6**
Aristides
See Epstein, Joseph
Aristophanes 450B.C.-385B.C.CMLC 4; DA;
DAB; DAC; DAM DRAM, MST; DC 2;
WLCS
See also DLB 176
Aristotle 384B.C.-322B.C. ... **CMLC 31; DA;
DAB; DAC; DAM MST; WLCS**
See also DLB 176
Arlt, Roberto (Godofredo Christophersen)
1900-1942TCLC 29; DAM MULT; HLC
See also CA 123; 131; CANR 67; HW 1, 2
Armah, Ayi Kwei 1939- . **CLC 5, 33; BLC 1;
DAM MULT, POET**
See also BW 1; CA 61-64; CANR 21, 64; DLB
117; MTCW 1
Armatrading, Joan 1950- .... **CLC 17**

See also CA 114
Arnette, Robert
See Silverberg, Robert
**Arnim, Achim von (Ludwig Joachim von
Arnim)** 1781-1831 ...... **NCLC 5; SSC 29**
See also DLB 90
Arnim, Bettina von 1785-1859 .... **NCLC 38**
See also DLB 90
Arnold, Matthew 1822-1888NCLC 6, 29; DA;
DAB; DAC; DAM MST, POET; PC 5;
WLC
See also CDBLB 1832-1890; DLB 32, 57
Arnold, Thomas 1795-1842 .... **NCLC 18**
See also DLB 55
Arnow, Harriette (Louisa) Simpson 1908-1986
CLC 2, 7, 18
See also CA 9-12R; 118; CANR 14; DLB 6;
MTCW 1, 2; SATA 42; SATA-Obit47
Arouet, Francois-Marie
See Voltaire
Arp, Hans
See Arp, Jean
Arp, Jean 1887-1966 .... **CLC 5**
See also CA 81-84; 25-28R; CANR 42, 77
Arrabal
See Arrabal, Fernando
Arrabal, Fernando 1932-.... **CLC 2, 9, 18, 58**
See also CA 9-12R; CANR 15
Arrick, Fran .... **CLC 30**
See also Gaberman, Judie Angell
Artaud, Antonin (Marie Joseph) 1896-1948
TCLC 3, 36; DAM DRAM
See also CA 104; 149; MTCW 1
Arthur, Ruth M(abel) 1905-1979 ...... **CLC 12**
See also CA 9-12R; 85-88; CANR 4; SATA 7,
26
Artsybashev, Mikhail (Petrovich) 1878-1927
TCLC 31
See also CA 170
Arundel, Honor (Morfydd) 1919-1973CLC 17
See also CA 21-22; 41-44R; CAP 2; CLR 35;
SATA 4; SATA-Obit 24
Arzner, Dorothy 1897-1979 .... **CLC 98**
Asch, Sholem 1880-1957 .... **TCLC 3**
See also CA 105
Ash, Shalom
See Asch, Sholem
Ashbery, John (Lawrence) 1927-CLC 2, 3, 4,
6, 9, 13, 15, 25, 41, 77; DAM POET; PC 26
See also CA 5-8R; CANR 9, 37, 66; DLB 5,
165; DLBY 81; INT CANR-9; MTCW 1, 2
Ashdown, Clifford
See Freeman, R(ichard) Austin
Ashe, Gordon
See Creasey, John
Ashton-Warner, Sylvia (Constance) 1908-1984
CLC 19
See also CA 69-72; 112; CANR 29; MTCW 1,
2
Asimov, Isaac 1920-1992 CLC 1, 3, 9, 19, 26,
76, 92; DAM POP
See also AAYA 13; BEST 90:2; CA 1-4R; 137;
CANR 2, 19, 36, 60; CLR 12; DLB 8; DLBY
92; INT CANR-19; JRDA; MAICYA;
MTCW 1, 2; SATA 1, 26, 74
Assis, Joaquim Maria Machado de
See Machado de Assis, Joaquim Maria
Astley, Thea (Beatrice May) 1925- ... **CLC 41**
See also CA 65-68; CANR 11, 43, 78
Aston, James
See White, T(erence) H(anbury)
Asturias, Miguel Angel 1899-1974 CLC 3, 8,
13; DAM MULT, NOV; HLC

Becker, Walter 1950- .... CLC 26

Beckett, Samuel (Barclay) 1906-1989 CLC 1, 2, 3, 4, 6, 9, 10, 11, 14, 18, 29, 57, 59, 83; DA; DAB; DAC; DAM DRAM, MST, NOV; SSC 16; WLC
See also CA 5-8R; 130; CANR 33, 61; CDBLB 1945-1960; DLB 13, 15; DLBY 90; MTCW 1, 2

Beckford, William 1760-1844 .... NCLC 16
See also DLB 39

Beckman, Gunnel 1910- .... CLC 26
See also CA 33-36R; CANR 15; CLR 25; MAICYA; SAAS 9; SATA 6

Becque, Henri 1837-1899 .... NCLC 3
See also DLB 192

Beddoes, Thomas Lovell 1803-1849 NCLC 3
See also DLB 96

Bede c. 673-735 .... CMLC 20
See also DLB 146

Bedford, Donald F.
See Fearing, Kenneth (Flexner)

Beecher, Catharine Esther 1800-1878 N C L C 30
See also DLB 1

Beecher, John 1904-1980 .... CLC 6
See also AITN 1; CA 5-8R; 105; CANR 8

Beer, Johann 1655-1700 .... LC 5
See also DLB 168

Beer, Patricia 1924- .... CLC 58
See also CA 61-64; CANR 13, 46; DLB 40

Beerbohm, Max
See Beerbohm, (Henry) Max(imilian)

Beerbohm, (Henry) Max(imilian) 1872-1956 TCLC 1, 24
See also CA 104; 154, 179; DLB 34, 100

Beer-Hofmann, Richard 1866-1945TCLC 60
See also CA 160; DLB 81

Begiebing, Robert J(ohn) 1946- .... CLC 70
See also CA 122; CANR 40

Behan, Brendan 1923-1964 CLC 1, 8, 11, 15, 79; DAM DRAM
See also CA 73-76; CANR 33; CDBLB 1945-1960; DLB 13; MTCW 1, 2

Behn, Aphra 1640(?)-1689 LC 1, 30, 42; DA; DAB; DAC; DAM DRAM, MST, NOV, POET; DC 4; PC 13; WLC
See also DLB 39, 80, 131

Behrman, S(amuel) N(athaniel) 1893-1973 CLC 40
See also CA 13-16; 45-48; CAP 1; DLB 7, 44

Belasco, David 1853-1931 .... TCLC 3
See also CA 104; 168; DLB 7

Belcheva, Elisaveta 1893- .... CLC 10
See also Bagryana, Elisaveta

Beldone, Phil "Cheech"
See Ellison, Harlan (Jay)

Beleno
See Azuela, Mariano

Belinski, Vissarion Grigoryevich 1811-1848 NCLC 5
See also DLB 198

Belitt, Ben 1911- .... CLC 22
See also CA 13-16R; CAAS 4; CANR 7, 77; DLB 5

Bell, Gertrude (Margaret Lowthian) 1868-1926 TCLC 67
See also CA 167; DLB 174

Bell, J. Freeman
See Zangwill, Israel

Bell, James Madison 1826-1902 ... TCLC 43; BLC 1; DAM MULT
See also BW 1; CA 122; 124; DLB 50

Bell, Madison Smartt 1957- ..... CLC 41, 102

See also CA 111; CANR 28, 54, 73; MTCW 1

Bell, Marvin (Hartley) 1937-CLC 8, 31; DAM POET
See also CA 21-24R; CAAS 14; CANR 59; DLB 5; MTCW 1

Bell, W. L. D.
See Mencken, H(enry) L(ouis)

Bellamy, Atwood C.
See Mencken, H(enry) L(ouis)

Bellamy, Edward 1850-1898 .... NCLC 4
See also DLB 12

Bellin, Edward J.
See Kuttner, Henry

Belloc, (Joseph) Hilaire (Pierre Sebastien Rene Swanton) 1870-1953 TCLC 7, 18; DAM POET; PC 24
See also CA 106; 152; DLB 19, 100, 141, 174; MTCW 1; YABC 1

Belloc, Joseph Peter Rene Hilaire
See Belloc, (Joseph) Hilaire (Pierre Sebastien Rene Swanton)

Belloc, Joseph Pierre Hilaire
See Belloc, (Joseph) Hilaire (Pierre Sebastien Rene Swanton)

Belloc, M. A.
See Lowndes, Marie Adelaide (Belloc)

Bellow, Saul 1915-CLC 1, 2, 3, 6, 8, 10, 13, 15, 25, 33, 34, 63, 79; DA; DAB; DAC; DAM MST, NOV, POP; SSC 14; WLC
See also AITN 2; BEST 89:3; CA 5-8R; CABS 1; CANR 29, 53; CDALB 1941-1968; DLB 2, 28; DLBD 3; DLBY 82; MTCW 1, 2

Belser, Reimond Karel Maria de 1929-
See Ruyslinck, Ward
See also CA 152

Bely, Andrey .... TCLC 7; PC 11
See also Bugayev, Boris Nikolayevich
See also MTCW 1

Belyi, Andrei
See Bugayev, Boris Nikolayevich

Benary, Margot
See Benary-Isbert, Margot

Benary-Isbert, Margot 1889-1979 .... CLC 12
See also CA 5-8R; 89-92; CANR 4, 72; CLR 12; MAICYA; SATA 2; SATA-Obit 21

Benavente (y Martinez), Jacinto 1866-1954 TCLC 3; DAM DRAM, MULT; HLCS 1
See also CA 106; 131; HW 1, 2; MTCW 1, 2

Benchley, Peter (Bradford) 1940- CLC 4, 8; DAM NOV, POP
See also AAYA 14; AITN 2; CA 17-20R; CANR 12, 35, 66; MTCW 1, 2; SATA 3, 89

Benchley, Robert (Charles) 1889-1945T C L C 1, 55
See also CA 105; 153; DLB 11

Benda, Julien 1867-1956 .... TCLC 60
See also CA 120; 154

Benedict, Ruth (Fulton) 1887-1948 TCLC 60
See also CA 158

Benedict, Saint c. 480-c. 547 .... CMLC 29

Benedikt, Michael 1935- .... CLC 4, 14
See also CA 13-16R; CANR 7; DLB 5

Benet, Juan 1927- .... CLC 28
See also CA 143

Benet, Stephen Vincent 1898-1943 . TCLC 7; DAM POET; SSC 10
See also CA 104; 152; DLB 4, 48, 102; DLBY 97; MTCW 1; YABC 1

Benet, William Rose 1886-1950 .... TCLC 28; DAM POET
See also CA 118; 152; DLB 45

Benford, Gregory (Albert) 1941- ..... CLC 52
See also CA 69-72, 175; CAAE 175; CAAS 27;

CANR 12, 24, 49; DLBY 82

Bengtsson, Frans (Gunnar) 1894-1954T C L C 48
See also CA 170

Benjamin, David
See Slavitt, David R(ytman)

Benjamin, Lois
See Gould, Lois

Benjamin, Walter 1892-1940 .... TCLC 39
See also CA 164

Benn, Gottfried 1886-1956 .... TCLC 3
See also CA 106; 153; DLB 56

Bennett, Alan 1934-CLC 45, 77; DAB; DAM MST
See also CA 103; CANR 35, 55; MTCW 1, 2

Bennett, (Enoch) Arnold 1867-1931TCLC 5, 20
See also CA 106; 155; CDBLB 1890-1914; DLB 10, 34, 98, 135; MTCW 2

Bennett, Elizabeth
See Mitchell, Margaret (Munnerlyn)

Bennett, George Harold 1930-
See Bennett, Hal
See also BW 1; CA 97-100

Bennett, Hal .... CLC 5
See also Bennett, George Harold
See also DLB 33

Bennett, Jay 1912- .... CLC 35
See also AAYA 10; CA 69-72; CANR 11, 42, 79; JRDA; SAAS 4; SATA 41, 87; SATA-Brief 27

Bennett, Louise (Simone) 1919-CLC 28; BLC 1; DAM MULT
See also BW 2, 3; CA 151; DLB 117

Benson, E(dward) F(rederic) 1867-1940 TCLC 27
See also CA 114; 157; DLB 135, 153

Benson, Jackson J. 1930- .... CLC 34
See also CA 25-28R; DLB 111

Benson, Sally 1900-1972 .... CLC 17
See also CA 19-20; 37-40R; CAP 1; SATA 1, 35; SATA-Obit 27

Benson, Stella 1892-1933 .... TCLC 17
See also CA 117; 155; DLB 36, 162

Bentham, Jeremy 1748-1832 .... NCLC 38
See also DLB 107, 158

Bentley, E(dmund) C(lerihew) 1875-1956 TCLC 12
See also CA 108; DLB 70

Bentley, Eric (Russell) 1916- .... CLC 24
See also CA 5-8R; CANR 6, 67; INT CANR-6

Beranger, Pierre Jean de 1780-1857NCLC 34

Berdyaev, Nicolas
See Berdyaev, Nikolai (Aleksandrovich)

Berdyaev, Nikolai (Aleksandrovich) 1874-1948 TCLC 67
See also CA 120; 157

Berdyayev, Nikolai (Aleksandrovich)
See Berdyaev, Nikolai (Aleksandrovich)

Berendt, John (Lawrence) 1939- ...... CLC 86
See also CA 146; CANR 75; MTCW 1

Beresford, J(ohn) D(avys) 1873-1947 T C L C 81
See also CA 112; 155; DLB 162, 178, 197

Bergelson, David 1884-1952 .... TCLC 81

Berger, Colonel
See Malraux, (Georges-)Andre

Berger, John (Peter) 1926- .... CLC 2, 19
See also CA 81-84; CANR 51, 78; DLB 14, 207

Berger, Melvin H. 1927- .... CLC 12
See also CA 5-8R; CANR 4; CLR 32; SAAS 2; SATA 5, 88

Berger, Thomas (Louis) 1924-CLC 3, 5, 8, 11,

See also BW 1, 3; CA 104; CANR 26; DLB 33

Bradley, John Ed(mund, Jr.) 1958- .. **CLC 55**
See also CA 139

Bradley, Marion Zimmer 1930-**CLC 30; DAM POP**
See also AAYA 9; CA 57-60; CAAS 10; CANR 7, 31, 51, 75; DLB 8; MTCW 1, 2; SATA 90

Bradstreet, Anne 1612(?)-1672**LC 4, 30; DA; DAC; DAM MST, POET; PC 10**
See also CDALB 1640-1865; DLB 24

Brady, Joan 1939- .... **CLC 86**
See also CA 141

Bragg, Melvyn 1939- .... **CLC 10**
See also BEST 89:3; CA 57-60; CANR 10, 48; DLB 14

Brahe, Tycho 1546-1601 .... **LC 45**

Braine, John (Gerard) 1922-1986**CLC 1, 3, 41**
See also CA 1-4R; 120; CANR 1, 33; CDBLB 1945-1960; DLB 15; DLBY 86;MTCW 1

Bramah, Ernest 1868-1942 .... **TCLC 72**
See also CA 156; DLB 70

Brammer, William 1930(?)-1978 .... **CLC 31**
See also CA 77-80

Brancati, Vitaliano 1907-1954 .... **TCLC 12**
See also CA 109

Brancato, Robin F(idler) 1936- .... **CLC 35**
See also AAYA 9; CA 69-72; CANR 11, 45; CLR 32; JRDA; SAAS 9; SATA 97

Brand, Max
See Faust, Frederick (Schiller)

Brand, Millen 1906-1980 .... **CLC 7**
See also CA 21-24R; 97-100; CANR 72

Branden, Barbara .... **CLC 44**
See also CA 148

Brandes, Georg (Morris Cohen) 1842-1927 **TCLC 10**
See also CA 105

Brandys, Kazimierz 1916- .... **CLC 62**

Branley, Franklyn M(ansfield) 1915-**CLC 21**
See also CA 33-36R; CANR 14, 39; CLR 13; MAICYA; SAAS 16; SATA 4, 68

Brathwaite, Edward (Kamau) 1930-**CLC 11; BLCS; DAM POET**
See also BW 2, 3; CA 25-28R; CANR 11, 26, 47; DLB 125

Brautigan, Richard (Gary) 1935-1984**CLC 1, 3, 5, 9, 12, 34, 42; DAM NOV**
See also CA 53-56; 113; CANR 34; DLB 2, 5, 206; DLBY 80, 84; MTCW 1; SATA 56

Brave Bird, Mary 1953-
See Crow Dog, Mary (Ellen)
See also NNAL

Braverman, Kate 1950- .... **CLC 67**
See also CA 89-92

Brecht, (Eugen) Bertolt (Friedrich) 1898-1956 **TCLC 1, 6, 13, 35; DA; DAB; DAC; DAM DRAM, MST; DC 3; WLC**
See also CA 104; 133; CANR 62; DLB 56, 124; MTCW 1, 2

Brecht, Eugen Berthold Friedrich
See Brecht, (Eugen) Bertolt (Friedrich)

Bremer, Fredrika 1801-1865 .... **NCLC 11**

Brennan, Christopher John 1870-1932**TCLC 17**
See also CA 117

Brennan, Maeve 1917-1993 .... **CLC 5**
See also CA 81-84; CANR 72

Brent, Linda
See Jacobs, Harriet A(nn)

Brentano, Clemens (Maria) 1778-1842**NCLC 1**
See also DLB 90

Brent of Bin Bin

See Franklin, (Stella Maria Sarah) Miles (Lampe)

Brenton, Howard 1942- .... **CLC 31**
See also CA 69-72; CANR 33, 67; DLB 13; MTCW 1

Breslin, James 1930-1996
See Breslin, Jimmy
See also CA 73-76; CANR 31, 75; DAM NOV; MTCW 1, 2

Breslin, Jimmy .... **CLC 4, 43**
See Breslin, James
See also AITN 1; DLB 185; MTCW 2

Bresson, Robert 1901- .... **CLC 16**
See also CA 110; CANR 49

Breton, Andre 1896-1966**CLC 2, 9, 15, 54; PC 15**
See also CA 19-20; 25-28R; CANR 40, 60; CAP 2; DLB 65; MTCW 1, 2

Breytenbach, Breyten 1939(?)- . **CLC 23, 37; DAM POET**
See also CA 113; 129; CANR 61

Bridgers, Sue Ellen 1942- .... **CLC 26**
See also AAYA 8; CA 65-68; CANR 11, 36; CLR 18; DLB 52; JRDA; MAICYA; SAAS 1; SATA 22, 90

Bridges, Robert (Seymour) 1844-1930**TCLC 1; DAM POET**
See also CA 104; 152; CDBLB 1890-1914; DLB 19, 98

Bridie, James .... **TCLC 3**
See also Mavor, Osborne Henry
See also DLB 10

Brin, David 1950- .... **CLC 34**
See also AAYA 21; CA 102; CANR 24, 70; INT CANR-24; SATA 65

Brink, Andre (Philippus) 1935- **CLC 18, 36, 106**
See also CA 104; CANR 39, 62; INT 103; MTCW 1, 2

Brinsmead, H(esba) F(ay) 1922- .... **CLC 21**
See also CA 21-24R; CANR 10; CLR 47; MAICYA; SAAS 5; SATA 18, 78

Brittain, Vera (Mary) 1893(?)-1970 . **CLC 23**
See also CA 13-16; 25-28R; CANR 58; CAP 1; DLB 191; MTCW 1, 2

Broch, Hermann 1886-1951 .... **TCLC 20**
See also CA 117; DLB 85, 124

Brock, Rose
See Hansen, Joseph

Brodkey, Harold (Roy) 1930-1996.... **CLC 56**
See also CA 111; 151; CANR 71; DLB 130

Brodskii, Iosif
See Brodsky, Joseph

Brodsky, Iosif Alexandrovich 1940-1996
See Brodsky, Joseph
See also AITN 1; CA 41-44R; 151; CANR 37; DAM POET; MTCW 1, 2

Brodsky, Joseph 1940-1996 **CLC 4, 6, 13, 36, 100; PC 9**
See also Brodskii, Iosif; Brodsky, Iosif Alexandrovich
See also MTCW 1

Brodsky, Michael (Mark) 1948- .... **CLC 19**
See also CA 102; CANR 18, 41, 58

Bromell, Henry 1947- .... **CLC 5**
See also CA 53-56; CANR 9

Bromfield, Louis (Brucker) 1896-1956**TCLC 11**
See also CA 107; 155; DLB 4, 9, 86

Broner, E(sther) M(asserman) 1930- **CLC 19**
See also CA 17-20R; CANR 8, 25, 72; DLB 28

Bronk, William 1918- .... **CLC 10**
See also CA 89-92; CANR 23; DLB 165

Bronstein, Lev Davidovich
See Trotsky, Leon

Bronte, Anne 1820-1849 .... **NCLC 71**
See also DLB 21, 199

Bronte, Charlotte 1816-1855 **NCLC 3, 8, 33, 58; DA; DAB; DAC; DAM MST, NOV; WLC**
See also AAYA 17; CDBLB 1832-1890; DLB 21, 159, 199

Bronte, Emily (Jane) 1818-1848**NCLC 16, 35; DA; DAB; DAC; DAM MST, NOV, POET; PC 8; WLC**
See also AAYA 17; CDBLB 1832-1890; DLB 21, 32, 199

Brooke, Frances 1724-1789 .... **LC 6, 48**
See also DLB 39, 99

Brooke, Henry 1703(?)-1783 .... **LC 1**
See also DLB 39

Brooke, Rupert (Chawner) 1887-1915 **TCLC 2, 7; DA; DAB; DAC; DAM MST, POET; PC 24; WLC**
See also CA 104; 132; CANR 61; CDBLB 1914-1945; DLB 19; MTCW 1, 2

Brooke-Haven, P.
See Wodehouse, P(elham) G(renville)

Brooke-Rose, Christine 1926(?)- .... **CLC 40**
See also CA 13-16R; CANR 58; DLB 14

Brookner, Anita 1928-**CLC 32, 34, 51; DAB; DAM POP**
See also CA 114; 120; CANR 37, 56; DLB 194; DLBY 87; MTCW 1, 2

Brooks, Cleanth 1906-1994 **CLC 24, 86, 110**
See also CA 17-20R; 145; CANR 33, 35; DLB 63; DLBY 94; INT CANR-35; MTCW 1, 2

Brooks, George
See Baum, L(yman) Frank

Brooks, Gwendolyn 1917- **CLC 1, 2, 4, 5, 15, 49; BLC 1; DA; DAC; DAM MST, MULT, POET; PC 7; WLC**
See also AAYA 20; AITN 1; BW 2, 3; CA 1-4R; CANR 1, 27, 52, 75; CDALB 1941-1968; CLR 27; DLB 5, 76, 165; MTCW 1, 2; SATA 6

Brooks, Mel .... **CLC 12**
See also Kaminsky, Melvin
See also AAYA 13; DLB 26

Brooks, Peter 1938- .... **CLC 34**
See also CA 45-48; CANR 1

Brooks, Van Wyck 1886-1963 .... **CLC 29**
See also CA 1-4R; CANR 6; DLB 45, 63, 103

Brophy, Brigid (Antonia) 1929-1995 **CLC 6, 11, 29, 105**
See also CA 5-8R; 149; CAAS 4; CANR 25, 53; DLB 14; MTCW 1, 2

Brosman, Catharine Savage 1934- ..... **CLC 9**
See also CA 61-64; CANR 21, 46

Brossard, Nicole 1943- .... **CLC 115**
See also CA 122; CAAS 16; DLB 53

Brother Antoninus
See Everson, William (Oliver)

The Brothers Quay
See Quay, Stephen; Quay, Timothy

Broughton, T(homas) Alan 1936- ..... **CLC 19**
See also CA 45-48; CANR 2, 23, 48

Broumas, Olga 1949- .... **CLC 10, 73**
See also CA 85-88; CANR 20, 69

Brown, Alan 1950- .... **CLC 99**
See also CA 156

Brown, Charles Brockden 1771-1810 **NCLC 22, 74**
See also CDALB 1640-1865; DLB 37, 59, 73

Brown, Christy 1932-1981 .... **CLC 63**
See also CA 105; 104; CANR 72; DLB 14

See also CA 41-44R; CANR 67

Clark, Curt
See Westlake, Donald E(dwin)

Clark, Eleanor 1913-1996 .... **CLC 5, 19**
See also CA 9-12R; 151; CANR 41; DLB 6

Clark, J. P.
See Clark, John Pepper
See also DLB 117

Clark, John Pepper 1935-.. **CLC 38; BLC 1; DAM DRAM, MULT; DC 5**
See also Clark, J. P.
See also BW 1; CA 65-68; CANR 16, 72; MTCW 1

Clark, M. R.
See Clark, Mavis Thorpe

Clark, Mavis Thorpe 1909- .... **CLC 12**
See also CA 57-60; CANR 8, 37; CLR 30; MAICYA; SAAS 5; SATA 8, 74

Clark, Walter Van Tilburg 1909-1971 **CLC 28**
See also CA 9-12R; 33-36R; CANR 63; DLB 9, 206; SATA 8

Clark Bekederemo, J(ohnson) P(epper)
See Clark, John Pepper

Clarke, Arthur C(harles) 1917-**CLC 1, 4, 13, 18, 35; DAM POP; SSC 3**
See also AAYA 4; CA 1-4R; CANR 2, 28, 55, 74; JRDA; MAICYA; MTCW 1, 2; SATA 13, 70

Clarke, Austin 1896-1974 ....**CLC 6, 9; DAM POET**
See also CA 29-32; 49-52; CAP 2; DLB 10, 20

Clarke, Austin C(hesterfield) 1934-**CLC 8, 53; BLC 1; DAC; DAM MULT**
See also BW 1; CA 25-28R; CAAS 16; CANR 14, 32, 68; DLB 53, 125

Clarke, Gillian 1937- .... **CLC 61**
See also CA 106; DLB 40

Clarke, Marcus (Andrew Hislop) 1846-1881 **NCLC 19**

Clarke, Shirley 1925- .... **CLC 16**

Clash, The
See Headon, (Nicky) Topper; Jones, Mick; Simonon, Paul; Strummer, Joe

Claudel, Paul (Louis Charles Marie) 1868-1955 **TCLC 2, 10**
See also CA 104; 165; DLB 192

Claudius, Matthias 1740-1815 .... **NCLC 75**
See also DLB 97

Clavell, James (duMaresq) 1925-1994**CLC 6, 25, 87; DAM NOV, POP**
See also CA 25-28R; 146; CANR 26, 48; MTCW 1, 2

Cleaver, (Leroy) Eldridge 1935-1998**CLC 30, 119; BLC 1; DAM MULT**
See also BW 1, 3; CA 21-24R; 167; CANR 16, 75; MTCW 2

Cleese, John (Marwood) 1939- .... **CLC 21**
See also Monty Python
See also CA 112; 116; CANR 35; MTCW 1

Cleishbotham, Jebediah
See Scott, Walter

Cleland, John 1710-1789 .... **LC 2, 48**
See also DLB 39

Clemens, Samuel Langhorne 1835-1910
See Twain, Mark
See also CA 104; 135; CDALB 1865-1917; DA; DAB; DAC; DAM MST, NOV; DLB 11, 12, 23, 64, 74, 186, 189; JRDA; MAICYA; SATA 100; YABC 2

Cleophil
See Congreve, William

Clerihew, E.
See Bentley, E(dmund) C(lerihew)

Clerk, N. W.
See Lewis, C(live) S(taples)

Cliff, Jimmy .... **CLC 21**
See also Chambers, James

Cliff, Michelle 1946- .... **CLC 120; BLCS**
See also BW 2; CA 116; CANR 39, 72; DLB 157

Clifton, (Thelma) Lucille 1936- **CLC 19, 66; BLC 1; DAM MULT, POET; PC 17**
See also BW 2, 3; CA 49-52; CANR 2, 24, 42, 76; CLR 5; DLB 5, 41; MAICYA; MTCW 1, 2; SATA 20, 69

Clinton, Dirk
See Silverberg, Robert

Clough, Arthur Hugh 1819-1861 ... **NCLC 27**
See also DLB 32

Clutha, Janet Paterson Frame 1924-
See Frame, Janet
See also CA 1-4R; CANR 2, 36, 76; MTCW 1, 2

Clyne, Terence
See Blatty, William Peter

Cobalt, Martin
See Mayne, William (James Carter)

Cobb, Irvin S. 1876-1944 .... **TCLC 77**
See also CA 175; DLB 11, 25, 86

Cobbett, William 1763-1835 .... **NCLC 49**
See also DLB 43, 107, 158

Coburn, D(onald) L(ee) 1938- .... **CLC 10**
See also CA 89-92

Cocteau, Jean (Maurice Eugene Clement) 1889-1963**CLC 1, 8, 15, 16, 43; DA; DAB; DAC; DAM DRAM, MST, NOV; WLC**
See also CA 25-28; CANR 40; CAP 2; DLB 65; MTCW 1, 2

Codrescu, Andrei 1946-**CLC 46; DAM POET**
See also CA 33-36R; CAAS 19; CANR 13, 34, 53, 76; MTCW 2

Coe, Max
See Bourne, Randolph S(illiman)

Coe, Tucker
See Westlake, Donald E(dwin)

Coen, Ethan 1958- .... **CLC 108**
See also CA 126

Coen, Joel 1955- .... **CLC 108**
See also CA 126

The Coen Brothers
See Coen, Ethan; Coen, Joel

Coetzee, J(ohn) M(ichael) 1940- **CLC 23, 33, 66, 117; DAM NOV**
See also CA 77-80; CANR 41, 54, 74; MTCW 1, 2

Coffey, Brian
See Koontz, Dean R(ay)

Cohan, George M(ichael) 1878-1942**TCLC 60**
See also CA 157

Cohen, Arthur A(llen) 1928-1986 . **CLC 7, 31**
See also CA 1-4R; 120; CANR 1, 17, 42; DLB 28

Cohen, Leonard (Norman) 1934- **CLC 3, 38; DAC; DAM MST**
See also CA 21-24R; CANR 14, 69; DLB 53; MTCW 1

Cohen, Matt 1942- .... **CLC 19; DAC**
See also CA 61-64; CAAS 18; CANR 40; DLB 53

Cohen-Solal, Annie 19(?)- .... **CLC 50**

Colegate, Isabel 1931- .... **CLC 36**
See also CA 17-20R; CANR 8, 22, 74; DLB 14; INT CANR-22; MTCW 1

Coleman, Emmett
See Reed, Ishmael

Coleridge, M. E.

See Coleridge, Mary E(lizabeth)

Coleridge, Mary E(lizabeth) 1861-1907**TCLC 73**
See also CA 116; 166; DLB 19, 98

Coleridge, Samuel Taylor 1772-1834**NCLC 9, 54; DA; DAB; DAC; DAM MST, POET; PC 11; WLC**
See also CDBLB 1789-1832; DLB 93, 107

Coleridge, Sara 1802-1852 .... **NCLC 31**
See also DLB 199

Coles, Don 1928- .... **CLC 46**
See also CA 115; CANR 38

Coles, Robert (Martin) 1929- .... **CLC 108**
See also CA 45-48; CANR 3, 32, 66, 70; INT CANR-32; SATA 23

Colette, (Sidonie-Gabrielle) 1873-1954**TCLC 1, 5, 16; DAM NOV; SSC 10**
See also CA 104; 131; DLB 65; MTCW 1, 2

Collett, (Jacobine) Camilla (Wergeland) 1813-1895 .... **NCLC 22**

Collier, Christopher 1930- .... **CLC 30**
See also AAYA 13; CA 33-36R; CANR 13, 33; JRDA; MAICYA; SATA 16, 70

Collier, James L(incoln) 1928-**CLC 30; DAM POP**
See also AAYA 13; CA 9-12R; CANR 4, 33, 60; CLR 3; JRDA; MAICYA; SAAS 21; SATA 8, 70

Collier, Jeremy 1650-1726 .... **LC 6**

Collier, John 1901-1980 .... **SSC 19**
See also CA 65-68; 97-100; CANR 10; DLB 77

Collingwood, R(obin) G(eorge) 1889(?)-1943 **TCLC 67**
See also CA 117; 155

Collins, Hunt
See Hunter, Evan

Collins, Linda 1931- .... **CLC 44**
See also CA 125

Collins, (William) Wilkie 1824-1889**NCLC 1, 18**
See also CDBLB 1832-1890; DLB 18, 70, 159

Collins, William 1721-1759 . **LC 4, 40; DAM POET**
See also DLB 109

Collodi, Carlo 1826-1890 .... **NCLC 54**
See also Lorenzini, Carlo
See also CLR 5

Colman, George 1732-1794
See Glassco, John

Colt, Winchester Remington
See Hubbard, L(afayette) Ron(ald)

Colter, Cyrus 1910- .... **CLC 58**
See also BW 1; CA 65-68; CANR 10, 66; DLB 33

Colton, James
See Hansen, Joseph

Colum, Padraic 1881-1972 .... **CLC 28**
See also CA 73-76; 33-36R; CANR 35; CLR 36; MAICYA; MTCW 1; SATA 15

Colvin, James
See Moorcock, Michael (John)

Colwin, Laurie (E.) 1944-1992**CLC 5, 13, 23, 84**
See also CA 89-92; 139; CANR 20, 46; DLBY 80; MTCW 1

Comfort, Alex(ander) 1920-**CLC 7; DAM POP**
See also CA 1-4R; CANR 1, 45; MTCW 1

Comfort, Montgomery
See Campbell, (John) Ramsey

Compton-Burnett, I(vy) 1884(?)-1969**CLC 1, 3, 10, 15, 34; DAM NOV**
See also CA 1-4R; 25-28R; CANR 4; DLB 36;

MTCW 1

Comstock, Anthony 1844-1915 ...... **TCLC 13**
See also CA 110; 169

Comte, Auguste 1798-1857 .... **NCLC 54**

Conan Doyle, Arthur
See Doyle, Arthur Conan

Conde, Maryse 1937- .... **CLC 52, 92; BLCS; DAM MULT**
See also Boucolon, Maryse
See also BW 2; MTCW 1

Condillac, Etienne Bonnot de 1714-1780 **LC 26**

Condon, Richard (Thomas) 1915-1996 **CLC 4, 6, 8, 10, 45, 100; DAM NOV**
See also BEST 90:3; CA 1-4R; 151; CAAS 1; CANR 2, 23; INT CANR-23; MTCW 1, 2

Confucius 551B.C.-479B.C. . **CMLC 19; DA; DAB; DAC; DAM MST; WLCS**

Congreve, William 1670-1729 **LC 5, 21; DA; DAB; DAC; DAM DRAM, MST, POET; DC 2; WLC**
See also CDBLB 1660-1789; DLB 39, 84

Connell, Evan S(helby), Jr. 1924- **CLC 4, 6, 45; DAM NOV**
See also AAYA 7; CA 1-4R; CAAS 2; CANR 2, 39, 76; DLB 2; DLBY 81; MTCW 1, 2

Connelly, Marc(us Cook) 1890-1980 .. **CLC 7**
See also CA 85-88; 102; CANR 30; DLB 7; DLBY 80; SATA-Obit 25

Connor, Ralph .... **TCLC 31**
See also Gordon, Charles William
See also DLB 92

Conrad, Joseph 1857-1924 **TCLC 1, 6, 13, 25, 43, 57; DA; DAB; DAC; DAM MST, NOV; SSC 9; WLC**
See also AAYA 26; CA 104; 131; CANR 60; CDBLB 1890-1914; DLB 10, 34, 98, 156; MTCW 1, 2; SATA 27

Conrad, Robert Arnold
See Hart, Moss

Conroy, Pat
See Conroy, (Donald) Pat(rick)
See also MTCW 2

Conroy, (Donald) Pat(rick) 1945- **CLC 30, 74; DAM NOV, POP**
See also Conroy, Pat
See also AAYA 8; AITN 1; CA 85-88; CANR 24, 53; DLB 6; MTCW 1

Constant (de Rebecque), (Henri) Benjamin 1767-1830 .... **NCLC 6**
See also DLB 119

Conybeare, Charles Augustus
See Eliot, T(homas) S(tearns)

Cook, Michael 1933- .... **CLC 58**
See also CA 93-96; CANR 68; DLB 53

Cook, Robin 1940- .... **CLC 14; DAM POP**
See also BEST 90:2; CA 108; 111; CANR 41; INT 111

Cook, Roy
See Silverberg, Robert

Cooke, Elizabeth 1948- .... **CLC 55**
See also CA 129

Cooke, John Esten 1830-1886 .... **NCLC 5**
See also DLB 3

Cooke, John Estes
See Baum, L(yman) Frank

Cooke, M. E.
See Creasey, John

Cooke, Margaret
See Creasey, John

Cook-Lynn, Elizabeth 1930-.. **CLC 93; DAM MULT**
See also CA 133; DLB 175; NNAL

Cooney, Ray .... **CLC 62**

Cooper, Douglas 1960- .... **CLC 86**

Cooper, Henry St. John
See Creasey, John

Cooper, J(oan) California (?)-**CLC 56; DAM MULT**
See also AAYA 12; BW 1; CA 125; CANR 55; DLB 212

Cooper, James Fenimore 1789-1851 **NCLC 1, 27, 54**
See also AAYA 22; CDALB 1640-1865; DLB 3; SATA 19

Coover, Robert (Lowell) 1932- **CLC 3, 7, 15, 32, 46, 87; DAM NOV; SSC 15**
See also CA 45-48; CANR 3, 37, 58; DLB 2; DLBY 81; MTCW 1, 2

Copeland, Stewart (Armstrong) 1952-**CLC 26**

Copernicus, Nicolaus 1473-1543 .... **LC 45**

Coppard, A(lfred) E(dgar) 1878-1957 **TCLC 5; SSC 21**
See also CA 114; 167; DLB 162; YABC 1

Coppee, Francois 1842-1908 .... **TCLC 25**
See also CA 170

Coppola, Francis Ford 1939- .... **CLC 16**
See also CA 77-80; CANR 40, 78; DLB 44

Corbiere, Tristan 1845-1875 .... **NCLC 43**

Corcoran, Barbara 1911- .... **CLC 17**
See also AAYA 14; CA 21-24R; CAAS 2; CANR 11, 28, 48; CLR 50; DLB 52; JRDA; SAAS 20; SATA 3, 77

Cordelier, Maurice
See Giraudoux, (Hippolyte) Jean

Corelli, Marie 1855-1924 .... **TCLC 51**
See also Mackay, Mary
See also DLB 34, 156

Corman, Cid 1924- .... **CLC 9**
See also Corman, Sidney
See also CAAS 2; DLB 5, 193

Corman, Sidney 1924-
See Corman, Cid
See also CA 85-88; CANR 44; DAM POET

Cormier, Robert (Edmund) 1925-**CLC 12, 30; DA; DAB; DAC; DAM MST, NOV**
See also AAYA 3, 19; CA 1-4R; CANR 5, 23, 76; CDALB 1968-1988; CLR 12, 55; DLB 52; INT CANR-23; JRDA; MAICYA; MTCW 1, 2; SATA 10, 45, 83

Corn, Alfred (DeWitt III) 1943- .... **CLC 33**
See also CA 104; CAAS 25; CANR 44; DLB 120; DLBY 80

Corneille, Pierre 1606-1684 .... **LC 28; DAB; DAM MST**

Cornwell, David (John Moore) 1931- **CLC 9, 15; DAM POP**
See also le Carre, John
See also CA 5-8R; CANR 13, 33, 59; MTCW 1, 2

Corso, (Nunzio) Gregory 1930- .... **CLC 1, 11**
See also CA 5-8R; CANR 41, 76; DLB 5, 16; MTCW 1, 2

Cortazar, Julio 1914-1984 **CLC 2, 3, 5, 10, 13, 15, 33, 34, 92; DAM MULT, NOV; HLC; SSC 7**
See also CA 21-24R; CANR 12, 32; DLB 113; HW 1, 2; MTCW 1, 2

CORTES, HERNAN 1484-1547 .... **LC 31**

Corvinus, Jakob
See Raabe, Wilhelm (Karl)

Corwin, Cecil
See Kornbluth, C(yril) M.

Cosic, Dobrica 1921- .... **CLC 14**
See also CA 122; 138; DLB 181

Costain, Thomas B(ertram) 1885-1965 **C L C 30**
See also CA 5-8R; 25-28R; DLB 9

Costantini, Humberto 1924(?)-1987 . **CLC 49**
See also CA 131; 122; HW 1

Costello, Elvis 1955- .... **CLC 21**

Costenoble, Philostene
See Ghelderode, Michel de

Cotes, Cecil V.
See Duncan, Sara Jeannette

Cotter, Joseph Seamon Sr. 1861-1949 **T C L C 28; BLC 1; DAM MULT**
See also BW 1; CA 124; DLB 50

Couch, Arthur Thomas Quiller
See Quiller-Couch, SirArthur (Thomas)

Coulton, James
See Hansen, Joseph

Couperus, Louis (Marie Anne) 1863-1923 **TCLC 15**
See also CA 115

Coupland, Douglas 1961-**CLC 85; DAC; DAM POP**
See also CA 142; CANR 57

Court, Wesli
See Turco, Lewis (Putnam)

Courtenay, Bryce 1933- .... **CLC 59**
See also CA 138

Courtney, Robert
See Ellison, Harlan (Jay)

Cousteau, Jacques-Yves 1910-1997 .. **CLC 30**
See also CA 65-68; 159; CANR 15, 67; MTCW 1; SATA 38, 98

Coventry, Francis 1725-1754 .... **LC 46**

Cowan, Peter (Walkinshaw) 1914- .... **SSC 28**
See also CA 21-24R; CANR 9, 25, 50

Coward, Noel (Peirce) 1899-1973 **CLC 1, 9, 29, 51; DAM DRAM**
See also AITN 1; CA 17-18; 41-44R; CANR 35; CAP 2; CDBLB 1914-1945; DLB 10; MTCW 1, 2

Cowley, Abraham 1618-1667 .... **LC 43**
See also DLB 131, 151

Cowley, Malcolm 1898-1989 .... **CLC 39**
See also CA 5-8R; 128; CANR 3, 55; DLB 4, 48; DLBY 81, 89; MTCW 1, 2

Cowper, William 1731-1800 . **NCLC 8; DAM POET**
See also DLB 104, 109

Cox, William Trevor 1928- .... **CLC 9, 14, 71; DAM NOV**
See also Trevor, William
See also CA 9-12R; CANR 4, 37, 55, 76; DLB 14; INT CANR-37; MTCW 1, 2

Coyne, P. J.
See Masters, Hilary

Cozzens, James Gould 1903-1978 **CLC 1, 4, 11, 92**
See also CA 9-12R; 81-84; CANR 19; CDALB 1941-1968; DLB 9; DLBD 2; DLBY 84, 97; MTCW 1, 2

Crabbe, George 1754-1832 .... **NCLC 26**
See also DLB 93

Craddock, Charles Egbert
See Murfree, Mary Noailles

Craig, A. A.
See Anderson, Poul (William)

Craik, Dinah Maria (Mulock) 1826-1887 **NCLC 38**
See also DLB 35, 163; MAICYA; SATA 34

Cram, Ralph Adams 1863-1942 ..... **TCLC 45**
See also CA 160

Crane, (Harold) Hart 1899-1932 **TCLC 2, 5, 80; DA; DAB; DAC; DAM MST, POET; PC 3; WLC**

113; HW 1, 2; MTCW 1, 2

Donovan, John 1928-1992 .... **CLC 35**
See also AAYA 20; CA 97-100; 137; CLR 3;
MAICYA; SATA 72; SATA-Brief 29

Don Roberto
See Cunninghame Graham, R(obert) B(ontine)

Doolittle, Hilda 1886-1961 **CLC 3, 8, 14, 31, 34, 73; DA; DAC; DAM MST, POET; PC 5; WLC**
See also H. D.
See also CA 97-100; CANR 35; DLB 4, 45; MTCW 1, 2

Dorfman, Ariel 1942- ...... **CLC 48, 77; DAM MULT; HLC**
See also CA 124; 130; CANR 67, 70; HW 1, 2; INT 130

Dorn, Edward (Merton) 1929- ... **CLC 10, 18**
See also CA 93-96; CANR 42, 79; DLB 5; INT 93-96

Dorris, Michael (Anthony) 1945-1997 .. **C L C 109; DAM MULT, NOV**
See also AAYA 20; BEST 90:1; CA 102; 157; CANR 19, 46, 75; DLB 175; MTCW 2; NNAL; SATA 75; SATA-Obit 94

Dorris, Michael A.
See Dorris, Michael (Anthony)

Dorsan, Luc
See Simenon, Georges (Jacques Christian)

Dorsange, Jean
See Simenon, Georges (Jacques Christian)

Dos Passos, John (Roderigo) 1896-1970 **C L C 1, 4, 8, 11, 15, 25, 34, 82; DA; DAB; DAC; DAM MST, NOV; WLC**
See also CA 1-4R; 29-32R; CANR 3; CDALB 1929-1941; DLB 4, 9; DLBD 1, 15; DLBY 96; MTCW 1, 2

Dossage, Jean
See Simenon, Georges (Jacques Christian)

Dostoevsky, Fedor Mikhailovich 1821-1881 **NCLC 2, 7, 21, 33, 43; DA; DAB; DAC; DAM MST, NOV; SSC 2, 33; WLC**

Doughty, Charles M(ontagu) 1843-1926 **TCLC 27**
See also CA 115; DLB 19, 57, 174

Douglas, Ellen .... **CLC 73**
See also Haxton, Josephine Ayres; Williamson, Ellen Douglas

Douglas, Gavin 1475(?)-1522 .... **LC 20**
See also DLB 132

Douglas, George
See Brown, George Douglas

Douglas, Keith (Castellain) 1920-1944 **T C L C 40**
See also CA 160; DLB 27

Douglas, Leonard
See Bradbury, Ray (Douglas)

Douglas, Michael
See Crichton, (John) Michael

Douglas, (George) Norman 1868-1952 **T C L C 68**
See also CA 119; 157; DLB 34, 195

Douglas, William
See Brown, George Douglas

Douglass, Frederick 1817(?)-1895 **NCLC 7, 55; BLC 1; DA; DAC; DAM MST, MULT; WLC**
See also CDALB 1640-1865; DLB 1, 43, 50, 79; SATA 29

Dourado, (Waldomiro Freitas) Autran 1926- **CLC 23, 60**
See also CA 25-28R; CANR 34; DLB 145; HW 2

Dourado, Waldomiro Autran

See Dourado, (Waldomiro Freitas) Autran

Dove, Rita (Frances) 1952-**CLC 50, 81; BLCS; DAM MULT, POET; PC 6**
See also BW 2; CA 109; CAAS 19; CANR 27, 42, 68, 76; CDALBS; DLB 120; MTCW 1

Doveglion
See Villa, Jose Garcia

Dowell, Coleman 1925-1985 .... **CLC 60**
See also CA 25-28R; 117; CANR 10; DLB 130

Dowson, Ernest (Christopher) 1867-1900 **TCLC 4**
See also CA 105; 150; DLB 19, 135

Doyle, A. Conan
See Doyle, Arthur Conan

Doyle, Arthur Conan 1859-1930 **TCLC 7; DA; DAB; DAC; DAM MST, NOV; SSC 12; WLC**
See also AAYA 14; CA 104; 122; CDBLB 1890-1914; DLB 18, 70, 156, 178; MTCW 1, 2; SATA 24

Doyle, Conan
See Doyle, Arthur Conan

Doyle, John
See Graves, Robert (von Ranke)

Doyle, Roddy 1958(?)- .... **CLC 81**
See also AAYA 14; CA 143; CANR 73; DLB 194

Doyle, Sir A. Conan
See Doyle, Arthur Conan

Doyle, Sir Arthur Conan
See Doyle, Arthur Conan

Dr. A
See Asimov, Isaac; Silverstein, Alvin

Drabble, Margaret 1939-**CLC 2, 3, 5, 8, 10, 22, 53; DAB; DAC; DAM MST, NOV, POP**
See also CA 13-16R; CANR 18, 35, 63; CDBLB 1960 to Present; DLB 14, 155; MTCW 1, 2; SATA 48

Drapier, M. B.
See Swift, Jonathan

Drayham, James
See Mencken, H(enry) L(ouis)

Drayton, Michael 1563-1631 ...... **LC 8; DAM POET**
See also DLB 121

Dreadstone, Carl
See Campbell, (John) Ramsey

Dreiser, Theodore (Herman Albert) 1871-1945 **TCLC 10, 18, 35, 83; DA; DAC; DAM MST, NOV; SSC 30**
See also CA 106; 132; CDALB 1865-1917; DLB 9, 12, 102, 137; DLBD 1; MTCW 1, 2

Drexler, Rosalyn 1926- .... **CLC 2, 6**
See also CA 81-84; CANR 68

Dreyer, Carl Theodor 1889-1968 ...... **CLC 16**
See also CA 116

Drieu la Rochelle, Pierre(-Eugene) 1893-1945 **TCLC 21**
See also CA 117; DLB 72

Drinkwater, John 1882-1937 .... **TCLC 57**
See also CA 109; 149; DLB 10, 19, 149

Drop Shot
See Cable, George Washington

Droste-Hulshoff, Annette Freiin von 1797-1848 **NCLC 3**
See also DLB 133

Drummond, Walter
See Silverberg, Robert

Drummond, William Henry 1854-1907 **T C L C 25**
See also CA 160; DLB 92

Drummond de Andrade, Carlos 1902-1987 **CLC 18**

See also Andrade, Carlos Drummond de
See also CA 132; 123

Drury, Allen (Stuart) 1918-1998 .... **CLC 37**
See also CA 57-60; 170; CANR 18, 52; INT CANR-18

Dryden, John 1631-1700 **LC 3, 21; DA; DAB; DAC; DAM DRAM, MST, POET; DC 3; PC 25; WLC**
See also CDBLB 1660-1789; DLB 80, 101, 131

Duberman, Martin (Bauml) 1930- ..... **CLC 8**
See also CA 1-4R; CANR 2, 63

Dubie, Norman (Evans) 1945- .... **CLC 36**
See also CA 69-72; CANR 12; DLB 120

Du Bois, W(illiam) E(dward) B(urghardt) 1868-1963 .. **CLC 1, 2, 13, 64, 96; BLC 1; DA; DAC; DAM MST, MULT, NOV; WLC**
See also BW 1, 3; CA 85-88; CANR 34; CDALB 1865-1917; DLB 47, 50, 91; MTCW 1, 2; SATA 42

Dubus, Andre 1936- **CLC 13, 36, 97; SSC 15**
See also CA 21-24R; CANR 17; DLB 130; INT CANR-17

Duca Minimo
See D'Annunzio, Gabriele

Ducharme, Rejean 1941- .... **CLC 74**
See also CA 165; DLB 60

Duclos, Charles Pinot 1704-1772 .... **LC 1**

Dudek, Louis 1918- .... **CLC 11, 19**
See also CA 45-48; CAAS 14; CANR 1; DLB 88

Duerrenmatt, Friedrich 1921-1990 **CLC 1, 4, 8, 11, 15, 43, 102; DAM DRAM**
See also CA 17-20R; CANR 33; DLB 69, 124; MTCW 1, 2

Duffy, Bruce 1953(?)- .... **CLC 50**
See also CA 172

Duffy, Maureen 1933- .... **CLC 37**
See also CA 25-28R; CANR 33, 68; DLB 14; MTCW 1

Dugan, Alan 1923- .... **CLC 2, 6**
See also CA 81-84; DLB 5

du Gard, Roger Martin
See Martin du Gard, Roger

Duhamel, Georges 1884-1966 .... **CLC 8**
See also CA 81-84; 25-28R; CANR 35; DLB 65; MTCW 1

Dujardin, Edouard (Emile Louis) 1861-1949 **TCLC 13**
See also CA 109; DLB 123

Dulles, John Foster 1888-1959 .... **TCLC 72**
See also CA 115; 149

Dumas, Alexandre (pere)
See Dumas, Alexandre (Davy de la Pailleterie)

Dumas, Alexandre (Davy de la Pailleterie) 1802-1870 .. **NCLC 11; DA; DAB; DAC; DAM MST, NOV; WLC**
See also DLB 119, 192; SATA 18

Dumas, Alexandre (fils) 1824-1895 **NCLC 71; DC 1**
See also AAYA 22; DLB 192

Dumas, Claudine
See Malzberg, Barry N(athaniel)

Dumas, Henry L. 1934-1968 .... **CLC 6, 62**
See also BW 1; CA 85-88; DLB 41

du Maurier, Daphne 1907-1989 **CLC 6, 11, 59; DAB; DAC; DAM MST, POP; SSC 18**
See also CA 5-8R; 128; CANR 6, 55; DLB 191; MTCW 1, 2; SATA 27; SATA-Obit 60

Dunbar, Paul Laurence 1872-1906 . **TCLC 2, 12; BLC 1; DA; DAC; DAM MST, MULT, POET; PC 5; SSC 8; WLC**
See also BW 1, 3; CA 104; 124; CANR 79; CDALB 1865-1917; DLB 50, 54, 78; SATA

40

Fisher, Rudolph 1897-1934 **TCLC 11; BLC 2;**
  DAM MULT; SSC 25
  See also BW 1, 3; CA 107; 124; CANR 80; DLB
  51, 102
Fisher, Vardis (Alvero) 1895-1968 ...... **CLC 7**
  See also CA 5-8R; 25-28R; CANR 68; DLB 9,
  206
Fiske, Tarleton
  See Bloch, Robert (Albert)
Fitch, Clarke
  See Sinclair, Upton (Beall)
Fitch, John IV
  See Cormier, Robert (Edmund)
Fitzgerald, Captain Hugh
  See Baum, L(yman) Frank
FitzGerald, Edward 1809-1883 .... **NCLC 9**
  See also DLB 32
Fitzgerald, F(rancis) Scott (Key) 1896-1940
  TCLC 1, 6, 14, 28, 55; DA; DAB; DAC;
  DAM MST, NOV; SSC 6, 31; WLC
  See also AAYA 24; AITN 1; CA 110; 123;
  CDALB 1917-1929; DLB 4, 9, 86; DLBD 1,
  15, 16; DLBY 81, 96; MTCW 1, 2
Fitzgerald, Penelope 1916- ... **CLC 19, 51, 61**
  See also CA 85-88; CAAS 10; CANR 56; DLB
  14, 194; MTCW 2
Fitzgerald, Robert (Stuart) 1910-1985 **CLC 39**
  See also CA 1-4R; 114; CANR 1; DLBY 80
FitzGerald, Robert D(avid) 1902-1987 **CLC 19**
  See also CA 17-20R
Fitzgerald, Zelda (Sayre) 1900-1948 **TCLC 52**
  See also CA 117; 126; DLBY 84
Flanagan, Thomas (James Bonner) 1923-
  CLC 25, 52
  See also CA 108; CANR 55; DLBY 80; INT
  108; MTCW 1
Flaubert, Gustave 1821-1880 **NCLC 2, 10, 19,**
  62, 66; DA; DAB; DAC; DAM MST, NOV;
  SSC 11; WLC
  See also DLB 119
Flecker, Herman Elroy
  See Flecker, (Herman) James Elroy
Flecker, (Herman) James Elroy 1884-1915
  TCLC 43
  See also CA 109; 150; DLB 10, 19
Fleming, Ian (Lancaster) 1908-1964 . **CLC 3,**
  30; DAM POP
  See also AAYA 26; CA 5-8R; CANR 59;
  CDBLB 1945-1960; DLB 87, 201; MTCW
  1, 2; SATA 9
Fleming, Thomas (James) 1927- .... **CLC 37**
  See also CA 5-8R; CANR 10; INT CANR-10;
  SATA 8
Fletcher, John 1579-1625 .... **LC 33; DC 6**
  See also CDBLB Before 1660; DLB 58
Fletcher, John Gould 1886-1950 .... **TCLC 35**
  See also CA 107; 167; DLB 4, 45
Fleur, Paul
  See Pohl, Frederik
Flooglebuckle, Al
  See Spiegelman, Art
Flying Officer X
  See Bates, H(erbert) E(rnest)
Fo, Dario 1926- **CLC 32, 109; DAM DRAM;**
  DC 10
  See also CA 116; 128; CANR 68; DLBY 97;
  MTCW 1, 2
Fogarty, Jonathan Titulescu Esq.
  See Farrell, James T(homas)
Folke, Will
  See Bloch, Robert (Albert)
Follett, Ken(neth Martin) 1949- ..... **CLC 18;**

DAM NOV, POP
  See also AAYA 6; BEST 89:4; CA 81-84; CANR
  13, 33, 54; DLB 87; DLBY 81; INT CANR-
  33; MTCW 1
Fontane, Theodor 1819-1898 .... **NCLC 26**
  See also DLB 129
Foote, Horton 1916- **CLC 51, 91; DAM DRAM**
  See also CA 73-76; CANR 34, 51; DLB 26; INT
  CANR-34
Foote, Shelby 1916- **CLC 75; DAM NOV, POP**
  See also CA 5-8R; CANR 3, 45, 74; DLB 2,
  17; MTCW 2
Forbes, Esther 1891-1967 .... **CLC 12**
  See also AAYA 17; CA 13-14; 25-28R; CAP 1;
  CLR 27; DLB 22; JRDA; MAICYA; SATA
  2, 100
Forche, Carolyn (Louise) 1950- **CLC 25, 83,**
  86; DAM POET; PC 10
  See also CA 109; 117; CANR 50, 74; DLB 5,
  193; INT 117; MTCW 1
Ford, Elbur
  See Hibbert, Eleanor Alice Burford
Ford, Ford Madox 1873-1939 **TCLC 1, 15, 39,**
  57; DAM NOV
  See also CA 104; 132; CANR 74; CDBLB
  1914-1945; DLB 162; MTCW 1, 2
Ford, Henry 1863-1947 .... **TCLC 73**
  See also CA 115; 148
Ford, John 1586-(?) .... **DC 8**
  See also CDBLB Before 1660; DAM DRAM;
  DLB 58
Ford, John 1895-1973 .... **CLC 16**
  See also CA 45-48
Ford, Richard 1944- .... **CLC 46, 99**
  See also CA 69-72; CANR 11, 47; MTCW 1
Ford, Webster
  See Masters, Edgar Lee
Foreman, Richard 1937- .... **CLC 50**
  See also CA 65-68; CANR 32, 63
Forester, C(ecil) S(cott) 1899-1966 ... **CLC 35**
  See also CA 73-76; 25-28R; DLB 191; SATA
  13
Forez
  See Mauriac, Francois (Charles)
Forman, James Douglas 1932- .... **CLC 21**
  See also AAYA 17; CA 9-12R; CANR 4, 19,
  42; JRDA; MAICYA; SATA 8, 70
Fornes, Maria Irene 1930- **CLC 39, 61; DC 10;**
  HLCS 1
  See also CA 25-28R; CANR 28; DLB 7; HW 1,
  2; INT CANR-28; MTCW 1
Forrest, Leon (Richard) 1937-1997 .. **CLC 4;**
  BLCS
  See also BW 2; CA 89-92; 162; CAAS 7; CANR
  25, 52; DLB 33
Forster, E(dward) M(organ) 1879-1970 **C L C**
  1, 2, 3, 4, 9, 10, 13, 15, 22, 45, 77; DA; DAB;
  DAC; DAM MST, NOV; SSC 27; WLC
  See also AAYA 2; CA 13-14; 25-28R; CANR
  45; CAP 1; CDBLB 1914-1945; DLB 34, 98,
  162, 178, 195; DLBD 10; MTCW 1, 2; SATA
  57
Forster, John 1812-1876 .... **NCLC 11**
  See also DLB 144, 184
Forsyth, Frederick 1938- **CLC 2, 5, 36; DAM**
  NOV, POP
  See also BEST 89:4; CA 85-88; CANR 38, 62;
  DLB 87; MTCW 1, 2
Forten, Charlotte L. .... **TCLC 16; BLC 2**
  See also Grimke, Charlotte L(ottie) Forten
  See also DLB 50
Foscolo, Ugo 1778-1827 .... **NCLC 8**
Fosse, Bob .... **CLC 20**

See also Fosse, Robert Louis
Fosse, Robert Louis 1927-1987
  See Fosse, Bob
  See also CA 110; 123
Foster, Stephen Collins 1826-1864 **NCLC 26**
Foucault, Michel 1926-1984 . **CLC 31, 34, 69**
  See also CA 105; 113; CANR 34; MTCW 1, 2
Fouque, Friedrich (Heinrich Karl) de la Motte
  1777-1843 .... **NCLC 2**
  See also DLB 90
Fourier, Charles 1772-1837 .... **NCLC 51**
Fournier, Henri Alban 1886-1914
  See Alain-Fournier
  See also CA 104
Fournier, Pierre 1916- .... **CLC 11**
  See also Gascar, Pierre
  See also CA 89-92; CANR 16, 40
Fowles, John (Philip) 1926- **CLC 1, 2, 3, 4, 6,**
  9, 10, 15, 33, 87; DAB; DAC; DAM MST;
  SSC 33
  See also CA 5-8R; CANR 25, 71; CDBLB 1960
  to Present; DLB 14, 139, 207; MTCW 1, 2;
  SATA 22
Fox, Paula 1923- .... **CLC 2, 8**
  See also AAYA 3; CA 73-76; CANR 20, 36,
  62; CLR 1, 44; DLB 52; JRDA; MAICYA;
  MTCW 1; SATA 17, 60
Fox, William Price (Jr.) 1926- .... **CLC 22**
  See also CA 17-20R; CAAS 19; CANR 11; DLB
  2; DLBY 81
Foxe, John 1516(?)-1587 .... **LC 14**
  See also DLB 132
Frame, Janet 1924- **CLC 2, 3, 6, 22, 66, 96; SSC**
  29
  See also Clutha, Janet Paterson Frame
France, Anatole .... **TCLC 9**
  See also Thibault, Jacques Anatole Francois
  See also DLB 123; MTCW 1
Francis, Claude 19(?)- .... **CLC 50**
Francis, Dick 1920- **CLC 2, 22, 42, 102; DAM**
  POP
  See also AAYA 5, 21; BEST 89:3; CA 5-8R;
  CANR 9, 42, 68; CDBLB 1960 to Present;
  DLB 87; INT CANR-9; MTCW 1, 2
Francis, Robert (Churchill) 1901-1987 **C L C**
  15
  See also CA 1-4R; 123; CANR 1
Frank, Anne(lies Marie) 1929-1945 **TCLC 17;**
  DA; DAB; DAC; DAM MST; WLC
  See also AAYA 12; CA 113; 133; CANR 68;
  MTCW 1, 2; SATA 87; SATA-Brief 42
Frank, Bruno 1887-1945 .... **TCLC 81**
  See also DLB 118
Frank, Elizabeth 1945- .... **CLC 39**
  See also CA 121; 126; CANR 78; INT 126
Frankl, Viktor E(mil) 1905-1997 ...... **CLC 93**
  See also CA 65-68; 161
Franklin, Benjamin
  See Hasek, Jaroslav (Matej Frantisek)
Franklin, Benjamin 1706-1790 .. **LC 25; DA;**
  DAB; DAC; DAM MST; WLCS
  See also CDALB 1640-1865; DLB 24, 43, 73
Franklin, (Stella Maria Sarah) Miles (Lampe)
  1879-1954 .... **TCLC 7**
  See also CA 104; 164
Fraser, (Lady) Antonia (Pakenham) 1932-
  CLC 32, 107
  See also CA 85-88; CANR 44, 65; MTCW 1,
  2; SATA-Brief 32
Fraser, George MacDonald 1925- ...... **CLC 7**
  See also CA 45-48; CANR 2, 48, 74; MTCW 1
Fraser, Sylvia 1935- .... **CLC 64**
  See also CA 45-48; CANR 1, 16, 60

12; DLB 14, 161; MAICYA; MTCW 1;
SAAS 9; SATA 39, 76; SATA-Brief 28

Gardner, Herb(ert) 1934- .... **CLC 44**
　See also CA 149

Gardner, John (Champlin), Jr. 1933-1982
　**CLC 2, 3, 5, 7, 8, 10, 18, 28, 34; DAM NOV,
　POP; SSC 7**
　　See also AITN 1; CA 65-68; 107; CANR 33,
　　73; CDALBS; DLB 2; DLBY 82; MTCW 1;
　　SATA 40; SATA-Obit 31

Gardner, John (Edmund) 1926-**CLC 30; DAM
　POP**
　　See also CA 103; CANR 15, 69; MTCW 1

Gardner, Miriam
　See Bradley, Marion Zimmer

Gardner, Noel
　See Kuttner, Henry

Gardons, S. S.
　See Snodgrass, W(illiam) D(e Witt)

Garfield, Leon 1921-1996 .... **CLC 12**
　　See also AAYA 8; CA 17-20R; 152; CANR 38,
　　41, 78; CLR 21; DLB 161; JRDA; MAICYA;
　　SATA 1, 32, 76; SATA-Obit 90

Garland, (Hannibal) Hamlin 1860-1940
　TCLC 3; SSC 18
　　See also CA 104; DLB 12, 71, 78, 186

Garneau, (Hector de) Saint-Denys 1912-1943
　TCLC 13
　　See also CA 111; DLB 88

Garner, Alan 1934-**CLC 17; DAB; DAM POP**
　　See also AAYA 18; CA 73-76; CANR 15, 64;
　　CLR 20; DLB 161; MAICYA; MTCW 1, 2;
　　SATA 18, 69

Garner, Hugh 1913-1979 .... **CLC 13**
　　See also CA 69-72; CANR 31; DLB 68

Garnett, David 1892-1981 .... **CLC 3**
　　See also CA 5-8R; 103; CANR 17, 79; DLB
　　34; MTCW 2

Garos, Stephanie
　See Katz, Steve

Garrett, George (Palmer) 1929-**CLC 3, 11, 51;
　SSC 30**
　　See also CA 1-4R; CAAS 5; CANR 1, 42, 67;
　　DLB 2, 5, 130, 152; DLBY 83

Garrick, David 1717-1779 .... **LC 15; DAM
　DRAM**
　　See also DLB 84

Garrigue, Jean 1914-1972 .... **CLC 2, 8**
　　See also CA 5-8R; 37-40R; CANR 20

Garrison, Frederick
　See Sinclair, Upton (Beall)

Garth, Will
　See Hamilton, Edmond; Kuttner, Henry

Garvey, Marcus (Moziah, Jr.) 1887-1940
　TCLC 41; BLC 2; DAM MULT
　　See also BW 1; CA 120; 124; CANR 79

Gary, Romain .... **CLC 25**
　　See also Kacew, Romain
　　See also DLB 83

Gascar, Pierre .... **CLC 11**
　　See also Fournier, Pierre

Gascoyne, David (Emery) 1916- .... **CLC 45**
　　See also CA 65-68; CANR 10, 28, 54; DLB 20;
　　MTCW 1

Gaskell, Elizabeth Cleghorn 1810-1865**NCLC
　70; DAB; DAM MST; SSC 25**
　　See also CDBLB 1832-1890; DLB 21, 144, 159

Gass, William H(oward) 1924-**CLC 1, 2, 8, 11,
　15, 39; SSC 12**
　　See also CA 17-20R; CANR 30, 71; DLB 2;
　　MTCW 1, 2

Gasset, Jose Ortega y
　See Ortega y Gasset, Jose

Gates, Henry Louis, Jr. 1950-**CLC 65; BLCS;
　DAM MULT**
　　See also BW 2, 3; CA 109; CANR 25, 53, 75;
　　DLB 67; MTCW 1

Gautier, Theophile 1811-1872 .. **NCLC 1, 59;
　DAM POET; PC 18; SSC 20**
　　See also DLB 119

Gawsworth, John
　See Bates, H(erbert) E(rnest)

Gay, John 1685-1732 ... **LC 49; DAM DRAM**
　　See also DLB 84, 95

Gay, Oliver
　See Gogarty, Oliver St. John

Gaye, Marvin (Penze) 1939-1984 ..... **CLC 26**
　　See also CA 112

Gebler, Carlo (Ernest) 1954- .... **CLC 39**
　　See also CA 119; 133

Gee, Maggie (Mary) 1948- .... **CLC 57**
　　See also CA 130; DLB 207

Gee, Maurice (Gough) 1931- .... **CLC 29**
　　See also CA 97-100; CANR 67; CLR 56; SATA
　　46, 101

Gelbart, Larry (Simon) 1923- .... **CLC 21, 61**
　　See also CA 73-76; CANR 45

Gelber, Jack 1932- .... **CLC 1, 6, 14, 79**
　　See also CA 1-4R; CANR 2; DLB 7

Gellhorn, Martha (Ellis) 1908-1998 **CLC 14,
　60**
　　See also CA 77-80; 164; CANR 44; DLBY 82,
　　98

Genet, Jean 1910-1986**CLC 1, 2, 5, 10, 14, 44,
　46; DAM DRAM**
　　See also CA 13-16R; CANR 18; DLB 72;
　　DLBY 86; MTCW 1, 2

Gent, Peter 1942- .... **CLC 29**
　　See also AITN 1; CA 89-92; DLBY 82

Gentlewoman in New England, A
　See Bradstreet, Anne

Gentlewoman in Those Parts, A
　See Bradstreet, Anne

George, Jean Craighead 1919- .... **CLC 35**
　　See also AAYA 8; CA 5-8R; CANR 25; CLR 1;
　　DLB 52; JRDA; MAICYA; SATA 2, 68

George, Stefan (Anton) 1868-1933**TCLC 2, 14**
　　See also CA 104

Georges, Georges Martin
　See Simenon, Georges (Jacques Christian)

Gerhardi, William Alexander
　See Gerhardie, William Alexander

Gerhardie, William Alexander 1895-1977
　CLC 5
　　See also CA 25-28R; 73-76; CANR 18; DLB
　　36

Gerstler, Amy 1956- .... **CLC 70**
　　See also CA 146

Gertler, T. .... **CLC 34**
　　See also CA 116; 121; INT 121

Ghalib .... **NCLC 39**
　　See also Ghalib, Hsadullah Khan

Ghalib, Hsadullah Khan 1797-1869
　　See Ghalib
　　See also DAM POET

Ghelderode, Michel de 1898-1962**CLC 6, 11;
　DAM DRAM**
　　See also CA 85-88; CANR 40, 77

Ghiselin, Brewster 1903- .... **CLC 23**
　　See also CA 13-16R; CAAS 10; CANR 13

Ghose, Aurabinda 1872-1950 .... **TCLC 63**
　　See also CA 163

Ghose, Zulfikar 1935- .... **CLC 42**
　　See also CA 65-68; CANR 67

Ghosh, Amitav 1956- .... **CLC 44**
　　See also CA 147; CANR 80

Giacosa, Giuseppe 1847-1906 .... **TCLC 7**
　　See also CA 104

Gibb, Lee
　See Waterhouse, Keith (Spencer)

Gibbon, Lewis Grassic .... **TCLC 4**
　　See also Mitchell, James Leslie

Gibbons, Kaye 1960-**CLC 50, 88; DAM POP**
　　See also CA 151; CANR 75; MTCW 2

Gibran, Kahlil 1883-1931 . **TCLC 1, 9; DAM
　POET, POP; PC 9**
　　See also CA 104; 150; MTCW 2

Gibran, Khalil
　See Gibran, Kahlil

Gibson, William 1914- .. **CLC 23; DA; DAB;
　DAC; DAM DRAM, MST**
　　See also CA 9-12R; CANR 9, 42, 75; DLB 7;
　　MTCW 1; SATA 66

Gibson, William (Ford) 1948- ... **CLC 39, 63;
　DAM POP**
　　See also AAYA 12; CA 126; 133; CANR 52;
　　MTCW 1

Gide, Andre (Paul Guillaume) 1869-1951
　**TCLC 5, 12, 36; DA; DAB; DAC; DAM
　MST, NOV; SSC 13; WLC**
　　See also CA 104; 124; DLB 65; MTCW 1, 2

Gifford, Barry (Colby) 1946- .... **CLC 34**
　　See also CA 65-68; CANR 9, 30, 40

Gilbert, Frank
　See De Voto, Bernard (Augustine)

Gilbert, W(illiam) S(chwenck) 1836-1911
　TCLC 3; DAM DRAM, POET
　　See also CA 104; 173; SATA 36

Gilbreth, Frank B., Jr. 1911- .... **CLC 17**
　　See also CA 9-12R; SATA 2

Gilchrist, Ellen 1935-**CLC 34, 48; DAM POP;
　SSC 14**
　　See also CA 113; 116; CANR 41, 61; DLB 130;
　　MTCW 1, 2

Giles, Molly 1942- .... **CLC 39**
　　See also CA 126

Gill, Eric 1882-1940 .... **TCLC 85**

Gill, Patrick
　See Creasey, John

Gilliam, Terry (Vance) 1940- .... **CLC 21**
　　See also Monty Python
　　See also AAYA 19; CA 108; 113; CANR 35;
　　INT 113

Gillian, Jerry
　See Gilliam, Terry (Vance)

Gilliatt, Penelope (Ann Douglass) 1932-1993
　CLC 2, 10, 13, 53
　　See also AITN 2; CA 13-16R; 141; CANR 49;
　　DLB 14

Gilman, Charlotte (Anna) Perkins (Stetson)
　1860-1935 .... **TCLC 9, 37; SSC 13**
　　See also CA 106; 150; MTCW 1

Gilmour, David 1949- .... **CLC 35**
　　See also CA 138; 147

Gilpin, William 1724-1804 .... **NCLC 30**

Gilray, J. D.
　See Mencken, H(enry) L(ouis)

Gilroy, Frank D(aniel) 1925- .... **CLC 2**
　　See also CA 81-84; CANR 32, 64; DLB 7

Gilstrap, John 1957(?)- .... **CLC 99**
　　See also CA 160

Ginsberg, Allen 1926-1997**CLC 1, 2, 3, 4, 6, 13,
　36, 69, 109; DA; DAB; DAC; DAM MST,
　POET; PC 4; WLC**
　　See also AITN 1; CA 1-4R; 157; CANR 2, 41,
　　63; CDALB 1941-1968; DLB 5, 16, 169;
　　MTCW 1, 2

Ginzburg, Natalia 1916-1991**CLC 5, 11, 54, 70**
　　See also CA 85-88; 135; CANR 33; DLB 177;

MTCW 1, 2

Giono, Jean 1895-1970 .... CLC 4, 11
See also CA 45-48; 29-32R; CANR 2, 35; DLB
72; MTCW 1

Giovanni, Nikki 1943- CLC 2, 4, 19, 64, 117;
BLC 2; DA; DAB; DAC; DAM MST,
MULT, POET; PC 19; WLCS
See also AAYA 22; AITN 1; BW 2, 3; CA 29-
32R; CAAS 6; CANR 18, 41, 60; CDALBS;
CLR 6; DLB 5, 41; INT CANR-18;
MAICYA; MTCW 1, 2, SATA 24, 107

Giovene, Andrea 1904- .... CLC 7
See also CA 85-88

Gippius, Zinaida (Nikolayevna) 1869-1945
See Hippius, Zinaida
See also CA 106

Giraudoux, (Hippolyte) Jean 1882-1944
TCLC 2, 7; DAM DRAM
See also CA 104; DLB 65

Gironella, Jose Maria 1917- .... CLC 11
See also CA 101

Gissing, George (Robert) 1857-1903TCLC 3,
24, 47
See also CA 105; 167; DLB 18, 135, 184

Giurlani, Aldo
See Palazzeschi, Aldo

Gladkov, Fyodor (Vasilyevich) 1883-1958
TCLC 27
See also CA 170

Glanville, Brian (Lester) 1931- .... CLC 6
See also CA 5-8R; CAAS 9; CANR 3, 70; DLB
15, 139; SATA 42

Glasgow, Ellen (Anderson Gholson) 1873-1945
TCLC 2, 7; SSC 34
See also CA 104; 164; DLB 9, 12; MTCW 2

Glaspell, Susan 1882(?)-1948TCLC 55; DC 10
See also CA 110; 154; DLB 7, 9, 78; YABC 2

Glassco, John 1909-1981 .... CLC 9
See also CA 13-16R; 102; CANR 15; DLB 68

Glasscock, Amnesia
See Steinbeck, John (Ernst)

Glasser, Ronald J. 1940(?)- .... CLC 37

Glassman, Joyce
See Johnson, Joyce

Glendinning, Victoria 1937- .... CLC 50
See also CA 120; 127; CANR 59; DLB 155

Glissant, Edouard 1928- . CLC 10, 68; DAM
MULT
See also CA 153

Gloag, Julian 1930- .... CLC 40
See also AITN 1; CA 65-68; CANR 10, 70

Glowacki, Aleksander
See Prus, Boleslaw

Gluck, Louise (Elisabeth) 1943-CLC 7, 22, 44,
81; DAM POET; PC 16
See also CA 33-36R; CANR 40, 69; DLB 5;
MTCW 2

Glyn, Elinor 1864-1943 .... TCLC 72
See also DLB 153

Gobineau, Joseph Arthur (Comte) de 1816-
1882 .... NCLC 17
See also DLB 123

Godard, Jean-Luc 1930- .... CLC 20
See also CA 93-96

Godden, (Margaret) Rumer 1907-1998 C L C
53
See also AAYA 6; CA 5-8R; 172; CANR 4, 27,
36, 55, 80; CLR 20; DLB 161; MAICYA;
SAAS 12; SATA 3, 36

Godoy Alcayaga, Lucila 1889-1957
See Mistral, Gabriela
See also BW 2; CA 104; 131; DAM MULT; HW
1, 2; MTCW 1, 2

Godwin, Gail (Kathleen) 1937- CLC 5, 8, 22,
31, 69; DAM POP
See also CA 29-32R; CANR 15, 43, 69; DLB
6; INT CANR-15; MTCW 1, 2

Godwin, William 1756-1836 .... NCLC 14
See also CDBLB 1789-1832; DLB 39, 104, 142,
158, 163

Goebbels, Josef
See Goebbels, (Paul) Joseph

Goebbels, (Paul) Joseph 1897-1945TCLC 68
See also CA 115; 148

Goebbels, Joseph Paul
See Goebbels, (Paul) Joseph

Goethe, Johann Wolfgang von 1749-1832
NCLC 4, 22, 34; DA; DAB; DAC; DAM
DRAM, MST, POET; PC 5; WLC
See also DLB 94

Gogarty, Oliver St. John 1878-1957TCLC 15
See also CA 109; 150; DLB 15, 19

Gogol, Nikolai (Vasilyevich) 1809-1852NCLC
5, 15, 31; DA; DAB; DAC; DAM DRAM,
MST; DC 1; SSC 4, 29; WLC
See also DLB 198

Goines, Donald 1937(?)-1974CLC 80; BLC 2;
DAM MULT, POP
See also AITN 1; BW 1, 3; CA 124; 114; DLB
33

Gold, Herbert 1924- .... CLC 4, 7, 14, 42
See also CA 9-12R; CANR 17, 45; DLB 2;
DLBY 81

Goldbarth, Albert 1948- .... CLC 5, 38
See also CA 53-56; CANR 6, 40; DLB 120

Goldberg, Anatol 1910-1982 .... CLC 34
See also CA 131; 117

Goldemberg, Isaac 1945- .... CLC 52
See also CA 69-72; CAAS 12; CANR 11, 32;
HW 1

Golding, William (Gerald) 1911-1993CLC 1,
2, 3, 8, 10, 17, 27, 58, 81; DA; DAB; DAC;
DAM MST, NOV; WLC
See also AAYA 5; CA 5-8R; 141; CANR 13,
33, 54; CDBLB 1945-1960; DLB 15, 100;
MTCW 1, 2

Goldman, Emma 1869-1940 .... TCLC 13
See also CA 110; 150

Goldman, Francisco 1954- .... CLC 76
See also CA 162

Goldman, William (W.) 1931- .... CLC 1, 48
See also CA 9-12R; CANR 29, 69; DLB 44

Goldmann, Lucien 1913-1970 .... CLC 24
See also CA 25-28; CAP 2

Goldoni, Carlo 1707-1793LC 4; DAM DRAM

Goldsberry, Steven 1949- .... CLC 34
See also CA 131

Goldsmith, Oliver 1728-1774 . LC 2, 48; DA;
DAB; DAC; DAM DRAM, MST, NOV,
POET; DC 8; WLC
See also CDBLB 1660-1789; DLB 39, 89, 104,
109, 142; SATA 26

Goldsmith, Peter
See Priestley, J(ohn) B(oynton)

Gombrowicz, Witold 1904-1969CLC 4, 7, 11,
49; DAM DRAM
See also CA 19-20; 25-28R; CAP 2

Gomez de la Serna, Ramon 1888-1963CLC 9
See also CA 153; 116; CANR 79; HW 1, 2

Goncharov, Ivan Alexandrovich 1812-1891
NCLC 1, 63

Goncourt, Edmond (Louis Antoine Huot) de
1822-1896 .... NCLC 7
See also DLB 123

Goncourt, Jules (Alfred Huot) de 1830-1870
NCLC 7

See also DLB 123

Gontier, Fernande 19(?)- .... CLC 50

Gonzalez Martinez, Enrique 1871-1952
TCLC 72
See also CA 166; HW 1, 2

Goodman, Paul 1911-1972 ...... CLC 1, 2, 4, 7
See also CA 19-20; 37-40R; CANR 34; CAP 2;
DLB 130; MTCW 1

Gordimer, Nadine 1923-CLC 3, 5, 7, 10, 18, 33,
51, 70; DA; DAB; DAC;DAM MST, NOV;
SSC 17; WLCS
See also CA 5-8R; CANR 3, 28, 56; INT CANR-
28; MTCW 1, 2

Gordon, Adam Lindsay 1833-1870 NCLC 21

Gordon, Caroline 1895-1981CLC 6, 13, 29, 83;
SSC 15
See also CA 11-12; 103; CANR 36; CAP 1;
DLB 4, 9, 102; DLBD 17; DLBY 81; MTCW
1, 2

Gordon, Charles William 1860-1937
See Connor, Ralph
See also CA 109

Gordon, Mary (Catherine) 1949-CLC 13, 22
See also CA 102; CANR 44; DLB 6; DLBY
81; INT 102; MTCW 1

Gordon, N. J.
See Bosman, Herman Charles

Gordon, Sol 1923- .... CLC 26
See also CA 53-56; CANR 4; SATA 11

Gordone, Charles 1925-1995CLC 1, 4; DAM
DRAM; DC 8
See also BW 1, 3; CA 93-96; 150; CANR 55;
DLB 7; INT 93-96; MTCW 1

Gore, Catherine 1800-1861 .... NCLC 65
See also DLB 116

Gorenko, Anna Andreevna
See Akhmatova, Anna

Gorky, Maxim 1868-1936TCLC 8; DAB; SSC
28; WLC
See also Peshkov, Alexei Maximovich
See also MTCW 2

Goryan, Sirak
See Saroyan, William

Gosse, Edmund (William) 1849-1928TCLC 28
See also CA 117; DLB 57, 144, 184

Gotlieb, Phyllis Fay (Bloom) 1926- .. CLC 18
See also CA 13-16R; CANR 7; DLB 88

Gottesman, S. D.
See Kornbluth, C(yril) M.; Pohl, Frederik

Gottfried von Strassburg fl. c. 1210- C M L C
10
See also DLB 138

Gould, Lois .... CLC 4, 10
See also CA 77-80; CANR 29; MTCW 1

Gourmont, Remy (-Marie-Charles) de 1858-
1915 .... TCLC 17
See also CA 109; 150; MTCW 2

Govier, Katherine 1948- .... CLC 51
See also CA 101; CANR 18, 40

Goyen, (Charles) William 1915-1983CLC 5, 8,
14, 40
See also AITN 2; CA 5-8R; 110; CANR 6, 71;
DLB 2; DLBY 83; INT CANR-6

Goytisolo, Juan 1931- . CLC 5, 10, 23; DAM
MULT; HLC
See also CA 85-88; CANR 32, 61; HW 1, 2;
MTCW 1, 2

Gozzano, Guido 1883-1916 .... PC 10
See also CA 154; DLB 114

Gozzi, (Conte) Carlo 1720-1806 .... NCLC 23

Grabbe, Christian Dietrich 1801-1836N C L C
2
See also DLB 133

See also CA 122; MTCW 2

Hayden, Robert E(arl) 1913-1980 . CLC **5, 9, 14, 37; BLC 2; DA; DAC; DAM MST, MULT, POET; PC 6**
See also BW 1, 3; CA 69-72; 97-100; CABS 2; CANR 24, 75; CDALB 1941-1968; DLB 5, 76; MTCW 1, 2; SATA 19; SATA-Obit 26

Hayford, J(oseph) E(phraim) Casely
See Casely-Hayford, J(oseph) E(phraim)

Hayman, Ronald 1932- .... CLC **44**
See also CA 25-28R; CANR 18, 50; DLB 155

Haywood, Eliza (Fowler) 1693(?)-1756 LC **1, 44**
See also DLB 39

Hazlitt, William 1778-1830 .... NCLC **29**
See also DLB 110, 158

Hazzard, Shirley 1931- .... CLC **18**
See also CA 9-12R; CANR 4, 70; DLBY 82; MTCW 1

Head, Bessie 1937-1986 CLC **25, 67; BLC 2; DAM MULT**
See also BW 2, 3; CA 29-32R; 119; CANR 25; DLB 117; MTCW 1, 2

Headon, (Nicky) Topper 1956(?)- ..... CLC **30**

Heaney, Seamus (Justin) 1939- CLC **5, 7, 14, 25, 37, 74, 91; DAB; DAM POET; PC 18; WLCS**
See also CA 85-88; CANR 25, 48, 75; CDBLB 1960 to Present; DLB 40; DLBY 95; MTCW 1, 2

Hearn, (Patricio) Lafcadio (Tessima Carlos) 1850-1904 .... TCLC **9**
See also CA 105; 166; DLB 12, 78, 189

Hearne, Vicki 1946- .... CLC **56**
See also CA 139

Hearon, Shelby 1931- .... CLC **63**
See also AITN 2; CA 25-28R; CANR 18, 48

Heat-Moon, William Least .... CLC **29**
See also Trogdon, William (Lewis)
See also AAYA 9

Hebbel, Friedrich 1813-1863 NCLC **43; DAM DRAM**
See also DLB 129

Hebert, Anne 1916- CLC **4, 13, 29; DAC; DAM MST, POET**
See also CA 85-88; CANR 69; DLB 68; MTCW 1, 2

Hecht, Anthony (Evan) 1923- CLC **8, 13, 19; DAM POET**
See also CA 9-12R; CANR 6; DLB 5, 169

Hecht, Ben 1894-1964 .... CLC **8**
See also CA 85-88; DLB 7, 9, 25, 26, 28, 86

Hedayat, Sadeq 1903-1951 .... TCLC **21**
See also CA 120

Hegel, Georg Wilhelm Friedrich 1770-1831 NCLC **46**
See also DLB 90

Heidegger, Martin 1889-1976 .... CLC **24**
See also CA 81-84; 65-68; CANR 34; MTCW 1, 2

Heidenstam, (Carl Gustaf) Verner von 1859-1940 .... TCLC **5**
See also CA 104

Heifner, Jack 1946- .... CLC **11**
See also CA 105; CANR 47

Heijermans, Herman 1864-1924 .... TCLC **24**
See also CA 123

Heilbrun, Carolyn G(old) 1926- .... CLC **25**
See also CA 45-48; CANR 1, 28, 58

Heine, Heinrich 1797-1856 NCLC **4, 54; PC 25**
See also DLB 90

Heinemann, Larry (Curtiss) 1944- ... CLC **50**
See also CA 110; CAAS 21; CANR 31; DLBD

9; INT CANR-31

Heiney, Donald (William) 1921-1993
See Harris, MacDonald
See also CA 1-4R; 142; CANR 3, 58

Heinlein, Robert A(nson) 1907-1988 CLC **1, 3, 8, 14, 26, 55; DAM POP**
See also AAYA 17; CA 1-4R; 125; CANR 1, 20, 53; DLB 8; JRDA; MAICYA; MTCW 1, 2; SATA 9, 69; SATA-Obit 56

Helforth, John
See Doolittle, Hilda

Hellenhofferu, Vojtech Kapristian z
See Hasek, Jaroslav (Matej Frantisek)

Heller, Joseph 1923- CLC **1, 3, 5, 8, 11, 36, 63; DA; DAB; DAC; DAM MST, NOV, POP; WLC**
See also AAYA 24; AITN 1; CA 5-8R; CABS 1; CANR 8, 42, 66; DLB 2, 28; DLBY 80; INT CANR-8; MTCW 1, 2

Hellman, Lillian (Florence) 1906-1984 CLC **2, 4, 8, 14, 18, 34, 44, 52; DAM DRAM; DC 1**
See also AITN 1, 2; CA 13-16R; 112; CANR 33; DLB 7; DLBY 84; MTCW 1, 2

Helprin, Mark 1947- CLC **7, 10, 22, 32; DAM NOV, POP**
See also CA 81-84; CANR 47, 64; CDALBS; DLBY 85; MTCW 1, 2

Helvetius, Claude-Adrien 1715-1771 .. LC **26**

Helyar, Jane Penelope Josephine 1933-
See Poole, Josephine
See also CA 21-24R; CANR 10, 26; SATA 82

Hemans, Felicia 1793-1835 .... NCLC **71**
See also DLB 96

Hemingway, Ernest (Miller) 1899-1961 C L C **1, 3, 6, 8, 10, 13, 19, 30, 34, 39, 41, 44, 50, 61, 80; DA; DAB; DAC; DAM MST, NOV; SSC 1, 25; WLC**
See also AAYA 19; CA 77-80; CANR 34; CDALB 1917-1929; DLB 4, 9, 102, 210; DLBD 1, 15, 16; DLBY 81, 87, 96, 98; MTCW 1, 2

Hempel, Amy 1951- .... CLC **39**
See also CA 118; 137; CANR 70; MTCW 2

Henderson, F. C.
See Mencken, H(enry) L(ouis)

Henderson, Sylvia
See Ashton-Warner, Sylvia (Constance)

Henderson, Zenna (Chlarson) 1917-1983 S S C **29**
See also CA 1-4R; 133; CANR 1; DLB 8; SATA 5

Henkin, Joshua .... CLC **119**
See also CA 161

Henley, Beth .... CLC **23; DC 6**
See also Henley, Elizabeth Becker
See also CABS 3; DLBY 86

Henley, Elizabeth Becker 1952-
See Henley, Beth
See also CA 107; CANR 32, 73; DAM DRAM, MST; MTCW 1, 2

Henley, William Ernest 1849-1903 .. TCLC **8**
See also CA 105; DLB 19

Hennissart, Martha
See Lathen, Emma
See also CA 85-88; CANR 64

Henry, O. .... TCLC **1, 19; SSC 5; WLC**
See also Porter, William Sydney

Henry, Patrick 1736-1799 .... LC **25**

Henryson, Robert 1430(?)-1506(?) ...... LC **20**
See also DLB 146

Henry VIII 1491-1547 .... LC **10**
See also DLB 132

Henschke, Alfred

See Klabund

Hentoff, Nat(han Irving) 1925- .... CLC **26**
See also AAYA 4; CA 1-4R; CAAS 6; CANR 5, 25, 77; CLR 1, 52; INT CANR-25; JRDA; MAICYA; SATA 42, 69; SATA-Brief 27

Heppenstall, (John) Rayner 1911-1981 C L C **10**
See also CA 1-4R; 103; CANR 29

Heraclitus c. 540B.C.-c. 450B.C. .. CMLC **22**
See also DLB 176

Herbert, Frank (Patrick) 1920-1986 CLC **12, 23, 35, 44, 85; DAM POP**
See also AAYA 21; CA 53-56; 118; CANR 5, 43; CDALBS; DLB 8; INT CANR-5; MTCW 1, 2; SATA 9, 37; SATA-Obit 47

Herbert, George 1593-1633 ..... LC **24; DAB; DAM POET; PC 4**
See also CDBLB Before 1660; DLB 126

Herbert, Zbigniew 1924-1998 ..... CLC **9, 43; DAM POET**
See also CA 89-92; 169; CANR 36, 74; MTCW 1

Herbst, Josephine (Frey) 1897-1969 CLC **34**
See also CA 5-8R; 25-28R; DLB 9

Hergesheimer, Joseph 1880-1954 .. TCLC **11**
See also CA 109; DLB 102, 9

Herlihy, James Leo 1927-1993 .... CLC **6**
See also CA 1-4R; 143; CANR 2

Hermogenes fl. c. 175- .... CMLC **6**

Hernandez, Jose 1834-1886 .... NCLC **17**

Herodotus c. 484B.C.-429B.C. ...... CMLC **17**
See also DLB 176

Herrick, Robert 1591-1674 LC **13; DA; DAB; DAC; DAM MST, POP; PC 9**
See also DLB 126

Herring, Guilles
See Somerville, Edith

Herriot, James 1916-1995 CLC **12; DAM POP**
See also Wight, James Alfred
See also AAYA 1; CA 148; CANR 40; MTCW 2; SATA 86

Herrmann, Dorothy 1941- .... CLC **44**
See also CA 107

Herrmann, Taffy
See Herrmann, Dorothy

Hersey, John (Richard) 1914-1993 CLC **1, 2, 7, 9, 40, 81, 97; DAM POP**
See also AAYA 29; CA 17-20R; 140; CANR 33; CDALBS; DLB 6, 185; MTCW 1, 2; SATA 25; SATA-Obit 76

Herzen, Aleksandr Ivanovich 1812-1870 NCLC **10, 61**

Herzl, Theodor 1860-1904 .... TCLC **36**
See also CA 168

Herzog, Werner 1942- .... CLC **16**
See also CA 89-92

Hesiod c. 8th cent. B.C.- .... CMLC **5**
See also DLB 176

Hesse, Hermann 1877-1962 CLC **1, 2, 3, 6, 11, 17, 25, 69; DA; DAB; DAC; DAM MST, NOV; SSC 9; WLC**
See also CA 17-18; CAP 2; DLB 66; MTCW 1, 2; SATA 50

Hewes, Cady
See De Voto, Bernard (Augustine)

Heyen, William 1940- .... CLC **13, 18**
See also CA 33-36R; CAAS 9; DLB 5

Heyerdahl, Thor 1914- .... CLC **26**
See also CA 5-8R; CANR 5, 22, 66, 73; MTCW 1, 2; SATA 2, 52

Heym, Georg (Theodor Franz Arthur) 1887-1912 .... TCLC **9**
See also CA 106

2

James, M. R.
See James, Montague (Rhodes)
See also DLB 156

James, Montague (Rhodes) 1862-1936 **T C L C 6; SSC 16**
See also CA 104; DLB 201

James, P. D. 1920- .... **CLC 18, 46**
See also White, Phyllis Dorothy James
See also BEST 90:2; CDBLB 1960 to Present; DLB 87; DLBD 17

James, Philip
See Moorcock, Michael (John)

James, William 1842-1910 .... **TCLC 15, 32**
See also CA 109

James I 1394-1437 .... **LC 20**

Jameson, Anna 1794-1860 .... **NCLC 43**
See also DLB 99, 166

Jami, Nur al-Din 'Abd al-Rahman 1414-1492 **LC 9**

Jammes, Francis 1868-1938 .... **TCLC 75**

Jandl, Ernst 1925- .... **CLC 34**

Janowitz, Tama 1957- .. **CLC 43; DAM POP**
See also CA 106; CANR 52

Japrisot, Sebastien 1931- .... **CLC 90**

Jarrell, Randall 1914-1965 **CLC 1, 2, 6, 9, 13, 49; DAM POET**
See also CA 5-8R; 25-28R; CABS 2; CANR 6, 34; CDALB 1941-1968; CLR 6; DLB 48, 52; MAICYA; MTCW 1, 2; SATA 7

Jarry, Alfred 1873-1907 .. **TCLC 2, 14; DAM DRAM; SSC 20**
See also CA 104; 153; DLB 192

Jarvis, E. K.
See Bloch, Robert (Albert); Ellison, Harlan (Jay); Silverberg, Robert

Jeake, Samuel, Jr.
See Aiken, Conrad (Potter)

Jean Paul 1763-1825 .... **NCLC 7**

Jefferies, (John) Richard 1848-1887 **NCLC 47**
See also DLB 98, 141; SATA 16

Jeffers, (John) Robinson 1887-1962 **CLC 2, 3, 11, 15, 54; DA; DAC; DAM MST, POET; PC 17; WLC**
See also CA 85-88; CANR 35; CDALB 1917-1929; DLB 45, 212; MTCW 1, 2

Jefferson, Janet
See Mencken, H(enry) L(ouis)

Jefferson, Thomas 1743-1826 .... **NCLC 11**
See also CDALB 1640-1865; DLB 31

Jeffrey, Francis 1773-1850 .... **NCLC 33**
See also DLB 107

Jelakowitch, Ivan
See Heijermans, Herman

Jellicoe, (Patricia) Ann 1927- .... **CLC 27**
See also CA 85-88; DLB 13

Jen, Gish .... **CLC 70**
See also Jen, Lillian

Jen, Lillian 1956(?)-
See Jen, Gish
See also CA 135

Jenkins, (John) Robin 1912- .... **CLC 52**
See also CA 1-4R; CANR 1; DLB 14

Jennings, Elizabeth (Joan) 1926- . **CLC 5, 14**
See also CA 61-64; CAAS 5; CANR 8, 39, 66; DLB 27; MTCW 1; SATA 66

Jennings, Waylon 1937- **CLC-21**

Jensen, Johannes V. 1873-1950 ...... **TCLC 41**
See also CA 170

Jensen, Laura (Linnea) 1948- .... **CLC 37**
See also CA 103

Jerome, Jerome K(lapka) 1859-1927 **TCLC 23**
See also CA 119; DLB 10, 34, 135

Jerrold, Douglas William 1803-1857 **NCLC 2**
See also DLB 158, 159

Jewett, (Theodora) Sarah Orne 1849-1909 **TCLC 1, 22; SSC 6**
See also CA 108; 127; CANR 71; DLB 12, 74; SATA 15

Jewsbury, Geraldine (Endsor) 1812-1880 **NCLC 22**
See also DLB 21

Jhabvala, Ruth Prawer 1927- **CLC 4, 8, 29, 94; DAB; DAM NOV**
See also CA 1-4R; CANR 2, 29, 51, 74; DLB 139, 194; INT CANR-29; MTCW 1, 2

Jibran, Kahlil
See Gibran, Kahlil

Jibran, Khalil
See Gibran, Kahlil

Jiles, Paulette 1943- .... **CLC 13, 58**
See also CA 101; CANR 70

Jimenez (Mantecon), Juan Ramon 1881-1958 **TCLC 4; DAM MULT, POET; HLC; PC 7**
See also CA 104; 131; CANR 74; DLB 134; HW 1; MTCW 1, 2

Jimenez, Ramon
See Jimenez (Mantecon), Juan Ramon

Jimenez Mantecon, Juan
See Jimenez (Mantecon), Juan Ramon

Jin, Ha 1956- .... **CLC 109**
See also CA 152

Joel, Billy .... **CLC 26**
See also Joel, William Martin

Joel, William Martin 1949-
See Joel, Billy
See also CA 108

John, Saint 7th cent. - .... **CMLC 27**

John of the Cross, St. 1542-1591 .... **LC 18**

Johnson, B(ryan) S(tanley William) 1933-1973 **CLC 6, 9**
See also CA 9-12R; 53-56; CANR 9; DLB 14, 40

Johnson, Benj. F. of Boo
See Riley, James Whitcomb

Johnson, Benjamin F. of Boo
See Riley, James Whitcomb

Johnson, Charles (Richard) 1948- **CLC 7, 51, 65; BLC 2; DAM MULT**
See also BW 2, 3; CA 116; CAAS 18; CANR 42, 66; DLB 33; MTCW 2

Johnson, Denis 1949- .... **CLC 52**
See also CA 117; 121; CANR 71; DLB 120

Johnson, Diane 1934- .... **CLC 5, 13, 48**
See also CA 41-44R; CANR 17, 40, 62; DLBY 80; INT CANR-17; MTCW 1

Johnson, Eyvind (Olof Verner) 1900-1976 **CLC 14**
See also CA 73-76; 69-72; CANR 34

Johnson, J. R.
See James, C(yril) L(ionel) R(obert)

Johnson, James Weldon 1871-1938 **TCLC 3, 19; BLC 2; DAM MULT, POET; PC 24**
See also BW 1, 3; CA 104; 125; CDALB 1917-1929; CLR 32; DLB 51; MTCW 1, 2; SATA 31

Johnson, Joyce 1935- .... **CLC 58**
See also CA 125; 129

Johnson, Judith (Emlyn) 1936- ..... **CLC 7, 15**
See also CA 25-28R; 153; CANR 34

Johnson, Lionel (Pigot) 1867-1902 **TCLC 19**
See also CA 117; DLB 19

Johnson, Marguerite (Annie)
See Angelou, Maya

Johnson, Mel

See Malzberg, Barry N(athaniel)

Johnson, Pamela Hansford 1912-1981 **CLC 1, 7, 27**
See also CA 1-4R; 104; CANR 2, 28; DLB 15; MTCW 1, 2

Johnson, Robert 1911(?)-1938 .... **TCLC 69**
See also BW 3; CA 174

Johnson, Samuel 1709-1784 **LC 15; DA; DAB; DAC; DAM MST; WLC**
See also CDBLB 1660-1789; DLB 39, 95, 104, 142

Johnson, Uwe 1934-1984 .. **CLC 5, 10, 15, 40**
See also CA 1-4R; 112; CANR 1, 39; DLB 75; MTCW 1

Johnston, George (Benson) 1913- ..... **CLC 51**
See also CA 1-4R; CANR 5, 20; DLB 88

Johnston, Jennifer 1930- .... **CLC 7**
See also CA 85-88; DLB 14

Jolley, (Monica) Elizabeth 1923- **CLC 46; SSC 19**
See also CA 127; CAAS 13; CANR 59

Jones, Arthur Llewellyn 1863-1947
See Machen, Arthur
See also CA 104

Jones, D(ouglas) G(ordon) 1929- ...... **CLC 10**
See also CA 29-32R; CANR 13; DLB 53

Jones, David (Michael) 1895-1974 **CLC 2, 4, 7, 13, 42**
See also CA 9-12R; 53-56; CANR 28; CDBLB 1945-1960; DLB 20, 100; MTCW 1

Jones, David Robert 1947-
See Bowie, David
See also CA 103

Jones, Diana Wynne 1934- .... **CLC 26**
See also AAYA 12; CA 49-52; CANR 4, 26, 56; CLR 23; DLB 161; JRDA; MAICYA; SAAS 7; SATA 9, 70

Jones, Edward P. 1950- .... **CLC 76**
See also BW 2, 3; CA 142; CANR 79

Jones, Gayl 1949- .... **CLC 6, 9; BLC 2; DAM MULT**
See also BW 2, 3; CA 77-80; CANR 27, 66; DLB 33; MTCW 1, 2

Jones, James 1921-1977 ...... **CLC 1, 3, 10, 39**
See also AITN 1, 2; CA 1-4R; 69-72; CANR 6; DLB 2, 143; DLBD 17; DLBY 98; MTCW 1

Jones, John J.
See Lovecraft, H(oward) P(hillips)

Jones, LeRoi .... **CLC 1, 2, 3, 5, 10, 14**
See also Baraka, Amiri
See also MTCW 2

Jones, Louis B. 1953- .... **CLC 65**
See also CA 141; CANR 73

Jones, Madison (Percy, Jr.) 1925- .... **CLC 4**
See also CA 13-16R; CAAS 11; CANR 7, 54; DLB 152

Jones, Mervyn 1922- .... **CLC 10, 52**
See also CA 45-48; CAAS 5; CANR 1; MTCW 1

Jones, Mick 1956(?)- .... **CLC 30**

Jones, Nettie (Pearl) 1941- .... **CLC 34**
See also BW 2; CA 137; CAAS 20

Jones, Preston 1936-1979 .... **CLC 10**
See also CA 73-76; 89-92; DLB 7

Jones, Robert F(rancis) 1934- .... **CLC 7**
See also CA 49-52; CANR 2, 61

Jones, Rod 1953- .... **CLC 50**
See also CA 128

Jones, Terence Graham Parry 1942- **CLC 21**
See also Jones, Terry; Monty Python
See also CA 112; 116; CANR 35; INT 116

Jones, Terry
See Jones, Terence Graham Parry

Author Index

Mangan, James Clarence 1803-1849NCLC 27
Maniere, J.-E.
   See Giraudoux, (Hippolyte) Jean
Mankiewicz, Herman (Jacob) 1897-1953
   TCLC 85
   See also CA 120; 169; DLB 26
Manley, (Mary) Delariviere 1672(?)-1724 **L C**
   1, 42
   See also DLB 39, 80
Mann, Abel
   See Creasey, John
Mann, Emily 1952- .... **DC 7**
   See also CA 130; CANR 55
Mann, (Luiz) Heinrich 1871-1950 ... **TCLC 9**
   See also CA 106; 164; DLB 66, 118
Mann, (Paul) Thomas 1875-1955 **TCLC 2, 8,**
   14, 21, 35, 44, 60; DA; DAB; DAC; DAM
   MST, NOV; SSC 5; WLC
   See also CA 104; 128; DLB 66; MTCW 1, 2
Mannheim, Karl 1893-1947 .... **TCLC 65**
Manning, David
   See Faust, Frederick (Schiller)
Manning, Frederic 1887(?)-1935 ... **TCLC 25**
   See also CA 124
Manning, Olivia 1915-1980 .... **CLC 5, 19**
   See also CA 5-8R; 101; CANR 29; MTCW 1
Mano, D. Keith 1942- .... **CLC 2, 10**
   See also CA 25-28R; CAAS 6; CANR 26, 57;
   DLB 6
Mansfield, KatherineTCLC 2, 8, 39; DAB; SSC
   9, 23; WLC
   See also Beauchamp, Kathleen Mansfield
   See also DLB 162
Manso, Peter 1940- .... **CLC 39**
   See also CA 29-32R; CANR 44
Mantecon, Juan Jimenez
   See Jimenez (Mantecon), Juan Ramon
Manton, Peter
   See Creasey, John
Man Without a Spleen, A
   See Chekhov, Anton (Pavlovich)
Manzoni, Alessandro 1785-1873 .... **NCLC 29**
Map, Walter 1140-1209 .... **CMLC 32**
Mapu, Abraham (ben Jekutiel) 1808-1867
   NCLC 18
Mara, Sally
   See Queneau, Raymond
Marat, Jean Paul 1743-1793 .... **LC 10**
Marcel, Gabriel Honore 1889-1973 . **CLC 15**
   See also CA 102; 45-48; MTCW 1, 2
Marchbanks, Samuel
   See Davies, (William) Robertson
Marchi, Giacomo
   See Bassani, Giorgio
Margulies, Donald .... **CLC 76**
Marie de France c. 12th cent. - **CMLC 8; PC**
   22
   See also DLB 208
Marie de l'Incarnation 1599-1672 ...... **LC 10**
Marier, Captain Victor
   See Griffith, D(avid Lewelyn) W(ark)
Mariner, Scott
   See Pohl, Frederik
Marinetti, Filippo Tommaso 1876-1944TCLC
   10
   See also CA 107; DLB 114
Marivaux, Pierre Carlet de Chamblain de 1688-
   1763 .... **LC 4; DC 7**
Markandaya, Kamala .... **CLC 8, 38**
   See also Taylor, Kamala (Purnaiya)
Markfield, Wallace 1926- .... **CLC 8**
   See also CA 69-72; CAAS 3; DLB 2, 28
Markham, Edwin 1852-1940 .... **TCLC 47**

See also CA 160; DLB 54, 186
Markham, Robert
   See Amis, Kingsley (William)
Marks, J
   See Highwater, Jamake (Mamake)
Marks-Highwater, J
   See Highwater, Jamake (Mamake)
Markson, David M(errill) 1927- .... **CLC 67**
   See also CA 49-52; CANR 1
Marley, Bob .... **CLC 17**
   See also Marley, Robert Nesta
Marley, Robert Nesta 1945-1981
   See Marley, Bob
   See also CA 107; 103
Marlowe, Christopher 1564-1593 **LC 22, 47;**
   DA; DAB; DAC; DAM DRAM, MST; DC
   1; WLC
   See also CDBLB Before 1660; DLB 62
Marlowe, Stephen 1928-
   See Queen, Ellery
   See also CA 13-16R; CANR 6, 55
Marmontel, Jean-Francois 1723-1799 .. **LC 2**
Marquand, John P(hillips) 1893-1960CLC 2,
   10
   See also CA 85-88; CANR 73; DLB 9, 102;
   MTCW 2
Marques, Rene 1919-1979 ..... **CLC 96; DAM**
   MULT; HLC
   See also CA 97-100; 85-88; CANR 78; DLB
   113; HW 1, 2
Marquez, Gabriel (Jose) Garcia
   See Garcia Marquez, Gabriel (Jose)
Marquis, Don(ald Robert Perry) 1878-1937
   TCLC 7
   See also CA 104; 166; DLB 11, 25
Marric, J. J.
   See Creasey, John
Marryat, Frederick 1792-1848 .... **NCLC 3**
   See also DLB 21, 163
Marsden, James
   See Creasey, John
Marsh, (Edith) Ngaio 1899-1982 **CLC 7, 53;**
   DAM POP
   See also CA 9-12R; CANR 6, 58; DLB 77;
   MTCW 1, 2
Marshall, Garry 1934- .... **CLC 17**
   See also AAYA 3; CA 111; SATA 60
Marshall, Paule 1929- .. **CLC 27, 72; BLC 3;**
   DAM MULT; SSC 3
   See also BW 2, 3; CA 77-80; CANR 25, 73;
   DLB 157; MTCW 1, 2
Marshallik
   See Zangwill, Israel
Marsten, Richard
   See Hunter, Evan
Marston, John 1576-1634LC 33; DAM DRAM
   See also DLB 58, 172
Martha, Henry
   See Harris, Mark
Marti (y Perez), Jose (Julian) 1853-1895
   NCLC 63; DAM MULT; HLC
   See also HW 2
Martial c. 40-c. 104 .... **PC 10**
   See also DLB 211
Martin, Ken
   See Hubbard, L(afayette) Ron(ald)
Martin, Richard
   See Creasey, John
Martin, Steve 1945- .... **CLC 30**
   See also CA 97-100; CANR 30; MTCW 1
Martin, Valerie 1948- .... **CLC 89**
   See also BEST 90:2; CA 85-88; CANR 49
Martin, Violet Florence 1862-1915 **TCLC 51**

Martin, Webber
   See Silverberg, Robert
Martindale, Patrick Victor
   See White, Patrick (Victor Martindale)
Martin du Gard, Roger 1881-1958 **TCLC 24**
   See also CA 118; DLB 65
Martineau, Harriet 1802-1876 .... **NCLC 26**
   See also DLB 21, 55, 159, 163, 166, 190; YABC
   2
Martines, Julia
   See O'Faolain, Julia
Martinez, Enrique Gonzalez
   See Gonzalez Martinez, Enrique
Martinez, Jacinto Benavente y
   See Benavente (y Martinez), Jacinto
Martinez Ruiz, Jose 1873-1967
   See Azorin; Ruiz, Jose Martinez
   See also CA 93-96; HW 1
Martinez Sierra, Gregorio 1881-1947TCLC 6
   See also CA 115
Martinez Sierra, Maria (de la O'LeJarraga)
   1874-1974 .... **TCLC 6**
   See also CA 115
Martinsen, Martin
   See Follett, Ken(neth Martin)
Martinson, Harry (Edmund) 1904-1978C L C
   14
   See also CA 77-80; CANR 34
Marut, Ret
   See Traven, B.
Marut, Robert
   See Traven, B.
Marvell, Andrew 1621-1678 ... **LC 4, 43; DA;**
   DAB; DAC; DAM MST, POET; PC 10;
   WLC
   See also CDBLB 1660-1789; DLB 131
Marx, Karl (Heinrich) 1818-1883 . **NCLC 17**
   See also DLB 129
Masaoka Shiki .... **TCLC 18**
   See also Masaoka Tsunenori
Masaoka Tsunenori 1867-1902
   See Masaoka Shiki
   See also CA 117
Masefield, John (Edward) 1878-1967CLC 11,
   47; DAM POET
   See also CA 19-20; 25-28R; CANR 33; CAP 2;
   CDBLB 1890-1914; DLB 10, 19, 153, 160;
   MTCW 1, 2; SATA 19
Maso, Carole 19(?)- .... **CLC 44**
   See also CA 170
Mason, Bobbie Ann 1940-CLC 28, 43, 82; SSC
   4
   See also AAYA 5; CA 53-56, CANR 11, 31,
   58; CDALBS; DLB 173; DLBY 87; INT
   CANR-31; MTCW 1, 2
Mason, Ernst
   See Pohl, Frederik
Mason, Lee W.
   See Malzberg, Barry N(athaniel)
Mason, Nick 1945- .... **CLC 35**
Mason, Tally
   See Derleth, August (William)
Mass, William
   See Gibson, William
Master Lao
   See Lao Tzu
Masters, Edgar Lee 1868-1950 **TCLC 2, 25;**
   DA; DAC; DAM MST, POET; PC 1;
   WLCS
   See also CA 104; 133; CDALB 1865-1917;
   DLB 54; MTCW 1, 2
Masters, Hilary 1928- .... **CLC 48**
   See also CA 25-28R; CANR 13, 47

See also AAYA 4, 23; BW 2, 3; CA 33-36R;
CANR 20, 42, 67; CLR 4, 16, 35; DLB 33;
INT CANR-20; JRDA; MAICYA; MTCW 2;
SAAS 2; SATA 41, 71; SATA-Brief 27
Myers, Walter M.
See Myers, Walter Dean
Myles, Symon
See Follett, Ken(neth Martin)
Nabokov, Vladimir (Vladimirovich) 1899-1977
**CLC 1, 2, 3, 6, 8, 11, 15, 23, 44, 46, 64;
DA; DAB; DAC; DAM MST, NOV; SSC
11; WLC**
See also CA 5-8R; 69-72; CANR 20; CDALB
1941-1968; DLB 2; DLBD 3; DLBY 80, 91;
MTCW 1, 2
Nagai Kafu 1879-1959 .... **TCLC 51**
See also Nagai Sokichi
See also DLB 180
Nagai Sokichi 1879-1959
See Nagai Kafu
See also CA 117
Nagy, Laszlo 1925-1978 .... **CLC 7**
See also CA 129; 112
Naidu, Sarojini 1879-1943 .... **TCLC 80**
Naipaul, Shiva(dhar Srinivasa) 1945-1985
CLC 32, 39; DAM NOV
See also CA 110; 112; 116; CANR 33; DLB
157; DLBY 85; MTCW 1, 2
Naipaul, V(idiadhar) S(urajprasad) 1932-
**CLC 4, 7, 9, 13, 18, 37, 105; DAB; DAC;
DAM MST, NOV**
See also CA 1-4R; CANR 1, 33, 51; CDBLB
1960 to Present; DLB 125, 204, 206; DLBY
85; MTCW 1, 2
Nakos, Lilika 1899(?)- .... **CLC 29**
Narayan, R(asipuram) K(rishnaswami) 1906-
CLC 7, 28, 47; DAM NOV; SSC 25
See also CA 81-84; CANR 33, 61; MTCW 1,
2; SATA 62
Nash, (Fredric) Ogden 1902-1971 . **CLC 23;
DAM POET; PC 21**
See also CA 13-14; 29-32R; CANR 34, 61; CAP
1; DLB 11; MAICYA; MTCW 1, 2; SATA 2,
46
Nashe, Thomas 1567-1601(?) .... **LC 41**
See also DLB 167
Nashe, Thomas 1567-1601 .... **LC 41**
Nathan, Daniel
See Dannay, Frederic
Nathan, George Jean 1882-1958 ... **TCLC 18**
See also Hatteras, Owen
See also CA 114; 169; DLB 137
Natsume, Kinnosuke 1867-1916
See Natsume, Soseki
See also CA 104
Natsume, Soseki 1867-1916 .... **TCLC 2, 10**
See also Natsume, Kinnosuke
See also DLB 180
Natti, (Mary) Lee 1919-
See Kingman, Lee
See also CA 5-8R; CANR 2
Naylor, Gloria 1950-**CLC 28, 52; BLC 3; DA;
DAC; DAM MST, MULT, NOV, POP;
WLCS**
See also AAYA 6; BW 2, 3; CA 107; CANR
27, 51, 74; DLB 173; MTCW 1, 2
Neihardt, John Gneisenau 1881-1973**CLC 32**
See also CA 13-14; CANR 65; CAP 1; DLB 9,
54
Nekrasov, Nikolai Alekseevich 1821-1878
NCLC 11
Nelligan, Emile 1879-1941 .... **TCLC 14**
See also CA 114; DLB 92

Nelson, Willie 1933- .... **CLC 17**
See also CA 107
Nemerov, Howard (Stanley) 1920-1991**CLC 2,
6, 9, 36; DAM POET; PC 24**
See also CA 1-4R; 134; CABS 2; CANR 1, 27,
53; DLB 5, 6; DLBY 83; INT CANR-27;
MTCW 1, 2
Neruda, Pablo 1904-1973**CLC 1, 2, 5, 7, 9, 28,
62; DA; DAB; DAC; DAM MST, MULT,
POET; HLC; PC 4; WLC**
See also CA 19-20; 45-48; CAP 2; HW 1;
MTCW 1, 2
Nerval, Gerard de 1808-1855**NCLC 1, 67; PC
13; SSC 18**
Nervo, (Jose) Amado (Ruiz de) 1870-1919
TCLC 11; HLCS 1
See also CA 109; 131; HW 1
Nessi, Pio Baroja y
See Baroja (y Nessi), Pio
Nestroy, Johann 1801-1862 .... **NCLC 42**
See also DLB 133
Netterville, Luke
See O'Grady, Standish (James)
Neufeld, John (Arthur) 1938- .... **CLC 17**
See also AAYA 11; CA 25-28R; CANR 11, 37,
56; CLR 52; MAICYA; SAAS 3; SATA 6,
81
Neville, Emily Cheney 1919- .... **CLC 12**
See also CA 5-8R; CANR 3, 37; JRDA;
MAICYA; SAAS 2; SATA 1
Newbound, Bernard Slade 1930-
See Slade, Bernard
See also CA 81-84; CANR 49; DAM DRAM
Newby, P(ercy) H(oward) 1918-1997 **CLC 2,
13; DAM NOV**
See also CA 5-8R; 161; CANR 32, 67; DLB
15; MTCW 1
Newlove, Donald 1928- .... **CLC 6**
See also CA 29-32R; CANR 25
Newlove, John (Herbert) 1938- .... **CLC 14**
See also CA 21-24R; CANR 9, 25
Newman, Charles 1938- .... **CLC 2, 8**
See also CA 21-24R
Newman, Edwin (Harold) 1919- .... **CLC 14**
See also AITN 1; CA 69-72; CANR 5
Newman, John Henry 1801-1890 .. **NCLC 38**
See also DLB 18, 32, 55
Newton, (Sir)Isaac 1642-1727 .... **LC 35**
Newton, Suzanne 1936- .... **CLC 35**
See also CA 41-44R; CANR 14; JRDA; SATA
5, 77
Nexo, Martin Andersen 1869-1954 **TCLC 43**
Nezval, Vitezslav 1900-1958 .... **TCLC 44**
See also CA 123
Ng, Fae Myenne 1957(?)- .... **CLC 81**
See also CA 146
Ngema, Mbongeni 1955- .... **CLC 57**
See also BW 2; CA 143
Ngugi, James T(hiong'o) .... **CLC 3, 7, 13**
See also Ngugi wa Thiong'o
Ngugi wa Thiong'o 1938- .. **CLC 36; BLC 3;
DAM MULT, NOV**
See also Ngugi, James T(hiong'o)
See also BW 2; CA 81-84; CANR 27, 58; DLB
125; MTCW 1, 2
Nichol, B(arrie) P(hillip) 1944-1988 **CLC 18**
See also CA 53-56; DLB 53; SATA 66
Nichols, John (Treadwell) 1940- .... **CLC 38**
See also CA 9-12R; CAAS 2; CANR 6, 70;
DLBY 82
Nichols, Leigh
See Koontz, Dean R(ay)
Nichols, Peter (Richard) 1927-**CLC 5, 36, 65**

See also CA 104; CANR 33; DLB 13; MTCW
1
Nicolas, F. R. E.
See Freeling, Nicolas
Niedecker, Lorine 1903-1970 .... **CLC 10, 42;
DAM POET**
See also CA 25-28; CAP 2; DLB 48
Nietzsche, Friedrich (Wilhelm) 1844-1900
TCLC 10, 18, 55
See also CA 107; 121; DLB 129
Nievo, Ippolito 1831-1861 .... **NCLC 22**
Nightingale, Anne Redmon 1943-
See Redmon, Anne
See also CA 103
Nightingale, Florence 1820-1910 ... **TCLC 85**
See also DLB 166
Nik. T. O.
See Annensky, Innokenty (Fyodorovich)
Nin, Anais 1903-1977 **CLC 1, 4, 8, 11, 14, 60;
DAM NOV, POP; SSC 10**
See also AITN 2; CA 13-16R; 69-72; CANR
22, 53; DLB 2, 4, 152; MTCW 1, 2
Nishida, Kitaro 1870-1945 .... **TCLC 83**
Nishiwaki, Junzaburo 1894-1982 .... **PC 15**
See also CA 107
Nissenson, Hugh 1933- .... **CLC 4, 9**
See also CA 17-20R; CANR 27; DLB 28
Niven, Larry .... **CLC 8**
See also Niven, Laurence Van Cott
See also AAYA 27; DLB 8
Niven, Laurence Van Cott 1938-
See Niven, Larry
See also CA 21-24R; CAAS 12; CANR 14, 44,
66; DAM POP; MTCW 1, 2; SATA 95
Nixon, Agnes Eckhardt 1927- .... **CLC 21**
See also CA 110
Nizan, Paul 1905-1940 .... **TCLC 40**
See also CA 161; DLB 72
Nkosi, Lewis 1936- .... **CLC 45; BLC 3; DAM
MULT**
See also BW 1, 3; CA 65-68; CANR 27; DLB
157
Nodier, (Jean) Charles (Emmanuel) 1780-1844
NCLC 19
See also DLB 119
Noguchi, Yone 1875-1947 .... **TCLC 80**
Nolan, Christopher 1965- .... **CLC 58**
See also CA 111
Noon, Jeff 1957- .... **CLC 91**
See also CA 148
Norden, Charles
See Durrell, Lawrence (George)
Nordhoff, Charles (Bernard) 1887-1947
TCLC 23
See also CA 108; DLB 9; SATA 23
Norfolk, Lawrence 1963- .... **CLC 76**
See also CA 144
Norman, Marsha 1947-**CLC 28; DAM DRAM;
DC 8**
See also CA 105; CABS 3; CANR 41; DLBY
84
Normyx
See Douglas, (George) Norman
Norris, Frank 1870-1902 .... **SSC 28**
See also Norris, (Benjamin) Frank(lin, Jr.)
See also CDALB 1865-1917; DLB 12, 71, 186
Norris, (Benjamin) Frank(lin, Jr.) 1870-1902
TCLC 24
See also Norris, Frank
See also CA 110; 160
Norris, Leslie 1921- .... **CLC 14**
See also CA 11-12; CANR 14; CAP 1; DLB 27
North, Andrew

See also CDBLB 1832-1890; DLB 57, 156

Paterson, A(ndrew) B(arton) 1864-1941
    TCLC 32
    See also CA 155; SATA 97

Paterson, Katherine (Womeldorf) 1932-**C L C 12, 30**
    See also AAYA 1; CA 21-24R; CANR 28, 59; CLR 7, 50; DLB 52; JRDA; MAICYA; MTCW 1; SATA 13, 53, 92

Patmore, Coventry Kersey Dighton 1823-1896
    NCLC 9
    See also DLB 35, 98

Paton, Alan (Stewart) 1903-1988 **CLC 4, 10, 25, 55, 106; DA; DAB; DAC; DAM MST, NOV; WLC**
    See also AAYA 26; CA 13-16; 125; CANR 22; CAP 1; DLBD 17; MTCW 1, 2; SATA 11; SATA-Obit 56

Paton Walsh, Gillian 1937-
    See Walsh, Jill Paton
    See also CANR 38; JRDA; MAICYA; SAAS 3; SATA 4, 72

Patton, George S. 1885-1945 .... **TCLC 79**

Paulding, James Kirke 1778-1860 ... **NCLC 2**
    See also DLB 3, 59, 74

Paulin, Thomas Neilson 1949-
    See Paulin, Tom
    See also CA 123; 128

Paulin, Tom .... **CLC 37**
    See also Paulin, Thomas Neilson
    See also DLB 40

Paustovsky, Konstantin (Georgievich) 1892-1968 .... **CLC 40**
    See also CA 93-96; 25-28R

Pavese, Cesare 1908-1950 ... **TCLC 3; PC 13; SSC 19**
    See also CA 104; 169; DLB 128, 177

Pavic, Milorad 1929- .... **CLC 60**
    See also CA 136; DLB 181

Pavlov, Ivan Petrovich 1849-1936 . **TCLC 91**
    See also CA 118

Payne, Alan
    See Jakes, John (William)

Paz, Gil
    See Lugones, Leopoldo

Paz, Octavio 1914-1998 **CLC 3, 4, 6, 10, 19, 51, 65, 119; DA; DAB; DAC; DAM MST, MULT, POET; HLC; PC 1; WLC**
    See also CA 73-76; 165; CANR 32, 65; DLBY 90, 98; HW 1, 2; MTCW 1, 2

p'Bitek, Okot 1931-1982 .... **CLC 96; BLC 3; DAM MULT**
    See also BW 2, 3; CA 124; 107; DLB 125; MTCW 1, 2

Peacock, Molly 1947- .... **CLC 60**
    See also CA 103; CAAS 21; CANR 52; DLB 120

Peacock, Thomas Love 1785-1866 . **NCLC 22**
    See also DLB 96, 116

Peake, Mervyn 1911-1968 .... **CLC 7, 54**
    See also CA 5-8R; 25-28R; CANR 3; DLB 15, 160; MTCW 1; SATA 23

Pearce, Philippa .... **CLC 21**
    See also Christie, (Ann) Philippa
    See also CLR 9; DLB 161; MAICYA; SATA 1, 67

Pearl, Eric
    See Elman, Richard (Martin)

Pearson, T(homas) R(eid) 1956- .... **CLC 39**
    See also CA 120; 130; INT 130

Peck, Dale 1967- .... **CLC 81**
    See also CA 146; CANR 72

Peck, John 1941- .... **CLC 3**

See also CA 49-52; CANR 3

Peck, Richard (Wayne) 1934- .... **CLC 21**
    See also AAYA 1, 24; CA 85-88; CANR 19, 38; CLR 15; INT CANR-19; JRDA; MAICYA; SAAS 2; SATA 18, 55, 97

Peck, Robert Newton 1928- ..... **CLC 17; DA; DAC; DAM MST**
    See also AAYA 3; CA 81-84; CANR 31, 63; CLR 45; JRDA; MAICYA; SAAS 1; SATA 21, 62

Peckinpah, (David) Sam(uel) 1925-1984 **C L C 20**
    See also CA 109; 114

Pedersen, Knut 1859-1952
    See Hamsun, Knut
    See also CA 104; 119; CANR 63; MTCW 1, 2

Peeslake, Gaffer
    See Durrell, Lawrence (George)

Peguy, Charles Pierre 1873-1914 .. **TCLC 10**
    See also CA 107

Peirce, Charles Sanders 1839-1914 **TCLC 81**

Pena, Ramon del Valle y
    See Valle-Inclan, Ramon (Maria) del

Pendennis, Arthur Esquir
    See Thackeray, William Makepeace

Penn, William 1644-1718 .... **LC 25**
    See also DLB 24

PEPECE
    See Prado (Calvo), Pedro

Pepys, Samuel 1633-1703 **LC 11; DA; DAB; DAC; DAM MST; WLC**
    See also CDBLB 1660-1789; DLB 101

Percy, Walker 1916-1990 **CLC 2, 3, 6, 8, 14, 18, 47, 65; DAM NOV, POP**
    See also CA 1-4R; 131; CANR 1, 23, 64; DLB 2; DLBY 80, 90; MTCW 1, 2

Percy, William Alexander 1885-1942 **TCLC 84**
    See also CA 163; MTCW 2

Perec, Georges 1936-1982 .... **CLC 56, 116**
    See also CA 141; DLB 83

Pereda (y Sanchez de Porrua), Jose Maria de 1833-1906 .... **TCLC 16**
    See also CA 117

Pereda y Porrua, Jose Maria de
    See Pereda (y Sanchez de Porrua), Jose Maria de

Peregoy, George Weems
    See Mencken, H(enry) L(ouis)

Perelman, S(idney) J(oseph) 1904-1979 **C L C 3, 5, 9, 15, 23, 44, 49; DAM DRAM; SSC 32**
    See also AITN 1, 2; CA 73-76; 89-92; CANR 18; DLB 11, 44; MTCW 1, 2

Peret, Benjamin 1899-1959 .... **TCLC 20**
    See also CA 117

Peretz, Isaac Loeb 1851(?)-1915 ... **TCLC 16; SSC 26**
    See also CA 109

Peretz, Yitzkhok Leibush
    See Peretz, Isaac Loeb

Perez Galdos, Benito 1843-1920 ... **TCLC 27; HLCS 1**
    See also CA 125; 153; HW 1

Perrault, Charles 1628-1703 .... **LC 2**
    See also MAICYA; SATA 25

Perry, Brighton
    See Sherwood, Robert E(mmet)

Perse, St.-John
    See Leger, (Marie-Rene Auguste) Alexis Saint-Leger

Perutz, Leo(pold) 1882-1957 .... **TCLC 60**
    See also CA 147; DLB 81

Peseenz, Tulio F.

See Lopez y Fuentes, Gregorio

Pesetsky, Bette 1932- .... **CLC 28**
    See also CA 133; DLB 130

Peshkov, Alexei Maximovich 1868-1936
    See Gorky, Maxim
    See also CA 105; 141; DA; DAC; DAM DRAM, MST, NOV; MTCW 2

Pessoa, Fernando (Antonio Nogueira) 1888-1935 **TCLC 27; DAM MULT; HLC; PC 20**
    See also CA 125

Peterkin, Julia Mood 1880-1961 .... **CLC 31**
    See also CA 102; DLB 9

Peters, Joan K(aren) 1945- .... **CLC 39**
    See also CA 158

Peters, Robert L(ouis) 1924- .... **CLC 7**
    See also CA 13-16R; CAAS 8; DLB 105

Petofi, Sandor 1823-1849 .... **NCLC 21**

Petrakis, Harry Mark 1923- .... **CLC 3**
    See also CA 9-12R; CANR 4, 30

Petrarch 1304-1374 **CMLC 20; DAM POET; PC 8**

Petrov, Evgeny .... **TCLC 21**
    See also Kataev, Evgeny Petrovich

Petry, Ann (Lane) 1908-1997 ... **CLC 1, 7, 18**
    See also BW 1, 3; CA 5-8R; 157; CAAS 6; CANR 4, 46; CLR 12; DLB 76; JRDA; MAICYA; MTCW 1; SATA 5; SATA-Obit 94

Petursson, Halligrimur 1614-1674 .... **LC 8**

Peychinovich
    See Vazov, Ivan (Minchov)

Phaedrus c. 18B.C.-c. 50 .... **CMLC 25**
    See also DLB 211

Philips, Katherine 1632-1664 .... **LC 30**
    See also DLB 131

Philipson, Morris H. 1926- .... **CLC 53**
    See also CA 1-4R; CANR 4

Phillips, Caryl 1958- .. **CLC 96; BLCS; DAM MULT**
    See also BW 2; CA 141; CANR 63; DLB 157; MTCW 2

Phillips, David Graham 1867-1911 **TCLC 44**
    See also CA 108; DLB 9, 12

Phillips, Jack
    See Sandburg, Carl (August)

Phillips, Jayne Anne 1952- **CLC 15, 33; SSC 16**
    See also CA 101; CANR 24, 50; DLBY 80; INT CANR-24; MTCW 1, 2

Phillips, Richard
    See Dick, Philip K(indred)

Phillips, Robert (Schaeffer) 1938- .... **CLC 28**
    See also CA 17-20R; CAAS 13; CANR 8; DLB 105

Phillips, Ward
    See Lovecraft, H(oward) P(hillips)

Piccolo, Lucio 1901-1969 .... **CLC 13**
    See also CA 97-100; DLB 114

Pickthall, Marjorie L(owry) C(hristie) 1883-1922 .... **TCLC 21**
    See also CA 107; DLB 92

Pico della Mirandola, Giovanni 1463-1494 **LC 15**

Piercy, Marge 1936- **CLC 3, 6, 14, 18, 27, 62**
    See also CA 21-24R; CAAS 1; CANR 13, 43, 66; DLB 120; MTCW 1, 2

Piers, Robert
    See Anthony, Piers

Pieyre de Mandiargues, Andre 1909-1991
    See Mandiargues, Andre Pieyre de
    See also CA 103; 136; CANR 22

Pilnyak, Boris .... **TCLC 23**
    See also Vogau, Boris Andreyevich

Pincherle, Alberto 1907-1990 ... **CLC 11, 18; DAM NOV**

Ragni, Gerome 1942-1991 .... CLC 17
  See also CA 105; 134
Rahv, Philip 1908-1973 .... CLC 24
  See also Greenberg, Ivan
  See also DLB 137
Raimund, Ferdinand Jakob 1790-1836NCLC
  69
  See also DLB 90
Raine, Craig 1944- .... CLC 32, 103
  See also CA 108; CANR 29, 51; DLB 40
Raine, Kathleen (Jessie) 1908- ...... CLC 7, 45
  See also CA 85-88; CANR 46; DLB 20; MTCW
  1
Rainis, Janis 1865-1929 .... TCLC 29
  See also CA 170
Rakosi, Carl 1903- .... CLC 47
  See also Rawley, Callman
  See also CAAS 5; DLB 193
Raleigh, Richard
  See Lovecraft, H(oward) P(hillips)
Raleigh, Sir Walter 1554(?)-1618 . LC 31, 39
  See also CDBLB Before 1660; DLB 172
Rallentando, H. P.
  See Sayers, Dorothy L(eigh)
Ramal, Walter
  See de la Mare, Walter (John)
Ramana Maharshi 1879-1950 .... TCLC 84
Ram****n y Cajal, Santiago 1852-1934
  TCLC 93
Ramon, Juan
  See Jimenez (Mantecon), Juan Ramon
Ramos, Graciliano 1892-1953 .... TCLC 32
  See also CA 167; HW 2
Rampersad, Arnold 1941- .... CLC 44
  See also BW 2, 3; CA 127; 133; DLB 111; INT
  133
Rampling, Anne
  See Rice, Anne
Ramsay, Allan 1684(?)-1758 .... LC 29
  See also DLB 95
Ramuz, Charles-Ferdinand 1878-1947T C L C
  33
  See also CA 165
Rand, Ayn 1905-1982CLC 3, 30, 44, 79; DA;
  DAC; DAM MST, NOV, POP; WLC
  See also AAYA 10; CA 13-16R; 105; CANR
  27, 73; CDALBS; MTCW 1, 2
Randall, Dudley (Felker) 1914-CLC1; BLC 3;
  DAM MULT
  See also BW 1, 3; CA 25-28R; CANR 23; DLB
  41
Randall, Robert
  See Silverberg, Robert
Ranger, Ken
  See Creasey, John
Ransom, John Crowe 1888-1974CLC 2, 4, 5,
  11, 24; DAM POET
  See also CA 5-8R; 49-52; CANR 6, 34;
  CDALBS; DLB 45, 63; MTCW 1, 2
Rao, Raja 1909- ..... CLC 25, 56; DAM NOV
  See also CA 73-76; CANR 51; MTCW 1, 2
Raphael, Frederic (Michael) 1931-CLC 2, 14
  See also CA 1-4R; CANR 1; DLB 14
Ratcliffe, James P.
  See Mencken, H(enry) L(ouis)
Rathbone, Julian 1935- .... CLC 41
  See also CA 101; CANR 34, 73
Rattigan, Terence (Mervyn) 1911-1977CLC 7;
  DAM DRAM
  See also CA 85-88; 73-76; CDBLB 1945-1960;
  DLB 13; MTCW 1, 2
Ratushinskaya, Irina 1954- .... CLC 54
  See also CA 129; CANR 68

Raven, Simon (Arthur Noel) 1927- .. CLC 14
  See also CA 81-84
Ravenna, Michael
  See Welty, Eudora
Rawley, Callman 1903-
  See Rakosi, Carl
  See also CA 21-24R; CANR 12, 32
Rawlings, Marjorie Kinnan 1896-1953TCLC
  4
  See also AAYA 20; CA 104; 137; CANR 74;
  DLB 9, 22, 102; DLBD 17; JRDA; MAICYA;
  MTCW 2; SATA 100; YABC 1
Ray, Satyajit 1921-1992 .. CLC 16, 76; DAM
  MULT
  See also CA 114; 137
Read, Herbert Edward 1893-1968 ..... CLC 4
  See also CA 85-88; 25-28R; DLB 20, 149
Read, Piers Paul 1941- .... CLC 4, 10, 25
  See also CA 21-24R; CANR 38; DLB 14; SATA
  21
Reade, Charles 1814-1884 .... NCLC 2, 74
  See also DLB 21
Reade, Hamish
  See Gray, Simon (James Holliday)
Reading, Peter 1946- .... CLC 47
  See also CA 103; CANR 46; DLB 40
Reaney, James 1926- .. CLC 13; DAC; DAM
  MST
  See also CA 41-44R; CAAS 15; CANR 42; DLB
  68; SATA 43
Rebreanu, Liviu 1885-1944 .... TCLC 28
  See also CA 165
Rechy, John (Francisco) 1934- CLC 1, 7, 14,
  18, 107; DAM MULT; HLC
  See also CA 5-8R; CAAS 4; CANR 6, 32, 64;
  DLB 122; DLBY 82; HW 1, 2; INT CANR-
  6
Redcam, Tom 1870-1933 .... TCLC 25
Reddin, Keith .... CLC 67
Redgrove, Peter (William) 1932- ..CLC 6, 41
  See also CA 1-4R; CANR 3, 39, 77; DLB 40
Redmon, Anne .... CLC 22
  See also Nightingale, Anne Redmon
  See also DLBY 86
Reed, Eliot
  See Ambler, Eric
Reed, Ishmael 1938-CLC 2, 3, 5, 6, 13, 32, 60;
  BLC 3; DAM MULT
  See also BW 2, 3; CA 21-24R; CANR 25, 48,
  74; DLB 2, 5, 33, 169; DLBD 8; MTCW 1,
  2
Reed, John (Silas) 1887-1920 .... TCLC 9
  See also CA 106
Reed, Lou .... CLC 21
  See also Firbank, Louis
Reeve, Clara 1729-1807 .... NCLC 19
  See also DLB 39
Reich, Wilhelm 1897-1957 .... TCLC 57
Reid, Christopher (John) 1949- .... CLC 33
  See also CA 140; DLB 40
Reid, Desmond
  See Moorcock, Michael (John)
Reid Banks, Lynne 1929-
  See Banks, Lynne Reid
  See also CA 1-4R; CANR 6, 22, 38; CLR 24;
  JRDA; MAICYA; SATA 22, 75
Reilly, William K.
  See Creasey, John
Reiner, Max
  See Caldwell, (Janet Miriam) Taylor (Holland)
Reis, Ricardo
  See Pessoa, Fernando (Antonio Nogueira)
Remarque, Erich Maria 1898-1970 CLC 21;

DA; DAB; DAC; DAM MST, NOV
  See also AAYA 27; CA 77-80; 29-32R; DLB
  56; MTCW 1, 2
Remington, Frederic 1861-1909 .... TCLC 89
  See also CA 108; 169; DLB 12, 186, 188; SATA
  41
Remizov, A.
  See Remizov, Aleksei (Mikhailovich)
Remizov, A. M.
  See Remizov, Aleksei (Mikhailovich)
Remizov, Aleksei (Mikhailovich) 1877-1957
  TCLC 27
  See also CA 125; 133
Renan, Joseph Ernest 1823-1892 ..NCLC 26
Renard, Jules 1864-1910 .... TCLC 17
  See also CA 117
Renault, Mary .... CLC 3, 11, 17
  See also Challans, Mary
  See also DLBY 83; MTCW 2
Rendell, Ruth (Barbara) 1930- . CLC 28, 48;
  DAM POP
  See also Vine, Barbara
  See also CA 109; CANR 32, 52, 74; DLB 87;
  INT CANR-32; MTCW 1, 2
Renoir, Jean 1894-1979 .... CLC 20
  See also CA 129; 85-88
Resnais, Alain 1922- .... CLC 16
Reverdy, Pierre 1889-1960 .... CLC 53
  See also CA 97-100; 89-92
Rexroth, Kenneth 1905-1982CLC 1, 2, 6, 11,
  22, 49, 112; DAM POET; PC 20
  See also CA 5-8R; 107; CANR 14, 34, 63;
  CDALB 1941-1968; DLB 16, 48, 165, 212;
  DLBY 82; INT CANR-14; MTCW 1, 2
Reyes, Alfonso 1889-1959TCLC 33; HLCS 1
  See also CA 131; HW 1
Reyes y Basoalto, Ricardo Eliecer Neftali
  See Neruda, Pablo
Reymont, Wladyslaw (Stanislaw) 1868(?)-1925
  TCLC 5
  See also CA 104
Reynolds, Jonathan 1942- .... CLC 6, 38
  See also CA 65-68; CANR 28
Reynolds, Joshua 1723-1792 .... LC 15
  See also DLB 104
Reynolds, Michael Shane 1937- .... CLC 44
  See also CA 65-68; CANR 9
Reznikoff, Charles 1894-1976 .... CLC 9
  See also CA 33-36; 61-64; CAP 2; DLB 28, 45
Rezzori (d'Arezzo), Gregor von 1914-1998
  CLC 25
  See also CA 122; 136; 167
Rhine, Richard
  See Silverstein, Alvin
Rhodes, Eugene Manlove 1869-1934TCLC 53
Rhodius, Apollonius c. 3rd cent. B.C.- C M L C
  28
  See also DLB 176
R'hoone
  See Balzac, Honore de
Rhys, Jean 1890(?)-1979 CLC 2, 4, 6, 14, 19,
  51; DAM NOV; SSC 21
  See also CA 25-28R; 85-88; CANR 35, 62;
  CDBLB 1945-1960; DLB 36, 117, 162;
  MTCW 1, 2
Ribeiro, Darcy 1922-1997 .... CLC 34
  See also CA 33-36R; 156
Ribeiro, Joao Ubaldo (Osorio Pimentel) 1941-
  CLC 10, 67
  See also CA 81-84
Ribman, Ronald (Burt) 1932- .... CLC 7
  See also CA 21-24R; CANR 46, 80
Ricci, Nino 1959- .... CLC 70

Sacastru, Martin
See Bioy Casares, Adolfo
Sacher-Masoch, Leopold von 1836(?)-1895
NCLC 31
Sachs, Marilyn (Stickle) 1927- .... **CLC 35**
See also AAYA 2; CA 17-20R; CANR 13, 47;
CLR 2; JRDA; MAICYA; SAAS 2; SATA 3,
68
Sachs, Nelly 1891-1970 .... **CLC 14, 98**
See also CA 17-18; 25-28R; CAP 2; MTCW 2
Sackler, Howard (Oliver) 1929-1982 **CLC 14**
See also CA 61-64; 108; CANR 30; DLB 7
Sacks, Oliver (Wolf) 1933- .... **CLC 67**
See also CA 53-56; CANR 28, 50, 76; INT
CANR-28; MTCW 1, 2
Sadakichi
See Hartmann, Sadakichi
Sade, Donatien Alphonse Francois, Comte de
1740-1814 .... **NCLC 47**
Sadoff, Ira 1945- .... **CLC 9**
See also CA 53-56; CANR 5, 21; DLB 120
Saetone
See Camus, Albert
Safire, William 1929- .... **CLC 10**
See also CA 17-20R; CANR 31, 54
Sagan, Carl (Edward) 1934-1996 **CLC 30, 112**
See also AAYA 2; CA 25-28R; 155; CANR 11,
36, 74; MTCW 1, 2; SATA 58; SATA-Obit
94
Sagan, Francoise .... **CLC 3, 6, 9, 17, 36**
See Quoirez, Francoise
See also DLB 83; MTCW 2
Sahgal, Nayantara (Pandit) 1927- .... **CLC 41**
See also CA 9-12R; CANR 11
Saint, H(arry) F. 1941- .... **CLC 50**
See also CA 127
St. Aubin de Teran, Lisa 1953-
See Teran, Lisa St. Aubin de
See also CA 118; 126; INT 126
Saint Birgitta of Sweden c. 1303-1373 **C M L C 24**
Sainte-Beuve, Charles Augustin 1804-1869
NCLC 5
Saint-Exupery, Antoine (Jean Baptiste Marie
Roger) de 1900-1944 **TCLC 2, 56; DAM NOV; WLC**
See also CA 108; 132; CLR 10; DLB 72;
MAICYA; MTCW 1, 2; SATA 20
St. John, David
See Hunt, E(verette) Howard, (Jr.)
Saint-John Perse
See Leger, (Marie-Rene Auguste) Alexis Saint-
Leger
Saintsbury, George (Edward Bateman) 1845-
1933 .... **TCLC 31**
See also CA 160; DLB 57, 149
Sait Faik .... **TCLC 23**
See also Abasiyanik, Sait Faik
Saki .... **TCLC 3; SSC 12**
See Munro, H(ector) H(ugh)
See also MTCW 2
Sala, George Augustus .... **NCLC 46**
Salama, Hannu 1936- .... **CLC 18**
Salamanca, J(ack) R(ichard) 1922- **CLC 4, 15**
See also CA 25-28R
Sale, J. Kirkpatrick
See Sale, Kirkpatrick
Sale, Kirkpatrick 1937- .... **CLC 68**
See also CA 13-16R; CANR 10
Salinas, Luis Omar 1937- ...... **CLC 90; DAM MULT; HLC**
See also CA 131; DLB 82; HW 1, 2
Salinas (y Serrano), Pedro 1891(?)-1951

TCLC 17
See also CA 117; DLB 134
Salinger, J(erome) D(avid) 1919- **CLC 1, 3, 8, 12, 55, 56; DA; DAB; DAC; DAM MST, NOV, POP; SSC 2, 28; WLC**
See also AAYA 2; CA 5-8R; CANR 39; CDALB
1941-1968; CLR 18; DLB 2, 102, 173;
MAICYA; MTCW 1, 2; SATA 67
Salisbury, John
See Caute, (John) David
Salter, James 1925- ....,....... **CLC 7, 52, 59**
See also CA 73-76; DLB 130
Saltus, Edgar (Everton) 1855-1921 . **TCLC 8**
See also CA 105; DLB 202
Saltykov, Mikhail Evgrafovich 1826-1889
NCLC 16
Samarakis, Antonis 1919- .... **CLC 5**
See also CA 25-28R; CAAS 16; CANR 36
Sanchez, Florencio 1875-1910 .... **TCLC 37**
See also CA 153; HW 1
Sanchez, Luis Rafael 1936- .... **CLC 23**
See also CA 128; DLB 145; HW 1
Sanchez, Sonia 1934- .... **CLC 5, 116; BLC 3; DAM MULT; PC 9**
See also BW 2, 3; CA 33-36R; CANR 24, 49,
74; CLR 18; DLB 41; DLBD 8; MAICYA;
MTCW 1, 2; SATA 22
Sand, George 1804-1876 **NCLC 2, 42, 57; DA; DAB; DAC; DAM MST, NOV; WLC**
See also DLB 119, 192
Sandburg, Carl (August) 1878-1967 **CLC 1, 4, 10, 15, 35; DA; DAB; DAC; DAM MST, POET; PC 2; WLC**
See also AAYA 24; CA 5-8R; 25-28R; CANR
35; CDALB 1865-1917; DLB 17, 54;
MAICYA; MTCW 1, 2; SATA 8
Sandburg, Charles
See Sandburg, Carl (August)
Sandburg, Charles A.
See Sandburg, Carl (August)
Sanders, (James) Ed(ward) 1939- .. **CLC 53; DAM POET**
See also CA 13-16R; CAAS 21; CANR 13, 44,
78; DLB 16
Sanders, Lawrence 1920-1998 **CLC 41; DAM POP**
See also BEST 89:4; CA 81-84; 165; CANR
33, 62; MTCW 1
Sanders, Noah
See Blount, Roy (Alton), Jr.
Sanders, Winston P.
See Anderson, Poul (William)
Sandoz, Mari(e Susette) 1896-1966 .. **CLC 28**
See also CA 1-4R; 25-28R; CANR 17, 64; DLB
9, 212; MTCW 1, 2; SATA 5
Saner, Reg(inald Anthony) 1931- .... **CLC 9**
See also CA 65-68
Sankara 788-820 .... **CMLC 32**
Sannazaro, Jacopo 1456(?)-1530 .... **LC 8**
Sansom, William 1912-1976 **CLC 2, 6; DAM NOV; SSC 21**
See also CA 5-8R; 65-68; CANR 42; DLB 139;
MTCW 1
Santayana, George 1863-1952 .... **TCLC 40**
See also CA 115; DLB 54, 71; DLBD 13
Santiago, Danny .... **CLC 33**
See also James, Daniel (Lewis)
See also DLB 122
Santmyer, Helen Hoover 1895-1986 . **CLC 33**
See also CA 1-4R; 118; CANR 15, 33; DLBY
84; MTCW 1
Santoka, Taneda 1882-1940 .... **TCLC 72**
Santos, Bienvenido N(uqui) 1911-1996 . **C L C**

22; DAM MULT
See also CA 101; 151; CANR 19, 46
Sapper .... **TCLC 44**
See also McNeile, Herman Cyril
Sapphire
See Sapphire, Brenda
Sapphire, Brenda 1950- .... **CLC 99**
Sappho fl. 6th cent. B.C.- ...... **CMLC 3; DAM POET; PC 5**
See also DLB 176
Saramago, Jose 1922- ...... **CLC 119; HLCS 1**
See also CA 153
Sarduy, Severo 1937-1993 **CLC 6, 97; HLCS 1**
See also CA 89-92; 142; CANR 58; DLB 113;
HW 1, 2
Sargeson, Frank 1903-1982 .... **CLC 31**
See also CA 25-28R; 106; CANR 38 79
Sarmiento, Felix Ruben Garcia
See Dario, Ruben
Saro-Wiwa, Ken(ule Beeson) 1941-1995 **C L C 114**
See also BW 2; CA 142; 150; CANR 60; DLB
157
Saroyan, William 1908-1981 **CLC 1, 8, 10, 29, 34, 56; DA; DAB; DAC; DAM DRAM, MST, NOV; SSC 21; WLC**
See also CA 5-8R; 103; CANR 30; CDALBS;
DLB 7, 9, 86; DLBY 81; MTCW 1, 2; SATA
23; SATA-Obit 24
Sarraute, Nathalie 1900- **CLC 1, 2, 4, 8, 10, 31, 80**
See also CA 9-12R; CANR 23, 66; DLB 83;
MTCW 1, 2
Sarton, (Eleanor) May 1912-1995 **CLC 4, 14, 49, 91; DAM POET**
See also CA 1-4R; 149; CANR 1, 34, 55; DLB
48; DLBY 81; INT CANR-34; MTCW 1, 2;
SATA 36; SATA-Obit 86
Sartre, Jean-Paul 1905-1980 **CLC 1, 4, 7, 9, 13, 18, 24, 44, 50, 52; DA; DAB; DAC; DAM DRAM, MST, NOV; DC 3; SSC 32; WLC**
See also CA 9-12R; 97-100; CANR 21; DLB
72; MTCW 1, 2
Sassoon, Siegfried (Lorraine) 1886-1967 **C L C 36; DAB; DAM MST, NOV, POET; PC 12**
See also CA 104; 25-28R; CANR 36; DLB 20,
191; DLBD 18; MTCW 1, 2
Satterfield, Charles
See Pohl, Frederik
Saul, John (W. III) 1942- **CLC 46; DAM NOV, POP**
See also AAYA 10; BEST 90:4; CA 81-84;
CANR 16, 40; SATA 98
Saunders, Caleb
See Heinlein, Robert A(nson)
Saura (Atares), Carlos 1932- .... **CLC 20**
See also CA 114; 131; CANR 79; HW 1
Sauser-Hall, Frederic 1887-1961 ...... **CLC 18**
See also Cendrars, Blaise
See also CA 102; 93-96; CANR 36, 62; MTCW
1
Saussure, Ferdinand de 1857-1913 **TCLC 49**
Savage, Catharine
See Brosman, Catharine Savage
Savage, Thomas 1915- .... **CLC 40**
See also CA 126; 132; CAAS 15; INT 132
Savan, Glenn 19(?)- .... **CLC 50**
Sayers, Dorothy L(eigh) 1893-1957 **TCLC 2, 15; DAM POP**
See also CA 104; 119; CANR 60; CDBLB 1914-
1945; DLB 10, 36, 77, 100; MTCW 1, 2
Sayers, Valerie 1952- .... **CLC 50**
See also CA 134; CANR 61

Sayles, John (Thomas) 1950- . CLC 7, 10, 14
See also CA 57-60; CANR 41; DLB 44
Scammell, Michael 1935- .... CLC 34
See also CA 156
Scannell, Vernon 1922- .... CLC 49
See also CA 5-8R; CANR 8, 24, 57; DLB 27;
SATA 59
Scarlett, Susan
See Streatfeild, (Mary) Noel
Scarron
See Mikszath, Kalman
Schaeffer, Susan Fromberg 1941- CLC 6, 11,
22
See also CA 49-52; CANR 18, 65; DLB 28;
MTCW 1, 2; SATA 22
Schary, Jill
See Robinson, Jill
Schell, Jonathan 1943- .... CLC 35
See also CA 73-76; CANR 12
Schelling, Friedrich Wilhelm Joseph von 1775-
1854 .... NCLC 30
See also DLB 90
Schendel, Arthur van 1874-1946 ... TCLC 56
Scherer, Jean-Marie Maurice 1920-
See Rohmer, Eric
See also CA 110
Schevill, James (Erwin) 1920- .... CLC 7
See also CA 5-8R; CAAS 12
Schiller, Friedrich 1759-1805 . NCLC 39, 69;
DAM DRAM
See also DLB 94
Schisgal, Murray (Joseph) 1926- .... CLC 6
See also CA 21-24R; CANR 48
Schlee, Ann 1934- .... CLC 35
See also CA 101; CANR 29; SATA 44; SATA-
Brief 36
Schlegel, August Wilhelm von 1767-1845
NCLC 15
See also DLB 94
Schlegel, Friedrich 1772-1829 .... NCLC 45
See also DLB 90
Schlegel, Johann Elias (von) 1719(?)-1749 L C
5
Schlesinger, Arthur M(eier), Jr. 1917- CLC 84
See also AITN 1; CA 1-4R; CANR 1, 28, 58;
DLB 17; INT CANR-28; MTCW 1, 2; SATA
61
Schmidt, Arno (Otto) 1914-1979 ...... CLC 56
See also CA 128; 109; DLB 69
Schmitz, Aron Hector 1861-1928
See Svevo, Italo
See also CA 104; 122; MTCW 1
Schnackenberg, Gjertrud 1953- .... CLC 40
See also CA 116; DLB 120
Schneider, Leonard Alfred 1925-1966
See Bruce, Lenny
See also CA 89-92
Schnitzler, Arthur 1862-1931 TCLC 4; SSC 15
See also CA 104; DLB 81, 118
Schoenberg, Arnold 1874-1951 ...... TCLC 75
See also CA 109
Schonberg, Arnold
See Schoenberg, Arnold
Schopenhauer, Arthur 1788-1860 . NCLC 51
See also DLB 90
Schor, Sandra (M.) 1932(?)-1990 ...... CLC 65
See also CA 132
Schorer, Mark 1908-1977 .... CLC 9
See also CA 5-8R; 73-76; CANR 7; DLB 103
Schrader, Paul (Joseph) 1946- .... CLC 26
See also CA 37-40R; CANR 41; DLB 44
Schreiner, Olive (Emilie Albertina) 1855-1920
TCLC 9

See also CA 105; 154; DLB 18, 156, 190
Schulberg, Budd (Wilson) 1914- ... CLC 7, 48
See also CA 25-28R; CANR 19; DLB 6, 26,
28; DLBY 81
Schulz, Bruno 1892-1942 TCLC 5, 51; SSC 13
See also CA 115; 123; MTCW 2
Schulz, Charles M(onroe) 1922- .... CLC 12
See also CA 9-12R; CANR 6; INT CANR-6;
SATA 10
Schumacher, E(rnst) F(riedrich) 1911-1977
CLC 80
See also CA 81-84; 73-76; CANR 34
Schuyler, James Marcus 1923-1991 CLC 5, 23;
DAM POET
See also CA 101; 134; DLB 5, 169; INT 101
Schwartz, Delmore (David) 1913-1966 CLC 2,
4, 10, 45, 87; PC 8
See also CA 17-18; 25-28R; CANR 35; CAP 2;
DLB 28, 48; MTCW 1, 2
Schwartz, Ernst
See Ozu, Yasujiro
Schwartz, John Burnham 1965- .... CLC 59
See also CA 132
Schwartz, Lynne Sharon 1939- .... CLC 31
See also CA 103; CANR 44; MTCW 2
Schwartz, Muriel A.
See Eliot, T(homas) S(tearns)
Schwarz-Bart, Andre 1928- .... CLC 2, 4
See also CA 89-92
Schwarz-Bart, Simone 1938-.. CLC 7; BLCS
See also BW 2; CA 97-100
Schwob, Marcel (Mayer Andre) 1867-1905
TCLC 20
See also CA 117; 168; DLB 123
Sciascia, Leonardo 1921-1989 . CLC 8, 9, 41
See also CA 85-88; 130; CANR 35; DLB 177;
MTCW 1
Scoppettone, Sandra 1936- .... CLC 26
See also AAYA 11; CA 5-8R; CANR 41, 73;
SATA 9, 92
Scorsese, Martin 1942- .... CLC 20, 89
See also CA 110; 114; CANR 46
Scotland, Jay
See Jakes, John (William)
Scott, Duncan Campbell 1862-1947 TCLC 6;
DAC
See also CA 104; 153; DLB 92
Scott, Evelyn 1893-1963 .... CLC 43
See also CA 104; 112; CANR 64; DLB 9, 48
Scott, F(rancis) R(eginald) 1899-1985 CLC 22
See also CA 101; 114; DLB 88; INT 101
Scott, Frank
See Scott, F(rancis) R(eginald)
Scott, Joanna 1960- .... CLC 50
See also CA 126; CANR 53
Scott, Paul (Mark) 1920-1978 .... CLC 9, 60
See also CA 81-84; 77-80; CANR 33; DLB 14,
207; MTCW 1
Scott, Sarah 1723-1795 .... LC 44
See also DLB 39
Scott, Walter 1771-1832 .. NCLC 15, 69; DA;
DAB; DAC; DAM MST, NOV, POET; PC
13; SSC 32; WLC
See also AAYA 22; CDBLB 1789-1832; DLB
93, 107, 116, 144, 159; YABC 2
Scribe, (Augustin) Eugene 1791-1861 N C L C
16; DAM DRAM; DC 5
See also DLB 192
Scrum, R.
See Crumb, R(obert)
Scudery, Madeleine de 1607-1701 .... LC 2
Scum
See Crumb, R(obert)

Scumbag, Little Bobby
See Crumb, R(obert)
Seabrook, John
See Hubbard, L(afayette) Ron(ald)
Sealy, I. Allan 1951- .... CLC 55
Search, Alexander
See Pessoa, Fernando (Antonio Nogueira)
Sebastian, Lee
See Silverberg, Robert
Sebastian Owl
See Thompson, Hunter S(tockton)
Sebestyen, Ouida 1924- .... CLC 30
See also AAYA 8; CA 107; CANR 40; CLR 17;
JRDA; MAICYA; SAAS 10; SATA 39
Secundus, H. Scriblerus
See Fielding, Henry
Sedges, John
See Buck, Pearl S(ydenstricker)
Sedgwick, Catharine Maria 1789-1867 N C L C
19
See also DLB 1, 74
Seelye, John (Douglas) 1931- .... CLC 7
See also CA 97-100; CANR 70; INT 97-100
Seferiades, Giorgos Stylianou 1900-1971
See Seferis, George
See also CA 5-8R; 33-36R; CANR 5, 36;
MTCW 1
Seferis, George .... CLC 5, 11
See also Seferiades, Giorgos Stylianou
Segal, Erich (Wolf) 1937- . CLC 3, 10; DAM
POP
See also BEST 89:1; CA 25-28R; CANR 20,
36, 65; DLBY 86; INT CANR-20; MTCW 1
Seger, Bob 1945- .... CLC 35
Seghers, Anna .... CLC 7
See also Radvanyi, Netty
See also DLB 69
Seidel, Frederick (Lewis) 1936- .... CLC 18
See also CA 13-16R; CANR 8; DLBY 84
Seifert, Jaroslav 1901-1986 .. CLC 34, 44, 93
See also CA 127; MTCW 1, 2
Sei Shonagon c. 966-1017(?) .... CMLC 6
Séjour, Victor 1817-1874 .... DC 10
See also DLB 50
Sejour Marcou et Ferrand, Juan Victor
See Séjour, Victor
Selby, Hubert, Jr. 1928- CLC 1, 2, 4, 8; SSC 20
See also CA 13-16R; CANR 33; DLB 2
Selzer, Richard 1928- .... CLC 74
See also CA 65-68; CANR 14
Sembene, Ousmane
See Ousmane, Sembene
Senancour, Etienne Pivert de 1770-1846
NCLC 16
See also DLB 119
Sender, Ramon (Jose) 1902-1982 CLC 8; DAM
MULT; HLC
See also CA 5-8R; 105; CANR 8; HW 1;
MTCW 1
Seneca, Lucius Annaeus c. 1-c. 65 . CMLC 6;
DAM DRAM; DC 5
See also DLB 211
Senghor, Leopold Sedar 1906- CLC 54; BLC
3; DAM MULT, POET; PC 25
See also BW 2, 3; CA 116; 125; CANR 47, 74;
MTCW 1, 2
Senna, Danzy 1970- .... CLC 119
See also CA 169
Serling, (Edward) Rod(man) 1924-1975 C L C
30
See also AAYA 14; AITN 1; CA 162; 57-60;
DLB 26
Serna, Ramon Gomez de la

See Crane, Stephen (Townley)
Smith, Joseph, Jr. 1805-1844 .... **NCLC 53**
Smith, Lee 1944- .... **CLC 25, 73**
See also CA 114; 119; CANR 46; DLB 143;
DLBY 83; INT 119
Smith, Martin
See Smith, Martin Cruz
Smith, Martin Cruz 1942- ..... **CLC 25; DAM
MULT, POP**
See also BEST 89:4; CA 85-88; CANR 6, 23,
43, 65; INT CANR-23; MTCW 2; NNAL
Smith, Mary-Ann Tirone 1944- .... **CLC 39**
See also CA 118; 136
Smith, Patti 1946- .... **CLC 12**
See also CA 93-96; CANR 63
Smith, Pauline (Urmson) 1882-1959**TCLC 25**
Smith, Rosamond
See Oates, Joyce Carol
Smith, Sheila Kaye
See Kaye-Smith, Sheila
Smith, Stevie .... **CLC 3, 8, 25, 44; PC 12**
See also Smith, Florence Margaret
See also DLB 20; MTCW 2
Smith, Wilbur (Addison) 1933- .... **CLC 33**
See also CA 13-16R; CANR 7, 46, 66; MTCW
1, 2
Smith, William Jay 1918- .... **CLC 6**
See also CA 5-8R; CANR 44; DLB 5; MAICYA;
SAAS 22; SATA 2, 68
Smith, Woodrow Wilson
See Kuttner, Henry
Smolenskin, Peretz 1842-1885 .... **NCLC 30**
Smollett, Tobias (George) 1721-1771**LC 2, 46**
See also CDBLB 1660-1789; DLB 39, 104
Snodgrass, W(illiam) D(e Witt) 1926-**CLC 2,
6, 10, 18, 68; DAM POET**
See also CA 1-4R; CANR 6, 36, 65; DLB 5;
MTCW 1, 2
Snow, C(harles) P(ercy) 1905-1980**CLC 1, 4,
6, 9, 13, 19; DAM NOV**
See also CA 5-8R; 101; CANR 28; CDBLB
1945-1960; DLB 15, 77; DLBD 17; MTCW
1, 2
Snow, Frances Compton
See Adams, Henry (Brooks)
Snyder, Gary (Sherman) 1930-**CLC 1, 2, 5, 9,
32, 120; DAM POET; PC 21**
See also CA 17-20R; CANR 30, 60; DLB 5,
16, 165, 212; MTCW 2
Snyder, Zilpha Keatley 1927- .... **CLC 17**
See also AAYA 15; CA 9-12R; CANR 38; CLR
31; JRDA; MAICYA; SAAS 2; SATA 1, 28,
75
Soares, Bernardo
See Pessoa, Fernando (Antonio Nogueira)
Sobh, A.
See Shamlu, Ahmad
Sobol, Joshua .... **CLC 60**
Socrates 469B.C.-399B.C. .... **CMLC 27**
Soderberg, Hjalmar 1869-1941 ..... **TCLC 39**
Sodergran, Edith (Irene)
See Soedergran, Edith (Irene)
Soedergran, Edith (Irene) 1892-1923 **T C L C
31**
Softly, Edgar
See Lovecraft, H(oward) P(hillips)
Softly, Edward
See Lovecraft, H(oward) P(hillips)
Sokolov, Raymond 1941- .... **CLC 7**
See also CA 85-88
Solo, Jay
See Ellison, Harlan (Jay)
Sologub, Fyodor .... **TCLC 9**

See also Teternikov, Fyodor Kuzmich
Solomons, Ikey Esquir
See Thackeray, William Makepeace
Solomos, Dionysios 1798-1857 .... **NCLC 15**
Solwoska, Mara
See French, Marilyn
Solzhenitsyn, Aleksandr I(sayevich) 1918-
**CLC 1, 2, 4, 7, 9, 10, 18, 26, 34, 78; DA;
DAB; DAC; DAM MST, NOV; SSC 32;
WLC**
See also AITN 1; CA 69-72; CANR 40, 65;
MTCW 1, 2
Somers, Jane
See Lessing, Doris (May)
Somerville, Edith 1858-1949 .... **TCLC 51**
See also DLB 135
Somerville & Ross
See Martin, Violet Florence; Somerville, Edith
Sommer, Scott 1951- .... **CLC 25**
See also CA 106
Sondheim, Stephen (Joshua) 1930- . **CLC 30,
39; DAM DRAM**
See also AAYA 11; CA 103; CANR 47, 68
Song, Cathy 1955- .... **PC 21**
See also CA 154; DLB 169
Sontag, Susan 1933-**CLC 1, 2, 10, 13, 31, 105;
DAM POP**
See also CA 17-20R; CANR 25, 51, 74; DLB
2, 67; MTCW 1, 2
Sophocles 496(?)B.C.-406(?)B.C. ... **CMLC 2;
DA; DAB; DAC; DAM DRAM, MST; DC
1; WLCS**
See also DLB 176
Sordello 1189-1269 .... **CMLC 15**
Sorel, Georges 1847-1922 .... **TCLC 91**
See also CA 118
Sorel, Julia
See Drexler, Rosalyn
Sorrentino, Gilbert 1929-**CLC 3, 7, 14, 22, 40**
See also CA 77-80; CANR 14, 33; DLB 5, 173;
DLBY 80; INT CANR-14
Soto, Gary 1952- **CLC 32, 80; DAM MULT;
HLC**
See also AAYA 10; CA 119; 125; CANR 50,
74; CLR 38; DLB 82; HW 1, 2; INT 125;
JRDA; MTCW 2; SATA 80
Soupault, Philippe 1897-1990 .... **CLC 68**
See also CA 116; 147; 131
Souster, (Holmes) Raymond 1921-**CLC 5, 14;
DAC; DAM POET**
See also CA 13-16R; CAAS 14; CANR 13, 29,
53; DLB 88; SATA 63
Southern, Terry 1924(?)-1995 .... **CLC 7**
See also CA 1-4R; 150; CANR 1, 55; DLB 2
Southey, Robert 1774-1843 .... **NCLC 8**
See also DLB 93, 107, 142; SATA 54
Southworth, Emma Dorothy Eliza Nevitte
1819-1899 .... **NCLC 26**
Souza, Ernest
See Scott, Evelyn
Soyinka, Wole 1934-**CLC 3, 5, 14, 36, 44; BLC
3; DA; DAB; DAC; DAM DRAM, MST,
MULT; DC 2; WLC**
See also BW 2, 3; CA 13-16R; CANR 27, 39;
DLB 125; MTCW 1, 2
Spackman, W(illiam) M(ode) 1905-1990**C L C
46**
See also CA 81-84; 132
Spacks, Barry (Bernard) 1931- .... **CLC 14**
See also CA 154; CANR 33; DLB 105
Spanidou, Irini 1946- .... **CLC 44**
Spark, Muriel (Sarah) 1918-**CLC 2, 3, 5, 8, 13,
18, 40, 94; DAB; DAC; DAM MST, NOV;**

SSC 10
See also CA 5-8R; CANR 12, 36, 76; CDBLB
1945-1960; DLB 15, 139; INT CANR-12;
MTCW 1, 2
Spaulding, Douglas
See Bradbury, Ray (Douglas)
Spaulding, Leonard
See Bradbury, Ray (Douglas)
Spence, J. A. D.
See Eliot, T(homas) S(tearns)
Spencer, Elizabeth 1921- .... **CLC 22**
See also CA 13-16R; CANR 32, 65; DLB 6;
MTCW 1; SATA 14
Spencer, Leonard G.
See Silverberg, Robert
Spencer, Scott 1945- .... **CLC 30**
See also CA 113; CANR 51; DLBY 86
Spender, Stephen (Harold) 1909-1995**CLC 1,
2, 5, 10, 41, 91; DAM POET**
See also CA 9-12R; 149; CANR 31, 54; CDBLB
1945-1960; DLB 20; MTCW 1, 2
Spengler, Oswald (Arnold Gottfried) 1880-1936
TCLC 25
See also CA 118
Spenser, Edmund 1552(?)-1599**LC 5, 39; DA;
DAB; DAC; DAM MST, POET; PC 8;
WLC**
See also CDBLB Before 1660; DLB 167
Spicer, Jack 1925-1965 **CLC 8, 18, 72; DAM
POET**
See also CA 85-88; DLB 5, 16, 193
Spiegelman, Art 1948- .... **CLC 76**
See also AAYA 10; CA 125; CANR 41, 55, 74;
MTCW 2
Spielberg, Peter 1929- .... **CLC 6**
See also CA 5-8R; CANR 4, 48; DLBY 81
Spielberg, Steven 1947- .... **CLC 20**
See also AAYA 8, 24; CA 77-80; CANR 32;
SATA 32
Spillane, Frank Morrison 1918-
See Spillane, Mickey
See also CA 25-28R; CANR 28, 63; MTCW 1,
2; SATA 66
Spillane, Mickey .... **CLC 3, 13**
See also Spillane, Frank Morrison
See also MTCW 2
Spinoza, Benedictus de 1632-1677 .... **LC 9**
Spinrad, Norman (Richard) 1940- ... **CLC 46**
See also CA 37-40R; CAAS 19; CANR 20; DLB
8; INT CANR-20
Spitteler, Carl (Friedrich Georg) 1845-1924
TCLC 12
See also CA 109; DLB 129
Spivack, Kathleen (Romola Drucker) 1938-
CLC 6
See also CA 49-52
Spoto, Donald 1941- .... **CLC 39**
See also CA 65-68; CANR 11, 57
Springsteen, Bruce (F.) 1949- .... **CLC 17**
See also CA 111
Spurling, Hilary 1940- .... **CLC 34**
See also CA 104; CANR 25, 52
Spyker, John Howland
See Elman, Richard (Martin)
Squires, (James) Radcliffe 1917-1993**CLC 51**
See also CA 1-4R; 140; CANR 6, 21
Srivastava, Dhanpat Rai 1880(?)-1936
See Premchand
See also CA 118
Stacy, Donald
See Pohl, Frederik
Stael, Germaine de 1766-1817
See Stael-Holstein, Anne Louise Germaine

See also CA 107

Vicar, Henry
See Felsen, Henry Gregor

Vicker, Angus
See Felsen, Henry Gregor

Vidal, Gore 1925-**CLC 2, 4, 6, 8, 10, 22, 33, 72; DAM NOV, POP**
See also AITN 1; BEST 90:2; CA 5-8R; CANR 13, 45, 65; CDALBS; DLB 6, 152; INT CANR-13; MTCW 1, 2

Viereck, Peter (Robert Edwin) 1916- . **CLC 4**
See also CA 1-4R; CANR 1, 47; DLB 5

Vigny, Alfred (Victor) de 1797-1863**NCLC 7; DAM POET; PC 26**
See also DLB 119, 192

Vilakazi, Benedict Wallet 1906-1947**TCLC 37**
See also CA 168

Villa, Jose Garcia 1904-1997 .... **PC 22**
See also CA 25-28R; CANR 12

Villaurrutia, Xavier 1903-1950 ...... **TCLC 80**
See also HW 1

Villiers de l'Isle Adam, Jean Marie Mathias Philippe Auguste, Comte de 1838-1889 **NCLC 3; SSC 14**
See also DLB 123

Villon, Francois 1431-1463(?) .... **PC 13**
See also DLB 208

Vinci, Leonardo da 1452-1519 .... **LC 12**

Vine, Barbara .... **CLC 50**
See also Rendell, Ruth (Barbara)
See also BEST 90:4

Vinge, Joan (Carol) D(ennison) 1948-**CLC 30; SSC 24**
See also CA 93-96; CANR 72; SATA 36

Violis, G.
See Simenon, Georges (Jacques Christian)

Virgil 70B.C.-19B.C.
See Vergil
See also DLB 211

Visconti, Luchino 1906-1976 .... **CLC 16**
See also CA 81-84; 65-68; CANR 39

Vittorini, Elio 1908-1966 .... **CLC 6, 9, 14**
See also CA 133; 25-28R

Vivekananda, Swami 1863-1902 .... **TCLC 88**

Vizenor, Gerald Robert 1934-**CLC 103; DAM MULT**
See also CA 13-16R; CAAS 22; CANR 5, 21, 44, 67; DLB 175; MTCW 2; NNAL

Vizinczey, Stephen 1933- .... **CLC 40**
See also CA 128; INT 128

Vliet, R(ussell) G(ordon) 1929-1984 **CLC 22**
See also CA 37-40R; 112; CANR 18

Vogau, Boris Andreyevich 1894-1937(?)
See Pilnyak, Boris
See also CA 123

Vogel, Paula A(nne) 1951- .... **CLC 76**
See also CA 108

Voigt, Cynthia 1942-........................... **CLC 30**
See also AAYA 3, 30; CA 106; CANR 18, 37, 40; CLR 13, 48; INT CANR-18; JRDA; MAICYA; SATA 48, 79; SATA-Brief 33

Voigt, Ellen Bryant 1943- .... **CLC 54**
See also CA 69-72; CANR 11, 29, 55; DLB 120

Voinovich, Vladimir (Nikolaevich) 1932-**CLC 10, 49**
See also CA 81-84; CAAS 12; CANR 33, 67; MTCW 1

Vollmann, William T. 1959- .. **CLC 89; DAM NOV, POP**
See also CA 134; CANR 67; MTCW 2

Voloshinov, V. N.
See Bakhtin, Mikhail Mikhailovich

Voltaire 1694-1778 . **LC 14; DA; DAB; DAC;**

DAM DRAM, MST; SSC 12; WLC

von Aschendrof, BaronIgnatz
See Ford, Ford Madox

von Daeniken, Erich 1935- .... **CLC 30**
See also AITN 1; CA 37-40R; CANR 17, 44

von Daniken, Erich
See von Daeniken, Erich

von Heidenstam, (Carl Gustaf) Verner
See Heidenstam, (Carl Gustaf) Verner von

von Heyse, Paul (Johann Ludwig)
See Heyse, Paul (Johann Ludwig von)

von Hofmannsthal, Hugo
See Hofmannsthal, Hugo von

von Horvath, Odon
See Horvath, Oedoen von

von Horvath, Oedoen
See Horvath, Oedoen von

von Liliencron, (Friedrich Adolf Axel) Detlev
See Liliencron, (Friedrich Adolf Axel) Detlev von

Vonnegut, Kurt, Jr. 1922-**CLC 1, 2, 3, 4, 5, 8, 12, 22, 40, 60, 111; DA; DAB; DAC; DAM MST, NOV, POP; SSC 8; WLC**
See also AAYA 6; AITN 1; BEST 90:4; CA 1-4R; CANR 1, 25, 49, 75; CDALB 1968-1988; DLB 2, 8, 152; DLBD 3; DLBY 80; MTCW 1, 2

Von Rachen, Kurt
See Hubbard, L(afayette) Ron(ald)

von Rezzori (d'Arezzo), Gregor
See Rezzori (d'Arezzo), Gregor von

von Sternberg, Josef
See Sternberg, Josef von

Vorster, Gordon 1924-........................ **CLC 34**
See also CA 133

Vosce, Trudie
See Ozick, Cynthia

Voznesensky, Andrei (Andreievich) 1933-**CLC 1, 15, 57; DAM POET**
See also CA 89-92; CANR 37; MTCW 1

Waddington, Miriam 1917- .... **CLC 28**
See also CA 21-24R; CANR 12, 30; DLB 68

Wagman, Fredrica 1937- .... **CLC 7**
See also CA 97-100; INT 97-100

Wagner, Linda W.
See Wagner-Martin, Linda (C.)

Wagner, Linda Welshimer
See Wagner-Martin, Linda (C.)

Wagner, Richard 1813-1883 .... **NCLC 9**
See also DLB 129

Wagner-Martin, Linda (C.) 1936- .... **CLC 50**
See also CA 159

Wagoner, David (Russell) 1926- **CLC 3, 5, 15**
See also CA 1-4R; CAAS 3; CANR 2, 71; DLB 5; SATA 14

Wah, Fred(erick James) 1939- .... **CLC 44**
See also CA 107; 141; DLB 60

Wahloo, Per 1926-1975 .... **CLC 7**
See also CA 61-64; CANR 73

Wahloo, Peter
See Wahloo, Per

Wain, John (Barrington) 1925-1994 . **CLC 2, 11, 15, 46**
See also CA 5-8R; 145; CAAS 4; CANR 23, 54; CDBLB 1960 to Present; DLB 15, 27, 139, 155; MTCW 1, 2

Wajda, Andrzej 1926- .... **CLC 16**
See also CA 102

Wakefield, Dan 1932- .... **CLC 7**
See also CA 21-24R; CAAS 7

Wakoski, Diane 1937- **CLC 2, 4, 7, 9, 11, 40; DAM POET; PC 15**
See also CA 13-16R; CAAS 1; CANR 9, 60;

DLB 5; INT CANR-9; MTCW 2

Wakoski-Sherbell, Diane
See Wakoski, Diane

Walcott, Derek (Alton) 1930-**CLC 2, 4, 9, 14, 25, 42, 67, 76; BLC 3; DAB; DAC; DAM MST, MULT, POET; DC 7**
See also BW 2; CA 89-92; CANR 26, 47, 75, 80; DLB 117; DLBY 81; MTCW 1, 2

Waldman, Anne (Lesley) 1945- .... **CLC 7**
See also CA 37-40R; CAAS 17; CANR 34, 69; DLB 16

Waldo, E. Hunter
See Sturgeon, Theodore (Hamilton)

Waldo, Edward Hamilton
See Sturgeon, Theodore (Hamilton)

Walker, Alice (Malsenior) 1944- **CLC 5, 6, 9, 19, 27, 46, 58, 103; BLC 3; DA; DAB; DAC; DAM MST, MULT, NOV, POET, POP; SSC 5; WLCS**
See also AAYA 3; BEST 89:4; BW 2, 3; CA 37-40R; CANR 9, 27, 49, 66; CDALB 1968-1988; DLB 6, 33, 143; INT CANR-27; MTCW 1, 2; SATA 31

Walker, David Harry 1911-1992 .... **CLC 14**
See also CA 1-4R; 137; CANR 1; SATA 8; SATA-Obit 71

Walker, Edward Joseph 1934-
See Walker, Ted
See also CA 21-24R; CANR 12, 28, 53

Walker, George F. 1947- . **CLC 44, 61; DAB; DAC; DAM MST**
See also CA 103; CANR 21, 43, 59; DLB 60

Walker, Joseph A. 1935- .... **CLC 19; DAM DRAM, MST**
See also BW 1, 3; CA 89-92; CANR 26; DLB 38

Walker, Margaret (Abigail) 1915-1998**CLC 1, 6; BLC; DAM MULT; PC 20**
See also BW 2, 3; CA 73-76; 172; CANR 26, 54, 76; DLB 76, 152; MTCW 1, 2

Walker, Ted .... **CLC 13**
See also Walker, Edward Joseph
See also DLB 40

Wallace, David Foster 1962- ..... **CLC 50, 114**
See also CA 132; CANR 59; MTCW 2

Wallace, Dexter
See Masters, Edgar Lee

Wallace, (Richard Horatio) Edgar 1875-1932 **TCLC 57**
See also CA 115; DLB 70

Wallace, Irving 1916-1990 **CLC 7, 13; DAM NOV, POP**
See also AITN 1; CA 1-4R; 132; CAAS 1; CANR 1, 27; INT CANR-27; MTCW 1, 2

Wallant, Edward Lewis 1926-1962**CLC 5, 10**
See also CA 1-4R; CANR 22; DLB 2, 28, 143; MTCW 1, 2

Wallas, Graham 1858-1932 .... **TCLC 91**

Walley, Byron
See Card, Orson Scott

Walpole, Horace 1717-1797 .... **LC 49**
See also DLB 39, 104

Walpole, Hugh (Seymour) 1884-1941**TCLC 5**
See also CA 104; 165; DLB 34; MTCW 2

Walser, Martin 1927- .... **CLC 27**
See also CA 57-60; CANR 8, 46; DLB 75, 124

Walser, Robert 1878-1956 **TCLC 18; SSC 20**
See also CA 118; 165; DLB 66

Walsh, Jill Paton .... **CLC 35**
See also Paton Walsh, Gillian
See also AAYA 11; CLR 2; DLB 161; SAAS 3

Walter, Villiam Christian
See Andersen, Hans Christian

Wambaugh, Joseph (Aloysius, Jr.) 1937-**C L C
3, 18; DAM NOV, POP**
 See also AITN 1; BEST 89:3; CA 33-36R;
 CANR 42, 65; DLB 6; DLBY 83; MTCW 1,
 2

Wang Wei 699(?)-761(?) .... **PC 18**

Ward, Arthur Henry Sarsfield 1883-1959
 See Rohmer, Sax
 See also CA 108; 173

Ward, Douglas Turner 1930- .... **CLC 19**
 See also BW 1; CA 81-84; CANR 27; DLB 7,
 38

Ward, Mary Augusta
 See Ward, Mrs. Humphry

Ward, Mrs. Humphry 1851-1920 .. **TCLC 55**
 See also DLB 18

Ward, Peter
 See Faust, Frederick (Schiller)

Warhol, Andy 1928(?)-1987 .... **CLC 20**
 See also AAYA 12; BEST 89:4; CA 89-92; 121;
 CANR 34

Warner, Francis (Robert le Plastrier) 1937-
 CLC 14
 See also CA 53-56; CANR 11

Warner, Marina 1946- .... **CLC 59**
 See also CA 65-68; CANR 21, 55; DLB 194

Warner, Rex (Ernest) 1905-1986 ...... **CLC 45**
 See also CA 89-92; 119; DLB 15

Warner, Susan (Bogert) 1819-1885 **NCLC 31**
 See also DLB 3, 42

Warner, Sylvia (Constance) Ashton
 See Ashton-Warner, Sylvia (Constance)

Warner, Sylvia Townsend 1893-1978 **CLC 7,
19; SSC 23**
 See also CA 61-64; 77-80; CANR 16, 60; DLB
 34, 139; MTCW 1, 2

Warren, Mercy Otis 1728-1814 ..... **NCLC 13**
 See also DLB 31, 200

Warren, Robert Penn 1905-1989**CLC 1, 4, 6,
8, 10, 13, 18, 39, 53, 59; DA; DAB; DAC;
DAM MST, NOV, POET; SSC 4; WLC**
 See also AITN 1; CA 13-16R; 129; CANR 10,
 47; CDALB 1968-1988; DLB 2, 48, 152;
 DLBY 80, 89; INT CANR-10; MTCW 1, 2;
 SATA 46; SATA-Obit 63

Warshofsky, Isaac
 See Singer, Isaac Bashevis

Warton, Thomas 1728-1790 ..... **LC 15; DAM
POET**
 See also DLB 104, 109

Waruk, Kona
 See Harris, (Theodore) Wilson

Warung, Price 1855-1911 .... **TCLC 45**

Warwick, Jarvis
 See Garner, Hugh

Washington, Alex
 See Harris, Mark

Washington, Booker T(aliaferro) 1856-1915
 TCLC 10; BLC 3; DAM MULT
 See also BW 1; CA 114; 125; SATA 28

Washington, George 1732-1799 .... **LC 25**
 See also DLB 31

Wassermann, (Karl) Jakob 1873-1934**T C L C
6**
 See also CA 104; 163; DLB 66

Wasserstein, Wendy 1950- ... **CLC 32, 59, 90;
DAM DRAM; DC 4**
 See also CA 121; 129; CABS 3; CANR 53, 75;
 INT 129; MTCW 2; SATA 94

Waterhouse, Keith (Spencer) 1929- . **CLC 47**
 See also CA 5-8R; CANR 38, 67; DLB 13, 15;
 MTCW 1, 2

Waters, Frank (Joseph) 1902-1995 .. **CLC 88**
 See also CA 5-8R; 149; CAAS 13; CANR 3,
 18, 63; DLB 212; DLBY 86

Waters, Roger 1944- .... **CLC 35**

Watkins, Frances Ellen
 See Harper, Frances Ellen Watkins

Watkins, Gerrold
 See Malzberg, Barry N(athaniel)

Watkins, Gloria 1955(?)-
 See hooks, bell
 See also BW 2; CA 143; MTCW 2

Watkins, Paul 1964- .... **CLC 55**
 See also CA 132; CANR 62

Watkins, Vernon Phillips 1906-1967 **CLC 43**
 See also CA 9-10; 25-28R; CAP 1; DLB 20

Watson, Irving S.
 See Mencken, H(enry) L(ouis)

Watson, John H.
 See Farmer, Philip Jose

Watson, Richard F.
 See Silverberg, Robert

Waugh, Auberon (Alexander) 1939- .. **CLC 7**
 See also CA 45-48; CANR 6, 22; DLB 14, 194

Waugh, Evelyn (Arthur St. John) 1903-1966
 **CLC 1, 3, 8, 13, 19, 27, 44, 107; DA; DAB;
DAC; DAM MST, NOV, POP; WLC**
 See also CA 85-88; 25-28R; CANR 22; CDBLB
 1914-1945; DLB 15, 162, 195; MTCW 1, 2

Waugh, Harriet 1944- .... **CLC 6**
 See also CA 85-88; CANR 22

Ways, C. R.
 See Blount, Roy (Alton), Jr.

Waystaff, Simon
 See Swift, Jonathan

Webb, (Martha) Beatrice (Potter) 1858-1943
 TCLC 22
 See also Potter, (Helen) Beatrix
 See also CA 117; DLB 190

Webb, Charles (Richard) 1939- .... **CLC 7**
 See also CA 25-28R

Webb, James H(enry), Jr. 1946- .... **CLC 22**
 See also CA 81-84

Webb, Mary (Gladys Meredith) 1881-1927
 TCLC 24
 See also CA 123; DLB 34

Webb, Mrs. Sidney
 See Webb, (Martha) Beatrice (Potter)

Webb, Phyllis 1927- .... **CLC 18**
 See also CA 104; CANR 23; DLB 53

Webb, Sidney (James) 1859-1947 .. **TCLC 22**
 See also CA 117; 163; DLB 190

Webber, Andrew Lloyd .... **CLC 21**
 See also Lloyd Webber, Andrew

Weber, Lenora Mattingly 1895-1971 **CLC 12**
 See also CA 19-20; 29-32R; CAP 1; SATA 2;
 SATA-Obit 26

Weber, Max 1864-1920 .... **TCLC 69**
 See also CA 109

Webster, John 1579(?)-1634(?) ... **LC 33; DA;
DAB; DAC; DAM DRAM, MST; DC 2;
WLC**
 See also CDBLB Before 1660; DLB 58

Webster, Noah 1758-1843 .... **NCLC 30**
 See also DLB 1, 37, 42, 43, 73

Wedekind, (Benjamin) Frank(lin) 1864-1918
 TCLC 7; DAM DRAM
 See also CA 104; 153; DLB 118

Weidman, Jerome 1913-1998 .... **CLC 7**
 See also AITN 2; CA 1-4R; 171; CANR 1; DLB
 28

Weil, Simone (Adolphine) 1909-1943**TCLC 23**
 See also CA 117; 159; MTCW 2

Weininger, Otto 1880-1903 .... **TCLC 84**

Weinstein, Nathan
 See West, Nathanael

Weinstein, Nathan von Wallenstein
 See West, Nathanael

Weir, Peter (Lindsay) 1944- .... **CLC 20**
 See also CA 113; 123

Weiss, Peter (Ulrich) 1916-1982**CLC 3, 15, 51;
DAM DRAM**
 See also CA 45-48; 106; CANR 3; DLB 69, 124

Weiss, Theodore (Russell) 1916-**CLC 3, 8, 14**
 See also CA 9-12R; CAAS 2; CANR 46; DLB
 5

Welch, (Maurice) Denton 1915-1948**TCLC 22**
 See also CA 121; 148

Welch, James 1940- ..... **CLC 6, 14, 52; DAM
MULT, POP**
 See also CA 85-88; CANR 42, 66; DLB 175;
 NNAL

Weldon, Fay 1931- . **CLC 6, 9, 11, 19, 36, 59;
DAM POP**
 See also CA 21-24R; CANR 16, 46, 63; CDBLB
 1960 to Present; DLB 14, 194; INT CANR-
 16; MTCW 1, 2

Wellek, Rene 1903-1995 .... **CLC 28**
 See also CA 5-8R; 150; CAAS 7; CANR 8; DLB
 63; INT CANR-8

Weller, Michael 1942- .... **CLC 10, 53**
 See also CA 85-88

Weller, Paul 1958- .... **CLC 26**

Wellershoff, Dieter 1925- .... **CLC 46**
 See also CA 89-92; CANR 16, 37

Welles, (George) Orson 1915-1985**CLC 20, 80**
 See also CA 93-96; 117

Wellman, John McDowell 1945-
 See Wellman, Mac
 See also CA 166

Wellman, Mac 1945- .... **CLC 65**
 See also Wellman, John McDowell; Wellman,
 John McDowell

Wellman, Manly Wade 1903-1986 .... **CLC 49**
 See also CA 1-4R; 118; CANR 6, 16, 44; SATA
 6; SATA-Obit 47

Wells, Carolyn 1869(?)-1942 .... **TCLC 35**
 See also CA 113; DLB 11

Wells, H(erbert) G(eorge) 1866-1946**TCLC 6,
12, 19; DA; DAB; DAC; DAM MST, NOV;
SSC 6; WLC**
 See also AAYA 18; CA 110; 121; CDBLB 1914-
 1945; DLB 34, 70, 156, 178; MTCW 1, 2;
 SATA 20

·Wells, Rosemary 1943- .... **CLC 12**
 See also AAYA 13; CA 85-88; CANR 48; CLR
 16; MAICYA; SAAS 1; SATA 18, 69

Welty, Eudora 1909- **CLC 1, 2, 5, 14, 22, 33,
105; DA; DAB; DAC; DAM MST, NOV;
SSC 1, 27; WLC**
 See also CA 9-12R; CABS 1; CANR 32, 65;
 CDALB 1941-1968; DLB 2, 102, 143;
 DLBD 12; DLBY 87; MTCW 1, 2

Wen I-to 1899-1946 .... **TCLC 28**

Wentworth, Robert
 See Hamilton, Edmond

Werfel, Franz (Viktor) 1890-1945 ... **TCLC 8**
 See also CA 104; 161; DLB 81, 124

Wergeland, Henrik Arnold 1808-1845**N C L C
5**

Wersba, Barbara 1932- .... **CLC 30**
 See also AAYA 2, 30; CA 29-32R; CANR 16,
 38; CLR 3; DLB 52; JRDA; MAICYA; SAAS
 2; SATA 1, 58; SATA-Essay 103

Wertmueller, Lina 1928- .... **CLC 16**
 See also CA 97-100; CANR 39, 78

Wescott, Glenway 1901-1987 .... **CLC 13**
 See also CA 13-16R; 121; CANR 23, 70; DLB

4, 9, 102

Wesker, Arnold 1932- .... **CLC 3, 5, 42; DAB; DAM DRAM**
See also CA 1-4R; CAAS 7; CANR 1, 33; CDBLB 1960 to Present; DLB 13; MTCW 1

Wesley, Richard (Errol) 1945- .... **CLC 7**
See also BW 1; CA 57-60; CANR 27; DLB 38

Wessel, Johan Herman 1742-1785 .... **LC 7**

West, Anthony (Panther) 1914-1987 **CLC 50**
See also CA 45-48; 124; CANR 3, 19; DLB 15

West, C. P.
See Wodehouse, P(elham) G(renville)

West, (Mary) Jessamyn 1902-1984 **CLC 7, 17**
See also CA 9-12R; 112; CANR 27; DLB 6; DLBY 84; MTCW 1, 2; SATA-Obit 37

West, Morris L(anglo) 1916- .... **CLC 6, 33**
See also CA 5-8R; CANR 24, 49, 64; MTCW 1, 2

West, Nathanael 1903-1940 **TCLC 1, 14, 44; SSC 16**
See also CA 104; 125; CDALB 1929-1941; DLB 4, 9, 28; MTCW 1, 2

West, Owen
See Koontz, Dean R(ay)

West, Paul 1930- .... **CLC 7, 14, 96**
See also CA 13-16R; CAAS 7; CANR 22, 53, 76; DLB 14; INT CANR-22; MTCW2

West, Rebecca 1892-1983 ... **CLC 7, 9, 31, 50**
See also CA 5-8R; 109; CANR 19; DLB 36; DLBY 83; MTCW 1, 2

Westall, Robert (Atkinson) 1929-1993 **CLC 17**
See also AAYA 12; CA 69-72; 141; CANR 18, 68; CLR 13; JRDA; MAICYA; SAAS 2; SATA 23, 69; SATA-Obit 75

Westermarck, Edward 1862-1939 . **TCLC 87**

Westlake, Donald E(dwin) 1933- **CLC 7, 33; DAM POP**
See also CA 17-20R; CAAS 13; CANR 16, 44, 65; INT CANR-16; MTCW 2

Westmacott, Mary
See Christie, Agatha (Mary Clarissa)

Weston, Allen
See Norton, Andre

Wetcheek, J. L.
See Feuchtwanger, Lion

Wetering, Janwillem van de
See van de Wetering, Janwillem

Wetherald, Agnes Ethelwyn 1857-1940 **TCLC 81**
See also DLB 99

Wetherell, Elizabeth
See Warner, Susan (Bogert)

Whale, James 1889-1957 .... **TCLC 63**

Whalen, Philip 1923- .... **CLC 6, 29**
See also CA 9-12R; CANR 5, 39; DLB 16

Wharton, Edith (Newbold Jones) 1862-1937 **TCLC 3, 9, 27, 53; DA; DAB; DAC; DAM MST, NOV; SSC 6; WLC**
See also AAYA 25; CA 104; 132; CDALB 1865-1917; DLB 4, 9, 12, 78, 189; DLBD 13; MTCW 1, 2

Wharton, James
See Mencken, H(enry) L(ouis)

Wharton, William (a pseudonym) **CLC 18, 37**
See also CA 93-96; DLBY 80; INT 93-96

Wheatley (Peters), Phillis 1754(?)-1784 **LC 3, 50; BLC 3; DA; DAC; DAM MST, MULT, POET; PC 3; WLC**
See also CDALB 1640-1865; DLB 31, 50

Wheelock, John Hall 1886-1978 .... **CLC 14**
See also CA 13-16R; 77-80; CANR 14; DLB 45

White, E(lwyn) B(rooks) 1899-1985 **CLC 10,**

34, 39; **DAM POP**
See also AITN 2; CA 13-16R; 116; CANR 16, 37; CDALBS; CLR 1, 21; DLB 11, 22; MAICYA; MTCW 1, 2; SATA 2, 29, 100; SATA-Obit 44

White, Edmund (Valentine III) 1940- **CLC 27, 110; DAM POP**
See also AAYA 7; CA 45-48; CANR 3, 19, 36, 62; MTCW 1, 2

White, Patrick (Victor Martindale) 1912-1990 **CLC 3, 4, 5, 7, 9, 18, 65, 69**
See also CA 81-84; 132; CANR 43; MTCW 1

White, Phyllis Dorothy James 1920-
See James, P. D.
See also CA 21-24R; CANR 17, 43, 65; DAM POP; MTCW 1, 2

White, T(erence) H(anbury) 1906-1964 **C L C 30**
See also AAYA 22; CA 73-76; CANR 37; DLB 160; JRDA; MAICYA; SATA 12

White, Terence de Vere 1912-1994 ... **CLC 49**
See also CA 49-52; 145; CANR 3

White, Walter
See White, Walter F(rancis)
See also BLC; DAM MULT

White, Walter F(rancis) 1893-1955 **TCLC 15**
See also White, Walter
See also BW 1; CA 115; 124; DLB 51

White, William Hale 1831-1913
See Rutherford, Mark
See also CA 121

Whitehead, E(dward) A(nthony) 1933- **CLC 5**
See also CA 65-68; CANR 58

Whitemore, Hugh (John) 1936- .... **CLC 37**
See also CA 132; CANR 77; INT 132

Whitman, Sarah Helen (Power) 1803-1878 **NCLC 19**
See also DLB 1

Whitman, Walt(er) 1819-1892 . **NCLC 4, 31; DA; DAB; DAC; DAM MST, POET; PC 3; WLC**
See also CDALB 1640-1865; DLB 3, 64; SATA 20

Whitney, Phyllis A(yame) 1903- ..... **CLC 42; DAM POP**
See also AITN 2; BEST 90:3; CA 1-4R; CANR 3, 25, 38, 60; JRDA; MAICYA; MTCW 2; SATA 1, 30

Whittemore, (Edward) Reed (Jr.) 1919- **CLC 4**
See also CA 9-12R; CAAS 8; CANR 4; DLB 5

Whittier, John Greenleaf 1807-1892 **NCLC 8, 59**
See also DLB 1

Whittlebot, Hernia
See Coward, Noel (Peirce)

Wicker, Thomas Grey 1926-
See Wicker, Tom
See also CA 65-68; CANR 21, 46

Wicker, Tom .... **CLC 7**
See also Wicker, Thomas Grey

Wideman, John Edgar 1941- **CLC 5, 34, 36, 67; BLC 3; DAM MULT**
See also BW 2, 3; CA 85-88; CANR 14, 42, 67; DLB 33, 143; MTCW 2

Wiebe, Rudy (Henry) 1934- .. **CLC 6, 11, 14; DAC; DAM MST**
See also CA 37-40R; CANR 42, 67; DLB 60

Wieland, Christoph Martin 1733-1813 **N C L C 17**
See also DLB 97

Wiene, Robert 1881-1938 .... **TCLC 56**

Wieners, John 1934- .... **CLC 7**
See also CA 13-16R; DLB 16

Wiesel, Elie(zer) 1928- **CLC 3, 5, 11, 37; DA; DAB; DAC; DAM MST, NOV; WLCS**
See also AAYA 7; AITN 1; CA 5-8R; CANR 8, 40, 65; CDALBS; DLB 83; DLBY 87; INT CANR-8; MTCW 1, 2; SATA 56

Wiggins, Marianne 1947- .... **CLC 57**
See also BEST 89:3; CA 130; CANR 60

Wight, James Alfred 1916-1995
See Herriot, James
See also CA 77-80; SATA 55; SATA-Brief 44

Wilbur, Richard (Purdy) 1921- **CLC 3, 6, 9, 14, 53, 110; DA; DAB; DAC; DAM MST, POET**
See also CA 1-4R; CABS 2; CANR 2, 29, 76; CDALBS; DLB 5, 169; INT CANR-29; MTCW 1, 2; SATA 9

Wild, Peter 1940- .... **CLC 14**
See also CA 37-40R; DLB 5

Wilde, Oscar 1854(?)-1900 **TCLC 1, 8, 23, 41; DA; DAB; DAC; DAM DRAM, MST, NOV; SSC 11; WLC**
See also CA 104; 119; CDBLB 1890-1914; DLB 10, 19, 34, 57, 141, 156, 190; SATA 24

Wilder, Billy .... **CLC 20**
See also Wilder, Samuel
See also DLB 26

Wilder, Samuel 1906-
See Wilder, Billy
See also CA 89-92

Wilder, Thornton (Niven) 1897-1975 **CLC 1, 5, 6, 10, 15, 35, 82; DA; DAB; DAC; DAM DRAM, MST, NOV; DC 1; WLC**
See also AAYA 29; AITN 2; CA 13-16R; 61-64; CANR 40; CDALBS; DLB 4, 7, 9; DLBY 97; MTCW 1, 2

Wilding, Michael 1942- .... **CLC 73**
See also CA 104; CANR 24, 49

Wiley, Richard 1944- .... **CLC 44**
See also CA 121; 129; CANR 71

Wilhelm, Kate .... **CLC 7**
See also Wilhelm, Katie Gertrude
See also AAYA 20; CAAS 5; DLB 8; INT CANR-17

Wilhelm, Katie Gertrude 1928-
See Wilhelm, Kate
See also CA 37-40R; CANR 17, 36, 60; MTCW 1

Wilkins, Mary
See Freeman, Mary Eleanor Wilkins

Willard, Nancy 1936- .... **CLC 7, 37**
See also CA 89-92; CANR 10, 39, 68; CLR 5; DLB 5, 52; MAICYA; MTCW 1; SATA 37, 71; SATA-Brief 30

William of Ockham 1285-1347 ..... **CMLC 32**

Williams, Ben Ames 1889-1953 ..... **TCLC 89**
See also DLB 102

Williams, C(harles) K(enneth) 1936- **CLC 33, 56; DAM POET**
See also CA 37-40R; CAAS 26; CANR 57; DLB 5

Williams, Charles
See Collier, James L(incoln)

Williams, Charles (Walter Stansby) 1886-1945 **TCLC 1, 11**
See also CA 104; 163; DLB 100, 153

Williams, (George) Emlyn 1905-1987 **CLC 15; DAM DRAM**
See also CA 104; 123; CANR 36; DLB 10, 77; MTCW 1

Williams, Hank 1923-1953 .... **TCLC 81**

Williams, Hugo 1942- .... **CLC 42**
See also CA 17-20R; CANR 45; DLB 40

Williams, J. Walker

See Wodehouse, P(elham) G(renville)

Williams, John A(lfred) 1925-**CLC 5, 13; BLC 3; DAM MULT**
See also BW 2, 3; CA 53-56; CAAS 3; CANR 6, 26, 51; DLB 2, 33; INT CANR-6

Williams, Jonathan (Chamberlain) 1929-**CLC 13**
See also CA 9-12R; CAAS 12; CANR 8; DLB 5

Williams, Joy 1944- .... **CLC 31**
See also CA 41-44R; CANR 22, 48

Williams, Norman 1952- .... **CLC 39**
See also CA 118

Williams, Sherley Anne 1944-**CLC 89; BLC 3; DAM MULT, POET**
See also BW 2, 3; CA 73-76; CANR 25; DLB 41; INT CANR-25; SATA 78

Williams, Shirley
See Williams, Sherley Anne

Williams, Tennessee 1911-1983**CLC 1, 2, 5, 7, 8, 11, 15, 19, 30, 39, 45, 71, 111; DA; DAB; DAC; DAM DRAM, MST; DC 4; WLC**
See also AITN 1, 2; CA 5-8R; 108; CABS 3; CANR 31; CDALB 1941-1968; DLB 7; DLBD 4; DLBY 83; MTCW 1, 2

Williams, Thomas (Alonzo) 1926-1990**CLC 14**
See also CA 1-4R; 132; CANR 2

Williams, William C.
See Williams, William Carlos

Williams, William Carlos 1883-1963**CLC 1, 2, 5, 9, 13, 22, 42, 67; DA; DAB; DAC; DAM MST, POET; PC 7; SSC 31**
See also CA 89-92; CANR 34; CDALB 1917-1929; DLB 4, 16, 54, 86; MTCW 1, 2

Williamson, David (Keith) 1942- ...... **CLC 56**
See also CA 103; CANR 41

Williamson, Ellen Douglas 1905-1984
See Douglas, Ellen
See also CA 17-20R; 114; CANR 39

Williamson, Jack .... **CLC 29**
See also Williamson, John Stewart
See also CAAS 8; DLB 8

Williamson, John Stewart 1908-
See Williamson, Jack
See also CA 17-20R; CANR 23, 70

Willie, Frederick
See Lovecraft, H(oward) P(hillips)

Willingham, Calder (Baynard, Jr.) 1922-1995 **CLC 5, 51**
See also CA 5-8R; 147; CANR 3; DLB 2, 44; MTCW 1

Willis, Charles
See Clarke, Arthur C(harles)

Willis, Fingal O'Flahertie
See Wilde, Oscar

Willy
See Colette, (Sidonie-Gabrielle)

Willy, Colette
See Colette, (Sidonie-Gabrielle)

Wilson, A(ndrew) N(orman) 1950- ... **CLC 33**
See also CA 112; 122; DLB 14, 155, 194; MTCW 2

Wilson, Angus (Frank Johnstone) 1913-1991 **CLC 2, 3, 5, 25, 34; SSC 21**
See also CA 5-8R; 134; CANR 21; DLB 15, 139, 155; MTCW 1, 2

Wilson, August 1945- ... **CLC 39, 50, 63, 118; BLC 3; DA; DAB; DAC; DAM DRAM, MST, MULT; DC 2; WLCS**
See also AAYA 16; BW 2, 3; CA 115; 122; CANR 42, 54, 76; MTCW 1, 2

Wilson, Brian 1942- .... **CLC 12**
Wilson, Colin 1931- .... **CLC 3, 14**

See also CA 1-4R; CAAS 5; CANR 1, 22, 33, 77; DLB 14, 194; MTCW 1

Wilson, Dirk
See Pohl, Frederik

Wilson, Edmund 1895-1972**CLC 1, 2, 3, 8, 24**
See also CA 1-4R; 37-40R; CANR 1, 46; DLB 63; MTCW 1, 2

Wilson, Ethel Davis (Bryant) 1888(?)-1980 **CLC 13; DAC; DAM POET**
See also CA 102; DLB 68; MTCW 1

Wilson, John 1785-1854 .... **NCLC 5**

Wilson, John (Anthony) Burgess 1917-1993
See Burgess, Anthony
See also CA 1-4R; 143; CANR 2, 46; DAC; DAM NOV; MTCW 1, 2

Wilson, Lanford 1937- **CLC 7, 14, 36; DAM DRAM**
See also CA 17-20R; CABS 3; CANR 45; DLB 7

Wilson, Robert M. 1944- .... **CLC 7, 9**
See also CA 49-52; CANR 2, 41; MTCW 1

Wilson, Robert McLiam 1964- .... **CLC 59**
See also CA 132

Wilson, Sloan 1920- .... **CLC 32**
See also CA 1-4R; CANR 1, 44

Wilson, Snoo 1948- .... **CLC 33**
See also CA 69-72

Wilson, William S(mith) 1932- .... **CLC 49**
See also CA 81-84

Wilson, (Thomas) Woodrow 1856-1924**TCLC 79**
See also CA 166; DLB 47

Winchilsea, Anne (Kingsmill) Finch Counte 1661-1720
See Finch, Anne

Windham, Basil
See Wodehouse, P(elham) G(renville)

Wingrove, David (John) 1954- .... **CLC 68**
See also CA 133

Wintergreen, Jane
See Duncan, Sara Jeannette

Winters, Janet Lewis .... **CLC 41**
See also Lewis, Janet
See also DLBY 87

Winters, (Arthur) Yvor 1900-1968 **CLC 4, 8, 32**
See also CA 11-12; 25-28R; CAP 1; DLB 48; MTCW 1

Winterson, Jeanette 1959-**CLC 64; DAM POP**
See also CA 136; CANR 58; DLB 207; MTCW 2

Winthrop, John 1588-1649 .... **LC 31**
See also DLB 24, 30

Wirth, Louis 1897-1952 .... **TCLC 92**
Wiseman, Frederick 1930- .... **CLC 20**
See also CA 159

Wister, Owen 1860-1938 .... **TCLC 21**
See also CA 108; 162; DLB 9, 78, 186; SATA 62

Witkacy
See Witkiewicz, Stanislaw Ignacy

Witkiewicz, Stanislaw Ignacy 1885-1939 **TCLC 8**
See also CA 105; 162

Wittgenstein, Ludwig (Josef Johann) 1889-1951 **TCLC 59**
See also CA 113; 164; MTCW 2

Wittig, Monique 1935(?)- .... **CLC 22**
See also CA 116; 135; DLB 83

Wittlin, Jozef 1896-1976 .... **CLC 25**
See also CA 49-52; 65-68; CANR 3

Wodehouse, P(elham) G(renville) 1881-1975 **CLC 1, 2, 5, 10, 22; DAB; DAC; DAM**

NOV; SSC 2
See also AITN 2; CA 45-48; 57-60; CANR 3, 33; CDBLB 1914-1945; DLB 34, 162; MTCW 1, 2; SATA 22

Woiwode, L.
See Woiwode, Larry (Alfred)

Woiwode, Larry (Alfred) 1941- ....**CLC 6, 10**
See also CA 73-76; CANR 16; DLB 6; INT CANR-16

Wojciechowska, Maia (Teresa) 1927-**CLC 26**
See also AAYA 8; CA 9-12R; CANR 4, 41; CLR 1; JRDA; MAICYA; SAAS 1; SATA 1, 28, 83; SATA-Essay 104

Wolf, Christa 1929- .... **CLC 14, 29, 58**
See also CA 85-88; CANR 45; DLB 75; MTCW 1

Wolfe, Gene (Rodman) 1931- **CLC 25; DAM POP**
See also CA 57-60; CAAS 9; CANR 6, 32, 60; DLB 8; MTCW 2

Wolfe, George C. 1954- .... **CLC 49; BLCS**
See also CA 149

Wolfe, Thomas (Clayton) 1900-1938**TCLC 4, 13, 29, 61; DA; DAB; DAC; DAM MST, NOV; SSC 33; WLC**
See also CA 104; 132; CDALB 1929-1941; DLB 9, 102; DLBD 2, 16; DLBY 85, 97; MTCW 1, 2

Wolfe, Thomas Kennerly, Jr. 1930-
See Wolfe, Tom
See also CA 13-16R; CANR 9, 33, 70; DAM POP; DLB 185; INT CANR-9; MTCW 1, 2

Wolfe, Tom .... **CLC 1, 2, 9, 15, 35, 51**
See also Wolfe, Thomas Kennerly, Jr.
See also AAYA 8; AITN 2; BEST 89:1; DLB 152

Wolff, Geoffrey (Ansell) 1937- .... **CLC 41**
See also CA 29-32R; CANR 29, 43, 78

Wolff, Sonia
See Levitin, Sonia (Wolff)

Wolff, Tobias (Jonathan Ansell) 1945- . **C L C 39, 64**
See also AAYA 16; BEST 90:2; CA 114; 117; CAAS 22; CANR 54, 76; DLB 130; INT 117; MTCW 2

Wolfram von Eschenbach c. 1170-c. 1220 **CMLC 5**
See also DLB 138

Wolitzer, Hilma 1930- .... **CLC 17**
See also CA 65-68; CANR 18, 40; INT CANR-18; SATA 31

Wollstonecraft, Mary 1759-1797 .... **LC 5, 50**
See also CDBLB 1789-1832; DLB 39, 104, 158

Wonder, Stevie .... **CLC 12**
See also Morris, Steveland Judkins

Wong, Jade Snow 1922- .... **CLC 17**
See also CA 109

Woodberry, George Edward 1855-1930 **TCLC 73**
See also CA 165; DLB 71, 103

Woodcott, Keith
See Brunner, John (Kilian Houston)

Woodruff, Robert W.
See Mencken, H(enry) L(ouis)

Woolf, (Adeline) Virginia 1882-1941**TCLC 1, 5, 20, 43, 56; DA; DAB; DAC; DAM MST, NOV; SSC 7; WLC**
See also Woolf, Virginia Adeline
See also CA 104; 130; CANR 64; CDBLB 1914-1945; DLB 36, 100, 162; DLBD 10; MTCW 1

Woolf, Virginia Adeline
See Woolf, (Adeline) Virginia

See also MTCW 2

Woollcott, Alexander (Humphreys) 1887-1943 **TCLC 5**
See also CA 105; 161; DLB 29

Woolrich, Cornell 1903-1968 .... **CLC 77**
See also Hopley-Woolrich, Cornell George

Wordsworth, Dorothy 1771-1855 .. **NCLC 25**
See also DLB 107

Wordsworth, William 1770-1850 .. **NCLC 12, 38; DA; DAB; DAC; DAM MST, POET; PC 4; WLC**
See also CDBLB 1789-1832; DLB 93, 107

Wouk, Herman 1915- **CLC 1, 9, 38; DAM NOV, POP**
See also CA 5-8R; CANR 6, 33, 67; CDALBS; DLBY 82; INT CANR-6; MTCW 1, 2

Wright, Charles (Penzel, Jr.) 1935- **CLC 6, 13, 28, 119**
See also CA 29-32R; CAAS 7; CANR 23, 36, 62; DLB 165; DLBY 82; MTCW 1, 2

Wright, Charles Stevenson 1932- ... **CLC 49; BLC 3; DAM MULT, POET**
See also BW 1; CA 9-12R; CANR 26; DLB 33

Wright, Frances 1795-1852 .... **NCLC 74**
See also DLB 73

Wright, Jack R.
See Harris, Mark

Wright, James (Arlington) 1927-1980 **CLC 3, 5, 10, 28; DAM POET**
See also AITN 2; CA 49-52; 97-100; CANR 4, 34, 64; CDALBS; DLB 5, 169; MTCW 1, 2

Wright, Judith (Arandell) 1915- **CLC 11, 53; PC 14**
See also CA 13-16R; CANR 31, 76; MTCW 1, 2; SATA 14

Wright, L(aurali) R. 1939- .... **CLC 44**
See also CA 138

Wright, Richard (Nathaniel) 1908-1960 **C L C 1, 3, 4, 9, 14, 21, 48, 74; BLC 3; DA; DAB; DAC; DAM MST, MULT, NOV; SSC 2; WLC**
See also AAYA 5; BW 1; CA 108; CANR 64; CDALB 1929-1941; DLB 76, 102; DLBD 2; MTCW 1, 2

Wright, Richard B(ruce) 1937- .... **CLC 6**
See also CA 85-88; DLB 53

Wright, Rick 1945- .... **CLC 35**

Wright, Rowland
See Wells, Carolyn

Wright, Stephen 1946- .... **CLC 33**

Wright, Willard Huntington 1888-1939
See Van Dine, S. S.
See also CA 115; DLBD 16

Wright, William 1930- .... **CLC 44**
See also CA 53-56; CANR 7, 23

Wroth, LadyMary 1587-1653(?) .... **LC 30**
See also DLB 121

Wu Ch'eng-en 1500(?)-1582(?) .... **LC 7**

Wu Ching-tzu 1701-1754 .... **LC 2**

Wurlitzer, Rudolph 1938(?)- .... **CLC 2, 4, 15**
See also CA 85-88; DLB 173

Wycherley, William 1641-1715 **LC 8, 21; DAM DRAM**
See also CDBLB 1660-1789; DLB 80

Wylie, Elinor (Morton Hoyt) 1885-1928 **TCLC 8; PC 23**
See also CA 105; 162; DLB 9, 45

Wylie, Philip (Gordon) 1902-1971 ... **CLC 43**
See also CA 21-22; 33-36R; CAP 2; DLB 9

Wyndham, John .... **CLC 19**
See also Harris, John (Wyndham Parkes Lucas) Beynon

Wyss, Johann David Von 1743-1818 **NCLC 10**

See also JRDA; MAICYA; SATA 29; SATA-Brief 27

Xenophon c. 430B.C.-c. 354B.C. ... **CMLC 17**
See also DLB 176

Yakumo Koizumi
See Hearn, (Patricio) Lafcadio (Tessima Carlos)

Yamamoto, Hisaye 1921- **SSC 34; DAM MULT**

Yanez, Jose Donoso
See Donoso (Yanez), Jose

Yanovsky, Basile S.
See Yanovsky, V(assily) S(emenovich)

Yanovsky, V(assily) S(emenovich) 1906-1989 **CLC 2, 18**
See also CA 97-100; 129

Yates, Richard 1926-1992 .... **CLC 7, 8, 23**
See also CA 5-8R; 139; CANR 10, 43; DLB 2; DLBY 81, 92; INT CANR-10

Yeats, W. B.
See Yeats, William Butler

Yeats, William Butler 1865-1939 **TCLC 1, 11, 18, 31, 93; DA; DAB; DAC; DAM DRAM, MST, POET; PC 20; WLC**
See also CA 104; 127; CANR 45; CDBLB 1890-1914; DLB 10, 19, 98, 156; MTCW 1, 2

Yehoshua, A(braham) B. 1936- .. **CLC 13, 31**
See also CA 33-36R; CANR 43

Yep, Laurence Michael 1948- .... **CLC 35**
See also AAYA 5; CA 49-52; CANR 1, 46; CLR 3, 17, 54; DLB 52; JRDA; MAICYA; SATA 7, 69

Yerby, Frank G(arvin) 1916-1991 . **CLC 1, 7, 22; BLC 3; DAM MULT**
See also BW 1, 3; CA 9-12R; 136; CANR 16, 52; DLB 76; INT CANR-16; MTCW 1

Yesenin, Sergei Alexandrovich
See Esenin, Sergei (Alexandrovich)

Yevtushenko, Yevgeny (Alexandrovich) 1933- **CLC 1, 3, 13, 26, 51; DAM POET**
See also CA 81-84; CANR 33, 54; MTCW 1

Yezierska, Anzia 1885(?)-1970 .... **CLC 46**
See also CA 126; 89-92; DLB 28; MTCW 1

Yglesias, Helen 1915- .... **CLC 7, 22**
See also CA 37-40R; CAAS 20; CANR 15, 65; INT CANR-15; MTCW 1

Yokomitsu Riichi 1898-1947 .... **TCLC 47**
See also CA 170

Yonge, Charlotte (Mary) 1823-1901 **TCLC 48**
See also CA 109; 163; DLB 18, 163; SATA 17

York, Jeremy
See Creasey, John

York, Simon
See Heinlein, Robert A(nson)

Yorke, Henry Vincent 1905-1974 ...... **CLC 13**
See also Green, Henry
See also CA 85-88; 49-52

Yosano Akiko 1878-1942 .... **TCLC 59; PC 11**
See also CA 161

Yoshimoto, Banana .... **CLC 84**
See also Yoshimoto, Mahoko

Yoshimoto, Mahoko 1964-
See Yoshimoto, Banana
See also CA 144

Young, Al(bert James) 1939- **CLC 19; BLC 3; DAM MULT**
See also BW 2, 3; CA 29-32R; CANR 26, 65; DLB 33

Young, Andrew (John) 1885-1971 ...... **CLC 5**
See also CA 5-8R; CANR 7, 29

Young, Collier
See Bloch, Robert (Albert)

Young, Edward 1683-1765 .... **LC 3, 40**
See also DLB 95

Young, Marguerite (Vivian) 1909-1995 **C L C 82**
See also CA 13-16; 150; CAP 1

Young, Neil 1945- .... **CLC 17**
See also CA 110

Young Bear, Ray A. 1950- ...... **CLC 94; DAM MULT**
See also CA 146; DLB 175; NNAL

Yourcenar, Marguerite 1903-1987 **CLC 19, 38, 50, 87; DAM NOV**
See also CA 69-72; CANR 23, 60; DLB 72; DLBY 88; MTCW 1, 2

Yurick, Sol 1925- .... **CLC 6**
See also CA 13-16R; CANR 25

Zabolotsky, Nikolai Alekseevich 1903-1958 **TCLC 52**
See also CA 116; 164

Zamiatin, Yevgenii
See Zamyatin, Evgeny Ivanovich

Zamora, Bernice (B. Ortiz) 1938- .. **CLC 89; DAM MULT; HLC**
See also CA 151; CANR 80; DLB 82; HW 1, 2

Zamyatin, Evgeny Ivanovich 1884-1937 **TCLC 8, 37**
See also CA 105; 166

Zangwill, Israel 1864-1926 .... **TCLC 16**
See also CA 109; 167; DLB 10, 135, 197

Zappa, Francis Vincent, Jr. 1940-1993
See Zappa, Frank
See also CA 108; 143; CANR 57

Zappa, Frank .... **CLC 17**
See also Zappa, Francis Vincent, Jr.

Zaturenska, Marya 1902-1982 ...... **CLC 6, 11**
See also CA 13-16R; 105; CANR 22

Zeami 1363-1443 .... **DC 7**

Zelazny, Roger (Joseph) 1937-1995 . **CLC 21**
See also AAYA 7; CA 21-24R; 148; CANR 26, 60; DLB 8; MTCW 1, 2; SATA 57; SATA-Brief 39

Zhdanov, Andrei Alexandrovich 1896-1948 **TCLC 18**
See also CA 117; 167

Zhukovsky, Vasily (Andreevich) 1783-1852 **NCLC 35**
See also DLB 205

Ziegenhagen, Eric .... **CLC 55**

Zimmer, Jill Schary
See Robinson, Jill

Zimmerman, Robert
See Dylan, Bob

Zindel, Paul 1936- **CLC 6, 26; DA; DAB; DAC; DAM DRAM, MST, NOV; DC 5**
See also AAYA 2; CA 73-76; CANR 31, 65; CDALBS; CLR 3, 45; DLB 7, 52; JRDA; MAICYA; MTCW 1, 2; SATA 16, 58, 102

Zinov'Ev, A. A.
See Zinoviev, Alexander (Aleksandrovich)

Zinoviev, Alexander (Aleksandrovich) 1922- **CLC 19**
See also CA 116; 133; CAAS 10

Zoilus
See Lovecraft, H(oward) P(hillips)

Zola, Emile (Edouard Charles Antoine) 1840-1902 **TCLC 1, 6, 21, 41; DA; DAB; DAC; DAM MST, NOV; WLC**
See also CA 104; 138; DLB 123

Zoline, Pamela 1941- .... **CLC 62**
See also CA 161

Zorrilla y Moral, Jose 1817-1893 .... **NCLC 6**

Zoshchenko, Mikhail (Mikhailovich) 1895-1958 **TCLC 15; SSC 15**
See also CA 115; 160

Zuckmayer, Carl 1896-1977 .... **CLC 18**

Literary Criticism Series
Cumulative Topic Index

This index lists all topic entries in Gale's *Classical and Medieval Literature Criticism, Contemporary Literary Criticism, Literature Criticism from 1400 to 1800, Nineteenth-Century Literature Criticism,* and *Twentieth-Century Literary Criticism.*

Topic Index

Contemporary Literary Criticism
Cumulative Nationality Index

Nationality Index

Nationality Index

Nationality Index

Nationality Index

CLC-120 **Title Index**

ISBN 0-7876-3195-7

90000